If you're wondering why you should buy this new edition of *Government by the People*, here are 10 good reasons!

1. The first two years of the **Obama administration** are explored throughout the book, including analysis of important legislation such as health care reform and financial reform, foreign policy decisions and developments in Iraq and Afghanistan, and Supreme Court appointments. Coverage has also been updated to include discussion of the **2010 midterm campaigns and elections,** and figures and tables have been updated with the latest data.

2. We have integrated the **latest examples and scholarship** on American politics and government, including recent Supreme Court decisions, the economic conditions at the end of 2010, and comparisons with countries around the world.

3. A **new Introduction chapter** provides brief historical background of the founding of our country and explains the book's thematic approach of a government by the people. Vital for students with little background in the discipline, it will help them to hit the ground running with the course. Bookended with the Introduction, the **Conclusion** summarizes our history of government by the people and emphasizes the importance of active citizenship.

4. **Chapter Learning Objectives are more fully integrated** into the chapters, providing stronger pedagogical guidance for navigating the chapter content. Objectives are also used to structure end-of-chapter content, which includes a **Summary and Self-Test,** allowing students to assess their understanding of each objective.

5. **New Part Openers preview the broad themes** of each group of chapters and help students step back from the details to understand the bigger picture. Organized around Course Learning Objectives, they summarize the important overall concepts students should master by the end of the course. A comprehensive **Course Exam,** appearing at the end of the text, allows students to test their mastery of the course material as a whole.

6. **New features** are built around the framework of a government of, by, and for the people. **Of the People** boxes explore the diversity of Americans and assess how they compare to the global community; **By the People** boxes demonstrate nontraditional and accessible ways students can participate in government and public service; and **For the People** boxes remind students of the important accomplishments achieved by our government. These features help today's students see the relevance of government and the important role that they as citizens play in this country's present and future.

7. Being part of a government by the people requires consideration of differing points of view. **You Will Decide** boxes, updated with the latest in-the-news topics, explore questions that citizens and policy analysts alike wrestle with, like the advantages and disadvantages of a national presidential primary, or the need for restrictions on civil liberties during the war on terror, and then ask students to weigh options for resolving these issues.

8. The **visual program,** updated for currency and relevance, has also been developed to be more pedagogically effective in helping students build their study skills and get more out of the visuals. Photo captions include analysis questions designed to promote critical thinking and stimulate class discussion, and figures are accompanied by visual literacy questions that ensure students are accurately reading and assessing the data.

9. All chapters revised with an emphasis on anticipating areas of student confusion and revising explanations to address those areas of common difficulty. In particular, the discussion in Chapter 13 on bureaucratic agencies and in Chapter 17 on the public policy process have been revised and reorganized for greater clarity and comprehension.

10. **MyPoliSciLab** has been revised and integrated with this edition to make learning more effective. This best-selling online resource offers a wide array of multimedia activities, including videos, simulations, exercises, and online newsfeeds.

PEARSON

ELECTORAL COLLEGE VOTES IN THE 2008 ELECTION

THE UNITED STATES
A political map showing the number of electoral votes per state

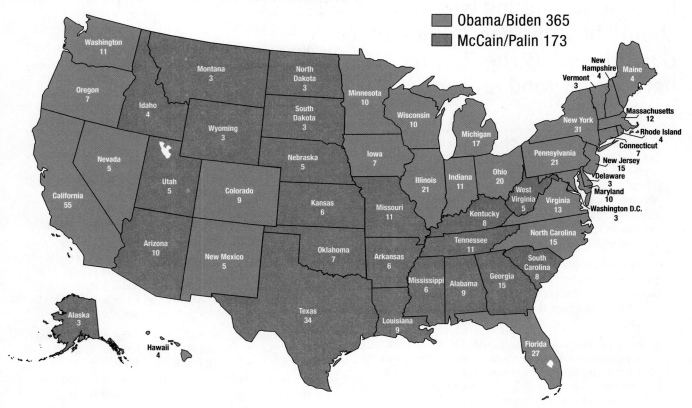

Obama/Biden 365
McCain/Palin 173

A political map with states drawn in proportion to the number of electoral votes

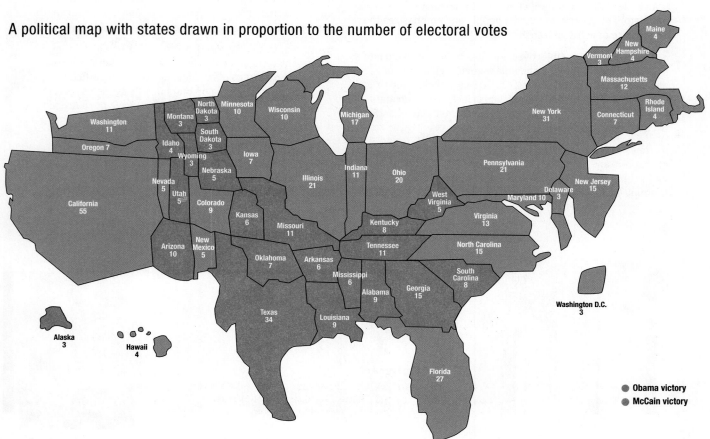

Obama victory
McCain victory

GOVERNMENT BY THE PEOPLE

DAVID B. MAGLEBY
Brigham Young University

PAUL C. LIGHT
New York University

CHRISTINE L. NEMACHECK
The College of
William and Mary

2011 National, State, and Local Edition

Longman
Boston   Columbus   Indianapolis   New York   San Francisco   Upper Saddle River
Amsterdam   Cape Town   Dubai   London   Madrid   Milan   Munich   Paris   Montreal   Toronto
Delhi   Mexico City   São Paulo   Sydney   Hong Kong   Seoul   Singapore   Taipei   Tokyo

EXECUTIVE EDITOR:	Reid Hester
DIRECTOR OF DEVELOPMENT:	Meg Botteon
EDITOR-IN-CHIEF:	Eric Stano
ASSOCIATE DEVELOPMENT EDITOR:	Donna Garnier
SUPPLEMENTS EDITOR:	Corey Kahn
EDITORIAL ASSISTANT:	Elizabeth Alimena
SENIOR MEDIA PRODUCER:	Regina Vertiz
SENIOR MARKETING MANAGER:	Lindsey Prudhomme
PRODUCTION MANAGER:	Bob Ginsberg
PROJECT COORDINATION, TEXT DESIGN, AND ELECTRONIC PAGE MAKEUP:	Integra Software Services, Inc.
COVER DESIGN MANAGER/COVER DESIGNER:	John Callahan
COVER ILLUSTRATION/PHOTO:	Michael Eudenbach/Aurora Photos
PHOTO RESEARCHER:	Teri Stratford
SENIOR MANUFACTURING BUYER:	Dennis J. Para
PRINTER AND BINDER:	RR Donnelley & Sons Company/Willard
COVER PRINTER:	Lehigh Phoenix

For permission to use copyrighted material, grateful acknowledgment is made to the copyright holders on pp. 799–801, which are hereby made part of this copyright page.

Library of Congress Cataloging-in-Publication Data

Magleby, David B.
    Government by the people: national, state, and local/David B. Magleby, Paul C. Light,
    Christine L. Nemacheck.—2011 ed.
        p. cm.
    Includes bibliographical references and index.
    ISBN 978-0-205-82843-2
    1. United States—Politics and government—Textbooks.   I. Light, Paul Charles.
    II. Nemacheck, Christine L.   III. Title.
    JK276.G68 2011
    320.473—dc22

                                                                                    2010045839

Longman
is an imprint of

www.pearsonhighered.com

2 3 4 5 6 7 8 9 10—DOW—14 13 12 11

ISBN-13: 978-0-205-82843-2
ISBN-10:   0-205-82843-4

BRIEF CONTENTS

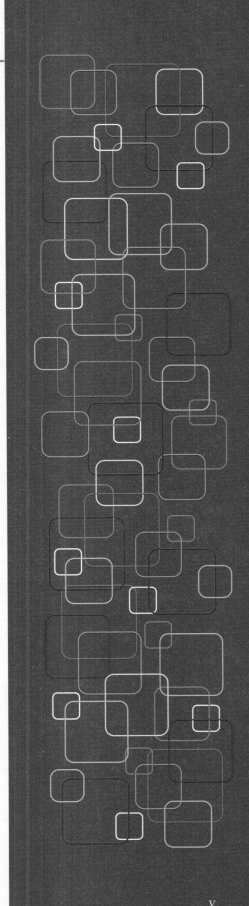

CONTENTS

COURSE **OBJECTIVES**

PART I Constitutional Principles

CHAPTER 1 Constitutional Democracy

Identify the philosophical principles on which our democratic republic is based.

CHAPTER 2 Constitutional Foundations

Describe the creation and adoption of the Constitution and the Bill of Rights, and identify the process for Amendments.

CHAPTER 3 American Federalism

Explain federalism in America, and analyze the relationship between the federal and state and local governments.

PART II The Political Process

CHAPTER 4 Political Culture and Ideology

Explain the role of political culture and ideology in American government.

CHAPTER 5 The American Political Landscape

Describe how American social and economic differences affect political beliefs and policy preferences.

CHAPTER 6 Interest Groups

Evaluate the efforts of different kinds of interest groups to influence elections and legislation.

CHAPTER 7 Political Parties

Explain the role of political parties, and assess the need for parties in American government.

CHAPTER 8 Public Opinion, Participation, and Voting

Explain differences in opinions and rates of participation, and evaluate the importance of public opinion and participation in a democracy.

CHAPTER 9 Campaigns and Elections

Compare and contrast the elections for president and Congress, and describe how elections have changed over time.

PART III Policy Making Institutions

CHAPTER 10 The Media and U.S. Politics

Describe the evolution of the media and evaluate its impact on public opinion, elections, and government.

CHAPTER 11 Congress

Identify the legislative powers of Congress, and compare and contrast the House of Representatives and the Senate.

CHAPTER 12 The Presidency

Identify the powers of the president for leading the nation.

CHAPTER 13 The Federal Bureaucracy

Describe the role of the federal bureaucracy in implementing the laws.

CHAPTER 14 The Judiciary

Explain the role of the courts in the system of checks and balances, and evaluate the challenges for judicial independence.

PART IV Rights and Liberties

CHAPTER 15 Civil Liberties

Describe the individual liberties protected in the Bill of Rights, and evaluate the limitations on these rights.

CHAPTER 16 Civil Rights

Explain how Congress and the Supreme Court have expanded and protected civil rights.

PART V The Politics of National Policy

CHAPTER 17 The Policy Process

Identify the steps in the policymaking process.

CHAPTER 18 Making Economic Policy

Describe the federal government's tools for making economic policy.

CHAPTER **19** Making Social Policy

Trace the evolution of social policy, and describe the government's recent challenges in protecting Americans from hardship.

CHAPTER **20** Making Foreign and Defense Policy

Describe the tools of foreign policymaking, and evaluate the status of America's current foreign policy interests.

PART **VI** State and Local Government

CHAPTER **21** State and Local Politics.

Identify the range of policy programs administered by state and local governments, and analyze the influences on state and local politics.

CHAPTER **22** State Constitutions

Compare and contrast the U.S. Constitution with state constitutions.

CHAPTER **23** Parties and Elections in the States

Assess the importance of parties and elections at the state level.

CHAPTER **24** State Legislatures

Describe the functions of state legislatures and evaluate their responsiveness to the people.

CHAPTER **25** State Governors

Explain how governors use their formal and informal powers to influence public policy.

CHAPTER **26** Judges and Justice in the States

Describe the judicial system at the state level, and evaluate the differences across the states in judicial selection and sentencing.

CHAPTER **27** Local Governments and Metropolitics

Identify the functions of local governments, including counties, cities, towns, and special districts.

CHAPTER **28** Making State and Local Policy

Evaluate the importance of state and local governments in implementing policy.

CHAPTER **29** Staffing and Financing State and Local Governments

Describe the challenges for state and local governments in organizing resources, raising funds, and managing expenditures.

PREFACE

We welcome you to the study of American government at the college level. The importance and relevance of the topics covered in our book have been reinforced by today's pressing economic, social, and foreign policy challenges. Governmental decisions made now will have lasting implications.

We title this book *Government by the People* because we want to emphasize the important role people play in our constitutional democracy. Understanding American politics and government must include an appreciation of the people, their similarities and differences, their beliefs and attitudes, and their behaviors.

The study of American government should be engaging, relevant, and rigorous. As authors of this book, we see politics and government as topics worthy of careful study. Constitutional democracy—the kind we have in the United States—is exceedingly hard to achieve, equally hard to sustain, and often hard to understand. Our political history has been an evolution toward an enlarged role for citizens and voters. Citizens have more rights and political opportunities in 2010 and 2011 than they had in 1800 or 1900. The framers of our Constitution warned that we must be vigilant in safeguarding our rights, liberties, and political institutions. But to do this, we must first understand these institutions and the forces that have shaped them.

We want you to come away from reading this book with a richer understanding of American politics, government, the job of politicians, and the important role you, as a citizen, play in this country's present and future. We hope you will participate actively in making this constitutional democracy more vital and responsive to the urgent problems of the twenty-first century.

What's New in This Edition

The new edition of *Government by the People* builds on the long-standing reputation of this book for strong coverage of the foundations of American government that is accurate, accessible, and current. We have integrated the latest in scholarship on American politics and government, the 2010 midterm elections, recent Supreme Court appointments and decisions, and comparisons with countries around the world into a book that introduces you to the subject and the discipline of political science.

Building on the theme of the people in government, we examine government through a new set of features that we have named *Of the People, By the People,* and *For the People.* These features explore who the American people are, how they compare to people and cultures around the world, the ways they are engaging in their government, and the important accomplishments that have resulted.

Growing from the success of the previous edition, this edition expands on the framework of learning pedagogy to help you navigate each chapter's discussion, focus on the most important concepts, and understand American politics and government. After surveying American government and politics courses taught around the country, we developed a list of Learning Objectives—the concepts professors teaching this course most often want their students to understand—to shape and guide the development of this edition. Each part opens with a list of Course Objectives, which provides students with a big picture overview of the broad concepts they will encounter, giving them a better understanding of how to focus their reading and studying for each section. At the end of the book, they will be able to test their mastery of the course material as a whole through the comprehensive Course Exam. Paralleling this structure, each chapter opens with a list of Chapter Objectives, highlighting the learning goals for that chapter. Chapter Objectives are called out in the text margins as the key concepts are discussed, and a summary and self-test at the end of each chapter provide students with a final check of their understanding of the chapter.

Chapter-by-Chapter Changes:

Introduction. New to this edition is an introductory chapter, which places in historical context the idea of self-government and introduces concepts that provide a foundation for understanding our distinctive constitutional democracy. Each of the features, designed to reinforce learning, are introduced in this chapter.

Chapter 1 is premised on the view that there is much about U.S. government that deserves praise, but at the same time, it remains a work in progress. In this chapter, we begin to explore the context of our experiment in constitutional democracy. In this edition, we have an expanded section on the conditions that help democracy endure. We also examine the American Revolution and Constitutional Convention and subsequent ratification debates, which continue to be central to understanding American government. A new feature explores the process for becoming an American citizen.

Chapter 2 uses the Supreme Court's recent rulings on the right to bear arms to examine the lack of specificity of the Constitution. The judiciary's role in interpreting the Constitution is explained, and students are challenged to consider how the document should be understood in light of current constitutional debates. Methods for proposing amendments include examples to clarify the two methods. A new feature encourages students to familiarize themselves with the U.S. Constitution, and immediately after this chapter, you will find a copy of it. We place it here rather than in an appendix at the back of the book because we think it is very important that you read and think about this remarkable document.

Chapter 3 uses the recent state regulations on texting while driving to introduce the chapter. The discussion of federalism has been expanded to compare the advantages and disadvantages of a federal system of government in the United States. Analysis of the centralist and decentralist arguments has been reorganized and clarified. A new feature shows students how to track and monitor distribution of funds from the national stimulus package.

Chapter 4 begins by looking at the struggle to establish Martin Luther King Jr. Day as a way of encouraging thought about how our political culture has changed over time. The section on liberalism, conservatism, and criticisms of both has been updated to reflect recent issues, elections, and events. The chapter also explores the implications of many Americans being middle-of-the road or not having thought much about ideology. Equality, one of the core elements of the American political culture, is examined in the context of the effort to provide access and opportunity for the disabled.

Chapter 5 opens with a new introduction on the parties' use of microtargeting to explore how and why people see politics and government differently. A more informed understanding of politics comes from an appreciation that social, economic, and other characteristics of people influence political behavior. Using the most current U.S. census and other data, we examine these relationships. Many people bring to their study of politics an assumption that other people see things the way they do, often not realizing the influences that have helped shape them. A new feature shows how students are spreading awareness of poverty in America.

Chapter 6 is about interest groups and the reality that as we become involved in politics, we generally do so as part of groups. The chapter begins with a discussion of the Tea Party Movement's involvement in recent campaigns and influence in framing issues. The role of the Internet in the forming and financing of interest groups receives added attention. The ways groups seek to influence public policy are also a central focus. In this new edition, we have expanded coverage of lobbying, including the diversity among lobbyists, recent efforts to regulate lobbying and common strategies used by lobbyists, and how students can get involved in lobbying for education policy.

Chapter 7 details the history of political parties in the American context. We explore the early antipathy toward parties among the founders, and the importance of parties generally and as part of the way elections are funded. A new feature encourages students to get involved with party organizations on their campus.

Chapter 8 has been updated throughout to reflect the events and outcomes of the 2008 and 2010 elections. The chapter begins with a discussion of the recent surge in use of absentee ballots and early voting and examines the implications of this for 2010 and 2012, and more generally. The role of the Internet and social networking sites has been added as well as a new feature explaining how to become a poll worker. We also analyze ways to further expand democracy and broaden participation.

Chapter 9 has been updated to reflect the 2008 and 2010 elections, including the substantial increase in individual contributions to candidates in 2008. The rules of elections matter in important ways that this chapter explores at the congressional and presidential levels. One important resource in elections is money. This area has seen significant changes in recent years, and this chapter has been revised accordingly, including a new feature exploring campaign contribution disclosure laws.

Chapter 10 begins with an examination of the role of the media in passage of health care legislation in 2009–2010. In this chapter, we discuss the declining importance of newspapers and the growing role of the Internet in campaigns and elections, and we explain the origins of the Internet in a new feature. Social networking is one place that young people in particular learn about news and discuss it with each other. Although where people go to get news is changing, the central importance of a free and attentive media has not changed.

Chapter 11 opens with Senator Evan Bayh's reflections on his time in Congress to introduce how the framers designed the legislative branch and how it actually works today. The chapter has been updated to reflect the 2010 congressional elections and recent congressional decisions on major legislation such as health care reform. The chapter also has new content on public approval of Congress, and new features discuss the agenda of Congress and how individuals can influence that agenda.

Chapter 12 begins by exploring presidential decision making through the example of President Obama's formulation of a strategy for the war in Afghanistan. The chapter includes updated information on Obama's use of the veto power and executive orders, use of executive privilege, and continued controversies over the war power and legislative signing statements. The chapter also addresses recent decisions involving the president's role during periods of economic and international crises.

Chapter 13 explains the factors that led to the British Petroleum (BP) oil spill in the Gulf to introduce the federal bureaucracy. It includes an updated section on defining bureaucracy, the organization of government, and the four types of bureaucratic organizations. The chapter also analyzes the types of federal government employees and the changing size of government. New features discuss how to bring transparency to the federal bureaucracy.

Chapter 14 uses the Supreme Court's decision in *Citizens United* v. *Federal Election Commission* and President Obama's critique of the decision at the 2010 State of the Union Address as a vehicle to consider the appropriate role of the courts in a separation-of-powers system. Appointments to the federal courts, and particularly the U.S. Supreme Court, increasingly focus attention on the judiciary and the important role judges play in American politics. The president's most recent Supreme Court appointments are discussed, as is diversity on the federal bench. The section on Supreme Court decision making has been revised to more clearly guide the students through the entire process.

Chapter 15 focuses on civil liberties, including an enhanced discussion on individual rights in an age of terrorism. The chapter includes a comprehensive overview of due process rights, property rights (as explored in *Kelo* v. *City of New London*) privacy rights, including abortion and sexual orientation, the rights of the accused, and the death penalty, with a focus on the Supreme Court's treatment of juvenile offenders, including the decision in *Graham* v. *Florida*. New features demonstrate how the federal government and students help guarantee Sixth Amendment rights.

Chapter 16 examines civil rights through a discussion of the Court's most recent decisions on the use of race in student assignment to public schools and through a historical overview of judicial and legislative action concerning discrimination based on race, sex, religion, ethnic origin, age, sexual orientation, and physical handicap. Barack Obama's victory in the 2008 presidential election is added to the discussion of racial equality, and Hillary Clinton's and Sarah Palin's campaigns are included in the discussion of women's rights. The chapter also includes an enhanced discussion of citizenship rights and the continuing debate over rights for same-sex couples.

Chapter 17 expands the last edition's brief introduction to public policy to provide a more thorough discussion of the process. It begins with a definition of public policy, including the various types of public policy. The chapter then explores the eight steps in making public policy, including more detail and examples.

Chapter 18 includes updated budget and expenditure data throughout the narrative and in figures and tables. The discussion of the Federal Reserve System includes analysis of the prime interest rate and the Federal Reserve's recent activity to stimulate the economy. The section on corporate responsibility has been updated.

Chapter 19 uses the health care bill negotiations to illustrate the difficulties in designing and enacting a major new federal social program. The chapter includes an expanded discussion of help for the unemployed, including a new figure on unemployment in the United States and discussion of low-income workers, the minimum wage, and the earned income tax credit. The section on education includes updated information on the impact of No Child Left Behind and Head Start.

Chapter 20 focuses on five key priorities in foreign policy today. The discussion of the war in Iraq has been updated to reflect events of the past two years and now incorporates coverage of the increased U.S. involvement in Afghanistan. A new feature shows students how to make a difference by ensuring their university is making ethical foreign investments.

Chapter 21 begins with an example of the current budget challenges faced by California. This and other new examples in the chapter illustrate how the economy and even international relations affect governments at all levels. The chapter has a new section on how individuals can influence state and local governments.

Chapter 22 has been updated to include a timely discussion of state constitutional efforts to deal with the question of same-sex marriage, one of the most hotly debated topics in politics today, and an excellent lens through which to analyze the importance of state constitutions. An expanded section on new judicial federalism addresses the important role state courts play in protecting individual liberties as they increasingly decide cases using protections in their own state constitutions rather than the U.S. Constitution.

Chapter 23 anticipates the reapportionment coming in 2011 and 2012 and provides a current and expanded discussion of the redistricting process. The chapter also explores the important agenda-setting role of ballot initiatives and referendums. With states experimenting with new ways to vote—by mail or electronically, for example—the chapter examines why these reforms were instituted and what has changed as a result of their adoption.

Chapter 24 places state legislatures in their historical context as predating the U.S. Constitution. The chapter explores similarities and differences between state legislatures and the U.S. Congress. One important similarity is a reliance on committees to do much of the work. New to this edition is information on how to contact your representative in the state legislature.

Chapter 25 has been updated to include results from the 2010 election in a broader analysis of the politics of becoming a governor. Although states vary in the power they give the governor, all governors have important formal and informal powers. For example, governors typically have the power to pardon criminals. As discussed in the new opener, former Illinois Governor Ryan exercised that power when he pardoned four death row inmates and commuted the sentence of all 167 death row inmates to life sentences.

Chapter 26 includes an updated and enhanced discussion of judicial elections and campaign contributions. State courts, like their federal counterparts, are becoming increasingly diverse, and this chapter also includes updated data on the presence of women and racial and ethnic minority judges on the state judiciary. The chapter also includes new discussions on the changing treatment of the death penalty in the states, the role of court monitoring groups, and efforts in some states to publicly fund judicial elections.

Chapter 27 taps into the controversy surrounding Arizona's immigration law by contrasting the responses of two county sheriffs to the new law. The impact of local differences in law and policy is also illustrated at the beginning of the chapter in a comparison of the different approaches local governments have taken in rules for posting bail for minor offenses. The chapter also presents an example of how people can make a difference in local zoning and school decisions.

Chapter 28 examines the broad sweep of policy making that occurs at the state and local levels. Using education as an example, the chapter includes a current examination of efforts by governments at all levels to improve public education. Of particular interest to college students is a section on higher education funding.

Chapter 29 includes an updated discussion of one of the consequences of the economic challenges faced by the United States in 2008–2011: the growing debt not only at the national level but in some states and many localities. There is also a renewed focus on lowering costs in local and state governments, exploring the challenges of adequately staffing government in a time of shrinking budgets.

Conclusion. We end the book with a concluding chapter returning to the broad themes of the book and calling on all citizens to take politics and government seriously.

A FOCUS ON
FOUNDATIONS . . .

Read by over one million students, this new edition of the classic *Government by the People* has been substantially rewritten and redesigned to assist you in your study of American government and politics.

PART I Constitutional Principles

THE BIG PICTURE

The U.S. Constitution provides our basic framework of government. It has resulted in great stability in governance for more than 220 years, but its success was in no way guaranteed. Indeed, its ratification came after significant debate and compromise and a previous governing document (The Articles of Confederation) that remained in effect for only eight years. Debates centered on such issues as the relative power of small and large states and the conflict between the ideal of individual freedom and the reality of slavery. In this section, we discuss the development of the U.S. Constitution, the debates and values that shaped the document and continue to shape our discussions about the appropriate role of government today, the genius of a separation-of-powers system, and the compromises that led to our unique balance of federal and state authority throughout the United States.

Throughout these first three chapters, we emphasize the importance of participation, politics, and compromise in developing and ratifying our founding document. We are a government by the people, but we are people with differing views and opinions on major issues of our day, just as the framers differed in their views of how our government should operate. Many of the issues about which we, as Americans, disagree today, such as health care reform, economic policy, and the United States' involvement in international affairs, mirror the kinds of debates that occurred in the founding era. They concern basic assumptions about the appropriate role of government, individual responsibility, and the degree to which the United States should be isolated from, or involved in, world affairs, including international conflict. As you read through this section, we challenge you to think about the ways you currently participate in our democratic system and perhaps consider a new way in which you might make your voice heard.

New! **Part Openers** identify the **Big Picture** themes and explain the overall **Course Learning Objectives** for each set of chapters. These will give you a better understanding of how to focus your reading and studying for the section, and will help you to integrate concepts across chapters.

New! At the end of the book you'll be able to test your mastery of the course material as a whole through the comprehensive **Course Exam.**

COURSE EXAM

Introduction: Government by the People

1. Who is considered to be the architect of the Constitution?
   a. Thomas Jefferson
   b. George Washington
   c. John Adams
   d. James Madison

2. How did the Mayflower Compact become an important model for government in America?

3. Which philosopher wrote that people once lived in a state of nature but could enter into self-government through a social contract?

   a. David Hume
   b. John Locke
   c. Jean-Jacques Rousseau
   d. Thomas Hobbes

4. For which of the terms is the following definition most appropriate? "The belief that the authority and legitimacy of government is based in the consent and authority of the individuals living within its boundaries."
   a. Pure democracy
   b. Popular sovereignty
   c. Individualism
   d. Freedom of speech

Part I Constitutional Principles

Chapter 1: Constitutional Democracy
Identify the philosophical principles on which our democratic republic is based.

   c. That Marbury was entitled to his commission and Madison should have delivered it to him
   d. That the proper court could issue a writ of mandamus, even against so high an official as the secretary of state

GUIDED LEARNING

American Federalism

The relationship of the national government to the states has been the subject of intense debate since the founding.[1] In 1787, members of what would become the Federalist Party defended the creation of a strong national government, whereas the Antifederalists warned that a strong national government would overshadow the states. The great debate over which level of government best represents the people continues to rage.

State governments have often complained that the national government is either taking over their responsibilities or controlling too much of what they do. Yet, in policy areas such as civil rights, educational opportunities for people with disabilities, and handgun control, the states have been slow to respond to citizens, and the national government has taken steps to deal with these issues.

At the same time, states retain enormous authority under the Constitution to regulate life within their borders. Working with the local governments they create, states police the streets, fight fires, impose their own taxes, create most of the laws that govern their citizens, define the meaning of marriage, set the rules for elections and register voters, run the public schools, and administer most of the programs to help the poor, even when the money for those programs comes from the national government.

In recent years, for example, states have become increasingly involved in regulating cell phone use and texting while driving. As the number of text messages sent in the United States increased from 57.2 billion in 2005 to more than 600 billion in 2008, states became increasingly concerned that texting was an even greater threat to safety than talking on cell phones. According to recent studies, drivers who are texting while driving are significantly more likely to drift out of their lane and look away from the cars in front of them. As a result, they are much more likely to be in life-threatening accidents than drivers who talk on cell phones, who themselves are already more likely to be in life-threatening accidents than those who keep their eyes on the road and hands on the wheel.[2] As with talking on cell phones, younger drivers are much more likely to text than older drivers.

The pressure to pass new laws banning texting while driving increased in 2009, when British television began running a public service advertisement showing the grizzly results of a fictitious accident. The four-minute advertisement is graphic, bloody, and terrifying. It is so disturbing that viewers must be 18 to watch the film on YouTube, although anyone can watch a 2009 *Today Show* story about the film at http://www.youtube.com/watch?v=vOTbAbKoL28.

States are reacting to the threat by passing new laws to ban texting while driving. By the end of 2009, 18 states were already imposing stiff fines for texting while driving under a general ban on distracted driving, and some were stripping driver's licenses from first-time drivers caught texting on the road. Delaware, Indiana, Kansas, Maine, Mississippi, and West Virginia now prohibit texting while driving for drivers with learning permits or probationary licenses, while Missouri prohibits texting while driving for anyone under age 21.

Enforcement is the problem with such bans. Police cannot be everywhere watching every possible violation, and text messaging is particularly hard to spot. This is why state-sponsored education campaigns built around the kind of intense messages in the British television advertisement may be the only way to frighten drivers away from the practice. Under the Constitution, it is mostly up to the states to figure out both what to do about texting while driving and how to enforce the laws they make.

3

CHAPTER OUTLINE & CHAPTER LEARNING OBJECTIVES

Defining Federalism

3.1 Interpret the definitions of federalism, and assess the advantages and disadvantages of the American system of federalism.

The Constitutional Structure of American Federalism

3.2 Differentiate the powers the Constitution provides to national and state governments.

The National Courts and Federalism

3.3 Assess the role of the national courts in defining the relationship between the national and state governments, and evaluate the positions of decentralists and centralists.

The National Budget as a Tool of Federalism

3.4 Analyze the budget as a tool of federalism, and evaluate its impact on state and local governments.

The Politics of Federalism

3.5 Evaluate the current relationship between the national and state governments and the future challenges for federalism.

CHAPTER OUTLINE & CHAPTER LEARNING OBJECTIVES

Defining Federalism

3.1 Interpret the definitions of federalism, and assess the advantages and disadvantages of the American system of federalism.

CHAPTER SUMMARY

3.1 Interpret the definitions of federalism, and assess the advantages and disadvantages of the American system of federalism.

A federal system is one in which the constitution divides powers between the central government and lower-level governments such as states or provinces. But, over time, there has been support for different balances between state and government power such

Each chapter begins with a **Chapter Outline** that breaks down larger subjects into important subparts and previews the topics to come. **Chapter Learning Objectives** help you identify the kinds of learning you will be expected to do with each chapter. We also integrate the Chapter Learning Objectives throughout the chapter and return to them at the end of the chapter in a short **Chapter Summary**. This closely knit pedagogical system helps you navigate through chapter discussions and demonstrate that you have mastered the concepts.

CHAPTER SELF-TEST

3.1 Interpret the definitions of federalism, and assess the advantages and disadvantages of the American system of federalism.

1. Match each term with its appropriate definition:

a. Dual federalism

b. Cooperative federalism

c. Marble cake federalism

i. The power of the national government is limited in favor of the broad powers reserved to the states

ii. All levels of government are engaged in a variety of policy areas, without rigid divisions between governmental jurisdictions

iii. Local governments, state governments, and the national government offer various "packages" of taxes and services, and citizens can choose which package they like best

a. A unitary state

b. A federalist state

c. A confederation

d. A territorial union

3. Federalism affords five be benefit along with a sente

3.2 Differentiate the power provides to national an

4. Determine whether the fo to the national governmen shared by both:

a. Power to establish court

b. Power to tax citizens an

c. Express powers stated i

d. Power to oversee prima education

To assist you in preparing for exams and make your learning experience more effective, we have prepared a **Chapter Self-Test** of multiple choice and essay questions. Before you take an exam, take this practice test to make sure you understand the chapter.

GOVERNMENT...

These features demonstrate how a government of, by, and for the people is put into practice, and highlight the important role of the people in our government.

OF THE PEOPLE
America's Changing Face

In important ways, the people of the United States today are much more diverse than at any previous time. This feature explores the impact of the ever-increasing level of diversity in the American political landscape, including how race and gender are changing the way the American government works. These unique boxes are designed to reflect the concerns and experiences of ethnic and minority groups in American politics.

Of the People
AMERICA'S CHANGING FACE

Where Americans Come From and Where They Live

The United States is a nation of immigrants who have arrived from many parts of the world. Throughout the decades, the portrait of immigrants has been changing from mostly white to mostly minority. In 2008, for example, 38 million Americans, or 12.5 percent, were foreign born, consisting of 16 million naturalized citizens, 10 million long-term visitors, and 12 million undocumented immigrants. The number of unauthorized, or illegal, immigrants has fallen somewhat in recent years due to the economic recession, which has depressed employment opportunities.

Many foreign-born residents live in the nation's largest cities. The New York City–area population includes more than 5 million foreign-born residents, while Los Angeles includes another 4.5 million; Miami, slightly more than 2 million; Chicago, 1.6 million; and San Francisco, 1.3 million. Although the inner cities host a majority of foreign-born residents, there has been recent movement of immigrants to the suburbs and some movement toward certain areas of the country such as the southwest.

The changing face of America brings great diversity in all aspects of life, from schools to farm fields and small businesses. It enriches the quality of life through the mix of new cultures and old and can often be a source of innovation in how the economy operates. Diversity also brings complaints about the national government's effort to close its borders to illegal immigrants. Some groups complain that illegal immigrants take jobs that should go to U.S. citizens, whereas others worry about the costs associated with high-poverty rates. Governments at all levels must reconcile these complaints with our history of welcoming immigrants from all around the world.

QUESTIONS
1. How are foreign-born citizens from different regions of the world different from each other?
2. Why do you think foreign-born citizens tend to live in our nation's largest cities?
3. How do foreign-born citizens contribute to the nation's quality of life?

The Statue of Liberty symbolizes America's long tradition of welcoming immigrants to its shores. The inscription at the base of the statue reads: "Give me your tired, your poor, Your huddled masses yearning to breathe free, The wretched refuse of your teeming shore. Send these, the homeless, tempest-tost to me, I lift my lamp beside the golden door!"

Asia 9%
Other areas 10%
Other Latin America
Europe

Other areas 7%
Europe 13%
Asia 27%
Mexico 30%
Other Latin America 23%

2007

...nographic Trends in Metropolitan America." Washington, D.C.:

Of the People
THE GLOBAL COMMUNITY

Global Opinion on the Role of Government

State and local governments are on the front lines of most programs for helping the needy. They provide much of the money and/or administration for unemployment insurance for the jobless, health care clinics and hospitals for the poor, school lunch programs for hungry children, and homeless shelters. Although many U.S. citizens see poverty firsthand as volunteers for local charities such as food pantries, some have doubts about how much government should do to help poor people who cannot take care of themselves. According to the Pew Global survey, citizens of other nations vary greatly on the question.

These opinions reflect very different social and economic conditions in each country. Japan has a culture of self-reliance that puts the burden on individuals to help themselves, while Nigeria continues to suffer from some of the highest poverty rates in the world. In this regard, U.S. citizens tend to mirror the Japanese—they want government to help the less fortunate but also want the less fortunate to help themselves. As a general conclusion, citizens of wealthier nations think poor people should take advantage of the opportunities that already exist in their economies, whereas citizens of poor nations believe that government should be more aggressive in providing support.

This does not mean wealthier nations are uncaring toward citizens in need, but it does suggest that they sometimes view

of race, gender, or circumstance have the same opportunity to participate in politics, self-government, and the economy. Most Americans want to help the less fortunate, but only when they are truly needy, not when they fail because they will not help themselves.

QUESTIONS
1. What are the advantages of having the government provide services for the poor? What are the advantages of relying on individual citizens to seize opportunities for themselves?
2. Why might more wealthy nations be more likely to believe that individuals ought to take care of themselves and not rely on the state?
3. Which level of government might be most effective in providing services to the poor?

Agreement with the statement:
It is the responsibility of the (state or government) to take care of the very poor people who can't take care of themselves.

70
60
50
40
30
20
10
0
Britain   China   India   Japan   Mexico   Nigeria   United

OF THE PEOPLE
The Global Community

speaks to the increasingly global context of American politics, examining public opinion from around the world on political issues and institutions. The experiences and opinions of people in other countries can both impact and provide insight into our own political system and culture.

...OF, BY, FOR
THE PEOPLE

By the People
MAKING A DIFFERENCE

Improving Health One Playground at a Time

Citizens can make an immediate difference on public policy by simply changing the way they behave. They can stop smoking, change their diets, and get more exercise every day. They can also lobby their local governments to build more sidewalks and bike paths so that other citizens can exercise safely. They can push school boards to remove sugary drinks and junk food from school vending machines and cafeterias, support efforts to bring full-service grocery stores such as Whole Foods to low-income neighborhoods, and even plant community gardens.

Playgrounds are an easy place to start. According to KaBoom!, which is a charitable organization that built more playgrounds in 2010 than any state or city in America, 60 minutes of exercise a day can reduce health care costs dramatically in the future. Yet, there are thousands of "play deserts" across the country, often in dense urban areas, in which there is no space for children to play. You can see what is in your community by visiting maps.kaboom.org.

Students can easily find a "play-space" where a new playground would improve the opportunity for healthy exercise for low-income children. They can then join the KaBoom! building team as volunteers.

CRITICAL THINKING QUESTIONS

1. What can you do today to reduce health care costs in the future?

2. Why are playgrounds so important to communities? And why are there so few playgrounds in low-income communities?

3. What other resources do low-income communities need to be healthier places to live?

First Lady Michelle Obama brings D.C. school children to her organic garden to educate them about locally grown, healthful food.

BY THE PEOPLE
Making A Difference.

Over the course of U.S. history, the people have become more and more involved in their own government. Active citizens have made real progress toward solving problems through involvement in government or public service. As you review this box, consider ways you can make a difference.

For the People
GOVERNMENT'S GREATEST ENDEAVORS

Clean Air and Water

One of the most visible forms of economic regulation involves nearly 60 years of effort to protect the nation's air and water from pollution. Although early laws such as the 1948 Water Pollution Act and the 1963 Clean Air Act established a federal role in protecting the environment, the 1970 Clean Air and 1972 Clean Water Acts provided much of the legal power to make progress in both areas.

During the past 30 years, the levels of most air pollution covered by the Clean Air Act have fallen dramatically as the U.S. Environmental Protection Agency has established ever-tighter rules promoting more efficient automobiles and cleaner-burning fuels. Although it is hard to find a single American city where the air quality has not improved, air pollution continues to spread to rural areas such as national parks where automobile pollution is concentrated as tourists arrive in record numbers.

Similarly, it is hard to find a single body of water or river that is not significantly cleaner because of the Clean Water Act. However,

The federal government is becoming more concerned about the global environment, including the melting of the polar ice caps, which may raise sea levels dramatically throughout the next 100 years.

as the nation has learned more about pollutants such as arsenic, the pressure to improve water quality has increased. The Obama administration has been moving to expand both acts to cover new pollutants, while tightening limits on acceptable levels

of exposure. It is also pushing for legislation to address the rising global temperature.

Despite these successes, there are many challenges ahead in keeping the air and water clean. The 2010 Gulf oil spill is a good example. As technology has become more sophisticated, the oil industry has been drilling at much greater depths below the water and in much more fragile environments. The Gulf oil spill shows how risky such drilling is, especially since the federal rules governing oil exploration were more than 30 years old when the spill occurred.

CRITICAL THINKING QUESTIONS

1. How clean should the air and water be in order to be declared "clean"?

2. How can the federal government protect the environment without hurting industry and creating unemployment when dirty factories must close?

3. What can citizens do to improve the environment through their own actions?

FOR THE PEOPLE
Government's Greatest Endeavors

Throughout the country's history, the government has achieved remarkable goals in the service of the people. This feature explores these important accomplishments, such as building an interstate highway system, fighting discrimination, and eradicating diseases.

RESOURCES IN PRINT AND ONLINE

NAME OF SUPPLEMENT	PRINT	ONLINE	AVAILABLE	DESCRIPTION
MyClassPrep 020511279X		✓	Instructor	This new resource provides a rich database of figures, photos, videos, simulations, activities, and much more that instructors can use to create their own lecture presentation. For more information visit *www.mypoliscilab.com*
Instructor's Manual 0205075673		✓	Instructor	Offers chapter overviews, lecture outlines, teaching ideas, discussion topics, and research activities. All resources hyperlinked for ease of navigation.
Test Bank 0205075568		✓	Instructor	Contains over 100 questions per chapter in multiple-choice, true-false, short answer, and essay format. Questions are tied to text Learning Objectives and have been reviewed for accuracy and effectiveness.
MyTest 0205075606		✓	Instructor	All questions from the Test Bank can be accessed in this flexible, online test generating software.
PowerPoint Presentation 0205075630		✓	Instructor	Slides include a lecture outline of the text, graphics from the book, and quick check questions for immediate feedback on student comprehension.
Transparencies 0205060471		✓	Instructor	These slides contain all maps, figures, and tables found in the text.
Pearson Political Science Video Program	✓		Instructor	Qualified adopters can peruse our list of videos for the American government classroom. Contact your local Pearson representative for more details.
Classroom Response System (CRS) 0205082289		✓	Instructor	A set of lecture questions, organized by American government topics, for use with "clickers" to garner student opinion and assess comprehension.
American Government Study Site		✓	Instructor/ Student	Online package of practice tests, flashcards and more organized by major course topics. Visit *www.pearsonamericangovernment.com*
You Decide! Current Debates in American Politics, 2011 Edition 020511489X	✓		Student	This debate-style reader by John Rourke of the University of Connecticut examines provocative issues in American politics today by presenting contrasting views of key political topics.
Voices of Dissent: Critical Readings in American Politics, Eighth Edition 0205697976	✓		Student	This collection of criticale essays assembled by William Grover of St. Michael's College and Joseph Peschek of Hamline University goes beyond the debate between mainstream liberalism and conservatism to fundamentally challenge the status quo.
Diversity in Contemporary American Politics and Government 0205550363	✓		Student	Edited by David Dulio of Oakland University, Erin E. O'Brien of Kent State University, and John Klemanski of Oakland University, this reader examines the significant role that demographic diversity plays in our political outcomes and policy processes, using both academic and popular sources.
Writing in Political Science, Fourth Edition 0205617360	✓		Student	This guide, written by Diane Schmidt of California State University—Chico, takes students through all aspects of writing in political science step-by-step.
Choices: An American Government Database Reader		✓	Student	This customizable reader allows instructors to choose from a database of over 300 readings to create a reader that exactly matches their course needs. For more information go to *www.pearsoncustom.com/database/choices.html.*
Ten Things That Every American Government Student Should Read 020528969X	✓		Student	Edited by Karen O'Connor of American University. We asked American government instructors across the country to vote for the ten things beyond the text that they believe every student should read and put them in this brief and useful reader. Available at no additional charge when packaged with the text.
American Government: Readings and Cases, Eighteenth Edition 0205697984	✓		Student	Edited by Peter Woll of Brandeis University, this longtime best-selling reader provides a strong, balanced blend of classic readings and cases that illustrate and amplify important concepts in American government, alongside extremely current selections drawn from today's issues and literature. Available at a discount when ordered packaged with this text.
Penguin-Longman Value Bundles	✓		Student	Longman offers 25 Penguin Putnam titles at more than a 60 percent discount when packaged with any Longman text. Go to *www.pearsonhighered.com/penguin* for more information.
Longman State Politics Series	✓		Student	These primers on state and local government and political issues are available at no extra cost when shrink-wrapped with the text. Available for Texas, California, and Georgia.

* Visit the Instructor Resource Center to download supplements at www.pearsonhighered.com/educator

Save Time and Improve Results with

PEARSON
mypoliscilab™

The most popular online teaching/learning solution for American government, MyPoliSciLab moves students from studying and applying concepts to participating in politics. Completely redesigned and now organized by the book's chapters and learning objectives, the new MyPoliSciLab is easier to integrate into any course.

✔ STUDY A flexible learning path in every chapter.

Pre-Tests. See the relevance of politics with these diagnostic assessments and get personalized study plans driven by learning objectives.

Pearson eText. Navigate by learning objective, take notes, print key passages, and more. From page numbers to photos, the eText is identical to the print book.

Flashcards. Learn key terms by word, definition, or learning objective.

Post-Tests. Featuring over 50% new questions, the pre-tests produce updated study plans with follow-up reading, video, and multimedia

Chapter Exams. Also featuring over 50% new questions, test mastery of each chapter using the chapter exams.

✔ APPLY Over 150 videos and multimedia activities.

Video. Analyze current events by watching streaming video from the AP and ABC News.

Simulations. Engage the political process by experiencing how political actors make decisions.

Comparative Exercises. Think critically about how American politics compares with the politics of other countries.

Timelines. Get historical context by following issues that have influenced the evolution of American democracy.

Visual Literacy Exercises. Learn how to interpret political data in figures and tables.

MyPoliSciLibrary. Read full-text primary source documents from the nation's founding to the present.

✔ PARTICIPATE Join the political conversation.

PoliSci News Review. Read analysis of—and comment on—major new stories.

AP Newsfeeds. Follow political news in the United States and around the world.

Weekly Quiz. Master the headlines in this review of current events.

Weekly Poll. Take the poll and see how your politics compare.

Voter Registration. Voting is a right—and a responsibility.

Citizenship Test. See what it takes to become an American citizen.

✔ MANAGE Designed for online or traditional courses.

Grade Tracker. Assign and assess nearly everything in MyPoliSciLab.

Instructor Resources. Download supplements at the Instructor Resource Center.

Sample Syllabus. Get ideas for assigning the book and MyPoliSciLab.

MyClassPrep. Download many of the resources in MyPoliSciLab for lectures.

✔ 📖 👁 ✳ The icons in the book and eText point to resources in MyPoliSciLab.

With proven book-specific and course-specific content, MyPoliSciLab is part of a better teaching/learning system only available from Pearson Longman.

✔ To see demos, read case studies, and learn about training, visit www.mypoliscilab.com.

✔ To order this book with MyPoliSciLab at no extra charge, use ISBN 0-205-07325-5.

✔ Questions? Contact a local Pearson Longman representative: www.pearsonhighered.com/replocator.

 Follow MyPoliSciLab on Twitter.

ACKNOWLEDGMENTS

The writing of this book has profited from the informed, professional, and often critical suggestions of our colleagues around the country. This and previous editions have been considerably improved as a result of reviews by the following individuals, for which we thank them all:

Scott Adler, *University of Colorado*

Wayne Ault, *Southwestern Illinois College–Belleville*

Paul Babbitt, *Southern Arkansas University*

Thomas Baldino, *Wilkes University*

Barry Balleck, *Georgia Southern University*

Robert Ballinger, *South Texas College*

Jodi Balma, *Fullerton College*

Jeff Berry, *South Texas College*

Cynthia Carter, *Florida Community College–Jacksonville, North Campus*

Leonard Champney, *University of Scranton*

Mark Cichock, *University of Texas at Arlington*

Alison Dagnes, *Shippensburg University*

Paul Davis, *Truckee Meadows Community College*

Ron Deaton, *Prince George's Community College*

Robert DeLuna, *St. Philips College*

Anthony Di Giacomo, *Wilmington College*

Richardson Dilworth, *Drexel University*

Rick Donohoe, *Napa Valley College*

Art English, *University of Arkansas, Little Rock*

Alan Fisher, *CSU–Dominguez Hills*

Bruce Franklin, *Cossatot Community College of the University of Arkansas*

Eileen Gage, *Central Florida Community College*

Richard Glenn, *Millersville University*

David Goldberg, *College of DuPage*

Nicholas Gonzalez, *Yuen DeAnza College*

Charles Grapski, *University of Florida*

Billy Hathorn, *Laredo Community College*

Max Hilaire, *Morgan State University*

James Hoefler, *Dickinson College*

Justin Hoggard, *Three Rivers Community College*

Gilbert Kahn, *Kean University*

Rogan Kersh, *Syracuse University*

Todd Kunioka, *CSU–Los Angeles*

La Della Levy, *Foothill College*

Jim Lennertz, *Lafayette College*

John Liscano, *Napa Valley College*

Amy Lovecraft, *University of Alaska–Fairbanks*

Howard Lubert, *James Madison University*

Lowell Markey, *Allegany College of Maryland*

Larry Martinez, *CSU–Long Beach*

Toni Marzotto, *Towson University*

Michael McConachie, *Collin County Community College*

Brian Newman, *Pepperdine University*

Adam Newmark, *Appalachian State University*

Randall Newnham, *Penn State University–Berks*

Keith Nicholls, *University of South Alabama*

Sean Nicholson-Crotty, *University of Missouri–Columbia*

Richard Pacelle, *Georgia Southern University*

William Parente, *University of Scranton*

Ryan Peterson, *College of the Redwoods*

Robert Rigney, *Valencia Community College–Osceola Campus*

Bren Romney, *Vernon College*

Jack Ruebensaal, *West Los Angeles College*

Bhim Sandhu, *West Chester University*

Gib Sansing, *Drexel University*

Colleen Shogan, *George Mason University*

Tom Simpson, *Missouri Southern*

Linda Simmons, *Northern Virginia Community College–Manassas Campus*

Dan Smith, *Northwest Missouri State University*

Jay Stevens, *CSU–Long Beach*

Lawrence Sullivan, *Adelphi University*

Halper Thomas, *CUNY–Baruch*

Jose Vadi, *CSU–Pomona*

Avery Ward, *Harford Community College*

Shirley Warshaw, *Gettysburg University*

Ife Williams, *Delaware County Community College*

Margie Williams, *James Madison University*

Christy Woodward-Kaupert, *San Antonio College*

Chris Wright, *University of Arkansas–Monticello*

Martha Burns, *Tidewater Community College*

David Caffey, *Clovis Community College*

Ann Clemmer, *University of Arkansas at Little Rock*

Ellen Creagar, *Eastern Wyoming College*

Robert Locander, *Lone Star College North Harris*

Sean Mattie, *Clayton State University*

Jerry Murtagh, *Fort Valley State University*

Tally Payne, *Casper College*

Mark Peplowski, *College of Southern Nevada*

Geoff Peterson, *University of Wisconsin–Eau Claire*

Dennis Pope, *Kean University*

Jonathan Reisman, *University of Maine at Machias*

Sean Savage, *Saint Mary's College*

Carolyn Schmidt, *Florida Community College Jacksonville*

Kevin Sims, *Cedarville University*

Melanie Young, *University of Nevada Las Vegas*

Government by the People began in 1948 when two young assistant professors, James MacGregor Burns of Williams College and Jack W. Peltason of Smith College, decided to partner and write an American government text. Their first edition had a publication date of 1952. Their aim was to produce a well-written, accessible, and balanced look at government and politics in the United States. As authors have become a part of this book, they have embraced that objective. Tom Cronin of Colorado College and David O'Brien of the University of Virginia have been coauthors and made important contributions to the book. As the current authors of *Government by the People*, we are grateful for the legacy we have inherited.

Writing the book requires teamwork—first among the coauthors who converse often about the broad themes, features, and focus of the book and who read and rewrite each other's drafts; then with our research assistants, who track down loose ends and give us the perspective of current students; and finally with the editors and other professionals at Pearson Longman. Important to each revision are the detailed reviews by teachers and researchers, who provide concrete suggestions on how to improve the book. Our revision of the chapters on state and local government especially benefited from the tremendous input of Tom Carsey at the University of North Carolina. We are grateful to all who helped with this edition.

Research assistants for the current edition of *Government by the People* are Rebecca Eaton, Jeff Edwards, Bret Evans, Maren Gardiner, Eric Hoyt, David Lassen, Virginia Maynes, Haley McCormick, Kristen Orr, and Case Wade of Brigham Young University.

We also express appreciation to the superb team at Longman, especially Political Science Editor Eric Stano, who has been wonderfully supportive. Donna Garnier, our Development Editor, kept us on schedule and added helpful insights all along the way. We also appreciate the work Bob Ginsberg for production, Heather Johnson at Elm Street Publishing for page layout, Teri Stratford for photo research, and John Callahan for cover design.

We also want to thank you, the professors and students who use our book, and who send us letters and email messages with suggestions for improving *Government by the People*. Please write us in care of the Political Science Editor at Pearson Longman, 51 Madison Avenue, New York, NY 10010, or contact us directly:

David B. Magleby Distinguished Professor of Political Science and Dean of FHSS, Brigham Young University, Provo, UT 84602, david_magleby@byu.edu

Paul C. Light Paulette Goddard Professor of Public Service at New York University and Douglas Dillon Senior Fellow at the Brookings Institution, pcl226@nyu.edu

Christine L. Nemacheck Alumni Memorial Distinguished Associate Professor of Government at The College of William & Mary, Williamsburg, VA 23187, clnema@wm.edu

ABOUT THE AUTHORS

David B. Magleby is nationally recognized for his expertise on direct democracy, voting behavior, and campaign finance. He received his B.A. from the University of Utah and his Ph.D. from the University of California, Berkeley. Currently Distinguished Professor of Political Science, Senior Research Fellow at the Center for the Study of Elections and Democracy, and Dean of the College of Family, Home and Social Sciences at Brigham Young University (BYU), Professor Magleby has also taught at the University of California, Santa Cruz, and the University of Virginia. He and his students have conducted statewide polls in Virginia and Utah. For the 1998–2008 elections, he has directed national studies of campaign finance and campaign communications in competitive federal election environments involving a consortium of academics from nearly 80 universities and colleges in 38 states. This research is summarized in seven edited books. In addition, he is coeditor of a long-standing series of books on financing federal elections. In partnership with colleagues, he has been studying the implementation of new voting technology, work funded in part by the National Science Foundation. He has been a Fulbright Scholar at Oxford University and a past president of Pi Sigma Alpha, the national political science honor society. Magleby is the recipient of many teaching awards, including the 1990 Utah Professor of the Year Award from the Council for the Advancement and Support of Education and the Carnegie Foundation, the 2001 Rowman & Littlefield Award for Innovative Teaching in Political Science, and several department and university awards. At BYU, he served as chair of the Political Science Department before being named dean. He is married to Linda Waters Magleby. They are the parents of four and grandparents of one.

Paul C. Light is the Paulette Goddard Professor of Public Service at New York University's Wagner School of Public Service. He received his B.A. from Macalester College and his Ph.D. from the University of Michigan. Professor Light has a wide-ranging career in both academia and government. He has worked on Capitol Hill as a senior committee staffer in the U.S. Senate and as an American Political Science Association Congressional Fellow in the U.S. House of Representatives. He has taught at the University of Virginia, University of Pennsylvania, and Harvard University's John F. Kennedy School of Government. He has also served as a senior adviser to several national commissions on federal, state, and local public service. He is the author of 15 books on government, public service, and public policy. Light's current research focuses on government reform, Congress, the presidency, and social entrepreneurship. His latest books are *A Government Ill Executed* (Harvard University Press, 2008) and *The Search for Social Entrepreneurship* (Brookings Institution Press, 2008). He was the founding director of the Brookings Institution's Center for Public Service and continues his research on how to invite Americans to serve their communities through public service. His work has been funded by the Douglas Dillon Foundation, the Pew Charitable Trusts, and the David and Lucille Packard Foundation, among many others. He is also an expert on preparing government, charitable organizations, and private corporations for natural and human-made disasters, and he was a recognized leader in the response to Hurricane Katrina in 2005. He has testified before Congress more than a dozen times in the last five years.

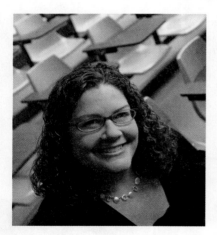

Christine L. Nemacheck is the Alumni Memorial Distinguished Associate Professor of Government at The College of William & Mary. She received her B.A. from the University of Michigan and her Ph.D. from The George Washington University. Professor Nemacheck has previously taught at Iowa State University. Her research focuses on judicial selection and the role of the courts in a separation-of-powers system. Her book, *Strategic Selection: Presidential Selection of Supreme Court Justices from Herbert Hoover through George W. Bush* was published in 2007. Other work on judicial selection has appeared in political science and law review journals. Her research, which is primarily archival, has been funded by numerous grants and awards from presidential library foundations. Nemacheck has received a number of awards for her teaching and research activity, including the Alumni Fellowship Award for excellence in teaching at The College of William & Mary, a Coco Faculty Fellowship, and she was named a Dean's Distinguished Lecturer in 2010. She is the coeditor of the Pi Sigma Alpha Undergraduate Journal of Politics, which will be housed at The College of William & Mary through the spring 2013 semester.

GOVERNMENT
BY THE PEOPLE

INTRODUCTION

Government by the People

In 1620, the *Mayflower*, with 102 passengers, including 19 adult women and 33 children, set sail for America. Earlier settlements like Jamestown had not initially included women and children, but the Pilgrim's colony at Plymouth would. Before embarking, the Pilgrims sought approval from the Virginia Company to establish a new colony and were granted an area of land, or patent, located south of the 41st parallel, near the Hudson River. Because of poor winds and a near shipwreck on shoals near Cape Cod, they came ashore a good deal north of their planned landing place. There they found an abandoned Native American settlement named Patuxet, whose inhabitants had died in 1617 from illnesses like small pox and yellow fever, which were attributed to contact with earlier European fishermen, traders, and explorers.

Because the terms of their patent did not apply to the place they decided to establish their settlement, there were concerns that some of the group, not feeling bound by their prior agreement, would leave. A contemporary account of the Pilgrims recorded, "This day, before we came to harbour, it was thought good there should be an association and agreement, that we should combine together in one body, and to submit to such government and governors as we should by common consent agree to make and choose."[1] On November 11, 1620, 41 of the male passengers on the *Mayflower* signed a document pledging to create a system of self-governance.[2] They stated:

> Having undertaken, for the glory of God, and advancement of the Christian faith and honor of our King and country, a voyage to plant the first colony in the northern parts of Virginia, do by these presents, solemnly and mutually in the presence of God, and one of another, covenant and combine ourselves together into a civil body politic, for our better ordering and preservation and furtherance of the ends aforesaid; and by virtue hereof to enact, constitute and frame such just and equal laws, ordinances, acts, constitutions and offices, from time to time, as shall be thought most meet and convenient and for the general good of the colony; unto which we promise all due submission and obedience.

This document, called the **Mayflower Compact,** is an enduring example of self-government. The compact was intended to unify the group for the arduous tasks before them of building a settlement, planting and harvesting crops so that they could survive the next winter, and defending themselves against potentially hostile Native Americans.[3] Although some historians view the compact as more about surviving than about self-government,[4] this voluntary action by the Pilgrims became an important model. For example, John Quincy Adams (president from 1825–1829) reflected that the signing was "perhaps the only instance in human history, of that positive, original social compact, which speculative philosophers have imagined as the only legitimate source of government. Here was a unanimous and personal assent by all the individuals in a community, to the association by which they became a nation."[5]

Although the debate about what motivated the signers of the Mayflower Compact continues, what may be more important is the fact that it became an important example to later settlers and revolutionaries of self-government and provided what some have called the "seeds" of later American constitutional government.[6] Scholar Louis Hartz described "the concept of a written constitution" as "the end product of a chain of historical experiences that went back to the Mayflower Compact and the Plantation Covenants of the New England towns."[7] American colonists celebrated Forefathers' Day, commemorating the landing of the Pilgrims at Plymouth, which came to be seen, in the words of one scholar, as "part of the repudiation of English Domination and as the inauguration of indigenous American government."[8] In the 1830s and 1840s, the Whig Party praised the Mayflower Compact "as a milestone in the growth of social order and cohesion."[9]

Mayflower Compact
A governing document created by the members of the *Mayflower* to temporarily establish self-government in the Mayflower Colonies in America.

3

The Idea of America

This book is about the continuing great experiment in self-government launched more than two centuries ago. We will examine the historical context and current practices of the institutions and political processes of American government. As the title to our book signals, a focus of the book is the role played by the people in their government. The idea of government by the people predated the Revolutionary War. It was important to the Pilgrims aboard the *Mayflower* who wrote and signed the Mayflower Compact, committing to a system of democratic government to promote the "general good of the colony."[10] Those who later signed the Declaration of Independence perceived government to derive its powers from the people, and when government violated that public trust, it was a legitimate cause for revolution.

In many respects, the early experience of the Pilgrims mirrors a set of enduring elements that form what we might call the idea of America. These elements include individualism, a desire for self-government, the pursuit of opportunity and a commitment to equality of opportunity, a commitment to freedom of religion, and the importance of economic liberty. A list of concepts like this was identified by Alexis de Tocqueville, the French aristocrat who visited the United States in the 1820s and whose book *Democracy in America* (written for French readers and published in 1835) remains insightful. Other writers more recently have identified a similar set of ideas as the enduring elements of the American political tradition.[11] We will focus here on five core values: individualism, popular sovereignty, equality of opportunity, freedom of religion, and economic liberty. We discuss these briefly here and then return to them again in Chapter 4.

Individualism

Although the term **individualism** was first used by de Tocqueville to describe the American focus on the importance of the individual in comparison to a focus on a group, society, or nation, the concept of individualism is much older. Individualism emphasizes the importance of individual rights, worth, freedom, and well-being. The idea of individualism is central to democracy, with the idea that each person has one vote, and to economic liberty, in which individuals may own property. In the United States, individual economic freedoms are protected, as are political freedoms. Consider the rhetoric of contemporary political campaigns and the arguments politicians make, which often center on individualistic themes.

Popular Sovereignty

As illustrated by the examples of the Mayflower Compact, the Declaration of Independence, and the Constitution, central to the American view of politics is the idea that the ultimate political authority rests with the people and that the people can create, alter, or abolish government. This idea is sometimes called **popular sovereignty.** On some occasions, as with the Mayflower Compact and Declaration of Independence, popular sovereignty is exercised by the people directly. More often, it is exercised through representative institutions, such as Congress or local decision-making bodies whose members are elected by the people. But self-government is practiced whenever people write, amend, or revise local, state, or federal constitutions or laws. Popular sovereignty is a political extension of individualism. The notion that individuals have rights, including most fundamentally political and economic rights, undergirds popular sovereignty.

Implicit in the idea of popular sovereignty is the idea of individual responsibility for self-government. If individuals in a constitutional democracy will not exercise self-government through participation in the governing process, the system ceases to function. Also important to American political thought is the enduring suspicion of political power, especially concentrated political power—a suspicion that should motivate but sometimes hinders civic involvement. As we frequently explore in this book, government

individualism
The moral, political, and ethical philosophy of life that emphasizes individual rights, effort, and independence.

popular sovereignty
The belief that the authority and legitimacy of government is based in the consent and authority of the individuals living within its boundaries.

by the people is both a right and a responsibility. As we will also show, Americans value popular rule while being critical of government.

Equality of Opportunity

In the lexicon of core American values, equality is important, but its meaning has changed dramatically over time and means different things to different people. In the early twenty-first century, political scientist Jack Citrin wrote: "If liberty is the most basic American political value, equality is a close second."[12] Yet the signers of the Mayflower Compact, Declaration of Independence, and Constitution did not include any women or persons of color—a contradiction of modern ideas about equality. And in what aspects can all persons be considered "equal," when individuals differ widely in such things as aptitude, motivation, and inheritance? A more functional objective for American government is **equality of opportunity:** all individuals regardless of race, gender, or circumstance have the same opportunity to participate in politics, self-government, and the economy.

Freedom of Religion

The framers understood the importance of freedom of conscience and freedom of worship to a free society. **Freedom of religion** has always been important to a large proportion of Americans. Indeed, as one author has noted, "American political culture celebrates freedom of religion, not freedom from religion."[13] Of course, freedom of religion does not extend to religious practice that is contrary to public peace or morality, or that causes harm to others. Central to the view of the founders was the importance of a separation of church and state, which requires, in part, that there be no religious test for public office, meaning that an individual need not belong to a particular church in order to hold office and, at least since passage of the Constitution, that there be no national church. The example of the Mayflower Pilgrims is informative, as the Separatists had fled England rather than accept King James's official state church.

Economic Liberty

The economic application of the idea of individualism is **economic liberty.** A driving force for much of the immigration to the United States from the Mayflower Pilgrims to the present day has been the pursuit of economic opportunity and the idea that, in this new world, individuals can shape their own destinies. Given the remnants of feudalism still existing in sixteenth- and seventeenth-century Europe, the possibility of owning property in the new world meant freedom and wealth for individuals. Property rights were also important to America's founders, as was protecting the functioning of a free market. To them, economic liberty came as a reaction to tariffs as well as trade and production restrictions imposed by governments under a system called mercantilism. The American Revolution was a reaction against these practices in favor of economic liberty for individuals and a view that government should have limited involvement in regulating the economy.

Economic liberty has been possible in the United States in part because of our initiative but also because of our resource advantages. As Benjamin Freedman has written, "There are many countries with abundant natural resources, and other physical advantages, but among large nations, only in America have they been used to produce such a consistently high level of income, and with consistent economic growth over time."[14] Today, government plays a larger role in economic affairs, but the idea that individuals are free to pursue their own self-interest and be rewarded for their innovations remains central.

Although the ideals of individualism, self-government, equality of opportunity, freedom of religion, and economic liberty were articulated early in our nation's history and have endured, the extent to which they have been put into practice has varied over time. Take the concept of equality, for example, which was one of the "self-evident" truths listed by Thomas Jefferson in the Declaration of Independence. The actual

equality of opportunity
All individuals, regardless of race, gender, or circumstance have the opportunity to participate in politics, self-government, and the economy.

freedom of religion
The belief that individuals living in a society should be free to exercise their personal religious convictions without government restrictions.

economic liberty
The belief that individuals should be allowed to pursue their economic self-interest without government restrictions.

The pilgrims' experiment in self-government encompassed many of the same values of our government today. ■ *What can you infer from the painting and from your knowledge of the conditions when the Pilgrims arrived about the importance of individual participation in government and society in early America?*

government
The processes and institutions through which binding decisions are made for a society.

politics
The process by which decisions are made and carried out within and among nations, groups, and individuals.

politician
An individual who participates in politics and government, often in the service of a group or political community.

political science
An academic discipline that studies the theory and practice of politics and government. It is one of the social sciences that use data and methods that overlap with Anthropology, Economics, Geography, History, Psychology, and Sociology.

practice of Jefferson and other founders in owning slaves was contrary to equality. Even after slavery was abolished, state-sanctioned discrimination against blacks continued and was clearly inegalitarian.[15] Although our constitutional democracy is imperfect in attaining the full measure of any of these values, Americans were path breakers in their effort to move toward them. As we examine American government in practice over time and especially today, these values remain important to contextualizing government and politics in the United States.

A Distinctive Constitutional Democracy

Before moving ahead, we need to define some of the basic terms we will be using throughout this book. **Government** refers to the procedures and institutions (such as elections, courts, and legislatures) by which a people govern and rule themselves. **Politics,** at least in our system of government, is the process by which people decide who shall govern and what policies shall be adopted. Such processes invariably require discussions, debates, and compromises about tactics and goals. **Politicians** are the people who fulfill the tasks of overseeing and directing a government. Some politicians—legislators, mayors, and presidents—come to office through election. Nonelected politicians may be political party officials or aides, advisers, or consultants to elected officials. **Political science** is the study of the principles, procedures, and structures of government and the analysis of political ideas, institutions, behaviors, and practices.

As we demonstrate throughout the book, an understanding of history is important to putting government and politics in context. That was also the case with the establishment of our Constitutional structure. Many of those who led the American Revolution and wrote the U.S. Constitution were familiar with the writings of thinkers like Locke, Hobbes, Hume, and Rousseau, who had written in the century or so before the 1770s, as well as with philosophers who wrote centuries earlier, like Aristotle.[16] These influential thinkers, like the founders themselves, relied on their understanding and reading of history, their observation of human behavior, and what they called "right reason," which essentially meant that an argument or idea seemed sensible.[17]

Out of this intellectual tradition had emerged a view that people have inherent rights. John Locke, the English philosopher, wrote that people were once free, living in what he called the "state of nature."[18] In this condition, according to Locke, they enjoyed rights to life, liberty, and property, and they could freely enter into what he called a "social contract" to govern themselves.[19] Louis Hartz explained, nearly a half-century ago, the appeal of Locke in the new world: "In America, one not only found a society sufficiently fluid to give a touch of meaning to the individualist norms of Locke, but one also found letter-perfect replicas of the very image he used. There was a frontier that was a veritable state of nature. There were agreements, such as the Mayflower Compact, that were veritable social contracts."[20] Indeed, Locke's ideas about inherent rights and the necessity of popular consent to government are echoed in Jefferson's words in the Declaration of Independence.[21]

The philosophical debate over human tendencies as either virtuous or evil was also important to the thinking of our republic's founders. Predisposition to do evil included such vices as pride, greed, superstition, injustice, bigotry, betrayal, and overweening self-interest. David Hume, the Scottish philosopher, warned that people following their self-interest could infringe on the rights and liberties of others. But Hume did not always see self-interest as a danger. Guided by law, self-interest could motivate work and innovation.[22] Designing a government that would not fall prey to humans' worst tendencies and might direct these tendencies to productive ends was thus a major aim of the Constitution. The founders were also influenced by philosophers like Jean-Jacques

Rousseau, who saw people as not inherently inclined to evil and as possessing a drive for public service. For Rousseau, citizen involvement was essential. He wrote, "As soon as any man says of the affairs of the State, 'What does it matter to me?' the State may be given up for lost."[23]

Unlike the governing systems in Europe, which grew out of centuries of feudalism, government as it developed in America was based on the idea that individuals have rights distinct from those granted by any government. Following Locke, the Constitution's founders believed that government derived its powers from the consent of the governed; in other words, individuals can agree to form a government with powers specified by those individuals. This type of agreement, sometimes called a **social contract**, had appeared in informal contexts throughout the world for centuries, and it was especially attributed to ancient Rome. At the same time, the American Revolution, the Constitution, and early governing conditions were something new in world history. As Peter Shuck and James Wilson have noted, "nobody then knew what it meant to live in a country where equality of condition was so widespread and where the common people actually ruled themselves."[24] A central and recurrent element of the idea of America then is that government by the people is preferred to other forms of government.

Understanding and applying lessons from history were important to those who signed the Declaration of Independence in 1776 and designed our distinctive Constitution in 1787. They were aware of the Mayflower Compact. More broadly, they knew of the successes and failures of past experiments with self-government, and they were well versed in political ideas. In today's world, as our generation works to sustain constitutional democracy, an understanding of history and politics is also critical.

The founders also shared a common perspective on the rule of law through courts and an idea of representation based on their background as Englishmen. The lack of responsiveness of Parliament and the King to their frequent petitions reinforced their sense that they needed to "throw off such Government, and to provide new Guards for their future security."[25] What the founders prescribed as *the structure of government* was written into the Constitution, and the *protections from government* became the Bill of Rights. The need for both structure and protection was reinforced by their common experience with monarchy under King George III and with ineffective governments under the Articles of Confederation.

The designers of our constitution were at least as unified in what they did *not* want to include in their design of government as in what they did want to include. They did not want to have a monarchy, they did not want to create a government so strong that it could threaten rights, and they did not want to establish a state religion. Nor did they wish to foster mob rule by providing too great a provision for democracy.

For James Madison and others who participated in creating our constitutional democracy, there were predictable patterns to human history and human nature. Taking into account these regularities was something Madison described as political science. But shouldn't science apply to things like gravity, motion, and molecules, and not to something like politics? You may be asked this question if you decide to major in political science.

Educated men of the period considered science, as well as politics and economics, within their sphere of knowledge. Influenced by Isaac Newton's discoveries, they were fascinated by machinery that operated by balancing forces one against another. The founders thought the Constitution should embody the principles of such machines, with each part of government exerting force upon the others. Newton's success in describing physical laws reinforced the founders' belief that they could identify, understand, and harness forces in human nature.

In a famous essay now known as Federalist Paper #10, Madison claims it is possible and important to understand and predict human nature because out of that understanding came ways to limit the negative tendencies of people. Madison identified the following aspects of human nature that need to be considered in designing a government: "zeal for different opinions,…attachment to different leaders,…[and the] propensity of mankind to fall into mutual animosities most commonly concerning the unequal distribution of property."[26] Madison, borrowing from Locke, connected understanding of human nature to constitutional structure, as follows: "If men were angels, no government would be necessary. If angels were to govern men, neither external nor internal controls on government would be

social contract
An agreement whereby individuals voluntarily commit to establish a government that will protect the common interests of all.

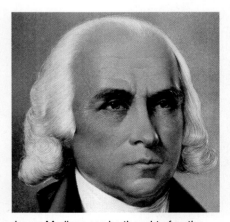

James Madison can be thought of as the architect of the constitution. He was its principle author and one of its strongest supporters as a contributing author of the *Federalist Papers*.

necessary."[27] In other words, human nature as Madison understood it required some type of government to regulate citizens' behavior and some type of control over that government to regulate citizen-politicians' behavior, as well.

Madison's idea of harnessing human capacity for evil found fullest expression in the provisions for dividing powers among the branches. The president cannot sit in the legislature; a senator cannot also be in the House. The president shares in legislation with the power to sign and veto bills. Congress shares in the executive power by providing all the money, but the spending is done by the executive branch. The president has the power to conduct foreign relations and wage war, but Congress must ratify treaties and provide declarations of war. Most appointments are made by the president, but Congress must concur. The judiciary can check both of the other branches by determining if executive or legislative actions are consistent with the Constitution. The executive has the power to appoint federal court judges and the Senate must consent to these appointments. Each branch thus is given ways to check the others. For Madison, there was a science of politics that included understanding human nature and designing constitutional mechanisms to channel power to good, and not bad, ends.

American Government Today

As important as the study of government and politics was to the founders, it is just as relevant today. Government and politics matter. Consider such areas as the economy, educational opportunity, and public health. One of the lessons from the government's poor response to Hurricane Katrina in 2005 is that in such times we all greatly depend on government to provide safety and security. Without that security, we face a world of anarchy. Even though government can fail, as it did in its response to Katrina, it can also succeed, as it did when the NASA space program placed astronauts on the moon, polio was largely eradicated, and the cold war was peacefully resolved. As referenced earlier, we title this book *Government by the People* because we want to emphasize the important role people play in our constitutional democracy. Understanding American politics and government must include an appreciation of the people, their similarities and differences, their beliefs and attitudes, and their behaviors. Examining such aspects of our population as race, ethnicity, gender, age, religion, income, and region helps us see how the diversity of our country is important politically.

Constitutional democracy—the kind we have in the United States—is exceedingly hard to achieve, equally hard to sustain, and often hard to understand. Our political history has been an evolution toward an enlarged role for citizens and voters. Citizens have more rights and political opportunities in 2011 and 2012 than they had in 1800 or 1900. The framers of our Constitution warned that we must be vigilant in safeguarding our rights, liberties, and political institutions. But to do this, we must understand these institutions and the forces that have shaped them.

Government Of, By, and For the People

Our emphasis on the important role people play in our constitutional democracy extends not only through the text but also through the features. The features—titled Of, By, and For the People—are intended to help you understand how the theory of self-government is put into practice and see the important role that you as a citizen play in this country's present and future.

This title of this book and these features are drawn from President Abraham Lincoln's famous Gettysburg Address in 1863. In his brief but powerful speech, Lincoln reminded Americans of their heritage of self-government. He began by referring to the Declaration of Independence and the enduring commitment to the principle of human equality, and he closed with the admonition that those who had died, giving "the last full measure of devotion" to preserve the United States, should lead the living to resolve "that government of the people, by the people, for the people, shall not perish from the earth." We use these

Of the People

From the Mayflower to Today

Understanding how the American population has changed is examined in boxes in each chapter, which we have labeled "Of the People: America's Changing Face." From the initial landing of the *Mayflower* to today, the people who make up America have changed, and these changes have affected government and society in the United States.

Of the 102 Pilgrims who started the Plymouth settlement, 52 were male, and in other early settlements like Jamestown the settlers were all male. Yet by the time the first census of the United States was conducted in 1790, the population was nearly equally divided between men and women, and has remained so since.

All of those on the Mayflower were European Caucasian, but the population of the area was largely native peoples. As many as 72,000 native people occupied New England in 1610, but by the time the Pilgrims arrived in 1621 that number had been reduced by epidemics.* The population of what became the United States grew more racially diverse with the arrival of African slaves in Jamestown in 1619. The number of slaves of African descent increased to more than 1.2 million in the 1810 census, two years after Congress banned the practice of importing slaves in 1808.†

The average age of the Mayflower settlers was 32. In the 1800 census of the United States, the median age was 16. Over time the median age rose to 22.9 in 1900 and 35.8 in 2000. The rise in median age over the course of U.S. history is due to advances in medical care, better hygiene, and nutrition.

Throughout the book we will examine how the changing population in the United States has affected our politics and government. It is important to understand the changing characteristics of the people in a government by the people.

CRITICAL THINKING QUESTIONS

1. Why might the age, race or gender of people be important to a study of government?

2. What are some of the implications of an increasingly older population?

3. What are the implications of America becoming more diverse?

---

* Sherburne F. Cook, "The Indian Population of New England in the Seventeenth Century," *Publications in Anthropology,* 12 (1976):84.

† James A. McMillon. *The Final Victims: Foreign Slave Trade to North America, 1783–1910.* University of South Carolina Press. (Columbia: South Carolina 2004), 56.

---

three important ways in which Lincoln defined American government as grounded in "the people" to drive our features.

Of the People

One interpretation of the phrase "of the people" is that our nation by design does not have a monarchy. The phrase answers the question "Who governs?" with the answer, "The people do." Political leaders in the United States are not born into positions of power, as political leaders have been for much of history. Moreover, as we explore in this book, "the people" have changed throughout the course of U.S. history and have come to be a more inclusive group. In each chapter, we explore the implications of the changing face of America for our experiment in self-government through the feature *Of the People: America's Changing Face* (see box above).

Although the subject of this book is government and politics in the United States of America, there are important lessons to be learned from how other societies are governed as well. Given our emphasis on the role of people in government, each chapter also includes a comparison of how people in different countries and cultures view the same question or challenge through the feature *Of the People: The Global Community* (see the box on the following page).

By the People

The phrase "government by the people" communicates that people are active or engaged in their self-government. Throughout the course of U.S. history, the people have become more and more involved in their own government. For example, U.S. senators, once elected by state legislatures, are now elected by the people. The right to vote has been dramatically expanded over time. The 2008 elections demonstrated the power of the Internet as a means to participate in politics. In addition to being active citizens, individuals can and do make a difference in their communities in

Of the People

Opinion of the United States

As Americans, we assume the world has a high regard for our country and what it stands for. Our history of freedom and our sustained constitutional democracy stand out in world history. But how do the people in other countries actually view the United States? The Pew Global Attitudes survey included a question that asked respondents the following question: "Please tell me if you have a very favorable, somewhat favorable, somewhat unfavorable, or very unfavorable opinion of the United States."

In the year following the election of Barack Obama, people's views toward the United States became more favorable in all of the countries in our sample. The most dramatic change in views toward the United States occurred in Mexico, which had a 22 percentage point rise in the proportion seeing the United States very or somewhat favorably in 2009 as compared to 2008. In the United States, the increase was insignificant, indicating that who currently occupies the White House matters less to Americans' views of their own country than to those in other countries.

The people of the world had a great deal of interest in the 2008 U.S. presidential election. The initial impact of that election and President Obama's early speeches and actions appears to have had a positive impact on how the world sees the United States. Over time, especially as President Obama and his administration make unpopular decisions, these numbers will likely drop.

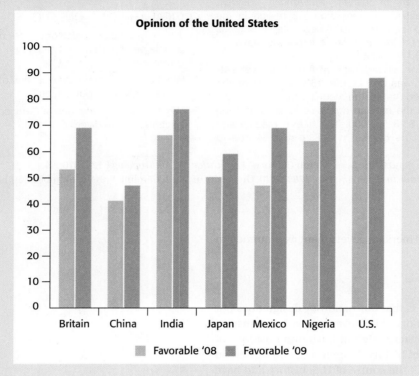

Opinion of the United States

Legend: Favorable '08, Favorable '09

Britain, China, India, Japan, Mexico, Nigeria, U.S.

CRITICAL THINKING QUESTIONS

1. Why is it important how the people in other countries view the United States?

2. Why do you think residents of China have the least favorable views toward the United States of our sample countries?

3. What about the election of Barack Obama in 2008 may explain why people in the nations presented here now view the United States more favorably?

addressing important problems. Seemingly small acts by individuals, many of them young people, have the potential to make real progress toward solving problems. In each chapter of the book, we include an example of how people are making a difference through involvement in government or public service. As you review this *By the People: Making a Difference* feature (see the box on the following page) in each chapter, consider ways you can make a difference.

For the People

Abraham Lincoln's final way of linking the people to their government implies that government exists for the people—and that what is good for the people should guide the government's aims. In the case of the United States, the Constitution's preamble spells out the government's assignments: to achieve justice, domestic tranquility, security ("common defense"), and general welfare. Throughout the country's history, the government has achieved remarkable goals in the service of the people, such as building an interstate highway system, promoting space exploration, fighting discrimination in public spaces and the workplace, and reducing the crime rate. In each chapter, we explore the

By the People

MAKING A DIFFERENCE

Greg Mortenson and Girls' Schools in Pakistan and Afghanistan

While recovering from an unsuccessful attempt to climb K2, the world's second-highest mountain, 36-year-old Greg Mortenson lived in Korphe, a small village in Pakistan. The people of the village could not afford to pay a school teacher's salary (valued at US $1 a day), so children met on their own and, lacking school supplies, wrote

with sticks in the dirt. Mortenson resolved to build a school for the people in Korphe.

Mortenson began his fundraising for the school by writing nearly 600 letters to American celebrities and business leaders. Only NBC's Tom Brokaw responded, sending a check for $100. It was a group of elementary school children in River Falls, Wisconsin—donating $623.40 in pennies—who helped Mortenson find a way to raise the money needed. That early donation led to many others, and Mortenson later founded Pennies for Peace, a program that raises money from school children to build schools in remote areas of Afghanistan and Pakistan.* So far, Mortenson has established 78 schools, and all of his schools offer education to girls as well as boys.

A striking aspect of Greg Mortenson's story is the difference an individual can make in the lives of others and in influencing the conversation about public policy. The Pennies for Peace website (http://www.penniesforpeace.org/) provides resources for setting up programs at local schools that would not only raise money but would also help American students broaden their cultural horizons and learn about their capacities as philanthropists. Visit the Central Asia Institute (CAI) Web site for additional ideas on how to help fundraise in your own community: www.ikat.org.

CRITICAL THINKING QUESTIONS

1. How did Mortenson get the idea to raise money for girls' schools in Pakistan and Afghanistan?

2. Might the "Pennies for Peace" idea be a model to raise money for other important needs?

3. Why would educating girls and boys in villages in Pakistan and Afghanistan foster a more peaceful society?

* Pennies for Peace, http://www.penniesforpeace.org/ (accessed November 30, 2009).

important accomplishments of government in the service of its citizens through the feature *For the People: Government's Greatest Endeavors* (see the box on the following page).

Learning Objectives

While we hope the thematic "Of, By, and For the People" approach shows you the importance of our constitutional democracy, we also employ a Learning Objectives framework to help you use this book to succeed in the course. Using the Course and Chapter Objectives can help you to systematically build your understanding of the fundamentals and develop the skills necessary to analyze, evaluate, and engage in the study of political science.

What are Learning Objectives? Your professor, the department, and the college faculty will often have identified key learning objectives as the important concepts, skills, motivation, and knowledge you should have acquired through completion of the course, major, or in your undergraduate education. Some examples of Learning Objectives for the Introduction to American Government course include understanding the historical foundations and development of American government, being able to identify and discuss the governmental and political institutions, and being able to think critically and analytically about important issues.

In this textbook, we list and explain these most common **Course Learning Objectives** at the beginning of each part of the book (for example, the Political Process). There, you will find a brief part opener in which we identify the **Big Picture** themes and explain the Course Learning Objectives for this part (see sample). This will give you a better understanding of how to focus your reading and studying for that section and will help you integrate information across chapters. Keep these Course Learning Objectives in mind as you make your way through the chapters in a section, and revisit them at the end of a section to make sure you

For the People

GOVERNMENT'S GREATEST ENDEAVORS

Making Government by the People More of a Reality

Moving from the idea that the people could govern themselves—as expressed by the Mayflower Pilgrims and the early colonists in North America—to actually accomplishing that ambition in the form of a government is a theme we will return to again and again in this book. Take the simple act of voting, for example. Owning property was commonly required of those who voted in the early years of the United States. By the election of Andrew Jackson in 1828, the right to vote had been extended to white males, without regards to owning property, at least in federal elections.

Later, as a result of the Civil War and the Fifteenth Amendment (1870), the Constitution was amended to say states could not deny the right to vote "on account of race, color, or previous condition of servitude." A half-century later, the Nineteenth Amendment (1920) was adopted granting the right to vote to women. More recently, the Constitution has been amended to prohibit poll taxes (Twenty-Fourth Amendment in 1964) and lowering the voting age to 18 (Twenty-Sixth Amendment (1971). There was resistance to each of these changes, with none more intense than the Civil War. And yet, 200 years after the signing of the Declaration of Independence, our notions of who may and who may not participate in elections has changed dramatically.

However, barriers to full participation still remain. The United States, in most states, retains a system of voter registration that requires people to complete a process of registering with local or state officials well in advance of the election. As recent elections taught us, the ballots or voting machines we use to cast our ballots are far from perfect.

An enduring debate centers on whether a goal of government should be to make voting easier. But when examined over the broad sweep of U.S. history, one of government's greatest successes is the expansion of voting to more and more people.

CRITICAL THINKING QUESTIONS

1. What have been the benefits to our democracy of extending the right to vote to more people?

2. Should the right to vote be extended to persons age 16 and older? Why or why not?

3. How does requiring people to register to vote before election day and register again each time they move discourage participation?

---

understand all of these big picture concepts. At the end of the book, you'll be able to test your mastery of the course material as a whole through the comprehensive **Course Exam**.

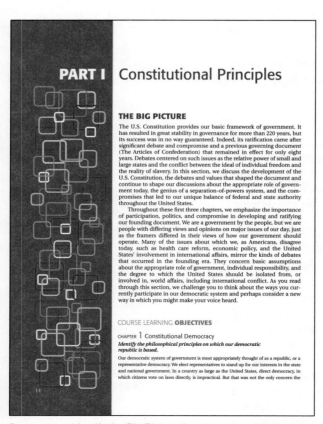

Part openers identify the Big Picture themes and explain the Course Learning Objectives for the section.

To understand these big picture concepts, you'll first need to understand the basics, so at the chapter level, there are **Chapter Learning Objectives.** These are the specific concepts you should understand after studying each chapter. For example, in the chapter on the Constitution, you'll see the objectives include such goals as being able to describe the basic structure of the Constitution and the Bill of Rights, comparing and contrasting the branches of government, explaining how we make changes to the Constitution, etc. These Chapter Learning Objectives appear as a list at the beginning of each chapter but also appear in the chapter where the concept is discussed. Refer to these Chapter Learning Objectives as you read through the chapters to make sure you understand the key concepts. We recap the objectives in a **Summary** at the end of the chapter, and we provide a set of review questions in the **Self-Test** to help you assess your progress in meeting the Chapter Learning Objectives and so that you know where to focus your studying (see sample).

Both the Course Learning Objectives and Chapter Learning Objectives can help guide you in your reading and studying of the course material, but asking your own questions as you read will also help you understand and apply the material. One way to prepare for exams is to turn chapter titles or major headings into possible essay questions. The chapter title "Making Economic Policy," for example, can be turned into a question like, "Explain how economic policy is made in the United States, and assess the strengths and weaknesses of that process in light of the economic crisis of 2008–2009." If you approach the book with questions in mind, you will often have better recall of the content and you will develop a capacity in critical thinking, which is one of the intellectual skills that can come from a college education. You can use the Course Learning Objectives and Chapter Learning Objectives as a good jumping off point and a model for this method of organization and study.

Conclusion

A text like *Government by the People* is intended to assist you in your study of American government. As authors of the book, we find the subject fascinating. As teachers of this course, we realize there is a great deal of material to learn. Our aim is to organize the subject matter and current research in a thorough, balanced, and engaging way. *Government by the People* provides a foundation for your course but also for other courses that will follow.[28] As we introduce you to American government at a college level, we are also introducing you to political science as a discipline. An academic discipline is a way of thinking about the world in a systematic and rigorous way. Yale Law School Dean Robert Post defined a discipline as "not merely a body of knowledge but also a set of practices by which that knowledge is acquired, confirmed, implemented, preserved, and reproduced."[29]

We want you to come away from reading this book with a richer understanding of American politics, government, the job of politicians, and the important role you, as a citizen, play in this country's present and future. We hope you will participate actively in making this constitutional democracy more vital and responsive to the urgent problems of the twenty-first century.

Finally, as you begin your American government course, and perhaps your study of the political science discipline, keep in mind the wisdom of early education reformer Horace Mann. Regarding Americans' quest for equality, he said, "Education, then, beyond all other devices of human origin, is the great equalizer of the conditions of men—the balance-wheel of the social machinery."[30]

CHAPTER SUMMARY

6.1 Explain the role of interest groups and social movements in American politics.

Interest groups form when a collection of people share similar political goals and organize to achieve them. Sometimes, these groups are based on a shared group identity, such as race, ethnicity, gender, or sexual orientation. Others are based on specific policy issues, such as reducing taxes or combating global warming. Still others claim to operate in the public interest on broad issues, such as educating voters or reducing the federal deficit. Interest groups sometimes begin as social movements, which consist of many people at the grassroots level who are interested in a significant issue, idea, or

include people with many other cross-cutting interests concern and take action to support or oppose it. ests, which both reduces and stabilizes their influence.

6.4 Describe lobbyists and the activities through which they seek to influence policy.

Lobbyists represent organized interests before government. Lobbying involves communicating with legislators and executive-branch officials, making campaign contributions, and assisting in election activity, especially through political action committees (PACs). Interest groups also communicate their message directly to the public through mass mailings, advertising, and online media.

CHAPTER SELF-TEST

6.1 Explain the role of interest groups and social movements in American politics.

1. Briefly explain the differences between *special interests* and *public interests*.
2. Describe what a social movement is and explain how it differs from an interest group or public interest.
3. In two or three sentences, analyze how the idea of pluralism explains the founders' method for protecting against overwhelming factions.

6.2 Categorize American interest groups into types.

4. Match each interest group with the category it most closely fits.
   a. American Gaming Association
   b. National Right to Life
   c. Project Vote Smart
   d. American-Israel Political Action Committee
   e. The State Department

   i. Public
   ii. Government
   iii. Economic
   iv. Ideological
   v. Foreign policy

End of chapter Summary and Self-Test can help you assess your progress in meeting the Chapter Learning Objectives.

KEY TERMS

Mayflower Compact, p. 3
individualism, p. 4
popular sovereignty, p. 4
equality of opportunity, p. 5

freedom of religion, p. 5
economic liberty, p. 5
government, p. 6
politics, p. 6

politician, p. 6
political science, p. 6
social contract, p. 7

ADDITIONAL RESOURCES

FURTHER READING

ALEXIS DE TOCQUEVILLE, *Democracy in America,* 2 vols. (1835).

ROBERT A. DAHL, *On Democracy* (Yale University Press, 1998).

LOUIS HARTZ, *The Liberal Tradition in America* (Harcourt, 1955).

PAULINE MAIER, *American Scripture: Making the Declaration of Independence* (Vintage Books, 1997).

PIPPA NORRIS, ED., *Critical Citizens: Global Support for Democratic Institutions* (Oxford University Press, 1999).

ROBERT PUTNAM, *Making Democracy Work* (Princeton University Press, 1993).

MICHAEL J. SANDEL, *Democracy's Discontent: America in Search of a Public Philosophy* (Belknap Press, 1996).

CASS R. SUNSTEIN, *Designing Democracy: What Constitutions Do* (Oxford University Press, 2001).

GARRY WILLS, *A Necessary Evil: A History of American Distrust of Government* (Simon & Schuster, 1999).

PETER H. SCHUCK and JAMES Q. WILSON, *Understanding America: The Anatomy of an Exceptional Nation* (Public Affairs, 2008).

WEB SITES

loc.gov The Library of Congress's Web site contains historical information on America's founding documents as well as general history information.

tocqueville.org This site explains the life and works of Alexis de Tocqueville.

Liberty Fund (libertyfund.org) Publishes books and materials and sponsors conferences related to freedom and personal responsibility.

Mayflower Society (themayflowersociety.com) The Mayflower Society has as one of its primary purposes furthering the understanding of the Mayflower Compact.

Philosophy Pages (philosophypages.com/ph/index.htm) This site provides information on a wide range of political philosophers.

bc.edu/centers/cloughcenter/ Located at Boston College, the Clough Center for the Study of Constitutional Democracy seeks to foster self-government and reflection on constitutional government.

PART I   Constitutional Principles

THE BIG PICTURE

The U.S. Constitution provides our basic framework of government. It has resulted in great stability in governance for more than 220 years, but its success was in no way guaranteed. Indeed, its ratification came after significant debate and compromise and a previous governing document (The Articles of Confederation) that remained in effect for only eight years. Debates centered on such issues as the relative power of small and large states and the conflict between the ideal of individual freedom and the reality of slavery. In this section, we discuss the development of the U.S. Constitution, the debates and values that shaped the document and continue to shape our discussions about the appropriate role of government today, the genius of a separation-of-powers system, and the compromises that led to our unique balance of federal and state authority throughout the United States.

Throughout these first three chapters, we emphasize the importance of participation, politics, and compromise in developing and ratifying our founding document. We are a government by the people, but we are people with differing views and opinions on major issues of our day, just as the framers differed in their views of how our government should operate. Many of the issues about which we, as Americans, disagree today, such as health care reform, economic policy, and the United States' involvement in international affairs, mirror the kinds of debates that occurred in the founding era. They concern basic assumptions about the appropriate role of government, individual responsibility, and the degree to which the United States should be isolated from, or involved in, world affairs, including international conflict. As you read through this section, we challenge you to think about the ways you currently participate in our democratic system and perhaps consider a new way in which you might make your voice heard.

COURSE LEARNING **OBJECTIVES**

CHAPTER 1 Constitutional Democracy

Identify the philosophical principles on which our democratic republic is based.

Our democratic system of government is most appropriately thought of as a republic, or a representative democracy. We elect representatives to stand up for our interests in the state and national government. In a country as large as the United States, direct democracy, in which citizens vote on laws directly, is impractical. But that was not the only concern the framers had with direct democracy. They also feared that a direct democracy would fall prey to the tyranny of the majority and the changing whims of the people.

Strongly held principles such as the importance of personal liberty, individualism, equality of opportunity, and popular consent motivate our democratic structures and policies. An educated public who share basic democratic values and have the freedom to own property make democratic governance possible. To ensure its continuity, it is necessary to maintain free, fair, and frequent elections, which guarantees individual freedom to express ideas and assemble with others and a system of majority or plurality rule.

CHAPTER 2 Constitutional Foundations

Describe the creation and adoption of the Constitution and the Bill of Rights, and identify the process for amendments.

The framers' success in writing a new constitution and getting it ratified was in no way guaranteed. There was a great deal of debate at the Constitutional Convention and during the drive for ratification over the relative authority of a new national government and the states about the protection of minority rights and individual liberties and about the relative power of the three branches of government. Debates between the Federalists and the Antifederalists raged in newspaper editorials as states considered whether to ratify the new Constitution. Such debates led to the development of a bicameral legislature to balance power between small and large states and to the separation of powers between three branches of government, with a built-in system of checks and balances, to prevent the rise of a tyrannical government. Although the document that emerged reflected many of the Federalists' goals, it was not ratified until it also included the Bill of Rights, which detailed some of our most prized individual liberties, as called for by the Anti-Federalists.

The Constitution also includes a process for amendments as would be needed over time to meet changing needs and circumstances. As an instrument of government, it is important that the document is capable of change as the nation and its values evolve. However, to ensure the stability of our democratic system, it should not be so easy to change as to be rendered meaningless as a governing document. Thus, the framers struck a balance, as they did on so many issues. In order to amend the Constitution, supermajorities are required in both houses of Congress (or in state conventions) and among the states.

CHAPTER 3 American Federalism

Explain federalism in America, and analyze the relationship between the federal and state and local governments.

Federalism is a system of government in which power is divided between a central government and subdivisional governments; in the United States, those subdivisions are referred to as states. Under a system of federalism, neither the national government nor the states depend on the other for power, and neither government can usurp the other's authority. Instead, the power for each is derived from the people, and in our case, their views as represented in the Constitution.

Although the Constitution describes the authority that belongs to the national government and the states, not everyone agrees on what the document means and the appropriate balance of power. Some argue for a more limited national government in favor of greater power for the states, whereas others prefer a stronger central government. Supreme Court cases have defined many aspects of the relationship between the national and state governments, and amendments to the Constitution have also affected this relationship. Over time, depending on conditions in the country and the parties in government, national and state power has ebbed and flowed.

CHAPTER

1

Constitutional Democracy

The peaceful transfer of power following elections is a process that U.S. citizens take for granted. Many people view elections with disdain, saying things like, "Voting does not matter," "Nothing ever changes," or "It's just all politics." But in fact, U.S. elections are remarkable and consequential. They conclude with a rare event in human history: the peaceful transfer of political power. What is unusual is what is *not* happening. Most of the time in most nations, those in power got there because either they were born to the right family or they killed or jailed their opponents. During most of history, no one, especially not an opposition political party, could openly criticize the government, and a political opponent was an enemy. England's King George III is reported to have said that George Washington would be "the greatest man alive in the world" if he were to voluntarily step down as president after two terms.[1]

This remarkably smooth transition of power was demonstrated again in the 2000 presidential election. Democrat Al Gore won the popular vote only to see George W. Bush declared the winner by the electoral college, after the Supreme Court effectively ruled 5 to 4 that Bush's slim Florida plurality should stand. Even in a highly contested election, Gore graciously conceded defeat: "I say to President-elect Bush that what remains of partisan rancor must now be put aside, and may God bless his stewardship of this country. Neither he nor I anticipated this long and difficult road. Certainly neither of us wanted it to happen. Yet it came, and now it has ended, resolved, as it must be resolved, through the honored institutions of our democracy."[2] The Democrats thus turned over the keys to the White House to George W. Bush and the Republicans. In many countries, the irregularities of the voting process in Florida and other states would have been sufficient excuse for the party in power to declare that a new election needed to be held.

After the 2008 election outcome appeared certain, John McCain graciously conceded defeat to Barack Obama and the process of organizing a new administration began. Obama's victory meant the eight-year Republican control of the presidency shifted to the Democrats. Even though the days before the election, John McCain, his running mate, Alaska Governor Sarah Palin, and their followers were insisting that if Barak Obama and his running mate, Delaware Senator Joe Biden, won the election, there would be dire economic and national security consequences, once the votes were counted, there was no serious consideration that anybody other than Barack Obama would become president. Outgoing president George Bush did not attempt to prolong his time in office by calling on the military to keep Obama from taking power. McCain's supporters did not take up arms or go underground to plan a revolution or leave the country. Instead, they almost immediately began planning how they could win the next election. Nor did Obama or his followers seriously think about punishing McCain and his supporters once they gained power. The Democrats wanted to throw the Republicans out of office, not in jail. In all these ways, the election of 2008 was a routine transfer—a constitutional democracy at work.

The peaceful transfer of power from one party and presidential administration to another is only one example of the successful functioning of our political system. In this chapter, we begin our exploration of the successful U.S. experiment with government by the people by taking a closer look at the meaning of democracy and the historical events that created the constitutional democracy of the United States.

CHAPTER **OUTLINE** & CHAPTER LEARNING **OBJECTIVES**

U.S. Government and Politicians in Context

1.1 Use the concept of constitutional democracy to explain U.S. government and politics.

Defining Democracy

1.2 Differentiate democracy from other forms of government, and identify conditions, values, political processes, and political structures conducive to a successful democracy.

The Roots of the American Constitutional Experiment

1.3 Show how politics before 1787 shaped the Constitution.

The Constitutional Convention of 1787

1.4 Assess the important compromises reached by the delegates to the Constitutional Convention of 1787.

To Adopt or Not to Adopt?

1.5 Evaluate the arguments for and against the ratification of the Constitution.

President Obama and Senator McCain were the two main candidates for president in 2008. Here they shake hands during the inauguration of Barack Obama.

U.S. Government and Politicians in Context

LEARNING OBJECTIVE

1.1 Use the concept of constitutional democracy to explain U.S. government and politics.

As the oldest constitutional democracy in the world, the United States of America has survived for more than two centuries, yet it is still a work in progress. We think of it as an enduring, strong government, but our constitutional political system is built on a fragile foundation. The U.S. Constitution and Bill of Rights survive not because we still have the parchment they were written on, but because each generation of U.S. citizens has respected, renewed, and worked to understand the principles and values found in these documents. Each generation has faced different challenges in preserving, protecting, and defending our way of government.

The U.S. constitutional democracy, founded on enduring values, has shown resilience and adaptability. We have held 112 presidential and midterm elections (including the 2010 election), and we have witnessed the peaceful transfer of power from one party to another on dozens of occasions. The United States has succeeded largely because its citizens love their country, revere the Constitution, and respect the free enterprise system. We also believe that debate, compromise, and free elections are the best ways to reconcile our differences. From an early age, we practice democracy in elementary school elections, and even though we may be critical of elected leaders, we recognize the need for political leadership. We also know there are deep divisions and unsolved problems in the United States. Many people are concerned about the persistence of racism, about religious bigotry, and about the gap in economic opportunities between rich and poor. And we want our government, in addition to defending us against terrorism and foreign enemies, to address domestic problems like basic health care and education.

But what is this government of which we expect so much? The reality is that "government by the people" is built on the foundation of hundreds of thousands of our fellow citizens: the people we elect and the people they appoint to promote the general welfare, provide for domestic tranquility, and secure the blessings of liberty for us.

More than any other form of government, the kind of democracy that has emerged under the U.S. Constitution requires active participation and a balance between faith and skepticism. Government by the people does not, however, mean that *everyone* must be involved in politics and policy making or that those who are involved need to do so through traditional avenues such as campaigning for a political candidate or interning in a representative's office. Some individuals, however, run for office seeking to represent the voters, many of whom will always be too busy doing other things, and some of whom will always be apathetic about government and politics. Moreover, the public must be sufficiently attentive, interested, involved, informed, and willing, when necessary, to criticize and change the direction of government.

Thomas Jefferson, author of the Declaration of Independence and one of our best-known champions of constitutional democracy, believed in the common sense of the people and in the possibilities of the human spirit. Jefferson warned that every government degenerates when it is left solely in the hands of the rulers. The people themselves, Jefferson wrote, are the only safe repositories of government. He believed in popular control, representative processes, and accountable leadership. But he was no believer in the simple participatory democracy of ancient Greece or revolutionary France, where all eligible citizens were directly involved in decision making in the political process. Even the power of the people, Jefferson believed, must be restrained from time to time.

Government by the people requires faith in our common human enterprise, a belief that the people can be trusted with their own self-government, and an optimism that when things begin to go wrong, the people can be relied on to set them right. But we also need a healthy skepticism. Democracy requires us to question our leaders and never entrust a group or institution with too much power. And even though constitutional advocates prize majority rule, they must think critically about whether the majority is always right.

Constitutional democracy requires constant attention to protecting the rights and opinions of others, to ensure that our democratic processes serve the principles of liberty, equality, and justice. Thus, a peculiar blend of faith and caution is warranted when dealing with the will of the people.

Constitutional democracy means government by representative politicians. A central feature of democracy is that those who hold power do so only by winning a free and fair election. In our political system, the fragmentation of powers requires elected officials to mediate among factions, build coalitions, and work out compromises among and within the branches of our government to produce policy and action. We expect our politicians to operate within the rules of democracy and to be honest, humble, patriotic, compassionate, well informed, self-confident, and inspirational. We want politicians, in other words, to be perfect, to have all the answers, and to have all the "correct" values (as we perceive them). We want them to solve our problems, yet we also make them scapegoats for the things we dislike about government: taxes, regulations, hard times, and limits on our freedom. Many of these ideals are unrealistic, and no one could live up to all of them. Like all people, politicians live in a world in which perfection may be the goal, but compromise, ambition, fund raising, and self-promotion are necessary.

U.S. citizens will never be satisfied with their political candidates and politicians. The ideal politician is a myth. Politicians become "ideal" only when they are dead. Politicians and candidates, as well as the people they represent, all have different ideas about what is best for the nation. Indeed, liberty invites disagreements about ideology and values. That is why we have politics, candidates, opposition parties, heated political debates, and elections.

Thomas Jefferson, author of the Declaration of Independence, third president of the United States, and founder of the University of Virginia.

democracy
Government by the people, both directly or indirectly, with free and frequent elections.

direct democracy
Government in which citizens vote on laws and select officials directly.

Defining Democracy

The distinguishing feature of democracy is that government derives its authority from its citizens. In fact, the word comes from two Greek words: *demos,* "the people," and *kratos,* "authority" or "power." Thus **democracy** means *government by the people,* not government by one person (a monarch, dictator, or priest) or government by the few (an oligarchy or aristocracy).

The word "democracy" is nowhere to be found in the Declaration of Independence or in the U.S. Constitution, nor was it a term the founders used. Ancient Athens, a few other Greek city-states, and the Roman Republic had a **direct democracy** in which citizens assembled to discuss and pass laws and select their officials. Most of these Greek city-states and the Roman Republic degenerated into mob rule and then resorted to dictators or rule by aristocrats. When this nation was founded, *democracy* was used to describe unruly groups or mobs, and a system that encouraged leaders to gain power by appealing to the emotions and prejudices of the people. In 1787, James Madison, in *The Federalist*, No. 10, reflected the view of many of the framers of the U.S. Constitution

LEARNING **OBJECTIVE**

1.2 Differentiate democracy from other forms of government, and identify conditions, values, political processes, and political structures conducive to a successful democracy.

when he wrote, "Such democracies [as the Greek and Roman]... have ever been found incompatible with personal security, or the rights of property; and have in general been as short in their lives, as they have been violent in their deaths" (*The Federalist*, No. 10, is reprinted in the Appendix at the back of this book). Madison feared that empowering citizens to decide policy directly would be dangerous to freedom, minorities, and property and would result in violence by one group against another.

Over time, our democracy has increasingly combined representative and direct democracy. The most important examples of direct democracy were added roughly a century ago and include the **direct primary,** in which voters, rather than party leaders or other elected officials, select who may run for office; the **initiative** and **referendum,** which allow citizens to vote on state laws or constitutional amendments; and the **recall,** which lets voters remove state and local elected officials from office between elections. Initiatives and referendums are not permitted in all states, but where they are available, they have been used frequently. In 2008, California's Proposition 8 divided the state on the issue of gay marriage. Proposition 8 was an initiative stating that "only marriage between a man and a woman is valid or recognized in California." Overall, $73.4 million was spent by the two sides in an intensely fought campaign. The measure was passed with 52 percent of the vote and was deemed constitutional by the California Supreme Court in 2009.

Today, it is no longer possible, even if it were desirable, to assemble the citizens of any but the smallest towns to make their laws or select their officials directly. Rather, we have invented a system of representation. Democracy today means **representative democracy,** or a *republic,* in which those who have governmental authority get and retain that power directly or indirectly by winning free elections in which all adult citizens are allowed to participate. These elected officials are the people who determine budgets, pass laws, and are responsible for the performances of government. The framers used the term "republic" to avoid any confusion between direct democracy, which they disliked, and representative democracy, which they liked and thought secured all the advantages of a direct democracy while curing its weaknesses.

Many of the ideas that came to be part of the Constitution can be traced to philosophers' writings—in some cases, centuries before the American Revolution and the constitutional convention. Among those philosophers the framers would have read and been influenced by were Aristotle, Hobbes, Locke, and Montesquieu. Aristotle, a Greek philosopher writing in the fourth century BC, had provided important ideas on a political unit

direct primary
An election in which voters choose party nominees.

initiative
A procedure whereby a certain number of voters may, by petition, propose a law or constitutional amendment and have it submitted to the voters.

referendum
A procedure for submitting to popular vote measures passed by the legislature or proposed amendments to a state constitution.

recall
A procedure for submitting to popular vote the removal of officials from office before the end of their term.

representative democracy
Government in which the people elect those who govern and pass laws; also called a *republic.*

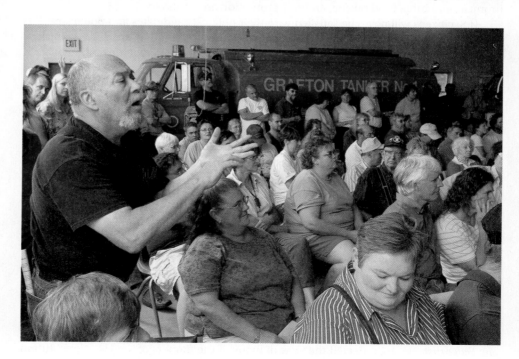

A New Hampshire man speaks at a local town meeting. Since Colonial times, many local governments in New England have held meetings in which all community members are invited to attend and discuss their opinions with public officials. ■ *Why is this form of direct democracy practiced primarily in small towns and communities?*

YOU WILL DECIDE

Should the United States Adopt a National Initiative Process?

Even though more than half the states have some form of initiative or popular referendum in which voters can petition to vote directly on policy issues, the national government does not provide for such a process. Those who wrote our constitution were not supporters of direct democracy, which is why it is not part of their document. They favored more indirect means of public involvement in making policy. Voters in many other democracies directly ratify constitutional changes like our constitutional amendments in a national election.

Proposals for a national initiative or referendum process have been put forward for more than a century. What might voters decide using a process for national petitions? They could, for example, petition to change the Senate so that instead of two senators, each state have a minimum of one and the remainder be apportioned by population. Others might petition to institute mandatory school prayer or to legalize medicinal marijuana as a guaranteed constitutional right. Do the possibilities for what might be decided by referendum affect your opinion on whether it should be used?

What do you think? Should the United States adopt a national initiative process? What are some of the arguments for or against this?

THINKING IT THROUGH

Involving voters directly in the process of deciding public policy is appealing and consistent with the move toward direct democracy the United States has experienced during the past century. Such votes may help legitimate major constitutional changes by demonstrating voter approval of them, and if a petition process were permitted, citizens could directly put before their fellow voters whatever constitutional changes they wanted. But as in the examples above, should some issues be out of bounds? If so, who decides? In most of the United States, these kinds of issues are decided by courts, but that puts courts in a politically charged position. Is that a good idea?

Although letting voters decide policy questions is an extension of direct democracy, in practice, the initiative and referendum may actually impede representative democracy. Congress and the president may evade tough issues by waiting for someone to put them to a vote of the people. An initiative also forces a "yes" or "no" vote, and compromise is not possible. Who decides how the question will be worded? How many signatures would be required to place a measure on the ballot? How many initiatives or referendums can we put before the voters in any single election?

When it comes to implementing a successful initiative or referendum, does that vote supersede the Constitution itself? Could the Supreme Court declare a national initiative unconstitutional, or is the vote of the people the final word on a matter? How would Congress and the president allocate tax money for implementing an initiative? The authors of our Constitution clearly preferred a more representative and deliberative form of democracy to the initiative. What were their reservations about direct democracy, and were they correct?

Critical Thinking Questions

1. Who should word the question put to voters in a referendum, and what effect does the way a question is worded have on the process?

2. Could a majority group vote to limit the rights of a minority in a referendum?

3. How is voters deciding a referendum different from legislators deciding legislation?

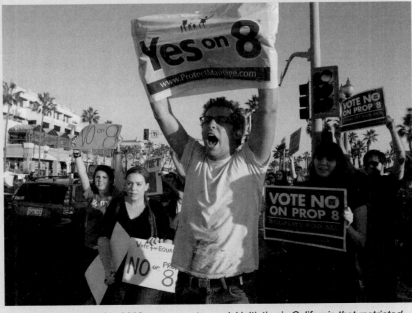

Proposition 8, passed in 2008, was a controversial initiative in California that restricted marriage to between a man and a woman.

called a state but also on the idea of a constitution and on various forms of governing.[3] John Locke, an English philosopher, also profoundly influenced the authors of the Declaration of Independence and Constitution. Locke rejected the idea that kings had a divine right to rule, advocated a constitutional democracy, and provided a philosophic justification for revolution.[4] Locke, like his fellow Englishman Thomas Hobbes, asserted that there was a social contract whereby people formed governments for security and to avoid what he called the state of nature, where chaos existed and where "everyone was against everyone."[5]

In defining democracy, we need to clarify other terms. **Constitutional democracy** refers to a government in which individuals exercise governmental power as the result of winning free and relatively frequent elections. It is a government in which there are recognized, enforced limits on the powers of all governmental officials. It also generally includes a written set of governmental rules and procedures—a constitution. The idea that constitutional provisions can limit power by having another part of the government balance or check it is one more good example of how the founders applied ideas from earlier thinkers—in this case, the French philosopher Charles de Montesquieu.[6]

Constitutionalism is a term we apply to arrangements—checks and balances, federalism, separation of powers, rule of law, due process, and a bill of rights—that require our leaders to listen, think, bargain, and explain before they make laws to prevent them from abusing power. We then hold them politically and legally accountable for the way they exercise their powers.

Like most political concepts, democracy encompasses many ideas and has many meanings. It is a way of life, a form of government, a way of governing, a type of nation, a state of mind, and a variety of processes. We can divide these many meanings of democracy into three broad categories: a system of interacting values, a system of interrelated political processes, and a system of interdependent political structures.

Democracy as a System of Interacting Values

A constitutional democracy is strengthened by an educated and prosperous public that has confidence in its ability to work out differences through the political process. A set of interacting values provides a foundation for that public confidence. As discussed in the Introduction, personal and economic liberty, individualism, equality of opportunity, and popular sovereignty are at the core of democratic values.

Personal Liberty The essence of liberty is *self-determination,* meaning that all individuals must have the opportunity to realize their own goals. Liberty is not simply the absence of external restraint on a person (freedom *from* something), it is also a person's freedom and capacity to reach his or her goals (freedom *to* do something). Moreover, both history and reason suggest that individual liberty is the key to social progress. The greater the people's freedom, the greater the chance of discovering better ways of life.

Individualism Popular rule in a democracy flows from a belief that every person has the potential for common sense, rationality, and fairness. Individuals have important rights; collectively, those rights are the source of all legitimate governmental authority and power. These concepts pervade democratic thought, and constitutional democracies make the *person*—rich or poor, black or white, male or female—the central measure of value.

Not all political systems put the individual first. Some promote **statism,** a form of government based on centralized authority and control, especially over the economy. China, Vietnam, and Cuba, for example, take this approach. In a modern democracy, the nation, or even the community, is less important than the individuals who compose it.

Equality of Opportunity The democratic value of *equality* enhances the importance of the individual: "All men are created equal and from that equal creation they derive rights inherent and unalienable, among which are the preservation of liberty and the pursuit of happiness." So reads Jefferson's first draft of the Declaration of Independence. But what does equality mean? And equality for whom? Does equality of opportunity mean that everyone should have the same place at the starting line? Or does it mean that society

constitutional democracy
Government that enforces recognized limits on those who govern and allows the voice of the people to be heard through free, fair, and relatively frequent elections.

constitutionalism
The set of arrangements, including checks and balances, federalism, separation of powers, rule of law, due process, and a bill of rights, that requires our leaders to listen, think, bargain, and explain before they act or make laws. We then hold them politically and legally accountable for how they exercise their powers.

statism
The idea that the rights of the nation are supreme over the rights of the individuals who make up the nation.

should try to equalize the factors that determine a person's economic or social well-being? These enduring issues often arise in American politics.

Popular Sovereignty   The animating principle of the American Revolution, the Declaration of Independence, and the resulting new nation was popular sovereignty—the idea that ultimate political authority rests with the people. This means that a just government must derive its powers from the consent of the people it governs, or **popular consent.** A commitment to democracy thus means that a community must be willing to participate and make decisions in government. These principles sound unobjectionable, but in practice, they mean that people must be willing to lose when more people vote the other way.

Democratic Values in Conflict   The basic values of democracy do not always coexist happily. Individualism may conflict with the collective welfare or the public good. Self-determination may conflict with equal opportunity. A media outlet's freedom to publish classified documents about foreign or defense policy may conflict with the government's constitutional requirement to "provide for the common defense."

Much of our political debate revolves around how to strike a balance among democratic values. How, for example, do we protect the Declaration of Independence's unalienable rights of life, liberty, and the pursuit of happiness, while trying to "promote the general Welfare" as the Constitution announces?

Democracy as a System of Interrelated Political Processes

In addition to meeting a few key conditions and having a consensus of core democratic values, a successful, democratic government requires a well-defined political process as well as a stable governmental structure. To make democratic values a reality, a nation must incorporate them into its political process, most importantly, in the form of free and fair elections, majority rule, freedom of expression, and the right of its citizens to peaceably assemble and protest.

In Cuba government is based on centralized control and loyalty to the state. Here, students attend a state-sponsored ceremony to mark the start of the school year.

Free and Fair Elections   Democratic government is based on free and fair elections held at intervals frequent enough to make them relevant to policy choices. Elections are one of the most important devices for keeping officials and representatives accountable to the voters. The United States actively supports such elections throughout the world.

Crucial to modern-day definitions of democracy is the idea that opposition political parties can exist, can run candidates in elections, and have a chance to replace those who currently hold public office. Thus *political competition and choice* are crucial to the existence of democracy. Although free and fair elections do not imply that everyone will have equal political *influence*, they do have equal voting power, and each citizen—president or plumber, corporate CEO or college student—casts only one vote.

Majority and Plurality Rule   Governance according to the expressed preferences of the majority, or **majority rule,** is a basic rule of democracy. The **majority** candidate or party is the one that receives *more than half* the votes and so wins the election and takes charge of the government until the next election. In practice, however, democracies often function by **plurality** rule. Here, the candidate or party with the *most* votes wins the election, even though the candidate or party may not have received more than half the votes because votes were divided among three or more candidates or parties.

Should the side with the most votes always prevail? American citizens answer this question in various ways. Some insist that majority views should be enacted into laws and

popular consent
The idea that a just government must derive its powers from the consent of the people it governs.

majority rule
Governance according to the expressed preferences of the majority.

majority
The candidate or party that wins more than half the votes cast in an election.

plurality
The candidate or party with the most votes cast in an election, not necessarily more than half.

Importance of Freedoms

As illustrated by the Pilgrims and those that followed, the United States has been known as a place where people value freedom. In today's world, what value do the people of the United States place on different freedoms, and how do they compare to the rest of the world? The respondents in the Pew Global survey were asked: "Thinking about your own personal life, which of these is MOST important to you: Being free to say whatever you want in public, Being free to practice your religion, Being free from hunger and poverty, Being free from crime and violence?"

To the worldwide population in the survey of 47 nations, the answer given most often to the question of what was most important was to be free from poverty (33 percent). This was also the most frequent response given in Britain (40 percent) and Nigeria (36 percent). In the United States, respondents are more evenly divided across the four competing values than in any other country.

In Japan, India, and Mexico, freedom to say whatever a person wanted to in public was the most frequently given response. Given the poverty in India and Mexico, this is a surprising answer. Both of these countries are relatively new democracies, so perhaps a political freedom like freedom of speech is more frequently cited there than in countries where it may be taken for granted. In Japan, this may be a reflection of the fact that the Japanese lost freedom of speech protections in the late nineteenth century and did not regain them until they were reinstated in the post–World War II constitution.

Being free to practice religion was most important to only 3 percent in Japan and 7 percent in Britain. In contrast, it was most important to 28 percent in the United States, where this value nearly tied for first place with being free from crime. The very clear differences in countries in what freedom they most valued is striking. Industrialized or wealthy countries do not always value the same things, nor do developing or less wealthy countries. When selecting from among these values, there is something distinctive about each country.

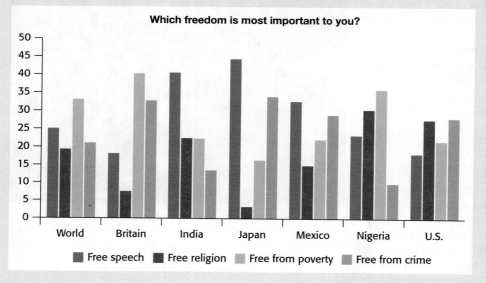

Which freedom is most important to you?

Legend: ■ Free speech ■ Free religion ■ Free from poverty ■ Free from crime

(X-axis: World, Britain, India, Japan, Mexico, Nigeria, U.S.)

CRITICAL THINKING QUESTIONS

1. Why do many Americans say that they personally value freedom of religion as the most important value? What are the implications of this for American politics?

2. How can we account for the vast difference in what the people in these different countries most highly value?

regulations. However, an effective representative democracy requires far more than simply counting individual preferences and implementing the will of most of the people. In a constitutional democracy, the will of a majority may run counter to the rights of individuals. For example, the Supreme Court struck down a 1964 California initiative where the majority voted to allow discrimination against minorities in the sale of residential housing.[7]

The framers of the U.S. Constitution wanted to guard society against oppression of any one faction of the people by any other faction. The Constitution reflects their fear of tyranny by majorities, especially momentary majorities that spring from temporary passions. They insulated certain rights (such as freedom of speech) and institutions (such as the Supreme Court and, until the Constitution was changed in 1913, even the Senate) from popular choice. Effective representation of the people, the framers insisted, should not be based solely on parochial interests or the shifting breezes of opinion.

Freedom of Expression Free and fair elections depend on voters having access to facts, competing ideas, and the views of candidates. This means that competing, nongovernment-owned newspapers, radio stations, and television stations must be allowed to flourish. If the government controls what is said and how it is said, elections cannot be free and fair, and there is no democracy. We examine free expression in greater detail in Chapter 15.

The Right to Assemble and Protest Citizens must be free to organize for political purposes. Obviously, individuals can be more effective if they join with others in a party, a pressure group, a protest movement, or a demonstration. The right to oppose the government, to form opposition parties, and to have a chance to defeat incumbents is a defining characteristic of a democracy.

Democracy as a System of Interdependent Political Structures

Democracy is, of course, more than the values and processes we have discussed so far. Its third characteristic is political structures that safeguard these values and processes. The Constitution and its first ten amendments—the Bill of Rights—set up an ingenious structure that both grants and checks government power. A system of political parties, interest groups, media, and other institutions that intercede between the electorate and those who govern reinforces this constitutional structure and thus helps maintain democratic stability.

The U.S. constitutional system has five distinctive elements: *federalism,* the division of powers between the national and state governments; *separation of powers* among the executive, judicial, and legislative branches; *bicameralism,* the division of legislative power between the House of Representatives and the Senate; *checks and balances* in which each branch is given the constitutional means, the political independence, and the motives to check the powers of the other branches so that a relative balance of power between the branches endures; and a judicially enforceable, written, explicit *Bill of Rights* that provides a guarantee of individual liberties and due process before the law. We will discuss all of these in more detail in Chapter 2.

Conditions Favorable for Constitutional Democracy

Although it is hard to specify the precise conditions essential for establishing and preserving a democracy, and it does not always flourish, we can identify some patterns that foster its growth.

Educational Conditions The exercise of voting privileges requires an educated citizenry. But a high level of education (measured by the number of high school diplomas and university degrees granted) does not guarantee democratic government. Still, voting makes little sense unless many of the voters can read and write and express their interests and opinions. The poorly educated and illiterate often get left out in a democracy. Direct democracy puts a further premium on education.[8]

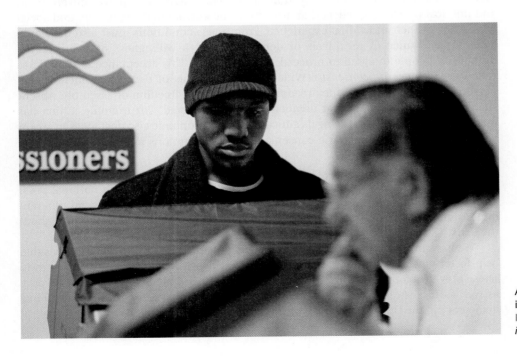

A student from Chicago casts an early vote in the 2008 Illinois presidential primary.
■ *Why is having an educated citizenry important for constitutional democracy?*

A woman casts her vote in Harare, Zimbabwe, where long lines formed at the polling stations hours before they opened.
■ *What factors make democratic government more difficult to maintain in countries such as Zimbabwe?*

Economic Conditions   A relatively prosperous nation, with an equitable distribution of wealth, provides the best context for democracy. Starving people are more interested in food than in voting. Where economic power is concentrated, political power is also likely to be concentrated; thus, well-to-do nations have a better chance of sustaining democratic governments than do those with widespread poverty. As a result, the prospects for an enduring democracy are greater in Canada or France than in Zimbabwe or Egypt.

Private ownership of property and a market economy are also related to the creation and maintenance of democratic institutions. Freedom to make economic choices is linked to other freedoms like freedom of religion and the right to vote. Democracies can range from heavily regulated economies with public ownership of many enterprises, such as Sweden, to those in which there is little government regulation of the marketplace, such as the United States. But there are no democracies with a highly centralized, government-run economy and little private ownership of property. When we examine experiments with democracy in other countries, we can find examples of democracies that struggled in settings in which conditions were not favorable. Economic challenges during the Weimar Republic in Germany (1919–1933) undermined that short-lived experiment in self-rule.[9]

Social Conditions   Economic development generally makes democracy possible, but proper social conditions are necessary to make it real.[10] In a society fragmented into warring groups that fiercely disagree on fundamental issues, government by discussion and compromise is difficult, as we have seen in Afghanistan and Iraq. When ideologically separated groups consider the issues at stake to be vital, they may prefer to fight rather than accept the verdict of the ballot box, as happened in the United States in 1861 with the outbreak of the Civil War.

In a society that consists of many overlapping associations and groupings, however, individuals are less likely to identify completely with a single group and give their allegiance to it. For example, Joe Smith is a Baptist, an African American, a southerner, a Democrat, an electrician, and a member of the National Rifle Association, and he makes $50,000 a year. On some issues, Joe thinks as a Baptist, on others as a member of the NRA, and on still others as an African American. Joe and his fellow Americans may differ on some issues and agree on others, but they share an overriding common interest in maintaining a democracy.[11]

Ideological Conditions   American adults have basic beliefs about power, government, and political practices—beliefs that arise from the educational, economic, and social conditions of their individual experience. From these conditions must also develop a general acceptance of the ideals of democracy and a willingness of a substantial number of people to agree to proceed democratically. This acceptance is sometimes called the *democratic consensus*. Widely accepted ideals of democracy include one person, one vote; majority rule; freedom of speech; and freedom of assembly. Absent such a consensus, attempts at democracy will be ill-fated. For example, China has made major strides in improving its educational and economic circumstances in recent years, but it lacks a democratic consensus or the institutions and liberties vital to a democracy.

Political scientists have long tried to determine what factors contribute to stability in a democracy. Comparative studies have often linked factors such as national prosperity, education, and literacy to democratic success. Table 1–1 lists several different dimensions for the countries that we will be comparing to the United States throughout the book.

We have now discussed the values, political processes, and political structures that help foster viable constitutional democracy, as well as the conditions conducive to it. These provide a foundation on which we can assess governments throughout the world, as well as the extraordinary story of the founding and enlargement of constitutional democracy in the United States, to which we turn next.

TABLE
1-1 | Conditions for Democratic Stability

	World	Britain	China	India	Japan	Mexico	Nigeria	United States
Population (millions; July 2007 est.)	6,790.06	61.11	1,338.61	1,156.90	127.08	111.21	149.23	307.21
Median Age	28.4	40.2	34.1	25.3	44.2	26.3	19	36.7
Life Expectancy	66.1	79.1	73.5	66.1	82.12	76.1	46.9	78.1
Literacy								
Male	87%	99	95.1	73.4	99	92.4	75.7	99
Female	77%	99	86.5	47.8	99	89.6	60.6	99
Government Type		Constitutional monarchy	Communist state	Federal republic	Constitutional monarchy	Federal republic	Federal republic	Federal republic
GDP[1]	57.53	2.20	4.76	1.24	5.05	0.87	0.17	14.27
Freedom House[2]		Free	Not Free	Free	Free	Free	Partly free	Free

■ These countries vary dramatically in many aspects. For example, note the extremely young population of Nigeria compared to the generally older population of Japan. *What are the implications of this difference for both governments?* Notice that the U.S. population is less than one-fourth that of China. *How might population size affect some of these factors?* Compare the differences in literacy between men and women in India, Nigeria, and China. *What do you think accounts for these differences?*

NOTES: (1) Calculated based on the country's official exchange rate in trillions of USD; (2) For more on Freedom House's Freedom Index, see www.freedomhouse.org/template.cfm?page=351&ana_page=333&year=2007.

SOURCE: Central Intelligence Agency, *The World Factbook,* at https://www.cia.gov/library/publications/the-world-factbook/geos/us.html; and Freedom House, *Freedom in the World 2009: The Annual Survey of Political Rights and Civil Liberties,* at www.freedomhouse.org/template.cfm?page=363&year=2009.

The Roots of the American Constitutional Experiment

Most of us probably consider having a democracy and a constitution as part of the natural order of history. Although we have essentially inherited a functioning system—the work of others, nine or ten generations ago—we take pride in our ability to make it work. Our job is not only to keep it going but to improve and adapt it to the challenges of our times. To do so, however, we must first understand it by recalling our democratic and constitutional roots.

LEARNING **OBJECTIVE**

1.3 Show how politics before 1787 shaped the Constitution.

The Colonial Beginnings

Our democratic experiment might well have failed. The 13 original states (formerly colonies) were independent and could have gone their separate ways. Differences between them, based on social and economic conditions, especially the southern states' dependence on slavery, were an obvious challenge to unity. Given these potential problems, how did democracy survive? The framers of the Constitution had experience to guide them. For nearly two centuries, Europeans had been sailing to the New World in search of liberty—especially religious liberty—as well as land and work. The experience of settling a new land, overcoming obstacles, and enjoying the fruits of their labors was also important to the spirit of independence in the colonies.[12]

But freedom in the colonies was limited. Ironically, given their concern for religious liberty, the Puritans in Massachusetts established a **theocracy,** a system of government in which religious leaders claimed divine guidance and in which other sects were denied religious liberty. Later, as that system was challenged, the Puritans continued to worry "about what would maintain order in a society lacking an established church, an attachment to place, and the uncontested leadership of men of merit."[13] Nine of the 13 colonies eventually set up a state church. Throughout the 1700s, Puritans in Massachusetts barred certain men from voting on the basis of church membership. Women, slaves, and Native Americans could not vote at all.

By the 1700s, editors in the colonies found they could speak freely in their newspapers, dissenters could distribute leaflets, and agitators could protest in taverns or in the

theocracy
Government by religious leaders, who claim divine guidance.

For the People

GOVERNMENT'S GREATEST ENDEAVORS

Creating a Lasting Government

To successfully design a government that protects basic liberties while incorporating popular sovereignty is a challenging task. Those who designed the U.S. Constitution in Philadelphia in 1787 could and did draw on the lessons learned in the drafting of the constitutions of the former colonies as they became states in 1776. From those experiences as well as other historical documents and political theory, the framers developed the fundamental values and principles of our government.

For example, the founders drew much inspiration on how to create the structures of their new government from the constitution of Virginia. The 1776 Virginia Constitution declared Virginia to be separate from Great Britain, and accused England's King George III of "detestable and insupportable tyranny."* To ensure a future executive could not wield such unilateral power, the structure of the new government included a separation of powers between the executive (Governor) and a two-house legislature (General Assembly). James Madison had participated in designing Virginia's Constitution, and he used those experiences to later incorporate separation of powers and a bicameral legislature into the federal constitution.

The Bill of Rights, essential for protecting the rights and liberties of the people, also benefited from the founders' use of a number of historical documents and experiences. George Mason, a statesman from Virginia, drew from the Magna Carta and the English Bill of Rights to write the "Virginia Declaration of Rights." This document guaranteed freedom of the press, civilian control of the military, and trial by jury; required search warrants; and prohibited cruel and unusual punishments. Mason went on to become a delegate from Virginia to the U.S. Constitutional Convention, and his document served as a model for other states and for the Bill of Rights for the U.S. Constitution.

Drawing from the lessons of history, the founders created a government that has endured drastic social, demographic, and economic change and that has served and protected the rights of the people for more than 200 years.

CRITICAL THINKING QUESTIONS

1. What criteria would you use to assess whether a constitution is successful or not?

2. Why did Mason, Madison, and the other Virginians rely on documents like the Magna Carta when they designed their state's founding documents?

3. What are some of the things the Virginia Constitution appears to have been designed to avoid?

---

* *The Constitution of Virginia*, June 29, 1776, http://www.nhinet.org/ccs/docs/va-1776.htm (accessed March 2, 2010).

---

streets. And yet dissenters were occasionally exiled, imprisoned, and even executed, and some printers were beaten and had their shops closed. In short, the colonists struggled with the balance between unity and diversity, stability and dissent, order and liberty.

The Rise of Revolutionary Fervor

As resentment against British rule mounted during the 1770s and revolutionary fervor rose, the colonists became determined to fight the British to win their rights and liberties. In 1776, a year after the fighting broke out in Massachusetts, the Declaration of Independence proclaimed, in ringing tones, that all men are created equal, endowed by their Creator with certain unalienable rights; that among them are "life, liberty, and the pursuit of happiness"; that to secure those rights, governments are instituted among men; and that whenever a government becomes destructive of those ends, it is the right of the people to alter or abolish it. (Read the full text of the Declaration of Independence in the Appendix.)

We have heard these great ideals so often that we take them for granted. Revolutionary leaders did not. They were deadly serious about these rights and willing to fight and pledge their lives, fortunes, and sacred honor for them. Indeed, by signing the Declaration of Independence, they were effectively signing their own death warrants if the Revolution failed.[14] In most cases, state constitutions guaranteed the underlying rights referred to in the Declaration: free speech, freedom of religion, and the natural rights to life, liberty, and property. All their constitutions spelled out the rights of persons accused of crime, such as knowing the nature of the accusation, confronting their accusers, and receiving a timely and public trial by jury.[15] Moreover, these guarantees were set out *in writing*, in sharp contrast to the unwritten British constitution.

Toward Unity and Order

As the war against the British widened to include all 13 colonies, the need arose for a stronger central government to unite them. In 1777, Congress established a new national government, the Confederation, under a written document called the **Articles of Confederation.**[16] Although they were established in 1777, the Articles were not approved by all the state legislatures until 1781, after Washington's troops had been fighting for six years.

The Confederation was more like a fragile league of friendship than a national government. There was no national executive, judiciary, or national currency. Congress had to work through the states and had no direct authority over citizens. It could not levy taxes, regulate trade between the states or with other nations, or prevent the states from taxing each other's goods or issuing their own currencies. The lack of a judicial system meant that the national government had to rely on state courts to enforce national laws and settle disputes between the states. In practice, state courts could overturn national laws. Moreover, with the end of the Revolutionary War in 1783, the sense of urgency that had produced unity among the states began to fade. Conflicts between states and between creditors and debtors within the various states grew intense. Foreign threats continued; territories ruled by England and Spain surrounded the weak new nation. As pressures on the Confederation mounted, many leaders became convinced that a more powerful central government was needed to create a union strong enough to deal with internal diversity and factionalism and to resist external threats.

In September 1786, under the leadership of Alexander Hamilton, supporters of a truly national government took advantage of the **Annapolis Convention**—a meeting in Annapolis, Maryland, on problems of trade and navigation attended by delegates from five states—to issue a call for a convention to consider basic amendments to the Articles of Confederation. The delegates were to meet in Philadelphia on the second Monday of May 1787, "to devise such further provisions as shall appear to them necessary to render the Constitution of the Federal Government adequate to the exigencies of the Union."[17] This meeting became the **Constitutional Convention.**

The American Revolutionary War was waged by militias and volunteers who overcame many challenges to prevail.

For a short time, all was quiet. Then, late in 1786, messengers rode into George Washington's plantation at Mount Vernon in Virginia with the kind of news he and other leaders had dreaded. Farmers in western Massachusetts, crushed by debts and taxes, were rebelling against foreclosures, forcing judges out of their courtrooms, and freeing debtors from jails. These actions came to be known as **Shays' Rebellion,** named for Daniel Shays, the leader of the insurrection. As a patriot and a wealthy landowner, Washington was appalled. "What, gracious God, is man?" he exclaimed.

Not all reacted as Washington did to Shays' Rebellion. When Abigail Adams, the politically knowledgeable wife of John Adams, the Revolutionary statesman from Massachusetts, sent news of the rebellion to Thomas Jefferson, the Virginian replied, "I like a little rebellion now and then," noting also that the "tree of liberty must be refreshed from time to time with the blood of patriots and tyrants. It is its natural manure."[18] But the rebellion highlighted the lack of a mechanism to enforce contractual obligations in the absence of a strong central government. Some, like historian Charles A. Beard, have argued that the primary motive of the authors of the U.S. Constitution was the protection of their economic interests more than a concern for other values.[19] Beard's views have been challenged.[20] Most agree that even though the early leaders of the United States were protecting their own economic interests, that was not their only motive.

Shays' Rebellion petered out after the farmers attacked an arsenal and were cut down by cannon fire. The uprising had threatened prosperity, the established order, and the rule of law, and it reinforced the view that a stronger national government was needed. Congress issued a cautiously worded call to all the state legislatures to appoint delegates for the "sole and express purpose of revising the Articles of Confederation."[21] The call for a convention specified that no recommendation would be effective unless approved by Congress and confirmed by all the state legislatures, as provided by the Articles.

Articles of Confederation
The first governing document of the confederated states, drafted in 1777, ratified in 1781, and replaced by the present Constitution in 1789.

Annapolis Convention
A convention held in September 1786 to consider problems of trade and navigation, attended by five states and important because it issued the call to Congress and the states for what became the Constitutional Convention.

Constitutional Convention
The convention in Philadelphia, from May 25 to September 17, 1787, that debated and agreed on the Constitution of the United States.

Shays' Rebellion
A rebellion led by Daniel Shays of farmers in western Massachusetts in 1786–1787 protesting mortgage foreclosures. It highlighted the need for a strong national government just as the call for the Constitutional Convention went out.

The Constitutional Convention of 1787

LEARNING OBJECTIVE

1.4 Assess the important compromises reached by the delegates to the Constitutional Convention of 1787.

The delegates who assembled in Philadelphia in May 1787 had to establish a national government powerful enough to prevent the young nation from dissolving but not so powerful that it would crush individual liberty. What these men did continues to have a major impact on how we are governed. It also provides an outstanding lesson in political science for the world.

The Delegates

The various states appointed 74 delegates, but only 55 arrived in Philadelphia. Of these, approximately 40 actually took part in the work of the convention. It was a distinguished gathering. Many of the most important men of the nation were there: successful merchants, planters, bankers, lawyers, and former and present governors and congressional representatives (39 of the delegates had served in Congress). Most had read the classics of political thought. Most had experience constructing local and state governments. Many had also worked hard to create and direct the national confederation of the states. And the Constitutional Convention also included eight of the 56 signers of the Declaration of Independence.

The convention was as representative as most political gatherings were at the time: the participants were all white male landowners. These well-read, well-fed, well-bred, and often well-wed delegates were mainly state or national leaders, for in the 1780s; ordinary people were not likely to participate in politics. (Even today, farm laborers, factory workers, and truck drivers are seldom found in Congress—although a haberdasher, a peanut farmer, and a movie actor have made their way to the White House.)

Although active in the movement to revise the Articles of Confederation, George Washington had been reluctant to attend the convention and accepted only when persuaded that his prestige was needed for its success. He was selected unanimously to preside over the meetings. According to the records, he spoke only twice during the deliberations, but his influence was felt in the informal gatherings as well as during the sessions. Everyone understood that Washington favored a more powerful central government led by a president. In fact, the general expectation that he would be the first president played a crucial role in the creation of the presidency. "No one feared that he would misuse power. . . . His genuine hesitancy, his reluctance to assume the position, only served to reinforce the almost universal desire that he do so."[22]

To encourage everyone to speak freely and allow delegates to change their minds after debate and discussion, the proceedings of the convention were kept secret and delegates were forbidden to discuss them with outsiders. The delegates also knew that if word of the inevitable disagreements got out, it would provide ammunition for the enemies of the convention.

Consensus

Critical to the success of the Constitutional Convention were its three famous compromises: the compromise between large and small states over representation in Congress, the compromise between North and South over the regulation and taxation of foreign commerce, and the compromise between North and South over the counting of slaves for the purposes of taxation and representation. There were other important compromises. Yet, on many significant issues, most of the delegates were in agreement.

All the delegates publicly supported a republican form of government based on elected representatives of the people. This was the only form the convention seriously considered and the only form acceptable to the nation. Equally important, all the delegates opposed arbitrary and unrestrained government.

Most of the delegates were in favor of *balanced government* in which no single interest would dominate and in which the national government would be strong enough to protect property and business from outbreaks like Shays' Rebellion.

Of the People

AMERICA'S CHANGING FACE

The Constitutional Convention

If the Constitutional Convention were convened today, how would the delegates compare to the all-white, all-male, property-owning delegates who drafted the Constitution in Philadelphia in 1787? One likely similarity is that they would be successful and generally well-educated individuals willing to engage in public service.

Many of those who drafted the Constitution had served in state legislatures. If the Constitutional Convention were held today and included state legislators, it would be much more diverse. Nearly 25 percent of most state legislators are now female, including at least a third in Maryland, Delaware, Arizona, Colorado, Kansas, Nevada, and Vermont. At the same time, state legislatures remain almost entirely white—only 9 percent were African American in 2009, and only 3 percent were Hispanic.[*]

Many of those who drafted the Constitution were also lawyers and successful business managers. If the Constitutional Convention were held today and included these professions, the proportion of women participating would be between 35 and 40 percent, and 15 percent of the delegates would not be white.[†] Although these proportions show a growing diversity among the delegates who might be called to Philadelphia today, they do not yet reflect the diversity of the population at large.

CRITICAL THINKING QUESTIONS

1. How would the recent changes in U.S. demographics translate into changes in the content of any constitution produced by a Constitutional Convention held today?

2. Why are lawyers disproportionately represented in politics, both today and at the Constitutional Convention? What difference does having so many lawyers as constitution makers have on the process and on the document they produce?

[*] Conference of State Legislators, "2009 African American Legislators," http://www.ncsl.org/Default.aspx?TabId=14767 (accessed February 16, 2010).
[†] U.S. Equal Employment Opportunity Commission, "Diversity in Law Firms," 2003, http://www.eeoc.gov/eeoc/statistics/reports/diversitylaw/lawfirms.pdf.

Benjamin Franklin, the 81-year-old delegate from Pennsylvania, favored extending the right to vote to all white males, but most of the delegates believed landowners were the best guardians of liberty. James Madison feared that those without property, if given the right to vote, might combine to deprive property owners of their rights. Delegates agreed in principle on limited voting rights but differed on the kind and amount of property owned as a prerequisite to vote. The framers recognized that they would jeopardize approval of the Constitution if they made the qualifications to vote in federal elections more restrictive than those of the states. As a result, each state was left to determine its own qualifications for electing members of the House of Representatives, the only branch of the national government that was to be elected directly by the voters.

Representing different constituencies and different ideologies, the Constitutional Convention devised a totally new form of government that provided for a central government strong enough to rule but still responsible to its citizens and to the member states.

31

Within five days of its opening, the convention voted—with only the Connecticut delegates dissenting—that "a national government ought to be established consisting of a supreme legislative, executive, and judiciary." This decision profoundly changed the nature of the union, from a loose confederation of states to a true nation.

Few dissented from proposals to give the new Congress all the powers of the old Congress, plus all other powers necessary to ensure that state legislation would not challenge the integrity of the United States. After the delegates agreed on the extensive powers of the legislative branch and the close connection between its lower house and the people, they also agreed that a strong executive, which the Articles of Confederation had lacked, was necessary to provide energy, direction, and a check on the legislature. They also accepted an independent judiciary without much debate. Other issues, however, sparked conflict.

Conflict and Compromise

Serious differences among the various delegates, especially between those from the large and small states, predated the Constitutional Convention. With the success of the War of Independence, the United States gained the formerly British land west of the colonial borders. States with large western borders such as Virginia claimed that their borders should simply be extended, as depicted in Figure 1–1. Colonies without open Western borders such as New Jersey and Connecticut took exception to these claims, reinforcing the tension between the colonies. The matter was resolved in the Land Ordinance of 1785 and the Northwest Ordinance of 1787, when all states agreed to cede the western lands to the national government and permit them to eventually become

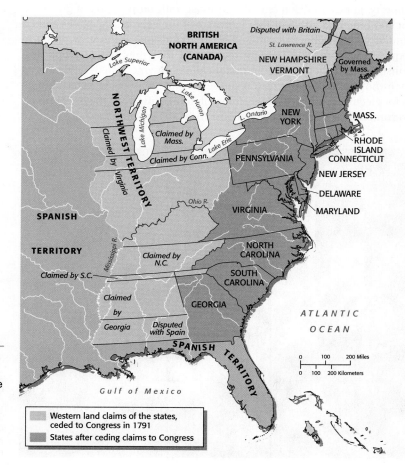

FIGURE 1–1 Western expansion, 1791.

Tension between small states and large states was intensified by the dispute over claims to Western land acquired after the Revolutionary War. ■ *Why might the size of a state be important in a federal system of government?*

part of new states rather than expand the borders of existing states. But the rivalries between the former colonies remained sharp at the convention in Philadelphia in 1787. For example, the large states also favored a strong national government (which they expected to dominate), while delegates from small states were anxious to avoid being dominated.

This tension surfaced in the first discussions of representation in Congress. Franklin favored a single-house national legislature, but most states had had two-chamber legislatures since colonial times, and the delegates were used to this system. **Bicameralism**—the principle of the two-house legislature—reflected delegates' belief in the need for balanced government. The Senate, the smaller chamber, would represent the states and to some extent the wealthier classes, and it would offset the larger, more democratic House of Representatives.

The Virginia Plan The Virginia delegation took the initiative. They presented 15 resolutions known as the **Virginia Plan.** This called for a strong central government with a legislature composed of two chambers. The voters were to elect the members of the more representative chamber, which would choose the members of the smaller chamber from nominees submitted by the state legislatures. Representation in both houses would be based on either wealth or population. Wealth was based on a 1783 law where "general expenses were apportioned on the basis of land values with their improvements." The more wealthy states were also the more populous ones—Massachusetts, Pennsylvania, and Virginia—which gave them a majority in the national legislature.

The Congress that the Virginia Plan would have created was to have all the legislative power of its predecessor under the Articles of Confederation, as well as the power "to legislate in all cases in which the separate States are incompetent," to veto state legislation that conflicted with the proposed constitution, and to choose a national executive with extensive jurisdiction. A national Supreme Court, along with the executive, would have a qualified veto over acts of Congress. In sum, the Virginia Plan would have created a strong national government with disproportionate power to the more populous states.

The New Jersey Plan The Virginia Plan dominated the discussion for the first few weeks. That changed when delegates from the small states put forward their plan. William Paterson of New Jersey presented a series of resolutions known as the **New Jersey Plan.** Paterson did not question the need for a strengthened central government, but he was concerned about how this strength might be used. The New Jersey Plan would give Congress the right to tax and regulate commerce and to coerce states, and it would retain the single-house or unicameral legislature (as under the Articles of Confederation) in which each state, regardless of size, would have the same vote.

The New Jersey Plan contained the germ of what eventually came to be a key provision of our Constitution: the *supremacy clause.* The national Supreme Court was to hear appeals from state judges, and the supremacy clause would require all judges—state and national—to treat laws of the national government and the treaties of the United States as superior to the constitutions and laws of each of the states.

For a time, the convention was deadlocked. The small states believed that all states should be represented equally in Congress, especially in the smaller "upper house" if there were to be two chambers. The large states insisted that representation in both houses be based on population or wealth, and that voters, not state legislatures, should elect national legislators. Finally, the so-called Committee of Eleven, a committee of 11 men, one from each of the member states, was elected to devise a compromise.[23] On July 5, it presented its proposals, including what came to be known as the great or Connecticut Compromise.

The Connecticut Compromise The **Connecticut Compromise** (so labeled because of the prominent role the Connecticut delegation played in constructing it) called for one

bicameralism
The principle of a two-house legislature.

Virginia Plan
The initial proposal at the Constitutional Convention made by the Virginia delegation for a strong central government with a bicameral legislature dominated by the big states.

New Jersey Plan
The proposal at the Constitutional Convention made by William Paterson of New Jersey for a central government with a single-house legislature in which each state would be represented equally.

Connecticut Compromise
The compromise agreement by states at the Constitutional Convention for a bicameral legislature with a lower house in which representation would be based on population and an upper house in which each state would have two senators.

TABLE

1–2 | The Constitutional Convention: Conflict and Compromise

Virginia Plan	New Jersey Plan	Connecticut Compromise
Legitimacy derived from citizens, based on popular representation	Derived from states, based on equal votes for each state	Derived from citizens and the states
Bicameral legislature, representation in both houses determined by population	Unicameral legislature, representation equal by state	Bicameral legislature with seats in the Senate apportioned by states and seats in the House apportioned by population
Executive size undetermined, elected and removable by Congress	More than one person, removable by state majority	Single executive elected by electoral college, not removable by state majority
Judicial life tenure, able to veto state legislation	No federal judicial power over states	Judicial life tenure, able to veto state legislation in violation of constitution
Legislature can override state laws	Government can compel obedience to national laws	
Ratification by citizens	Ratification by states	Ratification by states, with process open to citizen ratification

house in which each state would have an equal vote, and a second house in which representation would be based on population and in which all bills for raising or appropriating money—a key function of government—would originate. This proposal was a setback for the large states, which agreed to it only when the smaller states made it clear this was their price for union. After the delegates accepted equality of state representation in the Senate, most objections to a strong national government dissolved. (Table 1–2 outlines the key features of the Virginia Plan, the New Jersey Plan, and the Connecticut Compromise.)

North–South Compromises   Other issues split the delegates from the North and South. Southerners were afraid that a northern majority in Congress might discriminate against southern trade. They had some basis for this concern. John Jay, a New Yorker who was secretary of foreign affairs for the Confederation, had proposed a treaty with Great Britain that would have given advantages to northern merchants at the expense of southern exporters of agricultural products such as tobacco and cotton. To protect themselves,

The Connecticut compromise created a bicameral legislature, with seats in the Senate apportioned by states and seats in the House apportioned by population. ■ *How did this decision affect the relative sizes of the House chambers (left) and those of the Senate (right)?*

the southern delegates insisted that a two-thirds majority in the Senate be required to ratify a treaty.

One subject that appears not to have been open for resolution was slavery. The view widely shared among historians is that the states with a greater reliance on slaves would have left the convention if the document had reduced or eliminated the practice. The issue did arise on whether to count slaves for the purpose of apportioning seats in the House of Representatives. To gain more representatives, the South wanted to count slaves; the North resisted. After heated debate, the delegates agreed on the **three-fifths compromise.** Each slave would be counted as three-fifths of a free person for the purposes of apportionment in the House and of direct taxation. This fraction was chosen because it maintained a balance of power between the North and the South. The compromise also included a provision to eliminate the importation of slaves in 20 years, and Congress did so in 1808. The issue of balance between North and South would recur in the early history of our nation as territorial governments were established and territories that applied for statehood decided whether to permit or ban slavery.

Other Issues Delegates also argued about other issues. Should the national government have lower courts, or would one federal Supreme Court be enough? This issue was left to Congress to resolve. The Constitution states that there shall be one Supreme Court and that Congress may establish lower courts.

How should the president be selected? For a long time, the convention favored allowing Congress to pick the president, but some delegates feared that Congress would then dominate the president, or vice versa. The convention also rejected election by the state legislatures because the delegates distrusted the state legislatures. The delegates finally settled on election of the president by the **electoral college,** a group of individuals equal in number to the U.S. senators and representatives. Originally, it was thought electors would exercise their own judgment in selecting the president. But the college quickly came to reflect partisanship, and today, for most states, electors cast ballots for the candidate who wins the popular vote of that state. (We discuss the electoral college in greater detail in Chapter 9.) This was perhaps the delegates' most novel contribution as well as the most contrived, and it has long been one of the most criticized provisions in the Constitution.[24] (See Article II, Section 1 of the Constitution, which is reprinted between Chapters 2 and 3.)

After three months, the delegates stopped debating. On September 17, 1787, all but three of those still present signed the document they were recommending to the nation. Others who opposed the general drift of the convention had already left. Their work well done, the delegates adjourned to the nearby City Tavern to celebrate.

According to an old story, a woman confronted Benjamin Franklin as he left the last session of the convention.

"What kind of government have you given us, Dr. Franklin?" she asked. "A republic or a monarchy?"

"A republic, Madam," he answered, "if you can keep it."

three-fifths compromise
The compromise between northern and southern states at the Constitutional Convention that three-fifths of the slave population would be counted for determining direct taxation and representation in the House of Representatives.

electoral college
The electoral system used in electing the president and vice president, in which voters vote for electors pledged to cast their ballots for a particular party's candidates.

To Adopt or Not to Adopt?

The delegates had gone far. Indeed, they had disregarded Congress's instruction to do no more than revise the Articles of Confederation. In particular, they had ignored Article XIII, which declared the Union to be perpetual and prohibited any alteration of the Articles unless Congress and *every one of the state legislatures* agreed—a provision that had made it impossible to amend the Articles. The convention delegates, however, boldly declared that their newly proposed Constitution should go into effect when ratified by popularly elected conventions in nine states.

LEARNING **OBJECTIVE**

1.5 Evaluate the arguments for and against the ratification of the Constitution.

They turned to this method of ratification for practical considerations as well as to secure legitimacy for their proposed government. Not only were the delegates aware that there was little chance of winning approval of the new Constitution in all state legislatures, but many also believed that a constitution approved *by the people* would have higher legal and moral status than one approved only by a legislature. The Articles of Confederation had been a compact of state governments, but the Constitution was based on the will of the people (recall its opening words: "We the People...."). Still, even this method of ratification would not be easy. The nation was not ready to adopt the Constitution without a thorough debate.

Federalists Versus Antifederalists

Supporters of the new government, by cleverly appropriating the name **Federalists,** forced their opponents to be known as the **Antifederalists** and pointed out the negative character of the arguments opposing ratification. While advocating a strong national government but also retaining state prerogatives, the Federalists took some of the sting out of charges that they were trying to destroy the states and establish an all-powerful central government.

The split was in part geographic. Seaboard and city regions tended to be Federalist strongholds; backcountry regions from Maine (then part of Massachusetts) through Georgia, inhabited by farmers and other relatively poor people, were generally Antifederalist. The underlying regional and economic differences led to fears by those opposing the new form of government that it would not protect individual rights, and reinforced the "Antifederalist charge that the Constitution was an aristocratic document."[25] But as in most political contests, no single factor completely accounted for the division between Federalists and Antifederalists. Thus, in Virginia, the leaders of both sides came from the same general social and economic class. New York City and Philadelphia strongly supported the Constitution, yet so did predominantly rural New Jersey and Connecticut.

The great debate was conducted through pamphlets, newspapers, letters to editors, and speeches. It provides an outstanding example of a free people publicly discussing the nature of their fundamental laws. Out of the debate came a series of essays known as *The Federalist,* written under the pseudonym Publius by Alexander Hamilton, James Madison, and John Jay to persuade the voters of New York to ratify the Constitution. *The Federalist* is still "widely regarded as the most profound single treatise on the Constitution ever written and as among the few masterly works in political science produced in all the centuries of history."[26] (Three of the most important *Federalist* essays, Nos. 10, 51, and 78, are reprinted in the Appendix of this book.)

Antifederalists opposed the creation of a strong central government. They worried that, under the Constitution, Congress would "impose barriers against commerce," and they were concerned that the Constitution did not do enough to ensure "frequent rotation of office," meaning elected officials could not be recalled through elections and over time would become less concerned with their constituents.[27]

The Antifederalists' most telling criticism of the proposed Constitution was its failure to include a bill of rights.[28] The Federalists believed a bill of rights was unnecessary because the proposed national government had *only* the specific powers that the states and the people delegated to it. Thus, there was no need to specify that Congress could not, for example, abridge freedom of the press because the states and the people had not given the national government power to regulate the press in the first place. Moreover, the Federalists argued, to guarantee some rights might be dangerous, because rights not listed could be assumed to be denied. The Constitution itself already protected some important rights—the requirement of trial by jury in federal criminal cases, provided for in Article III, for example. Hamilton and others also insisted that paper guarantees were feeble protection against governmental tyranny.

Federalists
Supporters of ratification of the Constitution and of a strong central government.

Antifederalists
Opponents of ratification of the Constitution and of a strong central government generally.

The Federalist
Essays promoting ratification of the Constitution, published anonymously by Alexander Hamilton, John Jay, and James Madison in 1787 and 1788.

The Antifederalists were unconvinced. If some rights were protected, what could be the objection to providing constitutional protection for others? Without a bill of rights, what was to prevent Congress from using one of its delegated powers to abridge free speech? If bills of rights were needed in state constitutions to limit state governments, why did the national constitution not include a bill of rights to limit the national government? This was a government further from the people, they contended, with a greater tendency to subvert natural rights than was true of state governments.

The Politics of Ratification

The absence of a bill of rights in the proposed Constitution dominated the struggle over its adoption. In taverns, churches, and newspaper offices, people were muttering, "No bill of rights—no Constitution!" This feeling was so strong that some Antifederalists, though they were far more concerned with states' rights than individual rights, joined forces with those wanting a bill of rights in order to defeat the proposed Constitution.

The Federalists began the debate over the Constitution as soon as the delegates left Philadelphia in mid-September 1787. Their tactic was to secure ratification in as many states as possible before the opposition had time to organize. The Antifederalists were handicapped because most newspapers supported ratification. Moreover, Antifederalist strength was concentrated in rural areas, which were underrepresented in some state legislatures and in which it was more difficult to arouse the people to political action. The Antifederalists needed time to organize, while the Federalists moved in a hurry.

Most of the small states, now satisfied by getting equal Senate representation, ratified the Constitution without difficulty. Delaware was the first, and by early 1788, Pennsylvania, New Jersey, Georgia, and Connecticut had also ratified (see Table 1–3). In Massachusetts, however, opposition was growing. Key leaders, such as John Hancock and Samuel Adams, were doubtful or opposed. The debate in Boston raged for most of January 1788 and into February. But in the end, the Massachusetts Convention narrowly ratified the Constitution in that state, 187 to 168.

By June 21, 1788, Maryland, South Carolina, and New Hampshire had also ratified, giving the Constitution the nine states required for it to go into effect. But two big hurdles remained: Virginia and New York. It would be impossible to begin the new government without the consent of these two major states. Virginia was crucial. As the most populous state and the home of Washington, Jefferson, and Madison, Virginia was a link between North and South. The Virginia ratifying convention rivaled the Constitutional Convention in the caliber of its delegates. Madison, who had only recently switched to favoring a bill of rights after saying earlier that it was unnecessary, captained the Federalist forces. The fiery Patrick Henry led the opposition. In an epic debate, Henry cried that liberty was the issue: "Liberty, the greatest of earthly possessions ... that precious jewel!" But Madison promised that a bill of rights embracing the freedoms of religion, speech, and assembly would be added to the Constitution as soon as the new government was established. Washington tipped the balance with a letter urging ratification. News of the Virginia vote, 89 for the Constitution and 79 opposed, was rushed to New York.[29]

Patrick Henry's famous cry of "Give me liberty or give me death!" helped rally support for the revolution against Britain. Later, he was an outspoken opponent of ratification of the Constitution and was instrumental in forcing adoption of the Bill of Rights.

TABLE 1–3 Ratification of the U.S. Constitution

State	Date
Delaware	December 7, 1787
Pennsylvania	December 12, 1787
New Jersey	December 18, 1787
Georgia	January 2, 1788
Connecticut	January 9, 1788
Massachusetts	February 6, 1788
Maryland	April 28, 1788
South Carolina	May 23, 1788
New Hampshire	June 21, 1788
Virginia	June 25, 1788
New York	July 26, 1788
North Carolina	November 21, 1789
Rhode Island	May 29, 1790

■ *By what date did the Constitution have enough state support to go into effect? Why was it still important for the remaining states to ratify the Constitution?*

By the People

Becoming an American Citizen

Many Americans take their government for granted and have not thought much about the importance of their citizenship in this country. That is not the case for those who have gone through the process of securing U.S. citizenship. The process involves a detailed application, a criminal records search, information about your family, and an interview that includes an assessment of proficiency in English and knowledge of the U.S. government and Constitution. You can view samples of these civics questions by clicking on the "Naturalization Test" at http://www.uscis.gov/files/nativedocuments/M-685.pdf. How would you do on the oral exam? One current sample question, for example, asks applicants: "The idea of self-government is in the first three words of the Constitution. What are these three words?" The correct answer is "We the people." To pass the test,

an applicant must answer six of the ten questions correctly.*

For many people wanting to become U.S. citizens, the application process, interview, and examination are intimidating. The U.S. Committee for Refugees and Immigrants (USCRI) is a group that makes a difference in helping people attain U.S. Citizenship. USCRI is the nation's oldest (founded in 1911) and largest network of nonprofit organizations serving foreign-born people. USCRI has resettled a quarter million refugees in the past two decades. USCRI has a "Partnership for Citizenship Program" that helps individuals prepare to become citizens. Some of those seeking citizenship are refugees who also need assistance in such basics as writing resumes and preparing for job interviews, as well as information on where they can go for food, clothing, and housing.

You can make a difference by volunteering at an agency assisting refugees and others in your community. Some universities, like Harvard University, have programs where undergraduates tutor individuals to prepare them for the citizenship exam. If your institution does not have such a program, you might organize one. Given your study of American government, you will be especially prepared to assist in the English and Civics preparation for the citizenship screening interview.

CRITICAL THINKING QUESTIONS

1. Would all Americans take citizenship more seriously if they had to apply for citizenship and pass an oral exam on U.S. government?

2. How restrictive should the government be in extending citizenship?

* U.S. Citizenship and Immigration Services, "The Naturalization Test," http://www.uscis.gov/portal/site/uscis/menuitem (accessed April 27, 2010).

The great landowners along New York's Hudson River, unlike the southern planters, opposed the Constitution. They feared federal taxation of their holdings, and they did not want to abolish the profitable tax New York had been levying on trade and commerce with other states. When the convention assembled, the Federalists were greatly outnumbered, but they were aided by Alexander Hamilton's strategy and skill, and by word of Virginia's ratification. New York approved by a margin of three votes. Although North Carolina and Rhode Island still remained outside the Union (the former ratified in November 1789, the latter six months later), the new nation was created. In New York, a few members of the old Congress assembled to issue the call for elections under the new Constitution. Then they adjourned without setting a date for reconvening.

CHAPTER SUMMARY

1.1 Use the concept of constitutional democracy to explain U.S. government and politics.

The United States operates under a constitutional democracy. In our system, the Constitution lays out the basic rules of the game under which politicians act to accomplish their different agendas. "Politics" is a broad term that can be used to describe what happens between these politicians in pursuit of their goals. "Government" is another broad term that encompasses the many different institutions enumerated by the Constitution in which the politicians function. Political science studies the interaction among politics, politicians, the government, and, within the American context, our constitutional democracy.

1.2 Differentiate democracy from other forms of government, and identify conditions, values, political processes, and political structures conducive to a successful democracy.

In the United States, we often use the term "democracy" to describe our form of government. This is true to an extent, but a more accurate term would be "representative democracy" or "republic." The politicians in our system are elected representatives meant to stand up for the interests of their constituents. Representative democracy differs from direct democracy in the level of citizen participation.

Scholars have identified several conditions that may help democratic governments form and consolidate. Among these, educational, economic, social, and ideological conditions are the most important. These conditions further democratic values such as a belief in personal liberty, respect for the individual, equality of opportunity, and popular consent. Our representative democracy functions through political structures including courts, legislatures, the executive, administrative agencies, federalism, and the principle of limited government.

1.3 Show how politics before 1787 shaped the Constitution.

In the formative years of American democracy, several competing factions worked, sometimes at cross purposes, to develop the Constitution. Some of the most divisive issues that the framers had to address were the challenges presented by a federal system. Small states had real concerns about their role in a democratic system. There were also issues that had more to do with geography and economics. The divide between the North and the South on slavery was also important at the convention.

1.4 Assess the important compromises reached by the delegates to the Constitutional Convention of 1787.

The framers came up with some brilliant compromises to address these issues, such as the Connecticut Compromise that led to our current bicameral legislative branch. Other issues were put on hold. For example, the framers postponed dealing with slavery and compromised on counting slaves as three-fifths of a person for purposes of apportionment.

1.5 Evaluate the arguments for and against the ratification of the Constitution.

Some of the same themes that dominated the debate over ratification can still be heard today. Federalists argued for a central government that would be strong enough to make the newly united states capable of standing up to the great powers of the time. Antifederalists worried about what might come of a strong central government and were particularly concerned about the lack of any bill of rights in the document.

CHAPTER **SELF-TEST**

1.1 Use the concept of constitutional democracy to explain U.S. government and politics.

1. Write a short essay discussing the intersection between government and politics. In what ways are they similar? How are they different?
2. How would U.S. government be different if the Antifederalists had not been successful in pressing for a bill of rights?

1.2 Differentiate democracy from other forms of government, and identify conditions, values, political processes, and political structures conducive to a successful democracy.

3. Explain the differences between direct democracy and representative democracy. What concerns did the framers of the Constitution have about unlimited direct democracy?
4. Write a short essay explaining how democratic values are important to a successful democracy.
5. Write a short essay explaining how specific values have contributed to the relative longevity of democracy in the United States. Which values seem most important to U.S. citizens?
6. Identify three or four issues the United States faces today that the founders could not have foreseen. Discuss briefly how the Constitution is relevant to these issues.
7. Russia has a well-educated population and a fairly strong economy. However, its people do not have much experience with democracy and many are

suspicious of it. Given these facts, assess the prospects for democracy in Russia using the criteria listed in the chapter.

1.3 Show how politics before 1787 shaped the Constitution.

8. Put the following events in chronological order:
   a. Drafting of the Articles of Confederation
   b. Revolutionary War
   c. Declaration of Independence
   d. Constitutional Convention
   e. Shays' Rebellion
   f. Ratification of the Constitution

1.4 Assess the important compromises reached by the delegates to the Constitutional Convention of 1787.

9. Which state was the compromise that led to a bicameral legislature named after?
   a. Rhode Island
   b. Connecticut
   c. New Hampshire
   d. Maine
10. The critical compromise reached to accommodate concerns over how to count slaves for apportionment purposes was known as the _____ compromise:
    a. three-quarters
    b. three-fifths
    c. two-thirds
    d. five-sevenths

11. Match the following articles with their appropriate subject (see the Appendix):

a. Art. I   i. Interstate Relations
b. Art. II   ii. Ratification
c. Art. III   iii. Congressional
d. Art. IV   iv. Amending Power
e. Art. V   v. Executive
f. Art. VI   vi. Supremacy Act
g. Art. VII   vii. Judiciary

1.5 **Evaluate the arguments for and against the ratification of the Constitution.**

12. Identify three or four historical tensions that impeded ratification of the Constitution and that have persisted into present-day politics.

13. Write a brief persuasive essay adopting the Antifederalist position against ratification of the Constitution. In your essay, list two or three arguments that you feel Federalists would put forward and then counter those with your persuasive arguments.

Answers to selected questions: 8. The proper order is b, c, a, e, d, f; 9. b; 10. b; 11. a. iii, b. v, c. vii, d. i, e. iv, f. vi, g. ii.

mypoliscilab EXERCISES

Apply what you learned in this chapter on MyPoliSciLab.

Read on mypoliscilab.com

eText: Chapter 1

Study and Review on mypoliscilab.com

Pre-Test
Post-Test
Chapter Exam
Flashcards

Watch on mypoliscilab.com

Video: Mexico Border Security
Video: The Bailout Hearings
Video: Vaccines: Mandatory Protection

KEY TERMS

democracy, p. 19
direct democracy, p. 19
direct primary, p. 20
initiative, p. 20
referendum, p. 20
recall, p. 20
representative democracy, p. 20
constitutional democracy, p. 22
constitutionalism, p. 22
statism, p. 22

popular consent, p. 23
majority rule, p. 23
majority, p. 23
plurality, p. 23
theocracy, p.27
Articles of Confederation, p. 28
Annapolis Convention, p. 29
Constitutional Convention, p. 29
Shays' Rebellion, p. 29
bicameralism, p. 33

Virginia Plan, p. 33
New Jersey Plan, p. 33
Connecticut Compromise, p. 33
three-fifths compromise, p. 35
electoral college, p. 35
Federalists, p. 36
Antifederalists, p. 36
The Federalist, p. 36

ADDITIONAL RESOURCES

FURTHER READING

BERNARD BAILYN, ED., *The Debate on the Constitution: Federalist and Antifederalist Speeches, Articles, and Letters During the Struggle over Ratification,* 2 vols. (Library of America, 1993).

LANCE BANNING, *The Sacred Fire of Liberty: James Madison and the Founding of the Federal Republic* (Cornell University Press, 1995).
ROBERT A. DAHL, *How Democratic Is the American Constitution,* 2d ed. (Yale University Press, 2003).

STANLEY ELKINS AND **ERIC MCKITRICK,** *The Age of Federalism: The Early American Republic, 1788–1800* (Oxford University Press, 1994).
DAVID HACKETT FISCHER, *Washington's Crossing* (Oxford University Press, 2004).

ALAN GIBSON, *Understanding the Founding: Crucial Questions* (University Press of Kansas, 2007).

ALEXANDER HAMILTON, JAMES MADISON, AND JOHN JAY, *The Federalist Papers,* ed. Clinton Rossiter (New American Library, 1961). Also in several other editions.

PHILIP B. KURLAND AND **RALPH LERNER,** *The Founders' Constitution,* 5 vols. (University of Chicago Press, 1987).

SANFORD LEVINSON, *Our Undemocratic Constitution* (Oxford University Press, 2006).

AREND LIJPHART, *Patterns of Democracy: Government Forms and Performance in Thirty-Six Countries* (Yale University Press, 1999).

JACK N. RAKOVE, *Original Meanings: Politics and Ideas in the Making of the Constitution* (Vintage Books, 1997).

MICHAEL SCHUDSON, *The Good Citizen: A History of American Civic Life* (Harvard University Press, 1998).

GORDON S. WOOD, *The Radicalism of the American Revolution* (Knopf, 1992). See also the *Journal of Democracy* (Johns Hopkins University Press).

WEB SITES

www.usa.gov/Agencies/federal.shtml This site provides a variety of information on the government and its agencies.

www.constitutionfacts.com/ This site provides quotes, facts, and quizzes about the Constitution.

www.archives.gov/ This site provides information on America's key historical documents.

www.teachingamericanhistory.org/ This site is all about American history.

www.people.brandeis.edu/~teuber/ polphil.html This site provides resources for exploring the political philosophies important to the founders.

CHAPTER

2

Constitutional Foundations

The Constitution of the United States is the world's oldest written constitution. Some 224 other countries have written constitutions, but more than half (122) have been adopted or significantly revised since 1990, with 17 new ones ratified since 2000. Nine countries have no written constitution, including Oman, New Zealand, and the United Kingdom.[1]

Debate was critical in getting the signers' agreement to the initial document of the U.S. Constitution in 1787. Since then, the ambiguity and brevity of many constitutional provisions have spurred a great deal of additional debate, although there has not been a serious effort to alter our basic constitutional system of government since the Constitution went into effect in 1789. Indeed, the potential to alter the Constitution through the amendment process has created a remarkable democratic system of government capable of withstanding a civil war, two world wars, and internal and external security threats, all the while providing individual protections for an increasingly heterogeneous population.

Although the basic structures and processes that the Constitution set up have provided a consistent and stable foundation throughout the country's history, that does not mean that debate over what the Constitution means has ended. For example, what does the Second Amendment's protection of the "right to bear arms" mean? After 70 years of silence on the issue, the U.S. Supreme Court addressed it in a case in June 2008. By a 5-to-4 vote, the Court decided that the amendment meant that individual citizens, apart from any association with a state militia, had a constitutional right to own a gun. The Court's interpretation of the Second Amendment invalidated the District of Columbia's ban on registering (and thus owning) handguns.

Even though the Court invalidated one of the most strict gun-control laws in the nation in *District of Columbia* v. *Heller* (2008),[2] only two years later, the Court weighed in once again on the Second Amendment—this time to determine whether it also prohibits states from making such restrictive laws. In *McDonald* v. *Chicago* (2010),[3] the Court ruled that it did. Although the Court's decision did not specifically strike down the Chicago law, it did for the first time rule that states are barred from encroaching on citizens' Second Amendment rights. The Supreme Court then sent the case back to the lower federal courts to determine whether the Chicago law runs afoul of the Amendment's protections for individual citizens to own handguns.

The continuing debate regarding the Second Amendment's meaning highlights both the genius and a flaw in the Constitution—its lack of specificity. In composing the Constitution, the framers were conscious that they were writing a document that needed to withstand the test of time. By not specifying what is meant by the right to "keep and bear arms," they designed a document that others could apply to changing circumstances. However, this generality also results in continuing debates, which have included the appropriate authority of the governing branches and the extent of national government authority over the states. The power of the courts to determine what exactly the Constitution means has also led many to scrutinize the ways by which it reaches those decisions.

Understanding the Constitution and considering its strengths and weaknesses is a necessary step in studying and participating in U.S. government. After such a study, one student turned his college research paper at the University of Texas into a successful drive to ratify the Twenty-Seventh Amendment (concerning congressional salaries) in 1992. We may not all achieve such a result through our participation, but by being more knowledgeable about our system, we can better protect our own individual liberties, evaluate the appropriate authority of various elected and appointed governmental officials, and understand what it means to have a government with powers that are separated, shared, and checked.

In this chapter, we will discuss our constitutionally arranged system of separation of powers and checks and balances, as well as how special-interest groups and political parties try to circumvent these protections. We will see how the judiciary came to be widely accepted as the final interpreter of constitutional meaning and the way both the executive and the legislature have used the Constitution to pursue their own ends. Finally, we will examine the difficult process through which citizens can amend the Constitution. As the framers intended, that is no small feat, and one that is an important factor in the stability of our Constitution.

Views of the Constitution

LEARNING **OBJECTIVE**

2.1 Describe the basic structure of the Constitution and its Bill of Rights.

natural law
God's or nature's law that defines right from wrong and is higher than human law.

In addition to being the oldest written Constitution in the world, the U.S. Constitution is also one of the shortest. The original Constitution, excluding the Bill of Rights, contains only 4,543 words. In comparison, India's constitution is 117,000 words, and the longest state constitution—that of Alabama—is over 350,000 words. Its basic structure is straightforward. Article I establishes a bicameral Congress, with a House of Representatives and a Senate, and empowers it to enact legislation, for example, governing foreign and interstate commerce (as discussed further in Chapter 11). Article II vests the executive power in the president (as discussed in Chapter 12), and Article III vests the judicial power in the Supreme Court and other federal courts that Congress may establish (as discussed in Chapter 14). Article IV guarantees the privileges and immunities of citizens and specifies the conditions for admitting new states. Article V provides for the methods of amending the Constitution, and Article VI specifies that the Constitution and all laws made under it are the supreme law of the land. Finally, Article VII provides that the Constitution had to be ratified by 9 of the original 13 states to go into effect. In 1791, the first 10 amendments, the Bill of Rights, were added, and another 17 amendments have been added since.

The Bill of Rights, a hallmark of the U.S. Constitution, protects individual liberties. In comparison, some countries such as China might promise equality and the rule of law but fall short of meeting these goals. Some type of dictatorship has been the basis of the constitutional structure under all of China's several constitutions since 1949, and government officials have routinely been shielded from the law. In contrast, India used the U.S. Constitution as the basis for several aspects of its constitution, including the protection of individual rights and a system of federalism.

Despite its brevity, the Constitution firmly established the framers' experiment in free-government-in-the-making that each generation reinterprets and renews. That is why after more than 220 years we have not had another written Constitution—let alone two, three, or more, like other countries around the world. Part of the reason is the widespread acceptance of the Constitution across our population. But the Constitution has also endured because it is a brilliant structure for limited government and one that the framers designed to be adaptable and flexible. The entire Constitution and its amendments appear at the end of this chapter.

As the Constitution won the support of citizens in the early years of the Republic, it took on the aura of **natural law**—law that defines right from wrong, which is higher than human law. Like the crown in Great Britain, the Constitution became a symbol of national unity and loyalty, evoking both emotional and intellectual support from Americans,

Citizens can view the original U.S. Constitution at the National Archives in Washington DC. ■ *What effects might displaying the Constitution as it is pictured here have on the way citizens think about the document?*

regardless of their differences. The framers' work became part of the U.S. creed and culture.[4] The Constitution stands for liberty, equality before the law, limited or expanded government—indeed, it stands for just about anything anyone wants to read into it.

Even today, U.S. citizens generally revere the Constitution, although many do not know what is in it. A poll by the National Constitution Center found that nine of ten U.S. adults are proud of the Constitution and feel it is important to them. However, a third mistakenly believe the Constitution establishes English as the country's official language. One in six believes it establishes the United States as a Christian nation. Only one in four could name a single First Amendment right. Although two in three knew the Constitution created three branches of the national government, only one in three could name all three branches.[5]

The Constitution is more than a symbol, however. It is the supreme and binding law that both grants and limits powers. "In framing a government which is to be administered by men over men," wrote James Madison in *The Federalist*, No. 51, "the great difficulty lies in this: You must first enable the government to control the governed; and in the next place oblige it to control itself." (See *The Federalist*, No. 51, in the Appendix of this book.) The Constitution is both a positive instrument of government, which enables the governors to control the governed, and a restraint on government, which enables the ruled to check the rulers. How does the Constitution limit the power of the government? How does it create governmental power? How has it managed to serve as a great symbol of national unity and, at the same time, as an adaptable instrument of government? The secret is an ingenious separation of powers and a system of checks and balances that limits power with power.

James Madison was the fourth president of the United States (1809–1817) and an author of *The Federalist Papers.* Madison's view on a separated system of government in which each branch checks the power of other branches shapes our governmental structure. ■ *How did Madison's beliefs about the nature of man affect his views on the best structure for our federal government?*

Checking Power with Power

"If men were angels," James Madison argued in *The Federalist,* No. 51, "no government would be necessary. If angels were to govern men, neither external nor internal controls on government would be necessary."[6] But the framers knew well that men were not angels, and thus, to create a successful government, they would need to create a government of *limited* authority. How? Within the government, competing interests would check each other, and, externally, the governed would check the government through elections, petitions, protests, and amendments. The framers wanted a stronger and more effective national government than they had under the Articles of Confederation. But they were keenly aware that the people would not accept too much central control. Efficiency and order were important concerns, but liberty was more important. The framers wanted to ensure domestic tranquility and prevent future rebellions, but they also wanted to forestall the emergence of a homegrown King George III. Accordingly, they allotted certain powers to the national government and reserved the rest for the states, thus establishing a system of **federalism** (whose nature and problems we discuss in Chapter 3). Even this was not enough. The framers believed additional restraints were needed to limit the national government.

The most important means they devised to make public officials observe the constitutional limits on their powers was *free and fair elections,* through which voters could throw out of office those who abuse power. Yet the framers were not willing to depend solely on political controls because they did not fully trust the people's judgment. "Free government is founded on jealousy, and not in confidence," said Thomas Jefferson. "In questions of power, then, let no more be heard of confidence in man, but bind him down from mischief by the chains of the Constitution."[7]

No less important, the framers feared a majority might deprive minorities of their rights. This risk was certainly real at the time of the framing, as it is today. As *District of Columbia* v. *Heller* shows, even if there was sufficient public support for the District's legislation restricting gun ownership when it was enacted in 1976, the Second Amendment provides protection for citizens to own guns for their own self-protection. "A dependence

LEARNING **OBJECTIVE**

2.2 Analyze how the Constitution grants, limits, separates, and balances governmental power.

federalism
A constitutional arrangement in which power is distributed between a central government and subdivisional governments, called states in the United States. The national and the subdivisional governments both exercise direct authority over individuals.

By the People

MAKING A DIFFERENCE

Getting to Know Your Constitution

As discussed in this chapter, many Americans are woefully ignorant about our founding document. One way you can become involved in government is to understand this important document and help others understand it as well. By enrolling in this class, you have already taken the first step.

The U.S. Constitution was signed by 39 of our nation's founders on September 17, 1787. In 2004, Congress passed a statute requiring any school or college that receives federal money to recognize the Constitution on September 17, or a weekday immediately preceding or following that date if it falls on a weekend. There are many ways you or your school could celebrate Constitution Day. One way might be to actually read the document. You could pick up a pocket constitution or read the one we include at the end of this chapter.

Another great resource on the U.S. Constitution is the National Constitution Center in Philadelphia. It opened in 2003 and is a center for discussions about our founding document and its implications for governing. On the Center's Web site (http://ratify.constitution center.org/constitution/index_no_flash.php), you can read the Constitution and search it by using key words, topics, and even court cases related to different clauses. Try searching the document using the topic "Constitutional Convention" to learn more about the debate over the phrases included in the document. Understanding these arguments will help you become an informed participant in political debate with your peers, as well as in the political arena.

CRITICAL THINKING QUESTIONS

1. Should the fact that there was disagreement on the wording of the Constitution among the founders affect the way we should understand the document?

2. How might understanding these disagreements inform your own positions on political questions?

---

on the people is, no doubt, the primary control on the government," Madison contended in *The Federalist,* No. 51, "but experience has taught mankind the necessity of auxiliary precautions."[8] What were these "auxiliary precautions" against popular tyranny?

Separation of Powers

The first step against potential tyranny of the majority was the **separation of powers,** the distribution of constitutional authority among the three branches of the national government. In *The Federalist,* No. 47, Madison wrote, "No political truth is certainly of greater intrinsic value, or is stamped with the authority of more enlightened patrons of liberty, than that…the accumulation of all powers, legislative, executive, and judiciary, in the same hands…may justly be pronounced the very definition of tyranny."[9] Chief among the "enlightened patrons of liberty" to whose authority Madison was appealing were the eighteenth-century philosophers John Locke and Montesquieu, whose works most educated citizens knew well.

The intrinsic value of the dispersion of power, however, is not the only reason the framers included it in the Constitution. It had already been the general practice in the colonies for more than 100 years. Only during the Revolutionary period did some of

separation of powers

Constitutional division of powers among the legislative, executive, and judicial branches, with the legislative branch making law, the executive applying and enforcing the law, and the judiciary interpreting the law.

46

the states concentrate authority in the hands of the legislature, and that unhappy experience as well as that under the Articles of Confederation confirmed the framers' belief in the merits of the separation of powers. Many attributed the evils of state government and the lack of energy in the central government under the Articles of Confederation to the lack of a strong executive to check legislative abuses and to give energy and direction to administration.

Still, separating power by itself was not enough. It might not prevent the branches of the government and officials from pooling their authority and acting together, or from responding alike to the same pressures—from the demand of a majority to restrict handgun ownership, for example, or to impose confiscatory taxes on the rich. If separating power was not enough, what else could be done?

Checks and Balances: Ambition to Counteract Ambition

The framers' answer was a system of **checks and balances** (see Table 2–1). "The great security against a gradual concentration of the several powers in the same department," wrote Madison in *The Federalist*, No. 51, "consists in giving to those who administer each department the necessary constitutional means and personal motives to resist encroachments of the others.... Ambition must be made to counteract ambition."[10] Each branch therefore has a role in the actions of the others (see Figure 2–1).

Congress enacts legislation, which the president must sign into law or veto. The Supreme Court can declare laws passed by Congress and signed by the president unconstitutional, but the president appoints the justices and all the other federal judges, with the Senate's approval. The president administers the laws, but Congress provides the money to run the government. Moreover, the Senate and the House of Representatives have absolute veto power over each other because both houses must approve bills before they can become law.

Not only does each branch have some authority over the others, but also each is politically independent of the others. Voters in each local district choose members of the House; voters in each state choose senators; the president is elected by the voters in all the states through the electoral college. With the consent of the Senate, the president appoints federal judges, who remain in office until they retire or are impeached.

The framers also ensured that a majority of the voters could win control over only part of the government at one time. In an off-year (nonpresidential) election where a new majority might take control of the House of Representatives, the president still has at least two more years, and senators hold office for six years. Finally, there are independent federal courts, which exercise their own powerful checks.

checks and balances
A constitutional grant of powers that enables each of the three branches of government to check some acts of the others and therefore ensures that no branch can dominate.

TABLE

2–1	The Exercise of Checks and Balances, 1789–2010

Vetoes Presidents have vetoed more than 2,500 acts of Congress. Congress has overridden presidential vetoes more than 100 times.

Judicial Review The Supreme Court has ruled more than 175 congressional acts or parts thereof unconstitutional.

Impeachment The House of Representatives has impeached two presidents, one senator, one secretary of war, and 15 federal judges; the Senate has convicted seven of the judges but neither president.

Confirmation The Senate has refused to confirm nine cabinet nominations. Many other cabinet and subcabinet appointments were withdrawn because the Senate seemed likely to reject them.

SOURCE: The American Presidency Project, University of California, Santa Barbara, http://www.presidency.ucsb.edu/data/vetoes.php.
For additional resources on the Constitution, go to www.archives.gov/exhibits/charters/constitution.html.

■ *Does the relative infrequency of veto overrides surprise you? Why or why not? Are there other checks Congress can use against the president?*

FIGURE 2–1 **The Separation of Powers and Checks and Balances.**
■ *Does the fact that the judiciary has the fewest number of checks make it the least powerful?*

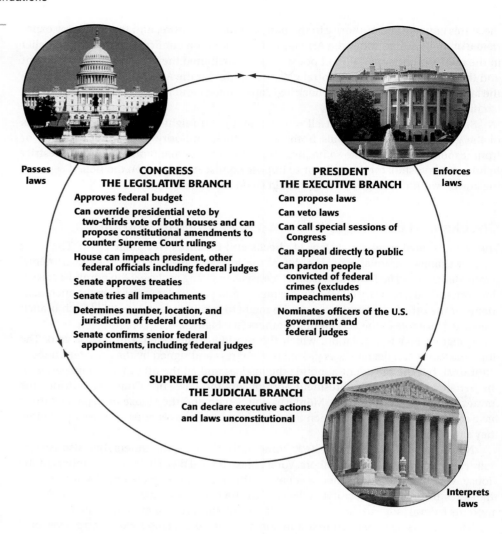

Passes laws

CONGRESS
THE LEGISLATIVE BRANCH
Approves federal budget
Can override presidential veto by two-thirds vote of both houses and can propose constitutional amendments to counter Supreme Court rulings
House can impeach president, other federal officials including federal judges
Senate approves treaties
Senate tries all impeachments
Determines number, location, and jurisdiction of federal courts
Senate confirms senior federal appointments, including federal judges

PRESIDENT
THE EXECUTIVE BRANCH
Can propose laws
Can veto laws
Can call special sessions of Congress
Can appeal directly to public
Can pardon people convicted of federal crimes (excludes impeachments)
Nominates officers of the U.S. government and federal judges

Enforces laws

SUPREME COURT AND LOWER COURTS
THE JUDICIAL BRANCH
Can declare executive actions and laws unconstitutional

Interprets laws

Distrustful of both the elites and the masses, the framers deliberately built into our political system mechanisms to make changing the system difficult. They designed the decision-making process so that the national government can act decisively only when there is a consensus among most groups and after all sides have had their say. "The doctrine of the separation of powers was adopted by the convention of 1787," in the words of Justice Louis D. Brandeis, "not to promote efficiency but to preclude the exercise of arbitrary power. The purpose was not to avoid friction, but, by means of the inevitable friction incident to the distribution of the governmental powers among three departments, to save the people from **autocracy**"[11]—a system in which one person has control over the populace. Still, even though the fragmentation of political power written into the Constitution remains, constitutional silences, or topics the Constitution does not address, and subsequent developments have modified the way the system of checks and balances works.

National Political Parties and Interest Groups

Political parties—the Republican and Democratic parties being the largest—can serve as unifying factors, at times drawing the president, senators, representatives, and sometimes even judges together behind common programs. When parties do this, they help bridge the separation of powers. Yet they can be splintered and weakened by having to work through a system of fragmented governmental power, and by the increasing influence of special-interest groups (discussed further in Chapter 6), so that they never become too strong or cohesive. When one party controls Congress or one of its chambers and the other party controls the White House, in a situation called **divided government, partisanship** is intensified, and Congress is inclined to more closely monitor the executive branch.

autocracy
A type of government in which one person with unlimited power rules.

divided government
Governance divided between the parties, especially when one holds the presidency and the other controls one or both houses of Congress.

partisanship
Strong allegiance to one's own political party, often leading to unwillingness to compromise with members of the opposing party.

Because his party controlled Congress during much of his presidency, President Bush was remarkably free from congressional investigations of his administration. However, when Democrats regained control in both the Senate and the House of Representatives in 2006, they quickly began congressional investigations into the use of intelligence leading up to the war in Iraq and the firing of U.S. Attorneys by the U.S. Justice Department. More conflict is certainly to be expected during divided government, but even when one party controls both branches, the pressures of competing interest groups may make cooperation among legislators difficult.

Because of this institutional competition between the legislative and executive branches, we find "each institution protecting and promoting itself through a broad interpretation of its constitutional and political status, even usurping the other's power when the opportunity presents itself."[12] Thus, we have had battles over the budget and angry confirmation hearings for the appointment of Supreme Court justices, lower federal court judges and members of the executive branch. The division of powers also makes it difficult for the voters to hold anyone or any party accountable. "Presidents blame Congress . . . while members of Congress attack the president. . . . Citizens genuinely cannot tell who is to blame."[13]

Yet when all the shouting dies down, political scientist David Mayhew concludes, there have been just as many congressional investigations and just as much important legislation passed when one party controls Congress and another controls the presidency as when the same party controls both branches.[14] And Charles Jones, a noted authority on Congress and the presidency, adds that divided government is precisely what the voters appear to have wanted through much of our history.[15] As we discuss in detail in Chapter 7, divided government frequently occurs when the president's party loses congressional seats in the midterm elections.

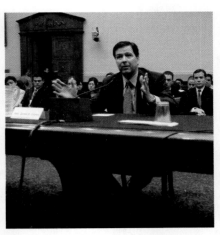

James Comey, former Deputy Attorney General of the United States, testifies in 2007 about the firing of eight U.S. Attorneys. Congress investigated whether the terminations were made for political reasons. ■ *Why might there be more frequent congressional investigations during periods of divided government?*

Expansion of the Electorate and the Move Toward More Direct Democracy

The electoral college was another provision of the Constitution meant to provide a buffer against the "whims of the masses" (see *Federalist,* No. 10, in the Appendix). The framers wanted the electoral college—wise, independent citizens free of popular passions and hero worship—to choose the president rather than leave the job to ordinary citizens. Almost from the beginning, though, the electoral college did not work this way.[16] Rather, voters actually do select the president because the presidential electors that the voters choose pledge in advance to cast their electoral votes for their party's candidates for president and vice president. Nevertheless, presidential candidates may occasionally win the national popular vote but lose the vote in the electoral college, as happened when Al Gore won the popular vote in the 2000 presidential election but lost the electoral college with 266 votes to George W. Bush's 271.

The kind of people allowed to vote has expanded from free, white, property-owning males to include all citizens over the age of 18. In addition, during the past century, U.S. states have expanded the role of the electorate, through such means as direct primaries, initiatives, and referendums and recalls, which are described in Chapter 1. And since the ratification of the Seventeenth Amendment in 1913, senators are no longer elected by state legislatures but are chosen directly by the people.

Changes in Technology

The system of checks and balances operates differently today from the way it did in 1789. Back then, there were no televised congressional committee hearings; no electronic communications; no *Larry King Live* talk shows; no *New York Times, USA Today,* CNN, Fox News, or C-SPAN; no Internet; no nightly news programs with national audiences; no presidential press conferences; and no live coverage of wars and of U.S. soldiers fighting in foreign lands. Nuclear bombs, television, computers, cellular telephones, and the Internet—these and other innovations create conditions today that are unimaginably different from those of two centuries ago. We also live in a time of instant communication

Although overall voter turnout remained largely unchanged in the 2004 and 2008 presidential elections, turnout among voters 18–24 years of age increased, as did the numbers of black, Hispanic, and Asian voters. ■ *What factors might have contributed to this increased turnout among younger voters and minorities?*

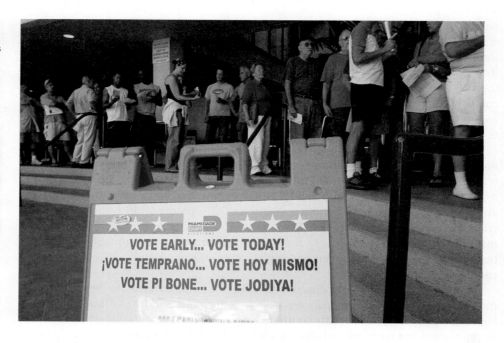

and polls that tell us what people are thinking about public issues almost from one day to the next.

In some ways, these new technologies have added to the powers of presidents by permitting them to appeal directly to millions of people and giving them immediate access to public opinion. And, in turn, they have enabled interest groups to target thousands of letters and calls at members of Congress, to orchestrate campaigns to write letters to editors, and to organize and mobilize on the Internet. New technologies have also given greater independence and influence to nongovernmental institutions such as special-interest groups and the press. They have made it possible for rich people to bypass political parties and carry their message directly to the electorate, as Meg Whitman, the billionaire former chief of eBay did, spending some $27 million of her own money during the first 11 weeks of her primary campaign to become the Republican gubernatorial candidate in California.[17]

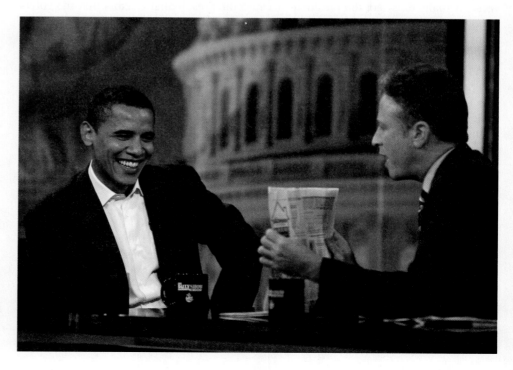

Government officials are able to express their views to the public through a variety of media outlets. Many have tried to target younger voters by appearing on programs like *The Daily Show,* as then-Senator Barack Obama did in October 2008. ■ *How have changes in technology affected citizens' abilities to check government?*

Groups like the American Center for Law and Justice use the Internet to encourage their members to "Take Action" by signing online petitions and connecting with elected officials. ■ *Have technological advances made elected officials more responsive to the public, or could it actually distance representatives from constituencies?*

The Growth of Presidential Power

Today, problems elsewhere in the world—Afghanistan, Israel, Pakistan, Iran, North Korea, and Iraq—often create crises for the United States. The need to deal with perpetual emergencies has concentrated power in the hands of the chief executive and the presidential staff. The president of the United States has emerged as the most significant player on the world stage, and media coverage of summit conferences with foreign leaders enhances the president's status. Headline-generating events give the president a visibility no congressional leader can achieve. The office of the president has on occasion modified the system of checks and balances, especially between the executive branch and Congress, and provided a measure of national unity. Drawing on constitutional, political, and emergency powers, the president can sometimes overcome the restraints the Constitution imposes on the exercise of governmental power—to the applause of some and the alarm of others. For example, President George W. Bush asserted that he had authority to use wiretaps to monitor communications of U.S. citizens without court-approved search warrants.[18]

judicial review
The power of a court to refuse to enforce a law or a government regulation that in the opinion of the judges conflicts with the U.S. Constitution or, in a state court, the state constitution.

Judicial Review and the "Guardians of the Constitution"

The judiciary has become so important in our system of checks and balances that it deserves special attention. Judges did not claim the power of **judicial review**—the power to strike down a law or a government regulation that judges believe conflicts with the Constitution—until some years after the Constitution had been adopted. From the beginning, however, judges were expected to check the legislature. "The independence of judges," wrote Alexander Hamilton in *The Federalist*, No. 78 (which appears in

LEARNING **OBJECTIVE**
2.3 Show how the use of judicial review strengthens the courts in a separation of powers system.

For the People

GOVERNMENT'S GREATEST ENDEAVORS

Increasing Access to Higher Education

The framers believed an educated public was essential to a strong government. As Thomas Jefferson wrote late in his life, "I know no safe depository of the ultimate powers of the society but the people themselves; and if we think them not enlightened enough to exercise their control with a wholesome discretion, the remedy is not to take it from them, but to inform their discretion by education. This is the true corrective of abuses of constitutional power."*

For most of American history, however, the federal government left college education to individuals and the states, and did not become involved in providing access to college until World War II. With more than 15 million soldiers about to return home in search of jobs and opportunity, Congress passed the Servicemen's Readjustment Act of 1944, popularly known as the GI Bill. It provided grants for college and other benefits to war veterans.

It was not until the late 1950s, though, that the federal government developed programs to help students from low-income families attend college. In 1958, Congress passed the National Defense Education Act in an effort to educate new scientists and engineers to fight the cold war with the Soviet Union. It provided money to fund students pursuing degrees in technical fields or modern languages, each considered essential for building weapons and collecting intelligence.

More recently, Congress has passed the Post 9/11 GI Bill to provide benefits to veterans who have been on active duty in the military for 90 or more days since September 10, 2001. As such, members of the National Guard and Reserve will qualify for benefits along with active duty service members. Through the new provisions, veterans can get up to 100 percent tuition reimbursement as well as funds for books and housing. Under this program and others, millions of college students have been able to finance their college education.

CRITICAL THINKING QUESTIONS

1. Why do you think it took so long for the federal government to become involved in education?

2. Are there public benefits to having federal tax dollars go toward such programs? Are there disadvantages?

* Thomas Jefferson, Letter to William Charles Jarvis, September 28, 1820.

---

the Appendix), "may be an essential safeguard against the effects of occasional ill humors in the society."[19]

Judicial review is a major contribution of the United States to the art of government, one that many other nations have adopted. In Canada, Germany, France, Italy, and Spain, constitutional courts review laws referred to them to ensure that the laws comply with their constitutions, including with the charter of rights that is now part of those constitutions.[20]

Origins of Judicial Review

The Constitution says nothing about who should have the final word in disputes that may arise over its meaning. Scholars have long debated whether the delegates to the Constitutional Convention of 1787 intended to give the courts the power of judicial review. The framers clearly intended that the Supreme Court have the power to declare state legislation unconstitutional, but whether they meant to give it the same power over *congressional* legislation and the president is not clear. Why didn't the framers specifically provide for judicial review? Probably because they believed justices could infer they had the power, from certain general provisions and the necessity of interpreting and applying a written constitution.

The Federalists—who urged ratification of the Constitution and controlled the national government until 1801—generally supported a strong role for federal courts and thus favored judicial review. Their opponents, the Jeffersonian Republicans (called *Democrats* after 1832), were less enthusiastic. In the Kentucky and Virginia Resolutions of 1798 and 1799, respectively, Jefferson and Madison (who by this time had left the Federalist camp) came close to arguing that state legislatures—and not the Supreme Court—had the ultimate power to interpret the Constitution. These resolutions seemed to question whether the Supreme Court even had final authority to review *state* legislation, a point about which there had been little doubt.

Chief Justice John Marshall (1755–1835) is our most influential Supreme Court justice. Appointed in 1801, Marshall served until 1835. Earlier he had been a staunch defender of the U.S. Constitution at the Virginia ratifying convention, a member of Congress, and a secretary of state. He was one of those rare people who served in all three branches of government. ■ *What might the federal courts look like today if the Marshall Court did not reach the outcome it did in Marbury v. Madison?*

When the Jeffersonians defeated the Federalists in the election of 1800, the question of whether the Supreme Court would actually exercise the power of judicial review was still undecided. Then in 1803 came *Marbury* v. *Madison,* the most path-breaking Supreme Court decision of all time.[21]

Marbury v. Madison

President John Adams and fellow Federalists did not take their 1800 defeat by Thomas Jefferson easily. Not only did they lose control of the executive office, they also lost both houses of Congress. That left the judiciary as the last remaining Federalist stronghold.

To further shore up the federal judiciary, the outgoing Federalist Congress created dozens of new judgeships. By March 3, 1801, the day before Jefferson was due to become president, Adams had appointed, and the Senate had confirmed, loyal Federalists to all of these new positions. Although the commissions were signed and sealed, a few, for the newly appointed justices of the peace for the District of Columbia, were not delivered. John Marshall, the outgoing secretary of state and newly confirmed chief justice of the Supreme Court, left the delivery of these commissions for his successor as secretary of state, James Madison.

This "packing" of the judiciary angered Jefferson, now inaugurated as president. When he discovered that some of the commissions were still lying on a table in the Department of State, he instructed a clerk not to deliver them. Jefferson could see no reason why the District needed so many justices of the peace, especially Federalist justices.[22]

William Marbury never received his commission and decided to seek action from the courts. Section 13 of the Judiciary Act of 1789 authorized the Supreme Court "to issue **writs of mandamus,**" orders directing an official, such as the secretary of state, to perform a duty, such as delivering a commission. Marbury went directly to the Supreme Court and, citing Section 13, made his request.

Marbury's request presented Chief Justice John Marshall and the Supreme Court with a difficult dilemma. On the one hand, if the Court issued the writ, Jefferson and Madison would probably ignore it. The Court would be powerless, and its prestige, already low, might suffer a fatal blow. On the other hand, by refusing to issue the writ, the judges would appear to support the Jeffersonian Republicans' claim that the Court had no authority to interfere with the executive. Would Marshall issue the writ? Most people thought he would; angry Republicans even threatened impeachment if he did so.

On February 24, 1803, the Supreme Court delivered what is still considered a brilliantly written and politically savvy decision. First, Marshall, writing for a unanimous Court, took Jefferson and Madison to task. Marbury was entitled to his commission, and Madison should have delivered it to him. Moreover, the proper court could issue a writ of mandamus, even against so high an officer as the secretary of state.

However, Marshall concluded that Section 13 of the Judiciary Act, giving the Supreme Court original jurisdiction to issue writs of mandamus, was in error. It impermissibly expanded the Court's original jurisdiction, which is detailed in Article III of the Constitution. Marshall concluded that the grant of original jurisdiction in Article III was meant to be limited to those cases explicitly mentioned: when an ambassador, foreign minister, or a state is a party. Because none of these was at issue in Marbury's request for the writ of mandamus, the Court deemed Section 13 of the Judiciary Act contrary to the Constitution. Given that Article VI provided that the Constitution is the "supreme Law of the Land," and judges took an oath to uphold the Constitution, any law in conflict with it could not withstand the Court's review.

Although the Federalists suffered a political loss in not seating all their "midnight judges" on the bench, Marshall and the Court gained a much more important power to declare laws passed by Congress unconstitutional. Subsequent generations might have interpreted *Marbury* v. *Madison* in a limited way, such as that the Supreme Court had the right to determine the scope of its own powers under Article III, but Congress and the president had the authority to interpret their powers under Articles I and II. But throughout the decades, building on Marshall's precedent, the Court has taken the commanding position as the authoritative interpreter of the Constitution.

writ of mandamus
A court order directing an official to perform an official duty.

Of the People

THE GLOBAL COMMUNITY

Increasing Concern over Government Control

Although our Constitution places limits on the reach of our federal government, citizens in the United States, as elsewhere in the world, show concern over government assuming too much control. According to the Pew Research Center's Global Attitudes surveys, majorities in most countries surveyed in 2007 agreed that their governments have too much control over their daily lives.* Respondents were asked how much they agreed with the statement: "The (state or government) controls too much of our daily lives." A Pew survey in 2002 asked the same question and allows us to compare the shift in concern between 2002 and 2007.

In the United States, for example, the percentage of respondents indicating that our government had too much control over our daily lives increased from 60 to 65 percent from 2002 to 2007. This trend was even more pronounced in Great Britain, where the percentage of respondents agreeing with that statement increased ten percentage points from 54 to 64 percent. This data may not be surprising given the kind of increased security measures governments have instituted since the September 11, 2001, attacks in New York and Washington, D.C.

These concerns are not confined to Western countries involved in the fight against terrorism. We also see an increase in India and Nigeria. In Japan, however, the percentage of survey respondents who are concerned about the government having too much control over their daily lives has decreased between 2002 and 2007 (from 42 to 34 percent). Given that our Constitution sets limits on the reach of government, citizens' perceptions that government has too much control over their daily lives might indicate an inconsistency between the theory and practice of constitutional government.

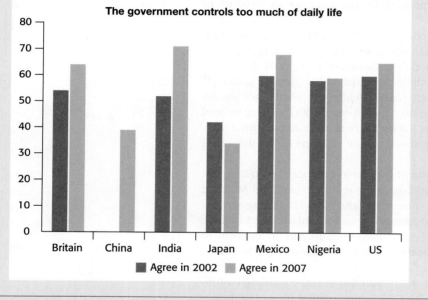

The government controls too much of daily life

■ Agree in 2002   ■ Agree in 2007

CRITICAL THINKING QUESTIONS

1. What factors might contribute to respondents' views that their governments have too much control over their lives?

2. How might a government's effort to become more open increase its citizens' views that it is too controlling?

3. In what ways does your federal government have control over your day-to-day life?

* Pew Research Center, "National Pew Global Attitudes Survey," October 4, 2007.

Once we accept Marshall's argument that judges are the official interpreters of the Constitution, several important consequences follow. The most important is that people can challenge laws enacted by Congress and approved by the president. Simply by bringing a lawsuit, those who lack the clout to get a bill through Congress can often secure a judicial hearing. And organized interest groups often find they can achieve goals through litigation that they could not attain through legislation. Litigation thus supplements, and at times even takes precedence over, legislation as a way to make public policy.[23]

Informal Change: The Unwritten Constitution

LEARNING **OBJECTIVE**

2.4 Illustrate how the Constitution has evolved through changes in the informal, unwritten Constitution.

As careful as the Constitution's framers were to limit the powers they gave the national government, the main reason they assembled in Philadelphia was to create a stronger national government. Having learned that a weak central government was a danger to liberty, they wished to establish a national government within the framework of a federal system with enough authority to meet the needs of all time. They made general grants of power, leaving it to succeeding generations to fill in the details and organize the structure of government in accordance with experience.

Hence our formal, written Constitution is only the skeleton of our system. It is filled out in numerous ways that we must consider part of our constitutional system in a larger sense. In fact, our system is kept up to date primarily through changes in the informal, unwritten Constitution. These changes exist in certain basic statutes and historical practices of Congress, presidential actions, and court decisions.

Congressional Elaboration

Because the framers gave Congress authority to provide for the structural details of the national government, it is not necessary to amend the Constitution every time a change is needed. Rather, Congress can create legislation to meet the need, with what we refer to as **congressional elaboration.** The Judiciary Act of 1789, for example, laid the foundations for our national judicial system, just as other laws established the organization and functions of all federal executive officials subordinate to the president and enacted the rules of procedure, internal organization, and practices of Congress.

Another example of this congressional elaboration of our constitutional system is the use of the impeachment and removal power. An **impeachment** is a formal accusation against a public official and the first step in removing him or her from office. Constitutional language defining the grounds for impeachment is sparse. Look at the Constitution and note that Article II, the Executive Article, calls for removal of the president, vice president, and all civil officers of the United States on impeachment for, and conviction of, "Treason, Bribery, or other High Crimes and Misdemeanors." But, what does that mean? The question is not an easy one as there is a general lack of consensus on its meaning. In fact, the last time the House of Representatives formally accused a president of an impeachable offense, President Bill Clinton in 1998, House members had nearly 20 scholars testify before them as to the clause's meaning, and they still did not find consensus on it. Although the Constitution provides for the basic procedural structure of impeachments, it leaves up to Congress determining when a president's actions amount to an impeachable offense.

congressional elaboration
Congressional legislation that gives further meaning to the Constitution based on sometimes vague constitutional authority, such as the necessary and proper clause.

impeachment
A formal accusation by the lower house of a legislature against a public official; the first step in removal from office.

President Bill Clinton was impeached by the House of Representatives in December 1998 for perjury and obstructing justice, but he was acquitted by the Senate. ■ *What kind of official wrongdoing should amount to an impeachable offense, and who should be responsible for determining this?*

Presidential Practices

Although the formal constitutional powers of the president have not changed, the office is dramatically more important and more central today than it was in 1789. Vigorous presidents—George Washington, Thomas Jefferson, Andrew Jackson, Abraham Lincoln, Theodore Roosevelt, Woodrow Wilson, Franklin Roosevelt, Harry Truman, Lyndon Johnson, Bill Clinton, and George W. Bush—have boldly exercised their political and constitutional powers, especially during times of national crisis such as the current war against international terrorism and the 2008 economic crisis. Their presidential practices have established important precedents, building the power and influence of the office.

A major practice is the use of **executive orders,** which carry the full force of law but do not require congressional approval. Executive orders direct the executive branch to take some action, such as President Franklin Roosevelt's 1942 order to intern Japanese-Americans during World War II or President Truman's order to integrate the armed forces in 1948. Presidents have long used these orders to achieve goals that may lack congressional support. Other practices include **executive privilege,** the right to confidentiality of executive communications, especially those that relate to national security; **impoundment** by a president of funds previously appropriated by Congress; the power to send armed forces into hostilities; and the authority to propose legislation and work actively to secure its passage by Congress.

Foreign and economic crises as well as nuclear-age realities and the war against international terrorism have expanded the president's role: "When it comes to action risking nuclear war, technology has modified the Constitution: the President, perforce, becomes the only such man in the system capable of exercising judgment under the extraordinary limits now imposed by secrecy, complexity, and time."[24] The presidency has also become the pivotal office for regulating the economy and promoting the general welfare through an expanded federal bureaucracy (as we discuss in Chapter 13). In addition, the president has become a leader in sponsoring legislation as well as the nation's chief executive.

Judicial Interpretation

In its decision in *Marbury* v. *Madison* (1803),[25] the Supreme Court established that it was the judiciary's responsibility to interpret the Constitution. Through this practice, the courts have made far-reaching decisions that have settled, at least for a time, what some of the vague clauses of the document mean. For example, the Supreme Court ruled that segregation by race, even when equal facilities were provided, violated the requirements of the equal protection clause (*Brown* v. *Board of Education* [1954]),[26] and that Americans have a constitutionally protected right to privacy, even though the word "privacy" appears nowhere in the Constitution (*Griswold* v. *Connecticut* [1965]).[27] In both of these cases and a myriad of others, the Court's definition of what the Constitution meant led to changes in our political system without any amendment to the document itself. Although there is relatively little current debate over the judiciary's authority to interpret the Constitution, there is substantial disagreement over *how* it should be read. (See the You Will Decide box.)

executive order
A directive issued by a president or governor that has the force of law.

executive privilege
The power to keep executive communications confidential, especially if they relate to national security.

impoundment
Presidential refusal to allow an agency to spend funds that Congress authorized and appropriated.

Changing the Letter of the Constitution

The idea of a constantly changing system disturbs many people. How, they contend, can you have a constitutional government when the Constitution is constantly being twisted by interpretation and changed by informal methods? This view fails to distinguish between two aspects of the Constitution. As an expression of *basic and timeless personal liberties,* the Constitution does not, and should not, change. For example, a government cannot destroy free speech and still remain a constitutional government. In this sense, the Constitution is unchanging. But when we consider

DECIDE
Should We Interpret the Constitution According to Original Intent or Today's Needs?

Debate about how to interpret the Constitution began almost immediately, and, as we have seen, it continues to this day, with very important practical implications for citizens.

One kind of constitutional interpretation is the **originalist approach**. Originalists believe that the Constitution should be understood according to the framers' intent. If the exact wording of the document does not provide a conclusive answer, most originalists consider the context of the times in which it was written and interpret it in light of that history. Especially important are writings or speeches by the founders themselves or by proponents of subsequent amendments.

A second approach to interpreting the Constitution sees it as a changing and evolving document that provides a basic framework for government but that allows, and even encourages, new generations to interpret ideas such as "equal justice" and "due process" in light of the needs of their time. This **adaptive approach** may mean that subsequent generations will interpret the same document differently from prior generations.

The adaptive approach makes the court a more powerful institution in U.S. government. The originalist approach forces people and institutions to adopt amendments if they want constitutional change.

What do you think? Should we interpret the Constitution according to the framers' original intent, or should it be considered in light of the needs of today's society? What are some of the arguments for or against each approach?

THINKING IT THROUGH

Differences between the adaptive and the originalist views do not necessarily align with political labels such as *conservative* or *liberal*, although they may in particular cases. For example, Justice Antonin Scalia, who tends to be originalist in his approach, voted in *District of Columbia* v. *Heller* to strike down the District's prohibition on registering handguns through a close reading of the original, literal meaning of the Second Amendment. Because the Amendment indicates that "the right of the people to keep and bear Arms, shall not be infringed," Justice Scalia, writing for the majority of the Court, determined that individual citizens had a constitutionally protected right to own handguns.

Justice Stephen Breyer typically favors a more adaptive approach. In his dissent to the Court's majority opinion, Justice Breyer argues that the Court must consider the District of Columbia's restriction on handguns in light of present day conditions, such as the public safety concerns raised by gun violence. Justice Breyer weighs an individual's right to own a handgun and the District's responsibility to protect its citizenry, and sided with the District of Columbia.

If the Constitution is indeed open to changing interpretations, are any constitutional principles absolute and *not* open to new interpretation? This danger in the adaptive approach worries some because the selection of judges is only indirectly democratic, and, with lifetime appointments, judges could lose the people's confidence yet retain their power. There are problems with the originalist approach as well. A global economy, electronic and mass media, and the need to respond immediately to national security threats are only some examples of circumstances the founders could not consider or address in the Constitution. In other instances, such as with privacy, for example, the original wording of the Constitution implies an interpretation but does not explicitly say it.

Critical Thinking Questions

1. How do you think we should interpret the Constitution? What are the best arguments of both sides of this question?

2. Why does it matter whether we take an originalist or an adaptive approach to interpreting the Constitution?

the Constitution as an *instrument of government* and a positive grant of power, we realize that if it did not grow with the nation it serves, it would soon be irrelevant and ignored.

The framers could never have conceived of the problems facing the government of a large, powerful, and wealthy nation of approximately 300 million people at the beginning of the twenty-first century. Although the general purposes of government remain the same—to establish liberty, promote justice, ensure domestic tranquility, and provide for the common defense—the powers of government that were adequate to accomplish these purposes in 1787 are simply insufficient more than 220 years later. The framers knew that future experiences would call for changes in the text of the Constitution and that it would need to be formally amended. In Article V, they gave responsibility for amending the Constitution to Congress and to the states. The president has no formal authority over constitutional amendments; presidential veto power does not extend to them, although presidential influence is often crucial in getting amendments proposed and ratified.

originalist approach
An approach to constitutional interpretation that envisions the document as having a fixed meaning that might be determined by a strict reading of the text or the framers' intent.

adaptive approach
A method used to interpret the Constitution that understands the document to be flexible and responsive to the changing needs of the times.

Proposing Amendments

The first method for proposing amendments—and the only one used so far—is by *a two-thirds vote of both houses of Congress*. Dozens of resolutions proposing amendments are introduced in every session, but Congress has proposed only 31 amendments, of which 27 have been ratified (see Figure 2–2).

Why is introducing amendments to the Constitution so popular? In part because groups frustrated by their inability to get things done in Congress hope to bypass it. In part because Congress, the president, interest groups, or the public may want to overturn unpopular Supreme Court decisions. In part because the nation needs to make government more responsive to changing times. Although amendments are debated rather frequently, very few have made it through Congress to begin the ratification process.

Congress, the president, interest groups, and the public were all involved in an effort to overturn the Supreme Court's decision to strike down a Texas law barring flag burning (*Texas v. Johnson* [1989]).[28] Though Congress attempted to bypass the decision with the Federal Flag Protection Act of 1989, which prohibited intentionally burning or defiling the flag, the Court struck down that law as well (*United States v. Eichman* [1990]).[29] In doing so, the Court ruled that the First Amendment protects burning the flag as a form of political speech.

Following its failure to overturn the decision through new laws, Congress has made repeated efforts to send a constitutional amendment banning flag burning to the states.[30] The House of Representatives has voted seven times since the early 1990s on an amendment prohibiting the "physical desecration of the flag of the United States," but the Senate has been unable to garner the necessary two-thirds vote. It came close to succeeding in June 2006, but the vote fell one short of the number required to send the amendment to the states for ratification.[31] See Table 2–2 on how the amending power has been used.

The second method for proposing amendments—*a convention called by Congress* at the request of the legislatures in two-thirds of the states—has never been used. Under Article V of the Constitution, Congress could call for such a convention without the concurrence of the president. This method presents difficult questions.[32] First, can state legislatures apply for a convention to propose specific amendments on one topic, or must they request a convention with full powers to revise the entire Constitution? How long do state petitions remain alive? How should delegates to a convention be chosen? How should such a convention be run? Congress has considered bills to answer some of these questions but has not

Outside the 1984 Republican National Convention, Gregory Johnson burned an American flag to protest the Reagan administration's policies. The U.S. Supreme Court upheld his right to do so as a protected form of expression under the First Amendment.
■ *Why do you think that legislators have been so persistent in proposing amendments to bar flag burning?*

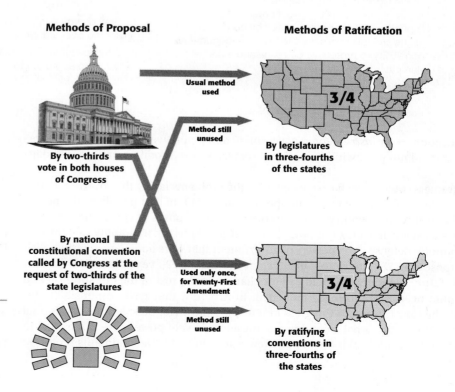

Methods of Proposal

Methods of Ratification

Usual method used

Method still unused

3/4

By legislatures in three-fourths of the states

By two-thirds vote in both houses of Congress

By national constitutional convention called by Congress at the request of two-thirds of the state legislatures

Used only once, for Twenty-First Amendment

3/4

Method still unused

By ratifying conventions in three-fourths of the states

FIGURE 2–2 **Four Methods of Amending the Constitution.**
■ *Why do you think Congress has been reluctant to call for a national constitutional convention?*

TABLE

2–2 | The Amending Power and How It Has Been Used

Leaving aside the first ten amendments (the Bill of Rights), the power of constitutional amendment has served a number of purposes:

To Increase or Decrease the Power of the National Government

The Eleventh took some jurisdiction away from the national courts.

The Thirteenth abolished slavery and authorized Congress to legislate against it.

The Sixteenth enabled Congress to levy an income tax.

The Eighteenth authorized Congress to prohibit the manufacture, sale, or transportation of liquor.

The Twenty-First repealed the Eighteenth and gave states the authority to regulate liquor sales.

The Twenty-Seventh limited the power of Congress to set members' salaries.

To Expand the Electorate and Its Power

The Fifteenth extended suffrage to all male African Americans over the age of 21.

The Seventeenth took the right to elect U.S. senators away from state legislatures and gave it to the voters in each state.

The Nineteenth extended suffrage to women over the age of 21.

The Twenty-Third gave voters of the District of Columbia the right to vote for president and vice president.

The Twenty-Fourth outlawed the poll tax, thereby prohibiting states from taxing the right to vote.

The Twenty-Sixth extended suffrage to otherwise qualified persons age 18 or older.

To Reduce the Electorate's Power

The Twenty-Second took away from the electorate the right to elect a person to the office of president for more than two full terms.

To Limit State Government Power

The Thirteenth abolished slavery.

The Fourteenth granted national citizenship and prohibited states from abridging privileges of national citizenship; from denying persons life, liberty, and property without due process; and from denying persons equal protection of the laws. This amendment has come to be interpreted as imposing restraints on state powers in every area of public life.

To Make Structural Changes in Government

The Twelfth corrected deficiencies in the operation of the electoral college that the development of a two-party national system had revealed.

The Twentieth altered the calendar for congressional sessions and shortened the time between the election of presidents and their assumption of office.

The Twenty-Fifth provided procedures for filling vacancies in the vice presidency and for determining whether presidents are unable to perform their duties.

■ *Overall, have constitutional amendments resulted in a stronger or weaker federal government than was established in the Constitution?*

passed any, in part because most members do not wish to encourage a constitutional convention for fear that once in session it might propose amendments on any and all topics.

Under most proposals, each state would have as many delegates to the convention as it has representatives and senators in Congress. Finally, and crucially, a constitutional convention would be limited to considering only the subject specified in the state legislative petitions and described in the congressional call for the convention. Scholars are divided, however, on whether Congress has the authority to limit what a constitutional convention might propose.[33]

Ratifying Amendments

After Congress has proposed an amendment, the states must ratify it before it takes effect. Again, the Constitution provides two methods, and Congress may choose: approval by the legislatures in three-fourths of the states or approval by special ratifying conventions in three-fourths of the states. Congress has submitted all amendments except one—the Twenty-First (to repeal the Eighteenth, the Prohibition Amendment)—to the state legislatures for ratification.

Seven state constitutions specify that their state legislatures must ratify a proposed amendment to the U.S. Constitution by majorities of three-fifths or two-thirds of each chamber. Although a state legislature may change its mind and ratify an amendment after it has voted against ratification, the weight of opinion is that once a state has ratified an amendment, it cannot "unratify" it.[34]

Of the People

Changing State Constitutions to Reflect Changing States

Although the United States Constitution has been amended only 27 times in more than 220 years of its existence, many of our state constitutions have experienced far greater change. Unlike the process to amend the U.S. Constitution, which requires supermajorities at both the proposal and ratification stages, some states allow their constitutions to be changed by simple majority vote of the citizens in a regularly scheduled election. In theory, then, these states' constitutions can be more responsive to the changing needs of its citizenry.

Proposed state constitutional amendments deal with a variety of issues. For example, in 2009 proposed amendments to the Texas Constitution ranged from establishing a state fund to provide money for scientific research in the state's universities to a provision allowing members of the Texas State Guard to hold other civil offices. Many other states have recently used the amendment process to establish constitutional prohibitions on same-sex marriage. California's Proposition 8, an initiative barring same-sex marriage in the state, passed by a 52-to-48 percent margin. Given that California requires only a majority vote to amend its constitution, a small majority of the state's citizens were able to invalidate the state supreme court's ruling allowing same-sex marriages. Although most initiatives do not succeed (only about one-third of all measures win voter approval), voters have approved more than 75 percent of proposed initiatives that restrict minority rights in areas such as housing, gay rights, and English language laws.*

However, the Californians voting on Proposition 8 looked quite different from the framers of the U.S. Constitution, and the process was arguably more democratic. The initiative process allows average citizens to have a direct vote on what their state constitutions look like. Instead of the white, male property owners at the convention in Philadelphia, a majority of voters on Proposition 8 were women (54 percent) and 28 percent were black, Hispanic, or Asian.†

CRITICAL THINKING QUESTIONS

1. Why might some states make their constitutions so easy to amend?

2. Should the U.S. Constitution be easier to amend?

3. Why might some groups lobby to change their state constitutions through an initiative process instead of lobbying their state legislatures to change the law?

---

* Barbara S. Gamble, "Putting Civil Rights to a Popular Vote," *American Journal of Political Science* (January 1997): 245–269.

† Patrick J. Egan and Kenneth Sherrill, "California's Proposition 8: What Happened, and What Does the Future Hold?," Report released by National Gay and Lesbian Task Force Policy Institute, 2009.

The Supreme Court has said that ratification must take place within a "reasonable time" so that it is "sufficiently contemporaneous to reflect the will of the people."[35] However, when Congress approved ratification of the Twenty-Seventh Amendment, it had been before the nation for nearly 203 years, so there seems to be no limit on what it considers a "reasonable time" (see Figure 2–3). In fact, ratification ordinarily takes place rather quickly—one-third of all amendments were ratified within about one year, and 80 percent were ratified within about two years. Congress will probably continue to stipulate that ratification must occur within seven years of the date it submits an amendment to the states.

Ratification Politics

The failure of the Equal Rights Amendment (ERA) to be ratified provides a vivid example of the pitfalls of ratification. First introduced in 1923, the ERA did not get much support until the 1960s. An influential book by Betty Friedan, *The Feminine Mystique* (1963), challenged stereotypes about the role of women. The National Organization for Women (NOW), formed in 1966, made passage of the ERA its central mission. By the 1970s, the ERA had overwhelming support in both houses of Congress and in both national party platforms. Every president from Harry Truman to Ronald Reagan, and many of their wives, endorsed the amendment. More than 450 organizations with a total membership of more than 50 million were on record in support of the ERA.[36] The ERA provided for the following:

Section 1. Equality of rights under the law shall not be denied or abridged by the United States or by any State on account of sex.

Section 2. The Congress shall have power to enforce, by appropriate legislation, the provisions of this article.

Section 3. This amendment shall take effect two years after the date of ratification.[37]

Soon after Congress passed the amendment and submitted it to the states in 1972, many legislatures ratified it—sometimes without hearings—and by overwhelming

FIGURE 2–3 **The Time for Ratification of the 27 Amendments to the Constitution.**
■ *What is an appropriate time for ratification of a proposed amendment? In thinking about your answer, should the length of elected legislators' terms play a role in your decision?*

majorities. By the end of that year, 22 states had ratified the amendment, and it appeared that the ERA would soon become part of the Constitution. But because of opposition organized under the leadership of Phyllis Schlafly, a prominent spokesperson for conservative causes, the ERA became controversial.

Opponents argued that "women would not only be subject to the military draft but also assigned to combat duty. Full-time housewives and mothers would be forced to join the labor force. Further, women would no longer enjoy existing advantages under state domestic relations codes and under labor law."[38] The ERA also became embroiled in the controversy over abortion. Many opponents contended that its ratification would jeopardize the power of states and Congress to regulate abortion and would compel public funding of abortions.[39]

State legislatures held lengthy hearings, and floor debates became heated. Legislators hid behind parliamentary procedures and avoided making a decision for as long as

People came from every state in the union to march in support of the passage of the Equal Rights Amendment in 1978. ■ *What factors led to the failure of the ERA? Do you think the ERA would be ratified if it were proposed today?*

possible. Opposition to ratification arose chiefly in the same cluster of southern states that had opposed ratification of the Nineteenth Amendment, which gave women the right to vote. As the opposition grew more active, proponents redoubled their efforts.

In the autumn of 1978, it appeared that the ERA would fall three short of the necessary number of ratifying states before the expiration of the seven-year limit on March 22, 1979. After an extended debate, and after voting down provisions that would have authorized state legislatures to change their minds and rescind ratification, Congress, by a simple majority vote, extended the time limit until June 30, 1982. Nonetheless, by the final deadline, the amendment was still three states short of the 38 needed for ratification.

The framers intended that amending the Constitution should be difficult, and the ERA ratification battle demonstrates how well they planned. Through interpretation, practices, usages, and judicial decisions, the Constitution has proved a remarkably enduring and adaptable governing document and one that is frequently used as a model for emerging democracies. But it is essential for citizens, individually and together, to keep watch that constitutional provisions are enforced and that change comes when necessary. Not all efforts for constitutional change are successful, but even failed drives for constitutional amendments can achieve a degree of success through the legislative process, influence on the executive, or calls for action by the judiciary.

CHAPTER **SUMMARY**

2.1 Describe the basic structure of the Constitution and its Bill of Rights.

The U.S. Constitution's first three articles establish the legislature, the executive, and the judiciary. The Bill of Rights, the first ten amendments to the Constitution, was added in 1791 and provides protections from federal government infringement on individual liberties.

2.2 Analyze how the Constitution grants, limits, separates, and balances governmental power.

The U.S. Constitution separates power vested in the legislature, which has the power to create law; the executive, with the power to enforce the law; and the judiciary, which interprets the law. None of the branches depends on the others for its authority, and each branch has the power to limit the others through the system of checks and balances.

Competing interests within this structure check and balance one another. Political parties may sometimes overcome the separation of powers, especially if the same party controls both houses of Congress and the presidency. Typically, this is not the case, however, and a divided government intensifies checks and balances. Presidential power, which has increased over time, has sometimes overcome restraints the Constitution imposes on it.

2.3 Show how the use of judicial review strengthens the courts in a separation of powers system.

Judicial review is the power of the courts to strike down acts of Congress, the executive branch, and the states as unconstitutional. This authority provides the judiciary a powerful check on the other branches of government. In deciding that it lacked the jurisdiction

to order a judicial commission be delivered, the Supreme Court, in *Marbury* v. *Madison*, established its authority to rule an act of the federal legislature unconstitutional. The Court's decision was politically savvy and greatly enhanced the role of the judiciary in a separation-of-powers system.

2.4 Illustrate how the Constitution has evolved through changes in the informal, unwritten Constitution.

The Constitution is the framework of our governmental system. The constitutional system has been modified over time, adapting to new conditions through congressional elaboration, presidential practices, and judicial interpretation.

Some jurists believe the Constitution is a static document with a set meaning, and they tend to interpret the Constitution according to a close reading of the text or according to what they think the framers' intended. Others consider the document's meaning to evolve with time and changing circumstances.

2.5 Outline the processes by which formal changes to the Constitution can be made.

Although adaptable, the Constitution itself needs to be altered from time to time, and the framers provided a formal procedure for its amendment. An amendment must be both proposed and ratified: proposed by either a two-thirds vote in each chamber of Congress or by a national convention called by Congress on petition of the legislatures in two-thirds of the states; ratified either by the legislatures in three-fourths of the states or by special ratifying conventions in three-fourths of the states.

CHAPTER **SELF-TEST**

2.1 **Describe the basic structure of the Constitution and its Bill of Rights.**

1. The Constitution reflects the founders' respect for _____ law, which implies a universal sense of right and wrong.
   a. natural
   b. formal
   c. federal
   d. corporal

2. How does the U.S. Constitution compare to other constitutions around the world?

2.2 **Analyze how the Constitution grants, limits, separates, and balances governmental power.**

3. Write two or three paragraphs to explain the ways the writers of the constitution attempted to limit the power of the branches in the federal government.

4. Draw a diagram that shows how the different branches of government check one another. (Table 2–1 can provide useful examples.)

5. What are some of the advantages of having a written constitution? List four or five. Can you think of any disadvantages?

2.3 **Show how the use of judicial review strengthens the courts in a separation of powers system.**

6. Describe the details of *Marbury* v. *Madison* and who the major actors were. Explain why the case was heard in the first place. Describe the impact of the decision.

7. Many people are uncomfortable with what they term "activist judges." Explain the constitutional grounds for and against judicial activism in four sentences or less.

2.4 **Illustrate how the Constitution has evolved through changes in the informal, unwritten Constitution.**

8. Write a persuasive essay (two to three paragraphs) justifying the use of executive privilege to protect the homeland. Be sure to address why this privilege might be questioned.

9. Explain why nominations to the Supreme Court are often so contentious.

10. Write a two-paragraph essay in which you evaluate the arguments for a static or evolving interpretation of the Constitution.

2.5 **Outline the processes by which formal changes to the Constitution can be made.**

11. The chapter lists two ways to propose amendments. Name these two ways, and describe how they are different. How is an amendment ratified?

12. How many states would need to agree to hold a new constitutional convention?

13. Write a brief essay detailing the difficulties that politicians would face in holding a new constitutional convention. Which individuals or groups might be opposed to a new convention? What are some of the procedural hurdles supporters would have to overcome?

Answers to selected questions: 1. a

---

mypoliscilab™ EXERCISES
Where participation leads to action!

Apply what you learned in this chapter on MyPoliSciLab.

Read on mypoliscilab.com

eText: Chapter 2

Study and Review on mypoliscilab.com

Pre-Test
Post-Test
Chapter Exam
Flashcards

Watch on mypoliscilab.com

Video: Animal Sacrifice and Free Exercise
Video: Polygamy and the U.S. Constitution

Explore on mypoliscilab.com

Simulation: You Are James Madison
Simulation: You Are Proposing a Constitutional Amendment
Comparative: Comparing Constitutions
Timeline: The History of Constitutional Amendments
Visual Literacy: The American System of Checks and Balances

KEY **TERMS**

natural law, p. 44
federalism, p. 45
separation of powers, p. 46
checks and balances, p. 47
autocracy, p. 48
divided government, p. 48

partisanship, p. 48
judicial review, p. 51
writ of mandamus, p. 53
congressional elaboration, p. 55
impeachment, p. 55
executive order, p. 56

executive privilege, p. 56
impoundment, p. 56
originalist approach, p. 57
adaptive approach, p. 57

ADDITIONAL **RESOURCES**

FURTHER READING

AKHIL REED AMAR, *America's Constitution: A Biography* (Random House, 2005).

CAROL BERKIN, *A Brilliant Solution: Inventing the American Constitution* (Harcourt, 2002).

STEPHEN BREYER, *Active Liberty: Interpreting Our Democratic Constitution* (Knopf, 2005).

JAMES MACGREGOR BURNS, *The Vineyard of Liberty* (Knopf, 1982).

MICHAEL KAMMEN, *A Machine That Would Go of Itself: The Constitution in American Culture* (Knopf, 1986).

KEN I. KERSCH, *Constructing Civil Liberties: Discontinuities in the Development of American Constitutional Law* (Cambridge University Press, 2004).

LIBRARY OF CONGRESS, CONGRESSIONAL RESEARCH SERVICE, JONNY KILLIAN, ED., *The Constitution of the United States of America: Analysis and Interpretation* (U.S. Government Printing Office, 2006).

ANTONIN SCALIA, *A Matter of Interpretation: Federal Courts and the Law* (Princeton University Press, 1997).

CASS SUNSTEIN, *Designing Democracy: What Constitutions Do* (Oxford University Press, 2001).

JOHN R. VILE, ED., *Encyclopedia of Constitutional Amendments, Proposed Amendments, and Amending Issues, 1789–2002* (ABC-Clio, 2003).

KEITH E. WHITTINGTON, *Political Foundations of Judicial Supremacy: The Presidency, the Supreme Court, and Constitutional Leadership in U.S. History* (Princeton University Press, 2007).

WEB SITES

www.constitutioncenter.org/ The National Constitution Center's Web site includes information on the Constitution and its framers as well as an interactive constitution, online exhibits, and news updates.

www.memory.loc.gov/ammem/amlaw/ lawhome.html This Library of Congress Web site is devoted to the Continental Congress and the Constitutional Convention. There are links to online documents contained in the Library's collection.

www.archives.gov/ The National Archives' Web site includes links to many online collections and historical documents.

On Reading the Constitution

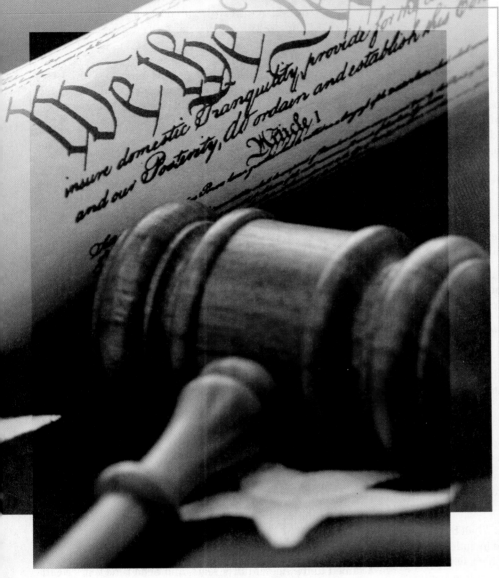

More than 218 years after its ratification, our Constitution remains the operating charter of our republic. It is neither self-explanatory nor a comprehensive description of our constitiutional rules. Still, it remains the starting point. Many Americans who swear by the Constitution have never read it seriously, although copies can be found in most American government and American history textbooks.

Justice Hugo Black, who served on the Supreme Court for 34 years, kept a copy of the Constitution with him at all times. He read it often. Reading the Constitution would be a good way for you to begin (and then reread again to end) your study of the government of the United States. We have therefore included a copy of it at this point in the book. Please read it carefully.

The Constitution of the United States

The Preamble

We the People of the United States, in Order to form a more perfect Union, establish Justice, insure domestic Tranquility, provide for the common defence, promote the general Welfare, and secure the Blessings of Liberty to ourselves and our Posterity, do ordain and establish this Constitution for the United States of America.

Article I—The Legislative Article

Legislative Power

SECTION 1   All legislative Powers herein granted shall be vested in a Congress of the United States, which shall consist of a Senate and House of Representatives.

House of Representatives: Composition; Qualifications; Apportionment; Impeachment Power

SECTION 2

Clause 1   The House of Representatives shall be composed of Members chosen every second Year by the People of the several States, and the Electors in each State shall have the Qualifications requisite for Electors of the most numerous Branch of the State Legislature.

Clause 2   No Person shall be a Representative who shall not have attained to the Age of twenty five Years, and been seven Years a Citizen of the United States, and who shall not, when elected, be an inhabitant of that State in which he shall be chosen.

Clause 3   Representatives and direct Taxes[1] shall be apportioned among the several States which may be included within this Union, according to their respective Numbers, which shall be determined by adding to the whole Number of free Persons, including those bound to Service for a Term of Years, and excluding Indians not taxed, three fifths of all other Persons.[2] The actual Enumeration shall be made within three Years after the first Meeting of the Congress of the United States, and within every subsequent Term of ten Years, in such Manner as they shall by Law direct. The Number of Representatives shall not exceed one for every thirty Thousand, but each State shall have at Least one Representative; and until such enumeration shall be made, the State of New Hampshire shall be entitled to chuse three, Massachusetts eight, Rhode-Island and Providence Plantations one, Connecticut five, New-York six, New Jersey four, Pennsylvania eight, Delaware one, Maryland six, Virginia ten, North Carolina five, South Carolina five, and Georgia three.

Clause 4   When vacancies happen in the Representation from any State, the Executive Authority thereof shall issue Writs of Election to fill such Vacancies.

Clause 5   The House of Representatives shall chuse their Speaker and other Officers; and shall have the sole Power of Impeachment.

Senate Composition: Qualifications, Impeachment Trials

SECTION 3

Clause 1   The Senate of the United States shall be composed of two Senators from each State, chosen by the Legislature thereof,[3] for six Years; and each Senator shall have one Vote.

Clause 2   Immediately after they shall be assembled in Consequence of the first Election, they shall be divided as equally as may be into three Classes. The Seats of the Senators of the first Class shall be vacated at the Expiration of the second Year, of the second Class at the Expiration of the fourth Year, and of the third Class at the Expiration of the sixth Year, so that one third may be chosen every second Year; and if Vacancies happen by Resignation, or otherwise, during the Recess of the Legislature of any State, the Executive thereof may make temporary Appointments until the next Meeting of the Legislature, which shall then fill such Vacancies.[4]

Clause 3   No person shall be a Senator who shall not have attained to the Age of thirty Years, and been nine Years a Citizen of the United States, and who shall not, when elected, be an Inhabitant of that State for which he shall be chosen.

Clause 4   The Vice President of the United States shall be President of the Senate, but shall have no Vote, unless they be equally divided.

Clause 5   The Senate shall chuse their other Officers, and also a President pro tempore, in the Absence of the Vice President, or when he shall exercise the Office of President of the United States.

---

[1]Modified by the 16th Amendment
[2]Replaced by Section 2, 14th Amendment

[3]Repealed by the 17th Amendment
[4]Modified by the 17th Amendment

Clause 6 The Senate shall have the sole Power to try all Impeachments. When sitting for that Purpose, they shall be on Oath or Affirmation. When the President of the United States is tried, the Chief Justice shall preside: And no Person shall be convicted without the Concurrence of two thirds of the Members present.

Judgment in Cases of Impeachment shall not extend further than to removal from Office, and disqualification to hold and enjoy any Office of honor, Trust or Profit under the United States: but the Party convicted shall nevertheless be liable and subject to Indictment, Trial, Judgment and Punishment, according to Law.

Congressional Elections: Times, Places, Manner

SECTION 4 The Times, Places and Manner of holding Elections for Senators and Representatives, shall be prescribed in each State by the Legislature thereof; but the Congress may at any time by Law make or alter such Regulations, except as to the Places of chusing Senators.

The Congress shall assemble at least once in every Year, and such Meeting shall be on the first Monday in December, unless they shall by Law appoint a different Day.[5]

Powers and Duties of the Houses

SECTION 5

Clause 1 Each House shall be the Judge of the Elections, Returns and Qualifications of its own Members, and a Majority of each shall constitute a Quorum to do Business; but a smaller Number may adjourn from day to day, and may be authorized to compel the Attendance of absent Members, in such Manner, and under the Penalties as each House may provide.

Clause 2 Each House may determine the Rules of its Proceedings, punish its Members for disorderly Behaviour, and, with the Concurrence of two thirds, expel a Member.

Clause 3 Each House shall keep a Journal of its Proceedings, and from time to time publish the same, excepting such Parts as may in their Judgment require Secrecy; and the Yeas and Nays of the Members of either House on any question shall, at the Desire of one fifth of those Present, be entered on the Journal.

Clause 4 Neither House, during the Session of Congress, shall, without the Consent of the other, adjourn for more than three days, nor to any other place than that in which the two Houses shall be sitting.

Rights of Members

SECTION 6

Clause 1 The Senators and Representatives shall receive a Compensation for their Services, to be ascertained by Law, and paid out of the Treasury of the United States. They shall in all Cases, except Treason, Felony and Breach of the Peace, be privileged from Arrest during their Attendance at the Session of their respective Houses, and in going to and returning from the same; and for any Speech or Debate in either House, they shall not be questioned in any other Place.

Clause 2 No Senator or Representative, shall, during the Time for which he was elected, be appointed to any civil Office under the Authority of the United States, which shall have been created, or the Emoluments whereof shall have been encreased during such time; and no Person holding any Office under the United States, shall be a Member of either House during his Continuance in Office.

Legislative Powers: Bills and Resolutions

SECTION 7

Clause 1 All Bills for raising Revenue shall originate in the House of Representatives; but the Senate may propose or concur with Amendments as on other Bills.

Clause 2 Every Bill which shall have passed the House of Representatives and the Senate, shall, before it become a Law, be presented to the President of the United States; if he approve he shall sign it, but if not he shall return it, with his Objections to that House in which it shall have originated, who shall enter the Objections at large on their Journal, and proceed to reconsider it. If after such Reconsideration two thirds of that House shall agree to pass the Bill, it shall be sent, together with the Objections, to the other House, by which it shall likewise be reconsidered, and if approved by two thirds of that House, it shall become a Law. But in all such Cases the Votes of both Houses shall be determined by yeas and Nays, and the Names of the Persons voting for and against the Bill shall be entered on the Journal of each House respectively. If any Bill shall not be returned by the President within ten Days (Sundays excepted) after it shall have been presented to him, the Same shall be a Law, in like Manner as if he had signed it, unless the Congress by their Adjournment prevent its Return, in which Case it shall not be a Law.

Clause 3 Every Order, Resolution, or Vote to which the Concurrence of the Senate and House of Representatives may be necessary (except on a question of Adjournment) shall be presented to the President of the United States; and before the Same shall take Effect, shall be approved by him, or being disapproved by him, shall be repassed by two thirds of the Senate and House of Representatives, according to the Rules and Limitations prescribed in the Case of a Bill.

Powers of Congress

SECTION 8

Clause 1 The Congress shall have Power To lay and collect Taxes, Duties, Imposts and Excises, to pay the Debts and provide for the common Defence and general Welfare of the United

---

[5]Changed by the 20th Amendment

States; but all Duties, Imposts and Excises shall be uniform throughout the United States;

To borrow Money on the credit of the United States;

To regulate Commerce with foreign Nations, and among the several States, and with the Indian Tribes;

To establish an uniform Rule of Naturalization, and uniform Laws on the subject of Bankruptcies throughout the United States;

To coin Money, regulate the Value thereof, and of foreign Coin, and fix the Standard of Weights and Measures;

To provide for the Punishment of counterfeiting the Securities and current Coin of the United States;

To establish Post Offices and post Roads;

To promote the Progress of Science and useful Arts, by securing for limited Times to Authors and Inventors the exclusive Right to their respective Writings and Discoveries;

To constitute Tribunals inferior to the supreme Court;

To define and punish Piracies and Felonies committed on the high Seas, and Offences against the Law of Nations;

To declare War, grant Letters of Marque and Reprisal, and make Rules concerning Captures on Land and Water;

To raise and support Armies, but no Appropriation of Money to that Use shall be for a longer Term than two Years;

To provide and maintain a Navy;

To make Rules for the Government and Regulation of the land and naval Forces;

To provide for calling for the Militia to execute the Laws of the Union, suppress Insurrections and repel Invasions;

To provide for organizing, arming, and disciplining the Militia, and for governing such Part of them as may be employed in the Service of the United States, reserving to the States respectively, the Appointment of the Officers, and the Authority of training the Militia according to the discipline prescribed by Congress;

Clause 2 To exercise exclusive Legislation in all Cases whatsoever, over such District (not exceeding ten Miles square) as may, by Cession of particular States, and the Acceptance of Congress, become the Seat of the Government of the United States, and to exercise like Authority over all Places purchased by the Consent of the Legislature of the State in which the Same shall be, for the Erection of Forts, Magazines, Arsenals, dock-Yards; and other needful Buildings;—And

Clause 3 To make all Laws which shall be necessary and proper for carrying into Execution the foregoing Powers, and all other Powers vested by this Constitution in the Government of the United States, or in any Department or Officer thereof.

Powers Denied to Congress

SECTION 9

Clause 1 The Migration or Importation of such Persons as any of the States now existing shall think proper to admit, shall not be prohibited by the Congress prior to the Year one

thousand eight hundred and eight, but a Tax or duty may be imposed on such Importation, not exceeding ten dollars for each Person.

Clause 2 The privilege of the Writ of Habeas Corpus shall not be suspended, unless when in Cases of Rebellion or Invasion the public Safety may require it.

Clause 3 No Bill of Attainder or ex post facto Law shall be passed.

Clause 4 No Capitation, or other direct, Tax shall be laid, unless in Proportion to the Census or Enumeration herein before directed to be taken.[6]

Clause 5 No Tax or Duty shall be laid on Articles exported from any State.

Clause 6 No Preference shall be given by any Regulation of Commerce or Revenue to the Ports of one State over those of another; nor shall Vessels bound to, or from, one State, be obliged to enter, clear, or pay Duties in another.

Clause 7 No Money shall be drawn from the Treasury, but in Consequence of Appropriations made by Law; and a regular Statement and Account of the Receipts and Expenditures of all public Money shall be published from time to time.

Clause 8 No Title of Nobility shall be granted by the United States: And no Person holding any Office of Profit or Trust under them, shall, without the Consent of Congress, accept of any present, Emolument, Office, or Title, of any kind whatever, from any King, Prince, or foreign State.

Powers Denied to the States

SECTION 10

Clause 1 No State shall enter into any Treaty, Alliance, or Confederation; grant Letters of Marque and Reprisal; coin Money; emit Bills of Credit; make any Thing but gold and silver Coin a Tender in Payment of Debts; pass any Bill of Attainder, ex post facto Law, or Law impairing the Obligation of Contracts, or grant any Title of Nobility.

Clause 2 No State shall, without the Consent of the Congress, lay any Imposts or Duties on Imports or Exports, except what may be absolutely necessary for executing its inspection Laws: and the net Produce of all Duties and Imposts, laid by any State on Imports or Exports, shall be for the Use of the Treasury of the United States; and all such Laws shall be subject to the Revision and Controul of the Congress.

Clause 3 No State shall, without the Consent of Congress, lay any Duty of Tonnage, keep Troops, or Ships of War in time of Peace, enter into any Agreement or Compact with another State, or with a foreign Power, or engage in War, unless actually invaded, or in such imminent Danger as will not admit of Delay.

[6]Modified by the 16th Amendment

Article II—The Executive Article

Nature and Scope of Presidential Power

SECTION 1

Clause 1 The executive Power shall be vested in a President of the United States of America. He shall hold his Office during the Term of four Years and, together with the Vice President, chosen for the same Term, be elected as follows:

Clause 2 Each State shall appoint, in such Manner as the Legislature thereof may direct, a Number of Electors, equal to the whole Number of Senators and Representatives to which the State may be entitled in the Congress: but no Senator or Representative, or Person holding an Office of Trust or Profit under the United States, shall be appointed an Elector.

Clause 3 The Electors shall meet in their respective States, and vote by Ballot for two Persons, of whom one at least shall not be an Inhabitant of the same State with themselves. And they shall make a List of all the Persons voted for, and of the Number of Votes for each; which List they shall sign and certify, and transmit sealed to the Seat of the Government of the United States, directed to the President of the Senate. The President of the Senate shall, in the Presence of the Senate and House of Representatives, open all the Certificates, and the Votes shall then be counted. The Person having the greatest Number of Votes shall be the President, if such Number be a Majority of the whole Number of Electors appointed; and if there be more than one who have such Majority and have an equal Number of Votes, then the House of Representatives shall immediately chuse by Ballot one of them for President; and if no Person have a Majority, then from the five highest on the List the said House shall in like Manner chuse the President. But in chusing the President, the Votes shall be taken by States, the Representation from each State having one Vote; A quorum for this Purpose shall consist of a Member or Members from two thirds of the States, and a Majority of all the States shall be necessary to a Choice. In every Case, after the Choice of the President, the Person having the greatest Number of Votes of the Electors shall be the Vice President. But if there should remain two or more who have equal Vote, the Senate shall chuse from them by Ballot the Vice President.[7]

Clause 4 The Congress may determine the Time of chusing the Electors, and the Day on which they shall give their Votes; which Day shall be the same throughout the United States.

Clause 5 No Person except a natural born Citizen, or a Citizen of the United States, at the time of the Adoption of this Constitution, shall be eligible to the Office of President; neither shall any Person be eligible to that Office who shall not have attained to the Age of thirty five Years, and been fourteen Years a Resident within the United States.

Clause 6 In Case of the Removal of the President from Office, or of his Death, Resignation, or Inability to discharge the Powers and Duties of the said Office, the Same shall devolve on the Vice President, and the Congress may by Law provide for the Case of Removal, Death, Resignation, or Inability, both of the President and Vice President, declaring what Officer shall then act as President, and such Officer shall act accordingly, until the Disability be removed, or a President shall be elected.[8]

Clause 7 The President shall, at stated Times, receive for his Services, a Compensation, which shall neither be increased nor diminished during the Period of which he shall have been elected, and he shall not receive within that Period any other Emolument from the United States, or any of them.

Clause 8 Before he enter on the Execution of his Office, he shall take the following Oath or Affirmation:—"I do solemnly swear (or affirm) that I will faithfully execute the Office of President of the United States, and will to the best of my Ability, preserve, protect and defend the Constitution of the United States."

Powers and Duties of the President

SECTION 2

Clause 1 The President shall be the Commander in Chief of the Army and Navy of the United States, and of the Militia of the several States, when called into the actual Service of the United States; he may require the Opinion, in writing, of the principal Officer in each of the executive Departments, upon any Subject relating to the Duties of their respective Offices, and he shall have the Power to grant Reprieves and Pardons for Offences against the United States, except in Cases of Impeachment.

Clause 2 He shall have Power, by and with the Advice and Consent of the Senate to make Treaties, provided two thirds of the Senators present concur; and he shall nominate, and by and with the Advice and Consent of the Senate, shall appoint Ambassadors, other public Ministers and Consuls, Judges of the supreme Court, and all other Officers of the United States, whose Appointments are not herein otherwise provided for, and which shall be established by Law: but the Congress may by Law vest the Appointment of such inferior Officers, as they think proper, in the President alone, in the Courts of Law, or in the Heads of Departments.

Clause 3 The President shall have Power to fill up all Vacancies that may happen during the Recess of the Senate, by granting Commissions which shall expire at the End of their next Session.

SECTION 3 He shall from time to time give to the Congress Information of the State of the Union, and recommend to their Consideration such Measures as he shall judge necessary and expedient; he may, on extraordinary Occasions, convene both Houses, or either of them and in Case of Disagreement between them, with Respect to the Time of Adjournment, he may adjourn them to such Time as he shall think proper; he shall receive Ambassadors and other public Ministers; he shall

---

[7]Changed by the 12th and 20th Amendments

[8]Modified by the 25th Amendment

take Care that the Laws be faithfully executed, and shall Commission all the Officers of the United States.

SECTION 4   The President, Vice President and all civil Officers of the United States, shall be removed from Office on Impeachment for, and Conviction of, Treason, Bribery, or other high Crimes and Misdemeanors.

Article III—The Judicial Article
Judicial Power, Courts, Judges

SECTION 1   The judicial Power of the United States shall be vested in one supreme Court, and in such inferior Courts as the Congress may from time to time ordain and establish. The Judges, both the supreme and inferior Courts, shall hold their Offices during good Behaviour, and shall, at stated Times, receive for their Services a Compensation, which shall not be diminished during their Continuance in Office.

Jurisdiction

SECTION 2   The judicial Power shall extend to all Cases, in Law and Equity, arising under this Constitution, the Laws of the United States, and Treaties made, or which shall be made, under their Authority;—to all Cases affecting Ambassadors, other public Ministers and Consuls;—to all Cases of admiralty and maritime Jurisdiction;—to Controversies to which the United States shall be a Party;—to Controversies between two or more States; between a State and Citizens of another State;[9]—between Citizens of different States;—between Citizens of the same State claiming Lands under Grants of different States, and between a State, or the Citizens thereof, and foreign States, Citizens, or Subjects.

In all Cases affecting Ambassadors, other public Ministers and Consuls, and those in which a State shall be Party, the supreme Court shall have original Jurisdiction. In all the other Cases before mentioned, the supreme Court shall have appellate Jurisdiction, both as to Law and Fact, with such Exceptions, and under such Regulations as Congress shall make.

The Trial of all Crimes, except in Cases of Impeachment, shall be by Jury; and such Trial shall be held in the State where the said Crimes shall have been committed; but when not committed within any State, the Trial shall be at such Place or Places as the Congress may by Law have directed.

Treason

SECTION 3   Treason against the United States, shall consist only in levying War against them, or in adhering to their Enemies, giving them Aid and Comfort. No Person shall be convicted of Treason unless on the Testimony of two Witnesses to the same overt Act, or on Confession in open Court.

The Congress shall have Power to declare the Punishment of Treason, but no Attainder of Treason shall work Corruption of Blood, or Forfeiture except during the Life of the Person attainted.

Article IV—Interstate Relations
Full Faith and Credit Clause

SECTION 1   Full Faith and Credit shall be given in each State to the public Acts, Records, and judicial Proceedings of every other State. And the Congress may by general Laws prescribe the Manner in which such Acts, Records and Proceedings shall be proved, and the Effect thereof.

Privileges and Immunities; Interstate Extradition

SECTION 2

Clause 1   The Citizens of each State shall be entitled to all Privileges and Immunities of Citizens in the several States.

Clause 2   A Person charged in any State with Treason, Felony or other Crime, who shall flee from Justice, and be found in another State, shall on Demand of the executive Authority of the State from which he fled, be delivered up, to be removed to the State having Jurisdiction of the Crime.

Clause 3   No person held to Service or Labour in one State, under the Laws thereof, escaping into another, shall, in Consequence of any Law or Regulation therein, be discharged from such Service or Labour, but shall be delivered up on Claim of the Party to whom such Service or Labour may be due.[10]

Admission of States

SECTION 3   New States may be admitted by the Congress into this Union; but no new State shall be formed or erected within the Jurisdiction of any other State; nor any State to be formed by the Junction of two or more States, or Parts of States, without the Consent of the Legislatures of the States concerned as well as of the Congress.

The Congress shall have Power to dispose of and make all needful Rules and Regulations respecting the Territory or other Property belonging to the United States; and nothing in this Constitution shall be so construed as to Prejudice any Claims of the United States, or of any particular State.

Republican Form of Government

SECTION 4   The United States shall guarantee to every State in this Union a Republican Form of Government, and shall protect each of them against Invasion; and on Application of the Legislature, or of the Executive (when the Legislature cannot be convened) against domestic Violence.

Article V—The Amending Power

The Congress, whenever two thirds of both Houses shall deem it necessary, shall propose Amendments to this Constitution, or, on the Application of the Legislatures of two thirds of several States, shall call a Convention for proposing Amendments,

[9]Modified by the 11th Amendment

[10]Repealed by the 13th Amendment

which, in either Case, shall be valid to all Intents and Purposes, as Part of this Constitution, when ratified by the Legislatures of three fourths of the several States, or by Conventions in three fourths thereof, as the one or the other Mode of Ratification may be proposed by the Congress; Provided that no Amendment which may be made prior to the Year One thousand eight hundred and eight shall in any Manner affect the first and fourth Clauses in the Ninth Section of the first Article; and that no State, without its Consent, shall be deprived of its equal Suffrage in the Senate.

Article VI—The Supremacy Act

Clause 1

All Debts contracted and Engagements entered into, before the Adoption of this Constitution, shall be as valid against the United States under the Constitution, as under the Confederation.

Clause 2

This Constitution, and the Laws of the United States which shall be made in Pursuance thereof; and all Treaties made, or which shall be made, under the Authority of the United States, shall be the supreme Law of the Land; and the Judges in every State shall be bound thereby, any Thing in the Constitution or Laws of any State to the Contrary notwithstanding.

Clause 3

The Senators and Representatives before mentioned, and the Members of the several State Legislatures, and all executive and judicial Officers, both of the United States and of the several States, shall be bound by Oath or Affirmation, to support this Constitution; but no religious Test shall ever be required as a Qualification to any Office or public Trust under the United States.

Article VII—Ratification

The Ratification of the Conventions of nine States, shall be sufficient for the Establishment of this Constitution between the States so ratifying the Same.

Done in Convention by the Unanimous Consent of the States present the Seventeenth Day of September in the Year of our Lord one thousand seven hundred and Eighty seven and of the Independence of the United States of America the Twelfth In Witness whereof We have hereunto subscribed our Names.

Amendments

The Bill of Rights

[The first ten amendments were ratified on December 15, 1791, and form what is known as the "Bill of Rights."]

Amendment 1—
Religion, Speech, Assembly, and Politics

Congress shall make no law respecting an establishment of religion, or prohibiting the free exercise thereof; or abridging the freedom of speech, or of the press; or the right of the people peaceably to assemble, and to petition the government for a redress of grievances.

Amendment 2—
Militia and the Right to Bear Arms

A well-regulated Militia, being necessary to the security of a free State, the right of the people to keep and bear Arms, shall not be infringed.

Amendment 3—Quartering of Soldiers

No Soldier shall, in time of peace be quartered in any house, without the consent of the Owner, nor in time of war, but in manner to be prescribed by law.

Amendment 4—Searches and Seizures

The right of the people to be secure in their persons, houses, papers, and effects, against unreasonable searches and seizures, shall not be violated, and no Warrants shall issue, but upon probable cause, supported by Oath or affirmation, and particularly describing the place to be searched, and the persons or things to be seized.

Amendment 5—Grand Juries,
Self-Incrimination, Double Jeopardy, Due Process, and Eminent Domain

No person shall be held to answer for a capital, or otherwise infamous crime, unless on a presentment or indictment of a Grand jury, except in cases arising in the land or naval forces, or in the Militia, when in actual service in time of War or public danger; nor shall any person be subject for the same offence to be twice put in jeopardy of life or limb; nor shall be compelled in any criminal case to be a witness against himself, nor be deprived of life, liberty, or property, without due process of law; nor shall private property be taken for public use, without just compensation.

Amendment 6—
Criminal Court Procedures

In all criminal prosecutions, the accused shall enjoy the right to a speedy and public trial, by an impartial jury of the State and district wherein the crime shall have been committed, which district shall have been previously ascertained by law, and to be informed of the nature and cause of the accusation; to be confronted with the witnesses against him; to have compulsory process for obtaining Witnesses in his favor, and to have the Assistance of Counsel for his defence.

Amendment 7—Trial by Jury in Common Law Cases

In Suits at common law, where the value in controversy shall exceed twenty dollars, the right of trial by jury shall be preserved, and no fact tried by a jury shall be otherwise re-examined in any Court of the United States, than according to the rules of the common law.

Amendment 8—Bail, Cruel and Unusual Punishment

Excessive bail shall not be required, nor excessive fines imposed, nor cruel and unusual punishments inflicted.

Amendment 9—Rights Retained by the People

The enumeration in the Constitution, of certain rights, shall not be construed to deny or disparage others retained by the people.

Amendment 10—Reserved Powers of the States

The powers not delegated to the United States by the Constitution, nor prohibited by it to the States, are reserved to the States respectively, or to the people.

Amendment 11—Suits Against the States

[Ratified February 7, 1795]

The Judicial power of the United States shall not be construed to extend to any suit in law or equity, commenced or prosecuted against one of the United States by Citizens of another State, or by Citizens or Subjects of any Foreign State.

Amendment 12—Election of the President

[Ratified June 15, 1804]

The Electors shall meet in their respective states, and vote by ballot for President and Vice-President, one of whom, at least, shall not be an inhabitant of the same state with themselves; they shall name in their ballots the person voted for as President, and in distinct ballots the person voted for as Vice-President, and they shall make distinct lists of all persons voted for as President, and of all persons voted for as Vice-President, and of the number of votes for each, which lists they shall sign and certify, and transmit sealed to the seat of the government of the United States, directed to the President of the Senate;—The President of the Senate shall, in presence of the Senate and House of Representatives, open all the certificates and the votes shall then be counted;—The person having the greatest number of votes for President, shall be the President, if such number be a majority of the whole number of Electors appointed; and if no person have such majority, then from the persons having the highest numbers not exceeding three on the list of those voted for as President, the House of Representatives shall choose immediately, by ballot, the President. But in choosing the President, the votes shall be taken by states, the representation from each state having one vote; a quorum for this purpose shall consist of a member or members from two-thirds of the states, and a majority of all states shall be necessary to a choice. And if the House of Representatives shall not choose a President whenever the right of choice shall devolve upon them, before the fourth day of March next following, then the Vice-President shall act as President, as in the case of the death or other constitutional disability of the President.[11] The person having the greatest number of votes as Vice-President, shall be the Vice-President, if such a number be a majority of the whole numbers of Electors appointed, and if no person have a majority, then from the two highest numbers on the list, the Senate shall choose the Vice-President; a quorum for the purpose shall consist of two-thirds of the whole number of Senators, and a majority of the whole number shall be necessary to a choice. But no person constitutionally ineligible to the office of President shall be eligible to that of Vice-President of the United States.

Amendment 13—Prohibition of Slavery

[Ratified December 6, 1865]

SECTION 1 Neither slavery nor involuntary servitude, except as a punishment for crime whereof the party shall have been duly convicted, shall exist within the United States, or any place subject to their jurisdiction.

SECTION 2 Congress shall have power to enforce this article by appropriate legislation.

Amendment 14—Citizenship, Due Process, and Equal Protection of the Laws

[Ratified July 9, 1868]

SECTION 1 All persons born or naturalized in the United States, and subject to the jurisdiction thereof, are citizens of the United States and of the State wherein they reside. No State shall make or enforce any law which shall abridge the privileges or immunities of citizens of the United States; nor shall any State deprive any person of life, liberty, or property, without due process of law; nor deny to any person within its jurisdiction the equal protection of the laws.

SECTION 2 Representatives shall be apportioned among the several States according to their respective numbers, counting the whole number of persons in each State, excluding Indians not taxed. But when the right to vote at any election for the choice of electors for President and Vice President of the United States, Representatives in Congress, the Executive and Judicial officers of a State, or the members of the Legislature thereof, is denied to any of the male inhabitants of such State, being twenty-one[12] years of age, and citizens of the United States, or in any way abridged, except for participation in rebellion, or other crime, the basis of representation therein shall be reduced in the proportion which the number of such

---

[11]Changed by the 20th Amendment
[12]Changed by the 26th Amendment

male citizens shall bear to the whole number of male citizens twenty-one years of age in such State.

SECTION 3   No person shall be a Senator or Representative in Congress, or elector of President and Vice President, or hold any office, civil or military, under the United States, or under any State, who, having previously taken an oath, as a member of Congress, or as an officer of the United States, or as a member of any State legislature, or as an executive or judicial officer of any State, to support the Constitution of the United States, shall have engaged in insurrection or rebellion against the same, or given aid or comfort to the enemies thereof. But Congress may by a vote of two-thirds of each House, remove such disability.

SECTION 4   The validity of the public debt of the United States, authorized by law, including debts incurred for payment of pensions and bounties for services in suppressing insurrection or rebellion, shall not be questioned. But neither the United States nor any State shall assume or pay any debt or obligation incurred in aid of insurrection or rebellion against the United States, or any claim for the loss or emancipation of any slave; but all such debts, obligations and claims shall be held illegal and void.

SECTION 5   The Congress shall have power to enforce, by appropriate legislation, the provisions of this article.

Amendment 15—The Right to Vote
[Ratified February 3, 1870]

SECTION 1   The right of citizens of the United States to vote shall not be denied or abridged by the United States or by any State on account of race, color, or previous condition of servitude.

SECTION 2   The Congress shall have power to enforce this article by appropriate legislation.

Amendment 16—Income Taxes
[Ratified February 3, 1913]

The Congress shall have power to lay and collect taxes on incomes, from whatever source derived, without apportionment among the several States, and without regard to any census or enumeration.

Amendment 17—Direct Election of Senators
[Ratified April 8, 1913]

The Senate of the United States shall be composed of two Senators from each State, elected by the people thereof, for six years; and each Senator shall have one vote. The electors in each State shall have the qualifications requisite for electors of the most numerous branch of the State legislatures.

When vacancies happen in the representation of any State in the Senate, the executive authority of such State shall issue writs of election to fill such vacancies: Provided, That the legislature of any State may empower the executive thereof to make temporary appointment until the people fill the vacancies by election as the legislature may direct. This amendment shall not be so construed as to affect the election or term of any Senator chosen before it becomes valid as part of the Constitution.

Amendment 18—Prohibition
[Ratified January 16, 1919. Repealed December 5, 1933 by Amendment 21]

SECTION 1   After one year from the ratification of this article the manufacture, sale, or transportation of intoxicating liquors within, the importation thereof into, or the exportation thereof from the United States and all territory subject to the jurisdiction thereof for beverage purposes is hereby prohibited.

SECTION 2   The Congress and the several states shall have concurrent power to enforce this article by appropriate legislation.

SECTION 3   This article shall be inoperative unless it shall have been ratified as an amendment to the Constitution by the legislatures of the several states, as provided in the Constitution, within seven years from the date of the submission hereof to the States by the Congress.[13]

Amendment 19—For Women's Suffrage
[Ratified August 18, 1920]

The right of the citizens of the United States to vote shall not be denied or abridged by the United States or by any State on account of sex.

Congress shall have power, by appropriate legislation, to enforce the provision of this article.

Amendment 20—The Lame Duck Amendment
[Ratified January 23, 1933]

SECTION 1   The terms of the President and Vice President shall end at noon on the 20th day of January, and the terms of the Senators and Representatives at noon on the 3rd day of January, of the years in which such terms would have ended if this article had not been ratified, and the terms of their successors shall then begin.

SECTION 2   The Congress shall assemble at least once in every year, and such meeting shall begin at noon on the 3rd day of January, unless they shall by law appoint a different day.

SECTION 3   If, at the time fixed for the beginning of the term of the President, the President elect shall have died, the Vice President elect shall become President. If a President shall not have been chosen before the time fixed for the beginning of his term, or if the President elect shall have failed to qualify, then the Vice President elect shall act as President until a President shall have qualified; and the Congress may by law provide for the case wherein neither a President elect nor a Vice President elect shall have qualified, declaring who shall then act as President, or the manner in which one who is to act shall be selected, and such person shall act accordingly until a President or Vice President shall have qualified.

---

[13]Repealed by the 21st Amendment

SECTION 4   The Congress may by law provide for the case of the death of any of the persons from whom the House of Representatives may choose a President whenever the right of choice shall have devolved upon them, and for the case of the death of any of the persons from whom the Senate may choose a Vice President whenever the right of choice shall have devolved upon them.

SECTION 5   Sections 1 and 2 shall take effect on the 15th day of October following the ratification of this article.

SECTION 6   This article shall be inoperative unless it shall have been ratified as an amendment to the Constitution by the legislatures of three-fourths of the several States within seven years from the date of its submission.

Amendment 21—Repeal of Prohibition
[Ratified December 5, 1933]

SECTION 1   The eighteenth article of amendment to the Constitution of the United States is hereby repealed.

SECTION 2   The transportation or importation into any State, Territory, or Possession of the United States for delivery or use therein of intoxicating liquors, in violation of the laws thereof, is hereby prohibited.

SECTION 3   This article shall be inoperative unless it shall have been ratified as an amendment to the Constitution by conventions in the several States, as provided in the Constitution, within seven years from the date of the submission hereof to the States by the Congress.

Amendment 22—Number of Presidential Terms
[Ratified February 27, 1951]

SECTION 1   No person shall be elected to the office of the President more than twice, and no person who has held the office of President, or acted as President, for more than two years of a term to which some other person was elected President shall be elected to the office of the President more than once. But this Article shall not apply to any person holding the office of President when this article was proposed by the Congress, and shall not prevent any person who may be holding the office of President, or acting as President, during the term within which this Article becomes operative from holding the office of President or acting as President during the remainder of such term.

SECTION 2   This Article shall be inoperative unless it shall have been ratified as an amendment to the Constitution by the legislatures of three-fourths of the several states within seven years from the date of its submission to the States by the Congress.

Amendment 23—Presidential Electors for the District of Columbia
[Ratified March 29, 1961]

SECTION 1   The District constituting the seat of government of the United States shall appoint in such manner as the Congress may direct:

A number of electors of President and Vice President equal to the whole number of Senators and Representatives in Congress to which the District would be entitled if it were a State, but in no event more than the least populous State; they shall be in addition to those appointed by the States, but they shall be considered for the purposes of the election of President and Vice President, to be electors appointed by a State; and they shall meet in the District and perform such duties as provided by the twelfth article of amendment.

SECTION 2   The Congress shall have power to enforce this article by appropriate legislation

Amendment 24—The Anti-Poll Tax Amendment
[Ratified January 23, 1964]

SECTION 1   The right of citizens of the United States to vote in any primary or other election for President or Vice President, for electors for President or Vice President, or for Senator or Representative in Congress, shall not be denied or abridged by the United States or any state by reason of failure to pay any poll tax or other tax.

SECTION 2   The Congress shall have power to enforce this article by appropriate legislation.

Amendment 25—Presidential Disability, Vice Presidential Vacancies
[Ratified February 10, 1967]

SECTION 1   In case of the removal of the President from office or his death or resignation, the Vice President shall become President.

SECTION 2   Whenever there is a vacancy in the office of the Vice President, the President shall nominate a Vice President who shall take the office upon confirmation by a majority vote of both Houses of Congress.

SECTION 3   Whenever the President transmits to the President pro tempore of the Senate and the Speaker of the House of Representatives his written declaration that he is unable to discharge the powers and duties of his office, and until he transmits to them a written declaration to the contrary, such powers and duties shall be discharged by the Vice President as Acting President.

SECTION 4   Whenever the Vice President and a majority of either the principal officers of the executive departments, or of such other body as Congress may by law provide, transmit to the President pro tempore of the Senate and the Speaker of the House of Representatives their written declaration that the President is unable to discharge the powers and duties of his office, the Vice President shall immediately assume the powers and duties of the office as Acting President.

Thereafter, when the President transmits to the President pro tempore of the Senate and the Speaker of the House of Representatives his written declaration that no inability exists, he shall resume the powers and duties of his office unless the Vice President and a majority of either the principal officers of the executive departments, or of such other body as Congress may by law provide, transmit within four days to the President pro tempore of the Senate and the Speaker of the House of Representatives their written declaration that the President is unable to discharge the powers and duties of his office. Thereupon Congress shall decide the issue, assembling within forty-eight hours for that purpose if not in session. If the Congress, within twenty-one days after receipt of the latter written declaration, or, if Congress is not in session, within twenty-one days after Congress is required to assemble, determines by two-thirds vote of both houses that the President is unable to discharge the powers and duties of his office, the Vice President shall continue to discharge the same as Acting President; otherwise, the President shall resume the powers and duties of his office.

Amendment 26—Eighteen-Year-Old Vote
[Ratified July 1, 1971]

SECTION 1   The right of citizens of the United States, who are 18 years of age, or older, to vote shall not be denied or abridged by the United States or by any state on account of age.

SECTION 2   The Congress shall have power to enforce this article by appropriate legislation.

Amendment 27—Congressional Salaries
[Ratified May 7, 1992]

No law, varying the compensation for the services of the Senators and Representatives, shall take effect, until an election of Representatives shall be intervened.

CHAPTER

3

American Federalism

The relationship of the national government to the states has been the subject of intense debate since the founding.[1] In 1787, members of what would become the Federalist Party defended the creation of a strong national government, whereas the Antifederalists warned that a strong national government would overshadow the states. The great debate over which level of government best represents the people continues to rage.

State governments have often complained that the national government is either taking over their responsibilities or controlling too much of what they do. Yet, in policy areas such as civil rights, educational opportunities for people with disabilities, and handgun control, the states have been slow to respond to citizens, and the national government has taken steps to deal with these issues.

At the same time, states retain enormous authority under the Constitution to regulate life within their borders. Working with the local governments they create, states police the streets, fight fires, impose their own taxes, create most of the laws that govern their citizens, define the meaning of marriage, set the rules for elections and voter registration, run the public schools, and administer most of the programs to help the poor, even when the money for those programs comes from the national government.

In recent years, for example, states have become increasingly involved in regulating cell phone use and texting while driving. As the number of text messages sent in the United States increased from 57.2 billion in 2005 to more than 600 billion in 2008, states became increasingly concerned that texting was an even greater threat to safety than talking on cell phones. According to recent studies, drivers who are texting while driving are significantly more likely to drift out of their lane and look away from the cars in front of them. As a result, they are much more likely to be in life-threatening accidents than drivers who talk on cell phones, who themselves are already more likely to be in life-threatening accidents than those who keep their eyes on the road and hands on the wheel.[2] As with talking on cell phones, younger drivers are much more likely to text than older drivers.

The pressure to pass new laws banning texting while driving increased in 2009, when British television began running a public service advertisement showing the grizzly results of a fictitious accident. The four-minute advertisement is graphic, bloody, and terrifying. It is so disturbing that viewers must be 18 to watch the film on YouTube, although anyone can watch a 2009 *Today Show* story about the film, also available on YouTube.

States are reacting to the threat by passing new laws to ban texting while driving. By the end of 2009, 18 states were already imposing stiff fines for texting while driving under a general ban on distracted driving, and some were suspending the driver's license of anyone caught texting on the road. Delaware, Indiana, Kansas, Maine, Mississippi, and West Virginia now prohibit texting while driving for drivers with learning permits or probationary licenses, while Missouri prohibits texting while driving for anyone under age 21.

Enforcement is the problem with such bans. Police cannot be everywhere watching every possible violation, and text messaging is particularly hard to spot. This is why state-sponsored education campaigns built around the kind of intense messages in the British television advertisement may be the only way to frighten drivers away from the practice. Under the Constitution, it is mostly up to the states to figure out both what to do about texting while driving and how to enforce the laws they make.

In 2009, a small city in Britain began running a graphic four-minute television advertisement about the dangers of texting while driving. Many U.S. states have passed or are considering legislation banning the practice. ■ *What are some of the potential difficulties for drivers when the regulation of texting while driving is handled on a state-by-state basis?*

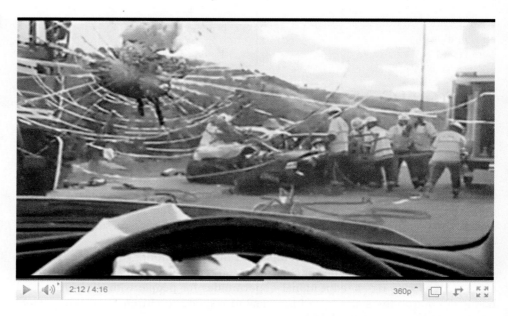

In this chapter, we first define federalism and its advantages and disadvantages. We then look at the constitutional basis for our federal system and how court decisions and political developments have shaped, and continue to shape, federalism in the United States. Throughout, you should think hard about how you influence the issues you care about, even in your local city council or mayor's office. The Constitution clearly encourages, and even depends on, you to express your view at all levels of government, which is why action in a single state can start a process of change that spreads to other states or the national government.

Defining Federalism

LEARNING **OBJECTIVE**

3.1 Interpret the definitions of federalism, and assess the advantages and disadvantages of the American system of federalism.

Scholars have argued and wars have been fought over what federalism means. One scholar recently counted 267 definitions of the term.[3]

Federalism, as we define it, is a form of government in which a constitution distributes authority and powers between a central government and smaller regional governments—usually called states, provinces, or republics—giving to both the national and the regional governments substantial responsibilities and powers, including the power to collect taxes and to pass and enforce laws regulating the conduct of individuals. When we use the term "federalism" or "federal system," we are referring to this system of national and state governments; when we use the term "federal government," here and in the other chapters of the book, we are referring to the national government headquartered in Washington, D.C.

The mere existence of both national and state governments does not make a system federal. What is important is that a *constitution divides governmental powers between the national government and smaller regional governments,* giving clearly defined functions to each. Neither the central nor the regional government receives its powers from the other; both derive them from a common source—the Constitution. No ordinary act of legislation at either the national or the state level can change this constitutional distribution of powers. Both levels of government operate through their own agents and exercise power directly over individuals.

Constitutionally, the federal system of the United States consists of only the national government and the 50 states. "Cities are not," the Supreme Court reminded us, "sovereign entities." This does not make for a tidy, efficient, easy-to-understand system; yet, as we shall see, it has its virtues.

federalism

A constitutional arrangement in which power is distributed between a central government and subdivisional governments, called states in the United States. The national and the subdivisional governments both exercise direct authority over individuals.

There are several different ways that power can be shared in a federal system, and political scientists have devised terms to explain these various kinds of federalism. At different times in the United States' history, our system of federalism has shared power based on each of the below interpretations.

- *Dual federalism* views the Constitution as giving a limited list of powers—primarily foreign policy and national defense—to the national government, leaving the rest to sovereign states. Each level of government is dominant within its own sphere.
- *Cooperative federalism* stresses federalism as a system of intergovernmental relationships in delivering governmental goods and services to the people and calls for cooperation among various levels of government.
- *Marble cake federalism* conceives of federalism as a mixed set of responsibilities in which all levels of government are engaged in a variety of issues and programs, rather than a layer cake, or dual federalism, with fixed divisions between layers or levels of government.[4]
- *Competitive federalism* views the national government, the 50 states, and the thousands of local governments as competing with each other over ways to put together packages of services and taxes.[5]
- *Permissive federalism* implies that, although federalism provides "a sharing of power and authority between the national and state government, the states' share rests on the permission and permissiveness of the national government."[6]
- *New federalism,* championed by former presidents Richard M. Nixon (1969–1974) and Ronald Reagan (1981–1989), presumes that the power of the federal government is limited in favor of the broad powers reserved to the states.

Alternatives to Federalism

Among the alternatives to federalism are **unitary systems** of government, in which a constitution vests all governmental power in the central government. The central government, if it so chooses, may delegate authority to constituent units, but what it delegates, it may take away. China, France, the Scandinavian countries, and Israel have unitary governments. In the United States, state constitutions usually create this kind of relationship between the state and its local governments.

At the other extreme from unitary governments are **confederations,** in which sovereign nations, through a constitutional compact, create a central government but carefully limit its authority and do not give it the power to regulate the conduct of individuals directly. The central government makes regulations for the constituent governments,

unitary system
A constitutional arrangement that concentrates power in a central government.

confederation
A constitutional arrangement in which sovereign nations or states, by compact, create a central government but carefully limit its power and do not give it direct authority over individuals.

State and local governments are responsible for policing the streets but not for enforcing federal laws. Nevertheless, they often work with national agencies such as the Federal Bureau of Investigation, Drug Enforcement Administration, or the Immigration and Customs Enforcement Bureau. ■ *What are some of the benefits of federal, state, and local law enforcement agencies working together against crime?*

Of the People

Global Opinion on the Role of Government

State and local governments are on the front lines of most programs for helping the needy. They provide much of the money and/or administration for unemployment insurance for the jobless, health care clinics and hospitals for the poor, school lunch programs for hungry children, and homeless shelters. Although many U.S. citizens see poverty firsthand as volunteers for local charities such as food pantries, some have doubts about how much government should do to help poor people who cannot take care of themselves. According to the Pew Global survey, citizens of other nations vary greatly on the question.

These opinions reflect very different social and economic conditions in each country. Japan has a culture of self-reliance that puts the burden on individuals to help themselves, while Nigeria continues to suffer from some of the highest poverty rates in the world. In this regard, U.S. citizens tend to mirror the Japanese—they want government to help the less fortunate but also want the less fortunate to help themselves. As a general conclusion, citizens of wealthier nations think poor people should take advantage of the opportunities that already exist in their economies, whereas citizens of poor nations believe that government should be more aggressive in providing support.

This does not mean wealthier nations are uncaring toward citizens in need, but it does suggest that they sometimes view poverty as the fault of the poor. In the United States, these opinions reflect the importance of equality of opportunity as a basic social value, meaning that all individuals regardless of race, gender, or circumstance have the same opportunity to participate in politics, self-government, and the economy. Most Americans want to help the less fortunate, but only when they are truly needy, not when they fail because they will not help themselves.

CRITICAL THINKING QUESTIONS

1. What are the advantages and disadvantages of having the government provide services for the poor?

2. Why might more wealthy nations be more likely to believe that individuals ought to take care of themselves and not rely on the state?

3. Which level of government might be most effective in providing services to the poor?

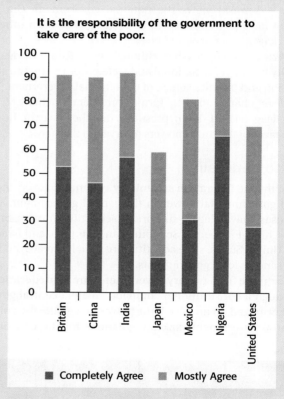

It is the responsibility of the government to take care of the poor.

■ Completely Agree   ■ Mostly Agree

---

but it exists and operates only at their direction. The 13 states under the Articles of Confederation operated in this manner, as did the southern Confederacy during the Civil War.

There is no single model for dividing authority between the national and smaller regional governments of the other nations. Indeed, even in the United States, we have seen shifts in the balance of federal-state power throughout our history. Some countries have no federal system at all, whereas others have different variations of power sharing between the national and smaller regional governments.

For example, Britain's government is divided into three tiers: national, county, and district governments. County and district governments deliver roughly one-fifth of all government services, including education, housing, and police and fire protection. As a rule, most power is reserved for the central government on the theory that there should be "territorial justice," which means that all citizens should be governed by the same laws and standards. In recent years, however, Great Britain has devolved substantial authority to Scotland, Wales, and Northern Ireland.

Why Federalism?

In 1787, federalism was a compromise between centrists, who supported a strong national government, and those who favored decentralization. Confederation had proved unsuccessful. A unitary system was out of the question because most people were too deeply attached to their state governments to permit subordination to central rule. Many scholars think that federalism is ideally suited to the needs of a diverse people spread throughout a large continent, suspicious of concentrated power, and desiring unity but not uniformity. Yet, even though federalism offers a number of advantages over other forms of government, no system is perfect. Federalism offered, and still offers, both advantages and disadvantages for such a people.

Advantages of Federalism

Federalism Checks the Growth of Tyranny   Although in the rest of the world federal forms have not always prevented tyranny (Germany's federal constitution did not, for example, prevent Hitler from seizing power in the 1930s), U.S. citizens tend to associate federalism with freedom.[7] When one political party loses control of the national government, it is still likely to hold office in a number of states and can continue to challenge the party in power at the national level. To the framers, who feared that a single interest group might capture the national government and suppress the interests of others, this diffusion of power was an advantage. There are now nearly 90,000 governments in the United States, including one national government, 50 state governments, and thousands of county, city, and town governments, as well as school boards and special districts that provide specific functions from managing hospitals or parks to mosquito control.[8] (See Figure 3–1 for the number of governments in the United States.)

Federalism Allows Unity Without Uniformity   National politicians and parties do not have to iron out every difference on every issue that divides us, whether the issue is abortion, same-sex marriage, gun control, capital punishment, welfare financing, or assisted suicide. Instead, these issues are debated in state legislatures, county courthouses, and city halls. Information about state action spreads quickly from government to government, especially during periods when the national government is relatively slow to respond to pressing issues.

Federalism Encourages Experimentation   As Justice Louis Brandeis once argued, states are "laboratories of democracy." If they adopt programs that fail, the negative effects are

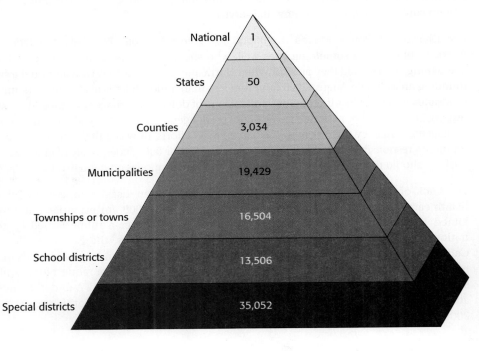

FIGURE 3–1 Number of Governments in the United States, 2009.
■ *How do the levels and numbers of governments in the United States help to prevent tyranny?*

SOURCE: U.S. Census Bureau, *Statistical Abstract of the United States*, www.census.gov/prod/2006pubs/07statab/stlocgov.pdf.

There are thousands of special districts in the United States that are responsible for providing specific services, such the Metropolitan Mosquito Control District in Minnesota. ■ *What are the advantages and disadvantages of dividing control of government services into local and special districts?*

limited; if programs succeed, they can be adopted by other states and by the national government. Georgia, for example, was the first state to permit 18-year-olds to vote; Wisconsin was a leader in requiring welfare recipients to work; California moved early on global warming; and Massachusetts created one of the first state programs to provide health insurance to all its citizens. Not all innovations, even those considered successful, become widely adopted.

Federalism Provides Training and Creates Opportunities for Future National Leaders Federalism provides a training ground for state and local politicians to gain experience before moving to the national stage. Presidents Jimmy Carter, Ronald Reagan, Bill Clinton, and George W. Bush previously served as governor of the respective states of Georgia, California, Arkansas, and Texas. In addition, three governors and one mayor ran for the Republican Party nomination for president in 2008, and another governor, Alaska's Sarah Palin, was selected as the Republican vice presidential candidate.

Federalism Keeps Government Closer to the People By providing numerous arenas for decision making, federalism provides many opportunities for Americans to participate in the process of government and helps keep government closer to the people. Every day, thousands of U.S. adults serve on city councils, school boards, neighborhood associations, and planning commissions. Federalism also builds on the public's greater trust in government at the state and local levels. The closer the specific level of government is to the people, the more citizens trust the government.

Disadvantages of Federalism

Dividing Power Makes It Much More Difficult for Government to Respond Quickly to National Problems There was a great demand for new efforts on homeland security after the September 11, 2001, terrorist attacks, and the national government created a new Department of Homeland Security in response. However, the department quickly discovered that there would be great difficulty coordinating its efforts with 50 state governments and thousands of local governments already providing fire, police, transportation, immigration control, and other governmental services.

The Division of Power Makes It Difficult for Voters to Hold Their Elected Officials Accountable When something goes well, who should voters reward? When something goes wrong, who should they punish? When Hurricane Katrina hit New Orleans and the surrounding areas in late August 2005 (and Rita less than a month later near Houston), many thousands of people lost their homes and billions of dollars in damage was done. Who was responsible? Did the national government and agencies like the Federal Emergency Management Agency (FEMA) drop the ball on relief efforts, or was it the state or local government's responsibility? Did the mayor and/or governor fail to adequately plan for such a crisis, or should the national government have had more supplies on hand in advance?

The Lack of Uniformity Can Lead to Conflict States often disagree on issues such as health care, school reform, and crime control. In January 2008, for example, California joined 15 other states in suing the national government over a ruling issued by the national Environmental Protection Agency (EPA). For decades, the EPA had allowed California to enact tougher air quality restrictions through higher mileage standards than required by the national Clean Air Act (first enacted in 1970). A similar request for permission to raise mileage standards was rejected in 2008, however, by the EPA under the Bush administration. The Obama Administration eventually approved California's request in 2009 and extended the higher mileage standards to all states.

Of the People

AMERICA'S CHANGING FACE

Where Americans Come From and Where They Live

The United States is a nation of immigrants who have arrived from many parts of the world. Throughout the decades, the portrait of immigrants has been changing from mostly white to mostly minority. In 2008, for example, 38 million Americans, or 12.5 percent, were foreign born, consisting of 16 million naturalized citizens, 10 million long-term visitors, and 12 million undocumented immigrants. The number of unauthorized, or illegal, immigrants has fallen somewhat in recent years due to the economic recession, which has depressed employment opportunities.

Many foreign-born residents live in the nation's largest cities. The New York City-area population includes more than 5 million foreign-born residents, while Los Angeles includes another 4.5 million; Miami, slightly more than 2 million; Chicago, 1.6 million; and San Francisco, 1.3 million. Although the inner cities host a majority of foreign-born residents, there has been recent movement of immigrants to the suburbs and some

movement toward certain areas of the country such as the southwest.

The changing face of America brings great diversity in all aspects of life, from schools to farm fields and small businesses. It enriches the quality of life through the mix of old and new cultures, and can often be a source of innovation in how the economy operates. Diversity also brings complaints about the national government's effort to close its borders to illegal immigrants. Some groups complain that illegal immigrants take jobs that should go to U.S. citizens, whereas others worry about the costs associated with high-poverty rates. Governments at all levels must reconcile these complaints with our history of welcoming immigrants from all around the world.

CRITICAL THINKING QUESTIONS

1. How are foreign-born citizens from different regions of the world different from each other?

The Statue of Liberty symbolizes America's long tradition of welcoming immigrants to its shores.

2. Why do you think foreign-born citizens tend to live in our nation's largest cities?

3. How do foreign-born citizens contribute to the nation's quality of life?

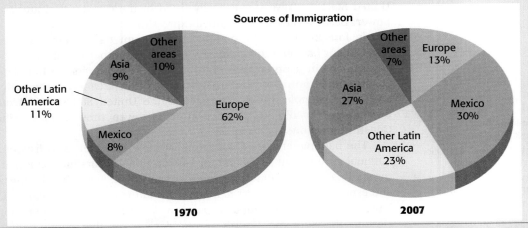

Sources of Immigration

1970
- Other areas 10%
- Asia 9%
- Other Latin America 11%
- Mexico 8%
- Europe 62%

2007
- Other areas 7%
- Europe 13%
- Asia 27%
- Mexico 30%
- Other Latin America 23%

SOURCE: William H. Frey, Alan Berube, Audrey Singer, and Jill H. Wilson, "Getting Current: Recent Demographic Trends in Metropolitan America," Washington, D.C.: The Brookings Institution, 2009.

Variation in Policies Creates Redundancies and Inefficiencies   The rules for environmental regulation, labor laws, teacher certification, gun ownership laws, and even the licensing requirements for optometrists vary throughout the 50 states, and this is on top of many federal regulations. Companies seeking to do business across state lines must learn and abide by many different sets of laws, while individuals in licensed professions must consider whether they face recertification if they choose to relocate to another state. One of the obstacles to health care reform debated throughout 2009 in Congress is the fact that each state has a different set of regulations for health insurance companies.

The Constitutional Structure of American Federalism

3.2 Differentiate the powers the Constitution provides to national and state governments.

The division of powers and responsibilities between the national and state governments has resulted in thousands of court decisions, as well as hundreds of books and endless speeches to explain them—and even then the division lacks precise definition. Nonetheless, it is helpful to have a basic understanding of how the Constitution divides these powers and responsibilities and what obligations it imposes on each level of government.

The constitutional framework of our federal system is relatively simple:

1. The national government has only those powers delegated to it by the Constitution (with the important exception of the inherent power over foreign affairs).
2. Within the scope of its operations, the national government is supreme.
3. The state governments have the powers not delegated to the central government except those denied to them by the Constitution and their state constitutions.
4. Some powers are specifically denied to both the national and state governments; others are specifically denied only to the states or to the national government.

Powers of the National Government

The Constitution explicitly gives legislative, executive, and judicial powers to the national government. In addition to these **delegated powers,** such as the power to regulate interstate commerce and to appropriate funds, the national government has assumed constitutionally **implied powers,** such as the power to create banks, which are inferred from delegated powers. The constitutional basis for the implied powers of Congress is the **necessary and proper clause** (Article I, Section 8, Clause 3). This clause gives Congress the right "to make all Laws which shall be necessary and proper for carrying into Execution the foregoing Powers, and all other Powers vested . . . in the Government of the United States." (Powers specifically listed in the Constitution are also called **express powers** because they are mentioned expressly.)

In foreign affairs, the national government has **inherent powers.** The national government has the same authority to deal with other nations as if it were the central government in a unitary system. Such inherent powers do not depend on specific constitutional provisions but exist because of the creation of the national government itself. For example, the government of the United States may acquire territory by purchase or by discovery and occupation, even though no specific clause in the Constitution allows such acquisition.

The national and state governments may have their own lists of powers, but the national government relies on four constitutional pillars for its ultimate authority over the states: (1) the *national supremacy article,* (2) the *war power,* (3) the *commerce clause,* and especially (4) the *power to tax and spend* for the general welfare. These authorities have permitted a tremendous expansion of the functions of the national government. Despite the Supreme Court's recent declaration that some national laws exceed Congress's constitutional powers, the national government has, in effect, almost full power to enact any legislation that Congress deems necessary, so long as it does not conflict with the provisions of the Constitution designed to protect individual rights and the powers of the states. In addition, Section 5 of the Fourteenth Amendment, ratified in 1868, gives Congress the power to enact legislation to remedy constitutional violations and the denial of due process or equal protection of the laws.

The National Supremacy Article   One of the most important constitutional pillars is found in Article VI: "This Constitution, and the Laws of the United States which shall be made in Pursuance thereof; and all Treaties made . . . under the Authority of the United States, shall be the supreme Law of the Land; and the Judges in every State shall be bound thereby; any Thing in the Constitution or Laws of any State to the Contrary notwithstanding." All officials, state as well as national, swear an oath to support the Constitution of the United States. States may not override national policies; this restriction also applies to local units of government because they are agents of the states.

delegated (express) powers
Powers given explicitly to the national government and listed in the Constitution.

implied powers
Powers inferred from the express powers that allow Congress to carry out its functions.

necessary and proper clause
The clause in the Constitution (Article I, Section 8, Clause 3) setting forth the implied powers of Congress. It states that Congress, in addition to its express powers, has the right to make all laws necessary and proper to carry out all powers the Constitution vests in the national government.

inherent powers
The powers of the national government in foreign affairs that the Supreme Court has declared do not depend on constitutional grants but rather grow out of the very existence of the national government.

National laws and regulations of federal agencies *preempt* the field, so that conflicting state and local regulations are unenforceable. States must abide by the national government's minimum wage laws, for example, but are allowed to set the minimum wage higher if they wish.

The War Power   The national government is responsible for protecting the nation from external aggression, whether from other nations or from international terrorism. The government's power to protect national security includes the power to wage war. In today's world, military strength depends not only on the presence of troops in the field but also on the ability to mobilize the nation's industrial might and apply scientific and technological knowledge to the tasks of defense. As Charles Evans Hughes, who became chief justice in 1930, observed: "The power to wage war is the power to wage war successfully."[9] The national government is free to create "no-fly" zones only for its military aircraft both within and across state borders, for example, and may use any airports it needs during times of war or peace.

The Power to Regulate Interstate and Foreign Commerce   Congressional authority extends to all commerce that affects more than one state. Commerce includes the production, buying, selling, renting, and transporting of goods, services, and properties. The **commerce clause** (Article I, Section 8, Clause 1) packs a tremendous constitutional punch; it gives Congress the power "to regulate Commerce with foreign Nations, and among the several States, and with the Indian Tribes." In these few words, the national government has found constitutional justification for regulating a wide range of human activity because few aspects of our economy today affect commerce in only one state and are thus outside the scope of the national government's constitutional authority.

The landmark ruling of *Gibbons* v. *Ogden* in 1824 affirmed the broad authority of Congress over interstate commerce. The case involved a New York state license that gave Aaron Ogden the exclusive right to operate steamboats between New York and New Jersey. Using the license, Ogden asked the New York state courts to stop Thomas Gibbons from running a competing ferry. Although Gibbons countered that his boats were licensed under a 1793 act of Congress governing vessels "in the coasting trade and fisheries," the New York courts sided with Ogden. Just as the national government and states both have the power to tax, the New York courts said they both had the power to regulate commerce.

commerce clause
The clause in the Constitution (Article I, Section 8, Clause 1) that gives Congress the power to regulate all business activities that cross state lines or affect more than one state or other nations.

The national military has the power to set restrictions on airspace so that it can fly anywhere across the country without approval of state or local governments.
■ *Why does the national government have the final say on national security issues?*

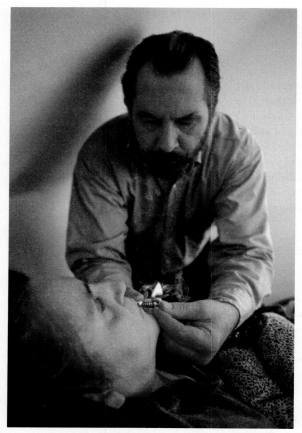

Though many states allow the use of medicinal marijuana, the Supreme Court decided that the national government could regulate its use in the states as a form of interstate commerce. ■ *Why did the Obama administration choose not to exercise this power to prohibit marijuana sales in states such as California that have legalized its use?*

federal mandate
A requirement the national government imposes as a condition for receiving federal funds.

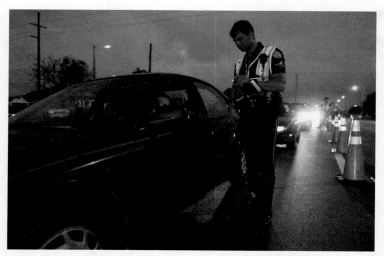

Under national pressure, states have raised the drinking age to 21. States are also under pressure to monitor drunk driving more aggressively.

Gibbons appealed to the Supreme Court and asked a simple question: Which government had the ultimate power to regulate interstate commerce? The Supreme Court gave an equally simple answer: The national government's laws were supreme.[10]

Gibbons v. *Ogden* was immediately heralded for promoting a national economic common market, in holding that states may not discriminate against interstate transportation and out-of-state commerce. The Supreme Court's brilliant definition of "commerce" as *intercourse among the states* provided the basis for national regulation of "things in commerce"[11] and an expanding range of economic activities, including the sale of lottery tickets,[12] prostitution,[13] radio and television broadcasts,[14] and telecommunications and the Internet.

The Power to Tax and Spend Congress lacks constitutional authority to pass laws solely on the grounds that they will promote the general welfare, but it may raise taxes and spend money for this purpose. For example, the national government lacks the power to regulate education or agriculture directly, but it does have the power to appropriate money to support education or to pay farm subsidies. By attaching conditions to its grants of money, the national government creates incentives that affect state action. If states want the money, they must accept the conditions.

When the national government provides the money, it determines how the money will be spent. By withholding or threatening to withhold funds, the national government can influence or control state operations and regulate individual conduct. For example, the national government has stipulated that federal funds should be withdrawn from any program in which any person is denied benefits because of race, color, national origin, sex, or physical handicap. The national government also used its "power of the purse" to force states to raise the drinking age to 21 by tying such a condition to federal dollars for building and maintaining highways.

Congress frequently requires states to provide specific programs—for example, provide services to indigent mothers and clean up the air and water. These requirements are called **federal mandates.** Often the national government does not supply the funds required to carry out "unfunded mandates" (discussed later in the chapter). Its failure to do so has become an important issue as states face growing expenditures with limited resources.

Powers of the States

The Constitution *reserves for the states all powers not granted to the national government,* subject only to the limitations of the Constitution. Only the states have the **reserve powers** to create schools and local governments, for example. Both are powers not given exclusively to the national government by the Constitution or judicial interpretation, so that states can exercise these powers as long as they do not conflict with national law.

The national and state governments also share powers. These **concurrent powers** with the national government include the power to levy taxes and regulate commerce internal to each state.

In general, states may levy taxes on the same items the national government taxes, such as incomes, alcohol, and gasoline, but a state cannot, by a tax, "unduly burden" commerce among the states, interfere with a function of the national government, complicate the operation of a national law, or abridge the terms of a treaty of the United States. Where the national government has not preempted the field,

TABLE 3–1 The Constitutional Division of National and State Powers

Examples of Powers Delegated to the National Government	Examples of Powers Reserved for State Governments	Examples of Concurrent Powers Shared by the National and State Governments
Regulate trade and interstate commerce	Create local governments	Impose and collect taxes and fees
Declare war	Police citizens	Borrow and spend money
Create post offices	Oversee primary and elementary education	Establish courts
Coin money		Enact and enforce laws
		Protect civil rights
		Conduct elections
		Protect health and welfare

states may regulate interstate businesses, provided these regulations do not cover matters requiring uniform national treatment or unduly burden interstate commerce.

Who decides which matters require "uniform national treatment" or what actions might place an "undue burden" on interstate commerce? Congress does, subject to the president's signature and final review by the Supreme Court. When Congress is silent or does not clearly state its intent, the courts—ultimately, the Supreme Court—decide whether there is a conflict with the national Constitution or whether a state law or regulation has preempted the national government's authority.

Constitutional Limits and Obligations

To ensure that federalism works, the Constitution imposes restraints on both the national and the state governments. States are prohibited from doing the following:

1. Making treaties with foreign governments
2. Authorizing private persons to interfere with the shipping and commerce of other nations
3. Coining money, issuing bills of credit, or making anything but gold and silver coin legal tender in payment of debts
4. Taxing imports or exports
5. Taxing foreign ships
6. Keeping troops or ships of war in time of peace (except for the state militia, now called the National Guard)
7. Engaging in war

In turn, the Constitution requires the national government to refrain from exercising its powers, especially its powers to tax and to regulate interstate commerce, in such a way as to interfere substantially with the states' abilities to perform their responsibilities. But politicians, judges, and scholars disagree about whether the national political process—specifically the executive and the legislature—or the courts should ultimately define the boundaries between the powers of the national government and the states. Some argue that the states' protection from intrusions by the national government comes primarily from the political process because senators and representatives elected from the states participate in congressional decisions.[15] Others maintain that the Supreme Court should limit the national government's power and defend the states.[16]

On a case-by-case basis, the Court has held that the national government may not command states to enact laws to comply with or order state employees to enforce national laws. In *Printz* v. *United States*, the Court held that states were not required to conduct instant national background checks prior to selling a handgun.[17] Referring broadly to the concept of dual federalism discussed early in this chapter, the Supreme Court said that the national government could not "draft" local police to do its bidding. But as previously discussed, even if the national government cannot force states to enforce certain national laws, it can threaten to withhold its funding if states do not comply with national policies, such as lowering the minimum drinking age or speed limit.

reserve powers
All powers not specifically delegated to the national government by the Constitution. The reserve power can be found in the Tenth Amendment to the Constitution.

concurrent powers
Powers that the Constitution gives to both the national and state governments, such as the power to levy taxes.

The U.S. Supreme Court ruled that the national government cannot demand that states enforce the national law requiring handgun dealers to run background checks on potential buyers. States are free, however, to use a national registry of criminals in doing background checks, which almost all do. ■ *Should the national government extend gun control laws to flea markets, where guns are still sold without first checking the national registry? Under what authority could these laws be imposed?*

The Constitution also obliges the national government to protect states against *domestic insurrection.* Congress has delegated to the president the authority to dispatch troops to put down such insurrections when the proper state authorities request them.

Interstate Relationships

Three clauses in the Constitution, taken from the Articles of Confederation, require states to give full faith and credit to each other's public acts, records, and judicial proceedings; to extend to each other's citizens the privileges and immunities of their own citizens; and to return persons who are fleeing from justice.

Full Faith and Credit   The **full faith and credit clause** (Article IV, Section 1), one of the more technical provisions of the Constitution, requires state courts to enforce the civil judgments of the courts of other states and accept their public records and acts as valid.[18] It does not require states to enforce the criminal laws or legislation and administrative acts of other states; in most cases, for one state to enforce the criminal laws of another would raise constitutional issues. The clause applies primarily to enforcing judicial settlements and court awards.

Interstate Privileges and Immunities   Under Article IV, Section 2, individual states must give citizens of all other states the privileges and immunities they grant to their own citizens, including the protection of the laws, the right to engage in peaceful occupations, access to the courts, and freedom from discriminatory taxes. Because of this clause, states may not impose unreasonable residency requirements, that is, withhold rights to American citizens who have recently moved to the state and thereby have become citizens of that state.

full faith and credit clause
The clause in the Constitution (Article IV, Section 1) requiring each state to recognize the civil judgments rendered by the courts of the other states and to accept their public records and acts as valid.

extradition
The legal process whereby an alleged criminal offender is surrendered by the officials of one state to officials of the state in which the crime is alleged to have been committed.

interstate compact
An agreement among two or more states. Congress must approve most such agreements.

Extradition   In Article IV, Section 2, the Constitution asserts that, when individuals charged with crimes have fled from one state to another, the state to which they have fled is to deliver them to the proper officials on demand of the executive authority of the state from which they fled. This process is called **extradition.** "The obvious objective of the Extradition Clause," the courts have claimed, "is that no State should become a safe haven for the fugitives from a sister State's criminal justice system."[19] Congress has supplemented this constitutional provision by making the governor of the state to which fugitives have fled responsible for returning them.

Interstate Compacts   The Constitution also requires states to settle disputes with one another without the use of force. States may carry their legal disputes to the Supreme Court, or they may negotiate **interstate compacts.** Interstate compacts often establish interstate agencies to handle problems affecting an entire region. Before most interstate compacts become effective, Congress has to approve them. Then the compact becomes binding on all signatory states, and the federal judiciary can enforce its terms. A typical state may belong to 20 compacts dealing with such subjects as environmental protection, crime control, water rights, and higher education exchanges.[20]

The National Courts and Federalism

LEARNING OBJECTIVE

3.3 Assess the role of the national courts in defining the relationship between the national and state governments, and evaluate the positions of decentralists and centralists.

Although the political process ultimately decides how power will be divided between the national and the state governments, the national court system is often called on to umpire the ongoing debate about which level of government should do what, for whom, and to whom. The nation's highest court claimed this role in the celebrated case of *McCulloch* v. *Maryland.*

McCulloch v. *Maryland*

In *McCulloch* v. *Maryland* (1819), the Supreme Court had the first of many chances to define the division of power between the national and state governments.[21] Congress had established the Bank of the United States, but Maryland opposed any national bank and levied a $10,000 tax on any bank not incorporated in the state. James William McCulloch, the cashier of the bank, refused to pay on the grounds that a state could not tax an instrument of the national government.

Maryland was represented before the Court by some of the country's most distinguished lawyers, including Luther Martin, who had been a delegate to the Constitutional Convention. Martin said the Constitution did not expressly delegate to the national government the power to incorporate a bank. He maintained that the necessary and proper clause gives Congress only the power to choose those means and to pass those laws absolutely essential to the execution of its expressly granted powers. Because a bank is not absolutely necessary to the exercise of its delegated powers, he argued, Congress had no authority to establish it. As for Maryland's right to tax the bank, the power to tax is one of the powers reserved to the states; they may use it as they see fit.

Equally distinguished counsel, including Daniel Webster, represented the national government. Webster conceded that the power to create a bank is not one of the express powers of the national government. However, the power to pass laws necessary and proper to carry out Congress's express powers is specifically delegated to Congress. Although the power to tax is reserved to the states, Webster argued that states cannot interfere with the operations of the national government. The Constitution leaves no room for doubt; when the national and state governments have conflicts, the national government is supreme.

Speaking for a unanimous Court, Chief Justice John Marshall rejected every one of Maryland's contentions. He summarized his views on the powers of the national government in these now-famous words: "Let the end be legitimate, let it be within the scope of the Constitution, and all means which are appropriate, which are plainly adapted to that end, which are not prohibited, but consist with the letter and spirit of the constitution, are constitutional."

Having established the presence of *implied national powers*, Marshall then outlined the concept of **national supremacy.** No state, he said, can use its taxing powers to tax a national instrument. "The power to tax involves the power to destroy.... If the right of the States to tax the means employed by the general government be conceded, the declaration that the Constitution, and the laws made in pursuance thereof, shall be the supreme law of the land, is empty and unmeaning declamation."

It is difficult to overstate the long-range significance of *McCulloch* v. *Maryland* in providing support for the developing forces of nationalism and a unified economy. If the contrary arguments in favor of the states had been accepted, they would have strapped the national government in a constitutional straitjacket and denied it powers needed to deal with the problems of an expanding nation.

National Courts and the Relationship with the States

The authority of national judges to review the activities of state and local governments has expanded dramatically in recent decades because of modern judicial interpretations of the Fourteenth Amendment, which forbids states to deprive any person of life, liberty, or property without *due process of the law.* States may not deny any person the *equal protection of the laws,* including congressional legislation enacted to implement the Fourteenth Amendment. Almost every action by state and local officials is now subject to challenge before a federal judge as a violation of the Constitution or of national law.

Preemption occurs when a national law or regulation takes precedence over a state or local law or regulation. State and local laws are preempted not only when they conflict directly with national laws and regulations but also when they touch on a field in which the "federal interest is so dominant that the federal system will be assumed to preclude enforcement of state laws on the same subject."[22] Examples of federal preemption include laws regulating hazardous substances, water quality, clean air standards, and many civil rights acts, especially the Civil Rights Act of 1964 and the Voting Rights Act of 1965.

Throughout the years, federal judges, under the leadership of the Supreme Court, have generally favored the powers of the national government over those of the states. Despite the Supreme Court's recent bias in favor of state over national authority, few would deny the Supreme Court the power to review and set aside state actions. As Justice Oliver Wendell Holmes of the Supreme Court once remarked, "I do not think the United

national supremacy
A constitutional doctrine that whenever conflict occurs between the constitutionally authorized actions of the national government and those of a state or local government, the actions of the national government prevail.

preemption
The right of a national law or regulation to preclude enforcement of a state or local law or regulation.

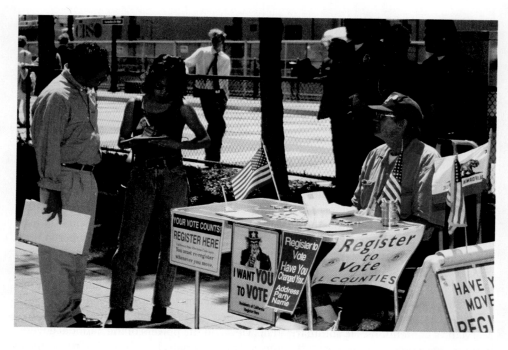

States are responsible for registering voters, but the national government is responsible for assuring that state registration rules are Constitutional. ■ *How and why might state voter registration rules vary from state to state? Does this highlight a strength or weakness of federalism?*

States would come to an end if we lost our power to declare an Act of Congress void. I do think the Union would be imperiled if we could not make that declaration as to the laws of the several States."[23]

The Supreme Court and the Role of Congress

From 1937 until the 1990s, the Supreme Court essentially removed national courts from what had been their role of protecting states from acts of Congress. The Supreme Court broadly interpreted the commerce clause to allow Congress to do whatever Congress thought necessary and proper to promote the common good, even if national laws and regulations infringed on the activities of state and local governments.

In the past 15 years, however, the Supreme Court has signaled that national courts should be more active in resolving federalism issues.[24] The Court declared that a state could not impose term limits on its members of Congress, but it did so by only a 5-to-4 vote. Justice John Paul Stevens, writing for the majority, built his argument on the concept of the federal union as espoused by the great Chief Justice John Marshall, as a compact among the people, with the national government serving as the people's agent.

The Supreme Court also declared that the clause in the Constitution empowering Congress to regulate commerce with the Indian tribes did not give Congress the power to authorize national courts to hear suits against a state brought by Indian tribes.[25] Unless states consent to such suits, they enjoy "sovereign immunity" under the Eleventh Amendment. The effect of this decision goes beyond Indian tribes. As a result—except to enforce rights stemming from the Fourteenth Amendment, which the Court explicitly acknowledged to be within Congress's power—Congress may no longer authorize individuals to bring legal actions against states to force their compliance with national law in either national or state courts.[26]

Building on those rulings, the Court continues to press ahead with its "constitutional counterrevolution"[27] and return to an older vision of federalism from the 1930s. Among other recent rulings, in *United States* v. *Morrison,* the Court struck down the Violence Against Women Act, which had given women who are victims of violence the right to sue their attackers for damages.[28] Congress had found that violence against women annually costs the national economy $3 billion, but a bare majority of the Court held that gender-motivated crimes did not have a substantial impact on interstate commerce and that Congress had thus exceeded its powers in enacting the law and intruded on the powers of the states.

By the People

Monitoring the National Stimulus Package

In early 2009, Congress and President Barack Obama passed a nearly $800 billion spending package designed to stimulate the national economy. The number of unemployed Americans was rising fast, small businesses were closing, consumers were spending less, sales of new and old homes alike had fallen, and the economy was in the worst recession in decades. Under the stimulus, states were given nearly $260 billion to invest in projects that would put unemployed Americans back to work and restart the economy.

Much of this money was designed to support highway construction, new building projects, and scientific research but has been difficult to track. According to ongoing monitoring by the national government and outside groups, thousands of small companies are still receiving national dollars for a broad mix of projects.

Citizens can track the spending as a form of public service—the more they pay attention to the projects, the more the states pay attention to them. One way to monitor the spending is to pick a project and see what is actually happening. The first step in this monitoring is to find the project through Web sites such as recovery.gov or propublica.org. Citizens can click on a specific state at

propublica.org, pick an individual county in that state, and see every project funded by the stimulus. Once citizens pick a project, they can visit the project and see what is actually happening. If the project is not even under way, citizens can report the inaction to the federal government through recovery.gov.

Colleges and universities have received a sizable amount of stimulus money. By early 2010, Florida's Alachua County had received more than $100 million. As home of the University of Florida, much of the money ended up in university research projects. According to the propublica.org list, the university received support for nearly 150 separate projects and student programs, while Santa Fe Community College received more than a dozen grants to support students with Pell Grants.

CRITICAL THINKING QUESTIONS

1. Why is monitoring the stimulus spending a form of public service?

2. What is the effect of visiting a project to see if it is working?

3. Does simply visiting the stimulus Web sites make any difference in telling Congress and the president that someone is watching?

University of Florida students conduct research with funds from the federal stimulus package.

These Supreme Court decisions—most of which split the Court 5 to 4 along ideological lines, with the conservative justices favoring states' rights—have signaled a shift in the Court's interpretation of the constitutional nature of our federal system. It is a shift that has been reinforced with the most recent Supreme Court appointments made by Presidents Bush and Obama. Chief Justice John Roberts and Justice Samuel Alito, each appointed by President George W. Bush, tend to favor the states, while justices Sonia Sotomayor and Elena Kagan, Obama appointees, tend to side with the national government.

The Great Debate Continues: Centralists Versus Decentralists

From the beginning of the Republic, there has been an ongoing debate about the "proper" distribution of powers, functions, and responsibilities between the national government and the states. Did the national government have the authority to outlaw slavery in the territories? Did the states have the authority to operate racially segregated schools? Could Congress regulate labor relations? Does Congress have the power to regulate the sale and use of firearms? Does Congress have the right to tell states how to clean up air and water pollution?

Today, the debate continues between **centralists,** who favor national action, and **decentralists,** who defend the powers of the states and favor action at the state and local levels on such issues as environmental and gun regulation.

centralists
People who favor national action over action at the state and local levels.

decentralists
People who favor state or local action rather than national action.

The Decentralist Position Among those favoring the decentralist or **states' rights** interpretation were the Antifederalists, Thomas Jefferson, the pre–Civil War statesman from South Carolina John C. Calhoun, the Supreme Court from the 1920s to 1937, and, more recently, Presidents Ronald Reagan and George H. W. Bush, the Republican leaders of Congress, former Chief Justice William H. Rehnquist, and current Justices Antonin Scalia and Clarence Thomas.

Most decentralists contend that the Constitution is basically a compact among sovereign states that created the central government and gave it limited authority. Thus the national government is little more than an agent of the states, and every one of its powers should be narrowly defined. Any question about whether the states have given a particular function to the central government or have reserved it for themselves should be resolved in favor of the states.

Decentralists believe that the national government should not interfere with activities reserved for the states. Their argument is based on the Tenth Amendment, which states: "The powers not delegated to the United States by the Constitution, nor prohibited by it to the States, are reserved to the States respectively, or to the people." Decentralists insist that state governments are closer to the people and reflect the people's wishes more accurately than the national government does.

Decentralists have been particularly supportive of the **devolution revolution,** which argues for returning responsibilities to the states.[29] In the 1990s, the Republican-controlled Congress gave states more authority over some programs such as welfare, and President Clinton also proclaimed, "The era of big government is over." However, he tempered his comments by adding, "But we cannot go back to the time when our citizens were left to fend for themselves," and despite its dramatic name, the revolution has fallen short of the hoped-for results.

Instead of a devolution revolution, the national government has actually grown stronger during the past decade. The national government has passed a number of laws that give states specific responsibilities in defending homeland security, including the implementation of national criteria for issuing driver's licenses. It has also ordered states not to sell any citizen's personal information to private companies, ended state regulation of mutual funds, nullified state laws that restrict telecommunication competition, and gave the national judiciary the power to prosecute a number of state and local crimes, including carjacking and acts of terrorism.

states' rights
Powers expressly or implicitly reserved to the states.

devolution revolution
The effort to slow the growth of the national government by returning many functions to the states.

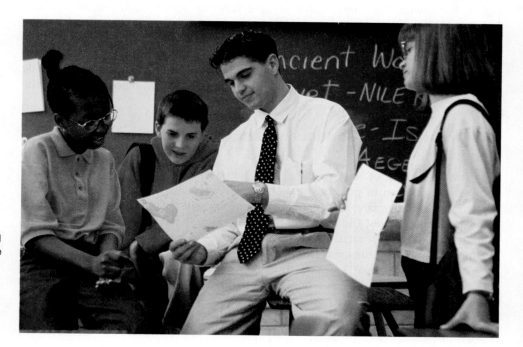

Decentralists believe that education should be a state responsibility. However, because the national government provides money to the states, it has the power to impose strings on how the money is spent.
■ *What are some of the arguments for greater or less federal government involvement in public education?*

The Centralist Position   The centralist position has been supported by presidents, Congress, and the Supreme Court. Presidents Abraham Lincoln, Theodore Roosevelt, Franklin Roosevelt, and Lyndon Johnson were particularly strong supporters, and the Supreme Court has generally ruled in favor of the centralist position.

Centralists reject the idea of the Constitution as an interstate compact. They view it as a supreme law established by the people. The national government is an agent of the people, not of the states, because it was the people who drew up the Constitution and created the national government. They intended that the national political process should define the central government's powers and that the national government be denied authority only when the Constitution clearly prohibits it from acting.

Centralists argue that the national government is a government of all the people, whereas each state speaks for only some of the people. Although the Tenth Amendment clearly reserves powers for the states, it does not deny the national government the authority to exercise all of its powers to the fullest extent. Moreover, the supremacy of the national government restricts the states because governments representing part of the people cannot be allowed to interfere with a government representing all of them.

The National Budget as a Tool of Federalism

LEARNING **OBJECTIVE**

3.4 Analyze the budget as a tool of federalism, and evaluate its impact on state and local governments.

Congress authorizes programs, establishes general rules for how the programs will operate, and decides whether room should be left for state or local discretion and how much. Most important, Congress appropriates the funds for these programs and generally has deeper pockets than even the richest states. Federal grants are one of Congress's most potent tools for influencing policy at the state and local levels.

Federal grants serve four purposes, the most important of which is the fourth:

1. To supply state and local governments with revenue
2. To establish minimum national standards for such things as highways and clean air
3. To equalize resources among the states by taking money from people with high incomes through federal taxes and spending it, through grants, in states where the poor live
4. To attack national problems but minimize the growth of federal agencies

Types of Federal Grants

The national government currently gives states three types of grants: *categorical-formula grants, project grants,* and *block grants* (sometimes called *flexible grants*). From 1972 to 1986, the national government also gave states a share of national tax revenues through *revenue sharing.* The program was terminated in an effort to reduce rising national budget deficits.

Categorical-Formula Grants   The national government provides grants for specific purposes, such as promoting homeland security. By definition, these grants are distributed to the states based on population. Many categorical-formula grants require state governments to provide at least some of the total funding, often on a matching basis. Categorical-formula grants are tightly monitored to ensure that the money is spent exactly as directed. There are hundreds of grant programs, but two dozen, including Medicaid, account for more than half of total categorical-formula spending.

Project Grants   The national government supports states through project grants for specific activities, such as scientific research, highway construction, and job training. Project grants are generally restricted to a fixed amount of time and can only be spent within tight guidelines. Many university-based medical schools rely on project grants to support their efforts to cure life-threatening diseases such as cancer and heart disease.

For the People

GOVERNMENT'S GREATEST ENDEAVORS

Supporting the States in Achieving National Goals

Throughout the decades, the national government has given state and local governments a long list of responsibilities for implementing national programs, such as health care for the poor, highway construction, and waste-water treatment. These programs involve important national goals for creating a healthy society and economy.

Most of these programs carry large amounts of national dollars, which allow the national government to set minimum standards for those who get unemployment insurance, public assistance, and medical care. National funds also offset state spending on both the administrative and program costs of achieving the national goals profiled throughout this book. But the national government relies on the states for the implementation of these programs.

Homeland security is a case in point. Following the 9/11 terrorist attacks on the World Trade Center and Washington, D.C. in 2001, the national government launched what President George W. Bush called the "war on terrorism." Local police departments are essential partners in the effort. They are linked to the national government through computer systems that contain the names of terrorist suspects and are often first at the scene of suspected terrorist acts such as the 2008 bombing of a Jewish center in New York City. The national government provides large amounts of funding to improve state and local defenses against terrorist attacks.

All totaled, the national government will spend nearly $600 billion in 2010 helping states achieve its broad goals for improving the quality of life in the United States, including $20 billion on transportation, $21 billion on education and job training, $43 billion on health care for the poor and substance abuse programs, and $36 billion on food and nutrition programs.* Although much of this money comes with tight restrictions on which citizens and projects qualify for funding, this spending indicates how much the national government is willing to invest in helping states help their citizens.

CRITICAL THINKING QUESTIONS

1. What are some of the advantages of national and local governments working

The national government works with state and local governments to ensure that airports are safe from terrorism. Baggage and passenger screeners are national government employees, but they work closely with local airports.

collectively on problems like airport security? What are the disadvantages?

2. Why might the national government prefer working in cooperation with state governments?

3. How is airport security a form of marble cake federalism? How is it a form of cooperative federalism?

---

*SOURCE: U.S. Census Bureau, The 2010 Statistical Abstract: National Data Book, Table 419 (Washington, D.C.: U.S. Census Bureau, 2010).

Block Grants   Block grants are broad grants to states for specific activities, such as public assistance, child care, education, social services, preventive health care, and health services. By definition, these blocks of funding are provided with very few requirements attached. States have great flexibility in deciding how to spend block grant dollars, but unlike programs such as national unemployment insurance that are guaranteed for everyone who qualifies for them, block grants are limited to specific amounts set by the national government.

The Politics of Federal Grants

Republicans "have consistently favored fewer strings, less federal supervision, and the delegation of spending discretion to the state and local governments."[30] Democrats have generally been less supportive of broad discretionary block grants, instead favoring more detailed, federally supervised spending. The Republican-controlled Congress in the 1990s gave high priority to creating block grants, but it ran into trouble when it tried to lump together welfare, school lunch and breakfast programs, prenatal nutrition programs, and child protection programs in one block grant.

The battle over national versus state control of spending tends to be cyclical. As one scholar of federalism explains, "Complaints about excessive federal control tend to be followed by proposals to shift more power to state and local governments. Then, when problems arise in state and local administration—and problems inevitably arise when any organization tries to administer anything—demands for closer federal supervision and tighter federal controls follow."[31]

94

The Americans with Disabilities Act of 1990 required state and local governments to improve access to buildings and public transportation for people with disabilities. The law covers all public colleges and universities. ■ *Why is enforcing the Americans with Disabilities Act so costly for state and local governments?*

Unfunded Mandates

Fewer federal dollars do not necessarily mean fewer federal controls. On the contrary, the national government has imposed mandates on states and local governments, often without providing federal funds. State and local officials complained about this, and their protests were effective. The Unfunded Mandates Reform Act of 1995 was championed by then-House Republican Speaker Newt Gingrich as part of the GOP's Contract with America. The act was considered part of what commentators called the "Newt Federalism."

The law requires Congress to evaluate the impact of unfunded mandates and imposes mild constraints on Congress itself. A congressional committee that approves any legislation containing a federal mandate must draw attention to the mandate in its report and describe its cost to state and local governments. If the committee intends any mandate to be partially unfunded, it must explain why it is appropriate for state and local governments to pay for it.

At least during its first 15 years, the Unfunded Mandates Reform Act has been mostly successful in restraining mandates.[32] According to the National Conference of State Legislatures, the national government has enacted only 11 laws that impose unfunded mandates. Three of these unfunded mandates involved increases in the minimum wage that apply to all state and local employees.

The Politics of Federalism

The formal structures of our federal system have not changed much since 1787, but the political realities, especially during the past half-century, have greatly altered the way federalism works. To understand these changes, we need to look at some of the trends that continue to fuel the debate about the meaning of federalism.

The Growth of National Government

Throughout the past two centuries, power has accrued to the national government. As the Advisory Commission on Intergovernmental Relations observed in a 1981 report, "No one planned the growth, but everyone played a part in it."[33]

LEARNING **OBJECTIVE**

3.5 Evaluate the current relationship between the national and state governments and the future challenges for federalism.

YOU WILL
DECIDE
Should the No Child Left Behind Act Be Renewed?

Early in 2002, President George W. Bush signed the No Child Left Behind Act into law, thereby creating one of the most significant mandates ever imposed on the states. Although primary and secondary education has long been considered an almost exclusive responsibility of state and local governments, the No Child Left Behind Act required states to create a new system of standardized testing for every public school. States could either implement the new mandate or lose their federal funding, which amounts to approximately 10 percent of all school budgets.

Under the No Child Left Behind Act, schools were required to adopt a number of separate reforms for improving student achievement. Students in grades three through eight were to be tested each year in reading and math, while students in high school were to be tested at least once in reading, math, and science. Based on the test results, schools were also required to show academic progress or risk the possibility of losing national funds.

Like many national laws, however, the No Child Left Behind Act is not permanent. It must be renewed every five years, which means that it can be changed. As they gain more experience with the act, parents and teachers will have more influence over the future of the tests and report cards that now govern their schools. Despite the five-year time limit, the law had not been formally reauthorized by September 2010, but continued to operate under a temporary extension.

What do you think? Should the No Child Left Behind Act be renewed? What arguments would you make for or against such an idea?

THINKING IT THROUGH

Parents and teachers already seem to agree that the No Child Left Behind Act created two problems that may need congressional attention.

First, some parents and teachers complain that instead of inspiring schools to focus on reading, math, and science, the act may encourage them to "teach to the test"—to prep students on how to take tests in reading, math, and science. There is no question, for example, that primary school students now spend enormous amounts of time practicing for the annual reading and math tests or that teachers are being encouraged to produce the highest scores possible, even if that occasionally means giving students extra practice on the test instead of instruction on basic skills. There have also been several highly publicized scandals in which schools cheated on the tests.

Second, parents and teachers worry that the national government has not provided enough funding to make the law work. Failing public schools cannot be improved simply by giving parents the right to remove their children, if only because they may not be able to find a better school. Moreover, new programs such as mentoring, afterschool tutoring, and summer school cost money that is often in short supply in large, urban school districts. These districts may also have much higher proportions of students who speak English as a second language, which can lead to lower test scores.

Despite these concerns, the act is almost certain to be renewed. Even though some say it focuses on testing, not learning, No Child Left Behind has created significant pressure for higher performance. The question is how its provisions might be changed to increase success.*

Actor Matthew McConaughey volunteers for Teach for America, a program that helps public schools by training young college graduates to spend two years teaching low-income students.

Critical Thinking Questions

1. What changes do you recommend when Congress and the president renew the No Child Left Behind Act?

2. Why does the support of teachers and parents matter to renewal of the No Child Left Behind Act?

3. Does the act ask too much of state and local governments given that the national government supplies only 10 percent of all school funding?

4. Should the national government be involved in issues like public education to make sure all states act the same way?

---

* Laura S. Hamilton et al., "Passing or Failing? A Midterm Report Card for 'No Child Left Behind,' " *RAND Review,* 31 (Fall 2007), pp. 16–25.Laura S. Hamilton et al., "Passing or Failing? A Midterm Report Card for 'No Child Left Behind,' " *RAND Review,* 31 (Fall 2007), pp. 16–25.

This shift occurred for a variety of reasons. One is that many of our problems have become national in scope. Much that was local in 1789, in 1860, or in 1930 is now national, even global. State governments could supervise the relationships between small merchants and their few employees, for instance, but only the national government can supervise relationships between multinational corporations and their thousands of worldwide employees, many of whom are organized in national unions.

As the economy grew rapidly during the early nineteenth century, powerful interests made demands on the national government. Business groups called on the government for aid in the form of tariffs, a national banking system, subsidies to railroads and the merchant marine, and uniform rules on the environment. Farmers learned that the national government could give more aid than the states, and they too began to demand help. By the beginning of the twentieth century, urban groups in general and organized labor in particular were pressing their claims. Big business, big agriculture, and big labor all added up to big government.

The growth of the national economy and the creation of national transportation and communications networks altered people's attitudes toward the national government. Before the Civil War, citizens saw the national government as a distant, even foreign, entity. Today, in part because of television and the Internet, most people know more about Washington than they know about their state capitals, and they know more about the president and their national legislators than about their governor, their state legislators, or even the local officials who run their cities and schools.

The Great Depression of the 1930s stimulated extensive national action on welfare, unemployment, and farm surpluses. World War II brought federal regulation of wages, prices, and employment, as well as national efforts to allocate resources, train personnel, and support engineering and inventions. After the war, the national government helped veterans obtain college degrees and inaugurated a vast system of support for university research. The United States became the most powerful leader of the free world, maintaining substantial military forces even in times of peace.

Although economic and social conditions created many of the pressures for expanding the national government, so did political claims. Once established, federal programs generate groups with vested interests in promoting, defending, and expanding them. Associations are formed and alliances are made. "In a word, the growth of government has created a constituency of, by, and for government."[34] The national budget can become a negative issue for Congress and the president if it grows too large, however. With the federal budget deficit rising rapidly in 2010, the Obama Administration was forced to back away from some of its largest spending programs and promise greater restraint.

The politics of federalism are changing, however, and Congress is being pressured to reduce the size and scope of national programs, while dealing with the demands for homeland security. Meanwhile, the cost of entitlement programs such as Social Security and Medicare are rising because there are more older people and they are living longer. These programs have widespread public support and to cut them is politically risky. "With all other options disappearing, it is politically tempting to finance tax cuts by turning over to the states many of the social programs...that have become the responsibility of the national government."[35]

The Future of Federalism

During recent decades, state governments have undergone a major transformation. Most have improved their governmental structures, taken on greater roles in funding education and welfare, launched programs to help distressed cities, expanded their tax bases by allowing citizens to deduct their state and local taxes from the national income tax, and assumed greater roles in maintaining homeland security and in fighting corporate corruption.

After the civil rights revolution of the 1960s, segregationists feared that national officials would work for racial integration. Thus, they praised local government, emphasized the dangers of centralization, and argued that the protection of civil rights was not a proper function of the national government. As one political scientist observed, "Federalism has a dark history to overcome. For nearly 200 years, states' rights have been asserted to protect slavery, segregation, and discrimination."[36]

Today, the politics of federalism, even with respect to civil rights, is more complicated than in the past. The national government is not necessarily more sympathetic to the claims of minorities than state or city governments are. Rulings on same-sex marriages and "civil unions" by state courts interpreting their state constitutions have extended more protection for these rights than has the Supreme Court's interpretation of the U.S. Constitution. Other states, however, are passing legislation that would eliminate such protections, and opponents are pressing for a constitutional amendment to bar same-sex marriages.

The national government is not likely to retreat to a more passive role. Indeed, international terrorism, the wars in Afghanistan and Iraq, and rising deficits have substantially altered the underlying economic and social conditions that generated the demand for federal action. In addition to such traditional challenges as helping people find jobs and preventing inflation and depressions—which still require national action—combating terrorism and surviving in a global economy based on the information explosion, e-commerce, and advancing technologies have added countless new issues to the national agenda.

Most American citizens have strong attachments to our federal system—in the abstract. They remain loyal to their states and show a growing skepticism about the national government. Yet, evidence suggests the anti-Washington sentiment "is 3,000 miles wide but only a few miles deep."[37] The fact is that we are pragmatists: We appear to prefer federal–state–local power sharing and are prepared to use whatever levels of government are necessary to meet our needs and new challenges.[38]

Federalism can be a source of great reward for the people, especially when it allows states to lead the nation in creating new programs to address problems such as global warming and health care access. If the people cannot move the national government toward action, they can always push their state and local governments. By giving them different leverage points to make a difference, the Constitution guarantees that government *is* by the people.

Federalism can also be a source of enormous frustration, especially when national and state governments disagree on basic issues such as civil rights and liberties. This is when the people need to step forward not as citizens of their states but as citizens of the nation as a whole. Even as they influence their state and local governments, the people must understand they have a national voice that often needs to be heard.

CHAPTER **SUMMARY**

3.1 Interpret the definitions of federalism, and assess the advantages and disadvantages of the American system of federalism.

A federal system is one in which the constitution divides powers between the central government and lower-level governments such as states or provinces. But, over time, there has been support for different balances between state and government power such as the shift from dual federalism to marble cake federalism. The federal system in the United States does protect us from tyranny, permit local variation in policy, and encourage experimentation, but it comes at the cost of greater complexity, conflict, and difficulty in determining exactly which level of government is responsible for providing which goods and services that citizens might demand.

3.2 Differentiate the powers the Constitution provides to national and state governments.

The Constitution provides three types of powers to the national and state governments: delegated powers to the national government, reserve powers for the states, and concurrent powers that the national and state

governments share. Beyond delegated powers, the national government also has implied powers under the necessary and proper clause and inherent powers during periods of war and national crisis.

The national government's power over the states stems primarily from several constitutional pillars: the national supremacy clause, the war powers, its powers to regulate commerce among the states to tax and spend, and its power to do what Congress thinks is necessary and proper to promote the general welfare and to provide for the common defense. These constitutional pillars have permitted tremendous expansion of the functions of the national government.

3.3 Assess the role of the national courts in defining the relationship between the national and state governments, and evaluate the positions of decentralists and centralists.

The national courts umpire the division of power between the national and state governments. The Marshall Court, in decisions such as *Gibbons* v. *Ogden* and *McCulloch* v. *Maryland*, asserted the power of the national government over the states and promoted a national economic common market. These decisions also reinforced the supremacy of the national government over the states.

Today, debates about federalism are less often about its constitutional structure than about whether action should come from the national or the state and local levels. Recent Supreme Court decisions favor a decentralist position and signal shifts in the Court's interpretation of the constitutional nature of our federal system.

3.4 Analyze the budget as a tool of federalism, and evaluate its impact on state and local governments.

The major instruments of national intervention in state programs have been various kinds of financial grants-in-aid, of which the most prominent are categorical-formula grants, project grants, and block grants. The national government also imposes federal mandates and controls activities of state and local governments by other means.

3.5 Evaluate the current relationship between the national and state governments and the future challenges for federalism.

The national government has grown dramatically throughout the past 200 years. Its budget dwarfs many state budgets combined. As it has grown, the national government has asked states to do more on its behalf. States have pressed back against the national government, however, and continue to fight for their authority to use powers that are reserved for them under the Constitution.

CHAPTER **SELF-TEST**

3.1 Interpret the definitions of federalism, and assess the advantages and disadvantages of the American system of federalism.

1. Match each term with its appropriate definition:

a. Dual federalism	i. The power of the national government is limited in favor of the broad powers reserved to the states
b. Cooperative federalism	ii. All levels of government are engaged in a variety of policy areas, without rigid divisions between governmental jurisdictions
c. Marble cake federalism	iii. Local governments, state governments, and the national government offer various "packages" of taxes and services, and citizens can choose which package they like best
d. Competitive federalism	iv. A system that requires intergovernmental support to deliver goods and services to the people
e. Permissive federalism	v. Limited powers are given to the national government, while the rest are retained by the states; the Supreme Court resolves disputes between the two
f. New federalism	vi. Power is shared between the state and national governments, but the national government determines what powers are given to the states

2. Canada has a central government in Ottawa, the nation's capital, along with ten provinces and three territories, each of which has its own government. According to Canada's constitution, both the provinces and the central government have powers to tax and regulate individual citizens. Which type of government best describes Canada?

a. A unitary state
b. A cooperative federalist state
c. A confederation
d. A territorial union

3. Federalism affords five benefits to its citizens. List each benefit along with a sentence or two that describes it.

3.2 Differentiate the powers the Constitution provides to national and state governments.

4. Determine whether the following powers are delegated to the national government, reserved for the states, or shared by both:
a. Power to establish courts
b. Power to tax citizens and businesses
c. Express powers stated in the Constitution
d. Power to oversee primary and elementary education
e. Inherent powers to present a united front to foreign powers

5. In one paragraph, explain the national supremacy article and discuss its consequences for state and local governments.

6. Create a diagram showing the relationships among *express, implied, inherent, reserved,* and *concurrent* powers.

3.3 Assess the role of the national courts in defining the relationship between the national and state governments, and evaluate the positions of decentralists and centralists.

7. In a few sentences, discuss the "constitutional counter-revolution" instigated by Chief Justice William Rehnquist and continued by Chief Justice John Roberts.

8. Discuss *McCulloch* v. *Maryland* and the reasons for its importance to federalism.

9. Write a persuasive essay appraising whether the balance of governmental power should lean more toward either

the national government or the states. Note the main arguments of both centralists and decentralists, and then refute the arguments of the side you disagree with.

3.4 Analyze the budget as a tool of federalism, and evaluate its impact on state and local governments.

10. Give an example of a program funded by (1) a *categorical-formula grant*, (2) a *project grant*, and (3) a *block grant*.

11. Identify which of the following is an example of a *federal mandate*:
   a. The New York state legislature passes a law requiring all New York school teachers to spend ten hours a year learning new teaching techniques.
   b. Congress passes a law requiring all coal plants in the United States to reduce their carbon emissions by 30 percent by 2015.
   c. The Supreme Court upholds a law requiring teenage women to get parental permission before having an abortion.

   d. The Federal Emergency Management Agency sends funds from the national government to help clean up after a tornado.

12. Explain why unfunded mandates can cause problems.

3.5 Evaluate the current relationship between the national and state governments and the future challenges for federalism.

13. Write an essay that explains the reasons for the growth of the national government since the founding and that outlines the pressures that exist today that encourage further expansion of the national government.

14. Analyze the arguments for and against turning over to the states many of the economic and social programs that have become the responsibility of the national government, and write a persuasive essay that advocates one of these positions.

Answers to selected questions: 1. a. i; b. iv; c. ii; d. iii; e. vi; f. v. 2. b 4. a. both; b. both; c. national; d. states; e. national 11. b

---

mypoliscilab EXERCISES
Where participation leads to action!

Apply what you learned in this chapter on MyPoliSciLab.

Read on mypoliscilab.com

    eText: Chapter 3

Study and Review on mypoliscilab.com

    Pre-Test
    Post-Test
    Chapter Exam
    Flashcards

Watch on mypoliscilab.com

    Video: The Real ID
    Video: Water Wars
    Video: Proposition 8

Explore on mypoliscilab.com

    Simulation: You Are a Federal Judge
    Simulation: You Are a Restaurant Owner
    Comparative: Comparing Federal and Unitary Systems
    Timeline: Federalism and the Supreme Court
    Visual Literacy: Federalism and Regulations

KEY **TERMS**

federalism, p. 78
unitary system, p. 79
confederation, p. 79
delegated (express) powers, p. 84
implied powers, p. 84
necessary and proper clause, p. 84
inherent powers, p. 84

commerce clause, p. 85
federal mandate, p. 86
reserve powers, p. 86
concurrent powers, p. 86
full faith and credit clause, p. 88
extradition, p. 88
interstate compact, p. 88

national supremacy, p. 89
preemption, p. 89
centralists, p. 91
decentralists, p. 91
states' rights, p. 92
devolution revolution, p. 92

ADDITIONAL **RESOURCES**

FURTHER READING

SAMUEL H. BEER, *To Make a Nation: The Rediscovery of American Federalism* (Harvard University Press, 1993).

MICHAEL BURGESS, *Comparative Federalism Theory and Practice* (Routledge, 2006).

CENTER FOR THE STUDY OF FEDERALISM, *The Federalism Report* (published quarterly by Temple University; this publication notes research, books and articles, and scholarly conferences).

CENTER FOR THE STUDY OF FEDERALISM, *Publius: The Journal of Federalism* (published quarterly by Temple University; one issue each year is an "Annual Review of the State of American Federalism"; Web site is www.lafayette.edu/~publius).

TIMOTHY J. CONLAN, *From New Federalism to Devolution: Twenty-Five Years of Intergovernmental Reforms* (Brookings Institution Press, 1998).

DANIEL J. ELAZAR AND **JOHN KINCAID,** EDS., *The Covenant Connection: From Federal Theology to Modern Federalism* (Lexington Books, 2000).

NEIL C. MCCABE, ED., *Comparative Federalism in the Devolution Era* (Rowman & Littlefield, 2002).

PIETRO NIVOLA, *Tense Commandments: Federal Prescriptions and City Problems* (Brookings Institution Press, 2002).

JOHN T. NOONAN, *Narrowing the Nation's Power: The Supreme Court Sides with the States* (University of California Press, 2002).

WILLIAM H. RIKER, *The Development of American Federalism* (Academic Press, 1987).

DENISE SCHEBERLE, *Federalism and Environmental Policy: Trust and the Politics of Implementation* (Georgetown University Press, 2004).

KEVIN SMITH, ED., *State and Local Government, 2008–2009* (CQ Press, 2008).

CARL VAN HORN, ED., *The State of the States,* 4th ed. (CQ Press, 2008).

WEB SITES

www.OPM.gov The national government's Web site for all information on the civil service system. It contains the Factbook of basic demographic information on every federal employee.

www.USAjobs.gov The national government's Web site listing all available jobs. Also provides application information and online application forms.

www.USASpending.gov The national government's summary of all spending activity. Includes charts and graphs on overall spending trends and amounts of funding dedicated to specific programs.

www.ourpublicservice.org The Partnership for Public Service Web site. The Partnership is dedicated to improving the national government's workforce.

www.govexec.com The Web site for *Government Executive* magazine. The magazine provides a news stream on current news affecting the national bureaucracy.

PART II | The Political Process

THE BIG PICTURE

Throughout the course of U.S. history, the role of the people in government has expanded significantly. In this section, we examine how people influence each other and impact their government. We begin by examining the U.S. political culture and the widely shared values people hold. Social and economic attributes of individuals like age, income, race, and education are often predictive of participation, vote choice, and attitudes. Although individual attributes and characteristics are important, much of politics is done through groups. How groups form and compete in our political system, their relative importance over time and across issues, and how government can harness the positive elements of groups without being captured by them are also main themes of this part of the book. Political parties are especially important to the functioning of democracy. How parties are formed and why they endure are important questions we explore.

The importance of measuring and understanding public opinion has grown as the role of people in our government has grown. How people see the political world is influenced by many factors, including their upbringing, peers, the media, and education. Americans vote more often and for more offices than do the citizens of any other democracy, and voting is only one of the modes of political participation people can engage in. Campaigns and elections seek to mobilize voters and persuade them to vote for one candidate or against the other, or to vote for or against a particular ballot measure. Understanding how elections are structured and conducted is important in assessing the strengths and weaknesses of our electoral democracy. One important source of information is the media. The media we turn to for news about the world has changed over time. An informed public is vital to meaningful participation.

COURSE LEARNING **OBJECTIVES**

CHAPTER 4 Political Culture and Ideology

Explain the role of political culture and ideology in American government.

The American political culture consists of shared values about the worth and importance of individuals; a commitment to majority rule; free and fair elections; freedom of speech, press, and religion; limited government; and economic liberty. Political culture is learned in the family, reinforced in schools, and influenced by the media. Also important to the American political culture is widespread respect for the Constitution. The United States is seen as a place where individuals can achieve the American dream of affluence and financial independence. To the extent that people think about politics in an ideological way, there are more conservatives than liberals in the United States. But few people are at the ideological extremes, and many people are more moderate and pragmatic than ideological.

CHAPTER 5 The American Political Landscape

Describe how American social and economic differences affect political beliefs and policy preferences.

The diversity of the U.S. population is important to American politics. Holding aside Native Americans and slaves who came here against their will, the remaining population descends from or are themselves immigrants. Such personal characteristics as ethnicity, gender, race, sexual orientation, income, education, occupation, and age are predictive of behaviors and attitudes that influence American politics. Where we live is also important because in our federal system people identify with their state. Differences also exist between those who live in rural, urban, or suburban areas.

CHAPTER 6 Interest Groups

Evaluate the efforts of different kinds of interest groups to influence elections and legislation.

Political life involves people associating with other people. These associations lead to groups built around work, religion, economic interests, and so on. Interest groups arise when people with similar political interests organize to pursue those objectives. Interest groups vary in their size, resources, cohesiveness, leadership, and the techniques the group uses in attempting to influence government. Many groups are represented before government by lobbyists, individuals knowledgeable about the group and how the government works. Groups also attempt to build relationships with elected officials by funding their campaigns and by providing information to them. Government has attempted to check the power of any particular interest group through regulations and by encouraging interest group competition.

CHAPTER 7 Political Parties

Explain the role of political parties, and assess the need for parties in American government.

Political parties facilitate much of the workings of democratic government. Parties recruit and help elect candidates, simplify voting choices, and help organize government. Our electoral rules foster a two-party system, which has been competitive and stable over time. Parties are responsive to the views of party adherents and change positions over time. Occasionally new parties arise, and the public realigns with the parties. Most people have a party preference, although the strength of that affiliation varies. Parties raise money from individuals and interest groups and spend money in ways designed to foster electoral competition.

CHAPTER 8 Public Opinion, Participation, and Voting

Explain differences in opinions and rates of participation, and evaluate the importance of public opinion and participation in a democracy.

Representative government is presumed to reflect the will of the people. Politicians, the media, and academics all want to measure public opinion. People have different levels of interest, awareness, and opinions on issues. To gauge public opinion accurately requires the application of scientific principles and care in asking questions. Opinions can change.

People in the United States have many ways they can participate in politics. Rates of participation are linked to education and age and vary by type of election or political activity. The most common form of participation is voting. Turnout varies by type of election and the interest of the voters. Better-educated and older persons vote more often. Party identification is an important predictor of how people vote, as are candidate appeal and issues.

CHAPTER 9 Campaigns and Elections

Compare and contrast the elections for president and Congress, and describe how elections have changed over time.

America's winner-takes-all rule in American elections encourages a two-party system. The electoral college system of choosing a president reinforces federalism but means the popular vote winner does not necessarily win the White House. Presidents are elected through state caucuses and primaries, a convention, and then the general election. Not all elections in the United States are competitive. Incumbents have important advantages and generally win in congressional contests. Successful candidates must be able to raise large amounts of money, much of it from individuals or groups with particular interests or agendas. Concerns over the influence of money on elections have led to reform efforts. Similarly, reforms of the electoral college and presidential nomination system arise regularly.

CHAPTER 10 The Media and U.S. Politics

Describe the evolution of the media, and evaluate its impact on public opinion, elections, and government.

How people learn about politics and what events become news are influenced by the news media. Over time, the media has evolved and now includes newspapers, radio, television, the Internet, and even social media, like Facebook. People selectively attend to and interpret what news they see and hear. The media are important to election campaigns and debates over public policy and can provide an important check on the government.

Political Culture and Ideology

CHAPTER **OUTLINE**
CHAPTER LEARNING
OBJECTIVES

Defining the American Political Culture

4.1 Identify the most important elements of and sources for the American political culture.

Political Ideology and Attitudes Toward Government

4.2 Compare and contrast political ideologies and evaluate the critiques of each ideology.

Political Ideology and the American People

4.3 Assess the importance of political ideology in light of competing ideas and the contemporary American context.

On the third Monday of January, the United States commemorates the birth of Dr. Martin Luther King Jr. as a federal holiday. Designated as a day of service, the holiday has come to celebrate the civil rights movement and progress toward Dr. King's dream of racial equality and social justice. Many have forgotten the controversy surrounding its creation, however. Legislation to create Martin Luther King Jr. Day was first introduced in Congress only days after Dr. King's assassination in 1968, but 15 years elapsed before Congress passed it and President Reagan signed the holiday into law.

Early support for the idea of the holiday came from labor unions, who pressed for the holiday in contract negotiations and at all levels of U.S. government. The entertainer Stevie Wonder helped advance the campaign with his single "Happy Birthday." A petition for the holiday with 6 million signatures was presented to Congress in 1982.[1]

Opposition centered on the costs of giving workers the day off, concerns about creating national holidays for persons other than U.S. presidents, the view that the importance of Dr. King's accomplishments would fade with time, and even attacks on Dr. King's reputation that linked him to communists.[2] When Arizona voters defeated a referendum to establish the holiday in 1990, the National Football League moved the 1993 Super Bowl from Arizona to Pasadena, California.[3] Some states adopted the holiday but at first named it "Human Rights Day" (Utah) or "Lee-Jackson-King Day" (oddly, Virginia combined the two confederate generals and Dr. King). In 2000, South Carolina became the last state to adopt the holiday, and all states now observe Martin Luther King Day.

During the 2008 presidential election, though racial tensions were never far from the headlines, candidates from both parties celebrated the accomplishments of Dr. King. During the campaign, controversy developed surrounding Barack Obama's African American minister Jeremiah Wright and his political views. In a speech on the topic of race in America, Obama spoke of his controversial pastor, Reverend Jeremiah Wright, when he said, "I can no more disown him than I can my white grandmother—a woman who helped raise me, a woman who sacrificed again and again for me, a woman who loves me as much as she loves anything in this world, but a woman who once confessed her fear of black men who passed by her on the street, and who on more than one occasion has uttered racial or ethnic stereotypes that made me cringe."[4] The speech served to distance Obama from Wright, and Obama won the election with strong support from African Americans (95 percent) and from whites (43 percent).[5]

Although substantial progress has been made in achieving Dr. King's dream of equal opportunity for all races, challenges remain. As we discuss in Chapter 5, significant differences persist among races in the rate of poverty, educational attainment, and income. Racial minorities and women continue to be underrepresented in Congress, on corporate boards, and as partners in law firms. Racial tensions persist in some neighborhoods and schools. Our society has not become free of racism, but we have seen substantial changes in voting rights, access to public accommodations, and educational opportunity as a result of the civil rights movement, one leader of which was Dr. King.

These changing attitudes toward civil rights and toward a holiday honoring one of the movement's central figures exemplify a shift in political culture in the United States. Dr. King's famous "I have a dream" speech expressed the idea that the American dream of freedom, opportunity, and tolerance for others should be open to everyone. The story of how Martin Luther King Jr. Day came about is not only a story of political persistence but also an example of how political attitudes can change over time. Political culture can also be understood in terms of attitudes and values, which when they are coherent and consistent are known as *ideology*. In this chapter, we look at political culture and ideology.

Defining the American Political Culture

LEARNING **OBJECTIVE**

4.1 Identify the most important elements of and sources for the American political culture.

Many American citizens' first experience with democracy is a school election, sometimes as early as in elementary school. Other elements of our political culture are learned in the family or from peers. Many important elements of our political culture are widely shared by Americans, others are evolving, and some are no longer widely shared. In this chapter, we examine our assumptions, beliefs, and values about politics, government, participation, freedom, and liberty.

Political scientists use the term **political culture** to refer to the widely shared beliefs, values, and norms citizens hold about their relationship to government and to one another. We can discover the specifics of a nation's political culture not only by studying what its people believe and say but also by observing how they behave. That behavior includes such fundamental decisions as who may participate in political decisions, what rights and liberties citizens have, how political decisions are made, and what people think about politicians and government generally.

Some elements of our political culture—such as our fear of concentrated power and our reverence for individual liberty—have remained constant over time. However, as discussed in the introduction, our ideas about **suffrage,** the right to vote, have changed from a belief that only property-owning white men should be allowed to vote to a conviction that all adults, excluding felons in some states, should have the right. Thus, citizens now vote in party primaries to select nominees for office, whereas for much of our history, party leaders determined who would run for office. The surge in political activity on the Internet in recent elections may be a harbinger of a new political culture in which citizens interact more with candidates, contribute money to campaigns, and mobilize each other.[6]

The idea of people coming together, listening to each other, exchanging ideas, learning to appreciate each other's differences, and defending their opinions is sometimes called **deliberation** and builds what has been called **social capital.** Such interaction is thought to foster and strengthen community and relationships in ways that do not happen when citizens only cast ballots. Political scientist Robert Putnam has defined social capital as "features of social organization such as networks, norms, and social trust that facilitate coordination and cooperation for mutual benefit."[7] In at least some respects, the Barack Obama campaign, through its extensive use of the Internet to network volunteers and donors, is an application of the social capital idea to political campaigning. As Obama's "new media" director put it, "The campaign tried to enable folks to take control of the process as much as they were willing at every stage. So if you made phone calls using the myBarackObama sound system or you made a donation or you sent a letter to the editor or joined a grassroots volunteer group…at each step you are prompted to not just tell someone but to upload your whole address book and tell everyone you know."[8]

political culture
The widely shared beliefs, values, and norms about how citizens relate to government and to one another.

suffrage
The right to vote.

deliberation
The process where people or elected officials meet together to discuss and consider public matters.

social capital
Democratic and civic habits of discussion, compromise, and respect for differences, which grow out of participation in voluntary organizations.

American political culture centers on democratic values such as liberty, equality, individualism, justice, the rule of law, patriotism, optimism, and idealism. There is no "official" list of American political values; however, and as we noted in Chapter 1, these widely shared democratic values overlap and sometimes conflict with each other.

Shared Values

Before the American and French Revolutions of the late eighteenth century, discussions about individual liberty, freedom, equality, private property, limited government, and popular consent were rare. Europe had been dominated by aristocracies, had experienced centuries of political and social inequality, and had been ruled by governments that often exercised power arbitrarily. Political philosophers rebelled against these traditions and proclaimed the principles of classical liberalism.

As discussed in the Introduction, the founders of our nation claimed that individuals have certain

Organizing for America, Barack Obama's Web site, was created during the 2008 presidential election and continues to spread information about causes important to the Obama administration.

natural rights—the rights of all people to dignity and worth—and that government must be limited and controlled because it was a threat to those rights. During this same period, the economic system was changing from a *mercantile system*, under which countries sought to strengthen the role of the state, establish colonies, and develop industry by encouraging exports and discouraging imports, to a *free market system* with the government taking a more "hands-off" approach to the economy and setting up fewer trade barriers.[9] People began to think they could improve their lot in life and enhance their political and social status. Radical new ideas like these influenced the thinking of the founders and shaped the values essential to the United States' political culture today.

Liberty   No value in the American political culture is more revered than liberty. "We have always been a nation obsessed with liberty. Liberty over authority, freedom over responsibility, rights over duties—these are our historic preferences," wrote the late Clinton Rossiter, a noted political scientist. "Not the good man but the free man has been the measure of all things in this sweet 'land of liberty'; not national glory but individual liberty has been the object of political authority and the test of its worth."[10] Not all students of U.S. political thought accept this emphasis on freedom and individualism over virtue and the public good, and in reality both sets of values are important.[11]

Equality   Thomas Jefferson's famous words in the Declaration of Independence express the strength of our views of equality: "We hold these truths to be self-evident, that all men are created equal, that they are endowed by their Creator with certain unalienable rights, that among these are life, liberty, and the pursuit of happiness." In contrast to Europeans, our nation shunned aristocracy, and our Constitution explicitly prohibits governments from granting titles of nobility. Although our rhetoric about equality was not always matched by our policy—slavery and racial segregation in schools—the value of social equality is now deeply rooted.

American citizens also believe in *political equality*, the idea that every individual has a right to equal protection under the law and equal voting power. Although political equality has always been a goal, it has not always been a reality. In the past, African Americans, Native Americans, Asian Americans, and women were denied the right to vote and otherwise participate in the nation's political life.

Equality encompasses the idea of *equal opportunity*, especially with regard to improving our economic status. American adults believe social background should not limit our opportunity to achieve to the best of our ability, nor should race, gender, or religion. The nation's commitment to public education programs such as Head Start for disadvantaged preschool children, state support for public colleges and universities, and federal financial aid for higher education reflects this belief in equal opportunity.

natural rights
The rights of all people to dignity and worth; also called *human rights*.

A teacher reads to her students as part of the Head Start program in Washington, D.C.   ■ *How does the education system in the United States, including programs like Head Start and Race to the Top, reflect the principle of equal opportunity?*

Increasing Access for the Disabled

People today take for granted that Americans restricted to a wheelchair can have access to public transportation and buildings, that hearing-impaired persons can use telecommunications, and that persons with disabilities are not subject to discrimination. But this was not always the case.

Prior to 1990, when President George H. W. Bush signed into law the Americans with Disabilities Act (ADA), discrimination and other barriers existed that greatly restricted disabled persons. For example, one of those who fought hard for the Americans with Disabilities Act was Justin W. Dart Jr. Born into affluence, Dart contracted polio at age 18, shortly before entering the University of Houston. That institution denied him a teaching certificate because of his disability. After a career in business, Dart became an advocate for the rights of people with disabilities.

By establishing requirements for buildings and public transportation, persons with disabilities are now able to travel and enjoy going to a restaurant, hotel, or theater. Although many changes still need to be made, the improvements have made it much easier for persons with disabilities to participate in daily activities. Similarly, employment regulations have helped prevent discrimination and allowed these individuals to participate more fully in society. As you consider your college campus and community, imagine how different it would be if persons with disabilities were denied access to public transportation, buildings, and employment.

CRITICAL THINKING QUESTIONS

1. How does the Americans with Disabilities Act foster equality of opportunity?

2. What are the advantages to society of making public transportation, accommodations and buildings, and employment more accessible to persons with disabilities?

3. What are arguments you could make against legislation like the ADA?

Individualism   The United States is characterized by a persistent commitment to the individual, who has both rights and responsibilities. As Peter Shuck and James Q. Wilson have recently written, "This belief in individualism causes Americans to place an unparalleled emphasis on the notion of individual rights in every area of social life and, correspondingly, to be suspicious of group rights."[12] Policies that limit individual choice generate intense political conflict. The debates over legalized abortion and universal health care are often framed in terms of our ability to exercise choices. Although American citizens support individual rights and freedoms, they also understand that their rights can conflict with another person's or with the government's need to maintain order or promote the general welfare.

Respect for the Common Person   Most American adults prefer action to reflection. We are often anti-expert and sometimes anti-intellectual, and an emphasis on practicality and common sense has become part of our national image. Poets such as Walt Whitman and Carl Sandburg and storytellers such as Mark Twain, Will Rogers, Eudora Welty, and Garrison Keillor helped shape this tradition. Reverence for the common people helps explain our ambivalence toward power, politics, and government authority. In the 2008 presidential primaries, for example, Democrat John Edwards made frequent reference to his father's work in textile mills, and Republican Mike Huckabee frequently mentioned that he was the first male in his family to graduate from high school.

Democratic Consensus   We are a people from many different cultural and ethnic backgrounds, histories, and religions. Despite these differences, our political culture includes a **democratic consensus,** a set of widely shared attitudes and beliefs about government and its values, procedures, documents, and institutions. We have strong opinions about fundamental "rules of the game" such as who has power to do what, how people acquire power, and how they are removed from power. But this shared commitment does not necessarily mean that people vote, keep up with public affairs, or believe government is always fair or just.

We believe in **majority rule**—governance according to the preferences of the majority as expressed through regular elections. Yet we also believe that people in the minority should be free to try to win majority support for their opinions. Even though many lack strong party attachments, we favor a two-party system and the idea of competition between the parties.

democratic consensus

Widespread agreement on fundamental principles of democratic governance and the values that undergird them.

majority rule

Governance according to the expressed preferences of the majority.

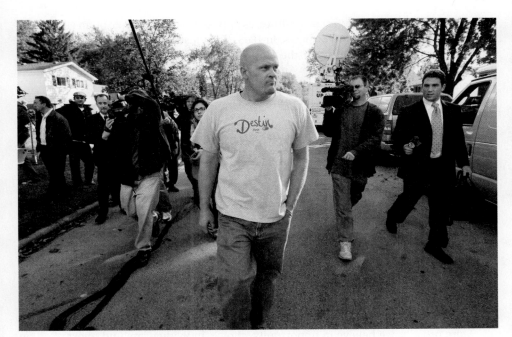

Joe the Plumber became a nationally recognized figure after Senator Obama and Senator McCain both referenced him repeatedly in the final presidential debate; he had previously directed a question to Senator Obama on the campaign trail in Ohio, and Senator McCain tried to use Joe the Plumber to prove that Obama did not understand the problems and needs of the average American. ■ *Considering the social and economic conditions in the country, as well as the background of the presidential candidates, why might the image of Joe the Plumber have been so resonant for many Americans in 2008?*

Our institutions are based on the principles of representation and consent of the governed. We believe in **popular sovereignty**—the idea that ultimate power resides in the people. Government exists to serve the people rather than the other way around. The government learns the will of the people through *elections*, the most important expression of popular consent and, to an extent, through public opinion polls (see Chapter 8). But sometimes other fundamental rights limit popular sovereignty and majority rule.[13]

The Constitution, especially the first ten amendments (the Bill of Rights) and the Thirteenth, Fourteenth, Fifteenth, and Nineteenth Amendments, spells out many of the limits on what governments can do. The Constitution is revered as a national symbol, yet we often differ about what it means, and we honor many constitutional rights more in the abstract than in the particular. Approximately half of us, for instance, think books with dangerous ideas should be banned from public school libraries (see Table 4–1). Americans with a college degree are about half as likely (23 percent) to hold this view.[14] Intolerance of dissenting or offensive views is amply demonstrated in public opinion polls and on college and university campuses. Still, most of us support democratic and constitutional values.

Justice and the Rule of Law   Inscribed above the entrance to the U.S. Supreme Court are the words "Equal Justice Under Law." The *rule of law* means government is based on a body

popular sovereignty
A belief that ultimate power resides in the people.

TABLE
4–1 | What Do You Mean by Rights and Freedoms? It Depends

	Agree	Disagree	Don't Know
There has been real improvement in the position of African Americans.	61%	31%	8%
Freedom of speech should not extend to groups that are sympathetic with terrorists.	49	45	6
Books that contain dangerous ideas should be banned from public school libraries.	46	49	5
Abortions should be more difficult to obtain.	41	54	6
The police should be allowed to search the houses of known terrorist sympathizers without a court order.	33	64	3
School boards ought to have the right to fire teachers who are known homosexuals.	28	67	5

■ *If Americans generally express support for the concept of individual rights and freedom, what concerns might they be balancing those beliefs against in some of the issues for which they express low levels of support?*

SOURCE: Used by permission of The Pew Research Center for the People & the Press. *Trends in Political Values and Core Attitudes: 1987–2009; INDEPENDENTS TAKE CENTER STAGE IN OBAMA ERA,* May 21, 2009, http://people-press.org/report/517/political-values-and-core-attitudes (accessed December 4, 2009); and responses to abortion question obtained from Harris Poll, July 7–14, 2009, http://pollingreport.com/abortion.htm (accessed April 23, 2010).

of law applied equally and by just procedures, as opposed to arbitrary rule by an elite whose whims decide policy or resolve disputes. In 1803, Chief Justice John Marshall summarized this principle: "The government of the United States has been emphatically termed a government of laws, not of men."[15] Americans strongly believe in fairness: Everyone is entitled to the same legal rights and protections.

To adhere to the rule of law, government should follow these five rules:

1. *Generality:* Laws should be stated generally and not single out any group or individual.
2. *Prospectivity:* Laws should apply to the present and the future, not punish something someone did in the past.
3. *Publicity:* Laws cannot be kept secret and then enforced.
4. *Authority:* Valid laws are made by those with legitimate power, and the people legitimate that power through some form of popular consent.
5. *Due process:* Laws must be enforced impartially with fair processes.

Patriotism, Optimism, and Idealism   The terrorist attacks of 2001 united the nation and reinforced American **nationalism.** As President George W. Bush said, "We are a different country than we were on September 10th: sadder and less innocent; stronger and more united; and in the face of ongoing threats, determined and courageous."[16] However, as the wars in Afghanistan and Iraq became less popular, the country became sharply divided on how best to confront the terrorism threat.

More broadly, we believe in opportunity, choice, individualism, and, most of all, in the freedom to improve ourselves and to achieve success with as little interference as possible from others or from government. U.S. citizens are more satisfied with their democratic government than are citizens of many other countries.[17] More than nine out of ten Americans are proud of their nationality.[18]

We know that our system is imperfect, yet we still believe in government by the people. We often grumble that elected officials have lost touch with us, we are disgusted by scandals, and we are impatient with how long the system takes to solve problems such as high gas taxes, crime, drug abuse, and terrorism. Despite the dissatisfactions, we believe that America is better, stronger, and more virtuous than other nations. Americans are known for this strong sense of **patriotism.** Like every country, the United States has interests and motives that are selfish as well as generous, cynical as well as idealistic. Still, our support of human needs and rights throughout the world is evidence of an enduring idealism.

Where We Learn the American Political Culture

One important source of political culture in the United States, as in other nations, is the family. Young children are taught what it means to be an American. They are curious about why people vote, what the president does, and whether Grandpa fought in Korea or Vietnam. The questions may vary from family to family, yet the themes of authority, freedom, equality, liberty, and partisanship are common. Families are the most important reference group, with parents and siblings orienting each other to politics, the media, and the community more generally. Compared to families in other cultures, American families are much more egalitarian, with children having more input in family decisions than in other cultures.[19]

Public schools are another source of the American political culture. Children and teachers often begin the school day by saluting the flag, reciting the Pledge of Allegiance, or singing the national anthem. Political and economic values are part of the curriculum. Not only are values taught in American history classes, but they are put into practice in school elections and newspapers and in everyday economic activities such as work and saving.[20]

Colleges and universities also help foster the American political culture. Students who attend college are often more confident than others in dealing with bureaucracy and politics generally and are more likely to participate in politics, vote, and know more about government.[21] Many states require students at state colleges and universities to take courses in American or state government, in part to instill a sense of civic duty.

American churches, synagogues, and mosques have long fostered a common understanding of right and wrong and of freedom—including freedom of religion, individualism, pluralism, and civic duty. Two scholars have recently written, "Surrounding and shaping

nationalism
An enduring sense of national identity or consciousness that derives from cultural, historic, linguistic, or political forces.

patriotism
Devotion to one's own country, often seeing it as better or stronger than other countries.

Of the People

AMERICA'S CHANGING FACE

Immigrants and Assimilation into American Political Culture

As a nation of immigrants, the United States has assimilated individuals from many countries. This process takes time as new immigrants learn the language, pursue education, and begin to understand the institutions and process of government, including elections.

The scholar Samuel Huntington and others have argued that immigrants from Mexico are less likely to support core American values or learn English and have "a strong resistance to acculturation...[and] persistence of their communal bonds."[*] Huntington's findings have been challenged. One study found that "nearly all Hispanic adults born in the United States of immigrant parents report they are fluent in English," suggesting assimilation after the first generation.[†] The data presented in the figure are from a survey of Latinos in the United States. Latinos who are not American citizens are more likely to

identify themselves with their country of birth and less likely to describe themselves as "American," but for both groups, the political focus is on the United States.

The immigration/assimilation debate inspires strong emotions on both sides. Some, like Huntington, fear that the influx of immigration will challenge "American" ideals. These groups and individuals are fearful that the immigration trends will mean the end of something—although they rarely specify what that will be. Fox News commentator John Gibson called on his presumably white viewers to "make more babies," otherwise, in "twenty-five years...the majority of the population [will be] Hispanic."[‡] The United States has been down this road before. In the 1850s, following a devastating period of famine due to a potato mold, Irish émigrés began arriving in the Americas in droves. Today, more than 34 million

Americans claim Irish ancestry—that number is more than nine times the population of Ireland today.[§] However, in the 1850s, these immigrants were held in contempt. They were predominantly Catholic and generally poor. In short, they represented—at least in the minds of their contemporaries—a threat to American culture.

CRITICAL THINKING QUESTIONS

1. What factors may make it more or less difficult to assimilate new waves of immigrants into U.S. society today?

2. How does the racial composition of the United States affect the country's political culture?

3. Is the comparison between the Irish immigration of the 1850s and our current situation valid?

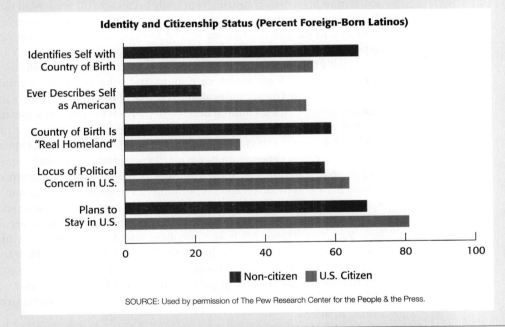

Identity and Citizenship Status (Percent Foreign-Born Latinos)

Legend: ■ Non-citizen ■ U.S. Citizen

SOURCE: Used by permission of The Pew Research Center for the People & the Press.

---

[*] Samuel P. Huntington, *Who Are We? The Challenges to America's National Identity* (Simon & Schuster, 2004), pp. 189–190.

[†] Shirin Hakimzadeh and D'Vera Cohn, "English Usage Among Hispanics in the United States," *Pew Hispanic Center*, November 29, 2007; see also Mary C. Water and Tomas R. Jimenez, "Assessing Immigrant Assimilation: Empirical and Theoretical Challenges," *Annual Review of Sociology* (2005), pp. 105–125; and Jack Citrin, Amy Lerman, Michael Murakami, and Kathryn Pearson, "Testing Huntington: Is Hispanic Immigration a Threat to American Identity?" *Perspectives on Politics*, March 2007.

[‡] John Gibson, "My Word," *Fox News*, May 11, 2006.

[§] U.S. Census Bureau, "Facts for Features: Irish-American Heritage Month," March 10, 2006, www.census.gov/Press-Release/www/releases/archives/facts_for_features_special_editions/006328.html.

American culture is a remarkably strong religious tradition and an inventive, though sometimes repellent, popular culture of religiosity."[22] Churches do not all take the same positions on political issues, but they have played important roles in such major social and political movements as the abolition of slavery, the expansion of civil rights, and opposition to war.

In modern times, the mass media have taken over some functions the family used to perform. By the time children leave high school, they will have spent more time watching television than talking to their parents. They may have learned more about politics from Comedy Central and Jon Stewart than from their parents, schools, or other media.[23] Finally, American adults educate each other about political values at work, at PTA meetings, and in more expressly political activities.

The American Dream

Many of our political values come together in the **American dream,** a complex set of ideas that holds that the United States is a land of opportunity where individual initiative and hard work can bring economic success. Whether fulfilled or not, this dream speaks to our most deeply held hopes and goals. Its essence is expressed in our enthusiasm for **capitalism,** an economic system based on private property, competitive markets, economic incentives, and limited government involvement in the production, pricing, and distribution of goods and services.[24]

The concept of *private property* enjoys extraordinary popularity in the United States. Most cherish the dream of acquiring property and believe that the owners of property have the right to decide how to use it. In many European democracies, the state owns and operates transportation systems and other businesses that are privately owned and operated in the United States. Even in Europe, though, some privatization has occurred in communications systems such as telephone companies and broadcast media.

The right to private property is only one of the economic incentives that cement our support for capitalism and fuel the American dream. Although it is difficult to compare social mobility across countries, especially because of differences in rates of immigration, the American dream is more attainable for middle-income persons in the United States than in Europe. But the bottom fifth of the economic distribution in the United States appears to be less upwardly mobile than in Europe.[25]

What explains these differences? We assume that people who have more ability or who work hard will get ahead, earn more, and enjoy economic rewards. We also believe that people in the United States should be able to pass most of the wealth they have accumulated along to their children and relatives. Even the poorest generally oppose high inheritance taxes or limits on how much someone can earn. American adults believe that the free market system gives almost everyone a fair chance, that capitalism is necessary, and that freedom depends on it. We reject communism and socialism—a rejection fortified in recent decades as most communist nations shifted toward capitalism. In the United States, individuals and corporations have acquired wealth and, at the same time, exercised political clout. Their power has in turn been widely criticized.

Wealthy individuals have used their assets to fund their campaigns for public office. New York City Mayor Michael Bloomberg spent $102 million on his successful 2009 reelection.[26] In 2005 and 2001, he spent $78 and $74 million.[27] New Jersey Governor Jon Corzine spent $60 million on his successful New Jersey Senate race in 2000 and another $43 million on his successful gubernatorial race in 2005.[28] In 2009, he spent another $22 million of his own money on the race, only to lose his bid for reelection to Republican Chris Christie.[29]

Wealthy individuals also spend their money hoping to influence elections or public policy (George Soros gave $27 million to organizations such as America Coming Together, the Media Fund, MoveOn.org, Joint Victory Campaign, Young Democrats of America, and a few other groups working to defeat George W. Bush in 2004).[30] In 2008, there was less activity by wealthy individuals funding outside groups. This decline may have been due to the requests from both presidential candidates that supporters not fund these kinds of groups.

The conflict in values between a *competitive economy,* in which individuals reap large rewards for their initiative and hard work, and an *egalitarian society,* in which everyone earns a decent living, carries over into politics. How the public resolves this tension changes over time and from issue to issue.

American dream

The widespread belief that the United States is a land of opportunity and that individual initiative and hard work can bring economic success.

capitalism

An economic system characterized by private property, competitive markets, economic incentives, and limited government involvement in the production, distribution, and pricing of goods and services.

DECIDE Is the American Dream Still Alive and Important?

The American dream holds that the United States is a land of opportunity, and individual initiative and hard work can bring economic success. Is the American dream alive, and is it important to people? Some argue that the wealth and prosperity so many have achieved in the United States means that, for most, the dream has been achieved and is no longer important as a motivating force or a way to explain behavior. Others contend that, for people in poverty, the hopelessness of their situation makes the American dream seem far-fetched and unattainable.

What do you think? Is the American dream still an important element of the political culture of the United States? What arguments would you make for or against this?

THINKING IT THROUGH

The persistence of poverty in a land of plenty is perplexing, but it does not change the reality that some are able to escape it. Examples of individuals who have achieved at least a portion of the American dream arise often enough to reinforce acceptance that the dream can come true. Although some achieve the dream because they win the lottery or make an NFL football team, more do so because of opportunities such as education.

The American dream does not have to be achieved by everyone to be an important motivator. New immigrant groups have long been an incubator of the American dream, and they continue to be so today. Parents working multiple low-paying jobs while stressing education for their children provide an example of both the work and the dream components of this aspiration. At the same time, it is also clear that the American dream is less available to some than to others and that access to it can be limited by larger forces such as recessions, unemployment, and illness. Some problems that many middle-class individuals can take in stride can derail the hopes and aspirations of those without a safety net.

The American dream also includes the idea that people in this country have more opportunity to pursue an education, to express themselves, and to associate with others as they see fit. In short, part of the dream is that the United States is a more open society. The extent to which the American dream persists in our political culture, despite its limitations, is evidence of its power and importance.

Oprah Winfrey came from humble beginnings, but is now one of the most influential and highest-paid people in the country.

Critical Thinking Questions

1. What examples can you identify of people who have achieved the American dream, and what difference has that success made to others who have the dream?

2. Is the American dream more attainable for some than others? If so, why is that the case?

3. Does the American dream encompass more than economic wealth? How important is religious or political freedom to the idea that the American dream is about opportunity?

As important as the American dream is as an aspiration, it remains unfulfilled. The gap between rich and poor has grown in recent years, and a sharp income difference between whites and blacks remains tenacious.[31] Figure 4–1 charts median household income for whites, blacks, Hispanics, and Asian and Pacific Islanders, as well as for all households over time.

For more people than we want to admit, chances for success still depend on the family they were born into, the neighborhood they grew up in, or the college they attended. An underclass persists in the form of impoverished families, malnourished and poorly educated children, and the homeless.[32] Many cities are actually two cities, where some residents live in luxury, others in squalor. This reality was starkly reinforced in the aftermath of Hurricane Katrina in 2005 as the world observed that poor people were much more likely to lack the transportation or resources to flee the hurricane-stricken city. National public opinion polls showed stark differences along racial lines in perceptions of whether the government's response would have been different if most of the victims had been white and not black. Two-thirds of African Americans held this view, compared with fewer than one in five whites.[33]

FIGURE 4–1 **Median Annual Household Income by Race.**

■ *Has there been much change in median household income over time? What are some reasons to explain this?*

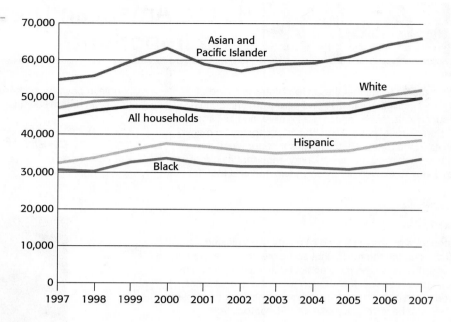

Political and Economic Change

Historical developments and economic and technological growth affect political values. The Declaration of Independence and the Constitution identified such important political values as individual liberty, property rights, and limited government.[34] These values have been shaped by events and political movements as have others such as political equality and more democratic forms of participation.

The Industrial Transformation By 1900, industrial capitalism and the growth of corporations had largely replaced the agrarian society of small farmers and plantations that the framers had known. These changes irreversibly transformed our political and social ideology. Large privately owned corporations changed not only the economic order but the role of government and the way people viewed each other. No one captures the implications of this shift better than political scientist Robert A. Dahl:

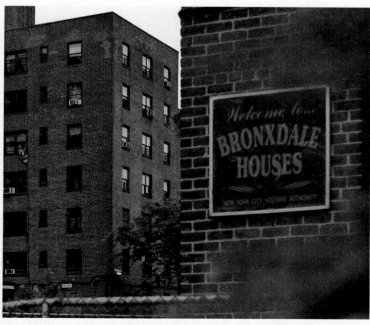

A contrast in housing can be seen in the two photos of New York City. On the left is the Plaza Hotel. On the right the Bronxdale houses, low-income public housing. ■ *Looking at the disparity of wealth that these images indicate, do you think they reaffirm that the American dream is still alive, or demonstrate that it's unattainable for most Americans?*

One of the consequences of the new order has been a high degree of inequality in the distribution of wealth and income—a far greater inequality than had ever been thought likely or desirable under an agrarian order by Democratic Republicans like Jefferson and Madison, or had ever been thought consistent with democratic or republican government in the historic writings on the subject from Aristotle to Locke, Montesquieu, and Rousseau. Previous theorists and advocates had, like many of the framers of our own Constitution, insisted that a republic could exist only if the citizen body contained neither rich nor poor. Citizens, it was argued, must enjoy a rough equality of condition.[35]

The success of the American economy led to the concentration of great wealth in the hands of a few—the "robber barons" or tycoons. Many had taken great risks or earned their fortunes through inventions and efficient production practices. But as disparities of income grew, so did disparities in political resources. People with more economic resources can invest time, energy, and money in political campaigns, parties, and candidates, which in turn enhance their power and influence.[36] The Supreme Court ruled in 2010 in a court case to allow corporations to spend their general funds, including profits as independent expenditures in federal elections.[37] This decision reversed earlier court decisions and a long-standing prohibition on such spending. Corporations continued to be named for giving their general funds to candidates or political parties (see Chapter 9).

Plumes of black smoke rise from steel mills in Homestead, Pennsylvania, behind a group of children on their way to school in the early 1900s. The rapid industrialization of the United States near the beginning of the twentieth century resulted in an increased disparity between the richest and the poorest Americans.

The Great Depression and the New Deal   The Great Depression of the 1930s and the near collapse of the capitalistic system that followed it shaped much of our thinking about the role of government in a capitalistic system. The Depression was largely blamed on unrestrained capitalism and an unregulated market. The collapse of the stock market, massive unemployment, and a failed banking system caused widespread suffering. Workers had no unemployment compensation, no guarantee for the money they put in banks, no federal regulation of the stock market, and no Social Security. People turned to the government to improve the lot of millions of jobless and homeless citizens. Beginning with President Franklin D. Roosevelt's New Deal in the 1930s, most people came to accept that governments, at both the national and state levels, should use their powers and resources to ensure some measure of equal opportunity and social justice.

Building on Roosevelt's policies, Presidents John F. Kennedy and Lyndon B. Johnson worked with the civil rights movement in the 1960s to pass civil rights and voting rights legislation and launch a "war on poverty." As the debate in Congress and the country over health care in 2009 illustrated, modern-day liberalism and conservatism turn, in large measure, on how much we believe that governments should help minorities, women, and others who have suffered discrimination or been left behind by the industrial or technological revolutions of the twentieth century.

Today, free enterprise is no longer unbridled. Government regulations, antitrust laws, job safety regulations, environmental standards, and minimum wage laws try to balance freedom of enterprise against the rights of individuals. This issue has come more sharply into focus with the collapse of Wall Street investment banking firms like Bear Stearns and Lehman Brothers in 2008. President Bush as well as both major party nominees—John McCain and Barack Obama—supported emergency legislation and

Bread lines like this provided handouts of food to thousands of unemployed and destitute people during the Great Depression.

TABLE

4–2	Attitudes About Business and Labor	

	Percentage Agreeing
There is too much power concentrated in the hands of a few big companies.	77%
The strength of this country is mostly based on the success of American business.	76
Labor unions are necessary to protect the working person.	61
Government regulation of business usually does more harm than good.	54
Business corporations generally strike a fair balance between making profits and serving the public interest.	37

■ *In what ways do you see these views being reflected in specific public policies or current policy debates in the news?*

SOURCE: Used by permission of The Pew Research Center for the People & the Press. *Trends in Political Values and Core Attitudes: 1987–2009; and INDEPENDENTS TAKE CENTER STAGE IN OBAMA ERA,* May 21, 2009, http://people-press.org/report/517/political-values-and-core-attitudes (accessed December 4, 2009).

charged the Treasury Department to shore up banks and other financial institutions. The initial cost of the Troubled Asset Relief Program (TARP) was $700 billion.[38] The action came to be seen as a bailout of Wall Street banks and other financial institutions that had made risky investments.[39] More broadly, the securities and banking industries were criticized by many as having operated without sufficient government oversight and regulation (see Chapter 18).[40]

Most people today support a semi-regulated or mixed free enterprise system that checks the worst tendencies of capitalism, but they reject excessive government intervention (see Table 4–2). Much of American politics centers on how to achieve this balance. Currently, most liberals and conservatives agree that some governmental intervention is necessary to assist those who fall short in the competition for education and economic prosperity and to encourage ventures that, though they have substantial public benefit, might not be undertaken without government assistance.

Political Ideology and Attitudes Toward Government

LEARNING OBJECTIVE

4.2 Compare and contrast political ideologies and evaluate the critiques of each ideology.

Political ideology refers to a consistent pattern of ideas or beliefs about political values and the role of government, including how it should work and how it actually does work.

Two major schools of political ideology dominate American politics: *liberalism* and *conservatism*. Two less popular schools of thought—*socialism* and *libertarianism*—also help define the spectrum of ideology. (See Table 4–3.)

Liberalism

In the eighteenth and nineteenth centuries, classical liberals favored *limited government* and sought to protect people from governmental harassment in their political and economic lives. Over time, the liberal emphasis on individualism has remained constant, but the perception of the need for government changed.

Contemporary Liberals In its current U.S. usage, **liberalism** refers to a belief that government can bring about justice and equality of opportunity. Modern-day liberals wish to preserve the rights of the individual and the right to own private property, but they believe that some government intervention in the economy is necessary to remedy the shortcomings of capitalism. Liberals advocate equal access to health care, housing, and education for all citizens. They generally believe in affirmative action programs, protections for workers' health and safety, tax rates that rise with a person's income, and unions' rights to organize and strike. Liberals are generally more inclined to favor greater environmental protection and individual choice in such matters as same-sex marriage and abortion.

Liberals generally believe that the future will be better than the past or the present—that obstacles can be overcome and the government can be trusted to, and should, play a role in that progress. They contend that modern technology and industrialization cry out for government programs to offset the loss of liberties that the poor and the weak suffer.

political ideology
A consistent pattern of beliefs about political values and the role of government.

liberalism
A belief that government can and should achieve justice and equality of opportunity.

TABLE

4-3 | Differences in Political Ideology

	Conservative	Moderate	Liberal	Don't Know/Haven't Thought About It
Sex				
Male	39%	23%	20%	18%
Female	31	24	22	23
Race				
White	39	24	21	17
Black	18	21	22	39
Asian	20	26	36	18
Hispanic	22	25	20	32
Age				
18–34	26	24	28	23
35–45	36	26	17	20
46–55	37	23	19	20
56–64	38	21	26	15
Religion				
Protestant	45	18	16	15
Catholic	31	28	18	23
Jewish	26	12	63	0
Education				
Less than high school	25	20	14	42
High school diploma	29	27	11	33
Some college	38	25	22	15
Bachelor's degree	42	21	32	5
Advanced degree	45	14	39	3
Party				
Democrat	13	27	37	23
Independent	14	35	11	40
Republican	70	15	5	11

This table displays how ideology is correlated to sex, race, age, religion, education, and political party. ■ *In which factors do you see the strongest and weakest correlations, and how might you account for that?*

SOURCE: Center for Political Studies, University of Michigan, *2008 American National Election Study Guide to Public Opinion and Electoral Behavior.*

Liberals such as Senator Charles Schumer and House Speaker Nancy Pelosi frequently stress the need for an involved and affirmative government.

Liberals led in expanding civil rights in the 1960s and 1970s and favor affirmative action today. Some liberals favor reducing the great inequalities of wealth that make equality of opportunity impossible. Most favor a certain minimum level of income for all. Rather than placing a cap on wealth, they want to build a floor beneath the poor. In short, liberals seek to extend opportunities to all, regardless of how poor they may be. If necessary, they favor raising taxes to achieve these goals. In the recent health care reform debate, liberals favored a public option insurance plan providing something like Medicare for all citizens.

Criticisms of Liberalism   Critics say liberals rely too much on government, higher taxes, and bureaucracy to solve the nation's problems. They argue that liberals have forgotten that government has to be limited if it is to serve our best interests. Power tends to corrupt, and too much dependence on government can corrupt the spirit, undermine self-reliance, and make people forget those cherished personal freedoms and property rights our Republic was founded to secure and protect. In short, critics of modern liberalism contend that the welfare and regulatory state liberals advocate will ultimately destroy individual initiative, the entrepreneurial spirit, and the very engine of economic growth that might lead to true equality of economic opportunity.

Patrick Leahy (D-Vermont) has promoted liberal programs and legislation for many years.

Since the late 1960s, Republicans have made liberalism a villain while claiming that their own presidential candidates represent the mainstream. Bill Clinton was careful not to label his programs liberal, focusing on the need for economic growth, jobs, and a balanced budget. He insisted he was a "New Democrat." In 2000, Al Gore also positioned himself as a centrist, not a liberal, but George W. Bush claimed that Gore was an advocate of "tax and spend" big government. This same charge is often made against Democratic congressional candidates.

The three major Democratic candidates for the presidency in 2008 (Hillary Clinton, Barack Obama, and John Edwards) rarely used the word "liberal." Barack Obama emphasized the need for change rather than ideology, especially with the war in Iraq, the economy, the environment, and health care. As two journalists summarized the mindset of the voters in the 2008 election: "voters were eager, almost desperate, to 'turn the page,' as Barack Obama's call for fundamental change put it—and they needed to rally behind a candidate who offered the best hope of delivering on that promise."[41] John McCain's campaign tried to shift the focus to Obama as a "tax and spend liberal" or paint him as "among the most liberal U.S. Senators." These arguments did not carry much sway with voters who were not already committed to McCain. Obama's campaign countered by linking John McCain to Bush's deficits and to deregulation, which Obama claimed was a major factor in the economic problems the country faced.

Conservatism

Belief in private property rights and free enterprise are cardinal attributes of contemporary **conservatism.** In contrast to liberals, conservatives want to enhance individual liberty by keeping government small, especially the national government, although they support a strong national defense. Conservatives take a more pessimistic view of human nature than liberals do. They maintain that people need strong leadership, firm laws, and strict moral codes. The primary task of government is to ensure order. Conservatives also believe that people are the architects of their own fortune and must solve their own problems and create their own successes.

Traditional Conservatives   Conservatives are emphatically pro-business. They favor tax cuts and resist all but the minimum antitrust, trade, and environmental regulations on corporations. They believe that the sole functions of government should be to protect the nation from foreign enemies, preserve law and order, enforce private contracts, encourage economic growth by fostering competitive markets and free and fair trade, and promote family values. Traditional conservatives favor dispersing power throughout the political and social systems to avoid an overly powerful national government; they believe that the market, not the government, should provide services. These views were tested by the Bush Administration's advocacy of a massive government bailout of financial institutions in 2008, leading GOP candidate John McCain to call for new regulation.

Conservatives opposed the New Deal programs of the 1930s, the War on Poverty in the 1960s, many civil rights and affirmative action programs, and the Obama Administration's push for a larger government role in health care in 2009 and 2010. Families and private charities, they say, can and should take care of human needs and social and economic problems. Conservatives are more inclined to trust the private sector and dislike turning to governments, especially the national government, to solve social problems. Government social activism, they say, has been expensive and counterproductive. State and local government should address those social problems that need a government response. For example, conservatives have long held abortion to be a matter for state and local governments to decide, as well as education. President Bush's education reform created under the No Child Left Behind Act of 2002 encountered opposition from some of the most conservative and Republican states because they saw the policy as interfering with the ability of states and local school districts to manage education.

Conservatives, especially those in office, do, however, selectively advocate government activism, often expressing a desire for a more effective and efficient government. Early in the 2000 presidential campaign, George W. Bush said, "Too often, my party has confused the need for a limited government with a disdain for government itself." Love of

conservatism
A belief that limited government ensures order, competitive markets, and personal opportunity.

country, he said, "is undermined by sprawling, arrogant, aimless government. It is restored by focused and effective and energetic government."[42]

Social Conservatives Some conservatives focus less on economics and more on morality and lifestyle. Social conservatives favor strong governmental action to protect children from pornography and drugs. They want to overturn or repeal judicial rulings and laws that permit abortion, same-sex marriage, and affirmative action programs. This brand of conservatism—sometimes called the New Right— emerged in the 1980s. The New Right shares traditional conservatism's love of freedom and backs an aggressive effort to defend American interests abroad. It favors the return of organized prayer in public schools and opposes policies such as job quotas, busing, and tolerance of homosexuality.

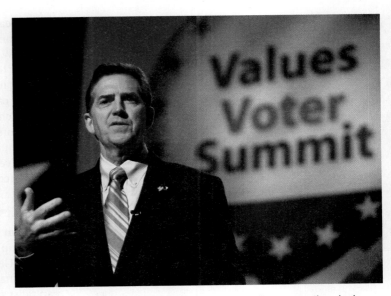

Senator Jim DeMint (R–South Carolina) is both socially conservative—he is opposed to same-sex marriage—and fiscally conservative—he opposes increases in federal spending and speaks against the federal bailout of banks and other corporations.

Accordingly, a defining characteristic of the New Right is a strong desire to impose *social controls*. Christian conservatives, who are disproportionately evangelical, want to preserve traditional values and protect the institution of the family. Groups promoting traditional marriage and committed parenting, like Focus on the Family, wax and wane in importance. In the 1980s and early 1990s, the Christian Coalition, founded by Reverend Pat Robertson, was an important political force that has become much less prominent in recent years.[43] Evidence of the decline of the coalition is the fact that the Republican Party created its own large-scale effort to mobilize conservative religious voters in the 2000 election and since.[44] In 2008, the connection between Christian conservatives and the GOP was further reinforced by the candidacy of former Arkansas governor and ordained Baptist minister Mike Huckabee, who emphasized his Christianity in his 2008 campaign.[45] In the 2008 Iowa caucuses, 60 percent of all Republican caucus goers were evangelicals who backed Huckabee 46 percent to Mitt Romney's 19 percent.[46]

Conservatives for decades have emphasized differences with liberals on social and moral matters. For example, in 2004, referendums in 13 states defining marriage as between a man and a woman forced moral values questions into the presidential election. Efforts by liberals to define the same-sex marriage issue as primarily about rights failed and all the referendums passed, providing Republicans with an issue that helped motivate conservatives to vote in key states such as Ohio.[47]

Criticisms of Conservatism Not everyone agreed with Ronald Reagan's statement that "government is the problem." Indeed, critics point out that conservatives themselves urge more government when it serves their needs—to regulate pornography and abortion, for example—but are opposed to government when it serves somebody else's. Conservatives may also have fewer objections to big government when individuals have a choice in determining how government will affect them. Vouchers for schools, choices in prescription drug benefit plans, and options to manage Social Security savings are examples of such choices.[48]

Their great faith in the market economy often puts conservatives at odds with labor unions and consumer activists and in close alliance with businesspeople, particularly large corporations. Hostility to regulation and a belief in competition lead conservatives to push for deregulation. This approach has not always had positive results, as the collapse of many savings and loan companies in the 1980s[49] and the 2008 financial crisis, brought about by troubled subprime mortgages and other risky lending practices, illustrates.[50] Conservatives counter that, overall, it is still best to rely on the free market.

The policy of lowering taxes is consistent with the conservative hostility to big government. Many conservatives embrace the idea that, if the rich pay fewer taxes, they will spend and invest more, and the benefits of this increased economic activity will "trickle down" to the poor. But Democrats argue that most of the growth in income and wealth that followed the Bush tax cuts was largely concentrated among the well-to-do and that reduced taxes and increased government spending, especially for defense, tripled the deficit during the 1980s, when conservatives were in control.[51] President George W. Bush pushed through tax cuts during his first term and pressed to make them permanent after his reelection in 2004. Republican nominee John McCain, who had initially opposed the Bush tax cuts, campaigned in 2008 on a platform to make them permanent. Liberals charge that some conservatives repeatedly fail to acknowledge and endorse policies that deal with racism and sexism. They cite conservative opposition to civil rights laws in the 1960s and more recently to affirmative action. They also blame conservatives for trying to weaken the enforcement of these laws by the executive branch and the courts.

Socialism and Communism

Socialism is an economic and governmental system based on public ownership of the means of production and exchange. The nineteenth-century German philosopher Karl Marx once described socialism as a transitional stage of society between capitalism and communism. In a capitalist system, the means of production and most property are privately owned; under **communism,** the state owns property in common for all the people, and a single political party that represents the working classes controls the government.

In communist countries such as Cuba and China, the Communist Party allows no opposition. Some countries, such as Sweden, have combined limited government ownership and operation of business with democracy. Most western European countries and Canada have various forms of socialized or government-run medical systems and sometimes telecommunications networks, while keeping most economic sectors private.

In one of the most dramatic transformations in recent times, Russia, its sister republics, and its former eastern European satellites abandoned communism in the early 1990s and have been attempting to establish free markets. These countries previously had a system of rigid state ownership and centralized government planning of the economy. The government arbitrarily set prices and production levels, which ultimately led to a very unstable economic system. But political and economic failure in the Soviet Union demoralized its communist leadership and weakened its hold over its satellite states. With the collapse of the Soviet Union in 1989, a tide of political and economic reform left communism intact in only a few countries, such as Cuba and North Korea. In addition, China and Vietnam, once also communist, now have growing private sectors and are thus not fully communist.

American socialists—of whom there are only a few prominent examples, including one United States senator, Vermont's Bernie Sanders—favor a greatly expanded role for the government but argue that such a system is compatible with democracy. They would nationalize certain industries, institute a public jobs program so that all who want to work could work, tax the wealthy much more heavily, and drastically cut defense spending.[52] Canada and most of the democracies of Western Europe are more influenced by socialist ideas than we are in the United States, but they remain, like the United States, largely market economies. Debate will continue about the proper role of government and what the market can do better than government can.[53]

Libertarianism

Libertarianism is a political ideology that cherishes individual liberty and insists on sharply limited government. It carries some overtones of anarchism, of the classical English liberalism of the nineteenth century (defined earlier in this chapter), and of a 1930s-style conservatism. The Libertarian Party has gained a small following among people who believe that both liberals and conservatives are inconsistent in their attitude toward the power of the national government.

Libertarians oppose nearly all government programs. They favor massive cuts in government spending and an end to the Federal Bureau of Investigation (FBI), the Central Intelligence Agency (CIA), the Internal Revenue Service (IRS), and most regulatory

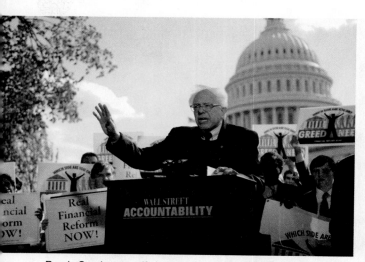

Bernie Sanders, a self-described socialist, represents Vermont in the U.S. Senate as an Independent.

socialism

An economic and governmental system based on public ownership of the means of production and exchange.

communism

A political, social and economic system in which land and capital are collectively owned and political power is exercised by the masses.

libertarianism

An ideology that cherishes individual liberty and insists on minimal government, promoting a free market economy, a noninterventionist foreign policy, and an absence of regulation in moral, economic, and social life.

Of the People

THE GLOBAL COMMUNITY

Free Market Economy

The Pew Global data provide an interesting contrast among countries in how the people express agreement with the statement: "Most people are better off in a free market economy, even though some people are rich and some are poor." The figure below plots the percent that completely or mostly agree or disagree.

For most of the world, nearly two-thirds completely or mostly agree "that most people are better off in a free market economy." In Nigeria, nearly four out of five hold this view. In Japan, however, under half of the respondents felt that a free market economy was preferable.

If we look at people who agree more strongly to the question, 37 percent of people in Nigeria and 40 percent of people in India completely agree that most people are better off in a free market economy, even though some people are rich and some are poor. In contrast, only 7 percent of people in Japan and 17 percent of those in Britain held this view. The U.S and World samples are between these two extremes with approximately one in four completely agreeing.

CRITICAL THINKING QUESTIONS

1. What elements of a political culture might help explain positive feelings toward a free market economy?

2. Conversely, what elements of a political culture explain a more cautious view of a free market?

3. Why might people in Nigeria or India more strongly agree that a free market economy is preferable, even in the presence of economic imbalances?

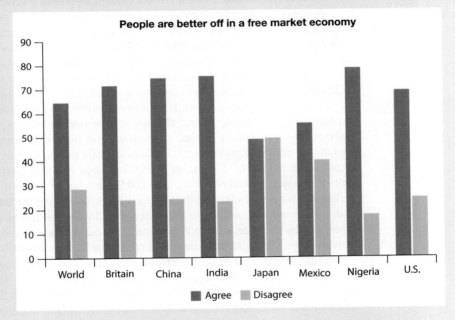

People are better off in a free market economy

commissions. They oppose American participation in the United Nations and favor armed forces that would defend the United States only if directly attacked. They oppose *all* government regulation, including, for example, mandatory seat-belt and helmet laws, in part because they believe individuals will all benefit more from an undistorted free market, and more generally because they embrace the attitude "live and let live." Unlike conservatives, libertarians would repeal laws that regulate personal morality, including abortion, pornography, prostitution, and illicit drugs.

A Libertarian Party candidate for president has been on the ballot in all 50 states in recent presidential elections, although the party has never obtained more than 1 percent of the vote, and in 2008, the party received less than one-half of 1 percent of the vote. The 2000 Libertarian platform called for immediate and complete removal of the federal government from education, energy, regulation, crime control, welfare, housing, transportation, health care, and agriculture; repeal of the income tax and all other direct taxes; decriminalization of drugs and pardons for prisoners convicted of nonviolent drug offenses; and withdrawal of overseas military forces. Libertarian positions are rarely timid; at the least, they prompt intriguing political debate.[54] In 2008, the Libertarian Party endorsed same-sex marriage, legalizing drugs, repealing the Patriot Act, withdrawing from

Former Republican Congressman Bob Barr accepts the 2008 Libertarian Party nomination with his wife, Jeri Barr, looking on.

Iraq, eliminating all gun control laws, repealing business regulations, and eliminating the Food and Drug Administration. Texas representative Ron Paul, an unsuccessful candidate for the 2008 Republican presidential nomination, had run as the Libertarian nominee for president in 1988, getting only 0.4 percent of the popular vote. His positions on several issues in 2008 embraced Libertarian ideals.[55] The competitive nature of the presidential campaign and the historic nature of the Obama candidacy meant minor parties were given even less attention in 2008 than in prior campaigns. Moreover, the centrality of the economic crisis pushed voters to find a candidate who could provide solutions and get things done. In such times, voters turn to established parties.

A Word of Caution

Political labels have different meanings across national boundaries as well as over time. To be a liberal in most European nations and Australia is to be on the right; to be a liberal in the United States and Canada is to be on the left. In recent elections, the term "liberal"—which had been popular while Franklin Roosevelt was president in the 1930s and 1940s—became "the L-word," a label most politicians sought to avoid. But liberalism is more than a label. On big questions—such as the role of government in the economy, in promoting equality of opportunity, and in regulating the behavior of individuals or businesses—real differences separate conservative and liberal groups. This does not mean, however, that people who are conservative in one area are necessarily conservative in another, or that all liberals always agree with each other.

Ideology both causes events and is affected by them. For example, World War II, which showed how government can work to defend freedom, increased support for the role of the national government. The Vietnam War had the opposite effect, producing disillusionment with government. The antigovernment sentiment in recent presidential elections is undoubtedly related to Vietnam, the Watergate scandal of the early 1970s, allegations of sexual and financial misconduct by political leaders, and the inadequate response to Hurricane Katrina in 2005. The surge in patriotism and sense of national unity in the war against terrorism after the September 11 terrorist attacks stands in sharp contrast to the national mood during the mid-1970s, during the final years of the Vietnam War. It reflected a view that government has an important role to play in responding to a crisis. But by the 2006 and 2008 elections, the country was increasingly opposed to the wars in Iraq and Afghanistan and looking for new leaders and different policies.

Unlike in 2000 and 2004, the 2008 election produced a winner with a large enough majority in the popular vote and electoral college to claim a mandate. Moreover, the Democrats began 2009 with expanded majorities in both houses of Congress. The extent to which the mandate was an ideological one will be debated. The major theme of the Obama campaign was change, and although he and his party provided some specifics as to what they wanted to change—for example, ending the war in Iraq, expanding health care coverage, and increasing educational opportunity—it was also the case that much of the rhetoric was couched in terms like "ending the failed Bush administration policies." Obama made clear that accomplishing the changes he proposes will require greater cooperation and bipartisanship. Obama also cautioned his supporters that the costs of dealing with the economic challenges the country faces will mean slowing the pace of change in other areas. Whether Obama can hold his coalition together when he must compromise will be a measure of his skill as a leader.

Political Ideology and the American People

LEARNING **OBJECTIVE**

4.3 Assess the importance of political ideology in light of competing ideas and the contemporary American context.

For some people, ideological controversy today centers on the role of the government in improving schools, encouraging a stronger work ethic, and stopping the flow of drugs into the country. For others, ideology focuses on whether to permit openly gay people into the military or sanction same-sex marriages and on the best ways to instill moral values, build character, and encourage cohesive and lasting families. Ideology has economic, social/lifestyle, environmental, civil rights/civil liberties, and foreign/defense policy dimensions. It is not surprising that some individuals are liberal or conservative in one dimension but not another.

By the People
MAKING A DIFFERENCE

Improving Literacy

In an extensive study released in 1993, between one-fifth and one-quarter of adult Americans were found to be illiterate, defined as being unable to "locate information in a text" or "make low-level inferences using printed material."* A follow-up study released in 2006 found no significant improvement in U.S. adult literacy.† Illiteracy, or the inability to use printed and written information effectively, is a significant problem for the illiterate individuals and for society as a whole. Most jobs require minimal literacy, as do daily activities like reading contracts or instructions on medications. Filling out governmental forms, including voter registration forms, and engaging in active citizenship in other ways is based on individuals being literate. Those not able to read often do not engage in active citizenship and exhibit a lack of confidence in dealing with other people and institutions.

You can make a difference in helping children and adults learn to read. Some college students have organized programs at their institutions to enhance literacy in their own communities. Baylor University, for example, has "Camp Success," which is a four-week language and literacy therapy camp for area children. Begun in 2003, the camp has had more than 500 children participate. Professor Michaela Ritter, who directs the camp, indicates that "most kids make from one to three years' progress" during the camp.‡

You do not have to find an organized program to make a difference in enhancing literacy. One-on-one reading with a child is something you can readily arrange in your local community. Most public schools are very eager for volunteers to read with struggling students, and local libraries often have such programs as well.

CRITICAL THINKING QUESTIONS

1. Does it surprise you that 20–25 percent of Americans are illiterate? Why or why not?

2. Why is literacy a condition of active citizenship?

3. Why do you think having a caring college student read with a younger person has such positive results?

---

* National Center for Education Statistics, *Adult Literacy in America* (April 2002), http://nces.ed.gov/pubs93/93275.pdf (accessed March 8, 2010).
† National Center for Education Statistics, *A First Look at the Literacy of America's Adults in the 21st Century* (2006), http://nces.ed.gov/NAAL/PDF/2006470.PDF (accessed March 8, 2010).
‡ http://www.wacotrib.com/news/content/news/stories/2009/07/03/07032009waccampsuccess.html

---

Despite the twists and turns of American politics, the distribution of ideology in the nation has been remarkably consistent (see Figure 4–2). Conservatives outnumber liberals, but the proportion of conservatives did not increase substantially with the decisive Republican presidential victories of the 1980s or the congressional victories of the 1990s.

Moreover, in the United States, most people are moderates or report not knowing whether they are liberal or conservative. In recent years, only 2–3 percent of the population saw themselves as extreme liberals, while extreme conservatives ranged from 2 to 4 percent

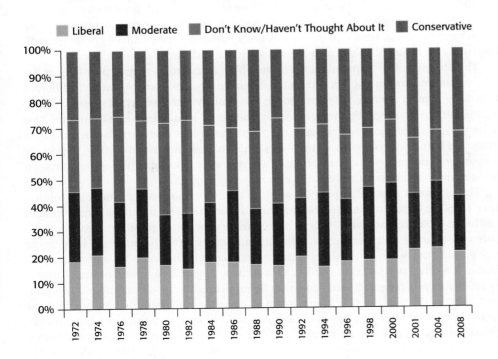

FIGURE 4–2 Ideology over Time.

■ *What factors might account for the stability in Americans' ideology over time?*

SOURCE: Center for Political Studies, University of Michigan, *2008 American National Election Study.*

FIGURE 4–3 **Distribution of Ideology in the United States.**

■ *How does the ideology of the American people compare to that of American politicians and pundits? In what ways might this difference matter?*

SOURCE: Center for Political Studies, University of Michigan, *2008 American National Election Study.*

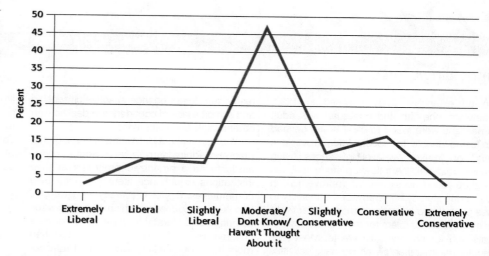

(see Figure 4–3). These percentages have changed little over time. Despite claims by ideological extremes in both parties of a move to the right or to the left, there are simply more voters in the middle who are moderate or do not have a preferred ideology.[56]

Both major parties target moderate or centrist voters, as reflected in the stands of the candidates on key issues, including their efforts to minimize ideological battles at the conventions. In 2008, John McCain won the GOP nomination despite opposition from some visible conservative leaders. At the same time, candidates from both parties also work hard to activate more ideological voters, sometimes called the "base" vote.

For those with a liberal or conservative preference, ideology provides a lens through which to view candidates and public policies. It helps simplify the complexities of politics, policies, personalities, and programs. However, most voters are selective or even inconsistent in their political views. A voter may support increased spending for defense but vote for the party that is for reducing defense spending because he or she has always voted for that party or prefers its stand on the environment. Or a person may favor tax cuts and a balanced budget while opposing substantial reductions in government programs.

The degree to which people have ideologically consistent attitudes and opinions varies but is often relatively low. Much of the time, people look at political issues individually and do not evaluate parties or candidates systematically or according to an ideological litmus test. Indeed, many citizens favor specific policies at variance with their broader political philosophy. This problem becomes more complex as government gets involved in more and more policy areas. Hence, many people, not surprisingly, have difficulty finding candidates who reflect their ideological preferences across a wide range of issues.

The absence of widespread and solidified liberal and conservative positions in the United States makes for politics and policy-making processes that are markedly different from those in most nations. Policy making in this country is characterized more by ad hoc coalitions than by fixed alignments that pit one set of ideologies against another. Our politics are marked more by moderation, pragmatism, and accommodation than by a prolonged battle between competing philosophies of government. Elsewhere, especially in countries such as Sweden or Germany, where a strong Socialist, Green, or Christian Democratic party exists, things are different.

This does not mean that policies or ideas are not important in American politics. Since 1995, for instance, there has been a shift to more partisan and ideological voting in the House of Representatives. Part of the explanation is that Republicans have become more conservative and Democrats more liberal. Conservative Republicans have made large gains in the South, while the remaining Democrats in the South have become more liberal;[57] in other parts of the country, such as New England and parts of the Midwest, liberal Democrats have replaced moderate Republicans. Perhaps even more important, congressional districts are now being drawn to make more of them safe for one party or the other, so Republican members of Congress tend to appeal to the more conservative wing of their party, whereas Democratic members of Congress tend to appeal to the more liberal wing of their party. We discuss these developments in greater detail in Chapter 11.

Ideologies have consequences. These sharp cleavages in political thinking stir opposing interest groups into action. A wide variety of groups promote their views of what is politically desirable. It is also these differences in ideological perspectives that reinforce party loyalties and divide us at election time. Policy fights in Congress, between Congress and the White House, and during judicial confirmation hearings also have their roots in our uneasily coexisting ideological values.

Our hard-earned rights and liberties are never entirely safeguarded; they are fragile and shaped by the political, economic, and social climate of the day. In later chapters, we examine the interest groups and political parties that are battling to advance their values and compete in the American political culture. But before turning to those topics, we examine the social and economic diversity of the American political landscape in Chapter 5 and see why agreement on shared democratic values is all the more remarkable.

CHAPTER **SUMMARY**

4.1 Identify the most important elements of and sources for the American political culture.

The American political culture consists of a widely held set of fundamental political values and accepted processes and institutions that help us manage conflict and resolve problems. American adults share a widespread commitment to classical liberalism, which embraces the importance of individual liberty, equality, individualism, power to the people, private property, limited government, nationalism, optimism, idealism, the democratic consensus, and justice and the rule of law. People respect the Constitution, the Bill of Rights, the two-party system, and the right to elect officials on the basis of majority rule. We learn American political culture in the family, schools, religious and civic organizations, and through the mass media and political activities. The American dream persists as an ideal, as American residents perceive this to be a land of opportunity and upward mobility.

4.2 Compare and contrast political ideologies and evaluate the critiques of each ideology.

The two most important ideologies in American politics are liberalism, a belief that government can and should help achieve justice and equality of opportunity, and conservatism, a belief in limited government to ensure order, competitive markets, and personal opportunity while relying on free markets and individual initiative to solve social and economic problems. Critics of liberalism contend that liberals, by favoring government solutions to problems, limit the capacity of markets to function well and create large and unmanageable bureaucracies. Critics of conservatism contend that some problems require government to become part of the solution and that too much faith in the market to solve the problem is misplaced. Socialism, which favors public ownership of the means of production, and libertarianism, which puts a premium on individual liberty and limited government, attract only modest followings in the United States.

4.3 Assess the importance of political ideology in light of competing ideas and the contemporary American context.

Few in the United States are extremists. There are more conservatives than liberals, and ideology has come to be more important in the nomination battles in both parties and Congress. Because a large fraction of the public is moderate or has not thought much about ideology, politicians can expand their coalition of voters and supporters by being pragmatic. Because nonideological persons are less likely to vote, they are not as important in elections as the more committed ideologues. However, in close elections, these pragmatic centrist voters can be critical.

CHAPTER **SELF-TEST**

4.1 Identify the most important elements of and sources for the American political culture.

1. Identify and define four shared political values.
2. For each of the five elements of the rule of law, describe a way government could violate that element or principle.
3. Which of the following "has taken over some functions the family used to perform" in terms of political socialization?
   a. Schools
   b. Churches
   c. The Internet
   d. The mass media
4. Which of the following statements best describes public opinion on the role of government after the Great Depression and New Deal?
   a. Government should focus on defense issues
   b. Government should only regulate moral issues
   c. Government should work to ensure social justice
   d. Government should not become involved in the private lives of its citizens

5. How widespread and how solid are political parties in the United States? With this in mind, how important are values like moderation, pragmatism, and accommodation in policy making?
6. What role do educational opportunity, economic wealth, and religious freedom play in achieving the American Dream?

4.2 Compare and contrast political ideologies and evaluate the critiques of each ideology.

7. Identify each belief as either conservative or liberal:
   a. Belief that government can bring about equality of opportunity
   b. Belief that some government intervention in the economy is necessary to remedy the defects of capitalism
   c. Pessimistic view of human nature
   d. Preference for greater environmental protection
   e. Belief in keeping government small, especially the national government
   f. Preference for business
   g. Preference for individual choice in moral issues such as same-sex marriage and abortion
   h. Belief that the primary task of government is to ensure order

8. Identify which of the following is a major tenet of libertarianism:
   a. Public ownership of business
   b. Opposition to all government regulation
   c. Government provision of universal health care
   d. Use of government regulation only for moral issues such as abortion
9. In a short essay, define three major criticisms of both conservatism and liberalism. Analyze these critiques and determine which criticism you find more persuasive.
10. In a short essay, compare and contrast the major beliefs of liberalism and conservatism. Consider each ideology's approach to moral, economic, and national defense issues. How are they alike? How are they different? Which do you think is more effective in today's world?

4.3 Assess the importance of political ideology in light of competing ideas and the contemporary American context.

11. In recent years, approximately how many people in the United States have identified themselves as "extreme" conservatives or liberals?
    a. 6%
    b. 23%
    c. 65%
    d. 80%

Answers to selected questions: 3. d. 4. c. 7. a. liberal, b. liberal, c. conservative, d. liberal, e. conservative, f. conservative, g. liberal, h. conservative 8. b. 11. a.

mypoliscilab EXERCISES

Apply what you learned in this chapter on MyPoliSciLab.

Read on mypoliscilab.com

eText: Chapter 4

Study and Review on mypoliscilab.com

Pre-Test
Post-Test
Chapter Exam
Flashcards

Watch on mypoliscilab.com

Video: Facebook Privacy Concerns
Video: The President Addresses School Children

Explore on mypoliscilab.com

Simulation: What Are American Civic Values?
Timeline: Major Technological Innovations that Have Changed the Political Landscape
Visual Literacy: Who Are Liberals and Conservatives? What's the Difference?

KEY TERMS

political culture, p. 106
suffrage, p. 106
deliberation, p.106
social capital, p.106
natural rights, p. 107
democratic consensus, p. 108

majority rule, p. 108
popular sovereignty, p. 109
nationalism, p.110
patriotism, p.110
American dream, p.112
capitalism, p.112

political ideology, p.116
liberalism, p.116
conservatism, p.118
socialism, p.120
communism, p.120
libertarianism, p.120

ADDITIONAL **RESOURCES**

FURTHER READING

E. J. DIONNE JR., *They Only Look Dead: Why Progressives Will Dominate the Next Political Era* (Simon & Schuster, 1996).

BRIAN DOHERTY, *Radicals for Capitalism: A Freewheeling History of the Modern American Libertarian Movement* (New York: Public Affairs, 2007).

JEAN BETHKE ELSHTAIN, *Democracy on Trial* (Basic Books, 1995).

E. H. H. GREEN, *Ideologies of Conservatism: Conservative Political Ideas in the Twentieth Century* (Oxford University Press, 2004).

AMY GUTMANN AND **DENNIS THOMPSON,** *Democracy and Disagreement: Why Moral Conflict Cannot Be Avoided in Politics, and What Should Be Done About It* (Harvard University Press, 1996).

CAROL A. HORTON, *Race and the Making of American Liberalism* (Oxford University Press, 2005).

GEORGE KLOSKO, *Democratic Procedures and Liberal Consensus* (Oxford University Press, 2000).

IRVING KRISTOL, *Neoconservatism: The Autobiography of an Idea* (Free Press, 1995).

HERBERT MCCLOSKY AND **JOHN ZALLER,** *The American Ethos: Public Attitudes Toward Capitalism and Democracy* (Harvard University Press, 1984).

MICHAEL NEWMAN, *Socialism: A Very Short Introduction* (Oxford University Press, 2005).

MARCUS G. RASKIN, *Liberalism: The Genius of American Ideals* (Rowman & Littlefield, 2004).

JOHN RENSENBRINK, *Against All Odds: The Green Transformation of American Politics* (Leopold Press, 1999).

GARRY WILLS, *A Necessary Evil: A History of American Distrust of Government* (Simon & Schuster, 1999).

WEB SITES

www.conginst.org A Web site that provides up-to-date survey data on the American political culture.

www.loc.gov The Library of Congress Web site; provides access to more than 70 million historical and contemporary U.S. documents.

www.stateline.org A University of Richmond/Pew Charitable Trust site dedicated to providing citizens with information on major policy issues.

www.tocqueville.org/ Includes biographical and other references to Alexis de Tocqueville and his writings.

www.politicalcompass.org A Web site that provides a typology of political opinion and ideology.

The American Political Landscape

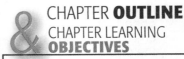
In recent elections, both parties have developed the ability to target their political communications to individual voters based on computer models they have developed from historic patterns and large sample-size polls that assess attitudes toward issues and candidates. This process is sometimes called data mining. Ohio Republican party chair Robert Bennett said, "We probably have more information about the average voter than they care for us to have."[1] The Republicans took the lead in this "microtargeting" activity in 2002 and 2004 with a massive voter file housed at the Republican National Committee named the "Voter Vault." Individuals who had been registered Republicans or who fit a certain profile in their age, gender, religion, and race were targeted for particular communications. New York U.S. Senator Charles Schumer, who headed the Democratic Senatorial Campaign Committee at the time, said of the GOP use of data in voter mobilization efforts: "In 2002 and 2004, the morning of Election Day, we thought we were going to win and we didn't. And the reason we didn't win the seats we thought we were going to win was because they had a much better get-out-the-vote operation."[2]

By 2008, the Democratic allies had heavily invested in their own voter files using a for-profit corporation called Catalist. Catalist lists among its clients Planned Parenthood, labor unions, Sierra Club, Rock the Vote, and other Democratic-leaning groups, and its files include more than 220 million names. Those doing the data mining and modeling can combine gender and age with consumer preferences—like the kind of cars a person owns or what types of magazines people read—to predict the message to which that voter will be most receptive. Among the variables in the Voter Vault and Catalist that are most important in predictive models are age, income, education, gender, religion, race, sexual orientation, partisanship, and ideology. In this chapter, we examine the political importance of several of these characteristics of individuals.

Do these social and economic differences still matter in American politics? The answer is clearly yes. In the United States, we celebrate our diversity and our immigrant past and proudly recite the words of Emma Lazarus, inscribed at the base of the Statue of Liberty: "Give me your tired, your poor, your huddled masses yearning to breathe free." Albert Einstein, who himself immigrated to the United States from Germany in the 1930s, once said that most people are incapable of expressing opinions that differ much from the prejudices of their social upbringing.[3] This **ethnocentrism**—selective perception based on our background, attitudes, and biases—is not uncommon. People often assume that others share their economic opportunities, social attitudes, sense of civic responsibility, and self-confidence, so in this chapter, we consider how our social environment explains, or at least shapes, our opinions and prejudices. In this chapter and Chapter 8, we will also discuss why some individuals have more political self-confidence than others, a characteristic called **efficacy.**

Specifically, this chapter explores the effects of regional or state identity on political perspectives; how differences in race, ethnicity, gender, family structure, religion, wealth and income, occupation, and social class influence opinions and voting choices; and the relationship among age, education, and political participation. Because people's personal characteristics or attributes are important to political interest groups (Chapter 6), we examine attitudes and behavior before discussing political parties (Chapter 7); public opinion, participation, and voting (Chapter 8); and campaigns and elections (Chapter 9). This chapter lays the foundation of how different aspects of who we are as people influence how we behave politically.

ethnocentrism
Belief in the superiority of one's nation or ethnic group.

efficacy
A sense of self-confidence in being able to produce a desired effect.

A Land of Diversity

LEARNING **OBJECTIVE**

5.1 Characterize the opportunities and challenges posed by the diversity of the American population and by the nation's geography.

Most nations consist of groups of people who have lived together for centuries and who speak the same language, embrace the same religious beliefs, and share a common history. Most Japanese citizens are Japanese in the fullest sense of the word, and this sense of shared identity is generally as strong in Sweden, Saudi Arabia, and China. The United States is different. We have attracted the poor and oppressed, the adventurous, and the talented from all around the world, and we have been more open to accepting strangers than many other nations.

In the pages that follow, we examine a variety of factors that shape individuals' political orientation and views on such issues as health care and economic policy. What becomes clear through this discussion is that, in a nation as geographically large and ethnically diverse as the United States, many characteristics differentiate us from each other. They can also unite us. In the late 1990s, for example, Orrin Hatch (R-Utah) and former Senator Ted Kennedy (D-Mass.), ideologically opposed on many policy issues, worked together to expand spending on health care for children.

Several elements of our diversity have political significance. Many retain an identity with the land of their ancestors, even after three or four generations. Families, churches, and other close-knit ethnic groups foster these ties. **Political socialization** is the process by which parents and others teach children about political values, beliefs, and attitudes. This teaching occurs in the home, in school, on the playground, and in the neighborhood. In addition to fostering group identities, political socialization also strongly influences how individuals see politics and which political party they prefer. Where we live and who we are in terms of age, education, religion, and occupation affect how we vote. Social scientists use the term **demography** to describe the study of such population characteristics. Persons in certain demographic categories tend to vote alike and to share certain **political predispositions** that can predict political behavior, despite individual differences within socioeconomic and demographic categories.

When social and economic differences reinforce each other, social scientists call them **reinforcing cleavages;** they can make political conflict more intense and society more polarized. In Italy, for example, the tendency of parts of the industrialized north to lean toward the Socialist or Communist Party, and of the poorer and more agrarian south to be politically conservative and Catholic, reinforces the divide between north and south that has existed for centuries.

Nations can also have **cross-cutting cleavages,** when, instead of reinforcing each other, differences pull people in different directions. To illustrate, if all the rich people in a nation belong to one religion and the poor to another, the nation would have reinforcing cleavages that would intensify political conflict between the groups. But if there are both rich and poor in all religions, and if people sometimes vote on the basis of their religion and sometimes on the basis of their wealth, the divisions would be cross-cutting. American diversity has generally been more of the cross-cutting than the reinforcing type. As a result, people have multiple allegiances that lessen political conflict. Winning in the American electoral system requires building a broad coalition that reinforces cross-cutting cleavages.

Geography and National Identity

The United States is a geographically large and historically isolated country. In the 1830s, French commentator Alexis de Tocqueville studied its early development and observed that the country had no major political or economic powers on its borders "and consequently no great wars, financial crises, invasions, or conquests to fear."[4] Geographic isolation from the major powers of the world during our government's formative period helps explain American politics.[5] The Atlantic Ocean served as a barrier to foreign meddling, giving us time to establish our political tradition and develop our economy. The western frontier provided room to grow and avoid some of the social and political tensions Europe experienced. American reluctance to become involved in foreign wars and controversies still emerges in debates over foreign policy.

political socialization
The process by which we develop our political attitudes, values, and beliefs.

demography
The study of the characteristics of populations.

political predisposition
A characteristic of individuals that is predictive of political behavior.

reinforcing cleavages
Divisions within society that reinforce one another, making groups more homogeneous or similar.

cross-cutting cleavages
Divisions within society that cut across demographic categories to produce groups that are more heterogeneous or different.

Of the People

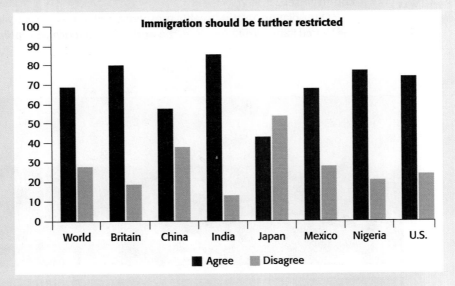

THE GLOBAL COMMUNITY

Restricting Immigration

Immigration is an issue in many countries, not only in the United States. The Pew Global Attitudes Project asked individuals: "Please tell me whether you completely agree, mostly agree, mostly disagree, or completely disagree with this statement: We should restrict and control entry of people into our country more than we do now." In the figure below, we have combined those who completely and mostly agree into one category and those who mostly and completely disagree into another.

In the worldwide sample, more than two-thirds of the people agree that immigration should be more restricted than it is today. The country that departs the most from this view is Japan, where more people disagree (53 percent) than agree (44 percent) with making immigration more restrictive. One possible explanation for this is that, as a matter of policy, Japan has historically had low levels of immigration. In China, a country that has also had very little immigration, a greater percentage of respondents favor further restrictions than in Japan (58 percent), but that percentage is significantly lower than in other countries in our sample of nations.

Nearly three-quarters of Americans favor further restrictions on immigration. But people in Nigeria, Britain, and India are even more uniformly of this view. A striking 86 percent of people in India favor more restrictions on immigration. This attitude may be a result of the perceived problems in India arising from immigrants from Bangladesh. Most illegal immigrants in the United States today come from Mexico, and yet in Mexico, 69 percent favor further restrictions on immigration. This may be explained in part by the presence of illegal immigrants in Mexico from other Central and South American countries.

CRITICAL THINKING QUESTIONS

1. Why are people outside of Japan generally inclined to want to further restrict immigration?

2. Why would so many people in Mexico favor further restrictions on immigration in their country?

3. On many questions we examine, as many as 10 percent or more do not know their views. That is not the case with immigration, where no more than 4 percent report not knowing their views. Why is this the case?

Immigration should be further restricted

Chart showing "Agree" and "Disagree" percentages by country: World, Britain, China, India, Japan, Mexico, Nigeria, U.S.

Legend: ■ Agree ■ Disagree

Remarkably few foreign enemies have successfully struck within U.S. continental borders: most notably, England in the War of 1812, terrorists in the World Trade Center bombing in 1993, and the attacks of September 11, 2001.[6] By contrast, Poland has been invaded repeatedly and was partitioned by Austria, Prussia, and Russia in the eighteenth century and by Nazi Germany and the Soviet Union in 1939. The difference is explained largely by location: Poland was surrounded by great powers. Had the United States been closer to Europe and not isolated by two oceans, it might have been overrun and its Constitution and institutions repeatedly changed or eliminated to suit the invaders. The presence of powerful and aggressive neighbors can impede the development of democracy in relatively weak nations.

Although geographic location may have previously provided a substantial buffer from foreign attack, technological advances make that less the case today. The ability of terrorists to harm the United States and other countries, especially if they are willing to die along with their victims, means that national defense and homeland security need to be rethought. The two oceans that protected the United States for so long cannot deter a small band of determined terrorists. Our newly recognized vulnerability to terrorist attacks on our own soil has changed the context in which we debate the balance between liberty and security and has led some to advocate the idea of preemptive war.

Size also confers an advantage. The landmass of the United States exceeds all but that of Russia and Canada. In contrast, India has a population more than three and one-half times that of the United States on a landmass one-third the size. Geographic space gave the expanding population of the United States room to spread out. This defused some of the political conflicts arising from religion, social class, and national origin because groups could isolate themselves from one another. Moreover, plentiful and accessible land helped foster the perspective that the United States had a **manifest destiny** to be a continental nation reaching from the Atlantic to the Pacific Ocean. Early settlers used this notion to justify taking land from Native Americans, Canadians, and Mexicans, especially the huge territory acquired after victory in the Mexican-American War.

The United States is also a land of abundant natural resources. We have rich farmland, which not only feeds our population but also makes us the largest exporter of food in the world.[7] We are rich in such natural resources as coal, iron, uranium, oil, and precious metals. All of these resources enhance economic growth, provide jobs, and stabilize government. As de Tocqueville observed, "Yet what takes place in the United States is much less attributable to the institutions of the country than to the country itself."[8]

Our isolation, relative wealth, prosperity, and sense of destiny have fostered a view that the United States is different from the world. This *American exceptionalism*, a term first used

manifest destiny
A notion held by nineteenth-century Americans that the United States was destined to rule the continent, from the Atlantic to the Pacific.

The diversity of its natural resources, including farmland, forests, waterways, and coal mines, is one of the advantages of the United States' large landmass. ■ *To what specific aspects of America's national identity do these images speak?*

by de Tocqueville in 1831, has historically been defined as "the perception that the United States differs qualitatively from other developed nations because of its unique origins, national credo, historical evolution, and distinctive political and religious institutions."[9] The term has long been used to describe not only the distinctive elements of the United States but the sense that the United States is a just and moral country. Exceptionalism can thus convey a sense of moral superiority or power that is not well received outside the United States, especially when the United States is seen to be acting in ways that other nations find objectionable or hypocritical.

Geography also helps explain our diversity. Parts of the United States are wonderfully suited to agriculture, others to mining or ranching, and still others to shipping and manufacturing. These differences produce diverse regional economic concerns, which in turn influence politics. For instance, a person from the agricultural heartland may see foreign trade differently from the way an automobile worker in Detroit sees it.

Where We Live

Unlike the case in many other countries, geography in the United States does *not* define an ethnic or religious division. All the Serbians in the United States do not live in one place, nor do all French-speaking Catholics and Hispanic immigrants reside in others. Sectional, or regional, differences in the United States are primarily geographic, not ethnic or religious.

LEARNING **OBJECTIVE**
5.2 Relate differences in political culture to where people live.

Regional Differences

The most distinct section of the United States remains the South, although its differences from other parts of the country are diminishing. From the beginning of the Republic, the agricultural South differed from the North, where commerce and later manufacturing were more significant. But the most important difference between the regions was the institution of slavery. Northern opposition to slavery, which grew increasingly intense by the 1850s, reinforced sectional economic interests. The 11 Confederate states, by deciding to secede from the Union, reinforced a common political identity. After the Civil War, Reconstruction and the problems of race relations reinforced regional differences.

The South is becoming less distinct from the rest of the United States. In addition to undergoing tremendous economic change, the large number of people moving to the South from other regions has diminished the sense of regional identity. The civil rights revolution of the 1960s eliminated legal and social barriers that prevented African Americans from voting, ended legal segregation, opened up new educational opportunities, and helped integrate the South into the national economy. African Americans still lag behind Southern white people in voter registration, but the gap is now no wider in the South than elsewhere and is explained more by differences in education than by race.[10] In economic terms, the South still falls below the rest of the country in per capita income and education but much less so than 50 years ago. The traditional religious and moral conservatism of the South, however, remains notable.

The Civil War made the Democratic party the party of the South, and the Republican party (the party of Lincoln), the party of the North. The Democratic "solid South" remained a fixture of American politics for more than a century. However, political alignment shifted as African Americans have been enfranchised and become overwhelmingly Democrats, and many white Southerners have become Republicans. As one respected observer of the region comments, "The decline of the South in the Democratic party would fundamentally reorder the American party system and realign the electorate."[11]

A Confederate flag flyes outside South Carolina's memorial for Confederate soldiers ■ *Are there still significant regional differences that distinguish the U.S. South from other parts of the country?*

Sun Belt

The region of the United States in the South and Southwest that has seen population growth relative to the rest of the country and which, because of its climate, has attracted retirees.

In 1992 and 1996, even with two southerners on the ticket—Bill Clinton and Al Gore—Democrats won only 4 of the 11 former Confederate states. In 2000 and 2004, Republican George W. Bush carried all 11 southern states, including Al Gore's home state of Tennessee in 2000 and vice presidential candidate John Edwards's home state of North Carolina in 2004. In 2008, Barack Obama made some inroads by winning in Florida, Virginia, and North Carolina, but in both North Carolina and Florida the margins were close.

Although Republican success in the South came first at the presidential level, gains in Congress and state legislatures have followed. The Republican share of state legislators in the House and Senate rose from 5 percent and 4 percent in 1960 to 48 percent and 50 percent, respectively, in 2009. In 2010, Republicans controlled 8 of the 11 governorships in the former Confederate states. In the state legislatures, remnants of the old Democratic "solid South" remain, but Republicans have made major inroads, and politics in the region are becoming more predictably Republican (see Figure 5–1).

Another sectional division is the **Sun Belt**—the 11 former Confederate states plus New Mexico, Arizona, Nevada, and the southern half of California. Sun Belt states are growing much more rapidly than the rest of the country. Arizona, California, Florida, Georgia, Nevada, North Carolina, and Texas gained 12 seats in the House of Representatives after the 2000 census.[12] Projected reapportionment after the 2010 census has Texas gaining four seats, with three other southern states and four western states gaining seats.[13] Moreover, population growth in the South and West is occurring in different age groups. In the South, growth is largest among those over the age of 65; in the West, younger persons provide the growth. Sun Belt states have also experienced greater economic growth as industries have headed south and southwest, where land and labor are cheaper and more abundant (see Figure 5–2). The shift of seats to the Sun Belt has helped Republicans, as the states picking up additional seats have tended to be more Republican. Other sectional groupings of states include the "rust belt" of states in the Midwest where industrial production and jobs have left the region, leaving rusting factories vacant. States in the rust belt include Ohio, Pennsylvania, Michigan, and parts of Indiana and New York. The interior western states are another section with economic and political similarities. Much of the land in the West is owned by the federal government, which provides tension between state and local governments and the federal government.

FIGURE 5–1 Republican Share of State Legislators in the Former Confederate States.

SOURCE: CQ Voting and Election Database; Todd Edwards, Council of State Governments, Southern Office, personal communication, December 22, 2000; Doris Smith, Council of State Governments, Southern Office, personal communication, November 10, 2004; and National Conference of State Legislatures, State Vote 2008, http://www.ncsl.org/statevote/StateVote2008.htm (accessed November 10, 2008).

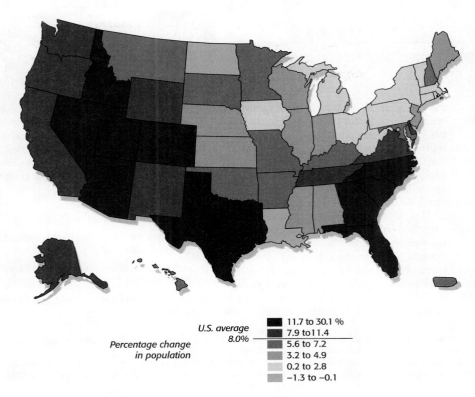

FIGURE 5–2 **Percentage Change in Resident Population, 2000–2008.**

■ *Which states saw the greatest shifts in population, and how might you account for some of those changes?*

SOURCE: U.S. Census Bureau, *Statistical Abstract of the United States: 2010* (U.S. Government Printing Office, 2009), p. 19.

Percentage change in population

U.S. average 8.0%

■	11.7 to 30.1 %
■	7.9 to 11.4
■	5.6 to 7.2
■	3.2 to 4.9
■	0.2 to 2.8
■	−1.3 to −0.1

State and Local Identity

States have distinctive political cultures that affect public opinion and policies. Individuals often have a sense of identification with their state.[14] Part of the reason for enduring state identities is that we elect members of Congress and the president at the state level. States such as Iowa and New Hampshire play important roles in narrowing the field of presidential candidates seeking their party's nomination. Differences in state laws relating to driving, drinking, gambling, and taxes reinforce the relevance of state identity. Colleges and universities may have the same effect while reinforcing competition between different states.

California also stands out in American politics today, if only because nearly one of eight U.S. citizens lives in the state.[15] In economic and political importance, California is in a league by itself; its 53 members of the House of Representatives exceed the number of representatives from the smallest 20 states combined. California's 55 electoral votes provide a large advantage for any presidential candidate who carries the state.[16] The state's reputation for distinctive politics was reinforced in 2003 when voters replaced Governor Gray Davis with former body builder and movie star Arnold Schwarzenegger in the first recall of a governor since North Dakota voters recalled Governor Lynn G. Frazier in 1921.[17]

Urban and Rural Populations

Where we live can be categorized as one of three types of areas: **urban,** which is defined by the U.S. Census Bureau as "densely settled territory," also often the central part of a city; **suburban,** which is typically less densely settled and surrounds the central city; and **rural,** which is more sparsely populated areas and where farmers often reside. Four of five people in the United States now live in urban areas.[18] During the early twentieth century, the movement of population was from rural areas to central cities, which we call *urbanization,* but the movement since the 1950s has been from the central cities to their suburbs. Today, the most urban state is California (more than 94 percent of its population lives in cities or suburbs).

urban
 A densely settled territory that is often the central part of a city of metropolitan area.

suburban
 An area that typically surrounds the central city, is often residential, and is not as densely populated.

rural
Sparsely populated territory and small towns, often associated with farming.

For the People

GOVERNMENT'S GREATEST ENDEAVORS

The Interstate Highway System

Beginning with early postal roads, highways have been a way to integrate the commerce and people of the states. The postal roads helped integrate the economy of the new nation, and they grew rapidly. In 1792, there were 5,642 miles of postal roads; by 1828, there were 114,546.* These roads were crucial in spreading news across the colonies.

Today, most people take for granted the Interstate Highway System, but in fact, it was a major initiative of government. Planning for the Interstate Highway System began in the late 1930s. Commissions in the period recommended a system of 33,900 miles in a National Interregional Highway System with an additional 5,000 miles of road for auxiliary urban routes. The name of the system changed to the Interstate Highway, and initial funding came in 1952. The source of funding for the massive project came from gas and motor vehicle taxes. The system was expanded in 1968 to nearly 47,000 miles.

The Interstate Highway System profoundly affected the American economy. It lowered freight costs but, at the same time, advantaged interstate trucking over railroads. It fostered the growth of towns and businesses along the route of the highways. It reduced travel time and fostered travel safety. Critics of freeways, including the interstate highways, see them as encouraging urban sprawl and longer commutes, which in turn add to air pollution. In addition to fostering commerce between states, the interstate highways, along with more leisure time, helped expand the scope of family vacations.†

CRITICAL THINKING QUESTIONS

1. How has the Interstate Highway System affected your life?

2. How should government pay for interstate highways?

3. Do interstate highways encourage motor vehicle use?

---

* Robert G. Cullen, "Early U.S. Postal Routes and the Communications Infrastructure," *American Association of State Highway and Transportation Officials*, April 26, 2009, http://www.transportation.org/sites/aashto/docs/Cullen-2009-04-26.pdf (accessed March 8, 2010).
† Wendell Cox and Jean Love, "40 Years of the U.S. Interstate Highway System: An Analysis," *American Highway Users Alliance*, June 1996, http://www.public-purpose.com/freeway1.htm#econ (accessed March 8, 2010); see also Susan Rugh, *Are We There Yet? The Golden Age of American Family Vacations* (University Press of Kansas, 2008).

Vermont is the least urban, with only 38 percent living in cities or suburbs.[19] Regionally, the West and Northeast are the most urban; the South and Midwest, the most rural.

People move from cities to the suburbs for many reasons—better housing, new transportation systems that make it easier to get to work, a lower cost of living, the desire for cleaner air and safer streets. Another reason is "white flight," the movement of white people away from the central cities so that their children can avoid being bused for racial balance and attend generally better schools. White, middle-class migration to the suburbs has made American cities increasingly poor, African American, and Democratic.

These proportions are nearly reversed for the suburbs, where more than half of all white American citizens reside. Slightly less than 40 percent of African Americans live in

Although four of five citizens live in urban areas, since approximately the 1950s, there has been a steady flow outward to the suburbs, particularly among the middle and upper classes.

TABLE
5–1 Cities with Populations of 100,000 or More That Are at Least 50 Percent African American, 2008

City	Population 2008	Percent African American 2008
Detroit, Mich.	808,398	83.0
Memphis, Tenn.	643,329	62.6
Baltimore, Md.	639,343	62.6
Washington, D.C.	588,373	54.4
Atlanta, Ga.	445,709	55.8
Newark, N.J.	262,313	53.6
New Orleans, La.	270,245	60.5
Birmingham, Ala.	209,639	74.1
Richmond, Va.	200,158	51.5
Jackson, Miss.	175,731	76.4
Savannah, Ga.	127,840	57.0

■ *How might having a high percentage of minority residents affect the kinds of public policies enacted in a city?*

SOURCE: U.S. Census Bureau, *American Community Survey: 2008.*

the suburbs, up from one-fifth in 1980.[20] In large cities such as Washington, D.C., Detroit, Baltimore, and Atlanta, the city population is now more than 50 percent African American (see Table 5–1). Hispanics constitute roughly 80 percent of the population of El Paso, Texas, and Santa Ana, California, and 65 percent of the population of Miami, Florida.[21]

Who We Are

Sectional distinctions, which separate populations by geography and regions, less prominently distinguish us from one another in the United States today than they did a century or even a half-century ago. Today, we are more likely to define ourselves by a number of other characteristics, each of which may influence how we vote or think about candidates, issues, or policies.

Race and Ethnicity

Racial and ethnic differences have always had political significance. **Race** groups human beings with distinctive physical characteristics determined by genetic inheritance. Some scholars define it as more culturally determined than genetic.[22] **Ethnicity** is a social division based on national origin, religion, and language, often within the same race, and includes a sense of attachment to that group. Examples of ethnic groups with enduring relevance to American politics include Italian Americans, Irish Americans, Polish Americans, and Korean Americans, although most race and ethnicity issues in the United States today focus primarily on African Americans, Asian Americans, Native Americans, and Hispanics.

There are more than 39 million African Americans in the United States, nearly 13 percent of the population. Asian Americans constitute 4.4 percent of the population, and Native Americans, 1 percent.[23] Most American Hispanics classify themselves as white, although Hispanics can be of any race. At 46.9 million, Hispanics are the fastest-growing U.S. ethnic group, constituting nearly 15 percent of the population.[24] Because of differences in immigration and birthrates, non-Hispanic whites will decrease to approximately 50 percent of the population by 2050.[25]

Native Americans The original inhabitants of what became the United States have played an important role in its history and continue to be important to the politics of states like South Dakota, New Mexico, and Oklahoma. More than half the names of states and hundreds of the names of cities, rivers, and mountains in the United States are Native

LEARNING **OBJECTIVE**
5.3 Analyze how demographic factors—including race and ethnicity, religion, gender, family structures, education, income, class, and age—affect American politics.

race
A grouping of human beings with distinctive characteristics determined by genetic inheritance.

ethnicity
A social division based on national origin, religion, language, and often race.

American. During much of our history, the policy of the U.S. government was to remove Native Americans from their tribal lands and relocate them to reservations. In recent U.S. Senate elections in South Dakota, the Native American vote has been important.[26] Ben Nighthorse Campbell from Colorado, who served in the U.S. Senate from 1993 to 2005, is a Native American. Representative Tom Cole from Oklahoma is the only registered Native American currently serving in the United States Congress, and he was first elected in 2002.[27]

One-third of Native Americans and Alaskan Natives have incomes below the federal poverty level. This percent is higher than those for African Americans and Hispanics.[28] The relative poverty of many Native Americans and Alaskan Natives has been a persistent problem that illustrates that these racial and ethnic distinctions have political consequences.

African Americans   Most immigrants chose to come to this country in search of freedom and opportunity. In contrast, most African Americans came against their will, as slaves. Although the Emancipation Proclamation and Thirteenth Amendment ended slavery in the 1860s, racial divisions still affect American politics. Until 1900, more than 90 percent of all African Americans lived in the South; a century later, that figure was 55 percent.[29] Many African Americans left the South hoping to improve their lives by settling in the large cities of the Northeast, Midwest, and West. But what many of them found was urban poverty. More recently, African Americans have been returning to the South, especially its urban areas.

Most African Americans are more vulnerable economically than most whites. African American median family income is close to $40,000, compared to about $64,000 for whites.[30] Approximately 22 percent of African American families live below the poverty level, compared to about 8 percent of white families.[31] However, African Americans have been doing better in recent years; 40 percent of African American households earned more than $50,000 in 2007 (compared to 62 percent of white households).[32] However, some African Americans, like Miami Heat basketball player LeBron James and syndicated talk-show host and corporate chief executive Oprah Winfrey, have risen to the top of their professions in terms of earnings.

Income is intimately related to education. Most African Americans and Hispanics have fewer resources to fall back on in hard times, and they are less likely to have the savings to help a child pay for college. The growing numbers of middle-class African Americans are role models for the young of all races, but their still comparatively small number is a reminder that most African Americans remain behind in an economy that relies more and more on education and job skills. Among recent high school graduates, 64 percent of white Americans go on to college, but only 58 percent of African Americans do.[33] Approximately 30 percent of whites graduate from college, whereas only about 20 percent of African Americans do.[34]

Finally, the African American population is much younger than the white population; the median age for whites in 2008 was 38.2 years, compared to 31.4 for African Americans.[35] The combination of a younger African American population, a lower level of education, and their concentration in economically depressed urban areas has resulted in a much higher unemployment rate for young African Americans. Unemployment can in turn contribute to social problems such as crime, drug and alcohol abuse, and family dissolution.

African Americans had little political power until after World War II. Owing their freedom from slavery to the "party of Lincoln," most African Americans initially identified with the Republicans, but this loyalty started to change in the 1930s and 1940s under President Franklin D. Roosevelt, who insisted on equal treatment for African Americans in his New Deal programs.[36] After World War II, African Americans came to see the Democrats as the party of civil rights. The 1964 Republican platform position on civil rights espoused *states' rights*—at the time, the creed of southern segregationists—in what appeared to be an effort to win the support of southern white voters. Virtually all African Americans voted for Lyndon Johnson in 1964, and in presidential elections between 1984 and 2008, their Democratic vote averaged more than 86 percent.[37] In 2008, with an African American running for president, 95 percent of blacks voted for Obama and their share of total votes rose from 11 percent in 2004 to 13 percent in 2008.[38]

African Americans have become much more important politically as their voting turnout has increased, particularly in certain regions. African Americans constitute only

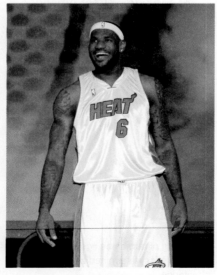

LeBron James, the two-time reigning NBA Most Valuable Player, earned nearly $15 million in salary last year, and earns millions more through lucrative endorsements.

Of the People

A More Diverse Population

The United States has become much more diverse throughout the past 60 years and will become even more so during the next half-century. In 1950, nearly nine of every ten persons in the United States were white, and Hispanics were not a category the U.S. Census Bureau reported. By 2008, only fewer than four in five persons in the United States were white, but that fraction included Hispanic whites. Non-Hispanic whites are now approximately two-thirds of the U.S. population. Groups projected to have the most growth between 2008 and 2050 are Asians, Pacific Islanders, and Hispanics. In the aggregate, about one in every four persons in the United States in 2025 will be Asian, Pacific Islander, or Hispanic. Although regional differences matter less to American politics than they once did, the emergence of "majority minority" communities and legislative districts, in which a majority of the population are from racial minorities, ensures that race will have a greater influence in some areas of the country than others.

The changing face of U.S. politics is increasingly diverse. Despite the surge in Hispanic population, there has not been a similar surge in political participation or representation. Researchers cite many reasons for this, including redistricting, low rates of citizenship and motivations for voting, and a lack of common party commitment.

Changing Racial Composition of the U.S. Polity, 1950–2050

	1950	1990	2008	2025	2050
White	89.4%	83.9%	79.8	77.3%	72.1%
Non-Hispanic White	—	75.7	65.6	59.5	50.1
African American	10.0	12.2	12.8	13.7	14.6
Native American, Inuit, Aleut	0.2	0.8	1.0	1.0	1.1
Asian and Pacific Islander	0.2	3.0	4.6	6.5	9.3
Hispanic	—	8.9	15.4	18.9	24.4

NOTE: Percentages do not equal 100 because Hispanics can be of any race. Figures for 2025 and 2050 are projections. Categories from the 1950 census are different from those used in the last several decades. For example, the 1950 census did not provide a classification for Hispanic, Native Americans were classified as "Indian," and Asians were separated into Japanese and Chinese.

SOURCE: 1950 figures from "U.S. Census Bureau" *Census of Population: 1950, Volume II Part I* (U.S. Government Printing Office, 1950), p. 106. 1990 figures from "U.S. Census Bureau" *Statistical Abstract of the United States: 2001* (U.S. Government Printing Office, 2001), pp. 16–17. 2008 figures from "U.S. Census Bureau" *Statistical Abstract of the United States: 2010* (U.S. Government Printing Office, 2010), p. 13. All other figures from "U.S. Census Bureau" *Projections of the Population by Sex, Race, and Hispanic Origin for the United States: 2010 to 2050," National Population Projections Released 2008 (Based on Census 2000)*, August 13, 2008, http://www.census.gov/population/www/projections/summarytables.html.

CRITICAL THINKING QUESTIONS

1. What does it say about our conceptions of race and ethnicity that Hispanic was not a category on the 1950 census?

2. How will U.S. politics be different in 2050 when 50.1 percent of the population will be non-Hispanic whites?

0.7 percent of the population in Montana and 0.9 percent in Idaho, but 37.2 percent in Mississippi, 30 percent in Georgia, and 28.5 percent in South Carolina.[39] Southern senators and representatives can no longer afford to ignore the African American vote.[40] Evidence of growing African American political power is the dramatic increase in the number of African American state legislators, which rose from 168 in 1970 to 623 in 2008.[41] Georgia has 55 African American state legislators, the most of any state. Alabama, Maryland, Mississippi, New York, and South Carolina all have more than 30.[42]

The dramatic success of President Obama in the 2008 election was due in part to his ability to secure large majorities of African American voters. But he also did well in states with few black voters such as Iowa, Utah, and Maine. Race was raised indirectly in the South Carolina primary by former President Bill Clinton,[43] and later by Clinton supporter Geraldine Ferraro, who said, "If Obama was a white man, he would not be in this position." Obama also confronted the issue of racism directly in a major speech after media reports of his pastor Reverend Jeremiah Wright's inflammatory statements generated widespread attention.

Even though Obama and his campaign did not make race a major theme of their campaign, pollsters and pundits speculated about what effect his race would have on voters. Exit polls found Obama did better among white voters than John Kerry had done in 2004 and substantially better among Latinos and African Americans. Among white voters age 18–29, Obama received 54 percent of the vote.[44] Obama got two-thirds of the Latino vote nationwide and, as noted, 95 percent of the African-American vote. In his victory speech on election night delivered to more than 200,000 people in Chicago's Grant Park, Obama recalled the events of the last century through the eyes of a 106-year-old voter,

Ken Salazar, elected to the U.S. Senate from Colorado in 2004, is the fourth U.S. senator of Latino descent in American history. Salazar replaced Ben Nighthorse Campbell, a Native American and Republican, who did not seek reelection. Salazar previously served two terms as Colorado attorney general.

Ann Nixon Cooper, who "was there for the buses in Montgomery, the hoses in Birmingham, a bridge in Selma, and a preacher from Atlanta who told a people that We Shall Overcome."

Hispanics   Hispanic Americans are not a monolithic group, and although they share a common linguistic heritage in Spanish, they often differ from one another depending on which country they or their forebears emigrated from. Cuban Americans, for instance, tend to be Republicans, whereas Mexican Americans and Puerto Ricans living on the mainland are disproportionately Democrats.[45] Hispanics are politically important in a growing number of states. Nearly two-thirds of Cuban Americans live in Florida, especially in greater Miami. Mainland Puerto Ricans are concentrated in and around New York City; many Mexican Americans live in the Southwest and California. More than 13 million Hispanics live in California.[46]

There are differences among Hispanics of Mexican, Puerto Rican, and Cuban descent in partisanship, ideology, and rates of political participation, but they share widespread support for a liberal domestic agenda, including increased spending on health care, crime and drug control, education, the environment, child services, and bilingual education.[47] But because Hispanics are not politically homogeneous, they are not a united voting bloc.

The many noncitizen Hispanics and the relative youth of the Hispanic population also diminish the group's political power. For example, 14.1 million foreign-born Hispanics are not citizens,[48] and of the estimated 11.6 million unauthorized immigrants, three-fifths are from Mexico.[49] This group cannot vote, nor can those under age 18, who make up a greater percentage of the Hispanic population than in other ethnic groups. The median age of Hispanics in 2008 was 27.7 years, more than ten years younger than whites (38.2 years), and younger than blacks (31.4 years).[50] Language problems also reduce Hispanic citizens' voter registration and turnout. The redrawing of legislative district boundaries after the 2000 census, despite their huge increase in population, disappointed Hispanic groups.[51] This has spurred lawsuits as Hispanic activists seek to eliminate gerrymandering (the drawing of district boundaries to benefit a group or party).

Both major parties are aggressively cultivating Hispanic candidates. Several Hispanics have been cabinet members. Mel Martinez resigned as secretary of the Department of Housing and Urban Development (HUD) to run successfully for the U.S. Senate from Florida in 2004. Ken Salazar, a Hispanic Democrat, was also elected to the Senate in 2004 from Colorado, and he became secretary of the Interior in the Obama administration. Bob Menendez, a Democrat, was appointed to the Senate from New Jersey and then elected in a contested race in 2006. He served as head of the Democratic Senatorial Campaign Committee in the 2009–2010 election cycle.

Asian Americans   The U.S. Census Bureau classifies Asian Americans together for statistical purposes, but like Hispanics, they show significant differences in culture, language, and political experience in the United States. Asian Americans include, among others, persons of Chinese, Japanese, Indian, Korean, Vietnamese, Filipino, and Thai origin, as well as persons from the Pacific Islands. As with Hispanics, there are differences among these subgroups.[52] For example, Japanese Americans were more likely to register as Democrats than Korean Americans or other Asian Americans. Japanese Americans also were somewhat more likely to vote than other Asian-ethnic groups.[53]

Many Asian Americans have done well economically and educationally. Their income is well above the national median, and 52.6 percent have graduated from college, compared to 29.8 percent of whites and 19.6 percent of African Americans.[54] Asian Americans are becoming more politically important and more visible in politics. Gary Locke, the first Chinese American governor of a state in the continental United States, served two terms in Washington. Elaine Chao, who emigrated from China at age 8, served as Secretary of Labor in the Bush administration, and Steven Chu, also of Chinese descent, is serving as Secretary of Energy in the Obama administration.

Chinese American and Nobel Prize laureate Steven Chu is the Secretary of Energy in the Obama Administration. He is the second Chinese American to serve in a Presidential Cabinet.

YOU WILL
DECIDE
Who Should the Census Count, and How Should They Be Counted?

As established in the Constitution, every ten years, the government conducts a count of all persons in the United States. For the 2000 census, the U.S. Census Bureau proposed using random sampling rather than attempting to count all households. The proposed sample approach would have contacted 90 percent of the households in a census tract consisting of roughly 1,700 individuals. The bureau would then check the accuracy of the sample by surveying 750,000 households throughout the nation and adjusting the final total accordingly. The sampling approach responded to complaints about the flawed 1990 census, which cost $2.6 billion (a 400 percent increase over the cost of the 1980 census) and failed to account for 10 million people while double-counting 6 million others, according to a study by the National Academy of Sciences.

In addition, although the census has always counted all individuals, citizens and noncitizens alike, it has not always asked about citizenship. Some members of Congress introduced legislation to require that citizenship be a question on the 2010 census and that illegal immigrants be excluded from the census count.

What do you think? As we assess the success of the 2010 census and look to future censuses, who should the census count, and how should they be counted? What arguments would you make for and against the use of sampling or questions about citizenship?

THINKING IT THROUGH

Both questions are really less about *how* to count as *whom* to count. The proposed sampling method would have produced a more accurate count of inner-city Hispanics and African Americans—the most difficult to count. Hispanics and African Americans are more likely to be homeless or living in poverty in urban areas. Using a sampling method would arrive at a more accurate count of these groups and would likely have resulted in a greater representation for Hispanics and African Americans in state legislatures and the U.S. House of Representatives. A more complete count of minorities could also mean that the Republican party would lose a few seats in the House to Democrats, which is one reason Republicans generally opposed the sampling approach while Democrats favored it.

The constitutionality of sampling is disputed, as the Constitution calls for an "actual enumeration" of the people. Democrats are quick to point out that under three presidents— Jimmy Carter, George H. W. Bush, and Bill Clinton—the Justice Department concluded that sampling is legal. Sampling as a method of determining population for congressional apportionment is not allowed under current law;* however, methods similar to sampling to fill in data missing from the "actual enumeration" has been upheld in the Supreme Court.†

Citizenship has been a question asked in the past in the census (1820–1960) but noncitizens have always been counted. Slaves counted as three-fifths of a person in the Constitution for apportionment purposes and the Fourteenth Amendment refers to the "whole number of persons" being counted without regards to citizenship. But counting illegal immigrants runs counter to our notions of political representation and is understandably unpopular. If illegal immigrants were excluded it could take away seats from states like California, Arizona, and Texas.

Critical Thinking Questions

1. Why do you think sampling may result in higher counts of minorities?

2. Do you think it is possible to decide questions about representation without considering partisan politics?

3. Should illegal immigrants and persons under age 18 be counted for purposes of apportioning seats in Congress or for counts of persons for distribution of federal monies to state and local governments?

---

* *Department of Commerce et al.* v. *U.S. House of Representatives et al.*, 119 S.Ct. 765 (1999).
† *Utah* v. *Evans*, 122 S.Ct. 2191 (2002).

The Ties of Ethnicity   Except for Native Americans and the descendants of slaves, all U.S. citizens have immigrant ancestors who chose to come to the American continent. There have been two large waves of new immigrants to the United States. The first, 17.3 million people, came between 1900 and 1924, primarily from Southern and Eastern Europe. The second large wave is now under way. From 1991 to 2008, the United States has seen nearly 17.4 million immigrants, primarily from the Caribbean, Mexico, and Asian countries such as the Philippines, Vietnam, and China. Of this group, an estimated 11.6 million came into the country illegally.[55]

The foreign-born population in the United States increased from 14 million in 1980 to more than 38.1 million in 2007. Today, there are more foreign-born people in the United States than ever before,[56] although at 11.7 percent, they represent a smaller proportion of the population than the 14.8 percent that was foreign born in 1890.[57]

Large numbers of immigrants can pose challenges to any political and social system. Immigrants are often a source of social conflict as they compete with more established groups for jobs, rights, political power, and influence.

Religion

In many parts of the world, religious differences, especially when combined with disputes over territory or sovereignty, are a source of violence. The conflict between Israelis and Palestinians has motivated suicide bombers who kill Israeli civilians along with themselves, and Israelis who attack Palestinian settlements and leaders. The war between India and Pakistan over Kashmir is largely a religious battle between Muslims and Hindus, as are the conflicts between Muslims and Christians in Indonesia and Nigeria. Afghanistan, Lebanon, Northern Ireland, Sri Lanka, and Sudan have also experienced intense religious conflicts in recent years. The Shi'ite–Sunni conflict among different branches of Islam threatens the stability of the new government in Iraq.

Jews have often been the target of religious discrimination and persecution (anti-Semitism), which reached its greatest intensity in the Holocaust of the 1940s, during which the Nazis murdered an estimated 6 million Jews.[58] The United States has not been immune from such hatred, despite its principle of religious freedom. In 1838, Governor Lilburn W. Boggs of Missouri issued an extermination order that made legal the killing of any Mormons in the state.[59]

fundamentalists
Conservative Christians who as a group have become more active in politics in the last two decades and were especially influential in the 2000 and 2004 presidential elections.

Our government is founded on the premise that religious liberty flourishes when there is no predominant or official faith, which is why the framers of the Constitution did not sanction a national church. In fact, James Madison wrote in *The Federalist*, No. 51, "In a free government the security for civil rights must be the same as that for religious rights. It consists in the one case in the multiplicity of interests, and in the other in the multiplicity of sects" (see the Appendix).

The absence of an official church does not mean that religion is unimportant in American politics; indeed, there were established churches in individual states in this country until the 1830s. Some observers contend that "the root of American political and social values…is the distinctive Puritanism of the early New England settlers."[60] Politicians frequently refer to God in their speeches or demonstrate their piety in other ways.

At one time, people thought voters' religious preferences could prevent a Catholic from being elected president. John F. Kennedy's election in 1960 resolved the issue of whether a Catholic would put aside religious teachings if they conflicted with constitutional obligations. He said, "I am not the Catholic candidate for President. I am the Democratic Party's candidate for President who happens also to be Catholic. I do not speak for my church on public matters, and the church does not speak for me."[61] Nevertheless, a candidate's religion may still become an issue today if the candidate's religious convictions on sensitive issues such as abortion threaten to conflict with public obligations.

Religion has also been an important catalyst for political change. The Catholic Church helped overthrow communism in parts of Eastern Europe. Black churches provided many of the leaders in the American civil rights movement. As Taylor Branch explains in his history of the civil rights movement, the Black church "served not only as a place of worship but also as a bulletin board to a people who owned no organs of communication, a credit union to those without banks, and even a kind of people's court."[62] African American ministers, such as the Reverend Martin Luther King Jr., became leaders of the civil rights movement; others, such as Jesse Jackson and, more recently, Al Sharpton, have run for national office. Hence, religion can be not only a source of personal values but also a foundation for political activity.

More recently, political activity among fundamentalist Christians has increased. Led by ministers such as Pat Robertson and Focus on the Family leader James Dobson, evangelicals, sometimes called **fundamentalists,** are an important force in

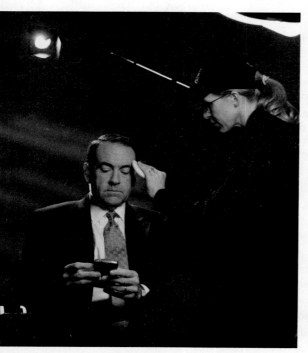

Former governor of Arkansas Mike Huckabee appealed to conservative Christians by keeping religion central to his campaign for president in 2008. The Southern Baptist minister now hosts the Fox News talk show *Huckabee*, and there are speculations that he's gearing up for a 2012 presidential run.

the Republican party and in some local governments.[63] Their agenda includes the return of school prayer, the outlawing of abortion, restrictions on homosexuals, opposition to gun control, and opposition to the teaching of evolution and sex education in public schools.

Many American adults take their religious beliefs seriously, more than do citizens of other democracies.[64] Thirty-seven percent attend houses of worship at least once a week; 16 percent, once or twice a month; and 18 percent more, at least several times a year.[65] Young Americans, ages 18–29, are the most likely of any age cohort *not* to claim a religious preference, with about one in four people in this category.[66] Religion, like ethnicity, is a *shared identity*. People identify themselves as Baptist, Catholic, Jewish, Buddhist, or no religion at all. Sometimes religious attendance or nonattendance, rather than belonging to a particular religion or denomination, determines attitudes toward issues. "Among both Catholics and Protestants, opposition to abortion increases with frequency of church attendance."[67]

The United States houses a tremendous variety of religious denominations. Approximately half the people in the United States describe themselves as Protestant (see Figure 5–3). The largest Protestant denomination is Baptist, followed by Methodists, Lutherans, Presbyterians, Pentecostals, and Episcopalians. Because Protestants are divided among so many different churches, Catholics have the largest single membership in the United States, constituting slightly more than a quarter of the population.[68] Jews represent less than 2 percent of the population.[69] Muslims number more than 1.3 million, which is approximately one-half of 1 percent of the U.S. population.[70]

Religion is important in American politics in part because people of particular religions are concentrated in a few states. Catholics number more than half the population of Rhode Island.[71] Baptists represent 16 percent of the American population; however, they account for roughly a third of the population of Mississippi and Alabama.[72] Mormons represent less than 2 percent of the American population but three-fifths of the population of Utah.[73] The state of New York has the highest percentage of Jews with 8.5 percent; the New York City metro area is 10.7 percent Jewish.[74]

In recent presidential elections, most Protestants voted Republican, whereas most Catholics and Jews voted Democratic.[75] In 2008, McCain got 54 percent of the Protestant vote, but Obama did better among Protestants than either Gore in 2000 or Kerry in 2004. Obama received a majority of the Catholic vote.[76] The perception among many Catholics and Jews that the Democratic party is more open to them helps explain the strength of their Democratic identification. For at least several decades, Democrats won the loyalty of many Catholics by their willingness to nominate Al Smith for the presidency in 1928 and John Kennedy in 1960. Jewish voters' long-standing identification with the Democratic party may have been reinforced by Al Gore's selection of Joseph Lieberman to be his running mate in 2000.

Religious groups vary in their rates of political participation. In recent elections, Jews have the highest rate of reported voter turnout, more than 90 percent in 2000 and 2004, whereas those who claim no religious affiliation have the lowest, an average of roughly 60 percent in 2000, 2004, and 2008.[77] In 2008, even with strong efforts by the McCain campaign to court Jewish voters, Obama received 78 percent of the Jewish vote.[78]

Gender

For most of U.S. history, politics and government were men's business. Women first gained the right to vote primarily in the western territories, beginning with Wyoming in 1869 and Utah in 1870, and then in Colorado and Idaho before 1900.[79] The right was not extended nationally to women until 1920 with passage of the Nineteenth Amendment. The fears of some opponents of *women's suffrage* (the right to vote)—that women would form their own party and vote largely for women or fundamentally alter our political system—have not been realized.

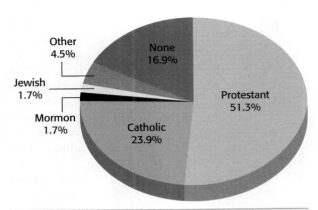

FIGURE 5–3 Religious Groups in the United States. Three-fourths of Americans describe themselves as Christian. ■ *In what areas of public policy do we see this playing a role? How important should religion be as a factor in making political decisions?*

SOURCE: U.S. Religious Landscape Survey, Pew Forum on Religion & Public Life, http://religions.pewforum.org. Copyright 2008 Pew Research Center.

FIGURE 5–4 Gender and the Vote for President.

■ *What were some of the issues raised in the 2008 election that may have led women to vote disproportionately democratic?*

SOURCE: 2008 CNN Exit Polls, http://www.cnn.com/ ELECTION/2008/results/polls/ (accessed November 5, 2008).

gender gap
The difference between the political opinions or political behavior of men and of women.

For a half-century after gaining the right to vote, American women voted at a lower rate than women in other Western democracies.[80] In 2008, as in the prior three presidential elections, slightly more women than men voted in the presidential elections, and there is no significant difference between the genders in rates of voting in midterm elections.[81] Because women outnumber men in the population, there are more potential female than male voters. Women have chosen to work within the existing political parties and do not overwhelmingly support female candidates, especially if they must cross party lines to do so.[82] Polls found a majority of women saying Sarah Palin was not qualified to be president, and men more likely to support Palin.[83]

The number of women in Congress reached new highs in the 1990s. At the beginning of 2010, there were six female governors, 17 women serving in the Senate, and 76 women in the House. The proportion of women serving in the House of Representatives is approximately the same as in the Senate: about 17 percent. In contrast, some state legislative chambers like those in Colorado, Vermont, and New Hampshire are nearly 40 percent female. The number of female officeholders is rising in part because women are increasingly running in contests in which there is no incumbent.[84]

Is there a **gender gap,** or a persistent difference between men and women in voting and in attitudes, on important issues? Women have typically divided their vote between the two major political parties. However, in recent elections, they have been more likely than men to vote for Democratic presidential candidates (see Figure 5–4). In 2000, Al Gore's share of the vote among women was 12 percent higher than among men.[85] In 2004, women preferred Kerry to Bush by 51 percent to 48 percent.[86] The gender gap was even wider in 2008, with women voting for Obama at 56 percent and McCain at 43 percent.[87] Men also gave Obama more votes than McCain, with 49 percent of men voting for Obama and 48 percent for McCain.

The women's movement in American politics seeks equal opportunity, education, jobs, skills, and respect in what has long been a male-dominated system.[88] Women are more likely than men to oppose violence in any form—the death penalty, new weapons systems, or the possession of handguns. Women, as a group, are more compassionate than men in that they are more likely to favor government that provides health insurance and family services. They also identify work and family issues such as day care, maternity leave, and equal treatment in the workplace as important.[89] Other gender issues, some of them focal points in recent elections, include reproductive rights and restrictions on pornography, gun control, and sexual harassment.[90]

There are serious income inequalities between men and women. Nearly twice as many women than men have an annual income of less than $15,000, and nearly three times as many men as women make more than $75,000 a year.[91] Because an increasing number of women today are the sole breadwinners for their families, the implications of this low income level are significant. Women earn on average less than men for the same work. Even among college graduates aged 25 to 34, women earn an average of 75 cents for every dollar earned by men of the same age and education level.[92] After controlling for characteristics such as job experience, education, occupation, and other measures of productivity, a U.S. Census Bureau study shows that wage discrimination between the genders is 77 cents on every dollar.[93] As age increases, the earnings gap widens. Women have reached parity with men in attending law schools, but only approximately 19 percent of partners in law firms are women.[94] In business schools, women constitute less than a third of entering classes,[95] and among the largest 100 companies in the United States, women make up only 17 percent of the boards of directors.[96]

Unemployment in the economic recession of 2008–2010 affected more men than women. Four out of the five jobs lost in the recession were jobs held by men in such industries as manufacturing and construction.[97] The result of this unequal impact of the recession is that for the first time the number of women working could surpass men, though this may be a temporary change as the recession ends and men again find jobs.[98]

Sexual Orientation

The modern movement for expanded rights for gays and lesbians traces its roots to 1969, when New York City police raided the Stonewall Inn, a bar in Greenwich Village, and a riot ensued.[99] Since then, gays and lesbians have become more active and visible in pushing for legal rights and protections.

The precise number of homosexuals in the United States is unclear. Estimates range from 2 to 10 percent of the U.S. population.[100] Whatever its overall size, the gay and lesbian community has become important politically in several cities, notably San Francisco. Its lobbying power has increased noticeably in many states as well, and being gay or lesbian is no longer a barrier to election in many places.

The political agenda for gay and lesbian advocacy groups includes fighting discrimination, such as laws barring same-sex marriage and the military's "don't ask, don't tell" policy. On some fronts, the groups have been successful. Many local governments and private employers now grant health care and other benefits for same-sex domestic partners. Several states have legalized same-sex marriage, including Massachusetts, Connecticut, New Hampshire, Vermont, and Iowa, as well as the District of Columbia, and a number of others provide for some types of civil unions for same-sex couples. Cities, counties, and states have passed antidiscrimination statutes protecting people from discrimination in housing and employment on the basis of sexual orientation. Groups like the Human Rights Campaign advocate eliminating restrictions based on sexual orientation. Hate crimes against gays and lesbians have led some to propose including sexual orientation in federal hate crimes legislation.[101] We discuss the movement to secure rights for gays and lesbians in Chapter 16.

Annise Parker became the mayor of Houston, Texas, on January 2, 2010. She is the first openly gay mayor of a city with more than 1 million people, as well as Houston's second female mayor.

Family Structure

Throughout the past half-century, the typical American family (mother and father married, with children in the home) has become anything but typical. The traditional family had several key characteristics: It married early, had children, and stayed together through thick and thin.

Marriage itself used to be essential to be a family at all. From 1996 to 2002, however, the number of American adults who live with someone of the opposite sex without being married increased by 50 percent.[102] In 2007, 5.5 percent of households had unmarried partners.[103] Living together raises public policy questions, such as whether the live-in partner is eligible for employment benefits and welfare payments.

Marriage also used to occur earlier in life, but people now marry later: The average age for first marriage for men is 28; for women it is 26.[104] Yet marrying later has not reduced divorce rates.

Children were also essential to the traditional families, but birthrates have been falling for decades. Birthrates in the United States dropped in the late 1960s and 1970s. In the early 1960s, a woman statistically averaged approximately 3.5 children. By 2009, that number was at 2.1 children, barely meeting the 2.1 needed to replace the population. In other words, if the current trend continues, the native-born population will actually decrease over time.[105] Some other countries have even lower average fertility rates per woman: Japan 1.21, Italy 1.3, Spain 1.3, and Sweden 1.7.[106]

Finally, the traditional family stayed together, but the divorce rate has nearly doubled since 1950.[107] Today, it is estimated that about half of all marriages will end in divorce.[108] Divorce is one reason why the number of households headed by women has risen. Attitudes about the role of women in marriage and the family have also changed. In 1972, one-third of American adults thought a woman belonged in the home and should not work outside it, but in 1998, only one-sixth felt this way.[109]

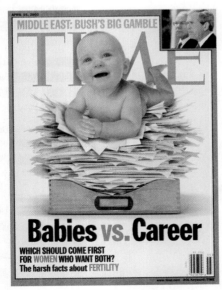

The risk of having children later in life has recently been the subject of cover stories in newsmagazines. ■ *In what areas might the political views of individuals from traditional versus nontraditional family structures differ?*

Education

Differences in education affect not only economic well-being but political participation and involvement as well. Thomas Jefferson wrote of education, "Enlighten the people generally, and tyranny and oppressions of body and mind will vanish like evil spirits at the dawn of day."[110] Most American students are educated in public schools. Nine of every ten students in kindergarten through high school attend public schools, and more than three of four college students are in public institutions.[111]

In 1992, for the first time, the number of American college graduates surpassed the number of persons who did not graduate from high school.[112] Slightly more than half of all U.S. adults have not gone to college, although many college students assume that nearly everyone goes to college. Approximately 30 percent of whites are college graduates, compared to 20 percent of African Americans and 13 percent of Hispanics; roughly 19 percent of African Americans and 41 percent of all Hispanics left school before completing high school (see Figure 5–5).[113]

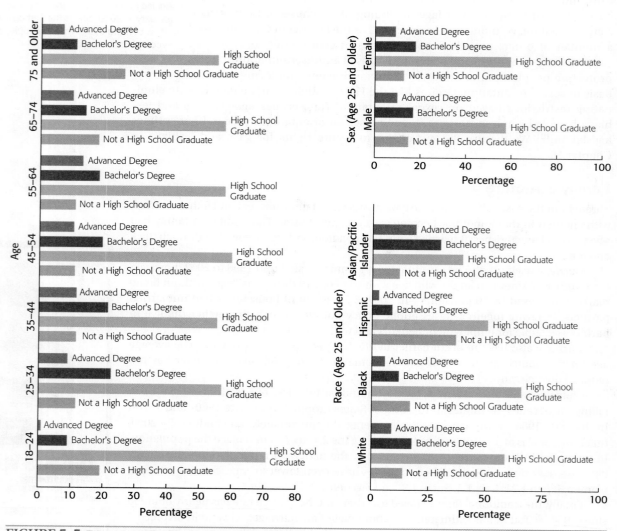

FIGURE 5–5 **Educational Attainment in the United States.**

■ *Based on the percentages of Americans who are high schools graduates in each age bracket, what assumptions might you make about how the educational system and culture in America has changed?*

SOURCE: U.S. Census Bureau, *Educational Attainment in the United States: 2009*, www.census.gov/population/www/socdemo/education/cps2009.html.

Education is one of the most important variables in predicting political participation, confidence in dealing with government, and awareness of issues. Education is also related to the acquisition of democratic values. People who have failed to learn the prevailing norms of American society are far more likely to express opposition to democratic and capitalist ideals than those who are well educated and politically knowledgeable.[114]

Wealth and Income

The United States is a wealthy nation. Indeed, to some knowledgeable observers, "the most striking thing about the United States has been its phenomenal wealth."[115] Most American citizens lead comfortable lives. They eat and live well and have first-class medical care. But the unequal distribution of wealth and income results in political divisions and conflicts.

Wealth, the total value of someone's possessions, is more concentrated than income (annual earnings). The wealthiest families hold most of the property and other forms of wealth such as stocks and savings. Historically, concentrated wealth fosters an aristocracy. Thomas Jefferson sought to break up the "aristocracy of wealth" by changing from laws based on *primogeniture* (which give the eldest son exclusive right to inherit his father's estate) to laws that encouraged or compelled people to divide their estates equally among all their children. Jefferson wanted to encourage an "aristocracy of virtue and talent" through a public school system open to all for the primary grades and for the best students through the university level.[116]

The framers of the Constitution recognized the dangers of an unequal concentration of wealth. "The most common and durable source of factions has been the various and unequal distribution of property," wrote James Madison in *The Federalist*, No. 10 (reprinted in the Appendix). "Those who hold, and those who are without property, have ever formed distinct interests in society." Madison was right. Economic differences often lead to conflict, and we remain divided politically along economic lines. Aside from race, income may be the single most important factor in explaining views on issues, partisanship, and ideology. Most rich people are Republicans, most poor people are Democrats, and this has been true since at least the Great Depression of the 1930s.

Between the 1950s and the 1970s, inflation-adjusted income doubled, but since then, it has fluctuated, with no substantial change over time.[117] Why has the pattern changed? Some economists cite higher energy costs, low levels of personal savings, and the worldwide slowdown in productivity.[118] Others point to the reduction of graduated income tax rates, the weakening of unions, and the shift from low-skill to high-skill jobs.[119]

As of 2007, 12.5 percent of the population fell below the poverty line and had the lowest per capita incomes, after factoring in family size.[120] In 2007, the official poverty level for a family of four with two children was an income below $21,027.[121] Families headed by a single female are more than two times as likely to fall below the poverty line than families headed by a single male, with 28.3 percent of all households headed by females falling below the poverty line.[122] Nearly 36 percent of the poor are children under age 18, and many appear to be trapped in a cycle of poverty where children raised in poverty are more likely to be poor as adults (see Figure 5–6).[123] African American and Hispanic children are more than twice as likely to be poor as white children.[124]

The definition of poverty is itself political, and a change in the definition of poverty can make it appear that there are more or fewer poor people than before. Whether we define poverty at a lower or higher level of income also determines who becomes eligible for some government programs. The poverty classification is intended to identify persons who cannot meet a minimum standard in such basics as housing, food, and medical care. Regardless of how we define poverty, however, the

FIGURE 5–6 **Percentage of Americans Living in Poverty, by Age, 1967–2009.**

In 2008-2009, a poor economy and high unemployment contributed to a rise in the poverty rate. ■ *What other factors could influence the percentage of Americans classified as living in poverty at any given time?*

SOURCE: U.S. Census Bureau, "Table 3—Poverty Status, by Age, Race, and Hispanic Origin," http://www.census.gov/hhes/www/poverty/histpov/perindex.html (accessed September 29, 2009); and U.S. Census Bureau, "Table 2—Poverty Status by Family Relationships, Race, and Hispanic Origin," http://www.census.gov/hhes/www/poverty/histpov/perindex.html (accessed September 29, 2009).

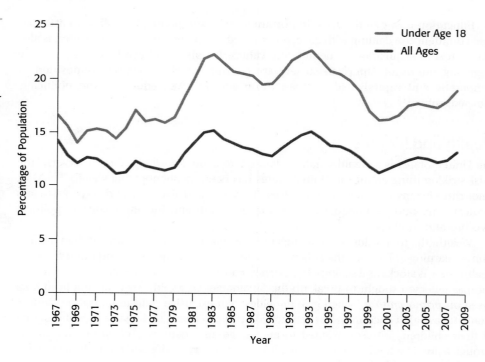

poor are a minority who lack political power. They vote less than wealthier people and are less confident and organized in dealing with politics and government. The gap between rich and poor has increased throughout the past 30 years.[125] Income is related to participation in politics. People who need the most help from government are the least likely to participate. They are also the most likely to favor social welfare programs.

The distribution of income in a society can have important consequences for democratic stability. If enough people believe that only the few at the top of the economic ladder can hope to earn enough for an adequate standard of living, domestic unrest and even revolution may follow.

In the United States, greater wealth and higher income is correlated with being Republican and favoring low taxes. There are, of course, wealthy Democrats. In 2008, higher-income Democrats and Independents favored Obama in the presidential nomination campaign.[126]

Occupation

In Jefferson's day and for several generations after, most people in the United States worked primarily on farms, but by 1900, the United States had become the world's leading industrial nation. As workers moved from farms to cities to find better-paying jobs, the cities rapidly grew. Labor conditions, including child labor, the length of the workweek, and safety conditions in mines and factories, became important political issues. New technology, combined with abundant natural and human resources, meant that the American **gross domestic product (GDP)** rose, after adjusting for inflation, by more than 460 percent from 1960 to 2007.[127] Gross domestic product is one measure of the size of a country's economy. It is the total market value of goods and services produced in that country in a specified period of time.

The United States has entered what Daniel Bell, a noted sociologist, labeled the "postindustrial" phase of its development. "A postindustrial society, being primarily a technical society, awards less on the basis of inheritance or property...than on education and skill."[128] *Knowledge* is the organizing device of the postindustrial era.

gross domestic product (GDP)
The total output of all economic activity in the nation, including goods and services.

Postindustrial societies have greater affluence and a class structure less defined along traditional labor-versus-management lines. Figure 5–7, which shows the percentage of American workers in various occupations, demonstrates the changing dynamics of the country's labor force.

The white-collar sector of our economy has grown tremendously throughout the past 50 years. This sector includes managers, accountants, and lawyers, as well as professionals and technicians in such rapid-growth areas as computers, communications, finance, insurance, and research. A dramatic decline in the number of people engaged in agriculture and a more modest decline in the number of people in manufacturing (which together make up the blue-collar sector) has accompanied this shift. Today, agriculture employs 1 percent of working adults, and manufacturing employs 11 percent.[129] Federal, state, and local governments employ 5 percent of jobholders, while government expenditures account for 20 percent of our gross domestic product.[130]

Men hold most blue-collar jobs.[131] We have already noted that women generally earn less than men of the same age and education. Occupations in which women predominate, such as teaching and clerical work, are generally lower-paying than industrial or management jobs. And as women try to advance in their careers, especially in management, they encounter a barrier that has been referred to as the "glass ceiling."

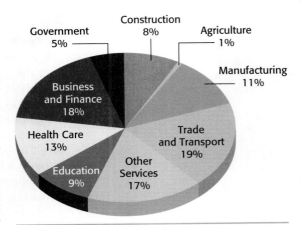

FIGURE 5–7 Employment by Occupational Groups, 2008.

SOURCE: U.S. Census Bureau, *Statistical Abstract of the United States: 2010* (U.S. Government Printing Office, 2010), p. 392.

Social Class

Why do U.S. citizens not divide themselves into social classes as Europeans do? American workers have not formed their own political party, nor does class seem to dominate our political life. Karl Marx's categories of *proletariat* (those who sell their labor) and *bourgeoisie* (those who own or control the means of production) are far less important here than they have been in Europe. Still, we do have social classes and what social scientists call **socioeconomic status (SES)**—a division of the population based on occupation, income, and education.

socioeconomic status (SES)
A division of population based on occupation, income, and education.

Most American adults say they are "middle class." Few admit to seeing themselves as lower class or upper class. In many other industrial democracies, large proportions of the population think of themselves as "working class" rather than middle class.[132]

What constitutes the "middle class" in the United States is highly subjective. For instance, some individuals perform working-class tasks (such as plumbing), but their income places them in the middle class or even the upper-middle class. A schoolteacher's income is below that of many working-class jobs, but in terms of status, teaching ranks among middle-class jobs.

People may define themselves as middle class because the American dream promises upward mobility. Or their responses may reflect the hostility many feel toward organized labor. In any case, compared to many countries, class divisions in the United States are less defined and less important to politics. As political scientist Seymour Martin Lipset has written, "The American social structure and values foster an emphasis on competitive individualism, an orientation that is not congruent with class consciousness, support for socialist or social democratic parties, or a strong union movement."[133]

School teachers in the U.S. remain disproportionately female. ■ *Why do you think this has not changed, despite opportunities in other professions becoming more available to women?*

Age

We are living longer, a phenomenon that has been dubbed the "graying of America" (Figure 5–8). This demographic change has increased the proportion of the population over the age of 65 and increased the demand for medical care, retirement benefits, and a host of other age-related services. Persons over the age of 65 constitute less than 13 percent of the population but account for more than 26 percent of the total medical expenditures.[134] With the decreasing birthrate discussed earlier, the graying of America has given rise to concern about maintaining an adequate workforce in the future. The median age in the world was 24 in 1950, rose to 27.9 in 2005, and is projected to be 38.4 in 2050. In the United States, the median age was 30 in 1950, rose to 36 in 2005, and is projected to be 41.7 in 2050. Countries like Japan and the United Kingdom have even older median ages.[135]

Older adults are more politically aware and vote more often than younger ones, making them a potent political force. Their vote is especially important in western states and in Florida, the state with the largest proportion of people over the age of 65. The "gray lobby" not only votes in large numbers but also has four political assets not found in other age groups that make it politically powerful: disposable income, discretionary time, a clear focus on issues, and effective organization. When older voters compete for their share of the budget pie, the young, minorities, and the poor often lose out.[136]

Age is important in terms of politics in two additional ways: lifecycle and generational effects. *Lifecycle effects* have shown that, as people become middle-aged, they become more politically conservative, less mobile, and more likely to participate in politics. As they age further and rely more on the government for services, they tend to grow more liberal.[137] Young people, in contrast, are more mobile and less concerned about the delivery of government services.

Several groups made registering younger voters and getting them to the polls a high priority in 2008. Exit polls from the 2008 election found that turnout among 18- to 29-year-olds rose from 48 percent in 2004 to 52 percent in 2008. An estimated 3.4 million more 18- to 29-year-olds voted in 2008.[138] Overall turnout was also higher in 2008, and so the proportion of the voters aged 18 to 29 increased only slightly from 17 percent to 18 percent.[139]

Generational effects in politics arise when a particular generation has had experiences that make it politically distinct. For example, for those who lived through it, the Great Depression of the 1930s shaped their lifelong views of political parties, issues, and political leaders. Some members of this generation saw Franklin D. Roosevelt as the leader who saved the country by pulling it out of the Depression; others felt he sold the country down the river by launching too many government programs. More recently and to a lesser extent, the baby boomers shared a common and distinctive political experience. These Americans came of age politically in the 1960s and 1970s during the civil rights movement and the Vietnam War.

FIGURE 5–8 **Percentage of Population Over the Age of 65, 1900–2050.**

■ *How will the population 30 years from now compare to that of today? In what areas of politics and society might that difference have an impact?*

SOURCE: U.S. Census Bureau; U.S. Census Bureau, http://www.census.gov/compendia/statab/cats/ population/estimates_and_projections_by_age_ sex_raceethnicity.htm; and U.S. Census Bureau, *Statistical Abstract of the United States: 2010* (U.S. Government Printing Office, 2010), p. 12.

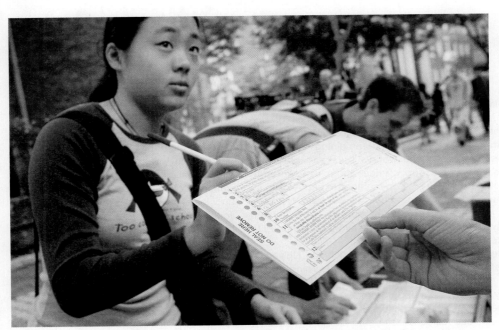

As was the case in 2004, the 2008 election cycle saw an increase in the number of young persons registering to vote. ■ *If young people were to turn out to vote at the same percentage as older people, in what areas of policy might the priorities of politicians change?*

Unity in a Land of Diversity

As remarkable as American diversity is, the existence of a strong and widely shared sense of national unity and identity may be even more remarkable. Economic and social mobility have unified much of the U.S. population. Education has been an important part of this, as was the nationalizing influence of World War II. We are united by our shared commitment to democratic values, economic opportunity, work ethic, and the American dream. Social scientists used to speak of the "melting pot," meaning that, as various ethnic groups associate with other groups, they are assimilated into U.S. society and come to share democratic values such as majority rule, individualism, and the ideal of the United States as a land of opportunity. Critics have argued that the melting pot idea assumes there is something wrong with differences between groups, and that these distinctions should be discouraged. In its place, they propose the concept of the "salad bowl," in which "though the salad is an entity, the lettuce can still be distinguished from the chicory, the tomatoes from the cabbage."[140]

As this chapter has demonstrated, regional, social, and economic differences have important political consequences. They influence public opinion, participation, voting, interest groups, and political parties. At the same time, our country has achieved a sense of unity despite our remarkable diversity.

More broadly, education and age are especially important predictors of citizen engagement and participation, and education predicts political efficacy. As we have shown, education is also associated with having confidence in dealing with government and asserting rights and liberties. As people move through the lifecycle, they become more involved in their communities and are more likely to vote. The 2008 election was noteworthy for the rise in proportions of young people who voted and sought to influence how others voted. Voters under 30 years of age were more than twice as likely to vote for Obama over McCain. Obama's vote share of these voters was the highest share of any candidate since exit polls reported the vote by age in 1976.[141]

LEARNING **OBJECTIVE**

5.4 Evaluate the degree to which America has achieved a measure of unity in a land of diversity.

By the People

Experiencing Poverty

As we have seen in this chapter, poverty is still a problem in the United States with direct political implications. The poor vote at lower rates and participate in other ways with less frequency than the wealthy. This reduces their political power and, among other things, threatens to weaken politicians' support of the social welfare programs on which the poor rely.

The enduring challenges of poverty have prompted some young people to take action to try and raise awareness of the enduring inequalities and difficulties of poverty.

Students at Ohio Wesleyan University, for example, hold a hunger banquet where participants are assigned to different socioeconomic classes, which determine their quality and quantity of food. The 15 percent of the students who are assigned to the upper class get a fully catered meal served at tables with linens. For the 30

percent of attendees who constitute the middle class, their meal consists of rice and beans served at tables without decoration or linens. The remaining 60 percent represent the world's poor and are fed a single scoop of rice and given water to drink. They sit on the floor to eat. A keynote speaker reinforces the contrast between different groups in society, and canned goods collected at the event are donated to the local shelter.

Students at Central Michigan University create a similar experiential learning opportunity in which they seek to raise public awareness about homelessness. To visually evoke the experience of Michigan's homeless residents, students create a makeshift "Shanty Town" out of cardboard in which they spend one night.* As people come to see the Shanty Town, they are encouraged to contribute to a homeless shelter in their area.†

For participants in these events, the contrast between the experiences of people at different socioeconomic levels is a powerful teaching moment. You might plan a hunger banquet at your campus if you do not already have one. Oxfam, a nonprofit organization dedicated to ending global poverty and injustice, provides a Hunger Banquet Toolkit with instructions and tips for how to host your own event: http://actfast.oxfam america.org/uploads/OA-HBToolkit.pdf.

CRITICAL THINKING QUESTIONS

1. What are some reasons why the poor participate less in politics?

2. Why is it hard for those who have not experienced hunger or poverty to relate to the difficulties faced by poor people?

3. Do events like "hunger banquets" help raise awareness of the issue being showcased?

---

* Michigan State Housing Development Authority, "The State of Homelessness in Michigan: 2008 Annual Summary," *Statistical Abstract: 2010*, p. 18, http://www.mpca.net/homeless.html.

† Maryellen Tighe, "Students Stay in Cardboard Boxes for 24 Hours for Homeless Awareness," *Central Michigan Life*, November 20, 2009, http://www.cm-life.com/ 2009/11/20/students-stay-in-cardboard-boxes-for-24-hours-for-homeless-awareness/.

CHAPTER **SUMMARY**

5.1 Characterize the opportunities and challenges posed by the diversity of the American population and by the nation's geography.

The character of a political society and its social environment are important to understanding its politics and government. Because the United States is a large continental nation with abundant natural resources, political freedom, and economic opportunity, immigrants from many nations have come here. These characteristics help explain American politics and traditions, including the notions of manifest destiny, ethnocentrism, and isolationism. Social and economic differences can foster conflict and violence. The continuing controversy over illegal immigration in the United States is an example of such a conflict. U.S. law has fostered religious diversity, and residential and settlement patterns have reinforced ethnic identify for some groups.

5.2 Relate differences in political culture to where people live.

For much of U.S. history, the South has been a distinct region in the United States, in large part because of its

agricultural base and its history of slavery and troubled race relations. Today, the region is Republican and Conservative. Recently, the most significant migration in the United States has been from cities to suburbs. Today, many large U.S. cities are increasingly poor, African American, and Democratic, surrounded by suburbs that are primarily middle class, white, and Republican.

5.3 Analyze how demographic factors—including race and ethnicity, religion, gender, family structures, education, income, class, and age—affect American politics.

Race has been and remains among the most important of the differences in our political landscape. Although we fought a civil war over freedom for African Americans, racial equality was largely postponed until the latter half of the twentieth century. Ethnicity, including the rising numbers of Hispanics, continues to be a factor in politics. The United States has many religious denominations, and these differences, including between those who are religious and those who are not, help explain public opinion and political behavior. Gender, sexual orientation, and family structures have become more important in politics. Although some achieve great wealth and there is a large middle class, poverty has grown throughout the past two decades, especially among African Americans, Native Americans, Hispanics, and single-parent households. Women as a group continue to earn less than men, even in the same occupations. Age and education are important to understanding political participation.

CHAPTER **SELF-TEST**

5.1 Characterize the opportunities and challenges posed by the diversity of the American population and by the nation's geography.

1. List four dimensions of diversity in the American population.
2. In a short paragraph, define ethnocentrism. Is it different from racism? Why or why not?
3. In a short essay, explain how the concept of manifest destiny relates to the current political geography of the United States.
4. Compared to other countries in the world, the United States does not have many deep cleavages. Why do you think this is? (Hint: Think about the differences between *cross-cutting cleavages* and *reinforcing cleavages*.) Explain your opinion in a short paragraph.

5.2 Relate differences in political culture to where people live.

5. Population growth patterns include all the following, *except:*
   a. In the West, population growth is occurring among younger persons.
   b. Growth in the South is occurring primarily in the population over the age of 65.
   c. There has been a resurgence of industrial growth in the New England states.
   d. Sun Belt states have experienced greater economic growth than most other areas.
6. Imagine you were a campaign consultant hired to advise a presidential candidate. List and describe three ways geography would affect your recommendations and decisions.
7. In a short essay, describe two or three ways in which urbanization has affected American politics.

5.3 Analyze how demographic factors—including race and ethnicity, religion, gender, family structures, education, income, class, and age—affect American politics.

8. List and describe seven demographic categories.

9. A study of the causes of diversity in the United States includes an analysis of the implications of all *except:*
   a. geography or demographics.
   b. social and ethnic background.
   c. economic or class divisions.
   d. politics and ideology.
10. Studies show that, after we control for socioeconomic status, many apparent racial divisions disappear. In a short essay, explain how race and socioeconomic status are related.
11. How might Figure 5–5 look if we were to add a section showing the relationship between income and education? Fill in the following table with some feasible numbers representing the percent of population in each category. Write two to three sentences justifying your table.

Income	Not a High School Graduate	High School Graduate	Bachelor's Degree	Advanced Degree
Less than $15,000				
$15,000–$34,999				
$35,000–$49,999				
$50,000–$99,999				
More than $100,000				

5.4 Evaluate the degree to which America has achieved a measure of unity in a land of diversity.

12. During the 2008 presidential election and nomination contest, much was made of "identity politics" in which individuals vote for the candidate most like them demographically. From what you know about the 2008 campaigns, how important was identity politics to the outcome?
13. Remembering that they are correlated, explain in a short essay whether you think regional or demographic distinctions are more important in how Americans see themselves.

Answers to selected questions: 5. c; 9. d

myp⊕liscilab™ EXERCISES
Where participation leads to action!

Apply what you learned in this chapter on MyPoliSciLab.

▭▭┤**Read** on **mypoliscilab.com**

eText: Chapter 5

✓•┤**Study** and **Review** on **mypoliscilab.com**

Pre-Test
Post-Test
Chapter Exam
Flashcards

◉┤**Watch** on **mypoliscilab.com**

Video: America's Aging Population
Video: Who is in the Middle Class?

✳┤**Explore** on **mypoliscilab.com**

Comparative: Comparing Political Landscapes
Visual Literacy: Using the Census to Understand Who
Americans Are

KEY **TERMS**

ethnocentrism, p. 129
efficacy, p. 129
political socialization, p. 130
demography, p. 130
political predisposition, p. 130
reinforcing cleavages, p. 130

cross-cutting cleavages, p. 130
manifest destiny, p. 132
Sun Belt, p.134
urban, p. 135
suburban, p. 135
rural, p. 135

race, p. 137
ethnicity, p. 137
fundamentalists, p. 142
gender gap, p. 144
gross domestic product (GDP), p. 148
socioeconomic status (SES), p. 149

ADDITIONAL **RESOURCES**

FURTHER READING

EARL BLACK AND **MERLE BLACK,** *The Rise of Southern Republicans* (Belknap Press, 2002).

DAVID T. CANON, *Race, Redistricting, and Representation: The Unintended Consequences of Black Majority Districts* (University of Chicago Press, 1999).

MAUREEN DEZELL, *Irish America: Coming into Clover* (Anchor Books, 2000).

JULIE ANNE DOLAN, MELISSA M. DECKMAN, AND **MICHELLE L. SWERS,** *Women and Politics: Paths to Power and Political Influence* (Prentice Hall, 2006).

LOIS DUKE WHITAKER, ED., *Women in Politics: Outsiders or Insiders?* 4th ed. (Prentice Hall, 2005).

RODOLFO O. DE LA GARZA, LOUIS DE SIPIO, F. CHRIS GARCIA, JOHN GARCIA, AND **ANGELO FALCON,** *Latino Voices: Mexican, Puerto Rican, and Cuban*

Perspectives on American Politics (Westview Press, 1992).

DONALD R. KINDER AND **LYNN M. SANDERS,** *Divided by Color: Racial Politics and Democratic Ideals* (University of Chicago Press, 1996).

MATTHEW D. LASSITER, *The Silent Majority: Suburban Politics in the Sunbelt South* (Princeton University Press, 2005).

TAEKU LEE, S. KARTHICK RAMAKRISHNAN, AND **RICARDO RAMIREZ,** *Transforming Politics, Transforming America: The Political and Civic Incorporation of Immigrants in the United States (Race, Ethnicity, and Politics)* (University Press of Virginia, 2006).

JAN E. LEIGHLEY, *Strength in Numbers? The Political Mobilization of Racial and Ethnic Minorities* (Princeton University Press, 2001).

PEL-TE LIEN, M. MARGARET CONWAY, AND **JANELLE WONG,** *The Politics of Asian Americans* (Routledge, 2004).

JEREMY D. MAYER, *Running on Race: Racial Politics in Presidential Campaigns, 1960–2000* (Random House, 2002).

NANCY E. McGLEN, KAREN O'CONNOR, LAURA VAN ASSENDELFT, AND **WENDY GUNTHER-CANADA,** *Women, Politics, and American Society,* 4th ed. (Longman, 2004).

S. KARTHICK RAMAKRISHNAN, *Democracy in Immigrant America: Changing Demographics and Political Participation* (Stanford University Press, 2005).

MARK ROBERT RANK, *One Nation, Underprivileged: Why American Poverty Affects Us All* (Oxford University Press, 2004).

ARTHUR M. SCHLESINGER JR., *The Disuniting of America* (Norton, 1992).

MARCELO M. SUAREZ-OROZCO AND **MARIELA PAEZ,** *Latinos: Remaking America* (University of California Press, 2002).

ALEXIS DE TOCQUEVILLE, *Democracy in America,* edited by J. P. Mayer, translated by George Lawrence (Doubleday, 1969). Originally published 1835.

KENNETH D. WALD, *Religion and Politics in the United States,* 5th ed. (Rowman & Littlefield, 2006).

JANELLE WONG, *Democracy's Promise: Immigrants and American Civic Institutions (The Politics of Race and Ethnicity)* (University of Michigan Press, 2006).

WEB SITES

www.census.gov The census provides demographic statistics for the country as a whole and for all 50 states.

www.usa.gov/Citizen/Topics/History_ Culture.shtml USA.gov provides information on a variety of subjects, including detailed information on America's cultural history.

www.religions.pewforum.org/reports The Pew Forum provides detailed information on the religious makeup of America.

www.pbs.org/peoplelikeus/ This PBS site gives stats, stories, and other information about class in America.

Interest Groups

The Politics of Influence

In early 2009, not long after Barack Obama took office, groups started forming to protest the $787 billion economic stimulus package, officially known as the American Recovery and Reinvestment Act of 2009. These groups adopted the name "tea party," a reference to the Boston Tea Party of 1773 when colonists rebelled against what they thought to be unfair British taxes on tea. The group's general concerns are about increasing government spending and growing government power. As Congress considered and the House of Representatives passed health care reform, that provided another issue for the tea party groups to protest. During the summer recess, many members of Congress faced heckling and protests in their home districts, in part the result of tea party organizing.[1] In the early 2010 special election to fill former Senator Ted Kennedy's Senate seat in Massachusetts, Republican Scott Brown staged an upset attributed by some in part to the Tea Party Movement. The British magazine, *The Economist*, said after Brown's victory, "America's most vibrant political force at the moment is the antitax tea-party movement."[2]

Tea party activists have held protests and rallies in cities throughout the country, where the number of participants ranges from a couple of dozen to thousands.[3] The movement has also organized national bus tours to call attention to their agenda.[4] This element of the Tea Party Movement was organized by the "Our Country Deserves Better PAC," founded by a political consulting firm in Sacramento.[5] In February 2010, a group called Tea Party Nation held a National Convention, which featured a speech by former Alaska Governor and Republican vice presidential nominee Sarah Palin.[6]

One additional organizational component of the Tea Party Movement is the Tea Party Patriots, a national organization, which claims more than one thousand local chapters. This group has been organized with the help of FreedomWorks, a conservative/libertarian nonprofit organization led by former Republican House Majority Leader Dick Armey.[7] FreedomWorks and Armey are credited with helping the Tea Party Movement's September 2009 march in Washington, D.C., in which 60,000 to 75,000 people participated.[8] Others have described "Armey and FreedomWorks as the invisible hand behind much of the recent conservative activism throughout the country."[9] FreedomWorks and its affiliated FreedomWorks Foundation raised an estimated "$7 million from donors in 2008, most of it in large donations—including gifts of $1 million and $750,000."[10]

In some ways, the Tea Party Movement has adopted many of the same tools used by the Obama campaign and Democratic leaning interest groups in 2008, such as using the Internet to coordinate, communicate, and recruit volunteers.[11] It remains to be seen if they will adopt the television and radio advertising strategies similar to the Swift Boat Veterans for Truth, a group that challenged Democratic presidential nominee John Kerry's patriotism and valor in ads run just after he accepted his party's 2004 nomination.

As the Tea Party Movement demonstrates, interest groups use a variety of strategies from local citizens spontaneously organizing for some political purpose, to more organized election-focused political action committees (PACs). Interest groups like these have long been important in electing and defeating candidates, in providing information to officeholders, and in setting the agenda of American politics. Similarly, U.S. citizens have been concerned about the power of "special interests" and the groups' focus on their self-interest at the expense of less well-organized groups or the general public. Restraining the negative tendencies of these interest groups while protecting their liberty is not easy. In this chapter, we examine the full range of interest group activities as well as efforts to limit their potentially negative influences, including reforming campaign finance regulations.

CHAPTER **OUTLINE**
CHAPTER LEARNING **OBJECTIVES**

Interest Groups Past and Present: The "Mischiefs of Faction"

6.1 Explain the role of interest groups and social movements in American politics.

Types of Interest Groups

6.2 Categorize American interest groups into types.

Characteristics and Power of Interest Groups

6.3 Analyze sources of interest group power.

The Influence of Lobbyists

6.4 Describe lobbyists and the activities through which they seek to influence policy.

Money and Politics

6.5 Identify ways interest groups use money in elections and assess efforts to regulate this spending.

How Much Do Interest Groups Influence Elections and Legislation?

6.6 Evaluate the effectiveness of interest groups in influencing elections and legislation.

Interest Groups Past and Present: The "Mischiefs of Faction"

LEARNING **OBJECTIVE**

6.1 Explain the role of interest groups and social movements in American politics.

The founders of the Republic were very worried about groups with common interests, which they called **factions.** (They also thought of political parties as factions.) For the framers of the Constitution, the daunting problem was how to establish a stable and orderly constitutional system that would both respect the liberty of free citizens and prevent the tyranny of the majority or of a single dominant interest.

As a talented practical politician and a brilliant theorist, James Madison offered both a diagnosis and a solution in *The Federalist*, No. 10 (reprinted in the Appendix). He began with a basic proposition: "The latent causes of faction are…sown in the nature of man." All individuals pursue their self-interest, seeking advantage or power over others. Acknowledging that we live in a maze of group interests, Madison argued that the "most common and durable source of factions has been the various and unequal distribution of property." Madison called a faction "a number of citizens, whether amounting to a majority or minority of the whole, who are united and actuated by some common impulse of passion, or of interest, adverse to the rights of other citizens, or to the permanent and aggregate interests of the community." For Madison, "the *causes* of faction cannot be removed, and…relief is only to be sought in the means of controlling its *effects*."[12]

James Madison played a critical role in drafting and enacting the Constitution, and many of its provisions are aimed at limiting the "mischiefs of faction." Separation of powers and checks and balances make it hard for a faction to dominate government. Staggered terms of office make it necessary for a faction to endure. But rather than trying to encourage one or another faction, the Constitution encourages competition between them. Indeed, checks and balances arguably function best when factions within the branches work to counter one another. The Constitution envisions a plurality of groups competing with each other, an idea that has been called **pluralism.**

How well pluralism has worked in practice is debated.[13] We will see that over time, government has sought to regulate factions as a response to the power some groups such as corporations, unions, and wealthy individuals have had in American government. The debate about how to check their power without damaging their liberty is an enduring one.

A Nation of Interests

Some U.S. citizens identify with groups distinguished by race, gender, ethnic background, age, occupation, religion, or sexual orientation. Others form voluntary groups based on their opinions about issues such as gun control or tax reduction. When such associations seek to influence government, they are called **interest groups.**

Interest groups are also sometimes called "special interests." Politicians and the media often use this term in a pejorative way. What makes an interest group a "special" one? The answer is highly subjective. One person's *special* interest is another's *public* interest. However, so-called public interest groups such as Common Cause or the League of Women Voters support policies that not everyone agrees with. Politics is best seen as a clash among interests, with differing concepts of what is in the public interest, rather than as a battle between the special interests on one side and "the people" or the public interest on the other.

In fact, the term "special interest" conveys a selfish or narrow view, one that may lack credibility. For this reason, we use the neutral term "interest groups." An interest group simply speaks for some, but not all, of us. A democracy includes many interests and many organized interest groups. The democratic process exists to decide among them. Part of the politics of interest groups is thus to persuade the general public that their interest is more important.

Social Movements

Interest groups sometimes begin as social movements. A social **movement** consists of many people interested in a significant issue, idea, or concern who are willing to take action to support or oppose it. Examples include the civil rights, environmental, antitax, animal

faction
A term the founders used to refer to political parties and special interests or interest groups.

pluralism
A theory of government that holds that open, multiple, and competing groups can check the asserted power by any one group.

interest group
A collection of people who share a common interest or attitude and seek to influence government for specific ends. Interest groups usually work within the framework of government and try to achieve their goals through tactics such as lobbying.

movement
A large body of people interested in a common issue, idea, or concern that is of continuing significance and who are willing to take action. Movements seek to change attitudes or institutions, not just policies.

rights, women's rights, Christian Right, gay rights, anti-immigration, and antiwar movements. In some respects, the tea party groups that formed in 2009 and 2010 are examples of social movements. They, like other social movements, represent a group that has felt unrepresented by government.

Social movements often arise at the grassroots level and spread throughout the nation. They tend to see their causes as morally right and their opponents as morally wrong. As movements mature, they develop interest groups that pursue public policies, as we will see later.

The Bill of Rights protects movements, popular or unpopular, by supporting free assembly, free speech, and due process. Consequently, those who disagree with government policies do not have to engage in violence or other extreme activities in the United States, as they do in some countries, and they need not fear persecution for demonstrating peacefully. In a democratic system that restricts the power of government, movements have considerable room to operate *within* the constitutional system.

After the controversial election in Iran, protestors took to the streets to call for change, and the government responded with violence and repression. ■ *What aspects of the American democracy, which are not present in Iran, allow for groups to engage in peaceful protests?*

Types of Interest Groups

Interest groups vary widely. Some are formal associations or organizations like the National Rifle Association (NRA); others have no formal organization. Some are organized primarily to persuade public officials on issues of concern to the group such as reducing greenhouse gases; others conduct research, or influence public opinion with published reports and mass mailings.

We can categorize interest groups into several broad types: (1) economic, including both business and labor; (2) ideological or single-issue; (3) public interest; (4) foreign policy; and (5) government itself. Obviously, these categories are not mutually exclusive. Most American adults are represented by a number of interest groups, even if they don't know it. For instance, people age 50 and older may not be aware that AARP (which began as the American Association of Retired Persons) claims to represent *all* older citizens, not only those who are actually members. Similarly, the American Automobile Association (AAA) claims to represent all motorists, not only those who join. The varied and overlapping nature of interest groups in the United States has been described as *interest group pluralism*, meaning that competition among open, responsive, and diverse groups helps preserve democratic values and limits the concentration of power in any single group. We look at each category of interest group next.

LEARNING OBJECTIVE

6.2 Categorize American interest groups into types.

Economic Interest Groups

There are thousands of economic interests: agriculture, consumers, plumbers, the airplane industry, landlords, truckers, bondholders, property owners, and more. Economic interests pursue what benefits them both financially and politically.

Business   The most familiar business institution is the large corporation. Corporations range from one-person enterprises to vast multinational entities. General Motors, AT&T, Microsoft, Coca-Cola, McDonald's, Walmart, and other large companies exercise considerable political influence, as do hundreds of smaller corporations. For example, as Microsoft and Walmart came under heightened government and public scrutiny, their political contributions expanded.[14] Corporate power and a changing domestic and global economy make business practices important political issues.

Cooperation between groups can increase their effectiveness, giving even small business an important voice in public policy. The Commerce Department includes a Small Business Administration. Small businesses are also organized into groups such as the National Federation of Independent Business that help elect pro-business candidates and persuade the national government on behalf of its members.

FIGURE 6–1 Union Membership in the United States Compared to Other Countries. ■ *How might aspects of American culture and ideology help explain the relatively low unionization of the American workforce?*

SOURCE: *European Foundation for the Improvement of Living and Working Conditions,* 2008 (Wyattville Road, Loughlinstown, Dublin 18, Ireland).

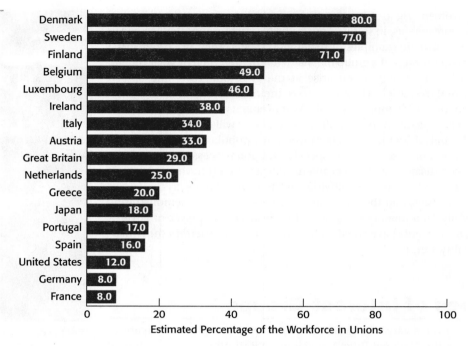

Trade and Other Associations Businesses with similar interests join together as *trade associations,* as diverse as the products and services they provide. Businesses of all types are also organized into large nationwide associations such as the National Association of Realtors and smaller ones like the American Wind Energy Association.

The broadest business trade association is the Chamber of Commerce of the United States. Organized in 1912, the Chamber is a federation of thousands of local Chambers of Commerce representing millions of businesses. Loosely allied with the Chamber on most issues is the National Association of Manufacturers, which, since 1893, has tended to speak for the more conservative elements of American business.

Labor Workers' associations have a range of interests, including professional standards and wages and working conditions. Labor unions are one of the most important groups representing workers, yet the American workforce is the least unionized of almost any industrial democracy.[15] (See Figure 6–1.) The level of unionization has policy consequences. For example, a nation's minimum wage rates increase with unionization. The United States' minimum wage of $7.25 per hour is lower than in the more unionized United Kingdom, whose minimum wage is $8.83 per hour.[16]

Throughout the nineteenth century, workers organized political parties and local unions. Their most ambitious effort at national organization, the Knights of Labor, registered 700,000 members in the 1890s. But by approximately 1900, the American Federation of Labor (AFL), a confederation of strong and independent-minded national unions mainly representing craft workers, was the dominant organization. During the 1930s, unions more responsive to industrial workers broke away from the AFL and formed a rival national organization organized by industry, the Congress of Industrial Organizations (CIO). In 1955, the AFL and CIO reunited. Recently, more than a third of AFL-CIO members (4.5 of 13 million members), affiliated with the Service Employees International Union (SEIU), the International Brotherhood of Teamsters, and two other unions, split off from the AFL-CIO, forming a new group named the Change to Win Federation.[17] Unions today are thus less unified, but by 2007, dues paid to the AFL-CIO exceeded levels before the division.[18]

The AFL-CIO speaks for approximately two-thirds of unionized labor,[19] but unions represent slightly more than 12 percent of the nation's workforce (see Figure 6–2).[20] The proportion of the U.S. workforce belonging to all unions has fallen, in part because of the

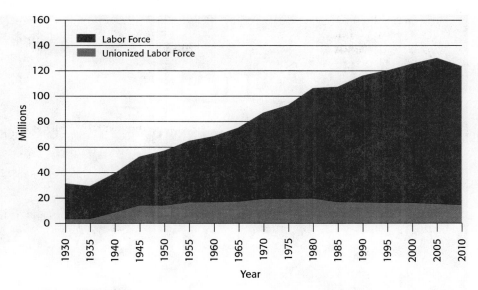

FIGURE 6–2 Labor Force and Union Membership, 1930–2010. ■ *How can you explain the steady upward growth of the labor force without a comparable growth in the unionized labor force?*

SOURCE: *The World Almanac and Book of Facts, 2000.* Copyright © 1999 Primedia Reference, Inc. Reprinted with permission, all rights reserved; and Barry Hirsch, Georgia State University, and David Macpherson, Florida State University, 1973–2007, "Union Membership, Coverage, Density, and Employment Among All Wage and Salary Workers, 1973–2007," http://www.unionstats.com.

shift from an industrial to a service and information economy. Dwindling membership limits organized labor's influence. Recently, however, some service and public sector unions have begun to expand, and even some doctors have unionized. Membership in SEIU rose from 1.58 million in 2006, a membership number little changed from 2003, to 2.2 million in 2009.[21]

Union membership is optional in states whose laws permit the **open shop,** in which workers cannot be required to join a union as a condition of employment. In states with the **closed shop,** workers may be required to join a union to be hired at a particular company if most employees at that company vote to unionize. In both cases, the unions negotiate with management, and all workers share the benefits the unions gain. In open-shop states, many workers may choose not to affiliate with a union because they can secure the same benefits that unionized workers enjoy without incurring the costs of joining the union. When a person benefits from the work or service of an organization like a union (or even a public TV or radio station) without joining or contributing to it, this condition is referred to as the **free rider** problem. We discuss how groups and government deal with the free rider challenge later in the chapter.

Since 1998, unions have emphasized direct contact with members and their families through mail, through e-mail, on the phone, and in person. They have organized get-out-the-vote drives and paid for television advertising. Unlike the case in 2000, when unions were important to securing Al Gore's nomination,[22] in the 2004 and 2008 Democratic presidential primaries they were divided. In 2008, some unions such as SEIU and the Change to Win Federation supported Senator Barack Obama, whereas the United Steel Workers supported John Edwards, and the American Federation of State, County, and Municipal Employees supported Senator Hillary Clinton. In the 2008 general election, unions were unified in backing Barack Obama for president and campaigned aggressively for pro-labor congressional, gubernatorial, and state legislative candidates.

Traditionally identified with the Democratic Party, unions have not enjoyed a close relationship with Republican administrations. Given labor's limited resources, one option for unions is to form temporary coalitions with consumer, public interest, liberal, and sometimes even industry groups, especially on issues related to foreign imports. Labor has been unsuccessful in blocking free trade agreements like the North American Free Trade Agreement (NAFTA).[23]

Professional Associations   Professional people join **professional associations** such as the American Medical Association (AMA) and the American Bar Association (ABA), which serve some of the same functions as unions. Other professions are divided into many

open shop
A company with a labor agreement under which union membership cannot be required as a condition of employment.

closed shop
A company with a labor agreement under which union membership can be a condition of employment.

free rider
An individual who does not join a group representing his or her interests yet receives the benefit of the group's influence.

professional associations
Groups of individuals who share a common profession and are often organized for common political purposes related to that profession.

Barack Obama meets with labor union members over breakfast while campaigning for the Democratic nomination for the presidency. Labor unions have traditionally identified with the Democratic party.
■ *What can you learn from this photo about the demographics of a typical labor union and the issues with which members would be most concerned?*

subgroups. Teachers and professors, for example, belong to the National Education Association, the American Federation of Teachers, and the American Association of University Professors, and also to subgroups based on specialties, such as the Modern Language Association and the American Political Science Association.

Government, especially at the state level, regulates many professions. Lawyers are licensed by states, which, often as a result of pressure from lawyers themselves, set standards of admission to the state bar. Professional associations also use the courts to pursue their agendas. In the area of medical malpractice, for example, doctors lobby hard for limited-liability laws, while trial lawyers resist them. Teachers, hairstylists, and marriage therapists work for legislation that concerns them. It is not surprising, then, that groups representing professional associations such as the AMA and the National Association of Home Builders are among the largest donors to political campaigns.

Ideological or Single-Issue Interest Groups

Ideological groups focus on issues—often a single issue. Members generally share a common view and a desire for government to pursue policies consistent with it. Such *single-issue* groups are often unwilling to compromise. Right-to-life and pro-choice groups on abortion fit this description, as do the National Rifle Association (NRA) and anti-immigration groups.

Countless groups have organized around other specific issues, such as civil liberties, environmental protection, nuclear energy, and nuclear disarmament.[24] Such associations are not new. The Anti-Saloon League of the 1890s was devoted solely to barring the sale and manufacture of alcoholic beverages, and it did not care whether legislators were drunk or sober as long as they voted dry. One of the best-known single-issue groups today is the NRA, with more than 4 million members committed to protecting the right to bear arms.[25] Other single-issue groups include the Club for Growth, a generally libertarian and antitax group.

One of the most influential interest groups, the National Rifle Association promotes issues related to Second Amendment gun ownership rights. The NRA also sponsors firearm safety courses and shooting competitions across the U.S. ■ *Why are single-issue groups like the NRA less willing to compromise on policy options than other kinds of interest groups?*

Public Interest Groups

Out of the political ferment of the 1960s came groups that claim to promote "the public interest." For example, Common Cause campaigns for electoral reform, for making the political process more open and participatory, and to stem media consolidation. Its Washington staff raises money through direct-mail campaigns, oversees state chapters of the group, publishes research reports and press releases on current issues, and lobbies Congress and government departments.

After uncovering design flaws in the Ford Pinto in 1977 resulting in 180 deaths, consumer activists like Ralph Nader charged Ford "with sacrificing human lives for profit."[26] Ralph Nader was instrumental in forming organizations to investigate and report on governmental and corporate action—or inaction—relating to consumer interests. Public interest research groups (PIRGs), as these groups are called, today seek to influence policy on Capitol Hill and in several state legislatures on environmental issues, safe energy, and consumer protection.

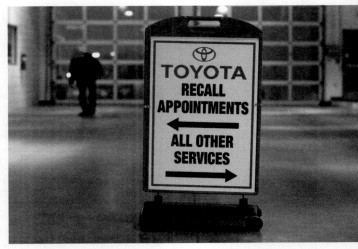

Fears about a defect in Toyotas that led to an uncontrolled acceleration of the car resulted in a safety recall of 3.8 million vehicles. U.S. PIRG, the federation of state Public Interest Research Groups, was vocal about the need for the recall, and played a role in the Senate hearings on product safety.

Foreign Policy Interest Groups

Interest groups also organize to promote or oppose foreign policies. Among the most prestigious is the Council on Foreign Relations in New York City. Other groups pressure Congress and the president to enact specific policies. For example, interest groups have been trying to influence American policy on China's refusal to grant independence for Tibet. Other groups support or oppose free trade. Foreign policy groups should not be confused with foreign governments and interest groups in other nations, which are banned from making campaign contributions but often seek to influence policy through lobbying firms.

One of the most influential foreign policy groups is the American Israel Political Action Committee (AIPAC), with more than 100,000 members.[27] Because AIPAC's primary focus is influencing government directly, not distributing campaign funds, it is not required to disclose where its money comes from or goes. Included in the long list of AIPAC successes are enactment of aid packages to Israel, passage of the 1985 United States–Israel Free Trade Agreement, and emergency assistance to Israel in the wake of the 1992 Gulf War. Its counterpart, the Arab American Institute, lobbies to support Arab causes. Efforts to secure a negotiated settlement between the Palestinians and Israel have kept U.S. interest groups on both sides visible and important.

nongovernmental organization (NGO)
A nonprofit association or group operating outside government that advocates and pursues policy objectives.

Nongovernmental organizations (NGOs), nonprofit groups that operate outside the institutions of government but often pursue public policy objectives and lobby governments are another type of foreign policy interest group. The most common are social, cultural, or environmental groups such as Greenpeace, Amnesty International, and the Humane Society of the United States.

Public Sector Interest Groups

Governments are themselves important interest groups. Many cities and most states retain Washington lobbyists, and cities also attempt to influence Congress and the executive branch of the federal government. Governors are organized through the National Governors Association, cities through the National League of Cities, and counties through the National Association of Counties. Other officials—lieutenant governors, secretaries of state, mayors—have their own national associations.

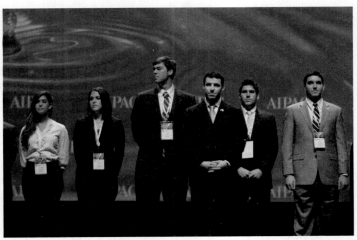

Students attend AIPAC's annual policy conference to learn more about what the organization will focus on in the coming year; AIPAC's decisions can have a large impact on policy. ■ *What issues or causes might motivate you to join an interest group?*

Global Warming

Much of the debate over global warming has been about the accuracy of the scientific claims about changes in the Earth's climate. Interest groups on both sides of the debate have cited studies supporting their point of view and a wide range of interest groups have a stake in what, if anything, governments should do about global warming.

Examples of such interests include oil companies, automobile manufacturers, and environmental groups like the Natural Resources Defense Council, the Environmental Defense Fund, and the Union of Concerned Scientists. Public opinion on whether global warming is a serious problem was part of the Pew Global Attitudes Survey. Respondents were asked: "In your view, is global warming a very serious problem, somewhat serious, not too serious, or not a problem?" The graph below plots responses from our sample countries to this question.

On this question, the United States stands apart in that fewer Americans think that global warming is a very or somewhat serious problem. Between 84 and 93 percent of people surveyed in our sample of countries outside the United States saw global warming as a very serious or somewhat serious problem. In the United States, the proportion was 74 percent. When we look only at those with the more strongly held view that global warming is a "very serious" problem, the United States is again lower than all other countries except China with 44 percent having that view. In contrast, roughly two-thirds of people in Mexico, Japan, and India think global warming is a very serious problem. In China, 30 percent think global warming is a very serious problem.

CRITICAL THINKING QUESTIONS

1. Why does public opinion on the severity of global warming differ between the United States and other countries?

2. Why would people in China be the least likely to respond that global warming is a very serious problem?

3. Do you think attitudes on this question are related to whether people would be willing to accept limitations in lifestyle to reduce the threat of global warming?

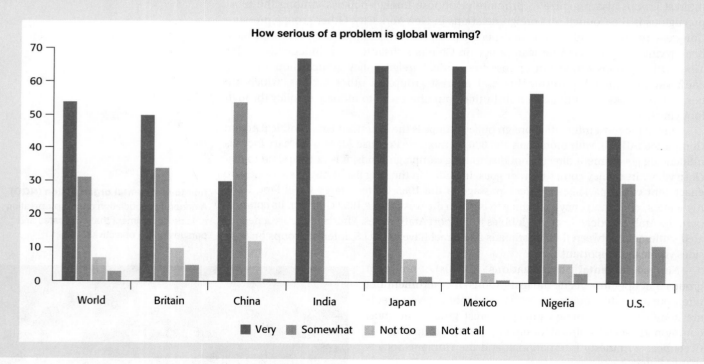

How serious of a problem is global warming?

Government employees form a large and well-organized group. The National Education Association (NEA), for example, has 3.2 million members.[28] The NEA endorses politicians from both parties but more typically supports Democrats. In 2008, the NEA endorsed Barack Obama for the presidency. The NEA fits the definition of a professional association, labor union, and public sector interest group. Public employees are increasingly important to organized labor because they constitute the fastest-growing unions.

Other Interest Groups

American adults are often emotionally and financially engaged by a wide variety of groups: veterans' groups, nationality groups, and religious organizations, among others.

TABLE 6-1 Environmental Groups' Resources and Strategies

Group	Membership	Issues	Activities
Sierra Club	1,300,000	Wilderness, pollution, global warming, human rights, population, suburban sprawl	Grassroots action; litigation; news releases
Natural Resources Defense Council	1,300,000	Resources, energy, global warming, pollution, nuclear weapons	Lobbying; litigation; watchdog; its scientists compete with experts from agencies and industry
Defenders of Wildlife	800,000	Imperiled wildlife and habitat, public lands, climate change impacts, international wildlife trade	Grassroots advocacy; litigation; hands-on conservation; lobbying
Greenpeace USA	250,000	Forests, global warming, genetically engineered foods, oceans, persistent organic pollutants, nuclear weapons	Media events; mass mailings; grassroots activity; does not lobby government
Wilderness Society	200,000	Wilderness areas, public lands, energy development	Scientific studies; analysis; advocacy group

SOURCE: Greenpeace USA, www.greenpeaceusa.org; Natural Resources Defense Council, www.nrdc.org; Sierra Club, www.sierraclub.org; and Wilderness Society, www.wilderness.org., Defenders of Wildlife, Rodger Schlickeisen, president, e-mail message to author, May 6, 2010.

Individuals join groups because of a common interest or concern, because of a shared identification, or because of an issue or concern. The American Legion or Veterans of Foreign Wars not only provide opportunities for military veterans to meet other veterans, but the groups provide an important advocacy function for veterans as they deal with Congress or the Veterans' administration bureaucracy.

Women's organizations have long been important in advocating for equal rights, most notably for the right to vote. Among the best-known group in the area of political rights for women is the League of Women Voters, formed in 1920 and with chapters in all 50 states. Other interest groups with a focus on gender include NARAL Pro-Choice America or Planned Parenthood. More broadly focused is the National Organization of Women (NOW).

An area of increasing activity is environmental groups (see Table 6–1). Among the best known of these groups is the Sierra Club. Founded in 1892, the Sierra Club is the oldest and largest environmental organization. The Sierra Club is active in environmental protection efforts in states and local communities, and it has a lobbying presence in Washington, D.C. Another group known for its efforts to elect pro-environment candidates is the League of Conservation Voters (LCV). The Defenders of Wildlife and the Wilderness Society have members and paid staff committed to protecting wildlife and securing preserving and protecting wilderness.

Characteristics and Power of Interest Groups

Political scientists, sociologists, and economists have described the differing ways groups form and organize to pursue their goals or objectives. Securing the participation of individuals in groups—what economist Mancur Olson labeled **collective action**,[29] and others describe as **public choice**[30]—is challenging because often the benefits from the group efforts are shared with everyone, including those who do not participate in the work of securing the benefit. This creates what is called the *free rider* problem. For example, unions that achieve wage concessions from management do so for all workers in and out of the union. This results in little incentive to join the union or support it financially. Groups sometimes attempt to sanction or punish free riders, which is why unions prefer that only union workers be employed in a given firm or industry. When this is not possible, group leaders try to reduce the free rider problem through persuasion or group pressure.

Groups vary in their goals, methods, and power. Among their most important characteristics are size, incentives to participate, resources, cohesiveness, leadership, and techniques. As we will demonstrate, these different resources and objectives help us understand the power and resources of interest groups.

LEARNING **OBJECTIVE**

6.3 Analyze sources of interest group power.

collective action

How groups form and organize to pursue their goals or objectives, including how to get individuals and groups to participate and cooperate. The term has many applications in the various social sciences such as political science, sociology, and economics.

public choice

Synonymous with "collective action," specifically studies how government officials, politicians, and voters respond to positive and negative incentives.

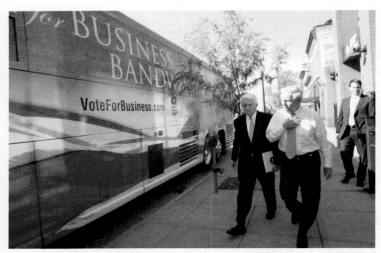

With a large membership and significant financial resources, the U.S. Chamber of Congress is active and influential in election campaigns. During the 2008 election the Chamber organized a "Vote for Business Bandwagon" to support candidates promoting economic policies beneficial to its members. Here, Chamber President and CEO Tom Donohue (left) meets with candidates in Denver.

Size and Resources

Obviously, size is important to political power; an organization representing 5 million voters has more influence than one speaking for 5,000. Perhaps even more important is the number of members who are active and willing to fight for policy objectives. Interest groups often provide tangible incentives to join, such as exclusive magazines, travel benefits, professional meetings and job opportunities, and discounts on insurance, merchandise, and admission to cultural institutions. Some are compelling enough to attract the potential free rider.[31]

Many government programs provide services that benefit everyone such as clean air, national defense, and public fireworks on July 4. One solution to the free rider problem is to pay for these widely shared benefits through taxes. Nongovernment service providers can require a number of people to pay for the service before providing it. It is then in everyone's interest to pay for the service or face the prospect that no one will have it. Groups rarely overcome the risk of free riders, but unless we offer some compensation for providing easily shared goods and services, they are not likely to be produced.

Although the size of an interest group is important to its success, so is its *spread*—the extent to which membership is concentrated or dispersed. Because automobile manufacturing is concentrated in Michigan and a few other states, the auto industry's influence does not have the same spread as the AMA, which has an active chapter in virtually every congressional district. Concentration of membership in a key battleground state, however, such as Cuban Americans in Florida or ethanol producers in Iowa, enhances that group's influence. Interest groups also differ in the extent to which they preempt or share a policy area.

Finally, groups differ in the extent of their *resources*—money, volunteers, expertise, and reputation. Some groups can influence many centers of power—both houses of Congress, the White House, federal agencies, the courts, and state and local governments—whereas others cannot.

Cohesiveness

Most mass-membership organizations include three types of members: (1) a relatively small number of formal leaders who may hold full-time, paid positions or devote much time, effort, and money to the group's activities; (2) a few hundred people intensely involved in the group who identify with its aims, attend meetings, pay dues, and do much of the legwork; and (3) thousands of people who are members in name only and cannot be depended on to vote in elections or act as the leadership wants.[32] When these groups share common views on the aims of the organization, the group is more cohesive.

Another factor in group cohesiveness is *organizational structure*. Some associations have a strong formal organization; others are local organizations joined into a loose state or national federation in which they retain a measure of separate power and independence.

Leadership

In a group that embraces many attitudes and interests, leaders may either weld the various elements together or sharpen their disunity. The leader of a national business association, for example, must tread cautiously between big business and small business, between exporters and importers, between chain stores and corner grocery stores, and between the producers and the sellers of competing products. The group leader is in the same position as a president or a member of Congress; he or she must know when to lead and when to follow.

Techniques for Exerting Influence

Our separation-of-powers system provides many access points for any group attempting to influence government. They can present their case to Congress, the White House staff, state and local governments, and federal agencies and departments. Efforts by individuals or groups to inform and influence public officials are called **lobbying.** Groups also become involved in litigation, protests, and election activities and even establish their own political parties. Groups vary in the extent to which they have widespread support that comes from the people (grassroots) vs. activity that is orchestrated or initiated centrally but looks to be grassroots (astroturf).[33]

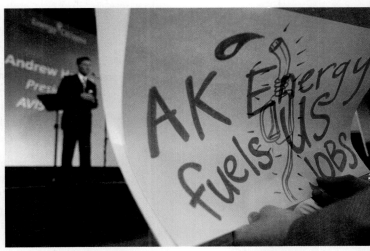

Energy Citizens, a interest group backed by the American Petroleum Institute, holds rallies against climate change legislation, which is under consideration by the Senate. ■ *Why might the oil and gas industry prefer using this technique of exerting influence?*

Publicity, Mass Media, and the Internet One way to attempt to influence policy makers is through the public. Interest groups use the media—television, radio, the Internet including Web sites, newspapers, leaflets, signs, direct mail, and word of mouth—to influence voters during elections and motivate them to contact their representatives between elections. Businesses enjoy a special advantage because, as large-scale advertisers, they know how to deliver their message effectively or can find an advertising agency to do it for them. But organized labor is also effective in communicating with its membership through shop stewards, mail, phone calls, and personal contact.

Mobilization increasingly occurs through the Internet, especially through social media such as Facebook. Business organizations like the Business and Industrial Political Action Committee (BIPAC) have used the Internet to communicate with members and employees of affiliated businesses. BIPAC's Web site provides downloadable forms to request absentee ballots and the roll call votes of legislators on issues of interest to their businesses.[34] Some groups, such as MoveOn.org, operate almost exclusively online, while massive forums such as DailyKos.com and Townhall.com act as a clearinghouse for left- and right-wing causes. As one scholar noted, much of what modern interest groups do "could not work without the Internet."[35]

The Internet helps interest groups in two ways. First, it allows citizens to easily organize themselves for rallies, marches, letter-writing drives, and other kinds of civic participation. Second, the Internet opens new, exclusively online forms of political action, such as sending mass e-mails, posting videos, joining Facebook groups, donating money online, commenting on articles, and blogging. We discuss these developments in greater detail in Chapter 10.

Mass Mailing One means of communication that has increased the reach and effectiveness of interest groups is computerized and targeted mass mailing.[36] Before computers, interest groups could either cull lists of people to contact from telephone directories and other sources or send mailings indiscriminately. Today's computerized mailing-list technology can target personalized letters to specific groups. Environmental groups make extensive use of targeted mail and e-mail.[37]

Direct Contact with Government Organized groups have ready access to the executive and regulatory agencies that write the rules implementing laws passed by Congress. Government agencies publish proposed regulations in the *Federal Register* and invite responses from all interested persons before the rules are finalized—in the "notice and comments period."[38] Well-staffed associations and corporations use the *Register* to obtain the specific language and deadlines for pending regulations. Lobbyists prepare written responses to the proposed rules, draft alternative rules, and make their case at the hearings.

Litigation When groups find the political channels closed to them, they may turn to the courts.[39] The Legal Defense and Educational Fund of the National Association for the Advancement of Colored People (NAACP), for example, initiated and won numerous court cases in its efforts to end racial segregation and protect the right to vote for African Americans. Urban interests, feeling underrepresented in state and national legislatures,

lobbying
Engaging in activities aimed at influencing public officials, especially legislators, and the policies they enact.

Federal Register
An official document, published every weekday, that lists the new and proposed regulations of executive departments and regulatory agencies.

turned to the courts to press for one-person, one-vote rulings to overcome the dispropor-tionate power rural interests had in legislatures and to otherwise influence the political process.[40]

In addition to initiating lawsuits, associations can gain a forum for their views in the courts by filing *amicus curiae* **briefs** (literally, "friend of the court" briefs), presenting arguments in cases in which they are not direct parties. It is not unusual for courts to cite such briefs in their opinions. Despite the general impression that associations achieve great success in the courts, groups are no more likely than individuals to win at the district court level.[41]

Protest   To generate interest and broaden support for their cause, movements and groups often use protest demonstrations. For example, after the House of Representatives passed new laws on illegal immigration in 2006, pro-immigrant groups mounted protests in cities such as Phoenix and Washington, D.C., with more than 1 million participants.[42] Two months later, in a protest called "A Day Without Immigrants," more than 600,000 protesters gathered in Los Angeles to focus greater media attention on the important role immigrants play in the economy; similar rallies in Chicago drew more than 400,000 people.[43] (The legislation died when differences between the Senate and House versions of the bill could not be reconciled.) Other movements or groups that have used protest include the civil rights movement and antiwar, environmental, and antiglobalization groups.[44]

Candidate Support   Most large organizations are politically engaged in some way, though they may be, or try to be, *nonpartisan*. Most organized interest groups try to work through *both* parties and want to be friendly with the winners, which often means they contribute to incumbents. But as competition for control of both houses of Congress has intensified and with presidential contests also up for grabs, many interest groups invest mostly in one party or the other.

Many interest groups publicly endorse candidates for office, either directly by is-suing a statement or hosting an event, or indirectly by publishing scorecards of how candidates responded to roll call votes or question-naires administered by the group. Some groups give candidates letter grades from A to F. The League of Conservation Voters names candidates it opposes to its "environmental dirty dozen," while praising others as "environmental champions."[45]

Ideological groups like Americans for Democratic Action and the American Conservative Union publish ratings of the voting records of members of Congress on liberal and conservative issues. Other interest groups, such as the U.S. Chamber of Commerce and the League of Conservation Voters, create scorecards of key legislative votes and report to their members how their representa-tive voted on those issues.

Contributions to Campaigns   Interest groups also form political action committees (PACs), which are the legal mechanism for them to contribute money to candidates, political party committees, and other political committees. One of the oldest PACs is the Committee on Political Education (COPE) of the AFL-CIO, but business groups and others have long existed to direct money to favored candi-dates. PACs also encourage other PACs to contribute to favored candidates, occasionally hosting joint fund-raisers for candidates. We discuss PACs in greater detail later in the chapter.

Individuals clearly associated with an interest group also contribute to campaigns as individuals in ways that

amicus curiae brief
Literally, a "friend of the court" brief, filed by an individual or organization to present arguments in addition to those presented by the immediate parties to a case.

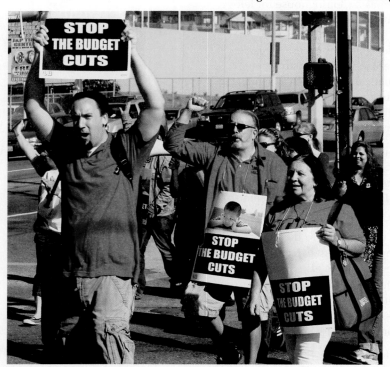

Teachers in downtown Los Angeles protest proposed state budget cuts for education. Groups often use protest as a way of generating interest and increasing support for their causes. ■ *What are some of the factors that might make government officials more or less likely to respond to protests or demonstrations?*

make clear to the candidate the interest of the donor. Often one party gathers contributions from several individuals and then gives the checks made out to the candidate's campaign in a bundle, a process called **bundling.** This can also be done via the computer.

New Political Parties   Another interest group strategy is to form a political party, not so much to win elections as to publicize a cause. Success in such cases may occur when a major party co-opts the interest group's issue. The Free Soil Party was formed in the mid-1840s to work against the spread of slavery into the territories, and the Prohibition Party was organized two decades later to ban the sale of liquor. Farmers have formed a variety of such parties. More often, however, interest groups prefer to work through existing parties.

Today, environmental groups and voters for whom the environment is a central issue must choose between supporting the Green Party, which has yet to elect a candidate to federal office, an Independent candidate such as Ralph Nader in 2008, or one of the two major parties. Sometimes minor-party candidates can spoil the chances of a major-party candidate. In a New Mexico congressional special election in 1997, the Green Party candidate won 17 percent of the vote, taking some votes from the Democrat and thereby helping to elect a Republican to what had been a Democratic seat. As discussed in the opener, the Tea Party Movement became a rallying cry for some candidates in 2010. However, although more closely identified with Republicans, the Tea Party Movement is not currently a party.

Cooperative Lobbying   Like-minded groups often form cooperative groups. In 1987, the Leadership Conference on Civil Rights and People for the American Way brought together many groups to defeat the nomination of outspoken federal judge Robert Bork to the U.S. Supreme Court.[46] Different types of environmentalists work together, as do consumer and ideological groups on the right and on the left. For example, although a large variety of groups that reflect diverse interests represent women, the larger the coalition, the greater the chance that members may divide over such issues as abortion. Another example of a cooperative group is the Business Roundtable, an association of chief executive officers of the 200 largest American corporations, which promotes policies that help large businesses, such as free trade and less government regulation.

The Influence of Lobbyists

Individuals who try to influence policy decisions and positions, often representing groups, are called **lobbyists.** The term "lobbying" was not generally used until around the mid-nineteenth century in the United States. These words refer to the lobby or hallway outside the House and Senate chambers in the U.S. Capitol and to those who hung around the lobby of the old Willard Hotel in Washington, D.C., when presidents dined there. The noun "lobby" is now used as a verb.

Despite their negative public image, lobbyists perform useful functions for government. They provide information for decision makers in all three branches of government, help educate and mobilize public opinion, help prepare legislation and testify before legislative hearings, and contribute a large share of the costs of campaigns. But many people fear that lobbyists have too much influence on government and add to legislative gridlock by stopping action on pressing problems.

Who Are the Lobbyists?

The typical image of policy making is of powerful, hard-nosed lobbyists who use a combination of knowledge, persuasiveness, personal influence, charm, and money to influence legislators and bureaucrats. Often former public servants themselves, lobbyists are experienced in government and often go to work for one of the interests they dealt with while in government, or for a lobbying firm.

Moving from a government job to a job with an interest group—or vice versa—is so common that this career path is called the **revolving door.** Although it is illegal for former national government employees to directly lobby the agency from which they came, their contacts made during government service are helpful to interest groups. Many former members of Congress use their congressional experience as full-time lobbyists. In 2007,

LEARNING **OBJECTIVE**
6.4 Describe lobbyists and the activities through which they seek to influence policy.

bundling
A tactic in which PACs collect contributions from like-minded individuals (each limited to $2,000) and present them to a candidate or political party as a "bundle," thus increasing the PAC's influence.

lobbyist
A person who is employed by and acts for an organized interest group or corporation to try to influence policy decisions and positions in the executive and legislative branches.

revolving door
An employment cycle in which individuals who work for government agencies that regulate interests eventually end up working for interest groups or businesses with the same policy concern.

Breaking into a Male-Dominated Profession

Relatively few women and even fewer minorities are lobbyists. The first woman to own a lobbying firm was Anne Wexler, who started her own firm after leaving the Carter administration in 1981. Wexler observed that when she started, "there were very few women in lobbying. It was completely male dominated."* More women head lobbying firms today. For example, April Burke, who was trained as a lawyer and spent time both on Capitol Hill and in the not-for-profit sector, heads Lewis-Burke Associates LLC. She has represented clients with interests in technology transfer, health policy, higher education, science, and energy sectors.

Women have begun to make inroads into the lobbying profession, especially in areas such as health care, reproductive rights, and education. Because the number of women serving in senior congressional and White House staffs has grown, the pool of women that would likely become lobbyists has similarly grown. Today, approximately 35 percent of Washington lobbyists are women, and a similar proportion of lobbyists at the state level are female.[†] While the number of female lobbyists has risen, the proportion of lobbyists who are white has remained at 95 percent.[‡]

April Burke, president and founder of Lewis-Burke Associates LLC.

CRITICAL THINKING QUESTIONS

1. Why have so few women become lobbyists?

2. Why are so few racial minorities lobbyists?

---

*Jeffrey H. Birnbaum, "Women, Minorities Make Up New Generation of Lobbyists," *Washington Post* (May 1, 2006), p. D1.

[†]Michael G. Bath, Jennifer Gayvert-Owen, and Anthony J. Nownes, "Women Lobbyists: The Gender Gap and Interest Representation," *Politics and Policy*, 33 (March 2005), pp. 136–152.

[‡]Jeffrey H. Birnbaum, "Number of Black Lobbyists Remains Shockingly Low," *Washington Post* (August 7, 2006), p. D01.

---

issue network

Relationships among interest groups, congressional committees and subcommittees, and the government agencies that share a common policy concern.

Congress passed the Honest Leadership and Open Government Act, which requires more disclosure of employment history of lobbyists, sets stricter limits on lobbyist activities, requires senators to wait two years before lobbying, and requires staff to wait one year before lobbying any Senate office. The Obama Administration used this lobbying list in prohibiting any registered lobbyists from serving in any White House or executive branch jobs.

Many lobbyists participate in **issue networks** or relationships among interest groups, congressional committees and subcommittees, and government agencies that share a common policy concern. Personal relationships among members of these groups can sometimes allow these networks to become so strong and mutually beneficial that they form a sort of subgovernment.

Legal and political skills, along with specialized knowledge, are so crucial in executive and legislative policy making that they have become a form of power in themselves. Elected representatives increasingly depend on their staffs for guidance, and these issue specialists know more about "Section 504" or "Title IX" or "the 2002 amendments"—and who wrote them and why—than most political and administrative leaders, who are usually generalists.[47] New laws often need specific rules and applications spelled out in detail by the agencies charged to administer them. In this rule-making activity, interest groups and issue networks assume even more significance.

After leaving his position as White House Counsel, Greg Craig, shown here between former Chief of Staff Rahm Emmanuel and Press Secretary Robert Gibbs, became a partner in a Washington, D.C. law firm. While lawyers do not face the same "revolving door" restrictions as lobbyists, concerns were still raised regarding his recent insider status when it was announced that he would be advising Goldman Sachs, which was facing a lawsuit from the SEC.

What Do Lobbyists Do?

Thousands of lobbyists are active in Washington, but few are as glamorous or as unscrupulous as the media suggest, nor are they necessarily influential. One limit on their

Disclosure of Lobbyist Activity

Obtaining meaningful and timely disclosure of interest group and lobbyist activities is an important way to protect the political process from the undue influence of interest groups. During the last few decades, the government has been engaged in reform efforts seeking to achieve more meaningful disclosure.

One of the problems of prior efforts at disclosing lobbying activities was an imprecise definition of lobbying. The Lobbying Disclosure Act of 1995 (LDA) requires all lobbyists to register with the Clerk of the House of Representatives or the Secretary of the Senate and provides a more detailed definition of exactly what is considered lobbying and who is considered a lobbyist. Lobbyists must file quarterly reports about their lobbying activity, the compensation they received, the time they spent, and the expenses they incurred.

Congress and the president went a step further in 2007 with passage of amendments to the 1995 law known as the Honest Leadership and Open Government Act of 2007 (HLOGA). This law made the lobbyist registration and their reports publicly available online and permits the House clerk and Senate secretary to review the reports for accuracy. The HLOGA includes further restrictions on gifts, on privately funded travel for members of Congress, and requires lobbyists who bundle contributions from individual donors to disclose that activity.[*]

Although it appears some progress has been made in achieving greater disclosure of lobbying activity, some substantial gaps remain. A 2008 Government Accounting Office study of lobbyist filings found that approximately two-thirds of the details in the reports could not be verified and the level of detail in the reports was sometimes lacking.[†] In addition, disclosure laws do not apply to people who only indirectly try to influence policy or legislation through activities such as organizing *others* to write letters or call decision makers. These individuals have come to be known as "strategists" and currently fall outside of lobbyist regulations.

CRITICAL THINKING QUESTIONS

1. Why is disclosure assumed to limit abuses by lobbyists?

2. Why is there resistance to full and complete disclosure by lobbyists and legislators?

[*] Anthony Corrado, "The Regulatory Environment," in David B. Magleby and Anthony Corrado, eds., *Financing the 2008 Election* (Washington, D.C.: Brookings Institution Press, forthcoming).

[†] United States Government Accountability Office, "2008 Lobbying Disclosure: Observations on Lobbyists' Compliance with Disclosure Requirements," April 2009.

---

power is the competition among interest groups. As we have seen, rarely does any one group have a policy area all to itself.

To members of Congress, the single most important thing lobbyists provide is money for their next reelection campaign. "Reelection underlies everything else," writes political scientist David Mayhew.[48] Money from interest groups is the most important source funding this driving need among incumbents. Interest groups also provide volunteers for campaign activity. In addition, their failure to support the opposition can enhance an incumbent's chances of being reelected.

Beyond their central role in campaigns and elections, interest groups provide information of two important types, political and substantive. *Political information* includes such matters as who supports or opposes legislation, including the executive branch, and how strongly they feel about it.[49] *Substantive information*, such as the impact of proposed laws, may not be available from any other source. Lobbyists often provide technical assistance for drafting bills and amendments, identifying persons to testify at legislative hearings, and formulating questions to ask administration officials at oversight hearings.

Interest groups sometimes attempt to influence legislators and regulators by going directly to the people and urging them to contact public officials. They sometimes do this through television advertising but also through mail, e-mail, and banner ads on the Internet. During the protracted debate over health care reform in 2009–2010, multiple groups took their message directly to the people, not only to influence public opinion on possible legislation but as a way to try to pressure Congress. In 2010, an estimated $200 million was spent in advertising on health care on television.[50]

Money and Politics

Interest groups also seek to influence politics and public policy by spending money on elections. They can do this in several ways. One way is by contributing money to candidates for their election campaigns; another is by contributing to political parties that

LEARNING OBJECTIVE

6.5 Identify ways interest groups use money in elections and assess efforts to regulate this spending.

assist candidates seeking office, especially in contested races. They can also contribute money to other interest groups; communicate to the members of their group, including employees; and spend money independently of the parties and candidates.

Helping to elect candidates creates a relationship between the interest group and the elected official that a group may exploit in the policy process. At a minimum, substantial involvement in the election process helps provide access to policy makers.[51] We discuss the dynamics of campaign finance and efforts to reform or regulate it in Chapter 9. Here, we discuss the most important ways interest groups organize and participate in funding campaigns and elections.

Political Action Committees (PACs)

A **political action committee (PAC)** is the political arm of an interest group legally entitled to raise limited and disclosed funds on a voluntary basis from members, stockholders, or employees in order to contribute funds to favored candidates or political parties. PACs link two vital techniques of influence—giving money and other political aid to politicians and persuading officeholders to act or vote "the right way" on issues. Thus, PACs are one important means by which interest groups seek to influence which legislators are elected and what they do once they take office.[52] We categorize PACs according to the type of interest they represent: corporations, trade and health organizations, labor unions, ideological organizations, and so on.

PACs grew in number and importance in the 1970s, in part because of campaign finance reform legislation enacted in that decade. The number of PACs registered rose from 608 in 1974 to 4,611 today.[53] Corporations and trade associations contributed most to this growth; today, their PACs constitute the majority of all PACs. Labor PACs, by contrast, represent less than 6 percent of all PACs.[54] But the increase in the number of PACs is less important than the intensity of PAC participation in elections and lobbying (see Figure 6–3).

Surprisingly, considering that the growth in numbers of PACs has occurred mainly in the business world, organized labor invented this device. In the 1930s, John L. Lewis, president of the United Mine Workers, set up the Non-Partisan Political League as the political arm of the newly formed Congress of Industrial Organizations (CIO). When the CIO merged with the American Federation of Labor (AFL), the new labor group established the Committee on Political Education (COPE), a model for PACs generally whose activities we have already described. Some years later, manufacturers formed the Business and Industry Political Action Committee (BIPAC), but the most active business PAC today is the one affiliated with the National Federation of Independent Business.[55] Table 6–2 lists the most active PACs in elections since 2000.

political action committee (PAC)
The political arm of an interest group that is legally entitled to raise funds on a voluntary basis from members, stockholders, or employees to contribute funds to candidates or political parties.

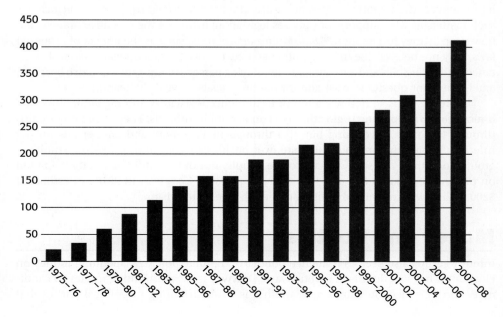

FIGURE 6–3 Total PAC Contributions to Candidates for U.S. Congress, 1975–2008 (in Millions).

SOURCE: Harold W. Stanley and Richard G. Niemi, *Vital Statistics on American Politics 2005–2006* (CQ Press), p. 103; and Federal Election Commission, "PAC Activity Continues to Climb in 2006," Press Release, October 5, 2007, www.fec.gov/press/press2007/20071009pac/ 20071009pac.shtml.

TABLE

6–2	PACs That Gave the Most to Federal Candidates, Cumulatively, 2000–2008 (Millions of Dollars)					
PAC	**2000**	**2002**	**2004**	**2006**	**2008**	**Total**
1. National Association of Realtors	$3.42	$3.65	$3.77	$3.75	$4.01	$18.61
2. National Auto Dealers Association	$2.50	$2.58	$2.58	$2.82	$2.86	$13.35
3. International Brotherhood of Electrical Workers	$2.46	$2.21	$2.30	$2.78	$3.33	$13.09
4. National Beer Wholesalers Association	$1.87	$2.07	$2.29	$2.95	$2.87	$12.04
5. National Association of Home Builders	$1.82	$1.92	$2.22	$2.90	$2.48	$11.35
6. International Brotherhood of Teamsters	$2.49	$2.33	$1.89	$2.07	$2.20	$10.99
7. American Federation of State, County, and Municipal Employees	$2.59	$2.42	$1.64	$2.05	$2.11	$10.81
8. United Auto Workers	$2.16	$2.34	$2.07	$2.22	$1.99	$10.77
9. Laborers Union	$1.79	$2.25	$2.25	$2.32	$2.05	$10.66
10. International Association of Machinists and Aerospace Workers	$2.18	$2.20	$1.91	$1.76	$2.33	$10.37

SOURCE: Federal Election Commission, "Growth in PAC Financial Activity Slows," Press Release, April 24, 2009, www.fec.gov/press/press2009/20090415PAC/20090424PAC.shtml (accessed March 15, 2010).

■ *What kinds of interests do the most active PACs support? What responsibility do candidates who receive funds have to those PACs?*

More recently, elected officials have begun to form their own PACs to collect contributions from individuals and other PACs and then make contributions to candidates and political parties.[56] These committees, called **leadership PACs,** were initially a tool of aspiring congressional leaders to curry favor with candidates in their political party. For example, House Speaker Nancy Pelosi has a leadership PAC that raised and spent between $900,000 and $1 million in each election cycle between 2000 and 2008.[57] She, in turn, contributed to other Democratic House candidates, which helped her win support when she campaigned to be Speaker of the House in 2007.

How PACs Invest Their Money

PACs take part in the entire election process, but their main influence lies in their capacity to contribute money to candidates. Candidates today need a lot of money to wage their campaigns. And as PACs contribute more, their influence grows. What counts is not only how much they give, but who gets it. PACs give to the most influential incumbents, to committee chairs, to party leaders and whips, and to the Speaker of the House. More pragmatic PACs give not only to the majority party but also to key incumbents in the minority party—because today's minority could be tomorrow's majority.

PACs are important not only because they contribute such a large share of the money congressional candidates raise for their campaigns but also because they contribute so disproportionately to incumbents. In the most recent election cycle, House incumbents seeking reelection raised 43 percent of the funds for their campaigns from PACs, compared to only 17 percent for the challengers opposing them. In total, House incumbents raised more than six PAC dollars for every one PAC dollar going to a challenger. Senate incumbents raise proportionately more from individuals but also enjoy a fundraising advantage among PACs compared to Senate challengers (see Figure 6–4). One reason

leadership PAC
A PAC formed by an officeholder that collects contributions from individuals and other PACs and then makes contributions to other candidates and political parties.

FIGURE 6–4 **PAC Contributions to Congressional Candidates, 1998–2008.**

■ *Over time, how has the distribution of PAC money changed? Why do PACs contribute so disproportionately to incumbents?*

SOURCE: Compiled from Federal Election Commission data, "Candidate Financial Summaries," www.fec.gov/finance/disclosure/ftpsum.shtml.

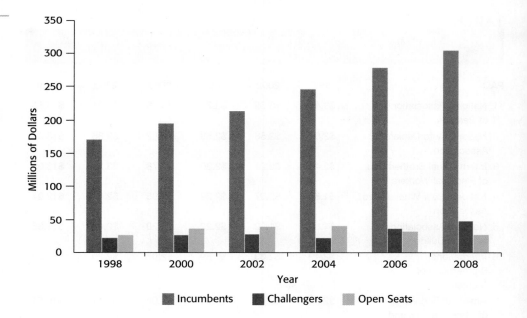

members of Congress become entrenched in their seats is that PACs fund them. Many members of Congress thrive on the present arrangements, and the leaders and members of both parties actively compete for PAC dollars.

The law limits the amount of money that PACs, like individuals, can contribute to any single candidate in an election cycle. But raising money from PACs is more efficient for a candidate than raising it from individuals. Since the 1970s, PAC contributions to any federal candidate have been limited to $10,000 per election cycle (primary and general elections), whereas individuals are limited to $4,800 per candidate in the 2009–2010 election cycle. The **Bipartisan Campaign Reform Act (BCRA)** doubled individual contribution limits and mandated that they increase with inflation while leaving PAC contribution limits unchanged. This probably reflected the view of the legislators that actual corruption or the appearance of it is more likely to come from organized interests such as unions, trade associations, and businesses than from individuals.

PAC contributions are especially made to committee chairs and party leaders. To reinforce this relationship, the Republicans developed a strategy, the "K Street Project," to do even better in getting PAC contributions. (K Street in Washington, D.C., houses many of the lobbying and law firms that represent trade associations and corporations that make contributions.) Former House Republican leader Tom DeLay, a prime mover in the K Street Project, once said, "If you want to play in our revolution, you have to live by our rules," meaning contribute to our candidates.[58] DeLay, under indictment in Texas for money laundering, resigned his seat in 2006.

Since the Democratic Party took control of Congress in 2007, some PACs have changed loyalties. In the House, approximately 60 percent of PAC money goes to Democrats and 40 percent to Republicans. Before Congress changed hands, just the opposite was true—approximately 60 percent of PAC money went to Republicans. In the Senate, Republicans still receive more PAC money than Democrats, but the gap is decreasing.

Mobilizing Employees and Members

Bipartisan Campaign Reform Act (BCRA)
Largely banned party soft money, restored long-standing prohibition on corporations and labor unions use of general treasury funds for electoral purposes, and narrowed the definition of issue advocacy.

Another way interest groups can influence the outcome of elections is by persuading their employees, members, or stockholders to vote in a way consistent with the interests of the group. They accomplish this mobilization through targeted communications at the workplace, through the mail, on the telephone, or on the Internet. As we discuss elsewhere in this chapter, labor unions have been especially effective in member communications. Corporations and business associations have been following labor's lead. Membership organizations such as the NRA have also been able to mobilize their members and allied individuals and groups.[59]

Other Modes of Electioneering

Until the 2004 election cycle, interest groups and individuals could avoid the contribution limitation to political parties by contributing so-called **soft money** to political parties. Originally justified as an exception to contribution limits to help the political parties by funding get-out-the-vote drives or party appeals that are not specific, soft money came to be used for candidate-specific electioneering.[60] We discuss party soft money in greater detail in Chapter 7 and BCRA in Chapter 9.

Between 1996 and 2002, interest groups could also help fund so-called issue ads supporting or opposing candidates as long as the ads did not use certain words. The Supreme Court in 2007 declared parts of BCRA relating to these kinds of ads unconstitutional, allowing corporations and unions to again spend their general funds on ads that advocate a point of view on political issues, which may affect elections.[61] The Supreme Court's 5-to-4 decision in 2010 to allow corporations to use general funds for election-specific ads will likely also result in the same kind of spending by unions and expand the amount of money spent by both types of organizations in competitive federal election contests.[62] Interest groups can avoid disclosure if they communicate with voters through the mail, in newspaper ads, on billboards, on the phone, and by e-mail.

Interest groups typically make the presidential campaign their highest priority. Some groups, such as the League of Conservation Voters (LCV), in the past had invested some of their resources in presidential races but made House and Senate races higher priorities. LCV did just the opposite in 2004.

Independent Expenditures

The Supreme Court in 1976 declared that limits on independent expenditures were unconstitutional when the contributions or expenditures were truly independent of a party or candidate. Hence, groups, like individuals, can campaign for or against a candidate, independent of a party or candidate committee and in addition to making contributions to candidates and party committees from their PAC. These **independent expenditures** are unlimited but must be disclosed to the Federal Election Commission (FEC). Interest-group independent expenditures fall well below PAC contributions to candidates and parties. Groups that have made heavy use of independent expenditures include MoveOn PAC, NRA, EMILY's List, several unions, National Right to Life PAC, the Club for Growth, and the National Association of Realtors. (See Table 6–3.) Independent expenditures enable groups to direct unlimited accounts of money to a particular race. In 2008, for example, the Service Employees International Union spent $1 million on television ads helping the Democrat in the New Hampshire U.S. Senate race. Republicans were benefited in Colorado where the Chamber of Commerce spent $1.9 million for the Republican candidate for U.S. Senate. Another GOP ally, Freedom's Watch, spent another $1.71 million in that race.[63] This spending dwarfs what groups can do through PAC contributions. Groups making independent expenditures receive credit with their members for their activity because the source of independent expenditures is clearly communicated.

Campaigning Through Other Groups

For more than a century, reformers had sought disclosure of money in politics. In campaigns and elections, disclosure was often incomplete, and groups quickly found ways to avoid it. Then, the disclosure provisions of the Federal Election Campaign Act of 1971, amended in 1974, defined electioneering ads as communications that used words such as "vote for" or "vote against" and made them subject to disclosure and spending limits.

For a time, citizens, journalists, and scholars had a complete picture of who was giving what to whom, and who was spending money and in what ways, to influence elections. That changed in 1996, when interest groups found a way to circumvent disclosure and contribution limits through **issue advocacy.** They simply made election ads without the words "vote for" or "vote against," and then they spent millions attacking or promoting particular candidates.

soft money
Money raised in unlimited amounts by political parties for party-building purposes. Now largely illegal except for limited contributions to state or local parties for voter registration and get-out-the-vote efforts.

independent expenditures
The Supreme Court has ruled that individuals, groups, and parties can spend unlimited amounts in campaigns for or against candidates as long as they operate independently from the candidates. When an individual, group, or party does so, they are making an independent expenditure.

issue advocacy
Unlimited and undisclosed spending by an individual or group on communications that do not use words like "vote for" or "vote against," although much of this activity is actually about electing or defeating candidates.

TABLE 6-3	Independent Expenditures by Top Interest Groups, 2008

Interest Group	Expenditure
Service Employees International Union COPE	$39,556,155
National Rifle Association of America Political Victory Fund	18,047,203
National Republican Trust PAC	9,384,714
AFSCME	6,992,408
National Association of Realtors PAC	6,737,055
MoveOn.org PAC	6,649,335
United Auto Workers	4,874,803
American Federation of Teachers	3,867,811
Club for Growth	3,614,053
National Right to Life	3,584,697
League of Conservation Voters Action Fund	3,332,140
EMILY's List	3,202,778
Republican Majority Campaign	3,089,333

NOTE: Expenditures for all national affiliates of an organization are combined, but expenditures for state affiliates are excluded.

SOURCE: Federal Election Commission, ftp://ftp.fec.gov/FEC (accessed March 12, 2009).

Labor unions were the first to exploit this tactic in a major way, spending an estimated $35 million in 1996, mostly against Republican candidates.[64] Corporations and ideological groups quickly followed labor's lead, spending millions on issue ads in 1996–2002.

In the post–campaign reform elections of 2004, 2006, and 2008, interest groups continued to mount their own campaigns against or for candidates in ways similar to the old issue advocacy. For example, a group of Vietnam War veterans formed a group they named Swift Boat Veterans for Truth and ran ads attacking Senator John Kerry's Vietnam War record.[65] Groups like Swift Boat Veterans for Truth are called **527 organizations** or groups because they are tax-exempt groups organized under section 527 of the Internal Revenue Service Code. They can run ads against or for candidates but under somewhat more restrictive conditions than existed before 2004.

527 organization

A political group organized under section 527 of the IRS Code that may accept and spend unlimited amounts of money on election activities so long as they are not spent on broadcast ads run in the last 30 days before a primary or 60 days before a general election in which a clearly identified candidate is referred to and a relevant electorate is targeted.

During the 2004 election cycle, 527 groups were much more active on the liberal or Democratic side than on the conservative or Republican side. Democratic activists and allied interest groups understood that the Bipartisan Campaign Reform Act ban on soft money would leave the party and its presidential candidate at a disadvantage against the fund-raising prowess of President Bush and the Republicans. As we discuss in Chapter 7, the Democrats were more dependent on soft money than the Republicans before BCRA. Thus, after BCRA, they started early and invested heavily in their 527 groups. Interest groups allied to Democrats, including 527 groups, were again more active in 2006 than Republican-allied groups. Labor unions, teachers' unions, trial lawyers, and 527 organizations such as America Votes were all active in competitive federal races. Corporations have been less likely to fund 527 groups. (See Table 6–4.)

Interest groups also used other sections of the tax code to involve themselves in the election. Section 501(c) of the tax code permits some groups to organize, and for some purposes such as nonpartisan voter registration drives, donations to the group are tax deductible. Contributions to partisan groups such as the NRA and MoveOn are not tax deductible. Nor are contributions to labor unions and business groups such as the Chamber of Commerce.[66] In 2004, Republicans found more allies in 501(c) organizations.[67] In 2006 and 2008,

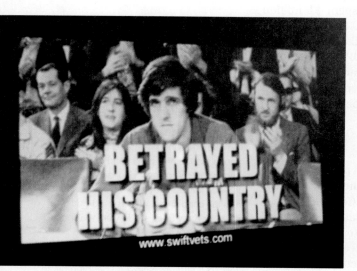

In this image from one of Swift Boat Veterans for Truth's television advertisements, then-presidential nominee John Kerry's patriotism and Vietnam War record are called into question. ■ *What methods do issues groups have to influence elections that individual campaigns do not?*

YOU WILL DECIDE

Should Corporations and Unions Be Unlimited in Funding Parties and in Running Issue Ads?

Does limiting the ability of corporations or unions to use their general or "treasury" funds for election-related expenditures violate the constitutional guarantee of freedom of speech? Corporations and unions, like other groups, are free to form political action committees to make contributions to candidates and parties. What has been at dispute is whether they could take their profits or general funds and spend those on electing or defeating candidates or in support of party efforts. For more than a century, federal law had banned unions and corporations from spending general or treasury funds on electoral politics.

These rules changed in 1979 when the Federal Election Commission allowed unions and corporations to give unlimited general treasury funds or profits to help political parties generally. This was called soft money. In 1996, unions and later corporations began spending unlimited and undisclosed amounts of money on "issue ads," which were really campaign commercials. The Bipartisan Campaign Reform Act banned soft money contributions to parties and more clearly defined election communications as to television or radio ads that refer to a specific candidate and that air within 30 days of the primary or 60 days of the general election. The Supreme Court initially upheld both bans but later reversed itself on election communications. Given this reversal, opponents of the soft money ban are likely to again challenge this provision in court.

What do you think? Should corporations and unions be unlimited in funding parties and in running issue ads? What are some arguments for or against this?

THINKING IT THROUGH

The Supreme Court in *McConnell* v. *FEC* cited a long list of precedents in upholding the limitation on unions and corporations using their general funds to influence elections.* The economic power of corporations such as Microsoft or major unions could, if unconstrained, drown out the voices of other participants and corrupt the electoral process.

But unions and corporations have a point in arguing that constraints on them are unfair when compared with the ability of wealthy individuals to spend unlimited amounts of their own money on politics via independent expenditures, which the Court allowed in its prior landmark decision, *Buckley* v. *Valeo*.[†] They would agree with Justice Scalia's dissent in *McConnell* v. *FEC* that restricting how much a group "can spend to broadcast [its] political views is a direct restriction on speech."[‡]

With respect to electioneering or issue ads, in 2007, the reconstituted Supreme Court in *FEC* v. *Wisconsin Right to*

Life, Inc. said the BCRA language was too broad in defining electioneering and that unions and corporations had a right to communicate with voters about political topics in the days and weeks before primary and general elections.[§] Chief Justice Roberts substituted a new, more loose definition of electioneering communication. In the past, language like that used by Chief Justice Roberts provided media consultants with enough latitude to craft election communications, arguing that they were about issues and not candidates. In 2010, the Supreme Court further broadened the opportunity for corporations and unions to engage in electioneering for or against candidates by reversing a long-standing ban on the use of corporate or union general funds, including profits.[**] This means that future elections could have substantial electioneering by unions and corporations on the eve of elections that is not subject to the other limitations of the law.

---

*McConnell v. *FEC*, 124 S. Ct. 533 (2003).

[†]*Buckley* v. *Valeo*, 96 S. Ct. 760 (1976).

[‡]Justice Antonin Scalia, dissenting in *McConnell* v. *FEC*, 124 S. Ct. 618 (2003).

[§]*Federal Election Commission* v. *Wisconsin Right to Life Inc.*, 466 F. Supp. 2d 195 (2007).

[**]*Citizens United* v. *Federal Election Commission*, 558 U.S. ___ (2010).

501(c) organizations were involved in activities that helped register and inform voters, often with an indirect benefit to one party. In 2008, groups on both sides of the partisan divide made use of 501(c) groups. Among those most active were Planned Parenthood, the League of Conservation Voters, and Defenders of Wildlife who mostly supported Democrats, and the Chamber of Commerce, which largely supported Republicans.[68]

Taken as a whole, interest groups spent more in 2007–2008 than they did in the prior presidential election cycle of 2003–2004. In 2007–2008, they spent an estimated $1.2 billion to influence federal elections.[69] Their level of 501(c) groups spending rose and PAC spending rose even more in 2007–2008, whereas their spending through Section 527 organizations declined.[70] Given the increase in PAC activity, Alan Cigler, an expert in interest groups, assesses the difference PACs made in 2008 and describes it as "robust" in contrast to spending activity by section 527 organizations. More broadly, 2008 saw a decline in Republican-ally involvement, especially at the end of the campaign, and a substantial effort by labor unions, especially the Service Employees International Union, in independent expenditure and 527 activities.[71]

TABLE

6–4	Top Ten 527 Committees Active in Recent Elections by Expenditures (millions of dollars)				
	Committee	**2004**	**2006**	**2008**	**Total**
1	Service Employees International Union	47.70	28.21	27.84	103.75
2	America Votes	3.65	14.11	24.49	42.25
3	College Republican National Committee	17.26	10.26	7.54	35.06
4	EMILY's List	8.10	11.13	12.91	32.14
5	Club for Growth	11.94	8.16	5.93	26.03
6	Intl Brotherhood of Electrical Workers	7.37	5.53	5.89	18.79
7	Gay & Lesbian Victory Fund	1.37	2.96	6.14	10.48
8	Laborers Union	3.29	3.76	2.55	9.60
9	National Federation of Republican Women	3.46	3.03	2.99	9.48
10	League of Conservation Voters	5.08	1.51	1.39	7.98

NOTES: This data is based on records released by the Internal Revenue Service on July 6, 2009.

SOURCE: Center for Responsive Politics, "Top 50 Federally Focused Organizations," www.opensecrets.org/527s/527cmtes.php?level=C&cycle=2008 (accessed August 25, 2009).

■ *What factors can account for fluctuations in 527 Committee spending from one election to the next?*

How Much Do Interest Groups Influence Elections and Legislation?

LEARNING **OBJECTIVE**

6.6 Evaluate the effectiveness of interest groups in influencing elections and legislation.

We have said that because PACs give more money to incumbents, challengers have difficulty funding their campaigns and have to rely more on individual contributors. Even with the larger individual contribution limits allowed in 2004 and since, most challengers still had less money than their incumbent opponents.

How much does interest group money influence election outcomes, legislation, and representation? Former U.S. senator Alan Simpson (R-Wyo.) said that "too often, members' first thought is not what is right or what they believe, but how it will affect fundraising. Who, after all, can seriously contend that a $100,000 donation does not alter the way one thinks about—and quite possibly votes on—an issue?"[72] Another former senator, Warren Rudman (R-N.H.), says, "You can't swim in the ocean without getting wet; you can't be part of this system without getting dirty."[73] In this area, as in others, money obviously talks. But it is easy to exaggerate its influence. Although a candidate may receive a great amount of interest group money, only a fraction of that total comes from any single group. It is also debatable how much campaign contributions affect elections, and there is no guarantee that money produces a payoff in legislation.

Numerous groups seek to mobilize their membership in elections. They create Web sites for members to obtain information about their view of candidates and provide voter registration materials and absentee ballot request forms. How effective is electioneering by interest groups? In general, mass-membership organizations fail to mobilize their full membership in elections, although they can effectively mobilize when their interests are directly attacked.[74] More typically, too many cross-pressures operate in the pluralistic politics of the United States for any one group to assume a commanding role. Some groups reach their maximum influence only by allying themselves closely with one of the two major parties. They may place their members on local, state, and national party committees and help send them to party conventions as delegates, but forming such alliances means losing some independence.

Curing the Mischiefs of Faction—Two Centuries Later

If James Madison were to return today, neither the existence of interest groups nor their variety would surprise him. However, the varied weapons of group influence, the deep investment of interest groups in the electoral process, and the vast number of lobbyists in Washington and the state capitals might come as a surprise. And doubtless, Madison

By the People MAKING A DIFFERENCE

Lobbying for Education Policy

Lobbying on education policy has important implications for college students. Numerous policies and laws enacted by Congress directly affect students and universities, and so it is important for students and universities to try to influence these policies for their own best interests.

For example, approximately two-thirds of college students graduating in 2008 with a bachelor's degree had some debt, with the average amount more than $22,000.* Approximately 6 million students received a Federal Pell Grant in 2007–2008.† Congress recently enacted changes in student loans and Pell grants through two pieces of legislation—the College Cost Reduction and Access Act and the American Recovery and Reinvestment Act. Under these acts, the maximum Pell Grant scholarship for the 2009–2010 school year will be $5,350—more than $600 higher than in 2008–2009. Among the groups active in lobbying Congress on this matter were Sallie Mae, the nation's largest student lender, but also the Consumer Bankers Association and the National Direct Student Loan Coalition.

Most universities and colleges retain a lobbyist to help them secure the support of government, either at the state level, the federal level, or both. Public institutions rely more on the state legislature than do private institutions. You can search online to learn about whether your institution has a lobbyist and how much the institution spent lobbying last year. Find a site on lobbyists in your state—such as http://cal-access.sos.ca.gov/lobbying/ for California or http://www.ethics.state.tx.us/main/search.htm for Texas—to get information on how your school lobbies the state government.

CRITICAL THINKING QUESTIONS

1. Why do you think your university or college hires lobbyists?

2. On matters like changes in the laws relating to student loans, do you think students' perspectives are adequately represented before Congress and the bureaucracy?

3. Is the money your school spent on lobbyists well spent? Why or why not?

* FinAid Page, "Student Loans," FinAid Page, LLC, 2010, http://www.finaid.org/loans/ (accessed March 15, 2010).
† Betsy Miller Kittredge, "Managing Your Student Loans: July 1 College Affordability Benefits Every Borrower Should Know About," *Committee on Education and Labor*, May 14, 2009, http://edlabor.house.gov/blog/2009/05/managing-your-student-loans-up.shtml (accessed March 15, 2010).

---

would still be concerned about the power or "mischiefs of faction," especially its tendency to foster instability and injustice.

Concern about the evils of interest groups has been a recurrent theme throughout U.S. history. President Ronald Reagan in his Farewell Address warned of the power of "special interests,"[75] and President Dwight Eisenhower used his Farewell Address to warn against the "military-industrial complex," the alliance of defense industries and the U.S. military formed to pursue more spending on weapons.

Single-issue interest groups organized for or against particular policies—abortion, handgun control, tobacco subsidies, animal rights—have aroused increasing concern in recent years. "It is said that citizen groups organizing in ever greater numbers to push single issues ruin the careers of otherwise fine politicians who disagree with them on one emotional issue, paralyze the traditional process of governmental compromise, and ignore the common good in their selfish insistence on getting their own way."[76] But which single issues reflect narrow interests? Women's rights—even a specific issue such as sexual harassment—are hardly "narrow," women's rights leaders contend, because women represent more than half the population. These issues may seem different from those related to subsidies for dairy farmers, for example.

One of the main arguments against interest groups is that they do not represent people equally. For example, fewer interest groups represent young or low-income people than represent senior citizens or corporations. Further, some groups are better organized and better financed, allowing them a decided advantage over more general groups. And the existence of a multiplicity of interests often leads to incoherent policies, inefficiency, and delay as lawmakers try to appease conflicting interests. In addition, the propensity of interest groups to support incumbents in elections increases the advantages of incumbency, which is often seen as undesirable.

What—if anything—should we do about factions? For decades, American citizens have tried to find ways to keep interest groups in check. They have agreed with James Madison that the "remedy" of outlawing factions would be worse than the disease. It would be absurd to abolish liberty simply because it nourished faction. And the Constitution solidly protects the existence and activity of interest groups and lobbies. Moreover, interest groups

An important part of campaigns is registering new voters and canvassing them about their views on issues. In this photo, a volunteer from an interest group focusing on get-out-the-vote efforts uses a palm pilot to record survey responses from a Minnesota family. ■ *In what ways can an interest group like this make America more democratic? Under what circumstances could they be accused of the "mischiefs of factions"?*

provide important services. They supply needed and accurate information to government officials. But by safeguarding the value of liberty, have we allowed interest groups to threaten equality, the second great value in our national heritage? The question remains: How can we regulate interest groups in a way that does not threaten our constitutional liberties?

The United States has generally responded to this question by seeking to regulate lobbying in general and political money in particular. Concern over the use of money—especially corporate funds—to influence politicians goes back more than a century, to the administration of Ulysses S. Grant in the 1870s, when members of Congress promoted the Crédit Mobilier construction company in exchange for the right to make huge profits by buying its stock below market value. In the Progressive Era during the first two decades of the twentieth century, Congress legislated against corporate contributions in federal elections and required disclosure of the use of the money.

In 1921, President Warren G. Harding's administration allowed private companies to secretly lease public land in order to extract oil that had been reserved for the navy. In response to this "Teapot Dome scandal," Congress passed the Federal Corrupt Practices Act of 1925. It required disclosure reports, both before and after elections, of receipts and expenditures by Senate and House candidates and by political committees that sought to influence federal elections in more than one state. Note that these were *federal* laws applying to *federal* elections; the states were left to regulate their own lobbying and elections.

But federal legislation was not very effective and was loosely enforced. Many candidates filed incomplete reports or none at all. The reform mood of the 1960s and the Watergate scandal of 1972 brought basic changes. The outcome was the Federal Election Campaign Act of 1971 (FECA), amended in 1974. We discuss FECA and the more recent Bipartisan Campaign Reform Act in greater detail in Chapter 9.

During President Bill Clinton's first term, and after the Republicans won control of Congress in 1994, Congress passed the first major overhaul of lobbying laws since 1946. Under the Lobbying Disclosure Act of 1995, the definition of a lobbyist was expanded to include part-time lobbyists, those who deal with congressional staff or executive branch agencies, and those who represent foreign-owned companies and foreign entities. The number of registered "clients" nearly doubled eight years after enactment of the act,[77] and more recent estimates show additional growth in numbers. The act also included specific disclosure and information requirements.

Interest groups provide important opportunities for individuals to work together to pursue common objectives. Sometimes, this means that individuals join existing groups; other times, they form new ones. Interest groups not only foster healthy competition in our politics, but they also teach important lessons about self-government.

CHAPTER **SUMMARY**

6.1 Explain the role of interest groups and social movements in American politics.

Interest groups form when a collection of people share similar political goals and organize to achieve them. Sometimes, these groups are based on a shared group identity, such as race, ethnicity, gender, or sexual orientation. Others are based on specific policy issues,

such as reducing taxes or combating global warming. Still others claim to operate in the public interest on broad issues, such as educating voters or reducing the federal deficit. Interest groups sometimes begin as social movements, which consist of many people at the grassroots level who are interested in a significant issue, idea, or concern and take action to support or oppose it.

6.2 Categorize American interest groups into types.

Interest groups can be categorized as economic, ideological or single-issue, public interest, foreign policy, and government itself. Economic groups include corporations, labor unions, and professional and trade associations; they lobby officials and campaign for candidates whose trade, tax, and regulation policies favor their financial situation. Ideological groups typically pursue a single policy goal through many means; for example, the ACLU litigates on behalf of clients whose civil liberties have been violated. Public interest groups claim to work on behalf of all citizens and include watchdog groups and charities. Foreign policy groups work to influence some area of the United States' international affairs and include organized lobbies such as AIPAC and grassroots movements such as Greenpeace. Finally, government groups include public sector unions such as the National Education Association and organizations that lobby on behalf of cities, states, and other government entities.

6.3 Analyze sources of interest group power.

Size, resources, cohesiveness, leadership, and techniques, especially the ability to contribute to candidates and political parties and to fund lobbyists, affect interest group power. But the actual power of an interest group stems from how these elements relate to the political and governmental environment in which the interest group operates. Interest groups typically include people with many other cross-cutting interests, which both reduces and stabilizes their influence.

6.4 Describe lobbyists and the activities through which they seek to influence policy.

Lobbyists represent organized interests before government. Lobbying involves communicating with legislators and executive-branch officials, making campaign contributions, and assisting in election activity, especially through political action committees (PACs). Interest groups also communicate their message directly to the public through mass mailings, advertising, and online media.

6.5 Identify ways interest groups use money in elections and assess efforts to regulate this spending.

Interest groups spend money to lobby government officials and to involve themselves in elections, especially through the expanded use of PACs. Groups that lack money typically struggle to get their message out to the public and fail to influence public officials.

Congress has enacted laws to regulate and reform excesses of interest groups in electoral democracy. The Federal Election Campaign Act (FECA) was passed in the 1970s in response to the Watergate scandal, and the Bipartisan Campaign Reform Act (BCRA) was passed in 2002 in response to soft money and other abuses by political parties and interest groups. In *WRTL* v. *FEC*, the Supreme Court ruled to remove some of the restrictions on interest group activities during elections.

6.6 Evaluate the effectiveness of interest groups in influencing elections and legislation.

Interest groups can be important in influencing elections. In 2004, groups helped George W. Bush by attacking John Kerry's heroism and patriotism and by promoting Bush's leadership. In 2006 and 2008, groups were important in competitive contests and in reinforcing the electorate's tendency to reelect incumbents. The influence of groups in the legislative process is greatest when there is an absence of strong groups on the other side of the issue and when members of Congress do not have a strong constituency interest.

CHAPTER **SELF-TEST**

6.1 Explain the role of interest groups and social movements in American politics.
1. Briefly explain the differences between *special interests* and *public interests*.
2. Describe what a social movement is and explain how it differs from an interest group or public interest.
3. In two or three sentences, analyze how the idea of pluralism explains the founders' method for protecting against overwhelming factions.

6.2 Categorize American interest groups into types.
4. Match each interest group with the category it most closely fits.

a. American Gaming Association
b. National Right to Life
c. Project Vote Smart
d. American-Israel Political Action Committee
e. The State Department

i. Public
ii. Government
iii. Economic
iv. Ideological
v. Foreign policy

5. In a few sentences, explain the free rider problem as it applies to labor unions.

6.3 Analyze sources of interest group power.
6. In a short essay, compare and contrast the three sources of interest group power: size, cohesiveness,

and leadership. In your answer, provide an example of at least one group that exhibits each of the three sources and assess how it uses that power to influence national policy, and why.

6.4 Describe lobbyists and the activities through which they seek to influence policy.

7. Associations can gain a forum for their views by filing _____ briefs with courts.

8. PACs that collect contributions from a number of individuals and present them as a single package to a candidate engage in the practice of _____.
   a. targeting
   b. bundling
   c. giving soft money
   d. influence peddling

9. Explain and assess at least five ways in which lobbyists attempt to influence policy.

6.5 Identify ways interest groups use money in elections and assess efforts to regulate this spending.

10. Describe what a PAC is and explain its characteristics.

11. A _____ PAC is a group formed by an office holder that collects contribution from individuals and other PACs and then makes contributions to other candidates and political parties.

12. List three or four arguments against allowing interest groups to donate money to political campaigns. Responding to those arguments, write a brief, persuasive essay explaining why interest groups should be allowed to donate money to political campaigns.

6.6 Evaluate the effectiveness of interest groups in influencing elections and legislation.

13. Write a short, persuasive essay that explains why it is important to allow well-funded groups to function at the expense of less well-funded groups.

Answers to selected questions: 4. a. iii; b. iv; c. i; d. v; e. ii. 7. amicus 8. b 11. Leadership

---

mypoliscilab EXERCISES

Where participation leads to action!

Apply what you learned in this chapter on MyPoliSciLab.

Read on **mypoliscilab.com**

eText: Chapter 6

✓ **Study** and **Review** on **mypoliscilab.com**

Pre-Test
Post-Test
Chapter Exam
Flashcards

Watch on **mypoliscilab.com**

Video: American Cancer Society Recommendation
Video: Murtha and the PMA Lobbyists

✳ **Explore** on **mypoliscilab.com**

Simulation: You Are a Lobbyist
Comparative: Comparing Interest Groups
Timelines: Interest Groups and Campaign Finance

KEY **TERMS**

faction, p.158
pluralism, p. 158
interest group, p. 158
movement, p.158
open shop, p.161
closed shop, p. 161
free rider, p. 161
professional associations, p. 161
nongovernmental organization (NGO), p. 163

collective action, p. 165
public choice, p. 165
lobbying, p.167
Federal Register, p.167
amicus curiae brief, p. 168
bundling, p.169
lobbyist, p. 169
revolving door, p.169
issue network, p.170

political action committee (PAC), p. 172
leadership PAC, p.173
Bipartisan Campaign Reform Act (BCRA), p. 174
soft money, p. 175
independent expenditures, p.175
issue advocacy, p. 175
527 organization, p. 176

ADDITIONAL **RESOURCES**

FURTHER READING

SCOTT H. AINSWORTH, *Analyzing Interest Groups: Group Influence on People and Policies* (Norton, 2002).

JEFFREY H. BIRNBAUM, *The Money Men: The Real Story of Fund-Raising's Influence on Political Power in America* (Crown, 2000).

ALLAN J. CIGLER AND **BURDETT A. LOOMIS,** EDS., *Interest Group Politics*, 8th ed. (CQ Press, 2010).

MARTHA A. DERTHICK, *Up in Smoke*, 2d ed. (CQ Press, 2004).

KENNETH M. GOLDSTEIN, *Interest Groups, Lobbying, and Participation in America* (Cambridge University Press, 1999).

GENE GROSSMAN AND **ELHANAN HELPMAN,** *Special Interest Politics* (MIT Press, 2001).

PAUL S. HERRNSON, RONALD G. SHAIKO, AND **CLYDE WILCOX,** *The Interest Group Connection: Electioneering, Lobbying, and Policymaking in Washington*, 2d ed. revised (CQ Press, 2005).

ALLEN D. HERTZKE, *Representing God in Washington: The Role of Religious Lobbies in the American Polity* (University of Tennessee Press, 1988).

KEVIN W. HULA, *Lobbying Together: Interest Group Coalitions in Legislative Politics* (Georgetown University Press, 1999).

DAVID B. MAGLEBY, *The Change Election* (Temple University Press, 2010).

DAVID B. MAGLEBY AND **ANTHONY D. CORRADO,** EDS., *Financing the 2008 Election* (Brookings Institution Press).

DAVID B. MAGLEBY AND **KELLY D. PATTERSON,** EDS., *The Battle for Congress: Iraq, Scandal, and Campaign Finance in the 2006 Election* (Paradigm, 2008).

ANTHONY J. NOWNES, *Total Lobbying: What Lobbyists Want (and How They Try to Get It)* (Cambridge University Press, 2006).

MANCUR OLSON, *The Logic of Collective Action* (Harvard University Press, 1965).

MARK J. ROZELL, CLYDE WILCOX, AND **DAVID MADLAND,** EDS., *Interest Groups in American Campaigns*, 2d ed. revised (CQ Press, 2006).

DAVID VOGEL, *Kindred Strangers: The Uneasy Relationship Between Politics and Business in America* (Princeton University Press, 1996).

JACK L. WALKER, JR., *Mobilizing Interest Groups in America: Patrons, Professions, and Social Movements* (University of Michigan Press, 1991).

WEB SITES

www.fec.gov The Federal Election Commission site provides information on elections, campaign finance, parties, voting, and PACs.

www.pirg.org This is the Web site of the Public Interest Research Group (PIRG); this group has chapters on many college campuses. PIRG provides state-by-state policy and other information.

www.townhall.com This Web site of the American Conservative Union (ACU) provides policy and political information.

www.adaction.org The Web site of the American for Democratic Action provides information and ratings on members of Congress.

Political Parties

Essential to Democracy

Some years ago, a community college district in Los Angeles held a nonpartisan election for its trustees in which any registered voter could run if he or she paid the $50 filing fee and gathered 500 valid signatures on a petition. Each voter could cast up to seven votes. Political parties were not allowed to nominate candidates, and party labels did not appear on the ballot. Party labels typically help voters get a sense for the candidates; without knowing anything about the individual candidate, voters can make reliable assumptions about the candidate's stance on issues based on his or her political party. In addition, because the community college district was newly created, none of the candidates were incumbents. As a result, incumbency—another frequently used voting cue—was also absent. A total of 133 candidates ran, and they were listed alphabetically.

So how do people vote in an election without parties? Based on the results of the election, having a Mexican American surname seemed to be an advantage. Those whose names began with the letters A to F did better than those later in the alphabet. Having a well-known name also helped. One of the winners, E. G. "Jerry" Brown Jr., was the son of a former governor. Winning this election launched his political career; later he was elected California governor in 1975 and then again in 2010. Endorsements by the *Los Angeles Times* also influenced the outcome, as did campaigning by a conservative group.

Clearly, parties play an important role in facilitating voting by organizing elections and simplifying choices. Rarely are American voters asked to choose from among 133 candidates. E. E. Schattschneider, a noted political scientist once said, "The political parties created democracy, and modern democracy is unthinkable save in terms of the parties."[1] This view that parties are essential to democracy runs counter to a long-standing and deeply seated distrust of parties. But without parties, voters would face the daunting challenge of choosing between scores of candidates for each office, as happened in Los Angeles. They would need to research the policy positions of each individual candidate in order to make an educated choice.

Parties are both a consequence of democracy and an instrument of it. They serve many functions, including narrowing the choices for voters[2] and making national and state elections work. American voters take for granted the peaceful transfer of power from one elected official to another and from one party to another, yet in new democracies where holding power may be more important than democratic principles, the transfer of power after an election is often problematic. Well-established parties help stabilize democracy.

This chapter begins by examining why parties are so vital to the functioning of democracy. We then examine the evolution of American political parties. Although U.S. political parties have changed over time, they remain important in three different settings: as institutions, in government, and in the electorate. We will look at the way parties facilitate democracy in all three. Finally, we discuss the strength of parties today and the prospects for party reform and renewal.

What Parties Do for Democracy

American political parties serve a variety of political and social functions, some well and others not so well. The way they perform them differs from place to place and time to time.

Party Functions

Political parties are organizations that seek political power by electing people to office who will help party positions and philosophy become public policy.

Organize the Competition Parties exist primarily as an organizing mechanism to win elections and thus win control of government. For some races, parties recruit and nominate candidates for office; register and activate voters; and help candidates by training them, raising money for them, providing them with research and voter lists, and enlisting volunteers to work for them.[3]

Local and judicial elections in most states are **nonpartisan elections,** which means no party affiliation is indicated. Such systems make it more difficult for political parties to operate—precisely why many jurisdictions have adopted this reform, contending that party affiliation is not important to being a good judge or school board member. Lacking a party cue as a simplifying device, voters turn to name familiarity of candidates or other simplifying devices like incumbency. These local elections are also often held at times other than when state or federal elections are held. As a result, fewer voters tend to turn out for nonpartisan elections than for standard partisan elections.[4]

Unify the Electorate Parties are often accused of creating conflict, but they actually help unify the electorate and moderate conflict, at least within the party. Parties have a strong incentive to fight out their internal differences but come together to take on the opposition. Moreover, to win elections, parties need to reach out to voters outside their party and gain their support. This action also helps unify the electorate, at least into the two large national political parties in the American system.

Parties have great difficulty building coalitions on controversial issues such as abortion or gun control. Not surprisingly, candidates and parties generally try to avoid defining themselves or the election in single-issue terms. Rather, they hope that if voters disagree with the party's stand on one issue, they will still support it because they agree on other issues. Deemphasizing single issues in this way helps defuse conflict and unify the electorate.

Help Organize Government Although political parties in the United States are not as cohesive as in some other democracies, they are important when it comes to organizing our state and national governments. Congress is organized along party lines. The political party with the most votes in each chamber elects the officers of that chamber, selects the chair of each committee, and has a majority on all the committees. State legislatures, with the notable exception of Nebraska, are also organized along party lines. The 2006 election gave the Democrats winning majorities in both houses of Congress, and as a result, Democrats took over all the committee chairs.

The party that controls the White House, the governor's mansion, or city hall gets **patronage,** which means it can select party members as public officials or judges. Such appointments are limited only by civil service regulations that restrict patronage typically to the top posts, but these posts, which number approximately 3,000 in the federal government (not including ambassadors, U.S. Marshals, and U.S. Attorneys), are also numerous at the state and local levels. Patronage provides an incentive for people to become engaged in politics and gives party leaders and elected politicians loyal partisans in key positions to help them achieve their policy objectives. Patronage, sometimes called the *spoils system*, has declined dramatically in importance due to civil service reform that we will discuss later in this chapter and in Chapter 13.

Translate Preferences into Policy One of the great strengths of our democracy is that even the party that wins an election usually has to moderate what it does to win

political party
An organization that seeks political power by electing people to office so that its positions and philosophy become public policy.

nonpartisan election
An election in which candidates are not selected or endorsed by political parties and party affiliation is not listed on ballots.

patronage
The dispensing of government jobs to persons who belong to the winning political party.

reelection. Thus, public policy seldom changes dramatically after elections. Nonetheless, the party that wins the election has a chance to enact its policies and campaign promises.

American parties have had only limited success in setting the course of national policy, especially compared to countries with strong parties. The European model of party government, which has been called a *responsible party system*, assumes that parties discipline their members through their control over nominations and campaigns. Officeholders in such party-centered systems are expected to act according to party wishes and vote along party lines—or they will not be allowed to run again under the party label, generally preventing their reelection. Candidates also run on fairly specific party platforms and are expected to implement them if they win control in the election.

Because American parties do not control nominations, they are less able to discipline members who express views contrary to those of the party.[5] The American system is largely *candidate-centered*; politicians are nominated largely on the basis of their qualifications and personal appeal, not party loyalty. In fact, it is more correct to say that in most contests, we have *candidate* politics rather than *party* politics. As a consequence, party leaders cannot guarantee passage of their program, even if they are in the majority.

Political parties help inform and motivate voters. Here a senior and political science major at Western Kentucky University makes calls from the local Republican Party headquarters urging voters to support GOP candidates.

Provide Loyal Opposition   The party out of power closely monitors and comments on the actions of the party in power, providing accountability. When national security is at issue or the country is under attack, parties restrain their criticism, as the Democrats in Congress did for some time after September 11, 2001. There is usually a polite interval following an election—known as the **honeymoon**—after which the opposition party begins to criticize the party that controls the White House, especially when the opposition controls one or both houses of Congress.[6] The length of the honeymoon depends in part on how close the vote was in the election, on how contentious the agenda of the new administration is, and on the leadership skills of the new president. Honeymoons have grown shorter throughout the past few decades as candidates from the president's own party and the opposition party get ready for the next presidential election. This puts pressure on the new president to move quickly to set the legislative agenda. Early success in enacting policy can prolong the honeymoon; mistakes or controversies can shorten it.

The Nomination of Candidates

From the beginning, parties have been the mechanism by which candidates for public office are chosen. The **caucus** played an important part in pre-Revolutionary politics and continued to be important in our early history as elected officials organized themselves into groups or parties and together selected candidates to run for higher office, including the presidency. This method of nomination operated for several decades after the United States was established.

As early as the 1820s, however, critics were making charges of "secret deals." Moreover, the caucus was not representative of people from areas where a party was in a minority or nonexistent as only officeholders took part in it. Efforts were made to make the caucus more representative of rank-and-file party members. The *mixed caucus* brought in delegates from districts in which the party had no elected legislators.

Then, during the 1830s and 1840s, a system of **party conventions** was instituted. Delegates, usually chosen directly by party members in towns and cities, selected the party candidates, debated and adopted a platform, and built party spirit by celebrating noisily. But the convention method soon came under criticism that it was subject to control by the party bosses and their machines.

To draw more voters and reduce the power of the bosses to pick party nominees, states adopted the **direct primary,** in which people could vote for the party's nominees for office. Primaries spread rapidly after Wisconsin adopted them in 1905—in the North,

honeymoon
The period at the beginning of a new president's term during which the president enjoys generally positive relations with the press and Congress, usually lasting about six months.

caucus
A meeting of local party members to choose party officials or candidates for public office and to decide the platform.

party convention
A meeting of party delegates to vote on matters of policy and, in some cases, to select party candidates for public office.

direct primary
An election in which voters choose party nominees.

as a Progressive Era reform, and in the South, as a way to bring democracy to a region that had seen no meaningful general elections since the end of Reconstruction in the 1870s because of one-party rule by the Democrats. By 1920, direct primaries were the norm for some offices in nearly all states.

Today, the direct primary is the typical method of picking party candidates. Primaries vary significantly from state to state. They differ in terms of (1) who may run in a primary and how he or she qualifies for the ballot; (2) whether the party organization can or does endorse candidates before the primary; (3) who may vote in a party's primary—that is, whether a voter must register with a party to vote; and (4) how many votes are needed for nomination—the most votes (a plurality), more than 50 percent (a majority), or some other number determined by party rule or state law. The differences among primaries are not trivial; they have an important impact on the role played by party organizations and on the strategy used by candidates.

In states with **open primaries,** any voter, regardless of party, can participate in the primary of whichever party he or she chooses. This kind of primary permits **crossover voting**—Republicans and Independents helping to determine who the Democratic nominee will be, and vice versa. Other states use **closed primaries,** in which only persons already registered in that party may participate. Some states, such as Washington and California, experimented with *blanket primaries*, in which all voters could vote for any candidate, regardless of party. Blanket primaries permitted voters to vote for a candidate of one party for one office and for a candidate from another party for another office, something that is not permitted under either closed or open primaries. In 2000, the Supreme Court held that California's blanket primary violated the free association rights of political parties, in part because blanket primaries permit people who have "expressly affiliated with a rival" party to have a vote in the selection of a nominee from a different party.[7] In a detailed study of California's blanket primary, political scientists found that fewer than 5 percent of voters associated with one party actually voted for nominees from another party. In 2010, California voters overwhelmingly passed an initiative to change the state's primary system to allow voters to cast their primary ballot for a candidate from any party, with the top two vote getters then running in the general election. Proponents of the "top two vote getter" primary see it as fostering more moderate politics.[8]

Along with modern communications and fund-raising techniques, direct primaries have diminished the influence of leaders of political parties. Many critics believe this change has had more undesirable than desirable consequences. Party leaders now have less influence over who gets to be the party's candidate, and candidates are less accountable to the party both during and after the election.

Direct primaries nominate most party candidates for most offices. Yet in some states, local caucuses choose delegates to attend regional meetings, which in turn select delegates to state and national conventions where they nominate party candidates for offices. The Iowa presidential caucuses, in which a record-setting 347,000 Iowans participated in 2008,[9] are highly publicized as the first important test of potential presidential nominees.[10]

Party Systems

Ours is a two-party system; most other democracies have a multiparty system. Although the United States has many **minor parties,** only the two major parties have much of a chance to win elections. Multiparty systems are almost always found in countries that have a parliamentary government, in contrast to our presidential system.

Parliamentary systems usually have a *head of state*, often called the president, but they also have a *head of the government*, often called the prime minister or chancellor, who is the leader of one of the large parties in the legislature. In Germany, the chancellor, currently Angela Merkel, is elected by parliament and holds the greatest share of executive power. Typically, the chancellor comes from the largest party of a coalition of two or more parties and maintains power throughout a four-year term. In Germany, the

open primary
A primary election in which any voter, regardless of party, may vote.

crossover voting
Voting by a member of one party for a candidate of another party.

closed primary
A primary election in which only persons registered in the party holding the primary may vote.

minor party
A small political party that persists over time, is often composed of ideologies on the right or left, or is centered on a charismatic candidate. Such a party is also called a *third party*.

Iowa's Democratic caucus is an unwieldy and complex process. Here, a precinct captain takes a head count to determine support for various candidates. ▪ *What kinds of voters do you think the caucus process would tend to exclude?*

president's responsibilities are mostly ceremonial, and he or she is expected to function in a politically neutral way. In democracies like Germany with multiparty systems, because no one party has a majority of the votes, *coalition* governments are necessary. Minor parties can gain concessions—positions in a cabinet or support of policies they want implemented—in return for joining a coalition. Major parties need the minor parties and are therefore willing to bargain. When parties are studied cross-nationally we see that they often form around class, religious, and economic interests and sometimes in response to particular politicians. An exception to this pattern is India where there are seven or eight parties based on regional identities.[11] Less democratic countries like China continue to only have one party.

Thus, the multiparty system favors the existence of minor parties by giving them incentives to persevere and disproportionate power if they will help form a government. In some multiparty parliamentary systems, parties run slates of candidates for legislative positions, and winners are determined by **proportional representation,** in which the parties receive a proportion of the legislators corresponding to their proportion of the vote. In our single-member district, **winner-take-all system,** only the candidate with the most votes in a district or state takes office.[12] Because a party does not gain anything by finishing second, minor parties in a two-party system can rarely overcome the assumption that a vote for them is a wasted vote.[13] For this reason, an election system in which the winner is the candidate in a single-member district with the plurality deciding the winner, there is tendency to have two parties. This regularity is called *Duverger's law.*[14]

proportional representation
An election system in which each party running receives the proportion of legislative seats corresponding to its proportion of the vote.

winner-take-all system
An election system in which the candidate with the most votes wins.

In multiparty systems, parties at the extremes are likely to have more influence than in our two-party system, and in nations with a multiparty system, legislatures more accurately reflect the full range of the views of the electorate. In contrast, our two-party system tends to create *centrist* parties that appeal to moderate elements and suppress the views of extremists in the electorate. Moreover, once elected, our parties do not form as cohesive a voting bloc as ideological parties do in multiparty systems.

Multiparty parliamentary systems often make governments unstable as coalitions form and collapse. In addition, swings in policy when party control changes can be dramatic.

Angela Merkel is the first female Chancellor of Germany. Because Germany has a multiparty system, she has presided over several coalition governments.

Of the People

THE GLOBAL COMMUNITY

A Competitive Two-Party System

Having a competitive two-party system is something that citizens of the United States take for granted, but not all countries place the same level of importance on it. In the Pew Global opinion survey in 2003 and 2009*, respondents were asked, "How important is it to you to live in a country where honest elections are held regularly with a choice of at least two political parties?"

Respondents from the United States were most likley to say that being able to choose from at least two political parties was very important, with 84 percent giving this response. In contrast, only 43 percent of respondents from Korea gave this answer, and slightly more than half in India thought a choice of at least two politial parties is very important. Mexico, a country which for many years was governed by one party, had slightly more than half of respondents thinking a choice between two parties is very important.

Germany, like many countries in Europe, has a strong party system and more than two competitive parties and had a similar pattern of opinion to the United States on the importance of a two-party system. When looking at a worldwide sample, approximately 60 percent think having a choice between two or more parties is very important.

CRITICAL THINKING QUESTIONS

1. What factors do you think explain people's belief that having a choice between at least two political parties is important?

2. Germany abandoned two parties with the rise to power of Hitler. To what extent do you think that experience influences the attitudes of Germans toward a competitive two-party system today?

3. South Korea is a neighbor to North Korea, one of the few remaining single-party states. Given this, why do you think South Koreans are not more inclined to see a competitive two-party system as very important?

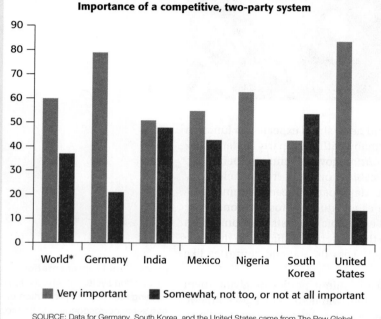

Importance of a competitive, two-party system

Legend: ■ Very important ■ Somewhat, not too, or not at all important

SOURCE: Data for Germany, South Korea, and the United States came from The Pew Global Attitudes Project, 2002. Data for the world average, India, Mexico, and Nigeria came from the Pew Global Attitudes Project, 2008. Note: Because not all countries were included in the 2009 Survey, we have included responses from the most recent survey for that country.

*The world average contains the average responses for the Pew sample for the question, which consists primarily of developing countries. It is not representative of the world as a whole.

*Some countries in our other *Global Community* boxes, such as China, were not included in the sample, in part because they do not have a competitive two or more party system.

In contrast, two-party systems produce governments that tend to be stable and centrist, and as a result, policy changes occur incrementally.

Minor Parties: Persistence and Frustration

Although we have a primarily two-party system in the United States, we also have minor parties, sometimes called *third parties*. Candidate-based parties that arise around a candidate usually disappear when the charismatic personality does. In most states, candidates can get their names on the ballot as an Independent or minor party candidate by securing the required number of signatures on a nomination petition. This is hard to do. In 1992, Ross Perot spent his own money to build an organization of volunteers who put his name on the ballot in all 50 states. Minor party candidates such as Ralph Nader in 2000 secured their nominations as candidates of existing minor parties.

TABLE

7–1	Minor Parties in the United States

Year	Party	Presidential Candidate	Percentage of Popular Vote Received	Electoral Votes
1832	Anti-Masonic	William Wirt	8	7
1856	American (Know-Nothing)	Millard Fillmore	22	8
1860	Democratic (Secessionist)	John C. Breckinridge	18	72
1860	Constitutional Union	John Bell	13	39
1892	People's (Populist)	James B. Weaver	9	22
1912	Bull Moose	Theodore Roosevelt	27	88
1912	Socialist	Eugene V. Debs	6	0
1924	Progressive	Robert M. La Follette	17	13
1948	States' Rights (Dixiecrat)	Strom Thurmond	2	39
1948	Progressive	Henry A. Wallace	2	0
1968	American Independent	George C. Wallace	14	46
1980	National Unity	John Anderson	7	0
1992	Independent	Ross Perot	19	0
1996	Reform	Ross Perot	8	0
2000	Reform	Pat Buchanan	0	0
2000	Green	Ralph Nader	3	0
2004	Reform	Ralph Nader	0	0
2008	Independent	Ralph Nader	0	0

There are 538 electoral votes cast in a presidential election. ■ *How does the percentage of popular vote received compare to the electoral votes received? How can you explain the difference in these numbers?*

SOURCE: C.Q. Press Voting and Elections Collection, 2010, http://library.cqpress.com/elections/search.php.

Minor parties that are organized around an ideology usually persist over a longer time than those built around a particular leader. Communist, Prohibition, Libertarian, Right to Life, and Green Parties are of the ideological type. Minor parties of both types come and go, and several minor parties usually run in any given election. Some parties arise around a single issue, like the Right to Life Party active in states like New York. The Green Party is another example of an ideological third party. Although they are often visible, minor parties have never won the presidency (see Table 7–1) or more than a handful of congressional seats.[15] They have done only somewhat better in gubernatorial elections.[16] They have never shaped national policy from *inside* the government, and their influence on national policy and on the platforms of the two major parties has been limited.[17] Minor parties operating in recent elections include the Libertarian, Green, and Reform Parties.

A Brief History of American Political Parties

To the founders of the young Republic, parties meant bigger, better-organized, and fiercer factions, which they did not want. Benjamin Franklin worried about the "infinite mutual abuse of parties, tearing to pieces the best of characters." In his Farewell Address, George Washington warned against the "baneful effects of the Spirit of Party." And Thomas Jefferson said, "If I could not go to heaven but with a party, I would not go there at all."[18]

How, then, did parties start?

Our First Parties

Political parties emerged largely out of practical necessity. The same early leaders who so frequently stated their opposition to them also recognized the need to organize

LEARNING OBJECTIVE

7.2 Trace changes in American political parties and identify four realigning elections.

YOU WILL DECIDE

Is a Vote for a Third-Party Candidate with Little Chance of Winning a Wasted Vote?

In several close elections, including the 2000 presidential election, the vote cast for one or another minor party, if cast for the likely second choice of those voters, would have changed the outcome of the election. This may have also been true in the 2009 special election in New York's 23rd Congressional District where the Conservative candidate Douglas Hoffman and Republican Dede Scozzafava together got more than 52 percent of the vote, but neither candidate could match the 48 percent of the vote the Democrat, Bill Owens, received. In such a situation, should voters care more about influencing who wins an election or more about casting a vote for a candidate whose views are closest to their own, even if that candidate has little chance of winning?

What do you think? Should voters ever cast votes for third-party candidates? What arguments would you make for or against your position?

THINKING IT THROUGH

How you answer this question depends on what you want to accomplish with your vote. Those who see the vote as a largely symbolic exercise will likely vote for a minor party candidate with little chance of winning. The problem is that the more electable candidate who is clearly preferred over the other more competitive alternative may not win office at all if a voter does not consider electability. The winner-take-all system makes this trade-off more consequential. In a system in which proportional representation is possible, a voter is more likely to be able to translate policy preferences into a vote for representatives. But in our system, voters must often vote for their second choice in order to avoid letting their third choice win office. Interest groups, like environmental groups, often find themselves not endorsing a minor party candidate who may be closer to their views because they want to avoid helping to elect a competitive alternative candidate whose views they abhor.

One way to lessen the influence of these candidates is to require a runoff election of the top two vote getters if no candidate gets a majority. Although this would force another election in some instances, it would also force people who vote to decide among the more viable options. A counterargument is that many people who support minor party candidates would opt out of an election without this chance to express their preferences, and so such a runoff is already accomplished with the plurality-winner system we now have.

Critical Thinking Questions

1. Was a vote for someone other than Bush or Gore in 2000 a wasted vote? Why or why not?

2. What are some issues a minor party might push that would affect the major parties, even if the minor party does not win an election?

3. What are the obstacles minor parties face that major parties do not?

---

officeholders who shared their views so that government could act. In 1787, parties began to form as citizens debated over ratifying the U.S. Constitution. To get Congress to pass its measures, the Washington administration had to fashion a coalition among factions. This job fell to Treasury secretary Alexander Hamilton, who built an informal Federalist party, while Washington stayed "above politics."

Secretary of state Jefferson and other officials, many of whom despised Hamilton and his aristocratic ways as much as they opposed the policies he favored, were uncertain about how to deal with these political differences. Their overriding concern was the success of the new government; personal loyalty to Washington was a close second. Thus, Jefferson stayed in the cabinet, despite his opposition to administration policies, during most of Washington's first term. When he left the cabinet at the end of 1793, many who joined him in opposition to the administration's economic policies remained in Congress, forming a group of legislators opposed to Federalist fiscal policies and eventually to Federalist foreign policy, which appeared "soft on Britain." This party was later known as Republicans, then as Democratic-Republicans, and finally as Democrats.[19]

Realigning Elections

American political parties have evolved and changed over time, but some underlying characteristics have been constant. Historically, we have had a two-party system with minor parties. Our parties are moderate and accommodative, meaning they are open to people with diverse outlooks. Political scientist V. O. Key and others have argued that our party system has been shaped in large part by **realigning elections.** Also called *critical elections*, these are turning points that define the agenda of politics and the alignment of voters within parties during periods of historic change in the economy and society.

Realigning elections are characterized by intense voter involvement, disruptions of traditional voting patterns, changes in the relationships of power within the broader political community, and the formation of new and durable electoral groupings. They have occurred cyclically, about every 32 years, and tend to coincide with expansions of suffrage or changes in the rate of voting.[20] Political scientists generally agree that there have been four realigning elections in American party history: 1824, 1860, 1896, and 1932. Although some argued that the United States was due for another in the 1970s and 1980s, there is little evidence that such an election occurred or is likely in the immediate future.

1824: Andrew Jackson and the Democrats   Party politics was invigorated following the election of 1824, in which the leader in the popular vote—the hero of the battle of New Orleans, Democrat Andrew Jackson—failed to achieve the necessary majority of the electoral college and was defeated by John Quincy Adams in the runoff election in the House of Representatives. Jackson, brilliantly aided by Martin Van Buren, a veteran party builder in New York State, later knitted together a winning combination of regions, interest groups, and political doctrines to win the presidency in 1828. The Whigs succeeded the Federalists as the opposition party. By the time Van Buren, another Democrat, followed Jackson in the White House in 1837, the Democrats had become a large, nationwide movement with national and state leadership, a clear party doctrine, and a grassroots organization. The Whigs were nearly as strong; in 1840, they put their own man, General William Henry Harrison ("Old Tippecanoe"), into the White House. A two-party system had been born.

1860: The Civil War and the Rise of the Republicans   Out of the crisis over slavery evolved the second Republican Party—the first being the National Republican Party that existed for barely a decade in the 1820s. The second Republican Party ultimately adopted the nickname "Grand Old Party" (GOP).[21] Abraham Lincoln was elected in 1860 with the support not only of financiers, industrialists, and merchants but also of many workers and farmers. For 50 years after 1860, the Republican coalition won every presidential race

realigning election
An election during periods of expanded suffrage and change in the economy and society that proves to be a turning point, redefining the agenda of politics and the alignment of voters within parties.

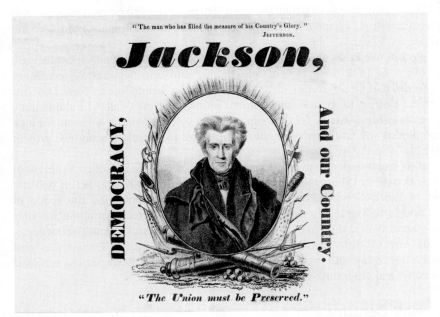

Campaigns are nothing new, dating back to the earliest days of the United States.
■ *Based on the imagery and quotations in this poster, what did the Jackson campaign seek to emphasize about this candidate? Do those themes still appear in today's campaigns?*

except for Grover Cleveland's victories in 1884 and 1892. The Democratic Party survived with its durable white-male base in the South.

1896: A Party in Transition   Economic changes, including industrialization and hard times for farmers, led to changes in the Republican Party in the late 1800s.[22] Some Republicans insisted on maintaining their party's Reconstruction policies into the 1890s until it became obvious it would jeopardize their electoral base.[23] A combination of western and southern farmers and mining interests sought an alliance with workers in the East and Midwest to "recapture America from the foreign moneyed interests responsible for industrialization. The crisis of industrialization squarely placed an agrarian-fundamentalist view of life against an industrial-progressive view."[24] The two parties also differed over whether American currency should be tied to a silver or gold standard, with Republicans favoring gold and Democrats silver. William Jennings Bryan, the Democratic candidate for president in 1896, was a talented orator but lost the race to William McKinley.[25] The 1896 realignment differs from the others, however, in that the party in power did not change hands. In that sense, it was a *converting realignment* because it reinforced the Republican majority status that had been in place since 1860.[26]

The Progressive Era, the first two decades of the twentieth century, was a period of political reform led by the Progressive wing of the Republican Party. Much of the agenda of the Progressives focused on the corrupt political parties. Civil service reforms shifted some of the patronage out of the hands of party officials. The direct primary election took control of nominations from party leaders and gave it to the rank-and-file. And a number of cities instituted nonpartisan governments, totally eliminating the role of a party. With the ratification of the Seventeenth Amendment to the Constitution in 1913, U.S. senators came to be popularly elected. Women obtained the right to vote when the Nineteenth Amendment was ratified in 1920. Thus, in a short time, the electorate changed, the rules changed, and even the stakes of the game changed. Democrats were unable to build a durable winning coalition during this time and remained the minority party until the early 1930s, when the Great Depression overwhelmed the Hoover administration.

1932: Franklin Roosevelt and the New Deal Alignment   The 1932 election was a turning point in U.S. politics. In the 1930s, the United States faced a devastating economic collapse. Between 1929 and 1932, the gross national product fell more than 10 percent per year, and unemployment rose from 1.5 million to more than 15 million, with millions more working only part-time.

With the economic crisis deepening, Franklin D. Roosevelt and the Democrats were swept into office in 1932 on a tide of anti-Hoover and anti-Republican sentiment. Roosevelt promised that his response to the Depression would be a "New Deal for America." After a century of sporadic government action, the New Dealers fundamentally altered the relationship between government and society by providing government jobs for the unemployed and using government expenditures to stimulate economic growth (see Chapter 18).

The dividing line between Republicans and Democrats was the role of government in the economy. Roosevelt Democrats argued that the government had to act to pull the country out of the Depression, but Republicans objected to enlarging the scope of government and intruding it into the economy. This basic disagreement about whether the national government should play an active role in regulating and promoting our economy remains one of the most important divisions between the Democratic and Republican Parties today, although, with time, the country and both parties accepted many of the New Deal programs.

The Last Half Century

Major shifts in party demographics have occurred in recent decades. The once "Solid South" that the Democrats could count on to bolster their legislative majorities and

For the People
GOVERNMENT'S GREATEST ENDEAVORS

Secret Ballots

The means by which people vote matters. We take for granted that voters cast their ballots in secret with no one seeing or knowing how we voted, but this has not always been the case. For most of the first century of U.S. history, ballots were not provided by the government but printed by the parties on different colored paper or distributed in partisan newspapers. In this system, voters turned in their ballots and observers knew how they voted, making it possible for parties to reward or punish individuals based on how they voted. Other voting systems in our early history included voting orally or casting a pebble or bean into a hat.*

Australia was the first country to adopt secret ballots in 1857; the trend later spread to other English-speaking countries and was first proposed in the United States in 1882. An article by Henry George, a writer and politician, published in the *North American Review*, argued that the secret ballot would prevent the bribery or intimidation of voters fostered by the party ballot system. Opponents of the reform contended that state printed ballots distributed at voting places would take too long, resulting in long lines, and would cost the taxpayers too much money.† Massachusetts was the first state to adopt the system in 1888 and by 1896, all but six states were using secret ballots.

Different states adopted different formats for their ballots. Some organized the ballots by party, while others by office. The organization of the ballot can be important in fostering more or less partisan voting. Later, some states permitted voters to vote via machines and today, many states use electronic voting machines. How people vote in other types of elections, like whether or not to unionize, has generated controversy in recent years. But providing, at state expense, voting systems that protect the privacy of the act of voting is now taken for granted.

CRITICAL THINKING QUESTIONS

1. Why might parties have been opposed to using the Australian ballot system in the United States?
2. What are the advantages and disadvantages of paper and electronic ballots?
3. How can ballot organization affect outcomes?

*Jill Lepore, "Rock, Paper, Scissors: How We Used to Vote," *The New Yorker*, October 13, 2008, http://www.newyorker.com/reporting/2008/10/13/ 081013fa_fact_lepore (accessed March 29, 2010).
†Ibid.

---

help win the White House has now become the "Republican South" in presidential elections and increasingly in congressional elections as well. Republican congressional leaders have often been from southern states that once rarely elected Republicans. This shift is explained by the movement of large numbers of white people out of the Democratic Party, in part because of the party's position on civil rights but also because of national Democrats' stand on abortion and other lifestyle issues. The rise of the Republican South reinforced the shift to conservatism in the GOP. This shift, combined with the diminished ranks of conservative southern Democrats, made the Democratic Party, especially the congressional Democrats, more unified and more liberal than in the days when more of its congressional members had "safe" southern seats.[27]

Since 1953, **divided government,** with one party controlling Congress and the other the White House, has been in effect twice as long as united government, in which one party controls both legislative and executive branches. At other times, Congress has had divided control with one party having a majority in the House and the other in the Senate. Although there have been significant periods of unified party control of government during the past half century, they have been more volatile and short-lived than earlier realignments.

The current system of party identification is built on a foundation of the New Deal and the critical election of 1932, events that took place three-quarters of a century ago. How can events so removed from the present still shape our party system? When will there be another realignment—an election that dramatically changes the voters' partisan identification? Or has such a realignment already occurred? The question is frequently debated. Most scholars believe that we have not experienced a major realignment since 1932.[28]

Elections during the past few decades have seen power change hands numerous times without any long-term shifts in the population in party allegiance. In the early 1980s, there seemed to be a possible voting realignment, when Republicans won several close Senate

divided government
Governance divided between the parties, as when one holds the presidency and the other controls one or both houses of Congress.

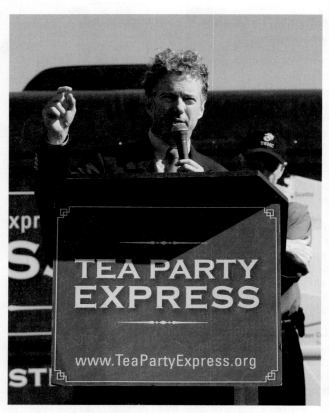

Rand Paul, a Tea Party favorite, was elected to the U.S. Senate from Kentucky. ■ *What factors help explain why some Tea Party candidates were so successful in 2010?*

elections and gained a majority in that body.[29] Democrats, however, won back the Senate in 1986, and until 1994, they appeared to have a permanent majority in the House. All that changed with the 1994 election, as Republicans won a congressional majority and then retained it in 1996 and 1998. In 2002, the Republicans secured unified party control of government, and in 2004, the GOP expanded its congressional majorities. However, in 2006, the Republicans lost control of both houses of Congress, and in 2008, the Democrats secured unified party control by gaining the presidency, a 60-to-40 advantage over Republicans in the Senate, and a 257-to-178 advantage in the House.

Could 2008 have been the long-awaited realigning election? A possible indicator is the expanding electorate. Throughout the course of the 2008 election, 20 states saw record-setting levels of voter registration.[30] Another sign that 2008 may have been a realigning election is the surge in turnout in the 2008 presidential primaries. The rate of participation was at historic highs in many states. Exit polls also found that more than 1-in-10 voters in 2008 were first-time voters. It is too soon to know if the enthusiasm evident in the 2008 contest is sustainable, but the 2008 election presented the Democrats with an opportunity to expand their share of the electorate.

In 2009, only months after Barack Obama took office, a organized opposition which later became known as the Tea Party Movement arose. As discussed in Chapter 6, the focus of the Tea Party included concerns about growing deficits, health care reform, illegal immigration, protecting gun rights, and big government in general.[31] Most people who saw themselves as part of the movement were also Republicans.[32] Tea Party supporters were seen as part of the coalition that elected Scott Brown to the U.S. Senate in the Massachusetts Special Election in January 2010, and they were active in denying renomination to Senator Bob Bennett in Utah.[33] Compared to the rest of the population, people who identify with the Tea Party are older, more likely to be white, and see themselves as very conservative.[34] Compared to other Republicans, they see Barack Obama even more unfavorably, favor reducing the deficit more than creating jobs, and watch Fox News.[35]

In the 2010 elections, Tea Party candidates were successful in some states, but their inexperience and mistakes hurt them in U.S. Senate races in states like Delaware, Nevada, and Colorado. However, the movement helped the Republicans muster energy and enthusiasm for the midterm election, and helped to focus attention on the two years of the Obama administration rather than the preceding eight years of the Bush administration.

American Parties Today

LEARNING **OBJECTIVE**

7.3 Differentiate the functions of parties as institutions, parties in government, and parties in the electorate.

American adults typically take political parties for granted.[36] If anything, most people are critical or distrustful of them. Some see parties as corrupt institutions, interested only in the spoils of politics. Critics charge that parties evade the issues, fail to deliver on their promises, have no new ideas, follow public opinion rather than lead it, or are just one more special interest.

Still, most people understand that parties are necessary. They want party labels kept on the ballot, at least for congressional, presidential, and statewide elections. Most voters think of themselves as Democrats or Republicans and typically vote for candidates from their party. They collectively contribute millions of dollars to the two major parties.[37] Thus, they appreciate, at least vaguely, that you cannot run a big democracy without parties.

Both the Democratic and Republican national parties and most state parties are moderate in their policies and leadership.[38] Successful party leaders must be diplomatic; to win presidential elections and congressional majorities, they must find a middle ground among competing and sometimes hostile groups. Members of the House of Representatives, to be elected and reelected, have to appeal to a majority of the voters from their own district. As more districts have become "safe" for incumbents, the House has had fewer moderates and is prone to more partisan ideological clashes than the Senate.

Parties as Institutions

Like other institutions of government—Congress, the presidency, and the courts—political parties have rules, procedures, and organizational structure. What are the institutional characteristics of political parties?

National Party Leadership   The supreme authority in both major parties is the **national party convention,** which meets every four years for four days to nominate candidates for president and vice president, to ratify the party platform, and to adopt rules.

In charge of the national party, when it is not assembled in convention, is the *national committee*. In recent years, both parties have strengthened the role of the national committee and enhanced the influence of individual committee members. The committees are now more representative of the party rank-and-file. But in neither party is the national committee the center of party leadership.

Each major party has a *national chair* as its top official. The national committee formally elects the chair, but in reality, this official is the choice of the presidential nominee. For the party that controls the White House, the chair actually serves at the pleasure of the president and does the president's bidding. Party chairs often change after elections. During the 2010 election cycle, the Republican National Committee (RNC) chair was Michael Steele, a former Maryland lieutenant governor who took the helm of the RNC after the 2008 election. Steele, an African American, became a visible spokesperson for the GOP and a critic of the Obama administration. The Democratic National Committee (DNC) is led by former Virginia governor Tim Kaine. His term of service at the DNC started in 2009, overlapping with his last year as governor. Kane was considered as a possible running mate by Obama in 2008.

The chair of the party without an incumbent president has considerable independence yet works closely with the party's congressional leadership. The national committee often elects a new head after an electoral defeat. Although chairs are the heads of their national party apparatus, they remain largely unknown to the voters. The chair may play a major role in running the national campaign; after the election, the power of the national chair of the victorious party tends to dwindle.

National party organizations are often agents of an incumbent president in securing his renomination. When there is no incumbent president seeking reelection, the national party committee is generally neutral until the nominee has been selected. National committees play an important role for the Republicans in organizing and coordinating the party get-out-the-vote (GOTV) efforts and were again significant in 2004 and 2008.[39] In 2008, the Democrats had invested in party chair Howard Dean's "50 State Strategy."[40]

In addition to the national party committees, there are national congressional and senatorial campaign committees. These committees work to recruit candidates, train them, make limited contributions to them, and spend independently in some of the most competitive contests.[41] The National Republican Senatorial Committee (NRSC) and Democratic Senatorial Campaign Committee (DSCC) are led by senators elected to two-year terms by their fellow party members in the Senate. The National Republican Campaign Committee (NRCC) and Democratic Congressional Campaign Committee (DCCC) have leaders chosen in the same manner by fellow partisans in the House. Chairs of campaign committees are nominated by their party leadership and typically ratified by their party caucus.

national party convention
A national meeting of delegates elected in primaries, caucuses, or state conventions who assemble once every four years to nominate candidates for president and vice president, ratify the party platform, elect officers, and adopt rules.

Michael Steele, Republican National Committee (RNC) Chairman, faced some opposition from within the party for his mismanagement of election spending and disappointing fundraising.

Party Platforms   Although national party committees exist primarily to win elections and gain control of government, policy goals are also important. Every four years, each party adopts a platform at the national nominating convention. The typical party *platform*—the official statement of party policy, that hardly anyone reads—is often a vague and ponderous document, the result of many meetings and compromises between groups and individuals. Platforms are ambiguous by design, giving voters few obvious reasons to vote against the party (see Figure 7–1).[42]

Many politicians contend that platforms rarely help elect anyone, but platform positions can hurt a presidential candidate. Because the nominee does not always control the platform-writing process, presidential candidates can disagree with their own party platform. But the platform-drafting process gives partisans, and generally the nominee through people he or she appoints, an opportunity to express their views and it spells out the most important values and principles on which the parties are based. Once elected, politicians are rarely reminded what their platform position was on a given issue. In reality, the winning party actually seeks to enact much of its party platform.[43] One major exception was former president George H. W. Bush's memorable promise not to raise taxes if elected in 1988, "Read my lips—no new taxes." He was forced to eat those words when taxes were raised in 1990.[44]

Neither of the party platforms in 2008 generated much attention or controversy. Both parties sought to reinforce the basic positions of their presidential standard bearers. Ideological groups in both parties did not use the platform in 2008 as a way to score points or generate media attention. Rather, the focus of the convention was on the nominees and those endorsing them. But in the year following the 2008 election, a group of Republican National Committee members headed by James Bopp of Indiana proposed a resolution for the 2010 meeting of the RNC that would have barred party support to any candidate whose past votes or positions ran counter to what the proposal called "party positions" on abortion, health care reform, and eight other issues. GOP opponents of this resolution called it a litmus test and the measure was voted down. But the episode illustrates the ideological tensions within parties, especially parties out of power.[45]

Parties at the State and Local Levels   The two major parties are decentralized. They have organizations for each level of government: national, state, and local; and organize for elections at each level. The state and local levels are structured much like the national level. Each state has a *state committee* headed by a *state chair.* State law determines the composition of the state committees and regulates them. Members of state committees are usually elected from local areas.

Powerful state parties have developed in recent years. Despite much state-to-state variation, the trend is toward stronger state organizations, with Republicans typically being much better funded.[46] Some states have significant third and fourth parties. New York, for instance, has a Conservative Party in addition to the Democratic and

FIGURE 7–1 Difference in Perception of What the Parties Stand For, 1984–2008.
A National Election survey tracks responses to the question, "Do you think there are any important differences in what the Republicans and Democrats stand for?" ■ *Why would people be more likely to see differences between parties in presidential election years than in midterm election years?*

SOURCE: *2004 National Election Study,* "Important Difference in What Democratic and Republican Parties Stand For, 1952–2004" (Center for Political Studies, University of Michigan, 2004); and *2008 National Election Study* (Center for Political Studies, University of Michigan, 2008).

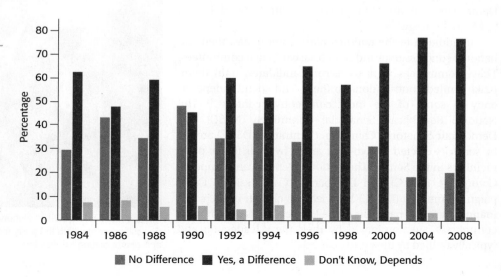

Republican Parties. The role that minor parties play in statewide elections can be important, even though they rarely win office themselves.

Below the state committees are *county committees*, which vary widely in function and power. These committees recruit candidates for such offices as county commissioner, sheriff, and treasurer. Often this means finding a candidate for the office, not deciding among competing contenders. For a party that rarely wins an election, the county committee has to struggle to find someone willing to run. When the chance of winning is greater, primaries, not the party leaders, usually decide the winner.[47] Many county organizations are active, distributing campaign literature, organizing telephone campaigns, putting up posters and lawn signs, and canvassing door-to-door. Other county committees do not function at all, and many party leaders are just figureheads.

Parties in Government

Political parties are central to the operation of our government. They help bridge the separation of powers and facilitate coordination between levels of government in a federal system.

In the Legislative Branch   Members of Congress take their partisanship seriously, at least while in Washington. Their power and influence are determined by whether their party is in control of the House or Senate; they also have a stake in which party controls the White House. The chairs of all standing committees in Congress come from the majority party, as do the presiding officials of both chambers. Members of both houses sit together with fellow partisans on the floor and in committee. (We discuss the role of parties in Congress in greater detail in Chapter 11.) Political parties help bridge the separation of powers between the legislative and executive branches by creating partisan incentives to cooperate. Partisanship can also help unify the two houses of Congress.

Congressional staffs are also partisan. Members of Congress expect their staff—from the volunteer intern to the senior staffer—to be loyal, first to them and then to their party. Should you decide to go to work for a representative or senator, you would be expected to identify yourself with that person's party, and you would have difficulty finding a job with the other party later. Employees of the House and Senate—elevator operators, Capitol Hill police, and even the chaplain—hold patronage jobs. With few exceptions, such jobs go to persons from the party that has a majority in the House or the Senate.

Members of Congress sit together by party during the annual State of the Union address and often respond to the speaker along partisan lines. As shown here during President Obama's 2010 address, they also tend to stand and applaud—or sit and not applaud—in unison as a party. ■ *Why do members of Congress choose to respond to an event like the State of the Union address as a party instead of as individuals?*

In the Executive Branch   Presidents select nearly all senior White House staff and cabinet members from their own party. In addition, presidents typically surround themselves with advisers who have campaigned with them and proved their party loyalty. Partisanship is also important in presidential appointments to the highest levels of the federal workforce. Party commitment, including making campaign contributions, is expected of those who seek these positions. However, presidents usually fill at least one or two senior posts with members of the opposition party. It is a time-honored way to emphasize bipartisanship.

In the Judicial Branch   The judicial branch of the national government, with its lifetime tenure and political independence, is designed to operate in an expressly nonpartisan manner. Judges, unlike Congress, do not sit together by political party. But the appointment process for judges has been partisan from the beginning. The landmark case establishing the principle of judicial review, *Marbury* v. *Madison* (1803), concerned the efforts of one party to stack the judiciary with fellow partisans before leaving office.[48] (See Chapter 2.) Today, party identification remains an important consideration when nominating federal judges.

At the State and Local Levels   The importance of party in the operation of local government varies among states and localities. In some states, such as New York and Illinois, local parties play an even stronger role than they do at the national level. In others, such as Nebraska, parties play almost no role. In Nebraska, the state legislature is expressly nonpartisan, although factions perform like parties and still play a role. Parties are likewise unimportant in the government of most city councils. But in most states and many cities, -parties are important to the operation of the legislature, governorship, or mayoralty. Judicial selection in most states is also a partisan matter. Much was made by the 2000 Bush campaign of the fact that six of the seven Florida Supreme Court justices deciding the 2000 ballot-counting case in favor of Gore were Democrats. Democrats noted that the five U.S. Supreme Court justices who decided the election in favor of Bush were nominated by Republican presidents.

Parties in the Electorate

Political parties would be of little significance if they did not have meaning to the electorate. Adherents of the two parties are drawn to them by a combination of factors, including their stand on the issues; personal or party history; religious, racial, or social peer grouping; and the appeal of their candidates. The emphases among these factors change over time, but they are remarkably consistent with those that political scientists identified more than 40 years ago.[49]

Party Registration   For citizens in most states, "party" has a particular legal meaning— **party registration.** When voters register to vote in these states, they are asked to state their party preference. They then become registered members of one of the two major parties or a third party, although they can change their party registration. The purpose of party registration is to limit the participants in primary elections to members of that party and to make it easier for parties to contact people who might vote for their party.

Party Activists   People who invest time and effort in political parties are often called party activists. They tend to fall into three broad categories: party regulars, candidate activists, and issue activists. *Party regulars* place the party first. They value winning elections and understand that compromise and moderation may be necessary to reach that objective. They also realize that it is important to keep the party together because a fractured party only helps the opposition.

Candidate activists are followers of a particular candidate who see the party as the means to elect their candidate. Candidate activists are often not concerned with the other operations of the party—with nominees for other offices or with raising money for the party. For example, people who supported Ron Paul in his unsuccessful run for the presidency as a Republican were candidate activists. Paul, a Libertarian Republican congressman from Texas, had previously run for the presidency as a Libertarian.

Issue activists wish to push the parties in a particular direction on a single issue or a narrow range of issues: the war in Iraq, abortion, taxes, school prayer, the environment, or civil rights, among others. To issue activists, the party platform is an important battleground because they want the party to endorse their position. Issue activists are also often candidate activists if they can find a candidate willing to embrace their position.

party registration
The act of declaring party affiliation; required by some states when one registers to vote.

Party Identification

Party registration and party activists are important, but many voters are not registered with a political party. Most American adults are mere spectators of party activity. They lack the partisan commitment and interest needed for active involvement. This is not to say that they find parties irrelevant or unimportant. For them, partisanship is what political scientists call **party identification**—a psychological attachment to a political party that most people acquire in childhood from their parents.[50] This type of voter may sometimes vote for a candidate from the other party, but without a compelling reason to do otherwise, most will vote according to their party identification. Peers and early political experiences reinforce party identification as part of the political socialization process described in Chapter 4.

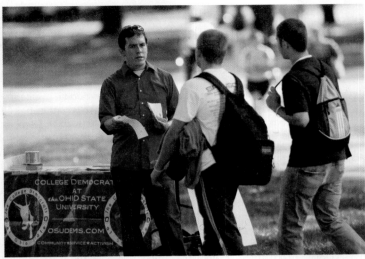

A member of the College Democrats at Ohio State University campaigns for Democratic candidates. While young people identify in greater numbers with the Democratic Party, exit polls suggest that many of the young Democratic voters newly registered in 2008 did not turn out for the 2010 election. ■ *Do You identify strongly with a political party?*

Political scientists and pollsters use the answers to the following questions to measure party identification: "Generally speaking, in politics, do you usually think of yourself as a Republican, a Democrat, an Independent, or what?" Persons who answer Republican or Democrat are then asked: "Would you call yourself a strong or a not very strong Republican/ Democrat?" Persons who answer Independent are asked: "Do you think of yourself as closer to the Republican or the Democratic Party?" Persons who do not indicate Democrat, Republican, or Independent to the first question rarely exceed 2 percent of the electorate and include those who are apolitical or who identify with one of the minor political parties.

When these questions are combined in a single measure, there are seven categories of partisan identification: strong Democrats, weak Democrats, Independent-leaning Democrats, pure Independents, Independent-leaning Republicans, weak Republicans, and strong Republicans. During the more than 50-year period in which political scientists have been conducting such surveys, partisan preferences of the public as a whole have remained remarkably stable, even though new voters have been added to the electorate—minorities and 18- to 21-year-olds (see Table 7–2). For some sub-populations like Protestants and Catholics, partisan allegiances have changed over time (see *Of the People: America's Changing Face* box).

Party identification is the single best predictor of how people will vote.[51] Unlike candidates and issues, which come and go, party identification is a long-term element in voting choice. The strength of party identification is also important in predicting participation and political interest. Strong Republicans and strong Democrats participate

party identification
An affiliation with a political party that most people acquire in childhood.

TABLE

7–2 | Party Identification, 1950s–2000s

Decade	Strong Democrat	Weak Democrat	Independent-Leaning Democrat	Independent	Independent-Leaning Republican	Weak Republican	Strong Republican	Other
1950*	23%	23%	8%	7%	7%	15%	13%	4%
1960	22	25	8	10	7	15	12	2
1970	17	24	12	14	10	14	9	2
1980	18	26	11	12	11	14	11	2
1990	18	19	13	10	12	15	13	1
2000†	18	16	16	10	12	13	14	2

* 1950s percentages based on years 1952, 1956, and 1958.
† 2000s percentages based on years 2000, 2002, 2004, and 2008.

NOTE: Data may not sum to 100 percent because of averaging.

■ *How has the strength of party identification changed over time?*

SOURCE: *National Election Study* (Center for Political Studies, University of Michigan, 2004).

Portrait of the Electorate

Throughout the 44-year period from 1964–2008, the demographic composition of the two major political parties has undergone some changes, while at the same time retaining some important similarities. Consistent with the Republican Party's having become stronger, we find slightly more Republicans than Democrats among men in 2008. In 1964, men were twice as likely to be Democrats as Republicans. Women are disproportionately Democratic in 2008, as they were in 1964. Lower-income voters have consistently been more Democratic, and higher-income voters more Republican. Younger voters in both 1964 and 2008 were more likely to be Democrats. In 1964, Democrats enjoyed strong support from Protestants, Catholics, and Jews. By 2008, Protestants were disproportionately Republican, and the Democratic margin among Catholics had dropped significantly. Jewish voters remained heavily Democratic. In 1964, 59 percent of whites were Democrats; by 2008, the white population was more Republican than Democratic. Blacks were heavily Democratic in both 1964 and 2008. The changing face of party composition has implications for electoral competition and campaign strategy.

CRITICAL THINKING QUESTIONS

1. Why have more white men become Republicans while white women have remained Democrats?

2. What might explain the shift to the GOP among Protestants and Catholics but not Jews?

3. How does the changing demographics of the two parties affect campaigns?

	1964			2008		
	Republican	Democrat	Independent	Republican	Democrat	Independent
Sex						
Male	30%	61%	8%	40%	46%	12%
Female	30	61	7	35	55	9
Race						
White	33	59	8	45	43	10
Black	8	82	6	6	85	8
Hispanic	—	—	—	22	63	14
Age						
18–34	26	64	9	30	56	12
35–45	32	59	8	41	47	10
46–55	26	65	8	41	49	9
56–64	28	66	6	35	54	11
65+	43	49	6	44	48	7
Religion						
Protestant	34	58	7	54	39	7
Catholic	22	70	9	39	51	10
Jewish	11	76	13	19	81	0
Other	28	55	16	28	58	13
Region						
Northeast	36	54	10	34	54	11
North-Central	36	55	8	36	51	11
South	20	71	7	42	46	11
West	30	63	7	32	60	7
Total	30	61	8	37	51	10

NOTE: Numbers may not add to 100 because of rounding. Independents that lean toward a party are classified with the party toward which they lean. Race is defined by the first race with which a respondent identifies. Income is classified as the respondent's household income.

SOURCE: *1964 National Election Study* (Center for Political Studies, University of Michigan, 1964); and *2008 National Election Study* (Center for Political Studies, University of Michigan, 2008).

more actively in politics than any other groups and are generally better informed about political issues. Pure Independents are just the opposite; they vote at the lowest rates and have the lowest levels of interest and awareness of any of the categories of party identification. This evidence runs counter to the notions that persons who are strong partisans are unthinking party adherents and that Independents are informed and ideal citizens.[52]

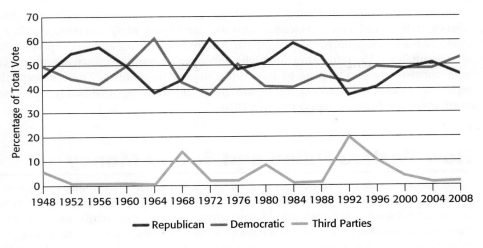

FIGURE 7–2 **Presidential Vote by Party.**
■ *Based on this graph, what share of the vote do third parties generally get? How many elections since 1952 have been exceptions to this?*

SOURCE: Stanley and Niemi, *Vital Statistics on American Politics 2009–2010*, pp. 20–21.

Partisan Dealignment?

As shown in Table 7–2, partisan identification has been stable for more than four decades, despite such changes to the electorate as adding minorities and 18- to 21-year-olds. In addition, as Figure 7–2 sugge sts, Americans have shown no consistent preference for one party over the other in their votes in presidential elections. In a time of electoral volatility, the basics of politics determine the winners and losers: who attracts positive voter attention, who strikes themes that motivate voters to participate, and who communicates better with voters.

However, some experts argue that Independents are increasing in number, suggesting that the party system may be in a period of **dealignment,** in which partisan preferences are weakening and there is a rise in the number of Independents. Indeed, the number of self-classified Independents has increased from 22 percent in the 1950s to 38 percent in 2009. However, two-thirds of all self-identified Independents are really partisans in their voting behavior and attitudes. Table 7–3 summarizes voting behavior

dealignment
Weakening of partisan preferences that point to a rejection of both major parties and a rise in the number of Independents.

TABLE

7–3	Voting Behavior of Partisans and Independents, 1992–2008

Percent Voting for Democratic Presidential Candidate

	1992	1996	2000	2004	2008
Strong Democrats	94%	96%	97%	98%	95%
Weak Democrats	69	84	85	85	86
Independent-Leaning Democrats	70	74	78	88	91
Pure Independents	41	39	45	58	55
Independent-Leaning Republicans	11	23	14	15	18
Weak Republicans	14	21	16	11	12
Strong Republicans	3	4	2	3	4

Percent Voting for Democratic House Candidate

	1994	1996	1998	2000	2002	2004	2008
Strong Democrats	90%	88%	83%	89%	92%	91%	92%
Weak Democrats	72	72	63	73	69	86	84
Independent-Leaning Democrats	66	72	65	73	68	80	83
Pure Independents	51	42	46	52	38	57	43
Independent-Leaning Republicans	25	20	25	26	28	34	21
Weak Republicans	22	20	27	17	27	17	22
Strong Republicans	8	3	8	12	8	10	7

■ *In years that were good for Democrats in congressional elections, like 2004 and 2008, what support did they have that they didn't in weaker elections, like 1994 and 1998?*

SOURCE: National Election Study Cumulative File (Center for Political Studies, University of Michigan, 2005); and 2008 National Election Study (Center for Political Studies, University of Michigan, 2008).

in recent contests for president and the House of Representatives. One-third of those who claim to be Independents lean toward the Democratic Party and vote Democratic in election after election. Another third lean toward Republicans and just as predictably vote Republican. The remaining third, who appear to be genuine Independents, do not vote consistently and appear to have little interest in politics. Thus, despite the reported growth in numbers, there are proportionately approximately the same number of pure Independents now as in 1956.

How Parties Raise and Spend Money

LEARNING **OBJECTIVE**

7.4 Explain party fundraising and expenditures, and assess their regulation.

Although parties cannot exert tight control over candidates, their ability to raise and spend money has had a significant influence. Political parties, like candidates, rely on contributions from individuals and interest groups to fund their activities. Because of the close connection political parties have with officeholders, the courts have long permitted regulation of the source and amount of money people and groups can contribute to parties, as well as the amount parties can spend with or contribute to candidates.

Under the post–Watergate reforms (Federal Election Campaign Act or FECA, as amended in 1974), contributions to the parties from individuals were limited to $20,000, whereas the limit for political action committees (PACs) was $15,000.[53] As we discuss in Chapter 6, PACs are more inclined to give to candidates than party committees.

After the 1976 election, both parties pressed for further amendments to FECA, claiming that campaign finance reforms resulted in insufficient money for generic party activities such as billboard advertising and get-out-the-vote drives. The 1979 amendments to FECA and the interpretations of this legislation by the Federal Election Commission (FEC) permitted unlimited **soft money** contributions to the parties by individuals and PACs for these party-building purposes. Unions and corporations were also allowed to give parties unlimited amounts of soft money. This unregulated money was thus easier to raise and could be spent in unlimited amounts as long as the parties could claim a party-building purpose.

In the 1996 election cycle, both parties found ways to spend this soft money to promote the election or defeat of specific candidates, effectively circumventing party spending limits.[54] In the 1998, 2000, and 2002 elections, congressional campaign committees, following the lead of the national party committees in the 1996 presidential election, raised unprecedented amounts of soft money. In 2000, all party committees combined raised $500 million in soft money. This money was spent in large amounts in the most competitive races. In many instances, this soft money paid for broadcast advertisements that did not even mention the party.[55]

After repeated defeats in one or both houses of Congress for 15 years, Congress regulated this unrestricted soft money under the Bipartisan Campaign Reform Act (BCRA) in 2002. As we will see in Chapter 9, soft money was almost entirely banned under the Act, whereas the limits on individual contributions to candidates and party committees were roughly doubled and indexed to inflation, and a more realistic definition of what constituted election communications by groups was enacted.

The new laws raised serious questions about how the parties would cope without this once-unregulated money in 2004 and thereafter. In 2004, individual giving to both parties set new records, and the DNC and RNC raised as much in **hard money** from individuals and PACs as they had raised in both hard and soft money combined in 2000 or 2002. Much of this money is coming from individuals, including many small contributions.

soft money

Money raised in unlimited amounts by political parties for party-building purposes. Now largely illegal except for limited contributions to state or local parties for voter registration and get-out-the-vote efforts.

hard money

Political contributions given to a party, candidate, or interest group that are limited in amount and fully disclosed. Raising such limited funds was harder than raising unlimited soft money, hence the term "hard money."

Party Expenditures

Party committees are permitted to make contributions to candidates and can also spend a limited amount of money in what are called "coordinated expenditures." In the last several election cycles, the party committees have concentrated their contributions and coordinated expenditures in the most competitive contests.

Former Alaska governor Sarah Palin speaks during the Republican 2010 Victory Fundraising Rally. Palin was instrumental in raising money for numerous winning Republican candidates. ■ *As Sarah Palin wasn't running in this election, why do you suppose she would campaign and raise money on behalf of Republican Party candidates?*

Parties, like individuals and groups, can now also spend unlimited amounts for and against candidates as long as the expenditures were independent of the candidate or a party committee.[56] Unlike soft money, **party-independent expenditures** had to use money raised with normal hard money contribution limits. As long as the party committees could use soft money, independent expenditures were of lesser importance, but with the BCRA ban on soft money, there has been a surge in party-independent expenditure activity (see Table 7–4).

Aside from the Democratic National Committee, all other party committees in Table 7–4 continued to spend heavily in independent expenditures in 2008. This money in 2008 was again spent in only a few competitive races. But where parties invest, they do so in substantial amounts.

During the debate over BCRA, and in the court case on its constitutionality, some such as political scientist Sidney Milkes speculated that BCRA's soft money ban would weaken political parties.[57] The surge in individual contributions has demonstrated

party-independent expenditures
Spending by political party committees that is independent of the candidate. The spending occurs in relatively few competitive contests and is often substantial.

TABLE 7–4 | Independent Expenditures by Party Committee, 1996–2008

	1996	1998	2000	2002	2004	2006	2008
DNC	$0	$0	$0	$0	$120,333,466	–$23,104	$1,104,113
DSCC	1,386,022	1,329,000	133,000	0	18,725,520	42,627,470	73,028,432
DCCC	0	0	1,933,246	1,187,649	36,923,726	64,141,248	81,641,424
RNC	0	0	0	500,000	18,268,870	14,022,675	53,459,386
NRSC	9,734,445	216,874	267,600	0	19,383,692	19,159,901	110,866,286
NRCC	0	0	548,800	1,321,880	47,254,064	82,059,161	30,971,545

NOTE: There was no independent spending by party committees before 1996. When party committees could spend soft money (1996–2002), they spent less in independent expenditures; when BCRA banned soft money in 2002, independent expenditures rose.

■ *Based on the data in this table, which election marked a substantial change in the amount of money spent independently by party committees? How did the spending between Democratic and Republican committees compare in 2008?*

SOURCE: Federal Election Commission, "Party Financial Activity Summarized for the 2004 Election Cycle," press release, March 2, 2005, www.fec.gov/press/press2005/20050302party/Party2004final.html; and David B. Magleby and Kelly D. Patterson, eds., *War Games: Issues and Resources in the Battle for Control of Congress*, monograph (Center for the Study of Elections and Democracy, 2007), p. 47.

the opposite; the DNC and RNC could and did find an alternative to unregulated money. It remains unclear whether the four congressional party committees can make up for the loss of soft money, but the surge in individual contributions to them is promising. The independent expenditure option allows parties to continue to direct money well in excess of the normal limits to races they thought were more competitive.

Compared to other countries, the United States has less public funding of political parties and candidates. Holding the United States aside, wealthier countries (by GDP per capita) have broader regulations than do less-wealthy countries. Britain and Japan, for example, both have limits on the sources of money allowed, disclosure, free television time to parties, and limits on paid television advertising.[58] In contrast, Nigeria only requires disclosure of donors, which could account for the overwhelming role that money plays in Nigerian elections.[59]

Are the Political Parties Dying?

LEARNING **OBJECTIVE**

7.5 Assess the effects of recent party reforms and the long-term prospects for the current party system.

Critics of the U.S. party system make three allegations against it: (1) parties do not take meaningful and contrasting positions on most issues, (2) party membership is essentially meaningless, and (3) parties are so concerned with accommodating the middle of the ideological spectrum that they are incapable of serving as an avenue for social progress. Are these statements accurate? And if they are accurate, are they important?

Some analysts fear that parties are in severe decline or even mortally ill. They point first to the long-run adverse impact on political parties of the Progressive movement reforms early in this century, reforms that robbed party organizations of their control of the nomination process by allowing masses of Independent and "uninformed" voters to enter the primaries and nominate candidates who might not be acceptable to party leaders. They also point to the spread of nonpartisan elections in cities and towns and to the staggering of national, state, and local elections that made it harder for parties to influence the election process.

Legislation limiting the viability and functions of parties was bad enough, say the party pessimists, but parties suffer from additional ills. The rise of television and electronic technology and the parallel increase in the number of campaign, media, and direct-mail consultants have made parties less relevant in educating, mobilizing, and organizing the electorate. Television, radio, the Internet, and telephones have strengthened the role of candidates and lessened the importance of parties. (See Chapter 10 for more on the media in this role.) Advocates of strong parties counter that there are signs of party revival, or at least the persistence of party. The national party organizations own permanent, modern buildings in Washington, D.C., located a few blocks from the U.S. Capitol, and remain capable of providing assistance to candidates in competitive races and to state and local party organizations.

Reform Among the Democrats

In Chicago in 1968, the Democratic National Convention saw disputes inside the hall and riots outside, largely because of protests against the country's policy in Vietnam. Responding to the disarray and to disputes about the fairness of delegate selection procedures, members of the party agreed to a number of reforms. They established a process that led to greater use of direct primaries for the selection of delegates to the national convention and greater representation of younger voters, women, and minorities as elected delegates. Another reform was the abolition of the winner-take-all rule (the *unit rule*) that gave all delegates to the primary or convention winner. This rule was replaced by a system of *proportionality* in which candidates won delegates in rough proportion to the votes they received in the primary election or convention in each state. These rule changes became important in 2008 as proportionality rules meant that neither Hillary Clinton nor Barack Obama could benefit from the "winner-take-all" rules that helped propel John McCain to his party's nomination.

The reforms following 1968 achieved greater diversity of representation among delegates and, as noted, meant that more states adopted primaries. But the new process also

By the People

MAKING A DIFFERENCE

Party Politics on Campus

Citizens gain a stronger voice in American politics by becoming involved in a political party. For all of the reasons discussed in this chapter, parties are vital to the functioning of democracy. Moreover, parties are highly permeable institutions, meaning they are open to influence by individuals like you. As with most Americans, you likely have a party preference or party identification, even if you are an Independent who leans toward one or the other of the political parties.

If your preference is with the Republican Party, you might become involved with the local affiliate of the College Republican National Committee (CRNC). This organization has been in existence for more than a century and has more than a quarter of a million members on more than 1,500 campuses. College Republicans pursue a variety of activities intended to help elect Republicans. You can learn more about the organization at www.cnrc.org. One well-known CRNC alum is Karl Rove, who served as executive director of the organization from 1971–1973.

If you identify more with Democrats, there is likely also a chapter of the College Democrats on your campus. College Democrats was founded in 1932 to help with FDR's campaign. CDA seeks to foster participation by college students in politics, often making use of twitter, blogs, Facebook, and other social networking sites to recruit other students. The national organization maintains an active Web site at www.collegedems.com.

Some students in both parties also become directly involved in campaigns of candidates they like. But as exciting as working for a candidate can be, becoming involved in making a political party stronger will serve many candidates. Groups like these help young voters get involved and learn how to make a difference.

CRITICAL THINKING QUESTIONS

1. Why do both parties invest in college student organizations?

2. What functions of a political party most interest you?

3. How could college students' participation in party politics affect the party system?

---

meant that elected officials who wanted a voice in determining presidential candidates had to run for delegate to the national convention. Some elected officials feared losing in their own party process, and others wanted to delay endorsing a candidate. Responding to this criticism, the party created "superdelegate" positions for elected officials and party leaders who were not required to run for election as delegates. Initially in 2008, most superdelegates favored Clinton, but by late May 2008, a majority of them supported Obama. They were decisive in determining the nominee, as neither Hilary Clinton nor Barack Obama had enough delegates selected in primaries or caucuses to win the nomination.

Reform Among the Republicans

Republicans have not been immune to criticism that their conventions and procedures were keeping out the rank-and-file. They did not make changes as drastic as those made by the Democrats, but they did give the national committee more control over presidential campaigns, and state parties were urged to encourage broader participation by all groups, including women, minorities, youth, and the poor.

The Republican Party has long been better organized than the Democrats. In the 1970s, the GOP emphasized grassroots organization and membership recruitment. Seminars taught Republican candidates how to make speeches and hold press conferences, and weekend conferences were organized for training young party professionals.[60] Until 2004, Republicans had cultivated a larger donor base and were less reliant on the large-donor soft money contributions that became so controversial in recent elections. In 2006, however, the Democratic committees closed the donor gap, with 45 percent of their money raised from small donors, compared to 46 percent from small donors among the Republican committees. The trend toward small donors continued in 2008, especially in the Obama campaign, which set new records not only for total contributions but also for the number of individuals contributing to the campaign. Many of these donors were new donors making contributions that did not exceed $200.

In the 2010 election cycle the Democratic Party committees all raised and spent more than the Republican Party committees, a gap that was filled in partly by interest groups which were more active on the Republican side. In 2010, all party committees raised substantial amounts ($29-$107 million) from donors giving in the aggregate $200 or less to a committee. Such small donors continue to give a larger proportion to the RNC than small donors give the DNC, but the DNC raised more from donors giving under $200 than donors giving more than $200. Small donors were important to tea party insurgent candidates like Rand Paul who was elected to the U.S. Senate from Kentucky.

Continued Importance of Parties

As we have demonstrated in this chapter, political parties are vital to the functioning of democracy. They organize electoral competition, unify large portions of the electorate, simplify democracy for voters, help transform individual preferences into policy, and provide a mechanism for opposition.

Parties are just as important in organizing the government. They help straddle the separation of powers as fellow partisans cooperate between the executive and legislative branches or between the House and Senate. Senior government appointees get their jobs in part because of their party loyalty.

Parties also provide an important way for citizens to influence government. Because they are the means by which politicians secure office, participation in the parties can help determine the course of American government. Parties also provide opportunities to learn about how other people see issues and to learn to compromise. Rather than being an impediment to democracy, they make government by the people possible.

CHAPTER **SUMMARY**

7.1 Identify the primary functions of parties in democracies and distinguish the U.S. party system from those in European democracies.

Political parties are essential to democracy. They simplify voting choices, organize electoral competition, unify the electorate, help organize government by bridging the separation of powers and fostering cooperation among branches of government, translate public preferences into policy, and provide loyal opposition.

American elections are based on single-member-district, winner-take-all election rules. Compared to some European parties, American parties remain organizationally weak. Party nominees are determined through primaries, caucuses, or mixed systems under rules determined by each state.

7.2 Trace changes in American political parties and identify four realigning elections.

Despite their reservations about political parties, the founders became early leaders of a two-party system. Since then, American parties have experienced critical elections and realignments. Most political scientists agree that the last realignment occurred in 1932. During the last half-century, the two parties have been fairly evenly matched, with both parties able to win elections and with divided government more common than unified government. Party identification has remained the best predictor of voting choice and most Americans have a party preference, especially if Independent leaners are included with partisans.

7.3 Differentiate the functions of parties as institutions, parties in government, and parties in the electorate.

Parties play many different roles. As institutions, they are governed by their national and state committees,

which are led by the party chairs, and they recruit and elect candidates, promote their party's principles, and keep the party organized. In government, Congress is organized around parties, and judicial and many executive branch appointments are based in large part on partisanship. In the electorate, parties actively seek to organize elections, simplify voting choices, and strengthen individuals' party identification. In recent years, there has been an increase in the number of persons who call themselves Independents. This trend is sometimes called dealignment, but most Independents are closet partisans who vote fairly consistently for the party toward which they lean.

7.4 Explain party fundraising and expenditures, and assess their regulation.

With the rise of soft money in recent elections, parties had more resources to spend on politics. In 2002, Congress passed the Bipartisan Campaign Reform Act (BCRA), which banned soft money except for some narrowly defined and limited activities. The parties adapted to BCRA by building a larger individual donor base. Donors wanting to spend more than the BCRA limits did so in 2008 through a range of interest groups, many of which ran parallel campaigns with the candidates and parties.

7.5 Assess the effects of recent party reforms and the long-term prospects for the current party system.

Frequent efforts have been made to reform our parties. The Progressive movement saw parties, as then organized, as an impediment to democracy and pushed direct primaries as a means to reform them.

Following the 1968 election, the Democratic Party took the lead in pushing primaries and stressing greater diversity among the individuals elected as delegates. Republicans have also encouraged broader participation, and they have improved their party structure and finances. There has been some party renewal in recent years as party competition has grown in the South and the parties themselves have initiated reforms.

CHAPTER **SELF-TEST**

7.1 **Identify the primary functions of parties in democracies and distinguish the U.S. party system from those in European democracies.**

1. Define the term *political party*, and explain the five major functions of political parties.

2. Keeping in mind the five functions of political parties, discuss in a few sentences why partisan fighting is an inevitable part of the party system.

3. From each pair, identify which feature is part of the U.S. party system and which is part of a typical parliamentary system.
   a. winner-take-all/proportional representation
   b. multimember districts/single-member districts
   c. party-centered campaigns/candidate-centered campaigns
   d. two dominant parties/many parties
   e. weak party organization/strong party organization
   f. ideological parties/centrist parties

4. In two or three sentences, explain why a vote for a third-party candidate in a U.S. election is typically considered a wasted vote.

7.2 **Trace changes in American political parties and identify four realigning elections.**

5. Place the following partisan realignments in chronological order and match them to the party that gained power as a result—Democratic, Republican, or Federalist.
   a. The Progressive Era
   b. Jackson and grassroots democracy
   c. The Founding
   d. The New Deal
   e. The Civil War

6. Analyze the chart on page 202 and identify three or four changes in partisan identification in the last 40 years. For example, far fewer men identify themselves as Democrats today.

7.3 **Differentiate the functions of parties as institutions, parties in government, and parties in the electorate.**

7. Match each of the following activities with the aspect of a political party it best represents—(a) parties as institutions, (b) in government, or (c) in the electorate.
   i. A student registers to vote, stating his party preference as Republican on the registration form before handing it to the county clerk
   ii. Howard Dean, chair of the Democratic National Committee, decides whether the votes of Democrats in Michigan and Florida should count during the 2008 presidential primaries
   iii. The Senate splits 55-to-45 on a bill authorizing funds for the Iraq War, with Republicans voting 44-to-5 in favor and Democrats voting 50-to-1 against

8. Many positions in the executive, legislative, and judicial branches of government are likely to be filled by loyal, active members of the political party in power. In one paragraph, discuss what problems may arise from this system.

7.4 **Explain party fundraising and expenditures, and assess their regulation.**

9. Describe why soft money was banned by the Bipartisan Campaign Reform Act.

10. From where do the national party committees get most of their money today?
    a. Soft money
    b. Individual donors
    c. The general funds of unions and corporations
    d. Their parties' candidates

7.5 **Assess the effects of recent party reforms and the long-term prospects for the current party system.**

11. Examine the tables on partisan identification, voting behavior, and party expenditures. In a paragraph, discuss which party, if either, you think will have the advantage in the coming years. Use specific numbers from the tables to support your argument.

12. In a short essay, describe two or three benefits and two or three problems of parties, then argue for keeping or doing away with our current party system.

Answers to selected questions: 3. a. U.S./parliamentary, b. Parliamentary/U.S., c. Parliamentary/U.S., d. U.S./parliamentary, e. U.S./parliamentary, f. Parliamentary/U.S.; 5. c. The Founding: Federalist, b. Jackson: Democratic, e. The Civil War: Republican, a. The Progressive Era: Republican, d. The New Deal: Democratic.; 7. i. c, ii. a. iii. b; 10. b.

mypoliscilab EXERCISES

Apply what you learned in this chapter on MyPoliSciLab.

Read on **mypoliscilab.com**

eText: Chapter 7

Study and **Review** on **mypoliscilab.com**

Pre-Test
Post-Test
Chapter Exam
Flashcards

Watch on **mypoliscilab.com**

Video: Republicans and Democrats Divide on Tax Cut
Video: Senator Specter Switches Parties
Video: Tea Party Victories Concern for GOP

Explore on **mypoliscilab.com**

Simulation: You Are a Campaign Manager: Help McCain Win Swing States and Swing Voters
Simulation: You Are an Environmental Activist
Comparative: Comparing Political Parties
Timeline: The Evolution of Political Parties in the United States
Timeline: Third Parties in American History
Visual Literacy: State Control and National Platforms

KEY TERMS

political party, p. 186
nonpartisan election, p. 186
patronage, p. 186
honeymoon, p. 187
caucus, p. 187
party convention, p. 187
direct primary, p. 187
open primary, p. 188

crossover voting, p. 188
closed primary, p. 188
minor party, p. 188
proportional representation, p. 189
winner-take-all system, p. 189
realigning election, p. 193
divided government, p. 195
national party convention, p. 197

party registration, p. 200
party identification, p. 201
dealignment, p. 203
soft money, p. 204
hard money, p. 204
party-independent expenditures, p. 205

ADDITIONAL RESOURCES

FURTHER READING

JOHN H. ALDRICH, *Why Parties? The Origin and Transformation of Party Politics in America* (University of Chicago Press, 1995).

JOHN F. BIBBY AND **BRIAN F. SCHAFFNER,** *Politics, Parties, and Elections in America,* 6th ed. (Wadsworth, 2007).

DAVID BOAZ, *Libertarianism: A Primer* (Free Press, 1998).

BRUCE E. CAIN AND **ELISABETH R. GERBER,** EDS., *Voting at the Political Fault Line: California's Experiment with the Blanket Primary* (University of California Press, 2002).

DONALD T. CRITCHLOW, *The Conservative Ascendancy: How the GOP Right Made Political History* (Harvard University Press, 2007).

LEON EPSTEIN, *Political Parties in the American Mold* (University of Wisconsin Press, 1986).

JOHN C. GREEN AND **DANIEL J. COFFEY,** EDS., *The State of the Parties: The Changing Role of Contemporary American Parties,* 6th ed. (Rowman & Littlefield, 2010).

MARJORIE RANDON HERSHEY, *Party Politics in America,* 14th ed. (Longman, 2010).

BRUCE E. KEITH, DAVID B. MAGLEBY, CANDICE J. NELSON, ELIZABETH ORR, MARK C. WESTLYE, AND **RAYMOND E. WOLFINGER,** *The Myth of the Independent Voter* (University of California Press, 1992).

MICHAEL S. LEWIS-BECK, HELMUT NORPOTH, WILLIAM G. JACOBY, AND **HERBERT F. WEISBERG,** *The American Voter Revisited* (University of Michigan Press, 2008).

DAVID B. MAGLEBY AND **ANTHONY D. CORRADO,** EDS., *Financing the 2008 Election* (Brookings Institution Press, 2011).

DAVID B. MAGLEBY, ED., *The Change Election: Money, Mobilization, and*

Persuasion in the 2008 Federal Elections (Temple University Press, 2011).

L. SANDY MAISEL AND **KARA Z. BUCKLEY,** *Parties and Elections in America: The Electoral Process,* 5th ed. (Rowman & Littlefield, 2007).

KELLY D. PATTERSON, *Political Parties and the Maintenance of Liberal Democracy* (Columbia University Press, 1996).

STEVEN J. ROSENSTONE, ROY L. BEHR, AND **EDWARD H. LAZARUS,** *Third Parties in America: Citizen Response to Major Party Failure,* 2d ed. (Princeton University Press, 1996).

JAMES SUNDQUIST, *Dynamics of the Party System: Alignment and Realignment of Political Parties in the United States,* rev. ed. (Brookings Institution Press, 1983).

WEB SITES

www.GOP.com; www.democrats.org These are the main Web sites of the Republican National Committee and Democratic

National Committee, respectively. These sites have information about each party's national party convention and platform as well as party history and information about how to volunteer for party activities.

www.nrsc.org; www.dscc.org These are the Web sites for the National Republican Senatorial Committee and Democratic Senatorial Campaign Committee, respectively. These committees focus on helping their party's candidates win election to the United States Senate. Individuals can volunteer for and contribute to candidates on each site.

www.nrcc.org; www.dccc.org These are the Web sites for the National Republican Congressional Committee and Democratic Congressional Campaign Committee, respectively. These committees focus on helping their party's candidates win election to the United States House of Representatives. Individuals can volunteer for and contribute to candidates on each site.

www.gp.org The Web site for the Green Party of the United States. The site has information about the party's platform, party history, and how to volunteer for party activists and contribute financially.

www.opensecrets.org/parties/index.php The Center for Responsive Politics maintains this Web site with a large amount of information about how parties raise money.

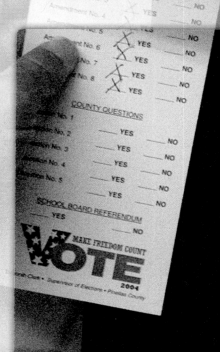

Public Opinion, Participation, and Voting

F or most of U.S. history, voting was something people did in person on a designated day during limited hours. Polling places included fire stations, schools, community centers, and a range of other locations. Under only very limited circumstances, like being out of town on election day, could a person request an *absentee ballot*, which allowed him or her to vote in advance of election day.

Beginning with some local elections in the 1970s, states like California and Oregon began to experiment with allowing voters to vote-by-mail in local elections.[1] In 1998, Oregon was the first state to switch to statewide elections done through the mail, an experiment that was widely seen as a success in that state. Voters who want to vote in person in Oregon can go to their county offices and vote in person, but relatively few do so. Election officials like vote-by-mail because it lowers cost and is easier to administer than an in-person voting process held on only one day. Vote-by-mail has been found to increase turnout, at least in the initial period after adoption,[2] and in Oregon, it continues to foster greater turnout in presidential general elections.[3] Opponents of vote-by-mail worry about potential abuses of the process where people might fraudulently cast the ballot of another person or bribe a person to vote a certain way and then mail in that person's ballot. Some see value in casting a ballot in public with other voters on a designated day. More fundamentally, some question the value of making it easier for people to vote, which voting by mail does. This viewpoint is based on the perceived importance of citizens being willing to invest time and effort, which in-person voting requires. To date, Oregon is the only state to have switched to vote-by-mail as its means to conduct elections.

Also during this same period, states liberalized their absentee voting rules to permit "no excuse" absentee voting, which meant people did not need to have a reason to request an absentee ballot. For voters who do not like to stand in line or prefer to cast their ballot as they study particular ballot propositions or candidate contests, this change was welcome news. In the last few elections, states have also permitted voters to vote early at designated voting places. This change again allows voters to avoid lines on election day and may be preferred by some to voting by absentee ballot through the mail. One advantage is voters do not have to request an absentee ballot—they can just show up to one of the early voting sites on an early voting day.

In 2008, 30 percent of all voters voted early or by absentee ballot, including virtually all of the votes cast in Oregon. This number is up from 22 percent in 2004 and 16 percent in 2000. In 2008, the percent of early or absentee votes was as high as 89 percent in Washington, 79 percent in Colorado, 67 percent in Nevada, and 62 percent in New Mexico.[4] With more and more voting happening before "election day," candidates have had to adapt their campaign strategies.

Making voting more accessible through vote-by-mail and "no-excuse" absentee voting is just the most recent reform intended to broaden electoral participation. In this chapter, we look at the nature and level of political participation in the United States and why people vote the way they do. We also explore public opinion, how to measure it, and what factors affect the formation of opinions. We begin by looking at how we get our political opinions and values.

CHAPTER **OUTLINE**
CHAPTER LEARNING
OBJECTIVES

Forming Political Opinions and Values

8.1 Identify the forces that create and shape individuals' political attitudes.

Public Opinion: Taking the Pulse of the People

8.2 Outline the key dimensions of public opinion, how public opinion is measured, and the relationship between public opinion and public policy.

Participation: Translating Opinions into Action

8.3 Identify forms of political participation, and assess the effect on voter turnout of demographic, legal, and electioneering factors.

Voting Choices

8.4 Analyze why people vote the way they do in elections.

Counting Votes

8.5 Identify problems associated with administering elections and evaluate proposed solutions to those problems.

Forming Political Opinions and Values

LEARNING **OBJECTIVE**

8.1 Identify the forces that create and shape individuals' political attitudes.

No one is born with political views. Rather, they are learned and acquired through experience and association with other people. Socialization—the way in which we come to see society and ourselves and learn to interact with other individuals and groups—lays the foundation for political beliefs, values, ideology, and partisanship. It is a process that continues throughout our lives. How people come to see the political world can change, but our core values and beliefs are resistant to change. More transitory opinions, say, on banking regulation, tend to be volatile, whereas core values on such things as liberty or freedom tend to remain more stable. Discerning this difference is important for understanding the varied levels on which people think about politics.

Political Socialization

We develop our political attitudes from many mentors and teachers through a process called **political socialization.** This process starts in childhood, and families and schools are usually our two most important political teachers. We learn about our culture in childhood and adolescence, but we reshape our opinions as we mature.[5] A common element of political socialization in most cultures is *nationalism,* a consciousness of the nation-state and of belonging to it.

The pluralistic political culture of the United States makes the sources of our views immensely varied. Political attitudes may stem from religious, racial, gender, or ethnic backgrounds or economic beliefs and values. But we can safely make at least one generalization: We form our attitudes through participation in *groups* (see Chapters 4 and 6). Close-knit groups such as the family are especially influential.

Children in the United States tend, at an early age, to adopt common values that provide continuity with the past and that legitimate the U.S. political system. Young children know what country they live in, and they quickly develop national loyalty. Although the details of our political system may elude them, most young citizens acquire a respect for the Constitution and for the concept of participatory democracy, as well as an initially positive view of the most visible figure in our democracy, the president.[6]

political socialization

The process—most notably in families and schools—by which we develop our political attitudes, values, and beliefs.

attitudes

An individual's propensity to perceive, interpret, or act toward a particular object in a particular way.

Family Most social psychologists agree that family is the most powerful socializing agent.[7] What we first learn in the family is not so much specific political opinions as basic **attitudes,** broad or general, that shape our opinions about our neighbors, political parties, other classes or types of people, particular leaders (especially presidents), and society in general. Attitudes are understood to be "a propensity in an individual to perceive, interpret, and act toward a particular object in particular ways."[8] Attitudes are often seen as positive or negative toward the object, person, or idea.

American children typically show political interest by age 10, and by the early teens, their awareness may be fairly high. Studies of high school students indicate a strong correlation between their partisan identification and their parents' political party that continues throughout life. In other words, people tend to belong to the same political party as their parents did. Does the direct influence of parents create the correspondence? Or does living in the same social environment—neighborhood, church, and socioeconomic group—influence parents and children? The answer is *both*. One influence often strengthens the other.

Presidents are important authority figures to children. Here a group of elementary school children watch a speech by President Obama on the importance of education. ■ *In what ways is this school functioning as an agent of political socialization?*

Schools Schools also mold young citizens' political attitudes. U.S. schools see part of their purpose as preparing students to be citizens and active participants in governing their communities and the nation. Especially important in fostering later political involvement are extracurricular activities such as student government and debate.[9]

From kindergarten through college, students generally develop political values consistent with the democratic process and supportive of the U.S. political system. In their study of U.S. history, they are introduced to our nation's heroes and heroines, important events, and the ideals of U.S. society. Other aspects of their experience, such as the daily Pledge of Allegiance and school programs or assemblies, reinforce respect for country. Children also gain practical experience in the way democracy works through elections for student government. In many states, high school and even college students are required by law to take courses in U.S. history or government to graduate.

Do school courses and activities give young people the skills needed to participate in elections and democratic institutions? A study of 18- to 24-year-olds commissioned by the National Association of Secretaries of State found that young people "lack any real understanding of citizenship…information and understanding about the democratic process…and information about candidates and political parties."[10] Furthermore, the Secretaries of State report noted that "most young people do not seek out political information and that they are not very likely to do so in the future."[11] You and your classmates are not a representative sample, in part because you have more interest and knowledge than most people.

Peers and Friends   People of all ages learn from peers and friends, but for younger people they are especially important. For example, friends help with adaptation to school, including college. The influence of friends and peers stems from the human desire to be like people around us.[12] Peer groups not only define fashion and social norms, they reinforce or may challenge what has been experienced in families. Technology has expanded the ways we interact with peers through Facebook or other social media.

The debate about whether there is peer pressure on college campuses to conform to certain acceptable ideas or to use particular language highlights how higher education can shape attitudes and values. One study suggests that college students are more likely than noncollege students of the same age to be knowledgeable about politics, more in favor of free speech, and more likely to talk and read about politics.[13]

Mass Media   Like everyone else, young people are exposed to a wide range of media—school newspapers, national and local newspapers, the Internet, movies, radio, and television—all of which influence what they think, and like everyone else, they often pick and choose the media with which they agree, a process called **selective exposure.** The mass media also serve as agents of political socialization by exposing individuals to the values and behavior of others. Media influence is greater on attitudes about issues and individual politicians than on underlying values.[14]

selective exposure
Individuals choosing to access media with which they agree or avoiding media with which they disagree.

Other Influences   Religious, ethnic, and racial backgrounds as well as the workplace can also shape opinions, both within and outside the family. Some scholars have found, for example, that the religious composition of a community has a direct impact on knowledge, discussion, and self-confidence among students in dealing with politics.[15] But although generalizations about how people vote are useful, we have to be careful about stereotyping. For example, not all African Americans vote Democratic, and many Catholics disagree with their church's opposition to abortion. It is a mistake to assume that because we know a person's religious affiliation or racial background, we know his or her political opinions.

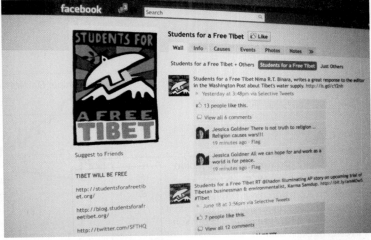

Facebook groups like Students for a Free Tibet allow peers to share their political interests and rally friends to their cause, all without leaving their dorm rooms. ■ *Has Facebook had an impact on your political opinions? How has it changed the way you interact with peers?*

Stability and Change

Adults are not simply the sum of their early experiences, but adults' opinions do tend to remain stable. Even if the world around us changes rapidly, we are slow to shift our loyalties or to change our minds about things that matter to us. In general, people who remain in the same place, in the same occupation, and in the same income group throughout their lives tend to have stable opinions. People often carry their attitudes with them, and families who move from cities to suburbs often retain their big-city attitudes after they have moved, at least for a time. Political analysts are becoming more interested in how adults modify their views. A harsh experience—a war, an economic depression, or an event like the terrorist attacks of September 11, 2001—may be a catalyst that changes attitudes and opinions. Political scientist Robert D. Putnam studied the public's greater confidence in political leaders and higher levels of community interaction following the terrorist attacks. Putnam has found that, for those aged 18 to 25, the post-2001 increase in civic engagement continues.[16]

Because they are part of our core values, views on abortion, the death penalty, and doctor-assisted suicide, for example, tend to remain stable over time. On issues less central to our values, such as how a president is performing, opinions can change substantially. Figure 8–1 contrasts the public's opinion toward President George W. Bush with its views on abortion over time. Although the electorate's opinion of President Bush changed noticeably over time, opinions on abortion remained remarkably stable. On many issues, opinion can change once the public learns more about the issue or perceives another side to the question. These are the issues politicians can help shape by calling attention to them and leading the debate.

Awareness and Interest

Many people find politics complicated and difficult to understand. And they should because democracy is complicated and difficult to understand. The mechanics and structures of our government, such as how the government operates, how the electoral college works, how Congress is set up, and the length of terms for the president and for members of the Senate and House of Representatives are examples of such complexity that are important to our constitutional democracy.

Younger adults who remember learning the details in school typically know most about how the government works. In general, however, adults fare poorly when quizzed about their elected officials.[17] Slightly more than 15 percent know the names of the congressional candidates from their district.[18] With so few voters knowing the candidates, it is not surprising that "on even hotly debated issues before Congress, few people know where their Congress member stands."[19]

The public knows even less about important public policy issues (see Figure 8–2). In 2004, only 28 percent could identify William Rehnquist as the then chief justice of the U.S. Supreme Court. Fortunately, not everyone is uninformed or uninterested. Approximately 25 percent of the public is interested in politics most of the time. This is

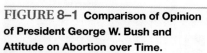

FIGURE 8–1 Comparison of Opinion of President George W. Bush and Attitude on Abortion over Time.
■ *Why is attitude on abortion so consistent in comparison to the fluctuation in opinion of President Bush over the same time period?*

SOURCE: Gallup and Gallup/USA Today polls, compiled by Polling Report, www.pollingreport.com/abortion and www.pollingreport.com/BushJob1.htm.

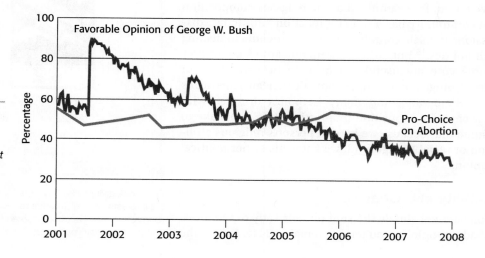

FIGURE 8–2 Political Interest and Knowledge

Do you know more than the average citizen? Test yourself!
(Answers at right)

1. How many votes are needed in the Senate to break a filibuster?
   51, 60, 67, or 75
2. How many GOP senators voted for the health bill?
   0, 5, 10, or 20
3. Who is the chair of the GOP National Committee?
   Sarah Palin, Howard Dean, Michael Steele, or Newt Gingrich
4. What is the Dow Jones Industrial Average currently closest to?
   3,000; 5,000; 10,000; or 20,000
5. Who is the majority leader of the U.S. Senate?
   Harry Reid, Al Franken, Mitch McConnell, or Hillary Clinton
6. Stephen Colbert is which of the following:
   congressman, athlete, comedian and TV host, or hip-hop artist
7. In 2009, were there more U.S. deaths in Iraq or Afghanistan?
8. Where was the attempted "Christmas day" bomber trained?
   Israel, Syria, Afghanistan, or Yemen
9. Which of the following is the unemployment rate closest to?
   5%, 10%, 15%, or 20%
10. How many women are on the U.S. Supreme Court?:
   0, 1, 2, or 3
11. The U.S. imports what percentage of the oil it consumes?
   one-quarter, one-third, half, or two-thirds
12. Who holds the most U.S. debt?
   Japan, China, Saudi Arabia, or Canada

SOURCE: Pew Research Center, January 28, 2010, news release, http://people-press.org/reports/pdf/586.pdf.

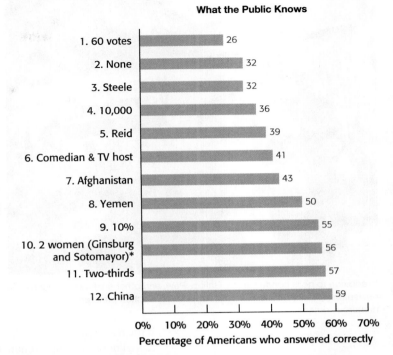

What the Public Knows

	Percentage
1. 60 votes	26
2. None	32
3. Steele	32
4. 10,000	36
5. Reid	39
6. Comedian & TV host	41
7. Afghanistan	43
8. Yemen	50
9. 10%	55
10. 2 women (Ginsburg and Sotomayor)*	56
11. Two-thirds	57
12. China	59

Percentage of Americans who answered correctly (0% to 70%)

*With the addition of Elena Kagan there are now three women on the Court

the **attentive public,** people who know and understand how the government works. They vote in most elections, read a daily newspaper, and talk politics with their families and friends. They tend to be better educated and more committed to democratic values than other adults.

At the opposite end of the spectrum are political know-nothings, people who are rarely interested in politics or public affairs and seldom vote. About one-third of American adults have indicated that they are interested in politics "only now and then" or "hardly at all."[20]

Between the attentive public and the political know-nothings are the *part-time citizens,* roughly 40 percent of the U.S. public. These individuals participate selectively in elections, voting in presidential elections but usually not in others. Politics and government do not greatly interest them, they pay only minimal attention to the news, and they rarely discuss candidates or elections with others.

Democracy can survive even when some citizens are passive and uninformed, as long as others serve as opinion leaders and are interested and informed about public affairs. Obviously, these activists will have much greater influence than their less-active fellow citizens.

attentive public
Citizens who follow public affairs carefully.

Public Opinion: Taking the Pulse of the People

All governments in all nations must be concerned with public opinion. Even in nondemocratic nations, unrest and protest can topple those in power. And in a constitutional democracy, citizens can express opinions in a variety of ways, including through demonstrations, in conversations, by writing to their elected representatives and to newspapers, and by voting in free and regularly scheduled elections. In short, democracy and public opinion go hand in hand.

LEARNING OBJECTIVE

8.2 Outline the key dimensions of public opinion, how public opinion is measured, and the relationship between public opinion and public policy.

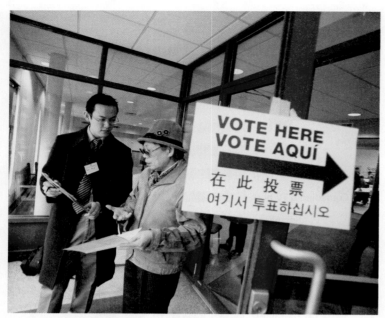

In addition to polls conducted by Gallup, Pew, and other such organizations, newspapers and TV networks conduct polls on election preferences and numerous other subjects.

public opinion

The distribution of individual preferences for or evaluations of a given issue, candidate, or institution within a specific population.

random sample

In this type of sample, every individual has a known and equal chance of being selected.

margin of error

The range of percentage points in which the sample accurately reflects the population.

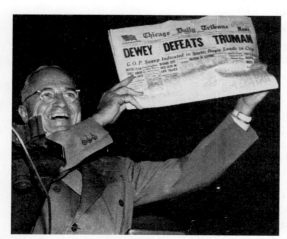

Chicago's *Daily Tribune* was so sure of its polling data in the 1948 election that it predicted a win for Republican Thomas Dewey before the results were final. A victorious Harry Truman displays the mistaken headline.

What Is Public Opinion?

Politicians frequently talk about what "the people" think or want. But social scientists use the term "public opinion" more precisely: **Public opinion** is the distribution of individual preferences for or evaluations of a given issue, candidate, or institution within a specific population as measured by public opinion surveys. *Distribution* means the proportion of the population that holds a particular opinion, compared to people who have opposing opinions or no opinion at all. The most accurate way to study public opinion is through systematic measurement in polls or surveys. For instance, final preelection polls in 2008 by the Gallup Poll found that, among likely voters and removing those with no opinion, 54 percent said they were voting for Barack Obama, 44 percent said they were voting for John McCain, and 2 percent said they were voting for someone else.[21] The actual vote was Obama, 52 percent; McCain; 46 percent; and 1 percent voted for all others.

Measuring Public Opinion

In a public opinion poll, a relatively small number of people can accurately represent the opinions of a larger population if the researchers use *random sampling*. In a **random sample**, every individual in the group has a known and equal chance of being selected. For instance, a survey of 18- to 24-year-olds should not consist solely of college students because nearly half of this age group does not attend college.[22] If only college students are selected, everyone in this age group does not have an equal chance of being included.

One classic example of a flawed poll was the 1936 *Literary Digest* poll, which predicted that Republican Alf Landon would defeat Democrat Franklin D. Roosevelt. However, *Literary Digest*'s Depression-era sample was drawn from subscribers to the magazine who owned cars and had telephones. In fact, Roosevelt decisively defeated Landon in the actual election, carrying every state except Vermont and Maine.[23] A much more reliable way to draw a sample today is with random-digit dialing, in which a computer generates phone numbers at random, allowing the researcher to reach unlisted numbers and cell phones as well as home phones. Exit polls, when properly administered, interview voters at random as they leave the polls at a randomly selected set of precincts.

Even with proper sampling, surveys have a **margin of error,** meaning the sample accurately reflects the population within a certain range—usually plus or minus 3 percent for a sample of at least 1,000 individuals. If, for example, a preelection poll had one candidate getting 50 percent of the vote and another 48 percent, and the margin of error was plus or minus 3 percent, the first candidate's share could be as high as 53 percent or as low as 47 percent, and the second candidate's could be as high as 51 percent or as low as 45 percent. In such a race, the result would be within the margin of error and too close to say who was ahead. If the sample is sufficiently large and randomly selected, these margins of error would apply in about 95 of 100 cases. The final preelection survey results in 2008 were within this margin of error for the actual vote.

The *art of asking questions* is also important to scientific polling. Questions can measure respondents' factual knowledge, their opinions, the intensity of their opinions, or their views on hypothetical situations. The type of questions asked should be determined by the kind of information desired by the researcher. The way questions are worded and the order in which they are asked can influence respondents' answers. Researchers should pretest their questions to be sure they are as clear and as specific as possible. Professional interviewers, who read the questions exactly as written and without any bias in their voices, should ask them.

TABLE

8-1 | The Way You Ask the Question Matters

The way you ask a polling question can make a lot of difference in the way people answer it. Consider the following questions about the Holocaust, each of which was asked during early 1994. Read each question and consider how you would have responded if asked by an interviewer.

1. The term Holocaust usually refers to the killing of millions of Jews in Nazi death camps during World War II. Does it seem possible or does it seem impossible to you that the Nazi extermination of the Jews never happened?

    Possible—36.8%   Impossible—58.2%   Unsure, do not know, etc.—5.0%*

2. The term Holocaust usually refers to the killing of millions of Jews in Nazi death camps during World War II. Do you doubt that the Holocaust actually happened or not?

    Yes, doubt it happened—8.8%   No, do not doubt it happened—87.0%   Unsure, etc.—4.2%**

3. Just to clarify, in your opinion, did the Holocaust definitely happen, probably happen, probably not happen, or definitely not happen?

    Definitely happened—77.8%   Probably happened—17.2%   Probably did not happen—2.2%   Definitely did not happen—0.1%   Do not know, etc.—2.7%†

4. Does it seem possible to you that the Nazi extermination of the Jews never happened, or do you feel certain that it happened?

    Possible it never happened—1.1%   Feel certain it happened—91.2%   Do not know—7.7%‡

* Gallup (January 1994)
** Gallup (January 1994)
† Gallup (January 1994)
‡ Roper (April 1994)

■ *What about the question wording might explain the very different results in these polls? Which of the questions do you think led to the most accurate measure of opinion? Why?*

Open-ended questions permit respondents to answer in their own words rather than by choosing responses from set categories. These questions are harder to record and compare, but they allow respondents to express their views more clearly and may provide deeper insight into their thinking. (See Table 8–1.)

Scientific polls also require thorough *analysis and reporting of the results.* Scientific polls must specify the sample size, the margin of error, and when and where the poll was conducted. Moreover, because public opinion can change from day to day and even from hour to hour, polls are really only snapshots of opinion at a particular point in time. One way to track opinion *change* is to interview the same sample more than once. Such surveys are called *panel surveys.* Although they can be informative, it can also be difficult and expensive to contact respondents for a second or third set of interviews, and those in the sample may know they will be interviewed again, which may influence their responses.

Defining public opinion as the distribution of *individual preference* emphasizes that the unit of measurement is *individuals*—not groups. The **universe** or *population* is the group of people whose preferences the researcher wants to measure. The sample of whom we ask the questions in the survey should be representative of this universe. The universe of subscribers to *Literary Digest* was not representative of the universe of all voters in 1936, for instance, a major reason the poll incorrectly predicted the election.[24] When a substantial percentage of a sample agrees on an issue—say, that we should honor the U.S. flag—there is a *consensus.* But on most issues, opinions are divided. When two opposing sides feel intensely about an issue and the difference between the major alternatives is wide, the public is said to be *polarized.* On such issues, it can be difficult to compromise or find a middle ground. The Vietnam War in the 1960s and 1970s was a polarizing issue. A more recent example is gay marriage. Neither those who favor legalizing gay marriage nor those who unequivocally oppose it see much room for compromise. Somewhere in the middle are those who oppose gay marriage but favor giving gay couples legal rights through "civil unions." (See Table 8–2.)

universe
The group of people whose preferences we try to measure by taking a sample; also called population.

TABLE
8–2 | Differing Opinions on Gay Marriage

	Gay Marriage Should Not Be Allowed	Gay Marriage Should Not Be Allowed, but Civil Unions Should Be Allowed (volunteered response)	Gay Marriage Should Be Allowed
Total Gender	35%	26%	39%
Men	37	27	36
Women	33	25	42
Region			
Northeast	24	28	49
Midwest	42	26	32
South	42	25	33
West	22	27	52
Age			
18-29	22	18	61
30–44	26	27	47
45–64	40	30	30
65+	53	28	19
Church Attendance			
Every week	59	26	15
Almost every week	44	24	32
Once or twice a month	34	31	36
A few times a year	21	28	51
Never	24	24	52
Race			
White	34	27	39
African American	47	20	33
Hispanic	31	22	47
Other	29	24	47
Party			
Republican	45	33	23
Democrat	27	22	51
Independent	36	22	42
Other	25	17	58
Political Philosophy			
Conservative	53	31	16
Moderate	27	29	44
Liberal	15	20	65
Do not know/Have not thought about it	35	22	43
Marital Status			
Married	39	30	31
Widowed	48	21	30
Divorced	35	28	37
Separated	33	18	50
Single, never married	23	19	58
Partnered, not married	18	33	49
Education			
High school or less	43	22	35
Some college	31	27	42
College degree or more	27	31	42

NOTE: Numbers may not add to 100 because of rounding. Independents who lean toward a party are classified with the party toward which they lean. Race is defined by the first race with which a respondent identifies.

SOURCE: *2008 National Election Study* (Center for Political Studies, University of Michigan, 2008).

■ *Why do you suppose more women than men support gay marriage? What might help explain the lack of support for gay marriage among African Americans, another disadvantaged group?*

Intensity   The degree to which people feel strongly about their opinions, or **intensity,** produces the brightest and deepest hues in the fabric of public opinion. For example, some individuals mildly favor gun control legislation, others mildly oppose it; some people are emphatically for or against it; and some have no interest in gun control at all. Others may not have even heard of it. People who lost their jobs or retirement savings because of corporate scandals are likely to feel more intensely about enhanced regulation of corporations and accounting firms than those not directly affected. We typically measure intensity by asking people how strongly they feel about an issue or about a politician. Such a question is sometimes called a *scale.*

Latency   When people hold political opinions but do not fully express them, they are described as **latent.** These opinions may not have crystallized, yet they are still important, because they can be aroused by leaders or events and thereby motivate people to support them. Latent opinions set rough boundaries for leaders who know that, if they take certain actions, they will trigger either opposition or support from millions of people. If leaders understand people's unexpressed wants, needs, and hopes, they will know how to mobilize people and draw them to the polls on election day. A recent example of a latent opinion is the concern for security from foreign enemies, which had not been an issue in the United States before the terrorist attacks of September 11, 2001. The need for homeland security has now become a **manifest opinion,** a widely shared and consciously held view.

Salience   Issues that people believe are important to them are **salient.** Most people are more concerned about personal issues such as paying their bills and keeping their jobs than about national issues, but if national issues somehow threaten their security or safety, their salience rises sharply. Salience and intensity, though different, are often correlated on the same issue.

The salience of issues may change over time. During the Great Depression of the 1930s, people were concerned mainly about jobs, wages, and economic security. By the 1940s, with the onset of World War II, foreign affairs came to the forefront. In the 1960s, problems of race and poverty were important to many. In the 1970s, Vietnam and then the Watergate scandals became the focus of attention. The economy took center stage in 2008 with the country in a recession and banks struggling to stay afloat, and in response, Congress enacted a $700 billion infusion of federal dollars into the banking system. In 2009 and 2010, the focus turned more to job creation and reform of the financial system.

intensity
A measure of how strongly an individual holds a particular opinion.

latency
Political opinions that are held but not yet expressed.

manifest opinion
A widely shared and consciously held view, such as support for abortion rights or for homeland security.

salience
An individual's belief that an issue is important or relevant to him or her.

Public Opinion and Public Policy

For much of human history, public opinion has been difficult to measure. "What I want," Abraham Lincoln once said, "is to get done what the people desire to be done, and the question for me is how to find that out exactly."[25] Politicians today do not face such uncertainty about public opinion—far from it.[26] Polling informs them about public opinion on all major policy issues. Politicians can commission polls themselves, or they can turn to public or media polls. All national and most local newspapers and television stations conduct or commission their own polls.[27]

Many examples from history show how public opinion can shape policy and, in turn, of how policies shape opinion. On May 3, 2003, the day after President Bush announced "Mission Accomplished" in the Iraq War, 72 percent of American adults approved of the way he had handled the situation in Iraq. About one year later, after revelations of torture by U.S. soldiers in the Abu Ghraib prison and repeated attacks on U.S. forces in Iraq, Bush's approval rating had fallen to 34 percent,[28] and in 2008, it

In Arizona, illegal immigration is a very salient issue, but one which divides the state. Sharon Angle, the Tea Party challenger for Harry Reid's Senate seat, came under fire from Latino rights groups for her "race-baiting" ads depicting threatening illegal immigrants. ■ *When should politicians simply respond to public opinion, and when should they try to shape it?*

fell to less than 30 percent.[29] Obama began his presidency with a 69 percent approval rating, only to see that drop to 49 percent in 2010, not long after Congress enacted health care reform.[30]

Typically, elected officials focus on issues of importance to the public.[31] In a sense, they follow public opinion by using polls to learn how to talk about issues in ways that resonate with the public. Members of Congress want to win reelection by showing greater attention to public opinion as election day looms.[32] Candidates use polls to determine where, how, and even whether to campaign. The decision in 2010 about which states and districts the two parties and allied interest groups most contested in U.S. House and Senate races was driven by the polls. In the 2008 presidential election, polls were important to both the Obama and McCain campaigns in how and where they campaigned.[33] Even smaller states such as New Hampshire and New Mexico received substantial attention. Larger states such as New York, California, Illinois, and Texas were taken for granted because one side or the other was so far ahead in them and gaining a plurality in the national popular vote was a secondary objective to securing 270 electoral votes.

Polls are no substitute for elections. With a choice between candidates before them, voters must now translate their opinions into concrete decisions and decide what is important and what is not. Democracy is more than the expression of views, a simple mirror of opinion. It is the thoughtful participation of people in the political process. Elections are the critical link between the many opinions "We the People" hold and how we select our leaders.

Participation: Translating Opinions into Action

U.S. citizens influence their government's actions in several ways, many of which the Constitution protects. In addition to voting in elections, they participate in Internet political blogs, join interest groups, go to political party meetings, ring doorbells, urge friends to vote for issues or candidates, sign petitions, write letters to newspapers, and call radio talk shows. This kind of "citizen-to-citizen" participation can be important and may become more so as more people use the Internet and its social capital-building applications, such as social networking sites.[34]

Protest is also a form of political participation. Our political system is remarkably tolerant of protest that is not destructive or violent. Boycotts, picketing, sit-ins, and marches are all legally protected. Rosa Parks and Martin Luther King Jr. used nonviolent protest to call attention to unfair laws (see Chapter 16). Relative to voting, few people participate in protests, but the actions of those who do can substantially shape public opinion as the Tea Party activities demonstrated in 2010.

Even in an established democracy, people may feel so strongly about an issue that they would rather fight than accept the verdict of an election. The classic example is the American Civil War. Following the election of 1860, in which Abraham Lincoln—an anti-slavery candidate who did not receive a single electoral vote from a slave state—won the presidency, most of the South tried to secede from the Union. The ensuing war marked the failure of democracy to resolve sectional conflict. Examples in our own time include antiabortion and animal rights groups that use violence to press their political agenda, and militia groups that arm themselves for battle against government regulations.

For most people, politics is a private activity. Some still consider it impolite to discuss politics at dinner parties. To say that politics is private does not mean that people do not have opinions or will not discuss them when asked by others, including pollsters. But many people avoid discussing politics with neighbors, coworkers, or even friends and family because it is too divisive or upsetting. Typically, less than one person in four attempts to influence how another person votes in an election,[35] and even fewer people contribute financially to a candidate.[36] Fewer still write letters to elected officials or to newspapers for publication or participate in protest groups or activities. Yet, despite the small number of people who engage in these activities, they can make a difference in politics and government. An individual or small group can generate media interest in an issue and thereby expand the issue's impact.

When the student pro-democracy protest was stopped by the Chinese government tanks in Tiananmen Square on June 5, 1989, one man stood up in defiance until he was pulled to safety by bystanders. ■ *In the United States, most protest is nonviolent, and dissidents work through the political system. Are there circumstances in which political violence is ever justified?*

Levels of political participation rose during the 2008 presidential election, in part because of increased use of the Internet (see Figure 8–3). In 2008, the proportion reporting that they tried to influence another person's vote rose to nearly 50 percent. Candidates' Web sites allowed individuals to register with the campaign and be connected with other politically active individuals in their area. They also provided calling lists for volunteers to call from their own phones. Local campaign leaders in turn used the Internet to contact individuals in the area who had expressed an interest in working with the campaign. The Internet helped campaigns organize more effectively and made it easier for interested people to participate. Supporters of several candidates in 2008 went so far as to create their own music videos and political advertisements, which they uploaded to YouTube and other video-hosting Web sites. Candidates and groups attempted to apply lessons learned in 2008 about internet communications in 2010.

More candidates and interest groups also used the Internet for fund raising in the 2008 campaign. Candidates' Web sites made it easy for individuals to donate and to invite their

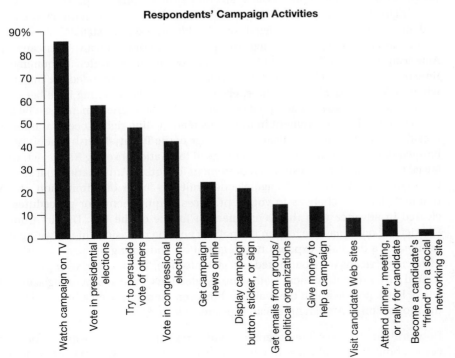

Respondents' Campaign Activities

FIGURE 8–3 **Political Participation and Awareness in the United States.**
■ *Ten years from now, which of these activities would you expect to become more prevalent, and which less so?*

SOURCE: U.S. Census Bureau, *Statistical Abstract of the United States: 2006* (U.S. Government Printing Office, 2006), p. 263; *2008 National Election Study*, Center for Political Studies, University of Michigan; NES Guide to Public Opinion and Electoral Behavior, http://www.electionstudies.org/studypages/2008prepost/2008prepost.htm; and Pew Research Center, "Social Networking and Online Videos Take Off," January 11, 2008, www.pewinternet.org/pdfs/Pew_Media.

Volunteers for the John McCain campaign call likely supporters, reminding them to vote. Many groups conduct get-out-the-vote operations in hopes of turning out people likely to vote for their favored candidate.

friends to donate through e-mail, Facebook, MySpace, and other social-networking Web sites. The Obama campaign was especially innovative in its use of the Internet. ActBlue, a liberal political action committee (see Chapter 6), has used the Internet to make it much easier for people to donate to the Democratic candidates of their choice, while Slatecard has tried to achieve the same for Republicans. Supporters of the Republican candidate Ron Paul independently organized Internet fund-raisers that netted him more than $10 million during two 24-hour periods.[37] Candidates in both parties attempted to use the Internet more in fundraising in 2010. Tea Party candidates and national figures had greater success with this tool.

Voting

Voting is our most typical political activity. The United States is a constitutional democracy with more than 200 years of free and frequent elections and a tradition of the peaceful transfer of power between competing groups and parties.

Originally, the Constitution left it to the individual states to determine who could vote, and qualifications for voting differed considerably from state to state. All states except New Jersey barred women from voting, most did not permit African Americans or Native Americans to vote, and until the 1830s, property ownership was often a requirement. By the time of the Civil War (1861–1865), however, every state had extended the franchise to all-white male citizens. Since that time, eligibility standards for voting have been expanded seven times by congressional legislation and constitutional amendments (see Table 8–3).

The civil rights movement in the 1960s made voting rights a central issue. In 1964, President Lyndon Johnson pushed for passage of the Twenty-Fourth Amendment, which banned poll taxes, and in 1965, for passage of the National Voting Rights Act, which outlawed the use of literacy tests as a requirement for voting. Anticipating that some state or local governments would change election rules to foster discrimination, the Act also required that any changes to voting practices, requirements, or procedures must be cleared in advance with the Department of Justice or the U.S. District Court for the District of Columbia. The ban on the poll tax and the provisions of the Voting Rights Act resulted in a dramatic expansion of registration and voting by black Americans. Once African Americans were permitted to register to vote, "the focus of voting discrimination shifted... to preventing them from winning elections."[38] In southern legislative districts where black people are in the majority, however, there has been a "dramatic increase in the proportion of African American legislators elected."[39]

voter registration
A system designed to reduce voter fraud by limiting voting to those who have established eligibility to vote by submitting the proper documents, including proof of residency.

Registration   One legal requirement—**voter registration**—arose as a response to concerns about voting abuses, but it also discourages voting. Most other democracies

TABLE
8–3 | Changes in Voting Eligibility Standards Since 1870

Timeline	Change
1870	Fifteenth Amendment forbade states from denying the right to vote because of "race, color, or previous condition of servitude."
1920	Nineteenth Amendment gave women the right to vote.
1924	Congress granted Native Americans citizenship and voting rights.
1961	Twenty-Third Amendment permitted District of Columbia residents to vote in federal elections.
1964	Twenty-Fourth Amendment prohibited the use of poll taxes in federal elections.
1965	Voting Rights Act removed restrictions that kept African Americans from voting.
1971	Twenty-Sixth Amendment extended the vote to citizens age 18 and older.

■ *How have "the people" included in our government by the people changed since the founding of the country?*

have automatic voter registration and some like Brazil, Greece, and the Philippines have mandatory voting. Average turnout in the United States, where voters must register before voting, is more than 30 percentage points lower than in countries such as Denmark, Germany, and Israel where voter registration is not required.[40] This was not always the case. In fact, in the 1800s, turnout in the United States was much like that of these countries today. It began to drop significantly around 1900, in part as a result of election reforms (see Figure 8–4). Voter registration requirements substantially affect rates of voting.[41] It requires voters to take an extra step—usually filling out a form at the county courthouse, when renewing a driver's license, or with a roving registrar—days or weeks before the election and every time they move to a new address.

Laws vary by state, but every state except North Dakota requires registration, usually in advance. Idaho, Maine, Minnesota, New Hampshire, Wisconsin, and Wyoming permit election-day registration. The most important provision regarding voter registration may be the closing date. Until the early 1970s, closing dates in many states were six months before the election. Now, federal law prevents a state from closing registration more than 30 days before a federal election.[42] Other important provisions include places and hours of registration and, in some states, a requirement that voters show photo identification before voting.[43]

Motor Voter   In 1993, the burdens of voter registration were eased a bit with the National Voter Registration Act—called the "Motor Voter" bill—which allows people to register to vote while applying for or renewing a driver's license. Offices that provide welfare and disability assistance can also facilitate voter registration. States may include public schools, libraries, and city and county clerks' offices as registration sites. The law requires states to allow registration by mail using a standardized form. To purge the voting rolls of voters who may have died or changed residence, states must mail a

FIGURE 8–4 Voter Turnout in Presidential Elections, 1789–2008.

SOURCE: Curtis Gans, Howard W. Stanley, and Richard G. Niemi, *Vital Statistics on American Politics, 2009–2010* (CQ Press, 2010), pp. 4–5.

questionnaire to voters every four years. But Motor Voter forbids states from purging the rolls for any other reasons, such as because a person has not voted in multiple previous elections.

As a result of this law, more new voters have registered.[44] Data on the impact of Motor Voter suggest that neither Democrats nor Republicans are the primary beneficiaries because most new voters who have registered claim to be Independent.[45] Yet, Motor Voter does not appear to have increased turnout.

Absentee and Early Voting As discussed at the beginning of the chapter, many people choose not to vote in person at their local voting places on election day. Instead they use *absentee voting* to vote early by mail. Absentee voting has been used since the Civil War[46] and has recently become more popular. Three in ten voters in 2008 cast their vote away from a traditional, election-day polling location, the most in the history of the United States.[47] Another innovation designed to make voting easier is allowing people to vote early but at a polling location. This change was in part the result of concerns about having insufficient voting machines for election day. By 2008, 31 states allowed early voting without needing to claim travel, work, or other reasons to vote early.[48]

Turnout

The United States holds more elections for more offices than any other democracy. That may be why U.S. voters tend to be selective about which elections they vote in. We elect office-holders in **general elections,** determine party nominees in **primary elections,** and replace members of the House of Representatives who have died or left office in *special elections.*

Elections held in years when the president is on the ballot are called **presidential elections;** elections held midway between presidential elections are called **midterm elections,** and elections held in odd-numbered calendar years are called *off-year elections.* Midterm elections (such as the ones in 2006 and 2010) elect one-third of the U.S. Senate, all members of the House of Representatives, and many governors, other statewide officeholders, and state legislators. Many local elections for city council members and mayors are held in the spring of odd-numbered years.

Turnout—the proportion of the voting-age public that votes—is higher in general elections than in primary elections, and higher in primary elections than in special elections. It is also higher in presidential general elections than in midterm general elections, and higher in presidential primary elections than in midterm primary elections (see Figure 8–5).[49] Presidential elections attract greater interest and awareness. Turnout is also higher in elections in which candidates for federal office are on the ballot (U.S. senator, member of the House of Representatives, and president) than in state elections in years when there are no federal contests. Some states—for example, New Jersey, Virginia, and Kentucky—elect their governor and other state officials in odd-numbered years to separate state from national politics. The result is generally lower turnout. Finally, local or municipal elections have lower turnout than state elections, and municipal primaries generally have the lowest rates of participation.

Turnout reached more than 65 percent of those eligible to vote in the presidential election of 1960, but it declined to slightly more than 60 percent in 2004, and rose to 61.7 percent in 2008.[50] In midterm elections, turnout was 40 percent nationally in 2006,

general election
Elections in which voters elect officeholders.

primary election
Elections in which voters determine party nominees.

presidential election
Elections held in years when the president is on the ballot.

midterm election
Elections held midway between presidential elections.

turnout
The proportion of the voting-age public that votes, sometimes defined as the number of registered voters that vote.

FIGURE 8–5 **Voter Turnout in Presidential and Midterm Elections, 1992–2010.**
■ *How can you explain the consistent pattern of voting demonstrated in the above graph?*

SOURCE: Curtis Gans, Howard W. Stanley, and Richard G. Niemi, *Vital Statistics on American Politics, 2009–2010* (CQ Press, 2010), pp. 4–5. U.S. Elections Project, George Mason University, http://elections.gmu.edu/Turnout_2010G.html.

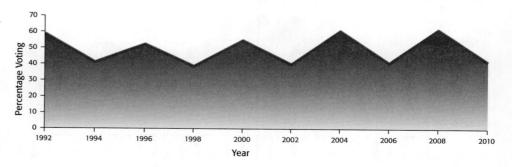

Helping America Vote

The exceedingly close Florida vote in the 2000 presidential election called attention to multiple problems with the voting process not only in that state but in many states. Among the problems were poorly maintained and outdated voting machines, confusing ballot designs, inconsistent rules for counting absentee ballots, and the need for more and better trained poll workers. In response to these and other problems, Congress enacted in 2002 the Help America Vote Act (HAVA).

HAVA for the first time established accessibility standards for voting systems in the United States. The Americans with Disabilities Act of 1990 required that voting places be accessible to persons with disabilities, but prior to HAVA, individuals with disabilities in some states could only vote with the assistance of a poll worker, which compromised the privacy of their vote. HAVA required that states provide voting machines for persons with disabilities, including the visually impaired, that allow these voters the same level of privacy as any other voter.

The system of voter registration in the United States is largely administered at the county level, and as such, there was widespread variability in the way counties maintained the list of registered voters. HAVA mandated the creation of statewide, computerized voter registration lists. The Act also mandated the creation of a toll-free phone number that individuals could use to learn about their registration status.

Poll workers are critical to the administration of elections. HAVA provides federal grants to help train poll workers and to involve college and high school students in assisting at the polls on election day (see "By the People: Be a Poll Worker" box later in this chapter). HAVA created the Election Assistance Commission to assist states with election administration and ensure that minimum federal standards in such areas as accessibility are met. Although problems remain in making elections work well, HAVA has helped state and local governments make substantial strides.

CRITICAL THINKING QUESTIONS

1. Why is the privacy of the voting act important to voters?

2. How would a common statewide list of registered voters enhance participation?

3. What are some other ways in which the voting process could be improved?

---

up about 1 percent from 2002 and up more than 2 percent since 1998. More competitive elections generate more interest among the public and more spending by the candidates, which in turn stimulate participation. However, more than 80 million eligible citizens failed to vote in the 2004 presidential election, and even more did not vote in midterm, state, and local elections.[51]

Who Votes?

The extent of voting varies widely among different groups. Level of education especially helps predict whether people will vote; as education increases, so does the propensity to vote. "Education increases one's capacity for understanding complex and intangible subjects such as politics," according to one study, "as well as encouraging the ethic of civic responsibility. Moreover, schools provide experience dealing with a variety of bureaucratic problems, such as coping with requirements, filling out forms, and meeting deadlines."[52]

Race and ethnic background are linked with different levels of voting, largely because they correlate with education. In other words, racial and ethnic minorities with college degrees vote at approximately the same rate as white people with college degrees. As a group, black people vote at lower rates than white people, although this is beginning to change.[53] In 2008, blacks were 13 percent of the vote, a 2 percent increase over 2004.[54]

In 2004, both parties mounted major efforts to register and mobilize Hispanic voters, as Hispanics have become the largest minority group in the United States. Despite these efforts, the proportion of Hispanics voting in 2008 was only slightly over 2004, 49.9 percent as compared to 47.2 percent.[55] As the illegal immigrant issue took center stage in 2006, Democrats, Republicans, and allied groups again sought to expand the number of Hispanic voters. Exit polls found that 9 percent of voters in 2008 were Latinos, with two-thirds of them voting for Obama.[56]

Women, another historically underrepresented group, have voted in greater numbers than men since 1984.[57] That was true again in 2008.[58] Women's higher turnout is

Voters wait to cast their ballots in a primary election. Voting reforms have led to more early voting, helping cut congestion on election day. ■ *What are the implications for political campaigns of greater levels of early voting?*

generally attributed to increasing levels of education and employment. Interest groups, including prominent pro-choice groups, have sought to mobilize female supporters of their agenda in recent elections.

Age is also highly correlated with the propensity to vote. As age increases, so does the proportion of persons voting. Older people, unless they are very old and infirm, are more likely to vote than younger people. The greater propensity of older persons to vote will amplify the importance of this group as baby boomers age and retire.

Young voters volunteered in large numbers for candidates in 2008, especially for the Obama campaign. Based on exit polls, their share of the vote also rose slightly. In 2004, 17 percent of all voters were 18 to 29 years of age. In 2008, they were 18 percent of all voters.[59] But because turnout was higher generally, the number of young people voting was up substantially.[60] In 2008, there were 3.4 million more voters under the age of 30 than had voted in 2004.[61] In 2010, President Obama held rallies on college campuses to encourage young people to vote. His party continued to do better among young voters than other voters, but turnout in this group was well below the 2008 level.

Mobilization

In a nation as evenly divided politically as the United States is now, candidates must also mobilize their most loyal supporters, or their "base." To do this, they reaffirm their support for issues or groups that matter to the base. In 2008, John McCain did this by calling for domestic offshore drilling, supporting continuing the Bush tax cuts, and by selecting Sarah Palin as his running mate. On the Democratic side, Barack Obama argued for greater investment in wind and solar energy and held to his position on a set timetable to end the war in Iraq.

In the 2008 "battleground" states where the vote seemed highly competitive, postcards urging residents to vote and phone calls reminding them it was election day bombarded voters who were already likely to vote and had already decided which candidate to support. In addition, the candidates and parties mobilized their supporters to vote early in states where it was possible. This effort, sometimes called "banking the vote," reduced the list of people the campaigns needed to mobilize on election day, when poll watchers would track those who had not yet voted and would urge those who had pledged support to vote.

Campaigners learn which issues matter to potential voters and which candidates these voters prefer by conducting interviews on the telephone or in person, a process called a *canvass.* Individuals who are undecided and probable voters in competitive races are likely to receive communications designed to persuade them to vote for a particular candidate. Interest groups and political parties may also conduct a canvass, followed by mail and phone calls that often reinforce the same themes the candidates themselves express.

Undecided or "swing voters" are a major focus of mobilization efforts, and they received a lot of attention in competitive states in recent elections. Both sides intensely courted these voters through numerous person-to-person contacts, mailings, telephone calls, and efforts to register new voters. Candidates, groups, and parties are all part of this "ground war." The volume of communication in competitive contests and battleground states in recent elections has been extraordinary. For example, there were 117 unique pieces of mail in New Mexico's

Of the People

Voter Turnout by Demographic Factors

Throughout the course of U.S. history, the right to vote has been extended and protected for women and racial minorities. Groups that did not have the franchise, or that had been effectively barred or discouraged from using it, have become as active in their rates of voting as white men.

In the following data, note that women have voted in higher percentages than men in each election since 1992. It took decades for women to reach this milestone and dismiss the old adage that "politics is men's business." The rate of voting among black persons was about 10 percentage points below white persons in 1992 and 1994, but more recently has lagged by only approximately 4 percentage points. Hispanics are not yet participating at rates similar to those of women and black persons. History suggests that over time this will change.

Percentage of People in Different Groups Who Voted

	1992	1994	1996	1998	2000	2002	2004	2006	2008
Sex									
Men	60%	44%	53%	41%	53%	41%	56%	42%	56%
Women	62	45	56	42	56	43	60	45	60
Race									
White	64	47	56	43	56	44	60	46	60
Black	54	37	51	40	54	40	56	39	61
Hispanic	29	19	27	20	28	19	28	19	32

SOURCE: U.S. Census Bureau, *Statistical Abstract of the United States: 2010* (U.S. Government Printing Office, 2009), p. 254.

CRITICAL THINKING QUESTIONS

1. Why might the rate of voting for women have increased over time?
2. How do presidential elections influence rates of voting? Why?
3. What factors might explain the change in the rate of voting among black persons?

1st Congressional District race sent by candidates, parties, and groups, and there were at least 112 unique pieces of mail in the Colorado U.S. Senate race in that same year.[62]

How Serious Is Nonvoting?

Although voters can hardly avoid reading or hearing about political campaigns, especially during an election as intensely fought as recent presidential elections, about 40 percent of all eligible citizens fail to vote. This amounts to approximately 80 million people.[63] Who are they? Why don't they vote? Is the fact that so many people choose not to vote a cause for alarm? If so, what can we do about it?

There is considerable disagreement about how to interpret low voter turnout. The simplest explanation is that people are lazy and voting takes effort, but there is more to it than that. Of course, some people are apathetic, but most are not. Paradoxically, we compare favorably with other nations in political interest and awareness, but for a variety of institutional and political reasons, we fail to convert this interest in politics into voting (see Table 8–4).

In the United States, voting is more difficult and takes more time and effort than in other democracies. In our system, as we have seen, people must first register to vote and then decide how to vote, not only for many different offices but also often for referendums on public policy or constitutional amendments. The United States also holds elections on weekdays, when people are at work, rather than on holidays or weekends as other countries often do. Another factor in the percentage decline of voter turnout since the 1960s is, paradoxically, the Twenty-Sixth Amendment, which increased the number of eligible voters by lowering the voting age to 18. But young people are the least likely to vote. After the amendment was ratified in 1971, turnout in the presidential election fell from 62 percent in 1968 to 57 percent in 1972.[64]

Some political scientists argue that nonvoting does not change the outcome, as nonvoters closely resemble voters in policy views.[65] "Nonvoting is not a social disease," wrote Austin Ranney, a noted political scientist. He pointed out that legal and extralegal denial of the vote

Voters in competitive elections receive large mailers like this one in the 2008 North Carolina 8th Congressional District Race. ■ *What do you see as the message of this mailer? Who is it likely targeting?*

to African Americans, women, Hispanics, persons over the age of 18, and other groups has been outlawed, so nonvoting is voluntary. The late Senator Sam Ervin of North Carolina provided a rationale for registration when he said "I don't believe in making it easy for apathetic, lazy people to vote."[66] Some may even contend that nonvoting is a sign of voter satisfaction.

Those who argue that nonvoting is a serious problem cite the "class bias" of those who do vote. The social makeup and attitudes of nonvoters differ significantly from those of voters and hence distort the representative system. "The very poor...have about two-thirds the representation among voters than their numbers would suggest." Thus, the people who need the most help from the government lack their share of electoral power to obtain it.[67] Some may contend that younger voters, the poor, and minority citizens do

TABLE

8–4 | Why People Do Not Vote

Too busy, conflicting schedule	17.5%
Illness or disability	14.9%
Other reason	11.3%
Not interested	13.4%
Did not like candidates or campaign issues	12.9%
Out of town	8.8%
Do not know or refused	7.0%
Registration problems	6.0%
Forgot to vote	2.6%
Inconvenient polling place	2.7%
Transportation problems	2.6%
Bad weather conditions	0.2%

■ *What reforms could you suggest to help negate the most often citing reason for not voting?*

SOURCE: U.S. Census Bureau, "Reasons for Not Voting, by Selected Characteristics: November 2008," www.census.gov/population/www/socdemo/voting/cps2008.html.

not vote because politicians pay less attention to them. But politicians understandably cater to people who vote more than to people who do not.

How might increased voter turnout affect national elections? It might make a difference because there are partisan differences between different demographic groups, and poorer persons are more likely to be Democrats. Candidates would have to adjust to the demands of this expanded electorate. A noted political scientist, while acknowledging that no political system could achieve 100 percent participation, pointed out that if the large nonvoter population decided to vote, it could overturn the balance of power in the political system.[68] However, others contend that the difference may not be that pronounced because, on many issues, nonvoters have much the same attitudes as voters. For example, nonvoters do not favor government ownership or regulation of industry more than voters do. Nor are nonvoters more egalitarian. They are, however, more inclined to favor additional spending on welfare programs.[69]

Finally, for better or worse, low voter turnout may indicate approval of the status quo, whereas high voter turnout may signify disapproval and widespread desire for change.

Voting Choices

Why do people vote the way they do? Political scientists have identified three main elements of the voting choice: party identification, candidate appeal, and issues. These elements often overlap.

Voting on the Basis of Party

Party identification is our sense of identification or affiliation with a political party (see Chapter 7). It often predicts a person's stand on issues. It is part of our national mythology that we vote for the person and not the party. But, in fact, we vote most often for a person *from the party we prefer.*

The number of self-declared Independents since the mid-1970s has increased dramatically, and today, Independents outnumber Republicans and Democrats. But two-thirds of all Independents are, in fact, partisans in their voting behavior. There are three distinct types of Independents: Independent-leaning Democrats, Independent-leaning Republicans, and Pure Independents. Independent-leaning Democrats are predictably Democratic in their voting behavior, and Independent-leaning Republicans vote heavily Republican. Independent "leaners" are thus different from each other and from Pure Independents. Pure Independents have the lowest rate of turnout, but most of them generally side with the winner in presidential elections. Independent leaners vote at about the same rate as partisans and more than Pure Independents. Independent leaners vote for the party toward which they lean at approximately the same rate, or even more so, than weak partisans do. This data on Independents only reinforces the importance of partisanship in explaining voting choice. When we consider Independent-leaning Democrats and Independent-leaning Republicans as Democrats and Republicans respectively, only 10 percent of the population were Pure Independents in 2004.[70] In 2008, that number had risen slightly to 11 percent.[71] This proportion is consistent with earlier election years. In short, there are few genuinely Independent voters.

Although party identification has fluctuated in the past 40 years, it remains more stable than attitudes about issues or political ideology. Fluctuations in party identification appear to come in response to economic conditions and political performance, especially of the president. The more information voters have about their choices, the more likely they are to defect from their party and vote for a candidate from the other party.

Voting on the Basis of Candidates

Although long-term party identification is important, it is clearly not the only factor in voting choices. Otherwise, the Democrats would have won every presidential election since the last major realignment in partisanship, which occurred during the Great Depression in the election of Franklin Roosevelt in 1932. In fact, since 1952, there have been five Democratic presidents elected and the same number of Republicans.[72] The

VOTE

BALLOT BOX

League of Women Voters

This poster, published by the League of Women Voters, urged women to use the vote the Nineteenth Amendment had given them.
■ *Is low voter turnout, particularly concentrated among certain demographic groups, a problem for democracy?*

LEARNING **OBJECTIVE**

8.4 Analyze why people vote the way they do in elections.

party identification
An informal and subjective affiliation with a political party that most people acquire in childhood.

YOU WILL DECIDE

Should We Allow Voting by Mail and on the Internet?

During the past two centuries of constitutional government, this nation has gradually adopted a more expansive view of popular participation. It seems logical that the next step in our democratic progress is permitting voters to cast ballots through the mail or via the Internet. Not only would such a reform make voting easier, but it would permit us to have more elections. For example, when a city council wants voters to decide whether to build a new football stadium or when there is need for a special election to fill the term of a member of Congress who has died or resigned, election officials could mail out the ballots and then in two or three weeks count up those that have been returned. The state of Oregon has already conducted several general elections by mail, and other states have considered adopting the Oregon system.

What do you think? Should we move toward replacing the ballot box with the mailbox or the computer? What arguments would you make for and against such an idea?

THINKING IT THROUGH

One of the problems with making elections more frequent is that voters will tire. Americans already vote more frequently and for more offices than citizens of any other democracy. Asking them to make voting choices even more frequently could result in lower turnout and less rational consideration. Many voters may be unaware that an election is going on. Yet the advantage of the vote-by-mail system employed by Oregon and some cities and counties is that it increases turnout, at least initially. What political scientists dispute is whether such increases in participation will continue when the novelty wears off.

Some critics of voting by mail or electronic democracy worry about fraud. Even when voters are required to sign their mailed-in ballots, the possibility of forgery still exists. Also, voting by mail or computer has the possibility of allowing people to pressure or harass voters. Another concern is late returns. Concerns about electronic voting have been reinforced by claims that the computer software is not secure and that some electronic voting fails to count all the votes.*

Another criticism is that mail and electronic voting could be skewed toward participation by better-educated and higher-income voters, who routinely pay their bills by mail, make purchases on their computer, and own a personal computer with Internet access. Advocates of these new voting procedures contend that voters who do not own computers can drop off their ballots in some public building and that eventually computers will be available widely enough that access will not be a problem.†

If the integrity of the vote can be protected and the new ways of voting become widely accessible, such changes are probably inevitable. With more people having access to computers and confidence using them for important transactions, the Internet is likely to be used for voting in the future. Electronic voting has been tested for military personnel overseas,‡ and states like Michigan and Washington have experimented with new applications of computer voting.

Critical Thinking Questions

1. What advantages do you see in allowing people to vote via the Internet?
2. What would be the disadvantages of allowing Internet voting?
3. If we move to voting by Internet, how often do you think voters would be likely to participate in an election?

---

*E. J. Dionne, Jr., "Election Dangers to Be Avoided," *The Washington Post*, May 25, 2004.
†Adam J. Berinsky, Nancy Burns, and Michael W. Traugott, "Who Votes By Mail? A Dynamic Model of the Indiviual-Level Consequences of Voting-by-Mail Systems," *Public Opinion Quarterly* 65 (Summer 2001), pp. 178–197.
‡http://www.servesecurityreport.org/DoDMay2007.pdf.

---

reason is largely found in a second major explanation of voting choice—**candidate appeal.**

Candidate-centered politics means that rather than relying on parties or groups to build a coalition of supporters for a candidate, the candidates make their case directly to the voters. In many races, the parties and groups also make the candidate the major focus of attention, minimizing partisanship or group identification.[73] The fact that we vote for officials separately—president/vice president, senator, governor, state attorney general, and so on—means voters are asked repeatedly to choose from among competing candidates. Although the party of the candidates is an important clue to voters, in most contested races, voters also look to candidate-specific information.

Candidate appeal often includes an assessment of a candidate's character. Is the candidate honest? Consistent? Dedicated to "family values"? Does the candidate have religious or spiritual commitments? In recent elections, the press has sometimes played the role of "character cop," asking questions about candidates' private lives and lifestyles. The press asks these questions because voters are interested in a political leader's background—perhaps even more interested in personal

candidate appeal
How voters feel about a candidate's background, personality, leadership ability, and other personal qualities.

character than in a candidate's political position on hard-to-understand health care or regulatory policy issues.

Candidate appeal, or the lack of it—in terms of leadership, experience, good judgment, integrity, competence, strength, and energy—is sometimes more important than party or issues. Many voters saw Bill Clinton in 1992 and 1996 as a regular working-class person who had risen against the odds. Dwight Eisenhower, who was elected president in 1952 and reelected in 1956, had great candidate appeal. He was a five-star general, a legendary hero of the Allied effort in World War II. His unmilitary manner, his moderation, his personal charm, and his appearance of seeming to rise above partisanship appealed across the ideological spectrum. In 2008, Republicans attempted to define Barack Obama as arrogant, aloof, and a celebrity. Democrats, while praising McCain as a war hero, tried to define him as out of touch and "more of the same [Bush]." John McCain, his running mate Sarah Palin, the Republican party, and outside groups all repeatedly called attention to Barack Obama's associations with William Ayers, now a college professor in Chicago. During the 1960s and 1970s, Ayers helped lead a radical group that bombed public buildings as a form of protest. Obama was also criticized for not objecting more strongly to the rhetoric of his former pastor, Reverend Jeremiah Wright. Obama denounced Wright's rhetoric and said his association with Ayers had been limited and came years after his radical activities. Neither association seemed to hold much sway with voters.

Increasingly, campaigns today focus on the negative elements of candidates' history and personality. Opponents and the media are quick to point out a candidate's limitations or problems. This was the case again in 2010.

Voting on the Basis of Issues

Most political scientists agree that issues, though important, have less influence on how people vote than party identification and candidate appeal do.[74] This occurs partly because candidates often intentionally obscure their positions on issues—an understandable strategy.[75] When he was running for president in 1968, Richard Nixon said he had a plan to end the Vietnam War, which was clearly the most important issue that year, but he would not reveal the specifics. By not detailing his plan, he stood to gain votes both from those who wanted a more aggressive war effort and those who wanted a cease-fire. In 2008, Obama and the Democrats emphasized change from the Bush administration, a general theme that exploited public sentiment.

For issue voting to become important, a substantial number of voters must find the issue itself important, opposing candidates must take opposite stands on the issues, and voters must know these positions and vote accordingly. Rarely do candidates focus on only one issue. Voters often agree with one candidate on one issue and with the opposing candidate on another. In such cases, issues will probably not determine how people vote. But voters' lack of interest in issues does not mean candidates can take any position they please.[76]

Political parties and candidates often look for issues that motivate particular segments of the electorate to vote and on which the opposing candidate or party has a less popular position. These issues are sometimes called *wedge issues*. In recent elections, wedge issues have been gay marriage, the minimum wage, and abortion. One way to exploit a wedge issue is to place on the ballot an initiative to decide a proposed law or amendment on the issue. Both parties and allied groups are expanding their use of ballot initiatives in this way.

More likely than **prospective issue voting,** or voting based on what a candidate pledges to do about an issue if elected, is **retrospective issue voting,** or holding incumbents, usually the president's party, responsible for past performance on issues, such as the economy or foreign policy.[77] In times of peace and prosperity, voters will reward the incumbent. If the nation falls short on either, voters are more likely to elect the opposition.

Because they do not have the benefits of a well-known party, third-party candidates must rely on their personal appeal to voters. Independent Ross Perot's fiery style and sense of humor helped him garner 19.8 percent of the vote in 1992, the best showing for a third-party presidential candidate since 1912.

prospective issue voting
Voting based on what a candidate pledges to do in the future about an issue if elected.

retrospective issue voting
Holding incumbents, usually the president's party, responsible for their records on issues, such as the economy or foreign policy.

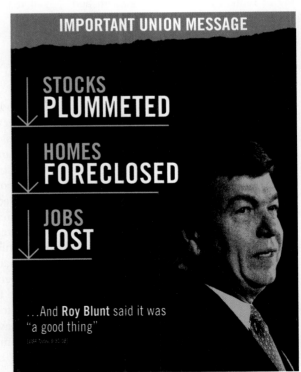

IMPORTANT UNION MESSAGE

STOCKS
PLUMMETED

HOMES
FORECLOSED

JOBS
LOST

...And **Roy Blunt** said it was "a good thing"

Exit polls indicated that the state of the economy was the most important issue to voters in 2010. In the Missouri Senate race, unions tried to portray House representative Roy Blunt as complicit in the failing economy, but the conservative Republican was nonetheless elected. ■ *What other issues in 2010 might have contributed to Blunt's win?*

Of the People

THE GLOBAL COMMUNITY

Corruption Among Political Leaders

In a free society where public opinion can be translated into action through elections and other means, there should in theory be less political corruption. In every country, there are corrupt individuals, but the ability to remove those people from office is enhanced through the expression of public opinion and the accountability afforded by elections. One Pew Global survey asked respondents the following question: "I am going to read you a list of things that may be problems in our country. As I read each one, please tell me if you think it is a very big problem, a moderately big problem, a small problem, or not a problem at all: corrupt political leaders."*

Corruption is seen as a very big problem for most people in India (73 percent) and Nigeria (82 percent) with Mexico not far behind (64 percent). Even though studies have found similar levels of corruption in the United States and Britain, people in Britain are much less likely to say it is a very big problem in their country. In China, which does not allow the free expression of public opinion nor have free elections, 44 percent say corruption is a very big problem and 40 percent saying it is a moderately big problem. Unlike democratic countries, individuals in China lack an electoral way to punish a corrupt government.

CRITICAL THINKING QUESTIONS

1. Why are people in the United States twice as likely to think corruption is a very big problem than people in Britain?

2. Is it possible that corruption may be such a part of the political culture that it is not seen as something elections or public opinion can do much about?

3. What checks are there on corruption in a country like China when the government acts as if there is no corruption?

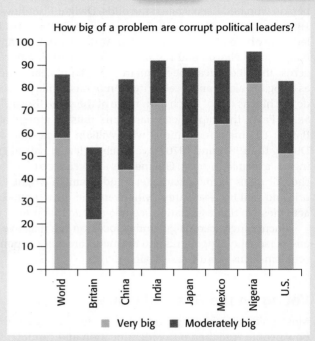

How big of a problem are corrupt political leaders?

Very big ■ Moderately big

*Pew Global Attitudes Project, 2007.

But good economic times do not always guarantee that an incumbent party will be reelected, as Vice President Al Gore learned in 2000 when he was the Democratic candidate for president. Part of Gore's problem in that election was that only half the public felt that their family's financial situation improved during the Clinton administration. Sixty-one percent of these voters voted for Gore.[78] But his inability to effectively claim credit for the good economic times hurt him, especially when Republicans contended that the American people, not the government under President Bill Clinton, had produced the strong economy.

The state of the economy is often the central issue in both midterm and presidential elections. Studies have found that the better the economy seems to be doing, the more congressional seats the "in" party retains or gains. The reverse is also true. The worse the economy seems to be doing, the more seats the "out" party gains.[79] Political scientists have been able to locate the sources of this effect in the way individual voters decide to vote. Voters tend to vote against the party in power if they perceive that their personal financial situations have declined or stagnated.[80] Anxiety over the economy and high unemployment were important to the vote in 2010, and the Democrats, as the party in power, were punished at the polls. Republicans also exploited fears about health care reform and growing federal budget deficits.

Unable to counter the Republican message on the economy, Democrats often resorted to attacking their opponent's record and policy positions. Harry Reid attacked his opponent Sharon Angle as a threat to Social Security, in Delaware Democratic allied groups sent a mailer reminding voters that Republican Christine O'Donnell had reported dabbling "into witchcraft" in high school, and in California Barbara Boxer reminded voters that Carly Fiorina had been fired as CEO of Hewlett-Packard. These personal contrasts in some states worked to the Democrats' advantage. In contests for the House of Representatives and Governorships, these candidate and issue comparisons tended to work more to the Republicans' advantage.

The Impact of Campaigns

Candidates and campaigns are important to the voting choice. Given the frequency of elections in the United States and the number of offices people vote for, it is not surprising that voters look for simplifying devices such as partisanship to help them decide how to vote. Effective campaigns give them reasons to vote for their candidate and reasons to vote against the opposition.

Campaigns are a team sport, with the political parties and interest groups also important to the process of persuading and motivating voters.[81] Groups and parties are heavily engaged in all aspects of campaigns, and their efforts are often indistinguishable from the candidates' campaigns.

Although having enough money is needed for a competitive campaign, spending more money does not guarantee that a candidate will win. Effective campaigners find ways to communicate with voters that are memorable and persuasive.

Campaigns are not for the faint of heart. Electoral politics is intensely competitive, and campaigns are often negative and personal. Campaigns give voters a sense of how politicians react to adversity because most competitive races involve adversity. Skills learned in the campaign environment, in some respects at least, carry over into the skill set needed to govern.

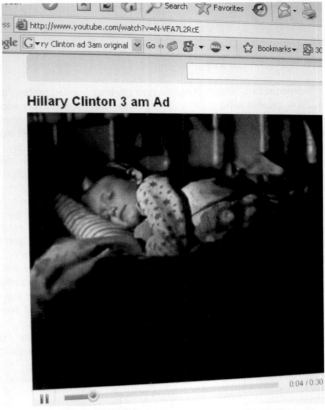

This advertisement from the Hillary Clinton campaign used a hypothetical national-emergency phone call at 3:00 AM to highlight her relative wealth of experience when compared to Barack Obama. ■ *What emotions does the imagery in this advertisement evoke?*

Counting Votes

Until the 2000 election, most people took the counting of ballots for granted. But with the closeness of that election and the controversy surrounding how the election was administered in Florida, the public became aware that counting votes is not a simple matter.

Votes are counted in the United States according to state law as administered by local officials. The technology used in voting varies greatly from state to state and in different parts of the same state. In Florida in 2000, some counties used paper ballots, others voting machines, and others punch-card ballots, and at least one county used ballots that a computer could scan. More recently, states have moved from touch-screen computerized voting systems to paper ballots that can be optically scanned.

Another lesson the recent ballot-counting controversies have reinforced is that in every election, in every jurisdiction, and with every technology, voting is imperfect. Touchscreen software can be manipulated; people can miscount paper ballots; punch cards may not always be completely perforated; and so on. The goal in election administration is to minimize errors and eliminate as much bias and outright fraud as possible.

But counting votes is more complicated than the means by which we vote. Election officials have to make judgment calls about incomplete or flawed ballots. Decisions about which ballots to count and which ones not to count matter in an election decided by only 537 votes, as Florida's presidential election was in 2000. With the growth in absentee voting, and with military personnel and civilians living abroad voting by mail, a close election may not be decided until days after the polls officially close.

The process of voting in person is administered by people from the neighborhood that serve as poll workers and arrive at the polls hours before voting starts to set up equipment and ensure that the voter lists, ballots, and physical facilities are in order. Recent research has found that poll workers can greatly influence the security, efficiency, and overall environment of polling locations. Those who receive high-quality training

LEARNING **OBJECTIVE**

8.5 Identify problems associated with administering elections and evaluate proposed solutions to those problems.

By the People

MAKING A DIFFERENCE

Be a Poll Worker

Some unsung heroes in our democracy are the people who staff voting places on election day. In most states, these individuals work long hours, often starting two hours before the polls open at around 7:00 AM and not completing their work until two or more hours after the polls close to transmit the vote. Although they are paid modest stipends, most poll workers report that they participate in this activity out of a deep sense of duty.

Studies of poll workers have found that 40 percent or more of poll workers are 65 or older.* As we have moved to the use of computers and technology at the voting place, election officials believe that they have a need for poll workers with more confidence dealing with technology. Your ability to use computers means you have a lot to offer as a poll worker. When poll workers are courteous and competent, voters report more confidence in the voting process and more satisfaction with the voting experience. Even though some training is required, what is really needed is a willingness to help make democracy function well on election day.

To watch democracy in action and help make it function more smoothly, contact your county election official to find out how you can become a poll worker. At some colleges like Muhlenberg College in Pennsylvania, there is an established partnership between the college and local election administrators. At Muhlenberg, participating students serve as poll workers or Spanish-language interpreters. You might inquire of faculty at your institution if they would be willing to create a college poll worker program and apply for funding from the U.S. Election Assistance Commission. For more information, go to http://www.eac.gov/voter/hava-college-poll-worker-program. Although an organized program at your campus would help facilitate the process, volunteering as a poll worker is something you can do yourself. You will find that you can truly make a difference and enjoy observing the inner-workings of democracy.

CRITICAL THINKING QUESTIONS

1. With computers more important in voting, why would having people like college students more involved as poll workers be important?

2. What are some things you might learn in a day working as a poll worker?

3. Why do studies show that poll workers can have a positive impact on how people feel about the voting experience?

---

*Stephen T. Mockabee, J. Quin Monson, and Kelly D. Patterson, "Evaluating Online Training," Center for the Study of Elections and Democracy, December 21, 2009, http://csed.byu.edu/Assets/OnlineFinalReport2.pdf (accessed April 29, 2010); and Kelly D. Patterson, J. Quin Monson, and David B. Magleby, "Evaluating the Quality of the Voting Experience," Center for the Study of Elections and Democracy, August 31, 2008, http://csed.byu.edu/Assets/Evaluating%20the%20Quality%20of%20the%20Voting%20Experience.pdf (accessed April 29, 2010).

---

and are confident in both their expertise and the accuracy of the polling location create an overall environment that makes voters feel more confident.[82]

Who is and who is not allowed to vote on election day is also a source of controversy. As discussed, in most states, persons must be registered voters in order to vote. Voters are expected to vote in designated voting places. In 2004, as a result of the 2002 redistricting, some voting places and precincts in parts of the country had changed, which confused some voters who voted only in presidential elections and had not voted since 2000. The law permits voters who think they should be allowed to vote but who are not on the rolls to cast what are called provisional ballots. These ballots are counted only if the voter is, in fact, registered to vote.

In the wake of the 2000 and 2004 elections, federal and state governments have invested billions of dollars in new voting technology, established new rules on provisional ballots, and modernized voting methods. Interest groups, political parties, and candidates have made the integrity of the voting process a high priority. In 2004 and 2008, thousands of people worked as poll watchers. Groups established toll-free hotlines for voters to call if they felt they were not being treated fairly, and in key jurisdictions, lawyers were on call to file immediate challenges when a person's right to vote was contested.

Who votes and how have changed dramatically throughout the course of U.S. history. Our process has become more democratic, and citizens today have a wider array of candidates and ballot referendums than ever before. Although progress has been made in making the process of voting more problem-free, important challenges remain. It is important to the confidence of the polity that every vote be counted and counted accurately. That goal has not yet been achieved.

Government by the people is most frequently exercised by voting. This is why, when younger persons do not vote, they leave to others decisions about important parts of their lives. Government, directly or indirectly, has a bearing on educational opportunity, taxes, and the environment, to name only a few examples. Elected officials are most attuned to the will of those who vote, and so when young persons fail to vote, they lessen their impact and enlarge the voice of those who do register and vote.

CHAPTER **SUMMARY**

8.1 **Identify the forces that create and shape individuals' political attitudes.**

People's political attitudes form early in life, mainly through the influence of family. Schools, the media, social groups, and changing personal and national circumstances can cause attitudes to change, although most of our political opinions remain constant throughout life. Most people do not follow politics and government closely and have little knowledge of political issues.

8.2 **Outline the key dimensions of public opinion, how public opinion is measured, and the relationship between public opinion and public policy.**

Public opinion is the distribution across the population of a complex combination of views and attitudes that individuals hold, and we measure it through careful, unbiased, random-selection surveys. Public opinion takes on qualities of intensity, latency, consensus, and polarization—each of which is affected by people's feelings about the salience of issues.

Sometimes, politicians follow prevailing public opinion on policy questions; in other cases, they attempt to lead public opinion toward a different policy option. Major events, such as economic crises and wars, affect both public opinion and government policy. Citizens who wish to affect opinion, policy, or both, can take action by voting or engaging in other forms of political participation.

8.3 **Identify forms of political participation, and assess the effect on voter turnout of demographic, legal, and electioneering factors.**

One of the hallmarks of democracy is that citizens can participate in politics in a variety of ways. Citizens who are dissatisfied with government can protest. Individual citizens participate by writing letters to elected officials, calling radio talk shows, serving as jurors, voting, or donating time and money to political campaigns. The Internet has allowed individuals to volunteer for campaigns in a wider variety of ways, to donate money more easily, and to produce content that can be uploaded onto the Internet and viewed by any interested people.

Better-educated, more affluent, and older people and those who are involved with parties and interest groups tend to vote more. The young vote the least. Voter turnout is usually higher in national elections than in state and local elections, higher in presidential elections than in midterm elections, and higher in general elections than in primary elections. Close elections generate interest and efforts to mobilize voters and thus have higher turnout than uncompetitive elections.

8.4 **Analyze why people vote the way they do in elections.**

Party identification remains the most important element in determining how most people vote. It represents a long-term attachment and is a "lens" through which voters view candidates and issues as they make their voting choices. Candidate appeal, including character and record, is another key factor in voter choice. Less frequently, voters decide on the basis of issues.

8.5 **Identify problems associated with administering elections and evaluate proposed solutions to those problems.**

Ballot-counting irregularities, equipment shortages and problems, and voter registration challenges have been problems with recent elections. Standardizing election administration; replacing old voting machines with computers, the Internet, and mail-only elections; and reforming registration procedures are all potential solutions to election problems.

CHAPTER **SELF-TEST**

8.1 **Identify the forces that create and shape individuals' political attitudes.**

1. Which of the following statements is true?
   a. Most people never change their political opinions.
   b. Most people change their political opinions quite often.
   c. Many people change their political opinions only when they meet new people.
   d. Many people change their political opinions after major experiences such as a war.

2. In a short essay, explain what the "attentive public" is. How are they different from part-time citizens and political know-nothings? Which group has greater influence on public policy?

3. In a short essay, identify and describe two major groups that influence the formation of individuals' political opinions and values. Which has had a greater influence in your life?

8.2 **Outline the key dimensions of public opinion, how public opinion is measured, and the relationship between public opinion and public policy.**

4. Which of the following was a major flaw in the 1936 *Literary Digest* poll?
   a. Biased questions
   b. A flawed sample
   c. Incorrectly counted results
   d. Poorly trained interviewers

5. What word describes opinions people may hold but have not fully expressed?
   a. Interest   c. Latency
   b. Salience   d. Intensity

6. In a short essay, explain why many politicians pay attention to public opinion. What are the public policy implications of this interest in public opinion?

8.3 Identify forms of political participation, and assess the effect on voter turnout of demographic, legal, and electioneering factors.

7. Which of the following is *not* a way individuals have used the Internet to participate in recent campaigns?
   a. Use candidate Web sites to participate in local caucuses
   b. Create campaign-centered music videos to upload to YouTube
   c. Call other individuals using calling lists provided on a candidate's Web site
   d. Invite other individuals to donate to campaigns through Facebook and MySpace

8. In a short essay, identify whether more women or more men have voted in recent elections. Has this always been the case? Why is it this way now?

9. In a short essay, analyze the impact voter registration laws have on turnout. Consider state-specific laws, Motor Voter, and automatic registration. What changes, if any, do you think should be made to increase registration?

8.4 Analyze why people vote the way they do in elections.

10. In a short essay, explain which is more common, prospective issue voting or retrospective issue voting, and why.

11. Think of the three main elements of vote choice—party identification, candidate appeal, and issues. In a short essay, evaluate which best explains the results of the 2008 presidential election.

8.5 Identify problems associated with administering elections and evaluate proposed solutions to those problems.

12. In a short essay, describe how Oregon has changed the way it administers elections since 1996. What two concerns have been raised about voting in this method?

Answers to selected Questions: 1. a; 4. b; 5. c; 7. a

---

mypoliscilab EXERCISES
Where participation leads to action!

Apply what you learned in this chapter on MyPoliSciLab.

📖—|Read on **mypoliscilab.com**

eText: Chapter 8

✓—|Study and Review on **mypoliscilab.com**

Pre-Test
Post-Test
Chapter Exam
Flashcards

👁—|Watch on **mypoliscilab.com**

Video: Obama Approval Rating
Video: Opinion Poll on the U.S. Economy
Video: Candidates Court College Students
Video: Chicago Worker Protest
Video: L.A. Riots: 15 Years Later
Video: Teen Sues for Equal Protection

✳—|Explore on **mypoliscilab.com**

Simulation: You Are a Polling Consultant
Simulation: You Are the Leader of Concerned Citizens for World Justice
Simulation: You Are an Informed Voter Helping Your Classmates
Comparative: Comparing Governments and Public Opinion
Timeline: War, Peace and Public Opinion
Visual Literacy: Voting Turnout: Who Votes in The United States?

KEY **TERMS**

political socialization, p. 214
attitudes, p. 214
selective exposure, p. 215
attentive public, p. 217
public opinion, p. 218
random sample, p. 218
margin of error, p. 218
universe, p. 219

intensity, p. 221
latency, p. 221
manifest opinion, p. 221
salience, p. 221
voter registration, p. 224
general election, p. 226
primary election, p. 226
presidential election, p. 226

midterm election, p. 226
turnout, p. 226
party identification, p. 231
candidate appeal, p. 232
prospective issue voting, p. 233
retrospective issue voting, p. 233

ADDITIONAL **RESOURCES**

FURTHER READING

R. MICHAEL ALVAREZ AND JOHN BREHM, *Hard Choices, Easy Answers: Values, Information, and American Public Opinion* (Princeton University Press, 2002).

R. MICHAEL ALVAREZ AND THAD E. HALL, *Electronic Elections: The Perils and Promises of Digital Democracy* (Princeton University Press, 2008).

HERBERT ASHER, *Polling and the Public: What Every Citizen Should Know,* 8th ed. (CQ Press, 2010).

BARBARA A. BARDES AND ROBERT W. OLDENDICK, *Public Opinion: Measuring the American Mind* (Wadsworth, 2006).

M. MARGARET CONWAY, *Political Participation in the United States,* 3d ed. (CQ Press, 2000).

ROBERT M. EISINGER, *The Evolution of Presidential Polling* (Cambridge University Press, 2002).

ROBERT S. ERIKSON AND KENT L. TEDIN, *American Public Opinion: Its Origins, Content, and Impact,* updated 8th ed. (Longman, 2010).

WILLIAM H. FLANIGAN AND NANCY H. ZINGALE, *Political Behavior of the American Electorate,* updated 12th ed. (CQ Press, 2009).

DONALD P. GREEN AND ALAN S. GERBER, *Get Out the Vote!: How to Increase Voter Turnout,* 2d ed. (Brookings Institution Press, 2008).

BRUCE E. KEITH, DAVID B. MAGLEBY, CANDICE J. NELSON, ELIZABETH ORR, MARK C. WESTLYE, AND RAYMOND E. WOLFINGER, *The Myth of the Independent Voter* (University of California Press, 1992).

V. O. KEY, JR., *Public Opinion and American Democracy* (Knopf, 1961).

RICHARD G. NIEMI AND HERBERT F. WEISBERG, *Classics in Voting Behavior* (CQ Press, 1993).

RICHARD G. NIEMI AND HERBERT F. WEISBERG, *Controversies in Voting Behavior,* 4th ed. (CQ Press, 2001).

FRANK R. PARKER, *Black Votes Count: Political Empowerment in Mississippi After 1965* (University of North Carolina Press, 1990).

JAMES A. THURBER AND CANDICE J. NELSON, EDS., *Campaigns and Elections American Style,* 3d ed. (Westview Press, 2010).

MICHAEL W. TRAUGOTT AND PAUL J. LAVRAKAS, *The Voter's Guide to Election Polls,* 4th ed. (Rowman & Littlefield, 2008).

MARTIN P. WATTENBERG, *Is Voting for Young People?* (Longman, 2007).

JOHN ZALLER, *The Nature and Origins of Mass Opinion* (Cambridge University Press, 1992). See also *Public Opinion Quarterly, The American Journal of Political Science,* and *American Political Science Review.*

WEB SITES

www.votesmart.org This is the Web site for Project Vote Smart. The site lists extensive nonpartisan information about candidates for both federal and state elections throughout the United States, including voting records and candidate positions.

www.govoteabsentee.org A collection of information and forms for individuals who would like to vote absentee in any state. This site is sponsored by an organization of current and recently graduated college students from around the country. You only need your home zip code in order to access the materials you will need to vote absentee in the next election.

www.rockthevote.org The home page for Rock the Vote, an organization that focuses on helping young people register to vote and participate in politics in general. The site includes voter registration materials, information on how to vote absentee, and information about other policy issues that young people may care about.

www.aapor.org As the home page of the American Association for Public Opinion Research, this site contains resources for both creators and users of polls and polling data. The site has information about how to accurately conduct a poll, how to understand polling data, and how to identify fake or poorly constructed polls.

Campaigns and Elections

Democracy in Action

The 2008 election set a new record for the most money raised and spent on federal elections. An estimated $6 billion was spent by candidates, political party committees, interest groups, and individuals on elections in 2007–2008.[1] This amounted to an increase of $1.4 billion over 2004 and more than $3 billion over 2000. Much of the increase came in spending by presidential candidates, who spent more than $1.8 billion, a nearly three-fold increase over what candidates spent in 2000.

Where does all this money come from? Under law, the nearly $6 billion spent on elections is reported to the Federal Election Commission (FEC) or Internal Revenue Service. In many cases, there are contributions limitations, or maximum amounts that individuals are allowed to donate, which means that candidates must find many donors. To maximize efficiency, candidates target individuals who could give the maximum allowable, which in 2007–2008 was $4,600. These donors provide an important jump-start to a campaign; their money helps fund the infrastructure of the campaign, such as the staff, early polling, and advertising, and helps the campaign raise more money. The media report the amount of money raised, which becomes a measure of how well or poorly a campaign is doing.

An unusual element of the 2008 election cycle was the success of the Obama campaign in raising money from individuals in relatively small amounts, under $200. Anthony Corrado, an expert on campaign finance, observed, "No previous presidential contender has ever raised as much money through small contributions as Obama did."[2] Roughly half of these small donors contributed for the first time during the last three months of the campaign, but many contributed several times during the election cycle.

Part of Obama's success in raising money was due to his innovative use of new media, especially the Internet. People were asked to volunteer, call or e-mail their friends, attend events, contribute money, and, most importantly, vote. It remains unclear whether the surge in numbers of individuals contributing money and the amount contributed in 2008 was a one-time event or if what happened can become part of American politics in the future. The Obama campaign combined a charismatic candidate with a compelling message who made skillful use of mass communications tools. Time will tell if others can learn from the way the 2008 campaign was financed in mounting future campaigns.

Money spent on elections is only one marker of their importance. Time devoted to campaigns by candidates, political parties, interest groups, and individuals is also substantial. Our system of federalism means we hold elections at the different levels of government. In the United States, citizens vote more often and for more offices than citizens of any other democracy. We hold thousands of elections for everything from community college directors to county sheriffs. Approximately half of a million persons hold elected state and local offices.[3] In 2010, we elected 37 U.S. senators,[4] all 435 members of the U.S. House of Representatives, 37 state governors, and, in many states, treasurers, secretaries of state, and judges.

In addition to electing people, voters in 27 states are allowed to vote on laws or constitutional amendments proposed by initiative petitions or on popular referendums put on the ballot by petition. In every state except Delaware, voters must approve all changes to the state constitution.

In this chapter, we explore our election rules. We note four important problems: the lack of competition for some offices, the complexities of nominating presidential candidates, the distortions of the electoral college, and the influence of money. We also discuss proposed reforms in each of these areas.

CHAPTER **OUTLINE**

CHAPTER LEARNING **OBJECTIVES**

Elections: The Rules of the Game

9.1 Assess the implications of election rules in the United States.

Running for Congress

9.2 Explain how congressional elections work and why they are generally not competitive.

Running for President

9.3 Outline the stages in U.S. presidential elections and the differences in campaigning at each stage.

Money in U.S. Elections

9.4 Evaluate the influence of money in American elections and the main approaches to campaign finance reform.

Improving Elections

9.5 Assess concerns regarding presidential elections and reforms that have been proposed.

Elections: The Rules of the Game

LEARNING **OBJECTIVE**

9.1 Assess the implications of election rules in the United States.

The rules of the game—the electoral game—make a difference. Although the Constitution sets certain conditions and requirements, state law determines most electoral rules. Our focus in this chapter is on presidential and congressional elections, although much of the discussion is also relevant to state and local elections.

Regularly Scheduled Elections

In our system, elections are held at fixed intervals that the party in power cannot change. It does not make any difference if the nation is at war, as we were during the Civil War, or in the midst of a crisis, as in the Great Depression; when the calendar calls for an election, the election is held. Elections for members of Congress occur on the first Tuesday after the first Monday in November of even-numbered years. Although there are exceptions (for special elections or peculiar state provisions), participants know *in advance* just when the next election will be. In most parliamentary democracies, such as Great Britain and Canada, the party in power can call elections at a time of its choosing. The predetermined timing of elections is one of the defining characteristics of democracy in the United States.

Fixed, Staggered, and Sometimes Limited Terms

Our electoral system is based on *fixed terms,* meaning the length of a term in office is specified, not indefinite. The Constitution sets the term of office for the U.S. House of Representatives at two years, the Senate at six years, and the presidency at four years.

Our system also has *staggered terms* for some offices; not all offices are up for election at the same time. All House members are up for election every two years, but only one-third of senators are up for election at the same time. Because presidential elections can occur two or four years into a senator's six-year term, senators can often run for the presidency without fear of losing their seat, as John Kerry did in 2004 and John McCain, Barack Obama, Hillary Clinton, and Joe Biden (for the vice presidency) did in 2008. But if their Senate term expires the same year as the presidential election, the laws of many states require them to give up their Senate seat to run for president, vice president, or any other position. An example of a state that permits a candidate to run for election to two offices is Connecticut, where Joseph Lieberman was reelected to the U.S. Senate in 2000 while being narrowly defeated in his race for vice president. Had he been victorious in both campaigns, he would have resigned his Senate seat.

Term Limits

The Twenty-Second Amendment to the Constitution, adopted in 1951, limits presidents to two terms. Knowing that a president cannot run again changes the way members of Congress, the voters, and the press regard the chief executive. A politician who cannot, or has announced he or she will not, run again is called a *lame duck.* Lame ducks are often seen as less influential because other politicians know that these officials' ability to bestow or withhold favors is coming to an end. Efforts to limit the terms of other offices have become a major issue in several states. The most frequent targets have been state legislators. One consequence of term limits is more lame ducks.

Term limits at the state level were largely adopted during the 1990s. Currently, 15 states have term limits for state legislatures. Six states have rescinded term limits. South Dakota voters were given the option of repealing term limits, and they overwhelmingly voted to keep them.[5] Despite their popularity at the state level, proposals for term limits on federal legislators have repeatedly been defeated when they have come to a vote in Congress. The Supreme Court, by a vote of 5-to-4, declared that a state does not have the constitutional power to impose limits on the number of terms for which its members of the U.S. Congress are eligible, either by amendment to its own constitution or by state law.[6] Congress has refused to propose a constitutional amendment to impose a limit on congressional terms.

Winner Take All

winner-take-all system
An election system in which the candidate with the most votes wins.

An important feature of our electoral system is the **winner-take-all system,** sometimes referred to as "first past the post" in other countries.[7] In most U.S. electoral settings, the candidate with the most votes wins. The winner does not need to have a *majority* (more than half the votes cast); in a multicandidate race, the winner may have only a *plurality* (the largest number of votes). An example is the 2009 special election held in New York's 23rd Congressional District. In a three-candidate race, Democrat Bill Owens won with 48 percent of the vote, a plurality, not a majority. The Conservative party candidate Doug Hoffman received 46 percent of the vote, and the Republican Dierdre Scozzafava received less than 6 percent.[8] Winner-take-all electoral systems tend to reinforce moderate and centrist candidates because they are more likely to secure a plurality or a majority. Candidates in a winner-take-all system often stress that a vote for a minor party candidate is a "wasted vote" that may actually help elect the voter's least desired candidate.

Most U.S. electoral districts are **single-member districts,** meaning that in any district for any given election—senator, governor, U.S. House, and state legislative seat—the voters choose *one* representative or official.[9] When the single-member-district and winner-take-all systems are combined, minor parties find it especially hard to win. For example, even if a third party gets 25 percent of the vote in several districts, it still gets no seats. As discussed in Chapter 7, the single-member districts and winner-take-all system is different from a **proportional representation** system, in which political parties secure legislative seats and power in proportion to the number of votes they receive in the election. Countries that practice some form of proportional representation include Germany, Israel, Italy, and Japan.

Proportional representation more accurately reveals the division of voter preferences and gives those who do not vote with the plurality some influence as a result of their vote. For this reason, proportional representation may encourage greater turnout for people who identify with parties that rarely win elections, such as Democrats in Utah or Republicans in Massachusetts. Proportional representation may also encourage issue-oriented campaigns and enhance the representation of women and minorities.

But proportional representation can cause problems. It may make it harder to have a clear winner, especially if minor parties are likely to win seats. As a result, it may encourage the proliferation of minor parties. Opponents of proportional representation worry that it can contribute to political instability and ideological extremism.

The Electoral College

We elect our president and vice president not by a national vote but by an indirect device known as the **electoral college.** The framers of the U.S. Constitution devised this system because they did not trust the choice of president to a direct vote of the people. Under this system, each state has as many electors as it has representatives and senators. California therefore has 55 electoral votes (53 House seats and two Senate seats), whereas seven states and the District of Columbia have three electoral votes each.

Each state legislature is free to determine how it selects its electors. Each party nominates a slate of electors, usually longtime party workers. They are expected to cast their electoral votes for the party's candidates for president and vice president if their party's candidates get a plurality of the vote in their state. In our entire history, no "faithless elector"—an elector who does not vote for his or her state's popular vote winner—has ever cast the deciding vote, and the incidence of a faithless elector is rare.[10]

Candidates who win a plurality of the popular vote in a state secure all of that state's electoral votes, except in Nebraska and Maine, which allocate electoral votes to the winner in each congressional district plus two electoral votes for the winner of the state as a whole. Winning electors go to their state capital on the first Monday after the second Wednesday in December to cast their ballots. These ballots are then sent to Congress, and early in January, Congress formally counts the ballots and declares who won the election for president and vice president.

It takes a majority of the electoral votes to win. If no candidate gets a majority of the electoral votes for president, the House chooses among the top three candidates, with each state delegation having one vote. If no candidate gets a majority of the electoral votes for vice president, the Senate chooses among the top two candidates, with each senator casting one vote.

When there are only two major candidates for the presidency, the chances of an election being thrown into the House are remote. But twice in our history, the House has had

single-member district
An electoral district in which voters choose one representative or official.

proportional representation
An election system in which each party running receives the proportion of legislative seats corresponding to its proportion of the vote.

electoral college
The electoral system used in electing the president and vice president, in which voters vote for electors pledged to cast their ballots for a particular party's candidates.

to act: in 1800, the House had to choose in a tie vote between Thomas Jefferson and Aaron Burr; and in 1824, the House picked John Quincy Adams over Andrew Jackson. The 1800 election prompted the Twelfth Amendment, ratified in 1804, requiring that electors in the electoral college vote for one person as president and for another as vice president.

As we were reminded in 2000, our electoral college system makes it possible for a presidential candidate to receive the most popular votes, as Al Gore did, and yet not get enough electoral votes to be elected president. Gore lost the electoral college vote 271 to 266, and George Bush became president.[11] This also happened in 1824, when Andrew Jackson won 12 percent more of the vote than John Quincy Adams; in 1876, when Samuel Tilden received more popular votes than Rutherford B. Hayes; and in 1888, when Grover Cleveland received more popular votes than Benjamin Harrison. It almost happened in 1916, 1960, and 1976, when the shift of a few votes in a few key states could have resulted in the election of a president without a popular majority.

Questions about the electoral college arise every time a serious third-party candidate runs for president. If no candidate receives a majority in the electoral college and the decision is left to Congress, which Congress casts the vote, the one serving during the election, or the newly elected one? The answer is the newly elected one, the one elected in November and taking office the first week in January. Because each state has one vote in the House, what happens if a state's delegation is tied, 2 to 2 or 3 to 3? The answer is, its vote does not count. Would it be possible to have a president of one party and a vice president of another? Yes, if the election were thrown into the House and Senate, and a different party controlled each chamber.

The electoral college sharply influences presidential politics. To win a presidential election, a candidate must appeal successfully to voters in populous states such as California, Texas, Ohio, Illinois, Florida, and New York. California's electoral vote of 55 in 2008 exceeded the combined electoral votes of the 14 least populous states plus the District of Columbia. Sparsely populated states such as Wyoming and Vermont also have disproportionate representation in the electoral college because each has one representative, regardless of population. When the contest is close, as it was in recent elections, every state's electoral votes are crucial to the outcome, and so greater emphasis is given to states in which the contest is close[12] (see Table 9–1).

In two of the four elections in which winners of the popular vote did not become president, the electoral college did not decide the winner. The 1824 election was decided by the U.S. House of Representatives. In the controversial 1876 presidential election between Rutherford B. Hayes and Samuel Tilden, the electoral vote in four states was disputed, resulting in the appointment of an electoral commission to decide how those votes should be counted. The Electoral Commission of 1877, depicted in the drawing, met in secret session, and after many contested votes, Hayes was elected.

TABLE

| 9–1 | 2004 and 2008 Battleground States |

As the table shows, many of the states that were battlegrounds in 2004, Obama took handily in 2008. In contrast, some states that voted strongly for Bush in 2004 became battlegrounds in 2008.

State	Electoral Votes in 2004 and 2008	Percent Difference in 2004 Popular Vote	Percent Difference in 2008 Popular Vote
Wisconsin	10	0.38 Kerry	13.91 Obama
New Mexico	5	0.79 Bush	15.13 Obama
Iowa	7	0.67 Bush	9.54 Obama
New Hampshire	4	1.37 Kerry	9.61 Obama
Pennsylvania	21	2.50 Kerry	10.32 Obama
Ohio	20	2.10 Bush	4.59 Obama
Nevada	5	2.59 Bush	12.50 Obama
Michigan	17	3.42 Kerry	16.47 Obama
Oregon	7	4.16 Kerry	16.35 Obama
Florida	27	5.01 Bush	2.81 Obama
Missouri	11	7.20 Bush	0.14 McCain
Virginia	13	8.20 Bush	6.30 Obama
North Carolina	15	12.44 Bush	0.32 Obama
Indiana	11	20.68 Bush	1.04 Obama

■ *Which states had the largest change in vote share to the two parties between 2004 and 2008? What do these states have in common?*

SOURCE: Federal Election Commission, "Election Results," http://www.fec.gov/pubrec/electionresults.shtml (accessed March 23, 2010).

Running for Congress

How candidates run for Congress differs depending on the nature of their district or state, on whether candidates are incumbents or challengers, on the strength of their personal organization, on how well known they are, and on how much money they have to spend on their campaign. There are both similarities and differences between House and Senate elections.

First, most congressional elections are not close (see Figure 9–1). In districts where most people belong to one party or where incumbents are popular and enjoy fundraising and other campaign advantages, there is often little competition.[13] Districts are typically drawn in ways that enhance the reelection prospects of incumbents or one party, a process called *partisan gerrymandering.* We explore this process in greater detail in Chapter 11, which deals with Congress. Those who believe that competition is essential to constitutional democracy are concerned that so many officeholders have **safe seats.** When officeholders do not have to fight to retain their seats, elections are not performing their proper role.[14]

Competition is more likely when both candidates have adequate funding, which is not often the case in U.S. House elections (see Chapters 7 and 11). Elections for governor and for the U.S. Senate are more seriously contested and more adequately financed than those for the U.S. House.

Presidential popularity affects both House and Senate races during both presidential and midterm elections. The boost candidates get from running along with a popular presidential candidate from their party is known as the **coattail effect.** But winning presidential candidates do not always provide such a boost. The Republicans suffered a net loss of six House seats in 1988, even though George H. W. Bush won the presidency, and the Democrats suffered a net loss of ten House seats in 1992 when Bill Clinton won

LEARNING **OBJECTIVE**

9.2 Explain how congressional elections work and why they are generally not competitive.

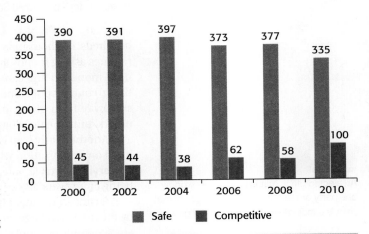

FIGURE 9–1 Safe and Competitive House Seats, 2000–2010.

SOURCE: Charlie Cook, "National Overview," *Cook Political Report*, October 16, 2008, p. 6; and Charlie Cook, "Competitive House Race Chart," *Cook Political Report*, http://www.cookpolitical.com/charts/house/competitive_2010-11-01_12-12-36.php.

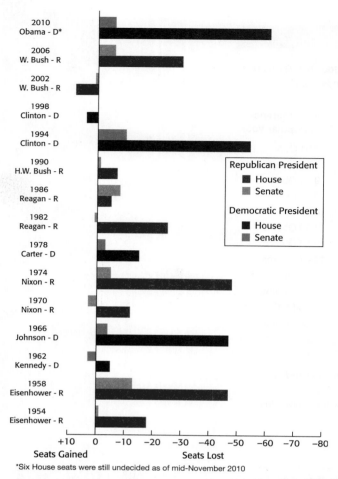

FIGURE 9–2 **Seats Gained or Lost by the President's Party in Midterm Elections, 1954–2010.**

■ *Based on past midterm elections, how does 2010 compare in terms of the seats lost by the President's party?*

SOURCE: Harold W. Stanley and Richard G. Niemi, *Vital Statistics on American Politics 2007–2008* (CQ Press, 2008), p. 54.

safe seat
An elected office that is predictably won by one party or the other, so the success of that party's candidate is almost taken for granted.

coattail effect
The boost that candidates may get in an election because of the popularity of candidates above them on the ballot, especially the president.

the presidential election. On the coattails of Barack Obama's convincing presidential win in 2008, the Democrats saw a net gain of 21 House seats and 8 Senate seats. Overall, "measurable coattail effects continue to appear," according to congressional elections scholar Gary Jacobson, but their impact is "erratic and usually modest."[15]

In midterm elections, presidential popularity and economic conditions have long been associated with the number of House seats a president's party loses.[16] These same factors are associated with how well the president's party does in Senate races, but the association is less strong.[17] Figure 9–2 shows the number of seats in the House of Representatives and U.S. Senate gained or lost by the party controlling the White House in midterm elections since 1954. In all of the midterm elections between 1934 and 1998, the party controlling the White House lost seats in the House. But in 1998 and 2002, the long-standing pattern of the president's party losing seats in a midterm election did not hold. In 2006, however, the long-standing pattern reemerged, with the Republicans losing 30 House seats and 6 Senate seats.[18] The net result of the Democrats success in 2006 and 2008 was that they had won many of the most competitive districts, making them vulnerable to the GOP in 2010.

In 2010, Republicans won a net gain of six U.S. Senate seats and more than sixty house seats. Putting this victory in historical perspective, this is the most house seats gained by a party since 1938 when the GOP had a net gain of 72 seats, and surpasses the 54 seats the Democrats lost in 1994 and 1946. Republicans did especially well in defeating centrist Democrats, sometimes called Blue Dog Democrats. More than half of this group in the House were defeated or retired in 2010.

The House of Representatives

Every two years, as many as 1,000 candidates—including approximately 400 incumbents—campaign for Congress. Incumbents are rarely challenged for renomination from within their own party, and when they are, the challenges are seldom serious. In the 1990s, for example, on average only two House incumbents were denied renomination in each election. In 2010, four House incumbents were denied renomination, and 29 ran unopposed.[19] Challengers from other parties running against incumbents rarely encounter opposition in their own party.[20] In 2010, Tea Party-supported candidates denied renomination to two senators and defeated the party leader's preferred Senate candidates in Kentucky, Nevada, and Delaware.

Mounting a Primary Campaign The first step for would-be challengers is to raise hundreds of thousands of dollars (or even more) to mount a serious campaign. This requires asking friends and acquaintances as well as interest groups for money. Candidates need money to hire campaign managers and technicians, buy television and other advertising, conduct polls, and pay for a variety of activities. Parties can sometimes help, but they shy away from giving money in primary contests. The party organization usually stays neutral until the nomination is decided.

Another early step is to build a *personal organization.* A congressional candidate can build an organization while holding another office, such as a seat in the state legislature, by serving in civic causes, helping other candidates, and being conspicuous without being controversial.

A candidate's main hurdle is gaining visibility. Candidates work hard to be mentioned by the media. In large cities with many simultaneous campaigns, congressional candidates are frequently overlooked, and in all areas, television is devoting less time to political news.[21] Candidates rely on personal contacts, on hand shaking and door-to-door campaigning, and on identifying likely supporters and courting their favor—the same techniques used in campaigns for lesser offices. Despite these efforts, the turnout in primaries tends to be low except in campaigns in which large sums of money are spent on advertising.

Of the People

Who Makes a Better Political Leader?

Voters in the United States have increasingly had the opportunity to vote for women for governor, president, vice president, senator, House representative, and other offices. How do people feel about women versus men serving in these offices? The Pew Global Attitudes survey asked respondents the following question: "Which of the following statements comes closest to your opinion about men and women as political leaders: Men generally make better political leaders than women, women generally make better political leaders than men, or, in general, women and men make equally good political leaders.

Holding aside Nigeria, the most common response in all countries in our sample is that men and women are equally qualified to be political leaders. In Britain, this response is given by 83 percent, perhaps a reflection of the fact that the position of prime minister in Britain has been held by a woman. Japan, Mexico, and the United States all have high proportions of respondents saying both genders make equally good leaders. However, in Nigeria, there is a preference for male leaders, with 48 percent saying they make better leaders. This likely stems from the political culture of Nigeria where women are often marginalized for social and religious reasons.*

Another way to look at these data is to compare the views of those who do not think men and women make equally good leaders. Of this group, people in India, Britain, Japan, and Mexico are about equally divided with some favoring men and others women. In the other countries and the world sample, men are preferred as leaders over women by about 3 to 1. Again, this is only among people who do not see the two genders as equally well-qualified.

CRITICAL THINKING QUESTIONS

1. What do you think the answer to this survey question would have been 100 years ago, 50 years ago, 20 years ago?

2. Why do we not see more women holding political office in the United States if 75 percent think men and women are equally well qualified?

3. If opinions have changed on this question over time, what factors might explain opinion change on this issue?

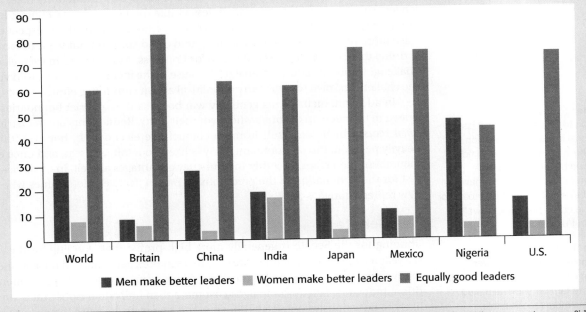

Legend: ■ Men make better leaders ■ Women make better leaders ■ Equally good leaders

*Muhammad Mustapha, "In the Shadows of Men: Women's Political Marginalisation," *Inter Press Service*, March 12, 2010, http://ipsnews.net/news.asp?idnews=50648 (accessed May 6, 2010).

Campaigning for the General Election   The electorate in a general election is different from that in a primary election. Many more voters turn out in general elections, especially the less-committed partisans and Independents. Partisanship is more important in a general election, as many voters use party as a simplifying device to select from among candidates in the many races they decide. Not surprisingly, candidates in districts where their party is strong make their partisanship clear, and candidates from a minority party deemphasize it. General elections also focus on the strengths and weaknesses of the candidates and their background, experience, and visibility. Political scientists describe this dimension as **candidate appeal.** Issues can also be important in general elections, but they are often more local than national issues. Occasionally, a major national issue arises that can help or hurt one party. Candidates

candidate appeal
The tendency in elections to focus on the personal attributes of a candidate, such as his or her strengths, weaknesses, background, experience, and visibility.

247

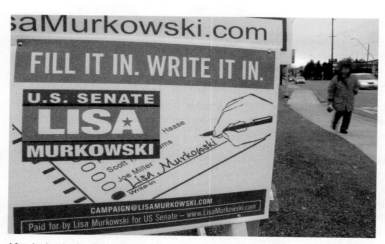

After losing in the Republican primary to Tea Party candidate Joe Miller, incumbent Senator Lisa Murkowski mounted a write-in campaign. While the results are still being tallied, Murkowski would be only the third Senator to be elected by write-in. ■ *Why is Murkowski's imcumbancy such an important factor in attempting a write-in campaign?*

who have differentiated themselves from their party or its leader can reduce the impact of such a **national tide** if it is negative. Some elections for Congress or the state legislature are in part referendums on the president or governor, but public opinion concerning the president or governor is rarely the only factor at play in these elections.

As we have mentioned, most incumbent members of Congress win reelection.[22] Since 1970, slightly more than 95 percent of incumbent House members seeking reelection have won, and since 2000, about 97 percent of incumbent House members running for reelection have been successful (see Figure 9–3).[23] This lends credibility to the charge that we have a "permanent Congress."

Why is reelection to a House seat so much easier than defeating an incumbent or winning an open seat? As we discuss in Chapter 11, incumbents have a host of advantages that help them win reelection. Incumbents are generally better known than challengers, something called **name recognition,** and benefit from years of media coverage of their generally positive efforts on behalf of the district.

Incumbents also win so often because they are able to outspend challengers in campaigns by approximately 3 to 1 in the House and about 2.37 to 1 in the Senate.[24] Most challengers run campaigns that are much less visible than incumbents, contact fewer voters, and lose badly. Many potential challengers are scared away by the prospect of having to raise more than $1 million in campaign funds, and some do not want to face the media scrutiny that comes with a serious race for Congress. Nonetheless, in each election, a few challengers mount serious campaigns because of the incumbent's perceived vulnerability, the challengers' own wealth, party or political action committee efforts, or other factors.

In addition, incumbents generally win because their district boundaries have been drawn to be made up of voters who favor their party. Retirements and redistricting create *open seats,* which can result in more competitive elections. If, however, the district is heavily partisan, the predominant party is likely to retain the seat, and once elected, the incumbent then reaps the other incumbency advantages as well. In these cases, the contest for the nomination in the predominant party effectively determines who will be the new representative.

The Senate

Running for the Senate is generally more high-profile than running for the House. The six-year term, the fact that there are only two senators per state, and the national exposure many senators enjoy make a Senate seat a glittering prize, leading to more intense competition. Individual Senate campaigns cost more than individual House races and are more likely to be seriously contested; though in the aggregate, because there are so many more

national tide
The inclination to focus on national issues, rather than local issues, in an election campaign. The impact of a national tide can be reduced by the nature of the candidates on the ballot who may have differentiated themselves from their party or its leader if the tide is negative, as well as competition in the election.

name recognition
Incumbents have an advantage over challengers in election campaigns because voters are more familiar with them, and incumbents are more recognizable.

FIGURE 9–3 **U.S. House Incumbents Reelected, 1960–2010.**

■ *Considering the advantages and disadvantages of continuity in office, do you think the high rate of reelection for incumbents is good or bad for our democracy?*

SOURCE: Harold W. Stanley and Richard G. Niemi, *Vital Statistics on American Politics 2009–2010* (CQ Press, 2010), pp. 45–47.

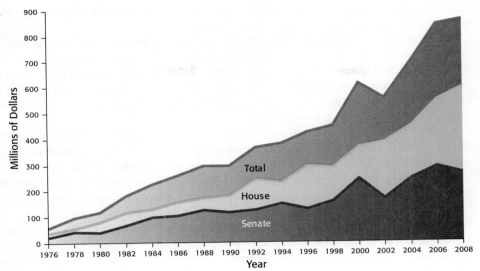

FIGURE 9–4 **Rising Campaign Costs in Congressional General Elections.**

■ *What are some of the ways in which the rising cost of campaigns might impact who runs for office, how campaigns are funded, and the priorities of candidates?*

SOURCE: 1976–2004, Harold W. Stanley and Richard G. Niemi, *Vital Statistics on American Politics 2007–2008* (CQ Press, 2008), p. 101; 2006–2008, Center for Responsive Politics, "Price of Admission: Winners," www.opensecrets.org/bigpicture/stats.php?cycle=2008&display=T&Type=W. Amounts are in 2006 dollars.

House races, overall spending on House races surpasses overall spending on Senate races (see Figure 9–4).[25] The essential tactics are to raise large amounts of money, hire a professional and experienced campaign staff, make as many personal contacts as possible (especially in states with smaller populations), avoid giving the opposition any positive publicity, and have a clear and consistent campaign theme. Incumbency is an advantage for senators, although not as much as it is for representatives.[26] Incumbent senators are widely known but often so are their opponents, who generally raise and spend significant amounts of money.[27]

When one party controls the Senate by only a few seats, as has been the case in recent years, both parties and the White House become more involved in recruiting competitive candidates. Sometimes, the party leadership attempts to "clear the field" for a preferred candidate by discouraging other candidates from running while endorsing a candidate it considers to be more competitive. In 2010, the Obama White House is reported to have cleared the field for Kristen Gillibrand in New York, asking Representative Steve Israel and former Representative Harold Ford not to run.[28]

The cost of Senate campaigns can vary greatly. California has nearly 70 times the number of potential voters as Wyoming; not surprisingly, running for a seat from Wyoming is much cheaper than running for a seat from California. As a result, interest groups and parties direct more money to competitive races in small states where their campaign dollars have a greater potential impact.[29]

Running for President

Presidential elections are major media events, with candidates seeking as much positive television coverage as possible and trying to avoid negative coverage. The formal campaign has three stages: winning the nomination, campaigning at the convention, and mobilizing support in the general election.

Stage 1: The Nomination

Presidential hopefuls must make a series of critical tactical decisions. The first is when to start campaigning. For the presidential election of 2008, some candidates began soon after the 2004 presidential election.[30] Some candidates formally announced in December 2006, and most had announced by the end of February 2007. Republican Fred Thompson delayed his entry until September 6, 2007, a decision that meant he was less competitive in recruiting staff, fundraising, and visibility.[31] Early decisions are increasingly necessary for candidates to raise money and assemble an organization. Campaigning begins well before any actual declaration of candidacy, as candidates try to line up supporters to win

LEARNING **OBJECTIVE**

9.3 Outline the stages in U.S. presidential elections and the differences in campaigning at each stage.

caucuses or primaries in key states and to raise money for their nomination effort. This period in the campaign has been called the "invisible primary."[32]

One of the hardest jobs for candidates and their strategists is calculating how to deal with the complex maze of presidential primaries and caucuses that constitutes the delegate selection system. The system for electing delegates to the national party convention varies from state to state and often from one party to the other in the same state. In some parties in some states, for example, candidates must provide lists of delegates who support them months before the primary.

Another decision candidates must make is whether to participate in partial public financing of their campaigns. The presidential campaign finance system provides funds to match small individual contributions during the nomination phase of the campaign for candidates who agree to remain within spending limitations. George W. Bush declined federal funds in the 2000 and 2004 nomination phase, as did Democrats John Kerry and Howard Dean in 2004. In 2008, Barack Obama, Hillary Clinton, Mitt Romney, Rudy Giuliani, Ron Paul, Mike Huckabee, and Fred Thompson all turned down matching funds. John McCain at one point said he would accept them and then later declined them. Forgoing the public matching funds allows greater flexibility in spending campaign money and removes the overall limit for this phase of the process. Most serious contenders for the White House are likely to decline federal matching funds in 2012 and beyond.

Presidential Primaries State presidential primaries, unknown before 1900, have become the main method of choosing delegates to the national convention. A delegate is a person chosen by local partisans to represent them in selecting nominees, party leaders, and party positions. Today, more than three-fourths of the states use presidential primaries. In 2008, 67 percent of the Democratic delegates and 77 percent of the Republican delegates were chosen in the primaries.[33] The rest of the delegates were chosen by state party caucuses or conventions or were party leaders who served as "superdelegates."

The states have different means of determining delegates, and state primaries allocate delegates using the following systems:[34]

- *Proportional representation:* Delegates to the national convention are allocated on the basis of the percentage of votes candidates win in the primary. This system has been used in most of the states, including several of the largest ones. The Democrats mandate proportional representation for all their primaries, with three-quarters of the states' delegates elected in primaries determined by the proportional vote in congressional districts.[35] In some states, Republicans use this same system, but Republicans are much more varied in how they select their delegates.[36]

- *Winner take all:* Whoever gets the most votes wins all that state's delegates or the share of delegates from each congressional district. Republicans still use the winner-take-all system at the state level, and in 2008, most states used this rule at either the state or congressional district levels.[37] To win all the delegates of a big state such as California is an enormous bonus to a candidate, as it was to John McCain in 2008.

- *Superdelegates and delegate selection without a commitment to a candidate:* New York Republicans allow the state committee to select 12 at-large delegates who are officially unpledged, as are the party chair and national committee representatives.[38] In 2008, a lot of attention was paid to Democratic superdelegates, who included party leaders, elected officials, and others who were selected for reasons other than which candidate they ended up backing. Following the 1972 election, there was an effort to give more influence in the selection of the presidential candidate to party leaders and elected officials. This led to the creation of superdelegates, which were delegates that were automatically selected due to their elected or party office or chosen by the state party committee. These superdelegates cast the deciding vote for Obama because no candidate secured a majority of all delegates through the primary and caucus process.

- *Delegate selection and separate presidential poll:* In several states, voters decide twice: once to indicate their choice for president and again to choose delegates pledged, or at least favorable, to a presidential candidate. In 2008, this was the process Democrats used in Texas, with a primary during the day to elect 126 delegates and a caucus that night electing 67 delegates. Republicans have long allowed a popularity vote or "beauty contest" in which votes indicate their preferred candidate but require a separate vote for delegates pledged to particular candidates.

Voters in states such as Iowa and New Hampshire, which are the first states to pick delegates, bask in media attention for weeks and even months before they cast the first ballots in the presidential sweepstakes. Because these early contests have had the effect of limiting the choices of voters in states that come later in the process, states have tended to move their primaries up in a process called "front loading." California, which traditionally held its primary in June, moved it to March in 2000 so that its voters would play a more important role in selecting the nominee. Other states did the same thing. Front loading was even more prominent in 2004 and 2008.[39] However, the parties have sought to prevent too much front loading. In 2008, when Florida and Michigan moved their primaries up to January 29 and January 15 (respectively), ahead of what party rules allowed, the Democratic National Committee (DNC) voted that delegates so selected would not be seated.[40] The controversy was resolved by giving each Florida and Michigan delegate a half vote, but at the convention, each delegate was given a full vote.

In 2008, the Republican nomination reached an early resolution, with John McCain effectively winning it after his victories in Ohio and Texas on March 4.[41] The Republican rules, which clearly advantage candidates who win states, even by narrow margins, helped McCain. The Democrats had a highly contested and protracted race that did not wrap up until June 2008, with voters in all states and territories voting in contested primaries and caucuses.

Caucuses and Conventions   A meeting of party members and supporters of various candidates who may elect state or national convention delegates, who in turn vote for the presidential nominee, is called a **caucus.** In about a dozen states, one or both parties use a caucus or convention system (or both) to choose delegates.[42] Each state's parties and legislature regulate the methods used.[43] The caucus or convention is the oldest method of choosing delegates, and unlike the primary system, it centers on staffing local party positions such as voting district chair and often includes party discussions of issues and candidates in addition to a vote on candidates or policies.

In caucus or convention states, delegates who will attend the national party conventions are chosen by delegates to state or district conventions, who themselves are chosen earlier in county, precinct, or town caucuses. The process starts at local meetings open to all party members, who discuss and take positions on candidates and issues and elect delegates to represent their views at the next level. This process is repeated until conventions of delegates from a district or state choose delegates to the national nominating convention.

The best-known example of a caucus is in Iowa, because Iowa has held the earliest caucuses in the most recent presidential nominating contests. Every January or February in a presidential election year, Iowans have the opportunity to attend Republican and Democratic precinct meetings.[44] In 2008, all Democratic caucus states except Nevada went heavily to Obama. Highlighting the distinction between the primary and caucus systems, Senator Clinton said that her campaign had "been less successful in caucuses because it brings out the activist base of the Democratic Party." Of these activists, she said, "I don't agree with them. They know I don't agree with them. So they flood into these caucuses and dominate them and really intimidate people who actually show up to support me."[45]

Strategies   Presidential hopefuls face a dilemma: To get the Republican nomination, a candidate has to appeal to the more intensely conservative Republican partisans, those who vote in caucuses and primaries and actively support campaigns. Democratic hopefuls have to appeal to the liberal wing of their party as well as to minorities, union members, and environmental activists. But to win the general election, candidates have to

caucus
A meeting of local party members to choose party officials or candidates for public office and to decide the platform.

By the People

Volunteering for a Campaign

You can make a difference in your community, state, or country by volunteering for a campaign. Campaigns are dependent on individuals like you to help make democracy happen. It is also a great way to learn about public opinion, representation, and the political process. If you decide to get involved, you may participate in a wide range of activities, including contacting voters in person, on the telephone, or through the Internet; helping with fundraising; or assisting in organizing events. Be sure to let the campaign know in what areas you have experience or expertise, such as database management or graphic design.

To have a good experience, it is important to understand that campaigns are hectic and intense. The election day cannot be postponed, and winning is the objective. But there is also an excitement and energy to campaigns that you will not forget. Because of the number and frequency of elections in the United States, there is likely a candidate or ballot measure campaign of some sort happening in your area that would welcome your assistance. Call, e-mail, or drop by the campaign office and inform the campaign manger of the kinds of things you would like to do and how you can assist.

You might also check on your campus to see if there is a possibility to do an internship with a campaign or if there is a clearing house for such opportunities. Occidental College, for example, had an internship program, "Campaign Semester," where a student could get a full semester's worth of college credit (16 credits) for volunteering full time with a presidential or U.S. Senate campaign.*

CRITICAL THINKING QUESTIONS

1. Why do many political leaders get their start in government or politics by volunteering in a campaign?

2. What aspect of campaigns most interests you?

3. If we judge a potential leader by the quality of his/her campaign, what are the markers of a good campaign?

* Peter Dreier and Caroline Heldman, "Campaign Semester Fall 2008," http://departments.oxy.edu/politics/campaignsemester.htm (accessed May 3, 2010).

---

win support from moderate and pragmatic voters, many of whom do not vote in the primaries. If candidates position themselves too far from the moderates in their nomination campaign, they risk being labeled extreme in the general election and losing these votes to their opponents.

Strategies for securing the nomination have changed throughout the years. Some candidates think it wise to skip some of the earlier contests and enter first in states where their strength lies. John McCain pursued such a strategy in 2000 and again in 2008, ignoring Iowa and concentrating on New Hampshire. In 2008, former New York City mayor Rudy Giuliani also bypassed Iowa, but unlike McCain, he did not win in New Hampshire and dropped out of the race after losing in Florida to McCain a few weeks later. Most candidates choose to run hard in Iowa and New Hampshire, hoping that early showings in these states, which receive a great deal of media attention, will move them into the spotlight for later efforts.

During this early phase, the ability of candidates to generate momentum by managing the media's expectations of their performance is especially important. Winning in the primaries thus centers on a game of expectations, and candidates may intentionally seek to lower expectations so that "doing better than expected" will generate momentum for their campaign. The media and pollsters generally set these expectations in their coverage of candidates. In 2008, polls consistently had Clinton in the lead in New Hampshire until the Iowa caucus the week before New Hampshire. With Obama's win in Iowa, however, Clinton's ability to win in New Hampshire was in doubt, and when she won, her victory was interpreted as a "stunner" by MSNBC.[46]

Stage 2: The National Party Convention

national party convention
A national meeting of delegates elected in primaries, caucuses, or state conventions who assemble once every four years to nominate candidates for president and vice president, ratify the party platform, elect officers, and adopt rules.

The delegates elected in primaries, caucuses, or state conventions assemble at their **national party convention** in the summer before the election to pick the party's presidential and vice presidential candidates. Conventions follow standard rules, routines, and rituals. Usually, the first day is devoted to a keynote address and other speeches touting the party and denouncing the opposition; the second day, to committee reports, including party and convention rules and the party platform; the third day, to presidential and vice presidential balloting; and the fourth day, to the presidential candidate's acceptance speech.

National party conventions used to be events of high excitement because there was no clear nominee before the convention. In the past, delegates also arrived at national nominating conventions with differing degrees of commitment to presidential candidates; some delegates were pledged to no candidate at all, others to a specific candidate for one or two ballots, and others firmly to one candidate only. Because of reforms encouraging delegates to stick with the person to whom they are pledged, there has been less room to maneuver at conventions. For a half century, conventions have ratified a candidate who has already been selected in the primaries and caucuses.

Despite the lack of suspense about who the nominee will be, conventions continue to be major media events. As recently as 1988, the major networks gave the Democratic and Republican national conventions gavel-to-gavel coverage, meaning that television covered the conventions from the beginning of the first night to the end of the fourth night. Now, the major networks leave comprehensive coverage to C-SPAN. The long-term decline in viewership and the reduced hours of coverage have altered the parties' strategies. The parties feature their most important speakers and highlight their most important messages in the limited time the networks give them. In 2008, coverage and viewership of the conventions increased; this was especially the case for the Obama, Palin, and McCain acceptance speeches. An estimated 40 million people viewed the McCain speech, slightly higher than the number who saw Obama's acceptance speech.[47]

Acceptance speeches provide the nominees with an opportunity to define themselves and their candidacy. An example of an acceptance speech that worked more to the benefit of the opposition was Barry Goldwater's speech to the Republican convention in 1964 when he said, "Extremism in the defense of liberty is no vice."[48] This only helped to define Goldwater as "dangerous" and "extreme," themes his opponent, Lyndon Johnson, exploited. Democrats hoped Ronald Reagan would also self-destruct in 1980. Instead, Reagan came off as warm and confident. At two places in his acceptance speech, he quoted Franklin D. Roosevelt, once by name. Candidates of one party rarely quote a president of the other party in favorable terms as Reagan did.[49] This was clearly an effort to reach out to Democrats.

The Party Platform   Delegates to the national party conventions decide on the *platform*, a statement of party perspectives on public policy. Why does anyone care what is in the party platform? Critics have long pointed out that the party platform is binding on no one and is more likely to hurt than to help a candidate by advocating positions unpopular to moderate or Independent voters, whose support the candidate may need to win in the general election. But presidential candidates, as well as delegates, take the platform seriously because it defines the direction a party wants to take. Also, despite the charge that the platform is ignored, most presidents try to implement much of it.[50]

The Vice Presidential Nominee   The choice of the vice presidential nominee garners widespread attention. Rarely does a person actually "run" for the vice presidential nomination because only the presidential nominee's vote counts. But there is a good deal of maneuvering to capture that one vote. Sometimes, the choice of a running mate is made at the convention—not a time conducive to careful and deliberate thought. But usually, it is made before, and the announcement is timed to enhance media coverage and momentum going into the convention. The last time a presidential candidate left the choice of vice president to the delegates was the Democratic convention in 1956.

In 2008, Barack Obama selected Delaware Senator Joe Biden to be his running mate. Biden, who himself had twice been a candidate for the presidency including a bid in 2008, was seen as adding extensive foreign policy experience to the ticket because of his long service on the Senate Foreign Relations Committee. Biden was also expected to assist in winning working class and Catholic support in his native Pennsylvania and other battleground states. John McCain's selection of Alaska Governor Sarah Palin surprised many but quickly helped energize the Republican party base. Later in the campaign, Palin became a liability to the campaign as her media interviews were seen as showing

Of the People

Diversity Among National Party Nomination Convention Delegates

One of the criticisms of the Democratic and Republican Parties in the contentious 1968 election was that the delegates to the national party nominating conventions were not representative of their parties as a whole. A commission was formed in the Democratic Party to reform the process of delegate selection. One result was a rise in the number of states holding presidential primaries rather than caucuses. Another consequence was a much more diverse group of delegates in nominating conventions.

In 1968, delegates were mostly older white males. By 1972, in response to the recommendations of the Democratic Party Reform Commission, the proportion of males had dropped from nearly 90 to 60 percent, the proportion of black delegates tripled, and the proportion of younger delegates rose from 4 to 21 percent. In all cases except young delegates, the 2008 Democratic delegates approximated the composition of the 1972 Democratic delegates.

Republicans have not become as diverse in their delegate composition. In 2008, one-third of GOP delegates were women, compared with 49 percent for Democrats. There were fewer minority and young delegates at the 2008 Republican convention than at the 2008 Democratic convention. Only 2 percent of GOP delegates were black compared with 23 percent for Democrats. Ninety-three percent of Republican delegates were white compared with 65 percent of Democratic delegates. In 2008, only 3 percent of Republican delegates were under 30 years of age compared with 7 percent for Democrats. But both parties are sensitive to the symbolism of diversity and showcase delegates and others who can help the party connect to different demographic groups.

CRITICAL THINKING QUESTIONS

1. Why have Republican delegates remained less diverse than Democratic delegates?
2. What kind of changes in a party delegation might you expect as a result of a shift from caucuses to primary elections?
3. Why might the percentage of younger delegates in 2008 have differed from 1972?

Demographic Makeup of Democratic National Delegates

*Note that the 2008 source lists "young" as 18 to 29 years old, whereas the 1968 source lists "young" as 30 years old and under.

SOURCE: 1968 data from Austin Ranney, *Curing the Mischiefs of Faction: Party Reform in America* (University of California Press, 1975), p. 155. 2008 data for Republicans from the *New York Times*/CBS Poll, "2008 Republican National Delegate Survey," July 23 – August 26, 2008. Available at http://graphics8.nytimes.com/packages/pdf/politics/20080901-poll.pdf. Data for the Democrats from the *New York Times*/CBS Poll, "2008 Democratic National Delegate Survey," July 16 – August 17, 2008. Available at http://graphics8.nytimes.com/packages/pdf/politics/demdel20080901-poll.pdf; from the *New York Times*/CBS News Poll, "2004 Republican National Delegate Survey," August 29, 2004; and "2004 Democratic National Delegate Survey," July 23, 2004, www.nytimes.com/packages/html/politics/20040829_gop_poll/2004_gop_results.pdf

---

a lack of knowledge and experience. Exit polls found that 60 percent of voters thought Palin was not qualified to be president, if necessary, compared with 31 percent having that view of Biden.[51]

The Value of Conventions   Why do the parties continue to have conventions if the nominee is known in advance and the vice presidential nominee is the choice of one person? What role do conventions play in our system? For the parties, they are a time of "coming together" to endorse a party program and to build unity and enthusiasm for the fall campaign. For candidates, as well as other party leaders, conventions are a chance to capture the national spotlight and further their political ambitions. For nominees, they are an opportunity to define themselves in positive ways. The potential exists to heal wounds festering from the primary campaign and move into the general election united, but it is not always achieved. Conventions can be potentially divisive, as the Republicans learned in 1964 when conservative Goldwater delegates loudly booed New York governor Nelson Rockefeller, and as the Democrats learned in 1968 in Chicago when the convention spotlighted divisions within the party over Vietnam, as well as ugly battles between police and protesters near the convention hotels.

Nomination by Petition   There is a way to run for president of the United States that avoids the grueling process of primary elections and conventions—if you are rich enough or well known enough to use it. Third-party and Independent candidates can qualify for the ballot by meeting each state's ballot access requirements. This takes time, organization, and money (see Chapter 7). In 2008, the petition process was as simple as submitting the signatures of 1,000 registered voters in Washington State[52] or by paying $500 in Colorado or Louisiana,[53] and as difficult as getting the signatures of currently registered voters equal to 2 percent of total votes cast in the last election in North Carolina (69,734 signatures).[54] Perennial third-party candidate Ralph Nader's name was on 45 state ballots plus the District of Columbia in 2008. He was not on the ballot in Georgia, Indiana, North Carolina, Oklahoma, and Texas.

Stage 3: The General Election

The national party convention adjourns immediately after the presidential and vice presidential candidates deliver their acceptance speeches to the delegates and the national television audience. Traditionally, the weeks between the conventions and Labor Day were a time for resting, for binding up wounds from the fight for the nomination, for gearing up for action, and for planning campaign strategy. In recent elections, however, the candidates have not paused after the convention but launched directly into all-out campaigning. In 2008, the Democratic race became a marathon with Senators Obama and Clinton campaigning in nearly every state and territory. This gave Obama some advantages in the general election as he was able to capitalize on late primaries and caucuses by easily carrying over his campaign organization into the general election. At the same time, the long nomination fight generated some hard feeling among Hillary Clinton supporters and gave Obama little time to refresh himself before the general election contest.

Presidential Debates   Televised presidential debates are a major feature of presidential elections. Presidential debates have come to be more of a joint appearance with opening and closing statements than a debate in which the candidates interact much with each other.

Since 1988, the nonpartisan Commission on Presidential Debates has sponsored and produced the presidential and vice presidential debates. The commission includes representatives from such neutral groups as the League of Women Voters. Before the commission became involved, there was often a protracted discussion about the format, the

Democratic presidential nominee Barack Obama campaigned unceasingly throughout the summer and fall of 2008 in hopes of winning the election. ■ *Based on the setting of this photo, what kind of voters was Obama likely targeting on this campaign stop?*

timing, and even whether to have debates. No detail seemed too small to the candidates' managers—whether the candidates would sit or stand, whether they would be able to ask each other questions, whether they would be allowed to bring notes, and whether a single journalist, a panel of reporters, or a group of citizens would ask the questions. By negotiating in advance many of the contentious details and arranging for debate locations, the commission now facilitates the presidential and vice presidential debates. The format of the 2008 presidential debates had one "town hall meeting" where the questions came from a group of citizens, which was preferred by McCain. The first and third debates had a journalist ask the questions, but with some encouragement of an exchange between the candidates. The vice presidential debate allowed for shorter answers without exchanges between candidates. Given the interest in Republican running mate Sarah Palin, the vice presidential debate had a large audience. None of the candidates made any major mistakes.

The 2008 presidential debates were widely watched and largely reinforced the candidate preferences of the viewers. Obama was seen as the "winner" by polls taken soon after all three debates. Obama in all three debates maintained a calm demeanor, even when it appeared McCain was trying to provoke him. McCain came out as more aggressive, especially in the third debate. But for voters who had not made up their minds, Obama made headway, denying McCain the chance to change the dynamic of the race. A recurrent theme in the debates was the economic crisis the country faced with home foreclosure, the collapse of large investment banks, and a looming recession. The economy became so central that in the last debate the war in Iraq was not mentioned by either candidate.

Minor party candidates often charge that those organizing debates are biased in favor of the two major parties. To be included in presidential debates, such candidates must have an average of 15 percent or higher in the five major polls the commission uses for this purpose. Candidates must also be legally eligible and on the ballot in enough states to be able to win at least 270 electoral votes.[55] In 2004 and 2008, Ralph Nader failed to meet these criteria for inclusion, as did both he and Patrick Buchanan in 2000. Neither Nader nor Libertarian Bob Barr was invited to participate in the 2008 presidential debates.[56] Including or excluding minor party candidates remains a contentious issue. Including them takes time away from the major party candidates, especially if two or more minor party candidates are invited. It may also reduce the likelihood of both major parties' candidates' participating. But excluding them raises issues of fairness and free speech.

Republican presidential nominee John McCain worked seemingly endless hours to attract voters during the 2008 campaign season. ■ *What does the event poster tell you about the intended message of McCain's campaign tour?*

The 2008 debate between the vice presidential candidates had a large audience. Prior to the debate, Republican nominee Sarah Palin had been criticized for her lack of knowledge in media interviews, which added to the voter interest. Both Democrat Joe Biden and Palin made no major mistakes in the debate. ■ *How important to an election are the debates? To what degree did the 2008 debates influence your opinion of the candidates?*

Although some critics are quick to express their dissatisfaction with presidential candidates for being so concerned with makeup and rehearsed answers, and although the debates have not significantly affected the outcomes of elections, they have provided important opportunities for candidates to distinguish themselves and for the public to weigh their qualifications. Candidates who do well in these debates are at a great advantage. They have to be quick on their feet, seem knowledgeable but not overly rehearsed, and project a positive image. Most presidential candidates are adept at these skills.

Television and Radio Advertising   Presidential candidates communicate with voters in a general election and in many primary elections through the media: broadcast television, radio, cable television, and satellite radio. Approximately 630,000 commercials were run across the country during the 2004 presidential election.[57] Spending on television has risen from $623 million in 2000 to $1.2 billion in 2004 to $1.6 billion in 2008.[58]

As with campaign activity generally—candidate visits and mail or phone calls about the candidates—the competitive or battleground states see much more activity. Candidates and their consultants believe that advertising on television and radio helps motivate people to vote and persuade voters to vote for them—or against their opponent. With the growth in cable television, candidates can target ads to particular audiences—people who watch the Golf Channel or Fox News, for instance. Political party committees and interest groups also run television and radio ads for and against candidates.

The Outcome   Though each election is unique, politicians, pollsters, and political scientists have collected enough information to agree broadly on a number of basic factors they believe affect election outcomes. Whether the nation is prospering probably has the most to do with who wins a presidential election, but as we have noted, most voters vote on the basis of party and candidate appeal.[59] Who wins thus also depends on voter turnout, and here the strength of party organization and allied groups is important. The Democrats' long-standing advantage in the sheer number of people who identify themselves as Democrats has declined in recent years and is mitigated by generally higher voter turnout among Republicans. Republican candidates also usually have better access to money, which means they can run more television ads in more places and more often.

In 2008, the tables were turned, and the Democratic nominee had a large advantage because he had raised so much more money than his Republican opponent. Obama outspent McCain in television advertising, campaign staffing, and get-out-the vote efforts. Obama had such a money advantage that he was able to purchase a primetime half-hour commercial slot on NBC, CBS, and FOX six days before the election, at the cost of $1 million per slot.[60]

After the votes are cast, they must be counted. And the way they are counted can be critical in close races. Even before the votes were counted in 2004 and 2008, both parties had deployed thousands of lawyers to observe the voting and ballot counting and to launch legal challenges if necessary. Although there were some problems with voting machines and long lines for people waiting to vote in 2008, there were not the kinds of legal challenges many had anticipated would arise over the use of provisional ballots or widespread challenges to voters because of home foreclosure or the voter not having a state-issued photo identification. The peaceful transfer of power from one individual or party to another, especially after such contested elections, is the culminating event in electoral democracy.

Money in U.S. Elections

LEARNING **OBJECTIVE**

9.4 Evaluate the influence of money in American elections and the main approaches to campaign finance reform.

Election campaigns cost money, and the methods of obtaining the money have long been controversial. Campaign money can come from a candidate's own wealth, political parties, interested individuals, or interest groups. Money is contributed to candidates for a variety of reasons, including ideology, group identification and support, and self-interest. Concern about campaign finance stems from the possibility that candidates or parties, in their pursuit of campaign funds, will decide it is more important to represent their contributors than their conscience or the voters. The potential corruption from politicians' dependence on interested money concerns many observers of U.S. politics.

Scandals involving the influence of money on policy are not new. In 1925, responding to the Teapot Dome scandal, in which a cabinet member was convicted of accepting bribes in 1922 for arranging for the lease of federal land in Wyoming and California for private oil developments,[61] Congress passed the Corrupt Practices Act, which required disclosure of campaign funds but was "written in such a way as to exempt virtually all [members of Congress] from its provisions."[62]

The 1972 Watergate scandal—in which persons associated with the Nixon campaign broke into the Democratic Party headquarters to steal campaign documents and plant listening devices[63]—led to media scrutiny and congressional investigations that discovered that large amounts of money from corporations and individuals had been deposited in secret bank accounts outside the country for political and campaign purposes. The public outcry from these discoveries prompted Congress to enact the body of reforms that still largely regulate the financing of federal elections.

Efforts at Reform

Reformers have tried three basic strategies to prevent abuse in political contributions: (1) imposing limits on giving, receiving, and spending political money; (2) requiring public disclosure of the sources and uses of political money; and (3) giving governmental subsidies to presidential candidates, campaigns, and parties to reduce their reliance on campaign contributors. Recent campaign finance laws have tended to use all three strategies.

The Federal Election Campaign Act In 1971, Congress passed the Federal Election Campaign Act (FECA), which limited amounts that candidates for federal office could spend on advertising, required disclosure of the sources of campaign funds and how they are spent, and required political action committees to register with the government and report all major contributions and expenditures.

In 1974, the Watergate scandal helped push Congress to amend FECA in what was the most sweeping campaign reform measure in U.S. history. These amendments established more realistic limits on contributions and spending by candidates and party committees, strengthened disclosure laws, created the **Federal Election Commission (FEC)** to administer the new laws, and provided for partial public funding for presidential primaries and a grant to major party presidential candidates in the general election. The money to fund the presidential candidates comes from an option that allows taxpayers to allocate $3 of their income taxes by checking a box on their tax returns.

The 1974 law was extensively amended after the Supreme Court's 1976 *Buckley* v. *Valeo* decision, which overturned several of its provisions on grounds that they violated the First Amendment free speech protection.[64] The *Buckley* decision still allowed limitations on contributions and full and open disclosure of all fundraising activities by candidates for federal office, as well as the system of public financing for presidential elections.[65] However, the Supreme Court made a distinction between campaign spending and campaign contributions, holding that the First Amendment protects spending; therefore, although Congress may limit how much people contribute to somebody else's campaign, legislatures may not limit how much of their own money people spend on their own campaigns independent of a candidate or political party.

One of the success stories of FECA was that presidential candidates of both parties for 20 years chose to accept the limitations on fundraising and campaign spending that were part of the public financing provisions. During the nomination phase, candidates receive federal matching funds for campaign contributions up to $250. Accepting the federal matching funds means candidates accept state-by-state spending limits for the caucuses and the primaries. Major party candidates receive a grant for the general election but also stop their own fundraising. Until 2000, presidential candidates (except a few wealthy, self-financed candidates) accepted the voluntary limitations that come with partial public financing of presidential nomination campaigns.

As noted, in 2008, the number of candidates in both parties turning down the matching funds in the primaries increased, although some candidates such as John Edwards still accepted them (see Figure 9–5). Obama, who originally indicated he would accept public funding in the general election, abandoned that position and ended up raising $639 million.[66] Obama was the first major party candidate since the system was created to reject taxpayers' money for the general election and ultimately had access to much higher funds for use in his campaign.

The Bipartisan Campaign Reform Act (BCRA)   After years of legislative debate, Senate filibusters, and even a presidential veto, Congress passed and President Bush signed into law in 2002 the **Bipartisan Campaign Reform Act (BCRA).** This legislation, often known as the McCain–Feingold bill after its two chief sponsors in the Senate, was written with the understanding that it would immediately be challenged in court—and it was. The Supreme Court upheld most of the provisions of BCRA in *McConnell* v. *FEC*.[67]

Federal Election Commission (FEC)
A commission created by the 1974 amendments to the Federal Election Campaign Act to administer election reform laws. It consists of six commissioners appointed by the president and confirmed by the Senate. Its duties include overseeing disclosure of campaign finance information, public funding of presidential elections, and enforcing contribution limits.

Bipartisan Campaign Reform Act (BCRA)
Largely banned party soft money, restored a long-standing prohibition on corporations and labor unions for using general treasury funds for electoral purposes, and narrowed the definition of issue advocacy.

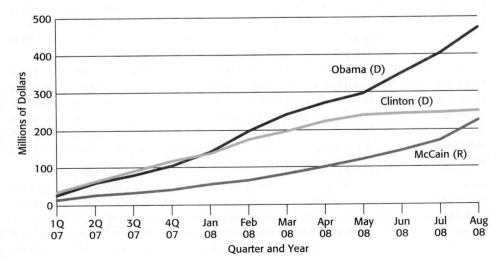

FIGURE 9–5 Presidential Primary Cumulative Receipts, 2007–2008 (millions of dollars).

■ *What are some of the benefits for a candidate of raising more money than a competitor?*

SOURCE: FEC reports from each campaign at www.fec.gov,http://fec.gov/finance/disclosure/efile_search.shtml.

BCRA is best understood as incremental change. It continued the public financing of presidential campaigns with funds from the income tax checkoff. It left unchanged the limits on spending by candidates for presidential nominations (on a state-by-state basis and in total) and in the presidential general elections for those candidates who accept public funding. Although recognizing that individuals are free to spend unlimited amounts on their own campaigns, BCRA provided increased contribution limits for candidates running against an opponent who was spending substantial amounts of his or her own money, a provision later declared unconstitutional in the Supreme Court.[68] Finally, it left unchanged the limits on the amounts the national parties can spend on presidential campaigns and on individual congressional and senatorial campaigns.

The limits under BCRA for 2007–2008 for individuals giving to candidates were $2,300 for each primary, general, or runoff election. Runoffs are rare in the United States, so for most individuals the contribution limit to a candidate in 2007–2008 was $4,600. Individuals can give $10,000 per cycle to a political action committee (PAC) or federal or state party committee. Contribution limits under BCRA are indexed to inflation. Individuals also have an aggregate two-year election cycle limit. In 2007–2008, they could give up to $42,700 to federal candidates and up to $65,500 to national party committees, federal PACs, and state party federal accounts. Of the $65,500, only $42,700 can be given to federal PACs and state party federal accounts. Individuals who want to give the maximum total of $108,200 in the 2007–2008 election cycle must thus allocate money to candidates, party committees, and PACs under the constraints noted.[69] BCRA thus gave party committees an opportunity to appeal to "max out" donors, something both parties pursued.

Soft Money   The 1976 and 1978 elections, the first after FECA, saw less generic party activity and prompted parties to seek legislation to allow for individuals or groups to avoid the contribution limits if the money they were giving was going to the political parties for "party-building purposes,"[70] such as voter registration drives or generic party advertising. This money came to be defined as **soft money,**[71] in contrast to the limited and more-difficult-to-raise **hard money** contributions to candidates and party committees that are committed to candidate-specific electoral activity. Over time, soft money became more important. The 1996 election saw aggressive soft money fundraising by the Clinton-Gore campaign, including opportunities for donors to have meetings with the president, to fly with him on Air Force One, and to spend the night in the Lincoln Bedroom at the White House. A congressional investigation into these and related concerns about campaign finance in the 1996 election cycle reinforced the case for reform.[72] From the perspective of the voter, the advertising purchased by soft money was indistinguishable from other campaign expenditures.[73]

Yet both parties continued to make raising and spending soft money a major priority, and soft money spending rose dramatically. All national party committees combined raised more than $509 million of soft money in the 1999-2000 election cycle, up from $110 million adjusted for inflation in 1991–1992.[74] And in 2002, the party committees raised more than $495 million combined in soft money.[75] Figure 9–6 plots the surge in soft money funds for the four congressional campaign committees.

Banning soft money became the primary objective of reformers and was one of the more important provisions in the BRCA. Soft money enabled large donors to be major players in campaign finance. It also strengthened the power of the national party committees, which allocated the money to state parties and indirectly to candidates. To the Supreme Court, which upheld the BCRA soft money ban, one of the major problems with soft money was that it purchased access to elected officials, and with that access came influence and the possibility or appearance of corruption.[76]

Issue Advocacy Advertising   Another way the post–Watergate election reforms were undermined was with the upsurge of interest groups running election ads. These ads typically attack a candidate, but the sponsor can avoid disclosure and contribution limitations because the ads do not use electioneering language, such as "vote for" or "vote against" a specific candidate. The Supreme Court in its 1976 *Buckley* v. *Valeo* decision

soft money
Money raised in unlimited amounts by political parties for party-building purposes. Now largely illegal except for limited contributions to state or local parties for voter registration and get-out-the-vote efforts.

hard money
Political contributions given to a party, candidate, or interest group that are limited in amount and fully disclosed. Raising such limited funds is harder than raising unlimited funds, hence the term "hard money."

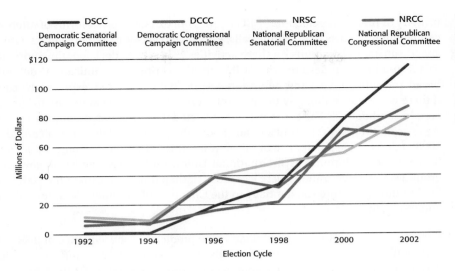

Legend:
- **DSCC** Democratic Senatorial Campaign Committee
- **DCCC** Democratic Congressional Campaign Committee
- **NRSC** National Republican Senatorial Committee
- **NRCC** National Republican Congressional Committee

FIGURE 9–6 Congressional Campaign Committee Soft Money Spending, 1994–2002.

NOTE: The totals for each party do not equal the sum of the party committee receipts because the numbers provided by the FEC have been adjusted to account for transfers between party committees so as not to double-count money in the total receipts.

SOURCE: Federal Election Commission, "Party Committees Raise More Than $1 Billion in 2001–2002," press release, March 20, 2003, http://www.fec.gov/press/press2003/20030320party/20030103party.html. In constant, 2008 dollars.

on FECA defined election communication as "communications containing express words of advocacy of election or defeat, such as 'vote for,' 'elect,' 'support,' 'cast your ballot for,' 'Smith for Congress,' 'vote against,' 'defeat,' and 'reject.'"[77] Communications that did not use these "magic words" were defined as issue ads, not subject to disclosure required by FECA restrictions. Not surprisingly, interest groups and media consultants found a way to communicate an electioneering message without using the magic words.

The 1996 election saw a surge in **issue advocacy.** Money spent on issue advocacy ads is unlimited and undisclosed because it presumably deals with issues not candidates. Issue ad spending in some U.S. House races exceeded $1 million in some elections. A prominent example of issue advocacy against a candidate was two Texans who formed a group named Republicans for Clean Air and ran ads in some 2000 presidential primaries attacking John McCain.[78] In the 1998, 2000, and 2002 elections, businesses, labor unions, health maintenance organizations, environmental groups, the Business Roundtable, pro- and antigun groups, pro- and antiabortion groups, and the pharmaceutical industry ran issue ads.

issue advocacy
Promoting a particular position or an issue paid for by interest groups or individuals but not candidates. Much issue advocacy is often electioneering for or against a candidate, avoiding words like "vote for," and until 2004 had not been subject to any regulation.

Campaign issue advertisements sponsored by interest groups are largely indistinguishable from candidate-run ads.[79] The same was also true for party ads paid for with soft money. In some competitive contests, interest groups and parties spent more money than the candidates did themselves. Typically, these party and group ads are even more negative than the ads run by candidates. Often the group identified as paying for the ad gave itself a nondescript name like "Citizens for…" or "Coalition Against…" Many candidates have disavowed ads intended to help them and hurt their opponent. One of the problems with noncandidate ads in an election context is determining who is accountable for the content of the ads.

BCRA only partially addressed the issue ads loophole of 1996–2002. It redefined "electioneering communications" to include much of what claimed to be issue ads. Under BCRA, an electioneering communication is "any broadcast, cable, or satellite communication which refers to a clearly identified candidate for Federal office [and in the case of House and Senate candidates is targeted to their state or district], is made within 60 days before a general, special, or runoff election for the office sought by the candidate; or 30 days before a

Presidential elections have a well-earned reputation for brutality. This advertisement exploits the relationship between Barack Obama and his former pastor Jeremiah Wright in order to raise fears of Obama being too extreme for most voters.

primary or preference election."[80] BCRA does not extend to other forms of interest group campaigning such as mail, phone calls, e-mail, and get-out-the-vote efforts. Groups can spend substantial amounts on these activities.[81] In a 2007 decision, the Supreme Court in a 5-to-4 decision declared the BCRA "electioneering communication" definition too broad and substituted a new definition that an ad is considered "express advocacy" only if there is no reasonable way to interpret it except "as an appeal to vote for or against a certain candidate."[82] The court also later rejected the BCRA ban on unions and corporations using their general funds on ads about the election or defeat of a candidate.[83] In 2008, unions made greater use of this new interpretation than did corporations. Unions like the Service Employees International Union (SEIU) were active in several battleground states. Corporations were less inclined than unions to exploit the 2007 court ruling but did contribute substantially to the Chamber of Commerce's large-scale effort to counteract the unions.

Section 527 and 501(c) Organizations   One predictable consequence of BCRA's ban on soft money, while leaving open the possibility of some electioneering communications, was increased interest-group electioneering through what are called 527 or 501(c) groups. These groups get their names from the section of the Internal Revenue Service code under which they are organized. Section **527 organizations** existed long before BCRA, but after BCRA, these groups had an incentive to expand their efforts. Section 527 groups are formed to influence elections. Section 501(c) groups include nonprofit groups whose purpose is not political. Money given to Section 501(c)(3) groups is tax deductible, and they can engage in nonpartisan voter registration and turnout efforts but cannot endorse candidates. Other 501(c) groups can be and are expressly political, and money contributed to them is not tax deductible. Disclosure of contributions to these groups and spending by them are less frequent than for Section 527 groups, political parties, or PACs.[84]

BCRA restricted the way 527 groups communicate with voters. Any 527 organization wishing to broadcast an electioneering communication within one month of a primary or two months of a general election must not use corporate or union treasury funds; it must report the expenditures associated with the broadcast; and it must disclose the sources of all funds it has received since January 1 of the preceding calendar year. Although contribution sources are restricted in this case, contribution amounts are not. Nor are people spending their own money individually, and not as part of a group. The Supreme Court permitted this exemption on free speech grounds.

In 2004, in the first post–BCRA election, the best-funded 527 organization was America Coming Together (ACT), which raised and spent an estimated $76 million in presidential battleground states to register and mobilize voters in 2004. However, the 527 group that may have had the greatest impact on the 2004 campaign was Swift Boat Veterans for Truth, which attacked Senator Kerry's war record. The modest initial budget for this group's ads generated widespread news coverage, especially on cable news stations. The message of the ads cut to the core of the persona that Kerry had presented at the Democratic National Convention.

The attack by the Swift Boat Veterans was effective in part because of the lack of a strong response and rebuttal from Kerry, his campaign, or his party. Nearly two years later, Kerry himself acknowledged his mistake by saying he should have responded and "we should have put more money behind it….I take responsibility for it; it was my mistake. They spent something like $30 million, and we didn't. That's just a terrible imbalance when somebody's lying about you."[85] Given the effectiveness of this attack on Kerry, similar attacks can be expected in the future, and candidates will likely respond much more aggressively to these attacks than Kerry did. These attacks led to a new term, being "swift-boated."[86]

Given the important role outside groups played in 2004 in attacking John Kerry and promoting George Bush as well in voter registration and mobilization, many anticipated they would play an even larger role in 2008. Although some groups ran ads for and against the presidential candidates, no group had the impact that Swift Boat Veterans for Truth had in 2004. Requests by both candidates that people not fund outside groups in 2008 may have

527 organizations
Interest groups organized under Section 527 of the Internal Revenue Code may advertise for or against candidates. If their source of funding is corporations or unions, they have some restrictions on broadcast advertising.

deterred these groups from playing a major role on either side. In terms of voter mobilization, outside groups remained important in 2008. On the Democratic side, a group called America Votes coordinated the voter mobilization efforts. On the Republican side, business, pro-life, and gun rights groups were active. Some groups like the Chamber of Commerce invested heavily in supporting Senate candidates; in the case of the Chamber, these were mostly Republicans. In competitive House and Senate races, groups like the League of Conservation Voters, Defenders of Wildlife, and Planned Parenthood were active, often for Democrats.[87]

Unlike 2004 and 2006 when Democratic groups were more visible and spent more money, Republican allied groups played an important role in making more contests competitive in 2010 and in helping elect Republicans. Former Bush political strategist Karl Rove and others organized American Crossroads and Crossroads Grassroots Policy Strategies, while other prominent Republicans organized American Action Network and other groups. Moreover, these groups coordinated their spending with other GOP allied groups like the Chamber of Commerce, Club for Growth and the National Rifle Association. Some groups organized under sections of the law that allow them to not disclose their donors, and all groups could tap corporation and union general funds for the first time in decades. The threat of secret outside money was frequently cited by President Obama in his 2010 campaign appearances.

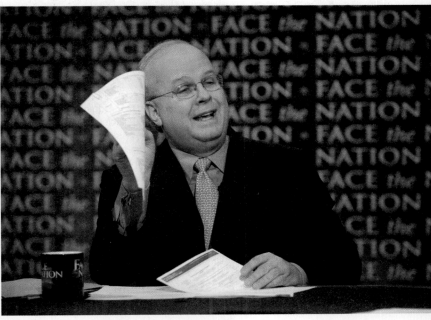

Former White House advisor and Fox TV commentator Karl Rove, seen here on "Face the Nation" discussing the mid-term elections, helped organize the 527 group American Crossroads, which aimed to spend over $50 million to help elect Republicans. Most of the group's funding came from billionaires. ■ *Should there be stricter laws regulating 527 and other outside group spending, or is political spending an extension of free speech?*

Independent Expenditures The Supreme Court made clear in its ruling on FECA in 1976 that individuals and groups have the right to spend as much money as they wish for or against candidates as long as they are truly independent of the candidate and as long as the money is not corporate or union treasury money. Some groups such as the American Medical Association, the National Education Association, and the National Rifle Association have long tried to influence elections independently rather than through a party committee or a candidate's campaign (see Chapter 6). As discussed in Chapter 7, the Supreme Court extended to political parties the same rights to make independent expenditures afforded to groups and individuals.[88]

Individuals have made large independent expenditures, such as Michael Goland, a California entrepreneur who spent $1.1 million against Senator Charles Percy (R-Ill.) in the 1984 election because he considered Percy unfriendly to Israel. In the 2000 presidential election, Stephen Adams, owner of an outdoor advertising firm, spent $2 million to support George W. Bush.[89] In 2004, billionaire George Soros, who gave millions to 527 organizations opposing the reelection of Bush, also spent $2.3 million in independent expenditures against the president. In 2008, groups did not have individual donors giving very large amounts to them as was the case in 2004.

BCRA does not constrain **independent expenditures** by groups, political parties, or individuals, as long as the expenditures by those individuals, parties, or groups are independent of the candidate and fully disclosed to the FEC. In 2008, independent expenditures by the party committee were important in some competitive contests. For example, in the North Carolina U.S. Senate race, the spending of $8.1 million by the Democratic Senatorial Campaign Committee helped Kay Hagan compete against Republican incumbent Elizabeth Dole, whose party spent $3.5 million independently.

Neither the DNC nor RNC made substantial independent expenditures in 2010 but the congressional campaign committees did. The Republicans and Democrats were at near parity in independent expenditures in U.S. House races, while the Democrats spent substantially more independently in U.S. Senate races than did the Republicans.

independent expenditures
Money spent by individuals or groups not associated with candidates to elect or defeat candidates for office.

Campaign Contribution Disclosure Laws

For much of the first half of U.S. history, campaigns were largely conducted through the political parties. As Frank Sorauf has written, "The parties dominated finance because they dominated the campaigns themselves."* When the parties needed large sums of money, they sought the help of wealthy individuals.

Starting in the 1890s, states began adopting campaign finance legislation, and, prompted by scandals, Congress limited the ability of corporations to contribute from their general funds. Later, Congress applied this same rule to unions. Early efforts to require disclosure of campaign contributions were only partly successful. In 1972, the Watergate scandal, which documented corporate and other money going in large and undisclosed amounts to the Committee to Reelect the President (Nixon), served as an impetus for more significant reform. Congress responded by amending the Federal Election Campaign Act (FECA) in 1974, requiring more complete and meaningful disclosure of campaign money.

As Justice Louis Brandeis had previously written about banking laws, "Sunlight is said to be the best of disinfectants."† Congress, the president, and the Supreme Court all embraced disclosure, or "sunlight," on where campaign money comes from and how it is spent. Although some provisions in FECA were declared unconstitutional and others have been criticized by one party or the other, disclosure has near universal support. Senate Republican leader Mitch McConnell, who has led efforts to defeat campaign finance reform, supports disclosure, saying, "The more disclosure, the better."‡

With disclosure, as with much of public policy, however, the details in the laws and their implementation are critical. Some groups will seek to escape disclosure, as was the case with the issue advocacy of the 1990s and early 2000s. The data on who is paying for what in campaigns must be accessible to the public and reporters and timely in its availability, or it is not meaningful. Passage and implementation of FECA was a major step forward in disclosure of how campaigns are financed, but the challenge of maintaining meaningful disclosure remains.

CRITICAL THINKING QUESTIONS

1. Why would some groups and individuals want to avoid disclosing their spending on campaigns?

2. What are some ways voters might access information on who is funding campaigns?

3. Should campaign communications be required to disclose who paid for them?

---

*Frank J. Sorauf , *Inside Campaign Finance* (Yale University Press, 1992), p. 2.

† Louis D. Brandeis, *Other People's Money* (New York: Frederick A. Stokes Co., 1914), p. 92.

‡Mitch McConnell, "*Meet the Press* Transcript for January 24, 2010," http://www.msnbc.msn.com/id/35014151/ns/meet_the_press/ (accessed May 3, 2010).

Continuing Problems with Campaign Finance

The continuing problems with federal election fundraising are easy to identify: dramatically escalating costs, a growing dependence on PAC money for congressional candidates, decreasing visibility and competitiveness of challengers (especially for the House), and the advantage wealthy individuals have in funding their own campaigns. BCRA reduced the danger of large contributions influencing lawmakers directly or indirectly through political parties. But large contributions can still influence the outcome of elections, as 527 and other groups have demonstrated. Supreme Court decisions have made campaign finance an increasingly deregulated activity. Interest groups like corporations and unions have been given much greater latitude to attempt to influence the outcome of elections.

Rising Costs of Campaigns   The U.S. ideal that anyone—even a person of modest or little wealth—can run for public office and hope to win has become more of a myth than a reality.[90] As discussed at the beginning of this chapter, federal elections have become increasingly expensive. Serious candidates in the future are likely to bypass public funding and instead try and replicate the kind of fundraising success Barack Obama had in 2007–2008. And rising costs also mean that incumbents spend more time raising funds and therefore less time legislating and representing their districts. Since FECA became law in 1972, total expenditures by candidates for the House of Representatives have more than doubled after controlling for inflation, and they have risen even more in Senate elections (see Table 9–2). One reason for escalating costs is television. Organizing and running a campaign is expensive, limiting the field of challengers to those who have their own resources or are willing to spend more than a year raising money from interest groups and individuals.

Declining Competition   Unless something is done to help finance challengers, incumbents will continue to have the advantage in seeking reelection. Nothing in BCRA addresses this problem. Challengers in both parties are typically underfunded. House Republican challengers averaged $375,000 in spending in 2004,[91] whereas incumbents in

TABLE 9–2 Average Campaign Expenditures of Candidates for the House of Representatives, 1988–2008 General Election (in thousands of 2008 dollars)

	Incumbent	Challenger	Open Seat
Republican			
1988	425.6	104.4	504.0
1990	414.0	115.2	471.6
1992	571.1	196.3	379.0
1994	478.8	252.9	666.9
1996	767.7	219.8	654.2
1998	725.4	270.7	843.4
2000	911.5	261.7	1289.9
2002	922.4	201.1	1234.9
2004	1129.5	259.3	1311.1
2006	1574.1	268.5	1422.4
2008	1456.2	375.8	1380.5
Democrat			
1988	372.6	148.5	464.9
1990	418.0	114.9	556.9
1992	629.0	167.2	501.4
1994	630.4	168.4	605.0
1996	594.4	308.2	653.2
1998	584.8	253.3	778.2
2000	765.1	372.8	1090.4
2002	844.7	336.9	1079.6
2004	963.4	299.5	993.6
2006	1010.4	574.5	1465.6
2008	1252.4	612.9	1637.5

■ *What are the patterns of spending for incumbents, challengers, and open seat candidates, across both parties?*

SOURCE: Federal Election Commission, "FEC Reports on Congressional Financial Activity for 2000," press release, May 15, 2001; Federal Election Commission, "Congressional Candidates Spend $1.16 Billion During 2003–2004," press release, June 9, 2005; and Federal Election Commission, "Congressional Candidates Raised $1.42 Billion in 2007–2008," press release, December 29, 2009.

both parties spent an average of more than $1.2 million each in 2008.[92] In today's expensive campaigns, candidates are generally invisible if they have less than $400,000 to spend.

The high cost of campaigns dampens competition by discouraging individuals from running for office. Potential challengers look at the fundraising advantages incumbents enjoy—at incumbents' campaign war chests carried over from previous campaigns that can reach $1 million or more and at the time it will take them to raise enough money to launch a minimal campaign—and they decide not to run. Moreover, unlike incumbents, whose salaries are being paid while they are campaigning and raising money, most challengers have to support themselves and their families throughout the campaign, which for a seat in Congress often lasts more than one year.

Increasing Dependence on PACs for Congressional Incumbents For most House incumbents, campaign money comes from political action committees (PACs), which we discussed in Chapter 6. In recent years, nearly two out of five incumbents seeking reelection raised more money from PACs than from individuals (see Figure 9–7).[93] Senators get a smaller percentage of their campaign funds from PACs, but because they spend so much more, they need to raise even more money from PACs than House incumbents do. PACs are pragmatic, giving largely to incumbents. Challengers receive little because PACs do not want to offend politicians in power. BCRA continued to cap PAC contributions at

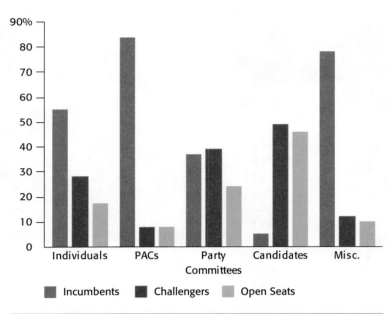

FIGURE 9–7 **How PACs and Others Allocated Campaign Contributions to House Candidates, 2007–2008.**

■ *Why might PACs be more apt than individuals or party committees to skew their funding so heavily to incumbents?*

SOURCE: Federal Election Commission, "PAC Activity Continues Climb in 2006," press release, October 5, 2007, http://www.fec.gov/press/press2007/20071009pac/20071009pac.shtml; and Federal Election Commission, "Growth in PAC Financial Activity Slows," press release, April 24, 2009, http://www.fec.gov/press/press2009/20090415PAC/20090424PAC.shtml.

$10,000 for the primary and general election combined. Incumbents will continue to rely on PACs because relatively few individuals have the means to give $4,600 to a campaign. It also often takes less time to raise money from PACs than from individuals.

To be sure, PACs and individuals spend money on campaigns for many reasons. Most of them want certain laws to be passed or repealed, certain funds to be appropriated, or certain administrative decisions to be rendered. At a minimum, they want access to officeholders and a chance to talk with members before key votes.

Defenders of PACs point out that there is no demonstrable relationship between contributions and legislators' votes. But influence in the legislative process depends on access to staff and members of Congress, and most analysts agree that campaign contributions give donors extraordinary access. PACs influence the legislative process in other ways as well. Their access helps them structure the legislative agenda with friendly legislators and influence the drafting of legislation or amendments to existing bills. These are all advantages that people outside PACs do not have.

Candidates' Personal Wealth Campaign finance legislation cannot constitutionally restrict rich candidates—the Rockefellers, the Kennedys, the Perots, the Clintons, the Romneys—from spending heavily on their own campaigns. Big money can make a big difference, and wealthy candidates can afford to spend big money. In presidential politics, this advantage can be most meaningful before the primaries begin. The personal wealth advantage also applies to congressional races. The 2000 New Jersey U.S. Senate race, for example, set new records for a candidate's personal spending in an election. Wall Street investment banker Jon Corzine, a newcomer to elections, spent a total of $60 million, $35 million of it on the primary alone.[94] Corzine was elected to the U.S. Senate and later spent another $45 million of his own money on his successful 2005 gubernatorial election in New Jersey.[95] He spent another $28.5 million on his unsuccessful reelection bid in 2009. Overall then, Corzine spent $133.5 million in one decade on his own campaigns.[96] BCRA included a millionaire's provision that allowed candidates running against self-financed opponents to have higher contribution limits from individuals or parties contributing to their campaigns. The Supreme Court later declared this provision unconstitutional. Meg Whitman, the unsuccessful Republican candidate for governor of California in 2010, spent over $140 million of her own money on her campaign, breaking the previous record held by New York Mayor Michael Bloomberg ($109 million). Other largely self financed U.S. Senate candidates like Linda McMahon, Republican in Connecticut, also lost in 2010.

Growth in Individual Contributions and Use of the Internet to Fund Campaigns BCRA made individuals more important as sources of money to candidates because it increased the amount they could give and indexed those limits to inflation. In the election cycles since BCRA took effect, there has been substantial growth in individual contributions, especially to the Democrats, who once were more reliant on soft money. As we have noted in the beginning of this chapter, the growth in individual contributions to both parties has been pronounced at the large and small donor levels.

Another development that has made individual donors more important is the Internet. Starting in 2000 with the McCain presidential campaign and then expanding with the Howard Dean candidacy for presidency in 2004, individuals started giving to candidates via the Internet. But it was the Obama campaign in 2008 that demonstrated the extraordinary power of the Internet as a means to reach donors and a way for people to contribute to a candidate. As former senator Tom Daschle said, the Internet "is an evolution away from Washington's control, away from the power that

After successfully running a self-financed campaign for the Senate, Jon Corzine spent millions of his own money on a successful bid for the governship of New Jersey, only to be defeated for reelection in 2009.

big money and big donors used to have a monopoly on."[97] It is clear that the Internet has the potential to change the way campaigns are funded.

Improving Elections

A combination of party rules and state laws determines how we choose nominees for president. Reformers agree that the current process is flawed but disagree about which aspects should be changed. Concern over how we choose presidents now centers on three issues:[98] how we fund presidential elections; the number, timing, and representativeness of presidential primaries and caucuses; and the role of the electoral college, including the possibility that a presidential election may be thrown into the House of Representatives.

LEARNING **OBJECTIVE**

9.5 Assess concerns regarding presidential elections and reforms that have been proposed.

Reforming Campaign Finance

The incremental reforms of BCRA and the subsequent Supreme Court decisions have not resolved the issues of campaign finance. Among the unresolved issues are how presidential campaigns will be financed, the role of Section 527 and 501(c) groups, the adequacy of disclosure, and the long-term strength and viability of the political parties. More broadly, the FEC's inability to reach decisions because of its partisan deadlock, as demonstrated by its inaction on Section 527 groups, has helped generate growing pressure to reform the agency.

The 2004 election cycle, with its substantial interest group activity through Section 527 and 501(c) organizations, was seen by those who favor deregulation of campaign finance as another example of the impossibility of limiting money in elections. The surge in individual donors in 2008 provides further evidence that public financing is unnecessary. This school of thought will continue to push for disclosure as the regulatory aim of government in this area.

Another group of reformers will press for more aggressive reforms than those found in BCRA. Included in this agenda will be reining in the 527 and 501(c) groups, restructuring the public financing of presidential elections, providing incentives for individuals to contribute to candidates and parties, and denying foreign corporations and those doing business with the government the ability to spend money on federal elections. Both sides are likely to agree that the FEC needs change but will not agree on how to change it.

Reforming the Nominating Process

In 2008, the importance of voters in early primary or caucus states such as Iowa and New Hampshire again generated controversy. Moreover, these early states are not broadly representative of the country or of their respective parties. Voters in primaries and caucuses also tend to be more ideological than voters generally, a further bias in the current nominating process. As noted, the relative representation of primaries and caucuses will likely be an enduring topic for discussion by party reformers. The 2008 contest pushed to the forefront controversy over whether the Democrats' proportionality rule made it more difficult to have a winner emerge from the process. Finally, the role of superdelegates in determining the 2008 nominee raised concerns about their role compared to delegates selected through a democratic process.

Only some of these concerns are new. What would the critics substitute for state presidential primaries (see Figure 9–8)? Some argue in favor of a *national presidential primary* that would take the form of a single nationwide election, probably held in May or September, or separate state primaries held in all the states on the same day.[99] Supporters contend that a one-shot national presidential primary (though a runoff might be necessary) would be simple, direct, and representative. It would cut down the wear-and-tear on candidates, and the media coverage would attract a large turnout. Opponents argue that such a reform would make the present system even worse. It would enhance the role of showmanship and gamesmanship, and because it would be enormously expensive, it would hurt the chances of candidates who lack strong financial backing. (See *You Will Decide* box.)

FIGURE 9–8 **Voter Turnout in the 2008 Presidential Primaries.**

FIGURE 9–8 **Voter Turnout in the 2008 Presidential Primaries.**

■ *What aspect of the presidential nomination process likely influenced the high voter turnout in New Hampshire compared to Delaware – a state of similar size and political leaning? What can help explain the higher turnout in California and Ohio?*

SOURCE: Michael McDonald, "2008 Presidential Primary Turnout Rates," United States Election Project at George Mason University, elections. gmu.edu/Voter_Turnout_2008_ primaries.htm.

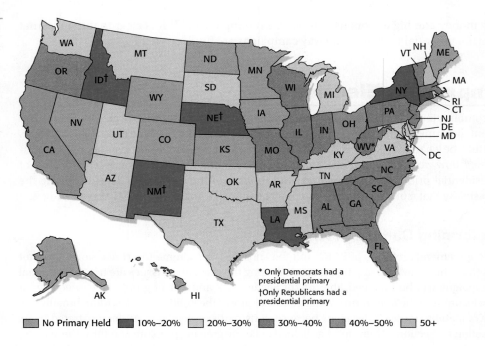

* Only Democrats had a presidential primary

†Only Republicans had a presidential primary

| No Primary Held | 10%–20% | 20%–30% | 30%–40% | 40%–50% | 50+ |

A more modest proposal is to hold *regional primaries,* possibly at two- or three-week intervals across the country. Regional primaries might bring more coherence to the process and encourage more emphasis on issues of regional concern. But such primaries would retain most of the disadvantages of the present system—especially the emphasis on money and media. Clearly, they would give an advantage to candidates from whatever region held the first primary, and this advantage would encourage regional candidates and might increase polarization among sections of the country. In recent years, many states have sought to move their primaries to the week(s) soon after the New Hampshire primary.

A different proposal is to drastically reduce the number of presidential primaries and make more use of the caucus system. The turnout of voters in Democratic caucuses in 2008 shows that participation can be high, and the time participants spent discussing candidates and issues shows that such participation can be thoughtful and informed. However, 2008 was unusual in its highly competitive prolonged competition. If more states adopted caucuses, their turnout would not likely be as high as in 2008 because they would lack the media and candidate attention that came that year. In caucus states, candidates are more dependent on convincing political activists, who will show up for a political meeting. By relying on party meetings to select delegates, the caucus system would also, some say, enhance the role of the party.[100]

Given the problems with the current nomination process, why has it not been reformed? Part of the answer is strong resistance from the states that benefit from the current system. In our federal system, imposing a national or regional primary means those states would lose power.

Does the present nominating process help or hurt candidates and parties? News coverage of candidates in nomination contests allows voters to evaluate the candidates' political qualities and their abilities to organize campaigns; communicate through the media; stand up under pressure; avoid making mistakes (or recover if they do make them); adjust their appeals to shifting events and to different regions of the country; control their staffs as well as make good use of them; and be decisive, articulate, resilient, humorous, informed, and ultimately successful in winning votes. In short, supporters of the current system claim primaries test candidates on the very qualities they must exhibit in the presidency.[101] The protracted 2008 Democratic nomination fight also meant that both Obama and Clinton registered and activated votes in most states and built a network of volunteers ready to go to work for them in the general election.

YOU WILL DECIDE
Should We Establish a National Presidential Primary?

States that have their caucuses or conventions early in the presidential selection process get more attention and have generally had a greater say in selecting the presidential candidates. For several election cycles prior to 2008, many states held presidential primaries after the nominee had effectively been selected. Continuing a trend from past election cycles, several states moved up their primary or caucus dates in 2008. The ordering of the states, with Iowa and New Hampshire first, has been disputed by other states that have proposed either a national primary or a set of regional primaries.

Another criticism of the current system is that the states asserting a claim to going first are not representative of their party or the country. Yet another problem is the threat of one party's voters participating in another's primary in hopes of nominating a weak candidate or prolonging the primary contest, such as when Rush Limbaugh urged Republicans, through his "Operation Chaos," to vote for Hillary Clinton to draw out the 2008 Democratic race for as long as possible. A national primary would give all U.S. voters an equal say as to whom their party nominee would be.

What do you think? Should we establish a national presidential primary? What are some of the arguments for or against it?

THINKING IT THROUGH

Our current system of state primaries or caucuses grows out of federalism and the rights of the states to govern elections. Mandating a national primary, though likely constitutional, would be a departure from federalism, and some may object to it as a step toward the federal government's controlling voter registration, voting technology, and other aspects of election administration that were long the province of the states. A national primary could force states that prefer the caucus system to adopt primaries. Because states sometimes combine the presidential primary with their primary for other offices, it may mean adding another election to the calendar.

A national primary would have the advantage of giving every voter an equal say in determining the nominee. It would also take away the kind of dispute that clouded the 2008 Democratic contest, in which Florida and Michigan voted earlier than the national party rules allowed, resulting in a disputed election.

A national primary would substantially change the nature of the campaign. Our current system means candidates with less money can spend more time meeting the voters of Iowa and New Hampshire and prove themselves in order to move on in the process. A national primary would help candidates with more money and greater name recognition because there would be little person-to-person campaigning.

Critical Thinking Questions

1. Do you think it is fair that Iowa and New Hampshire are always first in the nominating process?
2. What are the strengths and weaknesses of the current system?
3. When should a national primary be held, and why?

Reforming the Electoral College

The Florida ballot counting and recounting after the 2000 election and the fact that the winner of the popular vote did not become president prompted a national debate on the electoral college. The most frequently proposed reform is *direct popular election* of the president. Presidents would be elected directly by the voters, just as governors are, and the electoral college and individual electors would be abolished. Such proposals usually provide that, if no candidate receives at least 40 percent of the total popular vote, a *runoff election* would be held between the two contenders with the most votes. Supporters argue that direct election would give every voter the same weight in the presidential balloting in accordance with the one-person, one-vote doctrine. Plus, each voter would feel that his or her vote counts, even Republican voters in Massachusetts and Democratic voters in Utah. Winners would take on more legitimacy because their victories would reflect the will of the voters.

Opponents contend that the plan would further undermine federalism, encourage unrestrained majority rule and hence political extremism, and hurt the most populous and competitive states, which would lose some of their present influence. Others fear that the plan would make presidential campaigns more remote from the voters; candidates might stress television and give up their forays into shopping centers and city malls.[102]

From time to time, Congress considers proposals for a constitutional amendment to elect presidents directly.[103] Such proposals seldom get far, however, because of strong opposition from those who believe they may be disadvantaged by such a change, especially small states and minority groups whose role is enlarged by the electoral college.

Senator Barack Obama's campaign was characterized by his appeal to younger voters. In Oregon, he reportedly drew a crowd of 70,000–80,000.

Groups such as African Americans and farmers, for example, fear they might lose their swing vote power—their ability to make a difference in key states that may tip the electoral college balance.

Another alternative to the electoral college is sometimes called the National Bonus Plan. This plan would add another 102 electoral members to the current 538. These 102 members would be awarded on a winner-take-all basis to the candidate with the most votes, so long as that candidate received more than 40 percent of the popular vote. This system would avoid elections' being thrown into the House of Representatives and would help ensure that the candidate who won the popular vote became president. The most serious liabilities of the plan are that it is complicated and that it requires a runoff election if there is no winner.

Finally, two states, Maine and Nebraska, have already adopted a district system in which the candidate who carries each congressional district gets that electoral vote and the candidate who carries the state gets the state's two additional electoral votes. This quasi-proportional representation system has the advantage of not shutting out a candidate who is strong in some areas of a state but not others, but otherwise it does not address the larger concerns with the electoral college.

The failure of attempts to change the system of elections points to an important conclusion about procedural reform: U.S. voters normally do not focus on procedures. Even after the intense controversy on the outcome of the 2000 election, including the role of the electoral college, reform was not seriously considered.

The Importance of Elections

We have seen that elections matter in a constitutional democracy. They determine who holds office and what policies the government adopts. Elections are complex, and the rules of the game affect how it is played. Our winner-take-all system is an example of a rule that has influenced the nature of our party system, the strategy of candidates, and the stability of our institutions. Over time, the rules of the electoral game have been changed. Today, party nominees are largely selected by voters in primaries, whereas early in our nation's history, candidates were selected by party caucuses. Over time, our system has expanded the role of citizens and voters, as illustrated by the predominance of primaries.

Central to the functioning of a constitutional democracy like that in the United States is a system of fair elections that is well administered, so the outcome has legitimacy. Voter trust and confidence in elections centers on the kinds of issues we have examined in this chapter. Over time, we have learned ways to make elections better, including the secret ballot, disclosure and limitation of campaign contributions, and expansion of the role of citizens through primaries. As important as these structural and institutional changes are, without the participation of people in politics, the system will not function well.

Individual citizens can make a difference in elections in many ways. They do this through voting, being active in selecting candidates, working for political parties, and organizing groups around common interests. Because candidates, parties, and groups need money and volunteers to operate, donating money and time are also important ways in which people invest in elections. People also influence the votes of friends and neighbors, as voters are more likely to respond positively to a personal request to vote for a candidate or ballot proposition than they are to requests from other sources. As the

2008 election demonstrated, the Internet is a way for large numbers of individuals to donate money, volunteer time, and mobilize their friends. The Internet was used again in 2010 to organize people to make phone calls, contribute money, and vote. In key congressional and gubernatorial contests, candidates, party committees and interest groups were all engaged in these activities.

CHAPTER **SUMMARY**

9.1 Assess the implications of election rules in the United States.

The U.S. electoral system is based on winner-take-all rules, typically with single-member districts or single officeholders. These rules encourage a moderate, two-party system. Fixed and staggered terms of office add predictability to our electoral system. Although term limits have been popular with the public, Congress has not introduced any term limits to its members.

The electoral college is the means by which presidents are actually elected. To win a state's electoral votes, a candidate must have a plurality of votes in that state. Except in two states, the winner takes all. Thus, candidates cannot afford to lose the popular vote in the most populous states. The electoral college also gives disproportionate power to the largest and smallest states, especially if they are competitive. It has the potential to defeat the national popular vote winner.

9.2 Explain how congressional elections work and why they are generally not competitive.

Candidates for Congress must raise money, develop a personal organization, and increase visibility in order to be nominated for the election. Incumbents have significant advantages over their challengers, with House incumbents having stronger advantages than their Senate counterparts, whose challengers often have strong name recognition and more easily raise money. The cost of elections and incumbency advantages make congressional elections widely noncompetitive.

9.3 Outline the stages in U.S. presidential elections and the differences in campaigning at each stage.

The three stages in a presidential election are winning enough delegate support in presidential primaries and caucuses to secure the nomination, campaigning at

the national party convention, and mobilizing voters in enough states to get the most votes in the electoral college. The nomination phase is dominated by more partisan and often more ideological voters. Early contests are often important, which means candidates start early. The connection phase is important in defining candidates for less engaged voters. The general election concentrates candidate time and money in a relatively few contested states.

9.4 Evaluate the influence of money in American elections and the main approaches to campaign finance reform.

The rising costs of campaigns have led to declining competition for congressional seats and increasing dependence on PACs and wealthy donors. Because large campaign contributors are suspected of improperly influencing public officials, Congress has long sought to regulate political contributions. The main approaches to reform have been (1) imposing limitations on giving, receiving, and spending political money; (2) requiring public disclosure of the sources and uses of political money; and (3) giving governmental subsidies to presidential candidates, campaigns, and parties, including incentive arrangements. Present regulation includes all three approaches.

9.5 Assess concerns regarding presidential elections and reforms that have been proposed.

The present presidential selection system is under criticism because of its length and expense, because of uncertainties and biases in the electoral college, and because it seems to test candidates for media skills less needed in the White House than the ability to govern, including the capacity to form coalitions and make hard decisions. Reform efforts center on presidential primaries, the electoral college, and campaign finance.

CHAPTER **SELF-TEST**

9.1 Assess the implications of election rules in the United States.

1. Which system allows political parties to secure legislative seats and power in proportion to the number of votes they receive in the election?
   a. Cumulative voting
   b. Winner-take-all system
   c. Single-member districts
   d. Proportional representation
2. What other parts of the founders' design for our government does the electoral college reinforce? Why? Has the electoral college accomplished this objective?
3. Write two to three paragraphs detailing what would likely happen to the major and minor parties in

the United States if we adopted proportional representation.

9.2 Explain how congressional elections work and why they are generally not competitive.

4. The boost candidates from the president's party get from running along with a popular presidential candidate is known as the _____ .
   a. safe effect
   b. wave effect
   c. coattail effect
   d. proportional effect

5. List four reasons why congressional elections are generally not very competitive.

6. Many think it would be better for the country if congressional elections were more competitive. Write a short persuasive essay defending the current system.

9.3 Outline the stages in U.S. presidential elections and the differences in campaigning at each stage.

7. Choose from the following to complete the paragraph below: *strong partisans, moderates, win the nomination, win the election.*

   During the primary stage of the presidential campaign, candidates need to appeal to _____ in order to _____ . During the general election, however, they need to appeal to _____ in order to _____ .

8. List three important elements of the party convention.

9.4 Evaluate the influence of money in American elections and the main approaches to campaign finance reform.

9. Name and explain three ramifications of BCRA on political candidates and groups or individuals who contribute to their campaigns.

10. Describe how the FEC influences congressional and presidential fundraising.

9.5 Assess concerns regarding presidential elections and reforms that have been proposed.

11. In a paragraph, list and discuss two or three aspects of the 2008 presidential campaign that suggested potential reforms to the current electoral process.

12. Choose one potential reform to the current electoral process, and write a brief persuasive essay about why it should or should not be adopted. Be sure to address the issue from multiple perspectives.

Answers to selected questions: 1. d; 4. c; 7. strong partisans, win the nomination; moderates, win the election

---

mypoliscilab™ EXERCISES
Where participation leads to action!

Apply what you learned in this chapter on MyPoliSciLab.

▢▪ Read on mypoliscilab.com

eText: Chapter 9

✓▪ Study and Review on mypoliscilab.com

Pre-Test
Post-Test
Chapter Exam
Flashcards

◉▪ Watch on mypoliscilab.com

Video: Dissecting Party Primaries
Video: Oprah Fires Up Obama Campaign
Video: Money in the 2008 Presidential Race
Video: State Primary Race

✳▪ Explore on mypoliscilab.com

Simulation: You Are a Media Consultant to a Political Candidate
Simulation: You Are a Campaign Manager: Countdown to 270!
Simulation: You Are a Campaign Manager: Lead Obama to Battleground State Victory
Simulation: You Are a Campaign Manager: McCain Navigates Campaign Financing
Comparative: Comparing Political Campaigns
Comparative: Comparing Voting and Elections
Timeline: Nominating Process
Timeline: Close Calls in Presidential Elections
Timeline: Television and Presidential Campaigns
Visual Literacy: Iowa Caucuses
Visual Literacy: The Electoral College: Campaign Consequences and Mapping the Results

KEY **TERMS**

winner-take-all system, p. 242
single-member district, p. 243
proportional representation, p. 243
electoral college, p. 243
safe seat, p. 246
coattail effect, p. 246
candidate appeal, p. 247

national tide, p. 248
name recognition, p. 248
caucus, p. 251
national party convention, p. 252
Federal Election Commission (FEC), p. 259
Bipartisan Campaign Reform Act
  (BCRA), p. 259

soft money, p. 260
hard money, p. 260
issue advocacy, p. 261
527 organizations, p. 262
independent expenditures, p. 263

ADDITIONAL **RESOURCES**

FURTHER READING

R. MICHAEL ALVAREZ, *Information and Elections* (University of Michigan Press, 1998).

LARRY M. BARTELS, *Presidential Primaries and the Dynamics of Public Choice* (Princeton University Press, 1988).

EARL BLACK AND **MERLE BLACK,** *The Vital South: How Presidents Are Elected* (Harvard University Press, 1992).

BRUCE BUCHANAN, *Presidential Campaign Quality: Incentives and Reform* (Pearson, 2004).

ANN N. CRIGLER, MARION R. JUST, AND **EDWARD J. MCCAFFERY,** EDS., *Rethinking the Vote: The Politics and Prospects of American Election Reform* (Oxford University Press, 2004).

RONALD KEITH GADDIE, *Born to Run: Origins of the Political Career* (Rowman & Littlefield, 2004).

RODERICK P. HART, *Campaign Talk* (Princeton University Press, 2000).

PAUL S. HERRNSON, *Congressional Elections: Campaigning at Home and in Washington*, 5th ed. (CQ Press, 2007).

GARY C. JACOBSON, *The Politics of Congressional Elections*, 7th ed. (Longman, 2008).

KIM F. KAHN AND **PATRICK J. KENNEY,** *The Spectacle of U.S. Senate Campaigns* (Princeton University Press, 1999).

DAVID B. MAGLEBY AND **ANTHONY CORRADO,** EDS., *Financing the 2008 Election* (Brookings Institution Press, forthcoming).

DAVID B. MAGLEBY, ED., *The Change Election: Money, Mobilization, and Persuasion in the 2008 Federal Elections* (Temple University Press, 2011).

L. SANDY MAISEL AND **MARK D. BREWER,** *Parties and Elections in America: The Electoral Process*, updated 5th ed. (Rowman & Littlefield, 2009).

JEREMY D. MAYER, *Running on Race: Racial Politics in Presidential Campaigns, 1960–2000* (Random House, 2002).

WILLIAM G. MAYER AND **ANDREW E. BUSCH,** *The Front-Loading Problem in Presidential Nominations* (Brookings Institution Press, 2004).

STEPHEN K. MEDVIC, *Political Consultants in U.S. Congressional Elections* (Ohio State University Press, 2001).

SAMUEL L. POPKIN, *The Reasoning Voter: Communication and Persuasion in Presidential Campaigns*, 2d ed. (University of Chicago Press, 1994).

STEPHEN J. WAYNE, *The Road to the White House 2008* (Wadsworth, 2008). See also *Public Opinion Quarterly, The American Journal of Politics,* and *American Political Science Review.*

WEB SITES

www.fec.gov The Web site of the Federal Election Commission. This site contains information on elections, voting, parties, PACs, and campaign finance.

elections.gmu.edu/voter_turnout.htm The Web site of the United States Elections Project. This site contains voter turnout and registration data in primary and general elections.

www.politico.com This Web site focuses on political news and elections.

www.eac.gov The Web site of the United States Election Assistance Commission. This site contains information on voter registration, elections and election regulations, and other forms of election participation.

www.archives.gov/federal-register/ electoral-college/calculator.html An electoral college calculator that lets you tally different predictions for the electoral vote; a fun way to get a good understanding of how the electoral college works.

CHAPTER 10

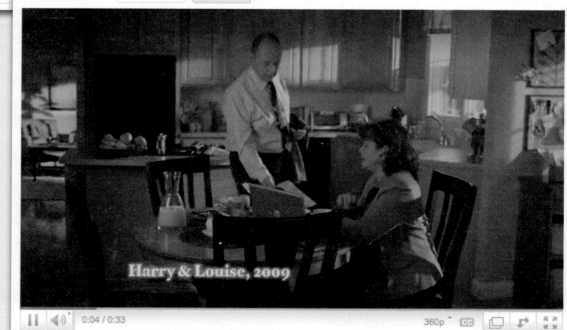

Harry and Louise on Clinton's health plan

danieljbmitchell 473 videos ⊗ Subscribe

SOMETIME IN THE FUTURE

Harry and Louise - "Get the Job Done"

harryandlouise 1 videos ⊗ Subscribe

Harry & Louise, 2009

0:04 / 0:33 360p ⌃ CC

The Media and U.S. Politics

As Congress debated and voted on health care reform in 2009 and 2010, interest groups on both sides mounted intense advertising campaigns urging people to contact their House representative or senator to advise them to take a particular action. Overall, an estimated $211 million was spent in television advertising from early 2009 to the final vote on the health care bill in March 2010.[1] One ad from Conservatives for Patients' Rights ran "115 times in 36 hours on network and cable television channels."[2]

It is not surprising that groups on both sides invested heavily in television advertising. The stakes in health care reform were high for several groups including doctors, lawyers, drug manufacturers, hospitals, unions, insurance companies, small businesses, and competing associations of retired persons. In one of the ads sponsored by the American Association of Retired Persons (AARP), a scene shows black SUVs blocking the path of an ambulance with the message that special interests are trying to block health care reform. A competing organization, the 60 Plus Association, ran an ad called "The Greatest Generation" about World War II veterans and other seniors who could lose health coverage if "the government, not doctors, will decide if older patients are worth the cost."[3]

Another reason groups took their message directly to the people via advertising is that when Congress last debated large-scale health care reform at the beginning of the Clinton administration (1993–1994), television advertising was seen as playing a pivotal role in its defeat. One particular ad came to symbolize the impact of advertising and its ability to influence public opinion. The ad is known as "Harry and Louise" and had a middle-age couple "lamenting the complexity of Clinton's plan and the menace of a new 'billion-dollar bureaucracy.'" It was sponsored by the Coalition for Health Insurance Choices (CHIC), which was a front group for the Health Insurance Industry Association.[4] The ad was seen as effective in communicating the complexity of the 1993–1994 health care legislation. Another reason the Harry and Louise ad was so important was that the proponents of health care reform did not effectively counter the claims made by opponents.[5] In 2009–2010, the same actors who appeared in Harry and Louise did an ad *supporting* health care reform. The ad was paid for by Families USA and PhRMA (Pharmaceutical Research and Manufacturers of America).[6]

In the 2009–2010 health care reform advertising, the sides were more evenly matched, and they presented starkly contrasting views. Opponents of health care reform highlighted increased governmental control over individuals' health care decisions; costs of the reform and the government deficits that would result, which in turn would lead to higher taxes; and increases in the cost of insurance.[7] Supporters of health care reform emphasized the problems of uninsured Americans, the lack of portability in health insurance, the ability of health insurance companies to deny claims, and higher premiums and overall costs for health insurance. Both sides in the legislative debate referred to the "false claims" of the opponents. Both sides also made use of the Internet and other forms of communication, including newspaper advertising. But the communications mechanism of choice remained broadcast and cable television advertising.

In this chapter, we explore the role of the media; its influence on public opinion, elections, institutions, and policy; and how it has changed over time.

LEARNING **OBJECTIVE**

10.1 Outline changes in the nature and extent of the political influence of the various news media.

The Influence of the Media on Politics

The media, in particular the print media, have been called the "fourth estate" and the "fourth branch of government."[8] Evidence that the media influence our culture and politics is plentiful. In one form or another, the **mass media**—newspapers and magazines, radio, television (broadcast, cable, and satellite), the Internet, films, recordings, books, and electronic communication—reach nearly everyone in the United States.[9] The **news media** are the parts of the mass media that tell the public what is going on in the country and the world, although the distinctions between entertainment and news have become increasingly blurred. News programs often have entertainment value, and entertainment programs often convey news. Programs in this latter category include TV newsmagazines such as *60 Minutes* and *Dateline*; talk shows with hosts such as Larry King and Sean Hannity; Jon Stewart's parody of the news, *The Daily Show*; and *The Colbert Report*.

By definition, and to make money, the mass media disseminate messages to a large and often heterogeneous audience. Because they must have broad appeal, their messages are often simplified, stereotyped, and predictable. But how much political clout do the media have? Two factors are important in answering this question: the media's pervasiveness, and their role as a link between politicians and government officials and the public.

The Internet has become a more important source of news in the United States, taking its place alongside print, radio, and television. The number of people who go online for news has grown dramatically and promises to become even more politically important as organizations and campaigns increasingly use the Internet to reach the public.[10] The Internet enables people to obtain information on any subject and from multiple sources—some of which may be unreliable—at any time of the day or night. The Internet also allows people to communicate and organize rapidly in response to political events.

The Pervasiveness of Television

Television has changed U.S. politics more than any other invention. With its visual imagery and drama, television has an emotional impact that print media can rarely match.[11] It cuts across age groups, educational levels, social classes, and races. In contrast, newspapers provide more detail about the news and often contain contrasting points of view, at least on the editorial pages, that help inform the public.

The average American watches more than four and one-half hours of television a day, and most homes have more than two television sets.[12] Television provides instant access to news from around the country and the globe, permitting citizens and leaders alike to observe events firsthand.

The growth of around-the-clock cable news and information shows is one of the most important developments in recent years. Until the late 1980s, the network news programs on CBS, NBC, and ABC captured more than 90 percent of the audience for television news in the morning and early evening. Although the "big three" networks have seen their audiences decline by about one million viewers a year since then, they still hold the majority of viewers. In 2010, the networks attracted on average approximately 22 million evening news viewers,[13] whereas the cable news networks CNN, Fox News, and MSNBC had average audiences of slightly less than 4 million evening viewers.[14]

Satellites, cable television, Internet search engines such as Google, and podcasts make vast amounts of political information available 24 hours a

mass media
Means of communication that reach the public, including newspapers and magazines, radio, television (broadcast, cable, and satellite), films, recordings, books, and electronic communication.

news media
Media that emphasize the news.

For more than 40 years, Americans have been getting their news primarily from television. Whenever there is a crisis, most people turn first to television for information. No event in recent history has done more to underscore the importance of television as the primary source of news in contemporary U.S. society than the terrorist attacks that took place on September 11, 2001.

day. These technologies eliminate the obstacles of time and distance and increase the volume of information that viewers can store, retrieve, and watch. They have also reduced the impact of single sources of broadcast or cable news. Competition from cable stations has put pressure on broadcast networks to remain profitable, which has both reduced budgets for broadcast news coverage and created the need to boost its entertainment value. For example, more viewers watched Barack Obama's acceptance speech at the Democratic Convention on cable stations than on ABC, CBS, and NBC. CNN had the most viewers.[15]

One of the biggest changes in U.S. electoral politics of the last half-century is that news stations devote less time to coverage of politics, making television commercials even more important as a source of information about candidates and issues.[16] The Court's recent decisions in campaign finance cases will likely foster more political advertising by groups running their own ads for and against candidates.[17] Successful candidates must be able to communicate with voters through this medium, attempting to define their opponent as well as themselves. To get their message across to television audiences, politicians rely on media advisers.

The amount of local television news devoted to politics has also been declining and now constitutes less than one minute per half-hour broadcast.[18] A major effort to get local television stations to devote a few minutes to candidate debate in their nightly local news ended up with stations averaging 45 seconds a night, or as one observer put it, just enough time to "let candidates clear their throats."[19]

In large urban areas, viewers rarely see stories about their member of Congress, in part because those media markets usually contain several congressional districts. Newspapers do a better job of covering politics and devote more attention to it than television stations do. The decline in news coverage of elections and voting, especially on television, has only increased the impact of political advertising on television, through the mail, and over the telephone.

The Persistence of Radio

Television and the Internet have not displaced radio. On the contrary, radio continues to reach more U.S. households than television does. Only 1 household in 100 does not have a radio, compared with 2 in 100 without a television.[20] More than eight in ten people listen to the radio every week,[21] and nearly seven in ten do so every day.[22] Many consider the radio an essential companion when driving. Certainly American adults get more than "the facts" from radio; they also get analysis and opinion from commentators and talk show hosts.

Political campaigns continue to use radio to communicate with particular types of voters. Because radio audiences are distinctive, campaigns can target younger or older voters, women, Hispanics, and so on. Many candidates in 2008 used radio to "microtarget" particular audiences in this way.[23] One particularly important source of news on the radio is National Public Radio (NPR). An estimated audience of 14 million listens to programs such as *Morning Edition*.[24] NPR even rivals conservative radio commentator Rush Limbaugh for size of audience.[25]

The Declining Importance of Newspapers and Newsmagazines

Despite vigorous competition from radio and television, newspapers remain important. Daily newspaper circulation has been declining for the past 20 years from more than 62 million in 1990 to less than 49 million nationwide currently—or less than one copy for every six people.[26] The circulation figures for newspapers reflect a troubling decline in readership among younger persons: The percentage of young people who read newspapers on a regular basis declined by more than half between 1967 and 2008.[27]

Newspapers have become less profitable because of declining circulation, in part because the Internet provides instantly available information for free.[28] The Internet has also hurt newspapers' bottom line most by providing an alternative medium for retail advertisers, and particularly for classified ads via sites such as Craigslist. Newspapers once earned about 40 percent of their revenue from classifieds; today, they receive only 20 percent.[29]

Rush Limbaugh, seen here during his daily talk show, is an outspoken conservative and opinion leader with a substantial following.

Of the People

Popular Sources for News

Do people in different countries turn to one medium more than another for news? This question is answered by the following question from the Pew Global survey: "Where do you most often turn to get news about national and international issues—television, newspapers, radio, magazines, or the Internet?"

There are substantial differences across countries in where the people "turn to get news about national and international issues." Television clearly dominates all other media around the world, but particularly in China, with 87 percent reporting they turn to television for news. More than 70 percent of people in India, Mexico, and Japan also rely more on television for news. The United States stands out from other countries in the

17 percent who turn to the Internet for news. This proportion is more than double that found in any other country. Another distinctive country is Nigeria, where 30 percent turn to radio, roughly double the share of the world sample that use radio for news. In Britain and India, one in five turn to newspapers for the news, and in Japan, a similar proportion rely on newspapers.

The reasons for these differences are probably based on what is most readily available to a population. Fewer people in Nigeria have access to television and newspapers, so radio is more important. Britain has a long history with newspapers, which helps explain the continued importance of newspapers in Britain, and the historic influence of the British on India may be part of

the relatively greater popularity of newspapers in India. Given its leadership in developing the Internet, it is not surprising that people in the United States use the Web more than people in any other country.

CRITICAL THINKING QUESTIONS

1. Does it make a difference where people turn to get their news?

2. In five or ten years, how do you think this question would be answered in the United States?

3. Is there an advantage to having competing sources of news—radio, television, newspaper, and the Internet?

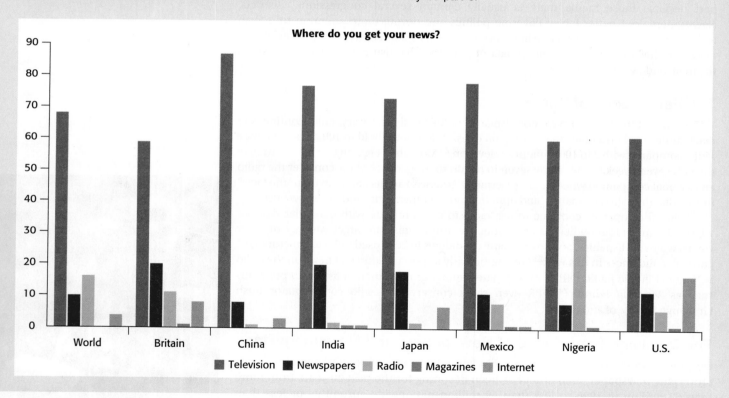

Where do you get your news?

■ Television ■ Newspapers ■ Radio ■ Magazines ■ Internet

In addition to metropolitan and local newspapers, Americans now have at least three national newspapers, *USA Today, The Wall Street Journal,* and *The New York Times.* With a circulation of nearly 2.1 million, *USA Today* has now replaced the *Wall Street Journal* as the top-circulating U.S. newspaper.[30] Newsmagazines, like newspapers, have also undergone major changes in recent years. Magazines such as *Time, Newsweek,* and *U.S. News and World Report* have experienced substantial declines in circulation and become less profitable. Declines in advertising revenue hurt the newsweeklies, as these magazines are called, just as it had hurt newspapers.[31]

The Growing Popularity of the Internet

From its humble beginnings as a Pentagon research project in the 1960s,[32] the Internet has blossomed into a global phenomenon. There are now more than 19 billion pages indexed by Yahoo on the Web,[33] and more than 117 million active domains have been registered worldwide.[34]

The Internet opens up resources in dramatic ways. One study found that nearly half of Internet users go online to search for news on a particular topic; somewhat smaller proportions go online for updates on stock quotes and sports scores. For approximately 37 percent of Internet users, the Internet is a primary source of news.[35] Internet users can also interact with politicians or other people about politics through e-mail, social networking sites, and blogs. Younger people, including teenagers, use the Internet extensively for schoolwork, and nearly three in four of them prefer it to the library.[36] A remarkable 63 percent of teenagers get news online, and the same proportion of teenagers use the Internet every day.[37]

The Internet provides an inexpensive way for candidates and campaigns to communicate with volunteers, contributors, and voters and promises to become an even larger component of future campaigns. Candidates' Web sites offer not only extensive information about the candidates themselves and their stands on issues but also tools for meeting fellow supporters, for receiving news and materials from the campaign, for volunteering, and for setting up personalized home pages, such as at my.barackobama.com and McCainSpace.com. This is in addition to candidates' YouTube channels, social networking profiles, and affiliated blogs. Although much is still unknown about the impact of the Internet, it has at least the potential to fragment the influence of other media.[38]

People can now access news and other information through their cell phones. They are also frequently invited by news organizations to upload photos and video from their cell phones to help cover news events. ■ *Is this spread of citizen journalism a positive democratization of the news, or a negative removal of the standards and source-checking for publication?*

During the past decade, there has been a dramatic increase in the use of social networking computer sites, and these have come to be important in American politics. Social networking sites allow individuals to create profiles and connect via the Web to other individuals via the site. Early sites had targeted populations like African Americans (BlackPlanet) or Asian Americans (AsianAvenue), but with the advent of Facebook, MySpace, and Twitter, social networking became a more generalized phenomenon. Since Facebook became available to more than only Harvard University students, the number of people with a Facebook profile has risen to an estimated 40 percent of all Americans over the age of 12,[39] and worldwide, there are nearly 500 million Facebook users.[40] Twitter has experienced similar growth.[41] Candidates like Barack Obama, political movements like the Tea Party Movement, and even law enforcement have all used social networking in recent years.

The Changing Role of the U.S. News Media

American adults spend on average 66 minutes per day consuming news, and the older they are, the more time they spend.[42] Yet media bashing has become a national pastime. We blame the media for phenomena as varied as increased tension between the races, biased attacks on public officials, sleaze and sensationalism, increased violence in our society, and the elevation of the profit motive over the job of conveying information. Many in the media agree with these charges and think the media are headed in the wrong direction.[43] But complaints may simply be a case of criticizing the messenger to avoid dealing with the message.

A Political Tool

The news media have changed dramatically throughout the course of U.S. history. When the Constitution was being ratified, newspapers consisted of a single sheet, often published irregularly by merchants to hawk their services or goods. Delinquent subscribers and high costs meant that newspapers rarely stayed in business more than a year.[44] But the framers understood the importance of the press as a watchdog of politicians and government, and the Bill of Rights guaranteed freedom of the press.

LEARNING **OBJECTIVE**

10.2 Trace the evolution of the news media over the course of U.S. history.

For the People

GOVERNMENT'S GREATEST ENDEAVORS

Creating the Internet

Presidential candidate Al Gore reaped some ridicule during the 2000 campaign when he claimed to have been instrumental in the "creation" of the Internet.* Gore had promoted the idea of a high-speed telecommunications network while in Congress and helped secure passage of legislation to expand the scope of the new technology in 1991, but the development of the Internet came from government agencies and government-funded researchers that predated Gore's activity. Private sector interests expanded and made the Internet more generally available, but the government was instrumental in its creation.

It began with the U.S. Air Force funding researchers at the RAND Corporation in the 1950s to develop technology to create a communications network that could survive nuclear attack. To avoid the problems that would result from an attack on what was a centralized communications system, researchers created a system that could function even if parts were destroyed, called distributed communications. Under the Defense Advanced Research Projects Agency (DARPA), government-funded researchers at the University of California, Los Angeles (UCLA), gave the concept its first large-scale test in 1969. The early system was intended for researchers and the military to be able to transmit information and share use of computers by granting remote access.

For decades, the government did not make access to the new technology generally available. Some entities like the National Science Foundation (NSF) developed NSFNET, linking much of the academic and research community. In 1993, Congress passed legislation allowing NSF to open NSFNET to commercial use, and by the mid-1990s, several commercial networks were in existence. Today, there are thousands of Internet service providers (ISPs) connecting an estimated 676 million computers worldwide to the Internet. More than half of these connected computers are in the United States, although China leads the world in estimated numbers of Internet users.† So the high-speed electronic communications network that you use for everything from e-mail to shopping to reading the latest news releases started as a government research endeavor.

CRITICAL THINKING QUESTIONS

1. How has the Internet changed your life?

2. What other inventions can be traced to government-funded research?

3. Does the Internet enhance national defense, the reason for its creation?

---

* CNN.com, "Transcript: Vice President Gore on CNN's 'Late Edition'," March 9, 1999 http://www.cnn.com/ALLPOLITICS/stories/1999/03/09/president.2000/transcript.gore/index.html (accessed June 8, 2010).

† CIA, "The World Factbook," https://www.cia.gov/library/publications/the-worldfactbook/rankorder/2184rank.html (accessed June 9, 2010).

POLITICO is a newspaper started by two former *Washington Post* reporters that focuses on issues related to Capitol Hill. While print versions of the paper are available in Washington, D.C., it is primarily accessed online. ■ *What are some of the impacts of newspapers transitioning to primarily online delivery?*

The new nation's political leaders, including Alexander Hamilton and Thomas Jefferson, recognized the need to keep voters informed. Political parties as we know them did not exist, but the support the press had given to the Revolution had fostered a growing awareness of the political potential of newspapers. Hamilton recruited staunch Federalist John Fenno to edit and publish a newspaper in the new national capital of Philadelphia. Jefferson responded by attracting Philip Freneau, a talented writer and editor and a loyal Republican, to do the same for the Republicans. (Jefferson's Republicans later became the Democratic Party.)

The two papers became the nucleus of a network of competing partisan newspapers throughout the nation. Although they competed in Philadelphia for only a few years, they became a model for future partisan papers. The early U.S. press served as a mouthpiece for political leaders. Its close connection with politicians and political parties offered the opportunity for financial stability—but at the cost of journalistic independence.

Financial Independence

During the Jacksonian era of the late 1820s and 1830s, the right to vote was extended to all free white adult males through the elimination of property qualifications. The press began to shift its appeal away from elite readers and toward the mass of less-educated and less politically interested readers. Thus, increased political participation by the common people—along with the rise of literacy—began to alter the relationship between politicians and the press.

Some newspaper publishers began to experiment with a new way to finance their newspapers. They charged a penny a paper, paid on delivery, instead of the traditional annual subscription fee of $8 to $10, which most readers could not afford. The "penny press," as it was called, expanded circulation and increased advertising, enabling newspapers to become financially independent of the political parties.

The changing finances of newspapers also affected the definition of news. Before the penny press, all news was political—speeches, documents, and editorials—directed at politically interested readers.[45] The penny press reshaped the definition of news as it sought to appeal to less politically aware readers with human interest stories and reports on sports, crime, trials, fashion, and social activities.

"Objective Journalism"

By the early twentieth century, many journalists began to argue that the press should be independent of the political parties. *New York Tribune* editor Whitelaw Reid eloquently expressed this sentiment: "Independent journalism! That is the watchword of the future in the profession. An end of concealments because it would hurt the party; an end of one-sided expositions…; an end of assaults that are not believed fully just but must be made because the exigency of party warfare demands them."[46] Objective journalism was also a reaction to exaggeration and sensationalism in the news media, something called *yellow journalism* at the time.

Journalists began to view their work as a profession, and they established professional associations with journals and codes of ethics. This professionalization reinforced the notion that journalists should be independent of partisan politics. Further strengthening the trend toward objectivity was the rise of the wire services, such as the Associated Press and Reuters, which remained politically neutral to attract more customers.

MAINE EXPLOSION CAUSED BY BOMB OR TORPEDO?

Capt. Sigsbee and Consul-General Lee Are in Doubt---The World Has Sent a Special Tug, With Submarine Divers, to Havana to Find Out---Lee Asks for an Immediate Court of Inquiry---Capt. Sigsbee's Suspicions.

The New York World a day after

As the nineteenth century progressed, literacy grew among the U.S. masses and more people began to get their news from newspapers. ■ *How did the popularization of the print media permanently change the way politicians and public officials relate with the press?*

The Impact of Broadcasting

Radio and television nationalized and personalized the news. People could now follow events as they were happening and not have to wait for the publication of a newspaper. From the 1920s, when radio networks were formed, radio carried political speeches, campaign advertising, and coverage of political events such as national party conventions.[47] Politicians could now speak directly to listeners, bypassing the screening of editors and reporters. Radio also increased interest in national and international news because it enabled its audience to follow faraway events as if they were actually there.

Beginning in 1933, President Franklin Roosevelt used radio with remarkable effectiveness. Before then, most radio speeches were formal orations, but Roosevelt spoke to his audience on a personal level, seemingly in one-on-one conversations. These "fireside chats," as he called them, established a standard that politicians still follow today. When Roosevelt began speaking over the microphone, he would visualize a tiny group of average citizens in front of him. He "would smile and light up," observers said, "as though he were actually sitting on the front porch or in the parlor with them."[48]

Television added a dramatic visual dimension, which increased audience interest in national events and allowed viewers to witness lunar landings and the aftermath of political assassinations, as well as more mundane events. By 1963, the two largest networks at the time, CBS and NBC, had expanded their evening news programs from 15 to 30 minutes. Today, news broadcasting has expanded to the point that many local stations provide 90 minutes of local news every evening as well as a half-hour in the morning and at noon. Programs such as *20/20* and other newsmagazine shows are among the most popular in the prime-time evening hours.

Cable television brought round-the-clock news coverage. During the Clinton impeachment hearings in 1998, the 2000 Florida ballot-counting controversy, and the "shock and awe" bombing of Iraq in March 2003, audiences around the world watched U.S. cable news for its instantaneous coverage. C-SPAN now provides uninterrupted coverage of congressional deliberations and presidential nominating conventions.

Franklin D. Roosevelt was the first president to recognize the effectiveness of radio to reach the public. His "fireside chats" were the model for later presidents.

In 2004, an investigative team at CBS News uncovered and aired this and other photos of prisoner abuse in Abu Ghraib. Although the military had been privately investigating the situation for several months, the actions of the CBS reporters brought the tragedy into the national spotlight. ■ *Does the decline of the traditional news industry and increased media consolidation weaken the capabilities of investigatory journalism? Why or why not?*

Investigatory Journalism

News reporters today do more than convey the news; they investigate it, and their investigations often have political consequences. An investigative team at *60 Minutes* of CBS News broke the story of torture of Iraqi prisoners held by U.S. soldiers at Abu Ghraib in 2004,[49] and Dana Priest of *The Washington Post* revealed the existence of secret CIA prisons in 2005 that were being used to hold and interrogate suspected terrorists.[50]

In many ways, the best example of the power of investigatory journalism is in the role the media played in the Watergate scandal.[51] Without persistent reporting by columnist Jack Anderson and two young *Washington Post* reporters, Robert Woodward and Carl Bernstein, the story would probably have been limited to a report of a failed burglary of the headquarters of the Democratic National Committee at the Watergate building.[52] The news reporting, coupled with congressional investigations, put a spotlight on the inner workings of the Nixon White House and the Nixon reelection committee, which had funded the attempted burglary and other political dirty tricks. Critical to the reporting on the broadening scandal, which ultimately brought down the president, was a confidential source, nicknamed Deep Throat by Woodward and Bernstein.[53] In 2005, more than 30 years after these events, the former deputy director of the FBI, W. Mark Felt, identified himself as Deep Throat.

Media Consolidation

Local firms used to own the regional newspapers, radio, and television stations. As in other sectors of the economy, media companies have merged and created large conglomerates of many newspapers and broadcasting stations. Some of these conglomerates are multinational. Rupert Murdoch, an Australian-born U.S. citizen and founder of the FOX Network, owns 35 television stations in the United States, DirecTV, 20th Century Fox, HarperCollins Publishers, MySpace.com, and *TV Guide*, which has the largest magazine circulation in the United States. His most recent acquisition is *The Wall Street Journal*, giving him one of the few national newspapers in the United States.[54] Murdoch also owns nine newspapers abroad and two television networks—one in Asia and one in Europe.[55]

When television was in its infancy, radio networks and newspapers were among the first to purchase television stations. These mergers established cross-ownership patterns that persist today. The Gannett Company, for example, owns 100 daily newspapers in the United States and United Kingdom and 23 television stations and cable television systems—assets that provide news coverage to more than 21 million households in the United States.[56] The Tribune Company, parent of the *Chicago Tribune*, purchased Times-Mirror, publisher of the *Los Angeles Times*, in 2000 and now has combined assets of ten newspapers, 23 television stations, one radio station, superstation WGN, and a growing online business.[57] In such acquisitions, some newspapers are subsequently sold to other conglomerates. At the same time, on the national level, the cable networks—CNN, Fox News, and others such as C-SPAN—have expanded the number of news sources available to the 90 percent of households receiving TV cable or satellite service.[58] The courts and the Federal Communications Commission (FCC)—an independent regulatory commission charged with licensing stations—are reinforcing the trend toward media conglomeration by relaxing and striking down regulations that limit cable and television network ownership by the same company.[59]

Will greater concentration of media ownership limit or restrict the free flow of information to the public? This concern is most evident in cities that once had two or more competing daily papers and now have only one newspaper. Although the number of local broadcast stations has not declined to the same extent, conglomerates without ties to the community now own more of these stations. The nationalization of media extends to some media personalities who have a large presence on television, radio, and through their books. Glenn Beck, for example, had two

Glenn Beck, seen here on FoxNews, reaches substantial audiences through his cable news show, radio program, books, and recently launched web site for political news and opinion. ■ *With which assessment of the nationalization of media do you agree more: that it allows for greater overall spread of information, or that it ensures only the loudest voices are heard?*

Of the People

AMERICA'S CHANGING FACE

Toward a More Representative Newsroom

The newspaper industry has worked hard to achieve greater diversity in the newsroom. The American Society of Newspaper Editors has stated that diverse newsrooms cover U.S. communities more effectively. Because many stories require contacts with a diverse public, the industry adopted a goal to make all newsrooms representative of the nation as a whole by 2025. Although the largest U.S. newspapers, such as *The New York Times* and *The Washington Post,* have made progress toward a more representative newsroom, smaller papers have had much more difficulty attracting and retaining minority reporters. Thus, less than 30 percent of smaller newspapers with circulations of less than 10,000 readers employ at least some minority reporters, compared with 100 percent of large newspapers with circulations of more than 500,000 readers. Moreover, the percentage of minority journalists varies greatly from one region of the country to another. Newspapers in the Midwest and New England have the smallest percentage of minority reporters, whereas newspapers in the western states have the highest percentage.

CRITICAL THINKING QUESTIONS

1. Why might more diverse newsrooms provide better news coverage?

2. Why are smaller newspapers less likely to have much diversity in their newsrooms?

3. What are some news topics where a more diverse newsroom might be important?

Diversity at U.S. Newspapers

Position	Women 1999	Women 2009	Minority* 1999	Minority* 2009
Supervisors	34%	35%	9%	11%
Copy-Layout Editors	40	42	11	13
Reporters	40	39	13	14
Photographers	26	27	15	17

* African American, Asian American, Native American, and Hispanic.

SOURCE: American Society of Newspaper Editors, "Newsroom Employment Census," http://204.8.120.192/index.cfm?id=5650 (accessed April 22, 2010).

best-selling books in 2010, plus he hosted a talk radio program and a cable news show on Fox, enabling a wide public following.

Regulation of the Media

The government has regulated the broadcast media in some form since their inception. Because of the limited number of television and radio frequencies, the national government oversees their licensing, financing, and even content through the FCC. The FCC continues to regulate licensing issues and occasionally fines or penalizes broadcasters that violate decency standards. For example, the FCC fined CBS for broadcasting as part of its 2004 Super Bowl half-time show an incident in which Justin Timberlake removed part of Janet Jackson's costume, exposing her right breast.[60] A federal appeals court later overruled the FCC fine.[61]

The Media and Public Opinion

When dramatic events such as the terrorist attacks on September 11, 2001, occur, we realize television's power to bring world events into our lives. Osama bin Laden, the purported mastermind behind those attacks, also understands the power of the media both inside and outside the United States, as evidenced by his release of videotapes of himself since the attacks.

The pervasiveness of newspapers, magazines, radio, and television confers enormous influence on the individuals who determine what we read, hear, and see because they can reach so many people so quickly. The news media have also assumed the role of speaking for the people. Journalists report what "the people" want and think, and then they tell the people what politicians and policy makers are doing about it. Politicians know they depend on the media to reach voters, and they are well aware that a hostile

LEARNING OBJECTIVE

10.3 Evaluate the media's influence on public opinion and attention.

Citizen Media

Newspapers have long published feedback from readers in the form of "letters to the editor." Other media also have long shared some form of public feedback and commentary. The published "letters" are often short, and of necessity the media outlet can only share a small fraction of what has been submitted.

In the Internet age there are more opportunities for citizens to communicate broadly on a wide range of topics. Some of these web-based tools are run by the media. An example is the CNN iReport, which is a CNN run website that allows people to post articles and videos. CNN is quick to make clear that stories posted at CNN iReport "are not edited, fact-checked, or screened before they post." Some of the postings at CNN iReport are verified by CNN and occasionally

they become a part of CNN news coverage. A prominent example of this is Virginia Tech graduate student Jamal Albarghouti, who captured dramatic video of the Virginia Tech shooting in 2007 which became part of CNN's coverage of the tragic incident.*

Citizens also use the web to post blogs, which if well written and relevant can generate a substantial audience. The Drudge Report has gone from relative obscurity to being what some have described as one of the most powerful blogs in the world.† YouTube adds a sound and video component to citizen reporting. The power of timely and newsworthy video clips first posted on YouTube to influence public discourse is now clear. The same can be said for citizens using Twitter. The media have relied on tweets to report on natural disasters like the earthquakes in

Mexico, the post-election revolts in Iran, and shootings in U.S. cities. The impact of citizen reporting through tweets, blogs or YouTube like postings is also substantial at the local level or on your college campus. If you observe an event that the media should cover you can pass it along. Expressing your views online is another way you can attempt to influence government.

CRITICAL THINKING QUESTIONS

1. How does citizen journalism broaden the reach of the media?

2. What are the advantages and disadvantages of using blogs as your primary news source?

3. In what ways might the use of Twitter change the way government functions?

* "CNN Celebrates Second Anniversary of iReport, More than 175,000 Contributions," TimeWarner, August 20, 2008, available at http://www.timewarner.com/corp/newsroom/pr/0,20812,1834490,00.html.

† Jessica Aldred, Amanda Astell, Rafael Behr, Lauren Cochrane, John Hind, Anna Pickard, Laura Potter, Alice Wignall, and Eva Wiseman, "The World's 50 Most Powerful Blogs," *The Observer*, March 9, 2008, available at http://www.guardian.co.uk/technology/2008/mar/09/blogs.

press can hurt or even destroy them. That explains why today's politicians spend so much time developing good relationships with the press.

Television's ability to present images and communicate events has influenced U.S. public opinion. Footage of the violence done to black and white protesters during the civil rights revolution of the 1950s and 1960s made the issue more real and immediate. News coverage of the war in Vietnam galvanized the antiwar movement in the United States because of the horrible images news shows brought into people's homes. The testimony of White House staff before the Senate about Watergate and later House Judiciary committees further weakened confidence in the Nixon administration. Television coverage of the terrorist attacks on the World Trade Center and the Pentagon and the devastation left by Hurricane Katrina and the earthquake in Haiti made indelible impressions on all who watched.

Natural disasters in a distant part of the world become part of global news coverage, as with this earthquake in China in 2010. ■ *How might this image have affected the world's reaction to the crisis? Do the media have obligations in how they present these kinds of stories?*

For a long time, analysts argued that political leaders wielded more influence in U.S. politics than the media did. Franklin D. Roosevelt's fireside chats symbolized the power of the politician over that of the news editor. Roosevelt spoke directly to his listeners over the radio in a way and at a time of his own choosing, and no network official could block or influence that direct connection. President John Kennedy's use of the televised press conference established similar direct contact with the public. President Ronald Reagan was nicknamed "the Great Communicator" because of his ability to talk with the people persuasively and often passionately about public policy issues through television.

Now the media are more aggressive in news gathering. Controversy over the justification for going to war with Iraq became a major focus of the media in George W. Bush's second term and helped explain the declining public assessment of his performance. In addition, the media can exert significant influence on public opinion through *agenda setting* and *issue framing*.

Agenda Setting

By calling public attention to certain issues, the media help determine what topics will become subjects of public debate and legislation.[62] However, the media do not have absolute power to set the public agenda. The audience and the nature of any particular issue limit it.[63] According to former Vice President Walter Mondale, "If I had to give up... the opportunity to get on the evening news or the veto power, ... I'd throw the veto power away. [Television news] is the president's most indispensable power."[64]

Communicating through the media works, especially when the communication is— or at least appears to be—natural and unscripted. When President Bush first visited the scene of the destruction of the World Trade Center in New York City in September 2001, he took a bullhorn and said, "I can hear you. The rest of the world hears you, and the people who knocked these buildings down will hear all of us soon."[65] This action projected presidential leadership and empathy to a nation that was still shocked by the attacks.

Issue Framing

Politicians, like everyone else, try to frame issues to win support, and they try to influence the "spin" the media will give to their actions or issues. The media provide the means. Opponents of U.S. intervention in Bosnia in the 1990s tried to portray it as another Vietnam. Objectors to normal trade relations with communist China frame that relationship as a human rights travesty. People who favor the right to have an abortion define the issue as one of freedom of choice; those who oppose it define it as murder. In referendum campaigns, the side that wins the battle of defining what the referendum is about, wins.[66]

Are the Media Biased?

We tend to blame the media for being either too conservative or too liberal. Conservatives often complain that the media are too liberal. For example, radio talk show host Rush Limbaugh even once said, "They all just happen to believe the same way.... They are part of the same culture as Bill Clinton."[67] Some liberal critics contend that the media reflect a conservative bias not only in what they report but also in what they choose to ignore. They point to Fox News as an example of conservative cable television.

In fact, most U.S. news media are committed to being unbiased. Newspapers and television management go to some lengths to insulate reporters from their advertising and business operations, in part to reduce criticism about favorable editorial treatment of large advertisers or the corporate owners. In 2007, when the management of the *Los Angeles Times* attempted to foster closer relationships between the business and news divisions, they were criticized out of a concern that advertisers would influence news coverage.[68]

Some commentators have suggested that a possible bias flows from the fact that reporters and editors become too friendly with the people and organizations they write about. According to David Broder of *The Washington Post*, many members of the print and television media have crossed the line that should divide objective journalism from partisan politics. Broder opposes the idea of journalists becoming government officials and vice versa.[69] Others argue that journalists with previous government service have close working relationships with politicians and can give us a valuable perspective on government without losing their professional neutrality.

The media's alleged political bias is also a frequent target of criticism, in part because the journalists tend to be more liberal than the rest of the public (see Table 10–1). Their worldview, some contend, may govern their choice of issues to cover and the way they cover them.[70] Critics counter that conservative forces in the media, such as corporate ownership, lead to disproportionate time and influence given to conservative pundits. The question of whether there is an ideological bias in the media has not been authoritatively

TABLE

10-1 Partisanship and Ideology of Journalists, Policy Makers, and the Public			
	Journalists	**Policy Makers**	**Public**
Party Identification			
Democrat	27%	43%	34%
Republican	4	24	28
Independent	55	26	21
Other	5	5	12
Do Not Know/Refused	9	2	4
Self-Described Ideology			
Liberal	25%	25%	21%
Moderate	59	52	37
Conservative	6	18	35
Do Not Know/Refused	11	5	7

■ *Why do you think journalists identify as Independent in a far greater percentage than policy makers or the public?*

SOURCE: The Kaiser Foundation, *The Role of Polls in Policy Making,* Combined Topline Results, June 2001, p. 27, www.kff.org/kaiserpolls/loader.cfm?url=/commonspot/security/getfile.cfm&PageID=13842.

answered. A further question is whether bias, if it exists and whatever its direction, seeps into the content of the news. The answer remains unclear.

One bias that does not have a partisan or ideological slant is the bias toward sensationalism. Scandals happen to liberals and conservatives, Republicans and Democrats. Once the province of tabloids like the *National Enquirer,* stories about these scandals involving celebrities, sex, or both have become commonplace in the mainstream media.

Factors That Limit Media Influence

Despite the varied means the media has for influencing public opinion, people are not just empty vessels into which politicians and journalists pour information and ideas. The

Bill O'Reilly, conservative TV and radio pundit, appeared as a guest on Comedy Central's show *The Colbert Report,* which mocks conservative pundits. ■ *Do you think media bias is a significant impediment to obtaining nonpartisan news and information?*

YOU WILL DECIDE

How Should the Media Report Sex Scandals?

Sex scandals involving politicians have always been an inviting media target. Most notably, President Bill Clinton was dogged by a series of accusations of unwanted sexual advances toward Paula Jones and Kathleen Willey and of a consensual affair with Monica Lewinsky. Ultimately, President Clinton was impeached for perjury connected to the Lewinsky scandal, although he was not removed from office. Media scrutiny of this scandal faded, however, and President Clinton still plays an active role in U.S. politics. New York Governor Eliot Spitzer resigned his office in March 2008 for his involvement in a high-priced prostitution ring. Photos of Spitzer littered the front pages of *The New York Times* for several days, the Web site of the prostitution ring registered 6 million page views the day after the scandal broke,[*] and the MySpace page of Spitzer's prostitute, Ashley Alexander Dupré, had received more than 10.5 million hits by late April.[†]

More recently, Democratic presidential candidate John Edwards admitted to an affair with his campaign videographer.[‡] South Carolina

Governor Mark Sanford's affair with a woman from Argentina led to his being censured by the state legislature in 2009 for misuse of state funds.[^] And Republican U.S. Senator John Ensign of Nevada in 2009 admitted to an affair with a staffer and that supporters provided the staffer and her husband with financial support.[**]

Sex scandals can have electoral consequences. Congressman Mark Foley (R-Fla.) resigned from Congress after allegations arose that he had sent sexually explicit e-mails and text messages to teenage boys serving as congressional pages. Foley had been known previously as a staunch fighter against child exploitation and abuse. Many feel the Foley scandal cost the Republicans the House and Senate in 2006. The cover of an October 2006 *Time* magazine read, "What a Mess. . . . Why a tawdry Washington sex scandal may spell the end of the Republican revolution."[††]

What do you think? Should the media report on political sex scandals? What are the arguments for and against this?

THINKING IT THROUGH

Some people dismiss reporting on sex scandals as sensationalist and unrelated to governing. Others, like Larry Sabato, a political scientist who has written on the media, disagree. Sabato criticized the press for not reporting "what most of them [the press] knew then about Clinton and all the other women. If the press had done its job in '92, the country would not be facing this horrible dilemma in '98."[§]

The question of how to report sexual misbehavior by political candidates is unresolved. It is debatable whether such matters ought to be reported at all. Some people, including some reporters, think sex scandals are not important. The public wants to know whether candidates meet high standards of personal conduct, but they react negatively to coverage that is too aggressive. Public reaction to the explicit details of the Starr report

about President Clinton's improper relationships is instructive: 84 percent of the public wanted to know the conclusions of the investigation, but 70 percent felt that Congress should have omitted the details of the sexual encounters.[^]

Critical Thinking Questions

1. What is the relevance to politics and elections of sex scandals like the one involving Governor Spitzer?

2. Why does the media give attention to the private lives of politicians?

3. Should politicians be held to a higher standard than other people in their private lives? Why or why not?

[*] Data from Alexa Internet Inc., www.alexa.com.

[†] Data from MySpace, www.myspace.com.

[‡] Kate Phillips, "Mistress of Edwards Ends Silence on Affair," *New York Times*, March 15, 2010, http://www.nytimes.com/2010/03/16/us/politics/16edwards.html (accessed May 26, 2010).

[§] Larry J. Sabato, quoted in William Power, "News at Warp Speed," *National Journal*, January 31, 1998, p. 220.

[^] Shaila Dewan, "S.C. Panel Kills Measure to Impeach Governor," *New York Times*, December 16, 2009, p. A32.

[**] David M. Herszenhorn, "Senator Says He Had Affair with an Aide," *New York Times*, June 16, 2009, p. A17.

[††] Frank Newport, "Initial Reaction Mixed on Delivery of Starr Report to Congress," *Gallup News Service*, September 12, 1998, http://www.gallup.com/poll/4168/Initial-Reaction-Mixed-Delivery-Starr-Report-Congress.aspx.

way we interpret political messages depends on a variety of factors: political socialization, selectivity, needs, and our ability to recall and comprehend the message.

Political Socialization   We develop our political attitudes, values, and beliefs through an education process social scientists call **political socialization.**[71] (See Chapters 4 and 8 for more detail on this process.) Although they are not as important as family in influencing our values and attitudes,[72] the media are a socializing force and help shape public perceptions and knowledge. Party identification is also a filter through which people view the media. Face-to-face contacts with friends and business associates (*peer pressure*) often have far more impact than the information or views we get from an impersonal television program or newspaper article. Strong identification with a party also acts as a powerful filter.[73] A conservative Republican from Arizona may watch the "liberal eastern networks" and complain about their biased news coverage while sticking to her own

political socialization
The process by which we develop our political attitudes, values, and beliefs.

FIGURE 10–1 Partisanship and Preferred News Source.

■ What do these figures imply about the practice of selective exposure?

SOURCE: Pew Research Center for the People & the Press, "July 2009 Political-Media Survey" dataset, people-press.org/data archive.

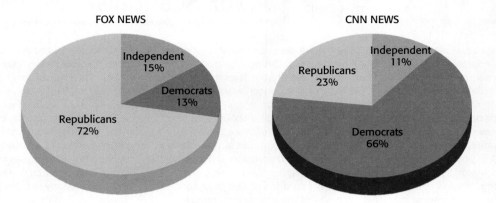

Party self-identification for regular viewers of:

opinions. A liberal from New York will often complain about right-wing talk radio, even if he listens to it occasionally (see Figures 10–1 and 10–2).

Selectivity   We all practice **selective exposure**—screening out messages that do not conform to our own biases. We subscribe to newspapers or magazines or turn to television and cable news outlets that support our views.[74] We also practice **selective perception**—perceiving what we want to in media messages.[75]

Needs   People read newspapers, listen to the radio, or watch television for different reasons.[76] Media affect people differently depending on whether they are seeking information about politics or want to be entertained. Members of the broader audience are also more likely to pay attention to news that directly affects their lives, such as interest rate changes or the price of gasoline.[77]

Audience Fragmentation   The growth of cable television and new media such as the Internet have reduced the dominance of broadcast media and newspapers in transmitting information. Because people are scattered across more press outlets and these outlets cover politics in varied ways, the impact of the press has become more diffuse. Fragmentation of the media audience has tended to counteract the impact of media conglomeration. But as media giants acquire both cable and broadcast stations and outlets and promote their own online sites, the importance of media conglomerates such as NBC, CNBC, and MSNBC will increase.

selective exposure
The process by which individuals screen out messages that do not conform to their own biases.

selective perception
The process by which individuals perceive what they want in media messages.

FIGURE 10–2 Partisanship and News Source Credibility.

SOURCE: Sacred Heart University poll on media and politics, November 2007; data compiled by Jerry Lindsay, April 30, 2008.

The Media and Elections

News coverage of campaigns and elections is greatest in presidential contests, less in statewide races for governor and U.S. senator, and least for other state and local races. Generally, the more news attention given the campaign, the less likely voters are to be swayed by any one source. Hence, news coverage is likely to be more influential in a city council contest than in an election for president or the Senate. For most city elections, there are only one or two sources of information about what candidates say and stand for; for statewide and national contests, there are multiple sources.

Diversification of the news media lessens the ability of any one medium to influence the outcome of elections. Newspaper publishers who were once seen as key figures in state and local politics are now less important because politicians and their media advisers are no longer so dependent on newspapers and other news media to communicate their messages. Candidates can use ads on radio and television, direct mail, phone, the Web, and cable television to reach voters. In local contests, or even in larger settings such as the Iowa caucuses or the New Hampshire primary, personal contact can also be important.

LEARNING **OBJECTIVE**

10.4 Describe the media's role in elections and the associated problems and benefits.

Choice of Candidates

The extensive use of television has made looking and sounding good on television much more important. It has also led to the growth of the political consulting industry and made *visibility* the watchword in politics. Television strongly influences the public's idea of what traits are important in a candidate. A century ago, successful candidates needed a strong pair of lungs; today, they need a telegenic appearance, a pleasing voice, and no obvious physical impairments.

Although the media insist that they pay attention to all candidates who have a chance to win, they also influence who gets such a chance. Consequently, candidates have to come up with creative ways to attract media attention. The late Paul Wellstone, in his 1996 campaign for the Senate in Minnesota, said in his advertisements that he did not have much money to pay for ads, so he would have to talk fast to cram what he had to say into fewer commercials. His witty commercial became a news event itself—it got Wellstone additional coverage. Sometimes, a limited ad buy can generate funding for a much larger one. This was the case with the group that attacked the credibility and heroism of John Kerry in the 2004 presidential election; the Swift Boat Veterans for Truth turned a $550,000 ad buy into millions of dollars in contributions, which funded the airing of additional ads.[78] Critical to this expanded campaign was the widespread news coverage generated by the controversy the first ad set off.[79]

Campaign Events

Candidates schedule events—press conferences, interviews, and "photo ops"—in settings that reinforce their verbal messages and public image. Barack Obama skillfully used a backdrop of young and diverse voters for his rallies and post-primary speeches. In contrast, other candidates were often surrounded by older and less diverse political leaders from the state or community. Many campaign events fail to receive attention from reporters because others are more newsworthy stories or the media may sense that they have been staged to generate news coverage.

The parties' national conventions used to capture national attention. However, because party primaries now select candidates, the conventions no longer provide much suspense or make news, except perhaps over who will be the vice presidential nominee. This is one reason the networks have cut back their coverage of presidential

These photos from the Obama and Clinton election night speeches following the Iowa caucuses contrast two different ways to stage such a speech. The Clinton staging included former Secretary of State Madeleine Albright, union leaders, and other notables. Obama, on the other hand, is surrounded by a sea of ordinary people, many of them more diverse and younger than in the Clinton staging. As the campaign progressed, Clinton adopted what later became the Obama staging.

nominating conventions. In 1952, the average television set was tuned to the political conventions for 26 hours, or an average of more than three hours a night for the eight nights of convention coverage.[80] During the last decade, by contrast, the major networks provided only one or two hours of prime-time coverage each evening. But cable channels now carry extensive coverage of the proceedings. The 2008 conventions had increased viewership in part because of excitement around the Obama and Palin candidacies. When Obama delivered his acceptance speech to a crowd of 80,000 at the Denver Bronco's football stadium, more than 38 million households tuned in. One week later, John McCain and Sarah Palin delivered speeches to audiences of similar sizes.[81]

Technology

Although the expense associated with television advertising has contributed to the skyrocketing costs of campaigning, it has also made politics more accessible to more people. Now with satellites, candidates can conduct local television interviews without having to travel to local studios. They can target specific voter groups through cable television or low-power television stations that reach homogeneous neighborhoods and small towns. DVDs and CDs with messages from the candidates further extend the campaign's reach.[82] All serious candidates for Congress and governor since 2000 have made themselves and their positions available through a Web page on the Internet.

Campaigns have primarily used the Internet and e-mail to reinforce voter preferences or help answer questions, more than to reach and persuade more passive citizens. But citizens can now interact with each other online on a wide range of political topics. In this sense, the Internet is like a town meeting, but one that people can attend without leaving their homes or offices. In recent elections, people have made greater use of blogs as sources of information, and campaigns have often created their own blogs. Of growing importance are political communications posted on YouTube or Facebook, as illustrated by the examples cited at the beginning of this chapter.

Image Making and Media Consultants

Consistent with the media's focus on personality is its highlighting of mistakes and gaffes by candidates and officeholders. Long before Jon Stewart and *The Daily Show,* print and broadcast media devoted considerable attention to such things as Gerald Ford mistakenly classifying Poland as a free country in the 1976 presidential debates.[83] More recently, Hillary Clinton's exaggeration about snipers shooting at her on a visit to Bosnia became the subject of ridicule by comedians and meant she had to repeatedly apologize for the mistaken statements.[84] The media also seized on Barack Obama's characterization during the Pennsylvania primary of residents of small, economically depressed towns as "bitter," stating, "They cling to guns or religion or antipathy to people who aren't like them…as a way to explain their frustrations."[85]

This ability of television to reach a mass audience and the power of the visual image on television has contributed to the rise of new players in campaign politics, most notably *media consultants*—campaign professionals who provide candidates with advice and services on media relations, advertising strategy, and opinion polling.[86] A primary responsibility of a campaign media consultant is to present a positive image of the candidate and to reinforce negative images of the opponent. Both parties have scores of media consultants who have handled congressional, gubernatorial, and referendum campaigns. These consultants have also been blamed for the negative tone and tactics of recent campaigns.

Today, consultants coach candidates about how to act and behave on television and what to discuss on the air. Consultants report the results of *focus groups* (small sample groups of people who are asked questions about candidates and issues in a discussion setting) and *public opinion polls,* which in turn determine what the candidate says and does. Some critics allege that political consultants have become a new "political elite" that can virtually choose candidates by determining in advance which men and women have the right images, or at least images that the consultants can restyle for the widest popularity.[87] But political consultants who specialize in media advertising and image making know their own limitations in packaging candidates. As one media consultant put it, "It is a very hard job to turn a turkey into a movie star; you try instead to make people like the turkey."[88]

Impact on Voter Choice

As television has become increasingly important to politics—and reforms such as primary elections have weakened the political parties and made news coverage of candidates more important—the question arises, what difference does the media make?

Personality over Substance Some critics think reporters pay too much attention to candidates' personality and background and not enough attention to issues and policy. Others say character and personality are among the most important characteristics for readers and viewers to know about. The public appetite for stories on candidates' personal strengths and weaknesses is not new and is likely to continue.

The influence of the media on the public varies by level of sophistication of the voters. Better-informed and more-educated voters are more sophisticated and therefore less swayed by new information from the media.[89] But for the public generally, other scholars contend that "television news is news that matters."[90]

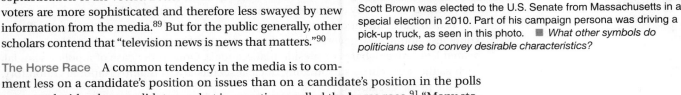

Scott Brown was elected to the U.S. Senate from Massachusetts in a special election in 2010. Part of his campaign persona was driving a pick-up truck, as seen in this photo. ■ *What other symbols do politicians use to convey desirable characteristics?*

The Horse Race A common tendency in the media is to comment less on a candidate's position on issues than on a candidate's position in the polls compared with other candidates—what is sometimes called the **horse race.**[91] "Many stories focus on who is ahead, who is behind, who is going to win, and who is going to lose, rather than examining how and why the race is as it is."[92] Reporters focus on the tactics and strategy of campaigns because they think such coverage interests the public.[93] The media's propensity to focus on the "game" of campaigns displaces coverage of issues.

Negative Advertising Paid political advertising, much of it negative in tone, is another source of information for voters. Political advertising has always attacked opponents, but recent campaigns have taken on an increasingly negative tone. A rule of thumb used to be to ignore the opposition's charges and thus avoid giving them, or the opposition, importance or standing. More recently, media advisers recommend responding quickly and aggressively to attacks.

Voters say the attack style of politics turns them off, but most campaign consultants believe that negative campaigning works. This seeming inconsistency may be explained by evidence suggesting that negative advertising may discourage some voters who would be inclined to support a candidate (a phenomenon known as *vote suppression*) while making supporters more likely to vote.[94] Other research suggests that negative advertising is more informative than positive advertising and does not discourage voter turnout, but it does alienate people from government.[95]

Information About Issues In recent elections, the media have experimented with a more issues-centered focus, what has been called *civic journalism*. With funding from charitable foundations, some newspapers have been identifying the concerns of community leaders and talking to ordinary voters and then writing campaign stories from their point of view.[96] Some newspaper editors and reporters disagree with this approach; they believe the media should stick to responding to newsworthy events.

Making a Decision Newspapers and television seem to have more influence in determining the outcome of primaries than of general elections,[97] probably because voters in a primary are less likely to know about the candidates and have fewer clues about how they stand. By the time of the November general election, however, party affiliation, incumbency, and other factors diminish the impact of media messages. The mass media are more likely to influence undecided voters, who, in a close election, can determine who wins and who loses.

Election Night Reporting Does television coverage on election night affect the outcome of elections? Election returns from the East Coast come in three hours before the polls close on the West Coast. Because major networks often project the presidential winner well

horse race
A close contest; by extension, any contest in which the focus is on who is ahead and by how much rather than on substantive differences between the candidates.

before polls close in western states, it can affect western voters. When one candidate appears to be winning by a large margin, it may make voters believe their vote is meaningless and dampen voter turnout. In a close presidential election, however, such early reporting may stimulate turnout because voters know their vote could determine the outcome.

Controversy over exit polls grew after the 2000 and 2004 elections when television networks projected that Al Gore had won Florida, only to later retract that prediction. Hours later, Fox News projected Bush winning Florida. The truth was that the vote in Florida was by every measure too close to judge. In 2004, leaks of early exit polls in the media showed John Kerry winning Ohio,[98] a state carried by Bush. Despite these problems, exit polls are generally accurate and inform the public about who voted and why people voted the way they did. Exit polls are one source of data used in this book, for example.

The Media and Governance

When policies are being formulated and implemented, decision makers are at their most impressionable.[99] Yet by that time, the press has moved on to another issue.

Lack of press attention to the way policies are implemented explains in part why we know less about how government officials go about their business than we do about heated legislative debates or presidential scandals. Only in the case of a policy scandal, such as the lax security surrounding nuclear secrets at Los Alamos National Laboratory, does the press take notice.

Some critics contend that the media's pressuring policy makers to provide immediate answers forces them to make hasty decisions, a particular danger in foreign policy: If an ominous foreign event is featured on television news, the president and his advisers feel bound to make a response in time for the next evening news broadcast. If he does not have a response ready by the late afternoon deadline, the evening news may report that the president's advisers are divided, that the president cannot make up his mind, or that while the president hesitates, his political opponents know exactly what to do.[100]

Political Institutions and the News Media

Presidents have become the stars of the media, particularly television, and have made the media their forum for setting the public agenda and achieving their legislative aims. Presidential news conferences command attention (see Table 10–2). Every public activity a president engages in, both professional and personal, is potentially newsworthy; a presidential illness can become front-page news, as can the president's vacations and pets.

A president attempts to manipulate news coverage to his benefit, as in the Bush administration's decision to embed reporters with U.S. forces during the early stages of the Iraq War. Presidents or their staff also selectively leak news to reporters. Presidents use speeches to set the national agenda or spur congressional action. Presidential travel to foreign countries usually boosts popular support at home, due to largely favorable news coverage. Better yet for the president, most coverage of the president—either at home or abroad—is favorable to neutral.[101]

Members of Congress have long sought to cultivate positive relationships with news reporters in their states and districts. They typically have a press relations staffer who informs local media of newsworthy events, produces press releases, and generally tries to promote the senator or representative.[102] Congress also provides recording studios for taping of news segments, and both parties have recording studios near the Capitol explicitly for electoral ads. Finally, politicians often appear on talk radio, which they can readily do from their offices in Washington. But the focus of this media cultivation is on the individual member and not on the institution of Congress as a whole.

Congress is more likely to get negative coverage than either the White House or the Supreme Court. Unlike the executive branch, it lacks an ultimate spokesperson, a single person who can speak for the whole institution.[103] Congress does not make it easy for the press to cover it. Whereas the White House attentively cares for and feeds the press corps, Congress does not arrange its schedule to accommodate the media; floor debates, for example, often compete with committee hearings and press conferences.[104] Singularly dramatic actions rarely occur in Congress; the press therefore turns to the president to

TABLE

| 10–2 | Presidential Press Conferences: Joint* and Solo Sessions, 1913–2010 |

President	Total	Solo	Joint	Joint as Percentage of Total	Months in Office
Wilson	159	159	0	0	96
Harding		No Transcripts Available			29
Coolidge	521	521	0	0	67
Hoover	268	267	1	0.4	48
Roosevelt	1020	984	33	3.2	145.5
Truman	324	311	13	4.0	94.5
Eisenhower	193	192	1	0.5	96
Kennedy	65	65	0	0	34
Johnson	135	118	16	11.9	62
Nixon	39	39	0	0	66
Ford	40	39	1	2.5	30
Carter	59	59	0	0	48
Reagan	46	46	0	0	96
G. H. W. Bush	143	84	59	41.3	48
Clinton	193	62	131	67.9	96
G. W. Bush	208	50	158	76	96
Obama[†]	39	17	22	56	21

* In a joint press conference, the president answers questions along with someone else, most often a foreign leader. In a solo session, only the president answers questions. There are three missing transcripts for Roosevelt and one for Johnson, which makes it impossible to determine whether those sessions were solo or joint ones.
[†] Obama through November 2010.

■ *How does President Obama's use of press conferences compare to his recent predecessors?*

SOURCE: Adapted from Martha Joynt Kumar, "Presidential Press Conferences: The Importance and Evolution of an Enduring Forum," *Presidential Studies Quarterly* 35, No. 1 (March 2005); and Kumar 2006, 2007, 2008, and 2010.

describe the activity of the federal government on a day-to-day basis and treats Congress largely as a foil to the president. Most coverage of Congress is about how it reacts to the president's initiatives.[105]

The federal judiciary is least dependent on the press. The Supreme Court does not rely on public communication for political support. Rather, it depends indirectly on public opinion for continued deference to or compliance with its decisions.[106] The Court does not allow television cameras to cover oral arguments, controls the release of audiotape, and bars reporters as well as anyone other than the justices when it meets to discuss cases. It has strong incentives to avoid being seen as manipulating the press, so it retains an image of aloofness from politics and public opinion. The justices' manipulation of press coverage is far more subtle and complex than that of the other two institutions.[107] For example, the complexity of the Supreme Court's decision in the 2000 Florida presidential vote recount case, with multiple dissents and concurrences and no press release or executive summary, made broadcast reporting on the decision difficult.

Not all who think the media are powerful agree that power is harmful. After all, they argue, the media perform a vital educational function. Nearly 70 percent of the public thinks the press is a watchdog that keeps government leaders from doing bad things.[108] At the least, the media have the power to mold the public agenda; at most, in the words of the late Theodore White, they have the power to "determine what people will talk and think about—an authority that in other nations is reserved for tyrants, priests, parties, and mandarins."[109]

U.S. President Barack Obama calls on reporters as he holds an impromptu news conference in the Brady Briefing Room of the White House in Washington on February 9, 2010. Obama urged compromise and bipartisanship with the Republican opposition on efforts such as health care and bringing down the deficit.

CHAPTER **SUMMARY**

10.1 Outline changes in the nature and extent of the political influence of the various news media.

The news media include newspapers, magazines, radio, television, films, recordings, books, and electronic communications in all their forms. These means of communication have been called the "fourth branch of government," for they are a pervasive feature of U.S. politics. The media provide and carry information among political actors, the government, and the public.

10.2 Trace the evolution of the news media over the course of U.S. history.

Our modern news media emerged from a more partisan and less professional past. Journalists today strive for objectivity and also engage in investigatory journalism. Corporate ownership and consolidation of media outlets raise questions about media competition and orientation. Radio and television broadcasting have changed the news media, and these are the sources from which most people get their news. The Internet has recently emerged as a new source of both information and political participation.

10.3 Evaluate the media's influence on public opinion and attention.

The mass media's influence over public opinion is significant but not overwhelming. People may not pay much attention to the media or may not believe everything they read, see, or hear. People tend to filter the news through their political socialization, selectivity, needs, and ability to recall or comprehend the news. Although conservatives charge that the media are too liberal and liberals charge that the media are captive to business interests, little evidence exists of actual, deliberate bias in news reporting. The media's influence is most strongly felt in their ability to determine what problems and events will come to the public's attention and how those issues are framed.

10.4 Describe the media's role in elections and the associated problems and benefits.

Media coverage dominates presidential campaigns, and candidates depend on media exposure to build name recognition, a positive image, and thereby votes. Because of the way the media cover elections, most people seem more interested in the contest as a game or "horse race" than as a serious discussion of issues and candidates. Another effect of media influence has been the rise of image making and the media consultant.

10.5 Assess the media's relationship to governance in the United States.

The press serves as both observer and participant in politics and as a watchdog, agenda setter, and check on the abuse of power, but it rarely gives much attention to the implementation or administration phases of the policy process. Exceptions include major mistakes such as the government's response to Hurricane Katrina.

CHAPTER **SELF-TEST**

10.1 Outline changes in the nature and extent of the political influence of the various news media.

1. Briefly explain the distinction between the *mass media* and the *news media*.
2. Describe the major changes during the past century in how Americans get their news.

10.2 Trace the evolution of the news media over the course of U.S. history.

3. True or False: The FCC has been relaxing regulations that limit cable and television network ownership by the same company.
4. In one or two paragraphs, define the "penny press" and discuss why its development was significant in the history of U.S. media.

10.3 Evaluate the media's influence on public opinion and attention.

5. The process by which individuals perceive what they want to in media messages is
   a. selective exposure.
   b. political alienation.
   c. selective perception.
   d. political socialization.

6. List four factors that limit the influence media have on public opinion, and explain each in a few sentences.

7. Explain how *issue framing* is different from *agenda setting*. In a few sentences, tell which of these two possible approaches by the media you think has a greater influence on national policy and why.

10.4 Describe the media's role in elections and the associated problems and benefits.

8. In a few sentences, explain how television and the media in general affect the choice of candidates for presidential elections.
9. Write a brief persuasive essay showing that the media's role in elections is a problem that calls for significant changes. Use the examples from the chapter as well as any personal experiences you have had.
10. In a short essay, discuss how presidential campaigns would differ without television. Would they be better or worse? Why?

10.5 Assess the media's relationship to governance in the United States.

11. In a short essay, discuss why the federal judiciary is the branch that is least dependent on the press.
12. In a short essay, describe how the president manipulates news coverage. In your opinion, is the president's ability to manipulate news coverage a positive or negative power?

Answers to selected questions: 3. true; 5. c

---

mypoliscilab EXERCISES
Where participation leads to action!

Apply what you learned in this chapter on MyPoliSciLab.

Read on **mypoliscilab.com**

eText: Chapter 10

Study and **Review** on **mypoliscilab.com**

Pre-Test
Post-Test
Chapter Exam
Flashcards

Watch on **mypoliscilab.com**

Video: YouTube Politics
Video: The Pentagon's Media Message

Explore on **mypoliscilab.com**

Simulation: You Are the News Editor
Comparative: Comparing News Media
Timeline: Three Hundred Years of American Mass Media
Visual Literacy: Use of the Media by the American Public

KEY TERMS

mass media, p. 276
news media, p. 276

political socialization, p. 287
selective exposure, p. 288

selective perception, p. 288
horse race, p. 291

ADDITIONAL RESOURCES

FURTHER READING

ERIC ALTMAN, *What Liberal Media? The Truth About Bias and the News* (Basic Books, 2004).

STEPHEN ANSOLABEHERE AND **SHANTO IYENGAR,** *Going Negative: How Attack Ads Shrink and Polarize the Electorate* (Free Press, 1996).

MATTHEW BAUM AND **TIM J. GROELING,** *War Stories: The Causes and Consequences of Public Views of War* (Princeton University Press, 2010).

BRUCE BIMBER AND **RICHARD DAVIS,** *Campaigning Online: The Internet in U.S. Elections* (Oxford University Press, 2003).

KEITH BYBEE, *Bench Press: The Collision of Courts, Politics, and the Media* (Stanford Law and Politics Press, 2007).

JEFFREY E. COHEN, *The Presidency in the Era of 24-Hour News* (Princeton University Press, 2008).

TIMOTHY E. COOK, *Making Laws and Making News: Press Strategies in the U.S. House of Representatives* (Brookings Institution Press, 1990).

RICHARD DAVIS, *Typing Politics: The Role of Blogs in American Politics* (Oxford University Press, 2009).

JOHN G. GEER, *In Defense of Negativity: Attack Ads in Presidential Campaigns* (University of Chicago Press, 2006).

DORIS A. GRABER, *Mass Media and American Politics,* 8th ed. (CQ Press, 2009).

RODERICK P. HART, *Campaign Talk: Why Elections Are Good for Us* (Princeton University Press, 2002).

MATTHEW S. HINDMAN, *The Myth of Digital Democracy* (Princeton University Press, 2009).

THOMAS A. HOLLIHAN, *Uncivil Wars: Political Campaigns in a Media Age* (Bedford/St. Martin's, 2009).

KATHLEEN H. JAMISON, *The Press Effect: Politicians, Journalists, and the Stories That Shape the Political World* (Oxford University Press, 2003).

PHYLLIS KANISS, *Making Local News* (University of Chicago Press, 1997).

DAVID D. PERLMUTTER, *Blog Wars: The New Political Battleground* (Oxford University Press, 2008).

DONALD A. RITCHIE, *Reporting from Washington: The History of the Washington Press Corps* (Oxford University Press, 2006).

CASS SUNSTEIN, *Republic.com 2.0* (Princeton University Press, 2007).

DARRELL M. WEST, *Air Wars: Television Advertising in Election Campaigns, 1952–2008,* 5th ed. (CQ Press, 2009).

WEB SITES

www.sunshineingovernment.org/ The Web site for the Sunshine in Government Initiative, which is a coalition of media groups that focus on ensuring open and accountable government.

www.mrc.org/public/default.aspx The Web site for the Media Research Center, which calls itself "America's Media Watchdog." It is an attempt to try and balance news media, originally trying to correct a "liberal bias."

mediamatters.org/p/about_us/ The Web site for Media Matters for America, which tries to correct "conservative misinformation in the U.S. media."

www.prwatch.org/cmd/index.html The Center for Media and Democracy Web site, which tries to investigate issues and inform the public as well as promote transparency and promote "open content" media.

PART III | Policy Making Institutions

THE BIG PICTURE

The U.S. Constitution established three branches of the federal government: Congress, the presidency, and the judiciary. The president also directs the federal bureaucracy, which implements the laws and enforces the court decisions that the three branches make. The three branches of government were designed to check and balance each other through a variety of mechanisms such as the presidential veto, judicial review, and congressional authority to pass, delay, or defeat legislation. Presidents are limited to two four-year terms; members of the Senate have six-year terms, but only a third of the Senate stands for election at a time; members of the House have two-year terms and all stand for election at the same time; and federal judges are appointed for life. Each branch also has different powers in the legislative process.

These checks and balances are part of a system of separate power, which is essential for controlling political ambition. James Madison believed that government must first control the people and then control itself. The Constitution was designed to pit each branch against the other in an effort to protect the nation from rapid swings in public policy. It allows Congress and the president to act only when there is great national consensus and then gives the judiciary the power to declare even popular laws unconstitutional.

The four chapters in this section describe each of the branches in detail and provide an introduction to the federal bureaucracy. Although the Constitution does not provide much detail on the bureaucracy, this "fourth branch" of government is responsible for converting laws into reality through a variety of techniques.

There are a number of ways that the public can influence decisions across these three branches, but citizens are up against a variety of forces, described in Part II of this book. Each of the three branches is built for stalemate unless citizens agree on the need for action.

COURSE LEARNING **OBJECTIVES**

CHAPTER **11** Congress

Identify the legislative powers of Congress, and compare and contrast the House of Representatives and the Senate.

Congress is the first branch of government mentioned in the Constitution. The founders believed that Congress would be the most active branch, except in times of great domestic and international threats to the survival of the nation. The Constitution gives Congress a long list of powers but divides authority in a bicameral, or two-house, system. Each house of Congress has its own responsibilities and operates under different calendars, leadership, and rules.

Because there are only 100 senators, the chamber is more flexible; because there are 435 representatives, the House has more rules for debate. Even as both chambers act together to check the president and the judiciary, each checks the other. The House of Representatives was given the power to initiate all revenue legislation, for example, whereas the Senate was given the power to confirm presidential appointees and approve treaties. Each also has the power to investigate the president and the federal bureaucracy, which puts pressure on executive decisions, and also to investigate violations of the law by citizens and private entities, such as businesses and charitable agencies.

As a general rule, members of Congress are usually reelected to their posts through the use of incumbency advantages such as name recognition. Nevertheless, there are times when the public turns strongly against incumbents, so members of Congress decide not to run for reelection or are defeated in primaries and the general election.

CHAPTER **12** The Presidency

Identify the powers of the president for leading the nation.

The U.S. president holds one of the most important jobs in the world. The Constitution gives the president a number of explicit and implied powers to protect the nation and provides the presidency with important checks on the legislature. The president also has a number of roles in drafting laws, negotiating international treaties, leading the federal bureaucracy, and building morale. Recent decades have produced a number of controversies surrounding the president's power, especially as commander in chief during wartime. These controversies often involve presidential assertions of significant implied powers to act in defense of the nation.

The president also has an important relationship with Congress. Although the two branches do pass important laws, they often disagree about the direction of the nation. The president has important tools for influencing Congress, but Congress has equally important tools for stopping the president. This is the essence of a separated powers system. Presidents often blame Congress for blocking key legislation, whereas Congress often argues that presidents claim powers that the Constitution gives to Congress.

CHAPTER **13** The Federal Bureaucracy

Describe the role of the federal bureaucracy in implementing the laws.

The Constitution left many of the key decisions about the future of the federal bureaucracy to the president and Congress. It instructs the president to appoint the senior political officers of government and gives Congress the power to create departments, independent stand-alone agencies, independent regulatory commissions, and quasi-government corporations. Several hundred presidential appointees lead the bureaucracy, but the civil service actually implements the laws, largely by making rules and regulations. The federal bureaucracy is also responsible for spending money on the programs that Congress and the president create.

Congress often delegates the implementation power to the bureaucracy by writing very general laws. This gives the bureaucracy great power to interpret congressional intent. The bureaucracy must translate general congressional intent into clear instructions that affect every American.

CHAPTER **14** The Judiciary

Explain the role of the courts in the system of checks and balances, and evaluate the challenges for judicial independence.

The Constitution created a single layer of the federal judiciary, the Supreme Court. It left the creation of "inferior courts" to Congress and the president through legislation. The Constitution gave the judiciary significant independence to make decisions on behalf of the nation. Over time, the Supreme Court expanded its role in checking the other branches by establishing its authority to decide whether even popularly enacted legislation was consistent with the Constitution. This role has evolved over time as the judiciary has taken a more active role in considering the constitutionality of the laws.

With life-terms, federal judges are theoretically insulated from political pressure. However, every federal judge must be nominated by the president and confirmed by the Senate, which creates political pressure on the appointments process. It is unusual that the Senate rejects the president's nominees, but the need for its approval influences the president's choices. Moreover, the president's choice of the Solicitor General, another appointment subject to Senate confirmation, affects the government's position on key cases. In addition, presidents appoint the U.S. Attorneys who initiate cases on behalf of the public and defend the government from citizens who challenge the laws.

Congress

The People's Branch

Indiana Democratic Senator Evan Bayh dropped a bombshell on Washington on February 13, 2010. Elected to the Senate in 1998, Bayh would have been eligible for reelection in 2010, but he decided to retire early. He was an important swing vote for Senate Democrats in trying to pass legislation, but in retiring, Bayh joined a growing list of Democrats and Republicans who have given up on the bitter congressional infighting that had frozen action on critical legislation such as economic recovery, health care reform, global climate change, and efforts to trim the huge federal budget deficit.

Bayh was not particularly nervous about his reelection chances in Fall 2010. He has $13 million in the bank to defend his seat against challengers from his own party and his potential Republican opponent. Although some in Washington immediately concluded that he was going to take a year or two off to prepare for his own campaign against President Barack Obama in 2012, he made no mention of his plans in making his tough announcement. As the son of former Senator Birch Bayh, a leader in the old Senate of bipartisan compromise, Bayh, 54, was simply tired of the battles. Writing in the *New York Times* Sunday edition on February 23, he did not mince any words about his decision to leave. As a moderate Democrat, he felt increasingly isolated in his own party:

> When I was a boy, members of Congress from both parties, along with their families, would routinely visit our home for dinner or the holidays. This type of social interaction hardly ever happens today and we are the poorer for it. It is much harder to demonize someone when you know his family or have visited his home. Today, members routinely campaign against each other, raise donations against each other, and force votes on trivial amendments written solely to provide fodder for the next negative attack ad. It's difficult to work with members actively plotting your demise.[1]

Bayh called Congress a dysfunctional institution in which moderates were increasingly isolated from both parties. "It shouldn't take a constitutional crisis or an attack on the nation to create honest dialogue in the Senate." The frustrations he voiced were probably shared by many other senators, but he was still harsh toward his colleagues: "Milton Berle famously joked: 'You can lead a man to Congress, but you can't make him think.' "

Bayh was simply saying what most Americans think. They are disgusted by politics in Washington and disappointed that Obama had not been able to honor his campaign promise to change the tone in Washington. The Senate and House, too, have engaged in the familiar politics of partisanship and anger. Absent fundamental reform in campaign finance and electoral politics, and with party divisions ever more personal, Bayh said it was time to go.

In this chapter, we examine how the framers designed the legislative branch and how it actually works today. We will also explore the role of interest groups, colleagues, congressional staff, the two parties, and the president in shaping decisions; discuss how a bill becomes a law; and explore the ethics issue in more detail.

Before turning to these questions, however, we will look at how members of Congress reach office in the first place. The way we elect members of the House and Senate has a great deal to do with how they behave once in office, and it influences everything from committee assignments to legislative interests. We will also ask why individual members of Congress win reelection so easily.

Readers should also note that the word "Congress" is used several ways in government. The words "a congress" is a two-year body of elected officials and is numbered for the two-year period dating all the way back to the first congress convened after the Constitution was ratified. Thus, the 112th Congress convened exactly 224 years after the first one. The words "the Congress" refer to the institution itself as part of the three branches of government. A congress may stand for two years, but the Congress is a never-ending institution.

Congressional Elections

LEARNING OBJECTIVE

11.1 Describe the congressional election process and the advantages it gives incumbents.

There is only one Congress in the Constitution, but the 435 House members and 100 senators serve in bodies that are significantly different. One important distinction is the different election calendars. The framers believed these calendars would make the House and its members much more sensitive than senators to the opinions of their **constituents,** meaning residents of their districts or states.

House members and senators also run for their first elections under slightly different entry rules. House members must be 25 years old at the time they take office and must have been citizens for seven years, whereas senators must be 30 years old and have been citizens for nine years. House and Senate candidates must be residents of the states from which they are elected, but House members do not need to reside in their district. The framers hoped that by setting the Senate's requirements higher and giving its members a six-year term, they would shape the Senate as a check against what they saw as the less predictable House. Concerned about the "fickleness and passion" of the House of Representatives, James Madison in particular saw the Senate as "a necessary fence against this danger."[2] This is why the founders decided that senators would be selected by their state legislatures. Although the Constitution was amended in 1913 to require the direct election of all senators, the Constitution allows state governors to appoint senators to fill vacant posts until the next scheduled election for their seats.

Senators are not free to ignore their constituents, however. Because the framers did not limit the number of terms House members or senators can serve, they must defend their records at some point if they want to stay in office.

constituents
The residents of a congressional district or state.

A campaign worker stays late after the Senator Arlen Specter's concession speech following his defeat in the Democratic Party's 2010 Pennsylvania Senate primary. Specter had often taken a moderate position on issues, and switched from the Republican to the Democratic party in 2009, citing that he was increasingly at odds with the Republican philosophy.

Drawing District Lines

The framers of the Constitution set the Senate and the House apart in terms of the populations they serve. Every state has two senators, each of whom represents the entire state. Members of the House of Representatives, on the other hand, serve districts within their states. A state's population determines the number of districts—hence, states with more citizens have more districts, and big states clearly have more influence in the House.

The exact number of districts in each state is determined by a national census of the population taken every ten years, which is also specified in the Constitution. The 2010 census is changing the distribution of congressional seats by giving growing states such as California and Texas more representatives. But the number of senators is fixed at two per state.

When the population changes, so does the potential number of districts, or seats in each state. This process of changing the number of seats allotted to each state is called **reapportionment.** Each seat in the House represents roughly 650,000 people. House members from small states often represent even fewer—Wyoming has only 580,000 people, for example, but each state is guaranteed one House member. Because the House limited the total number of districts to 435 after the 1910 census, the number of districts will not change after the 2010 census is completed, but the distribution of seats will.

The U.S. Congress has the power to change the number of seats per state, but the states have the power to determine the district lines. This process of converting the number of seats into districts is called **redistricting.**[3] Under the Constitution, states, not the federal government, are responsible for determining the time, place, and manner of elections, which includes district lines.

District lines can be drawn several ways to favor one party—a district can be "packed" with a large number of party voters, thereby diluting that party's strength in the districts next door, or a party stronghold can be dispersed into several districts, thereby possibly weakening that opposition party's strength in several districts. In extreme cases, this process is known as **gerrymandering,** a term dating to the early 1800s when Massachusetts governor Elbridge Gerry won passage of a redistricting plan that created a salamander-shaped district drawn to help his party win another seat.

Advantages of Incumbency

It only takes one defeat to end a House or Senate career, which is why so many House members and senators work so hard to create safe seats. A **safe seat** is almost certain to be won by the current officeholder, or **incumbent.** It usually occurs in a district where

reapportionment
The assigning by Congress of congressional seats after each census. State legislatures reapportion state legislative districts.

redistricting
The redrawing of congressional and other legislative district lines following the census, to accommodate population shifts and keep districts as equal as possible in population.

gerrymandering
The drawing of legislative district boundaries to benefit a party, group, or incumbent.

safe seat
An elected office that is predictably won by one party or the other, so the success of that party's candidate is almost taken for granted.

incumbent
The current holder of elected office.

Members of Congress often appear at ribbon-cuttings for important public projects. Here, Senator Hutchinson helps open The Women's Museum in Dallas. ■ *How does this photo show several of the advantages an incumbent has?*

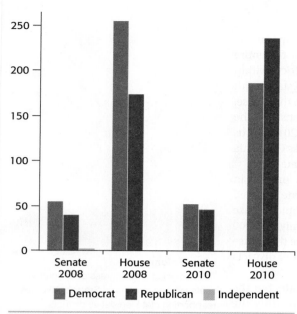

FIGURE 11–1 **Congressional Election Results, 2008 and 2010.**

■ *How did the party balance of Congress change after the 2010 elections, and what effect, if any, will that have on how Congress functions?*

NOTE: Some elections were still too close to call as of mid-November, 2010.

earmarks
Special spending projects that are set aside on behalf of individual members of Congress for their constituents.

one party has a clear majority of voters, virtually ensuring the election of the candidate from the dominant party.

Although there are still competitive seats in the House, most are considered invulnerable to challenge. Of 435 seats up for election in 2010, roughly one quarter were considered truly competitive two-party seats. In some districts where one party dominates, there is occasional competition within the dominant party for the nomination, most often when an incumbent retires or runs for a different office. In contrast, Senate seats are considered more vulnerable. Opponents are often well financed, in part because Senate elections are so visible nationally. With only a third of the Senate up for reelection at any one time, the public can pay closer attention to campaign issues and advertisements, and the two parties can invest more money in their candidates.[4]

Incumbents benefit from several advantages:

- Under the franking privilege, incumbents do not have to pay postage on their mail to their district, except during the last 90 days before an election.
- Incumbents are allowed to send bulk e-mails any time.
- Incumbents have greater access to the media, especially on local or state issues, and have very high name recognition in their districts.
- Incumbents have a natural advantage in raising campaign contributions over their challengers, in part because they have such high odds of victory.
- Incumbents are usually better candidates than their challengers, in part because they have more experience.
- Incumbents have great influence in helping their constituents solve problems with government, and they often take credit for federal spending in their districts or state.

Incumbents also control federal spending for pet projects through **earmarks,** which are usually slipped into large legislative packages at the last minute. These earmarks instruct the executive branch to spend money on specific items such as new highways or research centers in individual congressional districts.[5]

The 2010 Congressional Elections

The 2010 midterm elections produced dramatic gains for Republicans across the political landscape. They swept away dozens of incumbent Democrats in the House, made modest gains in the Senate, and emerged with much greater control of state governorships.

As the results rolled in on November 2, Democrats were not only shocked by the anger toward their candidates and president, but by the range of victories across the country. Republicans won more than sixty seats in the House, which was more than enough to recapture the majority they lost in 2006. Republicans also gained at least six seats in the Senate, which was still short of a majority, but enough to give them greater power in setting the agenda for the coming two years.

Republicans also gained at least eleven governorships, which gave them almost two-thirds of the key posts that will be so heavily involved in redistricting House seats in their states. Redistricting has already been scheduled in the wake of the 2010 census. Although state legislatures make the first decisions on where to draw the district lines, governors will have great influence in shaping the boundaries that will affect elections over the next decade.

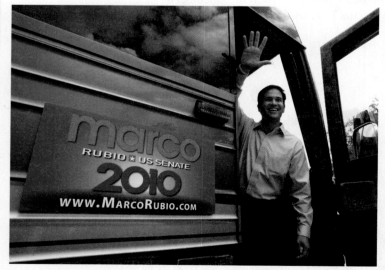

Conservative Republican Marco Rubio won a three-way way race for the Senate in Florida, easily defeating once seemingly unbeatable Republican Governor Charlie Christ, who ran as an independent after Rubio defeated him in the Republican primary. Rubio is a national leader in the Tea Party movement. ■ *What does Rubio's election signal about where Florida's electoral votes might go in the 2012 presidential election?*

Of the People

Members of Congress

Although the Constitution does not mention race, gender, or wealth among the qualifications for office, the framers expected members of Congress to be white male property owners. After all, women, slaves, and freed slaves could not vote, let alone hold office.

The framers would therefore be surprised at the face of Congress today. Recent Congresses have had record numbers of women and minorities. In 2008, New Hampshire's new Democratic senator Jeanne Shaheen became the 17th woman in the current Senate. All totaled, 95 women served in the 111th Congress, a record number.

[Hold for update]

These numbers would not have increased without the rise of a new generation of women and minority candidates. Although voting participation by women and minority groups has increased dramatically throughout the past half-century, it took time for women and minority candidates to gain the experience to increase the odds of their winning office.

Although Congress is becoming more diverse by race and gender, it still remains very different from the rest of the United States in income and occupation. Nearly one-third of the senators who served in the 111th Congress are millionaires, and more than half hold law degrees. At the current rate of change in the number of women, for example, it will take another 400 years before women constitute a majority in the House.

CRITICAL THINKING QUESTIONS

1. How does increasing diversity change the issues that Congress works on? Should Congress reflect the levels of diversity in the U.S. population in order to best represent our citizenry?

2. Does increasing diversity help strengthen public approval of Congress?

3. Did the election of Nancy Pelosi as Speaker of the House make any difference in the power of the office or the overall performance of Congress?

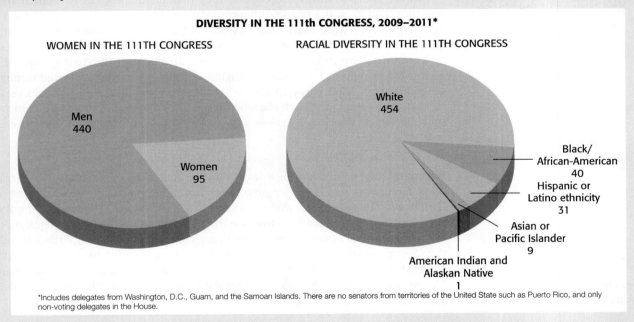

DIVERSITY IN THE 111th CONGRESS, 2009–2011*

WOMEN IN THE 111TH CONGRESS

Men 440
Women 95

RACIAL DIVERSITY IN THE 111TH CONGRESS

White 454
Black/African-American 40
Hispanic or Latino ethnicity 31
Asian or Pacific Islander 9
American Indian and Alaskan Native 1

*Includes delegates from Washington, D.C., Guam, and the Samoan Islands. There are no senators from territories of the United State such as Puerto Rico, and only non-voting delegates in the House.

SOURCE: Rutgers University, Eagleton Institute of Politics, Center for American Women and Politics, November 2008; updated by the authors.

The 2010 election involved record amounts of campaign spending, and the rise of a new corps of anti-government candidates who ran with the endorsement of the Tea Party, a highly conservative wing of the Republican Party. Although many Tea Party candidates were defeated in Republican primaries, their pressure for a radical turn toward more conservative policies resonated throughout the campaign. Many of the independents that had supported President Barack Obama in 2008 turned toward the Republicans in 2010.

The election was broadly interpreted as a rejection of the Obama administration's health bill, but also involved an angry reaction to the continued economic woes following the 2008 banking failures, economic collapse, and rising unemployment. The economy was the number one issue listed by voters in explaining their vote. But they were also angry at "business-as-usual" in Washington. Many were disgusted by the polarization in Congress and the failure to push the economy forward.

The president's party almost always loses seats during midterm elections, but rarely loses its majority. The 2010 midterms was only the third time since the end of World War II that Republicans were able to take the House majority from a Democratic president—the first was in 1946 and the second in 1994. With government under divided control, both parties began preparing for a tough election battle in 2012.

With divided control in Congress, Washington girded for stalemate on a host of issues. Republicans promised to repeal the new health care bill, cut government spending by 20 percent, and investigate waste in the economic stimulus package. There was little talk about working together across the party lines, suggesting that the 2012 election would involve more anger. However, Republicans were reminded that Democrats kept the presidency in both 1948 and 1996, suggesting that they need to do more than simply obstruct the president in order to win the presidency.

The Structure and Powers of Congress

LEARNING OBJECTIVE

11.2 Differentiate the powers of Congress, and compare and contrast the structure and powers of the House and Senate.

The framers expected that Congress, not the president or the courts, would be the most important branch of government, which is why it is defined in Article I, Section 1 of the Constitution. Hence, they worried most about how to keep Congress from dominating the other branches.

In an effort to control Congress, they divided the legislative branch into two separate chambers, the House of Representatives and the Senate, which would "be as little connected with each other as the nature of their common functions and their common dependence on the society will admit."[6] Not only would House members and senators have different terms of office and represent different groups of voters (districts versus states), the framers originally wanted them to be selected through very different means (House by popular election and the Senate by state legislatures).

The framers allowed each chamber to set its own rules. Because it is so much larger than the Senate, the House has less time allowed for debate and more rules governing it.

A Divided Branch

Bicameralism, or a two-house legislature, remains the most important organizational feature of the U.S. Congress. Each chamber meets in its own wing of the Capitol Building; each has offices for its members on separate sides of Capitol Street; each has its own committee structure, its own rules for considering legislation, and its own record of proceedings (even though the records are published together as the *Congressional Record*); and each sets the rules governing its own members (each establishes its own legislative committees, for example).[7] As James Madison explained in *The Federalist,* No. 51, "In order to control the legislative authority, you must divide it." (*The Federalist,* No. 51, is reprinted in the Appendix at the back of this book.)

bicameralism
The principle of a two-house legislature.

In the late 1970s, a handful of women members of the House created the Women's Caucus as a forum for discussing issues of concern to women. In the mid-1990s, the caucus was renamed the Caucus for Women's Issues and male members of the House were admitted. A history of women in Congress can be found at womenincongress.house.gov. ■ *Why do you think women still only make up about eighteen percent of Congress today?*

The Powers of Congress

The framers gave Congress a long list of express or **enumerated powers.** Because the Revolutionary War had been sparked by unfair taxation, the power "to lay and collect Taxes" was the very first of these powers. Another 17 express powers of Congress fall into five basic categories:

1. **The Power to Raise, Make, and Borrow Money.** Congress has the power to tax, borrow money, issue currency, and coin money.
2. **The Power to Regulate Commerce.** Congress has the power to regulate commerce between the United States and other nations, as well as between the states. It can also set standards for determining the value of products through weights and measures, establish uniform bankruptcy laws that govern private businesses, and promote the arts and sciences by granting copyright protection to authors and patents to inventors.
3. **The Power to Unify and Expand the Country.** Congress has the power to create post offices and postal roads, which link the states together; to determine the rules for becoming a citizen; and to acquire, manage, and dispose of federal land.
4. **The Power to Prepare and Declare War.** Alongside the power to declare war, Congress can raise, support, and regulate armies and a navy; provide for organizing, arming, disciplining, and calling on state militia (now called the National Guard); execute laws suppressing civil unrest; and repel foreign invasions.
5. **The Power to Create the Federal Judiciary.** Congress is responsible for creating all "inferior" courts below the Supreme Court and for determining their jurisdiction, as well as the appellate jurisdiction of the Supreme Court (discussed in Chapter 14).

Many of these powers are limited in some way, however. Congress has the power to collect taxes only for the common defense and general welfare of the nation, for example, and may not tax exports to other nations. Similarly, it may declare war, but only the president has the power to command the military.

The framers also gave Congress implied powers such as the power to "make all Laws which shall be necessary and proper for carrying into Execution the foregoing Powers, and all other Powers vested by this Constitution in the Government of the United States, or in any Department or Officer thereof."

Finally, the Constitution gave Congress important checks on government, including the power to remove the president and judges from office through the impeachment process. The House has the authority to charge, or impeach, a president or judge for committing "high crimes and misdemeanors," but the Senate has the responsibility to conduct the trial to determine guilt or innocence. Impeachment requires a majority vote in the House, but conviction requires a two-thirds vote of the Senate.

The Constitution gives different duties to each chamber (see Table 11–1). The Senate has the power to give its advice and consent in confirming or rejecting the president's nominees for senior executive branch positions and for the federal courts. The Senate also has the power to give its advice and consent in approving or rejecting treaties made by the president. All treaties must be ratified by a two-thirds vote in the Senate before they can be enforced by the president.

The House has its own responsibilities, too, most notably the power to author "all bills for raising revenues." But these powers are less significant than those given to the Senate, in part because the framers worried that House members would be too close to the people and therefore more likely to act in haste. Although all revenue bills must originate in the House, for example, the Constitution invites the Senate to propose amendments to revenue bills, even to the point of changing everything except the title.

Legislatures Around the World

Although the U.S. Congress is well known in other countries, Britain's parliament is the most visible legislature in the world. It is composed of two houses—the House of Commons, which is elected by the citizenry, and the House of Lords, which includes some individuals who have been given a lifelong title for achievement. Because the House of Lords has no durable legislative function beyond making small amendments in legislation, the British parliament is not considered a bicameral legislature.

enumerated powers
The powers explicitly given to Congress in the Constitution.

Alcee Hastings was one of only seven federal judges ever impeached and removed from office by Congress. He was impeached for corruption by the House in 1988 and removed by the Senate in 1989. Hastings was elected to the House in Florida's 23rd district in 1992, and continues to serve as a member of Congress today. ■ *Why is impeachment of judges and presidents so rare?*

TABLE 11–1 Differences Between the House of Representatives and the Senate

House	Senate
SIZE	**SIZE**
435 members	100 Members
ELECTIONS	**ELECTIONS**
Two-year term	Six-year term
All seats are open for election	One-third of seats are open for each election
Elected in districts	Elected in states
LEADERSHIP	**LEADERSHIP**
Strong leadership controls action by individual members	Weaker leadership provides more freedom to individual members
More powerful committee leaders	More equal distribution of power among committee members
LEGISLATION	**LEGISLATION**
Decision to consider legislation made by majority	Decision to consider legislation made by unanimous consent of all members; one senator can stop action
Responsible for moving first on raising revenues	Responsible for giving advice and consent on presidential appointees and treaties
All amendments to legislation must be approved for consideration in advance of legislative action	Amendments are generally allowed
DEBATE	**DEBATE**
Strict limits on debate	Flexible limits on debate approved by unanimous consent
Single member or group of members cannot stop debate once the bill is approved for action by the Rules Committee	Single member can stop action through the filibuster

■ *How are the rules for debate in the House and Senate related to their relative sizes and traditions?*

China has two legislatures, one controlled by the Communist Party and the other elected by the people for five-year terms. The People's Congress meets once a year and has up to 3,000 members. Although it has great formal powers, it yields to the party committees. Nevertheless, it has been asserting more power in recent years.

India has a parliamentary system, in no small measure because it was colonized by Britain. Its parliament has two chambers—the Lok Sabha (the House of the People) and Rajya Sabha (the Council of States). In recent years, the Council of States has become more influential to the point that the Indian system is bordering on a true bicameral legislature.

Mexico's legislature is one of the strongest in the world, at least in theory. Like the U.S. Congress, it is the first branch listed in the Mexican constitution. Like the U.S. Congress, too, it has two houses, both elected by the citizenry.

Congressional Leadership and Committees

LEARNING OBJECTIVE

11.3 Compare and contrast the leadership systems used in the House and Senate, and explain how work is done through congressional committees.

Given the differences between the chambers that are summarized in Table 11–1, we should not be surprised that the House and Senate have different kinds of leadership and rules. Whereas the House holds tight control over its large number of members, the Senate has much looser controls. This makes legislation easier to pass in the House and much more difficult in the Senate.

Leading the House of Representatives

The organization and procedures in the House are different from those in the Senate, largely because the House is more than four times as large as the Senate. A larger membership requires more rules, which means that *how* things are done affects *what* is done.

For the People

GOVERNMENT'S GREATEST ENDEAVORS

Building a Strong Defense

The United States spends more money on defense than any other nation in the world. In 2010 alone, the nation will spend more than $500 billion on defense. The Department of Defense, which houses all the military services, has invested heavily in sophisticated technologies that make the nation almost impossible to defeat in war. It is not clear, however, that these technologies assure that the nation can win a war against the kind of deeply committed insurgents now fighting in Iraq and Afghanistan.

Presidents support a strong national defense, but Congress is responsible for authorizing the spending. Defense spending is spread across most of the states, and many congressional districts and congressional incumbents eagerly seek spending in their districts. The interests of the nation and individual members of Congress can align, as when Senator Bayh (D-Ind.), discussed in the opener, helped push an amendment through Congress to provide more armored Humvees for the soldiers in Iraq. The troops needed the equipment, and Bayh secured a lucrative manufacturing contract for a plant in Indiana.

The military continues to work on new technologies that may make soldiers safer on the battlefield. Troops can now use drones to launch long-range attacks against targets, and they have a variety of high-technology tools to survey the battlefield. Nevertheless, the military has been highly susceptible to the unsophisticated improvised explosive devices used in Iraq and Afghanistan, suggesting that strengthening our defense still needs to be a top priority.

Congress has invested heavily in advanced warfighting technology such as pilotless predator drones. These remotely controlled aircraft have been used frequently in the Afghanistan War.

CRITICAL THINKING QUESTIONS

1. Why do many members of Congress support high levels of defense spending?

2. Does the military buy the right equipment or the equipment that is right for political support?

3. How does U.S. defense spending affect global views of our nation?

The Speaker of the House Again because of its size, the House gives its leaders more power than the Senate, where individual senators have more power to refuse to act at all. The most powerful leader on Capitol Hill is the **Speaker** of the House.[8] Although the Speaker is formally elected by the entire House, the post is always filled by the majority party, which gives the party even more power. The Speaker has the power to recognize members who rise to speak, rule on questions of parliamentary procedure, and

Speaker
The presiding officer in the House of Representatives, formally elected by the House but actually selected by the majority party.

Because its membership is so much larger than the Senate, the House uses an electronic voting board above the balcony to keep track of member votes. The Senate still uses voice votes recorded by the clerk of the Senate. ■ *What are some of the challenges that the House faces more acutely than the Senate because of its size?*

How the World Views the United Nations

The past half century has produced a long list of international organizations, such as the World Trade Organization, that are designed to encourage greater trade and economic coordination. In some ways, these organizations behave like a blend of legislatures and courts—they take votes on key issues and often impose penalties on nations that violate international rules.

The United Nations (U.N.) is the most visible of these international legislatures. With more than 190 member nations, the United Nations often makes decisions on war and peace, addresses international health, and draws on its members for its own peacekeeping forces that seek to maintain stability in war-torn countries. The United Nations has a general voting assembly of all members and a powerful Security Council that can veto action from the General Assembly. In a sense, the General Assembly is the legislature.

The world has different opinions on whether this "super-government" works. According to the Pew Global Survey, support for the United Nations has increased slightly throughout the past five years.

The Japanese remain skeptical of the United Nations, perhaps because their nation is not a permanent member of the Security Council. Moreover, Japan receives relatively little support from the United Nations' health programs and has been reluctant to contribute troops to U.N. peacekeeping forces.

CRITICAL THINKING QUESTIONS

1. In our sample of countries, people in Nigeria and Mexico have the most favorable opinions of the United Nations. Why might that be?

2. Why might Japan's not being a permanent member of the Security Council affect public opinion in Japan toward the United Nations?

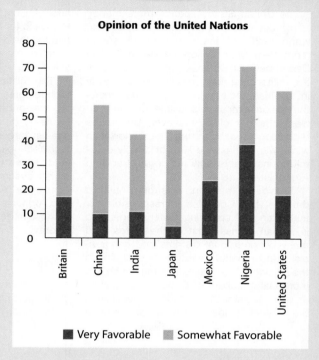

Opinion of the United Nations

Britain, China, India, Japan, Mexico, Nigeria, United States

■ Very Favorable   ■ Somewhat Favorable

---

party caucus
A meeting of the members of a party in a legislative chamber to select party leaders and to develop party policy. Called a *conference* by the Republicans.

majority leader
The legislative leader selected by the majority party who helps plan party strategy, confers with other party leaders, and tries to keep members of the party in line.

minority leader
The legislative leader selected by the minority party as spokesperson for the opposition.

whip
The party leader who is the liaison between the leadership and the rank-and-file in the legislature.

closed rule
A procedural rule in the House of Representatives that prohibits any amendments to bills or provides that only members of the committee reporting the bill may offer amendments.

appoint members to temporary committees (but not to the major committees that help make the laws).

The Speaker is usually selected on a vote by the majority **party caucus,** called *the party conference* by Republicans, which is all of the members of a party in the legislative chamber. The caucus also elects party officers and committee chairs, approves committee assignments, and often helps the Speaker decide which issues will come first on the legislative calendar. However, because the Speaker is always selected first, he or she has the most important voice in determining all these choices.

Other House Officers   The Speaker is assisted by the **majority leader,** who helps plan party strategy, confers with other party leaders, and tries to keep members of the party in line. The minority party elects the **minority leader,** who usually becomes Speaker when his or her party gains a majority in the House. (These positions are also sometimes called majority and minority *floor leaders.*) Assisting each floor leader are the party **whips.**

The House Rules Committee   The House Rules Committee is almost certainly the most powerful committee in either chamber. Under the much tighter rules that govern the larger House, the Rules Committee decides the rules governing the length of the floor debate on any legislative issue and sets limits on the number and kinds of floor amendments that will be allowed. By refusing to grant a *rule,* which is a ticket to the floor, the Rules Committee can delay consideration of a bill. A **closed rule** prohibits amendments altogether or provides that only members of the committee reporting the bill may offer amendments; closed rules are usually reserved for tax and spending bills. An **open rule** permits debate within the overall time allocated to the bill.

Leading the Senate

The Senate has the same basic committee structure, elected party leadership, and decentralized power as the House, but because the Senate is a smaller body, its procedures are more informal, and it permits more time for debate. It is a more open, fluid, and decentralized body now than it was a generation or two ago. Indeed, it is often said that the Senate has 100 separate power centers and is so splintered that party leaders have difficulty arranging the day-to-day schedule.[9]

The Senate is led by the Senate majority leader, who is elected by the majority party. When the majority leader is from the president's party, the president becomes the party's most visible leader on Capitol Hill and in the nation as a whole. However, when the majority leader and the president are from different parties, the Senate majority leader is considered his or her party's national spokesperson. Senator Harry Reid (D-Nev.) was elected as the current Senate majority leader in 2007 after Democrats persuaded the two Independents to help create a majority. Although that majority grew to 60 votes in 2009, it dropped to just a handful of seats after the 2010 midterm elections. Reid barely retained his seat after a tough reelection campaign against a well-financed opponent.

Although the majority leader has great authority, Senate floor debate is actually led by a **president pro tempore,** usually the most senior member of the majority party. Presiding over the Senate on most occasions is a thankless chore, so the president pro tempore regularly delegates this responsibility to junior members of the chamber's majority party. During controversial debates when there might be a tie vote, the vice president plays this role.

Party machinery in the Senate is similar to that in the House. There are party caucuses (conferences), majority and minority floor leaders, and party whips. Each party has a *policy committee,* composed of party leaders, which is theoretically responsible for the party's overall legislative program. In the Senate, the party policy committees help the leadership monitor legislation and provide policy expertise. Moreover, the Senate's rules allow individual senators to offer amendments on virtually any topic to a pending bill, occasionally allowing them to delay passage of a bill long enough to prevent passage.[10]

Individual senators also have the power to engage in unlimited debate, known as the **filibuster,** which was invented in the 1830s. A filibuster allows any individual senator to delay Senate proceedings by holding the floor continuously, thereby preventing action. Filibusters often begin with an individual senator issuing a legislative hold, putting a stop to all action. At one time, the filibuster was a favorite weapon of southern senators for blocking civil rights legislation.

A filibuster can be ended by invoking **cloture.** The rule specifies that the question of curtailing debate must be put to a vote two days after 16 senators sign a petition asking for cloture. If three-fifths of senators (60 of the 100 members) vote in favor of cloture, no senator may speak on the measure under consideration for more than one hour. Once invoked, cloture requires that the final vote on the measure be taken after no more than 30 hours of debate.[11]

open rule
A procedural rule in the House of Representatives that permits floor amendments within the overall time allocated to the bill.

president pro tempore
An officer of the Senate selected by the majority party to act as chair in the absence of the vice president.

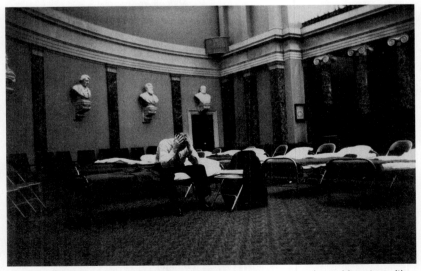

Old-fashioned filibusters went through the night. Here, a senator sits on his cot awaiting action to break a filibuster on the Civil Rights Act. Today, the threat alone of a filibuster can require that legislation has a supermajority in order to pass.

filibuster
A procedural practice in the Senate whereby a senator refuses to relinquish the floor and thereby delays proceedings and prevents a vote on a controversial issue.

cloture
A procedure for terminating debate, especially filibusters, in the Senate.

standing committee
A permanent committee established in a legislature, usually focusing on a policy area.

special or select committee
A congressional committee created for a specific purpose, sometimes to conduct an investigation.

joint committee
A committee composed of members of both the House of Representatives and the Senate; such committees oversee the Library of Congress and conduct investigations.

Congressional Committees

Committees are the workhorses of Congress. They draft legislation, review nominees, conduct investigations of executive branch departments and agencies, and are usually responsible for ironing out differences between House and Senate versions of the same legislation.

Types of Committees In theory, all congressional committees are created anew in each new Congress. But most continue with little change from Congress to Congress. **Standing committees** are the most durable and are the sources of most bills, whereas **special** or **select committees** come together to address both short-term and long-term issues such as investigating the September 11th terrorist attacks, but they rarely author legislation. **Joint committees** have members from both the House and the Senate and exist either to study an issue of interest to the entire Congress or to oversee congressional support agencies such as the Governmental Accountability Office (www.gao.gov).

Of the various types of committees, standing committees are the most important for making laws and representing constituents, and they fall into six types: (1) rules and administration, (2) budget, (3) authorizing, (4) appropriations, (5) revenue, and (6) oversight. (See Table 11–2.)

1. Rules and Administration Committees Rules committees in both chambers determine the basic operations of their chamber—for example, how many staffers individual members get and what the ratio of majority to minority members and staff will be. Again, because of the number of members it must control, the House Rules Committee is more powerful than its twin in the Senate. As noted earlier, the House Rules Committee has special responsibility

TABLE 11–2 Congressional Standing Committees, 2010–2011

House	Senate
RULES COMMITTEES	**RULES COMMITTEE**
House Administration	Rules and Administration
Rules	
Standards of Official Conduct	
BUDGET COMMITTEE	**BUDGET COMMITTEE**
Budget	Budget
AUTHORIZING COMMITTEES	**AUTHORIZING COMMITTEES**
Agriculture	Agriculture, Nutrition, and Forestry
Armed Services	Armed Services
Education and Labor	Banking, Housing, and Urban Affairs
Energy and Commerce	Commerce, Science, and Transportation
Financial Services	Energy and Natural Resources
Foreign Affairs	Environment and Public Works
Homeland Security	Foreign Affairs
Judiciary	Health, Education, Labor, and Pensions
Natural Resources	Judiciary
Science and Technology	Small Business and Entrepreneurship
Small Business	Veterans Affairs
Transportation and Infrastructure	
Veterans Affairs	
APPROPRIATIONS COMMITTEE	**APPROPRIATIONS COMMITTEE**
Appropriations	Appropriations
REVENUE COMMITTEES	**REVENUE COMMITTEES**
Budget	Budget
Ways and Means (Revenue and Budget)	Finance
OVERSIGHT COMMITTEES	**OVERSIGHT COMMITTEES**
Oversight and Government Reform	Homeland Security and Governmental Affairs

for giving each bill a rule, or ticket, to the floor of the House and determines what, if any, amendments to a bill will be permitted and how long the bill can be debated.

2. *Budget Committees*   There is one budget committee for the House and Senate each. They were created as permanent standing committees in 1974 to give each chamber greater information and discipline on the overall federal budget. They set broad targets for spending and taxes at the start of each session of Congress and push authorizing and appropriations committees to follow those guidelines as they work on legislation. In theory, everything that the House and Senate do with the budget must be reconciled against the targets that the budget committees set.

3. *Authorizing Committees*   Authorizing committees pass the laws that tell government what to do. The House and Senate education and labor committees, for example, are responsible for setting rules governing the federal government's student loan programs, including who can apply, how much they can get, where the loans come from, and how defaults are handled. Authorizing committees are also responsible for reviewing past programs that are about to expire. In the Senate, they also hold confirmation hearings for the president's political appointees.

4. *Appropriations Committees*   Appropriations committees make decisions about how much money government will spend on authorized programs. Although there is only one appropriations committee in each chamber, each appropriations committee has one subcommittee for each of the 13 appropriations bills that must be enacted each year to keep government running.

5. *Revenue Committees*   Revenue and budget committees deal with raising the money appropriating committees spend. Because it exists to raise revenues through taxes, the House Ways and Means Committee is one of the most powerful committee in Congress, for it both raises and authorizes spending. Although the appropriations committee determines how much is spent on specific programs, the Ways and Means Committee in the only committee in either chamber that can originate tax and revenue legislation. It is also responsible for making basic decisions on the huge Social Security and Medicare programs.

6. *General Oversight Committees*   There are two major oversight committees in Congress: the House Oversight and Government Reform Committee and the Senate Homeland Security and Governmental Affairs Committee. Both committees have wide latitude to investigate the performance of government. They are also free to authorize programs for fixing government-wide programs. The oversight committees do not generally have authority to authorize such reforms for individual departments and agencies of government, however. This responsibility belongs to the specific authorizing committee responsible for the individual department or agency.

Choosing Committee Members   Each political party controls the selection of standing committee members. Because some committees are more prestigious than others, the debate over committee assignments can be intense. These committees control more important programs or more money and give their members important advantages in helping their home districts.

Each chamber and party is responsible for choosing committee members. In the House, Republicans choose their committee members through their Committee on Committees, which is composed of one member from each state that has Republican representation in the House, whereas Democrats choose their committee members through their Steering and Policy Committee. In turn, Senate Republicans and Democrats both use their Steering Committees to make assignments. Both chambers make their selections based on an applicant's preferences, talent and party loyalty, and the needs of their district or state.

Most committee chairs are selected on the basis of the **seniority rule;** the member of the majority party with the longest continuous service on the committee becomes chair on the retirement of the current chair or a change in the party in control of Congress. The seniority rule lessens the influence of states or districts where the two parties are more evenly matched and where there is more turnover.[12]

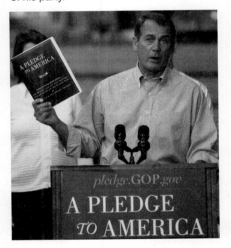

Nancy Pelosi (above), Speaker of the House since 2007, lost her position as a result of the 2010 elections in which Republicans won more than enough seats to take over the majority. The new Speaker of the House is Ohio Republican John Boehner (below), a much more conservative member of his party.

seniority rule
A legislative practice that assigns the chair of a committee or subcommittee to the member of the majority party with the longest continuous service on the committee.

Members of the Black Caucus often meet to decide what its members should do on particular issues. ■ *What are some of the advantages for members of Congress of organizing into caucuses based on shared interests?*

The choice of a committee chair in either chamber can make a very big difference on policy. Having decided not to run for reelection in 2010, Senate Banking Committee Chairman Chris Dodd (D-Conn.) turned over his chairmanship to Tim Johnson (D-S.D.). Dodd had been a passionate advocate of banking reform designed to protect consumers from credit card abuses. In contrast, Johnson was the only Democrat in the Senate to vote against Dodd's 2009 legislation to stop unreasonable credit-card interest rates. South Dakota is home to many of the nation's largest credit card companies, most notably CitiBank, so Johnson will likely take the Banking Committee in a very different direction as long as Democrats control the Senate.

The Special Role of Conference Committees Given the differences between the House and the Senate, it is not surprising that the version of a bill passed by one chamber may differ substantially from the version passed by the other. Only if both houses pass an absolutely identical measure can it become law. Most of the time, one house accepts the language of the other, but approximately 10–12 percent of all bills passed, usually major ones, must be referred to a **conference committee**—a special committee of members from each chamber that settles the differences between versions.[13] Both parties are represented on conference committees, but the majority party has more members.

Caucuses Caucuses are best defined as informal committees that allow individual members to promote shared legislative interests. There are caucuses for House members only, for senators only, and for members of both chambers together.[14]

How a Bill Becomes a Law

LEARNING **OBJECTIVE**

11.4 Identify the steps by which a bill becomes a law and the ways a bill can be stopped at each step.

Congress operates under a system of multiple vetoes. The framers intentionally dispersed powers so that no would-be tyrant or majority could accumulate enough authority to oppress the nation. Follow a bill through the legislative process, and there are dozens of ways it can be killed. Only approximately one out of ten bills even receives minimal attention. In 2010, members of Congress introduced more than 1,500 bills but passed less than 300.[15]

How Ideas Become Bills

Most members come to Washington to make a difference for their party and country. Members of Congress clearly care about national issues such as education, energy, the economy, and foreign policy. In choosing ideas for legislation, they often secure their reputations as leading thinkers far into the future. Fifteen years after leaving the Senate, David L. Boren continues to provide national leadership as president of the University of Oklahoma and is often called upon for advice on difficult issues.

How Bills Become Laws

A bill must win many small contests on the way to final passage. There are four broad steps from beginning to end: (1) introduction, which means putting a formal proposal before the House or the Senate; (2) committee review, which includes holding a hearing and "marking up" the bill; (3) floor debate and passage, which means getting on the legislative calendar, passing once in each chamber, surviving a conference to iron out any differences between the House and Senate versions, and passing once again in each chamber; and (4) presidential approval. These steps are summarized in Figure 11–2: How a Bill Becomes a Law.

Introducing a Bill House members introduce a bill by placing it into a mahogany box (called the *hopper*) on a desk at the front of the House chamber; senators introduce a bill by

conference committee
A committee appointed by the presiding officers of each chamber to adjust differences on a particular bill passed by each in different form.

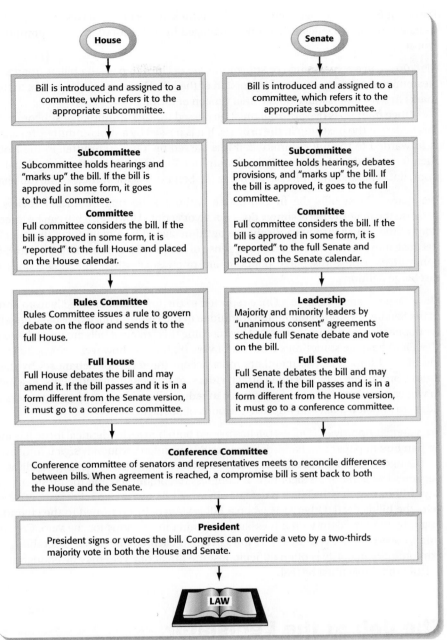

FIGURE 11–2 How a Bill Becomes a Law. ■ *Analyzing this legislative process, why is it so much easier for a bill to be killed than passed?*

either handing it to the clerk of the Senate or by presenting it to their colleagues in a floor speech. In the more informal Senate, members sometimes short-circuit the formalities by offering a bill as an amendment to pending legislation. A bill that comes from the House is always designated H.R. (House of Representatives) followed by its number, and a bill from the Senate is always designated S. (Senate) followed by its number. Presidents have no authority to introduce legislation, although they recommend many proposals.

Committee Review   Once a bill has been introduced in either chamber, it is read into the record as a formal proposal and referred to the appropriate committee—tax bills to Ways and Means or Finance; farm bills to Agriculture; technology bills to Science, Space, and Technology; small business to Small Business; and so forth. The parliamentarian in each chamber decides where to send each bill.

The Referral Decision   Although most bills are referred to a single committee, particularly complex bills may be referred simultaneously or sequentially to multiple committees.

President Bush's proposed Department of Homeland Security bill was so complicated and touched so many agencies that it was managed by a temporary special committee in the House.

Markup   Once a committee or subcommittee decides to pass the bill, it "marks it up" to clean up the wording or amend its version of the bill. The term *markup* refers to the pencil marks that members make on the final version of the bill.

Once markup is over, the bill must be passed by the committee or subcommittee and forwarded to the next step in the process. If it is passed by a subcommittee, for example, it is forwarded to the full committee; if it is passed by a full committee in the House, it is then forwarded to the House Rules Committee for a rule that will govern debate on the floor; if it is passed by a full committee in the Senate, it is forwarded to the full chamber.

Discharge   Most bills die in committee without a hearing or further review, largely because the majority party simply does not favor action. However, a bill can be forced to the floor of the House through a **discharge petition** signed by a majority of the membership. Because most members share a strong sense of reciprocity, or mutual respect toward other committees, House discharge petitions are rarely successful. The Senate does not use discharge petitions.

Floor Debate and Passage   Once reported to the full chamber directly from committee in the Senate or through the Rules Committee in the House, a bill will usually be scheduled for floor action or dropped entirely. Having come this far, most bills are passed into law.

Final passage sometimes comes at a very high price, however, especially for spending bills. Although House members must accept the terms of debate set by the House Rules Committee, senators often attach **riders,** or unrelated amendments, to a bill, either to win concessions from the sponsors or to reduce the odds of passage. Sponsors can use riders to sweeten a bill and improve the odds of passage.

Presidential Approval   Once a bill has passed both houses in identical form, it is inscribed on parchment paper and hand-delivered to the president, who may *sign* it into law or *veto* it. If Congress is in session and the president waits ten days (not counting Sundays), the bill becomes law *without* his signature. If Congress has adjourned and the president waits ten days without signing the bill, it is defeated by what is known as a **pocket veto.** After a pocket veto, the bill is dead. Otherwise, when a bill is vetoed, it is returned to the chamber of its origin by the president with a message explaining the reasons for the veto. Congress can vote to **override** the veto by a two-thirds vote in each chamber, but assembling such an extraordinary majority is often difficult. Just the threat of a veto may be enough to derail a bill, but the threat must be real.

discharge petition

A petition that, if signed by a majority of the members of the House of Representatives, will pry a bill from committee and bring it to the floor for consideration.

rider

A provision attached to a bill—to which it may or may not be related—in order to secure its passage or defeat.

pocket veto

A veto exercised by the president after Congress has adjourned; if the president takes no action for ten days, the bill does not become law and is not returned to Congress for a possible override.

override

An action taken by Congress to reverse a presidential veto, requiring a two-thirds majority in each chamber.

The Job of the Legislator

LEARNING OBJECTIVE

11.5 Characterize the two ways legislators represent their constituents, and identify the various influences on their votes.

Membership in Congress was once a part-time job. Legislators came to Washington for a few terms, averaged less than five years of continuous service, and returned to private life. Pay was low, and Washington was no farther than a carriage ride from home.[16]

Congress started to meet more frequently in the late 1800s, pay increased, and being a member became increasingly attractive.[17] In the 1850s, roughly half of all House members retired or were defeated at each election; by 1900, the number who left at the end of each term had fallen to roughly one-quarter; by the 1970s, it was barely a tenth. Even in the 1994 congressional elections, when Republicans won the House majority for the first time in 40 years, 90 percent of House incumbents who ran for reelection won.[18]

As members of Congress became attached to their careers, they began to abandon many of the norms, or informal rules, that once guided their behavior in office.[19] The old norms were simple. Members were supposed to specialize in a small number of issues (the norm of specialization), defer to members with longer tenure in office (the norm of seniority), never criticize anyone personally (the norm of courtesy), and wait their turn to speak and introduce legislation (the norm of apprenticeship). As longtime House Speaker

YOU WILL DECIDE: Should Congress Create a College Football Playoff?

Congress had many issues on its agenda in 2010, including health care reform, unemployment, the wars in Iraq and Afghanistan, and global climate change. But as with other congresses in history, it also had time for less important bills. In December 2009, Representative Joe Barton (R-Tex.) introduced a bill to require the National Collegiate Athletic Conference to create a national football playoff.

Barton was incensed that the undefeated Texas Christian University football team, champion of the Mountain West Conference, had been excluded from the Bowl Championship Series (BCS) championship game in 2009. He was supported by members of the Western Athletic Conference, which was incensed that Boise State had been excluded in 2009, too.

Barton's bill was quite simple. It prohibited any person to promote, market, or advertise a post-season NCAA Division I football bowl game as a championship or national championship game unless it was the final game of a single elimination post-season playoff system for which *all* NCAA Division I schools are eligible. Using the Federal Trade Commission Act as the enforcement tool, the bill would subject the BCS to stiff penalties if it continued to advertise or otherwise promote its final game as a championship. In HR 390, "College Football Playoff Act", Congress found that college football games involve and affect interstate commerce, and therefore Congress had the constitutional power to act on the issue, and the economic reasons to protect non-BCS schools.

What do you think? Should Congress create a college football playoff? What are the arguments for and against this?

THINKING IT THROUGH

Barton was clearly serious about the legislation, as was a newly created political action committee called Playoff PAC, which funded an advertisement supporting a national playoff that aired during halftime of the TCU-Boise State game on Monday, January 4, 2010. (The commercial can be viewed at www.youtube.com/user/Playoff PAC.) Moreover, the public was sympathetic to the proposal. According to a December 2009 Quinnipiac University Poll, 63 percent of Americans approved of a new playoff system.

However, many members of Congress objected to using scarce legislative time for such a seemingly trivial issue. "With all due respect," Representative John Barrow (D-Ga.) told Barton, "I really think we have more important things to spend our time on." As for the public, despite support for a national playoff, nearly half also said that they did not think Congress should resolve the issue.

The case for reform was well made—most pundits and members of Congress appear to want a playoff system. So does President Obama. Just after winning the 2008 presidential election and right before the 2008 BCS that Florida won, Obama said he was in favor of a playoff.

Furthermore, Congress can handle multiple issues, big and small, at the same time, especially because most bills pass with minimal debate or controversy. As Representative Bobby Rush (D-Ill.) said, "We can walk and chew gum at the same time." (Updates on the bill can be found at www.GovTrac.us/Congress. Just enter the bill number in the search field.)

Critical Thinking Questions

1. Should Congress take on issues such a national college playoff game and steroid abuse by baseball players?
2. Does the playoff bill help or hurt Congress's reputation among the American public?
3. Should the president have made any comments on the bill? Does his support increase the chances of eventual passage?

SOURCE: ESPN.com, "Subcommittee OKs College Playoff Bill," December 9, 2009, accessible at http://sports.espn.go.com/espn/print?id=4727426&type=story.

Sam Rayburn once said, new members were to go along in order to get along, and to be seen and not heard.

Legislators as Representatives

Congress has a split personality. On the one hand, it is a *lawmaking institution* that writes laws and makes policy for the entire nation. In this capacity, all the members are expected to set aside their personal ambitions and perhaps even the concerns of their own constituencies.

Individual members of Congress perceive their roles differently. Some believe they should serve as **delegates** from their districts, finding out what "the folks back home" want and acting accordingly. The word "delegate" refers to a member who tries to do what constituents want. Other members see themselves as **trustees** to act and vote according to their own view of what is best for their district and state, and the nation. The word refers to a member who acts on what he or she thinks is best for the district and country.

delegate
An official who is expected to represent the views of his or her constituents even when personally holding different views; one interpretation of the role of the legislator.

trustee
An official who is expected to vote independently based on his or her judgment of the circumstances; one interpretation of the role of the legislator.

Former Oklahoma Senator David Boren (D) at work in the Senate. Future Secretary of Defense Robert Gates and Senator Robert Dole sit to his right. Boren retired in 1994 and currently serves as the co-chairman of the President's Intelligence Advisory Board under Barack Obama.

Most legislators shift back and forth between the delegate and trustee roles, depending on their perception of the public interest, their standing in the last and next elections, and the pressures of the moment. Most also view themselves more as free agents than as instructed delegates for their districts. And recent research suggests they often *are* free. Although approximately half of citizens do not know how their representatives voted on major legislation, most still believe their representative voted with the district or state. Moreover, members of Congress spend a great deal of time helping their constituency, reaching out to swing voters, and worrying about how a vote on a controversial issue will "play" back home.[20]

Members cannot represent their constituents through their experiences as ordinary Americans, however. They are certainly very different from the rest of the public. They are older on average, more educated, and less diverse by gender and race. They are also much more likely to be lawyers.

Making Legislative Choices

Approximately 8,000 bills are introduced in the House and Senate during a two-year Congress, but only a handful receive hearings, even fewer reach the floor, and one in eight become law. Although House members and senators cast 1,000 votes each year, most are voice votes on noncontroversial legislation and procedures.[21] Because members pay attention to different factors depending on the bill at hand, they vote on the basis of a long list of varying influences that are presented in alphabetical order below.

Colleagues   Their busy schedules and the great number of votes force legislators to depend on the advice of like-minded colleagues and close friends in Congress. In particular, they look to respected members of the committee who worked on a bill.[22]

A member may also vote with a colleague in the expectation that the colleague will later vote for a measure about which the member is concerned—a practice called **logrolling,** meaning that members trade among themselves to get the legislation (log) moving. Some vote trading takes place to build coalitions so that members can "bring home the bacon" to their constituents. Other vote trading reflects reciprocity in congressional relations or deference to colleagues' superior information or expertise.

logrolling
Mutual aid and vote trading among legislators.

Congressional Staff   The complexity of the issues and increasingly demanding schedules created a demand for additional congressional staff. Because both chambers have roughly equal amounts of money for staff, the 100 senators and their committees have much larger staffs than their 435 House counterparts. Many congressional staffers work in district and state offices back home to create great incumbency advantage.

Constituents   Members of Congress rarely vote against the strong wishes of their constituents, but they often think their constituents are more interested in a particular issue than they really are.[23] Representatives mostly hear from the **attentive public**—meaning citizens who follow public affairs closely—rather than the general public. Members of Congress are generally concerned about how they will explain their votes, especially as election day approaches. Even if only a few voters are aware of their stand on a given issue, this group may make the difference between victory and defeat.

Ideology   Members of Congress are influenced by their own experiences and attitudes about the role of government.[24] Ideology is closely related to a member's party as a predictor of congressional voting.

Party allegiance is not a perfect predictor of ideology. In 1994, for example, moderate and conservative Democrats created the "Blue Dog Coalition" to work for budget cuts and increased defense spending. Members called themselves "blue dogs" because they felt they had been "choked blue" by liberals in their party. By 2009, the coalition had 54 members, including some of the most senior members in the House. The coalition also had enough votes to force major compromises on a long list of legislative proposals, including the economic stimulus package and health care reform.

Interest Groups   Interest groups influence the legislative process in many ways. They make contributions to congressional campaigns, testify before committees, provide information to legislative staff, and build public pressure for or against their cause. Congressional lobbying has existed since the early 1800s and is a perfectly legal exercise of the First Amendment right to petition government (see Chapter 6).

Interest groups often cancel each other out by taking opposing positions on issues, thereby killing a bill. Some of this maneuvering occurs at the subcommittee level and is almost invisible to the public. But it is always visible to the interest groups themselves and to Congress. "The result," says Senator Joe Lieberman (I-Conn.), "is that everyone on Capitol Hill is keeping a close eye on everyone else, creating a self-adjusting system of checks and balances."[25]

attentive public
Citizens who follow public affairs closely.

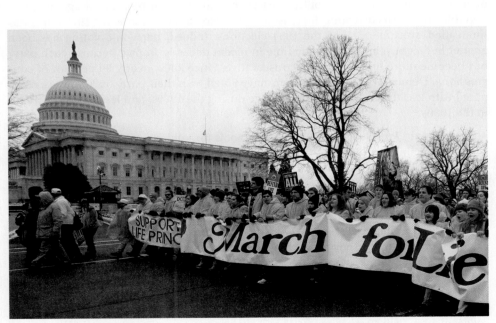

Constituents and interest groups often put pressure on Congress in person. Every January, opponents of abortion march on Washington. ■ *How does this march help citizens express their concerns? Do marches like this matter to congress?*

By the People

Staying in Touch with Congress

There are many ways that citizens can stay connected to Congress and their members, not the least of which are traditional means such as attending town hall meetings, sending letters, and voting.

More recently, however, members have started to use social networks such as Facebook to cultivate support and raise money. Some have even set up Twitter sites to keep their constituents informed on their work. As of January 2010, 19 members of the Senate and 51 members of the House were tweeting regularly with a mix of big and small news. They seem to accept TweetCongress.org's new version of the preamble to the Constitution: "We the Tweeple of the United States, in order to form a more perfect government, establish communication, and promote transparency do hereby tweet the Congress of the United States of America."

Their staffers keep track of the traffic, summarize the tweets, and provide advice on how to reach out more effectively to the kinds of people who tweet or use Facebook. Citizens can make a difference through these new media by commenting on blogs or setting up their own Twitter reviews.

QUESTIONS

1. Is social networking a new form of political participation? How did it affect President Obama's election chances?

2. Is tweeting an effective platform for sharing political ideas?

3. What other forms of social networking can be considered a form of public service? Do blogs qualify? What about Facebook?

Here is what Representative John Carter (R-Tex.) tweeted early in 2010:

R-TX John Carter: New year, same question: where are the jobs? http://ow.ly/Ud41 #jobs #tcot #tlot (via @replynnjenkins)

R-TX John Carter: If you're looking for work in the Austin area: Census Bureau plans to hire 4,000 in Central Texas for 2010 tally. http://shar.es/aQfEk

---

Party Members generally vote with their party. Whether as a result of party pressure or natural affinity, on major bills, most Democrats tend to be arrayed against most Republicans. Partisan voting increased in the House after the early 1970s and has intensified even more since the 1994 elections. Indeed, party-line voting has been greater in recent years than at any time in recent decades, in part because each party has become more liberal or more conservative. Since 2000, nearly 90 percent of congressional Democrats and Republicans have voted with their party on key votes, compared with less than 70 percent on average during the 1970s, and less than 80 percent in the 1980s.[26]

The President Presidents wield a variety of tools for influencing Congress, not least of which is the ability to distribute government resources to their friends. Presidents also help set the legislative agenda through their annual State of the Union Address, the budget, and assorted legislative messages, and they lobby Congress on particularly important issues.

When asked why they vote one way or the other, members of Congress tend to deny the president's influence. Presidents work hard to influence public opinion, and they have a long list of incentives to encourage congressional support, not the least of which are invitations to special White House dinners and federal grants to support key projects back home. Congress is also likely to rally around the president during times of national crisis, which is what helped Barack Obama win 97 percent of the congressional votes on which he took a clear position in 2009, easily besting every president since such scores were first collected more than 40 years ago.[27] (We will return to presidential influence in Congress in Chapter 12.)

Congressional Ethics

Members of Congress have never been under greater scrutiny regarding their conduct, in part because recent years have witnessed a parade of members accused and even convicted of trading their votes for cash and other gifts. "Super-lobbyist" Jack Abramoff admitted in 2006 that he had given several members of Congress free golfing trips, meals, and concert tickets in direct violation of congressional ethics rules.

Under the Constitution, Congress is responsible for punishing its own members. Although individual members are subject to federal prosecution for bribery and other criminal acts, the House and Senate set the more general rules for ethical conduct and investigate all complaints of misbehavior.

Under new rules enacted in September 2007, members of Congress may not accept any gifts or meals from any lobbyist. Although they can accept free admission at large meetings, conventions, discussions, and events where admission is free to other members, they may not accept free travel from any lobbyist.[28]

Finally, members may not accept any payment for making a speech, attending an event, or writing an article. Although they may accept free travel and expenses for making speeches and attending events, such travel must be related to their official duties as a member of Congress and publicly reported. These rules also apply to lobbyists, who may not offer gifts, free attendance, or travel.

The House and Senate enforce the rules through separate ethics committees (the House Committee on Standards of Official Conduct and the Senate Ethics Committee). Because the seats on both committees are equally divided between Democrats and Republicans (four on each side in the House, and three on each side in the Senate), and are filled through the normal committee selection process, members are under tremendous pressure not to hurt their own party.

Citizens can play an important role in monitoring congressional ethics, starting with careful monitoring of lobbying expenditures and campaign contributions. One of the best ways to get this information is from the Center for Responsive Politics, which operates a Web site called opensecrets.org. The Web site contains detailed information on what individual members of Congress spent on their campaigns, where the money came from, and how much they received from political action committees. The Web site also provides information on how much lobbyists spend each year trying to influence Congress. From 1989–2009, for example, AT&T spent more than $44 million lobbying Congress on cell phone issues, and state and local employee unions spent more than $41 million. By calling out their own reprsentatives on campaign spending and lobbying, citizens increase sensitivity to the issue that might lead to tighter regulations.

President Obama journeyed to Capitol Hill to address a joint session of Congress on the need for health care reform. Some Republicans booed the president during the speech, and one, Representative Joe Wilson (R-S.C.) was later reprimanded for shouting "you lie" in response to one of the president's explanations of the legislation. ■ *What are some of the reasons that the State of the Union address is such a good forum for the president to promote his legislative agenda?*

An Assessment of Congress

More than two centuries after its creation, Congress is a larger and very different kind of institution from the one the framers envisioned. It has become much more complex, more divided, and much more active. Although most incumbents are easily reelected, most campaign constantly to stay in office, creating what some observers have called the "permanent campaign." Members appear driven by their desire to win reelection, so that much of what takes place in Congress seems mainly designed to promote reelection. These efforts usually pay off: We have seen that those who seek reelection almost always win.

This *permanent campaign* also affects legislative progress. In an institution in which most members act as individual entrepreneurs, the task of providing institutional

LEARNING **OBJECTIVE**

11.6 Evaluate the influence of citizens in the legislative process.

House Republican majority leader Tom DeLay, otherwise known as "The Hammer," was driven out of office because of his connections to the Abramoff scandals. He later appeared on Dancing with the Stars in an effort to rehabilitate his reputation, but he lost in the early rounds.

leadership is increasingly difficult. With limited resources, and only sometimes aided by the president, congressional leaders are asked to bring together a diverse, fragmented, and independent institution. The congressional system acts only when majorities can be achieved. The framers clearly accomplished their original objective in creating a legislature that would rarely move quickly.

Citizens often complain about the lack of action, which is one reason why public approval of Congress is low. But citizens can play a role in speeding Congress up by demanding action from their own members. Even incumbents worry about losing elections. Indeed, as of late 2009, only 24 percent of Americans had a favorable view of Congress, compared with a 54 percent rating for President Obama. (See Figure 11–3 for the recent trend in public approval for Congress as measured by the NBC News/Wall Street Journal Poll.) By 2010, congressional approval remained at the all-time low.

Much of the public's recent discomfort with Congress involves the intense bargaining and conflict associated with passing major legislation such as health care reform. But in the longer term, it also reflects the performance of the economy. Americans are more favorable toward both Congress and the president when the economy is running smoothly, but they become understandably angry when the economy enters a downturn.

To the extent that citizens engage their members in tough conversations about the need to act on big issues such as health care, their members will listen. But individual citizens can be easily shouted down by organized interests and lobbyists. The question then is how to help citizens become more engaged in a constitutional system that sets checks and balances to stop action. Young Americans have a particular advantage in the effort—they understand the power of social networking.

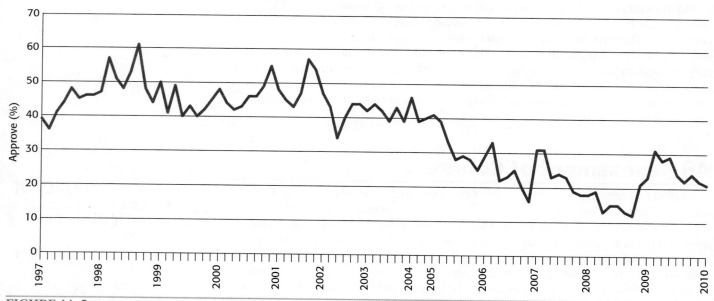

FIGURE 11–3 Favorability Toward Congress, 1997–2010. ■ *When were some of the highest and lowest points in Congressional approval? What reasons can you think of to explain these levels?*

SOURCE: http://pollingreport.com/congjob.htm, accessed May 16 2010.

CHAPTER **SUMMARY**

11.1 Describe the congressional election process and the advantages it gives incumbents.

The congressional election process requires decisions about who can run for office, when they run, and how long they serve. Most House elections concern local issues, whereas Senate elections are more likely to be about national concerns. Incumbents enjoy a variety of protections, including name visibility and the ability to send mail and other messages back home free of charge, to help constituents, and to raise money.

11.2 Differentiate the powers of Congress, and compare and contrast the structure and powers of the House and Senate.

Congress has express powers, implied powers, and checks and balances. The most important powers are the power to borrow and make money, regulate commerce, unify the country, declare and fund war, and create the inferior federal courts.

The most distinctive feature of Congress is its bicameralism, which the framers intended as a moderating influence on partisanship and possible error. The House has the power to propose legislation to raise revenue, whereas the Senate has the power to confirm presidential appointees (by a majority vote) and ratify treaties (by a two-thirds vote).

11.3 Compare and contrast the leadership systems used in the House and Senate, and explain how work is done through congressional committees.

The House is led by the Speaker, a majority and a minority leader, and whips in each party, whereas the Senate is led by a majority and a minority leader. The Senate is more difficult to lead because of its greater individualism, sometimes expressed through the use of holds and filibusters to control the legislative process.

Most of the work in Congress is done in committees and subcommittees, which are classified into six types: (1) rules and administration, (2) budget, (3) appropriations, (4) authorizing, (5) revenue, and (6) oversight. Authorizing committees author all legislation, whereas appropriations committees spend the money needed to implement the legislation.

11.4 Identify the steps by which a bill becomes a law and the ways a bill can be stopped at each step.

A bill moves through a tortuous process to become a law—an idea must first be converted into a proposal, then be introduced and referred to a committee, receive a hearing and markup, and move to the floor. Although all formal bills are referred to committees for consideration, very few receive a hearing, even fewer are marked up and sent to the floor, and fewer still are enacted by both chambers and signed into law by the president. In addition, the legislative obstacle course sometimes includes filibusters, riders, holds, and the occasional override of a presidential veto.

11.5 Characterize the two ways legislators represent their constituents, and identify the various influences on their votes.

Legislators must balance the needs of their constituents against the national good. In addressing constituent needs, they often act as representatives of public opinion in their home districts. In addressing national issues, they often act as trustees of the greater good. Members must balance these two roles.

Members of Congress vote on the basis of a long list of varying influences that include their colleagues, constituents, staff, ideology, their party, and the president. These influences vary in strength from issue to issue.

11.6 Evaluate the influence of citizens on the legislative process.

Citizens can influence Congress in many ways, not the least of which is voting in midterm elections, which have historically low turnout. They can also use a variety of methods to express their opinions, including Facebook and Twitter. And they register their concerns about the lack of progress on big issues such as health care through public opinion surveys and their level of congressional approval.

CHAPTER **SELF-TEST**

11.1 Describe the congressional election process and the advantages it gives incumbents.
1. How are congressional elections set, and where do they occur?
2. In a few sentences, outline the advantages an incumbent member of Congress has in elections.
3. HOLD FOR QUESTION ABOUT 2010 ELECTIONS

11.2 Differentiate the powers of Congress, and compare and contrast the structure and powers of the House and Senate.
4. List the five basic categories of congressional power.

5. Suggest three ways the two chambers of Congress check each others' power.
6. Write a brief essay explaining the major differences between the chambers of Congress and why the framers thought these differences were important.

11.3 Compare and contrast the leadership systems used in the House and Senate, and explain how work is done through congressional committees.
7. How is the leadership of the House different from the Senate?
8. How are members of Congress assigned to committees?

9. How do the differing committee structures in the House and Senate affect the way these bodies function?

11.4 Identify the steps by which a bill becomes a law and the ways a bill can be stopped at each step.

10. What are the steps in passing a law?
11. Why are conference committees so important to the legislative process?
12. Write a short essay on when and how to kill a bill.

11.5 Characterize the two ways legislators represent their constituents, and identify the various influences on their votes.

13. In a short essay, explain the major differences between a member of Congress acting as a trustee and acting as a delegate.
14. Imagine you are a member of Congress. In a paragraph, evaluate how you would determine your votes on bills. Would you vote the same way your constituency would, even if you disagreed? Would you vote against your party on a bad bill, even if it meant you would be barred from introducing legislation for your home state for the rest of the year?

11.6 Evaluate the influence of citizens on the legislative process.

15. Why are Americans often disappointed with the performance of Congress, and why do they give the president higher approval ratings than Congress? How might Congress improve its reputation?
16. Why would tweeting matter to a member of Congress?
17. Write a short essay on why voting is important. Are there times when voting is irrational?

---

mypoliscilab EXERCISES

Apply what you learned in this chapter on MyPoliSciLab.

📖 Read on **mypoliscilab.com**

eText: Chapter 11

✓ Study and **Review** on **mypoliscilab.com**

Pre-Test
Post-Test
Chapter Exam
Flashcards

👁 Watch on **mypoliscilab.com**

Video: Unknown Wins South Carolina Senate Primary
Video: Kagan Hearing

✳ Explore on **mypoliscilab.com**

Simulation: How a Bill Becomes a Law
Simulation: You Are a Member of Congress
Comparative: Comparing Legislatures
Timeline: The Power of the Speaker of the House
Visual Literacy: Congressional Redistricting
Visual Literacy: Why Is It So Hard to Defeat an Incumbent?

KEY **TERMS**

ADDITIONAL **RESOURCES**

FURTHER READING

E. SCOTT ADLER, *Why Congressional Reforms Fail: Reelection and the House Committee System* (University of Chicago Press, 2002).

SARAH A. BINDER, *Stalemate: Causes and Consequences of Legislative Gridlock* (Brookings Institution Press, 2003).

ROGER H. DAVIDSON, WALTER J. OLESZEK, AND **FRANCES E. LEE,** *Congress and Its Members,* 11th ed. (CQ Press, 2007).

CHRISTOPHER J. DEERING AND **STEVEN S. SMITH,** *Committees in Congress,* 3d ed. (CQ Press, 1997).

RICHARD F. FENNO, JR., *Home Style: House Members in Their Districts* (Little, Brown, 1978).

RICHARD F. FENNO, JR., *Senators on the Campaign Trail: The Politics of Representation* (University of Oklahoma Press, 1996).

MORRIS P. FIORINA, *Congress: Keystone of the Washington Establishment,* 2d ed. (Yale University Press, 1989).

PAUL HERRNSON, *Congressional Elections,* 54th ed. (CQ Press, 2007).

GODFREY HODGSON, *The Gentleman from New York: Daniel Patrick Moynihan* (Houghton Mifflin, 2000).

GARY JACOBSON, *Politics of Congressional Elections,* 7th ed. (Longman, 2008).

LINDA KILLIAN, *The Freshmen: What Happened to the Republican Revolution?* (Westview Press, 1998).

THOMAS MANN AND **NORM ORNSTEIN,** *The Broken Branch: How Congress Is Failing America and How to Get It Back on Track* (Oxford University Press, 2006).

DAVID R. MAYHEW, *America's Congress: Actions in the Public Sphere, James Madison Through Newt Gingrich* (Yale University Press, 2002).

WALTER J. OLESZEK, *Congressional Procedures and the Policy Process,* 6th ed. (CQ Press, 2004).

RONALD M. PETERS, JR., ED., *The Speaker: Leadership in the U.S. House of Representatives* (CQ Press, 1995).

BARBARA SINCLAIR, *Unorthodox Lawmaking: New Legislative Processes in the U.S. Congress,* 2d ed. (CQ Press, 2000).

WEB SITES

www.opencongress.org An easily accessible inventory of congressional activities and work, including lists of bills, members, committees, votes, issues, and campaign contributions.

www.GAO.gov The Web site for the Government Accountability Office, which provides studies on issues facing Congress.

www.CBO.gov The Web site for the Congressional Budget Office, which analyzes every bill for its costs and tracks key economic trends.

www.senate.gov The Senate's Web site. Pay particular notion to the historian's office and the oral histories section. Also click on "references," then "statistics and lists," "legislation and procedures," and "resume of congressional activity" to see how many bills have been introduced, have passed, how many days in sessions, and so forth.

www.house.gov The House's Web site. Links to all committees.

www.thomas.loc.gov The authoritative tracker of all legislation.

CHAPTER 17

The Presidency

The Personal Branch

President Barack Obama entered office with an extensive list of priorities for his first year. Name an international or domestic problem facing the nation, and Obama promised to address it. Within months of his inauguration on January 20, 2009, he had asked Congress for massive legislation to stimulate the sagging economy, health care for the nation's uninsured, action on global warming, new rules on credit card abuses, investments in the Interstate Highway System, action to curb tobacco use, expansion in volunteerism, greater openness in government, and improvements in education. It was the longest list of proposals since Lyndon Johnson pushed Congress to enact his "Great Society" reforms in the 1960s, and it reflected the president's extraordinary power to set the legislative agenda on Capitol Hill.

Obama's agenda included more than domestic proposals, however. His agenda also focused on the wars in Iraq and Afghanistan, both of which were central to his 2008 campaign for the presidency. He did not want the United States to withdraw its military forces immediately, but he clearly wanted to bring the wars to a successful end. Although military casualties were falling dramatically in Iraq, combat was increasing in Afghanistan. In 2009, 141 soldiers lost their lives in Iraq, compared with 491 deaths in Afghanistan. Half of the deaths in Iraq occurred in noncombat accidents, whereas nearly all of the deaths in Afghanistan came in firefights and bombings with insurgents.[1]

Obama came to his decision on Afghanistan after a long, often public process that involved a deep review of the situation. Unlike his predecessor, President George W. Bush, Obama rarely makes decisions on the spot. Rather, he tends to conduct what some critics call "seminars" on particular issues. He collects as much information as possible about a decision, seeks as many points of view as possible, and eventually reaches a decision based on his reading of the facts. His approach is admirable for its thoroughness but takes a great deal of time.

Obama used this long process in making his decision about Afghanistan. The process began with an initial request for 40,000 more troops from the U.S. military commander in Afghanistan. His hope was to bring enough troops to Afghanistan to pacify the entire country. Other advisors, including Vice President Joseph Biden, were skeptical about the effort. They proposed a much smaller increase in troops in the hope that the United States could help the Afghanistan government strengthen its military forces. As commander in chief under the Constitution, Obama had to make the final decision but was torn by the competing proposals.

The debate about the appropriate strategy dragged on for months as Obama worked through the issue. He finally decided to authorize 30,000 additional troops, but rather than focusing on defeating the Taliban, which had controlled Afghanistan when Osama bin Laden approved the terrorist attacks on New York City and Washington, D.C., in September 2001, Obama's objective was to "degrade" bin Laden's Al-Qaeda terrorist base. He also set a clear deadline for withdrawing the troops as quickly as possible. Obama wanted what he called a "faster surge" in U.S. troop strength and a much faster withdrawal.[2]

Obama's decision shows the extent of the president's authority to shape foreign policy through military action. Congress often complains about such decisions but is mostly unwilling to limit that action. As a result, citizens have few opportunities to influence foreign policy, and even less when the policies are secret. With so many other controversial issues confronting the country, the public did not react in any organized way to Obama's decision. There have been times in history, however, when citizen action has driven Congress and the president to alter foreign policy. Massive protests against the Vietnam War during the late 1960s clearly shaped the U.S. decision to end the conflict.

Being president is one of the most difficult jobs in the world. Here, President Barack Obama meets with the four living ex-presidents to discuss general issues of governing the nation from the White House. ■ *What kind of knowledge can ex-presidents share with the current president, especially at the start of the new president's term in office?*

The framers of the Constitution both admired and feared the centralized leadership of a president. Although they knew a strong president was needed to protect the nation against foreign and domestic threats, they also worried about the potential abuse of power. This chapter will examine the framers' intent in designing the presidency, review the president's powers, and then turn to the continuing controversies surrounding the exercise of these powers. We will also explore the many jobs of the president and ask how Congress and the president work together and against each other in making the laws. We conclude with a discussion of how history judges presidents.

The Structure and Powers of the Presidency

LEARNING **OBJECTIVE**

12.1 Describe the constitutional foundations of the presidency and of three presidential roles.

The framers wanted the president to act with "dispatch" against threats, but they also worried that the president could become too powerful. Although they gave the president the power to run the executive branch, which now includes the White House and all departments and agencies, they limited the president's other powers to a relatively short list, including the power to wage wars declared by Congress, report to the nation from time to time on the State of the Union, nominate judges and executive appointees for Senate confirmation, and negotiate treaties. They wanted a presidential office that would steer clear of parties and factions, enforce the laws passed by Congress, handle communications with foreign governments, and help states put down disorders. They wanted a presidency strong enough to match Congress but not so strong that it would overpower Congress.

The framers believed the "jarrings of parties" in Congress were perfectly appropriate in making the laws but not in fighting wars and running the executive branch. They did not believe the president should have unlimited freedom to act, however. Having given a much longer list of powers to Congress, they saw the president as a powerful check on legislative action and essential to the administration of government. As Alexander Hamilton argued in *The Federalist*, No. 70, which explains the presidency in detail, "A feeble executive implies a feeble execution of the government. A feeble execution is but another phrase for a bad execution: And a government ill executed, whatever it may be in theory, must be in practice a bad government."[3]

Young citizens massed at the Lincoln Memorial on May Day, 1970, vowing to shut down the federal government to protest the Vietnam War. ■ *How might these protests have affected the president's abilities to make executive decisions about the war?*

The Presidency and the Separation of Powers

Obama's power to act as commander in chief is part of the Constitution's separation of power. Even though Congress often gives the president the freedom to take action on foreign policy, it does retain the authority to cut off funding for foreign involvement, and the Senate is required to ratify all treaties with other nations.

Nevertheless, merely having three branches of a national government—legislative, executive, and judicial—does not by itself create a pure system of separated powers.

Unlike the United States, which has a separate path to the presidency through the electoral college, **parliamentary governments** elect their prime ministers from the parliament itself. In theory, this system makes the prime minister more influential—he or she controls both the executive and legislative branches. Great Britain is the oldest parliamentary government in the world, and its prime minister is possibly the most powerful. Becoming the prime minister is hardly easy—prime ministers must be members of Parliament, elected as their party's leader, and be able to lead their parties to a majority in a national election. Once in office, the prime minister has many of the same roles as the U.S. president.

India and Japan both follow this parliamentary system with several important differences. Like the British prime minister, the Indian prime minister can be removed from office through a vote of no confidence by the parliament. However, the Indian prime minister has the extraordinary power to suspend all political rights by declaring a national emergency. Even here, the parliament retains the power to overturn such declarations after two months. Also unlike the British system, the Indian system has often been governed by members of the same family. The Nehru family has ruled the country for nearly two-thirds of its 60 years of independence.

In the United States, however, the legislative, executive, and judicial branches are independent of one another. Although the legislative and executive branch are sometimes headed by the same political party, unified government can exist only if voters in enough states and districts vote for the same party over enough elections to control the House, Senate, presidency, and judiciary (whose members are nominated by the president and confirmed by the Senate).

The United States is one of the few world powers that is neither a parliamentary democracy nor a wholly executive-dominated government. Our Constitution plainly invites both Congress and the president to set policy and govern the nation.

parliamentary government
A form of government in which the legislature selects the prime minister or the president.

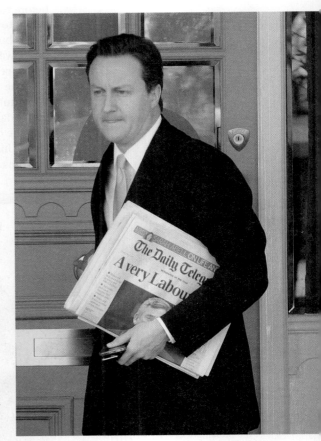

David Cameron was selected as prime minister of the United Kingdom after a May 2010 election. He became the leader of government after collecting enough votes in parliament from a coalition of parties, none of which had won a clear majority in the election.

Leadership and policy change are likely only when Congress and the president, and some-times the courts along with them, agree that new directions are desirable.

The Framers and the Presidency

The framers' most important decision about the presidency was also their first. Meeting on June 1, 1787, the Constitutional Convention decided there would be a single executive. Despite worries that a single president might lay the groundwork for a future monarchy, the framers also believed the new government needed energy in the executive. They were willing to increase the risk of tyranny in return for some efficiency.

Once past this first decision, the framers had to decide just how independent that executive would be from the rest of the national government. This meant finding an appro-priate method of selection or election. Had they wanted Congress to select the president from among its members, the framers would have created a parliamentary system that would look more like the European governments we discussed previously. The delegates were initially divided on how the president would be selected. A small number favored direct election by the people, which Pennsylvania's James Wilson thought would ensure that the president was completely independent of Congress. The delegates rejected direct election in favor of the electoral college: Voters would cast their ballots for competing slates of electors, who would in turn cast their electoral votes for president.

The framers also gave the executive a four-year term of office, further balancing the House with its two-year terms and the Senate with its six-year terms. Although the framers were silent on the number of terms a president could serve, the Twenty-Second Amendment to the Constitution, ratified in 1951, limits presidents to two terms in office.

The framers created the position of vice president just in case the president left office before the end of the term. With little debate, they decided to give the vice president the power to break tie votes in the Senate. Otherwise, the vice president has no constitutional duties but to wait for the president to be incapacitated or otherwise unable to discharge the powers and duties of the presidency. In recent years, however, presidents have given their vice presidents greater responsibilities.[4]

The framers also established three simple qualifications for both offices. Under the Constitution, the president and vice president must be (1) at least 35 years old on inaugu-ration day; (2) natural-born citizens of the United States, as opposed to immigrants who become citizens by applying to the U.S. government for naturalization; and (3) residents of the United States for the previous 14 years. The citizenship and residency requirements were designed to prevent a popular foreign-born citizen from capturing the office.

Presidents often make foreign policy and military decisions in the White House Situation Room. The room is in the basement of the White House and is completely secure. ■ *What might you expect in terms of the speed and cohesiveness of Situation Room decisions compared to legislative decisions?*

With this basic structure in place, the framers had to decide how the vice president would be selected. Once again, they created a remarkable electoral arrangement: The candidate who received the most electoral college votes would become president, and the candidate who came in second would become vice president. Any tie votes in the electoral college were to be broken by a majority vote in the House of Representatives.

It did not take long for the framers to discover the problem with this runner-up rule. The 1796 election produced Federalist President John Adams and Republican Vice President Thomas Jefferson. Because the two disagreed so sharply about the future of the country, Jefferson was rendered virtually irrelevant to government.

After a constitutional crisis in 1800, Congress decided to change the rule through a Constitution Amendment. Under the Twelfth Amendment, ratified in 1804, electors were allowed to cast separate votes for the president and vice president. This new practice encouraged candidates to run together as members of a **presidential ticket** that lists the presidential and vice presidential candidates first and second representatively.

Presidential Powers

Article II of the Constitution begins: "The executive Power shall be vested in a President of the United States of America." Presidents often use this **vesting clause** to argue that they control everything that happens in the executive branch after a bill becomes a law.[5] However, the Supreme Court has cast doubt on this breadth of the authority in a variety of past cases—presidents may control the executive branch, but they do not have unlimited command. The Supreme Court has also ruled that Congress cannot delegate powers to the president that the Constitution reserves for the legislative branch under Article I.

Although short, Article II does address foreign threats and the day-to-day operations of government, establishing the president's authority to play three central roles in the new government: (1) commander in chief, (2) diplomat in chief, and (3) administrator in chief.

It is important to note that the framers designed the presidency hoping George Washington would be the first to occupy the post. Washington commanded the public's trust and respect, and he was unanimously elected the first president of the new Republic. He understood that the people needed to have confidence in their fledgling government, a sense of continuity with the past, and a time of calm and stability free of emergencies and crises. He also knew that the new nation faced both domestic and foreign threats to its future.

As president, Washington set important precedents for the future. He not only established the legitimacy and basic authority of the office but negotiated the new government's first treaty, appointed its first judges and department heads, received its first foreign ambassadors, vetoed its first legislation, and signed its first laws, thereby demonstrating just how future presidents should execute and influence the laws.

Washington's most important precedent may have been his retirement after serving two terms. Although he would have been easily reelected to a third term, Washington believed two terms were enough and returned to his Mount Vernon estate in 1796. It was a precedent that held until Franklin Roosevelt's four terms and was finally enshrined in constitutional language under the Twenty-Second Amendment.

Commander in Chief The Constitution explicitly states that the president is to be commander in chief of the army and navy, but the framers were divided over which branch would both declare and make war.[6]

The framers initially agreed that Congress would make war, raise armies, build and equip fleets, enforce treaties, and suppress and repel invasions, but they eventually changed the phrase "make war" to "declare war." At the same time, the framers limited the presidential war power by giving Congress the power to appropriate money for the purchase of arms and military pay and by giving the Senate the power to approve military promotions. Although Congress has the sole authority to declare war, presidents have used their power as commander in chief to order U.S. troops into battle without formal

presidential ticket
The joint listing of the presidential and vice presidential candidates on the same ballot, as required by the Twelfth Amendment.

vesting clause
The president's constitutional authority to control most executive functions.

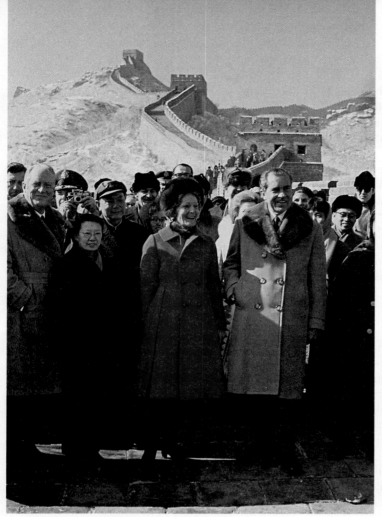

Richard Nixon shocked the world when he traveled to the People's Republic of China in 1972. As a young Republican member of Congress, Nixon had built his early career as an anti-communist. As president, he decided that only a Republican like himself could open the door to a future relationship with the communist nation. ■ *What do people mean when they say that a presidential decision is "like Nixon going to China?"*

declarations dozens of times throughout the past century, including the recent wars in Afghanistan and Iraq. Presidents have often interpreted the war power even more broadly, as the Bush administration did in authorizing the domestic eavesdropping program.

Diplomat in Chief Article II also makes the president negotiator in chief of treaties with foreign nations, which must be approved by the Senate by a two-thirds vote. A **treaty** is a binding and public agreement between the United States and one or more nations that requires mutual action toward a common goal. The United States has signed hundreds of treaties throughout the past 200 years, including limits on the number of nuclear, bio-logical, and chemical weapons. Although presidents cannot make treaties without Senate approval, past presidents have argued that they have the power to terminate treaties without Senate consent.

Presidents can also make **executive agreements** with the leaders of foreign nations. Unlike treaties, executive agreements are negotiated without Senate participation. In 2003, for example, the Bush administration negotiated a 22-item executive agreement with Mexico to create a "smart border" that would limit the movement of illegal aliens into the United States, while improving the flow of goods between the two nations. Although some executive orders are secret, most are made public.

Finally, presidents can make **congressional–executive agreements,** which are also negotiated between the president and leaders of other nations. Like treaties, congressional-- executive agreements require mutual action toward a common goal. Unlike treaties, they require approval by both houses of Congress by a simple majority vote.

Administrator in Chief By giving the president the power to require the opinion of the principal officer in each of the executive departments "upon any subject relating to the duties of their respective offices," the Constitution puts the president in charge of the day-to-day operations of the federal departments and agencies.

Additional Executive Powers The Constitution also gives the president five additional powers to lead government: (1) the power to appoint judges and officers of government; (2) the power to veto legislation, thereby serving as a check on Congress; (3) the power to grant pardons to individuals convicted of federal, but not state, crimes, thereby providing a check against the judiciary; (4) the power to take care that the laws are faithfully executed, thereby giving the president sweeping authority to oversee the executive branch; and (5) the power to inform and convene Congress.

1. *The Appointment Power.* The Constitution gives the president authority to appoint judges, ambassadors, and other officers of the executive branch subject to the advice and consent of the Senate, in the form of a simple majority of 51 votes.

This power gives presidents the ability to control what happens inside departments and agencies during their terms and to shape the federal judiciary far into the future. Presidents choose appointees on the basis of party loyalty, interest group pressure, and management ability. The Senate has failed to confirm only eight cabinet secretaries between 1789 and 2008, and only 36 of 159 nominations to the Supreme Court.

treaty

A formal, public agreement between the United States and one or more nations that must be approved by two-thirds of the Senate.

executive agreement

A formal agreement between the U.S. president and the leaders of other nations that does not require Senate approval.

congressional–executive agreement

A formal agreement between the U.S. president and the leaders of other nations that requires approval by both houses of Congress.

Of the People

THE GLOBAL COMMUNITY

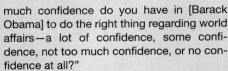

Opinions of Barack Obama

Presidents usually start their first terms in office with a burst of public support, both inside the United States and throughout the globe. Once they start making foreign policy decisions, their support tends to erode, especially if those decisions involve unpopular interventions such as the war in Iraq.

Almost without exception, they end their terms in office less popular than they were at the beginning.

The pattern is clear in the Pew Global Survey, which took an early snapshot of Obama's popularity throughout the world in April 2009. Respondents were asked, "How

much confidence do you have in [Barack Obama] to do the right thing regarding world affairs—a lot of confidence, some confidence, not too much confidence, or no confidence at all?"

Obama's extraordinary popularity in Nigeria reflects both his personal ties to Africa as the son of a Kenyan citizen and his commitment to improved diplomatic ties with the region. Eighty-eight percent of Kenyans reported a lot or some confidence in Obama.

Obama's popularity at the start of his first year was in sharp contrast to George W. Bush's popularity in 2007. Only 16 percent of British citizens had a lot or some confidence in Bush in the middle of his sixth year, compared with 30 percent of the Chinese, 25 percent of Japanese, 16 percent of Mexicans, 55 percent of Nigerians, and only 37 percent of Americans.

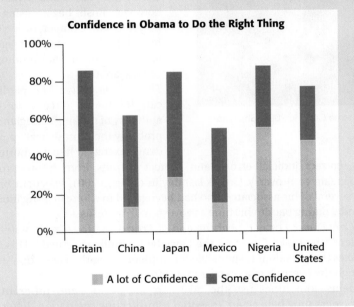

CRITICAL THINKING QUESTIONS

1. Why was the world so enthusiastic about Barack Obama's presidency?

2. How does Obama's popularity translate into more effective foreign policy?

3. How will the increase in the U.S. troops in Afghanistan affect Obama's popularity both at home and abroad?

Presidents also have the power to make **recess appointments** when Congress takes a formal recess, or break, during the year. Although the power was originally intended to be used only when a vacancy occurs during the break, presidents now use recess appointments regularly to appoint particularly controversial nominees to office without Senate confirmation. These appointments end at the start of the Congress that is elected after the appointment is made.[7] Obama did not make any recess appointments in his first year in office.

2. *The Veto Power.* The Constitution provides that bills passed by the U.S. House of Representatives and Senate "shall be presented to the President of the United States," and the president can then approve the measure or issue a **veto.** If a bill is vetoed by a president, it can be enacted only if the veto is overridden, which requires a two-thirds vote in each chamber of Congress.

A variation of the veto is the **pocket veto.** In the ordinary course of events, if a president does not sign or veto a bill within ten days after receiving it (not counting Sundays), the bill becomes law without the president's signature. But if Congress adjourns within the ten days, the president, by taking no action, can kill the bill with a pocket veto.

The power of a veto lies in the difficulty of overriding a president's decision. Recall that two-thirds of both houses must vote to overturn a veto. This requirement is a vital bargaining chip in the legislative process, in which the mere threat of a veto

recess appointment
Presidential appointment made without Senate confirmation during Senate recess.

veto
A formal decision to reject a bill passed by Congress.

pocket veto
A formal decision to reject a bill passed by Congress after it adjourns—if Congress adjourns during the ten days that the president is allowed to sign or veto a law, the president can reject the law by taking no action at all.

331

President Obama nominated Judge Sonia Sotomayor to the Supreme Court in 2009. She was easily confirmed as the first Hispanic to join the court.

can strengthen a president's hand. Historically, Congress has voted to override fewer than 10 percent of presidents' regular vetoes.

This veto threat is credible, however, only if the president is actually willing to use it. Whereas Ronald Reagan vetoed 78 bills in his two terms and Bill Clinton vetoed 37, George W. Bush issued only one veto during his first six years in office.

Once his Republican Party lost control of the House and Senate in 2007, however, Bush began using his veto power to stop Democratic legislation. In July, 2007, for example, he vetoed legislation to allow federal funding of stem cell research.

3. *The Pardon Power.* The pardon power can be traced directly to the royal authority of the king of England, and it is probably the most delicate power presidents exercise. It can shorten prison sentences, correct judicial errors, and protect citizens from future prosecution. It can also create controversy. On his last day in office in 2001, President Bill Clinton pardoned several of his associates who had been jailed in a long investigation of a real estate scandal dating back to his time as governor of Arkansas.

4. *The Take Care Power.* Located near the end of Article II is the simple statement that the president "shall take Care that the Laws be faithfully executed." This **take care clause** makes the president responsible for implementing the laws Congress enacts, even through the override of a presidential veto.

Presidents sometimes use the take care clause to claim **inherent powers,** meaning powers they believe are essential to protecting the nation. Jefferson drew on this broad notion in making the Louisiana Purchase in 1803, for example. Abraham Lincoln extended the concept early in the Civil War to suspend the rights of prisoners to seek judicial review of their detention, to impose a blockade of Confederate shipping, and to expand the size of the army beyond authorized ceilings, all without prior congressional approval as required under the Constitution's lawmaking power.

5. *The Power to Inform and Convene Congress.* Under Article II, presidents are required "from time to time to give to the Congress Information of the State of the Union, and recommend to their Consideration such Measures as he shall judge necessary." Throughout the years, the phrase "from time to time" has evolved to mean a constant stream of presidential messages, as well as the annual **State of the Union Address** in late January or early February. This power gives presidents a significant platform for presenting their legislative agenda to both Congress and the people.

The president also has the power to convene Congress in extraordinary circumstances and recommend "such Measures as he shall judge necessary and expedient." In August 2010, for example, Obama convened Congress to push for health care reform.

Presidents also believe they have unilateral powers that are not subject to traditional checks and balances. The most important unilateral power involves decisions not to implement a law. These **signing statements** often make the case that a certain provision of a law is either unconstitutional or so vague it cannot be implemented. Between 2001 and early 2008, Bush issued more than 150 statements promising not to follow the laws he was signing.[8]

take care clause
The constitutional requirement (in Article II, Section 3) that presidents take care that the laws are faithfully executed, even if they disagree with the purpose of those laws.

inherent powers
Powers that grow out of the very existence of government.

State of the Union Address
The president's annual statement to Congress and the nation.

signing statements
A formal document that explains why a president is signing a particular bill into law. These statements may contain objections to the bill and promises not to implement key sections.

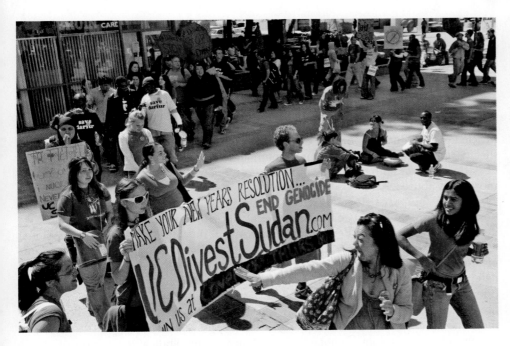

In his signing the Sudan Accountability and Divestment Act of 2007, President Bush noted that ordering states to jettison any investments made with companies doing business in Darfur conflicted with the president's authority to conduct foreign policy. His signing statement made clear Bush would implement the law selectively. ■ *Do signing statements such as this violate the constitution's requirement that the president faithfully execute the laws once they are signed?*

Presidential Removal and Succession

Having decided how a president would enter office and the length of the term of office, the framers also gave Congress the power to remove the president through **impeachment.** Under this constitutional check and balance, the House of Representatives is responsible for drafting the articles of impeachment that charge the president with treason, bribery, or other high crimes and misdemeanors. If the articles are approved by a majority vote in the House, the chief justice of the Supreme Court oversees a trial before the Senate. If two-thirds of the Senate vote to convict, the president is removed immediately from office.

impeachment
A formal accusation against the president or another public official; the first step in removal from office.

Impeachment charges have been filed against nine presidents in history, but the House has voted to impeach the president only twice: in 1868 against Andrew Johnson, and in 1998 against Bill Clinton. The Senate trials resulted in acquittals.

Although the framers did not limit the number of terms that a president could serve, the nation eventually ratified the Twenty-Second Amendment, which limits presidents to two terms in office. The ratification effort was led by Republicans who wanted to prevent a repeat of Franklin Roosevelt's four consecutive terms in office, which concentrated power in the White House and led to the great expansion of federal government power under the New Deal.

In 1967, the nation ratified the Twenty-Fifth Amendment, which allows for the temporary removal of the president due to illness or disability. The president can only be removed temporarily if (1) the vice president, and (2) a majority of either Congress or the president's own department secretaries declare the president to be unable to discharge the powers and duties of office. During the temporary removal of the president, the vice president becomes the acting president.

If the president dies or resigns from office, the vice president automatically becomes president and must nominate someone to be vice president. Under the Twenty-Fifth Amendment, the nominee for vice president must be confirmed by a majority vote in both houses of Congress.

Vice President Lyndon Baines Johnson takes the oath of office to become president on November 22, 1963, following the assassination of John F. Kennedy. In the wake of these events, the Twenty-Fifth Amendment was adopted to provide for replacing the vice president or removing a president from office for reasons of illness or disability.

Controversies in Presidential Power

LEARNING **OBJECTIVE**

12.2 Evaluate the controversies surrounding presidents' assertion of additional executive powers.

The president, today more visible than ever as a national and international leader, is still constrained by constitutional checks and balances. These do not stop presidents from asserting powers the framers intended for Congress or the judiciary, however.

The War Power

Article I of the Constitution gives Congress the power to declare war, but Article II gives the president the power to wage war as commander in chief. The framers recognized that declaring war was both one of the most important powers of government and one of the most easily abused. [9]

During the past half-century, U.S. presidents have ordered troops into battle in Korea, Vietnam, Grenada, Panama, Iraq (twice), Kosovo, and Afghanistan, all without asking Congress for a formal declaration of war. When they have asked for congressional approval, presidents have usually sought broad resolutions of support. In 2002, for example, Bush merely asked Congress to give him the authority to deploy U.S. forces as "he determines to be necessary and appropriate" to defend national security against the threat posed by Iraq. Although the request was eventually approved by wide margins in the House and Senate, White House lawyers also argued that the president already had the authority to act with or without congressional approval. [10]

Presidents and some scholars blame Congress for abdicating its constitutional authority to the presidency. Constitutional scholar Louis Fisher holds that Congress has repeatedly given up its fundamental war powers to the president. The framers knew what monarchy looked like and rejected it, writes Fisher. "Yet, especially in matters of the war power, the United States is recreating a system of monarchy while it professes to champion democracy and the rule of law abroad." [11]

Congress tried to reassert its role and authority in the use of military force at the end of the Vietnam War. In 1973, Congress enacted the War Powers Resolution over Nixon's veto. The law, still in place, declares that a president can commit the armed forces only (1) after a declaration of war by Congress, (2) by specific statutory authorization, or (3) in a national emergency created by an attack on the United States or its armed forces. After committing the armed forces under the third circumstance, the president is required to report to Congress within 48 hours. Unless Congress declares war, the troop commitment must be ended within 60 days.

This resolution signaled a new determination by Congress to take its prerogatives seriously, yet presidents have generally ignored it. And many leading scholars now believe that this earnest and well-intentioned effort by Congress to reclaim its proper role actually gave away more authority than previous practices had already done. Because presidents can declare a national emergency under almost any circumstances and often act under broad legislation that authorizes the use of force in ambiguous situations, the War Powers Resolution is almost always ignored.

The Power to Invoke Executive Privilege

executive privilege
The right to keep executive communications confidential, especially if they relate to national security.

The courts have recognized that presidents have the power, or **executive privilege,** to keep secrets, especially if doing so is essential to protect national security or confidential White House conversations about public policy.

Some experts argue that executive privilege has no constitutional basis. [12] Yet presidents have withheld documents from Congress at least as far back as 1792, when President George Washington temporarily refused to share sensitive documents with a House committee studying an Indian massacre of federal troops. Thomas Jefferson and the primary author of the Constitution, James Madison, also withheld information during their presidencies.

Most scholars, the courts, and even members of Congress agree that a president does have the implicit, if not constitutionally explicit, right to withhold information that could harm national security. Presidents must keep secrets, and they often fight hard to do so. However, they cannot assert executive privilege in either congressional or judicial proceedings when it means refusing to cooperate in investigations of personal wrongdoing.

Iranian president Mahmoud Ahmadinejad addresses the United Nations in 2007. Tensions began to rise dramatically between Iran and the United States late in the Bush administration. The Bush administration was particularly worried about the possibility that Iran was in the process of refining nuclear materials as part of a weapons program and threatened to use all powers in the U.S. arsenal to stop Iran's effort.

Nixon created enormous and continuing controversy over the term "executive privilege."[13] In an effort to hide his own role in the Watergate scandal, which involved a failed burglary of the Democratic National Committee offices during the 1972 election, Nixon refused to release the secret tapes of the White House meetings that led to a cover-up of the attempt. Nixon and his lawyers went so far as to claim that the decision to invoke executive privilege was not subject to review by Congress or the federal courts.

Ruling in an April 1974 unanimous decision, the Supreme Court acknowledged for the first time that presidents do indeed have the power to claim executive privilege if the release of certain information would be damaging to the nation's security interests. But the Court held that such claims are not exempt from review by the courts. More importantly for Nixon's future, the Court also held that national security was not threatened by the public release of the Watergate tapes. The Court ordered Nixon to yield his tapes, effectively dooming his presidency.[14]

The Bush administration formally invoked executive privilege four times between 2001 and 2007, and in late 2007, to prevent congressional testimony by two White House aides in a Justice Department scandal. As of early 2010, Obama has not invoked this power.

The Bush administration refused to release information on its use of "enhanced interrogation" techniques such as sleep deprivation at the Guantanamo interrogation facility. The decision was eventually reversed by the Obama administration, which released the Bush administration's "torture memos" in 2009.

The Power to Issue Executive Orders

Presidents execute the laws and direct the federal departments and agencies in part through **executive orders,** formal directives that are just as strong as laws and can be challenged in the courts. According to past Supreme Court decisions, executive orders are generally accepted as the law of the land unless they conflict with the Constitution or a federal law. Executive orders are numbered dating back to President George Washington's first order three months after his inauguration.

Beginning with George Washington, presidents have issued nearly 14,000 executive orders. Presidents have used executive orders to implement a variety of decisions, including a declaration of U.S. neutrality in the war between France and England (1793). President George W. Bush issued 270 executive orders during his eight-year term, while Obama issued 37 in his first year. (See Figure 12–1 for a comparison of the number of executive orders issued, by president.) Obama's first executive order, issued the day after his inauguration, was an ethics pledge that all future executive appointees must sign. (An indexed list of all executive orders dating back to 1933 can be found at http://www.archives.gov/federal-register/executive-orders/disposition.html.)

executive orders
Formal orders issued by the president to direct action by the federal bureaucracy.

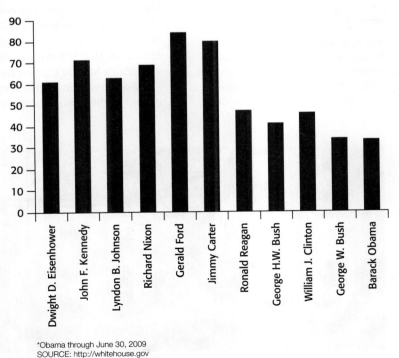

*Obama through June 30, 2009
SOURCE: http://whitehouse.gov

FIGURE 12–1 **Average Number of Executive Orders Issued Each Year, by President** ■ *Why has the average number of executive orders issued declined so much over the past six decades? What other tools might presidents now be using to influence policies and government?*

The Budget and Spending Power

The Constitution explicitly gives Congress the power to appropriate money, but presidents are responsible for actually spending it. Congress dominated the budget-making process until 1921, when it approved the Budget and Accounting Act. That law required the president to submit annual budgets to Congress, and it established the Bureau of the Budget, which in 1970 became the Office of Management and Budget. Although the 1921 act also created the General Accounting Office as an auditing and oversight arm of Congress, presidents have played an increasingly powerful role in shaping the federal budget. (A detailed look at current federal spending can be found at www.USAspending.gov.)

In 1974, Congress approved the Congressional Budget and Impoundment Control Act, which sharply curtailed the president's use of **impoundment,** or refusal to spend appropriations that had been passed into law. Enacted over Nixon's veto, the law gave Congress new powers to control its own budget process, created the Congressional Budget Office (CBO) to give the institution its own sources of economic and spending forecasts, and required the president to submit detailed requests to Congress for any proposed *rescission* (cancellation) of congressional appropriations.

In an effort to control its own tendency to overspend, Congress in 1996 voted to give the president greater budget power through the **line item veto,** which would have allowed presidents to strike out specific sections of an appropriations bill while signing the rest into law. In essence, the line item veto is a legal form of impoundment. Although many governors have the line item veto, the Supreme Court decided the law had disturbed the "finely wrought" procedure for making the laws and declared it unconstitutional in a 6-to-3 vote in 1998. If Congress wanted a new procedure for making the laws, Justice John Paul Stevens wrote for the majority, it would have to pursue a constitutional amendment.[15]

The Evolution of Presidential Power

The history of presidential power is one of steady, and uneven, growth. Of the individuals who have filled the office, approximately one-third have enlarged its powers. Andrew Jackson, Abraham Lincoln, Theodore Roosevelt, Franklin Delano Roosevelt, and Harry Truman all redefined the institution and many of its powers by the way they set priorities and responded to crises. Much of this expansion occurred during wartime or national crises such as the economic depression of the 1930s.

Nevertheless, today's presidency reflects precedents established by the nation's first chief executive, George Washington. The framers could not have anticipated the kinds of foreign and domestic threats that now preoccupy the office, but they did recognize the importance of the presidency in protecting the nation in times of trouble.

Today's presidency still bears the mark of George Washington, but also reflects the enormous expansion that occurred during the 1930s under Franklin Delano Roosevelt. During his 12 years in office, Roosevelt created an extraordinary record of achievement. He expanded the role of the president as commander, diplomat, and administrator in chief, while dominating Congress in both shaping and making the laws. Inaugurated for the first of his four terms in the midst of the Great Depression, Roosevelt took command, and his first 100 days in office in 1933 still stand as the most significant moment of presidential leadership in modern history. Most of his New Deal agenda for helping workers and the poor is still law today.

Roosevelt's impact extends well beyond the legislative agenda, however. He also exploited the powers of the presidency to build a highly personal relationship with the

impoundment
A decision by the president not to spend money appropriated by Congress, now prohibited under federal law.

line item veto
Presidential power to strike, or remove, specific items from a spending bill without vetoing the entire package; declared unconstitutional by the Supreme Court.

Franklin Roosevelt's Depression-era Works Progress Administration put millions of people to work on public projects, as depicted in this mural by Marvin Beerbohm, displayed at the Detroit Post Office. ■ *What does the mural tell you about the groups of people and industries that benefitted from the New Deal agenda?*

Should the Two-Term Limit Be Repealed?

The Twenty-Second Amendment was ratified in 1951 to limit the president's time in office to two terms whether served consecutively or not. If President Obama is defeated for reelection in 2012, for example, but ran again and won in 2016, he would still be limited to two terms total.

All of the presidents who have been elected since 1951 have supported repeal of the Twenty-Second Amendment. They argue that the amendment effectively renders them *lame ducks* in their

second terms. Because they cannot stand for reelection, Congress and the public tend to ignore them as thoughts turn to who will be the president after them. Nor can they be held accountable in the voting booth for their second-term decisions.

What do you think? Should the two-term limit be repealed? What arguments would you make for or against such an idea?

THINKING IT THROUGH

The founders clearly believed that elections serve to discipline presidents for their actions, while the four-year term provides enough time to achieve policy results. They believed that steadiness in administration would help the country survive its early years, while giving the president a reason to create policies that would help the nation long into the future. Presidents are arguably more effective if their allies and opponents assume they may be running for another term. Otherwise, they become "lame ducks" early in their second terms, meaning that they have little influence.

Much as they may have applauded Washington's two-term precedent, the founders did not support the idea of a formal term limit—such a limit would have weakened the public's voice in

keeping the president honest. Instead of starting a second term knowing they could not serve again, presidents would be able to keep Congress and the public guessing, thereby retaining influence until the last possible minute.

Critical Thinking Questions

1. Do presidents have so much power that they can almost guarantee reelection to more than two terms?
2. Does the two-term limit weaken the president's ability to influence the course of the nation in the second term?
3. What checks and balances ensure that presidents can be held accountable even if they are lame ducks?

U.S. public, using his "fireside chats" on radio to calm the public during the darkest days of the economic depression, while calling the nation to action during the early days of World War II. In doing so, he became the nation's communicator in chief, starting each broadcast with the simple phrase "My friends."

Managing the Presidency

Presidents cannot do their jobs without help. Although some of that help comes from their *inner circle,* composed of their closest advisers, including the first lady, presidents rely on a vast array of support that extends well beyond 1600 Pennsylvania Avenue to include the executive branch as a whole.

LEARNING **OBJECTIVE**

12.3 Outline the functions of the White House staff, Executive Office of the President, cabinet, and vice president.

The White House Staff

The president's most important advisers work inside the cramped confines of the West Wing of the White House.[16] Whereas presidents often view their cabinet secretaries as advocates of their departments, they view their White House staff as intensely loyal and responsive to the president, and the president alone.

Generally, the closer a staff member is to the president's Oval Office, the more power he or she has. However, power is also dependent on how the president organizes the staff for making decisions. Among modern presidents, Franklin Roosevelt and Lyndon Johnson both used the *competitive* approach for managing the White House staff, a "survival of the fittest" situation in which the president allows aides to fight each other for access to the Oval Office. Johnson sometimes gave different staffers the same assignment, hoping the competition would produce a better final decision.

In contrast, John Kennedy, Jimmy Carter, and Bill Clinton all used the *collegial* approach, encouraging aides to work together toward a common position. It is a

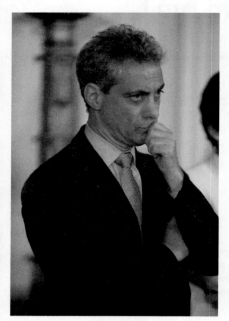

Rahm Emanuel resigned his seat in Congress to be Obama's chief of staff in 2009. Emmanuel left the White House late in 2010 to run for mayor of Chicago, a particularly powerful post in the Democratic Party given the city's strong Democratic base.

chief of staff
The head of the White House staff.

Executive Office of the President
The cluster of presidential staff agencies that help the president carry out his or her responsibilities. Currently, the office includes the Office of Management and Budget, the Council of Economic Advisers, and several other units.

friendlier way to work but may have the serious drawback of producing *groupthink,* the tendency of small groups to stifle dissent in the search for common ground.[17]

Finally, Dwight Eisenhower, Richard Nixon, Ronald Reagan, and George W. Bush all used the *hierarchical* approach, in which the president establishes tight control over who does what in making decisions. Presidents who use this approach usually rely on a "gatekeeper," or trusted adviser such as the chief of staff, to monitor the flow of information to and from the White House.

The White House Bureaucracy   The White House staff grew steadily from the early 1900s through the early 1990s, then stabilized at roughly 400 today. The **chief of staff,** the president's most loyal assistant, heads the staff, which also includes the president's chief lawyer, speechwriters, legislative liaison staff, and press secretary.

There are at least two kinds of White House offices. *Political* offices are designed to help the president run for reelection, control the national party, and shape the president's image through press conferences, television and radio addresses, polling, and travel.

Policy offices are designed to shape the president's foreign and domestic program. Like congressional committees, these offices collect information and often write legislation. The list of policy offices includes the National Economic Council, which coordinates the president's economic agenda; the National Security Council, which helps set foreign policy; and the Office of Faith-Based and Community Initiatives, which encourages the use of religious institutions to help address community problems.[18]

The Executive Office of the President

The **Executive Office of the President (EOP)** was created in 1939 to give the president more help running the federal departments and agencies. The EOP consists of the Office of Management and Budget, the Council of Economic Advisers, and several other staff units. It also includes the White House staff, which is a distinct organization of staff who report solely to the president and are not ordinarily subject to Senate confirmation.

No one is quite sure how many people work in the EOP—although many staffers are on the White House budget, the EOP staff also includes between 2,000 and 6,000 staffers who are *detailed* to the White House by departments and agencies of government. Because they are paid by their departments and agencies, they do not show up on the traditional head-counts of EOP staff. (Biographies of all White House staff can be found at http://www.whorunsgov.com/Departments/White_House_Organizational_Chart, and is illustrated in Figure 12–2.)

FIGURE 12–2 **Executive Office of the President.** ■ *Why are there so many separate offices under the president's direct command? And what do the kinds of offices President Obama includes in his Executive Office indicate about his policy priorities?*

Of the People

AMERICA'S CHANGING FACE

The President's Cabinet

As discussed above, the president's cabinet is composed of the Senate-confirmed secretaries and agency heads who are most important in giving the president advice. They meet regularly as a group with the president.

During the past 50 years, the president's cabinet has steadily become more diverse. Obama's first 20 cabinet appointees were the most diverse team in history but built on the gains made by women and minorities under Presidents Clinton and George W. Bush. The following chart shows the increasing diversity among the first round of cabinet appointments each president made.

This increasing diversity brings great assets to the White House. It provides greater creativity and life histories to the discussion of key issues such as economic growth, climate change, and health care reform. It also sends the message that a government of the people involves more than white males. With his appointments, Obama created the first cabinet with a majority of women and minorities.

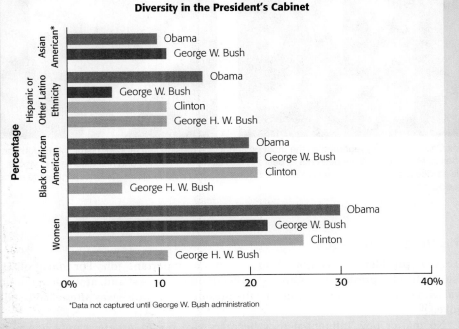

Diversity in the President's Cabinet

*Data not captured until George W. Bush administration

CRITICAL THINKING QUESTIONS

1. Does partisanship predict the level of diversity in the cabinet? Why or why not?

2. Does diversity matter to presidential decisions? Should it?

3. The federal government's workforce is very diverse. How does diversity in the cabinet affect the performance of the federal bureaucracy?

SOURCE: Author's analysis of appointment statistics.

The **Office of Management and Budget (OMB)** is the central EOP agency for making decisions about the budget. Its director advises the president in detail about the hundreds of government agencies—how much money they should be allotted in the budget and what kind of job they are doing. The OMB seeks to improve the planning, management, and statistical work of the agencies. It makes a special effort to see that each agency conforms to presidential policies in its dealings with Congress; each agency has to clear its policy recommendations to Congress through the OMB first.[19]

The Cabinet

It is hard to find a more unusual institution than the president's **cabinet.** The cabinet is not specifically mentioned in the Constitution, yet every president since 1789 has had one. Washington's consisted of his secretaries of state, treasury, and war, plus his attorney general.

Defining the Cabinet   Defining the cabinet is the first major job for the president-elect. Today, the cabinet consists of the president, the vice president, the heads of the 15 executive departments, and several others a president considers essential officials.

The cabinet has always been a loosely designated body, and it is not always clear who belongs in it. In recent years, certain executive branch administrators and White House counselors have been accorded cabinet rank. Nineteen officials had cabinet status in the George W. Bush administration, including the 15 cabinet secretaries, the vice president, the chief of staff, and the director of national intelligence.

Office of Management and Budget (OMB)
A presidential staff agency that serves as a clearinghouse for budgetary requests and management improvements for government agencies.

cabinet
The advisory council for the president, consisting of the heads of the executive departments, the vice president, and a few other officials selected by the president.

339

Dick Cheney is widely regarded as the most powerful vice president in modern history. Although Joe Biden is well respected, he does not appear to have as much influence and has taken a less visible role as vice president. ■ *What are some of the factors that might impact how much influence a vice president has?*

The Vice Presidency

The vice presidency has not always been an important job. For most of U.S. history, the vice president was an insignificant officer at best and, at worst, a political rival who sometimes connived against the president. The office was often dismissed as a joke.

No matter how influential they become, vice presidents have only one major responsibility: to be ready to take the oath of office in case the president cannot discharge his duties. Nevertheless, vice presidents enter office with substantial access, including an office just down the hall from the president in the West Wing of the White House, a substantial staff of their own, and access to all of the information flowing into the Oval Office.

Vice President Dick Cheney is generally considered the most influential vice president in modern times. He had more than just access to President Bush, however. He was a trusted adviser to the Bush family and had served in Congress and as secretary of defense under the first president Bush.

Joe Biden has a very different, but still powerful, role in the Obama Administration. He was a strong voice in the president's Afghanistan decision, and he is in charge of the effort to stimulate the economy. He also meets regularly with the president and is often consulted by the White House before the president makes his decisions. He has a regular and private weekly lunch with Obama to discuss anything on their minds and also sits just down the hallway from the president's Oval Office.

The Job of the President

LEARNING **OBJECTIVE**
12.4 Characterize the various roles that presidents play.

U.S. citizens want the chief executive to be an international peacemaker as well as a national morale builder, a politician in chief as well as a commander in chief. They want the president to provide leadership on foreign, economic, and domestic policy. They also want presidents to be crisis managers and role models of a kind. They want them to be able to connect with ordinary people, yet be smarter, tougher, and more honest than the rest of us. (See Table 12–1 for what U.S. adults thought presidents could change about the world in 2008.)

Presidents as Morale Builders

As chief of state, the president must project a sense of national unity and authority as the country's chief ceremonial leader. The framers of the Constitution did not fully anticipate the symbolic and morale-building functions a president must perform. But over time, presidents have become national celebrities and command media attention merely by jogging, fishing, golfing, or going to church. By their actions, presidents can arouse a sense of hope or despair, honor or dishonor.

Morale building means much more than just ceremonies or prayers. At its finest, presidential leadership radiates national self-confidence and helps unlock the possibility for good that exists in the nation. That is certainly what George W. Bush intended in the days and weeks that followed September 11, 2001. By his words and deeds, he sought to simultaneously calm the nation and warn the rest of the world that the United States would not tolerate further terrorist attacks.

Presidents as Agenda Setters

By custom and circumstance, presidents are now responsible for proposing initiatives in foreign policy and economic growth and stability. Presidential candidates searching for campaign issues seize on new ideas, and these are later refined and implemented by the executive office staff, by special presidential task forces, and by Congress.[20]

Economic Policy   Ever since the New Deal, presidents have been expected to promote policies to keep unemployment low, fight inflation, keep taxes down, and promote economic growth and prosperity. The Constitution does not specify these, but presidents know they will be held accountable for economic problems such as inflation and unemployment.

TABLE 12–1	What Can Presidents Change?

Percentage of Americans Who Said the President Has a Great Deal of Influence Over Each of the Following Issues

Housing prices	20%
Interest rates	23%
Inflation	30%
Gas prices	31%
Health care costs	38%
Federal budget deficit	48%
Taxes	48%
The way other countries view the United States	60%

SOURCE: Associated Press–Yahoo Poll, January 18, 2008.

President Bush, flanked by firefighters and rescue workers, addresses a crowd at the scene of the terrorist attacks on the World Trade Center in New York on September 11, 2001. In times of crisis, the nation often rallies around the president despite political differences. ■ *What messages does Bush convey in this photo solely through visual cues?*

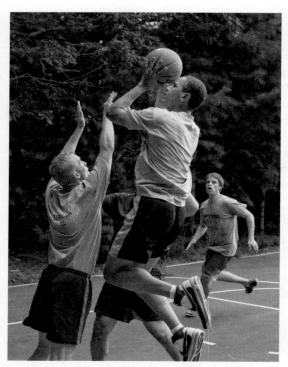

Presidents relax in many ways. President Ronald Reagan liked to chop wood at his California ranch, Bill Clinton liked to go jogging, George W. Bush went on frequent bike rides, and Obama likes to play pick-up games of basketball.

■ *How do images like this help presidents shape public perceptions of their human side?*

Social Policy   Leadership is often defined as the art of knowing what followers want. John Kennedy and Lyndon Johnson did not launch the civil rights movement, for example. Nor did Bill Clinton or George W. Bush create public pressure for national health insurance or prescription drug coverage. But they all responded to the public demand by supporting legislation on each issue.

National Security Policy   The framers foresaw a special need for speed and unity in dealing with other nations. The Supreme Court has upheld strong presidential authority in this area. In *United States* v. *Curtiss-Wright* (1936), the Court referred to the "exclusive power of the president as the sole organ of the federal government in the field of international relations—a power which does not require as a basis for its exercise an act of Congress, but which, of course, like every other governmental power, must be exercised in subordination to the applicable provisions of the Constitution."[21]

Presidents as Persuaders

Despite their formal powers, presidents spend most of their time *persuading* people. As Richard Neustadt argues, the power to persuade is the president's chief resource.[22] This power to persuade is based on the president's ability to communicate directly with members of Congress and the public through the skillful use of press conferences, speeches, and public events.

Presidents have reduced the number of their press conferences during the past five decades. Whereas Franklin Roosevelt averaged nearly seven press conferences a month during his dozen years in office, the past five presidents have averaged one. Although Barack Obama held three press conferences in his first six months, he did not hold another until 2010. "Going public" often means carefully staging events before friendly audiences that show strong support for the president.

Going public clearly fits with changes in the electoral process. Presidents now have the staff, the technology, and the public opinion research to tell them how to target their message, and they have nearly instant media access to speak to the public easily. And, as elections have become more image oriented and candidate centered, presidents have the incentive to use these tools to operate a permanent White House campaign.

Congress and the Presidency

LEARNING **OBJECTIVE**

12.5 Identify the sources of presidential-congressional conflict and the tools presidents use to influence Congress.

Congress and the presidency have a contentious relationship. They often work closely to address critically important problems but at other times are unable to reach agreement on equally difficult issues. They are most likely to agree in the first year of a president's first term and when one party controls both the White House and Congress, and they are more likely to fight late in the president's first term and off and on throughout the entire second term.

Given the separation of powers, it is a wonder that Congress and the president ever agree at all, which is exactly what the framers intended. The framers did not want the legislative process to work like an assembly line. Rather, they wanted ambition to counteract ambition as a way to prevent tyranny.

To the extent that they designed the legislative process to work inefficiently, the founders succeeded beyond their initial hopes. As hard as presidents work to win passage of their top priorities, they often complain that Congress is not listening. However, Congress listens more closely to its constituents, especially when the president's public approval is low. That is why so many of the Bush administration's second-term priorities never reached the floor of the House or Senate.

By the People

MAKING A DIFFERENCE

Public Service Through the White House Blog

Presidents pay attention to public opinion in many ways. Every president since the 1960s has appointed his own pollster to monitor public opinion. Presidents also travel frequently throughout the country lobbying for their programs, engaging citizens in town hall meetings, raising money for their political party, and campaigning for reelection.

Most of these activities are directed at relatively small numbers of citizens, which puts the burden on citizens to make contact with the president. Citizens are always welcome to send letters and e-mails to the president, but they rarely get a personal response. The White House receives 65,000 letters, 100,000 e-mails, 1,000 faxes, and between 2,500 and 3,500 phone calls per day, but only a handful of these messages end up on the president's desk.

At the start of his administration, however, Obama asked the White House mailroom to give him ten letters from ordinary Americans every day. Obama has been particularly interested in receiving real stories about the nation's current condition. "These letters, I think, do more than keep me in touch with what's happening around the country than anything else," Obama says in a White House video about the sorting process at http://www.whitehouse.gov/video/Inside-the- White-House-Letters-to-the-President. "Some of them are funny, some of them are angry, a lot of them are sad or frustrated about their current situation."

Under Obama, the White House established a series of forums for receiving public comments. On January 15, 2010, for example, the president's MySpace page had more than 160,000 friends, his Facebook page had nearly 500,000 friends, and his Twitter feed had more than 1.6 million followers. (All three destinations can be reached by entering MySpace.com, Facebook.com, or Twitter.com, followed by a backslash and the word "whitehouse.")

CRITICAL THINKING QUESTIONS

1. What kind of letter makes the most compelling reading in the White House and why?

2. Does a single hit on whitehouse.gov make any difference in the president's opinion?

3. What does the number of friends or followers actually tell the White House about public opinion? Are polls a better way for the president to understand what the country thinks?

Why Presidents and Congress Disagree

Congress and the president disagree for many reasons, not the least of which is the natural tendency of members of Congress to think about elections far into the future.

Competing Constituencies The framers guaranteed that members of Congress and the president would represent different constituencies, which often leads to conflict over major legislation. Members of Congress represent either states or local districts, whereas the president represents the nation as a whole. Although these constituencies often overlap, particularly in states that strongly support the president's election, members of Congress often worry most about how the laws and presidential actions will affect their home districts.

Competing Calendars The Constitution also ensures that Congress and the president will not share the same terms of office. Presidents can serve a maximum of eight years before leaving office, whereas senators and members of the House can serve for decades. Presidents enter office wanting everything passed at once, whereas members of Congress have plenty of time to wait.

President Jimmy Carter addresses the U.S. public in his first televised address to talk about energy policy. He made a deliberate choice to give the address sitting down near the fireplace dressed in a cardigan sweater as a way to calm the public's concern about increasing gasoline prices.

presidential support score
The percentage of times a president wins on key votes in Congress.

mandate
A president's claim of broad public support.

rally point
A rise in public approval of the president that follows a crisis as Americans "rally round the flag" and the chief executive.

Competing Campaigns   Finally, the Constitution ensures that Congress and the president will run different kinds of election campaigns. Most members of Congress finance their election campaigns with only minimal assistance from their national political party. They usually run independently of the president or national party platform. Even members of the president's own party have been known to ask the president not to visit their districts in particularly tight elections or when the president's public approval is falling. Whenever possible, members try to make elections about local, not national issues, which means the president is often completely ignored during the campaign.

Influencing Congress

Presidents have long had a substantial, if not always dominant, role in shaping what Congress does. Their primary vehicle for doing so is the president's agenda, an informal list of top legislative priorities. Whether through the State of the Union Address or through other messages and signals, presidents make clear what they think Congress should do.

It is one thing to proclaim a presidential priority, however, and quite another to actually influence congressional action. As Richard Neustadt argued in *Presidential Power*, a president's constitutional powers add up to little more than a job as the country's most distinguished office clerk. It is a president's ability to persuade others that spells the difference between being a clerk and being a national leader.[23]

The power to persuade on Capitol Hill is often measured through the **presidential support score,** calculated by counting the times the president wins key votes in Congress. Bush won more than 70 percent of his votes from 2001 to 2006, but only 38 percent in 2007.[24] Although his earlier high scores would seem to make him the most influential president in modern history, Bush earned the scores by taking relatively few positions on key votes that he knew he could win. Obama earned a record setting support score of almost 97 percent in 2009. Like Bush, Obama did so largely by limiting his positions to a handful of winnable votes.

Presidential Mandates   Presidents who enter office with a large electoral margin, high public approval, and a party majority in Congress often claim a **mandate,** or public support, to govern. The winner-take-all nature of the electoral-college system tends to make the president's popular vote look larger than it truly is.

Obama decided to spend his 2008 presidential election mandate on just two priorities: an economic stimulus package and health care reform. His mandate was relatively modest, however. Although he did win an overwhelming share of the electoral vote, his popular vote total was only 53 percent, which limited his ability to claim a sweeping mandate for change. Moreover, the economic calamity that started in 2008 reduced public support for most new programs.

Public Approval   The mandate to govern depends in part on public approval, which generally falls over time. (See Figure 12–3 for presidential approval trends throughout the past half-century.) Bush became the first incumbent president in modern history to win reelection despite starting his campaign with an approval rating below 50 percent. Although he regained ground after his second inauguration, his ratings continued to fall as his second term continued, which helps explain the declining number of congressional votes on which he took a position. He simply did not have enough *political capital* to take more positions.

Presidents also benefit from **rally points,** spikes in public approval following a domestic or international crisis. Rally points do not necessarily last long, however. George W. Bush's ratings jumped dramatically following the September 11, 2001, attacks when he called on the nation to support the war on terrorism but eventually fell back with the continued violence after the first months of the war in Iraq. His approval rating jumped 29 percent after the September 11 attacks and 12 percent after the start of the Iraq War in 2003.

Reputation   The longer presidents stay in office, the better they get at being president. They learn how Washington works, what powers they can use to influence congressional

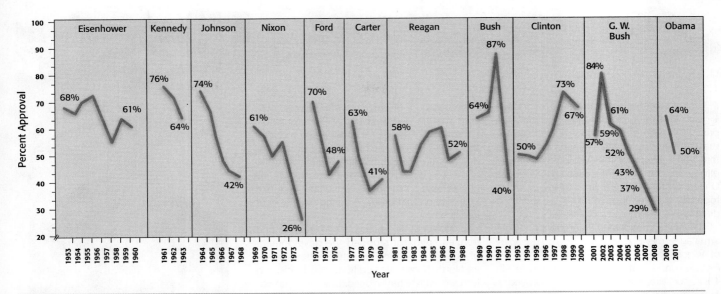

FIGURE 12–3 **Presidential Approval Ratings, 1953–2010.** ■ *How are all presidential approval ratings similar? Which president took office with the highest approval ratings, and which left with the lowest? What might explain the declines?*

NOTE: Percentage is from the first Gallup/*USA Today* poll taken each calendar year.

SOURCE: Gallup/*USA Today* poll, available at www.pollingreport.com.

action, and whom they need to convince to win passage of their top priorities. Presidents also learn how to use unilateral powers to accomplish some of their goals.

Nevertheless, presidents pay great attention to the steady erosion of public approval that occurs over time. As a result of this, they have the greatest potential influence at the very point when they know the least about being president, and they know the most about being president when they have the least influence.

Some experts believe the president's reputation has declined in recent years, in part due to political scandals. The controversy over the 2000 election raised questions about the legitimacy of the electoral process, and the war in Iraq led many to doubt President Bush's leadership in the war on terrorism. As a result, Congress may now be quicker to dismiss presidential positions.

Judging Presidents

Presidents rise and fall in the historical rankings based on a number of factors. Some rise because they led the nation through periods of intense domestic or international crisis; others rise because they had a distinctive vision of where the nation should go on issues such as civil rights, social policy, or the economy. Rankings also include at least some assessment of how presidents fared as political and moral leaders of the nation.

History tends to judge wars and international crises as the most significant test of a president's leadership. Wars that end in stalemate tend to diminish a president's greatness, whereas wars that end in victory raise a president's ranking, especially when the nation's survival is threatened. Abraham Lincoln (the Civil War), Woodrow Wilson (World War I), and Franklin Delano Roosevelt (World War II) rank among the great presidents because of their leadership during just such wars, whereas Lyndon Johnson ranks much lower because of his role in the Vietnam stalemate.

Corruption and inability to deal with economic problems are sure paths to presidential failure. Warren Harding and Richard Nixon both rank as failures because of scandals that tarnished their presidencies, while Herbert Hoover is ranked a failure because of his lack of leadership at the start of the Great Depression. Although Lyndon Johnson launched a number of great domestic programs such as Medicare for older citizens and

LEARNING **OBJECTIVE**

12.6 Identify factors that influence judgments about presidents.

Reducing Nuclear Weapons

Past presidents have invested enormous amounts of time and energy during the past 30 years to try to control and reduce the number of nuclear weapons throughout the world. Much of that work has involved efforts to stop the "arms race" between the United States and the Soviet Union, which together built enough nuclear weapons to destroy the world many times over.

Presidents negotiated a number of nuclear arms agreements during the long cold war, all of which had to be approved by the U.S. Senate under its treaty-making power. In 1972, for example, the Senate approved a freeze on the development of new weapons by the United States and Soviet Union that lasted through the 1970s. This Strategic Arms Limitation Treaty, negotiated by President Richard Nixon, froze the number of U.S. and Soviet missiles for five years.

In 1988, the Senate also approved a treaty banning the further development of shorter-range nuclear missiles that could be used in Europe and other "hot spots." This treaty, negotiated by President Ronald Reagan, marked the first time that the two nations also agreed to dismantle some of their existing weapons. Although both nations still have large numbers of nuclear weapons and missiles, further negotiations by Presidents Bill Clinton and George W. Bush have reduced the numbers of weapons and created a much safer world. Obama continued the effort by urging the world to destroy all nuclear weapons, but he was unable to make progress on that promise during his first year in office.

Unfortunately, these negotiations and treaties have not stopped the development of nuclear weapons by other nations, such as North Korea. In addition, Iran is moving forward with what it describes as a peaceful nuclear power program that foreign observers argue will produce the material for a nuclear weapon.

CRITICAL THINKING QUESTIONS

1. Why do nations seek nuclear weapons as part of their military strength?

2. What can the United States do to reduce the spread of nuclear weapons to other nations?

3. What can citizens do to put pressure on the United States and other nations to dismantle their nuclear weapons?

The U.S. and Russia negotiated a significant cut in nuclear weapons in May 2010 when they agreed to reduce the number of warheads to 1,500 in each country. However, the reduction still gives both nations the capacity to destroy each other many times over.

helped secure civil rights for African Americans, his role in the Vietnam War continues to cast a shadow on his presidential greatness.

It is too early to guess where George W. Bush will be ranked by history. His response to September 11, 2001, was steady and reassuring, and the nation rallied to his side in the first few weeks of the war in Iraq. At the same time, soaring budget deficits and questions about the war in Iraq undermined both his credibility and his public support. So did rising gasoline prices, the government's weak response to Hurricane Katrina in 2005, and the economic crisis that came at the end of his presidency in 2008.

At least for now, however, Bush seems destined for an average rating. According to public opinion polls taken in late 2006, only 19 percent of respondents rated Bush outstanding or above average, compared with 45 percent for Clinton, 32 percent for George H. W. Bush, 64 percent for Reagan, 38 percent for Jimmy Carter, and 23 percent for Gerald Ford. Of these presidents, only Reagan is likely to emerge as a great or near-great president in future polls.

Ultimately, a president's place in history is determined decades after he or she leaves office and varies over time. Reagan has moved up the charts with each passing survey, for example, as his role in ending the cold war takes on increasing visibility in an uncertain world. By remembering that there is a future accounting, presidents can find some inspiration for making the hard and sometimes unpopular choices that have led to greatness among their predecessors. Thus, the judgment of history may be one of the most important sources of accountability the nation has on its presidents.

CHAPTER **SUMMARY**

12.1 Describe the constitutional foundations of the presidency and of three presidential roles.

The framers wanted a presidency with enough authority to protect the nation from domestic and foreign threats but not so strong that it would become a threat to liberty. The framers gave the president three central roles in the new government: commander in chief, diplomat in chief, and administrator in chief. Presidents have expanded their powers in several ways throughout the decades. Crises, both foreign and economic, have enlarged these powers. When there is a need for decisive action, presidents are asked to supply it.

12.2 Evaluate the controversies surrounding presidents' assertion of additional executive powers.

The Constitution is not always clear on which branch has what powers, which creates controversies over the president's war power and authority to assert executive privilege, issue executive orders, and control the budget and spending process.

12.3 Outline the functions of the White House staff, Executive Office of the President, cabinet, and vice president.

Presidents manage the executive branch with the assistance of an intensely loyal White House staff, a much larger Executive Office of the President (EOP) that is anchored by the Office of Management and Budget (OMB), a cabinet of department secretaries that oversees the federal government's employees, and the vice president. The vice president's authority varies from president to president.

12.4 Characterize the various roles that presidents play.

We expect a great deal from our presidents. We want them to be crisis managers, morale builders, and agenda setters, but we also want them to be able to connect with average citizens. Presidents must also act as persuaders, using their staff, technology, and public opinion research to accomplish their agendas.

12.5 Identify the sources of presidential-congressional conflict and the tools presidents use to influence Congress.

The president and Congress often have a tense relationship because of different constitutional expectations and party divisions. Presidents have a variety of tools for influencing Congress, however, and use their political and personal resources to gain support for their policy proposals. Presidents have several powerful tools for influencing Congress. They can create mandates by helping members of Congress win elections, use their public approval to lobby Congress for action, and rely on the reputation of the presidency as a source of prestige.

12.6 Identify factors that influence judgments about presidents.

Presidential greatness is hard to define. Historians, political scientists, and the American public consider Washington, Jefferson, Lincoln, and Franklin Roosevelt as their greatest presidents. Greatness depends in part on how presidents deal with crisis and war.

CHAPTER **SELF-TEST**

12.1 Describe the constitutional foundations of the presidency and of three presidential roles.

1. Which of the following is NOT required for a person to be elected President of the United States?
   a. Be at least 35 years old
   b. Be a natural-born citizen of the United States
   c. Be affiliated with an officially organized political party
   d. Be a resident of the United States for the previous 14 years

2. What is the only constitutional duty of the Vice President aside from waiting to take the place of the President if needed?

3. In one or two paragraphs explain the president's responsibility in each of the three roles discussed in the chapter.

4. In a short essay, discuss how the framers addressed their concerns about the presidency

in the Constitution. In your opinion, have their protections worked?

12.2 Evaluate the controversies surrounding presidents' assertion of additional executive powers.

5. List and briefly explain the President's additional powers. Which of the president's additional executive powers are most important to the role as chief diplomat, chief lawmaker, manager in chief, and commander in chief?

6. Match each of the Presidents listed below with the precedents they set while in office.

1. George W. Bush	a. Establishing a two-term precedent
2. George Washington	b. Creating a strong Executive Office of the President
3. Franklin D. Roosevelt	c. Expanding the president's war power

7. Which of these precedents is the most important to the president's success in Congress? Which is the most threatening to the separation of powers?

12.3 Outline the functions of the White House staff, Executive Office of the President, cabinet, and vice president.

8. Write a brief sentence defining the following parts of the president's staff:
   a. The White House staff
   b. The Cabinet
   c. The Executive Office of the President
   d. The Office of Management and Budget
9. List the three ways of organizing the White House staff and the benefits and weaknesses of each.
10. Table 12–1 lists a set of issues over which the President might be assumed to have some control. Chose three and write a brief essay explaining how the president could influence each.

12.4 Characterize the various roles that presidents play.

11. Briefly explain each of the President's roles listed below.
    a. Persuader
    b. Agenda Setter
    c. Morale Builder

12. Which role do you think is the most important at the start of a president's first term? Which is the most important during times of national crisis? How do the three roles work together, and when do they conflict?

12.5 Identify the sources of presidential-congressional conflict and the tools presidents use to influence Congress.

13. List the three main causes of conflict between the president and Congress.
14. Write a persuasive essay explaining how the current relationship between the President and Congress fulfills the framers' intentions for their roles and interactions.

12.6 Identify factors that influence judgments about presidents.

15. In a short essay, discuss factors other than winning wars that you think make a president "great." How would the most two recent presidents rank in your determination of presidential greatness?
16. How much should presidents worry about their standing in history when they are making decisions?

Answers for selected questions: 1. b; 6. Bush: c; Washington: a; Roosevelt: b

---

mypoliscilab EXERCISES
Where participation leads to action!

Apply what you learned in this chapter on MyPoliSciLab.

📖 **Read** on **mypoliscilab.com**

eText: Chapter 12

✔ **Study** and **Review** on **mypoliscilab.com**

Pre-Test
Post-Test
Chapter Exam
Flashcards

👁 **Watch** on **mypoliscilab.com**

Video: Bush and Congress
Video: The Government Bails Out Automakers

✳ **Explore** on **mypoliscilab.com**

Simulation: Presidential Leadership: Which Hat Do You Wear?
Simulation: You Are a President During a Nuclear Power Plant Meltdown
Comparative: Comparing Chief Executives
Timeline: The Executive Order Over Time
Visual Literacy: Presidential Success in Polls and Congress

KEY **TERMS**

parliamentary governments, p. 327
presidential ticket, p. 329
vesting clause, p. 329
treaty, p. 330
executive agreement, p. 330
congressional–executive
  agreement, p. 330
recess appointment, p. 331
veto, p. 331
pocket veto, p. 331

take care clause, p. 332
inherent powers, p. 332
State of the Union Address, p. 332
signing statements, p. 332
impeachment, p. 333
executive privilege, p. 334
executive orders, p. 335
impoundment, p. 336
line item veto, p. 336
chief of staff, p. 338

Executive Office of the President
  (EOP), p. 338
Office of Management and Budget
  (OMB), p. 339
cabinet, p. 339
presidential support score, p. 344
mandate, p. 344
rally point, p. 344

ADDITIONAL **RESOURCES**

FURTHER READING

THOMAS E. CRONIN AND MICHAEL A. GENOVESE, *The Paradoxes of the American Presidency*, 2d ed. (Oxford University Press, 2004).

TERRY EASTLAND, *Energy in the Executive* (Free Press, 1992).

FRED GREENSTEIN, *The Presidential Difference: Leadership Style from FDR to George W. Bush*, 2d ed. (Princeton University Press, 2004).

GENE HEALY, *The Cult of the Presidency: America's Dangerous Devotion to Presidential Power* (Cato Institute, 2008).

CHARLES O. JONES, *The Presidency in a Separated System*, 2d ed. (Brookings Institution Press, 2005).

SAMUEL KERNELL, *Going Public: New Strategies of Presidential Leadership*, 4th ed. (CQ Press, 2006).

GARY KING AND LYN RAGSDALE, *The Elusive Executive: Discovering Statistical Patterns in the Presidency*, 2d ed. (CQ Press, 2002).

SIDNEY M. MILKIS, *The President and the Parties: The Transformation of the American Party System Since the New Deal* (Oxford University Press, 1993).

MICHAEL NELSON, ED., *The Presidency and the Political System*, 9th ed. (CQ Press, 2009).

RICHARD E. NEUSTADT, *Presidential Power and the Modern Presidents* (Free Press, 1991).

BRADLEY H. PATTERSON JR., *The White House Staff: Inside the West Wing and Beyond* (Brookings Institution Press, 2002).

JAMES PFIFFNER, *The Modern Presidency*, 5th ed. (Wadsworth, 2008).

STEPHEN SKOWRONEK, *Presidential Leadership in Political Time: Reprise and Reappraisal* (University of Kansas Press, 2008).

WEB SITES

whitehouse.gov Every fact possible on the Obama presidency, including speeches, blogs, videos, and links to all major EOP.

loc.gov The Library of Congress Web site. Click on the presidential history link for portraits and details on each presidency.

millercenter.org/academic/american president A huge inventory of resources on the American presidency, including research papers and oral histories from past administrations.

barackobama.com Information on Obama's call for citizen involvement.

presidency.org The Web site of the Center for the Presidency. Loaded with papers and facts.

presidency.ucsb.edu The largest inventory of information on what presidents do. Every State of the Union Address, executive orders, press conference transcripts, veto messages, and selected research papers. An invaluable resource for research papers.

The Federal Bureaucracy

Executing the Laws

E arly in the morning on April 20, 2010, British Petroleum was about to start producing oil from one of the deepest wells ever drilled in the Gulf of Mexico. Breaking through 5,000 feet below surface, the well was connected to a floating oil rig called the Deepwater Horizon. Hours before the Deepwater Horizon was to finish work, methane gas surged up the underwater pipe and exploded on the surface. Eleven oil workers were killed or lost at sea as the Deepwater Horizon was sinking. As it collapsed, the rig ripped free of the underwater oil pipe to the surface, which remained open because the underwater "blowout preventer" had failed. Within hours, the federal government discovered that the pipe was releasing thousands of gallons of oil per hour, creating the largest oil spill in U.S. history and threatening the entire Gulf coast.

The spill was caused by a number of failures, including British Petroleum's own haphazard safety precautions. However, the disaster was rooted in what President Barack Obama later called the "cozy relationship" between the federal government's Minerals Management Service (MMS) and the oil industry. Located within the Department of the Interior, the MMS was responsible for both regulating and promoting the industry. It set safety standards for offshore oil drilling even as it granted permits that allowed the industry to extract as much oil as possible. With the United States desperately trying to break its addiction to foreign oil, the MMS began to grant permits more freely and frequently waived safety requirements on deepwater drilling. For example, MMS decided that British Petroleum did not need an automatic cutoff valve on the Deepwater rig, waived the company's obligation to prove that its drilling would not cause environmental damage, and gave the company permission to test the Deepwater Horizon's blowout preventer at lower pressure standards than required under the MMS's own rules.

Confronted with these failures, Obama decided to overhaul MMS by breaking it into two new agencies, one for assuring safety and the other for granting permits. He also accepted the resignation of the political appointee heading the agency and gave the U.S. Coast Guard absolute authority to supervise British Petroleum's efforts to stop the spill. He also appointed a special commission to investigate the disaster, even as Congress launched its own investigations. Finally, Obama promised a new era of accountability at the MMS. However, MMS was the subject of numerous earlier investigations in previous decades, none of which had produced results. The fact that MMS continued to give the benefit of the doubt to the oil industry shows just how resistant some government agencies are to presidential and congressional control.

In this chapter, we examine the origins, functions, and realities of the federal bureaucracy as it works to faithfully execute the laws. We also explore how governmental departments, agencies, and employees are held accountable to the president, Congress, and the U.S. public.

This chapter uses the word "bureaucracy" to describe what political scientists call the federal administrative state. As we shall see, the word is sometimes used as a way to criticize government, while the word "bureaucrat" is often used to describe federal employees as poorly motivated and inefficient. Instead, we refer to federal employees as just that, federal employees. Some are very good at their work and are highly motivated to make a difference through their public service, but there are always a few employees in every organization, public or private, who do not work hard. The major difference is that private employees are relatively easy to fire, while poorly performing federal employees are protected against removal by a long list of laws.

Understanding the Federal Bureaucracy

LEARNING **OBJECTIVE**

13.1 Outline the constitutional roots of the federal bureaucracy and pros and cons of bureaucratic administration.

The framers clearly understood that the new national government would need an administrative system to protect the young Republic from foreign and domestic threats. They also understood that the new departments of government would need talented employees if they were to succeed. Although the framers hoped government employees would be motivated by the desire to serve their country, they knew government would have to pay those employees for their work.

Constitutional Controls

Under the Constitution, the federal bureaucracy is responsible for faithfully executing the laws on behalf of the president, Congress, and the judiciary. Although disagreements and factions were a normal and predictable part of making the laws, they were unacceptable when it came time for the laws to be executed. As Alexander Hamilton explained in *The Federalist,* No. 70, the new federal government would need a bureaucracy with the skill and motivation to convert laws into action, which he described as "the true test of a good government."[1]

The founders spent little time worrying about the administration of government, however. Instead, they left most of the details to future presidents. They believed that federal departments and agencies would be relatively small, and they expected Congress to establish the same departments that had existed under the Articles of Confederation, including the departments of war, state, and treasury, and the postal service.[2] Nevertheless, the framers made three key decisions about executing the laws that continue to shape federal administration to this day.

First, they prohibited members of the House and Senate from holding executive branch positions. They drew a sharp line on the issue in Article I, Section 6, of the Constitution: "No Senator or Representative shall, during the Time for which he was elected, be appointed to any civil Office under the Authority of the United States, which shall have been created, or the Emoluments whereof shall have been increased during such time, and no Person holding any Office under the United States, shall be a Member of either House during his Continuance in Office." Under this provision, Congress could not create executive jobs for its members, which was a common form of corruption in England before the Revolutionary War.[3]

Second, the framers decided to give the president complete authority to nominate the senior officers of government. Although they also gave the Senate authority to confirm or reject the president's appointees under the Constitution's "advice and consent" function, the framers made the president, not Congress, responsible for filling any vacancies in those jobs when the Senate is in recess. Although Article I does give Congress the power to create the departments of government and the Senate the power to confirm presidential appointees, both by a majority vote, the president emerged from the final days of the Constitutional Convention as the nation's *administrator in chief.* The framers saw direct presidential control of government as essential for faithfully executing the laws.

Third, the framers decided that the president, not Congress, is responsible for requiring the opinions of the "principal officer" of each executive department, which means the president is in charge of what presidential appointees do. The chief executive is not only responsible for hiring and supervising presidential appointees, however, but also has the power to fire appointees for any reason. Presidents routinely ask all their appointees to resign before the inauguration of a new president.

These decisions about presidential power did not give the president unlimited authority to execute the laws, however. Recall that Congress, not the president, has the power to create, reorganize, or abolish the departments and agencies of government in the first place and has the responsibility for appropriating the money to administer programs and hire government employees. They also gave the Senate the power to confirm certain presidential appointees, and they clearly expected both houses of Congress to monitor the workings of the executive branch.

Alexander Hamilton helped set many of the precedents that govern the federal bureaucracy today. He was a strong advocate of what he called "execution in detail," which involved detailed rules that federal employees must follow, and he argued for an expansion in the number of federal employees as the federal government's mission expanded.

Defining Bureaucracy

More than 200 years after the Constitution was written, the federal government is administered by one of the largest bureaucracies in the world. The federal bureaucracy is composed of 15 departments, 50 agencies, the U.S. Postal Service, and the armed services.

It also employs one of the largest workforces in the world. Nearly 4.5 million people worked for the federal government in 2010, including 700,000 postal workers, more than 2.2 million full-time federal employees, and 1.4 million military personnel. In addition, 7.6 million work for the federal government under contracts to private firms such as Lockheed Martin and Boeing, and 2.9 million work under federal grants to colleges, universities, and state and local governments. All told, the federal bureaucracy includes almost 15 million employees, only a handful of whom are visible to the public.[4] Figure 13–1 shows the numbers of full-time federal employees versus the number of contract employees. The former has been relatively stable throughout the last 20 years, whereas the latter has expanded rapidly.

At one time in history, **bureaucracy** actually meant fast, effective, and rational administration. In its ideal form, a bureaucracy made sure every job was carefully designed to ensure faithful performance by well-trained, highly motivated **bureaucrats,** or employees. According to German sociologist Max Weber, who wrote in defense of bureaucracy in the late 1800s, bureaucracies derive their strength from six characteristics:

1. *Specialization:* Bureaucracies break jobs into smaller and smaller parts so that every employee knows exactly what his or her job is. Because their jobs are so specialized, employees can be trained in enough detail to succeed.
2. *Centralization:* Bureaucracies concentrate authority at the top of the organization, where a single leader maintains control of all activity. This leader is in charge of every last person in the organization.
3. *Rules:* Bureaucracies implement policies through formal rules that govern everything that employees do.
4. *Standardization:* Bureaucracies make sure all decisions are the same—meaning every employee makes the same decisions in producing a product or making a ruling. Standardization assures customers and clients that they will be treated fairly whomever they talk to.
5. *Expertise:* Bureaucracies make sure all employees have the training and experience to do their jobs effectively and that they are given the tools such as information technology to succeed.
6. *Accountability:* Bureaucracies enforce these rules through a set of communication channels that allow the leaders of the organization to know exactly what is going on at all levels. The bureaucracy is structured so that employees follow orders or are fired.

bureaucracy
A form of organization that operates through impersonal, uniform rules and procedures.

bureaucrat
A career government employee.

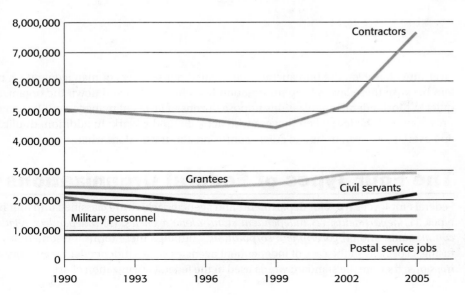

FIGURE 13–1 Measuring the Estimated Total Number of Federal Employees.

■ *Why has there been such a dramatic increase in the number of contracted employees?*

SOURCE: Paul C. Light, *A Government Ill Executed* (Harvard University Press, 2008).

Global Views of Bribery

Bribery is not a significant problem in the U.S. federal bureaucracy, but it is a way of doing business in many countries. A bribe is merely a way for ordinary citizens to speed up the bureaucracy so that they can get building permits, resolve traffic fines without going to court, and receive basic benefits such as aid for the needy. Bribes are a sign that a government is unwilling to faithfully execute the laws for all of its citizens and show significant corruption within the system. As the Pew Global Survey shows, countries vary greatly in the degree of this kind of corruption. Respondents were asked, "In the past year, how often, if ever, have you had to do a favor, give a gift, or pay a bribe to a government official in order to get services or a document that the government is supposed to provide?"

The Pew survey shows great variation throughout the world in bribery and corruption. Some nations such as India tolerate very high levels of bribery, whereas other Asian nations have been more successful in limiting the practice.

One way to avoid corruption is to impose strong limits on employee conduct through tight monitoring by special units of government such as the U.S. government's offices of inspector general. These offices, which can be found through www.ignet.gov, are responsible for detecting and punishing fraud, waste, and abuse. They create deterrence by making sure federal employees understand that they might be caught and punished if they take bribes or other payments for favorable treatment. Higher-level federal employees are also required to file annual financial disclosure reports showing their financial transactions

for the year. Citizens can also play a role in preventing fraud by reporting incidents of fraud, waste, and abuse through an inspector general's hotline.

CRITICAL THINKING QUESTIONS

1. What can international organizations such as the United Nations do to reduce government corruption throughout the world?

2. Do you have any theories about why the Pew Global Survey did not interview U.S., British, Chinese, and Japanese citizens about bribery?

3. Does financial exposure have any negative effects in discouraging people to take jobs in government?

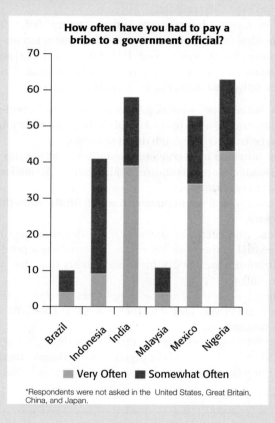

How often have you had to pay a bribe to a government official?

■ Very Often   ■ Somewhat Often

*Respondents were not asked in the United States, Great Britain, China, and Japan.

Over time, however, the bureaucracy has created dense layers of management—a problem because these layers keep information from moving up and down the organization quickly. Most federal organizations impose dozens of layers of management between the president and the federal employees who actually do the work. In addition, duplication and overlap between units can create confusion about who does what.

The Four Types of Federal Organizations

LEARNING OBJECTIVE

13.2 Identify the four types of federal organizations.

Federal employees work for departments and agencies, which are classified into four broad types: (1) *departments,* (2) *independent stand-alone agencies,* (3) *independent regulatory commissions,* and (4) *government corporations.* Although these terms are sometimes confusing, especially in the case of independent agencies versus independent regulatory commissions, they are the standard words used in the federal organization chart.

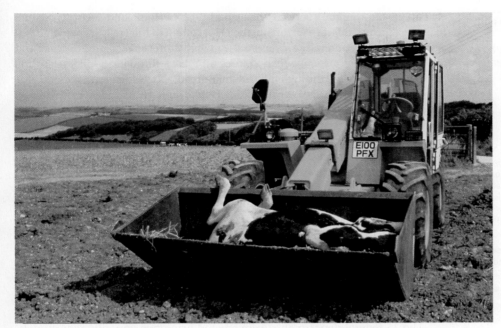

Duplication between agencies is evident in the procedures for protecting Americans from mad cow disease. The Department of Agriculture's Animal and Plant Health Inspection Service keeps diseased cattle out of the United States; the Department of Health and Human Services' Food and Drug Administration monitors cattle feed; and the Department of Agriculture's Food Safety and Inspection Service inspects cattle as they go to slaughter. ■ *Why is the federal bureaucracy, not the states, responsible for food safety?*

Departments tend to be the most common federal organizations, have the broadest missions, and usually have the largest number of federal employees. They are also the most visible organizations in government and are generally well known to the public.

Independent stand-alone agencies are also under the president's control but tend to have fewer federal employees and may have more focused missions than departments. In general, the word "independent" is used to distinguish agencies that exist outside a department from those that operate within a department such as the Department of Homeland Security. This chapter will generally use the term "independent stand-alone" agencies to describe what the federal government formally calls independent agencies.

Independent regulatory commissions are a special kind of independent agency. They are created to insulate the agency from congressional and presidential control through the appointment of a board of commissioners who serve for a fixed term of office and cannot be fired by the president.

Finally, **government corporations** are designed to operate much like private businesses and have special authorities to set the prices of their services. These corporations are quite rare and are often confused with departments and independent stand-alone agencies. The U.S. Postal Service is the biggest of the government corporations and is supposed to make money by delivering the mail. Amtrak is another example of a government corporation. It, too, is supposed to make money through ticket sales.

We will discuss each of the four types of federal organizations below.

Departments   Departments are the most visible organizations in the federal bureaucracy. Today's 15 departments of government employ more than 70 percent of all federal civil servants and spend 93 percent of all federal dollars. Fourteen of the departments are headed by secretaries; the 15th, the Justice Department, is headed by the attorney general. Many departments are collections of smaller agencies that are brought together under one organization chart. As Figure 13–2 shows, the Department of Health and Human Services contains more than a dozen smaller agencies as part of its overall structure.

Measured by the total number of employees, the five largest departments are the Defense Department; the Department of Veterans Affairs, which helps veterans return to

department
Usually the largest organization in government with the largest mission; also the highest rank in the federal hierarchy.

independent stand-alone agency
A government agency that operates outside a traditional government department, but under the president's direct control.

independent regulatory commission
A government agency or commission with regulatory power whose independence is protected by Congress.

government corporation
A government agency that operates like a business corporation, created to secure greater freedom of action and flexibility for a particular program.

FIGURE 13–2 **The Department of Health and Human Services.**

■ *What are the benefits and drawbacks of having all of these organizations housed within the Department of Health and Human Services?*

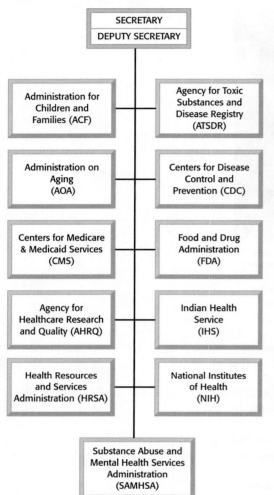

civilian life after military service; the Department of Homeland Security, created to protect the nation from terrorism; the Department of the Treasury, which manages the economy and raises revenues through the Internal Revenue Service; and the Department of Justice, which enforces the laws through the federal courts and investigates crime through the Federal Bureau of Investigation.

Measured by prestige, the Defense, Health and Human Services, Justice, State, and Treasury departments are considered part of the *inner cabinet* closest to the president, whereas the rest of the departments are considered part of the outer circle of departments that rarely receive the president's attention.

Measured by budget, the Department of Health and Human Services is the largest department of government and will become even larger as a result of health care legislation enacted in 2010. This department provides health insurance to the elderly through the huge Medicare program, helps states cover health care for the poor through the Medicaid programs, covers the cost of health insurance for children through the State Children's Health Insurance Program (SCHIP), and administers a variety of programs to help the poor. It also contains the Food and Drug Administration, the National Institutes of Health, and the Centers for Disease Control and Prevention, all of which protect the population from disease. The health care reforms signed into law in 2010 will be administered by the Centers for Medicare and Medicaid Services, which is also housed by this department.

The 15 federal departments were created using two very different models. The first approach to building a department focuses on creating an umbrella organization by combining a number of related independent agencies. The Department of Homeland Security, for example, was created by combining elements of 22 separate agencies, including the Immigration and Naturalization Service, the Customs Service, the Federal Emergency Management Agency, the Secret Service, portions of the Animal and Plant Health Inspection Service, and the Coast Guard, which is often viewed as a branch of the military.

The other approach to building a department is designed to create a single-purpose organization that owes its existence largely to the strength of an interest group. Congress created the Department of Veterans Affairs in 1989 under pressure from veterans' groups such as the American Legion and Veterans of Foreign Wars, who wanted their own advocate in the president's cabinet.

Independent Stand-Alone Agencies   The word "independent" means at least two things in the federal bureaucracy. Applied to a regulatory commission, it means the agency is outside the president's control. Applied to an agency of government, it merely means separate from a traditional department. Whereas independent regulatory commissions do not report to the president, independent agencies do.

As a general rule, independent stand-alone agencies are smaller than federal departments and work on specific problems. Becoming an agency is often the first step toward becoming a department. The Veterans Administration was created in 1930 as an agency, for example, but it became a department only in 1989. Independent stand-alone agencies are usually headed by an administrator, the second most senior title in the federal bureaucracy behind secretary or attorney general. There are more than 50 such agencies today.

The spread of independent stand-alone agencies can add to confusion about who is responsible for what in the federal government. For example, the federal government has 15 different intelligence agencies, which include the CIA, the Defense Intelligence Agency, the FBI, and the NSA. These 15 agencies had a history of keeping secrets not only from the people but also from each other, which contributed to the intelligence failures leading up to the war in Iraq. In late 2004, Congress created a new national intelligence director to oversee all of these agencies and foster greater collaboration.

Politically, independent stand-alone agencies can sometimes be more important to the president than some cabinet departments. The director of the CIA or the administrator of the EPA may get a higher place on the president's agenda than the secretary of HUD (the Department of Housing and Urban Development) or agriculture, particularly when an issue such as international spying or global warming is in the headlines.

The following independent stand-alone agencies are considered among the most important in the bureaucracy:

- *Central Intelligence Agency* collects and interprets international intelligence.
- *Director of National Intelligence* coordinates intelligence collected by other government agencies.
- *Environmental Protection Agency* regulates and enforces laws to reduce pollution.
- *National Aeronautics and Space Administration* manages the U.S. civilian space program.
- *Small Business Administration* monitors the state of U.S. small businesses.
- *Social Security Administration* administers the Social Security program.

Independent Regulatory Commissions Although independent regulatory commissions are part of the federal bureaucracy, they have a measure of independence from both Congress and the president. By definition, these commissions are headed not by a single executive but by a small number of commissioners appointed by the president, with Senate confirmation, for fixed terms of office. Unlike other presidential appointees, commissioners cannot be removed from office without cause, which is defined by law to mean "inefficiency, neglect of duty, or malfeasance in office." As a result, independent regulatory commissions are less responsive to political pressure from either Congress or the president.

Throughout the decades, Congress has created dozens of independent regulatory commissions with the power to protect consumers (the Consumer Product Safety Commission), regulate stock markets (the Securities and Exchange Commission), oversee federal election laws (the Federal Election Commission), monitor television and radio (the Federal Communications Commission), regulate business (the Federal Trade Commission), control the supply of money (the Federal Reserve Board), and watch over nuclear power plants (the Nuclear Regulatory Commission). Many experts contend that the Federal Reserve Board chair is the second most influential person in making economic policy, and others would argue that the current chair, Ben S. Bernanke, is the most important leader in influencing public confidence about the economy.[5] Bernanke was appointed to a four-year term as a member of the Board in 2006, and he was reappointed in 2010.

Independent regulatory commissions are not completely independent, however. Their commissioners are appointed by the president and are subject to Senate confirmation, their annual budgets must be approved by Congress, and their decisions are subject to judicial review. Moreover, presidents make most appointments on the basis of party, which means that commissions are often highly political.

Independent regulatory commissions tend to be much less visible than departments until a crisis occurs. The Securities and Exchange Commission was on the front pages for three years, for example, as one corporation after another disclosed accounting fraud in their annual reports to investors. The SEC was created in the 1930s to restore investor confidence in the stock market after the Great Depression, but it was accused of being negligent in monitoring accounting practices at big companies such as Enron and WorldCom in the early 2000s. It also failed to detect Bernie Madoff's investment fraud, which cost investors more than $18 billion. In May 2010, however, a newly rebuilt SEC filed suit against the financial giant Goldman Sachs, alleging that the firm bet against the very mortgages it was selling on the open market.

The following independent regulatory commissions are considered among the most important in the federal bureaucracy:

- *Commodity Futures Trading Corporation* regulates the markets for commodities such as corn, wheat, precious metals, and other products used in manufacturing.

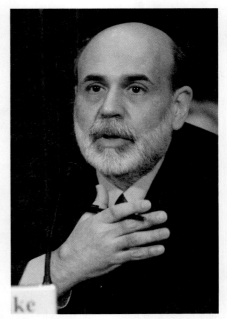

As Federal Reserve Board chair, Ben S. Bernanke is in charge of one of the most important independent regulatory commissions. Replacing Alan Greenspan, who had served for nearly 20 years, Bernanke has begun his second four-year term as chairman of the Federal Reserve Board. ■ *Why does the chairman of the Federal Reserve have a limited, four-year term when most presidential appointees do not?*

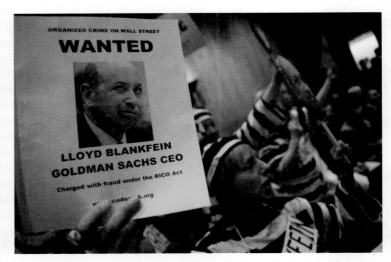

The giant investment firm Goldman Sachs came under fire for its behavior in the 2008 economic collapse. It was accused of betting against investment packages that it sold to clients, which allowed the firm to make money even as its clients lost. Congress began investigating the lack of federal oversight of the action in 2010.

Of the People

AMERICA'S CHANGING FACE

The Federal Workforce

The federal bureaucracy is more representative of the public now than it was in the 1950s, when most of its employees were white and most female employees were clerk-typists. Women held 44 percent of all federal jobs in 2007, whereas minorities held close to a third.

Even though the number of women and minorities in the federal workforce is at an all-time high, both groups still face barriers in rising to the top. First, women and minorities are not equally represented in all departments and agencies. They tend to be concentrated in departments with strong social service missions such as Education, Health and Human Services, Housing and Urban Development, and Veterans Affairs. Military and technical departments such as Defense, Energy, and Transportation have far fewer women employees.

Second, women and minorities are not represented at all levels of the federal bureaucracy. Women held 70 percent of lower-paying technical and clerical positions in 2007, and minorities were also heavily represented at the bottom

of government. Together, women and minorities held barely 15 percent of the top jobs. Nevertheless, they are moving into the top jobs at a fast rate. Between 1994 and 2007, the number of women and minorities in professional and managerial jobs jumped from 44 percent to roughly 60 percent. (Further statistics on the federal workforce can be found by searching for "factbook" at http://www.opm.gov.)

CRITICAL THINKING QUESTIONS

1. Why should the federal bureaucracy try to recruit more women and minorities to its top jobs?

2. Does increasing diversity improve the bureaucracy's performance and accountability? Why or why not?

3. How can the bureaucracy enhance diversity in scientific and technical fields?

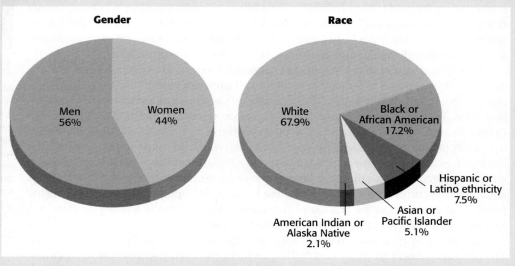

SOURCE: U.S. Office of Personnel Management, *Fact Book, 2007,* accessed at http://www.opm.gov/feddata/factbook/2007/2007FACTBOOK.pdf.

- *Consumer Product Safety Commission* monitors and regulates the safety of products released for public use, such as children's toys and cribs.
- *Equal Employment Opportunity Commission* regulates and enforces laws ensuring equality of access to jobs.
- *Federal Communications Commission* monitors and regulates use of the public airways for radio and television broadcasting, but its authority does not extend to cable television or satellite radio.
- *Federal Deposit Insurance Corporation* provides insurance for bank savings accounts up to $100,000.
- *Federal Election Commission* monitors and enforces federal campaign finance laws.
- *Federal Trade Commission* ensures that advertising for products is fair and truthful.
- *Federal Reserve Board* sets interest rates on borrowing.
- *Nuclear Regulatory Commission* regulates the nuclear power industry.
- *Securities Exchange Commission* regulates the stock markets that trade stocks in publicly held corporations.

Government Corporations Government corporations are perhaps the least understood organizations in the federal bureaucracy. Because they are intended to act more like businesses than like traditional government departments and agencies, they generally have more freedom from the internal rules that control traditional government agencies. They often have greater authority to hire and fire employees quickly and are allowed to make money through the sale of services such as train tickets, stamps, or home loans.[6]

Government corporations include organizations such as the Corporation for Public Broadcasting (which runs PBS television), the U.S. Postal Service, the National Railroad Passenger Corporation (better known as Amtrak), and AmeriCorps (which runs a national service program created by the Clinton administration), along with a host of financial enterprises that make loans of one kind or another.

Amtrak is a government corporation that is supposed to make money through its operations, but it lost more than $1 billion in 2009. Federal taxpayers must pick up the loss, which averaged $32 per Amtrak passenger. The U.S. Postal Service lost more than $3 billion in 2009, which was also covered by taxpayers. ■ *Do you think that the services these businesses provide justify allowing them to operate at a loss? Why might it be important that these services be provided by the government rather than a private business?*

Types of Federal Employees

The federal civilian workforce is composed of three different types of employees: (1) presidential appointees who run the bureaucracy; (2) members of the Senior Executive Service, which contains a mix of presidential appointees and civil servants; and (3) members of the civil service who execute the laws under the direction of presidential appointees and senior executives. (A full picture of the federal workforce would also include military personnel, but we will focus on civilian employees here.)

Presidential Appointees

Roughly 3,000 presidential appointees head federal departments and agencies, including 600 administrative officers subject to Senate confirmation and another 2,400 who serve entirely "at the pleasure of the president." As political officers, presidential appointees generally leave their posts at the end of that president's term in office. The president also appoints another 1,000 U.S. marshals, U.S. attorneys, and ambassadors to foreign nations but usually makes these appointments on a nonpolitical basis.

LEARNING OBJECTIVE
13.3 Differentiate three types of federal employees, and explain how each is selected.

Presidential appointees have some of the toughest jobs in the world. They work long hours, resolve complex disputes, and make important decisions about how the laws will be executed. Although many are selected on the basis of political connections, the top positions in the most important departments are generally reserved for individuals with significant leadership skills and experience.

Senior presidential appointees are selected through a four-step process. Except for individuals who are extraordinarily close to the president, the first step is to be selected by the White House Presidential Personnel Office. Most appointees are members of the president's party, and many contributed either time or money to the president's campaign.

The second step in becoming an appointee is to survive the White House clearance process, which is designed to ensure that candidates are legally qualified for office and pose no potential embarrassment to the president. All candidates receive a packet of forms that require detailed disclosure on every aspect of their personal and professional life, including job history, drug use, personal counseling, financial investments, and even traffic fines of more than $150.

The third step is the simplest: The president submits the name of the nominee on parchment paper to the clerk of the Senate. The document is placed in a special envelope, sealed with wax, and hand-delivered to the Senate when it is in session.

In the fourth step, the Senate refers each nomination to the appropriate confirmation committee, which conducts its own reviews. Depending on the position and the nominee, the Senate may ask to review the entire file developed by the White House, including the FBI's investigation. Once the review is complete, the committee holds a

Former Senate Majority Leader Tom Daschle was selected by President Obama as secretary of the Department of Health and Human Services. Daschle was forced to withdraw his name from consideration after reporting that he had underpaid his income taxes.

The Transportation Security Administration did not have an administrator in place when a terrorist attempted to blow up a Northwest Airlines flight on December 25, 2009. ■ *What other problems can arise when an agency doesn't have a senior official in place?*

hearing on the nomination and usually sends it to the floor of the Senate with a favorable recommendation. In turn, most nominations are approved by the Senate on voice votes.

Because the Senate acts through unanimous consent, individual senators can place *holds* on individual nominations to prevent confirmation. In 2009, for example, Senator Jim DeMint (R-S.C.) put a hold on Obama's choice for the top job at the Transportation Security Administration, which oversees airport security through its workforce of 45,000 baggage and passenger screeners. DeMint refused to release his hold unless the Obama administration promised not to allow the screeners to unionize. As a result, the Transportation Security Administration did not have an administrator in office when a terrorist attempted to explode a bomb on a flight from Amsterdam to Detroit on Christmas Day 2009.

The Senior Executive Service

Presidential appointees work closely with the 7,000 members of the **Senior Executive Service,** which includes roughly 6,400 career executives appointed through a rigorous review process and another 600 political executives appointed by the president without Senate confirmation. Career senior executives continue in their posts regardless of who happens to be president and are selected on the basis of merit. Except for a small number of political executives who are appointed for a limited time on the basis of political loyalty, members of the Senior Executive Service are selected through a highly competitive process that emphasizes their skills as managers.

When the number of presidential appointees and senior executives are added together, there are approximately 10,000 executives who run federal departments and agencies. The number has grown dramatically throughout the past three decades as the federal government has "thickened," with more layers of leadership and more leaders at each layer.[7] Some political scientists argue that Congress helped cause thickening by creating highly complex programs that demand close supervision, whereas others believe it is driven in part by a competition for power among competing organizations. According to this theory of public bureaucracy, bureaucratic organizations constantly seek to enhance their power, whether by creating new titles, adding more staff, or increasing their budgets.[8]

The Civil Service

The founders understood that the new federal government would need employees, and they would need to be paid. They also knew that most federal employees would not require Senate confirmation and that many of these employees would select government for their career. The founders believed that this **civil service** would outlast each administration, thereby providing steadiness for government.

For the first 100 years, however, members of the federal civil service were selected in part because of their political loyalty to the president's party. This **spoils system**—"to the

Senior Executive Service
Established by Congress in 1978 as a flexible, mobile corps of senior career executives who work closely with presidential appointees to manage government.

civil service
Federal employees who work for government through a competitive, not political selection process.

spoils system
A system of public employment based on rewarding party loyalists and friends.

victor belong the spoils"—was substantially expanded by President Andrew Jackson after his election in 1829. Jackson believed that every job in government was a potential opportunity for employing his political allies. Thus, every job was subject to presidential control and filled on the basis of political connections and even bribes. Actual ability to do the work had almost nothing to do with obtaining an appointment, and few employees outlasted their president.

The spoils system gave the president's party complete control over almost every government job, from cabinet secretaries down to post office clerks. Under its method of *patronage,* presidents would patronize, or support, their allies by providing jobs and other benefits after an election.

The spoils system began to unravel when Congress created the modern civil service in 1883. Indeed, it was a job seeker who started the federal bureaucracy down the road toward today's civil service system. Unfortunately for President James Garfield, that job seeker happened to be both disappointed and a good shot. Garfield's assassination prompted Congress to pass the Pendleton Act of 1883, which created an independent Civil Service Commission to ensure that most federal jobs were awarded under a **merit system,** meaning on the basis of an individual's ability to do the work, not political connections.[9] See Figure 13–3 for the different types of federal employees.

Ninety percent of federal employees are now selected on the basis of merit. Nearly all the rest are selected through hiring systems that emphasize a special skill such as medicine. The **Office of Personnel Management (OPM)** administers civil service laws and rules, whereas the independent **Merit Systems Protection Board** is charged with protecting the integrity of the federal merit system and the rights of federal employees. The Merit Systems Protection Board conducts studies of the merit system, investigates charges of favoritism, resolves employee complaints about unfair discipline, and orders corrective and disciplinary actions against an agency executive or employee when appropriate. (You can find a sampling of current federal job offerings at www.USAjobs.gov.)

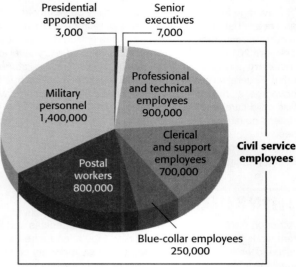

FIGURE 13–3 Types of Federal Employees.
■ *What are the advantages and disadvantages of having so many more federal employees be civil service employees rather than presidential appointees?*

The Hiring Process

Unlike appointees selected by the president, most federal employees are recruited through the civil service. The civil service system was designed to reduce political corruption by promoting merit in the hiring process. But hiring on the basis of merit is not the only way government seeks to reduce corruption. As we shall see, it also regulates the political activities of civil servants.

Under Office of Personnel Management rules, most prospective government employees apply the way private employees do, by submitting an application. Federal organizations cannot select just anyone, however. They must keep careful records about each candidate and justify their decisions when challenged. Federal Organizations must also give veterans special consideration for most jobs and ensure that all jobs are filled through a truly competitive process. Each candidate must also provide certain information about his or her past, including education, work history, and criminal violations. Candidates must also declare any potential conflicts of interest that might affect their performance.

These procedures are intended to protect the merit principle and to meet the bureaucracy's need for qualified personnel. In practice, the two objectives sometimes conflict. In general, the federal hiring process takes six months on average, far longer than in most private businesses. Although the federal government offers a range of recruitment incentives such as partial loan forgiveness, many potential employees are unwilling to wait for a decision, especially in a highly competitive job market.

Regulating the Civil Service

In 1939, Congress passed the Act to Prevent Pernicious Political Activities, usually called the **Hatch Act** after its chief sponsor, Senator Carl Hatch of New Mexico. The act was designed to ensure that the federal civil service did not have disproportionate influence in the election of presidents and members of Congress. In essence, it permitted federal employees to vote in

merit system
A system of public employment in which selection and promotion depend on demonstrated performance rather than political patronage.

Office of Personnel Management (OPM)
An agency that administers civil service laws, rules, and regulations.

Merit Systems Protection Board
An independent agency that oversees and protects merit in the federal government personnel system.

Hatch Act
A federal statute barring federal employees from active participation in certain kinds of politics and protecting them from being fired on partisan grounds.

YOU WILL
DECIDE
Should You Apply for a Federal Job?

The average federal employee was nearly 50 years old in 2010, and nearly half are within five years of retirement. As a result, the federal bureaucracy will hire nearly one million new employees between 2011 and 2020. Many will be offered entry-level jobs that carry good salaries and special benefits such as student loan relief. Federal employees also receive comprehensive health care coverage, signing bonuses, a retirement plan, vacation days, and free child care. It is little wonder many college seniors say the federal government is the place to go for pay, benefits, and job security.

The federal government also offers some of the most interesting jobs in the world. Scientists and engineers can work on leading-edge space technologies at the National Aeronautics and Space Administration, biochemists and physicians can find great reward at the National Institutes of Health and the Centers for Disease Control, lawyers can help enforce important civil and criminal laws at the Department of Justice, and environmentalists can deal with global warming at the National Oceanographic and Atmospheric Administration or the Environmental Protection Agency.

What do you think? Would you consider working for the federal government? What are the pros and cons of these jobs?

THINKING IT THROUGH

Although the federal government offers good benefits and important work, it also has a well-deserved reputation for being a difficult place to work. Most students say the most important consideration in taking a job is not pay or job security but the chance to make a difference, the opportunity for promotions, and meaningful work. They also say they want a simple, easy hiring process that makes decisions quickly.

The federal government has many problems meeting these goals. Getting a federal job is a complicated, often confusing process that takes months to complete, and new recruits often leave because they feel trapped by a bureaucracy that allows little room for advancement. The government's biggest problem with retaining talented employees appears to be a lack of resources to actually do meaningful work. Young recruits complain they do not have enough access to training or new technology, and their organizations do not have enough people to execute the laws. (For a list of many, but not all of, open federal jobs, visit www.USAJobs.gov.)

Many college seniors also say the federal government is a great place to work for anyone but them. They want the chance to make a difference *now,* not in 20 or 30 years. Although there are rewarding places to work in the federal bureaucracy, students rightly worry that they will land in a department or agency with little interest in giving them the tools to do their jobs well or the meaningful work they crave.

But public employment also provides opportunities to make a difference in a policy area of importance to the employee. Public employment may be open to people who lack the connections sometimes needed to secure jobs in the private sector. From auditing financial instutions for solvency to public health to the armed services, individuals can find job satisfaction in public employment.

Critical Thinking Questions

1. Why do college and university students put such a great emphasis on finding meaningful work?

2. Does the federal bureaucracy send the right message to students when it emphasizes the pay, benefits, and job security it can offer?

3. What can the federal bureaucracy do to make its jobs more attractive to this generation of employees?

---

government elections but not to take an active part in partisan politics. The Hatch Act also made it illegal to dismiss civilian employees for political reasons.[10]

In 1993, Congress, with the encouragement of the Clinton administration, overhauled the Hatch Act and made many forms of participation in partisan politics permissible. The revised act still bars federal officials from running as candidates in partisan elections, but it does permit most federal civil servants to hold party positions and involve themselves in party fund-raising and campaigning. This new law was welcomed by those who believed that the old act discouraged political participation by 3 million people who might otherwise be vigorous political activists.[11]

The new Hatch Act retains many restrictions on federal employees: They cannot raise campaign funds in their agencies, and those who work in such highly sensitive federal agencies as the CIA, the FBI, the Secret Service, and certain divisions of the IRS are specifically barred from nearly all partisan activity. Although public employees may in most cases express opinions about candidates and parties and contribute money to them, they *may not* be candidates for public office in partisan elections or use their jobs or authority for electoral purposes.

The vast majority of federal employees work outside of Washington, D.C., in regional federal offices, post offices, veterans medical centers, and a host of other big- and small-town federal service centers. In 1995, a homegrown antigovernment terrorist, Timothy McVeigh, bombed the federal building in Oklahoma City, killing 168 federal employees and some of their children who were in a federal day-care center in the building.

The Role of Government Employee Unions

Since 1962, federal civilian employees have had the right to form unions or associations that represent them in seeking to improve government personnel policies, and approximately one-third of them have joined such unions. Some of the most important unions representing federal employees today are the American Federation of Government Employees, the National Treasury Employees Union, the National Association of Government Employees, and the National Federation of Federal Employees.

Unlike unions in the private sector, federal employee unions lack the right to strike and are not able to bargain over pay and benefits. But they can attempt to negotiate better personnel policies and practices for federal workers, they can represent federal employees at grievance and disciplinary proceedings, and they can lobby Congress on measures affecting personnel changes. They can also vote in elections. This is why members of Congress from districts with large numbers of federal workers often sit on the House and Senate civil service subcommittees.

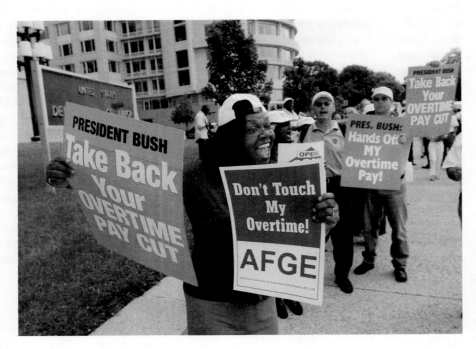

The National Treasury Employees Union represents thousands of federal employees who work within government. Although it started out as a union for Treasury Department employees, it has expanded throughout the years. ■ *Should federal employees be allowed to strike? How would a strike affect public confidence in government?*

The Job of the Federal Bureaucracy

implementation
The process of putting a law into practice through bureaucratic rules or spending.

administrative discretion
Authority given by Congress to the federal bureaucracy to use reasonable judgment in implementing the laws.

rule
A precise statement of how a law is implemented.

Federal Register
The official record of what the federal bureaucracy does.

Whatever their size or specialty, all federal organizations share one constitutional job: to faithfully execute, or implement, the laws.

Implementation covers a broad range of bureaucratic activities, such as writing checks at the Social Security Administration, inspecting job sites for the Occupational Safety and Health Administration, swearing in new citizens at the Immigration and Naturalization Service, or monitoring airline traffic for the Federal Aviation Administration. Some agencies implement the laws by spending money, others by raising revenues or issuing rules that govern what private citizens and businesses do, and still others by collecting information or conducting research. Whatever tool government uses, implementation is the act of converting a law into action.

Because Congress and the president could never pass laws detailed enough to deal with every aspect of their administration, they give federal departments and agencies **administrative discretion** to implement the laws in the most efficient and effective manner possible. This freedom varies from agency to agency, depending on both past performance and congressional politics. Political scientist Theodore Lowi believes that Congress often gives the federal bureaucracy vague directions because it is unable or unwilling to make the tough choices needed to resolve conflicts that arise in the legislative process. Congress gets the credit for passing a law, but the federal workforce gets the challenge of implementing an unclear law.[12]

Whether a law is clear or ambiguous, most agencies implement it through two means: administrative *regulations,* formal instructions for either running an agency or controlling the behavior of private citizens and organizations, and *spending,* the transfer of money to and from government. As noted earlier, the bureaucracy can only issue regulations that are authorized by Congress and the president through legislation, or ordered by the federal courts. In 2009, for example, Congress and the president gave the Food and Drug Administration formal authority to issue regulations governing the manufacturing of tobacco products such as cigarettes.

Making Regulations

As discussed in the chapter opener, **rules** are designed to convert laws into action. They tell people what they can and cannot do, as well as what they must or must not do. An Agriculture Department rule tells meat and poultry processors how to handle food; an Environmental Protection Agency rule tells automobile makers how much gasoline mileage their cars must get; a Social Security Administration rule tells workers how long they must work before they are eligible for a federal retirement check; an Immigration and Naturalization Service rule tells citizens of other nations how long they can stay on a student visa; and a Justice Department rule tells states what they must do to ensure that every eligible citizen can vote. All these rules can be traced back to legislation; they provide the details that laws leave out.

Rules are drafted and reviewed under the Administrative Procedure Act. Created in 1946 to make sure all rules are made visible to the public, the act requires that all proposed rules be published in the ***Federal Register.*** Publication in the federal government's newspaper marks the beginning of the "notice and comment" period, during which all parties affected by the proposed regulation are encouraged to make their opinions known to the agency. Because rules have the force of law and can become the basis for legal challenges, the process can take years from start to finish and consume thousands of pages of records. Some agencies even hold hearings and take testimony from witnesses in the effort to build a strong case for a particularly controversial rule.

The rule-making process does not end with final publication and enforcement. All rules are subject to the same judicial review that governs formal laws, thereby creating a check against potential abuse of power when agencies exceed their authority to faithfully execute the laws.

Spending Money

The federal bureaucracy also implements laws by spending money, whether by writing checks to more than 35 million Social Security recipients a year, buying billions of dollars'

Just before he left office on January 20, 2009, President George W. Bush approved a new federal rule allowing national park visitors to carry concealed loaded weapons. The rule was endorsed by Congress and signed into law by President Obama in 2009. The Interior Department's National Park Service enforces the rule.

For the People

Bringing Sunshine to Government

Congress, the president, and the federal judiciary have made many efforts to make government more open. Under the Administrative Procedure Act in 1946, for example, Congress required agencies to publish all proposed regulations in the *Federal Register* and give citizens a chance to make comments through direct access to government. Under the Sunshine Act in 1974, Congress required agencies to provide more access to records of key decisions and open their meetings to public participation. And under the Ethics in Government Act of 1978, Congress required presidential appointees to provide much more detailed information on their financial interests.

All of these laws promote the notion that sunshine is the best disinfectant for corruption, but none is more important than the Freedom of Information Act of 1966. Passed at the height of the Vietnam War, this law was designed to give citizens the power to demand the release of information from government through a Freedom of Information Act (FOIA) request. Such requests must be made through formal letters and notarized but force an agency such as the Federal Bureau of Investigation to make any information on any subject available. If the agency refuses to make the information available, it must provide a clear justification such as protecting national security.

Interest groups and the media often use FOIA requests to force the federal government to release particularly controversial documents. In October 2009, in response to a lawsuit brought by the American Civil Liberties Union, the federal courts ordered the Department of Justice to release hundreds of documents regarding the torture of suspected terrorists in U.S. custody overseas. The documents can be found at http://www.aclu.org/national-security/torture-documents-released-10302009.

The Obama Administration is trying tore-energize sunshine in government through a series of executive orders instructing the bureaucracy to provide more information to the public. Under a December 9, 2009, memorandum to the federal bureaucracy, the Obama administration ordered every department and agency to create separate Web sites for providing data to the public—the Web sites can be found at www.[agencyname].gov/open. The memorandum also ordered the bureaucracy to reduce the use of top-secret classifications to limit public access to information.

CRITICAL THINKING QUESTIONS

1. Would the framers support open government?

2. When should the bureaucracy refuse to release information? What rules should it use in making a decision to redact information?

3. Why do interest groups do much of the work on FOIA requests? Is their involvement good for citizen engagement?

Even when information is released, it can be difficult to understand. The federal government can "redact" portions of particularly sensitive information to the point that documents are nearly impossible to read.

---

worth of military equipment, or making grants to state governments and research universities. Viewed in relative terms as a percentage of gross domestic product (GDP), federal spending more than doubled throughout the past half-century but began to shrink with the end of the cold war in 1989.

Most government spending is **uncontrollable,** or *nondiscretionary*, which means it is not subject to congressional or presidential control without substantial and often unpopular changes in the law. The bulk of uncontrollable, mandatory spending goes to **entitlement programs** such as Social Security and Medicare for older citizens, college loans, and help for the victims of natural disasters such as floods and hurricanes. Everyone eligible for these programs is *entitled* to benefits—hence, spending often rises automatically. (The amount of this *uncontrollable spending* in the 1962 and 2010 federal budget is shown in Figure 13–4.)

The largest share of uncontrollable spending goes to Social Security and Medicare, which are guaranteed to anyone who has paid taxes into the program for enough years.

uncontrollable spending
The portion of the federal budget that is spent on previously enacted programs, such as Social Security, that the president and Congress are unwilling to cut.

entitlement program
Programs such as unemployment insurance, disaster relief, or disability payments that provide benefits to all eligible citizens.

FIGURE 13–4 **Uncontrollable Spending in 1962 and 2010.**

■ *Why do you think there are so many federal programs today with uncontrollable spending?*

SOURCE: Office of Management and Budget, *Budget of the U.S. Government, Fiscal Year 2009, Historical Tables* (U.S. Government Printing Office, February 2008).

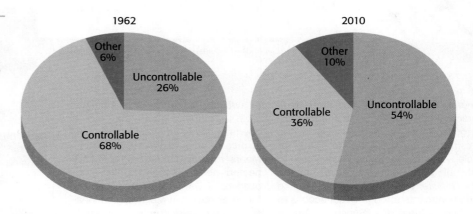

As a higher percentage of workers age throughout the next few decades, uncontrollable spending will almost certainly rise as Social Security and Medicare grow. The two programs are already the largest in the federal budget and will eventually account for more than half of all federal spending. In total, uncontrollable spending accounted for nearly $2 trillion in 2010, more than half of the federal government's spending.

A much smaller share of the uncontrollable budget goes to welfare for the poor and is linked to the performance of the economy. More unemployment, for example, means more federal unemployment insurance; more poverty means more food stamps, job training, temporary financial assistance, and other income support programs. On the other hand, spending for programs such as health research, highway construction, and defense weapons are discretionary.

Controlling the Federal Bureaucracy

LEARNING **OBJECTIVE**

13.5 Assess presidential and congressional efforts to control the federal bureaucracy.

Every president enters office promising to make federal agencies work better. Jimmy Carter, Ronald Reagan, Bill Clinton, George W. Bush, and Barack Obama all made bureaucratic reform a central part of their presidential campaigns. Carter promised to create a government as good as the U.S. people, Reagan promised to reduce waste in government, Clinton and Vice President Al Gore promised to reinvent government, Bush promised to make government friendlier to citizens, and Obama promised more government transparency.

Presidential Controls

Modern presidents invariably contend that they should be firmly in charge of federal employees because the chief executive is responsive to the broadest constituency. A president, they argue, must see that popular needs and expectations are converted into administrative action. The voters' wishes can be translated into action only if federal employees support presidential policies.

However, under the system of checks and balances, the party that wins the presidency does not acquire total control of the national government. The president is not even the undisputed master of the executive structure. Presidents come into an ongoing system over which they have little control and in which they have little leeway to make the bureaucracy responsive.

Still, the president has some control over federal departments and agencies through the powers of appointment, reorganization, and budgeting. A president can attempt to control the federal system by appointing or promoting sympathetic personnel, mobilizing public opinion and congressional pressure, changing the administrative apparatus, influencing budget decisions, using extensive personal persuasion, and if all else fails, shifting an agency's assignment to another department or agency (although such a shift requires tacit if not explicit congressional approval).[13]

Congressional Controls

Congress has a number of ways to control federal administration, whether by establishing agencies, formulating budgets, appropriating funds, confirming personnel, authorizing new programs or new shifts in direction, conducting investigations and hearings, or even terminating agencies.

Much of this authority is used to help constituents as they battle federal red tape. Members of Congress earn political credit by influencing federal agencies on behalf of their constituents. Still, Congress deserves at least some of the blame for having created the red tape in the first place, through such deeds as enacting pet programs, refusing to give federal agencies greater flexibility, delaying presidential appointments, and placing limits on bureaucratic discretion to protect some constituents but not others. Moreover, by demanding special attention for their constituents, members of Congress may undermine the fairness of the entire process. Like those who cut in line at a movie theater, they slow the progress for everyone but the special few who get their attention.

Individual committees generally specialize in the appropriations and oversight processes. They oversee policies of a particular cluster of agencies—often the agencies serving constituents in their own districts. Some legislators stake out a claim over specific areas. Members of Congress, who see presidents come and go, come to think they know more about particular agencies than the president does (and often they do). Some congressional leaders prefer to try to seal off "their" agencies from presidential direction and maintain their influence over public policy.

Shared Controls

Congress and the president spend a great deal of time and energy monitoring the federal bureaucracy through **oversight,** the technical term for their ongoing review.

Presidents use a number of tools for keeping a watchful eye. They can put loyal appointees into the top jobs at key agencies; they can direct White House aides to oversee the work of certain agencies; and they can always call cabinet meetings to learn more about what is happening in the various departments. However, presidents tend to use the Office of Management and Budget (OMB) for most routine oversight. Departments and agencies must get the president's approval before testifying before Congress on pending legislation, making legislative proposals, or answering congressional inquiries about their activities. Under this **central clearance** system, OMB tells Congress whether the bureaucracy's requests for legislation are "in accordance" with the president's program (indicating the highest presidential support), "consistent with" the president's program (indicating at least moderate presidential support), or without objection (indicating little or no presidential interest).

Congress also has a number of tools for overseeing the federal bureaucracy, not least of which are the individual members of Congress themselves, who are free to ask agencies for detailed information on just about any issue. However, most members and committees tend to use the General Accounting Office or the Congressional Budget Office to conduct a study or investigation of a particular program.

Oversight is often conducted through external investigations launched by Congress or the president. In 2009, for example, the Obama Administration created a special commission to investigate the banking scandals that led to the financial collapse in 2008 and the $700 billion federal bailout called the Troubled Asset Relief Program (TARP). Investigations have covered a range of issues including Vietnam War, the Watergate scandal, the space shuttle *Challenger* Disaster, and the September 11, 2001, terrorist attacks.

Together, Congress and the president conduct two basic types of oversight. One is "police patrol" oversight, in which the two branches watch the bureaucracy through a routine pattern. They read key reports, monitor the budget, and generally pay attention to the way the departments and agencies are running. The goal is to deter problems before they arise.

Former defense secretary Donald Rumsfeld resigned from office only days after the 2006 elections. His management of the war in Iraq had been widely criticized, and he was blamed for the deep Republican losses in the elections. In this way, citizens held government accountable through their votes against Republican candidates.

oversight
Legislative or executive review of a particular government program or organization that can be in response to a crisis of some kind or part of routine review.

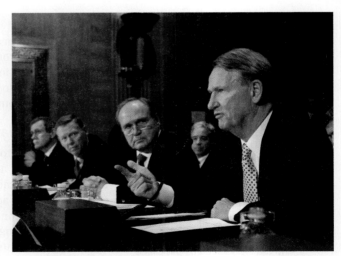

Congress often conducts oversight through very visible hearings with star witnesses. Congress did just that by bringing the chief executives of General Motors and Chrysler in 2009 to explain their use of federal bailout money to survive the economic downturn.
■ *Why do you suppose Congress brought the heads of the auto companies to the witness table in Capitol Hill, above, rather than conduct behind-the-scenes investigations?*

By the People

MAKING A DIFFERENCE

Joining the "Transparency Corps"

Under pressure from leading interest groups such as the Project on Government Oversight (www.pogo.org), OMB Watch (ombwatch.org), and the Sunlight Foundation (sunlightfoundation. com), the federal bureaucracy is releasing massive amounts of information to citizens. As the list of sources at www.data.gov shows, citizens can inspect virtually every corner of the bureaucracy except for national security and defense, which have tightly guarded Web sites.

There is also an enormous amount of information at private and interest group Web sites, including detailed information on congressional lobbying and fund-raising at the Center for Responsive Politics (www.opensecrets.org), lists of wasteful government programs at Citizens Against Government Waste (www.cagw.org), and detailed biographies of every Obama administration appointee at *The Washington Post's* dot-com Web site (www.whorunsgovernment.com)

The problem with the bureaucracy is no longer too little public information, however, but perhaps too much. There is so much information that citizens simply cannot put it together. The Sunlight Foundation is trying to solve the problem by creating virtual teams of citizens, most of whom are students, to analyze government information and collect additional data. Its "Transparency Corps" is designed to give each member a specific assignment such as

finding Twitter addresses for state legislators. "Use your Internet search 'kung fu' skills to track down whom among your state officials are on Twitter and what their usernames are," Sunlight tells its volunteers. "Don't know who your state officials are? No problem, you tell us your zip code, and we'll tell you who to look for."

The Transparency Corps is only one way citizens can monitor government. The more they do to make sense of government information, even by sorting information into graphs for data analysis at IBM's free Web site, http://manyeyes.alphaworks.ibm.com/manyeyes/, the more they can contribute to

the information that experts read for input to major policy debates.

CRITICAL THINKING QUESTIONS

1. Is there too much information now flowing from Washington? Can the flood of information be used to suppress citizen engagement or discourage people from looking?

2. Why does the concept of the "Transparency Corps" lessen this information overload?

3. Should citizens trust the bureaucracy's information?

The other form of oversight is "fire alarm" oversight, in which the two branches wait for citizens, interest groups, or the press to find a major problem and pull the alarm. The media play a particularly important role in such oversight, using the Freedom of Information Act to gain access to documents the federal bureaucracy keeps secret and often uncovering a scandal before a routine "police patrol" can discover the problem.

Can the Bureaucracy Regulate Itself?

Career administrators are in a good position to know when a program is not operating properly and what action is needed. But many people believe that federal employees care too much about their own pay, benefits, and job security to make things better. Some career employees act as if the expansion of their organization were vital to the public interest. They become more skillful at building political alliances to protect their organization than at building political alliances to ensure their programs' effectiveness.

Career administrators usually try hard to be objective, but they are inevitably political. Some have more bargaining and alliance-building skills than the elected and appointed officials to whom they report. In one sense, agency leaders are at the center of action in Washington. Over time, administrative agencies may become much closer to the interests they regulate than to the public they protect.

central clearance
Review of all executive branch testimony, reports, and draft legislation by the Office of Management and Budget (OMB) to ensure that each communication to Congress is in accordance with the president's program.

Vice President Al Gore took the Clinton administration's campaign to cut government waste to the people when he appeared on *The David Letterman Show.* Gore and Letterman both wore goggles as Gore showed how to smash an ashtray under federal rules. ■ *What makes this demonstration so effective at showing the Clinton administration's commitment to better government?*

Interest groups work hard to cultivate the bureau chiefs and agency staffs who have jurisdiction over their programs. They also work closely with the committees and subcommittees of Congress that authorize, appropriate, and oversee programs run by these key bureaucracies. Recognizing the power of interest groups, bureau chiefs frequently recruit them as allies in pursuing common goals. These officials, interest groups, and congressional allies share a common view that more money should be spent on their federal programs.

Does the Federal Bureaucracy Work?

Despite their complaints about the federal bureaucracy, U.S. citizens are reluctant to support cutbacks in what government does. Most say the federal bureaucracy's biggest problem is not setting the wrong priorities but allowing inefficiency. We may complain about the red tape and waste in Washington, but the federal bureaucracy continues to make progress in solving some of the most difficult problems of modern society.

In today's climate of promises to cut big government, it is useful to recall Alexander Hamilton's warning about the dangers of a government ill executed. As he argued in *The Federalist,* No. 70: "A feeble execution is but another phrase for a bad execution; and a government ill executed, whatever it may be in theory must be in practice, a bad government."[14]

More than 200 years later, however, the federal government seems plagued by bad execution. The failures are all too familiar: taxpayer abuse by the Internal Revenue Service, security breaches at the nation's nuclear laboratories, missing laptops at the Federal Bureau of Investigation, the *Challenger* and *Columbia* space shuttle disasters, breakdowns in policing everything from toys to cattle, the sluggish response to Hurricane Katrina, miscalculations about the war in Iraq, a cascade of fraudulent defense contracts, continued struggles to unite the nation's intelligence services, backlogs at dozens of agencies, shortages of air traffic controllers and food inspectors, mistakes on the passenger screening lines, the Christmas Day bombing plot, the Gulf of Mexico oil spill, and negligent veterans care.

As the federal government's agenda has expanded throughout the centuries, government has become increasingly difficult to manage. Its missions are critically important,

LEARNING **OBJECTIVE**

13.6 Evaluate the bureaucracy's effectiveness.

but its organizations are dense with layer upon layer of management, rules, red tape, and old technologies; the presidential appointments process is needlessly complex and slow; many civil servants are motivated more by their job security than their mission; and the faithful execution of the laws now involves a large and mostly hidden workforce of contract employees that is hard to control.

This is not to suggest that the federal government is a wasteland of failure. To the contrary, the federal government accomplishes the impossible every day. And over time, as demonstrated in the *For the People: Government's Greatest Endeavors* boxes, the federal bureaucracy has accomplished much for betterment of society, including reducing diseases, building a strong national defense, and increasing access to education. But even federal employees have concerns about how the bureaucracy functions. Interviewed in mid-2008 by the U.S. Office of Personnel Management, less than half of a random sample of federal employees said their agencies were able to recruit employees with the right skills, slightly more than a third said promotions were based on merit, and even fewer said their agencies took steps to deal with poor performers.

It is not surprising that the public has serious doubts about the federal bureaucracy's performance, too. As Figure 13–5 shows, public confidence in the executive branch of government has been generally declining throughout the past ten years. The only major breaks in the decline came in 2002–2004 when the nation was pulled together by the response to the September 11, 2001, terrorist attacks and early success in Iraq, and in September 2009, as the economy showed early signs of recovery. Other surveys show similar patterns—trust in the bureaucracy rises with the economy and the popularity of the president and declines to traditionally low levels as enthusiasm wears off.

Improving public confidence in the bureaucracy depends in large part on the public itself. Citizens can make a great difference in shaping rules, monitoring bureaucratic performance, and prompting Congress and the president to adopt needed reforms to prevent government breakdowns. Citizens can also support the many interest groups that lobby for good government and can now keep their own watchful eye over government by visiting government Web sites and collecting information. There is an old saying in politics that Americans get the government they deserve. The more that citizens demand better government, the better government they get.

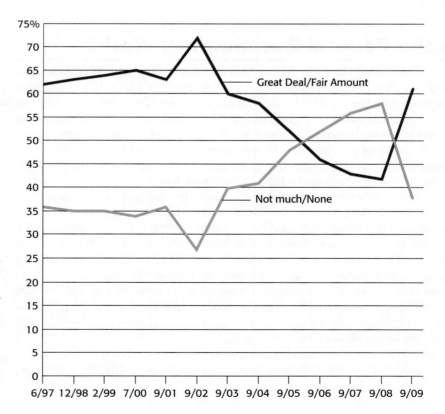

FIGURE 13–5 **Trust in the Bureaucracy.**

How much trust and confidence do you have at this time in the executive branch, headed by the president: a great deal, a fair amount, not very much, or none at all? ■ *What might explain the long-term decline in confidence in the federal bureaucracy? Why did confidence rise so dramatically in 2009?*

SOURCE: The Gallup Poll, available at http://pollingreport .com/institut.htm.

CHAPTER **SUMMARY**

13.1 Outline the constitutional roots of the federal bureaucracy and pros and cons of bureaucratic administration.

The founders assumed there would be a federal bureaucracy but that it would be small. Therefore, they left many of the details of the bureaucracy to the responsibility of future presidents. Although they did give the president the power to appoint the officers of government and require their opinions in writing, there are few constitutional rules for managing the bureaucracy. The chief benefits of bureaucracy are specialization, centralization, formal rules, standardization, expertise, and accountability. These factors create predictability by making sure all employees know their jobs. However, they can also create duplication and overlap, as well as needless levels of management.

13.2 Identify the four types of federal organizations.

There are four types of government organizations: (1) departments, (2) independent, stand-alone agencies, (3) independent regulatory commissions, and (4) government corporations. Departments are generally the largest organizations in government and are often divided into members of the inner and outer cabinet; independent stand-alone agencies are generally smaller than departments but conduct important enforcement and policy work; independent regulatory commissions are insulated from political control through the appointment of commissioners with fixed terms of office who cannot be easily removed from office; and government corporations are designed to work more like a business and make a profit.

13.3 Differentiate three types of federal employees, and explain how each is selected.

Most presidential appointees are appointed by the president with Senate confirmation. Nearly all of these appointees are selected on the basis of political connections and ability to do the job. The president does not appoint members of the civil service. Civil servants are selected on the basis of merit. The federal government's Office of Personnel Management sets policy for recruiting and evaluating federal workers. Various restrictions prevent federal workers from running for political office or engaging in political fund-raising activities.

13.4 Analyze the bureaucracy's tools of implementation and their effectiveness.

The federal bureaucracy generally uses regulations or spending to implement the laws. The rule-making process is governed by the Administrative Procedure Act, whereas the spending process is governed by the federal budget. Most of the federal budget is uncontrollable, meaning that anyone who qualifies for programs such as Social Security, unemployment insurance, health care for the poor, and Medicare must be given benefits regardless of the impact on the federal budget.

13.5 Assess presidential and congressional efforts to control the federal bureaucracy.

The federal bureaucracy has at least two immediate supervisors: Congress and the president. It must pay considerable attention as well to the courts and their rulings and to well-organized interest groups and public opinion. Despite their efforts to ensure accountability, Congress and the president often give vague instructions to the administrative system, which gives the system significant discretion in implementing the laws.

13.6 Evaluate the bureaucracy's effectiveness.

Americans generally favor more government activism on virtually every program but have serious concerns about big government. They also express concerns about fraud, waste, and abuse in government.

CHAPTER **SELF-TEST**

13.1 Outline the constitutional roots of the federal bureaucracy and pros and cons of bureaucratic administration.

1. List key decisions the framers made about executing the laws that continue to shape federal administration to this day.
2. Which of the following is a weakness of the modern federal bureaucracy?
   a. Communication within a large organization is difficult.
   b. Few qualified individuals want to work in the bureaucracy.
   c. Today's jobs are overly simplistic and not attractive to young workers.
   d. Rules are almost impossible to enforce within a very large workforce.

3. In a short essay, identify and describe three strengths of bureaucracy. Focus on experiences you or someone you know has had with the federal bureaucracy. How could those experiences have been improved?

13.2 Identify the four types of federal organizations.

4. Which type of federal organization is the Federal Reserve Board?
   a. Department
   b. Independent agency
   c. Government corporation
   d. Independent regulatory commission
5. Which types of federal organizations report directly to the president? Which do not? Why are independent regulatory commissions structured to insulate their work from the president?

13.3 Differentiate three types of federal employees, and explain how each is selected.

6. What are the three types of government employees? To whom does each report? How are they selected?
7. Identify whether each of the following describes the spoils or the merit system:
   a. Andrew Jackson substantially expanded the system after his election in 1829.
   b. Federal jobs are filled on the basis of personal connections.
   c. Ninety percent of federal employees are selected through this system.
   d. This system gave the president's party nearly complete control over almost every government job.
   e. Federal jobs are filled on the basis of ability.
8. What is the main duty of the Office of Personnel Management?
   a. Protect the integrity of the federal merit system
   b. Administer civil service laws, rules, and regulations
   c. Research and interview each potential presidential appointee
   d. Provide information to the Senate about presidential appointees
9. How does the Hatch Act limit civil service political participation? Should civil servants have more rights to participate in politics and unions?

13.4 Analyze the bureaucracy's tools of implementation and their effectiveness.

10. What is the constitutional job shared by all federal organizations regardless of their size or specialty?
    a. To faithfully execute the laws
    b. To protect the president from harm
    c. To cooperate with Congress in all legal matters
    d. To aid the president in electing members of his or her party to political office
11. What is uncontrollable spending? What two programs receive the majority of these funds? Why? What implications could this reason have for the way your future tax dollars are spent?
12. Write a short essay on why regulations are such an important tool of government action.

13.5 Assess presidential and congressional efforts to control the federal bureaucracy.

13. Why do many members of Congress prefer the current, complicated federal bureaucracy to a more efficient alternative?
    a. It creates greater incumbency advantages in elections.
    b. A more complicated system creates more jobs for politicians' friends.
    c. The bureaucratic red tape allows for greater back-room deals.
    d. A more complicated system allows politicians greater freedom with less oversight from constituents.
14. Do the constitutional controls actually work to limit bureaucratic discretion? Is oversight an effective means for changing bureaucratic behavior?

13.6 Evaluate the bureaucracy's effectiveness.

15. Write a brief essay on different ways of measuring bureaucratic effectiveness.
16. Write a brief essay on why citizens have such low approval toward the bureaucracy.

Answers to selected questions: 2. a; 4. d; 7. a: spoils, b: spoils, c: merit, d: spoils, e: merit; 8. b; 10. a; 13. a

mypoliscilab EXERCISES
Where participation leads to action!

Apply what you learned in this chapter on MyPoliSciLab.

📖┤Read on **mypoliscilab.com**

eText: Chapter 13

✓┤**Study** and **Review** on **mypoliscilab.com**

Pre-Test
Post-Test
Chapter Exam
Flashcards

👁┤Watch on **mypoliscilab.com**

Video: The CDC and the Swine Flu
Video: Internal Problems at the FDA

✳┤Explore on **mypoliscilab.com**

Simulation: You Are the President of MEDICORP
Simulation: You Are Deputy Director of the Census Bureau
Simulation: You Are a Federal Administrator
Simulation: You Are the Head of FEMA
Comparative: Comparing Bureaucracies
Timeline: The Evolution of the Federal Bureaucracy
Visual Literacy: The Changing Face of the Federal Bureaucracy

KEY **TERMS**

ADDITIONAL **RESOURCES**

FURTHER READING

ROBERT D. BEHN, *Rethinking Democratic Accountability* (Brookings Institution Press, 2001).

BARRY BOZEMAN, *Bureaucracy and Red Tape* (Prentice Hall, 2000).

SHELLEY L. DAVIS, *Unbridled Power: Inside the Secret Culture of the IRS* (Harper Business, 1997).

JAMES W. FESLER AND **DONALD F. KETTL,** *The Politics of the Administrative Process,* 4th ed. (CQ Press, 2008).

JANE E. FOUNTAIN, *Building the Virtual State: Information Technology and Institutional Change* (Brookings Institution Press, 2001).

STEPHEN GOLDSMITH AND **WILLIAM EGGERS,** *Government by Network: The New Shape of the Public Sector* (Brookings Institution Press, 2005).

CHARLES T. GOODSELL, *The Case for Bureaucracy,* 4th ed. (CQ Press, 2003).

AL GORE, *Creating a Government That Works Better and Costs Less: The Report of the National Performance Review* (Plume-Penguin, 1993).

WILLIAM T. GORMLEY AND **STEVEN J. BALLA,** *Bureaucracy and Democracy: Accountability and Performance,* 2d ed. (CQ Press, 2007).

PHILIP K. HOWARD, *The Death of Common Sense: How Law Is Suffocating America* (Random House, 1994).

ANDREW KOHUT, ED., *Deconstructing Distrust: How Americans View Government* (Pew Research Center for the People and the Press, 1998).

PAUL C. LIGHT, *A Government Ill Executed: The Decline of the Federal Service and How to Reverse It* (Harvard University Press, 2008).

G. CALVIN MACKENZIE AND **MICHAEL HAFKEN,** *Scandal Proof: Do Ethics Laws Make Government Ethical?* (Brookings Institution Press, 2002).

KENNETH J. MEIER AND **LAURENCE J. O'TOOLE, JR.,** *Bureaucracy in a Democratic State: A Governance Perspective* (Johns Hopkins University Press, 2006).

DAVID OSBORNE, *The Tools of Government: A Guide to the New Governance* (Oxford University Press, 2002).

JAMES Q. WILSON, *Bureaucracy: What Government Agencies Do and Why They Do It* (Basic Books, 1989). Four useful journals are the *Journal of Policy Analysis and Management, National Journal, Public Administration Review,* and *Government Executive.*

WEB SITES

www.omb.gov The source of information on the federal budget.

www.pogo.org The Project on Government Oversight, a source of investigations of the federal bureaucracy's performance.

www.washingpost.com Click on the "federal page" to find the latest news on what is happening in Washington.

www.ourpublicservice.org A source for information about the best places to work in the federal government.

www.USAJobs.gov Where federal agencies post federal jobs.

The Judiciary

The Balancing Branch

O n January 21, 2010, the U.S. Supreme Court announced its decision in a much-anticipated case dealing with federal campaign finance rules. The case, *Citizens United* v. *Federal Election Commission,*[1] dealt with the question of whether a documentary movie that was critical of Hillary Clinton, who was then running for the Democratic presidential nomination, violated the 2002 Bipartisan Campaign Reform Act's ban on corporation (and union) expenditures from their general funds—including profits—to advocate for the election or defeat of a candidate. In its 5-to-4 decision, the Court ruled that these expenditures cannot be limited under the First Amendment. This decision overturned long-standing restrictions on such spending and the Supreme Court's own precedent, which had allowed these restrictions due to the interest in preventing corruption, or the appearance of corruption, based on the potential for huge corporate general treasuries to disproportionately influence election outcomes.[2] As we discussed in Chapters 6 and 9, in *Citizens United,* the Supreme Court reaffirmed the free speech rights of corporations and ruled that the government had no right to limit that speech.

The Court's decision was met with a firestorm of criticism from commentators and politicians alike decrying the harm to the democratic process that would result from the Court's decision. Many members of Congress who had voted for the campaign reform legislation only eight years earlier disparaged the Court's opinion, arguing that the pro-business Roberts Court had struck yet another blow against the average citizen. The debate was amplified when, only six days later, President Obama openly criticized the Court's decision in his State of the Union Address. Six of the Court's nine justices attended the address and, as is their tradition, they sat mostly expressionless in the audience. That is, except for Justice Samuel Alito, who was caught on television cameras scowling and appearing to say "not true" in response to the president's remarks.

The unusual exchange between the president and justice provided extensive fodder for commentators and politicians and further criticism of both the president's comments in the State of the Union Address and Justice Alito's response. Debate over the exchange heated up again in early March when Chief Justice Roberts spoke about the event during a meeting with law students at the University of Alabama. Responding to a student's question, Roberts said he found the president's criticism of the Court at the State of the Union Address "very troubling" and suggested that event had turned into a "political pep rally" that perhaps the justices should not attend.[3]

The chief justice's remarks and the president's comments highlight a long-standing debate about the appropriate role of the Court in a separation-of-powers system. Is the Court part of the political process, or is it an apolitical institution operating outside the bounds of the political arena? In either case, it is clear that politics shape the courts, especially through the federal judicial appointment process, and the courts shape politics through the reach of their decisions.

In this chapter, we explore how the federal judiciary operates in a system of separated powers and examine the nomination process through which we staff the judiciary. The judicial branch is unlike the elected branches of government in several ways. We will first look at the way the framers envisioned the judiciary and discuss several of its important characteristics. After exploring the appointment process, we will discuss the Supreme Court in particular. Given that it is the court of last resort in the United States and has the final say on what the Constitution means, it is crucial to our understanding of the federal judiciary.

Understanding the Federal Judiciary

LEARNING **OBJECTIVE**

14.1 Determine characteristics of the federal judiciary and implications of the adversarial process.

The framers viewed the federal judiciary as an important check against both Congress and the president. But the judiciary lacked the institutional resources of the elected branches. As Alexander Hamilton wrote, "The Executive not only dispenses the honors, but holds the sword of the community. The legislature not only commands the purse, but prescribes the rules by which the duties and rights of every citizen are to be regulated. The judiciary, on the contrary, has no influence over either the sword or the purse."[4] So, in order to ensure the judicial check, the framers insulated the judiciary against both public opinion and the rest of government.

To protect the judiciary from shifts in public opinion, the framers rejected direct election. That was the method used to select many judges in the colonies, and it is still used today to choose some state and local judges. The framers also excluded the House, the more representative of the two bodies of Congress, from any role in either selecting or confirming federal judges. To protect the judiciary from Congress as a whole, no limits were allowed on judicial terms. Federal judges serve during good behavior, which typically means for life. And finally, to prevent Congress from assessing a financial penalty against the judiciary, judges' salaries cannot be reduced once confirmed.

These early decisions were essential to protect the judiciary's independence in resolving public disputes. Because it has no army or police force to enforce its will or make people obey its decisions, the judiciary must often rely on the public's respect to implement its decisions. This is sometimes a challenge, particularly when resolving controversial issues such as abortion rights or the rights of prisoners of war. Even in the face of these challenges, it is crucial that the judiciary maintain its independence.

However, in states where judges are chosen through popular elections, they are by definition accountable to the public. Although judicial elections arguably add accountability, some contend that it is accountability not to the average citizen but to the groups and corporations that contribute money to the judges' election campaigns. This is only one of the potential problems in systems that provide for greater accountability at the expense of judicial independence.

The appropriate balance between judicial independence and accountability is often at the forefront of debate about the best way to staff the judiciary. Some countries structure their appointment process so as to ensure independence. For example, in Japan, Great Britain, Germany, and France, individuals interested in the judiciary take a variety of competitive exams and go through specialized judicial training to become eligible for appointment to their country's courts. In other countries, like China, judicial independence has been difficult; many judges were simply transferred to the judiciary from military posts in the Communist Party. Since 1995, there have been efforts to improve the quality of the judiciary—judges must now have some basic legal education—but judicial independence is still not assured.

Characteristics of the Federal Judiciary

Civil and Criminal Law

Federal judges play a central role in U.S. life. They rule on controversial issues such as partial-birth abortion and race-conscious school assignment, and they often decide whether laws are constitutional. Many of these decisions are based on Chief Justice John Marshall's successful claim of **judicial review**—the power to interpret the Constitution (see Chapter 2). Only a constitutional amendment or a later Supreme Court can modify the Court's decisions.

Several important characteristics distinguish the judiciary from Congress, the presidency, and the administrative system. First, the federal judiciary is an **adversary system,** based on the theory that arguing over law and evidence guarantees fairness.[5] The courts provide a neutral arena in which two parties argue their differences and present evidence supporting those views before an impartial judge. Because the two parties in a case must bring their arguments before the judge, judges may not go looking for cases to decide; the adversary system thus imposes restraints on judicial power.

judicial review
The power of a court to refuse to enforce a law or government regulation that in the opinion of the judges conflicts with the U.S. Constitution or, in a state court, the state constitution.

adversary system
A judicial system in which the court of law is a neutral arena where two parties argue their differences.

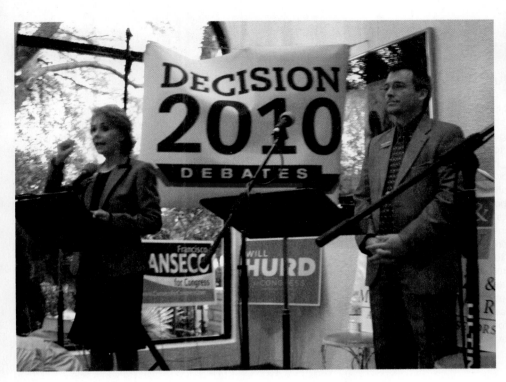

Texas uses a partisan election to determine its state supreme court justices. Here candidates Rick Green and Debra Lehman campaign for judicial office. ■ *What are the drawbacks to choosing judges through popular election? What are the advantages?*

The courts handle many kinds of legal disputes, but the most common are **criminal law,** which defines crimes against the public order and provides for punishment, and **civil law,** which governs relations between individuals and defines their legal rights. Here are several important distinctions between the criminal and civil law:

- In a criminal trial, a person's liberty is at stake (those judged guilty can be imprisoned); in a civil case, penalties are predominantly monetary.
- Criminal defendants who cannot afford attorneys are provided one by the government, but there is no right to a government-provided attorney in civil cases.
- Defendants generally have the right to a jury in criminal trials, but there is no constitutional right to a jury in state civil trials.

The federal government, not the judiciary, brings all federal criminal cases and can also be a party to a civil action. For example, when Martha Stewart was tried for securities fraud and obstruction of justice, the U.S. government brought the case. The federal judiciary decides the cases. Government **prosecutors,** acting on behalf of the public, choose whether and how to pursue a case against criminal **defendants** who may have violated the law. In some cases, they may decide to offer a **plea bargain,** an arrangement in which a defendant agrees to plead guilty to a lesser offense than he or she was charged with, to avoid having to face trial for a more serious offense and a lengthier sentence.

Cases and Controversies   Unlike the legislature and the executive, the federal judiciary is a *passive* and *reactive* branch. It does not instigate cases, nor can it resolve every issue that comes before it. Federal judges decide only **justiciable disputes**—according to the Constitution, they are to decide *cases and controversies*. It is not enough that a judge believe a particular law to be unconstitutional; a real case must be litigated for a judge to reach that decision. In addition, the parties that raise a civil case must have *standing to sue*. That is, the **plaintiff,** the person who begins a civil suit, must have experienced or be in immediate danger of experiencing direct and personal injury. Hypothetical harm is not enough to warrant court review. In an adversary system like ours, it is essential that each side bring forth the best possible arguments before the judge or jury. Because the decision makers depend on the adversaries to bring all the relevant information before them, if one side does not truly have a stake in the outcome, the adversarial process breaks down.

criminal law
A law that defines crimes against the public order.

civil law
A law that governs relationships between individuals and defines their legal rights.

prosecutor
Government lawyer who tries criminal cases, often referred to as a district attorney or a U.S. Attorney.

defendant
In a criminal action, the person or party accused of an offense.

plea bargain
An agreement between a prosecutor and a defendant that the defendant will plead guilty to a lesser offense to avoid having to stand trial for a more serious offense.

justiciable dispute
A dispute growing out of an actual case or controversy that is capable of settlement by legal methods.

plaintiff
The party instigating a civil lawsuit.

By the People

Serving on a Jury: Your Civic Duty and an Interesting Experience

Any time you would like to observe what is going on in Congress, you can turn on your television and watch C-SPAN's coverage of the House and Senate. But if you want to observe the workings of the judicial branch, it is not as easy. Although some states allow cameras into their courtrooms, typically only high-profile cases get any media attention, and cameras are not allowed in most federal courts. One way you can both fulfill your responsibilities of citizenship and get a better understanding of how our judiciary functions is to serve on a jury. Most states and the federal government use driver registration records as well as local records for city or county utilities to call residents to serve on juries. So, as long as you have a driver's license and pay for local services, you are in the pool to be called as a juror.

Serving on a jury can be an enlightening experience and is a necessity for carrying out justice in the United States. The Sixth Amendment to the U.S. Constitution guarantees people the right to a jury trial when they are accused of violating a criminal law. Thus, your service on a jury is essential to protecting that constitutional right. Next time you are called to serve on a jury, do not try to avoid this service; seize it as an opportunity to see our justice system firsthand.

In addition to serving on a jury, you can also get an understanding of how our court system works by visiting your local court for a day. In general, trials are open to the public and you are welcome to observe the courtroom work. Find your local court and visit it for a day. Your court's public relations office typically provides information on current trials, and some courts even have formal tours that allow you to observe a trial and engage in a follow-up discussion afterward. See your local court's Web site for information.

CRITICAL THINKING QUESTIONS

1. Why do you think many judges are reluctant to allow cameras in their courtrooms?

2. Do you think driver's registration rolls and utility records are a good way to develop a jury pool? How else might a pool of eligible citizens be determined?

3. Why might some people be reluctant to serve on a jury? What could be done to relieve their concerns?

The federal judiciary has also been reluctant to hear disputes on powers the Constitution explicitly assigns to Congress or the president. It resists intervening in foreign policy questions respecting the power to declare war or economic questions such as the fairness of the federal tax system. The federal judiciary does decide questions about whether the federal government followed the laws, but it generally allows Congress and the president to resolve their differences through the normal legislative process.

Prosecuting Cases

U.S. attorney general
The chief law enforcement officer in the United States and the head of the Department of Justice.

solicitor general
The third-ranking official in the Department of Justice who is responsible for representing the United States in cases before the U.S. Supreme Court.

public defender system
An arrangement whereby public officials are hired to provide legal assistance to people accused of crimes who are unable to hire their own attorneys.

The U.S. Department of Justice is responsible for prosecuting federal criminal and civil cases. The department is led by the United States **attorney general,** assisted by the **solicitor general,** 94 U.S. Attorneys, and approximately 1,200 assistant U.S. Attorneys. The solicitor general represents the federal government whenever a case appears before the Supreme Court, whereas U.S. Attorneys represent the government whenever a case appears before a lower federal court. U.S. Attorneys are appointed by the president with the advice and consent of the Senate, whereas the attorney general appoints each of the assistant U.S. Attorneys after consulting with the U.S. Attorneys in each district. Some districts have as few as 17 assistant U.S. Attorneys, as does the U.S. Attorney's Office for the district of North Dakota; the largest, the U.S. Attorney's Office for the District of Columbia, has more than 350.

The federal judiciary also provides help to defendants who cannot afford their own attorneys in criminal trials. Traditionally, private attorneys have been appointed to provide assistance, but many state and federal courts employ a **public defender system.** This system provides lawyers to any defendant who needs one and is supervised by the federal judiciary to ensure that public defenders are qualified for their jobs.

The Three Types of Federal Courts

LEARNING OBJECTIVE

14.2 Outline the structure of the federal court system.

Article III of the Constitution is the shortest of the three articles establishing the institutions of government. Yet as brief as it is, it instructs the judiciary to resolve several kinds of cases, including those to which the United States is a party in enforcing the laws, for example, and disputes between citizens of two or more states.

Article III is not the only part of the Constitution dealing with the federal judiciary, however. The framers also gave Congress the power to establish "all tribunals inferior to the Supreme Court," which meant that Congress could establish the lower courts we discuss next.

The first Congress used this power to create a hierarchy of federal courts. Under the Judiciary Act of 1789, which was the very first law Congress passed, the federal judiciary was divided into a three-tiered system that exists to this day. The first tier consists of **district courts,** the middle tier of **circuit courts of appeals,** and the highest tier of only one court, the **Supreme Court.** The Supreme Court has **original jurisdiction,** the authority to hear a case essentially as a trial court would, only in cases involving ambassadors, other public ministers, and other diplomats, and cases in which a state or states are a party.

In all other cases, the Supreme Court has **appellate jurisdiction** and reviews decisions of other federal courts and agencies and appeals from state supreme court decisions that raise questions of federal law. In general, federal courts may decide only cases or controversies arising under the Constitution, a federal law, a treaty, or admiralty and maritime law; cases brought by a foreign nation against a state or the federal government; and diversity suits—lawsuits between citizens of different states—if the amount of the controversy exceeds $75,000.

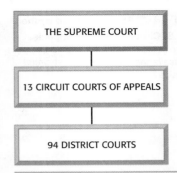

FIGURE 14–1 **The Structure of the U.S. Judiciary.**

■ *Why are there so many more district courts than there are circuit courts?*

Level One: District Courts

Although the Supreme Court and its justices receive most of the attention, the workhorses of the federal judiciary are the district courts in the states, the District of Columbia, and U.S. territories. In 2009, they heard more than 275,000 civil cases and more than 75,000 criminal cases.[6] There are 678 judgeships in the 94 district courts across the country, at least one in every state. (See Figure 14–1 for the three-tiered structure of the federal judiciary.)

District courts are the trial courts where nearly all federal cases begin. They make decisions on the death penalty, drug crimes, and other criminal violations. District judges normally hold trials and decide cases individually. However, because reapportionment of congressional districts and voting rights are so important to the nation, they hear cases concerned with these issues in three-judge panels.

Level Two: Circuit Courts of Appeals

All district court decisions can be *appealed,* or taken to a higher court for further review. Nearly all of these cases are reviewed by federal courts of appeals. Judges in these courts are bound by **precedent,** or decisions previously made by courts of appeals and the Supreme Court, but they have considerable discretion in applying these earlier decisions to specific new cases. Although most of their cases come upward from federal district courts, federal regulatory commissions bring their cases to the courts of appeals directly. For example, appeals of the Federal Energy Regulatory Commission's decisions may be heard by the U.S. Court of Appeals for the District of Columbia Circuit and by the U.S. Supreme Court.

Courts of appeals are located geographically in 11 *judicial circuits* that include all of the states and U.S. territories (see Figure 14–2 for a map of the states included in each of the 11 geographic circuits). A 12th is located in the District of Columbia and hears the largest number of cases challenging federal statutes, regulations, and administrative decisions. Circuit courts normally operate as panels of three judges; in 2009, they decided more than 57,000 cases.

Except in unusual circumstances, courts of appeals can resolve only cases that have been decided by district courts. Nevertheless, their decisions are usually final. Fewer than 1 percent of their decisions are appealed to the Supreme Court. (For more information about the federal judiciary, go to the Web site of the Administrative Office of the U.S. Courts at www.uscourts.gov.)

Level Three: The Supreme Court

The Constitution established only one court of appeals for the entire nation: the Supreme Court, or the "court of last resort." Once the Supreme Court decides, the dispute or case is over.

district courts
Courts in which criminal and civil cases are originally tried in the federal judicial system.

circuit courts of appeals
Courts with appellate jurisdiction that hear appeals from the decisions of lower courts.

Supreme Court
The court of last resort in the United States. It can hear appeals from federal circuit courts or state high courts.

original jurisdiction
The authority of a court to hear a case "in the first instance."

appellate jurisdiction
The authority of a court to review decisions made by lower courts.

precedent
A decision made by a higher court such as a circuit court of appeals or the Supreme Court that is binding on all other federal courts.

FIGURE 14–2 **States Covered by the Eleven U.S. Circuit Courts of Appeals.**
■ *Why are some circuits so much larger, geographically, than others? In what circuit do you reside?*

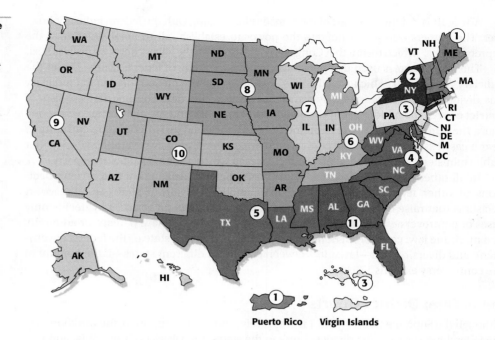

Puerto Rico   Virgin Islands

Compared with Congress and the presidency, the Supreme Court has changed the least since its creation. There are nine Supreme Court justices today, compared with six in 1789, and the Court moved into its own building only in 1935. Before then it had shared space with the House and Senate in the U.S. Capitol building. Unlike the current practice in both houses of Congress, oral arguments before the Court about individual cases are not televised, and the justices still appear in robes. Many of the Court's unique characteristics persist due to the constitutional protections the framers put in place. Given its importance, we will turn to a more in-depth discussion of the Supreme Court later in this chapter.

Judicial Federalism: State and Federal Courts

Unlike most countries, which have a single national judicial system that makes all decisions on criminal and civil laws, the United States has both federal and state courts. Each state maintains a judiciary of its own, and many large cities and counties have judicial systems as complex as those of the states. As in the federal system, state judicial power is divided between trial courts (and other special courts such as traffic courts) and one or more levels of appellate courts. State courts hear the overwhelming majority of cases in the U.S. legal system—approximately 90 million civil and criminal cases annually.

State courts primarily interpret and apply their state constitutions and law. When their decisions are based solely on state law, their rulings may not be appealed to or reviewed by federal courts. Only when decisions raise a federal question that requires the application of the Bill of Rights or other federal law are federal courts able to review them. Federal courts have **writ of *habeas corpus*** jurisdiction, or the power to release persons from custody if a judge determines they are not being detained constitutionally, and may review criminal convictions in state courts if they believe that an accused person's federal constitutional and legal rights have been violated (see Chapter 15). Except for habeas corpus jurisdiction, the Supreme Court is the only federal court that may review state court decisions, and only in cases presenting a conflict with federal law.

Other than the original jurisdiction the Constitution grants to the Supreme Court, no federal court has any jurisdiction except that granted to it by an act of Congress. Congress controls the Supreme Court's appellate jurisdiction (as we will discuss later in the chapter) and also established the three-tiered structure of the federal court system through legislation, beginning with the Judiciary Act of 1789. Congress could technically eliminate the lower federal courts, but that is entirely unlikely given the heavy caseloads under consideration.

writ of *habeas corpus*
A court order requiring explanation to a judge why a prisoner is being held in custody.

Reducing Crime

State and local governments are responsible for enforcing most laws against criminal activities such as murder, rape, and theft. However, the federal government provides money to help them do so, and it also enforces federal drug laws and gun controls. It has also helped fund larger police forces and imposed tougher sentences against federal crimes such as kidnapping and terrorism.

The federal government's biggest investment has been in providing money to help states control both street crimes and organized crime by the Mafia and other criminal organizations. In 1968, for example, Congress passed the Crime Control and Safe Streets Act, which gave millions of dollars to the states to increase their police forces and patrol the streets. The law also raised the minimum age for purchasing a handgun to 21 years of age.

The 1968 law set an important precedent for federal involvement in state and local crime control, which led to further controls on handguns and a new Crime Control and Safe Streets Act in 1994. Under the new law, the federal government gave states even more money to hire 100,000 new police officers and banned 19 types of assault weapons, such as the M-16 and AK-47, which are rapid-firing rifles often used by the military. The law also banned hate crimes such as painting Nazi slogans and swastikas on Jewish synagogues.

In part because of increased state and local action, national crime rates have fallen dramatically throughout the past quarter-century, particularly in large urban settings such as New York City. Crime fell through the 1990s and early 2000s, but there was an uptick in the number of violent crimes in 2005–2006. However, the rates in 2007–2008 have dropped back down below levels seen at the end of the 1990s but not yet to the lows of 2004. Preliminary rates for the first half of 2009 seem to indicate a further decline.*

CRITICAL THINKING QUESTIONS

1. Should the federal government be involved with state and local crime control?

2. What factors might drive the crime rate up or down?

3. How might criminal sentencing affect the crime rate?

* *Crime in the United States*, an annual publication of the Federal Bureau of Investigation, http://www.fbi.gov/ucr/ucr.htm#cius.

The Politics of Appointing Federal Judges

The Constitution sets absolutely no requirements for serving on the Supreme Court, nor did the first Congress create any requirements for the lower courts. Because judges were to be appointed by the president with the advice and consent of the Senate, the framers assumed that judges would be experienced in the law. As Alexander Hamilton explained, "there can be but few men in the society who will have sufficient skill in the laws to qualify them for the stations of judges. And making the proper deductions for the ordinary depravity of human nature, the number must be still smaller of those who unite the requisite integrity with the requisite knowledge."[7]

Much as the framers believed that the judiciary should be independent, the appointment process gives presidents and the Senate ample opportunity for influencing the direction of the courts. Indeed, George Washington established two precedents in judicial appointments. First, his appointees were his political and ideological allies—all of Washington's appointees belonged to his Federalist Party. Second, every state was represented on some court somewhere, thereby ensuring at least some representation across the nation.

Presidents have continued to follow Washington's lead on these two points. They nominate judges who are likely to agree with them on the key issues before the courts and tend to nominate judges from their own party. Presidents see these nominations as one of the most important legacies of their time in office. Indeed, if a president is able to appoint a 50-year-old justice, that person could continue to affect law in the United States for some 30 years beyond the president's time in office.

Presidents also routinely rely on the senators in a given state to make recommendations especially for district court appointments. Because judges serve for life, presidents see judicial appointments as an opportunity to shape the courts for decades to come. As Table 14–1 shows, federal court experience is the most common preparation for Supreme Court justices—in fact, 10 of the last 16 Supreme Court justices were federal lower-court judges at the time of their nomination. All of the current U.S. Supreme Court justices with the exception of the newest justice, Elena Kagan, have federal appeals court experience in particular.

LEARNING **OBJECTIVE**

14.3 Analyze the factors that play an important role in selecting judicial nominees.

TABLE

14–1	Moving Up to the Supreme Court

Job Experience	Number	Most Recent Example
Federal Judges	33	Sonia Sotomayor, 2009
Practicing Lawyers	22	Lewis F. Powell, 1971
State Court Judges	18	Sandra Day O'Connor, 1981
Cabinet Members	8	Labor Secretary Arthur Goldberg, 1962
Senators	7	Harold H. Burton (R-Ohio), 1945
Attorneys General	6	Tom C. Clark, 1949
Governors	3	Earl Warren (D-Calif.), 1953
Other	15	Solicitor General Elena Kagan, 2010

SOURCE: *CQ Weekly,* October 10, 2005, p. 2701, updated by authors.

■ *How might a justice's experience affect her work on the Court? Why do you think so many federal judges have won appointment to the U.S. Supreme Court?*

Making the Initial Choices

Article II of the Constitution gives the president the power to appoint federal judges with the advice and consent of the Senate. Although that language may seem straightforward, it has caused great controversy over the Senate's appropriate role in federal judicial selection. The result is a judicial selection process in which presidents are likely to consult with members of Congress and particularly senators, especially if they want a smooth confirmation.

The process through which the president consults with members of Congress is complex and may differ from appointment to appointment, but one particularly important norm is **senatorial courtesy**—the custom of submitting the names of prospective judges for approval to the senators from the states in which the appointees are to work. The home-state senators, particularly if they are of the president's party, may also develop a list of candidates for the president's consideration. If the senators approve the nomination, all is well. But if negotiations are deadlocked between them, or between the senators and the Department of Justice, a seat may stay vacant for years.[8]

The custom of senatorial courtesy is not observed with Supreme Court appointments, but presidents do strategically consult with members of Congress, as President Clinton did on his 1993 and 1994 appointments of Justices Ruth Bader Ginsburg and Stephen Breyer. Clinton was especially willing to consult with Republican senator Orrin Hatch, then the Senate Judiciary Committee chair, because the Senate was controlled by Republicans and he needed their support. Before selecting Solicitor General Elena Kagan as his candidate to replace Justice Stevens on the Supreme Court, President Obama met with Senate leaders and consulted with every member of the Senate Judiciary Committee.

Presidents are also advised by their own White House staffs and the Justice Department in compiling a list of potential nominees. Especially in more recent administrations, the Justice Department's Office of Legal Policy and the White House Counsel's Office begin formulating lists of potential court appointees as soon as the president assumes office.

In addition to this process within the government, nongovernmental actors try to influence the selection process. The American Bar Association (ABA) has historically rated candidates being considered for appointment, but conservative groups' concern that the ABA rankings were biased in favor of more liberal judges led the Bush administration to end its preappointment involvement.

Liberal and conservative interest groups also provide their own views of nominees' qualifications for appointment. People for the American Way and the Alliance for Justice often support liberal nominees and oppose conservatives, whereas the Heritage Foundation and a coalition of 260 conservative organizations called the Judicial Selection Monitoring Project often support conservative judges and oppose liberals. These organizations once waited to

senatorial courtesy
The presidential custom of submitting the names of prospective appointees for approval to senators from the states in which the appointees are to work.

In preparation for her confirmation hearings, then Solicitor General Elena Kagan met with Senate Judiciary Committee members. Here Kagan meets with Senator Patrick Leahy (D-VT), the Chair of the Senate Judiciary Committee.
■ *Why do nominees take the time to meet with senators before the confirmation hearings?*

express their opinions until after the president had sent the name of a nominee to the Senate, but now they are active before the choice is known, informing the media of their support or opposition to potential nominees.

Senate Advice and Consent

The normal presumption is that the president should be allowed considerable discretion in the selection of federal judges. Despite this presumption, the Senate takes seriously its responsibility in confirming judicial nominations, especially when the party controlling the Senate is different from that of the president. However, because individual senators can always threaten or actually mount a filibuster, even party control of the Senate is no guarantee that a nomination will succeed.

All judicial nominations are referred to the Senate Judiciary Committee for a hearing and a committee vote before consideration by the entire Senate. Like laws, judges are confirmed with a majority vote. Even before they receive a hearing, however, all district court nominees must survive a preliminary vote by the nominee's two home-state senators. Each senator receives a letter on blue paper, called a *blue slip,* from the committee asking for approval. If either senator declines to return the slip, the nomination is dead and no hearing will be held.

There are other ways to delay or defeat a judicial nominee, including the threat of a filibuster. Just as the Republican Senate majority had stalled Clinton nominations in the late 1990s, the Democratic majority stalled many of the Bush administration's nominees after it took control of the Senate in mid-2001. Democrats also stalled many of the Bush nominees even after Republicans regained control of the Senate following the 2002 midterm elections with both the threat and actual use of filibusters.[9] During his first 18 months in office, confirmation rates for President Obama's judicial nominees hit historic lows: only 37% of district court and 47% of appeals court nominees were confirmed. This compares to a confirmation rate of 85% for district court and 52% for appeals court nominees during President George W. Bush's first two years in office.[10] Even if the Senate delays or rejects a nomination, however, presidents always have the option of making *recess appointments* after the Senate adjourns at the end of a session. Presidents have made more than 300 recess appointments to the federal courts since 1789, including 15 Supreme Court justices who were initially seated as recess appointments.[11]

Before the mid-1950s, the Senate confirmation process was relatively simple and nonpartisan. Until then, the Senate Judiciary Committee did not even hold hearings to ask potential judges questions about their personal history and philosophy. However, as judges became more important in deciding civil rights and other controversial cases, the committee began interviewing candidates on various questions, sometimes imposing a *litmus test* by asking nominees about their positions on specific issues such as abortion. Nominees almost always refuse to answer such questions, to protect themselves from attack and reserve their judgment for actual future cases.

In 1987, however, Supreme Court nominee Robert Bork adopted a different and ultimately unsuccessful strategy. Because he had written so many law articles, made so many speeches, and decided so many cases as a circuit court judge, Bork sought to clarify his constitutional views in defending himself before the Judiciary Committee. His candor may well have contributed to the Senate's rejecting him, and that has made subsequent nominees even more reluctant to respond to similar questions.

Until recently, most judicial appointments, especially those for the district and circuit courts, were processed without much controversy. However, "now that lower-court judges are more commonly viewed as political actors, there is increasing Senate scrutiny of these nominees."[12] The battle over judicial confirmations ordinarily takes place in hearings before the Senate Judiciary Committee, although debates can also occur on the Senate floor after the committee has acted.[13] Supreme Court nominees have typically faced more

After a contentious confirmation process in 1987, the Senate rejected Judge Robert Bork by a vote of 58 to 42. ■ *Why might senators vote against a judicial nominee? Are there valid reasons for opposing judicial nominees?*

For the first time in the Supreme Courts's history, three of the court's nine justices are women: Justices Ginsburg, Sotomayor and Kagan. ■ *Is it important to have gender and racial diversity on the Supreme Court? Why or why not?*

Of the People

AMERICA'S CHANGING FACE

Diversity in the Federal Courts

The federal judiciary has long been dominated by white males. But diversity on the federal bench has been increasing during the last several decades, largely because of the judicial appointments of Presidents Jimmy Carter, George H. W. Bush, Bill Clinton, and George W. Bush. Although President Obama has only gotten 43% of his federal judges confirmed by the Senate through July 2010, he did appoint two women to the U.S. Supreme Court: Sonia Sotomayor, who is also the first Hispanic justice on the Court, and Elena Kagan, only the fourth woman ever to serve on the Court. He also appointed diverse candidates to the district and appellate courts. As of June 2010, President Obama had appointed 73 lower court judges. Twenty-five percent of those nominees are African-American, 10% are Hispanic, and 11% are Asian-American. Thirty-one of the nominees (42%) are women.

Although the number of women and minorities appointed to the federal courts has only recently increased significantly, the first female judge, Florence Allen, was appointed in 1934 by President Franklin D. Roosevelt. President Harry Truman named the first African American judge, William Henry Hastie, in 1950. President John F. Kennedy appointed the first Hispanic judge, Reynaldo G. Garza, in 1961, and President Richard M. Nixon in 1971 appointed the first Asian American judge, Herbert Choy. The first Native American

judge, Billy Michael Burrage, was appointed in 1994 by President Clinton.

There are several arguments for diversifying the federal judiciary. First, some scholars have argued that a diverse federal judiciary may reach decisions that more accurately reflect the views of our diverse populations. But research has not provided much support for the contention that female or minority judges decide cases differently than do white male judges, with the exception of discrimination suits. Even if there are no

differences in outcomes, others argue that simply having a federal judiciary that reflects the citizenry is important to maintaining the courts' legitimacy. In short, citizens place value in seeing someone like themselves on the federal judiciary.

CRITICAL THINKING QUESTIONS

1. How might a judge's race or gender affect decisions on the courts?

2. Should presidents consider judicial candidates' race or gender when making appointments to the federal courts?

3. What advantages or disadvantages might there be to having a diverse federal judiciary?

Justice Ruth Bader Ginsburg

Justice Sonia Sotomayor

Supreme Court Justices Clarence Thomas (left) and Anthony Kennedy.

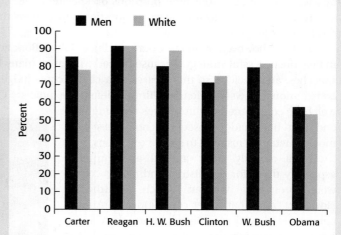

Demographic Characteristics of Federal District Court Judges by Appointing President

■ Men   ▨ White

SOURCE: Sheldon Goldman, Elliot Slotnick, Genard Gryski, and Sara Schiavoni, "Picking Judges in Time of Turmoil: W. Bush's Judiciary During the 109th Congress," *Judicature* (May–June 2007). Data updated by authors.

scrutiny in the confirmation process than have lower federal court judges. Indeed, the Senate has refused to confirm 31 of the 154 presidential nominations for Supreme Court justices since the first justice was nominated in 1789.

The Role of Ideology

Presidents so seldom nominate judges from the opposing party (only 10 percent of judicial appointments since the time of Franklin Roosevelt have gone to candidates from the opposition party) that partisan considerations are taken for granted. Today, more attention is paid to other characteristics, such as ideology, race, and gender.[14] (See *Of the People* box for more on the role of race and gender.)

Finding a party member is not enough; presidents want to pick the "right" kind of Republican or "our" kind of Democrat to serve as a judge. Thus judges picked by Republican presidents tend to be judicial conservatives, and judges picked by Democratic presidents are more likely to be liberals. Both these orientations are tempered by the need for judges to go through a senatorial confirmation process that must get bipartisan support.

As older, conservative judges appointed during the Reagan administration continued to retire, President George W. Bush worked hard to find younger conservative judges to fill the vacancies. Roberts and Alito were in their fifties when nominated for the Supreme Court and are likely to serve for decades. Many of the administration's lower-court appointees are also relatively young, which ensures their lasting impact. Like his recent predecessors, Bush had difficulty winning the support of opposition party senators for his judicial nominees. Democrats delayed Bush's most conservative nominees and held filibusters in order to prevent confirmation votes on ten circuit court nominees.

Alabama's Attorney General William Pryor was only 43 when he was confirmed for a life appointment as a federal judge on the 11th U.S. Circuit Court of Appeals. Here he testifies before the Senate Judiciary Committee. ■ *Are lifetime appointments to the federal courts problematic? Should there be term limits for these judges?*

The Role of Judicial Philosophy

A candidate's judicial philosophy also influences the selection process. Does a candidate believe that judges should interpret the Constitution to reflect what the framers intended and what its words literally say? Or does the candidate believe that the Constitution should be adapted to reflect current conditions and philosophies? Recall from our discussion in Chapter 2 that differences in constitutional interpretation can produce vastly different outcomes on the same legal question.

Presidents and senators also want to know how candidates see the appropriate role of the courts. Does the candidate believe that the courts should strike down acts of the elected branches if they violate broad norms and values that might not be explicitly stated in the Constitution? That is, does the candidate espouse the view of **judicial activism?** Or does the candidate believe in **judicial restraint,** which deems it appropriate for the courts to strike down popularly enacted legislation only when it clearly violates the letter of the Constitution? At the heart of this debate are competing conceptions of the proper balance between government authority and individual rights, and between the power of democratically accountable legislatures and that of courts and unelected judges.

Reforming the Selection Process

The televised confirmation hearings of Supreme Court nominees Robert Bork in 1987 and Clarence Thomas in 1991 provoked widespread complaints about the judicial selection process. Not only were the hearings lengthy and bitter, but they focused on personal issues that some critics believed were irrelevant to each nominee's qualification to serve. The hearings also included detailed questions about the nominees' positions on controversial issues, which neither was willing to answer.

The politics of judicial selection may shock those who like to think judges are picked strictly on the basis of legal merit and without regard for ideology, party, gender, or race. But as a former Justice Department official observed, "When courts cease being an instrument for political change, then maybe the judges will stop being politically selected."[15]

judicial activism
A philosophy proposing that judges should strike down laws that are inconsistent with norms and values stated or implied in the Constitution.

judicial restraint
A philosophy proposing that judges should strike down the actions of the elected branches only if they clearly violate the literal meaning of the Constitution.

YOU WILL DECIDE
Should the Federal Courts Be Active?

Given that a judicially active judge will be more willing to strike down the actions of the elected branches of government, it should not be surprising that legislators are interested to know how federal judicial candidates view judicial activism.

Throughout most of our history, federal courts have been more conservative than Congress, the White House, or state legislatures. Before 1937, judicial restraint was the battle cry of liberals who objected to judges' decisions to strike down many laws, such as state laws limiting the number of hours a person could work each week, that were passed to protect labor and women. These judges broadly construed the words of the Constitution to prevent what they thought were unreasonable regulations of property.

With Presidents Richard Nixon, Ronald Reagan, George H. W. Bush, and George W. Bush, however, these positions changed dramatically, and it was conservatives who advocated judicial restraint. What is needed, they argued, are judges who will step back and let Congress, the president, and the state legislatures regulate or forbid abortions, permit prayer in public schools, and not hinder law enforcement. Even though these presidents argued for restrained judges, many of the Supreme Court justices they appointed were quite active in overturning congressional legislation.

What do you think? Should the federal courts be judicially active? What arguments would you make for and against such a position?

THINKING IT THROUGH

Chief Justice John Marshall stated in 1803, "It is emphatically the province and duty of the judicial department to say what the law is."* The Court's decision in *Marbury* v. *Madison* established the use of judicial review to strike down congressional acts. Marshall saw this authority as essential to the Court's ability to check the other branches of government. Justices since Marshall have often been active in striking down legislation that infringes on the rights of minority groups. For example, the Supreme Court's decision in *Brown* v. *Board of Education of Topeka* (1954)† was an active one in that it struck down the state law requiring racial segregation in the public schools. The court's ability to take such action is often seen as an important check on the tyranny of the majority.

The courts have sometimes drawn criticism for too frequently striking down popularly supported legislation. The Roberts' Court decision to strike down restrictions on corporate and union spending from their general treasuries in *Citizens United* v. *Federal Election Commission*‡ resulted in substantial criticism by those who supported such limitations. One school of thought holds that the federal judiciary, composed of unelected judges secure from public pressure, has a responsibility to use restraint in reaching its decisions.

Many critics of judicial activism argue that although the Supreme Court has the authority of judicial review, the Court must also respect the elected branches' interpretations of the constitutionality of their own actions. These critics assert that Congress is especially well situated to determine whether it is acting under the appropriate grant of authority in Article I, and the executive branch is in a similarly good position to evaluate its power under Article II. According to this perspective, the Court's view on the constitutionality of executive or legislative action is that of only one coequal branch of government.

Critical Thinking Questions

1. Under what circumstances do you think the Supreme Court should be active and strike down state or federal legislation?
2. Might it be preferable to have an unelected body decide whether legislation is constitutional? Why or why not?
3. Why do you think most people associate judicial activism with a liberal court?

---

* *Marbury* v. *Madison*, 5 U.S. 137 (1803).
† *Brown* v. *Board of Education of Topeka*, 347 U.S. 483 (1954).
‡ *Citizens United v. Federal Election Commission*, 558 U.S. 50 (2010).

How the Supreme Court Decides

LEARNING **OBJECTIVE**
14.4 Trace the process by which Supreme Court decisions are reached, and assess influences on this process.

The Supreme Court is a unique institution. Its term runs from the first Monday in October through the end of June. The justices listen to oral arguments for two weeks each month from October to April and then adjourn for two weeks to consider the cases and to write opinions. By agreement, at least six justices must participate in each decision. Cases are decided by a majority vote. In the event of a tie, the decision of the lower court is sustained, although on rare occasions, the case may be reargued.

The Eight Steps to Judgment

When citizens vow to take their cases to the highest court of the land even if it costs their last penny, they underestimate the difficulty of securing Supreme Court review and misunderstand the Court's role. The rules for appealing a case are established by the Supreme Court and Congress. Since 1988, when Congress enacted the Act to Improve the Administration of Justice, the Supreme Court has not been obligated to grant review of most cases that come to it on appeal. Its *appellate jurisdiction* is almost entirely up to its discretion; the overwhelming majority of cases appealed to the Court will be denied review.

The process of deciding cases at the U.S. Supreme Court is substantially different than at other federal courts. The Court's first decision is to choose which of the thousands of appeals it will hear each year. Once it has decided to review a case, the Court must then decide the legal question at issue. Next, we discuss, step by step, the Court's process of accepting and deciding a case.

1. Reviewing Appeals   Today, the decision to grant nearly all appeals is at the Court's discretion. Many appeals come to the Court by means of a petition for a **writ of certiorari,** a formal petition seeking the Court's review, or through an **in forma pauperis** ("as a pauper") petition, which avoids the payment of Court fees. The great majority of in forma pauperis petitions come from prisoners. In either case, the appeals may arise from any state supreme court or from the federal court system (see Figure 14–3 for a simplified description of the two paths to the Supreme Court).

The writs, which the Court can grant or deny, produce its agenda, or **docket.** The docket has grown significantly since the 1970s as citizens have brought more lawsuits, states have imposed more death sentences (which are often appealed), federal regulation has increased, and federal punishment for crimes has become more severe. However, as the number of appeals has grown, the Supreme Court's discretion to decide which cases it will review has allowed it to hear fewer and fewer cases (see Figure 14–4 representing the size of the Supreme Court's docket over time).[16]

2. Granting the Appeal   The Supreme Court will review a case only if the claim raises a substantial question of federal or constitutional law with broad public significance— what kinds of affirmative action programs are permissible, whether individuals have a right to doctor-assisted suicide, or under what conditions women may have abortions. The Court also tends to review cases in which the courts of appeals disagree. Or a case may raise a constitutional issue on which a state supreme court has presented an interpretation with which the Court disagrees.

The Court decides whether to move forward based on the *rule of four.* If four justices are sufficiently interested in a petition, it will be granted and the case brought up for review. The justices' law clerks work as a group, in what is known as the *cert pool,* to read the petitions and write a memorandum on each, recommending whether a review should be granted. These memos circulate to all the justices except Justice Samuel Alito, who opted out of the cert pool in September 2008.

writ of certiorari
A formal writ used to bring a case before the Supreme Court.

in forma pauperis
A petition that allows a party to file "as a pauper" and avoid paying Court fees.

docket
The list of potential cases that reach the Supreme Court.

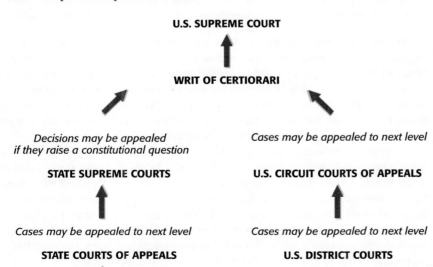

U.S. SUPREME COURT

WRIT OF CERTIORARI

Decisions may be appealed if they raise a constitutional question

Cases may be appealed to next level

STATE SUPREME COURTS   **U.S. CIRCUIT COURTS OF APPEALS**

Cases may be appealed to next level   *Cases may be appealed to next level*

STATE COURTS OF APPEALS   **U.S. DISTRICT COURTS**

Cases may be appealed to next level

STATE TRIAL COURTS

FIGURE 14–3 **How Most Cases Rise to the Supreme Court.**

■ *Under what conditions can a case that starts off in the state courts be appealed to the U.S. Supreme Court?*

FIGURE 14–4 **The Supreme Court Caseload.**

■ *Why do you think the Supreme Court's docket has gotten so much larger over time? Why has the number of cases decided declined at the same time?*

SOURCE: Lee Epstein, Jeffrey A. Segal, Harold J. Spaeth, and Thomas G. Walker, *The Supreme Court Compendium: Data, Decisions, and Developments* (CQ Press, 2007), figures updated by the authors.

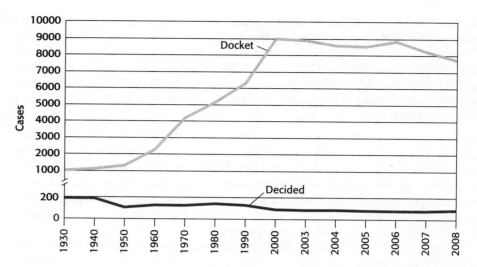

Denying a writ of certiorari does not mean the justices agree with the decision of the lower court, nor does it establish precedent. Refusal to grant a review can indicate all kinds of possibilities. The justices may wish to avoid a political "hot potato," or they may be so divided on an issue that they are not yet prepared to take a stand, or they may want to let an issue "percolate" in the federal courts so that the Court may benefit from their rulings before it decides.

3. Briefing the Case   After a case is granted review, each side prepares written *briefs* presenting legal arguments, relevant precedents, and historical background for the justices and their law clerks to study and on which to base their decisions. Prior decisions by the U.S. Supreme Court itself are most highly desirable as precedent; however, the Court may also consider cases decided by the lower federal courts as well as state supreme courts in reaching its decision, depending on the issue presented.

In writing these briefs, the appellants are often aware of the justices' views or concerns about their case, and they attempt to address those concerns. Indeed, attorneys readily admit that they sometimes frame their briefs to appeal to a particular justice on the Court, one they suspect may be the swing, or deciding, vote in the case. Often, outside groups interested in the case file ***amicus curiae* briefs** (Latin for "friend of the court"), through which they can make arguments specific to their members and of interest to the justices.

4. Holding the Oral Argument   After the Court grants review, a case is set for oral arguments—briefs must be filed according to a timely schedule and arguments are usually heard within three to four months. Lengthy oratory before the Supreme Court, once lasting for several days, is a thing of the past. As a rule, counsel for each side is now allowed only 30 minutes. In order to ensure compliance with this rule, lawyers use a lectern with two lights: A white light flashes five minutes before time is up. When the red light goes on, the lawyer must stop, even in the middle of a sentence.

The entire procedure is informally formal. Sometimes, to the annoyance of attorneys, justices talk among themselves or consult briefs or books during oral arguments. Other times, if justices find a presentation particularly bad, they will tell the attorneys so. Justices freely interrupt the lawyers to ask questions and request additional information. In recent years, "the justices seem barely able to contain themselves, often interrupting the answer to one question with another query."[17] Hence the 30-minute limit can be problematic, especially when the solicitor general participates, because his or her time comes out of the 30 minutes of the party he or she is supporting.

If a lawyer is having a difficult time, the justices may try to help out with a question. Occasionally, justices bounce arguments off an attorney and at one another. Justice Antonin Scalia is a harsh questioner. "When Scalia prepares to ask a question, he doesn't just adjust himself in his chair to get closer to the microphone like the others; he looks like a vulture, zooming in for the kill. He strains way forward, pinches his eyebrows, and

***amicus curiae* brief**
Literally, a "friend of the court" brief, filed by an individual or organization to present arguments in addition to those presented by the immediate parties to a case.

poses the question, like '... do you want us to believe?' "[18] Justice Ruth Bader Ginsburg is a particularly persistent questioner, frequently rivaling Scalia, whereas Justice Clarence Thomas almost never asks a question at all. (You can hear oral arguments in landmark cases [www.oyez.org] and argument transcripts are now made available on the Court's Web site on the same day as the case is heard [www.supremecourt.gov]).

5. Meeting in Conference   When in session, the justices meet on Friday mornings to discuss the cases they heard that week. These conference meetings are private; no one is allowed in the room except the justices themselves. As a result, much of what we know about the justices' conferences come from their own notes taken during the meetings.

The conferences are typically a collegial but vigorous give-and-take. The chief justice presides, usually opening the discussion by stating the facts, summarizing the questions of law, and suggesting how to dispose of each case. Each justice, in order of seniority, then gives his or her views and conclusions. The justices do not typically view this as a time to convince others of their views on the case; that will come later as drafts of the opinion are circulated between chambers. After each justice has given his or her view of the case, the writing of the majority opinion is assigned. By practice, if the chief justice is in the majority, he can either assign the opinion to a justice also in the majority or choose to write the opinion himself. If he is not in the majority, the most senior justice in the majority makes that determination.

6. Explaining the Decision   The Supreme Court announces and explains its decisions in **opinions of the Court.** These opinions are the Court's principal method of expressing its views and reasoning to the world. Their primary function is to instruct judges of state and federal courts how to decide similar cases in the future.

Although the writing is assigned to one justice, the opinion must explain the reasoning of the majority. Consequently, opinions are negotiated documents that require the author to compromise and at times bargain with other justices to attain agreement.[19]

A justice is free to write a **dissenting opinion** if desired. Dissenting opinions are, in Chief Justice Charles Evans Hughes's words, "an appeal to the brooding spirit of the law, to the intelligence of a future day."[20] Dissenting opinions are quite common, as justices hope that someday they will command a majority of the Court. If a justice agrees with the majority on how the case should be decided but differs on the reasoning, that justice may write a **concurring opinion.**

Judicial opinions may also be directed at Congress or at the president. If the Court regrets that "in the absence of action by Congress, we have no choice but to . . . " or insists that "relief of the sort that petitioner demands can come only from the political branches of government," it is asking Congress to act.[21] Justices also use opinions to communicate with the public. A well-crafted opinion may increase support for a policy the Court favors.

7. Writing the Opinion   Writing the opinion of the Court is an exacting task. The document must win the support of at least four—and more, if possible—intelligent, strong-willed persons. Assisted by the law clerks, the assigned justice writes a draft and sends it to colleagues for comments. If the justice is lucky, the majority will accept the draft, perhaps with only minor changes. If the draft is not satisfactory to the other justices, the author must rewrite and recirculate it until a majority reaches agreement.

The two weapons that justices can use against their colleagues are their votes and the threat of dissenting opinions attacking the majority's opinion. Especially if the Court is closely divided, one justice may be in a position to demand that a certain point or argument be included in, or removed from, the opinion of the Court as the price of his or her vote. Sometimes such bargaining occurs even though the Court is not closely divided. An opinion writer who anticipates that a decision will invite critical public reaction may want a unanimous Court and compromise to achieve unanimity. For this reason, the Court delayed declaring school segregation unconstitutional, in *Brown* v. *Board of Education* (1954), until unanimity was secured.[22] The justices understood that any sign of dissension on this major social issue would be an invitation to evade the Court's ruling.

8. Releasing the Opinion   In the past, justices read their entire opinions from the bench on "opinion days." Now, they generally give only brief summaries of the decision and their opinions. Occasionally, when they are unusually unhappy with an opinion, justices read

opinion of the Court
An explanation of a decision of the Supreme Court or any other appellate court.

dissenting opinion
An opinion disagreeing with the majority in a Supreme Court ruling.

concurring opinion
An opinion that agrees with the majority in a Supreme Court ruling but differs on the reasoning.

Of the People

Importance of an Impartial Judiciary

In the United States, as in most Western democracies, an independent judiciary serves a crucial role in maintaining democracy and protecting individual rights. In a separation-of-powers system like the United States, the judiciary maintains checks on the other branches of government and has the power to invalidate their actions when they violate the Constitution. It also ensures that the government treats all citizens fairly and impartially; no person is above the law. A Pew Global Attitudes Project survey asked respondents from around the world how important it was to live in a country where the judicial system treats everyone the same.

Even if it is not a present reality, most countries see an impartial judiciary where the judicial system treats everyone the same as an important goal. Nearly 90 percent of respondents in the United States indicated that it is very important that the judicial system treat everyone equally, and support in Germany nearly mirrors that in the United States. However, in other countries such as India, Mexico, Nigeria, and South Korea, there are fewer respondents who agree that an impartial judiciary is very important. It is, perhaps, not surprising that in countries where impartial justice is less assured that respondents value it less than in countries

such as the United States and Germany where impartiality is expected in the court systems.

CRITICAL THINKING QUESTIONS

1. In what ways could a judicial system show favoritism toward particular groups or individuals?

2. How do you think judicial elections might affect impartiality?

3. Would you expect greater or less impartiality of judges who gain their seats through popular elections?

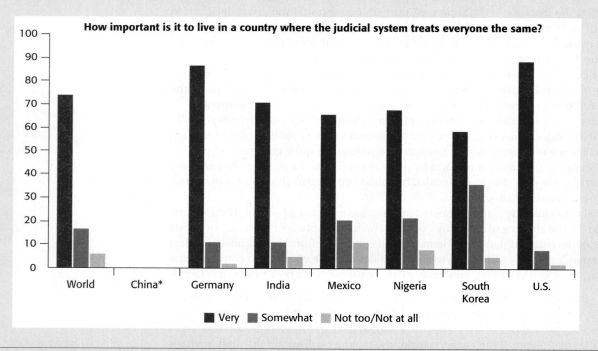

How important is it to live in a country where the judicial system treats everyone the same?

■ Very ■ Somewhat ■ Not too/Not at all

The Pew Global Attitudes Project, 2002. *Data was not collected in China, in part because they do not have an impartial judiciary.

portions of their dissenting opinions from the bench as Justice Stevens did in *Citizens United* v. *Federal Election Commission.*[23] Copies of the Court's opinions are immediately made available to reporters and the public and published in the official *United States Supreme Court Reports*. Since April 2000, the Court has made its opinions immediately available on its Web site (www.supremecourt.gov).

Influences on Supreme Court Decisions

Given the importance of cases that reach the U.S. Supreme Court, the complexity of the Court's decision-making process is not surprising. Supreme Court precedent is a primary influence, but if it were the only one, the lower courts could resolve the question themselves. Typically, there are conflicting precedents, and justices must decide which applies most closely to the legal question at hand.

Outside groups and other legal actors can also influence the Court's decisions. Interest groups' *amicus curiae* briefs may influence a justice's view of the case or the implications of a particular outcome. The chief justice can also affect decision making by the way he frames a case at the conference as well as by his choice of the justice to write the opinion based on the conference vote. Law clerks can affect the Court's decisions by the advice they give their justices, as well as by their role in reviewing the cases appealed to the Court.

The Chief Justice   The chief justice of the United States is appointed by the president and confirmed by the Senate, like other federal judges. Yet the chief justice heads the entire federal judiciary; as a result, he (so far in our history, all have been men) has greater visibility than if selected by rotation of fellow justices, as in the state supreme courts, or by seniority, as in the federal courts of appeals. The chief justice has special administrative responsibilities in overseeing the operation of the judiciary, such as assigning judges to committees, responding to proposed legislation that affects the judiciary, and delivering the Annual Report on the State of the Judiciary.

But within the Supreme Court, the chief justice is only "first among equals," even though periods in Court history (such as the Warren Court) are often named after the chief justice. As Rehnquist said when he was still an associate justice, the chief deals not with "eight subordinates whom he may direct or instruct, but eight associates who, like him, have tenure during good behavior, and who are as independent as hogs on ice."[24] As political scientist David Danelski observes, "The Chief Justiceship does not guarantee leadership. It only offers its incumbent an opportunity to lead." Yet the chief justice "sets the tone, controls the conference, assigns the most opinions, and usually, takes the most important, nation-changing decisions for himself."[25]

Law Clerks   Beginning in the 1920s and 1930s, federal judges began hiring the best recent graduates of law schools to serve as clerks for a year or two. As the judicial workload increased, more law clerks were appointed, and today, each Supreme Court justice is entitled to four. These are young people who have graduated from a leading law school and have previously clerked for a federal or state court.

Each justice picks his or her own clerks and works closely with them throughout the term. Clerks screen writs of certiorari and prepare draft opinions for the justices. As the number of law clerks and computers has increased, so has the number of concurring and dissenting opinions. Today's opinions are longer and have more footnotes and elaborate citations of cases and law review articles. This is the result of the greater number of law clerks and the operation of justices' chambers like "nine little law firms," often practicing against each other.[26]

Debate swirls about the degree to which law clerks influence the Court's decisions.[27] Some scholars contend that law clerks have had too much influence, especially as they help write early drafts of their justices' opinions. Others contend that justices select clerks with views very similar to their own, so to the extent law clerks are able to advance their views, they reflect those of the justice they serve. Regardless of this disagreement, however, there is widespread acceptance of law clerks' influence in the decision to grant certiorari. Law clerks' dominance at this stage of the decision-making process surely provides them with an opportunity at least to influence the Court's docket.

The Solicitor General   Attorneys in the Department of Justice and other federal agencies participate in more than

Chief Justice William Rehnquist (on the left) was very popular among his colleagues, both liberal and conservative. He was known for his general efficiency in running the Court and his fairness in assigning opinions. Here he meets with law clerks in his chambers. ■ *Should law clerks play such an important role in deciding which cases the Court will hear?*

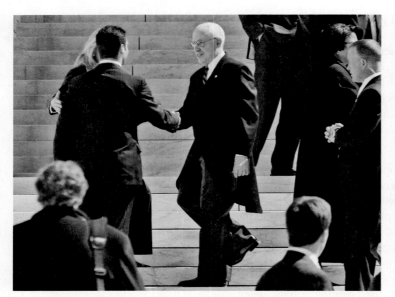

The U.S. Supreme Court is tradition bound. For example, when a male solicitor general appears before the Court, he wears a traditional vest, morning coat, and striped pants. The same applies on the rare occasion when the attorney general appears before the Court, as General Michael Mukasey did in 2008.

half of the cases the Supreme Court agrees to decide and therefore play a crucial role in setting its agenda. As we noted earlier in this chapter, the solicitor general is responsible for representing the federal government before the Supreme Court and is sometimes called the "tenth justice." Because the U.S. government may not appeal any case upward without the solicitor general's approval, the solicitor general has significant influence over the kinds of cases the Supreme Court eventually sees.[28]

The solicitor general also files *amicus curiae* briefs in cases in which the federal government is not a party. The practice of filing *amicus curiae* briefs guarantees that the Department of Justice is represented if a suit questions the constitutionality of an act of Congress or the executive branch. The solicitor general may also use these briefs to bring to the Court's attention the views of the current administration.

Citizens and Interested Parties   Citizens, interest groups, and organizations may also file *amicus curiae* briefs if they claim to have an interest in the case and information of value to the Court.[29] An *amicus* brief may help the justices by presenting arguments or facts the parties to the case have not raised. In recent decades, interest groups have increasingly filed such briefs in an effort to influence the Court and to counter the positions of the solicitor general and the government. For example, in *Grutter* v. *Bolinger* (2003), a case concerning affirmative action in college admissions, a record 102 *amicus* briefs were filed.[30] Although *Grutter* is an outlier, *amicus* briefs are regularly filed in cases before the U.S. Supreme Court. Between 1990 and 2001, at least one *amicus* brief was filed in nearly 90 percent of the cases. Cases involving civil liberties, which we will discuss in Chapter 15, are particularly likely to result in *amicus* participation.[31] Interest groups may also file *amicus curiae* briefs to encourage the Supreme Court to review a case, although this strategy has almost no influence on how the case is decided.[32]

After the Court Decides

Victory in the Supreme Court does not necessarily mean that winning parties get what they want. Although the Court resolves many issues, it also sometimes *remands* the case, sending it back to the lower court with instructions to act in accordance with its opinion. The lower court often has considerable leeway in interpreting the Court's mandate as it disposes of the case.

The impact of a particular Supreme Court ruling on the behavior of individuals who are not immediate parties to a lawsuit is more uncertain. The most important rulings require a change in the behavior of thousands of administrative and elected officials. Sometimes, Supreme Court pronouncements are simply ignored. For example, despite the Court's holding that it is unconstitutional for school boards to require students to pray within a school, some schools continue this practice.[33] And for years after the Supreme Court held public school segregation unconstitutional, many school districts refused to integrate or even closed their public school system, as in Prince Edward County, Virginia, so as to avoid integration.[34]

Judicial Power and Its Limits

LEARNING OBJECTIVE

14.5 Assess the limits on judicial action and the role of the judiciary in a constitutional democracy.

Although the framers worked hard to create an independent federal judiciary, judges are limited in that they cannot ignore earlier decisions unless they have a clear reason to break with the past.

Adherence to Precedent

Just because judges make independent decisions does not mean they are free to do whatever they wish. They are subject to a variety of limits on what they decide—some imposed by the political system of which they are a part and some imposed by higher courts and the legal profession. Among these constraints is the policy of **stare decisis,** the rule of precedent.

Stare decisis pervades our judicial system and promotes certainty, uniformity, and stability in the law. Drawn from the Latin phrase "to stand by that which is decided," the term means that judges are expected to abide by previous decisions of their own courts and by rulings of superior courts. However, the doctrine is not very restrictive.[35] Indeed, lower-court judges sometimes apply precedents selectively, to raise additional questions about an earlier higher-court decision or to give the higher courts a chance to change a precedent entirely.

Stare decisis is even less controlling in the field of constitutional law. Because the Constitution itself, rather than any one interpretation of it, is binding, the Court can *reverse* a previous decision it no longer wishes to follow, as it has done hundreds of times. Supreme Court justices are therefore not seriously restricted by stare decisis. Liberal Justice William O. Douglas, for one, maintained that stare decisis "was really no sure guideline because what did the judges who sat there in 1875 know about, say, electronic surveillance? They didn't know anything about it."[36] Anticipating Justice Stevens' strong dissent in *Citizens United* v. *Federal Election Commission* in which the Court overturned two of its previously decided cases, Chief Justice Roberts wrote that if stare decisis were an "inexorable command" or "mechanical formula of adherence to the latest decision… segregation would still be legal, minimum wage laws would be unconstitutional, and the Government could wiretap ordinary suspects without first obtaining warrants."[37] Since 1789, the Supreme Court has reversed nearly 200 of its own decisions and overturned more than 170 acts of Congress, as well as nearly 1,300 state constitutional and legislative provisions and municipal ordinances.[38]

Chief Justice John Roberts was appointed by President George W. Bush in 2005. He addressed students at the University of Alabama School of Law in 2010.
■ *What power does the Chief Justice have over the associate justices of the U.S. Supreme Court?*

Many Court observers expect the more conservative justices appointed during both Bush administrations to continue to move the law away from the right to abortion established in *Roe* v. *Wade* in 1973. Although they do not expect the Court to overturn the decision in a single, sweeping case, they do expect it to chip away at the precedent as more limited opportunities come before it.[39] The Court did just that when it upheld the federal Partial-Birth Abortion Ban Act in 2007. Although the act affected only late-term abortion procedures, the Court for the first time upheld an abortion restriction that did not provide an exception for the woman's health.[40]

Congressional and Presidential Action

Individual judges are protected from Congress and the president by their life tenure, but the judiciary as a whole can be affected by legislative decisions that alter both the number and the composition of the courts. Because the district and circuit courts are both created through legislation, they can be expanded or altered through legislation.

"Packing" the Court   When a political party takes control of both the White House and Congress, it may see an opportunity to increase the number of federal judgeships. With divided government, however, when one party controls Congress and the other holds the White House, a stalemate is likely to occur, and the possibility for new judicial positions is greatly decreased. During Andrew Johnson's administration, Congress went so far as to reduce the size of the Supreme Court to prevent the president from filling two vacancies. After Johnson left the White House, Congress returned the Court to its former size to permit Ulysses S. Grant to fill the vacancies.

stare decisis
The rule of precedent, whereby a rule or law contained in a judicial decision is commonly viewed as binding on judges whenever the same question is presented.

In 1937, President Franklin Roosevelt proposed an increase in the size of the Supreme Court by one additional justice for every member of the Court over the age of 70, up to a total of 15 members. Ostensibly, his proposal to "pack" the court with new supporters was aimed at making the Court more efficient. In fact, Roosevelt and his advisers were frustrated because the Court had declared much of the early New Deal legislation unconstitutional. Despite Roosevelt's popularity, his "court-packing scheme" aroused intense opposition and his proposal failed. Although he lost the battle, the Court began to sustain some important New Deal legislation, and subsequent retirements from the bench enabled him to make eight appointments to the Court.

Changing the Jurisdiction   Congressional control over the structure and jurisdiction of federal courts has been used to influence the course of judicial policy making. Although unable to get rid of Federalist judges by impeachment, Jefferson's Republican party abolished the circuit courts created by the Federalist Congress just before it lost control of Congress. In 1869, radical Republicans in Congress altered the Supreme Court's appellate jurisdiction in order to remove a case it was about to review weighing the constitutionality of some Reconstruction legislation.[41]

Each year, a number of bills are introduced in Congress to eliminate the jurisdiction of federal courts over cases relating to abortion, school prayer, and school busing, or to eliminate the appellate jurisdiction of the Supreme Court over such matters. These attacks on federal court jurisdiction spark debate about whether the Constitution gives Congress authority to take such actions. Congress has not yet decided to do so because it would amount to a fundamental shift in the relationship between Congress and the Supreme Court.

Judicial Power in a Constitutional Democracy

An independent judiciary is one of the hallmarks of a constitutional democracy and a free society. As impartial dispensers of equal justice under the law, judges should not depend on the executive, the legislature, parties to a case, or the electorate. But judicial independence is often criticized when judges make unpopular decisions. Perhaps in no other society do the people resort to litigation as a means of making public policy as much as they do in the United States. For example, the National Association for the Advancement of Colored People (NAACP) turned to litigation to get relief from segregation practices in the 1930s, 1940s, and 1950s. More recently, an increasing number of women's organizations, environmental groups, and religious and conservative organizations have also turned to the courts.[42]

Whether judges are liberal or conservative, defer to legislatures or not, try to apply the Constitution as they think the framers intended or interpret it to conform to current values, there are links between what judges do and what the people want. The people never speak with one mind and the links are not direct, but they are the heart of the matter.[43] In the first place, the president and the Senate are likely to appoint justices whose decisions reflect their values. Therefore, elections matter because the views of the people who nominate and confirm the judges are reflected in the composition and decisions of the courts. For instance, in *Planned Parenthood* v. *Casey* in 1992, the Supreme Court refused 5 to 4 to overturn *Roe* v. *Wade* and upheld its core ruling—that the Constitution protects the right of a woman to an abortion—although it also upheld state regulations that do not "unduly burden" that right.[44] This close vote made it clear that presidential elections could determine whether the right to abortion would continue to be protected.

If we as citizens oppose the Court's decisions, we have several avenues through which we can make our opposition known. By communicating with members of Congress, we can pressure them to pass legislation that limits the Court's ruling, as President Obama encouraged Congress to act to pare back the effects of the Court's decision in *Citizens United* during his 2010 State of the Union Address. We can organize to oppose a particular nomination to the federal judiciary, as many citizens did in response to Judge Robert Bork's nomination to the Supreme Court in 1986. When making our voting decisions, we can also consider the kinds of judges a presidential candidate is likely to appoint to the federal judiciary. In these ways and others, we can affect our federal courts. The Court's power rests, as former Chief Justice Edward White observed, "solely upon the approval of a free people."[45] No better standard for determining the legitimacy of a governmental institution has been discovered.

CHAPTER **SUMMARY**

14.1 Determine characteristics of the federal judiciary and implications of the adversarial process.

The courts provide a neutral arena in which two parties argue their differences and present evidence supporting those views before an impartial judge. As a result, the courts are largely *reactive*; judges have to wait for parties to a case to bring issues before the courts.

14.2 Outline the structure of the federal court system.

There are three levels of federal courts: (1) district courts, which hear original trials, (2) circuit courts of appeals, which can only review the process by which district courts made their decisions, and (3) the Supreme Court, which makes the final decision.

14.3 Analyze the factors that play an important role in selecting judicial nominees.

Partisanship and ideology are important factors in the selection of all federal judges. In making appointments to the federal courts, presidents must also consider the confirmation environment. They act strategically in selecting a candidate and consulting with Congress. In recent decades, candidates for the presidency and the Senate have made judicial appointments an issue in their election campaigns.

14.4 Trace the process by which Supreme Court decisions are reached, and assess influences on this process.

The Supreme Court has almost complete control over the cases it chooses to review as they come up

from the state courts, the courts of appeals, and district courts. Law clerks and the solicitor general play important roles in determining the kinds of cases the Supreme Court agrees to decide. Its nine justices dispose of thousands of cases, but most of their time is concentrated on the fewer than 90 cases per year they accept for review. The Court's decisions and opinions establish guidelines for lower courts and the country.

In addition to Supreme Court precedent and justices' own preferences, a number of actors may influence the decision-making process. Law clerks often write early drafts of justices' opinions. *Amicus curiae* participants and the solicitor general's office sometimes affect the opinion-writing process through the briefs they file, as well as through points made during oral argument before the Court.

14.5 Assess the limits on judicial action and the role of the judiciary in a constitutional democracy.

Although the federal judiciary is largely independent, factors such as stare decisis, the appointment process, congressional control over its structure and jurisdiction, and the need for the other branches of government to implement its decisions limit the degree to which the courts can or are likely to act without the support of the other branches. As impartial dispensers of equal justice under the law, judges should not depend on the executive, the legislature, the parties to a case, or the electorate. But judicial independence is often criticized when judges make unpopular decisions.

CHAPTER **SELF-TEST**

14.1 Determine characteristics of the federal judiciary and implications of the adversarial process.

1. List and explain three potentially negative consequences of the adversarial process.
2. In a criminal action, the _____ is the person or party accused of an offense.
   a. plaintiff
   b. defendant
   c. public defender
   d. judge magistrate
3. Match the following terms to their definitions:
   a. plea bargain
   b. adversary system
   c. standing
   i. The requirement that a person has experienced direct and personal injury in order to file a lawsuit.
   ii. System that holds arguing over law and evidence, which may or may not arrive at the

truth, guarantees fairness in the judicial system.
   iii. System whereby defendants agree to plead guilty to a lesser crime to avoid having to stand trial and face a sentence for a more serious crime.

14.2 Outline the structure of the federal court system.

4. Draw a diagram of the federal court system.
5. Match the following terms to their definitions:
   a. precedent
   b. original jurisdiction
   c. appellate jurisdiction
   i. The authority of a court to hear a case "in the first instance."
   ii. The authority of a court to review appeals of decisions made by the lower courts.
   iii. A decision made by a higher court, such as the Supreme Court, that is binding on all other federal courts.

14.3 Analyze the factors that play an important role in selecting judicial nominees.

6. In a short essay, explain why the judicial nomination process can be so contentious.

7. In two paragraphs, describe the way interest groups get involved in the nomination process.

14.4 Trace the process by which Supreme Court decisions are reached, and assess influences on this process.

8. Discuss two ways Supreme Court clerks can influence the outcomes in cases.

9. In one paragraph, explain why a justice would spend the time to write a dissenting opinion in a case decided by the Court.

10. Define *amicus curiae,* and describe a situation in which an *amicus* brief might be influential.

11. Write a brief essay distinguishing judicial activism from judicial restraint. How are they similar? In what ways are they different?

14.5 Assess the limits on judicial action and the role of the judiciary in a constitutional democracy.

12. Define stare decisis. Give one real-life example that illustrates this principle.

13. When Congress does not like a decision made by the Supreme Court, what kind of action can it take? In one paragraph, explain how Congress can constrain the Court.

14. Write a short essay detailing the role of the judiciary in our constitutional system. Could the system function without the judiciary? What adjustments would have to be made?

Answers to selected questions: 2. b; 3. a: iii, b: ii, c: i; 5. a: iii, b: i, c: ii

---

mypoliscilab EXERCISES

Apply what you learned in this chapter on MyPoliSciLab.

📖 **Read** on **mypolyscilab.com**

   eText: Chapter 14

✓ **Study** and **Review** on **mypoliscilab.com**

   Pre-Test
   Post-Test
   Chapter Exam
   Flashcards

👁 **Watch** on **mypoliscilab.com**

   Video: Court Rules on Hazelton's Immigration Laws
   Video: Prosecuting Corruption
   Video: Most Significant Abortion Ruling in 30 Years
   Video: Prosecuting Cyber Crime

✳ **Explore** on **mypoliscilab.com**

   Simulation: You Are a Young Lawyer
   Simulation: You Are the President and Need to Appoint a Supreme Court Justice
   Simulation: You Are a Clerk to Supreme Court Justice Judith Gray
   Comparative: Comparing Judiciaries
   Timeline: Chief Justices of the Supreme Court
   Visual Literacy: Case Overload

KEY **TERMS**

judicial review, p. 376
adversary system, p. 376
criminal law, p. 377
civil law, p. 377
prosecutor, p. 377
defendant, p. 377
plea bargain, p. 377
justiciable dispute, p. 377
plaintiff, p. 377
U.S. attorney general, p. 378

solicitor general, p. 378
public defender system, p. 378
district courts, p. 379
circuit courts of appeals, p. 379
Supreme Court, p. 379
original jurisdiction, p. 379
appellate jurisdiction, p. 379
precedent, p. 379
writ of *habeas corpus*, p. 380
senatorial courtesy, p. 382

judicial activism, p. 385
judicial restraint, p. 385
writ of certiorari, p. 387
in forma pauperis, p. 387
docket, p. 387
amicus curiae **brief,** p. 388
opinion of the Court, p. 389
dissenting opinion, p. 389
concurring opinion, p. 389
stare decisis, p. 393

ADDITIONAL **RESOURCES**

FURTHER READING

HENRY J. ABRAHAM, *Justices, Presidents, and Senators: A History of U.S. Supreme Court Appointments from Washington to Bush II,* 5th ed. (Rowman & Littlefield, 2008).

ROBERT A. CARP AND **RONALD STIDHAM,** *The Federal Courts* (CQ Press, 2001).

CORNELL CLAYTON AND **HOWARD GILMAN,** EDS., *Supreme Court Decision Making: New Institutionalist Approaches* (University of Chicago Press, 1999).

LEE EPSTEIN AND **JEFFREY A. SEGAL,** *Advice and Consent: The Politics of Judicial Appointments* (Oxford University Press, 2005).

LEE EPSTEIN, JEFFREY A. SEGAL, HAROLD SPAETH, AND **THOMAS WALKER,** EDS., *The Supreme Court Compendium,* 4th ed. (CQ Press, 2007).

SHELDON GOLDMAN, *Picking Federal Judges: Lower Court Selection from Roosevelt Through Reagan* (Yale University Press, 1997).

KERMIT L. HALL AND **KEVIN T. MCGUIRE,** EDS., *Institutions of American Democracy: The Judicial Branch* (Oxford University Press, 2005).

PETER IRONS, *A People's History of the Supreme Court* (Viking Press, 1999).

RANDOLPH JONAKAIT, *The American Jury System* (Yale University Press, 2003).

DAVID KLEIN, *Making Law in the U.S. Courts of Appeals* (Cambridge University Press, 2002).

FOREST MALTZMAN, JAMES F. SPRIGGS II, AND **PAUL J. WAHLBECK,** *Crafting Law on the Supreme Court: The Collegial Game* (Cambridge University Press, 2000).

CHRISTINE NEMACHECK, *Strategic Selection: Presidential Nomination of Supreme Court Justices from Herbert Hoover Through George W. Bush* (University of Virginia Press, 2007).

DAVID M. O'BRIEN, *Storm Center: The Supreme Court in American Politics,* 7th ed. (Norton, 2005).

J. W. PELTASON, *Federal Courts in the Political Process* (Doubleday, 1955).

TODD C. PEPPERS, *Courtiers of the Marble Palace: The Rise and Influence of the Supreme Court Law Clerk* (Stanford University Press, 2006).

TERRI JENNINGS PERETTI, *In Defense of a Political Court* (Princeton University Press, 1999).

GERALD N. ROSENBERG, *The Hollow Hope: Can Courts Bring About Social Change?* (University of Chicago Press, 1991).

PETER RUSSELL AND **DAVID M. O'BRIEN,** EDS., *Judicial Independence in the Age of Democracy: Critical Perspectives from Around the World* (University Press of Virginia, 2001).

ELLIOT E. SLOTNICK, *Judicial Politics: Readings from Judicature,* 3d ed. (American Judicature Society, 2005).

DONALD R. SONGER, REGINALD S. SHEEHAN, AND **SUSAN B. HAIRE,** *Continuity and Change on the United States Courts of Appeals* (University of Michigan Press, 2000).

ARTEMUS WARD AND **DAVID L. WEIDEN,** *Sorcerers' Apprentices: 100 Years of Law Clerks at the United States Supreme Court* (New York University Press, 2006).

WEB SITES

www.oyez.org Oyez is a Web site that contains links to audio recordings of Supreme Court oral arguments. It also provides an overview of the Court's decisions in many cases and links to other interesting Web sites on the judiciary.

www.supremecourt.gov This is a new Web site released by the Court in 2010. You can obtain oral argument transcripts, read the justices' biographies, and keep up to date with the Court's docket.

www.ncsconline.org The National Center for State Courts is an independent, nonprofit organization aimed at gathering data on state courts and improving the states' judicial administration.

PART IV Individual Rights and Liberties

THE BIG PICTURE

The original U.S. Constitution did not provide protections for an individual's right to express his or her views on the government or to worship freely. Nor did it affirm that all persons would be treated equally under the law. Today, we view these freedoms and rights as essential to democratic government, but this was not always the case. In this section, we discuss our basic freedoms, known as civil liberties, protected from improper government restriction in the Bill of Rights, as well as our civil rights, or the right to be free from irrational discrimination based on such factors as race, gender, or ethnic origin.

The struggle to protect and secure these rights and liberties has often been difficult, and even when protected appropriately, none of our rights are absolute. One of the most important constitutional developments that has occurred since the Constitution was ratified is known as incorporation—the act of applying the protections provided for in the Bill of Rights to the states. When it was ratified, the Bill of Rights applied only to the national government. The Anti-Federalists were mainly concerned with the new, powerful national government restricting individual rights. But, as the nation developed, it became clear that it was not only the national government that might impermissibly restrict these rights but also the states. The U.S. Supreme Court's decisions applying the protections found in the first ten amendments to the states have greatly changed the balance of power between the federal and state governments. The Court's rulings in these incorporation cases, as we discuss in Chapter 15, has made the federal courts largely responsible for protecting individual liberties against impermissible restriction by both the state and national governments.

The judiciary is the branch of government generally thought to protect these rights, and indeed the federal and state courts, and especially the U.S. Supreme Court, devote a good deal of time to doing just that. However, Congress has been especially important in providing protections against discrimination through the many pieces of civil rights legislation we discuss in Chapter 16. Many of the Supreme Court's most important civil rights decisions depended on congressional legislation prohibiting discrimination in voting, employment, housing, education, and federal financial assistance based on such factors as race, gender, age, national origin, or physical handicap.

COURSE LEARNING **OBJECTIVES**

CHAPTER 15 Civil Liberties

Describe the individual liberties protected in the Bill of Rights, and evaluate the limitations on these rights.

One of the major Anti-Federalist concerns over the new Constitution was its lack of explicit protections for individual liberties. As mentioned above, they were particularly concerned that a distant and powerful central government could trounce on the rights of individual citizens. Thus, they demanded that the Constitution include a Bill of Rights. In need of their votes for ratification, Federalists conceded to these demands.

The Bill of Rights provides protections for individuals' right to free speech, to practice religious beliefs freely, to petition government and assemble with like-minded individuals, to be free from unreasonable searches and seizures, to have a fair and speedy criminal trial, and to be free from cruel and unusual punishment, among others. But, these rights are not absolute. In certain circumstances, such as a national security threat, it may be necessary for the government to restrict speech. If one person's religious ritual threatens the life of another person, it too may be restricted. If there is a concern for a law enforcement officer's safety, searches that might otherwise be unreasonable may be permissible. In short, although our liberties are protected, these protections are not without exception. And, through our system of separated powers, it is the judiciary that decides the bound of such government restrictions.

CHAPTER 16 Civil Rights

Explain how Congress and the Supreme Court have expanded and protected civil rights.

Prior to the ratification of the Fourteenth Amendment, there was nothing in the Constitution that required states to treat all citizens equally. Indeed, even after the Fourteenth Amendment was ratified in 1868, providing for equal protection under the law, discrimination based on race and gender continued in the United States. Voting rights of former slaves were secured through the Fifteenth Amendment, ratified in 1870, and women's suffrage was garnered with the ratification of the Nineteenth Amendment in 1920. However, laws segregating society based on race and regulations that disadvantaged women in the workplace and property ownership continued well into the twentieth century. Through demonstrations and protests by civil rights activists supporting the rights of both African Americans and women, members of Congress finally felt the pressure necessary to pass civil rights legislation in the late 1950s and 1960s.

The federal courts have been an important institution in the fight for civil rights in the United States. They have heard cases challenging state and federal laws under the Fifth and Fourteenth Amendments, as well as cases challenging discrimination by private business owners who violated congressional civil rights legislation. The U.S. Supreme Court's decisions concerning equality of educational opportunity have been especially important to the civil rights movement, particularly the Court's decision in *Brown* v. *Board of Education* (1954) declaring that segregating students based on race was inherently unequal and thus violated the Fourteenth Amendment. However, the debate over the role of race in education continues. Today, the Court is more likely to confront affirmative action cases where universities, as well as elementary and secondary schools systems, have used race as a factor in admissions decisions.

Civil Liberties

Protections Under the Bill of Rights

Sixteen-year-old Terrance Graham attempted to rob a restaurant in July 2003. When the manager would not give Graham and his accomplices money, one of them hit the manager with a steel bar. Graham fled the scene but was later arrested and charged as an adult of a first-degree felony (burglary with assault or battery) with a maximum sentence of life in prison. Graham pled guilty to the crime and was sentenced to serve nine months in county jail and three years of probation.

But, six months after he was released from jail, Graham, then 17, was arrested on new felony charges: home invasion, robbery, and eluding police. He was also charged with violating his probation for his first criminal conviction. This time, Graham was sentenced to life in state prison without the possibility of parole. Graham's sentence was upheld by the Florida Court of Appeal and his attorney thus appealed to the U.S. Supreme Court arguing that Graham's sentence violated the Eighth Amendment ban on cruel and unusual punishment.

The Supreme Court has become more engaged recently in the way juveniles are treated in the criminal justice system, and the degree to which they are culpable in the same way as adults. The Eighth Amendment protects criminal suspects against cruel and unusual punishment, but the question facing the Court is whether there should be different standards for juvenile offenders. In *Roper* v. *Simmons* (2005), the Court relied on the decisions of state legislatures, scientific research on juvenile brain development, and international opinion against the death penalty for juveniles in deciding that the death penalty for minors violates the Eighth Amendment.[1] Would they apply a similar line of reasoning to Terrance Graham's case and rule that sentencing a juvenile offender to a life sentence without the possibility of parole also fails to meet the standards of the Eighth Amendment?

On May 17, 2010, the Supreme Court, for many of the same reasons it invalidated the death penalty for juvenile offenders, ruled that it did. They decided that life sentences without the possibility of parole for juveniles convicted of non-homicidal crimes violate the Eighth Amendment. Due to the potential for juveniles to mature and rehabilitate, the criminal justice system must provide juvenile offenders with some opportunity to show that they are "fit to rejoin society."[2] The Eighth Amendment is only one of several protecting the liberties of criminal suspects. Often these defendants are not the most sympathetic petitioners before the courts. But as Justice Felix Frankfurter observed, "The history of liberty has largely been the history of observance of procedural safeguards." Further, these safeguards have frequently "been forged in controversies involving not very nice people."[3] Our Constitution, and the Bill of Rights in particular, mandate that in order to deprive someone of their freedom, we must guarantee fairness and protect individual liberties.

In this chapter, we examine the fundamental liberties protected in a free society. These include freedom of speech and assembly, the right to practice one's religion without government interference, the right to bear arms, the right to be free from unreasonable searches and seizures, the right to be free from self-incrimination and double jeopardy, and the right to be represented by an attorney in a criminal proceeding. These freedoms are essential to self-determination and self-governance—government by the people. Yet they have also been vulnerable during times of war and, many would argue, are now threatened because of security measures put into place to combat international terrorism.[4] Regardless of the times, however, these liberties mean nothing if citizens do not challenge the government when they think it has impermissibly limited those freedoms. Unless we act as caretakers of our liberties, we lose them.

The Basis for Our Civil Liberties

LEARNING **OBJECTIVE**

15.1 Trace the roots of civil liberties in the original Constitution and their subsequent development in the Bill of Rights.

Before we delve into a discussion of freedoms, we will clarify several terms—*civil liberties, civil rights,* and *legal privileges*—often used interchangeably when discussing rights and freedoms.

Civil liberties are the constitutional protections of all persons against governmental restrictions on the freedoms of conscience, religion, and expression. Civil liberties are secured by the First Amendment and the due process clauses of the Fifth and Fourteenth Amendments, among others.

Civil rights are the constitutional rights of all persons to due process and the equal protection of the laws: the constitutional right not to be discriminated against by governments because of race, ethnic background, religion, or gender. These civil rights are protected by the due process and equal protection clauses of the Fifth and Fourteenth Amendments and by the civil rights laws of national and state governments. We discuss them further in Chapter 16.

Legal privileges, like the right to welfare benefits or to have a driver's license, are granted by governments and may be subject to conditions or restrictions.

Rights in the Original Constitution

Even though most of the framers did not think a bill of rights was necessary, they considered certain rights important enough to spell them out in the Constitution (see Table 15–1).

Foremost among constitutional rights, and deserving of particular mention here, is the **writ of *habeas corpus.*** Literally meaning "you have the body" in Latin, this writ is a court order directing any official holding a person in custody to produce the prisoner in court and explain why the prisoner is being held. Throughout the years, it developed into a remedy for any illegal confinement. People who are incarcerated have the right to appeal to a judge, usually through an attorney, stating why they believe they are being held unlawfully and should be released. The judge then orders the jailer or a lower court to justify why the writ should not be issued. If a judge finds that a petitioner is detained unlawfully, the judge may order the prisoner's immediate release.

The Supreme Court has recently underscored the fundamental nature of the right to a writ of *habeas corpus* in several decisions. In them, the Court rejected the Bush administration's position that it could indefinitely hold foreign nationals and U.S. citizens deemed "enemy combatants" in its war against terrorism. In *Hamdan* v. *Rumsfeld* (2006),[5] the Court rebuffed the Bush administration's position that it had the authority to try enemy combatants by military commissions, rather than in civilian courts or in court martial. The Court also rejected the argument that the Bush administration could ignore the

writ of *habeas corpus*
A court order requiring explanation to a judge as to why a prisoner is being held in custody.

TABLE
15–1 | Rights in the Original Constitution

1. Habeas corpus
2. No bills of attainder (legislative act that sentences a person or group to punishment without a trial)
3. No ex post facto laws
4. No titles of nobility (aristocratic titles that had also been barred by the Articles of Confederation)
5. Trial by jury in national courts
6. Protection for citizens as they move from one state to another, including the right to travel
7. Protection against using the crime of treason to restrict other activities; limitation on punishment for treason
8. Guarantee that each state has a republican form of government
9. No religious test oaths as a condition for holding a federal office
10. Protection against the impairment of contracts (forbids states from passing laws that effectively invalidate contracts)

■ *Why might some rights be mentioned both in the original Constitution and the Bill of Rights?*

Geneva Conventions, which specify that the accused has a right to see and hear the evidence for alleged crimes. In the aftermath of the Court's decision in *Hamdan,* Congress passed the Military Commissions Act of 2006, providing for enemy combatants' trial before military commission. Hamdan was tried by a military commission and although he was found guilty of supporting terrorism, a jury gave him only a 66-month sentence with credit for 61 months he had already served in the U.S. military prison at Guantanamo Bay, Cuba. He was sent back to his home country of Yemen in November 2008.[6]

In its 2008 decision in *Boumediene* v. *Bush,* the Supreme Court stood firm in its holding that Guantanamo Bay detainees have the right to pursue *habeas* review in the federal courts. In doing so, the Court struck down as unconstitutional the section of the Military Commissions Act barring the federal courts from hearing enemy combatants' *habeas corpus* petitions.[7]

Although the Court has emphasized the importance of *habeas corpus* generally, it has restricted its use, particularly for *habeas* appeals made by prisoners in the state criminal justice system. In these cases, the number of appeals has been restricted and the federal courts must defer to state judges unless their decisions were clearly "unreasonable."[8]

The Constitution also bars **ex post facto laws,** retroactive criminal laws making an act a crime that was not a crime when it was committed, increasing the punishment for a crime after it was committed, or reducing the proof necessary to convict for a crime after it was committed. However, the prohibition does not restrict retroactive application of a law that benefits an accused person, such as decreasing the punishment for a particular crime; nor does it apply to civil laws.

The Bill of Rights and the States

Most of the liberties we address in this chapter did not appear in the original Constitution. The Constitution drawn up in Philadelphia included guarantees of a few basic rights discussed previously, but it lacked a specific bill of rights similar to those in most state constitutions (see Chapters 1 and 2). Our civil liberties are found in the Bill of Rights, which is the first ten amendments to the Constitution, added in 1791.

The Bill of Rights originally applied *only to the national government,* not to state governments.[9] Why not to the states? The framers were confident that citizens could control their own state officials, and most state constitutions already had bills of rights. Furthermore, it would not have been politically feasible for the new Constitution to restrict state governments in this way. It was the new and distant central government the people feared. As it turned out, those fears were largely misdirected.

It was not until the Fourteenth Amendment was adopted in 1868 that there became a way for the restrictions in the Bill of Rights to be applied to the states. Because the Fourteenth Amendment applies explicitly to the states, supporters contended that its **due process clause**—declaring that no person shall be deprived by a state of life, liberty, or property without due process of law—limits states in precisely the same way the Bill of Rights limits the national government. But for decades, the Supreme Court refused to interpret the Fourteenth Amendment in this way. Then, in *Gitlow* v. *New York* (1925), the Court reversed this trend and decided that when fundamental liberties, such as the "freedom of speech and of the press—which are protected by the First Amendment from abridgment by Congress"—are at stake, the due process clause of the Fourteenth Amendment prohibits the state from infringing on those liberties just as the First Amendment prohibits Congress.[10]

Gitlow v. *New York* was a revolutionary decision. For the first time, the U.S. Constitution was interpreted to protect freedom of speech from abridgment by state and local governments. This landmark decision changed the balance of federalism in the United States. State actions that deprived citizens of fundamental liberties could now be challenged as a constitutional violation. In the 1930s and continuing at an accelerated pace during the 1960s, through the **selective incorporation** of provision after provision of the Bill of Rights into the due process clause, the Supreme Court applied the most important of these rights to the states.[11]

Today, the Fourteenth Amendment imposes on the states all the provisions of the Bill of Rights the Court has deemed essential to ordered liberty (see Figure 15–1). Although

ex post facto law
A retroactive criminal law that works to the disadvantage of a person.

due process clause
A clause in the Fifth Amendment limiting the power of the national government; a similar clause in the Fourteenth Amendment prohibiting state governments from depriving any person of life, liberty, or property without due process of law.

selective incorporation
The process by which provisions of the Bill of Rights are brought within the scope of the Fourteenth Amendment and so applied to state and local governments.

FIGURE 15–1 **Timeline of Selective Incorporation.**

■ *Examine the kinds of rights that the Court first began to incorporate. How are those different than the rights incorporated later, particularly in the 1960s?*

the Court had not incorporated a right since 1969, in 2010, it considered whether the Second Amendment ought to apply to the states as well as the federal government. In *McDonald* v. *Chicago,* the Court incorporated the Second Amendment protection of the right to bear arms to the states (*McDonald v. Chicago,* 561 U.S. ___ (2010)). As a result, state restrictions on handguns and other arms are now subject to strict constitutional review. Although the Supreme Court ruled that states have to abide by the Second Amendment, it left the decision as to whether or not Chicago's handgun restrictions violate the Second Amendment to the lower courts.

Selective incorporation of most provisions of the Bill of Rights into the Fourteenth Amendment is probably the most significant constitutional development that has occurred since the Constitution was written. It has profoundly altered the relationship between the national government and the states. It has made the federal courts, under the guidance of the Supreme Court, the most important protectors of our liberties—not the individual states. It has created a consistent national standard for interpreting the rights and liberties found in the Bill of Rights.

First Amendment Freedoms

Freedom of Religion

LEARNING OBJECTIVE

15.2 Outline the First Amendment freedoms and the limitations on them.

The first words of the First Amendment are emphatic and brief: "Congress shall make no law respecting an establishment of religion, or prohibiting the free exercise thereof." Though terse, it contains two important clauses: the *establishment* clause and the *free exercise* clause. Part of what makes religious liberties questions so interesting and difficult is that these clauses are often in tension with one another. Does a state scholarship for blind students given to a student who decides to attend a college to become a clergy member violate the establishment clause by indirectly aiding religion? Or would denying the scholarship violate the student's free exercise of religion? In dealing with the questions posed here, the Supreme Court ruled that providing such scholarship benefits does not go so far as to violate the establishment clause, but neither does the free exercise clause require that states provide the benefits.[12]

The Establishment Clause   In writing what has come to be called the **establishment clause,** the framers were reacting to the English system, wherein the crown was (and still is) the head not only of the government but also of the established church—the Church of England—and public officials were required to take an oath to support the established church as a condition of holding office. At least partly because of the brevity of the establishment clause, there is much debate as to its meaning. Some, such as the late Chief Justice William Rehnquist, contend it means *only* that the government cannot establish an official national religion nor prefer one sect or denomination to another.[13] Others argue that it requires the government to maintain neutrality, not only among religious denominations but also between religion and nonreligion.

establishment clause

A clause in the First Amendment that states that Congress shall make no law respecting an establishment of religion. The Supreme Court has interpreted this to forbid governmental support to any or all religions.

Separating Government from Religion

Throughout the world, there is substantial consensus that there ought to be some separation between religious beliefs and government policy. However, there are important differences between countries in which citizens believe more fully in such separation versus those in which citizens tend to agree with the idea. A Pew Global Attitudes Survey asked respondents for their level of agreement with the statement: "Religion is a matter of personal faith and should be kept separate from government policy." According to the survey, a majority of respondents in Great Britain, India, Nigeria, and the United States, completely agreed that government ought to be kept separate from religion.*

Although most countries' constitutions or laws provide for protections for religious liberties, enforcement of these rights vary, as does the degree to which government and religion are separate. For example, in Nigeria, in which tensions between Christians and Muslims have been on the rise, a separate court system exists for each group. Many Nigerian states use Shari'a courts in criminal and civil matters involving Muslims but common law courts for non-Muslims.† In other countries, such as India, there are differences between the national and state governments' involvement in religion. There, the national government has generally remained outside the religious sphere, but some state governments have enforced and enacted "anticonversion" laws.

The percentage of respondents completely agreeing that government policy and religion should be kept separate was significantly lower in China (21 percent), Japan (33 percent), and Mexico (38 percent). In China, the government sanctions only five religions known as "patriotic religious associations" (PRAs): Buddhist, Taoist, Muslim, Catholic, and Protestant. Only these PRAs can legally operate places of worship.

In Japan and Mexico, religious freedoms are constitutionally protected and the Mexican Constitution provides for a separation between church and state. However, particularly in Mexico, there is a great degree of religious homogeneity that might diminish the importance of separating government policy from religion in the eyes of many citizens. The great majority (approximately 88 percent) of Mexicans identify themselves, at least nominally, as Catholic.

CRITICAL THINKING QUESTIONS

1. Why might it be problematic to have the government involved in sanctioning religious groups as it does in China?

2. Do you think beliefs about separating government and religion depend on whether a person belongs to a religious minority? Should it?

3. How might religious homogeneity affect citizens' views of whether their government ought to be separate from the religion?

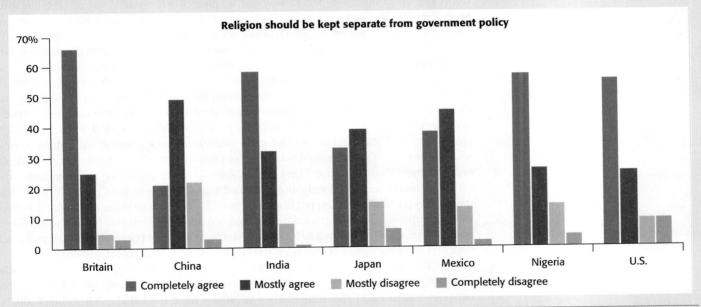

Religion should be kept separate from government policy

Legend: Completely agree · Mostly agree · Mostly disagree · Completely disagree

Countries: Britain, China, India, Japan, Mexico, Nigeria, U.S.

* Pew Research Center, "National Global Attitudes Survey," October 4, 2007.
† U.S. State Department, Bureau of Democracy, Human Rights, and Labor. "International Religious Freedom Report 2009," October 26, 2009, http://www.state.gov/g/drl/rls/irf/2009/index.htm.

Those who favor government neutrality regarding religion use the metaphor, coined by Thomas Jefferson, of a "wall of separation" to explain the strict separation between government and religion the clause requires. The metaphor was the basis for the Supreme Court's opinion in *Everson* v. *Board of Education of Ewing Township* (1947). The Court's 5-to-4 decision in the case, allowing government funds to reimburse parents for transporting children to private religious schools, is indicative of the confusion over

A singular religious display on government property, like this one of the nativity at City Hall in Dearborn, Michigan, might lead a reasonable observer to believe that the government was endorsing Christianity. Holiday displays with a variety of religious traditions represented along with some secular holiday symbols, such as a Christmas tree or Santa Claus, are considered acceptable. ■ *Why might displays that include references to several religious traditions pass constitutional scrutiny?*

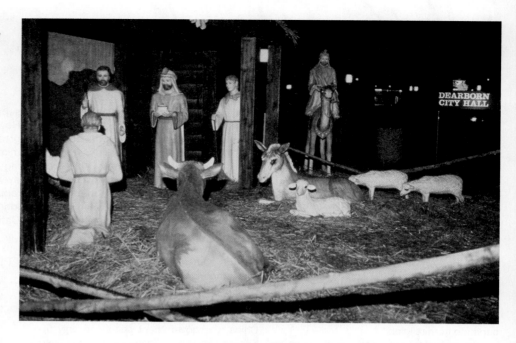

the establishment clause. All nine justices agreed that the wall of separation was the appropriate interpretation of the clause, yet they were divided five to four on whether the township's action violated that test.[14]

The Court's use of the wall of separation was hardly its last attempt at resolving debate over the establishment clause's interpretation. In *Lemon* v. *Kurtzman* (1971), the Court laid down the three-part *Lemon* test. To pass constitutional muster, (1) a law must have a secular legislative purpose, (2) it must neither advance nor inhibit religion, and (3) it must avoid "excessive government entanglement with religion."[15] Because the *Lemon* test has not been consistently used, however, the justices remain divided over how much separation between government and religion the First Amendment requires.

In addition to the *Lemon* test, former Justice Sandra Day O'Connor championed what is known as the *endorsement* test. She believed that the establishment clause forbids governmental practices that a reasonable observer would view as endorsing religion, even if there is no coercion.[16] For example, if a reasonable person would understand a crèche (nativity scene) displayed at the entrance to a county courthouse to be government endorsement of religion, Justice O'Connor would vote to strike down the practice.[17] Justices Antonin Scalia and Clarence Thomas joined Chief Justice Rehnquist in supporting a *nonpreferentialist* test.[18] As mentioned previously, they believed that the Constitution prohibits favoritism toward any particular religion but does not prohibit government aid to *all* religions. In their view, government may accommodate religious activities and even give nonpreferential support to religious organizations so long as government does not coerce individuals to participate in religious activities or give certain religious activities favorable treatment.[19]

By contrast, the more liberal justices—including John Paul Stevens, Ruth Bader Ginsburg, and Stephen Breyer—usually maintained that there should be *strict separation* between religion and the state.[20] They generally have held that even indirect aid for religion, such as scholarships or teaching materials and aids for students attending private religious schools, crosses the line separating the government from religion. But today, this view is not able to command a majority on the Court.

The Free Exercise Clause The right to hold any or no religious belief is one of our few absolute rights because it occurs solely within each person. The **free exercise clause** affirms that no government can compel us to accept any creed or to deny us any right because of what we do or do not believe. Requiring religious oaths as a condition of public employment or as a prerequisite for running for public office is unconstitutional. In fact, the original Constitution states, "No religious Test shall ever be required as a Qualification to any Office or public Trust under the United States" (Article VI).

free exercise clause
A clause in the First Amendment that states that Congress shall make no law prohibiting the free exercise of religion.

Of the People

AMERICA'S CHANGING FACE

Religious Diversity in the United States

From the beginning, religious freedom has been an important tenet of government in the United States. This was largely due to the fact that many of those who settled in the American colonies had experienced religious persecution in their former countries. Even so, many of those early immigrants were not so tolerant of those whose beliefs differed from their own. Respecting religious differences was difficult, even though those differences were largely between sects of Christianity.

Differences among religious beliefs today are substantially greater than when the United States was founded, and it appears that the country is on a path to even greater religious diversity. A report by the Pew Forum on Religion & Public Life provides evidence on religious affiliation in the United States.* Today, approximately 79 percent of adults identify themselves as Christian. However, that label masks substantial differences in beliefs among Protestants, Catholic, and other Christian groups. Other religious groups, including Jewish, Buddhist, Muslim, and Hindu, make up nearly 5 percent of the U.S. adult population. Approximately 16 percent of the adult population does not profess affiliation with any religious group.

Indications are that the United States is likely to become more religiously diverse in the coming years. Protestants, who currently make up a bare majority of the population, are more prevalent among the older population than among younger Americans. And immigrants to the United States tend to bring religious diversity with them. Approximately two-thirds of Muslims and more than 80 percent of those identifying themselves as Hindu are immigrants to the United States. As the country becomes more religiously diverse, protecting Americans' right to exercise their religious beliefs takes on greater importance and, in some cases, greater controversy.

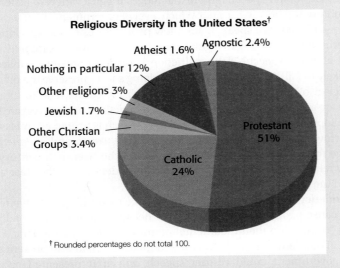

Religious Diversity in the United States†

Atheist 1.6%
Agnostic 2.4%
Nothing in particular 12%
Other religions 3%
Jewish 1.7%
Other Christian Groups 3.4%
Protestant 51%
Catholic 24%

† Rounded percentages do not total 100.

CRITICAL THINKING QUESTIONS

1. How might religious diversity in the United States affect the Supreme Court's decisions on religious liberties? Should it?

2. Do you think religious beliefs affect voting decisions? Why or why not?

* The Pew Forum on Religion & Public Life, *U.S. Religious Landscape Survey Religious Affiliation: Diverse and Dynamic*, February 2008, http://religions.pewforum.org/pdf/report-religious-landscape-study-full.pdf.

Although carefully protected, the right to practice a religion, which typically requires some action such as proselytizing or participating in a religious ritual, is more likely to be restricted than the right to hold particular beliefs. Before 1990, the Supreme Court carefully scrutinized laws allegedly infringing on religious practices and insisted that the government provide some compelling interest to justify actions that might infringe on someone's religion. Then, in *Employment Division* v. *Smith* (1990), the Court significantly altered the interpretation of the free exercise clause when it determined that the government does not always need to show a compelling interest if its laws infringe on religious exercise.[21] As long as a law is generally applicable and does not single out and ban religious practices, the law may be applied to conduct even if it burdens a particular religious practice.[22]

Free Speech and Free People

Government by the people is based on every person's right to speak freely, to organize in groups, to question the decisions of the government, and to campaign openly against them. Only through free and uncensored expression of opinion can government be kept responsive to the electorate and political power transferred peacefully. Elections, separation of powers, and constitutional guarantees are meaningless unless all persons have the right to speak frankly and to hear and judge for themselves the worth of what others have to say.

Even though the First Amendment explicitly denies Congress the power to pass any law abridging freedom of speech, the courts have never interpreted the amendment in

407

For many Native Americans, peyote is necessary to practice their religious beliefs. But the Supreme Court has ruled that states barring peyote do not need to create specific exceptions for its use in religious practices. ■ *Why do you think some states might not provide exemptions for the use of peyote in religious practices? Should they?*

Police arrested Scott Tyler of Chicago after he set fire to an American flag on the steps of the Capitol building in Washington, D.C. The Supreme Court afterward ruled that free speech covers even "symbolic speech" such as burning the U.S. flag. ■ *Would the Court's ruling on burning the flag differ if a riot were about to ensue as a result of that action?*

absolute terms. Like almost all rights, the freedoms of speech and of the press are limited. In discussing the constitutional power of government to regulate speech, we distinguish among *belief*, *speech*, and *action*.

At one extreme is the right to *believe* as we wish. Despite occasional deviations in practice, the traditional view is that government should not punish a person for beliefs or interfere in any way with freedom of conscience. At the other extreme is *action*, which the government may restrain. As the old saying goes, "Your right to swing your fist ends where my nose begins."

Speech stands somewhere between belief and action. It is not an absolute right, like belief, but neither is it as exposed to governmental restraint as is action. Some kinds of speech—libel, obscenity, fighting words, and commercial speech (discussed shortly)— are not entitled to constitutional protection. But many problems arise in distinguishing between what does and does not fit into the categories of unprotected speech. People disagree, and it usually falls to the courts to decide what free speech means and to defend the right of individual and minority dissenters to exercise it.

Plainly, questions of free speech require that judges weigh a variety of factors: What was said? In what context and how was it said? Which level of government is attempting to regulate the speech—a city council speaking for a few people, or Congress speaking for many? How is the government attempting to regulate the speech—by prior restraint (censorship) or by punishment after the speech? If the restriction is made to preempt publication (prior restraint), it is likely to fail. Why is the government doing so—to preserve the public peace or to prevent criticism of the people in power? Although the courts tend to be receptive to restrictions that are a genuine threat to public safety, restrictions on criticism are likely to fail.

Today, the Supreme Court generally holds that speech is protected unless it falls into one of four narrow categories—*libel, obscenity, fighting words,* and *commercial speech.* This is a change from its position at the beginning of the twentieth century, when the Court variously relied on one of three tests: the bad tendency test, the clear and present danger test, and the preferred position doctrine.

The **bad tendency test** presumed it was reasonable to forbid speech that tends to corrupt society or cause people to engage in crime. Because the test too broadly restricted speech and ran "contrary to the fundamental premises underlying the First Amendment as the guardian of our democracy,"[23] it was abandoned. The **clear and present danger test** provided that government could restrict speech *only* if it presented an immediate danger—for example, a false shout of "Fire!" in a crowded theater or speech leading to a riot, the destruction of property, or the corruption of an election. This clear and present danger test required the government to show the intended speech clearly resulting in imminent danger in order to restrict the important right of free speech.

The last of the three historic tests, the **preferred position doctrine,** was advanced in the 1940s when the Court applied all the guarantees of the First Amendment to the states (as discussed earlier). It comes close to the position that freedom of expression—the use of words and pictures—should rarely, if ever, be curtailed. This interpretation gives these freedoms, especially freedom of speech and of conscience, a preferred position in our constitutional hierarchy.

Although these tests are no longer applied, they provide a background for the current judicial approach to government regulation of speech, which represents an expansion of these more narrow constraints. Today, free speech and expression are constitutionally protected, and courts strictly scrutinize government regulation of such speech.

Protected Speech

Of all the forms of governmental interference with expression, judges are most suspicious of those that impose **prior restraint**—censorship before publication. Prior restraints include governmental review and approval before a speech can be made, before a motion picture can be shown, or before a newspaper can be published. Most prior restraints are unconstitutional, as the Court has said: "Any system of prior restraints of expression comes to this Court bearing a heavy presumption against its constitutional validity."[24] About the only prior restraints the Court has approved relate to military and national security matters—such as the disclosure of troop movements[25]—and to high school authorities' control over student newspapers.[26]

Even for an important purpose, a legislature may not pass a law that impinges on First Amendment freedoms if other, less drastic means are available. For example, a state may protect the public from unscrupulous lawyers but not by forbidding attorneys from advertising their fees for simple services. The state could adopt other ways to protect the public from such lawyers that do not impinge on their freedom of speech; it could, for example, disbar lawyers who mislead their clients.

Laws that regulate some kinds of speech but not others, or that regulate speech expressing some views but not others, are likely to be struck down. But those that are **content neutral or viewpoint neutral**—that is, laws that apply to *all* kinds of speech and to *all* views—are more likely to be safe. For example, the Constitution does not prohibit laws forbidding the posting of handbills on telephone poles. However, laws prohibiting only religious handbills or only handbills advocating racism or sexism would probably be declared unconstitutional because they would limit the content of handbills rather than restrict all handbills regardless of what they say.

Unprotected Speech

Unprotected speech lacks redeeming social value and is not essential to democratic deliberations and self-governance. The Supreme Court holds that all speech is protected unless it falls into one of four narrow categories: *libel, obscenity, fighting words,* or *commercial speech.* This does not mean that the constitutional issues relating to these kinds of speech are simple. How we prove *libel,* how we define *obscenity,* how we determine which words are *fighting words,* and how much *commercial speech* may be regulated remain hotly contested issues.

Libel   At one time, newspaper publishers and editors had to take considerable care about what they wrote to avoid prosecution by the government or lawsuits by individuals for **libel**—published defamation or false statements. Today, as a result of gradually rising constitutional standards, it has become more difficult to win a libel suit against a newspaper or magazine.

In *New York Times* v. *Sullivan* and subsequent cases, the Court established guidelines for libel cases and severely limited state power to award monetary damages in libel suits brought by public officials against critics of official conduct. Neither public officials nor public figures can collect damages for comments made about them unless they were made with *actual malice,* meaning that the "statements were made with a knowing or reckless disregard for the truth."[27] Nor can they collect damages even when subject to outrageous, clearly inaccurate parodies and cartoons. Such was the case when *Hustler* magazine printed a parody of the Reverend Jerry Falwell; the Court held that parodies and cartoons cannot reasonably be understood as describing actual facts or events.[28]

Obscenity and Pornography   Obscene publications are not entitled to constitutional protection, but members of the Supreme Court, like everyone else, have difficulty defining obscenity. As Justice Potter Stewart put it, "I know it when I see it."[29]

In *Miller* v. *California* (1973), the Court finally agreed on a constitutional definition of **obscenity.** A work may be considered legally obscene if (1) the average person, applying contemporary standards of the particular community, would find that the work, taken as a whole, appeals to a prurient interest in sex; (2) the work depicts or describes in a patently offensive way sexual conduct specifically defined by the applicable law or authoritatively construed (meaning that the legislature must define in law each obscene act); and (3) the work, taken as a whole, lacks serious literary, artistic, political, or scientific value.[30] As a result, cities such as New York City use zoning

bad tendency test
An interpretation of the First Amendment that would permit legislatures to forbid speech encouraging people to engage in illegal action.

clear and present danger test
An interpretation of the First Amendment that holds that the government cannot interfere with speech unless the speech presents a clear and present danger that it will lead to evil or illegal acts.

preferred position doctrine
An interpretation of the First Amendment that holds that freedom of expression is so essential to democracy that governments should not punish persons for what they say, only for what they do.

prior restraint
Censorship imposed before a speech is made or a newspaper is published; usually presumed to be unconstitutional.

content or viewpoint neutrality
Laws that apply to all kinds of speech and to all views, not only that which is unpopular or divisive.

unprotected speech
Libel, obscenity, fighting words, and commercial speech, which are not entitled to constitutional protection in all circumstances.

libel
Written defamation of another person. For public officials and public figures, the constitutional tests designed to restrict libel actions are especially rigid.

Internet bloggers pose an interesting twist on libel law. Bloggers can be sued for libel, just as print newspapers can, but bloggers' anonymity sometimes makes such suits more challenging. However, there are legal provisions to force Internet service providers to reveal the identity of a person who posts material online. ■ *Should the law treat bloggers differently than journalists? What other new media might pose difficult questions for the courts?*

New York City used zoning laws to eliminate adult entertainment and bookstores from Times Square. As a result, the area has once again become a vibrant center of the city and a prominent tourist attraction.
■ *Should states and cities be able to eliminate adult entertainment all together? Why or why not?*

obscenity
The quality or state of a work that, taken as a whole, appeals to a prurient interest in sex by depicting sexual conduct in a patently offensive way and that lacks serious literary, artistic, political, or scientific value.

fighting words
Words that by their very nature inflict injury on those to whom they are addressed or incite them to acts of violence.

commercial speech
Advertisements and commercials for products and services; they receive less First Amendment protection, primarily to discourage false and misleading ads.

laws to regulate where adult theaters and bookstores may be located,[31] and they may ban totally nude dancing in adult nightclubs.[32]

Fighting Words and Commercial Speech   **Fighting words** were held to be constitutionally unprotected because "their very utterance may inflict injury or tend to incite an immediate breach of peace."[33] That the words are abusive, offensive, and insulting or that they create anger, alarm, or resentment is not sufficient. Thus, a four-letter word worn on a sweatshirt was not judged to be a fighting word in the constitutional sense, even though it was offensive and angered some people. The word was not aimed at any individual, and those who were offended could look away.[34] In recent years, the Court has overturned convictions for uttering fighting words and struck down laws that criminalized "hate speech." However, hate crime statutes, which do not limit a person's expression but instead allow courts to consider motive in criminal sentencing, have been broadly upheld.[35]

Commercial speech—such as advertisements and commercials—used to be unprotected because it was deemed to have lesser value than political speech. But the Court has reconsidered and extended more protection to commercial speech, as it has to fighting words. In *44 Liquormart, Inc.* v. *Rhode Island* (1996), for instance, the Court struck down a law forbidding advertising the price of alcoholic drinks.[36] It now appears that states may forbid and punish only false and misleading advertising, along with advertising promoting the sale of anything illegal—for example, narcotics. Although the Supreme Court has not specifically removed commercial speech from the nonprotected category, it has interpreted the First, Fifth, and Fourteenth Amendments to provide considerable constitutional protection for it.

Freedom of the Press

We have seen that courts are immediately skeptical of prior restraints and have carefully protected the right to publish information, no matter how journalists get it. However, they have not recognized additional protections to allow journalists to withhold information from grand juries or legislative investigating committees. Without this right to withhold information, reporters insist they cannot assure their sources of confidentiality, and they will not be able to get the information they need to keep the public informed.

The Supreme Court, however, has refused to acknowledge that reporters, and presumably scholars, have a constitutional right to ignore legal requests such as subpoenas and to withhold information from governmental bodies.[37] In 2005, *New York Times* reporter Judith Miller was jailed for two months for refusing to disclose her sources to a grand jury. Many states have passed *press shield laws* providing some protection for reporters from state court subpoenas, and Congress is currently deliberating on a federal shield law known as the Free Flow of Information Act.

When the First Amendment was written, freedom of the press referred to leaflets, newspapers, and books. Today, the amendment protects other media as well, and much debate centers on the degree of protection that should be afforded to broadcast media and the Internet.

Broadcast and Cable Communications   Despite the rise of the Internet, television remains an important means of distributing news and appealing for votes. Yet of all the mass media, broadcasting receives the least First Amendment protection. Congress has established a system of commercial broadcasting, supplemented by the Corporation for Public Broadcasting, which provides funds for public radio and television. The Federal Communications Commission (FCC) regulates the entire system by granting licenses, regulating their use, and imposing fines for indecent broadcasts.

The First Amendment would prevent censorship if the FCC tried to impose it. The First Amendment does not, however, prevent the FCC from imposing sanctions on stations that broadcast indecent or filthy words, even if those words are not legally obscene.[38] Nor does the First Amendment prevent the FCC from refusing to renew a license if, in its opinion, a broadcaster does not serve the public interest. In the wake of Bono's 2003 Golden Globes acceptance speech including a certain indecent word and Janet Jackson's 2004

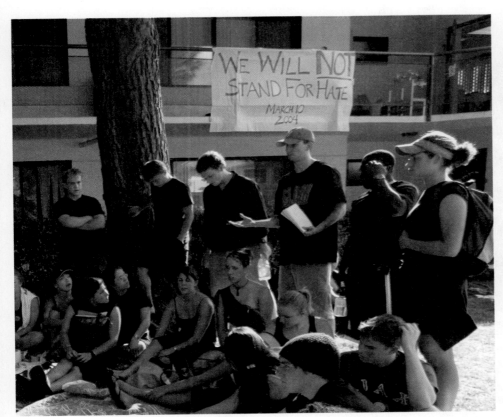

Although government may impose reasonable restrictions on the place and manner in which leaflets are posted, many college "hate speech" restrictions have been struck down because they unlawfully single out a certain kind of speech. ◾ *Why is it constitutionally impermissible to single out a particular kind of speech?*

Super Bowl performance in which her breast was exposed, heightened attention was focused on the issue of FCC sanctions. At least partly in response, President Bush signed a law in 2006 authorizing the FCC to fine broadcasters up to $325,000 for each instance of indecent broadcasting. Although the Court has continued to uphold restrictions on the broadcast media, cable operators are given greater latitude in their programming.[39]

The Internet   The Internet presents an interesting problem in determining the appropriate level of First Amendment protection. In many ways, it functions as a newspaper—providing news and information critical to an informed citizenry. But it is also a commercial marketplace where millions of U.S. consumers buy books, clothing, jewelry, airplane tickets, stocks, and bonds.

In general, attempts to regulate Internet content have been unsuccessful. In its major ruling on First Amendment protection for the Internet, *Reno* v. *American Civil Liberties Union* (1997), the Court struck down provisions of the Communications Decency Act of 1996 that had made it a crime to send obscene or indecent messages to anyone under the age of 18. In doing so, the Court emphasized the unique character of the Internet, holding that it is less intrusive than radio and broadcast television.[40] In response to *Reno* v. *ACLU*, Congress passed the Child Online Protection Act of 1998 (COPA), which made it a crime for a commercial Web site to knowingly make available to anyone under the age of 17 sexually explicit material considered "harmful to minors" based on "community standards." But the Supreme Court held that the law was unenforceable because imposing criminal penalties was not the least drastic means of achieving Congress's goals; Internet filters and adult checks could block minors' access to sites with sexually explicit material.[41]

Freedom of Assembly

Khallid Abdul Muhammad, a known racist and anti-Semite, organized what he called a "Million Youth March" in New York City in 1998. Mayor Rudolph

When Cher used profanity in reference to her critics as she accepted a Billboard Music Award, the FCC ruled that the broadcast was indecent, a determination upheld by the U.S. Supreme Court in 2009 (*Fox v. FCC*, 556 U.S. _____ (2009)). However, litigation on the FCC's policy on profanity is ongoing and a court of appeals has determined that its current policy is unconstitutionally vague. ◾ *Why does broadcast media receive comparatively little First Amendment protection?*

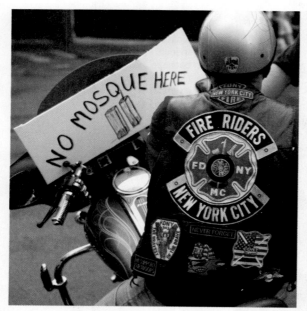

People who want to express their views, like this person protesting the construction of a Islamic community center near Ground Zero in New York City, must obtain the proper permits or paperwork. But the government may not deny their permit requests because it disagrees with the group's message. ■ *Under what circumstances might a government constitutionally deny a permit to assemble and protest?*

Giuliani denied a permit for the march on the grounds that it would be a "hate march." A federal appeals court upheld a lower-court ruling that denial of the permit was unconstitutional. However, a three-judge panel placed restrictions on the event, limiting its duration to four hours and scaling it back to a six-block area. The march proceeded, surrounded by police in riot gear who broke up the demonstration after Muhammad delivered a vitriolic speech against the police, Jews, and city officials. This is a classic free speech problem: The First Amendment protects speech regardless of whether it is popular. It is almost always easier, and certainly politically more prudent, to maintain order by curbing unpopular groups' public demonstrations.

Time, Place, and Manner Regulations   The Constitution protects the right to speak, but it does not give people the right to communicate their views to everyone, in every place, at every time they wish. No one has the right to block traffic or to hold parades or make speeches in public streets or on public sidewalks whenever he or she wishes. Governments may not censor what can be said, but they can make "reasonable" *time, place,* and *manner* regulations for protests or parades.

Depending on the place where the expressive activities are to occur, such as public parks, public school buildings, or government offices, the Court has been more or less willing to permit speech activities subject to reasonable time, place, and manner restrictions. It is essential, however, that any restriction be applied evenhandedly and that the government not act because of *what* is being said, rather than how, where, or by whom.

Does the right of peaceful assembly include the right to violate a law nonviolently but deliberately? We have no precise answer, but in general, **civil disobedience,** even if peaceful, is not a protected right. When Martin Luther King Jr. and his followers refused to comply with a state court's injunction forbidding them to parade in Birmingham, Alabama, without first securing a permit, the Supreme Court sustained their conviction, even though there was serious doubt about the constitutionality of the injunction and the ordinance on which it was based.[42]

More recently, the First Amendment right of antiabortion protesters to picket in front of abortion clinics has come into conflict with a woman's right to go to an abortion clinic. Protesters have often massed in front of clinics, shouting at employees and clients and blocking entrances to the clinic. The Supreme Court has struck down provisions that prohibit protesters from expressing their views. But it has upheld injunctions that keep antiabortion protesters outside a buffer zone around abortion clinics and also upheld injunctions that were issued because of the protesters' previous unlawful conduct.[43]

First Amendment freedoms are crucial for the survival of our republican form of democracy. It is of utmost importance that individuals be able to make their voices heard regardless of the political views they wish to express. However, these freedoms alone do not provide full protection from arbitrary or impermissible government infringements on our liberties more generally. Historically, U.S. political thinking and political institutions have emphasized the close connection between liberty and owning property, and between property and power. One of the framers' central goals was to establish a government strong enough to protect people's rights to use and enjoy their property. Next, we turn our attention to amendments in the Bill of Rights protecting property, due process, privacy, and the rights of criminal suspects.

civil disobedience
Deliberate refusal to obey a law or comply with the orders of public officials as a means of expressing opposition.

property rights
The rights of an individual to own, use, rent, invest in, buy, and sell property.

LEARNING **OBJECTIVE**
15.3 Explain how the Constitution protects property rights.

Property Rights

Property does not have rights; people do. People have the right to own, use, rent, invest in, buy, and sell property. The framers wanted to limit government so that it could not endanger that right. As a result, the Constitution has a variety of clauses protecting **property rights.**

Although the right of property ownership is highly regarded, both the national and state governments have the power of **eminent domain**—the power to take private property for public use—but the owner must be fairly compensated. What constitutes "taking" for purposes of eminent domain? Ordinarily, but not always, the taking must be direct, and a person must lose title and control over the property. Sometimes, especially in recent years, the courts have found that a governmental taking has gone "too far," and the government must compensate its owners even when title is left in the owner's name.[44] These are called **regulatory takings,** meaning the regulation has effectively taken the land by restricting its use. Thus, compensation is required when government creates landing and takeoff paths for airplanes over property adjacent to an airport, which makes the land unsuitable for its original use (say, raising chickens).[45] The government may, however, impose land use and environmental regulations, temporarily prohibiting the development of a property, without compensating the owners.[46]

In a controversial ruling with wide-ranging ramifications for urban planners and homeowners, a bare majority of the Court upheld the use of the government's power of eminent domain to condemn and take private property, with just compensation, for the purpose of advancing the economic development of a community. *Kelo* v. *City of New London* (2005) held that "public use" was not limited to eminent domain to build a road or a bridge but includes "promoting economic development," even if the property was taken and sold for development to private developers.[47] Public reaction to the Court's decision in *Kelo* was extremely negative. In a clear reminder that the Court is only one instrument of government, many states and localities acted swiftly to pass laws that barred authorities from taking private property for such purposes.

"Just compensation" is not always easy to define. When there is a dispute over compensation, the courts make the final resolution based on the rule that "the owner is entitled to receive what a willing buyer would pay in cash to a willing seller at the time of the taking."[48] An owner is not entitled to compensation for the personal value of an old, broken-down, dearly loved house—just the value of the old, broken-down house.

Major opposition to the Court's 2005 decision to allow New London, Connecticut, to take Susette Kelo's property led to many local ballot initiatives in the 2006 elections. ■ *How might ballot initiatives address citizens' concerns about the Court's decision in this case?*

Due Process Rights

Perhaps the most difficult parts of the Constitution to understand are the clauses in the Fifth and Fourteenth Amendments forbidding the national and state governments to deny any person life, liberty, or property without "due process of law." Cases involving these guarantees have resulted in hundreds of Supreme Court decisions. Even so, it is impossible to explain *due process* precisely. In fact, the Supreme Court has refused to do so and has emphasized that "due process, unlike some legal rules, is not a technical conception with a fixed content unrelated to time, place, and circumstances."[49] We define **due process** as rules and regulations that restrain those in government who exercise power. There are, however, basically two kinds of due process: procedural and substantive.

Procedural Due Process

Traditionally, **procedural due process** refers not to the law itself but to *how a law is applied.* To paraphrase Daniel Webster's famous definition, the due process of law requires a procedure that hears before it condemns, proceeds upon inquiry, and renders judgment only after a trial or some kind of hearing. Originally, procedural due process was limited to criminal prosecutions, but it now applies to most kinds of governmental proceedings.

The liberties that due process protects include "the right of the individual to contract, to engage in any of the common occupations of life, to acquire useful knowledge, to marry, to establish a home and bring up children, to worship God according to the dictates of his own conscience, and generally to enjoy those common law privileges long recognized as essential to the orderly pursuit of happiness by free men."[50]

LEARNING **OBJECTIVE**

15.4 Distinguish between procedural and substantive due process.

eminent domain

The power of a government to take private property for public use; the U.S. Constitution gives national and state governments this power and requires them to provide just compensation for property so taken.

regulatory taking

A government regulation that effectively takes land by restricting its use, even if it remains in the owner's name.

due process

Established rules and regulations that restrain government officials.

procedural due process

A constitutional requirement that governments proceed by proper methods; limits how government may exercise power.

Here a detainee is escorted by guards at the U.S. military prison at Guantanamo Bay, Cuba. Shortly after he took office, President Obama signed an executive order to close the facility in order to "restore the standards of due process and the core constitutional values that have made this country great even in the midst of war, even in dealing with terrorism."* ■ *Even with President Obama's executive order, why has it been so difficult to close the prison at Guantanamo Bay?*

*Susan Candiotti, Ed Hornick, and Jeanne Meserve, "What's Next for Guantanamo Bay Detainees?" CNN, *The First 100 Days*, January 26, 2009, http://www.cnn.com/2009/POLITICS/01/26/gitmo.next/index.html.

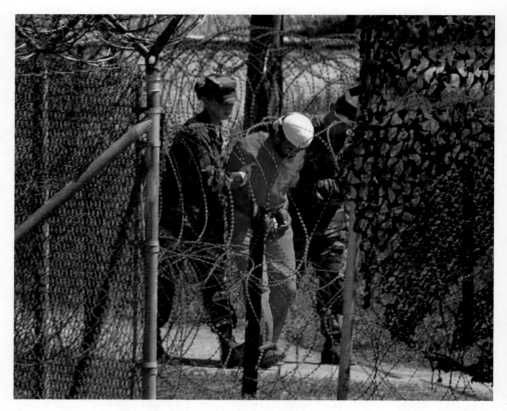

Substantive Due Process

Procedural due process limits *how* governmental power may be exercised; **substantive due process** limits *what* a government may do. Procedural due process mainly limits the executive and judicial branches because they apply the law and review its application; substantive due process mainly limits the legislative branch because it enacts laws. Substantive due process means that an "unreasonable" law, even if properly passed and properly applied, is unconstitutional. It means that governments *should not be allowed to do certain things.*

Substantive due process has deep roots in concepts of natural law and a long history in U.S. constitutional tradition. For most citizens most of the time, it is not enough merely to say that a law reflects the wishes of the popular or legislative majority. We also want our laws to be just, and we rely heavily on judges to decide what is just.

Privacy Rights

LEARNING **OBJECTIVE**

15.5 Assess the kinds of behavior that may be covered by a constitutional right to privacy.

substantive due process

A constitutional requirement that governments act reasonably and that the substance of the laws themselves be fair and reasonable; limits what a government may do.

The most important extension of substantive due process in recent decades has protected the right of privacy, especially marital privacy. Although the Constitution does not mention the right to privacy, in *Griswold* v. *Connecticut* (1965), the Supreme Court pulled together elements of the First, Third, Fourth, Fifth, Ninth, and Fourteenth Amendments to recognize that personal privacy is one of the rights the Constitution protects.[51] The decision remains highly controversial because the Bill of Rights does not specifically enumerate a right to privacy. Instead, the Court ruled that it was implied by the rights listed above.

This right has three aspects: (1) the right to be free from governmental surveillance and intrusion, especially with respect to intimate decisions on sexuality; (2) the right not to have the government make private affairs public; and (3) the right to be free in thought and belief from governmental regulations.[52] Thus, the right underlies our discussion later in this chapter of unreasonable searches and seizures, government surveillance, and self-incrimination. The right to privacy also encompasses two controversial issues: state regulation of abortion and private, adult consensual sexual conduct.

For the People

GOVERNMENT'S GREATEST ENDEAVORS

Protecting Sixth Amendment Rights of Indigent Defendants

Until 1963, defendants who could not afford an attorney to represent them in state criminal trials were left to defend themselves against charges brought by state prosecutors. Although the Sixth Amendment to the United States Constitution provided for an attorney in federal trials, it had not been incorporated against state infringement. However, all that changed when Clarence Earl Gideon appealed his conviction in the Florida state courts on the grounds that he was not provided with an attorney to fight charges that he had broken into a pool hall and stolen money from the cash register.

In *Gideon* v. *Wainwright*, the U.S. Supreme Court ruled that because of the complexities of the legal system and the potential for being deprived of one's basic liberty, the government must provide an attorney to a criminal defendant who

cannot afford one. This is particularly important in an adversarial legal system such as we have in the United States, where the judge or jury, as a neutral decision maker, depends on the attorneys to bring forth all of the relevant evidence in a case. The Court's decision in *Gideon* v. *Wainwright* resulted in public defender services being provided throughout the United States. Each state has its own method to provide counsel to indigent defendants. For example, in some states, they have a statewide public defender service, and, in others, they use a combination of state-employed defense attorneys and private attorneys whom the state pays by the case to represent indigent defendants.

Providing a defense for indigent persons accused of a crime is essential to fulfilling the requirements of the Sixth Amendment.

In 2007, more than 17,000 attorneys throughout some 964 public defender offices represented nearly 6 million cases involving indigent clients.[*] Although there are many concerns about the quality of representation provided to indigent defendants, including large caseloads and insufficient funding, indigent clients today are far better represented than they were some 40 years ago.

CRITICAL THINKING QUESTIONS

1. Why is it particularly important for indigent defendants to be represented by an attorney in an adversarial legal system?

2. Why might the Supreme Court have allowed the states to develop their own systems for providing indigent defendants with legal counsel?

* Public Defender Offices, 2007, Bureau of Justice Statistics, http://bjs.ojp.usdoj.gov/index.cfm?ty=pbdetail&iid=1758.

Abortion Rights

In *Roe* v. *Wade* (1973), the Supreme Court ruled that the right to privacy extended to a woman's decision, in consultation with her physician, to terminate her pregnancy. According to *Roe*'s "trimester framework," (1) during the first trimester of a woman's pregnancy, it is an unreasonable and therefore unconstitutional interference with her liberty and privacy rights for a state to set any limits on her choice to have an abortion or on her doctor's medical judgments about how to carry it out; (2) during the second trimester, the state's interest in protecting the health of women becomes compelling, and a state may make a reasonable regulation about how, where, and when abortions may be performed; and (3) during the third trimester, when the fetus becomes capable of surviving outside the womb, which the Court called "viability," the state's interest in protecting the unborn child is so important that the state can prohibit abortions altogether, except when necessary to preserve the life or health of the mother.[53]

The *Roe* decision led to decades of heated public debate and attempts by Presidents Ronald Reagan and George H. W. Bush to select Supreme Court justices who might reverse it. Nonetheless, *Roe* v. *Wade* was reaffirmed in *Planned Parenthood* v. *Casey* (1992). A bitterly divided Court upheld by a five-person majority (Justices O'Connor, Kennedy, Souter, Blackmun, and Stevens) the view that the due process clause of the Constitution protects a woman's liberty to choose an abortion prior to viability. The Court, however, held that the right to have an abortion prior to viability may be subject to state regulation that does not "unduly burden" it. In other words, the Court threw out the trimester framework and permitted states to make "reasonable regulations" on how a woman exercises her right to an abortion, so long as they do not prohibit any woman from making the ultimate decision on whether to terminate a pregnancy before viability.[54]

Applying the undue burden test, the Court has held, on the one hand, that states can prohibit the use of state funds and facilities for performing abortions; states may make a minor's right to an abortion conditional on her first notifying at least one parent

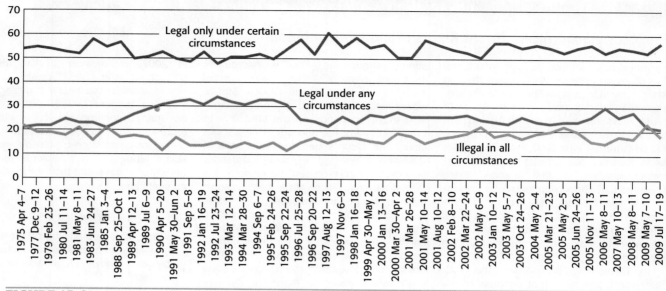

Do you think abortions should be legal under any circumstances, legal only under certain circumstances, or illegal in all circumstances?

FIGURE 15–2 **Public Opinion on Abortion Access.**
Although there is great controversy over the issue of abortion, a majority of Americans has consistently agreed that abortion access should be "legal only under certain circumstances." ■ *Are the Supreme Court's rulings on abortion access generally in line with public opinion?*

or a judge; and states may require women to sign an informed-consent form and wait 24 hours before having an abortion. On the other hand, a state may not condition a woman's right to an abortion on her first notifying her husband. The Court also struck down Nebraska's ban on "partial birth" abortions in *Stenberg* v. *Carhart* (2000) because it completely forbade one kind of medical procedure and provided no exception for when a woman's health is at stake and thus imposed an "undue burden" on women.[55] But, more recently (in 2007), the Court ruled five to four to uphold a federal ban on abortion procedures that was nearly identical to the one struck down in *Stenberg* v. *Carhart.* It reasoned that because of "medical uncertainty" about the banned procedure's necessity, Congress was not required to include a health exception.[56]

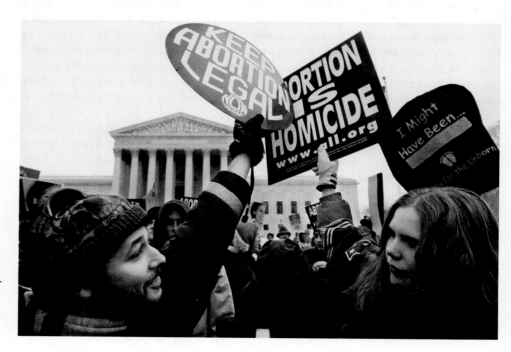

Abortion continues to be a hotly contested issue before the courts. Here protesters on both sides of the abortion debate demonstrate in front of the Supreme Court building.
■ *What impact might such protestors hope to have by demonstrating in front of the Supreme Court? Should justices pay attention to these protests?*

Sexual Orientation Rights

Although there is general agreement on how much constitutional protection is provided for marital privacy, in *Bowers* v. *Hardwick* (1986), the Supreme Court refused to extend such protection to private relations between homosexuals.[57] By a 5-to-4 vote in *Bowers*, the Court refused to declare unconstitutional a Georgia law that made consensual sodomy a crime. But several state supreme courts, including Georgia's, upheld privacy rights for homosexual couples based on their own state constitutions rather than relying on the U.S. Constitution. Finally, in *Lawrence* v. *Texas* (2003),[58] the Court struck down Texas's law making homosexual sodomy a crime. Writing for the Court and noting the trend in state court decisions that did not follow *Bowers*, Justice Kennedy held the law to violate personal autonomy and the right of privacy. Dissenting, Justice Scalia, along with Chief Justice Rehnquist and Justice Thomas, warned that the decision might lead to overturning laws barring same-sex marriages, as some state courts and Canadian courts had already done. We will explore this further in Chapter 16 under discussions of equal protection under the law.

The right of privacy as an element of substantive due process is one of the developing edges of constitutional law, one about which people both on and off the Court have strong disagreements. How the Supreme Court handles privacy issues has become front-page news.

search warrant
A writ issued by a magistrate that authorizes the police to search a particular place or person, specifying the place to be searched and the objects to be seized.

Rights of Criminal Suspects

Despite what you see in police dramas on television and in the movies, law enforcement officers have no general right to break down doors and invade homes. They are not supposed to search people except under certain conditions, and they have no right to arrest them except under certain circumstances. They also may not compel confessions, and they must respect other procedural guarantees aimed at ensuring fairness and the rights of the accused. Persons accused of crimes are guaranteed these and other rights under the Fourth, Fifth, Sixth, Eighth, and Fourteenth Amendments.

LEARNING **OBJECTIVE**
15.6 Characterize the constitutional rights of criminal suspects.

Freedom from Unreasonable Searches and Seizures

According to the Fourth Amendment, "The right of the people to be secure in their persons, houses, papers, and effects, against unreasonable searches and seizures, shall not be violated, and no Warrants shall issue, but upon probable cause, supported by Oath or affirmation, and particularly describing the place to be searched, and the persons or things to be seized."

Protection from unreasonable searches and seizures requires police, if they have time, to obtain a valid **search warrant**, issued by a magistrate after the police indicate under oath that they have *probable cause* to justify it. Magistrates must perform this function in a neutral and detached manner and not serve merely as rubber stamps for the police. The warrant must specify the place to be searched and the things to be seized. *General search warrants*—warrants that authorize police to search a particular place or person without limitation—are unconstitutional. A search warrant is usually needed to search a person in any place he or she has an "expectation of privacy that society is prepared to recognize as reasonable," including, for example, in a hotel room, a rented home, or a friend's apartment.[59] In short, the Fourth Amendment protects people, not places, from unreasonable governmental intrusions.[60]

The Fourth Amendment presents a complex area of the law that includes many possible exceptions to the warrant requirement. Beyond obtaining a search warrant, there are several other conditions in which a search might be considered "reasonable" according to the language of the Fourth Amendment. Key to determining whether a *warrantless search* is permissible are factors such as whether a person's consent to a search is coerced or whether an officer's or the public's safety is at risk. The Fourth Amendment does not apply to every encounter between individuals and law enforcement officials, however.

The Supreme Court ruled that it was permissible for police to use a drug-sniffing dog in a routine traffic stop without violating the Fourth Amendment protections against unreasonable search and seizure. (*Illinois v. Caballes*, 543 U.S. 405 (2005)). ■ *In what kinds of places might you have a reasonable expectation of privacy?*

Following September 11, 2001, airport security was tightened throughout the country. Such extensive searches are lawful because they are technically voluntary, meaning a person could choose not to fly.
■ *Should the same kind of searches be permissible before people board local public transportation such as buses or subways?*

If the police only ask questions or even seek consent to search an individual's person or possessions in a noncoercive atmosphere, and there is no detention, the person's physical liberty has not been limited. But if the person refuses to answer questions or consent to a search, and the police, by either physical force or a show of authority, restrain the movement of the person, even though there is no arrest, the Fourth Amendment comes into play.[61] For example, if police approach people in airports and request identification, this act by itself does not constitute a detention.[62]

The Supreme Court also upheld, in *Terry* v. *Ohio* (1968), a *stop and frisk* exception to the warrant requirement when officers have reason to believe someone is armed and dangerous or has committed or is about to commit a criminal offense. The *Terry* search is limited to a quick pat-down to check for weapons that may be used to assault the arresting officer, to check for contraband, to determine identity, or to maintain the status quo while obtaining more information.[63] If individuals who are stopped for questioning refuse to identify themselves, they may be arrested, although police must have a reasonable suspicion that they are engaged in criminal activities.[64] If an officer stops and frisks a suspect to look for weapons and finds criminal evidence that may justify an arrest, the officer can make a full search.[65]

Police and border guards may also conduct *border* searches—searches of persons and the goods they bring with them at border crossings.[66] The border search exception also permits officials to open mail entering the country if they have "reasonable cause" to suspect that it contains merchandise imported in violation of the law.[67]

The Exclusionary Rule   Before the development of the *exclusionary rule,* evidence obtained in violation of the Fourth Amendment might still be used at trial against a defendant. The remedy in such cases was the opportunity for the defendant to sue law enforcement. However, suing afterward did not resolve the denial of Fourth Amendment protection in the criminal action.

This changed in the federal courts in 1911 and was applied to the states in 1961. In *Mapp* v. *Ohio* (1961), the Supreme Court adopted a rule excluding from criminal trial evidence that the police obtained unconstitutionally or illegally.[68] This **exclusionary rule** was adopted to prevent police misconduct. Critics question why criminals should go free just because of police misconduct or ineptness,[69] but the Supreme Court has refused to abandon the rule. It has made some exceptions to it, however, such as cases in which police relied in "good faith" on a search warrant that subsequently turned out to be defective or granted improperly.[70]

The Right to Remain Silent   During the seventeenth century, special courts in England forced confessions by torture and intimidation from religious dissenters. The British

exclusionary rule
A requirement that evidence unconstitutionally or illegally obtained be excluded from a criminal trial.

privilege against self-incrimination developed in response to these practices. Because they were familiar with this history, the framers of our Bill of Rights included in the Fifth Amendment the provision that persons shall not be compelled to testify against themselves in criminal prosecutions. This protection against self-incrimination is designed to strengthen the fundamental principle that no person has an obligation to prove innocence. Rather, the burden is on the government to prove guilt.

The Miranda Warning Police questioning of suspects is a key procedure in solving crimes. Approximately 90 percent of all criminal convictions result from guilty pleas and never reach a full trial. Police questioning, however, can easily be abused. Police officers sometimes forget or ignore the constitutional rights of suspects, especially those who are frightened and ignorant. Unauthorized detention and lengthy interrogation to wring confessions from suspects, common practice in police states, have also occurred in the United States.

To put an end to such practices, the Supreme Court, in *Miranda* v. *Arizona* (1966), announced that no conviction could stand if evidence introduced at the trial had been obtained by the police during "custodial interrogation" unless suspects were notified that they have a right to remain silent and that anything they say can and will be used against them; to terminate questioning at any point; to have an attorney present during questioning by police; and to have a lawyer appointed to represent them if they cannot afford to hire their own attorney.[71] If suspects answer questions in the absence of an attorney, the burden is on prosecutors to demonstrate that suspects knowingly and intelligently gave up their right to remain silent. Failure to comply with these requirements leads to reversal of a conviction, even if other evidence is sufficient to establish guilt.

Critics of the *Miranda* decision believe the Supreme Court severely limited the ability of the police to bring criminals to justice. Throughout the years, the Court has modified the original ruling by allowing evidence obtained contrary to the *Miranda* guidelines to be used to attack the credibility of defendants who offer testimony at trial that conflicts with their statements to the police. But the Court has reaffirmed *Miranda*'s constitutional necessity as recently as 2000 (*Dickerson* v. *United States*).[72]

Fair Trial Procedures

Many people consider the rights of persons accused of a crime to be less important than other rights. Nonetheless, they guarantee that all persons accused of crimes will have the right to representation by counsel and to a fair trial by an impartial jury. Procedural

The case of Ernesto Miranda (right) led to the Supreme Court decision in 1966 requiring suspects in police custody to be advised of their constitutional right to remain silent and to have an attorney present during questioning. ■ *Why is it important that criminal suspects know their rights?*

protections are guaranteed at each of the stages in the criminal process: (1) pretrial, (2) trial, (3) sentencing, and (4) appeal.

Before a person can be forced to stand trial for a criminal offense (except for members of the armed forces or foreign terrorists), they must be *indicted* by a grand jury, or before a judge in what is called an *information* proceeding. A **grand jury** is concerned not with a person's guilt or innocence, as a **petit jury** would be, but merely with whether there is enough evidence to warrant a trial. The grand jury has wide-ranging investigatory powers and "is to inquire into all information that might bear on its investigations until it is satisfied that it has identified an offense or satisfied itself that none has occurred."[73] The strict rules that govern jury proceedings, and the exclusionary rule to enforce the Fourth Amendment, do not apply, and the grand jury may admit hearsay evidence. If a majority of the grand jurors agree that a trial is justified, they return a *true bill,* or **indictment.** During this stage of the criminal process and throughout the remaining stages, suspects have the right to an attorney, even if they cannot afford one on their own. Communication between the accused and counsel is privileged and cannot be revealed to a jury.

The Constitution guarantees the accused the right to be informed of the nature and cause of the accusation so that he or she can prepare a defense. After indictment, prosecutors and the defense attorney usually discuss the possibility of a **plea bargain** whereby the defendant pleads guilty to a lesser offense that carries a lesser penalty. Prosecutors, facing more cases than they can handle, like plea bargains because they save the expense and time of going to trial and they result in a conviction. Likewise, defendants are often willing to "cop a plea" for a lesser offense to avoid the risk of more serious punishment for the original indictment.

After indictment and preliminary hearings that determine bail and what evidence will be used against the accused, the Constitution guarantees a *speedy and public trial.* Do not, however, take the word "speedy" too literally. Defendants are given time to prepare their defense and often ask for delays because time works to their advantage. In contrast, if the government denies the accused a speedy trial, not only is the conviction reversed, but the case must also be dismissed outright.

An *impartial jury,* one that meets the requirements of due process and equal protection, consists of persons who represent a fair cross section of the community. Although defendants are not entitled to juries that reflect their own race, sex, religion, or national origin, government prosecutors cannot strike people from juries because of race or gender, and neither can defense attorneys use what are called *peremptory challenges* to keep people off juries because of race, ethnic origin, or sex.[74]

During the trial, the defendant has a right to obtain witnesses in his or her favor and to have the judge subpoena, or order, witnesses to appear at the trial and testify. Both the accused and witnesses may refuse to testify on the grounds that their testimony would tend to incriminate themselves. If witnesses testify, both the prosecution and the defense have the right to confront and cross-examine them.

The sentencing phase begins with the conclusion of the trial. Here, the jury recommends a verdict of guilty or not guilty. If the accused is found guilty, the judge usually hands down the sentence, although in some cases, juries also impose the sentence according to the judge's instructions. The Eighth Amendment forbids the levying of excessive fines and the inflicting of cruel and unusual punishment.

Although the crime rate has generally declined in the past few years, public concern about crime remains high. At the national and state levels, presidents, governors, and legislators vie with one another to show their toughness on crime. California, Virginia, Washington, and other states have "three strikes and you're out" laws, requiring a lifetime sentence without the possibility of parole for anyone convicted of a third felony, even if it is a minor offense. In some states, the felonies must be for violent crimes; in others, any three felonies will do. For example, the Supreme Court in *Ewing* v. *California* (2003) upheld California's tough law for committing three felonies, ruling that a 25-years-to-life sentence for a nonviolent third felony conviction for stealing three golf clubs did not violate the prohibition against cruel and unusual punishment.[75]

grand jury
A jury of 12 to 23 persons, depending on state and local requirements, who privately hear evidence presented by the government to determine whether persons shall be required to stand trial. If the jury believes there is sufficient evidence that a crime was committed, it issues an indictment.

petit jury
A jury of 6 to 12 persons that determines guilt or innocence in a civil or criminal action.

indictment
A formal written statement from a grand jury charging an individual with an offense; also called a *true bill*.

plea bargain
An agreement between a prosecutor and a defendant that the defendant will plead guilty to a lesser offense to avoid having to stand trial for a more serious offense.

By the People

MAKING A DIFFERENCE

Providing Legal Aid: Not Only for Law Students

Many law students spend time working at a legal aid clinic or volunteering for a legal aid society. They might provide legal advice, draft briefs, and even represent clients who cannot afford their own attorney. As discussed in this chapter's "For the People" box, criminal defendants who cannot afford to pay for their own legal representation are entitled through the Sixth Amendment to government-provided representation, but there are no constitutional requirements for attorneys in civil litigation and most states do not provide them.

Although many legal aid programs are aimed at law students, undergraduates also have the opportunity to provide legal help for those who cannot afford an attorney. Some legal aid societies welcome students as individual volunteers, and some court systems even cooperate with universities to provide organized programs for students as part of their service-learning programs.

For example, several California universities work with the Los Angeles Superior Court through a program called Justice Corps.* Through the program, the court trains students to work with self-represented litigants in court-based self-help programs. Some students with language skills are able to assist non-English speakers in navigating through the court system. Others conduct legal research and provide other assistance to people who may be fighting eviction or trying to obtain a civil restraining order. Programs like Justice Corps provide incredible opportunities to learn about the legal system and provide services to those in need.

In addition to organized programs, most local legal aid societies are continually looking for volunteers to help staff their offices, work with clients, and even perform routine maintenance. Lacking specialized legal skills need not prevent you from volunteering to make justice available to all citizens. Check to see if your college or university has an organized program for students to volunteer in the legal system. Does your community have a legal aid society? Sign up to volunteer your time for an hour or two a week.

CRITICAL THINKING QUESTIONS

1. Why are attorneys provided for indigent defendants in criminal cases but not for indigent litigants in civil case? Should attorneys be provided for those who cannot afford representation in civil cases?

2. What barriers might non-native English speakers encounter in the U.S. court system?

* See http://www.lasuperiorcourt.org/outreach/ui/#JusticeCorps.

In the final stage of the criminal process, defendants may *appeal* their convictions if they claim they have been denied some constitutional right or the due process and equal protection of the law. The Fifth Amendment also provides that no person shall be "subject for the same offense to be twice put in jeopardy of life or limb." **Double jeopardy** does not prevent punishment by the national and the state governments for the same offense, or for successive prosecutions for the same crime by two states. Nor does the double jeopardy clause forbid civil prosecutions, even after a person has been acquitted in a criminal trial for the same charge.[76]

The Death Penalty

The United States is unusual among industrialized nations in its retention and use of the death penalty. In December 2007, the United Nations General Assembly adopted a resolution calling for a worldwide moratorium on the death penalty. More than half of the countries throughout the world, 135, have abolished capital punishment for all or most crimes, and the trend has been growing. The United States and Japan are the only two industrialized countries that retain the death penalty. Most of the 62 countries that still impose capital punishment are in Africa, the Middle East, the Caribbean, and Central America.

After a ten-year moratorium on executions in the late 1960s and early 1970s, the U.S. Supreme Court ruled that the death penalty is not necessarily cruel and unusual punishment if it is imposed for crimes that resulted in a victim's death, if the courts "ensure that death sentences are not meted out wantonly or freakishly," and if these processes "confer on the sentencer sufficient discretion to take account of the character and record of the individual offender and the circumstances of the particular offense to ensure that death is the appropriate punishment in a specific case."[77]

The Rehnquist Court made it easier to impose death sentences, cut back on appeals, and carry out executions. More states have added the death penalty (35 states now have it),

double jeopardy
Trial or punishment for the same crime by the same government; forbidden by the Constitution.

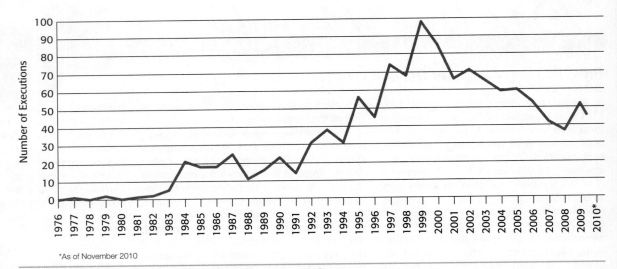

*As of November 2010

FIGURE 15–3 **Number of Executions by Year, 1976–2010.**
■ *What factors might explain the decline in the number of executions beginning in 2000?*

and the federal government has increased the number of crimes for which the death penalty may be imposed. As a result, the number of persons on death row has increased dramatically. Since capital punishment was reinstated in 1976, more than 1,000 people have been executed nationwide, and more than 3,300 are on death row.[78] (See Figure 15–3.) However, concerns have also grown about the fairness with which capital punishment is imposed. DNA tests that have established the innocence of a sizable number of those convicted of murder have increased these concerns.[79] Since 1973, more than 130 people who were convicted of murder and sentenced to death have been exonerated.[80] Much of this work has been done by the Innocence Project, which is a charitable organization that searches for wrongful convictions. (Visit the Innocence Project at innocenceproject.org.)

The prohibition against cruel and unusual punishment also forbids punishments grossly disproportionate to the severity of the crime. In 2002, the Supreme Court overruled an earlier decision and held that it is excessive and disproportionate to execute mentally retarded convicted murderers because they cannot understand the seriousness of their offense.[81] Using similar reasoning four years later, the Court ruled that executing minors also violated the Eighth Amendment.[82]

The Court continued its trend in limiting the use of the death penalty by deciding in *Kennedy* v. *Louisiana* (2008) that death could not be used when the defendant was convicted of child rape in which a death did not result, nor was it intended (the Court had previously ruled that the death penalty violated the Eighth Amendment in the case of adult rape).[83] In March 2008, however, the Court, in a 7-to-2 vote, upheld lethal injections as a constitutionally permissible means of carrying out executions.[84]

Protecting Our Civil Liberties in an Age of Terror: Whose Responsibility?

LEARNING **OBJECTIVE**

15.7 Evaluate the roles of institutions and the people in protecting civil liberties.

As the discussion regarding the appropriate venue for trying suspected terrorists illustrates (see "You Will Decide"), the debate over adequate protections of individual liberties is ongoing. Today, there is particular concern about how to protect those liberties in the face of terrorist threats. As Justice Oliver Wendell Holmes wrote in his famous decision in *Schenck* v. *United States* (1919), "when a nation is at war, many things that might be said in a time of peace" will not be permissible "so long as men fight."[85] How do we find the correct balance between security and protecting civil liberties?

Ensuring against another terrorist attack would be much easier if the government had open access to listen in on our conversations, search our possessions, and detain

YOU WILL DECIDE Should Terrorism Suspects Be Tried in Civilian Courts?

As the United States fights the war on terror, complex issues of national security and individual liberties continue to arise. One pressing issue is whether those arrested for plotting terrorist activities should be tried in our civilian court system or by military tribunals. The debate has important implications as defendants in the criminal court system are afforded protections that are not available in the military system. In general, military commissions allow some evidence against a defendant that would not be admitted into a civilian court and thus, in theory, provide an advantage to the prosecution. For example, prosecutors cannot use testimony obtained through coercion in civilian courts. However, in military courts, even statements that are made under coercion can be used in some circumstances. And, unlike military court judges, federal court judges have life tenure and there are protections to ensure judicial independence. On the other hand, some argue that accused terrorists should be tried in civilian courts because that system has proven capable of administering justice for more than two centuries, in other cases involving terrorism, and shows the world we will not compromise our system of justice in the face of terrorist attacks.

What do you think? Should terrorism suspects be tried in military or civilian courts? What argument would you make for or against either proposition?

THINKING IT THROUGH

There are a number of competing arguments regarding the appropriate venue for trying terror suspects. Underlying many of these debates is the question of whether suspected terrorists should be treated as soldiers caught on a new kind of battlefield, or whether they are more appropriately thought of as criminals who have violated criminal laws.

Those who argue that suspected terrorists ought to be tried in military tribunals cite the additional protections afforded to defendants in the criminal court system. They argue that suspected terrorists should not be privy to such additional protections when a soldier fighting in a traditional war would not be afforded those benefits. Proponents of military trials also argue that trying terror suspects in civilian courts would give them an opportunity to advance their ideology, provide incentives to attack civilian rather than military targets, and result in increased security concerns for cities in which the trials are held.

Those who argue for trying suspected terrorists in the civilian courts cite the relative success of such trials since September 11 and the relative lack of similar success in the military system. Military trials have led to only three convictions of suspected terrorists in eight years, and two of those three defendants are now free—one sent back to his native country of Australia and the other is in Yemen. Furthermore, legal changes have led many to question the validity of military commissions; those convicted through the military system are likely to challenge those outcomes. Supporters of civilian trials also argue that such trials will result in greater respect for the U.S. legal system and provide a platform for showing the horrors of terrorism. They also point to the fact that the federal courts have procedures for dealing with classified information, and prosecutors would not pursue these cases unless there was sufficient unclassified evidence to obtain convictions.

Critical Thinking Questions

1. What are the most important differences between civilian and military courts?
2. How should concerns for citizens' safety be weighed against the need to provide for a fair trial?
3. Should the relative success of the two court systems be considered when determining the most appropriate venue in which to try suspected terrorists?

---

or question suspects without having to show cause for doing so. The need to protect national security and gather foreign intelligence presents a special problem for Fourth Amendment protections. Endorsing the president's claim that he can authorize warrantless wiretaps and physical searches of agents of foreign countries, Congress created the Foreign Intelligence Surveillance Court to review requests for warrantless wiretaps. The court consists of federal district judges and meets in secret. The USA PATRIOT Act, of 2001 (Uniting and Strengthening America by Providing Appropriate Tools Required to Intercept and Obstruct Terrorism) expanded the size of the court, lowered the requirement to approve warrants in cases involving terrorism, and permits searches for foreign intelligence and evidence of terrorist activities. Congress overwhelmingly voted to extend the PATRIOT Act, and in February 2010, President Obama signed a one-year extension of the Act into law without additional protections for civil liberties sought by many Democrats. The extension continued to authorize "roving wiretaps" to monitor one individual's use of multiple communication devices.[86]

Although the U.S. Supreme Court is often seen as the guardian of our civil liberties and minority rights in the United States, the actions of the legislature and executive in fighting the war on terror make clear that the judiciary is not the only branch of government concerned with protecting liberties and it cannot do this work alone. In fact, some scholars contend that through the legislation it passes, Congress is as important as the Court in protecting individual liberties.[87] And, as we discussed in Chapter 14, the judiciary relies on the legislative and executive branches to enforce and provide funding to carry out its decisions. What does that imply for the role you play in protecting our civil liberties?

It is essential for citizens to be active in protecting our civil liberties. If we do not elect representatives who will uphold our civil liberties, enforce the Court's decisions, and appoint judges who will respect the individual guarantees in the Constitution, we cannot expect that they will be protected. Furthermore, if we do not act when we know civil liberties are being violated, the courts cannot make rulings. The judiciary is a reactive institution. It depends on individual citizens, or individuals working in cooperation through interest groups, to challenge government restrictions on civil liberties.

CHAPTER **SUMMARY**

15.1 Trace the roots of civil liberties in the original Constitution and their subsequent development in the Bill of Rights.

Antifederalists were concerned that the new national government would infringe on individual rights. Although many state constitutions already protected civil liberties, the Bill of Rights was to prevent the national government from infringing on civil liberties.

15.2 Outline the First Amendment freedoms and the limitations on them.

The First Amendment forbids the establishment of religion and also guarantees its free exercise. These two freedoms, however, are often in conflict with each other and represent conflicting notions of what is in the public interest. The Amendment also includes protections for speech, the press, and the right of assembly. However, each of these are limited: not all speech is protected, members of the press have no greater rights than do ordinary citizens, and the right to peaceably assemble is subject to reasonable time, place, and manner restrictions.

15.3 Explain how the Constitution protects property rights.

The framers saw private property rights as essential for maintaining a republican system of government. Although the government may take private property for public use, it must provide adequate compensation. And, even when the Constitution might allow such a "taking," the political process may prevent it.

15.4 Distinguish between procedural and substantive due process.

The Constitution imposes limits not only on the procedures government must follow but also on the ends it may pursue. Some actions are out of bounds no matter what procedures are followed. Legislatures have the primary role in determining what is reasonable and what is unreasonable. However, the Supreme Court exercises its own independent and final review of legislative determinations of reasonableness, especially on matters affecting civil liberties and civil rights.

15.5 Assess the kinds of behavior that may be covered by a constitutional right to privacy.

The right to privacy is implied by a number of the protections in the Bill of Rights, including protections against unreasonable searches and seizures, the protection against self-incrimination, and the right to associate (and not associate) with those you choose. It also protects a woman's right to terminate pregnancy and intimate relationships between consenting adults, regardless of sexual orientation.

15.6 Characterize the constitutional rights of criminal suspects.

The framers knew from their own experiences that in their zeal to maintain power and to enforce the laws, especially in wartime, public officials are often tempted to infringe on the rights of persons accused of crimes. To prevent such abuse, the Bill of Rights requires federal officials to follow detailed procedures in making searches and arrests and in bringing people to trial.

15.7 Evaluate the roles of institutions and the people in protecting civil liberties.

Although the judiciary is often seen as the guardian of civil liberties, it cannot carry out this function alone. Congress and the president also play an important role in protecting civil liberties through the laws they make and enforce. In addition, the judiciary is a reactive institution; without citizens who are willing to challenge improper restrictions on liberties, the courts are unable to act.

CHAPTER **SELF-TEST**

15.1 Trace the roots of civil liberties in the original Constitution and their subsequent development in the Bill of Rights.

1. Explain the Federalists concerns about adding a Bill of Rights to the Constitution. Were those concerns warranted?

2. In a few sentences, explain the significance of *Gitlow* v. *New York* and how it relates to the term *selective incorporation*.

3. List the four amendments in the Bill of Rights of which *no* part has been applied to states through the application of the Fourteenth Amendment. Why do you think these have not been incorporated?

15.2 Outline the First Amendment freedoms and the limitations on them.

4. In a paragraph, explain the tension that exists between the establishment and free exercise clauses of the First Amendment.

5. List the four categories of speech presently considered "unprotected," and give a brief definition of each.

6. Briefly define *prior restraint,* and explain the Supreme Court's position on it.

7. Imagine you are a newspaper editor who has just received a reliable tip that a prominent political leader fathered a child outside marriage. After checking the source, you run the story and are subsequently sued by the political leader. Write a short response defending your choice based on information in the chapter.

15.3 Explain how the Constitution protects property rights.

8. Your local city council has decided to develop a city park in your neighborhood. They offer you the fair market value for your home. If you prefer to stay in your house, can the city force you to move? In one paragraph, explain why or why not.

15.4 Distinguish between procedural and substantive due process.

9. Briefly define and contrast *procedural* and *substantive due process.*

15.5 Assess the kinds of behavior that may be covered by a constitutional right to privacy.

10. Which of the following is *not* an aspect of the right to privacy?
   a. The right to be free from government surveillance and intrusion
   b. The right not to have the government make private affairs public
   c. The right to be free in thought and belief from governmental regulations
   d. The right to perform religious acts as dictated by conscience on private property

11. Based on a credible tip, police officers obtain a search warrant to search your home. Can you deny them entry into your home based on your right to privacy? Explain your answer in one paragraph.

12. Match each of the following court cases with the significant precedent in the decision.

a. *Roe* v. *Wade*	i. Reaffirmed a woman's right to an abortion
b. *Romer* v. *Evans*	ii. Struck down a law criminalizing homosexual sodomy
c. *Lawrence* v. *Texas*	iii. Upheld Georgia law making consensual sodomy a crime
d. *Bowers* v. *Hardwick*	iv. Extended right to privacy to abortions
e. *Planned Parenthood* v. *Casey*	v. Struck down a constitutional amendment that banned state and local governments in Colorado from protecting homosexuals from discrimination

15.6 Characterize the constitutional rights of criminal suspects.

13. In a few sentences, describe the *exclusionary rule* and how it applies to the evolution of Fourth Amendment rights.

14. In a short essay, explain the procedures for a fair trial.

15.7 Evaluate the roles of institutions and the people in protecting civil liberties.

15. Write a paragraph discussing the limitations on the judiciary's ability to protect our civil liberties.

Answers to selected questions: 10. d; 12. a: iv, b: v, c: ii, d: iii, e: i

mypoliscilab EXERCISES

Apply what you learned in this chapter on MyPoliSciLab.

Read on mypoliscilab.com

eText: Chapter 15

Study and **Review** on mypoliscilab.com

Pre-Test
Post-Test
Chapter Exam
Flashcards

Watch on mypoliscilab.com

Video: Funeral Protestors Push the Limits of Free Speech
Video: D.C.'s Right to Bear Arms

Explore on mypoliscilab.com

Simulation: You Are a Police Officer
Simulation: You Are a Supreme Court Justice Deciding a Free Speech Case
Simulation: Balancing Liberty and Security in a Time of War
Comparative: Comparing Civil Liberties
Timeline: Civil Liberties and National Security

KEY **TERMS**

writ of habeas corpus, p. 402
ex post facto law, p. 403
due process clause, p. 403
selective incorporation, p. 403
establishment clause, p. 404
free exercise clause, p. 406
bad tendency test, p. 409
clear and present danger test, p. 409
preferred position doctrine, p. 409
prior restraint, p. 409

content or viewpoint neutrality, p. 409
unprotected speech, p. 409
libel, p. 409
obscenity, p. 410
fighting words, p. 410
commercial speech, p. 410
civil disobedience, p. 412
property rights, p. 412
eminent domain, p. 413
regulatory taking, p. 413

due process, p. 413
procedural due process, p. 413
substantive due process, p. 414
search warrant, p. 417
exclusionary rule, p. 418
grand jury, p. 420
petit jury, p. 420
indictment, p. 420
plea bargain, p. 420
double jeopardy, p. 421

ADDITIONAL **RESOURCES**

FURTHER READING

JEFFREY ABRAMSON, *We, the Jury: The Jury System and the Ideal of Democracy* (Harvard University Press, 2000).

STUART BIEGEL, *Beyond Our Control? Confronting the Limits of Our Legal System in the Age of Cyberspace* (MIT Press, 2001).

JAMES MACGREGOR BURNS AND **STEWART BURNS,** *A People's Charter: The Pursuit of Rights in America* (Knopf, 1991).

DAVID COLE AND **JAMES X. DEMPSEY,** *Terrorism and the Constitution,* 3d ed. (New Press, 2006).

LEE EPSTEIN and **THOMAS WALKER,** *Constitutional Law for a Changing America: Rights, Liberties, and Justice,* 7th ed. (CQ Press, 2009).

LOUIS FISHER, *The Constitution and 9/11: Recurring Threats to America's Freedoms* (University Press of Kansas, 2008).

LOUIS FISHER, *Religious Liberty in America: Political Safeguards* (University Press of Kansas, 2002).

ROBERT JUSTIN GOLDSTEIN, *Flag Burning and Free Speech: The Case of Texas v. Johnson* (University Press of Kansas, 2002).

ROGER HOOD, *The Death Penalty: A Worldwide Perspective,* 3d ed. (Oxford University Press, 2002).

LEONARD W. LEVY, *Emergence of a Free Press* (Oxford University Press, 1985).

ANTHONY LEWIS, *Gideon's Trumpet* (Random House, 1964).

CATHARINE A. MACKINNON, *Only Words* (Harvard University Press, 1993).

ALEXANDER MEIKLEJOHN, *Political Freedom: The Constitutional Powers of the People* (Harper & Row, 1965).

J. W. PELTASON AND **SUE DAVIS,** *Understanding the Constitution,* 16th ed. (Harcourt, 2004).

SHAWN FRANCIS PETERS, *Judging Jehovah's Witnesses: Religious Persecution and the Dawn of the Rights Revolution* (University Press of Kansas, 2002).

WILLIAM H. REHNQUIST, *All the Laws but One: Civil Liberties in Wartime* (Knopf, 1998).

BARRY SCHECK, PETER NEUFELD, AND **JIM DWYER,** *Actual Innocence: Five Days to Execution, and Other Dispatches from the Wrongly Convicted* (Doubleday, 2000).

NADINE STROSSEN, *Defending Pornography: Free Speech, Sex, and the Fight for Women's Rights* (Scribner, 1995).

MELVIN UROFSKY, ED., *100 Americans Making Constitutional History* (CQ Press, 2005).

MARY E. VOGEL, *Coercion to Compromise: Plea Bargaining, the Courts, and the Making of Political Authority* (Oxford University Press, 2001).

WELSH S. WHITE, *Miranda's Waning Protections: Police Interrogation Practices After Dickerson* (University of Michigan Press, 2001).

WEB SITES

www.law.cornell.edu/anncon/index.html
Congressional Research Service's Annotated U.S. Constitution. For each of the constitutional clauses, it describes the convention and/or ratification debate as well as court decisions dealing with the clause.

www.oyez.org Web site containing MP3 files of oral arguments before the U.S. Supreme Court in both current and historical cases. There also are links to other great Supreme Court resources.

www.deathpenaltyinfo.org The Death Penalty Information Center Web site. Up-to-date information on death penalty statistics in the United States, changing state laws concerning the death penalty, and data on its use internationally.

www.firstamendmentcenter.org The First Amendment Center is affiliated with Vanderbilt University and the Freedom Forum, a nonpartisan foundation supporting the First Amendment. Its Web site contains research and analysis on a multitude of First Amendment questions and cases.

Civil Rights

Equal Rights Under the Law

In 2000, Elizabeth Brose finished eighth grade in Seattle, Washington; the next fall, she would start high school. Under her school district's student assignment plan, Elizabeth, a white student, asked the district to assign her to Ballard High School, a newly remodeled school in her neighborhood with an excellent reputation. But race determined her assignment, and Brose was sent to Franklin High instead, a school eight miles away from her home where non-white students made up approximately 70 percent of the student body. When schools received too many applications, the Seattle School District used an "integration tiebreaker" to make schools more reflective of the district's racial composition as a whole.[1] Ballard would have had a heavily white student population without the tiebreaker, which meant Brose had to be assigned to Franklin.[2]

In 1978, Seattle became the first major U.S. city to use busing to integrate schools without a court order. Its plans had continued since, and although they clearly had popular support, it was not uniform. Some parents, especially those whose children were not placed in their chosen school, were strongly opposed to the program. Karen Brose, Elizabeth's mother, formed Parents Involved in Community Schools, a group opposed to Seattle's plan, and pursued the case in the courts.

Parents Involved in Community Schools was successful in its challenge. On June 28, 2007, the U.S. Supreme Court struck down Seattle's plan, as well as a similar plan used in Louisville, Kentucky. In its sharply divided (5-to-4) opinion, the Court ruled that Seattle had not shown that the goal of racial integration justified the method it used, which relied solely on race (and race broadly construed as white and non-white) as *the* factor in the admissions decision without other individualized assessment. In his opinion in the case, Chief Justice Roberts wrote, "The way to stop discrimination on the basis of race is to stop discriminating on the basis of race."[3]

The Seattle case highlights the United States' continuing dilemma concerning how to best ensure equality, and how to do so without violating the Constitution's protection from discrimination based on race. In this case, Elizabeth Brose's **civil rights** were at issue—her right not to be discriminated against because of race, religion, gender, or ethnic origin. The Constitution protects civil rights in two ways. First, it ensures that government officials do not impermissibly discriminate against us; second, it grants national and state governments the power to protect these civil rights against interference by private individuals.

Although the Constitution does not make any reference to "equality" (the Declaration of Independence proclaims "that all men are created equal," but equality is not mentioned in the Constitution or in the original Bill of Rights), we know that the framers believed all men—at least all white adult men—were equally entitled to life, liberty, and the pursuit of happiness. Although it took many years for the concept of equality to be extended to all people, the framers did create a system of government designed to protect what they called *natural rights*. (Today, we speak of *human rights,* but the idea is basically the same.) As we discussed in Chapter 1, by **natural rights,** the framers meant that every person, by virtue of being a human being, has an equal right to protection against arbitrary treatment and an equal right to the liberties the Bill of Rights guarantees.

These rights do not depend on citizenship; governments do not grant them. They are the rights of *all people.* In this chapter, we examine the protection of our rights from abuse *by government,* and the protection *through government* of our right to be free from abuse by our fellow citizens.

We will begin this chapter by discussing citizenship rights in general. Although natural rights do not depend on citizenship, the kinds of protections that can be denied based on citizenship have become increasingly important in recent years. We then discuss several groups'

efforts to secure their civil rights and examine what we mean by "equal protection of the law." In doing so, we will pay particular attention to two laws essential to securing civil rights protections: the Civil Rights Act of 1964 and the Voting Rights Act of 1965. Finally, we examine the controversy over affirmative action. We will see that the debate over civil rights is not over and that the way we deal with it today will direct the path of civil rights in the future.

Equality and Equal Rights

LEARNING **OBJECTIVE**

16.1 Explain the concept of equality and assess the rights of citizens.

Citizens of the United States are committed to equality. "Equality," however, is an elusive term. The concept of equality on which we have the greatest consensus is that everyone should have *equality of opportunity* regardless of race, ethnic origin, religion, and, in recent years, gender and sexual orientation.

There is not much equal opportunity if one person is born into a well-to-do family, lives in a safe suburb, and receives a good education, while another is born into a poor, broken family, lives in a run-down inner-city neighborhood, and attends inferior schools. Some argue that providing equalizing opportunities for the disadvantaged through federal programs such as Head Start, which helps prepare preschool children from poor families for elementary school, are necessary to bridge this gap.

Traditionally, we have emphasized *individual* achievement, but in recent decades, some politicians and civil rights leaders have focused attention on the concept of *equality between groups*. When large disparities in wealth and advantage exist between groups—as between black and white people or between women and men—equality becomes a highly divisive political issue. Those who are disadvantaged emphasize economic and social factors that exclude them from the mainstream. They champion programs like **affirmative action** that are designed to provide opportunities for those who have been disadvantaged because they belong to a certain group. As we will discuss later in this chapter, such programs have been and continue to be controversial.

Finally, equality can also mean *equality of results*. A perennial debate is whether social justice and genuine equality can exist in a nation in which people of one class have so much and others have so little, and in which the gap between them is growing wider.[4] There is considerable support for guaranteeing a minimum floor below which no one should be allowed to fall, but American adults generally do not support an equality of results.

civil rights
The rights of all people to be free from irrational discrimination such as that based on race, religion, gender, or ethnic origin.

natural rights
The rights of all people to dignity and worth; also called *human rights.*

affirmative action
Remedial action designed to overcome the effects of discrimination against minorities and women.

naturalization
A legal action conferring citizenship on an alien.

Citizenship Rights

Although natural rights do not depend on citizenship, important legal rights come with citizenship. Citizenship determines nationality and defines who is a member of, owes allegiance to, and is a subject of the nation. But in a constitutional democracy, citizenship is an *office,* and like other offices, it carries with it certain powers and responsibilities. How citizenship is acquired and retained is therefore important.

Proud naturalized citizens are sworn in at a Constitution Day naturalization ceremony. Many similar ceremonies are held throughout the year.

How Citizenship Is Acquired and Lost

The basic right of citizenship was not given constitutional protection until 1868, when the Fourteenth Amendment was adopted; before that, each state determined citizenship. The Fourteenth Amendment states, "All persons born or naturalized in the United States, and subject to the jurisdiction thereof, are citizens of the United States and of the State wherein they reside." This means that all persons born in the United States, except children born to foreign ambassadors and ministers, are citizens of this country regardless of the citizenship of their parents.

Naturalization People can also acquire citizenship by **naturalization,** a legal act conferring citizenship on an alien—someone who is living in the United States but is not

TABLE 16–1 | Requirements for Naturalization

An applicant for naturalization must:

1. Be over the age of 18.
2. Be lawfully admitted to the United States for permanent residence and have resided in the United States for at least five years and in the state for at least six months.
3. File a petition of naturalization with a clerk of a court of record (federal or state) verified by two witnesses.
4. Be able to read, write, and speak English.
5. Possess a good moral character.
6. Understand and demonstrate an attachment to the history, principles, and form of government of the United States.
7. Demonstrate that he or she is well-disposed toward the good order and happiness of the country.
8. Demonstrate that he or she does not now believe in, nor within the last ten years has ever believed in, advocated, or belonged to an organization that supports opposition to organized government, overthrow of government by violence, or the doctrines of world communism or any other form of totalitarianism.

For more information about immigration and naturalization, go to the Web site of the Federation for American Immigration Reform at www.fairus.org.

■ *How might the United States determine whether a potential citizen is of a "good moral character"?*

a citizen. Congress determines naturalization requirements (see Table 16–1 for the list of requirements). Today, with minor exceptions, nonenemy aliens over the age of 18 who have been lawfully admitted for permanent residence and who have resided in the United States for at least five years and in the state for at least six months are eligible for naturalization. Any state or federal court in the United States or the Immigration and Naturalization Service (INS) can grant citizenship. The INS, with the help of the FBI, makes the necessary investigations. Any person denied citizenship after a hearing before an immigration officer may appeal to a federal district judge.

Dual Citizenship   Because each nation has complete authority to define nationality for itself, two or more nations may consider a person a citizen. **Dual citizenship** is not unusual, especially for people from nations that do not recognize the right of individuals to renounce their citizenship, called the **right of expatriation.** Children born abroad to U.S. citizens may also be citizens of the nation in which they were born. Children born in the United States of parents from a foreign nation may also be citizens of their parents' country.

Rights of U.S. Citizens

A person becomes a citizen of one of the 50 states merely by residing in that state. *Residence* as understood in the Fourteenth Amendment means the place a person calls home. The legal status of residence is not the same as physical presence. A person may be living in Washington, D.C., but be a citizen of California—that is, consider California home and vote in that state.

Most of our most important rights flow from *state* citizenship. In the *Slaughter-House Cases* (1873), the Supreme Court carefully distinguished between the privileges of U.S. citizens and those of state citizens.[5] It held that the only privileges of national citizenship are those that "owe their existence to the Federal Government, its National Character, its Constitution, or its laws." These privileges have never been completely specified, but they include the right to use the navigable waters of the United States and to protection on the high seas, to assemble peacefully and petition for redress of grievances, to vote if qualified to do so under state laws and have your vote counted properly, and to travel throughout the United States.

In times of war, the rights and liberties of citizenship are tested and have been curbed. The Supreme Court overruled President Abraham Lincoln's use of military courts to try civilians during the Civil War,[6] but it upheld the World War II internment of Japanese Americans in "relocation camps"[7] and has approved the use of military tribunals to try captured foreign saboteurs[8] who were held abroad, but it ruled that citizens may not be subject to courts-martial or denied the guarantees of the Bill of Rights.[9]

In the war against international terrorism, President George W. Bush issued orders declaring U.S. citizens "enemy combatants" for plotting with the Al-Qaeda network and

dual citizenship
Citizenship in more than one nation.

right of expatriation
The right to renounce one's citizenship.

Although the Court upheld the internment of Japanese American citizens during World War II, it was later determined that the government had misrepresented information to the Court about the potential threat they posed. It was not until 1988 that the U.S. government officially apologized for its actions, and Congress awarded reparations to those interned during the war. ■ *Under what, if any, circumstances should the government be able to intern American citizens?*

authorized their and other captured foreign nationals' detention in military compounds, without counsel or access to a court of law. However, even in these cases, prisoners have a right to have their detention reviewed, and the Court's decision in *Boumediene* v. *Bush* (2008) reinforced this right. Even detainees designated as enemy combatants have the right to appeal their detention in the federal courts.[10] The tension over protecting citizens' rights while fighting the war on terror continued in the Obama Administration. Faisal Shahzad, a naturalized U.S. citizen, was arrested for attempting to detonate a car bomb in Times Square in May 2010. Under the Court's ruling in *Boumediene*, Shahzad's case was heard in the federal court system. Shahzad was indicted by a federal grand jury on 10 terror-related charges, several of which carried life sentences in federal prison. Shahzad pleaded guilty to each of the charges in Manhattan's federal district court. On October 5, 2010, U.S. District Court Judge Miriam Goldman Cedarbaum sentenced Shahzad to life in prison without the possibility of parole.

Rights of Resident Aliens

During periods of suspicion and hostility toward aliens, the protections of citizenship are even more precious. Congress enacted the Enemy Alien Act of 1798, which remains in effect, authorizing the president during wartime to detain and expel citizens of a country with which we are at war. U.S. citizens may not be expelled from the country, but aliens may be expelled for even minor infractions.[11] The Supreme Court also upheld the 1996 amendments to the Immigration and Naturalization Act, which require mandatory detention during deportation hearings of aliens accused of certain crimes,[12] though they may not be held longer than six months.[13]

Still, the Constitution protects many rights of *all persons* not only of American citizens. Only citizens may run for elective office, and their right to vote may not be denied, but all other rights are not so literally restricted. Neither Congress nor the states can deny to aliens the rights of freedom of religion or freedom of speech. Nor can any government deprive any person of the due process of the law or equal protection under the laws.[14]

However, Congress and the states may deny or limit welfare and many other kinds of benefits to aliens. Congress has denied most federally assisted benefits to illegal immigrants and has permitted states to deny them many other benefits, making an exception only for emergency medical care, disaster relief, and some nutrition programs. The Court has also upheld laws barring the employment of aliens as police officers, schoolteachers, and probation officers.[15] Although states have considerable discretion over what benefits they give to aliens, the Supreme Court has held that states cannot constitutionally exclude children of illegal immigrants from the public schools or charge their parents tuition.[16]

The Quest for Equal Justice

The rights of citizenship have been prominent throughout our country's history, but not all people in the United States were originally granted full rights of citizenship. Here, we review the political history and social contexts in which constitutional challenges to laws and other government actions relating to civil rights for women and minorities arose. This history involves more than court decisions, laws, and constitutional amendments, however. It encompasses the entire social, economic, and political system. And although the struggles of all groups are interwoven, they are not identical, so we deal briefly and separately with each.

LEARNING **OBJECTIVE**

16.2 Compare and contrast the efforts of various groups to obtain equal protection of the law.

Racial Equality

U.S. citizens had a painful confrontation with the problem of race at the time of the Civil War (1861–1865). As a result of the northern victory, the Thirteenth, Fourteenth, and Fifteenth Amendments became part of the Constitution. The Thirteenth Amendment ended slavery, the Fourteenth ensures that all people are treated equally and establishes citizenship, and the Fifteenth Amendment protects citizens' voting rights. During Reconstruction in the late 1860s and 1870s, Congress passed civil rights laws to implement these amendments and established programs to provide educational and social services for the freed slaves. But the Supreme Court struck down many of these laws, and it was not until the 1960s that legal progress was again made toward ensuring African Americans their civil rights.

Segregation and White Supremacy Before Reconstruction programs could have any significant effect, the white southern political leadership regained power, and by 1877, Reconstruction was ended. Northern political leaders abandoned African Americans to their fate at the hands of their former white masters; presidents no longer concerned themselves with enforcing civil rights laws, and Congress enacted no new ones. The Supreme Court either declared old laws unconstitutional or interpreted them so narrowly that they were ineffective. The Court also gave such a limited construction to the Thirteenth, Fourteenth, and Fifteenth Amendments that they failed to accomplish their intended purpose of protecting the rights of African Americans.[17]

For nearly a century after the Civil War, white supremacy went unchallenged in the South, where most African Americans then lived. They were kept from voting; they were forced to accept menial jobs; they were denied educational opportunities; they were segregated in public and private facilities.[18] Lynchings of African Americans occurred on an average of once every four days, and few white people raised a voice in protest.

During World War I (1914–1918), African Americans began to migrate to northern cities to seek jobs in war factories. The Great Depression of the 1930s and World War II in the 1940s accelerated their relocation. Although discrimination continued, more jobs became available, and African Americans made social gains. As their migration from the rural South shifted the racial composition of cities across much of the United States, the African American vote became important in national elections. These changes created an African American middle class opposed to segregation as a symbol of servitude and a cause of inequality. There was a growing demand to abolish color barriers, and by the mid-twentieth century, urban African Americans were active and gaining political clout.

Slow Government Response By the 1930s, African Americans were challenging the doctrine of segregation in the courts, and after World War II, civil rights litigation began to have a major impact. Beginning with the landmark 1954 ruling in *Brown* v. *Board of Education of Topeka*, the Supreme Court prohibited racially segregated public schools[19] and subsequently struck down most of the devices that state and local authorities had used to keep African Americans from voting.[20] We discuss *Brown* and voting rights in detail later in the chapter. Although the Court reached rulings ending segregation, achieving a significant level of desegregation would require the other branches of government to act.

In the late 1940s and 1950s, Presidents Harry S. Truman and Dwight D. Eisenhower used their executive authority to fight segregation in the armed services and the federal bureaucracy. They directed the Department of Justice to enforce whatever civil rights

A significant sign of integration was Jackie Robinson's debut with the Brooklyn Dodgers in 1947, breaking Major League Baseball's "color line." Robinson was active in the civil rights movement with the National Association for the Advancement of Colored People (NAACP) and its Freedom Fund Campaign. In 2005, he was posthumously awarded a Congressional Gold Medal, the highest honor a civilian can receive. ■ *How might breaking the "color line" in Major League Baseball affect other efforts to integrate society?*

laws were on the books, but Congress still held back. In the late 1950s, an emerging national consensus in favor of governmental action to protect civil rights, plus the political clout of African Americans in the northern states, began to influence Congress. In 1957, northern and western members of Congress from both parties overrode a southern filibuster in the Senate and enacted the first federal civil rights laws since Reconstruction, the Federal Civil Rights Act of 1957, which made it a crime to intimidate or threaten African Americans exercising their right to vote.

A Turning Point   Even after the Supreme Court declared racially segregated public schools unconstitutional, most African Americans still went to segregated schools, and there was widespread resistance to integration in the South. As we discuss in detail later in the chapter, many legal barriers to equal rights had fallen, yet most African Americans still could not buy houses where they wanted, compete fairly for the jobs they needed, send their children to well-equipped schools, eat in "white" restaurants, or walk freely on the streets of "white neighborhoods."

Still, change began to come by way of a massive social, economic, and political movement. It began in Montgomery, Alabama, on December 1, 1955, when Rosa Parks, an African American seamstress, refused to give up her seat to a white man on a bus as the law required her to do. She was removed from the bus, arrested, and fined. The black community responded by boycotting city buses.

The boycott worked and also produced a charismatic national civil rights leader, the Reverend Martin Luther King Jr. Through his doctrine of nonviolent resistance, King gave a new dimension to the struggle. Following a peaceful 1963 demonstration in Birmingham, Alabama, that was countered with fire hoses, police dogs, and mass arrests, more than a quarter of a million people converged on Washington, D.C., to hear King and other civil rights leaders speak. By the time the summer was over, hardly a city, North or South, had not had demonstrations, protests, or sit-ins; some cities erupted in violence.

This direct action had an effect. Many cities enacted civil rights ordinances, more schools were desegregated, and President John F. Kennedy urged Congress to enact a comprehensive civil rights bill. Late in 1963, the nation's grief over the assassination of President Kennedy, who had become identified with civil rights goals, added political fuel to the drive for decisive federal action to protect civil rights.[21] President Lyndon B. Johnson made civil rights legislation his highest priority. On July 2, 1964, after months of debate, he signed into law the Civil Rights Act of 1964, which forbids discrimination on the basis of race, color, religion, sex, or nationality.[22]

Rosa Parks's decision not to give up her seat on the bus in Montgomery, Alabama, sparked a boycott by African Americans who, for more than a year, refused to ride the segregated city buses. Rosa Parks died in 2006. ■ *How did the doctrine of non-violent resistance affect the civil rights movement?*

At the End of the Edmund Pettus Bridge On November 4, 2008, American voters elected Barack Obama president of the United States, the first time an African American candidate has been elected to the office. The historic election was one where the candidates, more so than at any time in the past, represented the diversity of the United States electorate. As President-Elect Obama discussed in his victory speech, this diversity was a direct result of the hard-won successes in our country's long battle over race and gender equality. Indeed, Congressman John Lewis, a long-time civil rights activist who was beaten by Alabama state police as he marched across Selma's Edmund Pettus Bridge in 1965, remarked that "Barack Obama is what comes at the end of that bridge in Selma."[23]

Congressman John Lewis (D-Ga.), then the chair of the Student Nonviolent Coordinating Committee, led civil rights activists in a 1965 march across the Edmund Pettus Bridge in Selma, Alabama. ■ *What effect did the response of the Alabama state police and other law enforcement officials have on the civil rights movement?*

Women's Rights

The 2008 election broke other barriers besides race. The Democrats' other major contender for the presidential nomination was Hillary Clinton, who would have been the first woman nominated by a major party for the presidency. Because of the historic nature of the Obama candidacy, less attention was paid to the fact that Senator Clinton was herself breaking barriers in her string of primary election victories and near majority of elected delegates. In 2008, Alaska governor Sarah Palin ran as the vice presidential candidate on the Republican ticket, the first Republican and only the second time a woman has gained her party's nomination for that office.

The Seneca Falls Women's Rights Convention (1848), which launched the women's movement, attracted men and women who actively campaigned to abolish slavery and to secure the rights of African Americans and women. But as the Civil War approached, women were urged to abandon their own cause and devote their energies to ending slavery.[24] The Civil War brought the women's movement to a halt.

By the turn of the twentieth century, however, a vigorous campaign was under way for **women's suffrage**—the right of women to vote. The first victories came in western states, where Wyoming led the way. But many suffragists were dissatisfied with this state-by-state approach. They wanted a decisive victory—a constitutional amendment that would force all states to allow qualified women to vote. Finally, in 1919, Congress proposed the Nineteenth Amendment. Many southerners opposed the amendment because it gave Congress enforcement power, which might bring federal officials to investigate elections and ensure that it was being obeyed—an interference that could call attention to how blacks were being kept from voting.

women's suffrage
The right of women to vote.

Women won the right to vote with the ratification of the Nineteenth Amendment in 1920, but they were still denied equal pay and equal rights, and national and state laws imposed many legal disabilities on them, such as the lack of comparable pay and health benefits. In the 1970s and 1980s, the unsuccessful struggle to secure the adoption of the Equal Rights Amendment occupied much of the attention of the women's movement. But now there are other goals, and women have mobilized their political clout behind issues that range from equal pay to world peace, an end to sexual harassment, abortion rights, and the election of more women to office.[25]

Since the late 1980s, the Supreme Court has been reluctant to expand the same level of Fourteenth Amendment protection against gender discrimination as it has against racial discrimination. But it did hold that Virginia could not create a separate military academy for women instead of admitting them into the all-male Virginia Military Institute, a 150-year-old state-run institution.[26]

And the courts have increasingly enforced the prohibition against sex discrimination in the 1964 Civil Rights Act and expanded it to forbid sexual harassment in the workplace. In 1986, the Court applied the Act to "quid pro quo" sexual harassment, in which an employer requires sexual favors from a person as a condition of employment (in hiring, promotions, and firing).[27] It has since ruled that the Act also forbids a "hostile environment," defined as a workplace "permeated" with intimidation, ridicule, and insult that is severe and pervasive, and this includes same-sex harassment.[28]

Susan B. Anthony and Elizabeth Cady Stanton were the two most influential leaders of the women's suffrage movement in the nineteenth century. ■ *Why might the women's suffrage movement have had early success in western states?*

Of the People

THE GLOBAL COMMUNITY

Educating Boys and Girls

Education is often seen as a necessary precondition to ensure equal opportunities for all members of society. A Pew Global survey asked respondents, "Which of the following statements comes closest to your opinion about educating children? It is more important for boys than girls, it is more important for girls than boys, or it is equally important for boys and girls."

Throughout the world, there is widespread consensus that it is important to provide educational opportunities for both boys and girls. In Western democracies such as Britain and the United States, this is particularly the case. In each country, 98 percent of respondents indicated that education was equally important for both boys and girls. Japanese respondents also indicated a very high level of support for equal educational opportunities; 95 percent of respondents thought education was equally important for both boys and girls.

Although there is general consensus on providing education to both boys and girls, there is some variation in the degree of that support. In China and India, 89 and 86 percent of respondents, respectively, indicated that education was important to both boys and girls. Even in regions of the world where there have not traditionally been educational opportunities for girls, such as in Nigeria, a full 84 percent of respondents indicated that it was equally important to provide these opportunities for both boys and girls, although there is still a fair number of respondents who indicate that it is more important to educate boys (14 percent).

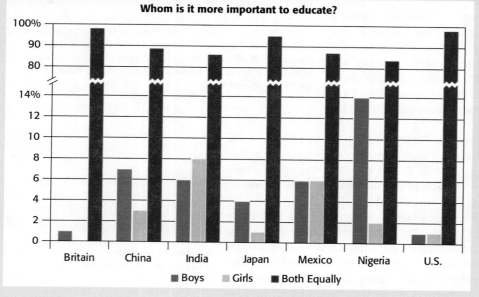

Whom is it more important to educate?

■ Boys ■ Girls ■ Both Equally

CRITICAL THINKING QUESTIONS

1. Why do you think some respondents indicated that it was more important to educate girls than boys?

2. Is it equally important that boys and girls should be educated together? Or, are separate educational facilities for boys and girls just as valuable as integrated facilities?

3. Is political equality possible without equal educational opportunities?

Many women still feel that a "glass ceiling" in large corporations prevents their advancement. But major progress has been made, with more and more women going to graduate and professional schools and into the media and business. Indeed, during the past three decades, more women have graduated from colleges and universities than men (see Figure 16–1).

Hispanics

The struggle for civil rights has not been limited to women and African Americans. Throughout U.S. history, many native-born citizens have considered new waves of immigrants suspect, especially if the newcomers were not white or English-speaking. Formal barriers of law and informal barriers of custom combined to deny equal rights to immigrants. But as groups established themselves—first economically and then politically—most barriers were swept away, and the newcomers or their children enjoyed the same constitutionally guaranteed rights as other citizens.

In many parts of the United States, Hispanics have not been able to translate their numbers into comparable political clout because of political differences among them and because many are not citizens or registered to vote. However, after California adopted Proposition 187 in 1994, which denied medical, educational, and social services to illegal immigrants, and Congress amended the federal welfare laws to curtail benefits to noncitizens, many immigrants rushed to become naturalized. Half of all Hispanic Americans live in

436

Total Degrees Awarded

9,371 12,896 15,539 27,410 37,199 48,622 122,484 186,500 432,058 392,440 792,316 929,417 1,051,344 1,237,875 1,622,000

1870 1880 1890 1900 1910 1920 1930 1940 1950 1960 1970 1980 1990 2000 2010*

■ Male ■ Female

FIGURE 16–1 Percentage of Bachelor's Degrees Awarded, by Gender.
■ *What factors might affect the variation in men's college attendance from the 1920s through the 1950s?*

* Projected Data.

SOURCE: U.S. Department of Education, National Center for Education Statistics, *Earned Degrees Conferred*, 1869–1870 through 1964–1965; *Projections of Education Statistics to 2016;* Higher Education General Information Survey (HEGIS), "Degrees and Other Formal Awards Conferred" surveys, 1965–1966 through 1985–1986; and 1986–1987 through 2005–2006, Integrated Postsecondary Education Data System, "Completions Survey" (IPEDS-C:87–99), and Fall 2000 through Fall 2006.

two states: California and Texas. In 2001, California became the first big state in which white people are in the minority, and Texas followed in 2005; a majority of the population are racial minorities (majority-minority) in Hawaii, New Mexico, and the District of Columbia as well.[29]

The difficulty Hispanics have had in gaining political clout at the state level was highlighted in April 2010 as the Arizona legislature enacted immigration reform that was widely viewed as the broadest and strictest in generations. The law makes it a crime to fail to carry immigration documentation and authorizes law enforcement officials to detain anyone whom they suspect of being in the country illegally.[30] The law was immediately met with criticism, including remarks by President Obama, who called for federal immigration reform.

Asian Americans

The term "Asian American" describes approximately 10 million people from many different countries and ethnic backgrounds. Most do not think of themselves as Asians but as U.S. citizens of Chinese, Japanese, Indian, Vietnamese, Cambodian, Korean, or other specific ancestry. Although Asian Americans are often considered a "model minority" because of their successes in education and business, the U.S. Civil Rights Commission found in 1992 that "Asian Americans do face widespread prejudice, discrimination, and barriers to equal opportunity" and that racially motivated violence against them "occurs with disturbing frequency."[31] Discrimination against Asian Americans is, unfortunately, nothing new. The Naturalization Act of 1906, for example, made it impossible for any Asian American to become a U.S. citizen. Although the Act was challenged, the Supreme Court upheld its provision that only white persons and aliens of African nativity or descent were eligible for citizenship.[32]

Chinese Americans The Chinese were the first Asians to come to the United States. Beginning in 1847, when young male Chinese peasants came to the American West to escape poverty and to work in mines, on railroads, and on farms, the Chinese encountered economic and cultural fears by the white majority, who did not understand their language or their culture. Chinese Americans were recruited by the Central Pacific Railroad to work on

Arizona Governor Jan Brewer signs a controversial bill aimed at identifying, prosecuting, and deporting illegal immigrants.
■ *What factors might contribute to current concerns about illegal immigration?*

the transcontinental railroad, but anti-Chinese sentiment grew. By the 1870s, attacks on "Chinatowns" began in cities throughout the United States. The Chinese Exclusion Act of 1882 restricted Chinese immigration and excluded Chinese immigrants already in the United States from the possibility of citizenship. It was not until 1943 that Congress repealed the Chinese Exclusion Act and opened the door to citizenship for Chinese Americans.

The 1965 amendments to the Immigration and Nationality Act went further to end the nationality criteria and thus equalize immigration criteria across race and ethnicity. Since that time, the Chinese have moved into the mainstream of U.S. society, and they are beginning to run for and win local political offices. Gary Locke, a Democrat and a graduate of Yale and Boston University Law School, became the first Chinese American to become governor of a continental state when, in 1996, he was elected to the first of two terms as governor of Washington.

Japanese Americans   The Japanese migrated first to Hawaii in the 1860s and then to California in the 1880s. By the beginning of the twentieth century, they faced overt hostility. In 1905, white labor leaders organized the Japanese and Korean Exclusion League, and in 1906, the San Francisco Board of Education excluded all Chinese, Japanese, and Korean children from neighborhood schools. Some western states passed laws denying the right to own land to aliens who were ineligible to become citizens—meaning aliens of Asian ancestry.

During World War II, anti-Japanese hysteria provoked the internment of West Coast Japanese—most of whom were loyal U.S. citizens guilty of no crimes—in prison camps in California, Colorado, and other states. Their property was often sold at deep discount rates, and many of them lost their businesses, jobs, and incomes. Although Japanese Americans challenged the curfews and internment policies, the U.S. Supreme Court upheld the government's actions. In *Korematsu* v. *United States* (1944), the Court ruled that under the threat to national security, it could not reject congressional and military judgment that disloyalty existed and must be segregated.[33] Following the war, the exclusionary acts were repealed, though discrimination against Japanese Americans persisted, such as the limits placed on Japanese American student enrollment at many colleges and universities. In 1988, President Ronald Reagan signed a law providing $20,000 restitution to each of the approximately 60,000 surviving World War II internees.

Other Asian Americans   Like other Asian Americans, Koreans faced overt discrimination in jobs and housing, but a Korean middle class has been growing, with many Korean Americans becoming teachers, doctors, and lawyers.[34]

When Filipinos first came to the United States in the early twentieth century, they were considered U.S. nationals because the Philippine Islands were a U.S. possession. Nonetheless, they were denied rights to full citizenship and faced discrimination and even violence, including anti-Filipino riots in the state of Washington in 1928 and later in California, where nearly one-third of the more than 1.5 million Filipinos in the United States live.[35] Their economic status has improved, but their influence in politics remains as small as their numbers.

The newest Asian arrivals consist of more than a million refugees from Vietnam, Laos, and Cambodia, who first came to the United States in the 1970s and settled mostly in California and Louisiana. Although this group included middle-class people who left Vietnam after the communist victory there in 1975, it also consisted of many "boat people," so called because they fled Vietnam in small boats, arriving in the United States without financial resources. In a relatively short time, most of these new Asian Americans established themselves economically. Although they are starting to have political influence, some remain socially and economically segregated.

Congressman Anh "Joseph" Cao (R-La.) escaped to the United States from Vietnam in 1975. He represents Louisiana's 2nd Congressional District. ■ *How might having greater representation of minority groups in Congress affect the kind of policy that is enacted?*

Native Americans

Nearly half of the more than 2 million Native Americans in the United States live on or near a *reservation*—a tract of land given to the tribal nations by treaties with the federal government—and are enrolled as members of one of the 550 federally recognized tribes, including 226 groups in Alaska.[36] Native Americans speak approximately 200 different languages, although most also speak English.

The history of discrimination against Native Americans in the United States is a great stain on our human rights record. Although discrimination against African Americans often gets more attention in civil rights discussions, legally sanctioned discrimination against Native Americans followed a similar path. Efforts to forcibly move Native American tribes off their land and farther west as more whites migrated to the Midwest and western states are well known. The Indian Removal Act, passed in 1830, required that all Native American tribes be moved from the East and Southeast. The Act also authorized the use of force to meet its goals. It is estimated that 4,000 of the 18,000 Cherokee Indians forced to move west into what became eastern Oklahoma in the late 1830s died on the "Trail of Tears."[37]

Native American rights organizations, including the American Indian Movement, protested discrimination against Native Americans in housing, employment, and health care. Over time, other civil rights groups, such as the American Civil Liberties Union (ACLU), have joined the fight to protect Native American civil rights. Currently pending suits allege discrimination against Native Americans in the public schools, as well as in the U.S. Department of Agriculture's farm-loan programs.

As a result of these efforts and of a greater national consciousness, most citizens are now aware that many Native Americans continue to face discrimination and live in poverty. Unemployment on many reservations continues to be 50 to 60 percent. Some reservations lack adequate health care facilities, schools, housing, and jobs. Congress has started to compensate Native Americans for past injustices and to provide more opportunities to develop tribal economic independence, and judges are showing greater vigilance in enforcing Indian treaty rights.

Equal Protection of the Laws: What Does It Mean?

The **equal protection clause** of the Fourteenth Amendment declares that no state (including any subdivision thereof) shall "deny to any person within its jurisdiction the equal protection of the laws." Although no parallel clause explicitly applies to the national government, courts have interpreted the Fifth Amendment's **due process clause,** which states that no person shall "be deprived of life, liberty, or property, without due process of law," to impose the same restraints on the national government as the equal protection clause imposes on the states.

Note that the clause applies only to the actions of *governments,* not to those of private individuals. If a private person performs a discriminatory action, that action does not violate the Constitution. Instead, it may violate federal and state laws passed to protect people from irrational discrimination by private parties.

The equal protection clause does not, however, prevent governments from discriminating in all cases. What the Constitution forbids is *unreasonable* classifications. In general, a classification is unreasonable when there is no relationship between the classes it creates and permissible governmental goals. A law prohibiting redheads from voting, for example, would be unreasonable. In contrast, laws denying persons under the age of 18 the right to vote, to marry without the permission of their parents, or to apply for a driver's license appear to be reasonable (at least to most persons over the age of 18).

Constitutional Classifications and Tests

One of the most troublesome constitutional questions is how to distinguish between constitutional and unconstitutional classifications. The Supreme Court uses three tests for this purpose: the *rational basis* test, the *strict scrutiny* test, and the *heightened scrutiny* test.

The Rational Basis Test   The traditional test to determine whether a law complies with the equal protection requirement—the **rational basis test**—places the burden of proof on the parties attacking the law. They must show that the law has no rational or legitimate governmental goals. Recall from Chapter 15 that when the court reviews the government's reason for legislating, it engages in substantive due process. Traditionally, the rational basis test applied only to legislation affecting economic interests and, with two exceptions in the last 70 years, the Court has upheld the legislation and deferred to legislative judgments.[38] But recently, the Court has applied the test when noneconomic interests are challenged.[39]

Suspect Classifications and Strict Scrutiny   When a law is subject to the **strict scrutiny test,** the burden is on the government to show that there is both a "compelling governmental interest" to justify such a classification and no less restrictive way to accomplish this compelling purpose. The Court applies the strict scrutiny test to suspect classifications. A *suspect classification* is one through which people have been deliberately subjected to severely unequal treatment or that society has used to render people politically powerless.[40] When a law classifies based on race or national origin, the legislation immediately raises a red flag regardless of whether it is intended to aid or inhibit a particular race or nationality. For example, the Supreme Court has held that laws that give preference for public employment based on race are subject to strict scrutiny.

Quasi-Suspect Classifications and Heightened Scrutiny   To sustain a law under the **heightened scrutiny test,** the government must show that its classification serves "important governmental objectives." Heightened scrutiny is a standard first used by the Court in 1971 to declare classifications based on gender unconstitutional. As Justice William J. Brennan Jr. wrote for the Court, "There can be no doubt that our nation has had a long and unfortunate history of sex discrimination. Traditionally, such discrimination was rationalized by an attitude of 'romantic paternalism,' which in practical effect put women, not on a pedestal, but in a cage."[41] In recent years, the Supreme Court has struck down most laws brought before it that were alleged to discriminate against women but has tended to do so on the basis of federal statutes like the 1964 Civil Rights Act (for other legislation, see Table 16–2).

rational basis test
A standard developed by the courts to test the constitutionality of a law; when applied, a law is constitutional as long as it meets a reasonable government interest.

strict scrutiny test
A test applied by the court when a classification is based on race; the government must show that there is a compelling reason for the law and no other less restrictive way to meet the interest.

heightened scrutiny test
This test has been applied when a law classifies based on sex; to be upheld, the law must meet an important government interest.

TABLE

16–2	Major Civil Rights Laws
• Civil Rights Act, 1957	Makes it a federal crime to prevent persons from voting in federal elections.
• Civil Rights Act, 1964	Bars discrimination in employment or in public accommodations on the basis of race, color, religion, sex, or national origin; created the Equal Employment Opportunity Commission.
• Voting Rights Act, 1965	Authorizes the appointment of federal examiners to register voters in areas with a history of discrimination.
• Age Discrimination in Employment Act, 1967	Prohibits job discrimination against workers or job applicants aged 40 through 65 and prohibits mandatory retirement.
• Fair Housing Act, 1968	Prohibits discrimination on the basis of race, color, religion, or national origin in the sale or rental of most housing.
• Title IX, Education Amendment of 1972	Prohibits discrimination on the basis of sex in any education program receiving federal financial assistance.
• Rehabilitation Act, 1973	Requires that recipients of federal grants greater than $2,500 hire and promote qualified handicapped individuals.
• Fair Housing Act Amendments, 1988	Gave the Department of Housing and Urban Development authority to prohibit housing bias against the handicapped and families with children.
• Americans with Disabilities Act, 1990	Prohibits discrimination based on disability and requires that facilities be made accessible to those with disabilities.
• Civil Rights Act, 1991	Requires that employers justify practices that negatively affect the working conditions of women and minorities or show that no alternative practices would have a lesser impact. Also established a commission to examine the "glass ceiling" that keeps women from becoming executives and to recommend how to increase the number of women and minorities in management positions.

■ *Do you think the "glass ceiling" still exists? Why or why not?*

Poverty and Age   Just as race and sex classifications receive elevated scrutiny, some argue that economic and age classification ought to be subject to some heightened review. The Supreme Court rejected the argument "that financial need alone identifies a suspect class for purposes of equal protection analysis."[42] However, some state supreme courts (Texas, Ohio, and Connecticut) have ruled that unequal funding for public schools, as a result of "rich" districts spending more per pupil than "poor" districts, violates their state constitutional provisions for free and equal education.[43]

Age is not a suspect classification. Many laws make distinctions based on age to obtain a driver's license, to marry without parental consent, to attend schools, to buy alcohol or tobacco, and so on. Many governmental institutions have age-specific programs: for senior citizens, for adult students, and for people in mid-career. As Justice Sandra Day O'Connor observed, "States may discriminate on the basis of age without offending the Fourteenth Amendment if the age classification in question is rationally related to a legitimate state interest."[44]

Nevertheless, Congress has attempted to extend the protections against age discrimination to cover state employees, but the Supreme Court ruled that Congress lacks the constitutional authority to open the federal courts to suits by state employees for alleged age discrimination. State employees are limited to recovering monetary damages under state laws in state courts.[45]

Sexual Orientation   In 1996, the U.S. Supreme Court struck down an initiative amending the Colorado Constitution that prohibited state and local governments from protecting homosexuals from discrimination.[46] The Court ruled in *Romer* v. *Evans* that this provision violated the equal protection clause because it lacked any rational basis and simply represented prejudice toward a particular group. Although in cases like *Romer* (1996) and *Lawrence* v. *Texas* (2003), discussed in Chapter 15, the Court found that state laws based on sexual orientation violated the U.S. Constitution, it has not elevated the level of scrutiny with which it reviews such classifications. However, as we discuss in the "You Will Decide" box, several state courts have ruled that their own state constitutions require at least the right to legal recognition of same-sex civil unions. The supreme courts of Massachusetts, California, Connecticut, and Iowa have gone even further to determine that their state constitutions require that marriage be open to same-sex as well as different-sex couples. Although the California Supreme Court's decision was negated by California voters in the 2008 election, a case challenging the CA initiative (Proposition 8) as a violation of the U.S. Constitution's equal protection clause is currently making its way through the federal courts.

Other countries provide more extensive protections from discrimination based on sexual orientation. The United Kingdom's Civil Partnership Act, which went into effect in December 2005, provides same-sex couples with the same Social Security and pension benefits, parental responsibility for partners' children, and next of kin rights in hospitals as married heterosexuals.[47] Mexico also prohibits discrimination based on sexual orientation, and same-sex unions are now recognized in Mexico City.[48] However, in other countries, homosexual behavior is a crime punishable by long prison sentences (in India) or by death (in Nigeria).[49]

Fundamental Rights and Strict Scrutiny   The Court also strictly scrutinizes laws impinging on *fundamental rights*. What makes a right fundamental in the constitutional sense? It is not the importance or the significance of the right but whether it is explicitly or implicitly *guaranteed by the Constitution*. Under this test, the rights to travel and to vote have been held to be fundamental. Rights to education, to housing, or to welfare benefits have not been deemed fundamental. Important as they may be, no constitutional provisions specifically protect them from governmental regulation.

As mentioned previously, the Constitution and particularly the Fourteenth Amendment's equal protection clause is only one of the legal bases for civil rights protections in the United States. Although we often think of court decisions when we think of the civil rights movement, many of the courts' rulings that upheld the civil rights of racial minorities and women were based on congressional legislation. Two pieces of legislation were particularly important to the civil rights movement: the Voting Rights Act of 1965 and the Civil Rights Act of 1964. We turn to these next.

Shelly Bailes and Ellen Pontac, who have been together for 34 years, were the first same-sex couple to marry in Yolo County, California, on June 16, 2008, after the California Supreme Court overturned a state statute banning same-sex marriage. On November 4 of that year, California voters passed Proposition 8, which amended the state constitution to bar same-sex marriage. However, the constitutionality of Proposition 8 is being challenged in the federal courts. A federal district court ruled that the proposition violated the 14th Amendment to the U.S. Constitution. The ruling is under appeal (*Perry v. Schwarzenegger*).

Voting Rights

LEARNING OBJECTIVE

16.4 Trace the evolution of voting rights and analyze the protections provided by the 1965 Voting Rights Act.

Under our Constitution, the states, not the federal government, regulate elections and voting qualifications. However, Article I, Section 4, gives Congress the power to supersede state regulations as to the "Times, Places, and Manner" of elections for representatives and senators. Congress has used this authority, along with its authority under Article II, Section 2, to set the date for selecting electors, to set age qualifications and residency requirements to vote in national elections, to establish a uniform day for all states to hold elections for members of Congress and presidential electors, and to give citizens who live outside the United States the right to vote for members of Congress and presidential electors in the states in which they are legal residents.

In spite of these protections, officials seeking to deny African Americans the right to vote developed biased registration requirements and even turned to intimidation and violence. Reports of violence and intimidation against black voters were frighteningly prevalent. One representative from Alabama described the efforts to deprive blacks of the right to vote this way: "At first, we used to kill them to keep them from voting; when we got sick of doing that, we began to steal their ballots; and when stealing their ballots got to troubling our consciences, we decided to handle the matter legally, fixing it so they couldn't vote."[50]

In many southern areas, **literacy tests** were used to discriminate against African Americans. Although poor white people often avoided registering out of fear of embarrassment from failing a literacy test, the tests were more often used to discriminate against African Americans.[51] White people were often asked simple questions; black people were asked questions that would baffle a Supreme Court justice. "In the 1960s, southern registrars were observed testing black applicants on such matters as the number of bubbles in a soap bar, the news contained in a copy of the Peking Daily, the meaning of obscure passages in state constitutions, and the definition of terms such as habeas corpus."[52] In Louisiana, 49,603 illiterate white voters were able to persuade election officials that they could understand the Constitution, but only two illiterate black voters were able to do so.

Local officials were also able to keep black voters from participating through the use of the **white primary.** In the one-party South of the early twentieth century, the Democratic party would hold whites-only primaries, effectively disenfranchising black voters because, in the absence of viable Republican candidates, the winner of the Democratic primary was guaranteed to win the general election.

literacy test
A literacy requirement some states imposed as a condition of voting, generally used to disqualify black voters in the South; now illegal.

white primary
A Democratic party primary in the old "one-party South" that was limited to white people and essentially constituted an election; ruled unconstitutional in *Smith* v. *Allwright* (1944).

YOU WILL

DECIDE — Should Marriage Be Limited to Heterosexual Couples?

On May 15, 2008, the California Supreme Court ruled that denying same-sex couples the opportunity to marry violated the state's constitutional guarantee of equal protection. The state supreme court's decision was immediately challenged by opponents who placed a constitutional amendment banning same-sex marriage on the 2008 ballot. The measure was narrowly approved by voters. However, that has not ended the legal battle. Citizens challenged the amendment, and the Federal District Court in the Northern District of California has struck down the ballot measure, ruling that it violates the 14th amendment's guarantee of equal protection under the law. That ruling is being appealed.

Proponents of same-sex marriage cite Supreme Court rulings that have upheld marriage as a fundamental right under the U.S. Constitution.* Under these rulings, supporters contend, depriving same-sex couples of the right to marry violates the basic concept of liberty. Others argue that same-sex marriage will provide the same sort of benefits to the community—having stable, caring families and children with two parents—as does heterosexual marriage.

Opponents of same-sex marriage feel equally strongly that such unions should be prohibited by law. They argue that allowing same-sex marriage will lessen the value of marriage and result in fewer heterosexual marriages. Furthermore, they argue that while heterosexual marriage furthers the state's legitimate interest in procreation, same-sex marriage does not and thus need not be sanctioned by the state.

California was only the second state to allow same-sex marriage. In November 2003, the Massachusetts Supreme Court held that the state constitution's guarantees of equality and due process were violated by a ban on same-sex marriage. On October 10, 2008, Connecticut's Supreme Court invalidated the state's civil union law to become the third state to legalize same-sex marriage. Iowa followed suit in April 2009. In the same month, Vermont became the first state to legalize same-sex marriage through the legislative process. New Hampshire did the same in June 2009. In December 2009, the District of Columbia also legalized same-sex marriage. In other states and localities, propositions and constitutional amendments providing for same-sex civil unions or barring any legal recognition of same-sex unions have been strongly debated.

What do you think? Should marriage be limited to heterosexual couples? What are the arguments for or against it?

THINKING IT THROUGH

The rights of homosexuals in the United States have never received the heightened protection against discrimination applied to classifications made on the basis of race or sex. The Court has ruled that government needs only a reasonable basis for legislating in order to permissibly classify individuals based on sexual orientation. Traditionally, legislation meant to uphold basic values and morals would pass such a test, and those opposed to same-sex marriage contend that it endangers the traditional notion of marriage and the value of the family unit. However, the Court, in *Romer* v. *Evans* (1996), struck down a Colorado constitutional amendment that made a distinction based on sexual orientation by ruling that it did not pass the test of rationality or reasonableness.

Opponents of same-sex marriage also object to state supreme courts' rulings on the basis of judicial activism (discussed in Chapter 14). Many opponents of state court decisions argue that same-sex marriage is not an issue for the courts to decide; instead, they contend, it should be decided through the democratic process, as it was in Vermont and New Hampshire.

Echoing arguments heard in the civil rights era, many who favor the right of same-sex couples to marry say that just as laws barring interracial marriage were declared to violate the Constitution's Fourteenth Amendment equal protection clause (in *Loving* v. *Virginia*, 1967), so do laws barring same-sex marriage. Supporters argue that once states provide an opportunity for legal recognition of marriage, they must do so equally. Although civil unions, an option provided for in four states (New Jersey, Washington, Oregon, and Nevada), typically offer many of the benefits afforded to married couples, they do not provide the equal recognition and legal rights of marriage.

Critical Thinking Questions

1. Why are state courts such an important part of the debate on same-sex marriage?
2. Why is the issue of same-sex marriage so hotly debated? What makes this issue such a difficult one?
3. When voters and courts disagree over a topic such as same-sex marriage, who should prevail?

* *Loving* v. *Virginia*, 388 U.S. 1 (1967); and *Zablocki* v. *Redhail*, 434 U.S. 374 (1978).

Protecting Voting Rights

After years of refusing to overturn racially discriminatory voting requirements, the Supreme Court in the 1940s began to strike down one after another of the devices that states and localities had used to keep African Americans from voting. In *Smith* v. *Allwright* (1944), the Court declared the white primary unconstitutional.[53] Later, it struck down other methods. In 1960, the Court held that **racial gerrymandering**—drawing election districts to ensure that African Americans would be a minority in all districts—was contrary to the Fifteenth Amendment.[54] We discuss legislative redistricting in greater detail in Chapter 11. In 1964, the Twenty-Fourth Amendment eliminated the **poll tax**—payment required as a condition for voting—in presidential and congressional elections. In 1966, the Court held that the Fourteenth Amendment forbade the poll tax as a condition in any election.[55]

racial gerrymandering
The drawing of election districts so as to ensure that members of a certain race are a minority in the district; ruled unconstitutional in *Gomillion* v. *Lightfoot* (1960).

poll tax
Tax required to vote; prohibited for national elections by the Twenty-Fourth Amendment (1964) and ruled unconstitutional for all elections in *Harper* v. *Board of Elections* (1966).

443

Protecting Student Voting Rights

Concern over student voting rights dates back to the 1940s and 1950s, when some states such as Kentucky and Georgia granted voting rights to 18-year-olds.* The Twenty-Sixth Amendment, which was ratified in 1971, grants all 18- to 21-year-old citizens the right to vote. There was substantial interest in increasing turnout among young voters in the 2008 presidential elections, and much of this effort was focused on college students. Throughout the United States, college students were urged to register to vote, and many sought to do so from their college campuses.

However, some states have strict residency and identification requirements that make it difficult for students to vote. Leading up to the 2008 election, congressional hearings were held to investigate reports that college students had been told they could not vote in the state in which they were attending college if their parents had claimed them as a dependent in another state.† Other reports included a local election official misleading students that registering to vote in their college town might result in losing their residency-based scholarships.‡

What efforts are made to encourage student voter registration on your college campus? In Ohio, Secretary of State Jennifer Bruner developed a Web site to assist students in the registration process whether they attend college in the place where they are a permanent resident or whether they are Ohio residents who attend college out of state and want to vote there.$ Do you have something similar in your state or through your college? Check your school's Web site and find out what you need to do to vote in the next election and help to protect students' voting rights. If you have more time, you might even become involved in a student voting registration campaign. Rock the Vote has volunteer Street Teams and Student Public Interest Research Groups (PIRGs) organize efforts to encourage student voting throughout the United States. You could get involved in PIRG's New Voters Project** or start up a group of your own.

CRITICAL THINKING QUESTIONS

1. Why might some local political leaders prefer it if college students did not vote in their local elections?

2. Why might you prefer to vote where you go to college instead of in your hometown?

3. Should voting rights be extended to 16-year-olds? Why or why not?

---

* Thomas H. Heale, "The Eighteen-Year-Old Vote: The Twenty-Sixth Amendment and Subsequent Voting Rates of Newly Enfranchised Age Groups" *Congressional Research Service*, May 20, 1983.

† "Members of Congress Worry That Students Are Being Misled About Voting Rights," *Chronicle of Higher Education*, September 24, 2008.

‡ Nikki Schwab, "Confusing Voter Registration Laws Could Affect Presidential Election," *US News and World Report*, September 24, 2008.

$ www.sos.state.oh.us/SOS/CollegeResources.aspx.

** www.studentpirgs.org/new-voters-project/#.

---

majority-minority district
A congressional district created to include a majority of minority voters; ruled constitutional so long as race is not the main factor in redistricting.

North Carolina's challenged "I-85 district" stretched more than 160 miles through the central region of the state. ■ *What changes did North Carolina have to make to comply with the Voting Rights Act?*

The Voting Rights Act of 1965

For two decades after World War II, under the leadership of the Supreme Court, many limitations on voting were declared unconstitutional, but as has often been the case, the Court acting alone was unable to open the voting booth to African Americans. Finally, Congress acted in passing the Voting Rights Act of 1965. It was renewed in 1982, and in 2006, it was extended for another 25 years.

The Voting Rights Act prohibits voting qualifications or standards that result in a denial of the right of any citizen to vote on account of race and color. It also bars any form of threats or intimidation aimed at preventing citizens from voting. Under the Act, the Department of Justice must also review changes in voting practices or laws that may dilute the voting power of these groups,[56] such as changes in candidacy requirements and qualifications or boundary lines of voting districts.[57] The requirement that states obtain Justice Department clearance was recently challenged in the federal courts. But in June 2009, the U.S. Supreme Court upheld the requirement.[58]

In a series of cases beginning with *Shaw* v. *Reno* (1993), the Supreme Court announced that state legislatures could consider race when they drew electoral districts to increase the voting strength of minorities. However, the Court ruled that states could not make race the sole or predominant reason for drawing district lines. A test case examined the North Carolina legislature's creation of a **majority-minority district** that was 160 miles long and in some places only an interstate highway wide. The Supreme Court ruled that it was wrong to force states to create as many majority-minority districts as possible. To comply with the Voting Rights Act, the Court explained, states must provide for districts roughly proportional to the minority voters' respective shares in the voting-age population.[59]

Rights to Equal Access: Accommodations, Jobs, and Homes

LEARNING **OBJECTIVE**

16.5 Describe congressional legislation against discrimination in housing, employment, and accommodations.

In 1883, the Supreme Court had declared unconstitutional an act of Congress that made it a federal offense for any operator of a public conveyance (such as a train or bus), hotel, or theater to deny accommodations to any person because of race or color, on the grounds that the Fourteenth Amendment does not give Congress such authority.[60] Until the Supreme Court finally moved to strike down such laws in the 1950s, southern states had made it illegal for white and black people to ride in the same train cars, attend the same theaters, go to the same schools, be born in the same hospitals, drink from the same water fountains, or be buried in the same cemeteries. **Jim Crow laws,** as they came to be called, blanketed southern life.

The Court reinforced legalized segregation under the Fourteenth Amendment's equal protection clause in *Plessy* v. *Ferguson* (1896). In the *Plessy* decision, the Supreme Court endorsed the view that government-imposed racial segregation in public transportation, and presumably in public education, did not necessarily constitute discrimination if "equal" accommodations were provided for the members of both races.[61] But the "equal" part of the formula was meaningless. African Americans were segregated in unequal facilities and lacked the political power to protest effectively.

Beginning in the 1960s, however, Congress began to act to prevent such segregation. Its constitutional authority to legislate against discrimination by private individuals is no longer an issue because the Court has broadly construed the **commerce clause**—which gives Congress the power to regulate interstate and foreign commerce—to justify action against discriminatory conduct by individuals. Congress has also used its power to tax and spend to prevent not only racial discrimination but also discrimination based on ethnic origin, sex, disability, and age.

Civil Rights Act of 1964 and Places of Public Accommodation The key step in establishing rights of equal access was the Civil Rights Act of 1964. Title II of the Act makes it a federal offense to discriminate against any customer or patron in a place of public accommodation because of race, color, religion, or national origin. It applies to any inn, hotel, motel, or lodging establishment (except those with fewer than five rooms and where the proprietor also lives—in other words, small boardinghouses); to any restaurant or gasoline station that serves interstate travelers or sells food or products that are moved in interstate commerce; and to any movie house, theater, concert hall, sports arena, or other place of entertainment that customarily hosts films, performances, athletic teams, or other sources of entertainment that are moved in interstate commerce. Within a few months after its adoption, the Supreme Court sustained the constitutionality of Title II.[62] As a result, public establishments, including those in the South, opened their doors to all customers.

Civil Rights Act of 1964 and Employment In addition to dealing with equal access in public accommodations, the Civil Rights Act also barred discrimination in employment. Title VII of the 1964 Act made it illegal for any employer or trade union in any industry affecting interstate commerce and employing 15 or more people (and, since 1972, any state or local agency such as a school or university) to discriminate in employment practices against any person because of race, color, national origin, religion, or sex. Employers must create workplaces that avoid abusive environments. Related legislation made it illegal to discriminate against persons with physical handicaps, veterans, or persons over the age of 40.

Jim Crow laws
State laws formerly pervasive throughout the South requiring public facilities and accommodations to be segregated by race; ruled unconstitutional.

commerce clause
The clause of the Constitution (Article I, Section 8, Clause 3) that gives Congress the power to regulate all business activities that cross state lines or affect more than one state or other nations.

Reducing Workplace Discrimination

The United States has one of the most diverse workforces in the world. As diversity has grown, so have calls for protection against workplace discrimination. Many of these calls have been answered by the federal judiciary, where women, older Americans, and the disabled have won a series of victories ensuring their basic rights. But the courts did not act alone. These victories also involved congressional action through the 1964 Civil Rights Act, the 1967 Age Discrimination Act, and the 1990 Americans with Disabilities Act. Together, these three acts have created protections that have made reducing workplace discrimination one of the federal government's greatest achievements.

The 1964 Civil Rights Act was particularly important for guaranteeing equal rights for women. Under the original bill, women were not included in the law. Ironically, it was a conservative Democrat who added the word "sex" to the prohibition against discrimination on the basis of "race, color, religion, or national origin" in the Act. He did so in the belief that Congress would not pass a bill guaranteeing equality of the sexes. However, the bill did pass, and women had the legislation that would provide the opportunity to take employers to court for sex discrimination.

Disabled Americans won similar protection under the 1990 Americans with Disabilities Act. The fight for passage was led by Senator Bob Dole (R-Kans.), who had lost the use of his right arm in World War II. In addition to providing protection from discrimination, this Act also mandates that all public buildings and transportation be handicap accessible.

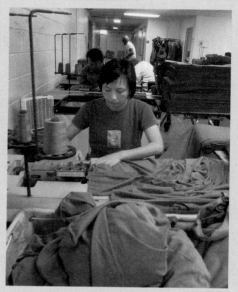

A worker at Delaware's Industries for the Blind sews desert scarves for the U.S. Military.

CRITICAL THINKING QUESTIONS

1. Are there other forms of workplace discrimination that should be protected but currently are not?

2. Might some victims of workplace discrimination be hesitant to bring a suit against their employers?

3. Sexual orientation is not listed in the Civil Rights Act. Should it be illegal to discriminate on the basis of sexual orientation?

There are a few exceptions. Religious institutions such as parochial schools may use religious standards. Employers may take into account the age, sex, or handicap of prospective employees when occupational qualifications are absolutely necessary to the normal operation of a particular business or enterprise—for example, hiring only women to work in women's locker rooms.

The Equal Employment Opportunity Commission (EEOC) was created under the Act to enforce Title VII. The commission works together with state authorities to try to ensure compliance with the Act and may seek judicial enforcement of complaints against private employers. The attorney general prosecutes Title VII violations by public agencies. Not only can aggrieved persons sue for damages for themselves, but they can also sue for other persons similarly situated in a **class action suit.** For example, a pending class action lawsuit against Walmart alleges that the company discriminates against women in promotions and pay. The vigor with which the EEOC and the attorney general have acted has varied throughout the years, depending on the commitment of the president and the willingness of Congress to provide an adequate budget for the EEOC.[63]

The Fair Housing Act and Amendments   Housing is the last frontier of the civil rights crusade, the area in which progress is slowest and genuine change most remote. Even after legal restrictions on segregated housing have been removed, housing patterns continue to be segregated. The degree to which housing also affects segregation in employment and the public schools makes it a particularly important issue. In 1948, the Supreme Court made racial or religious **restrictive covenants** (a provision in a deed to real property that restricts to whom it can be sold) legally unenforceable.[64] The 1968 Fair Housing Act forbids discrimination in housing, with a few exceptions similar to those mentioned in public accommodations. Owners may not refuse to sell or rent to any person because of race, color, religion, national origin, sex, or physical handicap or because a person has children. Discrimination in housing also covers efforts to deny mortgage loans to minorities.

class action suit

A lawsuit brought by an individual or a group of people on behalf of all those similarly situated.

restrictive covenant

A provision in a deed to real property prohibiting its sale to a person of a particular race or religion. Judicial enforcement of such deeds is unconstitutional.

The Department of Justice has filed hundreds of cases, especially against large apartment complexes, yet African Americans and Hispanics still face discrimination in housing. Some real estate agents steer African Americans and Hispanics toward neighborhoods that are not predominantly white and require minority renters to pay larger deposits than white renters. Yet victims complain about less than 1 percent of these actions because discrimination is so subtle that they are often unaware they are being discriminated against. However, more aggressive enforcement has increased the number of discrimination complaints the Department of Housing and Urban Development and local and state agencies receive.

Education Rights

Since the Court's decision in *Plessy*, segregated public as well as private facilities had become the norm. Separate public schools, buses, and bathrooms were commonplace. However, in the late 1930s, African Americans started to file lawsuits challenging *Plessy*'s "separate but equal" doctrine. The National Association for the Advancement of Colored People's (NAACP) Legal Defense Fund (LDF) was active in challenging segregated educational facilities. The LDF cited facts to show that in practice separate was anything but equal and generally resulted in discrimination against African Americans.

Initially, the LDF showed that so-called equal facilities were in fact not equal, or simply not provided. Many of their early successes addressed inequality in higher education. States were forced to either provide separate graduate and law schools for African American students, or integrate those they already had. A major success that laid the groundwork for the LDF's challenge in public secondary and elementary schools came when the Court ruled that, not only did segregated facilities themselves have to be equal, but they also had to provide the same quality of benefits to black students as their white counterparts.[65]

LEARNING **OBJECTIVE**
16.6 Evaluate the historical process of school integration and the current state of affirmative action.

The End of "Separate but Equal": *Brown* v. *Board of Education*

Once the LDF had adequately established that segregated facilities were far from equal, it challenged the *Plessy* doctrine of "separate but equal" head on. And, in *Brown* v. *Board of Education of Topeka* (1954), the Court finally agreed, ruling that "separate but equal" is a contradiction in terms. *Segregation is itself discrimination.*[66]

The question before the Court in *Brown* was whether separate public schools for black and white students violated the Fourteenth Amendment's equal protection clause. Relying heavily on arguments addressing the harm to all schoolchildren, black and white, caused by racial segregation, the Court struck down segregation in the public schools and, in so doing, overturned *Plessy* v. *Ferguson* (1896). A year later, the Court ordered school boards to proceed with "all deliberate speed to desegregate public schools at the earliest practical date."[67]

But many school districts moved slowly or not at all, and in the 1960s, Congress and the president joined even more directly to fight school segregation. Title VI of the Civil Rights Act of 1964, as subsequently amended, stipulated that federal dollars under any grant program or project must be withdrawn from an entire school or institution of higher education (including private schools) that discriminates "on the ground of race, color, or national origin," gender, age, or disability, in "any program or activity receiving federal financial assistance."

From Segregation to Desegregation—But Not Yet Integration

School districts that had operated separate schools for white children and black children now had to develop plans and programs to move from segregation to integration. Schools failing to do so were placed under court supervision to ensure that they were doing what was necessary and proper to overcome the evils of segregation. Simply doing away with laws mandating segregation would not be enough; school districts needed to actively integrate their schools.

Thurgood Marshall (center), George C. E. Hayes (left), and James Nabrit Jr. (right) argued and won *Brown* v. *Board of Education of Topeka* before the Supreme Court in 1954. ■ *Why do you think the NAACP Legal Defense Fund's strategy of using litigation to end segregation in education was successful?*

But because most white people and most African Americans continued to live in separate neighborhoods, merely removing legal barriers to school integration did not by itself integrate the schools. To overcome this residential clustering by race, some federal courts mandated busing across neighborhoods, moving white students to once predominantly black schools and vice versa. Busing students was unpopular and triggered protests in many cities.

The Supreme Court sustained busing only if it was undertaken to remedy the consequences of *officially* sanctioned segregation, **de jure segregation.** The Court refused to permit federal judges to order busing to overcome the effects of **de facto segregation,** segregation that arises as a result of social and economic conditions such as housing patterns.

After a period of vigorous federal court supervision of school desegregation programs, the Supreme Court in the 1990s restricted the role of federal judges.[68] It instructed some of them to restore control of a school system to the state and local authorities and to release districts from any busing obligations once a judge concludes that the authorities "have done everything practicable to overcome the past consequences of segregation."[69]

Political support for busing and for other efforts to integrate the schools also faded.[70] Many school districts eliminated mandatory busing, with the result that *Brown's* era of court-ordered desegregation drew to a close. As a result, the percentage of southern black students attending white-majority schools fell from a high of 44 percent in 1988 to 30 percent in 2001, or approximately the same level it had been in 1969.[71] In the wake of such resegregation, some school districts have attempted to increase integration through race-conscious admission plans such as the Seattle plan discussed at the beginning of the chapter. Another method some schools have pursued, which has the benefit of presumptive constitutionality, is integration based on socioeconomic factors rather than race.[72]

de jure segregation
Segregation imposed by law.

de facto segregation
Segregation resulting from economic or social conditions or personal choice.

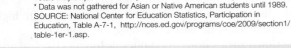

Of the People

AMERICA'S CHANGING FACE

Racial and Ethnic Diversity in U.S. Public Elementary and Secondary Schools

Since the 1970s, U.S. public schools as a whole have become more diverse. Over time, the percentage of white student enrollment in the public schools has dropped more than 20 percentage points, from 78 percent of schoolchildren between kindergarten and twelfth grade to slightly under 56 percent of the student population. The biggest increase for any minority group is certainly among Hispanic students, whose percentage of the student population has increased by more than 14 percentage points. One of many advantages of attending diverse schools is that students learn firsthand about differ-

ent cultures. Furthermore, diverse education opportunities lead to increased interaction between racial groups as adults.*

However, as you can see by looking at the data by region, this diversity is not evenly distributed across all areas of the country. In the West, for example, white students do not even make up the majority of the student population, and the Hispanic student population is twice as large as it is in any other region. Because of these kinds of regional differences, as well as differences among school districts, often based on housing patterns, the increasing level of

diversity across the student population is not necessarily reflected in individual schools or districts.

CRITICAL THINKING QUESTIONS

1. Why does diversity in the public school population vary by region?

2. Why have our public schools as a whole become more diverse over time?

3. Did the diversity in your school district reflect the overall diversity in your region of the country?

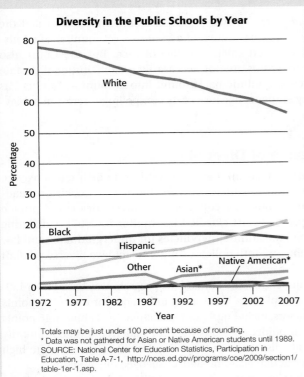

Diversity in the Public Schools by Year

Totals may be just under 100 percent because of rounding.
* Data was not gathered for Asian or Native American students until 1989.
SOURCE: National Center for Education Statistics, Participation in Education, Table A-7-1, http://nces.ed.gov/programs/coe/2009/section1/table-1er-1.asp.

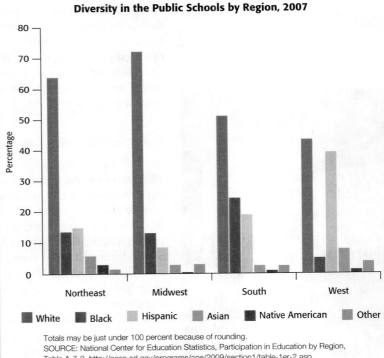

Diversity in the Public Schools by Region, 2007

Totals may be just under 100 percent because of rounding.
SOURCE: National Center for Education Statistics, Participation in Education by Region, Table A-7-2, http://nces.ed.gov/programs/coe/2009/section1/table-1er-2.asp.

* U.S. Commission on Civil Rights, "The Benefits of Racial and Ethnic Diversity in Elementary and Secondary Education, November 2006, http://www.usccr.gov/pubs/112806diversity.pdf.

The Affirmative Action Controversy

When white majorities were using government power to discriminate against African Americans, civil rights advocates cited with approval the famous words of Justice John Marshall Harlan when he dissented from the *Plessy* decision: "Our Constitution is color-blind and neither knows nor tolerates class among citizens."[73] But by the 1960s, a new set of constitutional and national policy debates raged. Many people began to assert that government neutrality is not enough. If governments, universities, and employers simply stopped discriminating but nothing else changed, individuals previously

449

discriminated against would still be kept from equal participation in U.S. life. Furthermore, when barriers to equality in education and employment advancement exist, we all suffer from a lack of diversity in society. Because discrimination had so disadvantaged some people and groups, they suffered disabilities that white males did not share in competing for openings in medical schools, for skilled jobs, or for their share of government grants and contracts.

Supporters call remedies to overcome the consequences of discrimination against African Americans, Hispanics, Native Americans, and women *affirmative action;* opponents call these efforts *reverse discrimination.* The Supreme Court's first major statement on the constitutionality of affirmative action programs came in a celebrated case relating to university admissions. Allan Bakke—a white male, a top student at the University of Minnesota and at Stanford, and a Vietnam War veteran—applied in 1973 and again in 1974 to the medical school of the University of California at Davis. In each of those years, the school admitted 100 new students, 84 in a general admissions program and 16 in a special admissions program created for minorities who had previously been underrepresented. Bakke was rejected in both years, while applicants with lower grade-point averages, test scores, and interview ratings were admitted through the special admissions program. Bakke brought suit in federal court, claiming he had been excluded because of his race, contrary to requirements of the Constitution and Title VI of the Civil Rights Act of 1964.

In *University of California Regents* v. *Bakke* (1978), the Supreme Court ruled the California plan unconstitutional[74] because it created a *quota*—a set number of admissions from which whites were excluded solely because of race. But the Court also declared that affirmative action programs are not necessarily unconstitutional. A state university may properly take race and ethnic background into account as "a plus," as one of several factors in choosing students because of its compelling interest in achieving a diverse student body.

Reaffirming the Importance of Diversity

For many years following the *Bakke* decision, the Court refused to hear challenges to affirmative action in higher education, despite conflicting lower-court decisions leading to confusion and uncertainty about how colleges and universities could pursue diverse student bodies. The Supreme Court clarified the matter in 2003, reaffirming *Bakke* in two cases that challenged the admission policies for undergraduates and law students at the University of Michigan. Both policies sought to achieve diverse student bodies but in different ways.

The University of Michigan's undergraduate admissions program was based on a 150-point "selection index" that ranked applicants' test scores and grades for up to 100 points and allocated 40 points for other factors, including 4 points for children of alumni, 16 points for residents of rural areas, and 20 points for students from underrepresented minority groups or socially and economically disadvantaged families. Jennifer Gratz, a white high school student with a 3.8 GPA who was denied admission, challenged the program.

In *Gratz* v. *Bollinger* (2003), the Court struck down the policy as too mechanical and not narrowly tailored to giving applicants "individualized consideration" as *Bakke* required.[75] However, a bare majority of the Court upheld the University's law school admissions program that was also challenged. In *Grutter* v. *Bollinger* (2003), the Court ruled that the law school made "special efforts" to achieve racial and ethnic diversity, but unlike the undergraduate program, it did not use a point system based in part on race.[76] Writing for the Court, Justice O'Connor held that law school admissions were based on a "highly individualized, holistic review of each applicant's file" and did not use race as a factor in a "mechanical way." For that reason, it was consistent with *Bakke*'s holding that race may be used as a "plus factor" to achieve a diverse student body.

Although the Court further clarified the requirements to render an affirmative action program permissible, its ruling did not end the debate. We have seen that the Court does not always have the final word on such questions. Motivated groups have

Americans debate whether affirmative action is the best way to address the issue of past racial and ethnic quotas. ■ *Why has the Supreme Court upheld the use of race as part of and individualized assessment in university admissions?*

spurred consideration of affirmative action programs at the polls, and several states have abolished affirmative action. Michigan is one example. In the aftermath of the Court's ruling in *Gratz* and *Grutter,* Jennifer Gratz formed the Michigan Civil Rights Initiative to place on the state's 2006 election ballot an initiative banning affirmative action in public colleges and government contracting. The initiative won approval with 58 percent of the vote.[77] In addition to effectively nullifying the Supreme Court's decision as it applied to the University of Michigan, the initiative's success also highlights a motivated group of citizens' success in mobilizing the electorate.

California's Proposition 209 and Other Plans

Michigan is not alone in its efforts to end affirmative action through the democratic process. In 1995, the Regents of the University of California voted to eliminate race or gender as factors in employment, purchasing, contracting, or admissions. The following year, Californians voted overwhelmingly for Proposition 209 to amend the state constitution to forbid state agencies to discriminate against or grant preferential treatment to any individual or group on the basis of race, sex, color, ethnicity, or national origin in public employment, public education, or public contracting, except where necessary to comply with a federal requirement.

Seven other states (Texas, Louisiana, Mississippi, Georgia, Florida, Washington, and Nebraska) have also abandoned affirmative action programs—some like California, Michigan, and Washington because of voter opposition, and others like Texas and Georgia because federal courts held that such programs were unconstitutional.[78] Some have also opted for a strategy of automatic admissions for a certain percentage of all high school graduates to maintain diversity in colleges and expand educational opportunities for minorities. California offers admission to the top 4 percent of high school graduates, Texas to the top 10 percent, and Florida to the top 20 percent.

Jennifer Gratz (right) was the successful plaintiff in *Gratz* v. *Bollinger*; Barbara Grutter (left) was unsuccessful in challenging the University of Michigan law school's admission program, which the Supreme Court upheld due to its individualized approach. ■ *Why did the Court uphold the University of Michigan's law school program but strike down its undergraduate admission program?*

Equal Rights Today

LEARNING **OBJECTIVE**

16.7 Assess the status of civil rights in the United States today.

Today, civil rights legislation, executive orders, and judicial decisions have lowered, if not fully removed, legal barriers to full and equal participation in society. Important as these victories are, according to civil rights leader James Farmer, "They were victories largely for the middle class—those who could travel, entertain in restaurants, and stay in hotels. Those victories did not change life conditions for the mass of blacks who are still poor."[79]

As prosperous middle-class African Americans have moved out of inner cities, the remaining black *underclass,* as they have been called, has become even more isolated from the rest of the nation.[80] There are similar trends in Hispanic communities in Los Angeles, Dallas, and Houston.[81] Children are growing up on streets where drug abuse and crime are everyday events. They live in "separate and deteriorating societies, with separate economies, diverging family structures and basic institutions, and even growing linguistic separation within the core ghettos. The scale of their isolation by race, class, and economic situation is much greater than it was in the 1960s, with impoverishment, joblessness, educational inequality, and housing insufficiency even more severe."[82]

Some contend that we should pay attention to the plight of the underclass, and that instead of focusing on issues of race, we need to focus on class differences and support policies that provide jobs and improve education.[83] Others say there has to be a revival of the civil rights crusade, a restoration of vigorous civil rights enforcement, more job training, and, above all, an attack on residential segregation.[84] In any event, questions about how best to provide equal opportunities for all citizens remain high on the national agenda.

One of the many important lessons of the civil rights movement is that individuals can affect our government process. Without people like Rosa Parks, one woman sitting on a bus who refused to give up her seat, or Karen Brose, who fought for her daughter's right to attend her school of choice without regard to her race, we would not have experienced the monumental changes in our country's protection of all citizens' rights that we have seen during the last 100 years. By participating in our democratic system and challenging the status quo, we each play a part in promoting equal rights for all citizens.

CHAPTER **SUMMARY**

16.1 Explain the concept of equality and assess the rights of citizens.

Although there is no one agreed-upon definition of equality in the United States, there is general consensus that everyone should have an equal opportunity to succeed. The Constitution protects the acquisition and retention of citizenship. It protects the basic liberties of citizens as well as aliens, although in times of war, foreign terrorists may be detained and tried without the rights accorded to citizens and other aliens.

16.2 Compare and contrast the efforts of various groups to obtain equal protection of the law.

Although African Americans' rights were finally recognized under the Thirteenth, Fourteenth, and Fifteenth Amendments, the government failed to act to prevent racial discrimination for nearly a century thereafter. The women's rights movement was born partly out of the struggle to abolish slavery, and the women's movement learned and gained power from the civil rights movements of the 1950s and early 1960s. Concern for equal rights under the law continues today for African

Americans and women as well as other groups, including Hispanics, Asian Americans, and Native Americans.

16.3 Analyze the Supreme Court's three-tiered approach used to evaluate discriminatory laws.

The Supreme Court uses a three-tiered approach to evaluate the constitutionality of laws that may violate the equal protection clause. The Court upholds most laws if they simply help accomplish a legitimate government goal. It sustains laws that classify people based on sex only if they serve important government objectives. It subjects laws that touch fundamental rights or classify people because of race or ethnic origin to strict scrutiny and sustains them only if the government can show that they serve a compelling public purpose.

16.4 Trace the evolution of voting rights and analyze the protections provided by the 1965 Voting Rights Act.

A series of constitutional amendments, Supreme Court decisions, and laws passed by Congress have now secured the right to vote to all citizens age 18 and older. Following the Voting Rights Act of 1965, the Justice Department can oversee practices in locales with a history of discrimination. Recent Supreme Court decisions have refined the lengths to which legislatures can go, or are obliged to go, in creating majority-minority districts.

16.5 Describe congressional legislation against discrimination in housing, employment, and accommodations.

By its authority under the interstate commerce clause (Article 1, Section 8), Congress has passed important legislation barring discrimination in housing and accommodations. The Civil Rights Act of 1964 outlawed discrimination in public accommodations. This Act also provided for equal employment opportunity. The Fair Housing Act of 1968 and its 1988 amendments prohibited discrimination in housing.

16.6 Evaluate the historical process of school integration and the current state of affirmative action.

Brown v. *Board of Education of Topeka* (1954) struck down the "separate but equal" doctrine that had

justified segregated schools, but school districts responded slowly. Full integration has proved elusive, as many white citizens have left the inner cities, and their schools, predominantly black or Hispanic.

The desirability and constitutionality of affirmative action programs that benefit members of groups subjected to past discrimination divide the nation and the Supreme Court. Remedial programs tailored to overcome specific instances of past discrimination are likely to pass the Supreme Court's suspicion of classifications based on race, national origin, and sex. The Court has also reaffirmed the importance of diversity in education and employment.

16.7 Assess the status of civil rights in the United States today.

Legal barriers to full and equal participation in American society have been largely eliminated. However, the fight to protect civil rights of women and minority groups continues. Some argue that in continuing to meet the challenges of inequality, we should focus on economic integration, job training, and better education opportunities.

CHAPTER **SELF-TEST**

16.1 Explain the concept of equality and assess the rights of citizens.

1. Naturalization requires new citizens to do all the following *except:*
   a. be able to read, write, and speak English.
   b. agree never to renounce their new citizenship.
   c. understand and have an attachment to the history and principles of the government of the United States.
   d. demonstrate they do not believe in, advocate, or belong to an organization that advocates violent overthrow of the government.
2. Americans determined to be enemy combatants in the war on terror have _____ .
   a. to be incarcerated indefinitely in a military detention facility.
   b. the right to have their detainment reviewed.
   c. the right to be immediately released and deported.
   d. no explicit rights because they do not fall under U.S. or international law.
3. Differences in the way people understand the term "equality" can have important implications for which policies get enacted to deal with the problem. In two paragraphs, compare and contrast equality of opportunity with equality of results.

16.2 Compare and contrast the efforts of various groups to obtain equal protection of the law.

4. Place the following events in correct chronological order.
   a. Violent riots erupt in many cities.
   b. Lyndon B. Johnson signs the Civil Rights Act.

   c. Barack Obama is elected president of the United States.
   d. Martin Luther King gives his "I Have a Dream" speech.
   e. African Americans migrate to northern and western cities.
   f. *Brown* v. *Board of Education* ends segregated public schools.
5. Different racial and ethnic groups in the United States have had different results in their struggles to achieve economic, political, and social equality and success. In a paragraph, explore possible reasons for these differences.
6. In a paragraph, list the historical events that impeded the progress of women's rights and discuss the gains made by women in the twentieth century, particularly in its last three decades.
7. Native Americans today suffer poor health and extremely high unemployment. Write a paragraph recommending what the Native American community can do to achieve equality.

16.3 Analyze the Supreme Court's three-tiered approach used to evaluate discriminatory laws.

8. In a paragraph, define *rational basis test, strict scrutiny,* and *heightened scrutiny,* and explain the relationships among them.
9. Imagine you are a judge. In a case before you, Isaac Johnson, a construction worker, age 60, has sued his company, United Builders, for discrimination because he was fired. United Builders explains it is company policy to cease employment of those over the age of 60

because they are usually unable to do the heavy work of construction. Write an essay determining whether this is a case of unfair discrimination.

10. The Supreme Court has placed sexual orientation as a classification for the rational basis test. In a paragraph, explain why the Court has ruled this way and evaluate whether the justification is correct, too lenient, or too severe.

16.4 Trace the evolution of voting rights and analyze the protections provided by the 1965 Voting Rights Act.

11. Which of the following is *not* a provision of the Voting Rights Act?
    a. Threats or intimidation in any form to prevent citizens from voting are barred.
    b. Voting criteria that result in a denial of the right to vote based on race or color are barred.
    c. Political parties must make a "reasonable effort" to nominate minority candidates for public office.
    d. The Justice Department must review changes in voting laws that may dilute the voting power of racial groups.

12. In a few sentences, discuss the rationale for creating majority-minority districts and judge whether they have been a wise public policy.

16.5 Describe congressional legislation against discrimination in housing, employment, and accommodations.

13. In one or two sentences, explain how Congress has used the commerce clause to fight discrimination in public accommodations.

14. Which of the following is *not* prohibited by the Fair Housing Act?
    a. A bank denies an African American man a mortgage because he has poor credit and no savings.
    b. A landlord denies a woman an apartment because he is concerned that her two young children will bother the other tenants.
    c. The owner of several apartment complexes charges handicapped tenants an extra $10 rent to help pay for the buildings' wheelchair lifts.
    d. A real estate agent shows a Hispanic family mostly Hispanic neighborhoods because, she assumes, they are most likely to feel comfortable with people of their own race.

16.6 Evaluate the historical process of school integration and the current state of affirmative action.

15. List and summarize the main points made by the Supreme Court in *University of California Regents* v. *Bakke, Gratz* v. *Bollinger,* and *Grutter* v. *Bollinger.*

16. In one paragraph, review the most recent court decisions and state laws on affirmative action and predict what will happen to the policy in the future.

16.7 Assess the status of civil rights in the United States today.

17. Consider civil rights leader James Farmer's statement that victories of the civil rights movement were "victories largely for the middle class...." In one paragraph, critique Farmer's statement. Do you agree with his assessment? Why or why not?

Answers for selected questions: 1. b; 2. b; 4. e, f, d, a, b, c; 11. c; 14. a

---

mypoliscilab EXERCISES

Apply what you learned in this chapter on MyPoliSciLab.

Read on **mypoliscilab.com**

eText: Chapter 16

Study and **Review** on **mypoliscilab.com**

Pre-Test
Post-Test
Chapter Exam
Flashcards

Watch on **mypoliscilab.com**

Video: Should Don't Ask Don't Tell Go Away?
Video: Supreme Court: No Race-Based Admissions

Explore on **mypoliscilab.com**

Simulation: You Are the Mayor and Need to Make Civil Rights Decisions
Comparative: Comparing Civil Rights
Timeline: The Civil Rights Movement
Timeline: The Mexican-American Civil Rights Movement
Timeline: The Struggle for Equal Protection
Timeline: Women's Struggle for Equality
Visual Literacy: Race and the Death Penalty

KEY **TERMS**

civil rights, p. 430
natural rights, p. 430
affirmative action, p. 430
naturalization, p. 430
dual citizenship, p. 431
right of expatriation, p. 431
women's suffrage, p. 435
equal protection clause, p. 439

due process clause, p. 439
rational basis test, p. 440
strict scrutiny test, p. 440
heightened scrutiny test, p. 440
literacy test, p. 442
white primary, p. 442
racial gerrymandering, p. 443
poll tax, p. 443

majority-minority district, p. 444
Jim Crow laws, p. 445
commerce clause, p. 445
class action suit, p. 446
restrictive covenant, p. 446
de jure segregation, p. 448
de facto segregation, p. 448

ADDITIONAL **RESOURCES**

FURTHER READING

RAYMOND ARSENAULT, *Freedom Riders: 1961 and the Struggle for Racial Justice* (Oxford University Press, 2006).

TAYLOR BRANCH, *At Canaan's Edge: America in the King Years, 1965–1968* (Simon & Schuster, 2006).

TAYLOR BRANCH, *Parting the Waters: America in the King Years, 1954–1963* (Simon & Schuster, 1988).

TAYLOR BRANCH, *Pillar of Fire: America in the King Years, 1963–1965* (Simon & Schuster, 1998).

GORDON H. CHANG, ED., *Asian Americans and Politics* (Stanford University Press, 2001).

CHARLES CLOTFELTER, *After Brown: The Rise and Retreat of School Desegregation* (Princeton University Press, 2004).

CLARE CUSHMAN, ED., *Supreme Court Decisions and Women's Rights* (CQ Press, 2000).

ARLENE M. DAVILA, *Latinos, Inc.: The Marketing and Making of a People* (University of California Press, 2001).

WILLIAM N. ESKRIDGE JR., *Gaylaw: Challenging the Apartheid of the Closet* (Harvard University Press, 2000).

RICHARD KAHLENBERG, *All Together Now: Creating Middle-Class Schools Through Public School Choice* (Brookings Institution Press, 2003).

RANDALL KENNEDY, *Race, Crime, and the Law* (Pantheon, 1997).

MICHAEL J. KLARMAN, *From Jim Crow to Civil Rights: The Supreme Court and the Struggle for Racial Equality* (Oxford University Press, 2006).

PHILIP A. KLINKER AND **ROGER M. SMITH,** *The Unsteady March: The Rise and Decline of Racial Equality in America* (University of Chicago Press, 2000).

PETER KWONG AND **DUSANKA MISCEVIC,** *Chinese America: The Untold Story of America's Oldest New Community* (New Press, 2006).

NANCY MCGLEN, KAREN O'CONNOR, LAURA VAN ASSELDFT, AND **WENDY GUNTHER-CANADA,** *Women, Politics, and American Society,* 3d ed. (Pearson/Longman, 2005).

GARY ORFIELD AND **CHUNGMEI LEE,** *Brown at 50: King's Dream or Plessy's Nightmare* (Civil Rights Project, Harvard University, 2004).

J. W. PELTASON, *Fifty-Eight Lonely Men: Southern Federal Judges and School Desegregation* (University of Illinois Press, 1971).

DAN PINELLO, *America's Struggle for Same-Sex Marriage* (Cambridge University Press, 2006).

RUTH ROSEN, *The World Split Open: How the Modern Women's Movement Changed America* (Viking Press, 2000).

JOHN DAVID SKRENTNY, ED., *Color Lines: Affirmative Action, Immigration, and Civil Rights Options for America* (University of Chicago Press, 2001).

GIRARDEAU A. SPANN, *The Law of Affirmative Action: Twenty-Five Years of Supreme Court Decisions on Race and Remedies* (New York University Press, 1999).

SUSAN F. VAN BURKLEO, *"Belonging to the World": Women's Rights and Constitutional Culture* (Oxford University Press, 2001).

WEB SITES

www.brennancenter.org/studentvoting This Web site for the Brennan Center for Justice, Student Voting Rights, contains state-by-state information on registration and voting requirements for students.

www.justice.gov/crt/ The Web site for the U.S. Department of Justice, Civil Rights Division; provides information on a variety of civil rights issues such as fair housing, hate crimes, and protecting voting rights.

www.uscis.gov The U.S. Citizenship and Immigration Services Web site provides an opportunity to test yourself on questions that could appear on a citizenship test. Click on the link to the "Naturalization Test" and see how well you do.

The Politics of National Policy

THE BIG PICTURE

The Constitution was created as an overall framework for making public policies about who gets what, when, where, and how from the federal government. A public policy is a specific course of action that government takes to manage the economy, social needs, or foreign issues. Defined this way, public policy is an important outcome of politics. Government makes public policy through laws, presidential orders, judicial opinions, and rules.

The Constitution assumes that government will intervene in these areas to protect the nation from domestic and foreign threats such as economic crises, internal unrest, and foreign attacks. In theory, federal policies are designed to assume that every American enjoys the promise of life, liberty, and the pursuit of happiness, which implies that the federal government will make and implement policies to assure opportunity for every citizen. However, there are strong disagreements about when and how the federal government should intervene. The Constitution clearly tells Congress, the president, and the judiciary to defend the nation from harm but does not tell these institutions what to do. Much of the contemporary conflict over issues such as health care and unemployment involve deep disagreements about what life, liberty, and the pursuit of happiness mean. Should government leave these pursuits to the individual citizen or try to set the rules that create equal opportunity for every American? As we will see in this section, the Constitution leaves the answer to the political process and the institutions of government.

Citizens play a prominent role in the great debates about what the government should do in response to perceived threats. They make their opinions known through elections, direct contact with their representatives, legal action, and more aggressive engagement in direct decisions by the federal bureaucracy. The nation's political leaders also pay great attention to what the public thinks through opinion surveys and the media.

COURSE LEARNING **OBJECTIVES**

CHAPTER **17** Public Policy

Identify the steps in the policy-making process.

The policy process is designed to act in response to economic, social, and foreign threats. The policy process produces different kinds of policies, including distributive, redistributive, and reverse distributive policies, which give and/or take benefits and resources from certain segments of society.

The process for making these choices is complex. It involves eight steps: (1) making assumptions about the problem, (2) setting the agenda, (3) deciding to act, which can involve decisions not to act at all, (4) deciding how much to do, (5) choosing a solution to the problem, (6) deciding who will deliver the goods or services, (7) making rules for implementation, and (8) running the program itself. The steps do not always occur in order. Some political scientists see problems, solutions, political actors, and so forth as "streams" that flow through the institutions of government and only occasionally come together.

Once government decides to act, it has a variety of choices about how to distribute or take away benefits. It can spend money collected through taxes or financed through borrowing. It can create taxes to reward or punish certain behaviors such as home ownership or smoking. It can also provide direct goods and services by building highways or hospitals, protecting its citizens from risks such as unemployment, and establishing rules for public conduct. These choices are often subject to intense debate among citizens and their representatives over the proper role of government in society.

CHAPTER **18** Making Economic Policy

Describe the federal government's tools for making economic policy.

The federal government has a significant role both in protecting the nation from economic crisis and promoting growth and stability. It can intervene in the economy through monetary policy, which affect the cost of borrowing. Increases in the cost of money tend to cool off the economy during times of high inflation in prices, whereas decreases tend to stimulate the economy during times of high unemployment. Monetary policy is made by the Federal Reserve Bank, which is insulated from politics.

The federal government intervenes in the economy through fiscal policy, which involves spending and taxing. Tax increases and budget cuts tend to cool off the economy, whereas tax cuts and budget increases tend to stimulate the economy. Fiscal policy is made by Congress and the president and involves intense political infighting as citizens, interest groups, and private businesses seek protection and benefits from the legislative process.

In addition to monetary and fiscal policy, the federal government plays a significant role in promoting and regulating business through rules.

CHAPTER **19** Making Social Policy

Trace the evolution of social policy, and describe the government's recent challenges in protecting Americans from hardship.

Along with state and local governments, the federal government is responsible for protecting Americans from hardship. This role involves great political conflict between citizens who believe that most Americans face hardship because they do not work hard enough and those who believe that Americans are often victims of forces beyond their control.

The greatest breakthroughs in protecting citizens from hardship came during Franklin Roosevelt's New Deal and Lyndon Johnson's Great Society. The economic collapse that began with the stock market crash in 1929 produced New Deal programs to insure Americans from economic hardship, including Social Security, unemployment and disability insurance, the first school lunch program, and other short-term public jobs programs. In turn, the Great Society produced health insurance for older Americans (Medicare), nutrition assistance, supplemental income for poor older Americans, and urban development programs. Most of these programs have expanded throughout the years and now cost more in total than the defense budget. Most are also entitlement programs that are available to citizens who meet a "means-test" of their need.

CHAPTER **20** Making Foreign and Defense Policy

Describe the tools of foreign policy making, and evaluate the status of America's current foreign policy interests.

Foreign policy is primarily concerned with protecting the United States from foreign threats. However, the term "threat" is broadly defined to include much more than potential attacks on the nation. It also includes concerns about environmental damage, humanitarian aid, peace in the Middle East, and the spread of nuclear weapons. Although the United States has been engaged in two wars during the past two decades, it has also been using a blend of "hard" (military) and "soft" (diplomatic) power to achieve its goals. These two forms of power involve a number of federal government agencies, including the State and Defense Departments, intelligence agencies such as the Central Intelligence Agency, and the president's National Security Council. The military plays a particularly powerful role in reinforcing U.S. foreign policy through its 1.5 million members of the Air Force, Army, Navy, and Marine Corps. Soft power is enhanced by a strong defense, just as hard power is held in reserve by soft power.

AMERICORPS

GETTING THINGS DONE

AMERICORPS

NATIONAL SERVICE

Public Policy

CHAPTER **OUTLINE**
CHAPTER LEARNING **OBJECTIVES**

Defining Public Policy

17.1 Relate politics and public policy, and differentiate three types of public policy.

The Eight Steps in Making Public Policy

17.2 Outline eight steps in making public policy, and assess types of policy solutions.

Citizens and Public Policy

17.3 Assess ways in which citizens can influence the public policy process.

Americans help shape and carry out public policy in many ways, but one of the most meaningful ways they can help influence and implement public policy is by volunteering. In 2008, more than 62 million Americans volunteered in their communities. They served soup to the hungry, tutored children, worked for advocacy organizations such as the American Civil Liberties Union (ACLU) and Americans for Tax Justice, and organized campus meetings on big issues such as health care reform.

The Serve America Act, which was enacted in 2009, has encouraged more volunteerism at just the right time in the economic downfall. Cosponsored by the late Democratic Senator Ted Kenney (D-Mass.) and Republican Senator Orrin Hatch (R-Utah), the bill won nearly unanimous support in both chambers. Under the Act, which was signed by President Barack Obama on April 21, 2009, Americans were given a variety of new ways to volunteer. For example, the Act designated September 11th as a day of service to commemorate the heroism of those who gave their lives in response to the terrorist acts on New York City and the Pentagon in Washington, D.C. Students on every campus will be asked to participate in this annual event, from cleaning up parks to repainting schools.

The Serve America Act also expanded AmeriCorps, the national program created in 1993 to provide volunteer opportunities for students both before and immediately after college. The number of AmeriCorps volunteers will rise from 75,000 per year in 2009 to 250,000 by 2015. The pay is very low—only $14,000 or so per year depending on local costs—but the rewards are enormous. Participants report that their two years as volunteers were the most important of their lives.

In addition, the Act selected some 25 colleges and universities as "campuses of service," providing them with special federal funding in recognition of their commitment to help students find meaningful opportunities to volunteer. Finally, the Act created an entirely new volunteer program for older Americans. Called the Encore Fellowship, the new initiative provides a small college tuition grant that can be transferred to children and grandchildren.

In signing the law, Obama emphasized the importance of volunteering to the quality of life in the United States: "I've met countless people of all ages and walks of life who want nothing more than to do their part. I've seen a rising generation of young people work and volunteer and turn out in record numbers. They're a generation that came of age amidst the horrors of 9/11 and Katrina; the wars in Iraq and Afghanistan; an economic crisis without precedent. And yet despite all this, or more likely because of it, they have become a generation of activists possessed with that most American of ideas—that people who love their country can change it."[1]

Volunteering is a form of civic engagement. The more that citizens give, the more they get. And their work is essential to public policy. The federal government often provides grants to charitable organizations such as Habitat for Humanity, Youth Build, and Teach for America to further its goals.

This chapter will explore the various ways in which citizens and government both work to create and implement public policy. We will start with some simple definitions of public policy. We will then examine the process for making public policy. Laws do not implement themselves. They must be converted into action. The public policy process is the method for making laws a reality in American life.

President Barack Obama signs the Serve America Act at a Washington, D.C. public school. He was joined by nonprofit leaders and members of Congress including the late Senator Kennedy, one of the bill's co-authors. ■ *Why do presidents hold public signing ceremonies for legislation?*

Defining Public Policy

LEARNING OBJECTIVE

17.1 Relate politics and public policy, and differentiate three types of public policy.

public policy
A specific course of action that government takes to address a problem.

politics
The interaction of the people and their government, including citizens, interest groups, political parties, and the institutions of government at all levels. Politics is concerned with who gets what, when, where, and how from government.

policy makers
Individuals and groups that make the actual choices to create a public policy.

distributive policy
A public policy such as Social Security that provides benefits to all groups in society.

When government decides to solve a problem, it does so through a **public policy,** a specific course of action that government takes to address a challenge such as global warming, health care, or unemployment. Government can convey a public policy to the nation in laws passed by Congress and signed by the president, in opinions issued by the Supreme Court, and/or in rules written by administrators.

But whatever its form, a public policy tells the nation and the world who is about to get what, when, and how from the federal government. As Table 17–1 shows, we can define **politics** as the interaction of the people and their government, whereas *policy* is the product of that give and take. If politics is a question of who gets what, when, where, and how from government, then policy is a formal statement of who has the greater power and what compromises have been reached. We define **policy makers** as the individuals and groups that make the actual choices to create a public policy—some policy makers are elected officials or government employees, whereas others are lobbyists and interest groups. Citizens are rarely considered to be policy makers.

Types of Public Policy

Public policies do not all have the same impact on society. Some benefit all groups of citizens, others benefit one group of citizens by taking something away from another, and still others take benefits from all groups in an effort to create a better society for everyone. These choices create three specific types of public policy.[2]

Federal policies that offer new benefits to all citizens are called **distributive policy.** National parks, air traffic control, the interstate highway system, education funding,

TABLE

17–1	Politics and Policy

The People →	Politics →	Policies →	Outcomes
Older Americans	Voting, joining AARP	Creating prescription drug coverage	Lower prescription drug costs
College students	Writing e-mails	Reducing college loan costs	Lower debt
Businesses	Contributing money to campaigns	Lower taxes	Higher profits
Environmental groups	Filing lawsuits	Enforcing smokestack rules	Cleaner air
Community	Setting up Facebook sites	Increasing police patrols	Safer neighborhoods

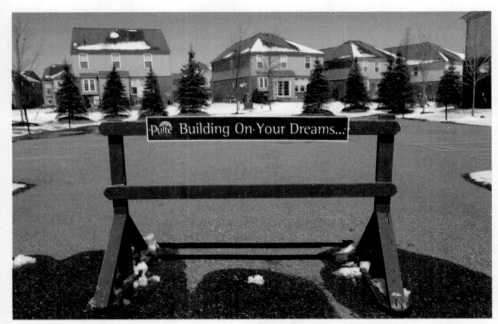

Citizens receive significant government support when they purchase their homes. They are allowed to reduce their taxes by subtracting the interest payments on their loans from their annual taxes and receive indirect federal funds for buying energy-efficient appliances. ■ *How does home ownership relate to the American dream, discussed in Chapter 4? Why does the federal government promote home ownership?*

national defense, and Social Security are all distributive. They help all groups at some level, whether rich or poor. Although some may get more benefit than others from a particular program such as Social Security, which reduces poverty among low-income beneficiaries, every group receives at least something through distributive policy.

In contrast, federal policies that take resources away from one or more groups in society (usually through taxes) so that another group can benefit (usually through an entitlement program) are **redistributive policy.** Such programs benefit the less fortunate. Welfare, poverty programs, Head Start for poor preschool children, and special programs to help minority groups are redistributive. Some political scientists call them **zero-sum games,** meaning one group's gain (the program's benefits) is another's loss (the program's cost in taxes).

Finally, federal policies that take resources from every group to solve a common problem by reducing benefits such as Social Security or raising taxes on all income levels are a form of **reverse distributive policy.**[3] When Social Security benefits are increased through annual cost-of-living-adjustments, it is a form of distributive policy, but when benefits are cut and taxes increased to provide more money for benefits, it becomes a reverse distributive policy by taking away something from all citizens.

We often use such *cost/benefit analysis* to compare and contrast policy proposals. For example, electric cars reduce the nation's need for oil (benefit) but increase the demand for the electricity produced by coal-fired plants (cost). Similarly, new restrictions on automobile pollution enacted in 2009 create important benefits for clean air and global warming but also add to the cost of every new automobile, and that may therefore reduce new purchases and weaken the economy. In turn, a weaker economy may raise unemployment, which has a cost to every taxpayer in increased federal government spending.

redistributive policy
A policy that provides to one group of society while taking away benefits from another through policy solutions such as tax increases to pay for job training.

zero-sum games
A policy that takes away exactly as much in benefits as another group gains.

reverse distributive policy
A policy that reduces benefits for all groups such as a tax increase in society, often by imposing rules that govern everyone.

The Eight Steps in Making Public Policy

Every public policy reflects a series of separate decisions leading to its creation. The process can be viewed as a staircase that moves upward toward final implementation. But like any very long staircase, there are times when policy makers simply run out of energy to keep going. The process can even go back down the staircase as new ideas are introduced and Congress and the president go back down to revisit their earlier decisions.

LEARNING **OBJECTIVE**

17.2 Outline eight steps in making public policy, and assess types of policy solutions.

Of the People

THE GLOBAL COMMUNITY

Opinions on Why People Succeed or Fail

Views about the individual's ability to determine life's success have an important role in shaping public policies designed to help the poor. The Pew Center's Global opinion survey asked respondents how much they agreed with the statement: "Success in life is pretty much determined by forces outside our control." According to the survey, there is enormous variation throughout the world regarding these basic beliefs.

In Japan, few citizens agree with the statement, reflecting their belief that individuals have a significant role in their own success. These views constrain the nation's willingness to support a variety of programs such as job training, unemployment assistance, and government support for the poor. On the other hand, citizens who believe that success in life is determined by forces outside an individual's control tend to support government programs that help the poor.

Despite our relatively strong economic position as one of the world's most powerful nations, many Americans are convinced that poor people suffer from the lack of access to equal opportunity and economic success.

In countries such as Nigeria, the economy is so poorly performing that even the most successful citizens wonder whether they can get ahead. In Bangladesh, for example, 80 percent of the public completely agrees that success in life is determined by forces outside

an individual's control, whereas only 34 percent of Canada's citizens believe the same.

CRITICAL THINKING QUESTIONS

1. What factors might contribute to beliefs that individual success is beyond a person's control?

2. How might the public's view about an individual's role in determining his or her own success affect public policy?

3. Why do respondents in the United States have such a different perspective than people in other countries on this question?

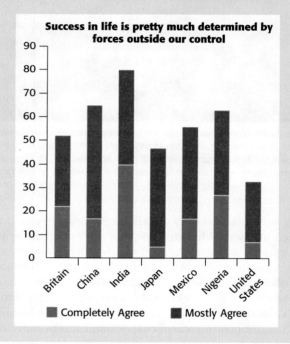

Success in life is pretty much determined by forces outside our control

Legend: Completely Agree, Mostly Agree

Countries: Britain, China, India, Japan, Mexico, Nigeria, United States

When the Obama administration entered office in 2009, for example, it reversed directions on many of the Bush administration's policies on issues such as global warming. Whereas the Bush administration had long argued that global warming was not a national threat, the Obama administration moved quickly to push for stricter limits on carbon emissions by automobiles and power plants.

The public policy staircase has eight steps: (1) making assumptions about the problem at the beginning, (2) setting the agenda of problems to be addressed, (3) deciding to act, (4) deciding how much to do, (5) choosing a solution to the problem, (6) deciding who will deliver the goods or services, (7) making rules for implementation, and (8) final implementation as an ongoing policy. Figure 17–1 presents the staircase.

We will discuss each step next, but note that by its very nature, the choice to move forward (in step 3) is the most difficult, largely because of the complexity of passing a bill, issuing an executive order, or making a Supreme Court decision. It is often far easier to make what political scientists call a **nondecision,** which means the policy process stops before final action. A nondecision can take place at any step on the staircase.

It is useful to note that the policy process does not vary greatly throughout the world. Virtually all policies are the product of making assumptions, setting the agenda, deciding to act, and so forth. However, other nations give their citizens different levels of influence in making policy decisions. In Great Britain, policy decisions are shaped by a tight bond

nondecision
A decision not to move ahead with the policy process. In short, it is a decision not to decide.

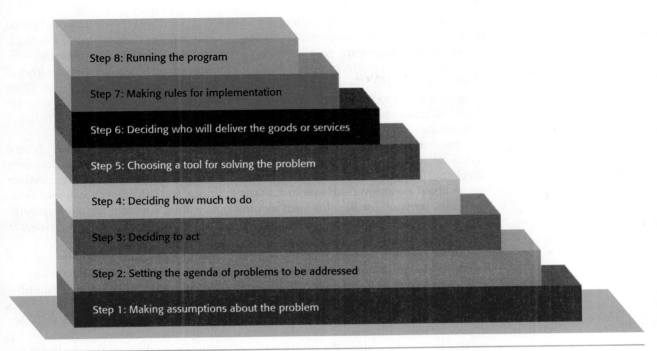

FIGURE 17–1 The Eight Steps in Making Public Policy.
■ *Why is step three the most difficult step?*

between the administrative agencies of government and Parliament. Indeed, it is said that the agenda is never set until a decision has already been made. "It's carrying democracy too far if you don't know the result of the vote before the meeting."[4] With 90 percent of the votes in Parliament decided along party lines, there is rarely any doubt about the outcome of debate. In Japan, all legislation originates in the administrative agencies. Ideas are submitted to the Japanese executive cabinet and usually sent forward to the Japanese legislature for formal action.

Making Assumptions About the Problem

Every government decision starts with assumptions about the future. Is the economy going to get stronger? If so, perhaps employment will go up and the costs of supporting the unemployed will go down. Is terrorism going to increase? If so, perhaps the federal government needs to inspect more cargo ships in search of bombs and other threats. Answers to questions about the future shape decisions about what the federal government might do.

Making even short-term assumptions about how the world will change is difficult, however. As one senior Reagan administration official once remarked, "I'm beginning to believe that history is a lot shakier than I thought it was. In other words, I think there are random elements, less determinism, and more discretion in the course of history that I ever believed before."[5] For example, the economy can change very quickly, which can increase joblessness overnight, which can put more pressure on the social safety net, which can demand higher taxes, and so on. Many experts were completely surprised in 2007–2008 when the mortgage market collapsed in the wake of billions of dollars of bad loans. They simply had not predicted it could happen.

Setting the Agenda

Choosing the problem to be solved is the essential decision in setting the **policy agenda.** The policy agenda, as political scientist John Kingdon defines it, "is the list of subjects or problems to which governmental officials, and people outside of government closely associated with those officials, are paying some serious attention at any given time."[6]

policy agenda
The list of issues that the federal government pays attention to.

Thus defined, the agenda is a direct product of politics and reflects broad social goals embraced by the people and their government, such as liberty, equality, individualism, and respect for the common person. These values are core to the ideology that shapes the policy agenda, but they often conflict with each other as ideas move toward public policies. Everyone wants the American dream, for example, but we often disagree on how to get it. Politics affects the rise and fall of these ideologies through elections, party identification, interest group pressure, and a variety of other political expressions.

Problems are distinct from politics and reach the list of possible agenda items from a variety of sources. Some arise from events such as the September 11, 2001, terrorist attacks or Hurricane Katrina. Others become prominent through newspaper or television stories about a controversial issue such as gay marriage, and still others because of interest group pressure for benefits such as prescription drug coverage for older citizens. Some emerge from congressional investigations of issues such as cigarette smoking, car safety, or government fraud.

Other possible problems are the subject of ongoing government monitoring. For example, the government regularly reports data on the state of the economy as measured by unemployment, inflation, or new housing starts. These markers can show the beginnings of an economic slowdown or of an improving economy. Readers need only visit www.fedstats.gov to see the range of information government provides to policy makers, investors, and the public. Through these different venues, policy makers latch on to particular problems or solutions depending on the readiness for action.

Nevertheless, the public's attention span can be very short. Problems identified through scientific research such as global warming may be the easiest to ignore, partly because there always seem to be numbers to refute a given analysis. Even as former Vice President Al Gore was accepting the Nobel Peace Prize for his work on global warming, a group of scientists challenged much of the evidence on which his work was based. The media can also play a role by magnifying or downplaying the impact of a particular story.

Policy makers set the agenda using many of the same criteria they apply to other political decisions—public opinion, interest group pressure, their own beliefs, ideology, party affiliation, and loyalty to their institution. In recent years, they have also come to rely on a small number of think tanks to help them sort through the stream of possible problems. A **think tank** is an organization composed of scholars who study public policy. Many are located in Washington, D.C., so that they can be closer to the national political process. Unlike a college or university, which also produces policy research, a think tank exists almost entirely to influence the immediate agenda. Thus, many are described as either liberal or conservative.

Deciding to Act

The fact that a problem exists does not automatically mean that Congress, the president, or the courts will try to solve it. Some problems help policy makers achieve their personal or political goals, such as reelection or a place in history, in which case they decide to act, whereas others do not, in which case they pick other problems to solve.

Policy makers also clearly understand that public pressure for action ebbs and flows over time. In fact, writes political scientist Anthony Downs, "American public attention rarely remains sharply focused upon any one domestic issue for very long—even if it involves a continuing problem of crucial importance to society." According to Downs, the public follows an **issue-attention cycle** in which each problem "suddenly leaps into prominence, remains there for a short time, and then—although still largely unresolved—gradually fades from the center of public attention."[7]

Global warming is a recent example. Public concern about the issue has gone up and down throughout the years, reflecting competing concerns about the economy and

think tank
A nongovernmental organization that seeks to influence public policy through research and education.

issue-attention cycle
The movement of public opinion toward public policy from initial enthusiasm for action to realization of costs and a decline in interest.

Former Vice President Al Gore clearly helped set the agenda for global warming with his Academy Award-winning documentary, *An Inconvenient Truth.* In the movie, Gore outlined what he believed were the negative impacts of global warming, and called citizens and policy makers to action.
■ *How else can citizens help set the policy making agenda?*

YOU WILL DECIDE

How Should We Fix Social Security?

Social Security is one of the most popular and important public policies. Created in 1934, it provides income to virtually every U.S. retiree and is widely credited with reducing poverty among older people to historic lows.

As the nation's 76 million baby boomers embark on retirement, however, Social Security will enter a major funding crisis. At the start of the program, there were approximately 160 workers paying FICA payroll taxes into the program for every one beneficiary; by 1998, there were approximately three workers per beneficiary; by 2030, there will be only two.

The result is a growing gap between the amount of money workers put into the program and the amount beneficiaries receive. The Social Security program does not keep worker taxes in individual accounts in some vault until they need them. Rather, it uses current taxes to pay for current benefits, pushing the money out almost as soon as it collects it.

Estimates suggest that Social Security will run out of money sometime in the 2020 or 2030s. By that point, the baby boom generation will simply overwhelm the system.

What do you think? How can we fix Social Security? What are the benefits and costs of different options?

THINKING IT THROUGH

There are only two ways to fix the Social Security program: increase revenues or cut benefits for retirees. Neither will be popular.

One way to help the program is to raise the basic tax rate on what workers earn and put more money into the system. Another way is to invest some Social Security funds in the stock market, where they might grow faster than they currently do in low-interest federal money accounts. Still another way is to allow younger workers to use their Social Security taxes to create their own personal savings accounts. Under this option, called privatization, workers would decide how much risk to take in investing their tax dollars—if they made good decisions, they would receive higher benefits; if they did poorly, they would receive lower benefits.

The options for cutting benefits are particularly unpopular. One way is to increase the retirement age again, which was increased from 65 to 67 when the program started losing money in 1983. An increase would delay retirement checks for a few years, saving money. Another way is to reduce the annual cost-of-living increases the government has always made in Social Security benefits. Beneficiaries would still get their checks, but the amount would no longer rise as fast as inflation.

It is not yet clear whether young Americans will accept a tax increase or higher retirement age given the state of the economy. After all, they are already having trouble getting mortgages and paying off college loans. Moreover, many young workers do not believe Social Security will exist when they retire—why put in more money now when they will not get anything back?

Critical Thinking Questions

1. Is Social Security a distributive or redistributive policy, or is it both?
2. How does the policy process create barriers to the changing Social Security? How can these barriers be lowered?
3. What political pressure can young workers exert to make sure fixing Social Security is fair to workers and beneficiaries alike?

---

doubt about specific solutions. Figure 17–2 shows the trends according to a variety of polls. As the polls show, the issue-attention cycle varies with a number of factors, most notably the economy. Citizens want government to act even when policy affects economic growth but not when the economy is in trouble. Although global warming is

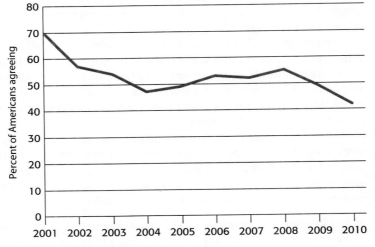

FIGURE 17–2 Concerns About the Environment, 2000–2010.

Agreement with the statement: "Protection of the environment should be given priority, even at the risk of curbing economic growth." ■ *What is one important reason why support for environmental action started to fall in 2008?*

SOURCE: Polls on global warming are available at http://www.polling-report.com.

465

still an issue for most Americans, it has been sliding somewhat throughout the past few years, suggesting that the issue-attention cycle is at work.

■ This cycle starts with what Downs described as the "pre-problem stage," the rise of some "highly undesirable social condition" such as global warming that has yet to capture public attention.

■ The issue-attention cycle continues with "alarmed discovery and euphoric enthusiasm," the sudden emergence of an issue as a topic for public debate. Books are written, documentaries made, speeches retooled, and campaigns rebuilt, all based on the sudden passion that generates public concern.

■ The cycle moves onward with the realization that change will incur significant cost. It is one thing to worry about greenhouse gases and quite another to pay more for clean electricity or buy smaller, more efficient cars. The greater the cost of solving a problem, especially if it means tax increases or benefit cuts, the more strongly people pull back from their euphoric view of change.

■ The cycle continues with the "gradual decline of intense public interest." Having pressed hard for action on an issue such as universal health insurance, the public may begin to realize that change is nearly impossible given the array of political forces fighting for a nondecision.

■ The cycle ends with what Downs calls the "post-problem stage." The problem moves into "prolonged limbo—a twilight realm of lesser attention or spasmodic recurrences of interest."

The ultimate decline of public interest is not inevitable. But if we expect problems to be solved immediately, we will only be disappointed. Civil rights took 100 years to become a reality, for example. Although issues such as global warming seem to demand that we take immediate action before the damage is beyond repair, we must acquire enough understanding of the problem, and of the policy process, to stay actively engaged for the long term.

Deciding How Much to Do

Once the federal government decides it *wants* to do something about a problem, the next difficult decision is *how much* to do. Government can launch a comprehensive program such as Social Security or Medicare, or it can expand a smaller program bit by bit over time.

Incremental or Comprehensive Policy An **incremental policy** makes a small-scale adjustment in an existing program, whereas a *comprehensive* or **punctuating policy** creates a dramatic change in the government's role. Incremental policies are generally the easiest to create, if only because they build on past decisions in very small ways, such as increasing the amount of federal support for colleges by a few hundred dollars. Punctuating policies, such as providing national prescription drug coverage for older adults, often require citizens, interest groups, political parties, and policy makers to mobilize in a broad movement for change.

Incremental policy is the most frequent response to calls for change. According to James L. True, Bryan D. Jones, and Frank R. Baumgartner, "American political institutions were conservatively designed to resist many efforts at change and thus to make mobilization necessary if established interests are to be overcome."[8] Because of constitutional protections such as separation of power and checks and balances, incremental policy often becomes the easiest way to advance an idea.

More fundamental change is sometimes possible. As True, Jones, and Baumgartner write, these "bursts" of change occur when a new image of a problem replaces the prevailing notion that incremental policy is the only answer. Such new images have shaped the way the government tests new drugs, regulates local education, attacks environmental pollution, and regulates the purchase of handguns and assault rifles.

Iron Triangles and Issue Networks Fundamental changes often depend on alliances of citizens, interest groups, political parties, private businesses, government agencies,

incremental policy
Small adjustments to existing public policies.

punctuating policy
Radical changes to public policy that occur only after the mobilization of large segments of society to demand action.

congressional committees, and others who come together to place an issue on the agenda and push for or against change. Alliances called **iron triangles** exist for decades; **issue networks** cooperate for a specific cause and then disband.

An iron triangle has three sides that hold together for long periods of time: (1) a federal department or agency, (2) a set of loyal interest groups, and (3) a House and/or Senate committee. Each side supports the other two. Loyal members of Congress work to protect or increase the agency's budget, allowing the agency to flourish, and pass legislation to support the interest groups, providing benefits for its members. Agencies give special services to the interest groups, keeping their members happy, and ensure the constituencies of members of Congress are provided for, aiding in congressional approval ratings. Interest groups give contributions and endorsements to loyal members of Congress, aiding in their reelection, and support the activities and requests of the agency, enhancing their legitimacy. Policy making for veterans, for example, is achieved through an iron triangle composed of the Department of Veterans Affairs, the House and Senate Veterans Committees, and a long list of interest groups that represent veterans, such as the American Legion and Veterans of Foreign Wars. The basic structure of this iron triangle is presented in Figure 17–3.

Iron triangles have been largely replaced by much looser collections of participants in issue networks. As political scientist Hugh Heclo has argued, the notion that iron triangles make all policy was "not so much wrong as it was disastrously incomplete" in today's complicated policy environment.[9] The increasing number of small, highly specialized interest groups makes an iron triangle nearly impossible to create, if only because Congress and federal agencies can no longer identify a steady occupant for the third corner of the triangle. They have to find temporary allies, depending on the issue. There is nothing "iron" about such coalitions: They last only as long as an issue is hot.

Issue networks concentrate power in the relatively small number of individuals who organize and maintain them. These people make the key decisions about who participates and what they say. Some political scientists thus refer to the rise of well-financed issue networks—such as those that promote prescription drug coverage for older consumers or tax cuts for business—as a form of elitism, not pluralism, in which a very small number of actors accelerate or delay action. Medicare prescription drug coverage, for example, engaged an issue network of drug companies, the AARP, and hospitals.

Choosing a Solution

The federal government has five tools to solve most public problems: (1) spending money, (2) using taxes to regulate the economy and encourage certain behaviors, (3) providing goods and services directly, (4) providing protection against risk, and (5) creating standards, incentives, or penalties.[10]

iron triangle
A policy-making instrument composed of a tightly related alliance of a congressional committee, interest groups, and federal department or agency.

issue network
A policy-making instrument composed of loosely related interest groups, congressional committee, presidential aides, and other parties.

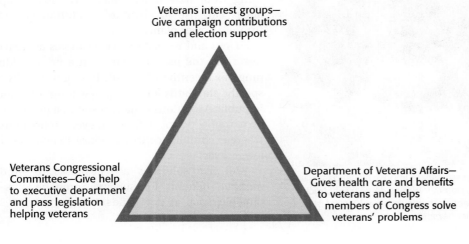

Veterans interest groups—
Give campaign contributions
and election support

Veterans Congressional
Committees—Give help
to executive department
and pass legislation
helping veterans

Department of Veterans Affairs—
Gives health care and benefits
to veterans and helps
members of Congress solve
veterans' problems

FIGURE 17–3 **Iron Triangle.**
■ *Why are iron triangles so hard to break?*

The first option is *federal spending* for direct payments to individuals, hospitals, corporations, and other nations. Social Security is still the largest direct payment to individuals, whereas Medicare for older citizens' medical care is the largest direct payment to hospitals. The federal government also buys a huge amount of material to support the military, including fighter jets, body armor, gasoline, and food. In 2007, the Defense Department spent more than $200 billion on such purchases.

The second public policy option is the *use of taxes* to regulate the economy—lower taxes may stimulate a weak economy, whereas higher taxes may slow down a hot economy. The federal government can use the tax system to encourage certain behaviors such as buying a house, making contributions to charity, or even having children. Businesses receive tax credits and deductions for activities such as energy conservation and the purchase of some U.S.-made goods. Advocates of policies designed to curb global warming argue that the federal government should impose taxes on the amount of carbon gases that private companies produce. By creating such taxes, companies would have incentives to reduce their pollution or lose profits.

The third option for solving a problem is *providing goods and services* to the public. National parks such as Yosemite and the Grand Canyon generally only charge a modest admission fee, the National Air and Space Museum on the Washington Mall is free, and we do not pay directly for national defense. Ultimately, of course, nothing the government does is completely free—the National Air and Space Museum is supported by general taxes, as is the Defense Department.

The fourth option of public policy is to *guarantee protection* against risk, with a range of devices to encourage activities the private sector might not otherwise undertake. The most familiar protections are federal loan guarantees, under which the government promises to cover losses if a student, farmer, small business, or other borrower fails to repay a debt. Student loan programs have become more difficult to get in recent years because of the economic collapse and fears that students will not be able to repay their loans.

The final option to solve a problem is through **regulation** to encourage or discourage certain behaviors such as smoking, using illegal drugs, polluting, and driving safely. Regulation involves **rules,** which are precise legal statements implementing a public policy. They can impose penalties or rewards enforceable by, and open to challenge in, the courts.

Thus, regulation and rules are best viewed as tactics for achieving a particular result. Advocates of action to reduce global warming believe that the federal government should increase mileage requirements for automobiles as a way to reduce the amount of pollution. In late 2009, for example, the Environmental Protection Agency was given the power to raise mileage standards as part of its general authority to protect the quality of the environment. These regulations are still being developed but are likely to affect everything from how much electricity kitchen appliances can use to curbs on pollution generated through power plants.

Laws and regulations cover topics as varied as terrorism, the use of firearms in a crime, kidnapping, tax incentives for contributing to charity, and specific standards for testing new drugs or smoking in public. Violations usually result in a penalty such as a traffic ticket, a fine, or even imprisonment, whereas compliance can produce benefits such as lower taxes.

All five solutions are designed to produce *material* benefits for society. Some benefits are tangible, such as new roads, bridges, schools, and

regulation
A policy that encourages or discourages certain behavior by imposing a legally binding rule. Rules are made through a long process that begins with an act of Congress and ends with issuance of a final rule.

rule
A precise statement of how a law is implemented.

California and other states sued the national government to impose higher gas mileage standards on automobiles and light trucks. The Hummer is considered a light truck.
■ *Is regulation the best policy option for protecting the environment? What other kinds of policy solutions might the government attempt?*

Public Service and Budgetball

Budgetball is a way to help citizens understand how to make tough choices about the federal budget. The game was designed by the Peter G. Peterson Foundation, a private charity committed to reducing the national debt. It is now being played on college campuses throughout the nation.

The rules of the game are complex, and we will not cover them all here, but the game is a blend of volleyball and analysis of the budget. It is played on a basketball court with two teams lined up against each other, and teams score points by passing a standard-size volleyball to the end zone. Strategy is the key to victory. Every period begins with a three-minute budget session. Teams start with zero "budgetbucks." They can earn budgetbucks by making sacrifices such as playing with oven-mitts on their hands or fewer team members on the floor; they can spend budgetbucks by adding power-ups such as extra players. If they run out of budgetbucks and enter negative territory, they must make sacrifices, which increase the odds that the other team will score more points. You can watch a short video about the game at budgetball .org, or by searching for "budgetball" on YouTube.

The point of the game is to reinforce the notion that the nation's debt is a function of spending and sacrifice. If policy makers want to cut the debt, they have to ask for sacrifice. By playing well with sacrifices, the

Budgetball is a brand new sport designed to raise awareness about the issue of the federal debt and encourage discussion and debate about America's fiscal future.

Budgetball is a non-contact sport played with a standard-size volleyball on a basketball court (or similarly sized outdoor field). It is played by two teams of 6 or more players each. Players must pass the ball to move it around the court and to a player in the end zone in order to score. The team with the most points at the conclusion of the game is the winner.

(Click on the image to get a full-size chart.)

This diagram illustrates some of the play as defined by the overview and rules.

more fiscally responsible team will almost always win. But sacrifices are painful in both budgetball and the public policy process.

CRITICAL THINKING QUESTIONS

1. Why might budgetball help citizens understand why the federal budget is so hard to balance?

2. How would budgetball encourage better financial management such as reducing credit card spending for individual players?

3. Is budgetball like the policy process? Who scores points in the real budget system? Leaders who spend money or ask for sacrifice?

---

hospitals; others, such as higher pay, greater safety, better education, and cleaner air and water, can only be felt. In theory, action to reduce global warming will produce less violent hurricanes throughout the coming decades. Scientists tend to believe that hurricanes have become more dangerous because of the rise in sea temperatures, which fuel hurricanes.

Other solutions produce *symbolic* benefits, such as efforts to educate the public, study an issue, appoint a blue-ribbon commission, or highlight the need for future action. In theory, symbolic benefits highlight an emerging issue and create citizen action. In reality, they are sometimes a way to make a nondecision as policy makers merely express their concern and move to other tangible policies. It is not yet clear, for example, just how much global warming is caused by sources beyond government's control, but action to reduce global warming through international treaties can give the public a sense that the world is getting better.

Deciding Who Will Deliver the Goods or Services

Part of selecting a solution to implement a policy is deciding who will actually implement the program. The answer is not always a federal employee.[11] Although federal employment has been steady at roughly 2 million workers since the early 1990s, the

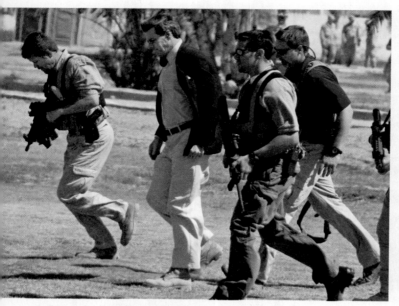

Private firms provided most security services to protect U.S. diplomats during the Iraq War. In 2007, employees of Blackwater, Inc., were charged with the unprovoked killings of Iraqi citizens during one of its patrols.
■ *Why does the U.S. military continue to use private contractors to guard diplomats?*

federal agenda has continued to grow. As a result, the government often depends on a largely hidden workforce of contractors, grantees, and state and local employees to achieve its policy goals.

There are four sources of what political scientists call *third-party government:* (1) private businesses, (2) colleges and universities, (3) state and local governments, and (4) charitable organizations.

Private Businesses Paid under contracts with federal departments and agencies, profit-making businesses do an increasing amount of federal work once done exclusively by federal employees. For example, the federal government uses contractors to serve meals in almost all of its cafeterias, make weather maps at the National Oceanographic and Atmospheric Administration, operate the passenger and baggage screening lines at airports as employees of the Transportation Security Administration, and sweep the floors at almost all federal buildings. In 2007 and 2008, the State Department became embroiled in a controversy over its use of private contractors such as Blackwater to provide security for diplomats in Iraq.

Colleges and Universities Colleges and universities are a second option for implementing public policy, especially if it includes research. Virtually every major university receives federal funding for education, environment, health, and space research, and many conduct research on behalf of the Defense Department or the Department of Homeland Security. Colleges and universities also receive federal funds for training scientists and engineers and often benefit from pet projects enacted by Congress. They have been the source of many scientific breakthroughs, including much medical research used to fight cancer and other life-threatening diseases.

State and Local Governments As the National Commission on the State and Local Government Service argued in 1993, state and local employees do much of the real work of governing. They collect the trash; provide safe drinking water; vaccinate children; administer the airports; run the public schools, universities, and community colleges; oversee environmental laws; run almost all public hospitals; staff most of the nation's prisons; prosecute most of the crimes; and provide police and fire protection.

Charities Finally, the federal government often relies on charities such as the American Red Cross, the Salvation Army, the American Cancer Society, and religious institutions to maintain the social safety net through contracts and grants. It also relies on charities to help the nation respond to crises such as Hurricane Katrina.

Charities are often called "social-benefit organizations" because of their role in battling problems such as poverty, illiteracy, hunger, and disease. But they also monitor and influence what the federal government does. Whatever their role in implementing federal policy, charities cannot be taxed by government if they are engaged in any legitimate educational, religious, or humanitarian purpose. Most gifts to charities are tax deductible, too, meaning that givers can deduct the amount of their contribution from their taxable income.

The number of charities has more than tripled throughout the past half-century. Today's 1.5 million charities employ approximately 11 million people and spend nearly a trillion dollars per year. Most private colleges and universities are considered charities under federal law, for example, as are many hospitals.

Making Rules for Implementation

Rule making comes at the very end of the policy-making process and is virtually invisible to most citizens. Nevertheless, it is the essential step in converting the abstract ideas and

For the People
GOVERNMENT'S GREATEST ENDEAVORS

Reducing Disease

Protecting the nation from foreign and domestic threats involves more than fighting wars and enforcing laws. It also involves protecting Americans from hidden threats such as disease, pollution, and unsafe foods. As we have learned more about preventing disease, the federal government's role has grown, whether through funding for advanced scientific research or programs to make sure all Americans are vaccinated against life-threatening disease.

Much of the federal government's progress against disease has been through incremental programs that have added up to very significant impacts. Some of the progress has been made through small research projects designed to discover the causes of illness, whereas other progress has occurred through efforts to conquer specific diseases.

The federal government subdued polio, for example, through legislation passed in 1955 to cover the cost of creating a vaccine against polio. Congress also provided the funding to help state governments immunize all children against diphtheria, whooping cough, and tetanus by the age of five.

As the inventory of infectious diseases grew, so did the federal government's involvement in health care research. Congress created the National Institute of Health (NIH) in 1930; added the National Cancer Institute in 1937; created a division of research grants to promote university research in 1946; added

new institutes for dental research, experimental biology, health disease, mental health, and microbiology in 1948; and expanded the federal government's health budget. Congress continued to create new research programs year after year. By 2001, the NIH had 27 separate institutes housed in its 75 buildings on a 300-acre campus in Bethesda, Maryland.

This investment has made a dramatic difference in the quality of life for most Americans. Deaths from heart disease is down by more than a third since the mid-1970s, five-year cancer survival rates are up by 60 percent, schizophrenia and depression are much more treatable, and dental sealants now prevent nearly 100 percent of cavities in children. Although there are still significant differences in disease rates between the rich and poor and among African Americans, Native Americans, and whites, Americans are living longer, healthier lives because of the federal effort to reduce disease.

CRITICAL THINKING QUESTIONS

1. How does a longer lifespan affect federal policy? What are the costs and benefits?

2. Why hasn't the number of deaths among infants decreased at the same time lifespan has increased?

3. Who do you think lives the longest? Poor people? Whites? People with health care coverage?

President Franklin D. Roosevelt had been stricken by polio as an adult, but he hid his dependence on a wheelchair and braces throughout his four-term presidency. In 1938 he created a private foundation now known as the March of Dimes to conduct research on the disease.

---

language of laws, presidential orders, and court rulings into precise rules governing what individual members of the public, companies, government, states, and localities must do to achieve the goals of a specific policy.

Rules can be extraordinarily detailed and are sometimes difficult for even regulated parties to understand. Because they are so complicated, interest groups have much greater influence over their construction than citizens and even members of Congress.

Although the federal government has been issuing rules since 1789, the number of rules jumped dramatically during World War II and again in the 1970s.[12] The number of rules did not increase because rule making became easier, however. On the contrary, Congress made it more difficult to create a rule under the 1946 Administrative Procedure Act. We can see the growth of rules in the number of pages in the *Federal Register*, which provides a daily record of all new and proposed rules. Figure 17–4 shows the number of pages by decade.

The process starts when a bill is passed and signed into law, which is sent to the appropriate department or agency for "faithful execution," as the Constitution requires. With the legislative history as a guide to what Congress wanted, the department or agency then drafts a proposed rule. The rule itself generally consists of a statement of purpose, the actual rule, and a review of any research or legislative language that shaped it.

471

FIGURE 17–4 **Pages in the**
Federal Register.

■ *Why do the pages in the Federal Register continue to rise even though Congress is passing fewer pieces of legislation?*

SOURCE: U.S. Office of the Federal Register, "Annual Federal Register Pages Published."

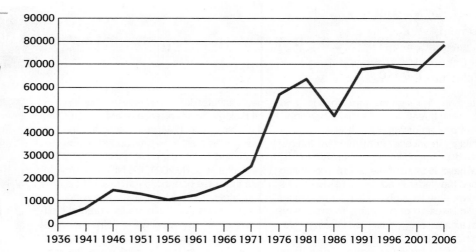

With the proposed rule in hand, the department or agency tells the public it is about to act. Under the Administrative Procedure Act, the department or agency must post a formal "Notice of Proposed Rulemaking" in the *Federal Register.*

Anyone affected by the rule has a short period of "notice and comment" to express concerns and suggest amendments through letters, e-mails, and personal testimony to government. After all the comments are reviewed, the department or agency publishes the final rule in the *Federal Register.* The rule goes into effect 30 days after it is published. Any citizen, including students, can provide comments regarding a proposed rule such as raising mileage standards, but they must first know when the proposed rule has been issued and when the notice-and-comment period starts and ends. The federal government publishes a list of all pending regulations and the timetable for action at http://www.regulations.gov/search/Regs/home.html#home. Under law, the federal government must review all comments and respond in a final summary of all comments.

Although the general rule making seems straightforward, it includes a number of leverage points at which a rule can be substantially altered. The process can also be

Citizens can monitor the rulemaking process and register their own comments on proposed rules at regulations.gov.

delayed—nothing in the Constitution or the Administrative Procedure Act says that a department or agency must propose a rule within a specific amount of time. Moreover, the department or agency retains great discretion to interpret information generated through the notice-and-comment period.

Rules are particularly important because Congress often leaves the details to the federal bureaucracy. Passing legislation requires many compromises, some of which are so vague that the bureaucracy can only act if it provides the details. In this regard, the bureaucracy has enormous *administrative discretion*. The bureaucracy exercised this discretion in 2009 when it implemented the Serve America Act. Under the Act, the federal government established a "Social Innovation Fund" of $50 million but left the details of how to spend the money to the Corporation for National and Community Service. The final structure of the program can be found at http://www.nationalservice.gov/about/serveamerica/innovation.asp.

Running the Program

Implementation does not end with release of a final rule. It continues with the day-to-day tasks of actually running a federal department or agency, making rules, supervising contractors, and evaluating impact. And as assumptions change and the issue-attention cycle takes hold, the policy-making process can begin again. As we shall see in the next chapter, successful execution of the laws is hardly easy. It requires millions of federal employees; a long list of departments and agencies; intense oversight by Congress, the president, and the judiciary; and money—more than $3 trillion in 2008 alone.

The Order of Action

Making public policy is an often unpredictable process. It can start with any step and skip back and forth as politics shapes everything from the decision to act to running the program. The result is a policy-making process that is almost always in flux.

Some political scientists such as John Kingdon even think of this process as taking place in a "primordial swamp" of competing problems, solutions, political actors, citizens, pressure, and resources such as dollars, public support, and administrative energy.[13]

These policy "streams" are shaped by citizens, interest groups, presidents, and members of Congress and move through the institutions in search of each other. Thus, an idea for solving a problem such as a new weapons system or an increase in the minimum wage may linger in waiting for a specific problem such as terrorism or an increase in unemployment. Politics ties these various streams together into a public policy. According to this view, one reason immigration reform has not yet passed is that the streams of problems, solutions, and interests have yet to come together, in part because the political stream is so divided.

Some policies are efforts to terminate a program. As opposed to a nondecision, which stops a policy before it can be made, termination stops a policy that is already running. The federal government once maintained a helium reserve in Texas to ensure a reliable supply of the gas for its military blimps. Even through the military stopped using blimps after World War II ended in 1945, it took 50 years for Congress and the president to halt the helium reserve program.

Citizens and Public Policy

LEARNING **OBJECTIVE**

17.3 Assess ways in which citizens can influence the public policy process.

Public policy is not made in a vacuum. Rather, it takes place in a sometimes confusing dance called politics that engages citizens, interest groups, political parties, legislators, judges, and government institutions.

Citizens are often anxious about participating in this process, not only because it can be complex, but also because they have many levers that give them influence. They can certainly vote—the higher the participation, the more the process will heed their voice.

The federal government once maintained a reserve of helium for its blimps. The reserve helped create jobs and income in Texas and was protected by the Texas congressional delegation. It was finally halted in the 1990s, long after the military had stopped using blimps. ■ *Why are federal programs so hard to kill once they are established?*

But voting is not enough. Citizens cannot vote on the basis of their policy positions if they do not have an opinion or if candidates do not tell the electorate where they stand. And because voting is a blunt instrument of participation that does not convey precise information about what they want, citizens must also find other pathways to influence, including joining interest groups, writing letters, sending e-mails, confronting legislators at community meetings, and even running for office themselves.

They can also join public interest groups that support or oppose government policy action. In this regard, Ralph Nader may have done more than any other person to influence the policy process on behalf of consumers.

Nader started his journey in 1965 with the publication of *Unsafe at Any Speed,* a damning attack on the poor state of automobile safety in the United States. Targeting General Motors and its Chevrolet Corvair, Nader demanded congressional action and got it. Today's airbags are directly traceable to Nader's early pressure for mandatory seat belts and crash-resistant passenger compartments. "You've got to keep the pressure on, even if you lose," he says about representing the public interest. "The essence of the citizen's movement is persistence." Nader went on to create the Center for Study of Responsive Law, the Freedom of Information Clearinghouse, and dozens of other Public Interest Research Groups (PIRGs).

There is no question that citizens want action on the big problems highlighted in this chapter. They know that safeguarding Social Security, reducing global warming, and fixing the economy so that everyone rises on the basis of merit will not happen without pressure. No citizen gets what he or she does not ask for. And asking is part of the politics that leads to ultimate action.

Citizen action is more successful when it involves clear ideas for an alternative policy. It is rarely enough to merely demand that government act. It is also important to tell government what to do. This means thinking through the options and making a clear, well-developed argument for change and pursuing it aggressively through our complicated policy process.

Ralph Nader was a major force in creating pressure for consumer protection. He created many of the tactics used to achieve public policy impact during his 40 years of public service.

$\mathcal{O}f$ the $\mathcal{P}eople$

AMERICA'S CHANGING FACE

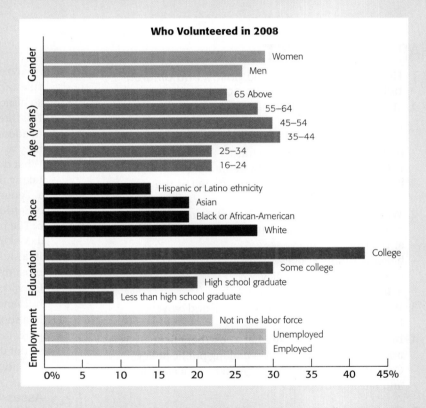

Who Volunteers?

The United States is a nation of volunteers. In 2008, 61 million Americans volunteered in one way or another, giving an average of 52 hours during the year. Valuing each hour at $22, Americans give more than $200 billion worth of energy to charity, thereby allowing federal, state, and local governments to focus more of their resources on the needy. Many charities rely on volunteers as mentors for children, ushers at religious services, counselors at job training programs, and campaign workers.

Not every American volunteers at equal levels, however. According to the U.S. Bureau of Labor Statistics, middle-aged Americans are the most likely to volunteer, in part because many are at the stage of life when they are more likely to engage in their local schools and communities. They may not have more time to give but are somewhat more motivated. Those with college degrees are also more likely to volunteer, largely because they know how to volunteer and have more income to pay for child care and other support when they take time to give time to charities.

Given these income and educational differences, it is not surprising that different groups of Americans are more or less likely to volunteer. As the following table shows, education and the income that goes with it is the single best predictor of whether Americans volunteer.

All of these percentages have declined since 2004 and may reflect the effect of the deep recession that began in 2008. People gave less money to charities during the recession and had less time to give. Interestingly, however, people who were unemployed in 2008 were just as likely to volunteer as people who were fully employed. Overall, the number of volunteers declined from 65 million in 2004 to 61 million in 2008. Younger

Americans showed the greatest increase in volunteering during that period, however, increasing from 41 hours per year to 48 hours on average.

Volunteering may have declined in part because some charities went out of business during the recession, whereas many others cut back on their ability to recruit and manage volunteers. Volunteers need fulfilling work to draw them into a charity. If their talents are not well used, many simply do not return. At least some volunteering among young Americans is for

service-learning programs at their local schools and colleges.

CRITICAL THINKING QUESTIONS

1. Why do you volunteer? What was your experience?

2. Why do college graduates volunteer more than citizens with less education? Why are young Americans less active than middle-aged Americans?

3. What can charities do to improve the volunteer experience?

Who Volunteered in 2008

(Bar chart showing percentage of volunteers by category)

- **Gender:** Women, Men
- **Age (years):** 65 Above, 55–64, 45–54, 35–44, 25–34, 16–24
- **Race:** Hispanic or Latino ethnicity, Asian, Black or African-American, White
- **Education:** College, Some college, High school graduate, Less than high school graduate
- **Employment:** Not in the labor force, Unemployed, Employed

Scale: 0%, 5, 10, 15, 20, 25, 30, 35, 40, 45%

SOURCE: U.S. Bureau of Labor Statistics, "Volunteering in the United States," January 2009, press release. The information is updated each year and can be found at http://www.bls.gov/cps/.

CHAPTER **SUMMARY**

17.1 Relate politics and public policy, and differentiate three types of public policy.

Public policy is the product of politics, which resolves the question of who gets what, when, where, and how from government. Politics involves the interaction of the people and their government. It affects policy through activities

such as voting, joining interest groups and political parties, congressional bargaining, ratifying treaties, signing laws, and administering laws. Policies are designed to produce certain outcomes, such as a healthier society.

There are three types of policy: distributive (which provides benefits to all groups in society), redistributive (which provides benefits to one group in society at the expense of another), and reverse distributive (which eliminates benefits to all groups in society).

17.2 Outline eight steps in making public policy, and assess types of policy solutions.

Every public policy emerges from a process that includes eight steps: (1) making assumptions about the problem, (2) setting the agenda, (3) deciding to act, which can involve nondecisions, (4) deciding how much to do, (5) choosing a solution to the problem, (6) deciding who will deliver the goods or services, (7) making rules for implementation, and (8) running the program itself. The steps do not always occur in order. Some political scientists see problems, solutions, political actors, and so forth as "streams" that flow through the institutions of government and only occasionally come together.

There are five solutions of policy: (1) spending, (2) taxing, (3) directly providing goods and services, (4) providing protection against risk, and (5) creating standards, incentives, or penalties. There are also different ways of delivering services through third-party government, which include private businesses, colleges and universities, state and local governments, and charities.

17.3 Assess ways in which citizens can influence the public policy process.

Citizens face significant obstacles to being heard in the policy process. But they may have more influence at certain stages of the process, and they can make their voices heard through both traditional and non-traditional means, including voting, joining interest groups, writing letters, sending e-mails, confronting legislators at community meetings, and even running for office themselves.

CHAPTER **SELF-TEST**

17.1 Relate politics and public policy, and differentiate three types of public policy.

1. Which is *not* a way government can convey public policy?
   a. A petition signed by voters
   b. Rules written by administrators
   c. Opinions issued by the Supreme Court
   d. A law passed by Congress and signed by the president

2. Which type of public policy includes programs like public assistance to poor people?
   a. Distributive policy
   b. Redistributive policy
   c. Semi-distributive policy
   d. Reverse distributive policy

3. What is reverse distributive policy, and why is it rare?

4. In a short essay, identify what a cost/benefit analysis is and how it has been used in making public policy. Consider proposals such as greater use of electric cars and reusable diapers.

17.2 Outline eight steps in making public policy, and assess types of policy solutions.

5. Which of the steps in making public policy is the most difficult?
   a. Deciding to act
   b. Running the program
   c. Making rules for implementation
   d. Making assumptions about the problem

6. During which of the following periods did the total size of the Federal Register decrease?
   a. 1936–1941
   b. 1956–1961
   c. 1981–1986
   d. 2001–2006

7. Analyze the ways that citizens can influence the rule-making process. Why is the real "budgetball" so difficult to win?

8. List three of the solutions the federal government uses to address public policy problems, and describe how they work in practice.

9. What does political scientist John Kingdon describe as taking place in a "primordial swamp"?
   a. Federal spending
   b. Setting the policy agenda
   c. The policy-making process
   d. Making assumptions about the world

10. In a short essay, describe what you think are the three most difficult steps of the policy-making process. Consider who is active in each step and how the step influences final policy decisions.

11. In a short essay, select three steps of the policy-making process and describe how a college student and a senior citizen can influence them. Consider each individual's desires and needs.

17.3 Assess ways in which citizens can influence the public policy process.

12. Which of the following is *not* a common way in which citizens seek action on public policy?
    a. Running for public office
    b. Joining an interest group
    c. Lobbying Congress through e-mails
    d. Stopping paying their taxes.

13. Why are volunteers so important to implementing policy decisions?

14. Select one of the major trends likely to influence public policy in the future. In a short essay, describe a possible way the government could address the problems associated with this trend. Use the eight steps and five solutions described in this chapter as a basis for your plan.

Answers for selected questions: 1. a; 2. b; 5. a; 6. c; 9. c; 12. d

mypoliscilab EXERCISES

Apply what you learned in this chapter on MyPoliSciLab.

Read on **mypoliscilab.com**

eText: Chapter 17

Study and **Review** on **mypoliscilab.com**

Pre-Test
Post-Test
Chapter Exam
Flashcards

Watch on **mypoliscilab.com**

Video: Making Environmental Policy
Video: Chicago Gun Laws

KEY TERMS

public policy, p. 460
politics, p. 460
policy makers, p. 460
distributive policy, p. 460
redistributive policy, p. 461
zero-sum games p. 461

reverse distributive policy, p. 461
nondecision, p. 462
policy agenda, p. 463
think tank, p. 464
issue-attention cycle, p. 464
incremental policy, p. 466

punctuating policy, p. 466
iron triangle, p. 467
issue network, p. 467
regulation, p. 468
rule, p. 468

ADDITIONAL RESOURCES

FURTHER READING

JAMES E. ANDERSON, *Public Policymaking: An Introduction* (Houghton Mifflin, 2005).

THOMAS A. BIRKLAND, *An Introduction to the Policy Process: Theories, Concepts, and Models of Public Policy Making* (Sharpe, 2005).

M. MARGARET CONWAY, DAVID W. AHERN, AND **GERTRUDE A. STEURNAGEL,** *Women and Public Policy: A Revolution in Progress* (CQ Press, 2004).

CORNELIUS KERWIN, *Rulemaking: How Government Agencies Write Law and Make Policy* (CQ Press, 2003).

JOHN W. KINGDON, *Agendas, Alternatives, and Public Policies* (Longman, 2002).

B. GUY PETERS, *American Public Policy: Promise and Performance* (CQ Press, 2006).

ANDREW RICH, *Think Tanks, Public Policy, and the Politics of Expertise* (Cambridge University Press, 2005).

MARK E. RUSHEFSKY, *Public Policy in the United States: At the Dawn of the Twenty-First Century* (Sharpe, 2007).

PAUL A. SABATIER, ED., *Theories of the Public Policy Process* (Westview Press, 2007).

JOE SOSS, JACOB S. HACKER, AND **SUZANNE METTLER,** EDS., *Remaking America: Democracy and Public Policy in an Age of Inequality* (Russell Sage Foundation, 2007).

DEBORAH STONE, *Policy Paradox: The Art of Political Decision Making* (Norton, 1997).

WEB SITES

www.volunteermatch.org A very large Web site for finding volunteer opportunities.
www.idealist.org The place to go for information on jobs in charities.
www.volunteer.gov The federal government's Web site on volunteering.
www.regulations.gov The place to go for basic information on the rule-making process.
www.POGO.org The Project on Government Oversight, which follows federal policy.

CHAPTER

18

Making Economic Policy

After two years of slow growth, the United States economy reached a crisis point in late September 2008. Consumers were increasingly anxious about making even small purchases, home prices and car sales were falling, and more than 750,000 Americans had lost their jobs in the first nine months of the year.

Most importantly, the credit market was beginning to freeze, sharply limiting the amount of money available for borrowing. Credit is the essential grease that keeps the economy moving—consumers borrow to buy homes and cars, students borrow to buy books and pay tuition, small businesses borrow to buy new goods to sell, banks borrow money from other banks to cover the ups and downs of borrowing itself, and Wall Street borrows money to buy businesses and finance big investments. But credit was quickly disappearing as nervous lenders decided to sit on their money rather than make what they thought were risky loans.

On Sunday, September 28, Treasury Secretary Henry M. Paulson Jr. went to Capitol Hill to ask lawmakers for unprecedented authority to ease the credit crisis, which had begun in 2007 with a surge in the number of homeowners who could no longer pay their debts. These loan defaults continued to grow through the year and eventually created billions of dollars of "toxic debt," meaning loans that banks could not cover.

Paulson's proposal to buy $700 billion of this bad debt and keep it in the federal government's hands for future action provoked intense anger. Many Americans saw his proposal as a bailout for Wall Street firms that had made so much money making the bad loans. Americans wondered how the bailout, or rescue, as Paulson called it, would help them pay for health insurance, college loans, gasoline, and groceries.

Paulson's proposal was not only unprecedented, it was complex. Members of Congress had difficulty explaining it back home and wondered how they could vote for such an expensive program when the federal government itself was already borrowing heavily to finance itself. With the economy teetering on what Paulson and other experts said was a complete breakdown, Congress only had days to make a decision on what to do. Moreover, the 2008 presidential election was in full swing with Democrat Barack Obama and Republican John McCain unwilling to take a position on the controversial idea. Under intense pressure as the stock markets fell dramatically, Congress passed the bill on October 3, only ten days after Paulson made his stunning proposal.

It will take several years to know whether Paulson's gamble will work. The U.S. economy no longer operates independently of other economies across the globe. If the U.S. economy failed, these other economies would fail, and vice versa. Much of the money that was loaned to banks by 2010 had been returned to the federal government, though the public remains intensely angry about the huge bonuses that bankers and Wall Street investors continue to receive.

Although economic policy is often viewed as artful management of predictable events, September 2008 showed just how complex economic policy has become. As president, Barack Obama now takes the lead on economic policy. He spent his first two years in office trying to jumpstart the economy through an assortment of spending programs designed to create new jobs, most of which were temporary. Economic policy, as with other elements of public policy, is no longer a matter of occasional tinkering when events go badly. It is a full-time job for a government by the people.

An Introduction to Economic Policy

LEARNING **OBJECTIVE**

18.1 Describe the federal government's economic policy making role and how economic performance is measured.

The federal government has been active in economic policy since the end of the Revolutionary War. The framers wanted a government strong enough to promote free trade, protect patents and trademarks, and enforce contracts between individuals and businesses. And they wanted a government with enough funding to build the postal roads, bridges, railroads, and canals that would allow the young economy to grow.

In part because the economy is so important, the framers did not concentrate economic policy in any one branch. Instead, they divided economic policy-making control between the legislative and executive branches and between the House and the Senate. Article I, Section 8, of the Constitution gives Congress the power to borrow, coin, and print money, while Article II, Section 2, gives the president the power to appoint the officers of government, including the secretary of the treasury.

In a similar vein, Article I gives Congress the power to regulate commerce with foreign nations, among the states, and with Native American tribes, while Article II gives the president authority to negotiate the treaties and enforce the laws. Finally, Article I gives Congress the power to establish post offices and build postal roads, which were as important to the free movement of commerce in the 1700s as the Internet is today. Article II gives the president the power to appoint executive officials such as the postmaster general of the United States.

By creating a national government of limited powers and providing constitutional guarantees to protect property from excessive regulation, the framers succeeded in protecting capitalism. Part of the government's role is to stay out of the way as individuals and businesses create wealth through new ideas and hard work, but part is to promote the national welfare through **fiscal policy,** which uses federal spending and taxation to stimulate or slow the economy, and **monetary policy,** which manipulates the supply of money that individuals and businesses have in their hands to keep the economy from swinging wildly from boom to bust. In addition, the federal government promotes economic growth and trade and controls many economic decisions through regulations against certain kinds of business, labor, and environmental practices.

These tools are designed to smooth the ups and downs of the normal *business cycle.* Economists tend to focus on four discrete stages of the cycle: (1) *expansion,* in which the economy produces new jobs and growth; (2) *contraction,* as the economy starts to slow down; (3) *recession,* in which the economy reaches a trough of slow growth; and (4) *recovery,* in which the economy rebounds. A *depression* is an extremely deep form of recession that lasts much longer than the average recession. Depressions also produce extremely high unemployment. The Great Depression of the 1930s began with a stock market crash on October 29, 1929, which is still called *Black Friday,* and lasted until the early years of World War II more than ten years later. The goal of effective economic policy today is to make sure the peaks are not too high and the troughs are not too low.

We use two yardsticks to measure the performance of the economy. The first is **inflation,** which we track by comparing the price of goods and services such as gasoline, food, and housing over time. Inflation, a rising price level, is the primary risk during expansion and recovery. The second measure is **unemployment,** or the number of people looking for work at any given time. Unemployment among the employable is the greatest problem during contraction and recession.

In theory, inflation increases when unemployment drops (an increase in the workforce creates more demand for products, which raises prices), whereas inflation declines when unemployment increases (fewer workers creates less demand for products, which lowers prices). This balance between the demand and supply of goods and services drives the business cycle: When supply is low and demand is high, prices rise; when supply is high and demand is low, prices fall. In reality, inflation and unemployment can rise or fall at the same time, as they did at the start of 2008. A simultaneous increase in inflation and unemployment is called **stagflation** (stagnation plus inflation). As of 2010, the economy was showing high levels of unemployment at approximately 10 percent but low levels of inflation.

fiscal policy
Government policy that attempts to manage the economy by controlling taxing and spending.

monetary policy
Government policy that attempts to manage the economy by controlling the money supply and thus interest rates.

inflation
A rise in the general price level (and decrease in dollar value) owing to an increase in the volume of money and credit in relation to available goods.

unemployment
The number of Americans who are out of work but actively looking for a job. The number does not usually include those who are not looking.

stagflation
A combination of an economic slowdown (stagnation) and a rise in prices (inflation).

The economic cycle runs from expansion to recovery. Fiscal and monetary policies are designed to make sure the cycle is relatively stable. Here, unemployed workers during the Great Depression of the 1930s (left) and the recession of today (right) stand in line to apply for jobs and other assistance.
■ *How do the workers of the 1930s compare to those of today? And why is unemployment such an important measure of the health of the economy?*

We measure inflation with the *consumer price index (CPI)*, which shows how much more or how much less consumers are paying for the same "basket of goods" over time. The major components of the CPI basket are food, shelter, fuel, clothing, transportation, and medical care. In turn, we measure unemployment simply by the percentage of able-bodied workers who are looking for jobs but cannot find them. This *unemployment rate* does not include able-bodied workers who have given up looking for work or taken jobs below their skill levels with lower pay.

Experts also use other measures to track the economy. These reveal whether the federal government is borrowing too much money (as measured by the budget deficit), whether it is selling too few goods and services to other nations (as measured by the balance of trade), and how much it is growing (as measured by year-to-year comparisons of the **gross domestic product [GDP]**). The gross domestic product, or GDP, shows the total value of all goods and services produced by the U.S. economy.

Fiscal Policy

Congress and the president make fiscal policy by taxing, borrowing, and spending money. Nothing reflects the growth of federal programs and the rise of big government more clearly than increased spending by the national government. The 2008 rescue plan discussed at the start of this chapter is an example of a particularly aggressive fiscal policy. Under the plan, the federal government used its tax dollars to buy $700 billion of bad debt as a way to unclog the credit markets.

In general, increased government spending and lower taxes are ways to stimulate the economy, whereas decreased spending and higher taxes tend to slow the economy. Higher spending and tax cuts put more money in the pockets of consumers, which increases demand for goods and services, which in turn increases inflation and reduces unemployment. Conversely, lower spending and tax increases take money away from consumers, which reduces demand for goods and services, which in turn reduces inflation and increases unemployment.

The Federal Budget

Today, federal, state, and local governments spend an amount equal to approximately one-third of the nation's GDP. The national government is the biggest spender of all—it spends more than all state and local governments combined, or approximately 23 percent of GDP annually—nearly one dollar of every four spent in the U.S. economy.

gross domestic product (GDP)
The value of all goods and services produced by an economy during a specific period of time such as a year.

Of the People

THE GLOBAL COMMUNITY

Protecting the Environment Versus Economic Growth

Governments sometimes have to choose between fostering economic growth and social progress. On the one hand, they want strong economies. On the other hand, they want to prevent environmental and other problems that might weaken their nations. When choices are linked in this way, they are called trade-offs. During economic crises, governments tend to relax many of their environmental and workplace protections to help stimulate the economy. When the economy recovers, they tend to restore or expand protections.

The Pew Global survey asked respondents their degree of agreement with the statement: "Protecting the environment should given priority, even if it causes slower economic growth and some loss of jobs." As these figures show, most nations share a broad commitment to protecting the environment, even during very tough economic times. (The survey was conducted in the summer of 2009 at the height of the international economic crisis.)

Citizens in India express the highest concerns about protecting the environment in part because pollution has been so damaging throughout the past decades, whereas Americans may perceive that there has already been good progress on environmental protection. When asked about other trade-offs between jobs and helping the needy, however, nations vary greatly. Some nations such as Japan are less likely to support programs for the unemployed in part because

their citizens believe that unemployment is due to an unwillingness to work.

CRITICAL THINKING QUESTIONS

1. Why do Americans put more emphasis on the economy than the environment today? Will these opinions change when the economy improves?

2. What can the federal government do that might help the environment and the economy at the same time?

3. Why is protecting the environment a possible problem for economic recovery?

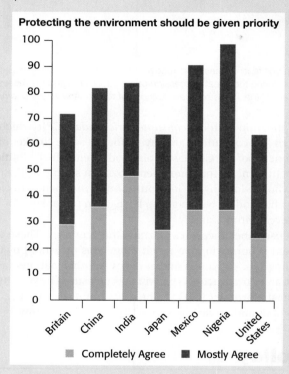

Protecting the environment should be given priority

Britain, China, India, Japan, Mexico, Nigeria, United States

■ Completely Agree   ■ Mostly Agree

The Federal Budget

Today, federal, state, and local governments spend an amount equal to approximately one-third of the nation's GDP. The national government is the biggest spender of all—it spends more than all state and local governments combined, or approximately 23 percent of GDP annually—nearly one dollar of every four spent in the U.S. economy.

Where the Money Comes From   Although Benjamin Franklin once said nothing is more certain than death and taxes, he would be surprised at the range of taxes and other revenue sources used to fund federal spending today (see Figure 18–1 for the percentages from each source):

1. *Individual income taxes.* Taxes on individuals account for the largest share of the federal government's tax revenue. The income tax was prohibited under the Constitution until the Sixteenth Amendment was ratified in 1913.

2. *Payroll taxes.* Payroll taxes to pay for social insurance (Social Security and Medicare) are the second-largest and fastest-rising source of federal revenue. Most workers pay more in Social Security taxes than in federal income taxes.

excise tax
A consumer tax on a specific kind of merchandise, such as tobacco.

5. *Other sources.* Smaller taxes and fees include admission to national parks and camping fees in national forests, taxes on large estates left behind after death, and interest payments on government loans to college students.

6. *Borrowing.* When the federal government does not raise enough revenue to cover all its services, the only way to cover the resulting **budget deficit** is to borrow from citizens, banks, and even foreign governments, by selling Treasury notes and other investments such as saving bonds. As Figure 18–2 shows, borrowing to cover the deficit accounted for an estimated $1.3 trillion in federal revenues in 2008.[1,2]

Giving the people power over taxation was a major achievement in the development of self-government. "No taxation without representation" had been a battle cry in the Revolutionary War. The Constitution clearly provided that Congress "shall have Power to lay and collect Taxes, Duties, Imposts, and Excises" and that **tariffs,** or taxes on imports from other countries, and excise taxes have to be levied, or collected, uniformly throughout the United States.

Taxes are not only a means of raising money, however. In a broad sense, all taxation implies decisions about who gets what, when, where, and how. For example, a **progressive tax** that places higher taxes on individuals and families with higher incomes tends to help individuals and families with lower incomes. In contrast, a **regressive tax,** such as a sales tax collected on everyone's purchases of food and clothing, tends to hurt individuals and families with lower incomes.

Taxes also carry certain costs—it costs money to raise money. Like people who carry large balances on their credit cards, the United States must pay interest on its deficits. Government borrowing adds to the total **national debt,** which is the cumulative total of all deficits over time. In spring 2006, Congress raised the amount of money the federal government could borrow to $9 trillion, which would generate nearly $200 billion in interest payments during the year.

Where the Money Goes   Much of the money the federal government takes in is spent on benefit payments to individuals and on national defense. Measured in absolute dollars spent in 2006, nearly half of federal spending went to required benefit payments for

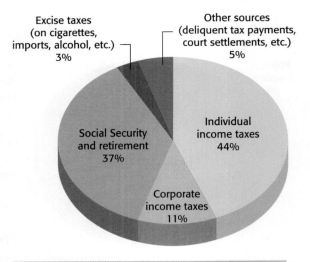

FIGURE 18–1 **Where the Money Comes From, 2010.**

■ *Are the majority of taxes collected by the government progressive or regressive?*

SOURCE: Summary Tables, *Budget of the United States, Fiscal Year 2011* (U.S. Government Printing Office, 2010).

budget deficit
The condition that exists when the federal government raises less revenue than it spends.

tariff
A tax levied on imports to help protect a nation's industries, labor, or farmers from foreign competition. It can also be used to raise additional revenue.

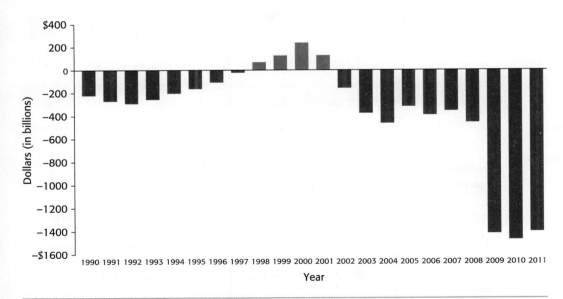

FIGURE 18–2 **The Federal Budget Deficit and Surplus.**

■ *Why has the budget deficit grown so rapidly in recent years?*

SOURCE: Summary Tables, *Budget of the United States, Fiscal Year 2011* (U.S. Government Printing Office, 2010).

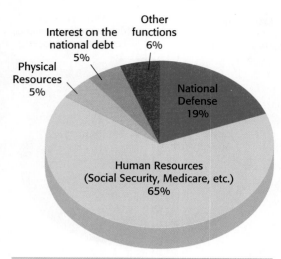

FIGURE 18–3 Where the Money Goes, 2008.

SOURCE: Summary Tables, *Budget of the United States, Fiscal Year 2009* (U.S. Government Printing Office, 2008).

individuals, such as Social Security, Medicare, Medicaid, and other major social programs. Most federal spending is **mandatory,** meaning that Congress and the president cannot use their discretion to change the spending rates. Mandatory programs include Social Security and Medicare for older people and other programs that pay any citizen who qualifies for support (see Figure 18–3). The rest of the spending is **discretionary,** meaning that Congress and the president can change the spending rates.

Two hundred years ago, revenues and spending were so small that neither had a significant impact on the overall economy. In the 2008 federal budget, even small changes in taxes and spending can alter the direction of the economy. However, because many federal programs are open to all eligible citizens, much of the federal budget is "uncontrollable" or nondiscretionary, meaning the bills must be paid regardless of the cost.

The Budget Process

Before Congress enacted the Budget and Accounting Act of 1921, each executive agency dealt with Congress on its own, requesting that the legislature appropriate funds for its activities with little or no presidential coordination. Today, the president is required by law to submit an annual budget proposal for all agencies together.

The Executive Branch The federal government's fiscal, or spending, year begins every October 1. But the budget process begins nearly two years in advance, when the various departments and agencies estimate their needs and propose their budgets to the president.[3] While Congress is debating the budget for the coming fiscal year, the agencies are making estimates for the year after that (see Table 18–1). Agency officials take into account not only their needs as they see them but also the overall presidential program and the probable reactions of Congress. Departmental budgets are detailed; they include estimates of expected needs for personnel, supplies, office space, and the like.

The **Office of Management and Budget (OMB)** is responsible for overseeing the budget process on behalf of the president. Once OMB receives each agency's budget request, its budget examiners review each agency's budget and reconcile it with the president's overall plans. OMB then holds informal hearings with every department and agency to give each one a chance to clarify and defend its estimates.

Once this give-and-take is over, the OMB director gives the president a single document that shows where the federal government's money will come from and where it will go.

progressive tax

A tax graduated so that people with higher incomes pay a larger fraction of their income than people with lower incomes.

regressive tax

A tax whereby people with lower incomes pay a higher fraction of their income than people with higher incomes.

national debt

The total amount of money the federal government has borrowed to finance deficit spending throughout the years.

mandatory spending

Required spending under the federal budget.

discretionary spending

Spending that can be altered by congressional and presidential action.

Office of Management and Budget (OMB)

The presidential staff agency that serves as a clearinghouse for budgetary requests and management improvements for government agencies.

TABLE 18–1	Steps in the Budget Process, Fiscal Year 2011
February–December 2009	Executive branch agencies develop requests for funds, which are reviewed by the Office of Management and Budget and forwarded to the president for final decision.
December 2009	The formal budget documents are prepared.
January–February 2010	The budget is transmitted to Congress as a formal message from the president.
March–September 2010	Congress reviews the president's proposed budget, develops its own budget, and approves spending and revenue bills.
October 1, 2010	Fiscal year 2011 begins (fiscal year is identified by the year that it ends).
October 1, 2010–September 30, 2011	Executive branch agencies execute the budget provided in law.
October–November 2011	Figures on actual spending and receipts for the completed fiscal year become available.

■ *Which step of the process is the most likely to produce budget cuts or increases? What conflicts would you anticipate at different steps?*

The president reviews these figures and makes adjustments. The president must submit the budget recommendations and accompanying message to Congress between the first Monday in January and the first Monday in February.

The Legislative Branch   The president's proposal is only the beginning of the budget process. Under the Constitution, Congress must appropriate the funds and raise the taxes. However, the White House also plays a role in all decisions, if only because all appropriations and tax proposals are subject to a presidential veto. Presidents often threaten to veto these bills as a way of winning passage of their priorities.

Congress acts on the budget in several steps. It starts its process by approving an initial budget resolution that sets the broad spending and revenue goals for the process. It then moves forward with hearings on the budget proposal.

Congress adopted the Budget and Impoundment Control Act of 1974 to strengthen its role in the budget process. This Act requires the president to include proposed changes in tax laws, estimates of amounts of revenue lost through existing preferential tax treatments, and five-year estimates of the costs of new and continuing federal programs. The Act also calls on the president to seek authorizing legislation for a program a year before asking Congress to fund it.

The 1974 Budget Act also created the **Congressional Budget Office (CBO),** an independent agency that prepares budget data on behalf of Congress, and Congress only. By February 15 of each year, the CBO director presents an analysis of the president's budget proposal to the House and Senate budget committees. The CBO director also provides Congress with biannual forecasts of the economy, analyzes alternative fiscal policies, prepares five-year cost estimates for bills proposed by congressional committees, and undertakes studies requested by committees.

Tax Expenditures

Tax expenditures are a final type of fiscal policy that uses the tax code to provide special tax incentives or benefits to individuals and businesses for economic goals such as homeownership, retirement savings, and college education. The federal government spent more than $900 billion in tax expenditures in 2008. Put another way, the federal government lost more than $900 billion in revenue it would have collected without these tax breaks.

Tax expenditures are one means by which the national government carries out public policy objectives. For example, instead of giving out federal grants for research and development (R&D), the government encourages investment in R&D by giving companies tax breaks to invest in innovation and expansion.

However, tax expenditures such as encouraging homeownership do not benefit all levels of society. In many instances, they lead investors to put their money into low-yield investments to obtain large tax benefits, which in turn pulls money out of more productive parts of the economy.

The Politics of Taxing and Spending

In addition to raising funds to run the government, taxes also promote economic growth and reward certain types of behavior, such as contributing to charities. Critics suggest that tax legislation helps individual members of Congress raise campaign funds—laws permitting several of the most popular corporate deductions must be renewed every year, for example, which gives Congress members a chance to show their support for corporations regularly, and corporations a chance to show their support for Congress, too.[4]

As much as taxpayers complain about taxes, most want more of virtually everything the federal government provides. However, there is considerable disagreement about the best type of tax. Some experts argue that a progressive income tax (also called a *graduated income tax*)

Congressional Budget Office (CBO)
An agency of Congress that analyzes presidential budget recommendations and estimates the costs of proposed legislation.

tax expenditure
A loss of tax revenue due to federal laws that provide special tax incentives or benefits to individuals or businesses.

All individual income taxes are due on April 15 of each year. Here, cars line up as taxpayers drop their tax returns at the U.S. Postal Service to make sure they are postmarked on April 15. Failure to pay income taxes on time can result in a fine.

is best because it is relatively easy to collect, takes most from those who are most able to pay, and hardly touches those with little income.

The **sales tax,** which is used only at the state and local levels in the United States, is widely used in Europe in a slightly different version. Called the **value-added tax (VAT),** it applies to the increased value of a product *at each stage of production and distribution* rather than just at the point where it is sold to a customer. A loaf of bread would thus have value added several times: The farmer would pay a value-added tax on the grain before selling to the miller, who would be taxed before selling to the baker, and so forth. Some see the value-added tax as a way to infuse a large amount of new revenue into the federal government.

sales tax
A general tax on sales transactions, sometimes exempting such items as food and drugs.

value-added tax (VAT)
A tax on increased value of a product at each stage of production and distribution rather than just at the point of sale.

Monetary Policy

LEARNING OBJECTIVE
18.3 Outline the way in which the federal government makes monetary policy and the role of monetary policy.

Monetary policy is the second way the federal government manages the economy. The core element of monetary policy is the idea that prices, incomes, and economic stability reflect growth in the amount of money that circulates through the economy at any one time. Advocates of aggressive monetary policy contend that the money supply is the key factor affecting the economy's performance. Even as the federal government used fiscal policy to buy bad debt in 2008, it also used monetary policy to pump more money into the economy to provide greater access to credit.

The Federal Reserve System

Monetary policy is not made by Congress or the president but by the Board of Governors of the **Federal Reserve System** (often simply called "the Fed"). The chair and six members of the Fed's Board of Governors are appointed by the president with Senate consent to 14-year terms; a different member's term expires every two years. As an independent regulatory commission, the Fed is effectively insulated from politics. The governors supervise 12 regional Federal Reserve banks located across the country, each headed by a president and run by a nine-member board of directors chosen from the private financial institutions in each region. The current Fed chair is Ben S. Bernanke, who is thus one of the most powerful policy makers in the world and may have more say over economic performance than the president and Congress.

The Fed has several basic tools for influencing the economy, but its most important involves changing the interest rates banks must pay the Fed for borrowing money, which is called the **federal funds rate.** Increasing the rate slows down the economy by increasing costs for money and credit; lowering the interest rate stimulates the economy by making money more easily available for investment and growth.

The cost of borrowing money is linked to the interest rate a bank's best customers receive on their short-term loans. In turn, this *prime rate* is linked to the interest rates on student loans, home mortgages, car loans, and credit card debt. As Figure 18–4 shows, during the last several years, the Fed has swung between trying to stimulate the economy, slow the economy, and stimulate the economy again.

The rate goes up and down through decisions by the Federal Reserve Board and is based on the current economic situation. In June 2010, the Federal Reserve Board announced that it would keep interest rates low because of continued unemployment. At that time, approximately 9.7 percent of Americans were unemployed, but the number only covered Americans who were actively looking for job, not those who had given up.

Federal Reserve System
The system created by Congress in 1913 to establish banking practices and regulate currency in circulation and the amount of credit available. It consists of 12 regional banks supervised by the Board of Governors. Often simply called "the Fed."

federal funds rate
The amount of interest banks charge for loans to each other.

FIGURE 18–4 Federal Funds Rate, 1998–2010.

■ *Why did the Federal Reserve Board reduce interest rates so drastically in 2007?*

SOURCE: The Federal Reserve Board, Open Market Operations, federalreserve.gov/monetarypolicy/fomc.htm, September 1, 2010.

By the People
MAKING A DIFFERENCE

Join Product Red

Citizens can affect corporate behavior in many ways. They can boycott products that they think are dangerous to the environment, organize protests against companies that treat their employees unfairly, or purchase products such as a cup of fair-trade coffee that help citizens in other countries.

In February 2006, (PRODUCT)RED was launched as a partnership between a group of artists, celebrities, and companies. With the GAP clothing stores in the lead, RED promised to give a portion of every purchase of a RED product such as a sweater, cell phone, laptop, or even car (all colored red, of course) to the Global Fund to Fight AIDS, Tuberculosis, and Malaria.

Corporations clearly had ample incentives to participate, if only because it created greater consumer demand for their products. But they also participated because of a commitment to corporate social responsibility, which is a term that refers to the role that corporations play in improving the quality of life through their own behavior.

Citizens can be involved in RED in many ways. They can join the RED information stream for updates on the fight against AIDS, tuberculosis, and malaria; "brand" their own Web sites by adopting the free RED logo and color scheme; buy RED products; and give money directly to RED. The list of products can be found at http://www.joinred.com. All contributions to RED can be deducted from individual and corporate income taxes.

Although RED was designed as a way to raise money for the Global Fund, it has expanded throughout the past five years to make sure that corporations honor the commitments they make in adopting the RED logo. It also works to make sure the money raised is actually transferred to the Global Fund.

Bono and Oprah Winfrey were the most visible celebrities leading RED.

CRITICAL THINKING QUESTIONS

1. Is RED a form of economic policy and, if so, why? Does it stimulate purchasing that would not have taken place otherwise?

2. How does the federal government support RED?

3. Is RED the best way that citizens can help the world fight AIDS, tuberculosis, and malaria?

Government and Economic Policy

The Great Depression of the 1930s tested competing theories about helping the economy. Some economists urged the government to reduce spending, lower taxes, curb the power of labor, and generally leave business and the economy alone. This first theory is called **laissez-faire economics.**

Another group, deeply influenced by the work of the English economist John Maynard Keynes,[5] recommended that when consumer spending and investment decline, government spending and investing should increase. Government must do the spending and investing during a recession because private enterprise will not or cannot.

This second theory is called **Keynesian economics.** When the economy is in a recession, Keynesians press for more government spending on goods and services to inject money into the economy and stimulate growth. Keynesians believe this spending will "prime the pump" for increased economic activity and stimulate new jobs for the unemployed. When people have more money in their pockets, Keynesians believe at least some of it will be spent—in economic terms, consumer demand will increase.

laissez-faire economics
A theory that opposes governmental interference in economic affairs beyond what is necessary to protect life and property.

Keynesian economics
An economic theory based on the principles of John Maynard Keynes stating that government spending should increase during business slumps and be curbed during booms.

Promoting the Economy

Federal economic policy does more than try to smooth the ups and downs of the business cycle. It also tries to promote economic growth, often measured by the number of new jobs or businesses created. Growth creates jobs for individual workers, which in turn produces higher revenues, which in turn produces either greater savings or more federal spending. U.S. economic policy has two goals: (1) to promote economic growth so that the

LEARNING **OBJECTIVE**

18.4 Identify ways in which the federal government seeks to promote economic growth.

World War II stimulated a huge rise in the production of weapons, airplanes, and tanks, and many women entered the workforce in manufacturing jobs while the men were at war. ■ *What impact did World War II have on the industrial economy? What is the relationship between war and the economy today?*

United States remains a world leader in terms of quality of life, and (2) to regulate business activity so that no single industry or company has an unfair edge in competing for success.

Promoting Economic Growth

The first goal of economic policy is promoting economic growth. The framers believed that developing a strong economy was part of securing the "blessings of liberty," and they encouraged U.S. exports by creating a navy to protect cargo ships. Throughout history, the federal government created a number of departments and agencies to protect that hoped-for growth, including the departments of Agriculture and Commerce and the Small Business Administration.

For example, the Department of Agriculture is a powerful advocate of the farming industry, supporting higher prices for basic products such as corn, barley, oats, wheat, soybeans, cotton, and rice. In 2008 alone, it spent more than $20 billion in *subsidies* by either guaranteeing a minimum price for crops or paying fees to farmers for not planting fields. By altering the supply and price of crops while promoting new products such as biofuels, these subsidies increase the cost of items such as bread, eggs, and soy milk.

Promoting International Trade

Worries about international competition often lead domestic producers to call for **protectionism,** which can take the form of special taxes, or tariffs, placed on imported goods to make them more expensive. Most economists oppose protectionism because it prevents efficient use of resources and because consumers pay much more for protected products than they otherwise would in the world economy. Tariffs merely divert attention from real solutions such as increased productivity and capital investments, and they inevitably invite retaliation from foreign countries.

Trade barriers are less severe today than they were in the 1930s. But restrictions still exist. Certain tariffs, limits on imported goods, and import regulations limit U.S. consumption of foreign products. Most exist to protect U.S. farmers, businesses, or workers in certain industries, but they often do more harm than good by leading other countries to put tariffs and other restrictions on U.S. goods. The result has been a persistent **trade deficit** in which the United States imports far more than it exports.

The United States experienced its first trade deficit in more than a century when the amount of imports exceeded the value of exports in 1971. In the forty years since then, the nation has faced billions of dollars in ever-growing trade deficits. Congress and the president are under continuing pressure from industry, unions, and regional political leaders to protect U.S. jobs, companies, and communities from foreign competition. These pressures come from the textile and auto industries as well as from glass, steel, shoes, lumber, electronics, book publishing, aluminum, farming, and domestic wine and spirit coalitions, to name only a few. Their leaders claim that the trade deficit justifies the imposition of trade sanctions.

Another unfair trade practice is *dumping*—selling products below the cost of manufacturing or below their domestic price with the intention of driving other producers out of the market and then raising prices to profitable levels. Governments might also *subsidize* certain industries. Some countries, for example, subsidize steel for export. Others require lengthy inspection procedures for imported goods. Japan has protected several of its industries—producers of automobiles, baseball bats, and even chopsticks, for example—by setting standards that are virtually impossible for U.S. manufacturers to meet. Japan also sets limits on rice imports.

The World Trade Organization   In 1947, a group of countries formed a trade organization to negotiate free trade by lowering tariffs, quotas (limits on the quantity of a particular

protectionism
A policy of erecting trade barriers to protect domestic industry.

trade deficit
An imbalance in international trade in which the value of imports exceeds the value of exports.

With its rapid growth and development, Dubai is one of the fastest-growing economies in the world. However, with the global recession, Dubai entered a debt crisis in 2010 that shook stock markets across the world, showing the power of individual nations to disrupt the global economy and its members.

World Trade Organization (WTO)
An international organization derived from the General Agreement on Tariffs and Trade (GATT) that promotes free trade around the world.

General Agreement on Tariffs and Trade (GATT)
An international trade organization with more than 130 members that seeks to encourage free trade by lowering tariffs and other trade restrictions.

North American Free Trade Agreement (NAFTA)
An agreement signed by the United States, Canada, and Mexico in 1992 to form the largest free trade zone in the world.

product that may be imported), and other disadvantages countries face when trading. Today, the **World Trade Organization (WTO)** enforces trade agreements that include more than 130 countries, and its membership accounts for four-fifths of the world's trade.

The WTO has conducted eight rounds of negotiations during the past six decades, all of which have amended the **General Agreement on Tariffs and Trade (GATT)** to encourage free trade. The WTO is responsible for overseeing GATT and resolving disputes; it can impose fines and penalties on nations that create protectionist policies.

Not everyone believes free trade should be unlimited, however. Labor unions, environmentalists, and human rights advocates argue that U.S. trade policies spur the creation of low-wage jobs abroad and encourage child labor, pollution, and worker abuse in countries such as China and India that export large quantities of goods to the United States.

The North American Free Trade Agreement In 1992, the United States, Canada, and Mexico signed the **North American Free Trade Agreement (NAFTA),** which formed the largest geographical free trade zone in the world. Although President George H. W. Bush signed NAFTA near the end of his presidency, the agreement could not become law until ratified by Congress. President Bill Clinton promoted NAFTA, even though many members of his own party were its most vigorous opponents. Congress passed it by a thin margin in a bipartisan vote with Democrats in the minority.

Though trade among the United States, Canada, and Mexico is not absolutely "free" or unimpeded, the agreement has had a tremendous impact on the economies of all three countries. Today, Mexico is the United States' third most important trading partner, and the United States is Mexico's most important. Critics remain concerned because Mexican antipollution laws are significantly less stringent than those in the United States, and Mexican workers receive considerably lower wages. Both these factors make relocation to Mexico attractive to many U.S. companies seeking to reduce labor and pollution control costs.

The growth of the global economy has produced efforts to protect U.S. workers from unfair dumping of low-priced products in the United States. Here, cargo containers filled with goods await delivery within the United States. Some goods are priced unfairly because of lower wages in other less-developed countries. ■ *Do you think the U.S. trade deficit is a problem? If so, what should be done?*

YOU WILL
DECIDE
Should the Federal Government Do More to Protect U.S. Jobs?

Workers in the United States receive much higher salaries and benefits than workers in less-developed nations. As U.S. labor costs have risen during the last 30 years, private corporations have moved hundreds of thousands of jobs to other countries. This process, called *offshoring*, creates wide swaths of unemployment in heavy industries such as steelmaking and service industries such as computer support. Although no one is certain how many jobs have left the United States, some estimates suggest more than one million U.S. jobs have been exported to

Mexico, other Central American countries, and China. The number may seem high, but it amounts to a fraction of the U.S. workforce of more than 140 million. Nevertheless, opposition to job migration remains a highly divisive issue between labor and management.

What do you think? Should the federal government do more to protect U.S. jobs? What arguments would you make for and against such an idea?

THINKING IT THROUGH

Most economists agree that efforts to stop the movement of jobs to other nations would hurt the U.S. economy in the longer term.

Liberals tend to agree but argue that the federal government should provide greater help for workers who lose their jobs to foreign nations. "The answer is not to try to stop outsourcing," says former Clinton administration Secretary of Labor Robert Reich, using a popular term for job migration, "but we do have to get serious about job retraining, lifetime learning, extended unemployment insurance, and wage insurance."[6]

Job migration may be the inevitable long-term cost of doing global business, but it has very visible consequences in the short term. Workers whose jobs move abroad often face years of unemployment, which is why the issue has been so controversial.

The United States' economic policy in the future will continue to combine free trade and selective protectionism. Although it shields highly visible industries from competition at home or abroad, protectionism often favors one industry over another, which reduces competition among those industries. In the short run, it helps protect U.S. jobs but may delay economic growth as companies spend more on pay than research and development.

Critical Thinking Questions

1. Why should the United States protect its workers from job migration?

U.S. companies have offshored thousands of jobs, including service call centers, to India and other low-wage nations.

2. Should workers be protected even if doing so results in higher prices for products such as clothing?

3. Do you know of any jobs that have been outsourced? Have you had any contact with a company that uses employees in other nations to deliver basic services?

Regulating the Economy

LEARNING OBJECTIVE

18.5 Categorize ways in which the federal government seeks to regulate the economy.

The second goal of U.S. economic policy is to regulate business activities that may create unfair advantages. U.S. workers believe in competition among businesses, but they also want a level playing field, meaning no industry or company cheats its way to the top or abuses its employees or the environment along the way.

The Constitution explicitly authorizes Congress to regulate commerce among the states and with foreign nations. In our earliest years, Congress used this regulatory power to impose or suspend tariffs on imports from other nations. In the nineteenth century, the federal government created a number of agencies to regulate the conduct of citizens and commercial enterprises with an eye toward promoting economic development. Among these were the Army Corps of Engineers (1824), the Patent and Trademark Office (1836), the Steamboat Inspection Service (1837), and the Copyright Office of the Library of Congress (1870). In 1887, Congress created the Interstate Commerce Commission to deal with widespread dissatisfaction over the practices of railroads.

Regulating Corporations

In a broad sense, regulation is any attempt by the government to control the behavior of corporations, other governments, or citizens. Regulation by government interjects political goals and values into the economy in the form of rules that direct behavior in the marketplace. These rules have the force of law and are backed by the government's police powers.

Congress has created two types of regulatory agencies: independent agencies under the president's control and independent regulatory commissions insulated from Congress and the president. The heads of independent agencies are nominated by the president and confirmed by the Senate, but they do not have terms of office and serve at the pleasure of the president. Independent regulatory commissioners are also appointed by the president and confirmed by the Senate, but they serve for specific terms of office and cannot be removed by a president except for cause.

Although the national government has been regulating interstate commerce since 1789, it was generally reluctant to regulate private businesses until after the Civil War. As the U.S. economy grew, so did the need for rules governing business and labor. Congress created the Interstate Commerce Commission (ICC) in 1887; the first of many independent regulatory commissions, the ICC regulated railroads and other transportation industries but was abolished in the late 1970s as part of the deregulation movement, which we discuss later in this chapter.

Additional regulations were created to end monopolies, increase food safety, prevent environmental pollution, improve automobile safety, and prevent employment discrimination on the basis of race, color, national origin, religion, sex, and age. Estimates vary on how much compliance with these federal regulations costs consumers and businesses, but the amount is in the hundreds of billions of dollars. All economies are regulated by their governments, but the amount of government regulation varies. The United States has a competitive market economy, with relatively little government regulation. It allows wages, prices, and the allocation of goods and services to follow the laws of supply and demand, even when that produces unpopular results, such as the dramatic increase in gasoline prices in 2005–2006. The nation relies on private enterprise and market incentives to carry out most production and distribution.

monopoly
Domination of an industry by a single company; also the company that dominates the industry.

Nevertheless, even opponents of regulation recognize that the market does not always solve every problem. Both political parties say regulatory overkill threatens to overwhelm entrepreneurs and divert them from building vital, innovative companies. The question is not whether there are both costs and benefits from regulation, however, but whether the balance is right. Conservatives tend to overstate the costs of many regulations and understate the benefits, whereas liberals tend to overstate the benefits and understate the costs.

antitrust legislation
Federal laws (starting with the Sherman Antitrust Act of 1890) that try to prevent a monopoly from dominating an industry and restraining trade.

Regulating Competition

Business regulation increased in three major waves during the past century. The first came in the 1910s, the second in the 1930s, and the third in the late 1960s through 1980. In each case, changing circumstances gave rise to the legislation.

Perhaps the most important responsibility of government regulation in a free market system is to maintain competition. When one company gains a **monopoly,** or several create an *oligopoly,* the market system operates ineffectively. The aim of **antitrust legislation** is to prevent monopolies, break up those that exist, and ensure competition. In the past, so-called natural monopolies, such as electric utilities and telephone companies, were protected by the government because it was assumed that in these fields, competition would be grossly inefficient.

In the late nineteenth century, social critics and populist reformers believed that the oil, sugar, whiskey, and steel industries were deceiving consumers, in large part because of the rise of large monopolies called

In August 2010, the Food and Drug Administration ordered grocery stores to remove almost 25 million eggs from their shelves due to an outbreak of salmonella, a deadly disease. ■ *Why does the federal bureaucracy, not state and local governments, regulate the food system?*

trusts. Once they became aware of abuses in these industries, citizens began to call for more government regulation. In 1890, Congress responded by passing the Sherman Antitrust Act, designed "to protect trade and commerce against unlawful restraints and monopolies." However, the Sherman Antitrust Act had little immediate impact; presidents made few attempts to enforce it, and the Supreme Court's early interpretation of the Act limited its scope.[7]

Congress added the Clayton Act to the antitrust arsenal in 1914. This Act outlawed such specific abuses as charging different prices to different buyers in order to destroy a weaker competitor, granting rebates, making false statements about competitors and their products, buying up supplies to suppress competition, and bribing competitors' employees. In addition, *interlocking directorates* (in which an officer or director in one corporation served on the board of a competitor) were banned, and corporations were prohibited from acquiring stock in competing companies if such acquisitions substantially lessened interstate competition. That same year, Congress established the Federal Trade Commission (FTC), run by a five-person board, to enforce the Clayton Act and prevent unfair competitive practices. The FTC was to be the "traffic cop" for competition.[8]

Regulating the Use of Labor

Most laws and rules curb business practices and steer private enterprise into socially useful channels. But regulation cuts two ways. In the case of U.S. workers, most laws in recent decades have tended not to restrict labor but to confer rights and opportunities on it. Actually, many labor laws do not touch labor directly; instead, they regulate labor's relationship with employers.

Federal regulations protect workers in the following important areas, among others:

1. *Public contracts.* The Walsh-Healey Act of 1936, as amended, requires that most workers employed under contracts with the federal government be paid at least the average or prevailing wage for that job, and that they be paid overtime for all work in excess of 8 hours per day or 40 hours per week.
2. *Wages and hours.* The Fair Labor Standards Act of 1938 set a maximum workweek of 40 hours for all employees engaged in interstate commerce or in the production of goods for interstate commerce (with certain exemptions). Work beyond that amount must be paid for at 1.5 times the regular rate.
3. *Child labor.* The Fair Labor Standards Act of 1938 prohibits children from working in any industry that engages in interstate commerce, which essentially means that all child labor is illegal.
4. *Industrial safety and occupational health.* The Occupational Safety and Health Act of 1970 created the first comprehensive federal industrial safety program. It gave the secretary of labor broad authority to set safety and health standards for companies engaged in interstate commerce.

Federal regulations also protect employees' right to organize unions. Under the 1935 National Labor Relations Act (usually called the Wagner Act), for example, the federal government gave workers significant new rights to organize unions, while prohibiting businesses from discriminating against union members or refusing to bargain in good faith with union representatives.

Congress passed a major modification of the labor laws in 1947, the Labor-Management Relations Act, commonly called the Taft-Hartley Act. The Act outlawed the **closed shop,** a company in which only union members in good standing may be hired; permitted the **union shop,** a company in which new employees are obligated to join the union within a stated period of time; prohibited employers from refusing to bargain with employees; allowed courts to issue **labor injunctions** forbidding specific individuals or groups from performing acts considered harmful to the rights or property of an employer or community; and structured the process of **collective bargaining** between unions and employers to set wages, benefits, and working conditions.

trust
A monopoly that controls goods and services, often in combinations that reduce competition.

closed shop
A company with a labor agreement under which union membership is a condition of employment.

union shop
A company in which new employees must join a union within a stated time period.

labor injunction
A court order forbidding specific individuals or groups from performing certain acts (such as striking) that the court considers harmful to the rights and property of an employer or a community.

collective bargaining
A method whereby representatives of the union and employer determine wages, hours, and other conditions of employment through direct negotiation.

Of the People

Female and Minority Board Members

All corporations have boards of directors that wield great power—they oversee executive salaries and compensation, approve major decisions such as mergers and acquisitions of other companies, and attest to the honesty of corporate financial reports.

Although women and minorities now constitute a significant percentage of the U.S. workforce, they occupy relatively few of the seats on the boards of the country's largest corporations. As of 2005, only 12 percent of board members at the nation's 1,500 largest companies were women, and 10 percent were minorities. These percentages have grown slightly during the past decade, but they remain well below the percentage of women and minorities in the workforce. They are also well below the number of women and minorities who work as managers and executives in the largest U.S. corporations.

These percentages may increase in coming years as corporations seek to add more board members under new federal rules adopted in the wake of the accounting scandals at Enron, WorldCom, and other leading corporations. The problem is not a lack of candidates—in 2002, for example, the New American Alliance, a nonprofit association of Latino business leaders, and the Hispanic Association for Corporate Responsibility together created a database of more than 1,000 Hispanic candidates for board openings. If the numbers do not grow, advocacy groups have promised to pressure the Securities and Exchange Commission for a rule requiring greater diversity.

Percentage of Women and Minorities in the Workforce and Board Room, 2005

	Percentage of Women	Percentage of Racial Minorities
U.S. workforce	47%	30%
Executives and managers	35	16
Seats on the boards of the 1,500 largest companies	12	10

SOURCE: Data from Susan Williams, "Board Diversity," Investment Responsibility Resource Center, 2006 Background Report A, March 1, 2006.

CRITICAL THINKING QUESTIONS

1. How do women and minorities improve the performance of major corporations?

2. Why are so few women and minorities appointed to these boards?

3. Should the federal government require that boards be more representative of the population or workforce as a whole?

Regulating Corporate Markets

The stock market crash of 1929 did more than devastate the U.S. economy and usher in the Great Depression. It also revealed deep problems in the way companies sold their stock to investors. Millions of new investors entered the stock market in the 1920s, only to find that the companies in which they had invested were virtually worthless.

Before 1934, investors themselves had to determine whether a company was telling the truth about its stock. Since 1934, that responsibility has fallen to the Securities and Exchange Commission (SEC). Under the Securities Exchange Act of 1934, which established the SEC, and a long list of later laws, companies that offer their stock for sale to the public must tell the truth about their businesses, which means full disclosure of their financial condition.

The Act also required that anyone in the business of selling stocks, including brokers, dealers, and stock exchanges such as the New York Stock Exchange and NASDAQ, must treat investors fairly and honestly, putting investors' interests first. That means, for example, that individuals who know about a new stock offering in advance, or who have other insider information on events that might increase or decrease the value of a given stock, are prohibited from using that information to benefit themselves.

Congress passed a corporate reform bill in 2002 that strengthened the SEC, created a new oversight board to monitor accounting practices, and set new disclosure requirements for reporting corporate profits. The Enron collapse was only one of many highly visible corporate scandals of the early 2000s that included communications companies such as WorldCom and Adelphia. In 2006, Enron executive Kenneth Lay went on trial for stealing money from his company, while WorldCom became part of Verizon Corporation, and Adelphia went out of business.

Clean Air and Water

One of the most visible forms of economic regulation involves nearly 60 years of effort to protect the nation's air and water from pollution. Although early laws such as the 1948 Water Pollution Act and the 1963 Clean Air Act established a federal role in protecting the environment, the 1970 Clean Air and 1972 Clean Water Acts provided much of the legal power to make progress in both areas.

During the past 30 years, the levels of most air pollution covered by the Clean Air Act have fallen dramatically as the U.S. Environmental Protection Agency has established ever-tighter rules promoting more efficient automobiles and cleaner-burning fuels. Although it is hard to find a single American city where the air quality has not improved, air pollution continues to spread to rural areas such as national parks where automobile pollution is concentrated as tourists arrive in record numbers.

Similarly, it is hard to find a single body of water or river that is not significantly cleaner because of the Clean Water Act. However,

The federal government is becoming more concerned about the global environment, including the melting of the polar ice caps, which may raise sea levels dramatically throughout the next 100 years.

as the nation has learned more about pollutants such as arsenic, the pressure to improve water quality has increased. The Obama administration has been moving to expand both acts to cover new pollutants, while tightening limits on acceptable levels

of exposure. It is also pushing for legislation to address the rising global temperature.

Despite these successes, there are many challenges ahead in keeping the air and water clean. The 2010 Gulf oil spill is a good example. As technology has become more sophisticated, the oil industry has been drilling at much greater depths below the water and in much more fragile environments. The Gulf oil spill shows how risky such drilling is, especially since the federal rules governing oil exploration were more than 30 years old when the spill occurred.

CRITICAL THINKING QUESTIONS

1. How clean should the air and water be in order to be declared "clean"?

2. How can the federal government protect the environment without hurting industry and creating unemployment when dirty factories must close?

3. What can citizens do to improve the environment through their own actions?

---

environmental impact statement
A statement required by federal law from all agencies for any project using federal funds to assess the potential effect of the new construction or development on the environment.

Bernie Madoff was convicted of stealing billions of dollars through his stock-market investment fund. Madoff headed his own investment corporation. ■ *What might explain the SEC's failure to catch Madoff's scheme?*

Protecting the Environment

Until the 1960s, the United States did little to protect the environment, and the little that was done was by state and local governments. Recently, the federal government has taken on new responsibilities, starting with passage of the Clean Air and Water Acts in the early 1970s. These put new limits on the amount of pollution companies could release into the environment and launched a long list of laws regulating things, such as leaking underground storage tanks, garbage, and encouraging energy conservation and recycling. Congress also created the Environmental Protection Agency (EPA) to enforce the new laws.

Perhaps the most controversial environmental regulations are **environmental impact statements,** which assess the potential effects of new construction or development on the environment. Most projects using federal funds must prepare such statements, and since 1970, thousands have been filed. Supporters contend that the statements reveal major environmental risks in new construction projects and can lead to cost savings and greater environmental awareness. Critics claim that they represent more government interference, paperwork, and delays in the public and private sectors.

Environmental impact statements are only one form of environmental regulation, however. In 1990, Congress amended the Clean Air Act to tighten controls on automobiles and the fuel they use. Building on earlier mileage regulation, the 1990 amendments required automakers to install pollution controls to reduce emissions of hydrocarbons and nitrogen oxides and set stiff standards for the kinds of gasoline that can be sold. The 1990 Act also required power companies to cut pollution from coal-burning power plants, phased out the use of certain chemicals that harm the earth's protective ozone layer and may contribute to global warming, and set new limits on a long list of cancer-causing pollutants. In 2005, the Bush administration implemented a new set of relatively loose regulations supporting its Clear Skies initiative, but most of these regulations were repealed and replaced by more stringent limits by the Obama administration.

Corporate Responsibility

Many corporations have been dealing with the increased pressure to be more responsible by creating programs to give money and volunteer time to their communities. The Gap has pledged to provide a portion of every sale to charities through "Product Red," and other corporations have promised to be more environmentally conscious. These efforts at **corporate social responsibility** have increased public confidence in big business.

There are three forms of corporate social responsibility. The first is corporate giving to charities. Many corporations have foundations that give 1 or 2 percent of their annual profits to specific causes. The second is free consulting and advertising to help charities become more effective in making their voices heard. The third pairs corporations and charities in partnership activities such as annual walks for cancer. Many corporations also give their employees paid time off to volunteer.

The Deregulation Movement

One response to criticisms of government regulation of the economy is **deregulation,** the reduction or abolition of federal regulation in a particular sector of the economy. Deregulation began in 1977 with the airline, trucking, and railroad industries and has continued with banking and telecommunications.

At the same time that the federal government has been working to deregulate certain industries, it has also created new procedures to limit the amount of regulation it can impose. In 1993, for example, President Clinton issued an executive order prohibiting agencies from issuing regulations unless the benefits of the regulations (in lives saved, for example) outweighed the costs. In 2001, President Bush followed suit by imposing a 60-day hold on all regulations published by the Clinton administration until his administration could ensure that they passed the benefit/cost test.

Deregulating Transportation

No industry has undergone more extensive deregulation than the transportation industry. During the past generation, airlines, trucking, and railroads have been granted considerable freedom in conducting their operations. No deregulation effort has been more visible to consumers than airline deregulation.

The federal government began regulating aviation when it established the Civil Aeronautics Board (CAB) in 1938 to control rates and fares, protecting airlines from unreasonable competition. Critics charged that under regulation, airlines competed only in the frequency of flights and in the services they offered, forcing consumers to pay higher fares than needed.

After years of debate, Congress abolished the CAB in 1978, allowing the market to set fares through competition. The end of airline regulation has created problems but has resulted in generally lower fares, greater choice of routes and fares in most markets, and more efficient use of assets by the industry.[9] If an airline is overcharging passengers, a competitor will eventually steal those travelers away. Carriers have thus had to streamline their operations in order to survive in a competitive market. Southwest, AirTran, and JetBlue Airlines are examples of discount airlines that took advantage of deregulation to take on larger airlines.[10]

But recent mergers of major airlines have worsened the problems that deregulation and cancellation of service brought to small and medium-sized cities in many

LEARNING **OBJECTIVE**

18.6 Evaluate the advantages and disadvantages of the deregulation movement.

corporate social responsibility
Efforts by corporations to improve their reputations by paying attention to their contributions to the social good.

deregulation
A policy promoting cutbacks in the amount of federal regulation in specific areas of economic activity.

JetBlue offers its customers numerous amenities, including free snacks and personal televisions for in-flight entertainment. ■ *How did the deregulation movement allow for the rise of companies such as JetBlue? How has JetBlue been so successful as a start-up airline?*

states and localities. The post–September 11 collapse in travel pushed several airlines toward bankruptcy, which in turn prompted Congress to provide loans to many airlines to help them through the crisis. Under economic pressure, many airlines stopped providing basic services such as meals, and some have demanded deep cutbacks in wages and benefits from their employees. However, some newer airlines such as Jet Blue and Southwest have been highly profitable offering low-cost services across the nation.

A Continued Federal Role

Despite campaign promises to reduce the federal government's economic role and give more money back to citizens and corporations, members of Congress and the president understand that the federal government must be active in the economic life of the nation. It will continue to collect taxes, regulate the money supply, prevent monopolies that would hurt consumers, and promote free trade. It will do all this while trying to let the market, not government regulators, shape the demand for and the price of products and services. Most U.S. adults want their government to play only a limited role in the economy, but competing values such as fairness, equality, protection of workers and the environment, and support of healthy competition inevitably encourage elected officials to take on referee responsibilities in order to promote the common good.

Citizens exert a great deal of influence on economic policy, if only by purchasing goods and services. But they can also influence policy through pressure on their representatives. The economy was a top concern in the 2008 presidential elections and led both the Democratic and Republican parties to push hard for action to protect homeowners from unscrupulous lenders and stimulate energy production.

CHAPTER **SUMMARY**

18.1 Describe the federal government's economic policy making role and how economic performance is measured.

Inflation and unemployment are considered the two most important measures of economic performance, although we also use the size of the federal budget deficit, the U.S. trade deficit or surplus with other nations, and gross domestic product (GDP). Inflation and unemployment tend to move together in opposite directions—inflation rises as unemployment drops, and it falls as unemployment rises. Other measures of economic performance include the amount of government spending and the balance of trade.

18.2 Outline the way in which the federal government makes fiscal policy and the role of fiscal policy.

Fiscal policy consists of economic policies made by Congress, the president, and the judiciary. There are two basic types—collecting revenues through taxes and fees and spending money through the federal budget. Increasing government spending stimulates

the economy, thereby reducing unemployment, whereas increasing taxes generally slows economic growth, thereby curtailing inflation. The federal government also spends money through tax expenditures hidden from public view.

18.3 Outline the way in which the federal government makes monetary policy and the role of monetary policy.

Monetary policy, made by the Federal Reserve Board (the Fed), is designed to affect the flow of money through the economy. The Fed's most important tool is the federal funds rate, the amount of interest it allows banks to charge each other on short-term loans. Raising the cost of money is generally a way to slow down the economy and reduce inflation; lowering the cost of money ignites the economy and reduces unemployment.

18.4 Identify ways in which the federal government seeks to promote economic growth.

The federal government has long promoted the economy and specific industries. It also promotes trade and commerce with other nations, including efforts to reduce barriers to imports and exports, stabilize prices of certain goods and services, and encourage innovation through patents and other protections.

18.5 Categorize ways in which the federal government seeks to regulate the economy.

Economic regulation is designed to control the behavior of the economy in a variety of ways such as preventing monopolies, reducing environmental pollution, and protecting workers. Many regulations were designed to curb specific abuses and promote competition.

18.6 Evaluate the advantages and disadvantages of the deregulation movement.

The deregulation movement is driven by the belief that regulations are too costly and often fail to achieve their desired ends. Democrats and Republicans have both supported deregulation of key industries during the past four decades, but it sometimes produces new problems that create a backlash in favor of reregulation. Although air fares dropped immediately after airline deregulation, for instance, they have moved upward as many airline companies have merged to reduce competition.

CHAPTER **SELF-TEST**

18.1 Describe the federal government's economic policy making role and how economic performance is measured.

1. Explain the interaction between *inflation* and *unemployment*. Define the terms, and draw a diagram to demonstrate their relationship.
2. Differentiate fiscal policy from monetary policy.
3. Match the following definitions to their terms
   a. Rising prices on goods and services.
   b. Joblessness among employable workers.
   c. Uses federal spending and taxation to stimulate or slow the economy.
   d. Manipulates the supply of money to keep the economy from swinging wildly from boom to bust.
      i. Fiscal policy
      ii. Monetary policy
      iii. Unemployment
      iv. Inflation

18.2 Outline the way in which the federal government makes fiscal policy and the role of fiscal policy.

4. What are the main sources of income and biggest expenditures of the federal government?
5. Examine Table 18–1: Steps in the Budget Process. Identify the important actors at each step of the process, and analyze the roles of the executive and legislative branch in the budget process.

18.3 Outline the way in which the federal government makes monetary policy and the role of monetary policy.

6. When the Federal Reserve Board lowers the federal funds rate, what is the intended consequence?

7. In one or two paragraphs, explain why it is so difficult for the Fed to anticipate the full consequences of its decisions.
8. Write a brief persuasive essay explaining what you believe the government's proper role in the economy should be.

18.4 Identify ways in which the federal government seeks to promote economic growth.

9. Define protectionism, and provide examples.
10. Why does the federal government promote industries such as agriculture but not industries such as computers? Is federal promotion of certain industries fair to American consumers and taxpayers?

18.5 Categorize ways in which the federal government seeks to regulate the economy.

11. In two or three paragraphs, explain the relationship between the real economic situation and economic theory. For example, when are people more likely to argue for *more* or *less* regulation?
12. Why does the federal government encourage corporate social responsibility? Why would corporate social responsibility help reduce federal spending?

18.6 Evaluate the advantages and disadvantages of the deregulation movement.

13. In a few paragraphs, describe the process and results of the deregulation of the airline industry.

Answers to selected questions: 3. a. iv; b. iii; c. i; d. ii

mypoliscilab EXERCISES

Apply what you learned in this chapter on MyPoliSciLab.

Read on mypoliscilab.com

eText: Chapter 18

Study and Review on mypoliscilab.com

Pre-Test
Post-Test
Chapter Exam
Flashcards

Watch on mypoliscilab.com

Video: Recession Hits Indiana
Video: The Stimulus Breakdown
Video: Economic Policy Debate at the G20
Video: Fed Approves Mortgage Crackdown

Explore on mypoliscilab.com

Simulation: You Are the President and Need to Get a Tax Cut Passed
Simulation: Making Economic Policy
Comparative: Comparing Economic Policy
Timeline: Growth of the Budget and Federal Spending
Visual Literacy: Evaluating Federal Spending and Economic Policy
Visual Literacy: Where the Money Goes

KEY TERMS

fiscal policy, p. 480
monetary policy, p. 480
inflation, p. 480
unemployment, p. 480
stagflation, p. 480
gross domestic product (GDP), p. 481
excise tax, p. 482
budget deficit, p. 483
tariff, p. 483
progressive tax, p. 484
regressive tax, p. 484
national debt, p. 484
mandatory spending, p. 484
discretionary spending, p. 484

Office of Management and Budget (OMB), p. 484
Congressional Budget Office (CBO), p. 485
tax expenditure, p. 485
sales tax, p. 486
value-added tax (VAT), p. 486
Federal Reserve System, p. 486
federal funds rate, p. 486
laissez-faire economics, p. 487
Keynesian economics, p. 487
protectionism, p. 488
trade deficit, p. 488
World Trade Organization (WTO), p. 489
General Agreement on Tariffs and Trade (GATT), p. 489

North American Free Trade Agreement (NAFTA), p. 489
monopoly, p. 491
antitrust legislation, p. 491
trust, p. 492
closed shop, p. 492
union shop, p. 492
labor injunction, p. 492
collective bargaining, p. 492
environmental impact statement, p. 494
corporate social responsibility, p. 495
deregulation, p. 495

ADDITIONAL RESOURCES

FURTHER READING

STEPHEN G. BREYER, *Breaking the Vicious Circle: Toward Effective Risk Regulation* (Harvard University Press, 1993).

GARY BRYNER, *Blue Skies, Green Politics: The Clean Air Act of 1990 and Its Interpretation,* 2d ed. (CQ Press, 1995).

GARY BURTLESS, ROBERT J. LAWRENCE, ROBERT E. LITAN, AND ROBERT J. SHAPIRO, *Globaphobia: Confronting Fears About Open Trade* (Brookings Institution Press, 1998).

THOMAS W. CHURCH AND ROBERT T. NAKAMURA, *Cleaning Up the Mess:*

Implementation Strategies in Superfund (Brookings Institution Press, 1993).

ROBERT W. CRANDALL AND HAROLD FURCHTGOTT-ROTH, *Cable TV: Regulation or Competition?* (Brookings Institution Press, 1996).

ROBERT M. ENTMAN, *Competition, Innovation, and Investment in Telecommunications* (Aspen Institute, 1998).

THOMAS L. FRIEDMAN, *The World Is Flat: A Brief History of the Twenty-First Century* (Farrar, Straus, & Giroux, 2005).

PHILIP K. HOWARD, *The Death of Common Sense: How Law Is Suffocating America* (Random House, 1994).

CORNELIUS M. KERWIN, *Rulemaking: How Government Agencies Write Law and Make Policy,* 2d ed. (CQ Press, 1998).

PAUL KRUGMAN, *The Return of Depression Economics and the Crisis of 2008* (W.W. Norton, 2009).

ROBERT KUTTNER, *Everything for Sale: The Virtues and Limits of Markets* (Knopf, 1997).

MICHAEL LEWIS, *The Big Short: Inside the Doomsday Machine* (W.W. Norton, 2010).

PETER G. PETERSON, *Facing Up: Paying Our Nation's Debt and Saving Our Children's Future* (Simon & Schuster, 1994).

ANDREW ROSS SORKIN, *Too Big to Fail: The Inside Story of How Wall Street and Washington Fought to Save the Financial System and Themselves* (Viking, 2010).

ALLEN SCHICK, *The Federal Budget: Politics, Policy, Process,* rev. ed. (Brookings Institution Press, 2007).

JOSEPH E. STIGLITZ, *Globalization and Its Discontents* (Norton, 2002).

DANIEL YERGIN AND **JOSEPH STANISLAW,** *The Commanding Heights: The Battle Between Government and the Marketplace That Is Remaking the Modern World* (Simon & Schuster, 1998).

WEB SITES

OMB.gov All the information on what the federal government has spent in the past and will spend in the future. Specific information on historical trends can be found in the historical tables section of the federal budget.

Federalreserve.gov The key Web site for information on monetary policy.

Spending.gov An easily accessible source of information on where the federal dollars go.

ConcordCoalition.org A nonpartisan interest group that promotes reductions in the federal deficit.

CTJ.org The Citizens for Tax Justice (CTJ) Web site. CTJ is a conservative interest group that promotes reductions in federal taxes.

CBPP.org The Web site for the Center on Budget and Policy Priorities. CBBP is a liberal interest group that provides analysis of fiscal policy and programs.

npr.org National Public Radio offers a free series of podcasts on our rapidly changing global economy called Planet Money.

CHAPTER 19

Making Social Policy

President Barack Obama entered office with one of the largest domestic policy agendas since Lyndon Johnson in the 1960s. Alongside the need for quick action on stimulating the economy, he had promised health insurance for the poor, a complete overhaul of the No Child Left Behind Act, expansion of AmeriCorps and volunteerism, and a jobs program for the unemployed.

No priority was more contentious than health insurance for the millions of Americans without coverage for either hospital or physician care. Obama started the process with a dramatic proposal to establish a new government insurance plan called the "public option" that would give all Americans, insured or not, the chance to participate in a new national insurance program modeled on the Medicare program discussed later in this chapter. His bill would have also forced employers to pay for insurance, guaranteed citizens the right to keep their physicians, prohibited insurance companies from denying coverage because of preexisting medical conditions, and provided a host of benefits for specific problems such as elder care.

Facing mounting resistance from the public toward the plan, Obama eventually moved to what his chief of staff called the "skinny bill;" Speaker of the House Nancy Pelosi derided the scaled-back bill as "kiddie care."[1] She demanded something bigger, arguing that this was a once-in-a-lifetime chance to complete the work that Franklin Delano Roosevelt and Harry S. Truman had begun in the 1930s and 1940s.

After months of negotiations, Obama and congressional Democrats reluctantly agreed to drop the public option. In its place, the final bill required every American to purchase health insurance or face a stiff federal penalty. The bill also included new taxes on "Cadillac" private insurance plans that give higher-income Americans almost complete coverage for nearly every medical, dental, and home-health care service. As enacted, the Patient Protection and Affordable Health Care for America Act included most of Obama's original requests, but at more modest levels. In the end, the Act provided insurance coverage for nearly 32 million citizens but still left 5 percent of the population uncovered.

Last-minute bargaining produced just enough votes for passage, and the $1 trillion program became law with the president's signature in March 2010. It is still too early to know whether the bill will cost or save money. Democrats argued that the final bill would produce $150 billion per year in savings, but Republicans argued it would cost $50 billion more per year. However, no one is sure how Americans will respond to the law, which will determine whether the federal government will have to spend more or less money.

The health care negotiations illustrate the difficulties in both designing and enacting a major new federal social program. No matter how well intended new legislation may be, new programs require time to take hold and do not always work as intended. Unfortunately for low-income older adults, time is of the essence if the federal government is to guarantee the Constitution's promise to promote the general welfare of its citizens.

This chapter will explore how the federal government promotes the general welfare through a range of social programs, how that promise has expanded throughout the past century, and what remains to be done to protect low-income Americans. It will also examine three areas of social policy likely to be active throughout the next few years: health, education, and crime control.

Citizens have a clear interest in social policy, if only because the federal government and its state and local partners are there to protect them in crisis. But as members of interest groups large and small, such as the Children's Defense Fund or the American Association of Retired Persons (AARP), with nearly 40 million dues-paying members, all over the age of 50, they can make their voices heard on major issues such as health care reform.

CHAPTER OUTLINE & CHAPTER LEARNING OBJECTIVES

The Role of the Federal Government in Social Policy

19.1 Outline the goals of the federal government's social policy and the forms of protection it provides.

The Expansion of Social Policy in the Twentieth Century

19.2 Outline the evolution of social policy throughout the twentieth century.

Social Policy Challenges for the Future: Health, Education, and Crime

19.3 Evaluate the current status of and challenges for federal government policy in the areas of health care, education, and crime.

The Politics of Social Policy

The Role of the Federal Government in Social Policy

19.1 Outline the goals of the federal government's social policy and the forms of protection it provides.

Most Western governments expanded their social programs long before the United States did. American adults generally believed that people who could not succeed in a nation as big, rich, and open as the United States simply weren't working hard enough. This commitment to *rugged individualism* meant that government, whether local, state, or federal, played only a limited role in people's lives. Rather grudgingly, state governments in the early twentieth century extended relief to low-income groups, especially the old, the blind, and the orphaned. But government aid was limited, and most low-income people relied on charity for help, as many still do.[2]

This is not to suggest that the federal government ignored domestic policy, however. From its founding, the government took care of its military veterans. Indeed, with the Revolutionary War barely over, the Continental Congress established the nation's first programs to help soldiers disabled in battle and to provide retirement pensions for officers, well before the new government was even created.

Established in the 1780s, the financial security system for veterans expanded slowly but steadily as the soldiers aged into disability and poverty. Citizens could not stand to see their veterans in tattered clothing and felt obliged to provide support for the less fortunate. In 1818, for example, Congress expanded retirement benefits to cover all veterans of the Revolutionary War, whether officers or not, and created the first old soldiers' homes for poor veterans. In 1840, Congress expanded the veterans program again to provide financial relief to the widows of soldiers killed in battle.[3]

These early programs set two important precedents for contemporary domestic policy. First, they established the notion that some people would be automatically entitled to certain government benefits on the basis of an eligibility requirement such as service in the nation's armed forces. Thus, veterans' relief was the nation's first **entitlement,** under which the government provides benefits to any citizen who is eligible regardless of need. Throughout the decades since, Congress and the president have created dozens of entitlement programs, including Social Security and Medicare. Both programs provide benefits to anyone who has paid taxes for them and are available once an individual reaches retirement age.

Second, these early programs also established government's right to restrict some benefits to only those citizens who could actually prove their need for help. In the original program, for instance, only poor veterans could go to old soldiers' homes. These were early examples of what we now call **means-tested entitlements,** under which citizens must

entitlements
Programs such as unemployment insurance, disaster relief, or disability payments that provide benefits to all eligible citizens.

means-tested entitlements
Programs such as Medicaid and welfare under which applicants must meet eligibility requirements based on need.

Although the federal government has become much more involved in helping the needy, private charities still provide nearly three-quarters of the free food for the hungry in the United States. ■ *Why are both private charities and government programs important for social welfare in America?*

prove they are poor enough to deserve the government's help. Throughout the decades since, Congress and the president have created dozens of means-tested entitlement programs, including Supplemental Security Income and food stamps. Both programs provide benefits only to those who can prove they are below a certain income level.

Having entered the twentieth century with only a handful of domestic programs, most of which were built around helping veterans, the federal government left the century with a deep inventory of such programs. According to the 2008 *Catalog of Federal Domestic Assistance,* which lists every one of the federal government's approximately 1,250 domestic funding programs in a searchable database (www.cfda.gov), there are at least 38 separate programs for farmers, another 35 for college and university students, 34 for women, and 44 for infants.

The Goals of Social Policy

Because most of these programs are restricted to one group of citizens only, they are often described as *categorical* aid. Simply typing a search term online such as "students," "elderly," "children," "disabled," "workers," "farmers," "women," or "veterans" reveals just how much help the federal government provides in each category. But regardless of category, federal domestic policy focuses on two broad goals.

The first goal is to protect citizens against social and economic problems by creating a **social safety net,** whether through relief for unemployed workers, health care for the elderly, emergency shelter for the homeless, or school lunches for poor children, most of which are available to citizens only on the basis of a means test that proves they need help. Although almost all citizens are covered by federal unemployment insurance through a payroll tax, only workers who have been laid off from their jobs through no fault of their own can qualify for benefits, and then only for a relatively brief period of time.

The second goal of federal social policy is to raise the quality of life for all, whether by improving air and water quality, building roads and bridges, regulating air traffic, fighting crime, or strengthening local schools through federal aid. Nearly all federal aid to the states for these purposes is distributed by formula on the basis of population, not need.

Types of Protection

Most scholars trace the federal government's effort to protect citizens against economic and personal hard times to the Great Depression and the Social Security Act of 1935. Although Franklin Roosevelt's New Deal agenda stimulated a remarkable expansion in

social safety net
The many programs that the federal government provides to protect Americans against economic and social misfortune.

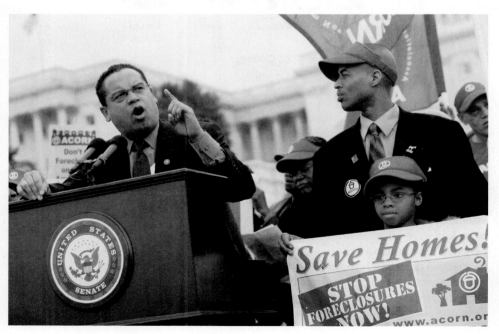

The collapse of the economy in 2008 meant that millions of people lost their homes because they could not pay their mortgages. Here, citizens ask government for action to help keep their homes.

Of the People

THE GLOBAL COMMUNITY

Experience with Poverty

The social safety net is a response to continuing problems such as hunger, disease, and poverty. Although countries vary greatly in the amount of need, the Pew Global Survey shows that significant percentages of citizens go without access to basic human needs every year.

The survey asked respondents, "Have there been times during the last year when you did not have enough money to (a) buy food your family needed, (b) pay for medical care your family needed, (c) and buy clothing your family needed?"

These answers provide a barometer of economic and social progress. All nations were hard hit by the 2008 recession, but the safety net appears to have been stronger in Britain, China, India, and Japan than it was in Mexico, Nigeria, and the United States.

China shows the greatest variation in the strength of its safety net—whereas its citizens report fewer problems buying food and clothing, a third said they had problems with access to health care in 2009. The problem lies in the rapid expansion of the Chinese population, which is putting pressure on the health system. Although the Chinese economy is growing rapidly too, the country has faced difficulty converting its growth into health care access.

CRITICAL THINKING QUESTIONS

1. Besides the economy, why might citizens in some countries have greater problems getting access to basic necessities such as food, health care, and clothing?

2. Does this lack of access have an impact on trust in government and other measures of citizen participation? What is the effect of hunger and poverty on how citizens think of other freedoms?

3. Why do so many Americans report lack of access to basic necessities? Are you surprised?

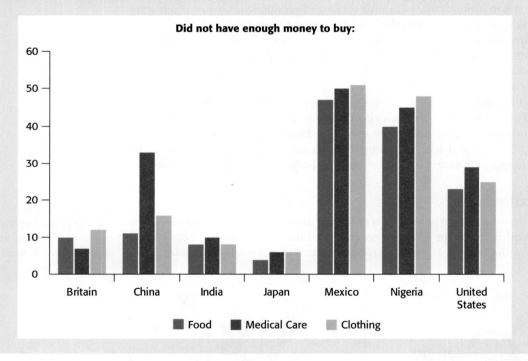

Did not have enough money to buy:

■ Food ■ Medical Care ■ Clothing

the federal government's domestic policy role, federal, state, and local governments were helping citizens long before the Depression hit. However, as the nation sunk deeper into economic distress, Congress and the president soon invented two very different types of federal programs to protect citizens against hardship, both of which continue today.

Public Assistance   One type of help for the poor is called **public assistance,** or "welfare." The first public assistance programs were actually created in the late 1800s, when states established aid programs to help poor single mothers and their children. Although these programs were often described as "mothers' pensions" to create the impression that the beneficiaries had earned the benefits through some contribution, they created a precedent for many of the federal government's later antipoverty programs.

Most of these programs are means-tested entitlement programs. As noted earlier, such programs require applicants to disclose all financial assets and income to prove they fall below the poverty line, generally calculated as three times the amount of money an individual

public assistance
Aid to the poor; "welfare."

or family needs to purchase the food for a nutritious diet. This poverty level changes with the size of the family and the cost of living. For 2008, individuals who made slightly more than $10,000 and families of four who made slightly more than $21,000 were eligible for means-tested assistance.[4]

Public assistance in the United States today incorporates elements of job training, transportation subsidies, housing subsidies, free school lunches, food aid for poor families and pregnant mothers with young children, and tax credits for low-income people. The federal government also provides what some critics label "corporate welfare" to favored industries such as agriculture and corporate bailouts to businesses like investment bank Bear Stearns, as well as "middle-class welfare" to college students, home buyers, and the citizenry as a whole in the form of college loans, tax deductions for home mortgages, and access to national parks and forests (supported by taxpayers but rarely used by poor people). However, the term "welfare" is generally reserved for public assistance to the low-income Americans.

In absolute numbers, most poor people are white. As a percentage within their own population, however, a larger proportion of African Americans and Hispanics are poor. Moreover, in both absolute and proportional terms, more women than men are poor. Indeed, some scholars refer to the relatively recent rise in poverty among women as the "feminization of poverty."[5]

CDMM2080000   Austin, TX: Food stamps ready for mailing. Replaced by Lone Star card. ©Bob Daemmrich / The Image Works   NOTE: The copyright notice must include "The Image Works"
DO NOT SHORTEN THE NAME OF THE COMPANY

Food stamps, which today are often distributed as debit cards for food purchases, allow needy families to purchase nutritious food. In 2010, the food stamp program fed 1 in 8 Americans and 1 in 4 children in America.
■ *Why were food stamps created as an entitlement program?*

Social Insurance   The second type of protection against hardship is **social insurance,** government programs that provide benefits to anyone who is eligible because of either past service (veterans, miners, merchant marines) or prepayments of some kind (payroll taxes for Social Security and Medicare or insurance premiums).

Many federal assistance programs are partnerships with state governments. There are two reasons for the connection. First, except for veterans' policy, states have been responsible for protecting their citizens against hardship since the United States was formed. Second, state and local governments have the administrative agencies to stay in touch with recipients of aid, whether to make sure they are actually eligible for support or to provide services such as job training or school lunches.

Because states vary greatly in their generosity, most federal assistance is designed to set a minimum floor of support that individual states can raise on their own. The most generous states in the country tend to be located in the Northeast and West, where living costs tend to be higher and legislatures more liberal, whereas the least generous tend to be found in the South. In this way, states act as a check on the federal government's ability to raise benefits too far, frustrating those who believe that the federal government should set a uniform level of benefits for all citizens. (Table 19–1 shows the amount of federal payments to individuals in 2010.)

The Expansion of Social Policy in the Twentieth Century

The federal government's commitment to helping the poor and improving the quality of life expanded rapidly during the Great Depression, which followed the stock market crash of 1929. The social safety net built by state and local governments and private charities at that time simply could not meet the needs of the huge increase in the homeless, unemployed, and poor.

The New Deal

Franklin Roosevelt was responsible for the expansion of social programs during the 1930s. As part of his New Deal agenda, the federal government began making loans to

LEARNING **OBJECTIVE**

19.2 Outline the evolution of social policy throughout the twentieth century.

social insurance
Programs in which eligibility is based on prior contributions to government, usually in the form of payroll taxes.

For the People

GOVERNMENT'S GREATEST ENDEAVORS

Helping the Working Poor

The federal government has passed many laws to help low-income workers make ends meet, including increasing the minimum wage, providing help for day care centers, and creating job-training programs.

Between the end of World War II and today, the federal government has increased the minimum wage from 40 cents an hour in 1945 to $4.25 in 1989 and $5.15 in 1997. Although the federal minimum wage was increased to $7.25 an hour in 2007, many states have raised the amount even higher on their own. Connecticut's minimum wage is $8.25 an hour, while Oregon's is $8.40. States are free to pay more than the federal minimum wage, but not less.

The federal government's greatest contribution to helping low-income workers came in 1975 with the creation of the Earned Income Tax Credit (EITC), which reduces or completely eliminates all taxes for the working poor. Under the EITC, low-income workers also receive money back from the federal government to help raise their income. Because the money comes in the form of a tax refund, not a welfare check, many experts

EHVZ049000 Wallingford, Connecticut: Hispanic seventeen (17) year old McDonald's Restaurant employee serving customers hamburgers, french fries and other fast food from behind the counter and cash register. October 16, 2002 ©Peter Hvizdak / The Image Works

NOTE: The copyright notice must include "The Image Works" DO NOT SHORTEN THE NAME OF THE COMPANY

Many restaurant workers earn minimum wage. But some employers such as McDonald's pay slightly higher wages to make sure their workers stay longer on the job.

believe that low-income workers are less embarrassed to take the federal support.

The EITC has clearly reduced poverty rates among low-income workers. In 2010, for example, nearly 25 million low-income workers received more than $50 billion

through the program, which lifted more than 5 million Americans above the poverty line. The program has been particularly effective in helping unmarried working mothers, who often take minimum-wage jobs in the service industry (fast-food restaurants, dry cleaners, day care centers, grocery stores, and so forth). The maximum credit for the 2009 tax year, which can be used to pay taxes owed or taken as a refund, was $5,657 for a family with three or more children, $5,028 for a family with two children, $3,043 for a family with one child, and $457 if there are no children.

CRITICAL THINKING QUESTIONS

1. Besides raising the minimum wage and increasing the EITC, what other ways might the federal government help low-income workers?

2. Have you ever held a minimum-wage job? Was it or do you think it would be enough to live on by yourself?

3. What would Americans think about the EITC if they knew how much it paid?

---

states and localities to help the poor, and soon it launched a long list of programs to help older workers (Social Security), the jobless (unemployment insurance), and the poor (Aid to Families with Dependent Children).

The First 100 Days Before creating these signature New Deal programs, however, the Roosevelt administration moved quickly to help low-income Americans. The first

TABLE

19–1 | Federal Payments to Individuals, 2010

Major Public Assistance Programs, 2010

Medicaid	$275 billion
Food stamps (now called SNAP)	72 billion
Earned Income Tax Credit	50 billion
Supplemental Security Income	44 billion
Family support payments to states	22 billion
Child nutrition	17 billion
State Children's Health Insurance Program	9 billion
Social Insurance	
Social Security	$721 billion
Medicare	520 billion
Unemployment insurance	190 billion
Disability insurance	124 billion

■ *Why is social security so expensive, and why is its cost increasing rapidly?*

SOURCE: Summary Tables, *Historical Tables, Budget of the United States, Fiscal Year 2011* (U.S. Government Printing Office, February 2009).

100 days of 1933 produced the most significant list of legislation ever passed in U.S. history, including the Federal Emergency Relief Administration (FERA), which was established to give unemployed workers cash grants to get them through the summer.

The list of "alphabet agencies" grew longer as the administration created a host of new programs to help the poor, including the Works Progress Administration (WPA), which was created in 1935 to provide work for millions of unemployed, and the Civilian Conservation Corps (CCC), which put millions of young people to work clearing trails and building roads in the national forests and parks. Between 1933 and 1945, for example, the WPA put 8.5 million people to work at a cost of $10 billion. All told, the WPA built 650,000 miles of roads, 125,000 public buildings, 8,200 parks, and 850 airports. Though the wages were hardly generous, these and other New Deal programs created a national safety net to catch those in need. It is little wonder that scholars describe the New Deal as the "big bang" of social policy.[6] Although the distinction between the worthy and unworthy poor still remained, joblessness was no longer defined as merely a problem of individual idleness or the unwillingness to work.

Help for Older Citizens   Once past the immediate crisis, the Roosevelt administration began designing the flagship programs of the New Deal. First on the list was **Social Security,** enacted in 1935 and still the federal government's most popular social program. Social Security was designed to meet two goals: (1) provide a minimum income for poor beneficiaries, and (2) ensure that benefits bear a relationship to the amount of payroll taxes a beneficiary actually paid. Supported by equal contributions from employers and employees, the program now covers more than 90 percent of the U.S. workforce.[7] Employees pay half of the annual Social Security tax, which applies to income up to $102,000 per year. The tax is identified on pay stubs as FICA, which stands for the Federal Insurance Contribution Act, and also covers disability insurance for injuries on the job.

Social Security was expanded in 1939 to include financial support for survivors of workers covered by Social Security when the retired worker died, and in 1954, it was expanded again to include support for disabled workers and the children of deceased or disabled workers. Benefit levels were raised repeatedly during the first 40 years of the program, often just before an election. The increases became so frequent and so costly that in 1975, Congress finally indexed benefits to rise only with inflation. Under legislation enacted in 1983, the Social Security retirement age started to rise in 2003 and will reach 67 by the year 2027.

Until the 1970s, steady growth in Social Security benefits was relatively uncontroversial, largely because "the costs were initially deceptively low," making the system politically painless.[8] It is now the world's largest insurance program for retirees, survivors, and people with disabilities. In 2008, Social Security and Medicare expenditures totaled $966 billion.

Employees now pay more in annual Social Security payroll taxes than in income tax. Employees paid a 6.2 percent FICA tax on all wages up to $102,000 in 2010, and an additional 1.45 percent on all of their wages, both above and below $94,200 for Medicare health coverage. All employee taxes are matched dollar for dollar by employers. People who are self-employed pay both the employee and employer taxes.

The aging of the U.S. population (discussed in Chapter 5) would not affect Social Security and Medicare if the payroll taxes coming into the two programs from today's workers were deposited in individual savings accounts for their eventual retirement. But much of the revenue actually goes to payments for *today's* retirees. Social Security is thus a "pay-as-you-go" system, in which today's young workers finance the retirement of today's elderly. At some point, in the not-too-distant future, there will not be enough workers paying taxes to cover the benefits. Sooner or later, Congress will have to decide whether to raise taxes on workers, cut benefits for retirees, increase the retirement age, or some combination of all three. Experts differ on when the next Social Security funding crisis will come, but they agree that something will have to be done to ensure the viability of Social Security for young people now paying into the system.[9]

Help for the Poor   The federal government began protecting women and children against poverty when Congress passed the Infancy and Maternity Protection Act of 1921. Supported by many of the same women's groups that had just won ratification of the Nineteenth Amendment, which gave women the right to vote, the Act gave the newly

Social Security
A combination of entitlement programs, paid for by employer and employee taxes, that includes retirement benefits, health insurance, and support for disabled workers and the children of deceased or disabled workers.

Many senior citizens rely on Social Security benefits to see them through their retirement years. This entitlement program covers more than 90 percent of the American workforce. ■ *What are the arguments for and against making Social Security a means-tested program?*

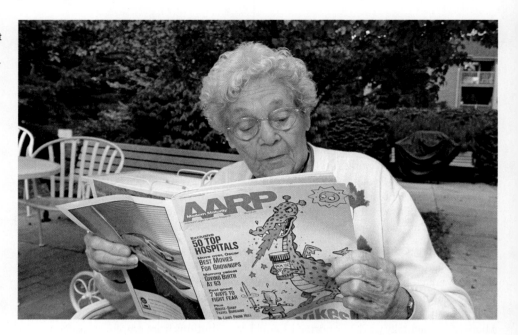

created federal Children's Bureau funds to encourage states to create new maternal, infant, and early childhood health programs.

This precedent eventually produced the Aid to Families with Dependent Children (AFDC) program in 1935.[10] As its name suggests, AFDC tried to reduce public opposition to expanded benefits by shifting the focus away from what the mother had done or not done to deserve poverty, and onto the children, who suffered whatever the cause. Under the program, states were given federal money to establish cash grants for poor families under two conditions: states had to (1) match the federal funds with some contribution of their own and (2) establish a means-test for all families receiving benefits.

Congress also established the school lunch program during the New Deal as a way to both feed the hungry and strengthen the ailing farm economy. The Federal Surplus Relief Corporation began purchasing surplus agriculture products for low-income families in 1935 and launched the nation's first school lunch programs for poor children shortly thereafter. By 1941, more than 5 million children were receiving free school lunches, consuming more than 450 million pounds of surplus pork, dairy products, and bread. Although the program was disbanded during World War II because of food shortages, it was restored under the 1946 National School Lunch Act. As President Harry Truman said at the signing ceremony, "No nation is any healthier than its children." He could have added that many draftees had been rejected for service in World War II because of malnutrition.

Help for the Disabled and Unemployed   The New Deal created two new federal programs to help disabled workers and the unemployed. Both were established under the Social Security Act in 1935.

Under the Disability Insurance program, workers can apply for government benefits if they have been injured on the job. They must have been disabled for at least five months and be unable to continue on the job. The process for earning a disability payment, which covers part of a worker's monthly salary, is very strict. Only 20 percent of applications are approved. The worker has to present detailed evidence that the disability was work, not age related, for example, and must prove that the disability is long term. Approximately 3 million Americans received disability support in 2009.

Unemployment insurance is available to workers who have lost their jobs because of economic conditions. Workers cannot receive benefits if they quit their jobs by their own choice—for example, if they have children, get married, move to another part of the country—or are fired for poor performance. Federal unemployment insurance is jointly administered by the federal government and the 50 states and is covered by monthly premiums that are automatically deducted from paychecks. Employers also pay monthly

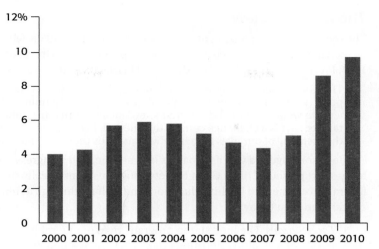

FIGURE 19–1 Unemployment in the United States.

■ *How does the unemployment rate today compare to the average rate over the last decade? What percentage unemployment is acceptable?*

SOURCE: U.S. Bureau of Labor Statistics.

premiums for their employees. Unemployed workers cannot receive more than half their monthly pay, up to specific limits—in New York, for example, the maximum payment is approximately $500 a month, but it is less than half that amount in Arizona. During normal economic times, the benefit is paid for 26 weeks.

There are exceptions to the length of coverage, however. The length of coverage was extended as unemployment began to rise in 2008. Under legislation signed by President George W. Bush in mid-2008, the federal government provided the money to give unemployed workers an extra 13 weeks of coverage. The extension was renewed in 2009 and again in 2010. As of September 2010, nearly 25 million Americans were unemployed. Most received at least some unemployment coverage. Between January 2000 and March 2010, the unemployment rate increased from 4 percent of employable adults to 9.7 percent. (See Figure 19–1, and visit the Bureau of Labor Statistics at www.bls.gov for the latest information on unemployment.)

Although these programs sound generous, and are sometimes abused by employees who invent disabilities, they provide the bare minimum for survival. They are often the only sources of income that stand between a family and homelessness, hunger, and the loss of health care.

The federal government has several programs to make sure that women, children, and infants receive nutritious food. School lunch programs sometimes provide the only full meal of the day for the nation's poorest children. ■ *Why does federal spending on early childhood health save money in the longer term?*

The Great Society

The second major expansion of social policy came in the 1960s with what became known as the Great Society. At a commencement speech at the University of Michigan in May 1964, President Lyndon Johnson described his vision of the Great Society:

> The Great Society rests on abundance and liberty for all. It demands an end to poverty and racial injustice....But that is just the beginning. The Great Society is a place where every child can find knowledge to enrich his mind and to enlarge his talents....It is a challenge constantly renewed, beckoning us toward a destiny where the meaning of our lives matches the marvelous products of our labors.[11]

Johnson's agenda was as broad as his rhetoric, and Congress enacted much of it in a fairly short period of time. Great Society programs dramatically increased the role of the federal government in health, education, and welfare through a number of programs that continue to exist today:

■ *Food Stamps.* The food stamp program gives poor families coupons to purchase the basics of a healthy, nutritious diet. The average benefit is approximately $90 per person per month. The program was renamed SNAP in 2009 (Supplemental Nutrition Assistance Program).

■ *Head Start.* Head Start is a preschool program designed to help poor children get ready for kindergarten. The program serves more than 900,000 children each year at a cost of approximately $7,000 per child. Nearly 30 percent of Head Start teachers and staff are parents of Head Start children or were Head Start children themselves.

■ *Medicare.* As noted earlier, **Medicare** was created in 1965 to provide health care to older citizens. It provides all reasonable hospital, medical, and prescription drug insurance. The hospital insurance is funded by a 1.42 percent tax on employees and employers. Medicare pays for inpatient hospital care, skilled nursing care, and other services. Individuals can purchase additional Medicare insurance to cover some expenses not traditionally covered by Medicare. With enactment in 2010 of Obama's health care plan, Medicare will become the largest federal spending program by 2015, if not sooner.

■ *Medicaid.* **Medicaid** was created in 1965 to provide basic health services for poor families. The program is administered and partially funded by state governments and covers items such as hospital care and family planning. Obama's health care plan expanded Medicaid dramatically as a way to provide more coverage for the poor.

■ *Supplemental Security Income.* The SSI program was created in 1972 to provide an extra measure of support for the elderly, the poor, and the blind or disabled. Levels of SSI support vary by state to reflect cost-of-living differences, so the program provides monthly benefit checks ranging from only $1 to approximately $800. SSI benefits are financed by general tax revenues and administered by the Social Security Administration.

■ *Housing Assistance.* The Department of Housing and Urban Development, which was created in 1965, administers a number of programs designed to help low-income families find affordable, safe housing, in part by giving property owners subsidies to make up the difference between what tenants can pay and what the local housing market will bear.

Medicare

A national health insurance program for the elderly and disabled.

Medicaid

A federal program that provides medical benefits for low-income people.

Social Security and Medicare taxes are withdrawn from regular paychecks and are called payroll taxes. The FICA (Federal Insurance Contribution Act) tax is collected on all payroll checks up to certain limits on income. ■ *How much do you pay in taxes in each of your paychecks?*

Reforming Welfare

Republicans have not been the only critics of the New Deal and Great Society welfare programs. President Bill Clinton made welfare reform a centerpiece of his reelection agenda in 1996, promising to "end welfare as we know it."[12]

Working with the new Republican congressional majority, Clinton won passage of the Personal Responsibility and Work Opportunity Reconciliation Act in 1996, which replaced the New Deal's AFDC with Temporary Assistance for Needy Families (TANF).

YOU WILL DECIDE
Should the Federal Government Promote Marriage?

Although the 1996 welfare reform legislation focused on replacing welfare with work, it also ordered the federal government to promote marriage. Advocates argue that marriage improves the lives of both children and parents. Married adults, whether women or men, are happier, healthier, and wealthier than their unmarried peers and are more likely to give their children a healthier start in life. Some advocates even argue that more marriages would reduce health costs by reducing depression and crime.*

The federal government can promote marriage in two ways. First, it can reduce the penalties it imposes on welfare recipients who get married. Under current law, for example, a single mother working full time at a minimum-wage job who marries stands to lose as much as $8,000 per year in cash and noncash benefits. Second, it can promote marriage through advertising, counseling, or even providing cash grants for getting married.

What do you think? Should the federal government enact policies that promote marriage? What are the arguments for both sides of the issue?

THINKING IT THROUGH

Although the federal government has long engaged in activities designed to promote vaccinating children, quitting smoking, wearing seat belts, and driving under 55 miles per hour, not everyone believes that promoting marriage is the answer to reducing the welfare rolls.

Critics note, for example, that domestic violence and child abuse occur almost as frequently in married as in unmarried households. They also worry that government grants for marriage would promote a rash of false marriages designed to get the cash. Most important, opponents believe that the best way to improve conditions for welfare recipients is to find them good-paying jobs. They look to states such as Minnesota that have created strong welfare-to-work programs that do not punish married women for getting a job.

Nevertheless, marriage appears to affect income. Two paychecks are better than one, and married couples may be more likely to save money for the future. Marital stability also positively influences child well-being on several measures, and marriage fosters healthier living habits as the marriage partners help monitor each other in such areas as smoking, weight gain, and drug use. These effects can be benefits to society in general.

The question, however, is whether they are a consequence of marriage or simply a product of adults living together. Absent a solid answer, support for marriage may be more an indicator of a person's ideology and religion than a position based on careful research.

Critical Thinking Questions

1. Should the federal government promote social values such as marriage?

2. How is promoting marriage similar to and different from other federal programs such as its campaign to stop smoking?

3. Why is marriage considered a way to reduce poverty? Are there other or better ways to achieve the same goal?

* See, for example, Ron Haskins and Isabel V. Sawhill, *Work and Marriage: The Way to End Poverty and Welfare*, Welfare Reform & Beyond Brief No. 28 (Brookings Institution, 2003).

Under the new rules, federally funded public assistance is limited to five years during a person's lifetime, and all recipients must enter some kind of work training program within two months of receiving initial benefits. Although states can exempt up to 20 percent of cases from the work requirements and time limits—an exemption intended for blind and disabled persons—the message to recipients is clear: Find work soon.

The law originally excluded legal immigrants from many welfare programs, but at the strong urging of the governors, most welfare benefits were later restored to legal immigrants. To discourage people on welfare from moving to states with more generous assistance payments, the law gave states the option of limiting welfare to newcomers from other states. This provision was declared unconstitutional by a federal district court judge, however, who said it "denies 'equal protection of the laws' to indigent families moving from one state to another."[13] The decision was not appealed.

Social Policy Challenges for the Future: Health, Education, and Crime

Even if states take on a greater social policy role, the federal government is sure to remain the greatest source of funding for the safety net. As Figure 19–2 shows, human resource spending for programs such as Social Security, Medicare, Medicaid, and child nutrition has doubled since 1950. The figure also shows a very slight increase in

FIGURE 19–2 Changing Priorities in the Federal Budget.

■ *What parts of the federal government have seen the greatest change over the last 50 years? What explains these changes in spending priorities?*

SOURCE: Historical Tables, *Budget of the United States, Fiscal Year 2011* (U.S. Government Printing Office, February 2011).

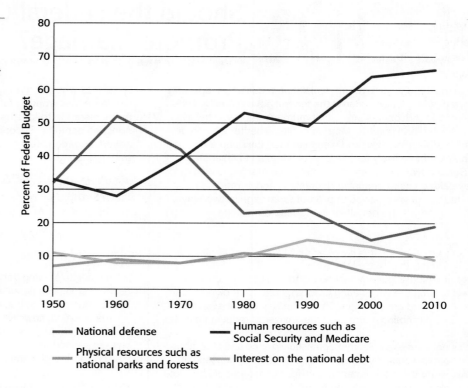

National defense — Human resources such as Social Security and Medicare — Physical resources such as national parks and forests — Interest on the national debt

spending on physical resources, such as roads and bridges, due to the large, one-time infusion of money through the economic stimulus package. However, the figure does not show the projected interest on the national debt beyond 2010—according to the White House Office of Management and Budget, estimated interest payments will swell to $551 billion in 2015.

The Federal Role in Health Care

Medicare is only one of the federal government's many health programs. The federal government has been instrumental in reducing disease since 1887, when then it opened a one-room laboratory on Staten Island, New York, to study infectious diseases carried to the United States on passenger ships. In time, that one-room laboratory expanded into the National Institutes of Health (NIH), a conglomeration of 37 separate institutes on a 300-acre campus in Bethesda, Maryland.

The surgeon general of the United States is arguably the most visible health care official in government. As head of the Public Health Service (PHS), the surgeon general oversees a diverse array of health care researchers at NIH and elsewhere. Federally funded researchers study causes and seek cures for serious diseases. The PHS also grants fellowships for health research to scientists and physicians and administers grants to states and local communities to help improve public health. Another federal agency promoting health is the Food and Drug Administration (FDA), which oversees the development of new drugs and ensures food safety through inspections of the nation's food supply.

Dozens of other federal agencies work to improve public health. The Centers for Disease Control and Prevention (CDC) in Atlanta is also actively engaged in preventing disease. The CDC and its 7,800 "disease detectives" have been at the forefront of identifying a host of mystery illnesses, including the respiratory disease that attacked attendees at an American Legion convention in 1976 (Legionnaire's disease), toxic shock syndrome in 1980, and hepatitis C in 1989, as well as tracking down the causes of major health disasters, including the outbreak of swine flu in 2009. The swine flu outbreak produced a massive effort to vaccinate Americans against the virus, which was especially threatening to young adults.

Despite its success in improving the nation's health, the federal government faces two major health care challenges in the future: containing costs and expanding coverage.

The Rising Cost of Health Care Health care costs in the United States have nearly quadrupled, after controlling for inflation, since 1970.[14] Although costs slowed with the rest of the economy in 2001, they are expected to escalate rapidly as the nation ages throughout the next two decades. Health costs rose 4.4 percent in 2007 and another 6.0 percent in 2008.[15] It's too early to know if the Patient Protection and Affordable Health Care Act will reduce these increases.

All workers pay for the increasing health care costs. Although employers provide insurance to three of five working adults, they have steadily increased the share of insurance that employees must pay, including increased premiums, higher deductibles, and partial payments for services. Taxpayers also pay for these increases through federal dollars that might otherwise go to other programs such as homeland security, college loans, or highway construction. (Figure 19–3 shows where health care dollars are spent. The figures are not expected to change dramatically with the federal government's health care program.)

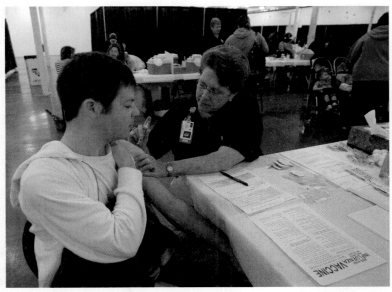

Young adults proved particularly susceptible to the new swine flu virus that emerged in 2009. The federal government accelerated development of the vaccine to prevent the spread of the disease on college campuses.

The good news is that costs have risen in part because people are living longer. Average life expectancy increased by more than five years between 1970 and 1995. In 1900, only 1 of every 25 American adults was over the age of 65. By 1950, the number was 1 in 12, and by 1985, 1 in 9. According to experts, the number will rise to 1 in 5 by 2030. In 1900, the average American adult lived to age 47; by 2000, the average had increased to 79. Again according to experts, the number will rise into the mid-80s by 2030.

As people live longer, of course, they place greater demands on the health care system, as well as on the Social Security program. New and advanced medical technology—life-support systems, ultrasound, sophisticated X-ray equipment, and genetic counseling—have all increased the costs of health care. Longer life expectancies also place greater demands on other social policies, subtracting from funding for public assistance and other forms of social insurance.

In addition, costs have risen because of new technologies that are now widely available. Nuclear magnetic imaging, or as it is more commonly known, magnetic resonance imaging (MRI), is now routinely used to diagnose a host of diseases easily detected through more traditional tests. Once a medical center purchases this kind of expensive technology, its physicians are given incentives to use it, which increases patients' health care costs.

At least part of the cost crisis is avoidable. Medicare alone spends billions of dollars each year treating smoking-related diseases, and throughout the next 20 years, the costs to treat such diseases will continue to rise. Other illnesses at least partly related to lifestyle choices include heart disease, liver disease, HIV/AIDS, and the epidemic of health disorders caused or made worse by obesity, such as diabetes.

Covering the Uninsured Despite passage of the Medicare program in 1965, the United States did not provide comprehensive insurance to the rest of the uninsured until 2010. Until then, most uninsured Americans either relied on public clinics, emergency room care, or simply lived without health or dental care.[16]

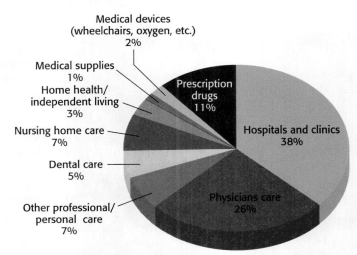

FIGURE 19–3 **Where the Health Care Dollar Was Spent, 2008.**

■ *On what aspect of health care is the most money spent? How might you expect the new health care program to change where Americans go for preventive medical care?*

SOURCE: Centers for Medicare and Medicaid Services, Office of the Actuary, National Statistics Group, http://www.cms.hhs.gov/NationalHealthExpendData/downloads/highlights.pdf.

The Patient Protection and Affordable Health Care Act was designed to cover as many of these Americans as possible but was one of the most complicated laws passed in recent history. The bill was more than 1,200 pages long and contained a long list of changes in how health care is delivered and to whom. Its key provisions involved expansions of existing health care programs such as Medicaid for the poor and the creation of new health insurance "exchanges" in each state as a source of insurance for Americans who could not buy insurance from private companies. It also contained tax increases and benefit cuts for Medicare. The main provisions of the Act are:

■ Most Americans will be required to buy health insurance starting in 2014 and will be fined by the federal government if they do not do so.

■ Individuals who cannot buy affordable insurance will be able to purchase insurance from a state insurance exchange.

■ Insurance companies will be prevented from denying coverage to people for any reason, including preexisting conditions, such as high blood pressure, cancer, or mental illness.

■ Insurance companies will have to extend coverage for young Americans up to 26 years of age under their parents' insurance.

■ The Medicaid program will be expanded to all poor Americans under the age of 65, including the unemployed and unmarried individuals.

■ General Medicare benefits will not be cut, and all older Americans will qualify for free preventive care, but the special Medicare Advantage program for higher-income beneficiaries will be frozen, and some benefits will be abolished.

■ Individual Americans will pay a tax on "Cadillac" insurance plans that offer broader coverage at a much higher cost.

■ The Medicare payroll tax will rise 0.9 percent for Americans who make more than $200,000 per year.

Because these changes will be phased in throughout the next decade, it is not clear just how much the new reforms will cost on a yearly basis. Moreover, it is not clear that older Americans will accept the changes in Medicare. Some argue that the Medicare changes will be repealed as they approach full implementation in 2011. Moreover, the reforms are extremely difficult to implement, in part because they rely on the states to form the new insurance exchanges on their own. At least for now, the health care reform is a work in progress and will rely on faithful execution to have its full effects.

Nevertheless, the program reflects a 50-year effort to expand the social safety net. Although there will still be a small number of Americans who will not qualify for any coverage because they already receive benefits through other federal programs such as Supplemental Security Income and Veterans hospitals, the reform represents the final achievement of the New Deal vision of health care for the uninsured.

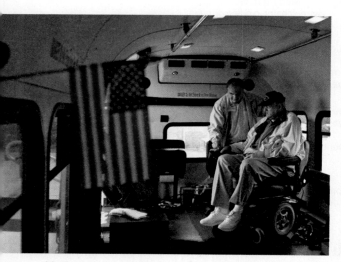

Medicare is not the only federal government health program. The federal government has dozens of health programs, including the Department of Veterans Affairs hospital system, which is open only to veterans.

The Federal Role in Education

The federal government has been a partner in education at least since the Northwest Ordinance of 1785, in which Congress set aside land in every township for a public school. In 1862, the Morrill Land-Grant Colleges Act provided grants of land to states for universities specializing in the mechanical or agricultural arts. The U.S. Office of Education was established in 1867 to oversee these programs, but the scope of federal involvement was modest by today's standards. Even the G.I. Bill, which helped provide a college education for approximately 20 million World War II veterans, was seen more as an employment program than an educational one.

During the Cold War, however, education became one part of the national defense. When the Soviet Union launched *Sputnik*—the first

By the People

MAKING A DIFFERENCE

Improving Health One Playground at a Time

Citizens can make an immediate difference on public policy by simply changing the way they behave. They can stop smoking, change their diets, and get more exercise every day. They can also lobby their local governments to build more sidewalks and bike paths so that other citizens can exercise safely. They can push school boards to remove sugary drinks and junk food from school vending machines and cafeterias, support efforts to bring full-service grocery stores such as Whole Foods to low-income neighborhoods, and even plant community gardens.

Playgrounds are an easy place to start. According to KaBoom!, which is a charitable organization that built more playgrounds in 2010 than any state or city in America, 60 minutes of exercise a day can reduce health care costs dramatically in the future. Yet, there are thousands of "play deserts" across the country, often in dense urban areas, in which there is no space for children to play. You can see what is in your community by visiting maps.kaboom.org.

Students can easily find a "play-space" where a new playground would improve the opportunity for healthy exercise for low-income children. They can then join the KaBoom! building team as volunteers.

CRITICAL THINKING QUESTIONS

1. What can you do today to reduce health care costs in the future?

2. Why are playgrounds so important to communities? And why are there so few playgrounds in low-income communities?

3. What other resources do low-income communities need to be healthier places to live?

First Lady Michelle Obama brings D.C. school children to her organic garden to educate them about locally grown, healthful food.

---

human-made satellite to orbit the earth—in 1957, Congress responded in 1958 by passing the National Defense Education Act to upgrade science, language, and mathematics courses.

Elementary and Secondary Education   Kindergarten through high school education is generally seen as a state and local responsibility. Most children go to public schools run by local school boards and funded, at least partly, by property taxes. Because school districts vary greatly in the wealth of their residents, children from poor districts are much more likely to have lower-quality public schools than those from wealthier districts. As a result, public schools vary in the quality of teacher preparation, student performance, dropout rates, and educational opportunities provided to minority students.

Although the federal government has been reluctant to make direct investments in poor school districts, it has tried to help the children those districts serve. For example, in 1964, Congress created the Head Start program to help low-income children learn to read and understand numbers. Head Start centers also provide healthy meals and snacks and monitor child health care. Many also work with parents to encourage greater involvement and literacy.

Recent evaluations suggest that Head Start does increase learning but needs improvement. In 2010, Head Start provided funding to more than 20,000 child care centers, some of which reported chronic shortages of well-trained teachers. The student–teacher ratio also varied significantly across centers. Moreover, the program is not an entitlement, meaning funding covers only approximately a third of eligible children. When the dollars run out, Head Start centers stop enrolling participants.

Head Start is not the federal government's only education program, however. In 1965, Congress passed the Elementary and Secondary

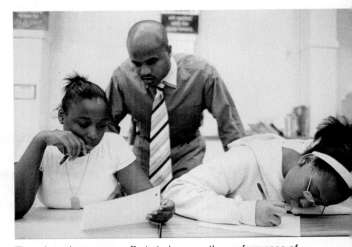

There have been many efforts to improve the performance of public schools, including the No Child Left Behind Act. Here, a teacher for the nongovernmental Knowledge Is Power Program (KIPP) works with poor children to improve their performance.

515

Education Act (ESEA), which supplied educational materials for underprivileged public school students and provided funding for research on how to help children from disadvantaged backgrounds.

As concerns about the quality of public education increased during the 1990s, however, the federal government became more engaged in local education, first by setting national goals for student achievement, then by passing the No Child Left Behind Act in 2002. Under the Act, in return for federal funding, states were required to annually test at least 95 percent of all third and eighth graders in reading and mathematics. In addition, states were required to grade schools as passing or failing, to set higher standards for teachers, and to give students in failing schools the option to move to higher-performing schools. Schools must either improve test scores each year or risk being labeled "in need of improvement." Under the Act, all students are supposed to be proficient in reading and mathematics by 2014.

Although the No Child Left Behind Act set higher standards, it increased federal spending for education by only a tiny percentage. Under great pressure during the economic downturn, many states complained that they did not have enough funding to test every student every year or to meet the law's requirement for teacher training and certification. In addition, schools with many disabled or special-needs students were being unfairly categorized as "failing" because they could not meet the test-score requirement. As of late 2010, Congress was still working to change the Act to put a greater emphasis on teacher performance. At the same time, the Obama Administration launched an effort to reward states for increasing the number of charter schools.

Parents ask more of their schools than just to educate their children. Schools are now a major means of providing basic nutrition to millions of poor children. They screen at-risk children and attempt to get them medical and psychological assistance; they seek to socialize students into acceptable behaviors, often in the face of increasing violence in the surrounding neighborhoods; and they often reach out to families to provide basic help in parenting.

Higher Education   The federal government also provides help to colleges and universities. In 2010, the federal government provided approximately $90 billion of the financial aid that college students receive. Pell grants for low-income students and low-interest guaranteed student loans continue to be the biggest source of college costs for low-income students.

In 1998, Congress added three new programs to improve the odds that low-income children will make it to college: (1) GEAR UP, which supports early interventions to help students complete high school; (2) the Learning Anytime Anywhere Partnerships (LAAP), which provide federal funding for distance learning through the Internet; and (3) a new initiative designed to improve teacher quality in primary and elementary schools. Although the three programs account for less than 1 percent of federal spending for education, they acknowledge the link between the quality of primary and elementary education and college success, as well as the need to act early to increase the odds of success for low-income students.

The Federal Role in Crime Control

Like education, controlling crime is primarily a state and local matter. The federal government has passed sweeping legislation helping state and local governments pay for crime control. Often, the federal government acts more as a banker than a police officer, providing grants to states and local governments to hire their own police officers, build more prisons, improve drug enforcement, and prosecute organized crime. The federal government must also enforce its own laws against activities such as counterfeiting and pollution, while protecting the borders and preventing drugs from flowing into the country.

The federal government enforces its laws primarily through the Department of Justice, which contains the Federal Bureau of Investigation (FBI). The FBI was created

Of the People

Access to College

Federal aid to education has increased access to college for all American students, but it has had a particularly significant effect on women and people of color at both the community college and four-year levels. Women now earn the majority of both associate and bachelor degrees. In 2000, women earned 48 percent of associate's degrees awarded and 46 percent of bachelor's degrees; in 2008, they earned 60 percent of associate's degrees and nearly 58 percent of bachelor's degrees.

Students of color have more than doubled throughout the decades at both community colleges and four-year colleges and universities. Under the 1998 Higher Education Act, the number of students of color should increase even faster as the federal government puts more dollars into preparing students for college. Although two-year and four-year colleges have seen an increase in enrollments by both women and minority students, growth has been fastest at two-year colleges, which tend to have lower tuition. They are increasingly the destination of choice for many students unable to afford four-year colleges, or who start at two-year colleges to save money, then transfer to four-year institutions.

CRITICAL THINKING QUESTIONS

1. Why has there been such a sudden change in the number of women attending college?

2. Has diversity increased at your college or university? Why or why not?

3. Thinking back to Chapter 5 of this book, what do changes in education mean for U.S. government and politics?

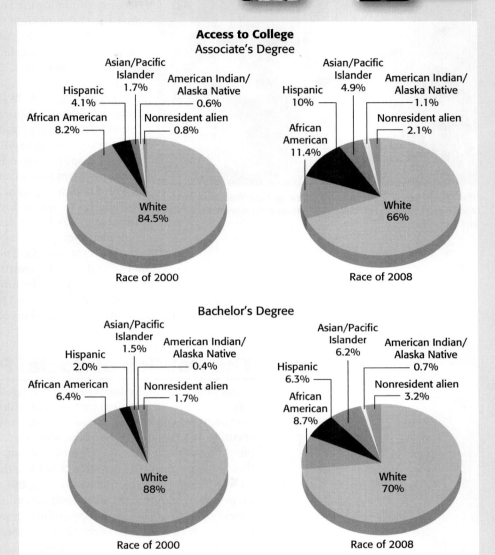

Access to College
Associate's Degree

Race of 2000:
- Hispanic 4.1%
- Asian/Pacific Islander 1.7%
- American Indian/Alaska Native 0.6%
- African American 8.2%
- Nonresident alien 0.8%
- White 84.5%

Race of 2008:
- Hispanic 10%
- Asian/Pacific Islander 4.9%
- American Indian/Alaska Native 1.1%
- African American 11.4%
- Nonresident alien 2.1%
- White 66%

Bachelor's Degree

Race of 2000:
- Hispanic 2.0%
- Asian/Pacific Islander 1.5%
- American Indian/Alaska Native 0.4%
- African American 6.4%
- Nonresident alien 1.7%
- White 88%

Race of 2008:
- Hispanic 6.3%
- Asian/Pacific Islander 6.2%
- American Indian/Alaska Native 0.7%
- African American 8.7%
- Nonresident alien 3.2%
- White 70%

SOURCE: U.S. Department of Education, National Center for Education Statistics, *Postsecondary Institutions in the United States: Fall 2003 and Degrees and Other Awards Conferred: 2002–04* (U.S. Government Printing Office, 2007), www.nces.ed.gov/fastfacts.

in 1908 and charged with gathering and reporting evidence in matters relating to federal criminal laws. In addition, the FBI provides fingerprint identification and laboratory services to local law enforcement on a cooperative basis and has new responsibilities in the war on terrorism. Other law enforcement agencies of the federal government include the Drug Enforcement Agency (DEA), which is responsible for preventing the flow of illegal narcotics and other illegal drugs into the United States, patrolling U.S. borders, and conducting joint operations with countries where drugs are produced. The Bureau of Alcohol, Tobacco, Firearms, and Explosives monitors the sale of destructive weapons and guns inside the United States, regulates alcoholic beverage production, and oversees the collection of taxes on alcohol and tobacco.

The September 11, 2001, terrorist attack on New York City and Washington, D.C., sparked a massive federal investment in homeland security.

Terrorism is clearly the federal government's top crime priority today. Only weeks after the September 11, 2001, terrorist attacks on New York City and Washington, D.C., Congress passed a massive antiterrorism law, and it created the new Department of Homeland Security the following summer. For his part, President Bush created the Office of Homeland Security within the White House in October 2001, merging 22 agencies and 180,000 federal employees, and ordered a complete reorganization of the Federal Bureau of Investigation in early 2002 to create a stronger focus on preventing terrorism.

Under the USA PATRIOT Act of 2001 (the letters stand for Uniting and Strengthening America by Providing Appropriate Tools Required to Intercept and Obstruct Terrorism), the federal government was given sweeping authority to conduct secret investigations of suspected terrorists. Those investigations may use "roving wiretaps" to intercept conversations on any phones a suspect may use and detain any noncitizens believed to be a national security risk for up to seven days without charging them with a crime. Although the PATRIOT Act expired on December 31, 2005, the Bush administration made its renewal a centerpiece of the president's second-term agenda. The administration also asked Congress to expand the government's authority to investigate what it called "lone-wolf" terrorists who are not affiliated with a foreign government or known terrorist organization such as Al-Qaeda, which planned the September 11 attacks. President Obama signed a short-term reauthorization of the main provisions of the Act in February 2010.

The Politics of Social Policy

Social policy is a major focus of American politics. Welfare, health care, education, and crime—and their costs—are important political battlegrounds between the parties and between contending interest groups, second only to the economy and national security. The nation long ago answered questions about whether the national government has a role in providing decent housing, adequate health care, and a solid education for all citizens. The question is not whether the nation will provide a safety net for its low-income citizens but how strong the net will be and who will be responsible for providing it. Although most American adults support Social Security and Medicare, for example, they are sharply divided over how much the nation should do for its poorest citizens. They are also increasingly divided about reforms such as the No Child Left Behind Act and its mandatory testing, which have prompted some states to sue the federal government to recover some of the costs of implementing the unfunded mandate portions of the Act.

Nevertheless, social policy will be part of the federal agenda far into the future. Although presidents and Congress cannot always know what voters will support and how much they are willing to pay, they can be sure that most want government to take care of citizens who are low-income through no fault of their own. As the earlier figures on payments to individuals show, the economic recession has cost the federal government billions in payments to unemployed Americans—spending on unemployment soared from $35 billion in 2007 to $191 billion in 2010.

Citizens can influence social policy in several ways. One is to join interest groups that represent low-income Americans or taxpayers. Another is to write letters to their members of Congress when significant legislation such as prescription drug coverage comes to a vote. They can also volunteer for specific programs that are designed to help the needy such as KaBoom!, especially programs that are administered by charities. Although the federal government has created dozens of programs to help the needy, the nation still relies heavily on charities to fill gaps in coverage, whether through food pantries and soup kitchens or early childhood programs. In turn, these programs rely on volunteers.

CHAPTER **SUMMARY**

19.1 Outline the goals of the federal government's social policy and the forms of protection it provides.

The goals of social policy are to create a safety net to protect citizens against social and economic problems and to raise the quality of life for all. The two types of social policy are public assistance (usually means-tested) and social insurance. Public assistance takes many forms, including direct payments to the poor, the unemployed, and the disabled; food stamps; job training; housing subsidies; free school lunches; tax credits; and subsidized medical care. Social insurance (usually an entitlement), such as Social Security, is provided to anyone who has paid enough in contributions to receive support after meeting certain requirements, such as reaching retirement age.

19.2 Outline the evolution of social policy throughout the twentieth century.

The greatest expansion in the federal government's social programs occurred in two eras: (1) Franklin Roosevelt's New Deal from 1933 to 1945, and (2) Lyndon Johnson's Great Society from 1964 to 1969. The New Deal created a number of public assistance and social insurance programs such as job training for

the unemployed, Social Security, and Aid to Families with Dependent Children; the Great Society produced help for the homeless, more job training, and Medicare.

19.3 Evaluate the current status of and challenges for federal government policy in the areas of health care, education, and crime.

Health care is well on track to becoming the federal government's largest social program, in part because health care costs are rising rapidly with the increasing lifespan, new technologies, and access to promising new treatments for life-threatening diseases such as cancer. In 2010, Congress passed a new health insurance program to provide greater access for millions of uninsured Americans.

Education and crime continue to be primarily state and local government functions in the United States. However, the federal government plays an important role in funding public schools and pushing national goals for better education and is also heavily engaged in helping finance college and university education. Crime control has also been part of the national agenda for decades, especially related to drugs, but has become much more visible as part of the war on terrorism.

CHAPTER **SELF-TEST**

19.1 Outline the goals of the federal government's social policy and the forms of protection it provides.

1. Which are means-tested entitlement programs?
   a. Programs that have exhibited financial viability
   b. Programs that have been researched by a congressional committee
   c. Programs that give funds only to those who have a proven individual need
   d. Federal programs that have been successfully used at the state level
2. Which of the following is *not* a social insurance program?
   a. Medicare
   b. Food stamps
   c. Social Security
   d. Disability Insurance
3. In a short essay, identify the two types of programs the federal government uses to protect citizens against hardship. What are the requirements to receive each type of protection? On which type did the government spend more money in 2008? Analyze the connection between eligibility requirements and levels of spending.

19.2 Outline the evolution of social policy throughout the twentieth century.

4. Which of the following was a major goal of Social Security when it was created in 1935?
   a. To provide an alternative to welfare programs
   b. To help veterans transition financially after active duty
   c. To provide elderly citizens with a consistent income
   d. To provide a minimum income floor for poor beneficiaries
5. Identify each social program with the appropriate period—the New Deal or the Great Society.
   a. Food stamps
   b. Social Security
   c. Disability Insurance
   d. Medicare
   e. Head Start
   f. Unemployment Insurance
6. What is one way the government can promote marriage?
   a. Increase welfare funds for children
   b. Increase welfare funds for those who are married
   c. Reduce the penalties on welfare recipients who get married
   d. Provide expanded Social Security benefits for those who are married

7. In a short essay, analyze the future of Social Security. Consider how it is funded and what steps Congress may have to take to ensure its continued existence.

19.3 **Evaluate the current status of and challenges for federal government policy in the areas of health care, education, and crime.**

8. What was the largest category of health care spending in 2006?
   a. Hospital care
   b. Prescription drugs
   c. Nursing home care
   d. Unnecessary surgery
9. What are the most important provisions of the new health care reform?
10. How will the new health care reform help lower-income Americans, older Americans, and young Americans?

11. What has been one of the main criticisms of the No Child Left Behind Act, passed in 2002?
   a. It reduced the amount of federal funding available to states.
   b. It made it more difficult for illegal immigrants to obtain an education.
   c. It changed the requirements for students to graduate from high school.
   d. It increased federal spending on education by only a tiny percentage.
12. In a short essay, compare the circumstances that prompted the No Child Left Behind Act with those that gave rise to an earlier social program—food stamps, Head Start, or Social Security, for instance. Identify and analyze concerns with No Child Left Behind in light of U.S. experience with long-running social programs.

Answers to selected questions: 1.c; 2.b; 4.d; 5.a: Great Society, 5b: New Deal, 5c: New Deal, 5d: Great Society, 5e: Great Society, 5f: New Deal, 6.c; 8.a; 11.d.

mypoliscilab EXERCISES

Apply what you learned in this chapter on MyPoliSciLab.

Read on mypoliscilab.com

eText: Chapter 19

Study and Review on mypoliscilab.com

Pre-Test
Post-Test
Chapter Exam
Flashcards

Watch on mypoliscilab.com

Video: Raising The Minimum Wage
Video: Health Care Plan

Explore on mypoliscilab.com

Comparative: Comparing Health Systems
Comparative: Comparing Social Welfare Systems
Timeline: The Evolution of Social Welfare Policy

KEY TERMS

entitlements, p. 502
means-tested entitlements, p. 502
social safety net, p. 503

public assistance, p. 504
social insurance, p. 505
Social Security, p. 507

Medicare, p. 510
Medicaid, p. 510

ADDITIONAL **RESOURCES**

FURTHER READING

JOHN BALDOCK, NICHOLAS MANNING, AND SARAH VICKERSTAFF, EDS., *Social Policy* (Oxford University Press, 2007).

DONALD L. BARLETT AND **JAMES B. STEELE,** *Critical Condition: How Health Care in America Became Big Business—and Bad Medicine* (Broadway Books, 2005).

BARBARA EHRENREICH, *Nickel and Dimed: On (Not) Getting By in America* (Metropolitan Books, 2001).

MICHAEL HILL, *Social Policy in the Modern World: A Comparative Perspective* (Wiley, 2006).

CHRISTOPHER JENCKS, *The Homeless* (Harvard University Press, 1994).

PAUL C. LIGHT, *Still Artful Work: The Continuing Politics of Social Security Reform* (McGraw-Hill, 1995).

DANIEL PATRICK MOYNIHAN, *Miles to Go: A Personal History of Social Policy* (Harvard University Press, 1996).

CHARLES MURRAY, *Losing Ground: American Social Policy, 1950–1980* (Basic Books, 1984).

PAUL E. PETERSON AND **MARTIN R. WEST,** EDS., *No Child Left Behind: The Politics and Practice of School Accountability* (Brookings Institution Press, 2004).

MARK ROBERT RANK, *One Nation Underprivileged: Why American Poverty Affects Us All* (Oxford University Press, 2005).

DAVID K. SHIPLER, *The Working Poor: Invisible in America* (Vintage Books, 2005).

R. KENT WEAVER, *Ending Welfare as We Know It* (Brookings Institution Press, 2001).

MARGARET WEIR, ED., *The Social Divide: Political Parties and the Future of Activist Government* (Brookings Institution Press, 1998).

BOB WOODWARD, *Agenda: Inside the Clinton White House* (Simon & Schuster, 1994).

WEB SITES

Healthiergeneration.org The Web site for the Alliance for a Healthier Generation, an organization founded to promote healthier lives and sponsored by First Lady Michelle Obama.

CMS.gov The Web site for the Centers for Medicare and Medicaid Services, which administer the largest health programs in the federal government.

Health.gov A portal to every federal program that deals with health care.

www2.ed.gov/about/offices/list/fsa/index.html The Web site for the federal government's student loan programs.

FBI.gov The destination for finding details on crime, including statistics on major crimes (http://www.fbi.gov/ucr/cius2008/index.html).

Making Foreign and Defense Policy

The conflict in Darfur, Sudan, began in 2003 when a small rebel group attacked Sudanese government targets. Frustrated by drought and unrelenting poverty in a territory the size of Texas, the people of Darfur did not demand independence but clearly demanded aid. The Sudanese government, however, seemed more concerned with driving black Africans out of Darfur than with ending poverty. If they could not be driven out, the Sudanese government decided they would be killed.

The government sent troops into battle backed by its air force. At the same time, it began arming its own rebel army called the Janjaweed, who soon took up the fight against the people of Darfur. Riding into villages and towns on camels and horses, the Janjaweed ravaged the population, raping and killing men, women, and children.

By the beginning of 2008, international aid groups put the number of dead at 200,000 and the number in refugee camps along the border with Chad at 2 million. Although the warring groups had signed a peace agreement in 2006, that quickly collapsed. And although the United Nations sent a peacekeeping force to the area, its 26,000 members were unarmed and unable to protect refugees who strayed from the camps in search of food and firewood. So the killing went on. The anti-Darfur rebels soon took their violence to the southern Sudan, where they opened a new war on black Africans.

Because the attacks have concentrated on the systematic elimination of a specific population, the black Africans in Sudan, many activists have accused the Sudanese government of engaging in genocide. Human rights groups such as the International Crisis Group and SaveDarfur.org, college students throughout the United States, and entertainers such as Don Cheadle and George Clooney have been among the most vocal advocates of a much stronger international response that would include a well-armed U.N. force. They have also demanded a much stronger stand by the United States against the warfare. They often refer to the lack of U.S. response to the Rwanda genocide in April 1994 and the failure to stop the killing in Kosovo in 1998. If these kinds of international atrocities cannot provoke international outrage and action, they ask, what will?

The question for the United States' foreign policy and defense agenda is, what kind of power could be used to stop the genocide?[1] The United States tried creating international pressure on the Sudanese government to halt the arming of the Janjaweed and other anti-Darfur rebel groups, but those efforts mostly failed. As much as activists demand action, the U.S. public has been mostly unwilling to support the use of military force in distant lands.

Thus, despite continued pressure from students throughout the United States and the world, the suffering in Darfur continues today. The problem with preventing atrocities is that the international community may know where atrocity is most likely to occur, but it rarely knows when. And once genocide begins, it can move very quickly, forcing the community to choose between quick but unpopular military action and painfully slow diplomatic persuasion.

This chapter will ask how we make choices in planning and executing foreign and defense policy. We will first examine key debates in making foreign and defense policy, look at basic terms and concepts, and examine some of today's greatest foreign policy challenges, such as the increased U.S. presence in fighting the war in Afghanistan. Then, we will turn to a discussion of the key actors in making U.S. foreign policy and appraise the range of tools the United States uses to accomplish its international goals. The chapter concludes with a more detailed assessment of defense policy.

Citizens clearly play a role in foreign and defense policy, whether through their advocacy and pressure or through their own decisions to join the public service or armed forces. They can also create change through voting, especially if a foreign policy such as the war in Iraq becomes a national issue as it did in the 2006 congressional elections. Of course, citizens also can affect policy by their unwillingness to act, as has widely been the case regarding Darfur. That said, citizens often feel that the foreign policy and defense bureaucracy is immune to criticism and that Congress gives too much freedom to the president.

Understanding Foreign Policy and Defense

In the broadest sense, the primary goal of U.S. foreign and defense policy is to protect the nation from harm. Doing so requires more than building strong borders, however. The United States does not have the luxury of avoiding the rest of the world. As one of the world's great superpowers, it has accepted a range of obligations, including promoting democracy abroad in nations such as Iraq, providing help to victims of disaster such as the 2010 earthquake in Haiti, promoting greater economic ties across all nations, and fighting terrorism.

Although the United States supports greater freedom in the world, it has long been divided about its own role in international affairs. Some believe that the United States should defend itself against its enemies but remain isolated from the rest of the world; others question whether it should assume that other nations will act in their own self-interest, or if it should maintain a more hopeful vision of a peaceful world; still others debate whether the United States should use its substantial military strength to force other nations to support its positions, versus using its own history of civil liberties and rights to lead the world through example.

In general, these debates start with five basic questions: (1) Should the United States view the world realistically or idealistically? (2) Should it isolate itself from the world or accept a role in the international community? (3) Should it act on its own or only with the help of other nations? (4) Should it act first against threats to its safety or wait until it is attacked? and (5) Should it use its military and economic hard power or its diplomatic soft power? We will discuss each of these issues next.

realism
A theory of international relations that focuses on the tendency of nations to operate from self-interest.

idealism
A theory of international relations that focuses on the hope that nations will act together to solve international problems and promote peace.

Realism Versus Idealism

Historically, U.S. foreign and defense policy has been built on two very different views of the world. The first relies on **realism,** a belief that other nations are interested first and foremost in their own advancement, whether economic, political, or social, and in strengthening their own power.

Critics of realism argue that nations seek cooperation and stability, not power. This view invokes **idealism,** a belief that nations can work together to solve common problems such as global hunger and poverty with peace, not war, as the ultimate aim. Idealists view national power as a tool for good and for promoting democracy in other nations, not merely as a way to amass more military and economic resources.

Although realism and idealism represent two competing views of the world, they can become part of a broader, more integrated foreign and defense policy. Thus, the United States could be realistic about the need to work with dictators (realism) yet still believe that democracy is the best form of government (idealism). As President Bush often argued in the months leading to the war in Iraq, the United States had to be realistic about Iraq's interest in building biological, chemical, and nuclear weapons, even as he also argued that democracy would lead nations such as Iran and North Korea toward international cooperation and peace. Thus far, the Obama administration has taken a more idealistic approach to nuclear weapons, arguing that it is in the world's best interests to limit access to nuclear materials.

Aung San Suu Kyi has been a tireless supporter of human rights in Myanmar, which was formerly known as Burma. She has been under house arrest by the Myanmar government for 14 of the last 20 years in an effort to silence her advocacy.

Isolationism Versus Internationalism

Whether it is based on realism or idealism, U.S. foreign policy has reflected very different views of how it should respond to the rest of the world. Some back an approach based on

By the People

Promoting Ethical Investments by Colleges and Universities

Students who care about the tragedy in Darfur have many options for making their voices heard. They can certainly join organizations that are campaigning against the human rights abuse and can contribute time and money to organizations such Save Darfur (savedarfur.org). Save Darfur is an alliance of more than 100 organizations that are working to stop the violence.

Students can also put pressure on their own colleges and universities to stop investing in businesses that operate in Sudan. Colleges and universities have endowment funds, which they invest to generate income for everything from faculty to financial aid. Some of these investments might be with businesses that have ties to or interests with the Sudanese government. Products bought by universities could be made by businesses that do business with Sudan. Because these purchases and investments are helping these businesses, even indirectly, opponents of the Sudanese government argue that

colleges and universities should cut off their support so that they do not support the Darfur oppression in any way.

The University of California system prohibited all such investments in Sudan in 2006, and many colleges and universities have followed suit. Much of the effort has come from students who have worked hard to understand how their colleges and universities invest their endowment money.

The first step in stopping such investments is to know which companies actually operate in Sudan, which is sometimes very difficult. Multinational corporations often operate through subsidiaries that might do business with a specific country. The only way to know is to get a list of all companies in an endowment portfolio or sponsor a general resolution ordering the endowment's investment managers to sell all investments in Sudan.

This is what students have done at colleges such as Amherst, Hampshire, and

Smith College. Students at all three colleges pushed for socially responsible investing, which is the term for removing all questionable investments in activities that might harm the environment, undermine human rights, or violate generally accepted codes of ethics.

CRITICAL THINKING QUESTIONS

1. Should colleges divest in unethical investments even if doing so costs money that could support students?

2. How can a college know when it is making an unethical investment? Are broad policies that prohibit such investments enforceable?

3. How can students make sure that their colleges take action on issues such as Darfur? What kinds of political participation might work on your campus?

---

isolationism, a belief that the United States should stay out of international affairs unless other nations constitute a direct threat to its existence. The term was first used during the years leading up to World War I, when many Americans believed that the United States should stay out of the global conflict.

But isolationism is alive and well in the debate about whether the United States should remain in Iraq and Afghanistan. Isolationists argue that the United States should follow George Washington's advice to avoid international "entanglements," lest those entanglements lead the United States into wars that either cannot be won or have a high cost in American lives. They also argue that the United States should always focus first on its own interests.

Other citizens, including most foreign and defense policy experts, believe in **internationalism,** which says the United States must be engaged in international affairs to protect its own interests. Realists and idealists can disagree on the goals of U.S. foreign and defense policy, but they can still agree that the United States should engage the world on economic, political, and social issues such as human rights for oppressed people, global hunger, and the war on terrorism. Internationalists tend to view themselves as citizens of the world, not only the United States. They feel there are times when the United States should intervene, even when not directly threatened by another nation.

Unilateralism Versus Multilateralism

Although internationalists agree that the United States should participate in world affairs, they have two very different views about how. Supporters of **unilateralism** believe that the United States has the right to act alone in response to threats, even if other nations are unwilling to help. They argue that it should never give other nations (or the United

isolationism
The desire to avoid international engagement altogether.

internationalism
The belief that nations must engage in international problem solving.

unilateralism
A philosophy that encourages individual nations to act on their own when facing threats from other nations.

In early 2009, the United States received satellite photos of Iran's nuclear development. The United States responded by demanding more international penalties against Iran in an effort to strangle the country's economy. Iran continues to develop nuclear weapons and shows no readiness to negotiate. ■ *Why is the U.S. so concerned about Iran's effort to acquire a nuclear weapon?*

Nations) a veto over its actions, even if that means it acts alone in using its great military power.

In fact, President Bush announced a new unilateral policy immediately after the September 11, 2001, terrorist attacks on New York City and Washington, D.C. Under the **Bush Doctrine,** any nation that threatened the United States was automatically a potential target for unilateral action. The Bush Doctrine was built on three basic concepts:

1. The United States reserves the right to attack any nation that either harbors terrorists or constitutes a serious threat to the United States.
2. The United States reserves the right to act unilaterally against other nations even if it does not have the support of its allies.
3. The United States reserves the right to use massive force against its enemies, including nuclear weapons if needed.

Opponents of the Bush Doctrine support **multilateralism,** a belief that the United States should act only with the active support of other nations. According to its advocates, multilateralism not only increases the odds that other nations will share the burdens of war with the United States, but it also increases the potential that other nations will support the U.S. position once a war is over. At least partly because of the advantages of multilateralism, the Bush administration began backing away from the Bush Doctrine only three years after announcing it. Faced with mounting costs of rebuilding Iraq and reducing international tension with other Middle Eastern nations, the administration began working to bring other nations such as Russia, France, and Germany into the debate.

The Obama administration immediately renounced the Bush Doctrine. For example, it decided early on that it would not use nuclear weapons against Iran's nuclear program, even though those weapons could be used against the United States. However, the administration continues the long-standing U.S. practice of promising retaliation for attacks on U.S. citizens in other countries. It is particularly concerned about terrorist attacks around the world and inside the United States and is ready to respond immediately with strong military force.

Preemption Versus Provocation

For most of its history, the United States has waited to be provoked before going to war. Although there is considerable debate about what constitutes a provocation to war, **preemption** assumes the United States can attack first when it believes another nation constitutes a very serious threat. This approach was a centerpiece of the Bush Doctrine discussed above, based on the notion that the proliferation of **weapons of mass destruction** such as chemical, biological, or nuclear arms makes waiting for provocation much more dangerous than it once was. However, Iraq's weapons of mass destruction were never found despite an intense search—U.S. intelligence agencies were widely blamed for providing misleading intelligence perhaps under pressure from the Bush administration and Vice President Dick Cheney.

The war in Iraq is an example of preemption, which some experts call the nation's first "war of choice." Prior to Iraq, the United States only engaged in war in direct response to a first attack by an adversary. Believing that Iraq continued to hold weapons of mass destruction, the Bush administration decided to force Saddam Hussein from his dictatorship before he could use those weapons against the United States. Then-national security adviser Condoleezza Rice argued that the United States had a moral obligation to remove Hussein from power, even if doing so meant war. "This is an evil man who, left to his own devices, will wreak havoc again on his own population, his neighbors, and, if he gets weapons of mass destruction and the means to deliver them, on all of us," Rice told the British Broadcasting Corporation in August 2002. "There is a very powerful moral case for regime change. We certainly do not have the luxury of doing nothing."[2]

Bush Doctrine

A policy adopted by the Bush administration in 2001 that asserts America's right to attack any nation that has weapons of mass destruction that may be used against U.S. interests at home or abroad.

multilateralism

A philosophy that encourages individual nations to act together to solve international problems.

preemption

A policy of taking action before the United State is attacked rather than waiting for provocation.

weapons of mass destruction

Biological, chemical, or nuclear weapons that can cause a massive number of deaths in a single use.

Hard Power Versus Soft Power

Internationalists have different views of just how the United States should influence other nations in protecting itself. Some favor the use of **hard power,** or military and economic strength, whereas others favor **soft power,** or negotiation and diplomacy.[3]

Hard power depends almost entirely on a nation's ability to threaten or force another nation to act a certain way to avoid an attack. It relies on military strength as measured by the number of soldiers in uniform, their preparation for war, the quality of their equipment, and their nation's willingness to put them in harm's way.

We often associate hard power with the **theory of deterrence,** under which a nation creates enough military strength to ensure a massive response to any attack. During the cold war, the United States maintained more than enough nuclear weapons to deter the Soviet Union from using its nuclear weapons first and argued that sufficient bombs would survive any Soviet attack to ensure the destruction of the Soviet Union. This notion of *mutual assured destruction,* sometimes called MAD, was enough to keep both nations from using their nuclear weapons, but it kept each on constant alert just in case the other dared to act first.

Soft power is based on more traditional diplomacy and a nation's reputation for keeping its word in honoring treaties, its readiness to provide financial aid, and its ability to find consensus by bargaining with allies and adversaries alike. The Obama administration has been a strong supporter of more diplomacy in international affairs, although it has shown a willingness to use hard power in Afghanistan.

Nations can use hard and soft power at the same time to resolve disputes. In fact, the threat of military force is often enough to produce a negotiated settlement, as was the case throughout the cold war.

President Jimmy Carter, Egyptian President Anwar El Sadat, and Israeli Prime Minister Menanchem Begin share a famous handshake in 1978 agreeing to negotiate for peace in the Middle East. The three met at the U.S. president's retreat at Camp David, Maryland.
■ *How is this meeting an example of soft power?*

The Foreign Policy and Defense Agenda

The United States does not always have a choice about whether to act in world affairs. Many issues reach its borders that the country cannot avoid. These constitute the foreign and defense policy agenda, which currently focuses on seven major issues, presented here in alphabetical order: (1) controlling weapons of mass destruction, (2) ending the wars in Iraq and Afghanistan, (3) fighting terrorism, (4) negotiating peace in the Middle East, (5) promoting free trade abroad, (6) reducing global warming, and (7) strengthening democracy and international understanding. Just because an issue such as global diseases like HIV/AIDS is not on the list does not mean it is off the agenda. Rather, we focus here on the issues that appear to be at the top of the agenda today.

Controlling Weapons of Mass Destruction

The international community has been working for decades to reduce the threat of weapons of mass destruction. Although the world is particularly concerned about the development of such weapons in North Korea and Iran, the effort to reduce the spread of nuclear weapons actually started with nuclear disarmament talks between the United States and the Soviet Union in the 1970s.

With the end of the cold war in 1989, the United States and Russia began to look for new ways of reducing their nuclear arsenals, and in 2010, they agreed to reduce the number of nuclear warheads dramatically. Meeting in Prague on April 8, Russia and the United States agreed that each would reduce the number of nuclear warheads to 1,500, down from 2,200–2,700, respectively.

The world is still threatened by biological, chemical, and nuclear weapons, however. Although chemical weapons were outlawed by international agreement after World War I, at least nine countries say they have developed chemical weapons, such

LEARNING OBJECTIVE
20.2 Assess the status of each of the issues that currently dominate the foreign policy and defense agenda.

hard power
Reliance on economic and military strength to solve international problems.

soft power
Reliance on diplomacy and negotiation to solve international problems.

theory of deterrence
A theory that is based on creating enough military strength to persuade other nations not to attack first.

as nerve gases, that kill on contact. Others continue to develop biological weapons that spread disease or poisons, and still others already have or intend to develop nuclear weapons.

The United States has been particularly concerned in recent years about Iran and North Korea's recent efforts to develop nuclear weapons, which the United States and many other nations believe they may use against Israel. In April 2006, for example, Iran declared its intent to continue building its nuclear power program, which could generate uranium for nuclear weapons. There is also concern about the possibility that terrorists could build and explode some kind of nuclear weapon in the United States.

Fighting Terrorism

The war on terrorism is a broad term used to describe efforts to control terrorist acts sponsored by other nations, such as Afghanistan, or acts undertaken by independent groups that operate without any connection to a government.

Although the war is most often associated with Osama bin Laden and his Al-Qaeda terrorist organization, dozens of other terrorist organizations exist. These groups have executed bombings in London, Madrid, Moscow, the Middle East, and throughout Southeast Asia, including Thailand, Malaysia, the Philippines, and Indonesia, where terrorists have carried out several bombings at or near popular tourist hotels. For example, in November 2008, terrorists conducted a coordinated attack on major hotels in Mumbai, India, that killed 172 citizens. The attack was followed in December with the attempted Christmas Day bombing of a Northwest Airlines flight from Amsterdam to Detroit. These attacks showed the power of violence as a tool of terrorism, and the media's widespread coverage of terrorist incidents like these also (unwittingly or not) spreads this fear. Groups that were once small and unknown can achieve widespread notoriety, which helps with fund raising and recruiting.

Negotiating Peace in the Middle East

Long before the September 11, 2001, terrorist attacks, the United States was working to secure peace between Israel and its neighbors, in part because the Middle East is such an

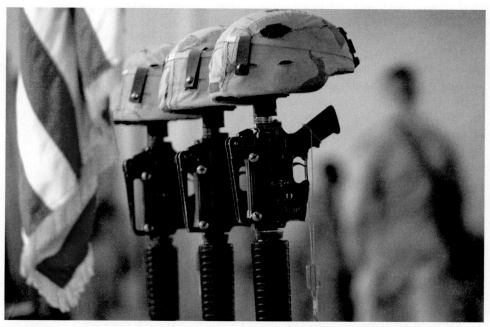

The war in Iraq, part of the ongoing war on terrorism, has cost the lives of more than 4,400 U.S. soldiers and more than 100,000 Iraqi civilians. ■ *Alongside the loss of life, what are the other costs of hard power?*

important source of the world's oil and in part because the United States has long considered Israel an ally. However, despite decades of U.S. efforts to promote peace in the region, the Middle East remains locked in a violent struggle over Israel's right to exist. Progress toward peace has been threatened by ongoing conflict with Arab nations and terrorist groups.

In 2002, however, the United States, Israel, and most Arab nations embraced "The Road Map to Peace." Under this agreement, signed in April 2003, Israel and its adversaries agreed to two broad steps toward peace. The Palestinian Authority, which represents citizens in territories captured by Israel in past wars, agreed to arrest, disrupt, and restrain individuals and groups that plan and conduct violent attacks on Israel. Israel in turn agreed to start dismantling settlements of Israeli citizens in the occupied territories to its south and east. Israel honored part of its end of the agreement starting in 2005 by beginning to dismantle settlements and turn over control of these territories to the Palestinian Authority. However, the dismantling of settlements happened in Gaza only; the settlements in East Jerusalem and the West Bank continue to expand. The dispute continues under the Obama administration, which is working toward a "soft power" resolution.

The Israeli-Palestian conflict involves continued resistance to the creation of Israel, but it also involves ongoing international opposition to the construction of Israeli settlements in Palestinian territory.

Promoting Free Trade Abroad

As the world economy has grown, so has international competition with the United States. The United States has generally responded to this *globalization* with a basic policy of free trade, meaning a commitment to the free movement of goods across international borders. But it does not allow the unrestricted export of technologies that can be used to build nuclear weapons, and it has long protected certain defense industries that would be essential should it ever be forced into another world war. The United States has also used trade as a tool to promote human rights and democratic reform.

Conflicting goals have characterized the U.S. debate over free trade with China. On the one hand, China has a long history of violating basic human and democratic rights. But it also has one of the fastest-growing economies in the world. U.S. exports to China have tripled during the past decade, and imports from China have grown rapidly. The conflict between concern for human rights and a desire to benefit from China's growing economy became especially prominent when the Clinton administration asked Congress to grant **normal trade relations** status to China. Under normal trade relations, China would be given the same favorable trading terms, such as low tariffs on imports and exports, that other favored nations receive.

Typically, Congress grants normal trade relations under a "fast-track," or accelerated, basis by limiting its own debate to a simple yes-or-no, up-or-down vote with no amendments. Although Congress initially refused to use this process for China, it eventually approved the status and extended the president's authority to negotiate such trade agreements in the Trade Act of 2002.

Reducing Global Warming

The United States has a mixed record in efforts to control the global climate change often associated with greenhouse gases that trap heat in the environment and raise the world's temperature. Much of the recent increase in greenhouse gases is related to the release of carbon dioxide from the burning of fossil fuels such as gasoline and coal by automobiles and power plants.

Experts do not all agree that global warming is a problem. Nevertheless, rising temperatures appear to threaten the world's climate in two ways. First, as the average temperature rises, the polar ice caps and glaciers melt. As the water melts, the oceans rise, threatening low-lying areas across the world. By some estimates, New York City, the

normal trade relations
Trade status granted as part of an international trade policy that gives a nation the same favorable trade concessions and tariffs that the best trading partners receive.

Of the People

THE GLOBAL COMMUNITY

International Support for Ties with Business

Global citizens have very different views of ties between business and their countries. Some see the ties as essential for economic growth, whereas others worry that business is only interested in profits. In addition, some global citizens appear to worry about corruption in business dealings with their countries. They many even view business as too involved in local affairs.

Nevertheless, international trade is usually seen as a way to help nations reduce poverty. The Pew Global Survey shows that the world's citizens generally believe that global trade is very or somewhat good for their nation. Respondents were asked: What do you think about the growing trade and business ties between your country and other countries—do you think it is a very good thing, somewhat good, somewhat bad, or a very bad thing for your country?

Favorability toward global trade has fallen in most countries during the past three years, in part because of the economic recession. Although Indians have become more supportive of trade as their economy grows, Americans remain skeptical about business ties. Worries about the recession have driven these concerns higher within the nation as Americans blame business and trade for the high unemployment that has

followed the economic collapse. However, most Americans understand that trade is one way to rebuild the economy as long as it flows both ways. They want more free trade between all nations.

In general, support for trade varies by the economic conditions of the world's nations. Poorer nations tend to see trade as a way out of poverty, but it is not always clear that trade has benefited them.

CRITICAL THINKING QUESTIONS

1. Why are less developed countries more supportive of international trade, and should they be so favorable?

2. What are the advantages of international trade in creating peaceful relations around the world?

3. How can trade damage a developing nation?

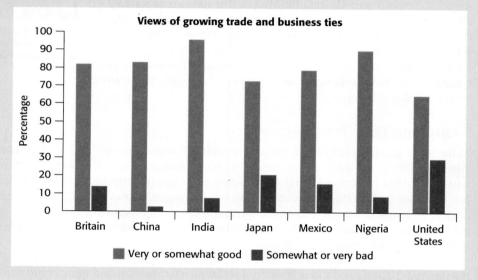

state of Washington, Florida, Louisiana, and other coastal areas could be completely under water within several hundred years. Second, as the average temperature rises, the weather becomes more unpredictable and potentially severe. Some experts attribute the recent increase in violent hurricanes such as Hurricane Katrina to global warming and predict more violent storms in the future.

The world acknowledged these problems when it adopted an international treaty called the Kyoto Protocol in 1997. Under the treaty, all participating nations agreed to reduce their emission of greenhouse gases by set amounts during the coming decades. Although 85 nations signed the agreement and 190 have ratified it, the United States has never ratified the treaty and has yet to embrace limits on burning fossil fuels, even though it produces a significant amount of the world's greenhouse gases. The United States has argued that the limits imposed by the Kyoto Protocol would weaken its economy. There is considerable debate today regarding the scientific evidence underpinning the call for action on global warming. Many of the world's largest carbon-producers met in Copenhagen in early 2010 but were unable to reach an agreement in setting targets.

In late 2009, the world's leaders met in Copenhagen to discuss targets for reducing global warming. The meeting failed to produce a formal agreement. ■ *Why is it so difficult to produce international agreements for reducing global warming?*

Ending the Wars in Iraq and Afghanistan

Iraq moved rapidly up the list of foreign-policy priorities in the days and weeks following the September 11, 2001, terrorist attacks. Convinced that Iraq possessed weapons of mass destruction that it was ready and willing to use against the United States, President Bush ordered the military to start planning for a preemptive war only six days after the attacks.[4] He also began building the case for action with the U.S. public and later made his argument before the United Nations.

> The United States has no quarrel with the Iraqi people; they've suffered too long in silent captivity. Liberty for the Iraqi people is a great moral cause, and a great strategic goal. The people of Iraq deserve it; the security of all nations requires it. Free societies do not intimidate through cruelty and conquest, and open societies do not threaten the world with mass murder. The United States supports political and economic liberty in a unified Iraq.[5]

The Bush administration also argued that Iraq was manufacturing weapons of mass destruction such as nuclear missiles and poisons that it intended to use against the United States and its allies in the Middle East. In March 2003, the United States launched a massive attack on Iraq. U.S. troops quickly reached the outskirts of the nation's capital city and secured it during the next two days. On May 1, 2003, President Bush stood on the deck of the USS *Abraham Lincoln* underneath a banner that read "MISSION ACCOMPLISHED" and told the nation that "Major combat operations in Iraq have ended."

However, the United States never found any weapons of mass destruction in Iraq. More troubling, violence and political unrest increased following the early military victory. Under pressure from congressional Democrats and Republicans to do something to quell the violence, the president announced a "surge" of 28,000 troops in early 2007, raising the total U.S. presence to 160,000. The troops were deployed to Iraq's capital city, Baghdad, and other "hot spots" where terrorists were most active. The Obama administration continued the surge but promised to remove all U.S. combat troops as soon as possible. Nonetheless, the Obama administration also committed to leaving at least some troops in Iraq to train Iraqi soldiers.

However, the war in Iraq may have distracted the United States from maintaining pressure against Afghan terrorists, prompting calls for more troops.[6] The Obama administration answered these calls in 2009 by sending 40,000 more troops into battle. By March 2010, the number of U.S. troops killed had crossed 1,000 and was larger than the troops killed in Iraq during the same period.

As discussed at the beginning of Chapter 12, the United States is currently committed to a "surge" strategy in which U.S. troops work with Afghan troops to stabilize key cities in the country. The U.S. and Afghan troops enter the city with massive force and move a civilian government into place as quickly as possible. The Obama administration hopes that this strategy will defeat terrorist forces that are seeking to recapture the country and has promised to end the surge in 2011.

Strengthening Democracy and International Understanding

The United States has long engaged in promoting democracy and its freedoms. It does so mostly through economic sanctions to increase the pain that might bring its adversaries to negotiations. However, some efforts conflict with other U.S. goals such as promoting international trade and fighting the war on terrorism. For example, the United States continues to promote international trade with China,

President Bush, on the deck of the USS *Abraham Lincoln* on May 1, 2003, declares an end to major combat operations in Iraq. Since that time, thousands of injuries and deaths have occurred on both sides of the conflict. ■ *How is Bush's message reinforced visually by elements in this photograph?*

Part of the peacemaking strategy in Afghanistan involves building a stronger Afghanistan government and military. The Obama administration's strategy is to train the Afghanistan military to take a greater role in fighting its adversaries. ■ *What are some of the difficulties in training and transferring authority to the Afghanistan military?*

Celebrities work together on many humanitarian fundraising efforts. In 2009, George Clooney organized a celebrity telethon to raise money for the victims of the Haitian earthquake. ■ *How can humanitarian aid help promote democracy abroad?*

one of the world's fastest-growing economies, even though China continues to deny its citizens basic rights such as a free press. In addition, the United States still provides aid to many Middle Eastern nations ruled by dictatorships in order to gain their help on the war on terrorism.

The United States also provides humanitarian aid to nations affected by natural disasters such as the 2010 earthquakes in Chile, Haiti, and China. Although dictators led many of the countries affected, the United States has long believed that citizens should not suffer during crises even though their governments are not free.

Finally, the United States uses programs such as the Peace Corps to promote international understanding. Peace Corps volunteers are expected to serve in another nation for two years and become part of the community they are serving. They work on a variety of projects, such as teaching mathematics and science, doing community development work, and improving water and sanitation systems. Most have a college degree, specific international experience, or both. Approximately 10 percent of the 7,300 current volunteers are over the age of 50. The Peace Corps covers travel and a minimum salary and typically trains volunteers in language and job skills for approximately three months before their service abroad.[7]

The Foreign Policy and Defense Bureaucracy

LEARNING OBJECTIVE

20.3 Outline the structure of the foreign policy and defense bureaucracy.

Even in troubled times, the president does not have absolute authority to act. Congress has the power to declare war, to appropriate funds for the armed forces, and to make rules that govern them. But the president is commander in chief and is authorized to negotiate treaties and receive and send ambassadors—that is, to recognize or refuse to recognize other governments. The Senate confirms U.S. ambassadorial appointments and gives consent (by a two-thirds vote) to treaty ratification.

Officially, the president's principal foreign policy adviser is the secretary of state, although others, such as the national security adviser or the vice president, are sometimes equally influential. In practice, the secretary of state delegates the day-to-day responsibilities for running the State Department and spends most of the time negotiating with the leaders of other countries.

However, foreign policy requires more than only one adviser. The application of hard and soft power is the responsibility of several major departments and agencies, including State, Defense, Treasury, Agriculture, Commerce, Labor, Energy, the Central Intelligence Agency (CIA), and the Department of Homeland Security.

The National Security Council

The key coordinating agency for the president is the National Security Council (NSC). Created by Congress in 1947, it serves directly under the president and is intended to help integrate foreign, military, and economic policies that affect national security. By law, it consists of the president, vice president, secretary of state, and secretary of defense. Recent presidents have sometimes also included the director of the CIA, the White House chief of staff, and the national security adviser as assistants to the NSC.

The national security adviser, appointed by the president, has emerged as one of the most influential foreign policy makers, sometimes rivaling the secretary of state in influence. Presidents come to rely on these White House aides both because of their proximity (down the hall in the West Wing of the White House) and because they owe their primary loyalties to the president, not to any department or program. Each president has shaped the NSC structure and adapted its staff procedures to suit his personal preferences. Throughout the years, however, the NSC, as both a committee and a staff, has taken on a major role in making and implementing foreign policy.

The State Department

The State Department is responsible for the diplomatic realm of foreign and defense policy. It is organized around a series of "desks" representing different parts of the world and foreign policy missions.

Duties   The State Department is responsible for negotiating treaties with other nations and international organizations, protecting U.S. citizens abroad, promoting U.S. commercial interests in other nations, and granting visas to foreign visitors. The State Department also runs all U.S. embassies and consulates abroad. Embassies provide full diplomatic services on behalf of the United States and its citizens; consulates are smaller branch offices of embassies that help foreign citizens enter the United States through visas, or entry papers.

The State Department also plays a significant role in homeland security. Many of the September 11, 2001, attackers had entered the United States on student visas granted by the State Department's Bureau of Consular Affairs. Although their movements once in the United States were supposed to be monitored by the Justice Department's Immigration and Naturalization Service, the State Department was criticized for being too lax in granting visas to almost anyone with enough money to purchase an airline ticket.

The Foreign Service   U.S. embassies are staffed largely by members of the U.S. Foreign Service. Although part of the State Department, the service represents the entire government and performs jobs for many other agencies. Its main duties are to carry out foreign policy as expressed in the directives of the secretary of state; gather political, economic, and intelligence data for U.S. policy makers; protect U.S. citizens and interests in foreign countries; and cultivate friendly relations with host governments and foreign peoples.

The Foreign Service is a select group of approximately 4,000 highly trained civil servants, comparable to army officers in the military and expected to take assignments anywhere in the world on short notice. Approximately two-thirds of U.S. ambassadors to approximately 160 nations come from the ranks of the Foreign Service. The others are usually presidential appointees confirmed by the senate.

The Foreign Service is one of the most prestigious, and most criticized, career services of the national government. Criticism sometimes comes as much from within as from outside. Critics claim that the organizational culture of the Foreign Service stifles creativity; attracts officers who are, or at least become, more concerned about their status than their responsibilities; and requires new recruits to wait 15 years or more before being considered for positions of responsibility. Like other federal agencies, most notably the CIA and the FBI, the Foreign Service has had great difficulty recruiting officers with Arabic-language skills, which clearly weakens each agency's ability to interpret, let alone collect, intelligence about the terrorist networks that have emerged in the Middle East and Asia.

Intelligence Agencies

Accurate, timely information about foreign nations is essential for making wise decisions. As the Senate Intelligence Committee and the national commission created to investigate the September 11, 2001, attacks both noted, the intelligence community failed to provide that information in time to prevent the attacks or change the course of the Iraq War.[8]

The Central Intelligence Agency   The most important intelligence agency is the Central Intelligence Agency, created in 1947 to gather and analyze information that flows into various parts of the U.S. government from all around the world. In recent years, the CIA has had approximately 20,000 employees, who both collect information and shape the intelligence estimates that policy makers use to set priorities.

Although most of the information the CIA gathers comes from open sources such as the Internet, the CIA does use spies and undercover agents to monitor foreign threats. This secret intelligence occasionally supplies crucial data. But it is not all glamour; much is routine. Intelligence work consists of three basic operations: reporting, analysis, and dissemination. *Reporting* is based on close and rigorous observation of developments around the world; *analysis* is the attempt to detect meaningful patterns in what was observed in the past and to understand what appears to be going on now; *dissemination* means getting the right information to the right people at the right time.

The Broader Intelligence Community   The CIA is only one of 15 intelligence agencies in the federal government, including the State Department's Bureau of Intelligence and Research; the Defense Department's Defense Intelligence Agency (which combines the intelligence operations of the Army, Navy, Air Force, and Marine Corps); the Federal Bureau of Investigation; the Treasury Department's Office of Terrorism and Finance Intelligence; the Energy Department's Office of Intelligence; the Homeland Security Department's Directorate of Information Analysis and Infrastructure Protection and Directorate of Coast Guard Intelligence; the National Security Agency (which specializes in electronic reconnaissance and code breaking); the National Reconnaissance Office (which runs the U.S. satellite surveillance programs); and the National Geospatial-Intelligence Agency (which collects and analyzes photographic imagery). Together, the 15 agencies constitute the *intelligence community.*

Because each was created to collect unique information (imagery, electronic intelligence, and so forth) for a unique client (the president, the secretary of defense, or others), historically, the agencies rarely shared information with each other. The lack of cooperation clearly affected the government's ability to prevent the September 11, 2001, attacks. "Many dedicated officers worked day and night for years to piece together the growing body of evidence on Al-Qaeda and to understand the threats," the 9/11 Commission concluded. "Yet, while there were many reports on bin Laden and his growing Al-Qaeda organization, there was no comprehensive review of what the intelligence community knew and what it did not know, and what that meant."[9]

Congress responded by creating a national intelligence director in 2004 to oversee all the intelligence offices. Under its legislation, the new director was responsible for providing the primary advice to the president on intelligence issues and was given the authority to increase or decrease the budgets of all other intelligence agencies. The director also oversees a new federal counterterrorism center, responsible for making sense of all national intelligence on potential terrorist threats to the United States. Despite the promise of more coordination, however, congressional critics in both parties complained that the new director merely added a layer of bureaucracy to an already cumbersome system.

The spirit of bipartisanship is reflected in the report of the 9/11 Commission, issued on July 22, 2004. The commission was made up of both Democrats and Republicans who managed to put their ideological differences aside and issue a report that is critical of both the Clinton and Bush administrations in their handling of terrorism. Shown here are 9/11 Commission co-chairs Thomas Kean and Lee Hamilton.

The Department of Defense

The president, Congress, the National Security Council, the State Department, and the Defense Department all make overall defense policy and attempt to integrate U.S. national security programs, but the day-to-day work of organizing for defense is the job of the Defense Department. Its headquarters, the Pentagon, houses within its 17.5 miles of corridors 23,000 top military and civilian personnel. The offices of several hundred generals and admirals are there, as is the office of the secretary of defense, currently Robert Gates, who provides civilian control of the armed services.

The Joint Chiefs of Staff   The committee known as the Joint Chiefs of Staff serves as the principal military adviser to the president, the National Security Council, and the secretary of defense. It includes the heads of the Air Force, Army, Navy, and Marine Corps, and the chair and vice chair of the Joint Chiefs. The president, with the consent of the Senate, appoints all the service chiefs to four-year nonrenewable terms. Note that the twice-renewable two-year term of the chair of the Joint Chiefs is part of the process of ensuring civilian control over the military.

The Department of Defense Reorganization Act of 1986 shifted considerable power to the chair of the Joint Chiefs. Reporting through the secretary of defense, the chair now advises the president on military matters, exercises authority over the forces in the field, and is responsible for overall military planning. In theory, the chair of the Joint Chiefs can even make a military decision that the chiefs of the other services oppose.

Note, however, that the chair of the Joint Chiefs is *not* the head of the military. The chair and the Joint Chiefs are advisers to the secretary of defense and the president, but the president can disregard their advice and on occasion has done so. A president must weigh military action or inaction against the larger foreign and security interests of the nation.

As chair of the Joint Chiefs of Staff, Admiral Mike Mullen is the highest-ranking officer in the U.S. military. The chair and the Joint Chiefs are advisers to the secretary of defense and the president. ■ *Why does the military report to the president?*

The All-Volunteer Force The Constitution authorizes Congress to do what is "necessary and proper" in order to "raise and support Armies," "to provide and maintain a Navy," and "to provide for calling forth the Militia." The Joint Chiefs and the presidential appointees who serve as secretaries of the Air Force, Army, Navy, and Marine Corps oversee the 1.5 million soldiers who currently serve in what the founders might call the national militia.

During most of its history, the United States has used military conscription to raise and support its armed services. The draft, as it is called, was first used in 1862, during the Civil War, and again during World War I, World War II, and Vietnam. Shortly before the Vietnam War ended, Congress replaced the draft with an *all-volunteer force,* composed entirely of citizens who choose to serve.

Contractors The tools of war include contracts with private businesses. The U.S. defense budget reached $555 billion in 2008, not counting the costs of the wars in Afghanistan and Iraq. More than $400 billion of that total is for private business contracts, such as military equipment, computer programming, and housing for troops.

Defense spending fell dramatically at the end of the cold war as weapons systems were canceled or postponed, bases closed, ships retired, and large numbers of troops brought home from Germany, the Philippines, and elsewhere. The army was cut by more than 30 percent, and the National Guard and the military reserve were cut back by approximately 25 percent. As a result, defense spending also fell, dropping from 25 percent of total federal spending at the height of the cold war in the mid-1980s to 15 percent in 2000. It has been rising since, as has spending for the effort to curb terrorism.

Weapons are, in fact, a major U.S. industry, one that members of Congress work hard to promote and protect. As former World War II hero Dwight Eisenhower warned in his presidential Farewell Address in 1960, the United States must be wary of the *military-industrial complex* that supports increased defense spending as a way to protect jobs. Eisenhower's words are well worth rereading today:

> This conjunction of an immense military establishment and a large arms industry is new in the American experience. The total influence—economic, political, even spiritual—is felt in every city, every State house, and every office of the Federal government. We recognize the imperative need for this development. Yet we must not fail to comprehend its grave implications. Our toil, resources, and livelihood are all involved; so is the very structure of our society.
>
> In the councils of government, we must guard against the acquisition of unwarranted influence, whether sought or unsought, by the military industrial complex. The potential for the disastrous rise of misplaced power exists and will persist.[10]

Despite Eisenhower's warning, the military-industrial complex has grown dramatically since the 1950s.

Of the People

AMERICA'S CHANGING FACE

Diversity in the Military

The U.S. military has become much more diverse during the past three decades, in part because of much more aggressive recruiting of women and minorities. In 1990, for example, only 11 percent of all military personnel were women, and 28 percent were people of color. By 2006, which is the latest information available, 15 percent were women, and 39 percent were people of color.

The four armed services—the army, navy, Marine Corps, and air force—vary greatly in terms of diversity, however. Looking at new recruits in 2006, approximately 34 percent of the navy, 25 percent of the army, 23 percent of the air force, and 15 percent of the Marine Corps were African American, Hispanic, Asian American, or another minority group. At the same time, 24 percent of the air force, 19 percent of the navy, 17 percent of the army, and only 7 percent of the Marine Corps were women.

Several reasons explain why the armed forces have done better recruiting people of color than recruiting women. First, the military has worked hard to improve its reputation as an equal opportunity employer. Colin Powell's rise to the highest post in the armed services has often been used to show recruits of color that anything is possible in the military. Powell entered the military as a second lieutenant in 1958, served two tours of duty in Vietnam, and eventually became the first African American officer to chair the Joint Chiefs of Staff.

Second, the military has long focused on recruiting high school graduates who are not college-bound, which is a group that contains more people of color. The military has

also developed several new programs that set aside substantial amounts of funding for future college tuition, which has also been effective in recruiting people of color.

CRITICAL THINKING QUESTIONS

1. What may explain the large percentages of minority soldiers in the military?

2. What may explain the much smaller percentages of women in the military?

3. Should the military represent all groups in society? Should combat soldiers be equally representative?

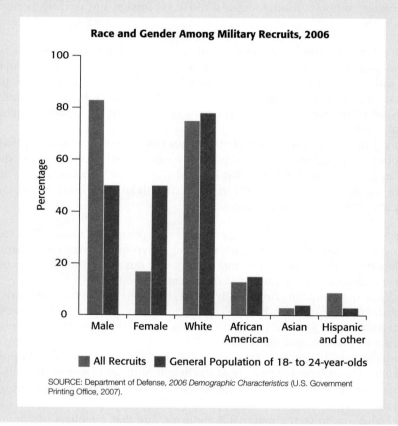

Race and Gender Among Military Recruits, 2006

■ All Recruits ■ General Population of 18- to 24-year-olds

SOURCE: Department of Defense, *2006 Demographic Characteristics* (U.S. Government Printing Office, 2007).

Foreign Policy and Defense Options

LEARNING OBJECTIVE

20.4 Evaluate the options for achieving foreign policy and defense goals.

The United States has a number of tools for achieving foreign policy success, not the least of which is military might. But military might, or hard power as we discussed earlier, is no longer enough to ensure success, or even deter foreign threats. Without other forms of soft and hard power, such as conventional diplomacy to send its message clearly, foreign aid to help nations in need, economic sanctions to isolate its adversaries, and public diplomacy to help other nations understand its agenda, the nation will not succeed in reaching its foreign policy goals.

Conventional Diplomacy (Soft Power)

Much of U.S. foreign policy is conducted by the Foreign Service and ambassadors in face-to-face discussions across the world. International summit meetings, with their high-profile pomp and drama, are another form of conventional diplomacy. Even though traditional diplomacy appears more subdued and somewhat less vital in this era of personal leader-to-leader communication by telephone, fax, and teleconferencing, it is still an important, if slow, process by which nations can gain information, talk about mutual interests, and try to resolve disputes.

Conventional diplomacy can become hard power when the United States breaks diplomatic relations with another nation. Doing so greatly restricts tourist and business travel to a country and in effect curbs economic as well as political relations with the nation. Breaking diplomatic relations is a next-to-last resort (force is the last resort), for it undermines the ability to reason with a nation's leaders or use other diplomatic strategies to resolve conflicts. It also hampers our ability to get valuable information about what is going on in a nation and to have a presence there.

Secretary-General Ban Ki-moon plays a central role in leading the United Nations. His job is to find common ground among nations of the world.

The United Nations is one of the most important arenas for traditional diplomacy. Established in 1945 by the victors of World War II, it now has 189 nation members. Despite its promise as a forum for world peace, the United Nations has been frustrated during its first 65 years. Critics contend that it has either ducked crucial global issues or was politically unable to tackle them. During much of that time, the U.N. General Assembly, dominated by a combination of Third World and communist nations, was hostile to many U.S. interests.

More recently, the five permanent members of the U.N. Security Council—the United States, China, Russia (which replaced the Soviet Union), Britain, and France—have usually worked in harmony. Moreover, the United Nations' assumption of responsibilities in the Persian Gulf War and its extensive peacekeeping missions in Cyprus and Lebanon have been notable examples of the effort to build the United Nations' respect. Several of the United Nations' specialized agencies—including the World Health Organization, the United Nations High Commission for Refugees, and the World Food Program—are considered major successes. But the review is much more mixed with respect to the United Nations' 63 peacekeeping efforts throughout its history. As of early 2010, the United Nations was engaged in at least 16 different peacekeeping missions, including the effort to protect civilians in the Darfur region of Sudan discussed at the beginning of this chapter.

Public Diplomacy (Soft Power)

In July 2002, President George W. Bush created the White House Office of Global Communications to address the question he asked before a joint session of Congress only a week after the terrorist attacks on New York City and Washington, D.C.: "Why do they hate us?" The Office of Global Communications is designed to enhance the United States' reputation abroad, countering its image as the "Great Satan," as some of its enemies describe it.[11]

Bush was not the first president to worry about the U.S. image abroad. President Franklin Roosevelt created the Office of War Information early in World War II, which in turn established the Voice of America program to broadcast pro-U.S. information into Nazi Germany. President Harry Truman followed suit early in the cold war with the Soviet Union by launching the Campaign of Truth, which eventually led to the creation of the U.S. Information Agency under President Dwight Eisenhower. Both agencies exist today and are being strengthened as part of the "new public diplomacy."

Public diplomacy is a blend of age-old propaganda techniques and modern information warfare. It has three basic goals: (1) to cast the enemy in a less favorable light among its supporters, (2) to mold the image of a conflict such as the war in Afghanistan, and (3) to clarify the ultimate goals of U.S. foreign policy. For example, the United States has tried to convince the people of Afghanistan that Osama bin Laden is the true enemy of the people, and that the war is not between Muslims and Western democracies but about preventing the deaths of innocent women and children in Afghanistan and the United States.

Foreign Aid (Soft Power)

The United States offers aid to more than 100 countries directly and to other nations through contributions to various U.N. development funds. Since 1945, the United States has provided approximately $400 billion in economic assistance to foreign countries. In recent years, however, its foreign aid spending has amounted to approximately $15 billion per year, or less than 50 percent of what it spent in inflation-adjusted dollars back in 1985.[12]

Most foreign aid goes to a few countries the United States deems to be of strategic importance to national security: Israel, Egypt, Ukraine, Jordan, India, Russia, South Africa, and Haiti. That list is sure to change in the future as the nation reallocates its budget to nations central to the war on terrorism. However, regardless of which nation receives the aid, most foreign aid is actually spent in the United States, where it pays for the purchase of U.S. services and products being sent to those countries. It thus amounts to a hefty subsidy for U.S. companies and their employees.

The American public thinks the United States spends much more on foreign aid than it actually does and therefore opposes increased spending. Although the United States is one of the largest foreign aid contributors in terms of total dollars, it ranks low among developed countries when aid is measured as a percentage of gross national income. A recent poll of U.S. citizens found that few supported increased foreign aid, and approximately half favored reducing it. The rest favor keeping foreign aid at the same level.[13] State Department officials are invariably the biggest advocates of foreign aid. Presidents also recognize the vital role foreign aid plays in advancing U.S. interests and have wanted to maintain the leverage with key countries that economic and military assistance provides. One major debate today is how much debt relief to provide for the world's poorest nations, especially ones that are hard hit by war and natural disasters such as Haiti.

Despite these arguments, Congress invariably trims the foreign aid budget, responding in part to polls that show most people erroneously believe that the United States spends more on foreign aid than it does on Medicare and other domestic priorities. Members of Congress often criticize foreign aid as a "Ghana versus Grandma" case. How, they say, can you give away taxpayers' money to some foreign country when we have poor older people who cannot afford their prescription drugs and decent medical help?[14]

Critics also note that U.S. foreign aid has subsidized the most autocratic and most corrupt of dictators. And there are plenty of instances in which foreign aid money has been stolen or misspent. Defenders counter that some corruption is inevitable.

Economic Sanctions (Hard Power)

The United States has frequently used economic pressure to punish other nations for opposing its interests. Indeed, it has employed economic sanctions more than any other nation—more than 100 times in the past 50 years. **Economic sanctions** deny export, import, or financial relations with a target country in an effort to change that country's policies. Those imposed on South Africa doubtless helped end apartheid and encourage democracy in that nation; sanctions on Libya helped end its nuclear weapons program. But sanctions imposed on Cuba have not had much effect in dislodging that nation's dictatorial regime.

The use of economic sanctions has varied throughout the years. They are especially unpopular among farmers and corporations that have to sacrifice part of their overseas markets to comply with government controls, and they rarely work as effectively as intended. They can also be costly to U.S. businesses and workers while intensifying anti-U.S. sentiment.

economic sanctions
Denial of export, import, or financial relations with a target country in an effort to change that nation's policies.

Military Intervention (Hard Power)

War is not merely an extension of diplomacy but rather the complete and total breakdown of diplomatic efforts. The United States has used military force in other

For the People

GOVERNMENT'S GREATEST ENDEAVORS

Rebuilding Europe After World War II

Approximately 50 years after the United States completed its most significant work rebuilding Europe after World War II, this endeavor still resonates as one of the its greatest achievements for the people. The roads, railroads, bridges, and factories that had been bombed into rubble were rebuilt; the economies that had been devastated by labor shortages were rekindled; and the

A young West German boy clutches new shoes received from foreign aid after WWII.

hunger, homelessness, and unemployment that marked the end of war were dispatched as the war-torn continent healed.

By strengthening the economies of Western Europe, this endeavor simultaneously helped alleviate suffering abroad, contain communism, and create a vibrant market for American goods. It also created new economic competition that made the U.S. economy stronger, while forging a bond with future allies in the war against terrorism.

The centerpiece of rebuilding Europe was the 1948 Marshall Plan, named for its champion, General George C. Marshall, who had served as Army chief of staff during World War II and who had just joined the Truman administration as secretary of state. The essence of the Marshall Plan was simple: Inject billions in economic aid to get Europe moving again. The program, which was formally titled the European Recovery Plan, provided approximately $12 billion in aid to increase economic production, expand European trade, encourage new economic ties between former enemies, and put an end to the rampant economic chaos of the time.

The program was limited to four years and demanded cooperation from the

nations it was designed to help. Nations could only receive help if they created a new organization to distribute the funding. Twenty-two European nations were invited to the first planning meeting in the summer of 1947, but only 16 showed up. The Soviet Union and its communist allies in Eastern Europe refused to attend, choosing instead to revive the Comintern, an international organization pledged to destroying world capitalism.

The Marshall Plan was a stunning foreign policy success, particularly in helping the United States contain communism. But it was also a great moral victory for America, prompting British Prime Minister Winston Churchill to call it "the most unsordid act in history."

CRITICAL THINKING QUESTIONS

1. Why was rebuilding Europe so important to the United States?

2. How is this kind of soft power being used today around the world?

3. Should the United States spend money helping future competitors such as Europe become self-sufficient?

---

nations on the average of almost once a year since 1789, although usually in short-term initiatives such as NATO's military activities in Bosnia and Kosovo. Although presidential candidate John Kerry argued that the Iraq War was the first time in history the United States had gone to war because it chose to, not because it had to, the country has actually sent forces into combat many times without a clear threat. It did not have to go to war against Spain in 1898 or send troops to Cuba, Haiti, the Dominican Republic, Lebanon, Mexico, Nicaragua, Somalia, South Vietnam, or even Europe in World War I.[15] (See Table 20–1 for the number of troops killed in the nation's major wars.)

Experts tend to agree that the use of force is most successful in small and even medium-sized countries for short engagements (Grenada, Panama, Kuwait, Kosovo, and Afghanistan). They also agree that it "often proves ineffective in the context of national civil wars (the United States in Vietnam; Israel in Lebanon)."[16]

Not all military action is visible to the public or even the intended target. Covert activities are planned and executed to conceal the identity of the sponsor. The United States repeatedly engaged in covert operations during the cold war, including early intervention in Vietnam and Central America, as well as in Afghanistan, where it supported rebels fighting the Soviet invasion. But covert activities in Cuba, Chile, and elsewhere have backfired, and support for this strategy has cooled in the post–cold war era.[17] Ironically, U.S. covert aid to the Afghan rebels eventually led to the Soviet withdrawal, which in turn led to the establishment of the Taliban, which allowed Osama bin Laden and his followers to establish training bases in its territory.

TABLE

20–1 | The Costs of War

War	Number Killed
Revolutionary War	4,435
War of 1812	2,260
Civil War	214,939
Spanish-American War	385
World War I	53,402
World War II	291,557
Korean War	35,516
Vietnam War	58,516
Persian Gulf War	382
Iraq War	4,416*
Afghanistan War	1,233*

* Estimated figures as of August 2010.

SOURCE: *The Washington Post*, May 26, 2003; figures updated by authors.

YOU WILL
DECIDE Should Women Engage in Combat?

As the number of women in the armed forces has increased, so has the number of women who serve in combat zones. Whereas women constituted 6 percent of U.S. forces in the first war in Iraq in 1991, they made up 15 percent of forces in Iraq in 2008.

Although their jobs were in noncombat positions, Iraq and Afghanistan have been very dangerous places to serve—by July 2010, 113 female soldiers had been killed. Technically, the women killed in Iraq and Afghanistan did not die in combat operations. Under a 1994 order, women can fly combat aircraft to and from airfields, protect convoys, guard prisoners of war, and rescue wounded soldiers, but they may not participate in any "direct combat on the ground." Although the military is redesigning assignments to ensure that women have an equal opportunity to participate in noncombat operations, women are allowed to serve only in support units.

The military has changed dramatically in recent years—combat uses high-technology weapons and requires tight coordination of air, land, and sea operations, which can blur the lines between support and combat units. As war has become more complicated, experts are asking whether women should be given the order to engage in combat.

What do you think? Should women be engaged in direct ground combat? What are some of the arguments for or against this?

THINKING IT THROUGH

Opponents argue that men are physically superior to women—although there are many high-tech jobs in combat, there is nothing high-tech about a face-to-face encounter with a deadly enemy. These opponents believe that men are better suited to win these encounters. There is also concern that men and women would form personal relationships in combat units that might distract them as they enter battle, or that female soldiers might be in the early stages of pregnancy when called for combat.

Moreover, opponents feel women would be much more vulnerable to sexual harassment in combat units, which is obviously harder to police during battle.* There is already plenty of evidence that women in the military face discrimination and harassment. According to a recent investigation, approximately 3,000 women experienced some kind verbal and physical abuse in 2008 alone.[†]

Advocates of a combat role for women argue that physical differences are mostly irrelevant. All soldiers must meet certain physical qualifications such as height, weight, and conditioning. If women meet these criteria, they argue, they should be allowed to fight. After all, they go through the same boot camps as men and learn how to use the same weapons. With the armed services struggling to recruit new soldiers, advocates also argue, women constitute an important source of future volunteers.

Women now make up approximately 15 percent of the total enlistment in the U.S. armed forces.

Critical Thinking Questions

1. What are the political barriers against allowing women in combat?
2. Are women just as able to win the face-to-face battles that often arise in combat?
3. How can the military ensure that personal relationships do not affect combat decisions on the battlefield?

---

* Evan Thomas and Gregory L. Vistica, "Falling Out of the Sky," *Newsweek,* March 17, 1997, p. 26.
[†] http://www.time.com/time/magazine/article/0,9171,1968110,00.html.

Prospects for the Future

The world has become a much more uncertain place since the end of the cold war, if only because the United States now faces many potential "hot spots" where individual nations and groups can challenge its views. Moreover, the Internet has increased access to information around the world, the global economy has increased competition for jobs and markets, and the war on terrorism has increased anti-U.S. sentiment in many nations.

The United States is clearly struggling to address this uncertainty without frustrating the public or compromising basic democratic principles. On the one hand, for example, citizens favor open borders, easy movement of imports and exports, short lines at airports, quick access to information, and protection of their privacy. On the other hand, they want government to monitor terrorists, detect dangerous cargo, ensure airport security, keep secrets from the enemy, and make sure no one slips through the border to bring harm to the nation.

Osama bin Laden became America's number one public enemy after his Al-Qaeda organization took credit for destroying the World Trade Center on 9/11.
■ *What do Americans think when they see this image year after year? How important is it to capture bin Laden?*

Although these goals are not necessarily contradictory, they do require a careful balance of individual liberty and national interest. They also call for an effort to prevent the spread of terrorism by promoting global peace and understanding. The war on terrorism will not be won in a single battle with a single adversary, nor will weapons of mass destruction disappear without a broad international commitment to action. As the United States has learned during the hard months of combat in Iraq, coalition building may be difficult, frustrating, and most certainly time-consuming, but, ultimately, it may be the only option available. Having fought the Iraq War largely on its own, the United States has come to realize that it needs help to accomplish its goals.

Citizens can help the United States achieve its goals in many ways, whether by contributing or volunteering to provide humanitarian aid, serving in the military, or trying to improve the nation's reputation by addressing problems at home. At the same time, citizens can help change the foreign policy and defense agenda through active engagement in the political process. Their voices can be and have been heard on many issues, including Darfur. By putting pressure on the federal government, citizens can influence the priorities given to our foreign policy goals, while holding the nation's elected leaders accountable for what they do.

CHAPTER **SUMMARY**

20.1 Analyze the questions and responses that shape approaches to U.S. foreign policy and defense.

Views of foreign policy address five basic questions: Should the United States view the world realistically or idealistically? Should the United States isolate itself from the world or accept a role in the international community? Should the United States act on its own or only with the help of other nations? Should the United States act first against threats to its safety or wait until it is attacked? And should the United States use its military and economic hard power or its diplomatic soft power? Hard power relies on military and economic strength, whereas soft power uses diplomacy.

20.2 Assess the status of each of the issues that currently dominate the foreign policy and defense agenda.

The foreign policy and defense agenda contains a long list of issues, but seven are currently at the top of the list: controlling weapons of mass destruction such as nuclear missiles, fighting terrorism, negotiating peace in the Middle East, promoting free trade abroad, reducing global warming, ending the wars in Iraq and Afghanistan, and strengthening democracy and international understanding. Congress and the president do not always agree on the specific issues but tend to spend most of their time and the federal budget on them.

20.3 Outline the structure of the foreign policy and defense bureaucracy.

The defense bureaucracy involves a set of interlocking agencies that engage in many of the same issues. The National Security Council, State Department, intelligence agencies, and Defense Department all play a role in setting and administering foreign policy and defense. The Defense Department is designed to ensure civilian control of the U.S. military but seeks advice from the military through the Joint Chiefs of Staff, who oversee the all-volunteer force. Contractors deliver a large amount of goods and services to the department and are part of what President Eisenhower called the military-industrial complex.

20.4 Evaluate the options for achieving foreign policy and defense goals.

Foreign policy and defense options involve a mix of hard and soft power, including conventional diplomacy and foreign aid, economic sanctions, and military intervention.

CHAPTER **SELF-TEST**

20.1 Analyze the questions and responses that shape approaches to U.S. foreign policy and defense.

1. A policy of viewing the world idealistically requires accepting a role in the international community. In a few sentences, make two or three more connections between the five questions shaping U.S. foreign policy.
2. List and define the three components of the Bush Doctrine.
3. Decide whether the following are aspects of hard power or soft power.
   a. Negotiating with other nations
   b. Providing aid to developing countries
   c. Maintaining powerful military forces
   d. Using battlefield forces to defeat enemies
   e. Participating in international treaties and institutions

20.2 Assess the status of each of the issues that currently dominate the foreign policy and defense agenda.

4. List and describe five of the seven issues dominating the U.S. international agenda.
5. In a few sentences, explain two problems and two opportunities related to granting normal trade relations status to China.
6. In a few sentences, explain what the "surge" is, why it has been implemented, and its results so far.
7. Write a short essay discussing which of the seven issues on the U.S. agenda deserves the most attention. Explain how attention to it will most likely ensure peace and prosperity and why the other issues are less important.

20.3 Outline the structure of the foreign policy and defense bureaucracy.

8. Match each of the following government organizations with its appropriate description:

   a. Contractor
   b. State Department
   c. Joint Chiefs of Staff
   d. National Security Council
   e. Central Intelligence Agency

   i. The organization charged with gathering information from around the world
   ii. A private business that develops and manufactures technology for the military
   iii. The organization responsible for negotiating treaties, protecting U.S. citizens abroad, and staffing embassies and consulates
   iv. A council consisting of the heads of the Army, Navy, Air Force, and Marine Corps
   v. A committee of the president, vice president, secretaries of defense and state, and often others that make foreign policy

9. The foreign policy and defense bureaucracy is extremely complex and employs thousands of people. In a paragraph, suggest some of the problems that may arise from its size and complexity.
10. In two or three sentences, explain how the president is truly the commander in chief of the armed forces.

20.4 Evaluate the options for achieving foreign policy and defense goals.

11. Which of the following is an example of public diplomacy?
    a. Diplomats from Japan, China, and the United States negotiate with North Korea over ending its nuclear weapons program
    b. President Bush addresses the U.S. people about the Iraq War
    c. The State Department creates Web sites in Arabic showing that Al-Qaeda has killed thousands of fellow Muslims
    d. Executives from the United States' General Motors and Japan's Toyota discuss an auto industry trade agreement
12. In a few sentences, define conventional diplomacy and explain how it is related to hard power.
13. In an essay, discuss which foreign policy and defense tools, such as foreign aid or military force, would best keep the United States safe and improve its relationship with Iran. Also discuss which tools would likely *not* work or would make the situation worse.

Answers to selected questions: 3. a. soft, b. soft, c. hard, d. hard, e. soft; 8. a. ii, b. iii, c. iv, d. v, e. i; 11. c

mypoliscilab EXERCISES

Where participation leads to action!

Apply what you learned in this chapter on MyPoliSciLab.

Read on mypoliscilab.com

eText: Chapter 20

Study and **Review** on mypoliscilab.com

Pre-Test
Post-Test
Chapter Exam
Flashcards

Watch on mypoliscilab.com

Video: NYC's Subway Surveillance System
Video: Sanctions on Iran

Explore on mypoliscilab.com

Simulation: You Are President John F. Kennedy
Simulation: You Are the Newly Appointed Ambassador to the Country of Dalmatia
Simulation: You Are the President of the United States
Comparative: Comparing Foreign and Security Policy
Timeline: The Evolution of Foreign Policy
Visual Literacy: Evaluating Defense Spending

KEY TERMS

realism, p. 524
idealism, p. 524
isolationism, p. 525
internationalism, p. 525
unilateralism, p. 525

Bush Doctrine, p. 526
multilateralism, p. 526
preemption, p. 526
weapons of mass destruction, p. 526
hard power, p. 527

soft power, p. 527
theory of deterrence, p. 527
normal trade relations, p. 529
economic sanctions, p. 538

ADDITIONAL RESOURCES

FURTHER READING

KIMBERLY ANN ELLIOTT, GARY CLYDE HUFBAUER, AND **JEFFREY J. SCHOTT,** *Economic Sanctions Reconsidered,* 3d ed. (Peterson Institute, 2008).

LOUIS FISHER, *Presidential War Power,* 2d ed. (University Press of Kansas, 2004).

JOHN LEWIS GADDIS, *The Cold War: A New History* (Penguin, 2005).

OLE HOLSTI, *Public Opinion and American Foreign Policy,* rev. ed. (University of Michigan Press, 2004).

STEVEN W. HOOK AND **JOHN SPANNIER,** *U.S. Foreign Policy Since World War II,* 18th ed. (CQ Press, 2010).

LOCH K. JOHNSON, *Secret Agencies: U.S. Intelligence in a Hostile World* (Yale University Press, 1996).

JOYCE P. KAUFMAN, *A Concise History of U.S. Foreign Policy,* 2d ed (Rowman & Littlefield, 2010).

STEVEN KULL AND **I. M. DESTLER,** *Misreading the Public: The Myth of a New*

Isolationism (Brookings Institution Press, 1999).

ROBERT S. LITWAK, *Rogue States and U.S. Foreign Policy: Containment After the Cold War* (Johns Hopkins University Press, 2000).

NATIONAL COMMISSION ON TERRORIST ATTACKS ON THE UNITED STATES, *The 9/11 Commission Report* (Norton, 2004).

JOSEPH NYE, *Soft Power: The Means to Success in World Politics* (Public Affairs, 2005).

MICHAEL E. O'HANLON, *How to Be a Cheap Defense Hawk* (Brookings Institution Press, 2002).

PAUL R. PILLAR, *Terrorism and U.S. Foreign Policy* (Brookings Institution Press, 2004).

ROSEMARY RIGHTER, *Utopia Lost: The United Nations and World Order* (Twentieth Century Fund, 1995).

STEPHEN R. WEISSMAN, *A Culture of Deference: Congress's Failure of Leadership in Foreign Policy* (Basic Books, 1995).

GEORGE C. WILSON, *This War Really Matters: Inside the Fight for Defense Dollars* (CQ Press, 2000).

WEB SITES

State.gov The State Department's Web site.

Defense.gov The Defense Department's Web site.

Foreignaffairs.com A leading magazine about foreign policy. Many articles are free.

Freedomhouse.org Freedom House is a charitable organization that follows threats to freedom around the world. It also provides news feeds on specific events.

Foreignpolicy.com Another leading magazine about foreign policy. Many articles are also free.

careers.state.gov/officer/index.html The place to go to apply to the foreign service.

PART VI

State and Local Government

THE BIG PICTURE

A distinguishing feature of American government is federalism. State and local governments help define our politics and shape our political identities. They administer most public programs, have been the laboratories for experiments in public policy, and are the proving grounds for many leaders who go on to serve at the national level. As with the federal government, the states have constitutions that detail the powers and prerogatives of government. Electoral competition is state centered because all elective offices in the United States honor state boundaries. Although the executive, legislative, and judicial institutions of state government have some similarities with their federal counterparts, they do vary across the states. There are even more varieties in the ways local governments are organized. Local governments provide many of the services most important to citizens. The relationship between local and state governments is influenced by different legal structures and budgetary policies.

COURSE LEARNING **OBJECTIVES**

CHAPTER 21 State and Local Politics
Identify the range of policy programs administered by state and local governments, and analyze the influences on state and local politics.

Most government programs, including those funded in part by federal programs, are administered by state and local governments. The range of policy issues dealt with by state and local governments is broad and important. As a result, interest groups are organized and active at the state and local levels. Because of the closer proximity of local and state government and the tradition in many localities and states of more direct citizen participation, there is a perception that state and local governments are more responsive to the people. Other factors that impact local government are the political structure, the local traditions, the social structure, and the local economy.

CHAPTER 22 State Constitutions
Compare and contrast the U.S. Constitution with state constitutions.

State constitutions are often patterned after the U.S. Constitution in providing both a separation and sharing of powers among the legislative, executive, and judicial branches. They differ from each other and from the U.S. Constitution in some of the ways they structure these branches. State constitutions are typically longer and more detailed than the U.S. Constitution. Constitutional change occurs by different means, ranging from wholesale change at a constitutional convention to specific amendments, which in some states may be proposed by a petition process and then voted on by the people.

CHAPTER 23 Parties and Elections in the States
Assess the importance of parties and elections at the state level.

States are where the action is in American campaigns and elections. Presidential, congressional, gubernatorial, and legislative elections all have substantial state components. State laws determine who may vote, the means by which people vote, how nominees are selected, and which candidates may appear on ballots. Political parties are organized around the units of competition, which are most typically state and local elections. The strength of parties varies across states.

CHAPTER 24 State Legislatures
Describe the functions of state legislatures, and evaluate their responsiveness to the people.

With the exception of Nebraska's unicameral and nonpartisan legislature, all other state legislatures are bicameral and organized along party lines. State legislatures, like Congress, rely on committees, staff, and seniority in doing business. Most legislators are white, middle-aged, and male. Voters and the courts have attempted to make legislatures more representative and responsive by requiring that legislative districts have equal numbers of people and, in some states, by enacting term limits. In approximately half of the states, voters may effectively veto legislation through the popular referendum or initiative process.

CHAPTER 25 State Governors
Explain how governors use their formal and informal powers to influence public policy.

The executive branch in state government often includes several elected office holders, including the governor, lieutenant governor, secretary of state, attorney general, and state treasurer. Although the formal powers of governors differ across states, governors typically have appointment, budgetary, veto, and pardon powers. Governors also have informal powers and substantial visibility in their states. The power of governors has grown in recent years.

CHAPTER 26 Judges and Justice in the States
Describe the judicial system at the state level, and evaluate the differences across the states in judicial selection and sentencing.

Although the names given to particular courts vary by state, states generally have trial courts, appellate courts, and a court of last resort. Judges are selected or elected by different means in different states. The justice system includes lawyers who serve as prosecutors, defenders, and judges; citizens who serve as jurors; and state employees who serve as corrections officials. States differ in their sentencing practices and use of incarceration as they attempt to find a balance in protecting the rights of the accused and the victim.

CHAPTER 27 Local Governments and Metropolitics
Identify the functions of local governments, including counties, cities, towns, and special districts.

Local governments are typically agents of state governments with limited independence. The size, population density, structure, and role of county governments vary dramatically. Some counties are effectively like large cities, whereas others are largely administrative structures to manage state and federal policies. Cities can also be very different from each other, but share in common such aims as economic development and providing services like public safety and sanitation. Suburbs, which may or may not be incorporated with the nearby city, have been fast growing and increasingly share the same challenges as cities. Mayors are the most visible leader of cities.

CHAPTER 28 Making State and Local Policy
Evaluate the importance of state and local governments in implementing policy.

State and local governments are essential in implementing policy in such areas as health care, education, welfare, and transportation. The ability of states to implement policy is dependent on revenue, which comes from grants or transfers from the federal government, and from taxes at the state and local level. Revenue shortfalls have forced state governments to scale back spending in recent years. In higher education, for example, this has often resulted in increasing students' tuition. Rising costs of providing services, especially health care, have also constrained state and local governments. States influence national policy by taking the lead in areas such as health care (Massachusetts) and the environment (California).

CHAPTER 29 Staffing and Financing State and Local Governments
Describe the challenges for state and local governments in organizing resources, raising funds, and managing expenditures.

Most of state spending is on education and health. The revenue to pay for these and other services comes from taxes, user fees, and transfers from other levels of government. Some states utilize sales, income, or excise taxes, but states vary in how much they tax the people and businesses in their state. States generally are prohibited from deficit spending, so they must either adjust taxes or spending to keep their budgets balanced. Much of the spending by state and local governments goes to pay for public employees. Hoping to reduce costs, states have increasingly privatized the delivery of services.

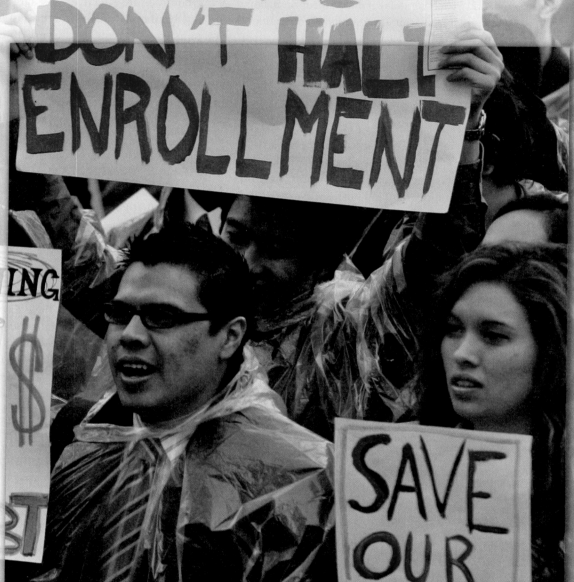

State and Local Politics

On May 19, 2009, voters in California went to the polls for a special election. Like nearly every state, California's budget was running large deficits ($25 billion) because of the national economic recession. The Democratically controlled legislature had passed a budget in February 2009, which Republican Governor Arnold Schwarzenegger had signed, that contained several proposals to manage this crisis. However, that budget depended on voters approving constitutional amendments on how the state collects and distributes revenue. Thus, voters could endorse the actions of their elected officials or effectively scuttle the deal. This was literally government by the people. By overwhelming margins, voters defeated every proposed change except the largely symbolic one that prohibited the state from giving pay raises to the governor, legislators, or other state officials.

For those unfamiliar with California politics, this outcome might seem bizarre. Serious repercussions were at stake for the state—state workers faced unpaid furloughs or being fired; school teachers at every level faced larger classes, pay freezes or reductions, and substantial layoffs; and many government services, particularly those directed at California's neediest citizens, faced drastic cuts or elimination. From this crisis, a Democratic legislature and a Republican governor had crafted a deal that neither side loved, but that both sides could live with—the kind of political compromise that voters supposedly want when they complain about partisan bickering leading to gridlock. How could voters say "No" so emphatically to this compromise?

Those more familiar with California's political history, however, would tell you that this simply marked the most recent in a long line of ballot initiatives that have effectively tied the hands of state officials in dealing with budgetary matters. In 1978, for example, voters approved Proposition 13, which capped state property tax rates and required future increases in any state tax to receive a two-thirds majority in both legislative chambers. Voters have used other initiatives to tie a fixed percentage of the budget to education spending (1988). Add to this a 1933 provision requiring that a two-thirds majority in both chambers in the state legislature is needed to pass a budget, and you are left with a system where elected officials have little room to maneuver and where minorities can block nearly all attempts to change the fiscal situation.

The situation in California is not entirely unique, as states across the country face similar budgetary problems. However, no two states face exactly the same situation, and no two states have exactly the same set of rules and institutions in place to deal with policy problems. Some states have very professional state legislatures, whereas others have legislatures that meet part time and lack professional staff support. Some states have voter initiatives, while others do not. Some governors have strong veto and line-item veto powers, while others do not. Thus, a full understanding of the United States' political system requires exploring this variation across the states and how that shapes the way states respond to the very real policy problems facing their citizens.

Who Governs?

State and local governments flourished long before there was a national government. Indeed, the framers of our Constitution shaped the national government largely according to their practical experience with colonial and state governments. What happens today in state and local governments continues to influence the policies of the national government, and the national government and its policies have an important impact on local

CHAPTER **OUTLINE**
CHAPTER LEARNING
OBJECTIVES

Who Governs?

21.1 Contrast the functions of federal, state, and local governments, and evaluate the theories of decision-making in local governments.

Influences on State and Local Governments

21.2 Analyze the activities and influence of interest groups and lobbyists at the state and local levels.

Participation Patterns in Local Government

21.3 Assess the level and consistency of involvement of the major participants in local communities.

Challenges for State and Local Governments

21.4 Evaluate the challenges facing state and local governments.

LEARNING **OBJECTIVE**
21.1 Contrast the functions of federal, state, and local governments, and evaluate the theories of decision-making in local governments.

and state governments. The federal government, 50 state governments, and the more than 89,000 cities, counties, towns, villages, school districts, water control districts, and other local governments all interact to govern and make policy for the country.

The Role of State and Local Governments

The national government has become the driving force behind the nation's economic strength and security. It assumes major responsibility for protecting civil rights, fighting inflation and unemployment, regulating economic sectors, funding scientific research, and subsidizing weaker sectors of the economy. The national government also operates some of the nation's largest social programs, such as Social Security, Medicare, student loans and grants, and various forms of food and nutritional assistance. It funds recovery efforts after natural disasters, it dominates issues of international trade and relations, and it exercises exclusive authority over matters of war and peace.

However, many of the critical domestic and economic issues facing the United States are confronted by state and local officials. State and local governments make most of the decisions about how schools are run, where roads and bridges are built, how land is used, and what social services are provided and to whom. They regulate our driving, our occupations, and our families (through marriage and divorce laws, among others). They decide, for the most part, what constitutes criminal behavior and how it should be charged, tried, and punished, and they have custody of more than 91 percent of the nation's nearly 2.4 million prison and jail inmates.[1]

State and local governments administer most of our laws and domestic programs, including many programs funded by the federal government. Through Medicaid and related programs, state governments provide health care coverage for approximately half of all poor children and a quarter of all poor adults, and, with federal assistance, they finance half of all nursing home expenditures and more than one-third of all births.[2] They pay for 79 percent of the total costs of building and maintaining our public highway system, and they are responsible for building and maintaining most of our bridges, water and sewage systems, and other elements of our nation's infrastructure.[3] State and local colleges and universities educate nearly three of every four students enrolled in higher education.[4]

Some of the most beautiful buildings and parks in the United States were built with the support of state and local governments, including Central Park in New York City, the University of Virginia's original campus, and Pasadena City Hall. ■ *Are you surprised by the amount and variety of services provided by state and local governments? Why or why not?*

State and local governments are a very large part of our economy. The nation's more than 89,000 state and local governments spent slightly more than $2 trillion in 2008, which equals approximately 14 percent of the United States' gross domestic product (GDP).[5] (GDP is a good measure of the size of the country's economy; it measures the total market value of all final goods and services produced in the nation.) That is less than the federal government's expenditures of nearly $3 trillion in 2008, which were approximately 21 percent of GDP that year. State and local expenditures as a percentage of national GDP have steadily grown during the last 30 years, while federal spending has held steady or slightly declined,[6] although the massive federal spending in 2009 and 2010 in response to the recession runs counter to this trend. The critical point to remember is that state and local government spending combined has nearly the same total impact on our country's economy as does that of the national government.

State and local governments employ more than 19 million people, which is slightly more than seven times the 2.7 million civilians the federal government employs.[7] This ratio has increased in recent decades as the federal government has downsized, while state and local governments have grown. Most state and local employees work in education (10.9 million), hospitals (1.1 million), police protection (997,000), and corrections (743,000).[8] In fact, from 2001 onward, state and local governments have employed more workers than the entire manufacturing sector.

As these many functions suggest, state and local governments deal more directly with the average person than the national government does. The points at which people come into contact with government services and officials most often relate to schools, streets and highways, parks and playgrounds, police and fire protection, zoning, and health care—activities that are typically managed by state and local officials. However, even in these areas, the mix of national, state, and local programs and responsibilities is such that it is often hard to isolate what each level of government is doing. State and local employees are the face of government for many of us—but that face may be responsible for complying with rules and carrying out programs established by multiple levels of government.

Who Has the Power?

Every government system is part of a larger social system. Each one operates in the context of a particular economic system, class structure, racial and religious differences, political party structure, and set of lifestyles. The diversity of social systems surrounding state and local governments, along with their complex interconnections with each other and the federal government, affect how these many different state and local governments recognize problems, manage conflict, make decisions about what actions to take, and benefit some people and institutions and not others.

How can we grasp the complex operations and problems of so many state and local governments? We can do so by focusing on the core components of democratic governance: *citizen participation, liberty, constitutional checks and balances, representation, and responsible leadership.* Further, we can address several questions that throw light on all these problems: *Who governs?* How much influence or control is in the hands of the business community? Does political power gravitate toward a small number of people? If so, who are these people? Do they work closely together, or do they oppose each other? Do the same people or factions shape the agenda for public debate and dominate all decision making? Or do some sets of leaders decide certain questions and leave other questions to other leaders or influences?

In 1924, two sociologists from Columbia University, Robert and Helen Lynd, decided to study a typical U.S. city as though they were anthropologists. For two years, they lived in Muncie, Indiana—at that time, a city of 38,000 residents. They asked questions and watched how people made their living, raised their children, used their leisure time, and joined in civic and social associations. The Lynds reported that despite the appearance of democratic rule, a social and economic elite actually ran things.[9] Their work stimulated studies in all kinds of communities to find out whether

YOU WILL DECIDE — Should States Exercise Authority over Climate Change Policies?

Many states have struggled over what, if anything, they should do to combat climate change, particularly because the federal government has done little in recent years to address or even recognize the problem.

In late 2007, the federal government denied a request from California to permit the state to implement its own law aimed at reducing greenhouse gas emissions from motor vehicles. The California law was stricter than relevant federal laws, and the federal law allowed California to set antipollution standards stronger than those of the federal government, if the federal Environmental Protection Agency (EPA) gave its approval. At least 16 other states were expected to adopt California's standards if the EPA granted the state a "waiver."

However, the head of the EPA denied California's request. He argued that it was better to adopt a unified federal standard than a state-by-state approach. A lobbyist for automobile manufacturers agreed and said that a "patchwork quilt of inconsistent and competing fuel economy programs at the state level would only have created confusion, inefficiency, and uncertainty for automakers and consumers."

What do you think? Should states be allowed to create stricter laws to help regulate climate change? What arguments would you make for and against such an idea?

THINKING IT THROUGH

This question raises many issues about who ought to govern efforts in the United States to deal with climate change. Those who support state discretion say global warming has different effects on different localities. California may be especially vulnerable because of its reliance on snowpack for water storage, its long coastline, its agricultural industry, and its severe air-quality problems. By contrast, some northern inland states may see gains from climate change—for instance, by having longer warm seasons for agriculture and recreation. Also, although the economies of some states, such as Michigan, depend on industries such as motor vehicle manufacturing that would be greatly affected by the proposed regulations, the economies of other states, such as California, are not so dependent on them.

Others claim that allowing California and other states to write their own emissions laws means some groups (such as motor vehicle manufacturers) are poorly represented in political processes even though they are strongly affected by the state's decisions. If every state set its own standards, it would make producing cars more expensive and distributing cars across states more complicated, which may lead to California regulations becoming the national standard. These opponents argue that such regulations should be made at the national level, where policy decisions are more likely to reflect the wider, more pluralistic array of competing interests found in the United States as a whole. In response, advocates for state control may say that this pluralism at the federal level contributes to political gridlock and the absence of vigorous and effective policies.

California's state government has played a leading role in climate change and other environmental issues, in part because its environmental problems are so severe. This picture shows Los Angeles.

Critical Thinking Questions

1. Should states have discretion over environmental policies, or should the federal government have exclusive control over efforts to deal with this global issue? Why?

2. If states dominated climate change policies in the United States, which groups or interests do you think would be advantaged, and which would be disadvantaged, when compared with a situation in which the federal government dominated policies?

---

power is concentrated in the hands of a few people, is dispersed among many, or operates in some other way.

Relying on a mix of research methods, social scientists since the Lynds' time have studied patterns of power in communities and arrived at a variety of findings. Floyd Hunter, a sociologist who analyzed Atlanta in the 1950s, found a relatively small and stable group of top policy makers drawn largely from the business class. This elite group operated through secondary leaders who sometimes modified policy, but the power of the elite was almost always important.[10] Clarence Stone's seminal study of Atlanta, *Regime Politics*, reaffirmed much of what Hunter first uncovered.[11] In contrast, Robert Dahl and his graduate students at Yale University studied New Haven, Connecticut, and concluded that although some people had a great deal of influence, there was no permanent group of elites. Instead, they found shifting coalitions of leaders who sometimes disagreed among themselves but who kept in mind what the public would accept when making decisions.[12]

Rule by a Few or Rule by the Many?

One group of investigators, chiefly sociologists such as Hunter, have been concerned with **social stratification** in the political system—how politics is affected by divisions among socioeconomic groups or classes in a community. These social scientists assume that political influence is a function of social stratification. They try to find out who governs particular communities by asking various citizens to identify the people who are most influential. Then they study those influential people to determine their social characteristics, their roles in decision making, and the interrelations among them and between them and the rest of the citizens. Using this technique, they find that the upper socioeconomic groups make up the **power elite.** Elected political leaders are subordinate to that elite, and the major conflicts within the community are between the upper and the lower socioeconomic classes.

In contrast, other investigators argue that the evidence of a power elite is merely a reflection of the research methods used by those scholars and the assumptions they made about social stratification. Instead of studying the activities of those thought to have "clout," these critics insist, we should study how decisions are actually made.

Researchers conducting *community power* studies that analyze the making of decisions usually find a relatively open, pluralistic power structure. Some people do have more influence than others, but that influence is shared among many people and tends to be limited to particular issues and areas. For example, those who decide how the public schools are run may have little influence over economic policies. These studies also find that, in the fight for influence, competing elites often appeal to the public, especially voters, and thus draw larger groups into local politics. Importantly, these studies find that local governments tend to be nonresponsive to those groups of citizens who are not engaged at all in local politics—those who are uninformed, apathetic, and do not vote.[13] Furthermore, scholars have also noted that political activism by citizens alone may not be enough to get local governments to respond to their needs. Rather, it often takes full political incorporation of representatives from the group to generate meaningful policy change.[14]

social stratification
Divisions in a community among socioeconomic groups or classes.

power elite
A group composed of community, business, and other leaders who determine public policy or block changes in policy without themselves necessarily holding office.

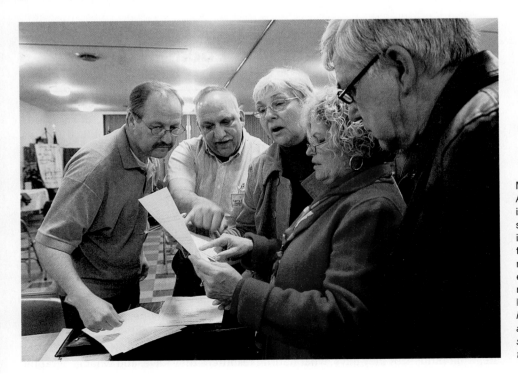

Members of Dover C.A.R.E.S. (Citizens Actively Reviewing Educational Strategies) in Dover, Pennsylvania, examine a list of school board candidates. The group formed in response to the school board's decision to require biology teachers to read a statement in class saying that Darwin's theory of evolution is not fact and that alternate theories exist, including "intelligent design."
■ *Who should be responsible for determining what is taught in schools? What are the arguments for or against citizen groups, school boards, or local governments making these decisions?*

Comparing power elite and community power studies highlights the fact that how we ask questions often influences the answers we get. If we ask highly visible and actively involved citizens for their opinions of who is powerful, we find they often name a small number of people as the real brokers of power. But if we study dozens of local events and decisions, we typically find that a variety of people are active, usually different people in different policy areas—a theory called **pluralism.**

Other studies of local politics suggest that local values, traditions, and the structure of governmental organizations affect which issues get on the local agenda.[15] Tobacco, mining, or steel interests may be so dominant in some areas that tax, regulation, environmental, or job safety policies are kept off the local policy agenda for fear of offending the "powers that be." Those "powers" may indeed go to great lengths to prevent what they deem to be adverse policies. Defenders of the status quo can mobilize power resources in such a way that nondecisions may be more important than decisions. In effect, these researchers tell us not only to study who governs but also to study the procedures and rules of the game. They urge us to determine which groups or interests would gain and which would lose if certain decisions are not made or even seriously considered.[16]

On many economic policy matters, local corporations and business elites have input. Studies of cities in Michigan and Georgia, employing refined and contextual analyses of political decision making, concluded that business elites are indeed important but are not necessarily the controlling factor in city governance:

> There is, then, no controlling hand in community politics. No conspiracy of business and government exists. Business interests do not invariably dominate government policy even where a single industry dominates the community. However, the giant industrial companies do provide the backdrop against which the public policy process operates in the industrial city. They are always there, seldom intervening in specific policy matters but never far from the calculations of policy makers.[17]

In summary, studies of states and communities reveal that political power is often highly unequal, and that local traditions, institutions, and social and economic factors frequently constrain what state and local governments can do. However, the studies also find pluralism and change, as different elites dominate different issues at different times. Also, conflicts often spill out and engage larger publics when competing elites seek to gain allies and legitimacy for their positions.

Influences on State and Local Governments

LEARNING **OBJECTIVE**

21.2 Analyze the activities and influence of interest groups and lobbyists at the state and local levels.

Because state and local governments are powerful institutions in the United States, it is important to understand what affects their actions. Similar to the federal level, individuals, parties, interest groups, elections, the beliefs and skills of political leaders, and media coverage can exert significant influence over state and local governments, although their importance varies greatly across different governments and types of government actions.

Who Are the Constituents?

pluralism
A theory of government that holds that open, multiple, and competing groups can check the asserted power of any one group.

Every state and local community is different. A town of 1,800 residents in rural Nebraska and a city of millions such as New York City present their elected leaders with very different opportunities and obstacles. California has more than 36 million residents, whereas 29 states have fewer than 5 million each. It is not only a question of size, either—many states and cities serve tremendously diverse populations, whereas others have populations that are much more homogeneous. For example, the population of Asian descent in California alone exceeds the total population of more than 26 states. States and localities also show tremendous differences in how urbanized they are, what industries they have, what natural resources they have, and what geographic

Of the People

The Growing Diversity of State Populations

The U.S. Census Bureau estimates for 2008 showed significant changes in both the number and location of minority residents. The percentage of whites declined from 76 percent of the population in 1990 to 66 percent in 2008, whereas the percentage of Hispanics increased from 9 to 15 percent, African-Americans from 12 to 13 percent, and Asian–Pacific Islanders from 3 to 4.5 percent. Nearly 2 percent of residents refer to themselves as members of two or more races.

The growing minority population in the United States is not equally distributed across the states and cities. Approximately three-quarters of all Hispanics live in the West or South, accounting for a quarter of the population in the West and 12 percent of the population in the South. In turn, more than half of all African-Americans live in the South, making up 20 percent of the total population; whereas half of the Asian–Pacific Islander population live in only three states (California, New York, and Hawaii), and two-fifths of all Native Americans live in the West.

Although Hispanics are counted as a single minority group, nearly 60 percent of Hispanics identified themselves in the 2000 census as Mexican, 10 percent as Puerto Rican, and 4 percent as Cuban. Similarly, the Asian–Pacific Islander population includes Asian Indians, Chinese, Filipinos, Japanese, Koreans, Native Hawaiians, and Samoans; Native Americans include members of American Indian tribes, including Cherokee, Navajo, Latin American Indian, Choctaw, Sioux, and Chippewa—as well as Eskimo.

CRITICAL THINKING QUESTIONS

1. As racial and ethnic "minority" groups become majorities in more and more states, do you expect these changes to increase or decrease political divisions in the United States?

2. What kinds of public policies might be most affected by the growing diversity of state populations?

Top Ten States by Minority Population in 2008	
Hawaii	75%
New Mexico	58%
California	58%
Texas	53%
Nevada	43%
Maryland	42%
Georgia	42%
Arizona	42%
Mississippi	41%
New York	40%

SOURCE: U.S. Census Bureau, *Statistical Abstract of the United States: 2010* (U.S. Government Printing Office, 2010), Table 19, http://www.census.gov/compendia/statab/2010/tables/10s0019.pdf.

---

advantages and obstacles they face. They also have different political cultures and political histories that influence politics.[18] And, as this and the remaining chapters will make clear, they all operate within a different set of political institutions. All of this diversity provides the backdrop for how politics and policy making unfolds across states and localities.

The Maze of Interests

A wide range of organized special-interest groups are typically very important at the state and local levels. Even industrial Rhode Island has farm organizations, and rural Wyoming has trade unions. Influential economic pressure groups and political action committees, organized to raise and disburse campaign funds to candidates for public office, operate in the states much as they do nationally. They try to build up the membership of their organizations, they lobby at state capitols and city halls, they educate and organize voters, and they support their political friends in office while opposing their enemies. They also face the same internal problems all groups face: maintaining unity, dealing with subgroups that break off in response to special needs, and balancing democracy with discipline.

One great difference, however, is that group interests can be concentrated and highly influential in states and localities, whereas their strength tends to be diluted in the national government. No single industry or business runs things in Washington, D.C., but in some states and localities, certain interests dominate because they represent the social and economic majorities of the area or because many people rely on a particular industry or corporation for their jobs and livelihood.

The range and variety of these groups give politics in each individual state its own special flavor, excitement, and challenge: auto unions and manufacturers in Michigan, corn and hog farmers in Iowa, gas and oil companies in Texas and Louisiana, tobacco farmers in North Carolina and Virginia, poultry growers and processors in Arkansas, Microsoft in Washington State, the banking and finance industries in Delaware and New York, wineries in California, and tourism in Utah. If there is one group that is present in nearly every state and locality, it is the various public school teachers' unions and associations.

Differences among groups and group representation are often reflected in state policies. State cigarette tax rates vary widely, from $2.70 per pack in New Jersey to $0.07 per pack in South Carolina.[19] Lower cigarette taxes are found among other southeastern and border states, such as Virginia, North Carolina, Tennessee, and Kentucky, where smoking is more common and tobacco farming is economically and politically significant. High cigarette taxes are found among states in the Northeast and Northwest, where neither of these conditions is true.[20]

Still, we should not exaggerate the power of interest groups. Because all groups have internal divisions, we have to be cautious about lumping all workers, all businesspeople, all teachers, or all Hispanics together. The union movement is sometimes sharply divided among truckers, building trades people, machinists, and auto workers. The business community is often divided between big industrial, banking, and commercial firms on the one hand and small merchants on the other. Hispanic voters with different family backgrounds—some more closely associated with Cuba, some with Puerto Rico, and some with Mexico—may also express very different political preferences.

Business interests are inevitably active in city and county politics and policy making. As one study of Atlanta found, the business elite is rarely a passive or reluctant partner in setting local priorities. "Atlanta's postwar political experience is a story of active business-elite efforts to make the most of their economic and organizational resources in setting the terms on which civic cooperation occurs."[21] Businesses everywhere depend on local governments for parking facilities, good roads and transportation, safety, urban renovations, and much more. Business elites become active in long-range community planning, are keenly interested in who gets elected, and are ever watchful of changes in taxes.

Another type of interest group intimately concerned with public policy is the professional association. States license barbers, beauticians, architects, lawyers, doctors,

Boston's "Big Dig" completely changed the way drivers got around the city by burying a major highway in a 3.5-mile tunnel under downtown. It was the largest urban construction project in modern history, cost $14.6 billion, and took 30 years to complete.
■ *What interest groups are likely active in planning and executing projects like this one?*

teachers, accountants, dentists, and many other occupational groups. At the statehouse, you will find lobbying representatives from the Beauticians Aid Association, the Funeral Directors and Embalmers Association, the Institute of Dry Cleaning, and the Association of Private Driver-Training Schools. Such lobbies are naturally interested in the nature of the regulatory laws and the makeup of boards that do the regulating. Stiffening licensing requirements for physicians will decrease the supply of new doctors, for example, and thereby raise the incomes of those in practice. Bar associations, for the same reason, closely monitor licensing standards for the legal profession and the appointment of state and local judges.

Today, other groups of citizens are also likely to organize to influence decisions in the state capital: those who are pro-life and those who are pro-choice; those who support laws permitting same-sex marriages and those who oppose such unions; those who want to keep illegal immigrants out of their state and businesspeople who rely on such workers; and those who want more wind farms to reduce reliance on nonrenewable energy and those who oppose them as damaging blights on our coasts and mountains. Environmental and antismoking groups; animal rights activists; and prison guards are also well organized. Antitax groups have also been common and have re-emerged as part of the so-called "Tea Party" movement that began in 2009.

Lobbyists at the Statehouse

Many businesses, especially large corporations, employ lobbyists, public relations specialists, political consultants, or law firms to represent them.[22] For a fee, lobbyists push desired bills through the legislature or block unwanted ones. This kind of activity again raises the question of who has clout or who governs. Clearly, those who can hire skilled lobbyists and other experts to shape the public agenda often wield more influence than unorganized citizens, who rarely follow state and regional governmental decision making. Public interest, religious, senior citizen, and other groups also have lobbyists, many of whom are not highly paid.

Lobbyists are present in every state capital, and they are there to guide through the legislature a small handful of bills their organization wants passed or to stop those their organization wants defeated.[23] Some observers believe that lobbyists have freer rein in state legislatures than they do in the U.S. Congress. Although there is little direct evidence either for or against this claim, there are a few reasons why we might assume it to be true. Compared with most members of Congress, state legislators typically have few professional staff and have shorter electoral careers, so they may rely more on lobbyists for information about public policies, problems, and political risks and opportunities. Also, lobbying regulations in most states are more relaxed than at the federal level.[24] Media coverage of state politics is often weak and spotty in many states, especially when compared with the attention focused on national politics in Washington, D.C.

Some of these factors may be changing. In response to some prominent scandals,[25] several legislatures enacted comprehensive financial disclosure laws, and today, most state governments are more open, professional, and accountable than in the past.[26] Now five states ban lobbyists from contributing to campaigns at any time, and 22 states prohibit contributions during a legislative session. Four states ban gifts of any sort to state officials—this is

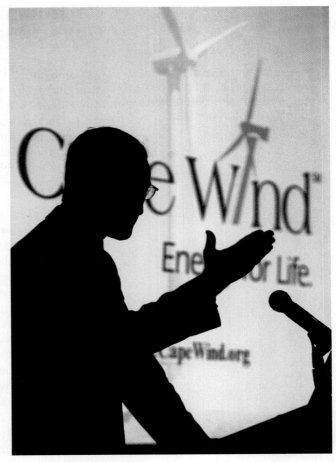

The Cape Wind energy company has proposed building a wind farm in Nantucket Sound off the coast of Massachusetts. Interest groups, most notably the Alliance to Protect Nantucket Sounds, have fought to stop this project, citing environmental concerns. ■ *Should interest groups and lobbyists at the state level have the same regulations as those at the federal level? Why or why not?*

sometimes called the "no cup of coffee" rule—and approximately half of the states prohibit gifts to public employees above a certain monetary value, ranging from $3 (Iowa) to $500 (Texas).[27]

We have already noted that some states have diverse populations and economies, while others have a more limited range of central interests. In most states, many organizations compete, and in no state does only one organization control legislative politics. Political scientist Diane Blaire writes, "It is still true that ordinarily those with greater economic resources, greater numbers, and higher status have far more impact than those who lack these attributes. Nevertheless, an increasingly complex economy has produced many more actors in the political system, and especially when there is division among the economic elite, some of the lesser voices can be heard."[28]

Not to be overlooked is the growing number of groups and media outlets that view themselves as "watchdogs" of the public policy process. State PIRGs (Public Interest Research Groups, often staffed by students or recent college graduates), the League of Women Voters, Common Cause, and various citizens' groups regularly monitor state politics for questionable fund-raising or lobbying practices. Their "watchdog" efforts are sometimes aided by reporters who cover state capitals.

Participation Patterns in Local Government

LEARNING OBJECTIVE

21.3 Assess the level and consistency of involvement of the major participants in local communities.

Citizens feel closer to local governments than to the more remote national government in Washington, D.C. When the public was surveyed regarding its confidence in different governments in 2006, 69 percent of the respondents said they had a "great deal" or a "fair amount" of trust in local governments, compared with 65 percent for state governments, and only 54 percent for the federal government.[29] These numbers have all dropped more recently. A 2009 Gallup poll showed only 51 percent trusted state governments a "great deal" or a "fair amount."[30] A 2010 report by the Pew Center on the States demonstrated public confidence in the national government had reached all-time lows, with fewer than one in four Americans saying they can trust the government in Washington.[31]

Nonetheless, citizens generally take less interest in, vote less often in, and are less informed about their local governments than about the national government. Although decisions about where to locate a garbage dump or a prison or how to deal with police brutality can arouse considerable attention, most of the time, local governments are preoccupied with relatively noncontroversial routine matters, such as keeping the roads in shape, providing fire and police services, attracting businesses that can create more jobs, or applying for state and federal financial assistance. In addition, the news media devotes considerably more time and resources to reporting on national news events and national political leaders than they do state and local issues.

Local communities want to keep their tax rates down and promote their cities as "nice places" in which to live, work, and raise families. Mayors and city officials generally try to avoid controversy and criticism that will divide a community. Although they do not always succeed, they go to considerable lengths to be reasonable and work for the good of the community. Few aggressively seek to alter the status quo. They do not, as a rule, try to promote equality by redistributing various resources to needier citizens. **Redistributive policies** are programs to shift wealth or benefits from one segment of the population to another, usually from the rich to the poor. Local officials tend to believe that this is the task of national or state authorities—if they think it should be done at all. Typically, they say their communities do not have the funds for such programs. They might add, "Go see the governor," or "Go talk to your member of Congress." This may be good advice because various

redistributive policies
Governmental tax and social programs that shift wealth or benefits from one segment of the population to another, often from the rich to the poor.

programs (educational loans, unemployment compensation, disability assistance, and so on) explicitly designed to help the less fortunate are administered at the state or federal level.

Neighborhood groups sometimes become engaged in protecting their neighborhoods and petitioning for improvements. One concern that often activates them is the possibility that "undesirable" facilities may be located in their neighborhood, such as drug treatment clinics, prisons, dumps, or homeless shelters. Although attendance at local government meetings is usually low, the announcement of a landfill or a prison construction project often stimulates the reaction that local officials call NIMBY, an acronym for "Not In My Back Yard!" This response can have the perverse effect of forcing facilities such as airports to remain in densely populated areas because it is too difficult to find alternative sites for them. Of course, sometimes the need for economic development trumps concerns about possibly undesirable facilities. For example, when President Obama announced a plan for sending military detainees held by the U.S. government at its Guantanamo Bay facility to an underutilized facility in Thomson, Illinois, local officials touted the nearly 3,000 jobs the move was expected to create for the local community.[32] Illinois's governor, Pat Quinn, reportedly suggested the move, knowing that region of his state faced an unemployment rate of more than 10 percent at the time.

The Role of Local Media

Most communities have only one newspaper (and associated Web site), and in small communities it is often only published once a week. Some newspapers and local radio and television stations do a good job of covering city and county politics, but this is the exception rather than the rule. Reporters assigned to cover local politics are often inexperienced, yet they provide the only news that citizens get about their city council or zoning board. Even the best of them have difficulty conveying the full complexities of what is going on in a column or two of newsprint.

Some local newspapers enjoy a cozy relationship with elected local officials. Sometimes, the owners or editors are social friends or golfing buddies of local officials. Friendships and mutual interests develop, and close scrutiny of what goes on in city hall takes a back seat to city boosterism. In effect, "newspapers boost their hometown, knowing that its prosperity and expansion aid their own. Harping on local

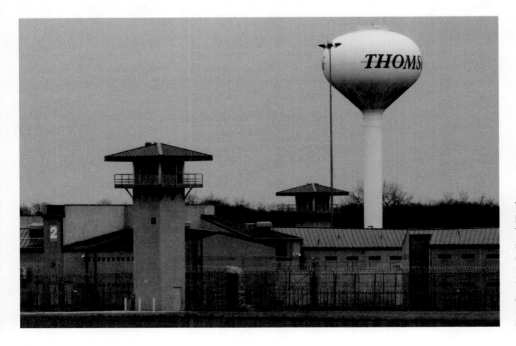

When Illinois Governor Quinn suggested housing Guantamano detainees at the Thomson Correctional Center's maximum security prison, he touted the jobs it would create. However, residents exhibited the "not in my backyard" reaction, opposing the proposal. ■ *How should state and local officials balance the inevitable trade-offs involved with any economic development policy?*

faults, investigating dirty politics, revealing unsavory scandals, and stressing governmental inefficiencies only provide readily available documentary material to competing cities."[33]

Editors and station managers recognize that their readers, viewers, or listeners are more interested in state or national news, and especially in sports, than in what is going on at municipal planning meetings or county commission sessions. Also, although we have dozens of ways to find out about Congress and the White House, we usually have fewer sources for stories about the mayor or sheriff or school board. Many local newspapers have gone out of business in recent decades, and the remaining papers and local TV stations often ignore local political and economic issues. Some local governments have established Web sites to make information more accessible to residents, but the quality of the sites varies greatly, and many are not very useful in helping citizens understand and participate in local government.[34]

Grassroots Apathy

Voter turnout in local elections is substantially lower on average than turnout in most state and national elections. Much of the difference in turnout stems from the fact that a large number of local governments hold elections separate from state and federal elections; turnout is much higher when cities and other local governments hold their elections at the same time when voters select governors or presidents. Also, many local elections are uncontested, and voting turnout is lower when no competition exists for some of the races on a particular ballot.[35]

Voter apathy about local politics may also depress turnout. Charter revision and taxation often galvanize only those directly affected by the new taxes or regulations. Even New England town meetings have difficulty getting people to participate—despite the fact that decisions made at these meetings have major consequences for local tax rates and the quality of the schools, the police force, and the parks and recreational areas. Thomas Jefferson once proclaimed the town meeting to be the noblest, wisest instrument yet devised for the conduct of public affairs, but today, most towns find that only a very small percentage of the population has the time, interest, or ability to participate in local government meetings.[36]

Although apathy may be widespread under most circumstances, issues emerge from time to time that draw intense public interest—and that increases participation in local governments. For instance, one study of Massachusetts town meetings found that although only 4 percent of citizens reported they attended all annual meetings during the previous five years, nearly three out of four citizens attended at least one of the meetings during the five-year period—probably meetings that dealt with controversial issues.[37] This level of participation would be high by national standards. Sometimes, local political processes even see citizen protests—mass demonstrations, economic boycotts, and even civil disorders—that make demands on government. People become politically active when certain issues become intense, especially issues they think will affect their families, property, and deeply held values, such as severe cuts in school budgets, sharp increases in taxes, the building of an "undesirable" facility (such as a "big box" store or extensive housing for low-income families). Most of the time, large groups of citizens may constitute less of a real, concrete presence in local government decision making than a threat to mobilize if and when officials make unpopular choices.

Civic Initiatives in Communities

Because participation at the local level is more limited, the impact an individual can have is likely even greater than at the state or national level. States such as Oregon and Minnesota seem to encourage a climate of innovation and civic enterprise, and a wider look at the United States finds buoyant, optimistic, creative problem solvers in nearly every corner of the nation. The Internet may make it easier for these "innovators" to network and share ideas.

By the People
MAKING A DIFFERENCE

Holding State Governments Accountable

We all want our state governments to perform well and operate efficiently, but how can we measure their performance and track their progress? The Government Performance report produced by the Pew Center on the States and *Governing* magazine graded all 50 states in how their governments manage themselves in four key areas: people, information, money, and infrastructure. States receive performance grades of A through F in each area, plus an overall grade. You can find the most recent report here: http://www.pewcenteronthestates.org/uploadedFiles/Grading-the-States-2008.pdf.

How does your state stack up compared to others? The overall national average was a B-. Three states—Utah, Virginia, and Washington—received the highest grade awarded (A-) for their innovations to manage information about state services, retain state workers, and budget for short- and long-term needs. For example, Alabama has a single Web site where citizens can go to find information on all of the social services provided by the state (http://camellia.alabama.gov/default.aspx), and Washington produces six-year budget forecasts that are widely available and updated every quarter. States receiving low grades did not manage their resources well or lacked sufficient communication and transparency. Some state workers in Rhode Island are still working on typewriters rather than computers, and New Hampshire, which received the lowest grade awarded (a D+) "has such weak data-sharing systems that it doesn't know how much it spends each month."*

States differ in how they manage their operations. However, studies like this of the best and worst practices employed by states show citizens how their states are performing, and they provide opportunities for states to learn from each other. Find out whether your state makes the grade. Knowing what areas your state excels in and what areas it needs to improve is the first step to getting involved and making a difference.

CRITICAL THINKING QUESTIONS

1. How should citizens measure government performance? How do the factors we use reflect our priorities for government performance?

2. What can citizens do to encourage stronger and more efficient performance from their government?

* Pew Center on the States, "Grading the States, 2008" p. 27. http://www.pewcenteronthestates.org/uploadedFiles/Grading-the-States-2008.pdf.

Enterprising local activists have advocated and implemented cost-saving energy programs, environmental cleanup campaigns, recycling and solar energy initiatives, job training centers, AIDS prevention efforts, housing for the elderly, tutoring for the illiterate, housing for the poor, and hundreds of other problem-solving and opportunity-enhancing community efforts.[38] In almost every case, they create partnerships with elected officials at city hall, sometimes with the Urban League or Chamber of Commerce, and often with local foundations and business corporations.

Sometimes, it takes a tragedy to get community groups mobilized. Such an event happened in Boston when gang members burst into the funeral of a young man. "In the presence of the mourners, the gang killed one of those in attendance," writes the Reverend Eugene Rivers of the Azusa Christian Community:

> That brazen act told us we had to do more. Now. That young man's death galvanized us, and soon the Ten Point Coalition was reaching out to at-risk youth. Our mission was to pair the holy and the secular, to do whatever it took to save our kids. The black churches worked hand-in-hand with the schools, courts, police, and social service agencies. We called on anyone and everyone who had the means to help our children. We formed programs for teens, neighborhood watches, and patrols...We established ourselves in the neighborhood, standing on the same street corner where the drug dealers once stood. We tracked down the thieves, dealers, and gangs. We tried to give people a chance, but if they wouldn't take it, we staked our claim and ran them out of our neighborhood.[39]

The aftermath of the devastation produced by hurricanes Katrina and Rita in 2005 to the Gulf Coast also revealed the importance of community groups. Local governments varied greatly in their effectiveness in dealing with the disasters, but the consensus among close observers was that "nonprofit, community-based, and faith-based organizations as well as individual volunteers...responded to the rebuilding challenge beyond all expectation."[40]

Debates persist about how to solve social, economic, and racial problems in our large metropolitan areas. Some people contend that government cannot undertake this task and that private initiatives will be more effective. Others insist that state and local governments are best suited to deal with these challenges. Still others believe that imaginative public–private collaboration is needed to fashion the strategies and mobilize the resources needed to revive cities and bring about greater opportunity. Whatever the merits of such contending interpretations, it is clear that neighborhood organizations and spirited civic renewal are critical to the vitality of local government.[41]

Challenges for State and Local Governments

Most states and communities are confronting difficult times. People want better schools, a clean environment, and safe roads and bridges. Many of our inner-city governments and school systems are in financial distress. The cycle of poverty in many inner cities remains one of the greatest threats to the economic health of the country. Cities, though, usually cannot raise enough funds through local taxes to create jobs and to provide adequate educational opportunities and housing. Federal and state initiatives have attempted to create economic opportunities for inner-city residents. Community development banks, "empowerment zones," Head Start, charter schools, and national service (AmeriCorps) programs have all been tried in an attempt to bring residents of depressed inner cities into the economic mainstream. However, these efforts have been inadequate, and support for them must compete with other demands on financially pressed states and localities. Meanwhile, federal officials are proposing cuts in many of the domestic programs that aid state and local governments.[42]

The following central issues in state and local communities command the attention of the country. They vary depending on location, of course, but these urgent challenges are part of the unfinished business of a government by the people:

■ *People want more services but at the same time would like to see their taxes cut.* Voters in many states and communities have enacted spending limits that constrain growth in public budgets, yet state and local governments struggle with many long-run problems in raising revenues to pay for programs the public demands—problems such as shifts to Internet purchasing and the consumption of services rather than goods, trends that make it harder for state and local governments to collect sales taxes. On the spending side, states are further squeezed by hard-to-control increases in costs, such as health care and energy prices and pensions for retired government workers.[43]

■ *Intense political divisions over new immigrants exist in many communities.* As our nation has become more diverse, most U.S. citizens have learned to appreciate the strength that comes from multiple cultures and races, and many of our businesses have come to rely on immigrant labor, both legal and illegal. However, in many communities where foreign-born residents have settled in large numbers, longtime residents have resented the changing racial, linguistic, and ethnic composition of their communities and have pushed state and local officials to stem or even reverse the growth of immigrants. New immigration laws passed in Arizona in 2010 reignited a national debate on how all levels of government might address this problem.

■ *Much of the nation's infrastructure needs to be repaired or rebuilt.* The collapse of the Interstate 35W bridge in Minneapolis in 2007 and the failure of the levees in New Orleans in 2005 highlight the poor conditions of many of the nation's roads, highways, bridges, dams, levees, water and sewage systems, and other elements of our infrastructure. But the enormous cost of

Not all citizens are apathetic. These young people are spending their free time rehabilitating a community center. ■ *What, if any, responsibility do you think citizens have to their community?*

Improving Access to Information

Sometimes, the hardest part of interacting with a government is knowing where to start. States are using the Internet to help make that first step easier. States have made tremendous strides in providing their citizens with more information about their state's government and access to government agencies and officials. The state of Nebraska provides a good example. The official Web site of the state, http://www .nebraska.gov/, provides users with instant access for citizens, businesses, education, those relocating to the state, and tourists. From the main page, users can check on the status of their income tax refund, renew their license plates, or apply for financial aid to any of the state's colleges and universities. Citizens can also search the campaign

contribution records for all public officials or track the use of federal funds received as part of the American Recovery and Reinvestment Act of 2009 (the federal stimulus program).

Another innovation is the link to what the state calls the Reference Desk, which advertises, "When you just can't find the answers...we can help." This link takes you to the Government Information Services of the Nebraska Library Commission. Among the features on this Web page is a live chat window where you can ask a librarian on staff any question you have, and the librarian will help you track down an answer. Inquiring with the Reference Desk about the history of the program generated a response within about two minutes reporting

that the service has been available since 2006 and that it gets used daily. Efforts like this demonstrate how at least some states go the extra mile to try to serve their citizens.

CRITICAL THINKING QUESTIONS

1. In a state where citizens have easy access to information about government, which groups or interests do you think would be advantaged, and which would be disadvantaged?

2. How might the development of a Web site like Nebraska's help state and local governments address some of the current challenges they face that are discussed in this chapter?

repairs or replacements is well beyond the current fiscal capacities of state and local governments.

- *The costs of corrections and prisons have skyrocketed in recent years,* driven by the rapid growth of prison populations as well as the costs of caring for an aging population of prisoners. In 2007, nearly 7 percent of state expenditures went to corrections.[44] Many states are trying to cut costs with new policies and programs, including stronger efforts to divert inmates to rehabilitation facilities; "good-time" credits to low-risk offenders, who would then be allowed to shorten their prison terms; shorter sentences at the discretion of judges; more effective systems of parole and probation; and greater use of privately run (and often out-of-state) prison facilities.

- *Poverty in the inner cities persists.* We have extremes of rich and poor within metropolitan regions, and many feel that wealthier suburbs often turn their backs on the problems and poverty of the older cities. Indifference to these inequalities and lack of opportunities undermine a sense of community and fairness—and limit the nation's capacity to develop a skilled and internationally competitive workforce.

- *We need to guarantee the best possible education for all our young people.* Parents are demanding better education and more parental involvement. Communities have been experimenting with educational choice and competition, school vouchers, charter schools, expanded hours, and prekindergarten programs. Improving the public schools is necessary, but their resources and the salaries of teachers are often too low to attract and retain the best-qualified educators. Many states also object to the federal No Child Left Behind program as a costly and ineffective way of using standardized tests to improve the accountability and quality of schools.

- *Environmental regulation, land use, and recycling are also major challenges at the local level.* Every city and state wants economic growth and economic opportunities for its workers and businesses, but many forms of economic development impose costs in terms of the quality of air, water, landscapes, and health. Local officials face tough decisions about the need to balance economic and environmental concerns. Governors of both political parties are trying to formulate laws to combat global

Harlem Children's Zone (www.hcz.org) is a non-profit organization that runs education programs designed to engage families and communities in the development and education of children. ■ *What are the pros and cons of organizations like this providing services instead of the public school district doing so?*

warming—by promoting renewable sources of energy, by creating multistate agreements to cut emissions from power plants, and by adopting California's greenhouse-gas limits for cars.

■ *Health care costs and delivery are challenges to all levels of government.* Health care costs have been rising rapidly for several years, while at the same time, citizens have faced greater obstacles to gaining access to care. Some states have responded by developing programs to cover the growing number of uninsured. Massachusetts succeeded in enacting its attempt at universal health insurance, and now it is trying to put this complicated system into effect. In the meantime, the uninsured often fail to get adequate health care, and many turn to emergency rooms in local public hospitals, which in turn seek funding from local and state governments. It remains to be seen how the reforms adopted at the national level in 2010 will affect the states.

Our political system does not rely exclusively on one level of government to take up these formidable challenges. If leadership is lacking at the federal level for a time, it may be found in at least some of our state and local governments, as citizens bring their concerns to whichever governments are willing to hear them and take action. As former governor of New York Nelson A. Rockefeller said in 1962, "By providing several sources of political strength and creativity, a federal system invites inventive leadership—on all levels—to work toward genuine solutions to the problems of a diverse and complex society."[45]

CHAPTER **SUMMARY**

21.1 Contrast the functions of federal, state, and local governments, and evaluate the theories of decision-making in local governments.

Although the federal government has enacted a large number of major domestic programs, state and local governments face many of the most critical domestic and economic issues facing the United States. State and local governments also administer most public programs, including those funded in large part by the federal government. Finally, most interactions between citizens and government involve employees of state and local governments.

Studies of states and communities have investigated how formal government institutions, social structure, economic factors, and local traditions interact to create a working political system. Some studies find that a power elite dominates, whereas community power studies find pluralism and diverse interest groups competing for influence over a range of policy areas. These different findings may reflect in part differences in research methods.

21.2 Analyze the activities and influence of interest groups and lobbyists at the state and local levels.

Special-interest groups operate in every state and locality, but their composition and influence vary a great deal, and the politics of some states and localities are dominated by a small number of major, usually economic interests. In some ways, the types of interest groups found at the state and local levels are similar to what we find at the national level, as are their activities and paths to influence. But the influence of groups is often greater at the state and local levels, as there is often less competition between diverse groups and as legislators typically have fewer sources of alternative information.

21.3 Assess the level and consistency of involvement of the major participants in local communities.

Although local governments command more public trust and are widely viewed as "closer to the people" than the national government, voting and other forms of participation at the local level are low. Nonetheless, local civic action often does occur, and it frequently produces innovative and flexible approaches to problems in education, the environment, crime and violence, and recovery from natural disasters.

21.4 Evaluate the challenges facing state and local governments.

State and local governments face severe challenges now and in the near future—in raising sufficient revenues, resolving conflicts over recent immigrants, rebuilding infrastructure, paying the costs of a fast-growing prison population, alleviating urban poverty, providing quality education, solving environmental problems, and ensuring that all residents have access to good-quality and affordable health care.

CHAPTER **SELF-TEST**

21.1 Contrast the functions of federal, state, and local governments, and evaluate the theories of decision-making in local governments.

1. Match the following functions with the appropriate level of government—either national or state and local.
   a. Hospitals
   b. Highways
   c. Universities
   d. Social Security
   e. Regulating the economy
   f. Elementary, middle, and high schools
2. Which of the following accurately defines *social stratification*?
   a. Direct democracy in small communities
   b. The division of government leaders into specialized policy areas
   c. The division of people in a community by social or economic class
   d. The fiscal relationship between local, state, and federal governments
3. List and briefly explain at least three theories about who actually has power in communities.
4. Write a paragraph suggesting three reasons why some responsibilities are best left to the national government, while others are best met by state and local government. Use examples in your answer.

21.2 Analyze the activities and influence of interest groups and lobbyists at the state and local levels.

5. Give three examples of state and local interest groups, and show how state and local government policies affect them.
6. In a paragraph, suggest why lobbyists and interest groups might be more effective at the state and local level than at the national level.

21.3 Assess the level and consistency of involvement of the major participants in local communities.

7. Which is closest to the size of typical turnout in local-only elections?
   a. Less than 20 percent
   b. 20 to 40 percent
   c. 40 to 60 percent
   d. More than 60 percent
8. In an essay, explore the reasons why citizens are typically apathetic toward their local government. Suggest two or three ideas that would help solve this problem.

21.4 Evaluate the challenges facing state and local governments.

9. List three areas of government spending in which costs have risen dramatically during the last few years.
10. Which of the following states has successfully enacted a program to provide its citizens with universal health insurance?
    a. Florida
    b. Kansas
    c. California
    d. Massachusetts

11. Select one of the challenges facing state and local government and, in one paragraph, argue which level of government—local, state, or national—is best equipped to face the challenge.

12. Write a short essay identifying which of the current challenges facing state and local governments deserves the most attention. Explain how emphasizing it will best help the U.S. people and why the other challenges are less important.

Answers to selected questions: 1. a. state & local, b. state & local, c. state & local, d. national, e. national, f. state & local; 2. c; 7. a; 10. d

---

mypoliscilab EXERCISES

Apply what you learned in this chapter on MyPoliSciLab.

📖—┤●├─Read on **mypoliscilab.com**

   eText: Chapter 21

✓●├─**Study** and **Review** on **mypoliscilab.com**

   Pre-Test
   Post-Test
   Chapter Exam
   Flashcards

👁—┤●├─Watch on **mypoliscilab.com**

   Video: L.A. Billboards
   Video: California Teachers Stage Sit-Ins

✳—┤├─Explore on **mypoliscilab.com**

   Comparative: Comparing State and Local Governments
   Visual Literacy: Explaining Differences in State Laws

KEY **TERMS**

social stratification, p. 551
power elite, p. 551

pluralism, p. 552
redistributive policies, p. 556

ADDITIONAL **RESOURCES**

FURTHER READING

PETER L. BERNSTEIN, *Wedding of the Waters: The Erie Canal and the Making of a Great Nation* (Norton, 2005).

BUZZ BISSINGER, *A Prayer for the City* (Random House, 1997).

FRANK J. COPPA, *County Government* (Praeger, 2000).

E. J. DIONNE JR., ED., *Community Works: The Revival of Civil Society in America* (Brookings Institution Press, 1998).

ROBERT S. ERIKSON, GERALD C. WRIGHT, AND **JOHN P. McIVER,** *Statehouse Democracy: Public Opinion and Policy in the American States* (Cambridge University Press, 1993).

LARRY N. GERSTON AND **TERRY CHRISTENSEN,** *Recall! California's Political Earthquake* (Sharpe, 2004).

STEPHEN GOLDSMITH, *The Twenty-First Century City* (Regnery, 1997).

VIRGINIA GRAY AND **RUSSELL HANSON,** EDS., *Politics in the American States: A Comparative Analysis,* 9th ed. (CQ Press, 2007).

VALERIE C. JOHNSON, *Black Power in the Suburbs* (State University of New York Press, 2002).

ANDREW KARCH, *Democratic Laboratories: Policy Diffusion Among the American States* (University of Michigan Press, 2007).

V. O. KEY, JR., *Southern Politics in State and Nation* (Alfred A Knopf, 1949; reprinted by the University of Tennessee Press).

PAUL E. PETERSON, *The Price of Federalism* (Brookings, 1995).

DOUGLAS W. RAE, *City: Urbanism and Its End* (Yale University Press, 2003).

ALAN ROSENTHAL, *The Third House: Lobbyists and Lobbying in the States,* 2d ed. (CQ Press, 2001).

JON C. TEAFORD, *The Rise of the States* (Johns Hopkins University Press, 2002).

SUSAN W. THRANE AND **TOM PATTERSON,** *State Houses: America's 50 State Capitol Buildings* (Boston Mills Press, 2005).

JOSEPH F. ZIMMERMAN, *The New England Town Meeting: Democracy in Action* (Praeger, 1999).

ROBERT DAHL, *Who Governs: Democracy and Power in an American City* (Yale University Press, 1961).

WEB SITES

www.pewcenteronthestates.org/ The Pew Center for the States non-profit organization conducts research on state government performance and numerous state policy issues.

www.statelocalgov.net/ State and Local Government on the Net provides a directory of official state, county, and city government websites.

www.loc.gov/rr/news/stategov/stategov. html Library of Congress State Government Page provides information and government publications from all 50 states.

http://sppq.sagepub.com The official website of the academic journal *State Politics and Policy Quarterly*, which publishes research articles on state politics.

www.governing.com/ *Governing Magazine* provides news articles and analysis of political and policy issues facing the states.

State Constitutions

Charters or Straitjackets?

CHAPTER **OUTLINE**
CHAPTER LEARNING
OBJECTIVES

The Roots of State Constitutions

22.1 Compare and contrast the U.S. Constitution and state constitutions.

Amending State Constitutions

22.2 Outline the processes used to amend state constitutions.

The Politics of Constitutional Revision

22.3 Evaluate the states' recent attempts at constitutional revision.

On May 1, 1991, three couples filed a lawsuit against the state of Hawaii challenging the state's law that limited marriage to opposite-sex couples. Hawaii's state Supreme Court ruled that such a law would be presumed to be unconstitutional unless the state could show it has a compelling interest in barring same-sex marriages and that it could do so without unnecessary abridgments of citizens' rights. This ruling triggered a firestorm of political and media attention. Certainly, same-sex marriage was (and remains) a controversial topic, but why would folks in the rest of the country be so concerned about how Hawaii's Supreme Court interpreted Hawaii's state constitution? The reason centers on what is called the "Full Faith and Credit" clause of the U.S. Constitution, which generally requires every state to recognize the "public Acts, Records, and judicial Proceedings" of every other state. In other words, those opposed to same-sex marriage were concerned that if Hawaii legalized it, all others would have to treat any same-sex couple lawfully married in Hawaii as lawfully married if or when they came to any other state to visit, work, or reside.

The national government responded by passing the so-called Defense of Marriage Act (DOMA) in 1996. This act defined marriage with regard to federal law as between one man and one woman, and it granted states the authority to refuse to recognize same-sex marriages performed in other states. There have been several challenges to DOMA in the federal court system, but so far, it has been upheld and the U.S. Supreme Court has yet to accept an appeal of one of these cases for review.

On November 18, 2003, the Massachusetts Supreme Judicial Court ruled that discriminating against same-sex marriages violated the state constitution. That ruling has survived several attempts to amend the state's constitution to ban same-sex marriage. Since that time, four other states: New Hampshire, Connecticut, Iowa, and Vermont, along with Washington, D.C., have legalized same-sex marriages. Same-sex marriages were legal in California for a short time under a state supreme court ruling, but voters passed Proposition 8 in the 2008 election to amend the state's constitution to ban them. There is a case in the federal court system, *Perry v. Schwarzenegger*, seeking to overturn this ban. In August of 2010, a federal judge ruled that Prop 8 violated the U.S. Constitution, but the Ninth Circuit Court of Appeals ordered no change in the policy pending an appeal.

Except for DOMA, and now *Perry v. Schwarzenegger*, virtually the entire battle surrounding same-sex marriage has been fought in the states, and the major battleground has centered on state constitutions. Does a state's constitution permit the legislature to ban or approve same-sex marriage? Can the state's constitution be amended to either permit or ban such marriages? Since all of this began back in 1991, the U.S. Supreme Court has yet to review a case or rule on the constitutionality of same-sex marriage bans, although some experts believe the *Perry* v. *Schwarzenegger* case may make it that far.

What the history of same-sex marriage makes clear is that state constitutions (a) can play a central role in defining meaningful rights for citizens and (b) vary a great deal from one state to another. Take a look at your state's constitution and see what sorts of rights and restrictions it contains that differ from the U.S. Constitution. Constitutions are foundational documents that establish the basic scope and structure of a government. They both empower governments to take actions and limit the actions they can take. Our U.S Constitution holds a revered place in our country's history and culture, but our state constitutions do not generally enjoy the same iconic status. On a trip to your state capitol, you are unlikely to find the state constitution "displayed [like] the federal Constitution, in a setting similar to a Shinto shrine."[1] Still, our state constitutions are powerful documents that affect our government and our lives as citizens in more ways than we typically realize.

In this chapter, we examine the roots of state constitutions and some of the reasons for constitutional rigidity. Then, we look at methods of amending state constitutions, ending with a few case studies of states that have tried, for the most part unsuccessfully, to adopt new constitutions.

The Roots of State Constitutions

LEARNING **OBJECTIVE**

22.1 Compare and contrast the U.S. Constitution and state constitutions.

The first state constitutions were outgrowths of colonial charters. Massachusetts and New Hampshire can boast of charters still in effect that are older than the federal Constitution. Virginia added a bill of rights to its constitution in 1776—13 years before the national one was proposed by Congress. In 1787, the framers of the U.S. Constitution drew heavily on their experience with these state charters. "What is the Constitution of the United States but that of Massachusetts, New York, and Maryland!" remarked John Adams, who drafted the Massachusetts Constitution in 1779. "There is not a feature in it," he said, "which cannot be found in one or the other."[2]

Subject only to the broad limitations of the U.S. Constitution, the people of each state are free to create whatever kind of republican government they wish. All state constitutions are similar in general outline (see Figure 22–1). A state constitution typically

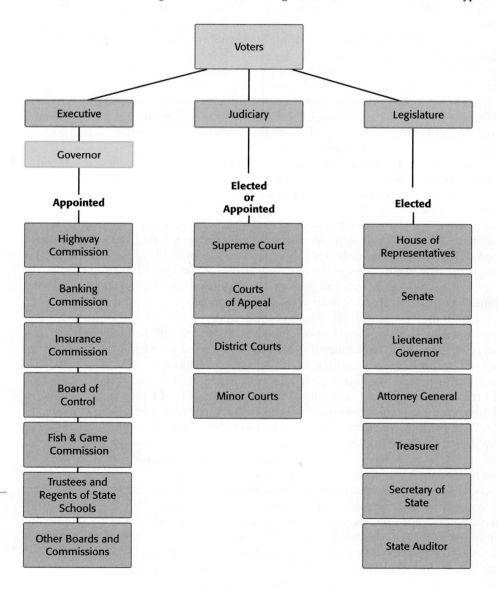

FIGURE 22–1 Government Under a Typical State Constitution.

■ *How does this figure help explain why state constitutions are typically so much longer than the U.S. Constitution?*

Exploring Your State Constitution

Although state constitutions are generally not permitted to restrict rights beyond the U.S. Constitution, they routinely provide for additional rights for their citizens beyond those included in the U.S. Constitution. Although the Equal Rights Amendment barring discrimination based on gender was never added to the U.S. Constitution, 22 state constitutions include at least partial guarantees of equal rights based on sex.

These provisions have been used by state supreme courts to expand the rights of women beyond those provided for in the U.S. Consti-tution. For example, the Colorado Supreme Court in 1988 ruled that an insurance policy that excludes coverage for pregnant women but is otherwise comprehensive constituted a violation of Colorado's Consti-tution.* Of course, there is considerable variance in the wording of individual state equal rights provisions. Montana's expressly includes the actions of government as well as private individuals while five states—Virginia, Colorado, Illinois, Hawaii, and New Hampshire—limit the scope of their equal rights protections to only the actions of governments.

What rights regarding gender discrimination does your state's constitution provide, and how does your state's constitution compare to those of other states? Several Web sites make it easy for you to find out. At Cornell University Law School's Legal Information Institute (LII), you can find constitutions, statutes, and legislative information by state, and you can also search state statutes by topic at http://www.law.cornell.edu/statutes.html#state. Knowing what rights are provided by your state constitution will help you become a more informed participant in political debate and a better protected citizen.

CRITICAL THINKING QUESTIONS

1. What do you think about the notion that the rights citizens enjoy in this country depend at least in part on the state in which they happen to reside?

2. Why would states differ in the constitutional rights they provide?

* Linda J. Wharton. "State Equal Rights Amendments Revisited: Evaluating Their Effectiveness in Advancing Protection Against Sex Discrimination." *Rutgers Law Journal* 36 (2004–2005): 1201–1294.

consists of a preamble, a bill of rights, articles providing for the separation of powers, a two-house legislature, an executive branch, and an independent judiciary with the power of judicial review. It will also have a description of the form and powers of local units of government, an article on how to amend the constitution, and miscellaneous provisions dealing with election procedures, corporations, railroads, finances, education, and other specific topics.

The bills of rights in state constitutions are, in general, similar to the federal Bill of Rights, although they sometimes use different language. However, the bills of rights in many state constitutions go beyond the protections the federal government offers, covering more recently emerging protections, such as the right to an equal public education and the rights of crime victims. Fourteen states adopted the Equal Rights Amendment even though it was never ratified to become part of the U.S. Constitution. (See the box, By the People: Exploring Your State Constitution.)

State constitutions contain more details than the U.S. Constitution does. They have to deal with a much wider range of functions, educational provisions, and criminal codes than the U.S. Constitution, which created a national government of intentionally limited powers to deal with a limited range of functions.[3] Thus, state constitutions often include articles with statute-like details that concern specific substantive policies. As a result, state constitutions are longer than the U.S. Constitution, which has only 7,400 words. The median state constitution has approximately 26,000 words,[4] ranging from the 9,200 words of New Hampshire's to the 365,000 words of Alabama's. Alabama's Constitution is nearly 40 times as long as the U.S. Constitution.

Constitutions as Straitjackets

The earliest state constitutions granted authority to the legislatures without much restriction on how they should exercise it. However, after many legislatures gave special privileges to railroads, canal builders, and other business interests, reform groups began to insist on certain controls in state constitutions. In time, state constitutions became encrusted with layer on layer of procedural detail.

Although most state constitutional provisions deal with matters of significance, some deal with subjects more appropriate for legislative statute. California's much-amended constitution (more than 500 amendments since it was adopted in 1879) goes into great detail about the internal organization of various departments.[5] The South Dakota Constitution declares that providing hail insurance is a public purpose and authorizes the legislature to levy a tax to do so.[6] The Alabama Constitution authorizes the legislature to indemnify peanut farmers for losses incurred as a result of *Aspergillus flavus* (a fungus) and freeze damage in peanuts.[7]

What does this mean for democratic government? It means that state constitutions—intended as charters of self-government—are often like straitjackets imposed on the present by the past. Some outdated provisions do no harm, but others are roadblocks to effective government. For example, fixed salaries do not reflect changing economic conditions, and a rigidly organized administrative structure is incapable of adjusting to new needs. When a constitution allocates revenues, elected officials are deprived of discretion to deal with budget difficulties as they arise. Under such conditions, the legislature cannot act, and the constitution must be amended or provisions interpreted to reflect contemporary circumstances.

Because state constitutions are long and often specific, they require more frequent amendment and revision[8] (see Figure 22–2). Louisiana has had 11 constitutions; Georgia has had ten; South Carolina, seven; and Alabama, Florida, and Virginia, six.[9] Only 19 states have their original constitution. The average state constitution is more than 100 years old and has been amended approximately 140 times, with Alabama's leading the way at more than 800 adopted amendments.[10]

The New Judicial Federalism Amendments are one way to alter constitutions. But another device for constitutional change is **judicial interpretation,** whereby judges modify a constitutional provision by giving a new interpretation of its meaning. One reason for the growing length of some constitutions is that amendments are often required to *reverse* judicial interpretations. In addition, some sections of state constitutions have been invalidated by federal action, especially in the areas of civil rights and suffrage.

In what is called **new judicial federalism,** state constitutions have taken on greater importance than in the past. For decades, state judges tended to look only to the U.S. Constitution and Bill of Rights and how the U.S. Supreme Court interpreted these documents. But since the 1970s, as the Supreme Court has become more conservative, some state

judicial interpretation
A method by which judges modify the force of a constitutional provision by reinterpreting its meaning.

new judicial federalism
The practice of some state courts using the bill of rights in their state constitutions to provide more protection for some rights than is provided by the Supreme Court's interpretation of the Bill of Rights in the U.S. Constitution.

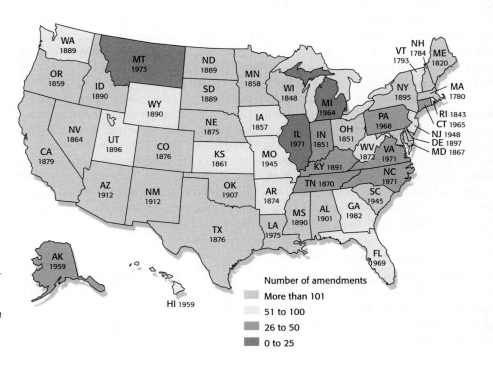

FIGURE 22–2 **Amending State Constitutions.**

■ *What factors might influence how often a state's constitution is amended?*

NOTE: Dates indicate year state constitution was ratified.

For the People

GOVERNMENT'S GREATEST ENDEAVORS

Providing for Quality Education in the States

Every state provides for some level of public education in its constitution. In fact, 36 of the 37 states in the United States in 1868 already had provisions in their state constitutions regarding public education.* Several states have interpreted their state's constitution to define access to public education as a fundamental right for their state's citizens. In contrast, the U.S. Supreme Court has expressly rejected the argument that access to public education is a fundamental right protected by the Fourteenth Amendment.[†]

Some state courts have even gone so far as to declare state education funding systems that allow for large discrepancies in funding between schools or that simply underfund the school system as a whole as unconstitutional. For example, early in 2010,

a judge in Washington state ruled that the state's low level of funding failed to meet its constitutional obligation to make "ample provision" for the education of all children residing within the state a "paramount duty."[††] In this particular case, the plaintiffs and their supporters cited the lack of textbooks, overcrowding, dilapidated and inadequate facilities, and the extensive use of class time for activities associated with fund-raisers as evidence that the state had failed to meet its constitutional obligation.[$] In his decision, Judge Erlick ordered the state to determine the actual cost of providing basic education and then to adequately fund it through stable and reliable sources.

Cases like this one in Washington show the value of state constitutions and the protections they can provide beyond those provided for by the national government.

Students in Washington state stand to benefit to the tune of an additional $1 billion a year for better educational resources due entirely to the state's constitution and how judges in Washington have interpreted it.

CRITICAL THINKING QUESTIONS

1. As the national government begins playing a bigger role in providing for public education, should we consider amending the U.S. Constitution to provide for a right to public education? What might be the pros and cons of such an amendment?

2. Do the differences among states in the rights and protections they offer conflict with the national constitutional provisions designed to provide all citizens with equal protection under the law?

---

* Steven Calabresi and Sarah E. Agudo. "Individual Rights Under State Constitutions When the Fourteenth Amendment Was Ratified in 1868: What Rights Are Deeply Rooted in American History and Tradition?" *Texas Law Review* 87 (November 2008), No. 1.

[†] *San Antonio Independent School District* v. *Rodriguez* (1973).

[††] Linda Shaw, "King County Judge Rules That State Isn't Providing Enough Money for Schools," *The Seattle Times*, February 4, 2010, http://seattletimes.nwsource.com/html/localnews/2010981329_webschoollawsuit05m.html.

[$] *McCleary* v. *State of Washington*, No. 07-2-02323-2 SEA.

---

supreme courts have been relying on their own state constitutions and state bills of rights in overruling state laws and the actions of state and local officials. Recall that although states must provide citizens the minimum protection guaranteed by the U.S. Constitution, they can and sometimes do provide even more in areas such as equal protection and privacy. Based on the U.S. Constitution, the U.S. Supreme Court has allowed governments to adopt sobriety checkpoints for drivers,[11] random drug testing of public employees,[12] and restrictions on minors who seek abortions.[13] However, these rulings do not force states to adopt such policies. In fact, several state supreme courts have ruled that such policies are unconstitutional violations of privacy provisions included in their own state's constitution.

This trend takes its inspiration from the U.S. Supreme Court, which sent clear messages to state supreme court judges that they are free to interpret their own state constitutions to allow greater protections for citizens against government action than the U.S. Constitution does. The U.S. Supreme Court and the U.S. Constitution set the floor, not the ceiling, for the protection of rights.[14] As a result, some state judges are now using their constitutions to require state legislatures to provide better schools for children living in poor neighborhoods, build low-income housing, provide public financing of abortions for poor women, and regulate business enterprises to protect the environment.[15]

When state judges rely on their own state constitutions to protect rights beyond those required by the U.S. Constitution, they do so at some political peril. Many such rulings protect minorities and/or run counter to popular opinion and current state law. Because most state judges depend on voter approval to keep their office, making unpopular rulings risks voter backlash. This risk has increased now that the U.S. Supreme Court requires state judges who wish to escape its review of their decisions to make it clear that they have decided a case on adequate and independent state constitutional grounds.[16]

571

Amending State Constitutions

Amendments to state constitutions may be proposed by state legislatures, citizen-initiated ballot petitions, or constitutional conventions. After an amendment has been proposed, it must be ratified. In all states except Delaware, where the legislature can ratify as well as propose amendments, ratification is by the voters. In most states, an amendment becomes part of the constitution when approved by a majority of those who actually vote on it. In a 2003 special election in New Mexico, voters approved by only 195 votes constitutional amendments that created a cabinet-level secretary of education and authorized more spending for public education.[17] In some other states—such as Minnesota—approval by a majority of all those voting in the election is required. This provision makes ratification more difficult because some people who vote for candidates do not vote on amendments. In recent years, state voters have typically adopted approximately 75 percent of all constitutional amendments proposed by legislatures, but voter approval increased in 2006, when 85 percent of the amendments proposed by legislatures were adopted.[18] That figure dropped to only 60 percent in 2008.[19]

Legislative Proposals

All states permit their legislatures to propose constitutional amendments; in fact, this is the most common method. Although provisions vary, the general practice is to require the approval by a supermajority, usually two-thirds or three-fifths, of each chamber of the legislature. Some states, however, permit proposal of an amendment by a simple majority in two successive legislatures.

A legislature may appoint a **revision commission** to make recommendations for constitutional change that, except in Florida, have no force until acted on by the legislature and approved by the voters. The legislature creates a commission of a relatively small number of people—some selected by the governor and some by the legislature—and charges it with presenting proposals for constitutional revision. A commission is less expensive than a full-blown constitutional convention, does not require initial voter approval, and gives the legislature final control of what is presented to the electorate.

California, for instance, turned to a revision commission to overcome its budgetary gridlock after its senate rejected a 1992 proposal asking voters whether they wanted a constitutional convention (the first in 113 years). California's constitution has been so frequently amended to require certain expenditures that approximately 85 percent of the state's annual revenues are allocated before the governor and legislature even start working on the budget! Eventually, if this trend were to continue, *all* state revenues could be allocated in this way, and there might be no state funds available for programs such as higher education and health care.[20] A 23-member revision commission was created in 1993 to examine the budget process and the configuration of state and local duties. Two years later, the commission made its recommendations. However, the legislature failed to act on any of them, in part because it was an election year. Also, because the state senate was Democratic and the state assembly Republican, it proved impossible to work out any compromise.

Constitutional commissions are, in fact, infrequently used. Utah is the only state that had such a commission in operation in 2004.[21] Voters in three states—Connecticut, Hawaii, and Illinois—voted on whether to call constitutional conventions in their states in 2008, but more than 60 percent of voters in all three states said no.[22] The recommendations of revision commissions are also seldom implemented quickly, perhaps because the commissioners have not been responsive to political currents or are not representative of broad enough interests. Still, a commission may be less partisan and more resistant to single-interest groups than either the legislature or a convention. Mississippi has tried, so far unsuccessfully, to use a commission for changing its 1890 constitution, which was designed to keep African Americans out of the political process.[23]

Nonetheless, Florida, Virginia, and Louisiana have used the commission procedure to bring about significant constitutional change. Utah's Constitutional Revision Commission is a permanent body, required by law to submit recommendations for constitutional revision to the legislature 60 days before each regular session.[24] It has initiated revisions

revision commission
A state commission that recommends changes in the state constitution for action by the legislature and vote by the voters.

relating to the rights of crime victims as well as to changes in revenue and taxation. Florida has a Taxation and Budget Reform Commission that is called into session every ten years. Unlike other such commissions, in addition to making recommendations to the legislature, it may propose constitutional amendments directly to the voters. In 1998, the commission recommended nine amendments; Florida voters approved eight of them.

Initiative Petitions

At the end of the nineteenth century, revelations of corruption diminished the prestige of state governments, especially state legislatures. From this disillusionment and the Progressive Movement came a variety of reforms. Among them was the **constitutional initiative petition,** a device that permits voters to place specific constitutional amendments on the ballot by petition. Eighteen states allow amendments to their constitutions to be proposed by initiative petitions.

The number of signatures required on petitions varies from 4 to 15 percent of either the total electorate or the number who voted in the last election.[25] Although it takes more signatures to propose a constitutional amendment than to place other kinds of initiatives on the ballot, "the higher threshold is no longer a significant impediment to well-financed special-interest groups."[26] Once the appropriate state official (attorney general or secretary of state) approves the precise wording of a petition, the amendment goes on the ballot at the next general election. (California allows initiatives to appear even on primary election ballots.)

In some states, initiative proposals are limited to *amending* the state constitution, not to *revising* it. The distinction between revision and amendment is that revision refers to a comprehensive change in the basic governmental plan, a substantial alteration in the basic governmental framework, or a substantial alteration of the entire constitution, rather than to a less extensive change in one or more of its provisions.[27] Some states exclude certain subjects from amendment by initiative. Massachusetts, for example, does not allow amendments by popular initiative that concern religion, the judiciary, or judicial decisions; that are restricted to a particular town, city, or political division; that appropriate money from the state treasury; or that restrict rights such as freedom of speech.

In recent years, voters have approved slightly more than a third of amendments proposed by initiative petitions. This figure compares with a slightly more than 75 percent approval rate for amendments proposed by state legislatures.[28] In 2008, 78 amendments were proposed to voters by their legislatures, and 52 were approved.

constitutional initiative petition
A device that permits voters to place specific amendments to a state constitution on the ballot by petition.

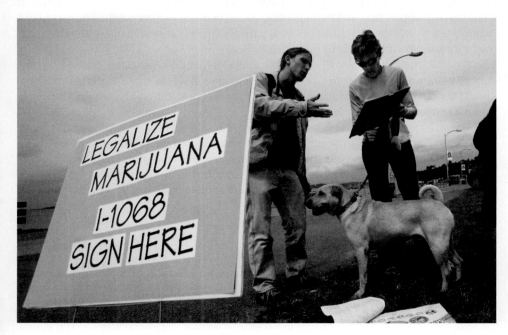

A citizen in Seattle stops to consider signing a petition to legalize marijuana. If the petition gets enough signatures, it can appear on the ballot for Oregon voters. ■ *Are there issues that should not be permitted to be considered by citizen initiative? Why?*

In contrast, only 29 amendments were proposed to voters through the citizen initiative process, and only 12 of them were approved.[29] A variety of factors may account for the lower adoption rate of initiative measures. Initiatives tend to be used for controversial issues that have already been rejected by the legislature and engender an organized opposition. Initiatives are also often proposed by narrow-based groups or by reform-minded elites who lack broad support for their views. Sometimes initiatives are proposed in order to launch educational campaigns rather than to actually win adoption.

Use of the initiative process is spreading among people who are anxious to limit the power of state and local governments. Since 1978, when California adopted Proposition 13 limiting property taxes, other states have followed suit. In addition, these "new reformers" have produced "a series of state constitutional amendments that, taken together, fundamentally altered the character and powers of state governments by limiting the tenure of governmental officials, reducing their powers, and transferring policy-making responsibilities to the people."[30] In addition, "the focus of constitutional initiatives...has shifted from questions of governmental structure...to questions of substantive policy," such as initiatives on tort liability, the rights of gays, affirmative action, and the rights of immigrants.[31]

Constitutional Conventions

Voters once loved state constitutional conventions: they held 144 in the nineteenth century. But the twentieth century produced only 63 constitutional conventions, and only one has been convened in the twenty-first century so far.[32] One scholar noted that calling conventions of the people is a uniquely American idea, emphasizing that legislators cannot be trusted and that the supreme power belongs to the people.[33]

Forty-one state constitutions authorize their legislature to submit the calling of a convention to the voters; the other states assume that the legislature has the power to do so. Fourteen state constitutions require the legislature to question voters about a convention at fixed intervals. For example, Missouri is required to submit the question to the voters every 20 years; Hawaii, every 9 years; and Michigan, every 16 years.

If the voters approve, the next step is to elect delegates. Some state constitutions contain elaborate procedures governing the number of delegates, the method of election, and the time and place of the convention. Others leave the details to the legislature. The way convention delegates are selected seems to affect the kind of document the convention proposes. Selection by nonpartisan, multimember districts is more likely to result in a reform convention that makes major changes than one in which political parties play a major role because the two major political parties generally resist changing any rules that might threaten their standing or influence.[34]

The chosen delegates usually assemble at the state capital, prepare a draft of the new constitution, and submit it to the voters. First, they have to make a difficult choice: Should they ask the voters to accept or reject the new constitution as a whole? Or to vote on each section separately?

The advantage of the first method is that each provision of a constitution ties in with another, and to secure all the advantages of revision, voters should adopt the entire document. The disadvantage is that those who oppose only a particular provision may vote against the entire constitution. Delegates may decide to submit separately a provision they know is controversial. Whichever method they choose, supporters of change must rally their forces to gain voter approval.

The Politics of Constitutional Revision

LEARNING **OBJECTIVE**

22.3 Evaluate the states' recent attempts at constitutional revision.

Constitutions are not a neutral set of rules perched above the world of everyday politics. Rather, they significantly affect who gets what from government. Changes can thus help or hinder various groups.

YOU WILL DECIDE

Should States Require a Supermajority to Approve a Constitutional Amendment?

Florida's constitution has been changed considerably since the state was first admitted to the Union in 1845. Constitutional changes were required when the state seceded from the Union in 1861, was readmitted to the Union in 1865, and grappled with Reconstruction. Yet the state's constitution has also been used to change public policy, through amendments that reduce class size in public schools or construct high-speed rail lines.

Legislators worried that amendments restricting legislative flexibility and straining the state's budget were passed too easily and pressed for a constitutional amendment that would make it more difficult for amendments to pass by raising the threshold of adoption from a simple majority, 50 percent plus one, to a supermajority, or 60 percent plus one. In 2006, this amendment received 58 percent of the vote and thus did not reach the threshold it establishes for future amendments.

What do you think? Should states require a supermajority to approve a constitutional amendment? What arguments would you make for and against such an idea?

THINKING IT THROUGH

Supporters of the amendment argued that Florida's Constitution was too easily changed. They were concerned that well-funded special-interest groups could advance their own narrow self-interests by posing as grassroots organizations, hiring people to gather signatures on petitions, and then bankrolling advertising campaigns that never told the full story about the consequences of a particular amendment. "A spot on the ballot can be purchased for $2 million and takes only six months of work," lamented Protect Our Constitution, Inc., a group formed to advocate for the amendment.*

Legislators also grumbled that amendments too often involved proposals they had already rejected as not in the state's best interest. The state needed to rely on representative democracy, they asserted, and allow the legislature to do its job. Requiring a higher threshold for adoption of a constitutional amendment would preserve the people's right to amend the constitution yet ensure that amendments reflected "the collective will of folks and not just a whim."†

Opponents responded that the supermajority requirements subverted democracy. It blocked the will of the people by allowing a minority to block the majority position. Moreover, they said, Florida needed direct democracy to check the abuse of representative democracy. A coalition of citizen groups that formed to fight against the amendment, Trust the Voters, alleged that the amendment was "nothing short of a power grab by a Legislature that is already unresponsive to popular will." Pointing out that all the money raised by Protect Our Constitution, Inc., came from major corporations and business interests, opponents charged that those supporting the amendment were the special interests and had far too much influence in the legislature. Amendments such as those that banned smoking in restaurants, raised the state minimum wage, and reduced class size reflected the public will and were necessary because the legislature had refused to enact them.

Critical Thinking Questions

1. Should states use a threshold greater than 50 percent plus one to determine whether the people have approved an amendment to the constitution? Why or why not?

2. In establishing the charter for the state government, should state constitutions strengthen direct democracy or rely more heavily on representative democracy?

* www.protectourconstitution.org/mx/hm.asp?id=home.
† Sen. Jim King (R-Jacksonville, Flor.), quoted in J. Taylor Rushing, "Amending State's Top Document Could Be Tougher," *(Jacksonville) Florida Times-Union,* September 22, 2006, p. B1.

There are generally two types of proposed amendments: those focused on streamlining or modernizing the constitution and those targeting specific policy issues rather than institutional reforms. Proponents of the first type generally find that people might favor such measures in the abstract, but only special-interest groups are likely to get invested in the debate and outcome, and they are more likely to oppose than to favor reform.[35] Supporters of the status quo thus have a systemic advantage: "To be successful, revision requires gubernatorial as well as legislative leadership.... An effective political campaign is essential.... Success at the polls is not assured. Constitutional revision can be a high-risk endeavor."[36] Amendments aimed at specific policy issues are often initially promoted by a more focused interest group or constituency with intense preferences. For example, same-sex marriage bans have often been based on a motivated group of citizens organized in favor of such bans working against a less-organized opposition. The following case studies illustrate the risky nature of constitutional revision.

Rhode Island Amends Its Constitution

Rhode Island's biennial constitutional convention began in 1984 and produced 14 separate propositions for amending its 1843 constitution. On November 4, 1986, voters approved 8 of the 14 provisions, rejecting attempts to increase compensation of state legislators, to provide for merit selection of judges, and to create a paramount right to life that would have banned abortions or public funding of them. The voters approved provisions strengthening free speech, due process, and equal protection rights, and expanding fishing rights and access to the shore; they also approved a statement that the rights protected by the Rhode Island Constitution are independent of the U.S. Constitution.[37]

The Rhode Island Constitution calls for voters to be asked every ten years whether they want to convene a constitutional convention. In November 1994, the voters rejected a convention by a vote of 173,693 to 118,545.[38] Despite this defeat, in November 2001, voters approved by a 2-to-1 margin a nonbinding ballot question calling for a constitutional convention focused on separation-of-powers issues. This was a response to a decision of the Rhode Island Supreme Court ruling that the Rhode Island Constitution allowed the state legislature to both make and execute state laws. After continued pressure from Common Cause and 30 other organizations, in 2003, Rhode Island's legislature approved a constitutional amendment strengthening the separation of powers and placed it on the 2004 ballot for voters' approval. State voters passed the separation-of-powers amendment by a 78 percent vote, and in 2005, the state's legislature began developing legislation implementing the new constitutional provisions.[39]

Changing the Hawaii Constitution

More than 800 proposals for constitutional changes were submitted to the Hawaii state constitutional convention of 1978. The League of Women Voters and other groups conducted extensive information and discussion meetings, and the convention held many public hearings on key issues. The 102 delegates met for nearly three months and eventually narrowed the proposals to 34 questions for the fall ballot.

The delegates endorsed a two-term limit for governor and lieutenant governor, moved to make Hawaii's party primaries more open by allowing voters to cast ballots without declaring party preference, and authorized the state legislature to provide partial public funding for election campaigns and to establish spending limits. The convention reflected concern over government spending by setting tougher overall debt and spending limits for the state. It also strengthened environmental safeguards and gave further constitutional and financial protection to the special status of native Hawaiians. In November 1978, 74 percent of the voters went to the polls and adopted all 34 amendments.

However, in 1986, Hawaiians narrowly rejected the periodic question of whether to call a convention. The decision was put to them again in 1996, and the vote was 163,869 in favor and 160,153 against, but 45,245 people left the question unanswered. Blank ballots were tallied as a no, in response to a decision of the state supreme court that the Hawaii Constitution required approval by a majority of all ballots cast. The Ninth U.S. Circuit Court of Appeals, which refused to order a new election, sustained this decision.

Since 1996, additional proposals for a convention have been backed by several interests, including those who wanted to ban same-sex marriage after learning of the Hawaii Supreme Court's ruling in 1993 suggesting that the current constitution would not support such a ban, those who wanted to impose term limits on state legislators, and those who wanted to limit the power of state courts to restrict police searches. Other groups, including the League of Women Voters, have argued that there is no compelling need for a constitutional convention and that these hot-button issues would dominate and polarize the delegates, hindering deliberative discussion about other equally important issues.

In November 2008, Hawaiian voters were asked again to decide whether the state should hold a constitutional convention. Controversial issues included rights and legal protections for native Hawaiians, same-sex marriage, public finance of election campaigns, and term limits. Typical of many drives for state conventions, the effort in Hawaii failed by nearly a 30 percentage-point margin.[40]

Of the People

Affirmative Action via State Amendment

Although most American adults believe everyone should be given an equal start in achieving a good education, job, housing, and so forth, they do not agree on how to remedy past discrimination. They are especially divided on affirmative action, which has sometimes been upheld by the U.S. Supreme Court due to the state's compelling interest in providing a diverse educational experience.

In 2006, Michigan voters spoke on the issue in the elections by enacting an amendment to their state constitution to "ban public institutions from using affirmative action programs that give preferential treatment to groups or individuals based on their race, gender, color, ethnicity, or national origin for public employment, education, or contracting purposes." The amendment also contained a specific list of public institutions affected by the ban, including the University of Michigan. Prior to 2006, the university had waged a long fight to consider diversity in admission decisions. In those battles, the U.S. Supreme Court struck down the university's point system for undergraduate admission that included awarding points to minorities, but it upheld the university's broader interest in including race as part of evaluating diversity among its law school applicants.

The Michigan amendment banning affirmative action passed, 58 to 42 percent. Although it may not survive another Supreme Court challenge, the ban did reflect a statewide sentiment that all applicants should be treated the same and specifically rejected any preference in state job and university applications. Michigan voters were not saying that the demographics of state institutions should remain mostly white or male but rather that they did not want to give any group special status.

The vote itself reflected a division over just how important these programs aimed at increasing diversity were. According to exit polls of voters, the vote was clearly split on whether to end affirmative action in the state, with white men providing the most support for the amendment (see the table that follows).

The Michigan amendment echoes similar bans in California and Washington state but was much more specific. It is no surprise that nonwhite women expressed the greatest opposition to banning affirmative action because they are likely to be the most affected, but the University of Michigan was also intensely opposed. Like many colleges and universities, Michigan has used a variety of tools to increase the number of minority students and made clear its intent to fight the ban through the federal court system. Michigan voters may want the face of American politics to continue changing but not if it involves affirmative action.

CRITICAL THINKING QUESTIONS

1. Why do you think there is opposition to affirmative action programs?

2. Should affirmative action programs in university admissions be treated differently from programs aimed at public employment or government contracts? Why or why not?

Proposition 2: Restrict Affirmative Action		
Vote by Race and Gender	Yes	No
White Men	70%	30%
White Women	59	41
Nonwhite Men	30	70
Nonwhite Women	18	82

SOURCE: www.cnn.com/ELECTION/2006/ pages/results/states/MI/I/01/epolls.O.html.

Texas Keeps Its Old Constitution

Texas has a lengthy constitution adopted in 1876 and amended more than 430 times. The most recent effort to thoroughly revise it occurred in 1972, after political scandals brought in a new governor, Dolph Briscoe, and a reform-oriented state legislature. After pushing through a variety of reforms dealing with the ethics of officeholders, campaign practices, and registration of lobbyists, the legislature called an unusual convention of members of the legislature, rather than a specially elected body, to revise the constitution.

After 17 months, the legislator-delegates came up with a much revised and shortened document intended to modernize many obsolete governmental practices. The convention deadlocked, however, over whether to give constitutional status to the state's right-to-work law, which prohibits labor contracts that require union membership as a condition of employment, so this issue was referred to the voters. In the end, neither the AFL-CIO nor Governor Briscoe supported all the convention's recommendations. The governor was especially opposed to the proposal that legislative sessions be held annually, rather than every two years, because he thought yearly sessions would lead to higher taxes. Advocates of the revised constitution tried to salvage their work by offering voters substantial parts of the new charter as amendments to the existing constitution.

Conservatives praised the old constitution, claiming that it had served Texas well for 100 years. Progressives complained that it was elitist, permitted only the narrowest governmental objectives, and made real change nearly impossible. In November 1975,

The Alabama Citizens for Constitutional Reform (constitutionalreform.org) is promoting a new film that shows a re-enactment of Alabama's 1901 Constitutional Convention, based on actual transcripts, in which delegates openly discussed ways to disenfranchise black and poor white voters. ■ *Do you think the creation of the Alabama Citizens' Constitutional Commission was a good idea? What are the strengths and weaknesses of putting a group like this in charge of constitutional reform?*

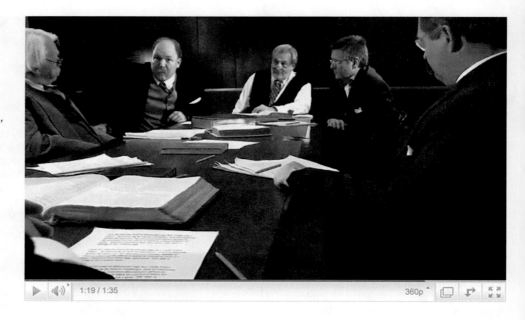

amid charges and countercharges, Texas voters rejected the amendments by a 2-to-1 margin.[41] Since then, they have approved 143 amendments and rejected 33 but have not held another convention.

Alabama Considers a New Constitution

Alabama has had six constitutions. The most recent, written in 1901 and adopted in 1902, was "a document of the Old South,"[42] unashamedly designed to keep African Americans segregated in public schools and prevent them from voting or participating in governmental matters.[43] It has been amended more than 740 times and survived many attempts to modernize and replace it.

The issue of constitutional reform remains on the state's agenda. The 21-member independent commission, called Alabama Citizens for Constitutional Reform, has been pushing the idea for years[44] and proposed putting the question of holding a constitutional convention to a statewide vote.

Although one poll showed that 61 percent of Alabamans favored reform, in November 2002, that proposal was nonetheless defeated in the Alabama House of Representatives by a vote of 33 to 105.[45, 46] However, the Democratic and Republican candidates for governor that year both supported constitutional reforms and a statewide vote on the matter. Shortly after his inauguration in 2003, Governor Bob Riley established a 35-member Alabama Citizens' Constitutional Commission to propose constitutional reforms in several areas: strengthening the governor's line-item veto power, giving more home rule back to counties, requiring more than a simple majority of the legislature to raise taxes, changing provisions that earmark 90 percent of all tax revenues for specific purposes, eliminating racist provisions, and studying how the constitution might be shortened and reformed. Based on the commission's recommendations and Governor Riley's leadership, major revisions of the constitution were encapsulated into one amendment, which was resoundingly defeated. Despite the defeat, Governor Riley was praised for his political courage and leadership.

In 2004, the legislature pressed forward with one of the reform areas and proposed an amendment eliminating language in the constitution that requires segregated schools and poll taxes, which remain even though federal courts invalidated them more than 40 years ago. Opponents claimed that the proposed changes in language would have established a right to a public education, opening the door to activist judges demanding that taxes be raised to increase school spending.[47] Voters defeated the amendment by only 1,850 of the more than 1.3 million votes cast. Nonetheless, the issue has not died: Many in Alabama still want to call a convention to reform the constitution and are pushing to get the question placed on the ballot.[48]

The Future of State Constitutions

Unlike the federal Constitution, amended only 27 times in more than 220 years, most state constitutions are amended on a regular basis. Although no entirely new state constitution has been adopted since the 1980s, the process of constitutional amendment allows state governments and voters to modify and modernize constitutions to fit changing conditions. Nearly 1,100 amendments were proposed between 1998 and 2006, affecting nearly every state constitution. Many were limited in scope, concerning only local issues or specific state agencies. However, others affected states' bills of rights, broad finance and taxation issues, and electoral processes.[49]

State constitutions will continue to be modified as new issues arise and conditions change in the states. The recent trend to add bans on same-sex marriages to state constitutions is not exceptional. Indeed, it reflects the fact that voters are the ultimate judges of the meaning and content of their state's constitution, which rights the state will recognize, and which policies it will follow.

CHAPTER **SUMMARY**

22.1 Compare and contrast the U.S. Constitution and state constitutions.

Like the U.S. Constitution, state constitutions usually have a preamble, a bill of rights, and articles providing for a legislature, an executive branch, and an independent judiciary. State constitutions are longer and more detailed than the U.S. Constitution, and their bills of rights often include new and expanded rights not mentioned in the U.S. Constitution. In the past 20 years, state constitutions have become instruments for protecting and expanding rights in what is known as the new judicial federalism. Some state supreme courts have relied on their own state constitutions and bills of rights to provide their citizens greater protections than those found in the U.S. Constitution.

22.2 Outline the processes used to amend state constitutions.

State constitutions can be amended by voters' ratifying proposals submitted by the legislature, by popular

initiative petitions, or by constitutional conventions. Conventions tend to revise the entire constitution rather than amend only portions of it. The Progressive Movement advanced initiative petitions as a reform measure to control legislatures thought to be beholden to special interests. In recent decades, initiative petitions have become a popular means to amend state constitutions by people anxious to limit the power of state and local governments.

22.3 Evaluate the states' recent attempts at constitutional revision.

States rarely call full-blown constitutional conventions, as they expose current elected officials to substantial risk. Thus, most revisions of state constitutions happen via individual amendments proposed either by the legislature or directly by citizens. Citizen-led initiatives can produce an array of proposals, which often deal less with constitutional issues, such as fundamental rights or the basic structure of government, and more with very narrow policy questions.

CHAPTER **SELF-TEST**

22.1 Compare and contrast the U.S. Constitution and state constitutions.

1. Which of the following statements is true?
   a. The U.S. Constitution is longer than all state constitutions.
   b. The U.S. Constitution is shorter than all state constitutions.
   c. The U.S. Constitution is longer than some state constitutions and shorter than others.

2. In a few sentences, explain what is meant by referring to state constitutions as "straitjackets."
3. Imagine a judge serving in your state recently ruled that according to the state constitution, the government must provide a free college education to all of its residents. In one or two paragraphs, explain how this decision is an example of "new judicial federalism," and tell why it is or is not appropriate for judges to make rulings in such a way.

4. Decide whether state constitutions should be as specific as they are. Write a short essay (one to two paragraphs) explaining your decision and attempting to persuade a person who is unfamiliar with the issue.

22.2 Outline the processes used to amend state constitutions.

5. Explain the distinction between *amending* and *revising* a constitution.

6. List the three ways in which state constitutions can be amended. Which of these methods do you feel will provide the highest-quality amendments? In two or three paragraphs, defend your position and explain some shortcomings of the other methods.

7. In a few paragraphs, argue that states should have constitutional conventions more frequently than they currently do.

8. List some amendments more likely to be proposed by petition of the general population than by the legislature. Write a short paragraph arguing why states should or should not be able to propose amendments through petitions.

22.3 Evaluate the states' recent attempts at constitutional revision.

9. Write a few paragraphs comparing efforts at constitutional changes in two of the following states: Rhode Island, Hawaii, Texas, and Alabama. Give your opinion on how each case did or did not improve the state's constitution.

10. In one or two paragraphs, explain why state constitutions are amended much more frequently than the U.S. Constitution. Describe any major problems or benefits you see in the frequent amending of state constitutions.

Answers for selected questions: 1. b

---

mypoliscilab™ EXERCISES
Where participation leads to action!

Apply what you learned in this chapter on MyPoliSciLab.

Read on mypoliscilab.com

    eText: Chapter 22

Study and **Review** on mypoliscilab.com

    Pre-Test
    Post-Test
    Chapter Exam
    Flashcards

Explore on mypoliscilab.com

    Simulation: You Are Attempting to Revise the California Constitution
    Simulation: You Are Attempting to Revise the Texas Constitution

---

KEY **TERMS**

judicial interpretation, p. 570
new judicial federalism, p. 570

revision commission, p. 572
constitutional initiative petition, p. 573

ADDITIONAL **RESOURCES**

FURTHER READING

WILLI PAUL ADAMS, *The First American Constitutions: Republican Ideology and the Making of State Constitutions in the Revolutionary Era* (Rowman & Littlefield, 2001).

RICHARD J. ELLIS, *Democratic Delusions: The Initiative Process in America* (University Press of Kansas, 2003).

PAUL FINKELMAN AND **STEPHEN E. GOTTLIEB,** EDS., *Toward a Usable Past: Liberty Under State*

Constitutions (University of Georgia Press, 1991).

JENNIFER FREISEN, *State Constitutional Law* (Michie, 1996).

SANFORD LEVINSON, ED., *Responding to Imperfection: The Theory and Practice of Constitutional*

Amendment (Princeton University Press, 1995).

CHARLES LOPEMAN, *The Activist Advocate: Policy Making in State Supreme Courts* (Praeger, 1999).

ROBERT L. MADDEX, *State Constitutions of the United States,* 2d ed. (CQ Press, 2005).

G. ALAN TARR, *Understanding State Constitutions* (Princeton University Press, 2000).

G. ALAN TARR AND **ROBERT F. WILLIAMS,** *State Constitutions for the Twenty-First Century* (State University of New York Press, 2006).

ROBERT F. WILLIAMS, *State Constitutional Law: Cases and Materials* (Michie, 1993). See also the quarterly review *State Constitutional Commentaries and Notes,* published by the Edward McNail Burns Center for State Constitutional Studies at Rutgers University.

WEB SITES

www.greenwood.com/catalog/series/ Reference%2bGuides%2bto%2bthe% 2bState%2bConstitutions%2bof%

2bthe%2bUnited%2bStates.aspx The Greenwood Publishing Group has commissioned reference guides for the constitution of each state, written by an expert on the state.

www.constitution.org/ The Constitution Society Web site includes links to every state's constitution.

www.stateconstitutions.umd. edu/index.aspx The NBER/University of Maryland State Constitutions Project Web site includes search functions for the text of state constitutions.

CHAPTER 23

Parties and Elections in the States

On May 6, 2008, voters in North Carolina and Indiana went to the polls to cast ballots in the presidential primaries. Three years earlier, Indiana had adopted laws requiring voters to provide valid identification (ID) before they would be allowed to vote. According to Indiana Public Law 109-2005, a valid ID is one that: (1) displays a photo, (2) displays your current name, (3) displays an expiration date that is current, and (4) was issued by the State of Indiana or the U.S. government. Student IDs could only be used if they met all four criteria, which automatically excluded students from private schools.

The law was adopted to limit potential voter fraud, but critics feared it would lead to many eligible voters being discouraged from voting or being turned away at the polls. On that day in May, news sources reported that several nuns were blocked from voting—they were in their 80s or 90s and did not have driver's licenses or up-to-date passports. Several students from private colleges were also turned away from the polls. Voters in North Carolina casting ballots that same day faced no such obstacles unless they had never voted before and had registered to vote by mail rather than in person. How can there be such differences between the two states? Doesn't the U.S. Constitution provide for equal voting rights for all citizens?

Actually, the U.S. Constitution and a series of U.S. Supreme Court decisions throughout the years have made it quite clear that states have the power to regulate the conduct of elections, even for national offices. As such, considerable variation exists across the states regarding when elections are held, how citizens cast ballots, how candidates qualify to get on the ballot, and who is eligible to vote. About one month before the Indiana primary, the U.S. Supreme Court, in *Crawford* v. *Marion County Election Board*, upheld the Indiana law as constitutional by a vote of 6 to 3.[1] The majority of the justices argued that the state's interest in preventing fraud was sufficient grounds for adopting the policy and that the identification requirement did not place an undue burden on voters. However, in 2009, an Indiana appeals court struck down the law, finding that it violated Indiana's constitution by not treating all voters equally. The appeal of this decision was heard by the Indiana Supreme Court on March 4, 2010 (*The League of Women Voters et al* v. *Todd Rokita*; you can watch video of the oral arguments online at https://mycourts.in.gov/arguments/default.aspx?view=detail&id=1007). At that hearing, the state supreme court set aside the appeals court ruling and agreed to take over the case. As we learned in the previous chapter, state constitutions can and often do provide for more broadly defined rights than does the U.S. Constitution.

These recent events in Indiana illustrate the central role that states play in conducting elections in the United States for offices at the local, state, and national levels. In this chapter, we focus on state elections in general, leaving detailed discussions of gubernatorial, state legislative, and judicial elections to subsequent chapters. As we will see, states have made very different decisions about how to manage elections and regulate participation, so "democracy" varies significantly across states. Though state differences are large and many problems remain, our state and local governments have seen major advances in democratic government in recent decades—in who is permitted to vote, in the ease of voting, in the openness of party primaries and caucuses to diverse voters, in the administration of elections, in the regulation of campaigns, and in the spread of party competition.

CHAPTER **OUTLINE** CHAPTER LEARNING **OBJECTIVES**

The Constitutional Context: State and Federal Roles in Regulating Elections

23.1 Compare and contrast the constitutional roles of state and federal governments in regulating elections.

Elections at the State and Local Levels

23.2 Describe differences among the states in laws regulating voting, elections, and campaign finance, and assess federal influence on these regulations.

The Role of Political Parties

23.3 Outline the organization of state parties and their major functions with respect to elections, voters, and government.

Party Balance and Imbalance

23.4 Assess how party competition has changed in recent decades.

The Constitutional Context: State and Federal Roles in Regulating Elections

Although we often speak of national elections for the U.S. Congress or the presidency, in fact there are no purely national elections in the United States. All elections for national offices are held by and within the states. Senate elections are statewide contests; elections to the House of Representatives are held within states and in districts drawn by the states, and even presidential elections are actually a set of statewide contests for electoral votes. The U.S. Constitution gives states the leading role in regulating the conditions under which elections for members of the U.S. Congress are held. Article I, Section 4, says, "The Times, Places and Manner of holding Elections for Senators and Representatives, shall be prescribed in each State by the Legislature thereof; but the Congress may at any time by Law make or alter such Regulations, except as to the Places of choosing Senators."[2] The language regarding presidential elections also gives states a leading role: "Each State shall appoint, in such Manner as the Legislature thereof may direct, a Number of Electors."[3]

Nonetheless, the federal government also exercises considerable control over the circumstances under which national elections are held. As already noted, although Article I, Section 4, gives states the leading role in regulating congressional elections, it also gives the Congress the authority to "make or alter such Regulations." *The Federalist*, No. 59, defended this provision by arguing that, although state control over elections was preferable under most circumstances, the national government had to have the authority to intervene "whenever extraordinary circumstances might render that interposition necessary to its safety."[4] That is, control over elections was so important, giving states exclusive control would have made the national government's very existence vulnerable to state regulation. By sharing authority over elections, the original Constitution set up an ever-shifting tug-of-war between state variation and national standards.

The U.S. Constitution says little about state and local elections—the elections of governors, lieutenant governors, attorneys general, state legislators, mayors, city council members, and many other public officials. It seems to require only that states actually use and abide by elections, as some sort of popular sovereignty is implied by the clause in Article IV, which says "the United States shall guarantee to every State in this Union a Republican Form of Government."[5] As a result, states differ even more in the ways they regulate elections that fill state and local offices than in the laws they apply to congressional and presidential elections.

Amendments to the original Constitution maintained the primacy of states in regulating elections, although they placed constraints on how states could exercise that authority. The Fifteenth Amendment prohibits states from denying the franchise on the basis of "race, color, or previous condition of servitude." The Seventeenth Amendment requires that U.S. senators be chosen directly by a state's voters rather than its legislators. The Nineteenth Amendment guarantees women the right to vote. The Twenty-Fourth Amendment prohibits states from requiring voters to pay a poll tax. And the Twenty-Sixth Amendment prevents states from denying the vote to otherwise qualified persons age 18 or older.

These amendments do not necessarily represent triumphs of national over state powers to control elections because national action was often a culmination of state flexibility and innovation. For instance, the ratification of the Nineteenth Amendment in 1920 came after a half-century of change at the subnational level, which eventually forced national action. In 1869–1870, the Wyoming territory gave women the rights to vote and hold office, rights that continued after Wyoming became a state 20 years later. Soon afterward, Colorado, Utah, and Idaho also gave women equal political rights. Between 1910 and 1914, seven more states in the West and Midwest gave women full voting rights, followed by large states such as New York in 1917 and Michigan in 1918. By the end of 1918,

Women in several western states were given the right to vote and hold public office before they won the right to vote at the national level in 1920. ■ *What examples can you think of in how regulations for conducting elections differ across the states today?*

women had full voting rights in 15 states and partial rights (that is, they were eligible to vote in presidential elections only) in a dozen others.[6] Thus, when Congress considered the proposed Nineteenth Amendment, many members were understandably reluctant to vote against it and face the prospect of having to explain to female voters in their own districts why they thought women were unqualified to participate in the nation's politics. In this instance, then, as in others, shared state and national authority over elections created pathways for change that would not have been available if either the states or the federal government had exclusive control.

Elections at the State and Local Levels

Each year, there are thousands of state and local elections. Europeans, used to voting for one or two candidates at the national and local levels and only once every two or three years, are flabbergasted to learn that we engage in so many elections. Selection of town and local officials in the late winter may be followed in the spring by **primary elections,** which are used to determine who will run in the general elections under the party labels. Actual officeholders are chosen in **general elections** in the fall. These elections may be interspersed with **special elections,** which are generally held to fill vacant offices or address one-time issues, or elections for school boards or to adopt school budgets. Some states allow for **recall elections,** which are used to throw unpopular officials out of office, as in California in 2003 when voters removed Gray Davis from the governorship and replaced him with Arnold Schwarzenegger.[7] Voters in all states but Delaware must ratify changes to the state constitution in a referendum, and approximately half the states allow public **initiatives** and **referendums** to be put on the ballot by petition. A public referendum occurs when enough citizens petition to hold an election to vote on a bill that has already been approved by the legislature. A public initiative allows citizens to petition to propose a law to be voted on in an election without requiring any action by the legislature. Just as bewildering to some observers is the number of offices we vote on, from president to probate judge, from senator to sheriff, from governor to noxious weed control superintendent. By contrast, Europeans elect only a handful of key officials, who in turn appoint career officials.

For the most part, control over this vast electoral process in the United States is *decentralized* in its rules and administration. States, for example, differ in the hours the polls are open, how close to the voting place campaigning may be conducted, and whether and when they require voters to register. Furthermore, many states delegate a number of responsibilities to county or other local governments. Such delegation was why voters in Palm Beach County, Florida had the infamous "butterfly" ballot in the 2000 presidential election while others did not (see Figure 23–1). Due to overriding federal legislation, some of the differences among the states in their electoral laws have diminished in recent years. Yet new differences open up as new options and issues emerge, such as mail-in ballots and extended voting periods. The remainder of this section discusses these differences as well as occasional federal efforts to reduce them.

Differences in Who May Vote

States determine, for the most part, who is eligible to vote—and their laws can exclude large numbers of people from the polls and create considerable variation in voting throughout the country. All states but Maine and Vermont, for example, prohibit prison inmates from voting. Most states also refuse to register citizens on parole or probation, and ten states permanently ban some or all convicted felons from voting (see the "You Will Decide" box).[8] Thirty-six states have a "mental competency" requirement for voter registration. States must keep accurate and up-to-date lists of registered voters and those ineligible to register. States could also extend the right to vote further, but most do not exercise this authority. If a state wanted to permit 16-year-olds to vote, it could do so—yet none has chosen that option.[9]

Voter registration rules are important because they can exclude or discourage people from participating in elections. All states except North Dakota require citizens to register

LEARNING OBJECTIVE
23.2 Describe differences among the states in laws regulating voting, elections, and campaign finance, and assess federal influence on these regulations.

primary elections
Elections in which voters choose party nominees.

general elections
Elections in which voters elect officeholders.

special elections
Elections in which voters decide on ballot initiatives, vote on statewide constitutional changes or new constitutions, or elect a senator or representative to replace one who has died or resigned.

recall elections
A procedure for submitting to popular vote the removal of officials from office before the end of their term.

initiative
A procedure whereby a certain number of voters may, by petition, propose a law or constitutional amendment and have it submitted to the voters.

referendum
A procedure for submitting to popular vote measures passed by the legislature or proposed amendments to a state constitution.

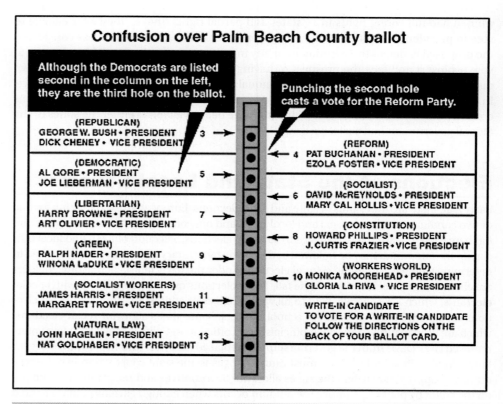

FIGURE 23–1 **Sample Butterfly Ballot.**

■ *What are some of the pros and cons of decentralized control over elections?*

before voting, and states vary greatly in how easy they make registration. More than 20 states require persons to live in a state or locality for one month before they can register or vote, but about the same number have no minimum residency period. Although most states require citizens to register as much as 30 days before the election in which they plan to vote, nine states allow citizens to register at the polls on election day. Voter turnout is generally higher in states where getting registered is easier. A common reason people do not register is that they have moved. Fifteen percent of U.S. citizens change their residence every year.[10] After moving, they may not realize they need to register at their new address until only a few days before the election, when it may be too late. Early registration deadlines may thus cause some people not to vote.

Voter registration became somewhat easier when Congress passed the National Voter Registration, or Motor Voter, Act in 1993. The Act tried to reduce disparities in voter registration throughout income groups by, among other things, requiring states to offer voter registration when people apply for or renew their driver's license, or when they visit government agencies offering public assistance benefits. The eight states that permit election day registration or do not require voter registration are exempt from the law.

What difference has Motor Voter made? During 2005 and 2006, nearly 21 million people registered through motor vehicle or other agencies, approximately 43 percent of total registrations in that period.[11] However, scholars suggest that many of those would likely have registered anyway and also that Motor Voter has had only a limited impact on reducing disparities in voter registration or subsequent turnout.[12] Also, many of these new registrants are registering as Independents. Motor Voter thus does not appear to have made much difference in party balance, contrary to expectations that it would result in a bias in favor of Democrats.[13]

Taken together, states' voter eligibility and registration rules can have important effects on **voter turnout,** which we typically measure as the percentage of a state's voting-age

voter turnout
The proportion of the voting-age public that votes.

population who actually vote in a particular election. (The U.S. Census Bureau annually estimates the voting-age population.) More restrictive voting registration laws may lower turnout, according to one study, by as much as 9 percent.[14]

Voter turnout may also be influenced by *voter identification laws,* which affect how registered voters can demonstrate to poll workers that they are who they say they are. The issue of voter identification received a push from a section of the federal Help America Vote Act of 2002 (HAVA), which attempted to combat fraud by requiring new registrants to show or prove identification, either when they registered or when they first showed up to vote. However, as discussed in the opener of this chapter, many states, such as Indiana, decided to go beyond these minimal requirements and demanded that all registrants identify themselves using strict criteria before casting a ballot in any election.

Although not much is known about the effects of strict voter identification requirements, early studies suggest that such requirements may depress voter turnout for registered voters, especially persons with little education and low incomes, perhaps because such individuals are less likely to own cars or travel and thus are less likely to have up-to-date driver's licenses or passports.[15] Now that the states have some flexibility on this issue, the debate over voter identification laws—and the trade-offs they suggest between preventing fraud and ensuring widespread and unbiased voter access—will probably be intense for several years into the future.

States' voter turnouts vary enormously, even for the same elections. In the 2008 presidential election, fewer than 50 percent of the voting-age population in four states—Hawaii, Texas, Arizona, and California—cast votes, whereas more than 65 percent voted in ten states.[16] Although registration and other voting rules affect these rates, many other factors affect turnout. States whose residents have individual characteristics associated with voting—such as being older and better educated—have higher turnout rates. States with more competitive elections also have higher rates, in part because such elections draw more public interest, though perhaps also because competitive elections spur candidates and parties to work harder to get voters to the polls.

Voter eligibility and registration laws may seem like mundane matters, but they have stirred some of the greatest controversies in the history of U.S. politics. Voter registration laws were at the heart of the struggle for civil rights in the South in the 1950s and 1960s. Southern states disenfranchised African American citizens by selectively enforcing poll taxes, literacy tests, and vouchers of "good character." Even attempting to register was dangerous for blacks in some parts of the South, sometimes resulting in severe harassment and death.

To combat disenfranchisement, President Lyndon Johnson pushed for and signed the Voting Rights Act of 1965 into law. The Act prohibited the denial or abridgment of the right to vote by means of literacy tests throughout the nation. It also contained special enforcement provisions aimed at parts of the country where discriminatory laws and administrative practices were prevalent. These mostly southern states and localities were prohibited from implementing any changes affecting voting unless the federal government reviewed the proposed changes and found them to be nondiscriminatory. The Act gave the federal government authority to monitor and review local elections, voter qualifications, and registration procedures.

The Voting Rights Act had an enormous effect on voter registration and participation. In Mississippi, registration among African Americans climbed from 6.7 percent in 1965 to 74.2 percent in 1988. In Alabama, it went from 19.3 percent in 1965 to 68.4 percent in 1988. Voting rates among black citizens also increased enormously, and southern politics became multiracial, with significant new competition between parties in many parts of the region.[17]

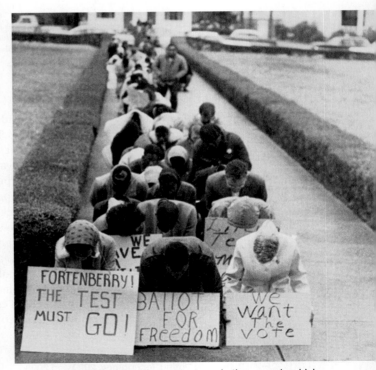

Students protested against literacy tests and other ways in which public officials prevented black citizens from voting in this 1962 demonstration in McComb, Mississippi.

DECIDE
Should Former Felons Be Allowed to Vote?

All states except Maine and Vermont prohibit citizens in prison from voting, and most states also withhold voting rights from persons on parole or probation. Ten states permanently ban some or all ex-felons from voting, even those not on parole or probation. It is estimated that approximately 5.3 million Americans are not allowed to vote due to state laws restricting the voting rights of some felons.* However, some states are reconsidering such laws. Nebraska eliminated its lifetime ban in 2006 in favor of one that ends two years after felons complete their sentences. In Iowa, the governor signed an executive order in 2005 restoring voting rights to felons who have completed their sentences.

What do you think? Should former felons be allowed to vote? What arguments would you make for and against such an idea?

THINKING IT THROUGH

One argument in favor of restoring voting rights to felons after they complete their prison sentences is that the voting bans affect too many people. The American Civil Liberties Union claims that hundreds of thousands of people are disenfranchised by Florida's ban on voting by former felons.† The United States' high rate of incarceration, including many people convicted of nonviolent crimes, reduces the vote for large parts of low-income and minority communities. Laws prohibiting former inmates from voting may, for instance, affect as many as 20 to 30 percent of African Americans in some states. Advocates for former inmates say state governments ought to stress their reintegration into society, not their permanent separation. Another reason not to withhold the vote is that the administration of such laws has had negative side effects. In Florida's 2000 elections, many black voters may have been wrongly prevented from voting by the former-felon ban, due to mistakes in identity.

On the other hand, some argue that the bans should stay. A Tennessee state representative said, "I don't believe we need to have a voting bloc that comes out of prison angry at the sheriff's department . . . and angry at the prosecutor's office."‡ One can also make the argument that simply because a law is badly administered—resulting in too many black voters disqualified—does not mean that the law itself is bad; instead, the law should be better implemented. The central difference, however, remains whether a convicted felon permanently forfeits the right to vote.

Critical Thinking Questions

1. Are there other arguments for or against laws that prevent U.S. citizens from voting after they have completed their prison terms?
2. What information or research would you need to make an appropriate decision on these arguments?
3. How is it fair that former felons may vote for president in one state but not in another?

---

* Estimate provided by The Sentencing Project, http://www.sentencingproject.org/template/page.cfm?id=133.
† See American Civil Liberties Union, "State Legislative and Policy Reform to Advance the Voting Rights of Formerly Incarcerated Persons: ACLU Policy Activities and Legislative Accomplishments: 2007," www.aclu.org/votingrights/exoffenders/statelegispolicy2007.html#text.
‡ Charisse Jones, "Rhode Island to Revisit Felons' Voting Rights," *USA Today,* May 31, 2006, www.usatoday.com/news/nation/2006-05-31-felons-voting-rights_x.htm.

Used old technology (lever machines, punch cards, hand-counted ballots)

Used optically scanned paper ballots

Used electronic screens

FIGURE 23–2 Changes in Voting Technology, 2000 and 2008.

■ *How has the way we vote changed since 2000? What are some potential advantages and drawbacks of these changes?*

Differences in How We Vote

As a result of widespread problems in election administration in 2000, Congress passed HAVA, which provided federal funds to help states replace punch cards, paper ballots, and lever voting machines. Since HAVA was enacted, big changes have occurred in the way citizens vote. In 2000, nearly half of all registered voters in the United States (49 percent) voted in counties that used lever machines, punch cards, or hand-counted paper ballots. Punch-card ballots can be subject to problems such as dangling or dimpled chads (the little pieces of paper voters punch out to make machine-readable holes) that do not clearly indicate the voter's intent.[18] Only 29 percent used optically scanned paper ballots, and 12 percent used electronic touchscreen machines. Eight years later in 2008, only 7 percent of registered voters voted in counties that used the older methods, while 56 percent used optically scanned ballots and 33 percent used electronic screens (see Figure 23–2).[19]

The spread of computerized voting prompted new debates about the accuracy and accountability of computerized voting machines. Unlike punch cards, optical scanners, and paper ballots, touchscreen voting machines do not permit an audit of the vote.[20] To deal with this accountability problem, many states require all of their voting machines to print paper ballots that they can check in case of problems in the electronic tally. Others use optical scan technologies, in which voters mark paper ballots that are then scanned, allowing quick and accurate tallies but still preserving a paper record. Yet even these systems—called a "voter-verified paper trail"—can malfunction or be tampered with.[21]

These changes reduced some of the uncertainty over vote counts. The biggest voting problem in 2004 was long lines at polling locations in several states. However, this was more the result of an insufficient number of voting machines and booths than a breakdown in voting technology. The 2006 elections appeared to be quite successful, with few reports of problems or controversies. Voting went smoothly in the 2008 elections as well, although some "early voters" (people who voted before election day, in states where that is allowed) stood in long lines.

There are still, however, many issues for voting systems in the future. The new technologies are harder and more expensive to maintain; local governments may not have the funds to keep them in good condition and will rely more on state and federal dollars.[22] Also, at least one study found that older, less-educated voters may make more mistakes than others when using various computerized voting or optical scanning machines.[23] So long as the nation relies on a highly decentralized system—often underfunded, staffed not by professionals but by partisan volunteers, and strained by intense party competition—problems and future changes are likely to occur.

A critical and often overlooked aspect of voting is poll workers. Poll workers implement the rules on who may and may not vote, manage the entire process of voting, and have a strong impact on citizens' experience at the polls. With the new voting technology, poll workers also manage the machines, explain their operation to voters, and at the end of the day ensure that they are properly stored. The competence of the poll worker is correlated to voters' overall satisfaction with the voting experience.[24]

State election ballots also vary widely and with important implications. Ballots are of two basic kinds. The **party column ballot** (also known as the *Indiana ballot*) is organized by parties, with the party name and symbol at the top of a column that lists all the party's candidates running for offices in that election. Typically, there is an option at the top of the ballot column that allows voters to cast votes for all candidates of that party. When voters choose this option, they cast a **straight ticket** vote. Voters may also have to work their way through any state constitutional amendments, referendums, and initiatives on the ballot.

Partly to discourage straight ticket voting, some states use the **office block ballot** (also known as the *Massachusetts ballot*), which lists all the candidates running for an office together in one block or on one screen, all those running for another office in another block/screen, and so on. Office block ballots encourage **split ticket** voting, or voting for candidates from more than one party. One consequence of computerized ballots will be a shift to office block formats. The sample ballot in Figure 23-3 allows the voter to either cast a straight ticket or to select each vote independently by office.

Voting by Mail and Absentee Ballot Modern technology makes it possible to vote by other means than appearing in person at a voting place on election day. Cities such as San Diego and Berkeley first experimented with holding *elections by mail*. The government mails voters a pamphlet that describes the questions to be decided in the election and gives instructions on how to complete the ballot and return it by mail. Voters sign the return envelope, and their signatures are compared against their signatures on the voter registration form. There have been no major problems administering local mail ballot elections, and the turnout has been higher than the norm for in-person special elections.[25]

In January 1996, Oregon voters elected a U.S. senator in a special election through the mail rather than in person. Oregonians had 20 days from the date the ballots were mailed to return them to county clerks, and two-thirds of those who received ballots returned them. In 1998, Oregon voters approved an initiative to conduct all elections by mail. Vote-by-mail elections have proved popular there and show little evidence of fraud.[26]

Nonetheless, opponents of the vote-by-mail system worry about fraud, and they worry that voters may be pressured to vote a certain way. One person in a household may try to direct the votes of others. Another problem is that supporters of a candidate may visit voters at home soon after the ballots are delivered and pressure people to vote on the spot,

Touchscreen voting machines typically present candidates in office blocks, not party columns, and may thus discourage straight ticket voting.

party column ballot
A type of ballot that encourages party-line voting by listing all of a party's candidates in a column under the party name.

straight ticket
A vote for all of one party's candidates.

office block ballot
A ballot on which all candidates are listed under the office for which they are running.

split ticket
A vote for some of one party's candidates and some of another party's.

OFFICIAL BALLOT
PIUTE COUNTY, UTAH
TUESDAY, NOVEMBER 4, 2008

Valeen H. Brown
COUNTY CLERK

INSTRUCTIONS TO VOTERS: To vote for the candidate of your choice, completely darken the OVAL ● next to the candidate's name. To vote for a person whose name is not on the ballot, darken the OVAL next to "Write-In" and write in the candidate's name on the Write-in line. To vote on a measure, fill in the oval ● next to your choice. Use ballpoint pen with dark ink (not red). All distinguishing marks or erasures are forbidden and make the ballot void. If you tear, deface, or wrongly mark this ballot, contact the County Clerk's office or Poll Worker. **VOTE LIKE THIS:** ●
VOTE BOTH SIDES OF THE BALLOT

Voting this Straight Party Race is optional. It is permissible to vote for candidates of various political parties in this election.	FEDERAL RACES	STATE RACES
STRAIGHT PARTY	**UNITED STATES PRESIDENT VICE PRESIDENT** (Vote for One)	**GOVERNOR / LT. GOVERNOR** (Vote for One)
○ REPUBLICAN PARTY REP	○ JOHN McCAIN SARAH PALIN REP	○ JON M. HUNTSMAN, JR. GARY R. HERBERT REP
○ DEMOCRATIC PARTY DEM	○ BARACK OBAMA JOE BIDEN DEM	○ BOB SPRINGMEYER JOSIE VALDEZ DEM
	○ BOB BARR WAYNE A. ROOT LIB	○ "SUPERDELL" DELL SCHANZE JOEY HOBBS LIB
○ LIBERTARIAN PARTY LIB	○ CHARLES O. "CHUCK" BALDWIN DARREL CASTLE CON	○ Write-In
		STATE ATTORNEY GENERAL (Vote for One)
○ CONSTITUTION PARTY CON	○ RALPH NADER MATT GONZALEZ * PEACE AND FREEDOM	○ MARK L. SHURTLEFF REP
		○ JEAN WELCH HILL DEM
		○ W. ANDREW McCULLOUGH LIB
		○ Write-in
	○ GLORIA LA RIVA ROBERT MOSES * PARTY FOR SOCIALISM AND LIBERATION	**STATE TREASURER** (Vote for One)
		○ RICHARD K. ELLIS REP
		○ DICK CLARK DEM
		○ Write-in

FIGURE 23–3 Sample ballot with straight party option

■ *Why would the major parties prefer to keep the "straight party vote" option on the ballots? What interests might prefer solely office block ballots?*

perhaps offering to mail the ballot. However, supporters point to the higher turnout and lower costs in administering vote-by-mail elections. They also cite the absence of observed and documented fraud or abuse in vote-by-mail elections.

A less dramatic reform of election laws is the *absentee ballot.* In most of the country, voters may request a ballot by mail. In some states, voters must give an acceptable reason why they cannot reach the polls on election day, such as a planned trip or a physical disability (though these reasons are almost never verified). But in an increasing number of states—28 in 2008—voters may ask for and get an absentee ballot without giving any excuse or reason at all.[27] Absentee balloting is especially useful for initiative measures. In states such as California or Washington, where voters may face 20 or more complicated ballot questions, those who vote by absentee ballot can take their time researching and pondering how they are going to vote instead of deciding within the few minutes they have in a voting booth.

Increased ease in obtaining ballots has significantly expanded the rate of absentee voting in California. It has been used especially by Republicans to activate retirees and other voters who find it difficult to get to polling places. In Washington state, absentee ballots made up nearly 89 percent of all ballots in 2008.[28] Other forms of *early voting* have also spread widely in recent years. In 2008, 35 states permitted voters to cast their ballots in person several days before an election at several locations in each county, and only 4 of those states required voters to give an excuse for not showing up on election day.[29] Michael McDonald, a political scientist at George Mason University, estimates that nearly 32 million citizens cast early votes in 2008.[30]

Differences in Nomination Processes

State law establishes the process by which party nominees are selected. Most states use primary elections, but some permit the parties to nominate their candidates through a *caucus* or *convention*. In the caucus system, party delegates elected in local voting district meetings decide on the party nominee. In some states, a convention narrows the field to two candidates if no candidate gets a set percentage of delegate votes at the party convention.

The dynamics of winning a nomination in states with a caucus system are different from those in states with a primary. In a caucus system, having a grassroots organization or an intense appeal that can mobilize politically active, better-educated voters to attend a neighborhood meeting is essential for candidates. In the 2008 presidential primaries, Barack Obama did especially well in caucuses in part because, as one political scientist argued, "He's got a middle-class base. They're more likely to be turning out (for caucuses), and he's turning them out."[31] The state best known for the caucus system is Iowa, whose party caucuses yield the first decision in our presidential election system and are covered extensively by the media. In presidential elections, about a dozen states use some form of the caucus or convention system. For state offices, nearly all states use primaries or some combination of primaries and conventions.[32]

There are two kinds of party primaries. In a **closed primary,** only voters registered in a party may vote in that party's primary. Such a primary discourages **crossover voting**—allowing voters from outside the party to help determine the party's nominee—which is why partisans prefer closed primaries. In an **open primary,** any voter can participate in any party's primary. Candidates whose policy positions or leadership styles appeal to independent voters (those without party affiliation), or even to people who are registered or generally vote with the opposite party, are likely to benefit from open primaries. In the 2008 Republican presidential primaries, John McCain did particularly well in states with open primaries. In fact, he failed to get pluralities from Republican voters in the crucial primaries of New Hampshire and South Carolina, but he won both states because of his strong support among Independents choosing to vote in these open primaries.[33]

Louisiana has a unique system. All candidates, regardless of party, run in a single election. If no candidate gets a majority of the votes, a runoff election determines the winner between the two candidates with the most votes. It is not uncommon for both candidates in a runoff to be from the same party. Washington has a similar top-two primary system in place. Voters in California voted on June 8, 2010, on a ballot initiative that would create a similar system for primaries in their state. This proposal was supported by outgoing Republican Governor Arnold Schwarzenegger but opposed by both the Republican and Democratic parties of California. Voters approved the measure by a margin of 54 percent to 46 percent, which will go into effect for primaries held in 2012, assuming the measure survives expected legal challenges in the courts.

closed primary
A primary election in which only persons registered in the party holding the primary may vote.

crossover voting
Voting in another party's primary.

open primary
A primary election in which any voter, regardless of party, may vote.

These absentee ballots will be sent to voters in Missouri as an alternative to the conventional practice of going to the polls to vote. ■ *What are the advantages and disadvantages of widespread use of absentee ballots?*

Differences in the Timing and Frequency of Elections

Federal law sets the date of the presidential election as "the Tuesday next after the first Monday in November, in every fourth year," with similar language applying to elections for the House and Senate. States are free to determine the dates of all other elections, but for ease of administration, they usually consolidate gubernatorial and state general elections on the first Tuesday after the first Monday in November.

Two-thirds of the states elect governors in presidential midterm years, halfway between presidential elections; only 11 states hold their gubernatorial elections in presidential election years. Vermont and New Hampshire elect their governor every two years. Five states conduct their primary and general elections for governor, other state officials, and the state legislature in odd-numbered years, leaving the even-numbered years for federal elections.

Separating state elections from presidential or federal elections permits voters to focus more closely on state issues than if they had to vote for state and federal candidates at the same time. Separating elections also means state and local officials are less likely to be hurt by an unpopular presidential candidate at the top of the ticket. Of course, even in off-year elections, national political forces are sometimes strong enough to have a big impact on state and local elections. In the 1994 congressional elections, for instance, when Republicans mobilized around the conservative "Contract with America" and many voters reacted against unpopular policies and economic problems during the first years of the Clinton administration, Democrats in state governments were turned out of office in large numbers. A similar situation in the 2010 midterm elections saw even greater gains by the Republicans at the state level. Energized by tea party activists and supported with record spending made possible in part by the U.S. Supreme Court's ruling in *Citizens United* v. *Federal Election Commission* (2010), the GOP rode low approval of President Obama and the poor national economy to electoral success. The GOP emerged with control of at least 29 governorships, both legislative chambers in at least 25 states, and one chamber in another 5 states. Overall, Republicans captured about 700 seats in state legislatures, leaving them with an outright majority of state legislative seats nationally and the party's largest such majority since 1928. Still, the 1994 and 2010 elections were exceptional. Most off-year elections are not as strongly affected by national issues, though presidential evaluations and "coattails" generally remain.[34]

State law establishes the rules for local elections but often allows cities and towns some discretion in setting the dates of elections. Many municipal elections are held in the spring of odd-numbered years, again to avoid any positive or negative carryover from candidates running for federal or statewide office. Counties usually conduct their elections at the same time state officials are elected.

State governments can also hold *special elections* to vote on a ballot initiative, a statewide constitutional change or a new constitution, or to replace a U.S. senator who has died or resigned. Participation in special elections varies greatly, depending on what is being decided, but turnout is generally lower than in midterm general elections.

What are the consequences of holding so many elections at so many different times? One is that voters pick and choose which elections, if any, they participate in. Primaries ordinarily draw fewer voters than general elections, and sometimes the turnout is very low, less than 10 percent. General election turnout is also lower in nonpresidential years, and generally lower still if a state lacks a hotly contested race for governor or U.S. senator at the top of the ballot. Low turnout raises concerns about whether the voters who participate are representative of the general public.

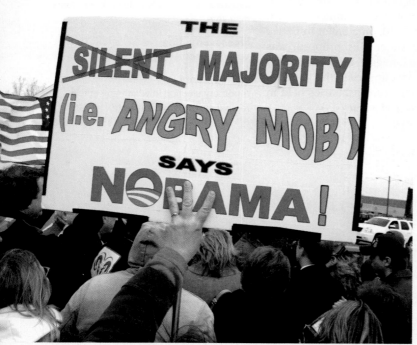

Rallies designed to capitalize on Democratic President Obama's low approval ratings and the weak economy were held across the country leading up to the 2010 midterm elections. Republicans rode this wave of discontent to major electoral gains. ■ *What role should national political and economic conditions play in elections for state and local offices?*

Differences in What We Vote On

When we think about elections in the United States, we generally think about voting for candidates for a particular set of offices. However, citizens in many states and communities frequently face a range of other choices as well when they go to the polls. For example, approximately half of the states permit citizens to vote on initiatives and public referendums. Some states and many cities also have recall elections, and many localities use elections to gain approval for special projects or initiatives.

Voting on Ballot Questions   After California voters passed Proposition 13 in June 1978, which amended the state's constitution to cut property taxes and keep them low, ballot questions have become increasingly popular among the states. There are many types of ballot questions. Some, like Proposition 13, are citizen initiatives, which may be placed before the state's voters if proponents collect a minimum number of signatures from registered voters on a petition. Referendums are questions typically proposed by state legislatures. Both types of questions may be used to amend the state's constitution or to enact ordinary legislation. Each decade since the 1970s, more and more citizen initiatives have been placed on the ballot, and more have been approved. Since 1998, around 200 initiatives and referendums appear on state ballots every even-numbered year, two-thirds of which are generally legislative referendums.[35]

Conservative groups have used initiatives to reduce taxes, cut government spending, deny public benefits to immigrants, and restrict same-sex marriages. Liberal groups have backed them to increase taxes on tobacco, ban smoking in public places, expand Medicaid coverage, raise the minimum wage, and promote stem cell research. One concern about ballot questions is that voting may hinge on factors having little to do with the merits of the proposals.

Voters typically do not have much information about the proposals or their likely consequences, and many simply vote no. Others suffer from "ballot fatigue" when there are too many contests and questions on the ballot, and they refuse to vote on the questions at all.[36] Because voters typically have little information about the questions and their views are not deeply rooted in party affiliation, feelings toward an incumbent, or party appeal, there may also be greater opportunities for campaign advertising to shape public opinion on ballot questions.[37]

Because many initiatives are supported by well-funded interests and because a vote in one state can start a national movement on an issue, initiative campaigns can attract large sums of money. For example, more than $101 million was spent in California in the late 1990s on five initiatives that dealt with automobile insurance reform.[38]

Voting in Recall Elections   Recall elections permit citizens to attempt to remove elected public officials from office before the end of their term. Eighteen states permit the recall of at least some state-level officials.[39] Like initiatives and referendums, recalls require sufficient petition signatures from registered voters to meet a preestablished threshold. Recall elections have been relatively rare at the statewide level. For example, before the successful 2003 recall of Governor Gray Davis, there had been 31 unsuccessful attempts to recall California governors, none of which made it to the ballot.[40] Only one other governor in U.S. history has ever been recalled (Lynn Frazier in North Dakota in 1921). Although there were significant political problems in California at the time of the Davis vote, including large budget deficits, it has been argued that Davis was recalled largely because of negative views of his political character, which caused him to lose the goodwill and trust of voters.[41]

The 2003 California recall ballot consisted of two questions: the first asking whether to remove Governor Davis from office, the second asking who should replace him if he were recalled.[42] If a majority had voted no on the first question, the results of the second question would not have mattered. Because a majority voted yes on the first question, the person who got the most votes on the second question became the new governor. Other states divide the questions, first having an election to decide whether to recall the official. If a majority votes yes, a second election determines the replacement. Although still relatively rare, recall elections are more common and have been more likely to succeed for local elected officials.[43]

Voting on Bond Issues   Maybe the most common elections voters throughout the country are involved with that do not involve specific candidates revolve around bond issues.

For the People

GOVERNMENT'S GREATEST ENDEAVORS

Improving the Election Process

The chaos in the counting of ballots in Florida in the 2000 presidential election surprised many citizens, who assumed that vote counting was simple and precise. They were wrong. The problems were not isolated to Florida's clogged voting machines or poorly designed ballots. Ballots were misplaced in New Mexico; voting machines broke down in several states; people's names were incorrectly purged from voting lists; and long lines of people waiting to vote led to court challenges. In the weeks and months following the election, at least half the states launched efforts to study the problems and propose solutions. In addition, national commissions, advisory groups, and experts undertook extensive analyses of our voting procedures. How have governments responded?

In 2002, Congress passed the Help America Vote Act (HAVA). HAVA helped states replace antiquated punch-card and lever voting machines with optical scanners and video touchscreen systems. Many states also made it easier for voters to vote early. Thirty-two states now allow voters to vote early without needing to provide a reason for why they might not be able to vote on election day. The remaining 18 states have some form of absentee voting as well.* Other states make it possible to vote by mail, and Oregon has been conducting all of its elections by mail for a decade. HAVA has also led to improved voter registration lists, better trained poll workers, and improved information access for voters.

Of course, even changes designed to make it easier for us to vote come with controversy. The spread of touchscreen voting prompted new debates about the accuracy and accountability of computerized voting machines. How could election outcomes be checked and verified if electronic systems fail to provide a paper record? Other efforts targeted at reducing the potential for fraud by requiring stricter forms of identification might discourage some voters from participating. For years to come, states will debate how best to conduct elections, as elections are central to how our democracy works.

CRITICAL THINKING QUESTIONS

1. When it comes to regulating elections, should we be more concerned about maximizing participation or minimizing fraud?

2. What other aspects of the regulation of elections should be addressed by the states?

* Information available at http://www.ncsl.org/LegislaturesElections/ElectionsCampaigns/AbsenteeandEarlyVoting/tabid/16604/Default.aspx.

States, cities, school boards, and other governmental organizations routinely issue bonds as a way to raise funds for a project now that can be paid off gradually over time. When the government sells the bond to investors, it agrees to pay the purchaser back for the price of the bond plus some amount of interest. The money collected from selling the bonds is then used for some purpose, such as building a new school, expanding a highway, or something similar. In many cities throughout the country, city officials need the approval of voters before they can issue such bonds. Voter participation in such elections is frequently quite low, and information about the issues at hand is generally scarce.

Differences in Campaign Finance

By the early 1980s, nearly all states had campaign finance **disclosure laws.** Disclosure is a fundamental element of campaign finance regulation that asks candidates to file statements specifying who contributed money to their campaigns, and how much the individuals or organizations gave and when. Interest groups are often required to file reports on how they distribute their campaign contributions as well. By making public which individuals and interest groups support a candidate, disclosure laws help voters understand how a candidate may behave in office and help prevent corrupt relationships by making all potential connections public and open to investigation.

Contribution limits are also widespread among the states. These are intended to prevent politicians from relying on a small number of large contributors who might, as a result, exert undue influence. Approximately three-fourths of the states have enacted contribution limits for individual donors—usually limits on how much an individual may give to a particular candidate in a single election or year. All but six states restrict corporate contributions, and most also limit or ban direct contributions from unions.[44] Of course, this may change in the wake of the U.S. Supreme Court's 5-to-4 ruling in January of 2010 that the government may not ban political spending by corporations and unions in candidate elections.[45] This ruling immediately brought laws governing similar kinds of contributions into question in half of the states.[46] Businesses and labor organizations that want to give money to candidates must usually establish political action committees (PACs)—separate political agencies that raise money from employees or union members

disclosure laws
A requirement that candidates specify where the money came from to finance their campaign.

contribution limits
Limits on how much a single contributor may give to a candidate in an election or period of time.

594

according to clear rules and disclosure requirements. State contribution laws often resemble federal regulations, but some states (and a few cities) have much lower and stricter contribution limits than those allowed in federal elections, whereas five states have virtually no restrictions at all.[47]

Public financing laws aim to replace or supplement private donations with public dollars. The laws have several purposes: to reduce the potential for corruption in relationships between donors and elected officials; to give candidates who are not wealthy or who have no access to rich donors an opportunity to run strong campaigns; and to keep total campaign spending down. The two basic types of public financing programs for candidates are matching grants and flat grants. *Matching grant programs* provide funds to candidates in proportion to every qualifying private contribution the candidates raise and report. In New York City, for example, qualifying candidates for mayor, borough president, and city council seats receive $4 for every $1, up to $250, contributed by a New York City resident. In exchange for accepting public matching money, candidates agree to limit their total campaign spending. This clause is important because, under the U.S. Supreme Court's interpretation of the First and Fourteenth Amendments, involuntary **candidate expenditure limits** are unconstitutional infringements on free speech.[48] *Flat grant programs* provide funds to qualifying candidates in lieu of their raising additional private donations. In Maine, candidates qualify for public subsidies by raising a minimum number of $5 contributions from eligible voters in their state or district.[49] The idea behind this requirement is to determine which candidates are serious, with real voter support. After they raise this "seed money," candidates get a grant from the state to pay all the costs of their primary and general elections campaigns.[50]

Although there are few studies of the effects of public financing programs, evidence suggests they are more important in expanding opportunities to run for office and mounting competitive campaigns than in reducing the role of private contributors.[51] One reason is that private donors, whether individuals or organizations, have many other ways to become active in campaigns and politics, and many candidates who have access to a lot of private money usually forgo using public money. Another challenge for public financing laws is the chronic difficulty states face in raising sufficient public money to support the programs.[52] Maine's legislators, for example, borrowed large sums from the state's Clean Election Fund after the state's general revenues dropped.[53] Thus, although 16 states offer public funds to candidates, many of the programs have few resources to give to candidates, and serious candidates typically refuse to accept public money because the amounts are not sufficient to fund a strong campaign. Public financing has also been advocated for judicial elections as a way to insulate candidates from the potential influence of money from individuals, businesses, or groups that might have cases pending before the court. North Carolina's recent program in this area has been touted by supporters as a model for other states to follow.[54]

public financing laws
Laws authorizing grants of government funds to qualifying candidates for elective office, to be used in their campaigns.

candidate expenditure limits
Limits on how much money a candidate may spend in support of a campaign for elective office.

The Role of Political Parties

Although political parties are not mentioned in the U.S. Constitution, they are vital to our national government and to the functioning of the electoral system within the states. Parties organize electoral competition by recruiting and nominating candidates, function as the loyal opposition when out of power, unify and organize the electorate, and provide a link between the people and their government. Many state constitutions acknowledge their existence.

State parties are, in many ways, more important than national parties. Indeed, national parties, aside from their congressional campaign committees, are largely federations of autonomous state parties. The independence of state parties also helps explain why, for instance, Democratic voters in one state can be so different from those in another, and why Republicans from different states can come down on opposite sides of some major issues.

LEARNING **OBJECTIVE**

23.3 Outline the organization of state parties and their major functions with respect to elections, voters, and government.

Most states prescribe the organization of the state parties, the means by which their officers are elected, the nomination process for president and other offices, and the requirements that party candidates must meet to get on the ballot.[55] Election rules in general favor the two major parties over minor parties. Although Republican and Democratic candidates can count on being placed on the ballot, state laws typically require minor parties to garner a minimum number of votes in the previous election or submit a prescribed number of signatures of registered voters in order to appear on the ballot. States vary in the difficulty of ballot access for minor parties, depending on three factors: the number of signatures required, the time allowed to collect them, and whether signatures must be distributed across several counties. A handful of states, such as New York, make it easier for minor parties to get on the ballots by allowing them to cross-endorse major-party candidates for office. For example, a candidate for governor in New York might appear on the ballot twice—once as the Republican Party nominee and a second time as the Conservative Party nominee. The candidate's vote total will simply be the sum of the votes he or she gets regardless of which party line a voter marks. In a similar vein, Oregon adopted a system in 2009 that will allow candidates to list up to three political parties next to their names on the ballot.

Party Organization and Officers

Political party organizations have changed enormously throughout the last century, from urban machines dominated by political bosses who often did not serve in elective office, to modern organizations with professional staff able to provide extensive and often technical support to state party candidates.

An Earlier Era: Machines and Bosses In the nineteenth century, political *machines* became established in a number of U.S. cities. Typically, one political party dominated the political life of the city, often by recruiting new immigrants as supporters and voters by offering them patronage jobs and social welfare benefits. For many years, the epitome of a political machine in the United States was Tammany Hall, the building where the Tammany Society (named after a Delaware Indian chief) met and ran New York City politics. Tammany Hall was closely identified with Democrats and was ruled by William Tweed, the boss of New York City politics.

A *boss* is a party leader who uses patronage, government contracts, and access to power to dictate policy. Some bosses, like Tweed, were never elected to office but rather were powers behind the scenes. Party bosses were common after the Civil War and well into the twentieth century. Other cities with powerful political machines and bosses were Los Angeles, Boston, Pittsburgh, Cincinnati, Philadelphia, Indianapolis, San Francisco, and Baltimore. Maybe the last real political machine boss was Chicago's Mayor Richard J. Daley. Daley, first elected mayor in 1955, served 21 years before his death. Reviled by some as corrupt, brutal, and racist,[56] he was also ranked by a group of historians as the sixth best mayor in American history.[57] His oldest son, Richard M. Daley, served as Chicago's mayor from 1989 to 2011.

The principal objective of the urban reform movement in the early twentieth century was to overthrow the bosses and political machines. Reformers advocated nonpartisan local elections, competitive bids for projects, and civil service in place of patronage. They achieved most of their goals, although it is not clear whether the power of political machines was reduced by these reforms or by other social and economic forces in play at the time.

Party Organizations Today Although state party organizations vary greatly from one state to another, they differ in several ways from the old political machines. First, instead of being dominated by city bosses, political party organizations are typically under the influence of top state-elected officials, such as the governor or state legislative leaders. These elected officials usually play important, though often informal, roles in selecting the party chair. In all states, a *party chair* is elected by the party's central committee or delegates to a party convention. Other statewide party officers include the *vice chair*, who by state law or party bylaws often must be of the opposite gender from the party chair,[58] plus officers such as treasurer and secretary. Party leaders generally answer to a *central committee,* which consists of 20 or more persons elected or otherwise chosen for specified terms.

The state party chair is the spokesperson for the party, especially when the party does not control the governorship. He or she raises money for the party and its candidates. Because overt expressions of partisanship are thought to be unbecoming in elected officials, often the party chair defends the party and, when necessary, goes on the offensive against the opposition party.

Second, contemporary political parties are more likely to have large, paid, and professional staffs. They often provide assistance to candidates in raising campaign money, developing ads, obtaining and using data on voters and party activists, conducting polls, calling prospective voters to get them to vote, and many other activities. The day-to-day operations of the party are usually carried out by the party's *executive director,* a full-time employee who oversees the staff, assists the chair, coordinates the work of the central committee and other party officials, and serves as a liaison with the national organizations.[59]

Third, political parties do not rely as much as the political machines did on ethnic ties and the promise of material benefits, such as jobs and contracts, to motivate large numbers of people to work on campaigns and support the party's candidates and interests. Most activists are now likely to be motivated by policy or ideological goals or by strong support for a particular candidate. Although some party activists may hope for a job in a new administration if their candidate for governor wins, most party workers are more likely to support the party's candidates because of their positions on issues or because the candidate has considerable personal charisma.

At the local level, political parties are generally patterned after the state party organization. In some counties, party organizations are fully staffed and functioning, but in most, they are run by volunteers and are mostly inactive until just before an election. Local parties provide opportunities for ordinary citizens to become active in politics, a first step that can eventually lead to running for office. Some states, such as Minnesota, have congressional district parties as well.[60]

Although party bosses and strong party machines are a thing of the past, local politics is still organized on a partisan basis in many of our largest cities. Outside these cities, local politics is typically nonpartisan, with three-quarters of U.S. cities having nonpartisan elections.[61]

Party Activities in Elections

U.S. parties used to dominate electoral politics through control of the nomination process, the ballot itself, and political patronage. Beginning with the widespread use of primaries to nominate candidates in the 1960s, our system shifted to a more candidate-centered process. Candidates created their own campaign organizations, appealed directly to potential voters, raised their own funds, and pushed the parties into the background. Starting in the 1980s and accelerating in the 1990s, parties began to enjoy a resurgence as they dramatically improved their fund-raising skills and expanded the campaign services they could provide to voters and, as activists, realized that working within the parties might be an easier path to success than by trying to go around them. In some places, parties recruit candidates, register voters, and mobilize voters on election day.

Structure for Elections   Our election system would function in quite a different way if we had no political parties to organize the competition. Parties narrow the field of candidates through a primary election or convention process, providing voters with fewer and more focused choices in the general election. Candidates must secure the support of fellow partisans to win a place on the ballot as the party's nominees for the offices they are seeking.

Candidate Recruitment   State party officials often seek out candidates to run for office. Many offices go uncontested, especially as you go down the ballot. Party leaders thus often try to identify potential candidates, even if that candidate will be a "sacrificial lamb" because they want to maintain some presence in a district. The most common place to find potential candidates for state office is among former candidates, local officeholders, or by getting

Former governor Sarah Palin was a force for the Republican party in the 2010 primaries, and her support was bolstered the campaigns of a number of Republican Congressional candidates. ■ *How might strong party affiliation in a primary become a disadvantage for a candidate in a general election?*

names from local groups generally supportive of the party, such as a chamber of commerce or teachers association.

Voter Registration   Helping register sympathetic voters is important to candidates, parties, and interest groups. These efforts are typically aimed at citizens they anticipate will vote for their preferred candidate. Interest groups with active voter registration efforts include organized labor, business groups, and groups concerned about the environment and abortion.

Political parties favor laws requiring voters to disclose their party preference at the time they register. This requirement permits parties in states with closed primaries to limit participation to registered party members. Party registration also creates voter registration lists, which parties find extremely useful for campaigning and fund raising. *List vending*—selling voter lists with addresses, phone numbers, and party preferences—is a multimillion-dollar industry. Finally, voter registration helps the parties in the redistricting process because state legislators, using party registration, voting, and other data, can draw new congressional and state legislative district boundaries in ways that give their party an advantage.

Voter Mobilization   Slightly more than three-quarters of eligible voters are registered, and of that number, only approximately two-thirds vote in presidential elections, meaning that *as few as half of the voting-age population bothers to vote* in a presidential election, and still fewer in midterm elections.[62] Turnout in the 2004 presidential election was heavier than in any election since 1968 but was still only 55 percent of the voting-age population. Only 36 percent of the voting-age population voted in the 2006 congressional midterm elections, and only 17 percent of the voting-age population in the 1998 state and local primaries.[63] Turnout for the hotly contested presidential election in 2008 reached 57 percent of the voting-age population.[64]

Elections are often decided by which party does better at turning out its supporters. Get-out-the-vote drives are therefore a major activity of candidates and parties. But what works? The best research has found that a "personal approach to mobilizing voters is generally more effective than an impersonal approach."[65] Door-to-door canvassing, for instance, or telephone calls from neighbors and friends are much more effective than automatically dialed, prerecorded messages. Where resources permit, the parties may even provide transportation to the polls or baby-sitting services.[66]

Campaign Resources   In better-organized states, parties provide extensive campaign funds and campaign help. They raise funds for their party organization and finance voter registration and mobilization efforts, often with the help of national parties.

Well-organized parties train the candidates they have recruited. Wisconsin and New York have strong state legislative campaign committees that distribute resources to candidates, as the national party committee does to congressional candidates.[67] In many states, the state parties provide in-kind contributions to candidates, such as polling data for state and local candidates, advice on campaign themes and strategies, and generic advertisements to use in several state legislative districts. In some states, parties have come to dominate the campaign finance system. For instance, various New Jersey state party organizations provided 59 percent of all contributions to state legislative candidates in the 2005 elections.[68]

Political parties also make direct campaign contributions to candidates in most states. Although they do not typically provide large amounts, their contributions can have an important electoral impact by concentrating resources in support of candidates in the small number of legislative districts where elections are expected to be most competitive. Such districts are typically "open seats," where no incumbent is running for

By the People

Registering to Vote

Because elections are the central institution of representative democracy, the best way to participate in your government is to get registered and vote. Getting registered is now easier than it has ever been. Every state government operates a Web site that contains information on how to register to vote. Numerous other Web sites provide similar information, such as Rock the Vote (http://www.rockthevote.com/), the National Register to Vote Web site (http://register-vote.com/), and the League of Women Voters (http://www.lwv.org/). The laws are different in every state. Also, the rules regarding whether college students can register in the place where they attend school versus where their home address is located also vary. Most states require that voters get registered 30 days before the election takes place, so you need to plan in advance.

Once you are registered, you will be assigned a voting precinct. When an election is held, a location within that precinct will be designated as your polling place. It might be a school or an office building, but it might also be an apartment lobby or a local church. Most state Web sites where you can register to vote will also inform you of your polling location, although if you register well in advance of the election, you may need to check for voting location at a date closer to the election. Again, the League of Women Voters sponsors a Web site that helps voters find their polling sites: http://www.vote411.org/pollfinder.php. Find out how to register in your state, where your polling location is, and when the next election is scheduled. What do you need to bring with you when you go to vote? Can you vote early? Participation in governing ourselves is a fundamental right in a representative democracy, and there is no easier way to exercise that right than getting registered and voting.

CRITICAL THINKING QUESTIONS

1. Why might states require voters to register in advance of an election? What are the pros and cons of having voters register weeks in advance compared with doing so on election day?

2. What are the arguments for making voter registration easier? Are there any arguments for making registration more difficult? How do you think voter registration requirements affect young voters?

---

office, or legislative districts where the incumbent is widely viewed as vulnerable. By contrast, interest groups and individual contributors often direct their funds toward incumbents, even when they face weak challengers or none at all.[69]

Parties and Voting Choices

Voters generally base their election decisions on three factors, listed in decreasing order of importance: political party identification, candidate appeal, and issues. In many local elections, because party labels are absent from the ballot, voters rely more on candidate appeal, issues, and factors such as incumbency, media endorsements, and name recognition.

Party Identification Party identification is the most important predictor of voting behavior. Parties provide a label for candidates that guides voters in making decisions. Party labels are especially important in elections in which voters have little information about candidates, as in contests for attorney general, state senator, state representative, or county commissioner.

People who identify themselves as strong Democrats and strong Republicans are remarkably loyal to their party when voting for state and local offices. Independent-leaners have clear partisan preferences in the direction of one party or the other. Pure Independents have no party preference and are most inclined to vote for one party and then another with changing circumstances, but there are few Pure Independents in the total electorate, and their turnout rates are often low, particularly when there is not a presidential race taking place.[70]

Candidate Appeal Although party identification is important, it is not decisive. Candidate appeal can be crucial. For example, in the 2003 California recall election, voters not only viewed Governor Gray Davis negatively[71] but viewed Arnold Schwarzenegger positively because of his success in business, the independence from special interests his personal wealth allowed, and his sponsorship of a ballot initiative that provided for afterschool programs.[72] In the 1998 Minnesota gubernatorial election, Reform Party candidate Jesse Ventura was elected largely because his style and approach

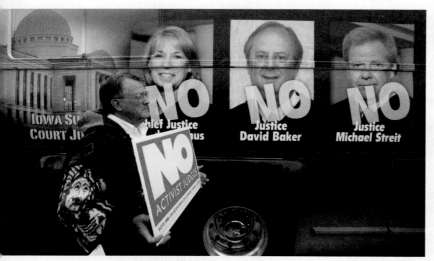

Three Iowa Supreme Court justices facing a retention election were defeated in 2010, the first time anyone had lost their seat on the Iowa bench since the current system began in 1962. All three were targeted by a conservative group called "Iowa for Freedom" because they were part of the Court's unanimous decision in 2009 that permitted same-sex marriages in Iowa. The group spent several million dollars on its campaign, most of which came from individuals and groups outside of Iowa. ■ *Should state Supreme Court Justices be held accountable to the electorate for their rulings?*

generated interest among voters, and a plurality preferred him over the established candidates in the major parties.

In state and local elections, name identification and the advantages of incumbency—such as campaign resources and the ability to point to constituent service—are important. Incumbency advantages at the state level have been especially high for executive offices—governors and attorneys general, for instance—but they have been large factors in state legislative races as well.[73] In primary elections, when all the candidates are from the same party, voters cannot use party affiliation to make their choices and must rely on candidate appeal, issues, and incumbency. They may also vote for the candidate they perceive has the best chance of winning the general election.[74]

Issue Voting   Issues can be very important to the outcome of elections. Economic conditions are as important a factor in state and local elections as they are in national ones. William Weld, a Republican, was able to win his first Massachusetts gubernatorial election in 1990, despite the fact that Massachusetts is a very strong Democratic state, because the state's economy at the time was so bad. Former New Jersey Governor Christine Todd Whitman won election in part because her incumbent opponent had raised state taxes and she promised a 30-percent tax cut. Although issues are important in state and local elections, it is fair to say that they are probably less important than at the national level.[75] Research shows that gubernatorial candidates can affect the issues voters use to evaluate them on election day by what issues the candidates choose to stress during their campaigns.[76]

Judicial Elections   Judicial elections in some states are partisan and resemble campaigns for other offices in intensity. More than $16 million was spent on television ads in state judicial campaigns in 2006, with candidates increasingly stating positions and using negative advertisements against their opponents on issues such as gay marriage, school vouchers, abortion, gun control, and school choice.[77] Many states used to regulate the conduct of judicial candidates to limit such behavior, but the U.S. Supreme Court, in *Republican Party* v. *White* (2002) ruled such restrictions unconstitutional. This ruling has fueled the trend toward judicial campaigns looking more like races for other offices. A lot of campaign money comes from corporations concerned about liability, environmental, and other economic regulatory issues. The trend toward expensive and divisive judicial elections has prompted criticism by good-government groups and efforts to extend the use of alternative means of selecting and retaining judges. We will take up this issue in greater detail in Chapter 26 when we discuss state courts and the judicial branch.

Nonpartisan Local Elections   Arguing that political parties had little to contribute to the administration of local government, reformers during the first half of the twentieth century introduced nonpartisan elections. The two parties were, in effect, blocked from exerting an open influence on local politics.

Some observers contend that nonpartisan local elections make it more difficult for less-affluent and less-educated citizens to participate effectively. For such people, the party label serves to identify politicians who share their values and perspectives on government. Well-educated and wealthy voters know more about who is running and what they stand for, even without party labels. Nonpartisan elections sometimes help Republican candidates, especially in cities with populations of more than 50,000, because Republican voters tend to vote in low-turnout elections and are more likely to know which candidates are Republicans.[78] Others have found that there is not generally an advantage to Republican candidates in nonpartisan elections.[79]

Parties in State Government

Political parties are not only critical in conducting elections and campaigns; they also help organize our governmental institutions, particularly the state executive and legislative branches.

Parties in the Executive Branch   Just as winning the presidency is the big prize at the national level, so is winning the governorship at the state level. The party that controls the governorship has the power to appoint executive department officials and some state judges. Governors are usually perceived as the state leaders of their party, and they establish the political agenda and help define the party for their state.

Governors usually campaign on behalf of their party, even when they are not on the ballot for reelection. Presidential candidates often seek the help of governors. In fact, presidential candidates are often former governors, as were four of the last six presidents. Governors raise money for campaigns as well as for the state party. They have wide latitude in appointing boards, commissions, judges, and state administrators, and they almost always take party affiliation and activity into account when making appointments.

Parties in the Legislature   Like Congress, state legislatures (excluding Nebraska, which is nonpartisan) are organized largely along party lines. The *speaker of the house or assembly* and the *president of the senate* are elected by the majority party in most states. They preside over floor proceedings and make key assignments to standing committees and study committees. Most state legislatures have floor leaders, called *majority leaders* and *minority leaders* and majority and minority *whips*.

In most states, parties sit on different sides of the aisle in the legislative chambers and are separated in committee meetings as well. Committee chairs in most state legislatures go to members from the majority party in that chamber, and most committees have more members from the majority party than from the minority party. As a result, leaders of the majority party wield great power in deciding what bills are considered and ultimately passed in state legislatures. The **party caucus** is often important in state legislatures. The caucus is a meeting of party leaders and legislators to discuss party policy. Because some state legislatures meet for only a few months a year, the party caucus can help hammer out agreements rapidly.

Political parties also structure the decision making of state legislators when casting their votes on bills. In most states, when a legislative proposal is controversial and the outcome is close, most Democrats find themselves on one side of an issue with most Republicans on the other side.[80] Political scientists Gerald Wright and Brian Schaffner demonstrate the importance of party in state legislatures by comparing the unicameral in Nebraska, in which members are elected on a nonpartisan ballot, to the state senate in neighboring Kansas. The party affiliation of legislators clearly structures the coalitions formed in the Kansas Senate but plays little role in shaping how senators in Nebraska's state legislature behave.[81]

One area in which legislatures are predictably partisan is **redistricting.** Each decade, following the national census, state legislatures are constitutionally required to realign congressional and state legislative district boundaries to make them equal in population and reflect population changes. In a series of decisions in the 1960s, the U.S. Supreme Court required states to equalize the population size within state legislative districts just as they are required to do for districts for the U.S. House of Representatives.[82] Previously, it was common for districts to follow other established boundaries, such as county lines. Industrialization and the resulting concentration of population in urban centers meant that many states had some urban legislative districts that included ten times as many voters as several rural districts. This forced **reapportionment**—the reallocation of legislative seats based on population—shifted power to urban areas and helped create pressure to modernize state legislatures.[83]

The redistricting following the 2000 census was especially important because the two parties were so evenly divided in numbers of legislative chambers controlled, that is, the upper and lower houses in 49 states, and the single unicameral in Nebraska. However, the 2006 elections altered this balance by shifting control of many state legislatures toward the Democratic Party. Going into the 2008 elections, the Democrats controlled 57 chambers, the Republicans 39, and two were tied.[84] Of course, redistricting will occur again following the 2010 census. Going into the 2010 elections, Democrats controlled both

party caucus
A meeting of the members of a party in a legislative chamber to select party leaders and develop party policy. Called a *conference* by the Republicans.

redistricting
The redrawing of congressional and other legislative district lines following the census, to accommodate population shifts and keep districts as equal as possible in population.

reapportionment
The redistribution of seats in a legislature. In the United States, this occurs in order to equalize the size of populations within legislative districts and happens as part of the redistricting process.

With the election of Governor Mary Fallin, Republicans control the governership and both legislative houses in Oklahoma for the first time ever.

two-party state

A state in which the two major parties alternate in winning majorities.

one-party state

A state in which one party wins all or nearly all of the offices and the other party receives only a small proportion of the popular vote.

LEARNING **OBJECTIVE**

23.4 Assess how party competition has changed in recent decades.

chambers in 27 states, Republicans in only 8 states, with 14 states having split control (and Nebraska being nonpartisan).[85] The elections in 2010 dramatically reversed party control of state legislatures. Republicans emerged with control of both chambers in at least 25 states and one chamber in another 5 states. This shift will give Republicans an opportunity to use redistricting to solidify their electoral gains.

The way district lines are drawn can help or hurt a party. When one party controls both houses and the governorship or has a veto-proof majority in the legislature, the majority party can do what it wants with district boundaries, so long as it keeps the districts equal in population and respects the rights of racial minorities. For instance, Democratic legislators may try to pack as many Republican voters as possible in a small number of districts so that the remaining districts in the state have majorities of Democratic voters. The importance of state redistricting to the national parties is so great that the parties are establishing and funding special organizations devoted to influencing state redistricting processes.[86] Where power is divided between the parties, redistricting that protects incumbents is often the result.

Although, traditionally, it has been the practice to redistrict only once per decade, usually right after the decennial census data become available, redistricting may become more frequent and sensitive to shifts in party control of the state legislatures. In 2003, Texas replaced a congressional districting plan that a state court had drawn up the previous year with one much more favorable to Republicans. The new plan was challenged in court, eventually reaching the Supreme Court, which upheld the constitutionality of most of the second plan, overturning only one district's boundaries that were held to dilute Hispanic votes in violation of the Voting Rights Act.[87] However, a similar attempt to replace a court-drawn plan in Colorado was struck down by the state supreme court because the state constitution allowed redistricting only once a decade.[88]

In five states, commissions rather than the legislatures do the redistricting. Commissions tend to be more neutral and often create districts that are more competitive. This was the case in Arizona with the last redistricting. Arizona's new congressional district, the First District, had nearly equal numbers of registered Democrats and Republicans and was seen as a toss-up by political prognosticators. The Republican candidate has won this district most years, but three times with less than 55 percent of the vote, and the Democrat won in 2008.

Party Balance and Imbalance

We can classify state politics according to how the parties share public offices. In a **two-party state,** the Republican and Democratic parties can each regularly assemble winning majorities. Two-party states include Indiana, Michigan, and Missouri. In a **one-party state,** one party wins all or nearly all the offices, and the second party usually receives only one-third or less of the popular vote. One-party Republican states currently include Utah, Idaho, and Kansas. Massachusetts and Rhode Island are examples of Democratic one-party states. It is possible for Democrats to win in Utah, and the same is true for Republicans in Massachusetts, but the more predictable tendency is for state voters to support the predominant party. Of course, the classic examples of one-party dominance of states in the United States are the Democratic party dominance that characterized southern states from the end of Reconstruction into the 1970s and 1980s.[89]

Since the end of World War II, there has been an accelerating trend toward two-party politics. The Democratic Party lost its previously solid support in the South as more and more white southerners moved to the Republican Party. Since the mid-1970s, the number of Republicans in southern state legislatures has increased from approximately 12 percent to nearly 50 percent in 2008.[90] In the 2008 elections, the South was the only region of the country where Republicans gained state legislative seats.

Of the People

Youth Voting

Numerous reports following the 2008 presidential election credited a strong turnout among young voters as pivotal to Barack Obama's victory. Using data from the U.S. Census Bureau, the Center for Information and Research on Civic Learning and Engagement reported that approximately 51 percent of those under 30 years old voted, equivalent to approximately 22 million voters nationwide.* This marked an increase of 2 percentage points over the 2004 presidential election and a full 12 percentage points compared with 2000. Of course, turnout among older voters remained substantially higher in 2008 compared with younger voters (67 percent to 51 percent), but many wondered if 2008 signified a new and sustained high level of participation among younger citizens.

Higher turnout was not uniform across all younger voters. Among younger citizens, women were more likely to vote than were men (55 percent compared with 47 percent). African American youth turnout reached 58 percent, compared with 52 percent among non-Hispanic whites, with Asian and Latino voting rates at approximately 41 percent each. A major division among young people is whether they have attended college or not. While 62 percent of those who have attended at least some college voted, only 36 percent of those with no college experience did so.

Most important for this chapter, there were substantial differences across the states in terms of youth turnout. Youth turnout in Minnesota, Iowa, and New Hampshire exceeded 60 percent, whereas less than 40 percent of young people voted in Hawaii, Arkansas, Utah, and Texas. Although a variety of factors may explain these differences across states, a critical factor is whether or not states allow for election day registration (EDR). Youth voting was a full 9 percentage points higher in states with EDR compared with states without it. Early voting options, the distribution of sample ballots and polling place information, and no-excuse absentee balloting also appear to increase turnout among young voters.

CRITICAL THINKING QUESTIONS

1. Why are young people less likely to vote than older voters? Which of these factors could be affected by reforms to election laws and practices?

2. What might be the consequences for the policies different states adopt if youth voter participation rates are substantially different from one state to the next?

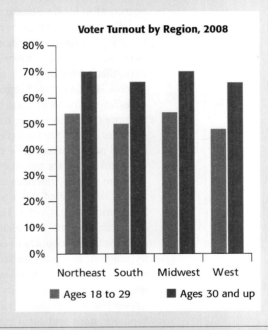

Voter Turnout by Region, 2008

Ages 18 to 29 ◼ Ages 30 and up

* The Center for Information and Research on Civic Learning and Engagement, Youth Voting (http://www.civicyouth.org/?page_id=241), their Presidential Election fact sheet (http://www.civicyouth.org/PopUps/FactSheets/FS_youth_Voting_2008_updated_6.22.pdf), and their State Election Law Reform and Youth Voter Turnout fact sheet (http://www.civicyouth.org/PopUps/FactSheets/State_law_and_youth_turnout_Final.pdf) provide all the information for this section.

Republican gains have also been evident in contests for governor and president. Since 1966, all southern states have elected a Republican governor at least once, and in 2010, Republican governors led seven southern states. In terms of the popular vote for president, since 1964, the only Democratic candidate for president to win more than 4 of the 11 former Confederate states was Jimmy Carter in 1976, who at the time was governor of Georgia. In 2000 and 2004, all 11 former Confederate states went to George W. Bush. Democrat Barack Obama won three southern states in 2008, although three other southern states (Arkansas, Louisiana, and Tennessee) increased their support for the Republican ticket between 2004 and 2008.

Outside the South, there has also been a gradual spread of two-party politics, with the rise of Democratic strength in the formerly solid Republican states of Iowa, Maine, and New Hampshire. Democrats had been losing strength in parts of the Rocky Mountain area, though they gained four House seats, two Senate seats, and three governorships in these states in the 2004 and 2006 elections. Democrats gained another six House seats and two Senate seats in 2008. Democrats have also been winning most seats in Congress in the Northeast and Pacific Coast states.

What are the consequences of party balance? When parties and their candidates compete vigorously, they are more likely to be sensitive to public opinion, for the loss of even a fraction of the voters can tip the scales to the other side in the next election. Party competition may lead opposing candidates to compete for the middle ground on issues, at least the middle ground in their particular districts. Strong party competition may also generate more service to constituents by legislators.

In a one-party state, party imbalance may have a serious effect on the accountability that is part of electoral competition. Voters do not participate as much as they do in two-party contests, and voters who do cannot rely on party labels to help them differentiate between candidates. Competition that otherwise would occur *between* the major parties occurs among factions *within* the majority party. The most important contests in some states such as Massachusetts are generally not between Democrats and Republicans but among Democrats in the primary; the same is true for Republicans in Utah. In these intraparty fights, personalities dominate the campaign. This was evident in 2010, when incumbent U.S. Senator Bob Bennett was defeated in his bid for the GOP nomination for his Senate seat by a coalition of conservatives and Tea Party supporters.

If party imbalance disorganizes the dominant party, it pulverizes the minority party. With faint hope of winning, minority party leaders do not put up much of a fight. Extreme forms of party imbalance are more commonly found in cities and towns than at the state level. Republicans, for instance, hardly ever carry Chicago; Boston; Washington, D.C.; Baltimore; Albany; Hartford; Pittsburgh; and many other cities throughout the industrial North. In such cases, minority parties find it difficult to raise money for campaigns and persuade people to become candidates. They have no state or local patronage to give out. Volunteers are slow to come forward. Young people wishing to succeed in politics drift into the dominant party. The second party is likely to be concerned only with national politics, where it may win an election, and the patronage that could come its way if its candidate wins the White House.

The great differences in party balance across state and local governments remind us that while we talk of a two-party system in the United States, the reality is we have more than 50 distinct party systems. Because parties are organized to compete for elective office, parties adapt to state and local political cultures, which vary enormously due to differences throughout the country in economic conditions, social classes, race, ethnicity and nationality, religion, and many other factors. The resulting differences across state parties and party systems give rise to divisions within each of the major parties when the "national" parties make nationwide decisions, such as whom to nominate for presidential elections. But it is important for our democracy that these differences are expressed forcefully by the many separate state and local parties throughout the country, as they typically represent real differences in citizens' opinions. Thus, state political parties straddle between the varied (and often changing) opinions and circumstances of each state's citizens and the imperative to make national decisions regarding leadership and government policies in the federal government. As such, state parties help to ensure that when national decisions are made, those decisions are responsive to a wide range of citizen viewpoints.

CHAPTER **SUMMARY**

23.1 Compare and contrast the constitutional roles of state and federal governments in regulating elections.

In the United States, there are no national elections, only state elections. Even the presidential election is a set of 51 different elections to choose electors, who will in turn cast their ballots for president. The U.S. Constitution gives states the lead role in determining the conditions under which elections for U.S. senators and representatives are held, although it also authorizes the national government to make or alter those

regulations. States have even more authority to regulate elections to state and local governments. Amendments to the U.S. Constitution have generally extended access to the vote.

23.2 Describe differences among the states in laws regulating voting, elections, and campaign finance, and assess federal influence on these regulations.

States are primarily responsible for defining who may vote, conditions under which they may register, when elections will be held (other than elections to national offices), how voting occurs, how party nominees are chosen, and which candidates appear on the ballot. Unlike the federal government, most states have some provisions for direct forms of democracy, including citizen initiatives, referendums, or recall elections. States have also developed a wide variety of campaign finance regulations; some impose virtually no restrictions other than disclosure requirements, whereas other states and some cities have extensive regulations on private money combined with public financing programs. States share authority over election law with the federal government, which has sometimes imposed constraints on state election laws.

23.3 Outline the organization of state parties and their major functions with respect to elections, voters, and government.

Contemporary political parties are often dominated by top state officeholders who have extensive professional staff. Political parties play important roles in candidate recruitment, voter registration, voter mobilization, and fund raising, and they provide a link between people and government. Voters usually vote along party lines, although candidate characteristics and issues also influence them. Parties are also important to the operation of most state legislatures. The governor is the head of his or her party. Governors consider party loyalty when appointing people to executive and judicial openings.

23.4 Assess how party competition has changed in recent decades.

States vary in whether the two parties are competitive. In one-party states, elections are generally won by one party, whereas in two-party states, the parties often alternate in holding power. More states have become competitive in recent years.

CHAPTER **SELF-TEST**

23.1 Compare and contrast the constitutional roles of state and federal governments in regulating elections.

1. True or false: "The presidential election is the only purely national election in the United States."
   a. True
   b. False
2. Match the following Constitutional articles and amendments to their results:

   a. Article I — i. States must have a republican form of government.
   b. Article IV — ii. States may not deny voting rights on the basis of race.
   c. Fifteenth Amendment — iii. Senators are elected by each state's people rather than by its legislators.
   d. Seventeenth Amendment — iv. Each state may decide its own way of electing senators and representatives, but Congress can intervene if it wants.

23.2 Describe differences among the states in laws regulating voting, elections, and campaign finance, and assess federal influence on these regulations.

3. In a paragraph, identify three or four factors that influence voter turnout and explain how each increases or decreases it.
4. States are making it increasingly easy for people to vote, such as through vote-by-mail, absentee ballots, and pre-election day voting. In a paragraph, discuss the benefits and potential problems of these measures.

5. In two or three sentences, explain why strong supporters of the Republican and Democratic parties prefer closed primaries to open primaries.
6. In one or two paragraphs, suggest two reasons for campaign finance disclosure laws, and discuss the effects of these laws.

23.3 Outline the organization of state parties and their major functions with respect to elections, voters, and government.

7. In one or two sentences, describe the tools used by political machines to maintain their power.
8. In a few sentences, delineate three differences between the old political machines and today's political parties.
9. Which proportion of the voting-age population has turned out to vote for recent presidential elections?
   a. Approximately 35 percent
   b. Approximately 55 percent
   c. Approximately 75 percent
   d. Approximately 90 percent
10. In an essay, describe how the political parties help mobilize voters, simplify voting choices, and provide resources to candidates. Also, suggest how local elections might be different without political parties.

23.4 Assess how party competition has changed in recent decades.

11. List three areas of the country that have seen major shifts in party competition, and describe those shifts.
12. In a paragraph, list and discuss three problems that arise when one party dominates state politics.

Answers to selected questions: 1. b (False; there is no truly national election); 2. a. iv, b. i, c. ii, d. iii; 9. b

mypoliscilab EXERCISES
Where participation leads to action!

Apply what you learned in this chapter on MyPoliSciLab.

📖● Read on **mypoliscilab.com**

    eText: Chapter 23

✓● Study and Review on **mypoliscilab.com**

    Pre-Test
    Post-Test
    Chapter Exam
    Flashcards

👁● Watch on **mypoliscilab.com**

    Video: New Ballots Bring New Complications in New York
    Video: Green Party Candidates Stay on Ballot

KEY **TERMS**

primary elections, p. 585
general elections, p. 585
special elections, p. 585
recall elections, p. 585
initiative, p. 585
referendum, p. 585
voter turnout, p. 586
party column ballot, p. 589

straight ticket, p. 589
office block ballot, p. 589
split ticket, p. 589
closed primary, p. 591
crossover voting, p. 591
open primary, p. 591
disclosure laws, p. 594
contribution limits, p. 594

public financing laws, p. 595
candidate expenditure limits, p. 595
party caucus, p. 601
redistricting, p. 601
reapportionment, p. 601
two-party state, p. 602
one-party state, p. 602

ADDITIONAL **RESOURCES**

FURTHER READING

R. MICHAEL ALVAREZ AND **THAD E. HALL,** *Electronic Elections: The Perils and Promises of Digital Democracy* (Princeton University Press, 2008).

R. MICHAEL ALVAREZ, THAD E. HALL, AND **SUSAN HYDE,** EDS., *Election Fraud: Detection, Prevention, and Consequences* (Brookings Institution Press, 2008).

EARL BLACK AND **MERLE BLACK,** *Politics and Society in the South* (Harvard University Press, 2005).

BRUCE E. CAIN, TODD DONOVAN, AND **CAROLINE J. TOLBERT,** EDS., *Democracy in the States: Experiments in Election Reform* (Brookings Institution Press, 2008).

THOMAS M. CARSEY, *Campaign Dynamics: The Race for Governor* (University of Michigan Press, 2000).

JEFFREY E. COHEN, ED., *Public Opinion in State Politics* (Stanford University Press, 2006).

GARY W. COX AND **JONATHAN N. KATZ,** *Elbridge Gerry's Salamander: The Electoral Consequences of the Reapportionment Revolution* (Cambridge University Press, 2002).

THOMAS E. CRONIN, *Direct Democracy: The Politics of Initiative, Referendum, and Recall* (Replica Books, 2000).

LARRY N. GERSTON AND **TERRY CHRISTENSEN,** *Recall! California's Political Earthquake* (Sharpe, 2004).

V. O. KEY, JR., *Southern Politics in State and Nation* (Knopf, 1949; reprinted by University of Tennessee Press).

NORMAN R. LUTTBEG, *The Grassroots of Democracy* (Lexington Books, 1999).

DAVID B. MAGLEBY, *Direct Legislation: Voting on Ballot Propositions in the United States* (Johns Hopkins University Press, 1984).

L. SANDY MAISEL, *American Political Parties and Elections: A Very Short Introduction* (Oxford University Press, 2007).

MARK MONMONIER, *Bushmanders and Bullwinkles: How Politicians Manipulate*

Electronic Maps and Census Data to Win Elections (University of Chicago Press, 2001).

DANIEL SMITH AND **CAROLINE TOLBERT,** *Educated by Initiative: The Effects of Direct Democracy on Citizens and Political Organizations in the American States* (University of Michigan Press, 2004).

JON WINBURN, *The Realities of Redistricting: Following the Rules and Limiting Gerrymandering in State Legislative Redistricting* (Lexington Books, 2008).

LINDA WITT, KAREN M. PAGET, AND **GLENNA MATTHEWS,** *Running as a Woman: Gender and Politics in American Politics* (Free Press, 1994).

WEB SITES

www.democrats.org/local.html Links to the 50 state Democratic parties.
our.gop.com/app/render/go.aspx? xsl=search.xslt&searchTerm=*:*& searchFilter=SearchObjectType:OUR.

GOP.COM_STATES Links to the 50 state Republican parties.

www.nass.org/ This is the site for the National Association of Secretaries of State. The secretary of state in most states is the top official who oversees the conduct of elections in the state.

elections.gmu.edu/ This site for the United States Elections Project, hosted by Professor Michael McDonald at George Mason University, contains information on recent national and statewide elections.

www.ncsl.org/default.aspx?tabid=16580 This site for the National Conference of State Legislatures Ballot Initiative Database can be searched for information on any statewide ballot initiative that has been held.

CHAPTER

24

State Legislatures

Although state legislatures play a vital role in state politics and policy making, they are not simply smaller versions of the U.S. Congress. State legislators face unique challenges related to the nature and resources of their positions. In addition, the experience of a state legislator can vary dramatically from state to state, as does the number of people legislators in different states represent. Some California state legislators represent more people than another state's U.S. Representative.

In some states, being a legislator can be a full-time job. These state legislatures pay good salaries, have numerous support staff and resources, meet year-round, and attend to a robust scope of activities. State legislators in California, Michigan, New York, and Pennsylvania earn annual salaries of nearly $80,000 or more. Many other states pay members poorly, provide little staff, and only meet part-time. Legislators in Maine, Mississippi, Nebraska, North Carolina, and Texas, among others, make less than $15,000 per year. In Vermont, legislators make $625 per week when the legislature is in session, which is typically for about 16 weeks from January through April. In contrast, the legislature in California has more than 2,000 staff members assisting the legislators, while members in Vermont share a common pool of around 20 clerks and 15 lawyers.[1] These states with part-time legislatures embody the ideal of the "citizen" legislature—a body of representatives who are not full-time career politicians but are instead part-time legislators serving as citizen representatives.

Another difficulty faced by legislators is balancing the need to represent the sometimes narrow interests of their districts with responding effectively to all of the major policy issues that affect residents of the entire state. State legislators decide on issues from taxes to health care to education to economic development, but they still cannot forget about the neighbors and local businesses in their own district that are holding them accountable. Former state legislator Ralph G. Wright was the Speaker of the House in Vermont for a record-setting ten years before being defeated for reelection in 1994. Wright reflects, "I got beat that November [because] I had forgotten my roots. Montpelier [the state capital] had become more important than my district, and like an army that outruns its supply line, I had outrun my reservoir of good will back home."[2] Thus, service as a state legislator is both broadly important for the entire state and deeply personal and local.

Faced with difficult tasks, few resources, and varying levels of professionalism, why would anyone want to serve in a state legislature? Wright suggests that people serve in legislatures like Vermont's for many reasons, but at least part of the draw is the desire to be part of the great "game" of politics: to be where the action is and to be in a place where you can effect some good for others. Serving in a state legislature can be an opportunity for average citizens to have a bigger impact on the policies that affect their own communities.

This chapter will examine state legislatures in greater detail by asking what they do, how they are organized, and how they have adapted to a much more complex world. As they have grown into more professional bodies, state legislatures are claiming a greater role in the workings of government and are becoming important partners in both state policy and federal action.

The Legislative Branch

State legislatures existed long before the Continental Congress was formed in 1776. They exerted great power under the Articles of Confederation and were reluctant to give up their power to either the national government or their own governors. Most states had relatively weak executives, and several had no executive at all. Although state legislatures

CHAPTER OUTLINE
CHAPTER LEARNING OBJECTIVES

The Legislative Branch

24.1 Explain how state legislatures are organized, and describe state legislators and their responsibilities.

Influences on State Legislators

24.2 Identify the factors that influence state legislators' voting decisions.

Modernization and Reform

24.3 Evaluate recent changes in state legislatures.

Drawing Legislative District Lines

24.4 Analyze the controversies over redistricting.

Direct Legislation: Policy Making by the People?

24.5 Evaluate the debate regarding the methods of direct democracy available to some states.

LEARNING OBJECTIVE

24.1 Explain how state legislatures are organized, and describe state legislators and their responsibilities.

today do not dominate state policy making the way they did in 1787, they do play a vital role in state politics and policy.

State legislatures make laws and modify and approve budgets. They strive to solve problems and provide services without raising taxes or creating larger bureaucracies. They make or modify policies by balancing conflicting political pressures, while forging compromises among political factions, interest groups, or different parts of the state. Legislatures also perform countless constituency services and, along with the governor and the courts, help keep state agencies accountable to both the laws and the citizens.

The 50 state legislatures share many characteristics—all states except Nebraska have a two-house **bicameral legislature.** Nebraska has a one-house **unicameral legislature.**[3] The larger chamber is generally called the *house of representatives,* or in a few states, the *assembly* or *house of delegates.* It contains as few as 40 members in Alaska and as many as 400 in New Hampshire; the average number is about 100. In all but five states, representatives serve two-year terms; in Alabama, Louisiana, Maryland, Mississippi, and North Dakota, they serve four years. The smaller chamber, known as the *senate,* is typically composed of approximately 40 members who serve four-year terms, though senators in 11 states serve only two-year terms.[4]

How Are Legislatures Organized?

State legislatures look very much like the U.S. Congress. A *speaker,* usually chosen by the majority party, presides over the lower house. In many states, speakers have more power to control proceedings than their national counterpart has. For example, most state speakers have the right to appoint committees and thus play a key role in determining policy. However, their power varies greatly: Speakers in West Virginia, New Hampshire, Arizona, and more than a dozen other states have strong formal powers,[5] whereas Speakers in Alaska, Mississippi, Hawaii, and Wyoming have minimal powers.[6] In 25 states, lieutenant governors preside over the senate, though they are usually mere figureheads; in other states, the majority party in the senate chooses its presiding officer, the *president of the senate.*[7]

As in the U.S. Congress, the committee system prevails. Every state has a series of standing, or permanent, committees as well as some temporary or ad hoc committees. In several states, such as Maine and Massachusetts, *joint committees* can speed up legislative action. However, state legislative committees usually do not have the same power over bills as their national counterparts: Some still lack adequate professional staffs, the seniority system is not as closely followed as in Congress, and turnover is usually higher, especially where term limits have taken effect. Still, legislators themselves report that committees play an important part in legislative decision making in nearly every state legislative chamber.[8]

Every legislature has committees on education, transportation, agriculture, and energy or natural resources. Most also have important committees on rules, appropriations, and taxes (sometimes called the Ways and Means Committee). The number of standing committees varies widely across states. The lower houses of states including Colorado, Maryland, and Rhode Island have ten or fewer standing committees, whereas the lower houses of Illinois, Mississippi, North Carolina, Texas, and Wisconsin have 40 or more standing committees.[9] Legislators generally specialize and become experts on one or two substantive matters, such as education, crime, taxation, or the budget process.

Legislatures differ in the way members interact and conduct legislative politics—differences that stem from historical or ethnic traditions, or from regional divisions or differences. Here is how one expert on state politics viewed some of the more distinctive characteristics shaping state politics in the United States:

> In New York professional politics, political wheeling and dealing and frantic activity are characteristic. In Virginia, one gets a sense of tradition, conservatism, and gentility.... Louisiana's politics are wild and flamboyant. By contrast, moderation and caution are features of Iowa. A strong disposition of compromise pervades Oregon, with politicians disposed to act as brokers and deal pragmatically rather than dogmatically. In Kansas, hard work, respect for authority, fiscal prudence, and a general conservatism and resistance to rapid social change are pervasive features of the state environment. Indiana is intensely partisan. Wyoming is mainly individualistic, and Ohio is fundamentally

bicameral legislature
A two-house legislature.

unicameral legislature
A one-house legislature.

conservative. In Hawaii, the relatively recent political dominance of Japanese and the secondary status of Chinese, native Hawaiians, and Haoles (whites) makes for tough ethnic politics. Yankee Republicans used to run Massachusetts, but now the Irish dominate. Their personalized style, which blends gregariousness and political loyalty, results in a politics of the clan. Mormonism of course dominates Utah.[10]

Who Serves in the State Legislature?

Like members of the U.S. Congress, most state legislators run for reelection and win. Indeed, nearly 95 percent of incumbents who seek reelection succeed. Approximately one-third of state legislative elections are uncontested, especially in smaller, one-party states and in the South.[11] Although 67 percent are contested, only about 25 percent of state legislative elections are closely contested—with "closely" defined as the winner receiving 60 percent of the votes or less.[12] An incumbent seeking reelection has many advantages over a challenger: name recognition, better access to campaign funds, experience in running campaigns, and a record of helping constituents with problems.

Despite this apparent advantage, in an incumbent's mind, there is seldom such a thing as a "safe district" and a sure reelection. "Whatever their margins of victory in prior elections, however 'safe' their district may appear to the analyst, incumbents know that lightning can strike.... They have seen colleagues relax their efforts and subsequently lose their seats. They live in perpetual danger of casting a roll-call vote that upsets their constituency or mobilizes a key interest group to seek their defeat."[13]

Personal Profile   The typical U.S. state legislator is a 53-year-old white male, well-educated and well-off, often a business executive or lawyer of Anglo-Saxon origin who has had some type of previous political experience—not always elective—at the city or county level. Some have worked as staff members in the legislature or in state government.[14] Most have held some type of local party position and have been active in political campaigns. Surprisingly, approximately one-third were born in some other state, a reflection of our increasingly mobile population.

State legislators tend to have more education and higher incomes than other citizens in their states. They are usually hard-working, public-spirited citizens who believe that being in the legislature is a good opportunity for service. Yet state legislators enjoy less prestige than members of Congress, especially in states that have large legislatures. Discouraged by modest salaries and long hours, many serve a few terms and then either retire voluntarily or run for higher office. As one one-termer explained, "A great deal in the political process does not—repeat, does not—involve the glamorous policy issues. Most of the work is sheer routine and hardly awe-inspiring."[15] And some leave because term limits in their states prevent more than two or three terms.

Party Affiliation   After the 2008 elections, Democrats had an edge over Republicans in the state legislatures. Democrats occupied 3,023 of the 5,411 House seats, whereas Republicans occupied 2,356; similarly, Democrats held 1,020 of the 1,971 Senate seats, whereas Republicans held 893. Only 70 of the nation's state legislators consider themselves Independents or nonpartisan, including all 49 members of Nebraska's unicameral legislature.[16] As a result of the 2008 election, Democrats controlled both houses in 27 states, the Republicans held both houses in 14 states, and 8 states had divided control.

Occupation   Business owners or managers has surpassed lawyers in recent years as the largest occupational group in most state legislatures. Business owners or managers account for approximately 18 percent of state legislators nationwide, with lawyers down to 15 percent. There has been an increase in those who consider themselves full-time legislators, from about 3 percent in 1976 to slightly more than 16 percent in 2007. There has also been a slight increase as well of teachers, homemakers, retirees, and students.[17] Because legislators must have flexible schedules, the job often attracts retired people and those whose businesses or professional practices have been so successful that they can afford to take time off. Real estate and insurance dealers and sales representatives are also commonly found. The number of farmers continues to fall, declining from about 10 percent of state legislators in 1976 to nearly 5 percent in 2007. This has

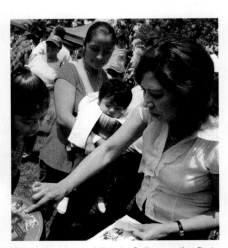

Congresswoman Hilda L. Solis was the first Latina elected to the California State Senate. In 2009, she was named U.S. Secretary of Labor.

Of the People

AMERICA'S CHANGING FACE

Diversity in the Statehouse

In the late 1960s, state legislatures were dominated by white men and often had the look of a "good old boys' club." This has begun to change in recent years, and there is more diversity in legislatures now than at any time previously.

Diversity in State Legislatures, 2009

Male: 5,594 (76%)
Female: 1,788 (24%)
_____
White: 6,350 (86%)
African American: 628 (8.5%)
Latino: 242 (3.3%)
Asian: 85 (1.2%)
Native American: 77 (1%)

The largest growth has occurred among women. In 1971, only 4.5 percent of state legislators were female, whereas today, that number has reached 24 percent. In four states—Colorado, Minnesota, New Hampshire, and Vermont—more than 35 percent of legislators are women. The states with the largest number of African American legislators include Georgia, Maryland, and Mississippi. The largest numbers of Hispanic legislators reside in New Mexico, Texas, and California. More than half of all Asian legislators serve in Hawaii, and more than a quarter of all Native American legislators serve in Oklahoma.

Although scholarly research is a bit mixed, diversity appears to have both procedural and substantive consequences for how state legislatures operate. Several state legislatures have well-organized and influential black caucuses that help shape legislation. Some research suggests that female legislators may have somewhat different policy preferences than their male counterparts, and that women may also practice a more consensus-oriented politics. Evidence also suggests that female and minority citizens feel more efficacious toward government when they see members of their own group serving in office. Such *descriptive representation*, as it is called, allows some citizens to feel like they have an advocate representing their perspective on political issues facing the state.

CRITICAL THINKING QUESTIONS

1. How important is it for the legislature to reflect the demographic makeup of its population? How well does your state legislature reflect your state's demographic makeup?

2. Does descriptive representation have consequences for how your state legislature operates? Do you think it should?

SOURCE: National Conference of State Legislatures, "Legislator Demographics," http://www.ncsl.org/default.aspx?tabid=14850.

---

resulted from redistricting shifting power away from rural areas and a decline in the number of farms and farmers in the population (see Figure 24–1).

Prospects Many state legislators go on to fill other elected offices. About half of the members of the U.S. Congress in 2008 were former state legislators—229 of the 435 members of the House of Representatives and 40 of the 100 U.S. senators.[18] Many statewide elected officials are also former state legislators.

What State Legislators Do

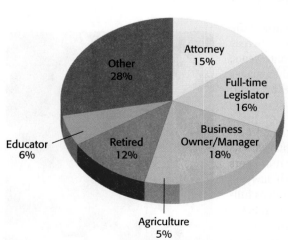

FIGURE 24–1 **Professions of State Legislators.**

■ *Why do you suppose only 16% are full-time legislators?*

SOURCE: National Conference of State Legislatures.

The nation's 7,382 state legislators engage in many of the same lawmaking and oversight activities as members of the U.S. Congress: They enact laws that create state parks; specify salaries for state officials; draw up rules governing state elections; fix state tax rates; set workers' compensation policies; determine the quantity and quality of state correctional, mental health, and educational institutions; and oversee welfare programs. State legislators approve all appropriations and thereby confirm or modify a governor's proposed budget. In most states, they are also responsible for overseeing the administration of public policy. Although they do not administer programs directly, legislators determine through hearings, investigations, audits, and the budgetary process whether programs are being carried out according to legislative intentions. Bill passage rates vary greatly from state to state, depending on a variety of factors, including procedural necessities, constitutional requirements, and local culture. Figure 24–2 outlines the steps in passing state laws.

State legislatures perform various functions within the larger federal system, such as ratifying proposed amendments to the U.S. Constitution, calling for a constitutional convention to propose an amendment to the U.S. Constitution, and approving interstate compacts on matters affecting state

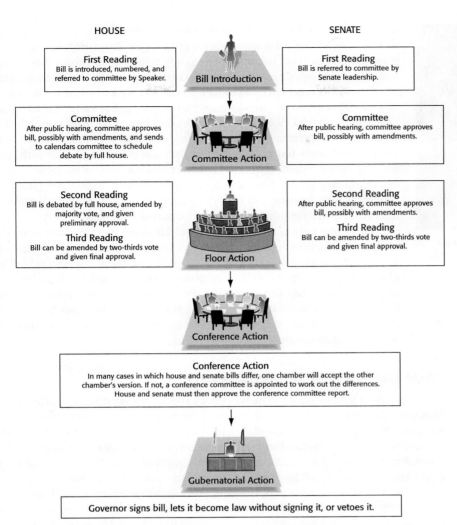

HOUSE

SENATE

First Reading
Bill is introduced, numbered, and referred to committee by Speaker.

Bill Introduction

First Reading
Bill is referred to committee by Senate leadership.

Committee
After public hearing, committee approves bill, possibly with amendments, and sends to calendars committee to schedule debate by full house.

Committee Action

Committee
After public hearing, committee approves bill, possibly with amendments.

Second Reading
Bill is debated by full house, amended by majority vote, and given preliminary approval.

Third Reading
Bill can be amended by two-thirds vote and given final approval.

Floor Action

Second Reading
After public hearing, committee approves bill, possibly with amendments.

Third Reading
Bill can be amended by two-thirds vote and given final approval.

Conference Action

Conference Action
In many cases in which house and senate bills differ, one chamber will accept the other chamber's version. If not, a conference committee is appointed to work out the differences. House and senate must then approve the conference committee report.

Gubernatorial Action

Governor signs bill, lets it become law without signing it, or vetoes it.

FIGURE 24–2 How a Bill Becomes a State Law.

■ *What similarities and differences do you notice between the process for creating a state versus a federal law?*

policies and their implementation. Each state's constitution prescribes the procedures its legislatures must follow and sets limits on the rate of taxation, the kinds of taxes, the subjects that may be taxed, and the purposes of taxation. State legislatures participate in amending their states' constitutions by proposing amendments for voter ratification (see Chapter 22). Legislatures also have authority to impeach and try state officials, and they confirm or reject individuals nominated by governors for executive and judicial posts.

State legislators help translate public wants and aspirations into laws and regulations. In addition to their lawmaking functions, they also try to be ombudsmen—to listen, learn, and find solutions to problems. Invariably, state legislators wind up doing a lot of favors: getting a merchant a license to sell lottery tickets, persuading a state agency to look into safety standards at the local hospital, pushing for funds to repair county roads, arranging for a campaign supporter to be appointed to the state labor commission, and so on. State legislators are accessible. Citizens and students can almost always contact their legislators directly and communicate with them in person, by telephone, or via e-mail.

The agenda of issues that legislators confront varies over time and from state to state. Some budget issues have severely challenged many states' legislatures in recent years. Rapid increases in health care costs and the growing number of people without health insurance have made it very difficult for state legislatures to slow government spending in this area. Public demands for state spending have also been strong for the building and repair of roads and highways; for environmental protection, particularly as the federal government has cut back its support for such functions; for correctional facilities, as more criminals have been given lengthy sentences; and for primary and secondary education,

State Senator Russell Pearce authored Arizona's immigration reform legislation, SB1070, which has been criticized for encouraging racial profiling. A federal judge has already blocked some of the more controversial portions of the state law.

■ *Is immigration a national issue, that should be handled by the federal government, or should states adopt laws that they deem appropriate?*

as society has come to expect greater performance from schools in a competitive world economy. Yet these demands for public spending are often hard to meet, as state politicians have become increasingly reluctant to raise taxes, or they are unable to because of new constitutional restrictions on their powers of taxation.

Legislators have also had to face some difficult and divisive issues of fundamental rights in recent years—issues that are not going away. The nomination of new justices on the U.S. Supreme Court has led some state legislators to believe that states may now exercise greater control over access to abortions. The growing number of immigrants has put pressure on state legislatures to deal with questions about the enforcement of immigration laws and the rights of undocumented workers. Competing groups have also been fighting in state legislatures about whether couples of the same sex may marry or join in civil unions and enjoy some or all of the rights typically granted to heterosexual married couples.

With the growth of state functions, legislators are spending increasing amounts of time on casework or constituency services. Constituent relations are often the most time-consuming aspect of a legislator's job. Local city and school officials always need the help of legislators, and interest groups back home are always pressing their views. Legislators usually try hard to perform constituent casework because they recognize its political value. The more help they give home-district citizens and businesses, they reason, the more they will earn respect, win reelection, or perhaps gather support for election to higher office.

What Legislative Committees Do

To paraphrase a famous quote, "The two things you do not want to see made are laws and sausages." The idea is that lawmaking is a messy business not for the faint of heart. The bulk of legislative "sausage-making" takes place within legislative committees. Committees consider and amend legislation, oversee the implementation of the laws, interview judges, and serve as the major access point for citizens, interest groups, and lobbyists. The functions of a legislative committee are advisory; all its proposals are subject to review, approval, or rejection by the legislative body of which it is a part. However, committees are where most of the critical decisions, compromises, and details of proposed legislation are hammered out, and the full body rarely adopts a bill that a committee has not screened and favorably reported on.

Committees vary in power and influence from state to state. In less populous states, committees are pale shadows of their counterparts in the U.S. Congress because of short sessions, limited staffing, and turnover of both staff and legislators. In other states, however, their influence has increased in recent decades. Committees process and shape hundreds or even thousands of bills and resolutions every year.[19] In many of the more professionalized legislatures, they may also meet between sessions of the legislature, conducting hearings and preparing for the next session.

The committee system allows members to concentrate their energies on specific areas of governmental operations. Over time, legislative committees and their members develop extensive knowledge about particular activities and provide their colleagues with greatly valued information about the content and desirability of proposed bills. Because it is impossible for everybody to be an expert on all aspects of state government, properly staffed and run committees can evaluate the merits and faults of a proposed law more effectively than any individual legislator can.

So just how powerful are committees? It is hard to tell because most committees are controlled by the majority party in a chamber, and committee members are appointed by chamber leaders. Thus, separating the power of committees from the power of parties and chamber leaders is difficult. Still, surveys show that the vast majority of state legislators believe that committees are important centers of power in the legislature.[20] Another way scholars look for evidence of committee power is by considering how many bills die in committees, arguing that killing bills is evidence of committees exercising *gatekeeping power*—the power to prevent proposals from being considered or passed by the entire chamber.[21]

Contacting Your Representative

State legislators generally work very hard to represent the view of their constituents. However, they often have very limited information on exactly how their constituents feel about a given issue. They do not have the time or resources for extensive public opinion polling, and a surprisingly small number of citizens contact their representatives directly to express their views. In fact, most of the letters, phone calls, and e-mails legislators receive come from organized efforts by interest groups. Thus, when legislators do get a genuine contact from a constituent, they are often eager to respond. This is where you come in.

Every state legislature operates a Web site for both its upper and lower house. They are easy to find using an Internet search of your state's name and the term "legislature." You can also find them on the following NCSL Web

site, which provides links to chambers in all 50 states: http://www.ncsl.org/?tabid=17173. Now, find your own state representatives in both the upper and lower chamber of your state's legislature. What are their names, occupations, and party affiliations? On what committees do they serve, or what bills are they currently sponsoring?

You can write your representatives a personal letter or e-mail expressing your views on an issue currently under consideration by the legislature. This might be something your representative has sponsored, something under consideration in one of their committees, or just an issue that is of concern to you. Most legislators want to hear from their constituents. As a follow-up, keep track of how long it takes your representative to respond, whether that response looks like it came directly from him or her or from a staff

person, and whether it specifically addresses the issue you mentioned or looks more like a generic "thank you for contacting me" letter. Compare your experience with your classmates, and discuss what this implies for the quality of representation you are receiving.

CRITICAL THINKING QUESTIONS

1. Why do you think legislators respond to personal letters and e-mails from individuals? What is their motivation?

2. How do you think the responses you might get from legislators would be affected by whether they serve in a professional or part-time legislature, whether they face term limits or not, or whether you are a member of the same political party as your legislators or not? Why might these factors matter?

Influences on State Legislators

State legislators are influenced by many of the same factors that affect members of the U.S. Congress, including legislators' personal ideology and policy positions and the views of their constituencies.

Political Parties

Except in Nebraska, candidates for state legislatures are nominated by political parties in primaries or by party conventions and caucuses, and they are elected *as party members*. Although the official party organization is sometimes not a dominant influence in recruiting state legislative candidates, a candidate nonetheless has to go through the party to gain the nomination. Figure 24–3 shows the current party control of the state legislatures.

The role of political parties in the governance of legislatures and in policy making varies widely from state to state. Gerald Wright and Tracy Osborn report that party unity—the degree to which members of the same party vote together on bills and differently from members of the other party—varies substantially across states.[22] In fact, party unity scores in many state legislative chambers exceed those observed in the U.S. House of Representatives. Legislators in California, Washington, Colorado, Minnesota, Wisconsin, and Texas are among the most polarized, whereas those from Oregon, Louisiana, Rhode Island, and West Virginia are among the least polarized.[23]

In nearly every state where there are two active parties, the political party selects legislative leaders and assigns members to committees. **Party caucuses**—meetings of all the members of one party in the chamber—also distribute campaign funds to their members and to specifically targeted districts.

The party caucus is a principal instrument for legislative decision making in about half the states, including Colorado, Delaware, Idaho, Montana, California, and Utah. In states where a party holds a slim majority of the seats in a legislative chamber, representatives are more likely to feel pressure to "toe the party line" than where a party commands a large majority.[24] Similarly, legislators are more likely to vote with their party in states where the political party plays an important role in recruiting and nominating candidates.

LEARNING **OBJECTIVE**

24.2 Identify the factors that influence state legislators' voting decisions.

party caucus
A meeting of the members of a party in a legislative chamber to select party leaders and develop party policy.

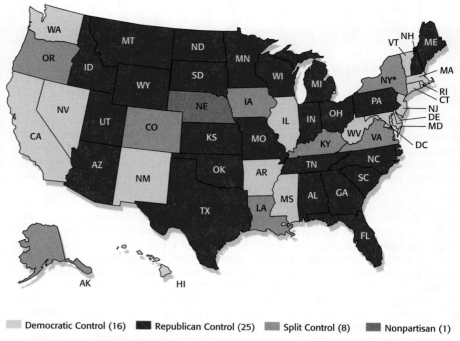

FIGURE 24–3 **Party Control of State Legislatures, 2011**
After the 2010 elections, at least eighteen legislative chambers switched from Democratic control to Republican control. ■ *How would public policy making under a single-party state legislature differ from policy making in a state legislature under split control?*

Democratic Control (16)　Republican Control (25)　Split Control (8)　Nonpartisan (1)

*Based on projections as of mid-November 2010.

In legislatures in which a single party has had long-standing dominance or control, as used to be true in most southern states, parties are less important in conducting and shaping legislative business. However, the re-emergence and success of the Republican party in the South was accompanied by a strengthening of parties both inside and outside legislative chambers.

Interest Groups

Interest groups are a significant and growing source of influence on state legislatures. One group of scholars concludes, based on surveys of public officials and political scientists, that interest groups have a dominant impact in Alabama, Florida, Hawaii, and Nevada, whereas they are weakest in Kentucky, Michigan, Minnesota, South Dakota, and Vermont.[25] Teacher organizations, trade associations, labor groups, trial attorneys, taxpayer associations, insurance, mining, real estate, road builders, and banking interests are often the most visible single-interest groups. In states with a dominant major economic interest, such as agriculture, mining, lumbering, or fishing, legislators pay close attention to the needs of that interest, regardless of whether the group employs lobbyists.

Most state interest groups use lobbying as a major tool of influence. **Lobbying** is attempting to influence the decisions of public officials, especially legislators. The right to lobby is secured by the First and Fourteenth Amendments to the Constitution, which protect the right of the people to petition the government for redress of grievances. State constitutions provide similar protections.

Anyone can try to influence how a state legislator votes. States usually define a professional **lobbyist** as someone paid to influence legislators on behalf of a client or clients. States now require lobbyists to register annually, either with the secretary of state's office or with an election or lobbyist commission. In most states, lobbyists must pay a fee for lobbying. The more populated states register thousands of lobbyists.

Most lobbyists are regular employees of corporations, unions, or trade associations. Many are members of law firms; others are former state employees. Effective lobbyists are specialists in both subject matter and legislative procedure. They know the schedule of general hearings, committee meetings, floor debates, and social events. They also know as much as possible about the legislators, their electoral support, their values, their hobbies, and who has their "ear." Lobbyists live by two important rules: First, remember that it is a lot easier to kill a bill than to pass it. And second, have no permanent allies and no permanent enemies. Today's opponent may be your supporter on the next issue for which you are lobbying.[26]

lobbying
Engaging in activities aimed at influencing public officials, especially legislators, and the policies they enact.

lobbyist
A person who is employed by and acts for an organized interest group or corporation to influence policy decisions and positions in the executive and legislative branches.

Some of the most effective lobbyists are retired state legislators. They not only have good contacts with their former colleagues but also know where the leverage points are in the legislative process. "If you happen to know the four people on a certain senate committee," said one Colorado legislator, "it's pretty damn easy to kill a bill."[27]

Lobbyists have two sources of influence: information and campaign resources. Information is usually the key ingredient in gaining or losing a vote. Effective lobbyists typically explain how the sometimes complicated laws or proposals are likely to affect the businesses, institutions, and individuals in a legislator's own district. Although the popular impression of lobbyists suggests that they will say and do anything to win, that is generally not true. A lobbyist who wants a long career must protect his or her reputation for dealing honestly with legislators. If a lobbyist tricks, misleads, or lies to a legislator, or does something that embarrasses a legislator or gets a legislator in hot water with his or her constituents, word will spread quickly that the lobbyist in question cannot be trusted.

In addition, interest groups are usually major financial backers of incumbent legislators, and in return, the lobbyists for those groups get unusual access. As the costs of state legislative races climb, so does the dependence of legislators, legislative leaders, and political parties on organized interests.[28]

Illegal use of lobbying techniques, primarily bribery, has been found in some states. Scandals have been exposed in Arkansas, Arizona, Kentucky, Massachusetts, New Mexico, and South Carolina, among others, in recent years. Still, bribery is not a widespread problem in most states. Writing about his own experiences in the Vermont Senate, Frank Smallwood observed that as a rule, most of the lobbyists "were articulate, hard-working, and extremely well-informed in their particular areas of expertise. This last attribute—information—represented their chief weapon and gave them real clout. As far as I could find out, the lobbyists didn't offer legislators any money or other direct inducements, at least, they never offered me anything, not even a sociable drink. Instead they relied on information."[29]

In recent years, states have sought to regulate lobbying activities, conflicts of interest, and the financing of political campaigns. For example, several states have enacted laws that prohibit contractors or executives from their companies from contributing to officials who could influence state contracts. In addition to adopting this pay-to-play law, Connecticut also bans campaign contributions from the children and spouses of candidates.[30] At the beginning of his term in 2008, Governor Bobby Jindal pushed through the Louisiana legislature a package of tough ethics rules, including financial disclosure, restrictions on lobbyist spending, and prohibitions on state-financed or disaster-related contracts with legislators and executive branch officials.[31]

Laws that control lobbying and campaign contributions are difficult to enforce. First Amendment rights severely limit a government's ability to regulate lobbying activities.[32] There are two schools of thought on lobbyist regulations. One says that creating more complex and difficult lobbying and campaign-funding regulations merely drives the process further away from the public eye to the advantage of those with the resources and skills needed to navigate the rules. The other school of thought is embodied in a quote by former Texas Governor Anne Richards, who said, "I'm all for…reform…just to slow things down. If you can create an atmosphere in which you got to learn new tricks to cheat…" it at least makes moneyed interests work harder.[33]

Constituents

Usually the greatest influence on legislators comes from the people who elect them, their constituents. Former state legislator John E. Brandl says state legislators understand that on election day, their constituents who are grateful for favors received "are more apt to express positive sentiments on the ballot than those not receiving benefits from the capitol…. A former colleague of mine in the Minnesota House of Representatives seemed bewildered when he heard the suggestion that his first responsibility as a legislator might not be to look out for his district but rather to be concerned for the good of the whole state. 'Nobody who thinks like that could ever get elected from my district,' he maintained."[34]

Still, if state legislators are elected to represent the people and their views at the statehouse, few lawmakers think they should merely mirror or "re-present" the views of their district's constituents. Most legislators like to consider themselves **trustees** of their

trustee
An official who is expected to vote independently, based on his or her judgment of the circumstances; one interpretation of the role of a legislator.

For the People

GOVERNMENT'S GREATEST ENDEAVORS

Promoting Trust in Government

Of importance to a constitutional democracy is that citizens understand what their governments are doing and have trust in their leaders. The National Conference of State Legislatures (NCSL) launched a program several years ago to promote civics education and citizen participation in order to foster greater trust. The program includes the "America's Legislators Back to School Program," in which more than 1,200 legislators reach out to more than 1 million students every year through classroom visits. NCSL has also produced several public service announcements targeted at young people designed to "tackle cynicism and common misconceptions about representative democracy." NCSL has partnered with other organizations to produce a nonpartisan television effort called "American Democracy Television," which also targeted school-aged children. Finally, NCSL has organized the "Democracy in America" seminars designed to provide training and support for teachers.

All these programs are designed to provide more information about how representative government in the states works and how citizens can get involved. Programs like this put a human face on government, making it easier for young people to relate to the political process and see a role for themselves in it. More information about the program, several additional documents, and video clips of the public service announcements can be found online here: http://www.ncsl.org/default. aspx?tabid=15390.

CRITICAL THINKING QUESTIONS

1. What kinds of activities or events do you think would influence the level of trust or cynicism young people might have toward government in their state? What kinds of things would work? What kinds of things would likely fail or even backfire?

2. Are teachers or representatives in your state participating in these "back-to-school" programs? What role should they have in promoting democratic values and trust in government?

constituents, claiming to rely on their own conscience or on their considered judgments in making decisions. Legislators who view themselves as **delegates,** by contrast, adhere more closely to instructions from their constituents. Not surprisingly, the trustee role is not only more popular among legislators, but it is also easier and more realistic to practice. Given the complexity of government and the difficulty of finding out where citizens stand on a wide variety of issues, the trustee role is a more workable one in the day-to-day decision making of a legislator during legislative sessions. Only on issues of keen local interest do legislators tend to assume the role of a trustee.

Learning from Other Governments

Another aspect of state politics that often fuels legislation is action taken by other states. Legislators frequently ask their staffs, "What is California, Minnesota, or Oregon doing on

delegate

An official who is expected to represent the views of his or her constituents even when personally holding divergent views; one interpretation of the role of a legislator.

this problem?" They are always on the lookout for innovative tax, educational, or welfare policies implemented elsewhere and keenly interested in how their state compares with others—on sales taxes, teenage driving privileges, high school dropout rates, air quality, the minimum wage, or federal monies coming to the state. The press often uses such rankings in headlines and editorials.

The National Conference of State Legislatures, a nonpartisan professional organization funded by all 50 state legislatures, acts as an effective clearinghouse for new ideas (www.ncsl.org). With approximately 180 staff members located mainly in Denver, Colorado, it distributes studies to legislators across the country. A rival yet smaller and more conservative group, the American Legislative Exchange Council, has developed in recent years (www.alec.org). The Council of State Governments (www.csg.org) and the State Legislative Leaders Foundation (www.sllf.org) are two groups that also help serve state legislative leaders.

Actions taken by the federal government also influence state laws and regulations. During the past 30 years, states have accepted federal grants for many programs, such as Medicaid and primary and secondary education. In exchange, they must dedicate state funding to the programs and meet certain federal requirements. The need to allocate state money and structure state-administered programs to meet these federal requirements is a sore point for many state legislators.

Finally, just as states sometimes serve as laboratories for other states and the national government, local governments sometimes serve as laboratories for the states. For example, many cities banned smoking in restaurants before most states considered taking such action. Local governments have also been innovators in policies as diverse as public education and public funding of elections.

Modernization and Reform

As states are asked to take on increasing responsibility, their legislatures face greater pressure to modernize, which has also changed how legislators act. According to state legislative scholar Alan Rosenthal, "Earlier, leaders were truly in command, and power was tightly held. Partly as a consequence of modernization and reform, legislatures have been democratized. Resources are more broadly distributed, and the gap between leaders and other legislators is narrower."[35]

State legislatures in the past were criticized as inefficient, ineffective, poorly staffed, scandal-ridden, secretive, sexist, unrepresentative, and often dominated by rural interests. Most had little or no staff and high rates of turnover among members. They were often run by factions that could not be held accountable, and parliamentary procedures and inadequate committee systems either prevented action or served narrow or specially favored interests. Legislators had to rely primarily on information from lobbyists or the governor's office.

Given the goals of members, the demands of groups, and the heavy workload, deliberation gives way to expediency. Members frequently are unwilling to say no to their colleagues, lest their colleagues say no to them. They also are averse to saying no to constituents, lest their constituents withdraw support. The process has become porous; much seeps through that probably should not. Standing committees do not screen the wheat from the chaff as diligently as they might.[36]

Most state legislatures have adopted internal reforms to address these shortcomings. Legislatures typically now have longer annual sessions, expanded and more competent staffs, more effective committee systems, streamlined procedures such as automated bill status and statute retrieval systems, higher salaries, and modern information systems.[37] In 1979, for example, state legislatures had 16,930 permanent staffers; by 1996, the number had climbed to 27,882, where it has held steady up through 2009.[38]

Legislatures have also become more sensitive to new technologies. Every legislature now has a colorful Web site with detailed information about the workings of the lawmaking body. Hawaii has a fully equipped and staffed "public access room," making it easy for citizens to lobby their state legislators.[39] Michigan, Missouri, Utah, Virginia, and Washington were scored by the Pew Center for the States as best in applying data and technology to measure the effectiveness of government services, to make decisions,

YOU WILL DECIDE

Should Legislators Be Paid Higher Salaries?

The idea of a citizen legislature, an assembly populated by ordinary citizens who meet periodically to discuss the needs of their community and decide how they should address them, is appealing to many. Idaho boasts that the success of the state's legislative chamber in guiding the state is due to its citizen legislators. "Farmers and ranchers, businessmen and businesswomen, lawyers, doctors, salespeople, loggers, and teachers" are in session for only three months each year. Their part-time status, the state asserts, enables them to "maintain close ties to their communities and a keen interest in the concerns of the electorate."*

In citizen legislatures, politics is not supposed to be a career, and elected officials are expected to work only part time.

Compensation for these state legislatures reflects this belief. In states with less professional legislatures, members spend approximately half their time on the job, and their compensation, including salary, per diem, and any other expense payments averages $15,984 a year. In states with professional legislatures, however, members work full time or close to it, and their higher compensation, averaging $68,599, allows them to make a living as a state legislator without having another source of income.**

What do you think? Should states provide higher compensation for their legislators? What arguments would you make for and against such an idea?

THINKING IT THROUGH

Raising legislative salaries is almost always a contentious issue in the states. The public tends to be skeptical of salary increases, doubtful that they are warranted, and inclined to believe that legislators enact them out of self-interest. Opponents of higher salaries argue that professional politicians do not necessarily do a good job, and they point to problems in a state with a professional legislature as evidence in favor of citizen assemblies. Debating a salary hike in Arizona, ultimately denied by the voters, Republican Senator Robert Blendu moaned, "Look at California—they're professional politicians and they've run that state into oblivion."[†]

Proponents of higher salaries counter that legislators work more hours than people realize, even in states with acknowledged part-time legislators. When the legislature is not in session, members attend meetings, work on legislation, and help their constituents. The work is complicated and demanding, especially as the federal government has given more responsibilities to the states and as citizens have come to expect more from their state governments. If legislators do not do this work, power is likely to shift to other government offices, such as the governorship and administrative agencies.

When compensation to legislators is low, proponents continue, the assembly resembles a citizen's body in name only. Many people cannot afford to serve in the legislature, and the opportunity is limited to those who are retired or independently wealthy, or whose occupations provide sufficient flexibility that they can leave their jobs for several months at a time. "No one goes into politics to get rich," notes former Massachusetts State Senator Tom Birmingham. "But you can't have a system where only the rich get into politics."[‡]

Critical Thinking Questions

1. What are the strengths and weaknesses of a citizen legislature, and how do they compare with the strengths and weaknesses of a professional legislature?

2. Is higher compensation for legislators likely to foster a more diverse and representative body? Why or why not?

---

* www.legislature.idaho.gov/about/citizenlegislature.htm.
** "NCSL Backgrounder: Full- and Part-Time Legislature," updated January 2008, National Conference of State Legislatures, 204.131.235.67/programs/press/2004/backgrounder_fullandpart.htm.
[†] Phil Riske, "Arizona Lawmakers Seek 50% Salary Hike—Again," *Arizona Capitol Times*, September 29, 2006.
[‡] Tom Birmingham, quoted in Karen Hansen, "Legislator Pay: Baseball It Ain't," *State Legislatures* (July–August 1997), p. 20.

---

and to communicate with their citizens.[40] In short, amateur, part-time state legislatures are much less common now than a few decades ago. The new professionalism reflects a determination on the part of most legislators—especially the leaders—to take charge of their own branch as a major player in shaping state public policy.

The movement to encourage full-time professional legislatures with substantial staffs, however, has not been universally praised. In fact, in recent years, some political scientists and some citizens have contended that we were better off when we had part-time citizen-legislators. The groundswell in the early 1990s to enact term limits was in many ways a voters' protest against professionalized legislators who appeared to be making their job of representation into a career.

Legislative Term Limits: Problem or Solution?

Although the complexity of state problems may well require professional legislators who devote full-time attention to legislative issues, this professionalism "runs counter to the traditional theory of American politics in which citizens come together, conduct the public's business, and return to their other occupations."[41] In the 35 states without term limits, many legislators have served for a very long time—and hence are perceived by some as less connected to the people they represent.

Term limits were the most talked-about legislative "reform" in the 1990s. Reform began in 1990 when voters in California, Colorado, and Oklahoma approved the first term-limit restrictions through citizen-instigated ballot initiatives. Two years later, another 11 states enacted voter initiatives along the same lines. Several more approved term-limit provisions of some type, but voters in three states rejected them. In addition, state legislators in Utah and Louisiana voted to impose term limits on themselves. State supreme courts in five states—Massachusetts, Nebraska, Oregon, Washington, and Wyoming—have struck down term limits as unconstitutional. Note, however, that in 2000, four years after their court nullified voter-approved limits, Nebraskans voted to reinstate them. In 2004, voters in Arkansas and Montana rejected ballot measures that would have relaxed term limits.

There is some evidence that the term-limit movement has run out of energy. In 2002, Idaho legislators repealed term-limit provisions that voters had approved on several occasions. Term-limit supporters complained that this legislative repeal constituted "a slap in the face to all Idaho voters. The arrogance of the Legislature to repeal an issue that has been supported by four separate votes is unconscionable."[42] But Idaho legislative leader Bruce Newcomb responded that term limits won approval only because out-of-state money influenced the votes: "We were a cheap state to buy; it was not in the public interest.... There was never a real debate.... They had no opposition."[43] In 2003, the Utah legislature followed suit, repealing the limits it had imposed on itself only five years earlier.[44] Oregon voters in 2006 rejected an attempt to reinstate term limits after a court ruling had struck them down, and in 2007, Maine lengthened term limits from four to six terms.[45]

Nevertheless, term-limit provisions exist in 15 states (see Table 24–1). These limit state legislators to service of 6 to 12 years. In some states, lawmakers are barred from serving in the same office beyond a set number of years. In nine other states, they must skip one term (more in some states) before running again. In 2002, for example, 71 percent of Michigan's

TABLE
24–1 | Term Limits in the States

State	Year Enacted	House		Senate		Popular Vote in Favor
		Limit (years)	Year of Impact	Limit (years)	Year of Impact	
Maine	1993	8	1996	8	1996	67.6%
California	1990	6	1996	8	1998	52.2
Colorado	1990	8	1998	8	1998	71.0
Arkansas	1992	6	1998	8	2000	59.9
Michigan	1992	6	1998	8	2002	58.8
Florida	1992	8	2000	8	2000	76.8
Missouri*	1992	8	2002	8	2002	75.0
Ohio	1992	8	2000	8	2000	68.4
South Dakota	1992	8	2000	8	2000	63.5
Montana	1992	8	2000	8	2000	67.0
Arizona	1992	8	2000	8	2000	74.2
Oklahoma	1990	12	2004	12	2004	67.3
Nevada†	1996	12	2008	12	2008	70.4
Louisiana	1995	12	2007	12	2007	76.0
Nebraska‡	2000	8	2008	—	—	55.8

* Because of special elections, term limits became effective in 2000 for eight current members of the House and one senator in 1998.
† The Nevada Legislative Council and attorney general have ruled that Nevada's term limits cannot be applied to legislators who were elected in the same year that term limits were passed (1996). They first apply to persons elected in 1998.
‡ Nebraska has a unicameral legislature.

■ *During what period of time were most term limits enacted, and how many years on average were legislators limited to serving? Do you support or oppose term limits?*

SOURCE: National Conference of State Legislatures, "The Term-Limited States," www.ncsl.org/programs/legman/about/states.htm.

legislators were forced out of office under term limits. The California statute goes even further. It slashed legislative staffs, curbed legislative pensions, limited the number of terms legislators could serve, and prohibited legislators from ever running again for the legislature.

Thus far, term limits have not changed the general profile of state legislators.[46] Yet, term limits have serious consequences for state legislative activity. In a comprehensive study, political scientist Thad Kousser finds that the gains produced by "a higher level of professionalism" are wiped out by term limits.[47] Kousser argues that this gets at the fundamental question of whether we want professional politicians as our representatives. In California, novice lawmakers now chair committees and hold leadership positions, and signs there and elsewhere suggest that term limits discourage legislative cooperation, decrease institutional expertise, and generally weaken legislatures relative to governors, bureaucrats, and lobbyists. It takes several years for new legislators to become acquainted with rules, procedures, and regulations; to jettison politicians just as they begin to feel comfortable, confident, and knowledgeable is to lose a wealth of accumulated experience.

redistricting
The redrawing of congressional and other legislative district lines following the census to accommodate population shifts and keep districts as equal as possible in population.

gerrymandering
The drawing of legislative district boundaries to benefit a party, group, or incumbent.

malapportionment
Having legislative districts with unequal populations.

LEARNING **OBJECTIVE**
24.4 Analyze the controversies over redistricting.

Drawing Legislative District Lines

State legislatures are required by their state constitutions, by federal laws, and by court rulings to draw district boundaries for both their state legislature and U.S. House of Representative seats after each population census to ensure that each district represents essentially the same number of voters. The 2010 census will once again trigger this mandatory redistricting of congressional and state legislative lines. However, most states are free to redraw district boundaries more frequently, and several have done so in recent years either for political reasons or in response to court orders.

Redistricting is the action of a state legislature or other body in redrawing legislative electoral district lines. About a dozen states delegate these responsibilities to independent redistricting or reapportionment commissions. In Alaska, the governor's office draws the legislative districts. Most legislatures consider these once-a-decade responsibilities so important, however, that they are unwilling to turn over control of the task to anybody else.

Drawing legislative district boundaries has always been controversial, in large part because redistricting decisions are made by partisan majorities in legislatures. The highly political nature of the undertaking is usually reflected in the results. "Redistricting is the political equivalent," says one observer, "of moving the left field fence for a right-handed pull hitter. By changing the boundaries, redistricting helps some, hurts others—and leaves just about everyone else scrambling."[48] Computers and mapping software have made the politics of redistricting even more precise and sophisticated.

In 2003, Republicans in the Texas state legislature introduced a redistricting plan designed to help the party gain a majority of the state's seats in the U.S. House for the first time since Reconstruction. Democratic legislators tried to block the plan by leaving town, preventing the legislature from being able to vote. These eleven Democratic state senators spent a month in Albuquerque, New Mexico. Eventually one returned, the plan was passed, and the Republicans succeeding in winning a majority of Texas's U.S. House seats in 2004. ■ *Should redistricting be affected by partisanship? Should elected officials use the chamber's rules to block legislation that will otherwise pass?*

Drawing district boundaries to benefit a party, group, or incumbent is called **gerrymandering.** The term was first used in 1811 to describe a strange, salamander-shaped legislative district drawn in northeastern Massachusetts when Elbridge Gerry was governor. A district does not need to be odd in shape, however, to be gerrymandered.

As a result of huge differences in population among the districts, state legislative districts used to face problems of **malapportionment.** State legislatures for decades had given rural and small-town voters more votes in the legislature than they were entitled to based on population alone. In Georgia, for instance, the 1960 reapportionment gave the largest county, with 556,326 inhabitants, no more representation than the three smallest counties, whose *combined* population was 6,980.[49] City officials complained bitterly that small-town and farmland-dominated legislators were unsympathetic to their problems and had different legislative priorities.

No matter how much they protested, people who were underrepresented in the state legislatures made little progress. Legislators from small towns and farm areas naturally did not wish to reapportion themselves out of jobs, and their constituents did not wish to lose their influence. Even though the failure of state legislatures to reapportion often violated express provisions of state constitutions and raised serious questions under the U.S. Constitution, state and federal judges took the position that issues having to do with legislative districting were "political questions" and outside the scope of judicial authority.

Finally, the U.S. Supreme Court stepped in. In 1962, in *Baker* v. *Carr,* the Court held that voters have standing to challenge legislative apportionment and that the federal courts should consider such questions. Arbitrary and capriciously drawn districts deprive people of their constitutional rights of representation, and federal judges may take jurisdiction over such cases.[50]

One Person, One Vote

In *Wesberry* v. *Sanders* (1964), the U.S. Supreme Court announced that "as nearly as practicable one man's vote in a congressional election is to be worth as much as another's."[51] The Court extended this principle to representation in the state legislatures, although it subsequently modified this decision to allow for somewhat larger population discrepancies among state legislative districts than for congressional districts.

In *Reynolds* v. *Sims* (1964), the Court held that "the fundamental principle of representative government in this country is one of equal representation for equal numbers of people, without regard to race, sex, economic status, or place of residence within a state." In the Court's view, this principle should be applied to both the more numerous house of the state legislature, which was usually based on population, *and* to the state senate, where representation was often based on area, such as the county. Defenders of this pattern had argued that as long as the more numerous chamber represented population, the senate could represent geographical units. Looking at the federal system embodied in the U.S. Constitution, they said: Isn't representation in the U.S. Senate based on area? Although many thought this a compelling argument, a majority of the Court did not. Chief Justice Earl Warren explained: "Legislators represent people, not trees or acres. Legislators are elected by voters, not farms or cities or economic interests.... The right to elect legislators in a free unimpaired fashion is a bedrock of our political system."[52]

The Supreme Court has been especially strict about how states draw districts for the U.S. House of Representatives. A state legislature must justify any variance from absolute equality by showing that it made a good-faith effort to come as close as possible to the standard. The Supreme Court is, however, less insistent on absolute equality for state legislative districts. Thus, in 1983, the Court upheld a Wyoming plan that allocated at least one state legislative seat per county, saying that Wyoming's policy was rational and appropriate to the special needs of that sparsely populated state.[53] This ruling was a rare exception to the general principle of allowing at most a 10 percent deviation between state legislative districts. The "reapportionment revolution" triggered by U.S. Supreme Court cases like *Baker* v. *Carr* (1962) and *Reynolds* v. *Sims* (1964) produced a seismic shift in state legislatures, more so than any reform adopted since the end of Reconstruction.[54]

New Rules for Redrawing the Districts

Even though the one-person, one-vote principle is firmly established, many issues affecting the nature of legislative representation continue to be hotly debated. In northern metropolitan areas, for instance, the general pattern has been for the center city to be Democratic and the outlying suburbs Republican. If legislative district lines in these areas are drawn like spokes from the center city to the suburbs, fewer Republicans will probably be elected than if district lines are drawn in concentric circles.

In recent decades, African Americans and Hispanics have begun to charge that state legislatures have an obligation under the Voting Rights Act of 1965 to redraw legislative districts to avoid dilution of the influence of minorities at the ballot box. They have gone to court to force legislators to create **majority-minority districts.** These are districts in which the majority of residents come from a minority population. The goal of creating such districts produced an otherwise unlikely coalition between Republican and African American legislators in many states. That is because creating a district that is majority African American generally also results in a district that is overwhelmingly Democratic. This leaves fewer Democratic voters in neighboring districts, which increases the chances for electoral victory for Republicans in those neighboring districts. The U.S. Supreme Court, however, has put restraints on implementation of the Act. The Court has held that although legislatures may take race into account in drawing state and federal legislative district lines and must act to avoid diluting the voting strength of minorities, a legislature violates the constitutional rights of white voters if race becomes the overriding motive.[55]

A case can be made that most state legislative elections offer little meaningful competition. Whether legislative party leaders or redistricting commissioners, those who carve up legislative districts every ten years do so primarily with the intent to protect incumbents or create districts that at least leave their party no worse off than it was before. The Supreme Court has ruled that partisan gerrymandering can be challenged in court as a violation of the Constitution. However, the Court did not find that a particularly controversial redistricting plan in Texas was an unconstitutional gerrymander, and it has not yet stated a standard by which to judge exactly what would make a gerrymander unconstitutional.[56]

Direct Legislation: Policy Making by the People?

LEARNING OBJECTIVE

24.5 Evaluate the debate regarding the methods of direct democracy available to some states.

Many states provide citizens with the power to create legislation through the initiative and referendum. This "direct democracy" movement began with populist reformers in Utah in 1900 and spread quickly to Oregon in 1902, Montana in 1904, Maine and Michigan in 1908, and Arizona and Colorado in 1910. Of the nearly 2,200 initiatives the public has placed on the ballot in the 24 states that allow this form of direct democracy, nearly 1,100 have been in five states: Oregon, California, Colorado, North Dakota, and Arizona.

Reformers had good reason to bypass their legislatures in the early 1900s—legislatures in several states were either incompetent or under the domination of political machines. For example, the Southern Pacific Railroad's political machine in California had dominated the selection of state legislators, governors, and U.S. senators for years.[57] The Progressives placed enormous trust in the wisdom of the people, assuming that voters would inform themselves about issues and make responsible decisions on a variety of policy questions put before them.

Initiative

The **initiative** permits a designated minimum number of voters to propose a law or constitutional amendment by petition. It becomes law if approved by a majority of the voters at a subsequent election, although Florida voters recently approved an initiative to require all subsequent initiatives to receive 60 percent of the vote to earn passage. As noted above, 24 states, mostly in the West, authorize the making of laws by means of the initiative petition (see Figure 24–4).

In some states, the *direct initiative* applies to constitutional amendments and to legislation; in others, it can be used only for one or the other. Thus, in Florida, voters can use

majority–minority district
A legislative district created to include a majority of minority voters; ruled constitutional as long as race is not the main factor in redistricting.

initiative
A procedure whereby a certain number of voters may, by petition, propose a law or constitutional amendment and have it submitted to the voters.

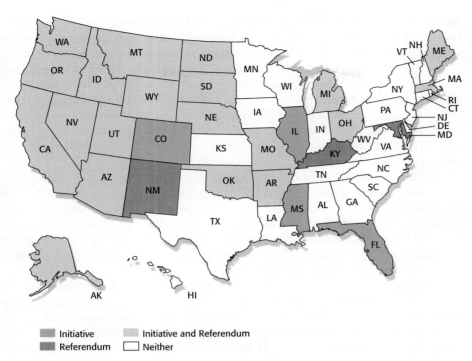

FIGURE 24–4 Citizen-Initiated Initiative and Referendum at the State Level.

■ *What parts of the country are more likely to allow citizen initiative and referendum? How does that relate to the overall political culture of those states?*

Initiative   Initiative and Referendum
Referendum   Neither

the direct initiative only to change the state constitution, whereas in Idaho, they can apply it only to statutory lawmaking. In a state that permits the direct initiative, any individual or interest group may draft a proposed law and file it with a designated state official, usually the secretary of state. Supporters have only to secure a certain number of signatures (between 2 and 15 percent of the vote total from the last election) to place the measure on the next general election ballot. Only California permits initiatives on primary election ballots.

The *indirect initiative* exists in a few states, including Alaska, Maine, and Massachusetts. After supporters have collected a certain number of petition signatures, the state legislature has an opportunity to act on the measure without altering it; if approved, the law simply goes into effect. If not, the proposed legislation is placed on the ballot, although in some states, additional signatures are required first.

Referendum

A **referendum** permits citizens to vote on, and possibly overturn, recently passed laws. More broadly, referendums can be on legislatively proposed amendments to a state's constitution. A majority vote is required to overturn legislatively approved laws. Every state except Delaware requires the referendum for the ratification of constitutional amendments.

Legislation may be subject to mandatory or optional referendums. The *mandatory referendum* calls for a waiting period, usually 60 to 90 days, before legislation goes into effect. If during this period, a prescribed number of voters sign a referendum petition requesting that the act be referred to the voters, the law does not go into effect unless a majority of voters give their approval at the next election. The *optional referendum* permits the legislature, at its discretion, to provide that a measure shall not become law until approved by voters at an election. This type is more common.

Although statewide initiatives and referendums get the most attention, the same processes also flourish at the local level in many states. Nearly 90 percent of cities have some form of referendum process.[58] The annual volume of measures presented to voters in school districts, cities, and counties runs to several thousand and covers a wide range of issues: bonds for school buildings, fluoridation of water, banning of glass bottles, restrictions on nuclear power facilities, and approval or rejection of convention facilities or sport stadiums.

The Debate Over Direct Democracy

Citizens have turned to the initiative process to try to regulate handguns in California, to protect moose in Maine, to encourage the death penalty in Massachusetts, to approve the

referendum
A procedure for submitting to popular vote measures passed by the legislature or proposed amendments to a state constitution.

sale of wine in grocery stores in Colorado, to abolish daylight saving time in North Dakota, to limit inhumane treatment of pregnant pigs in large hog production operations, and in several states, to allow marijuana to be used for specific medicinal purposes.

Voters approved 58 percent of the 174 ballot propositions considered across 37 states in 2008.[59] The highest profile issue associated with initiatives in 2008 continued to be same-sex marriage, where voters in Arizona, California, and Florida all approved bans on same-sex marriage. More than $85 million was spent by opponents and supporters combined in the California contest alone.[60] Also interesting in 2008, voters approved 15 of 16 statewide bond issues, authorizing their states to borrow more than $13.5 billion even as the economy was clearly already in decline.

In 2010, nearly 200 propositions will be on the ballot. Voters in Colorado will decide on tax and borrowing issues that could reduce the state's general fund by 25 percent. Voters in California will decide if the state should legalize personal marijuana use, if the current two-thirds majority needed to pass a budget in the legislature should be reduced to a simple majority, and if authority for redistricting should be returned to the legislature. Florida voters will decide if any changes made by local governments to their comprehensive land use plans must be approved by voters.

The initiative process has become a powerful tool used by interest groups, politicians, and ideologues, becoming what one author calls "a veritable fourth branch of government" in some states.[61] A vote on an issue in a single state can propel an issue onto the national agenda because of the widespread media attention given to some controversial initiatives.[62] Interest groups have set state policy by means of the initiative and have used it to reduce local government options in taxing, zoning and planning, and related matters. "One reason for this tendency to take on matters that were previously local and decide them at the statewide level is interest group efficiency. It is easier to restrict local taxing powers, strike local rent control laws, and eliminate ordinances protecting gays and lesbians by mobilizing a single statewide vote" rather than by campaigning to reverse or defeat local initiatives.[63]

The results of direct democracy have been mixed. Historically, direct legislation by initiative has resulted in progressive victories on many consumer and economic issues and conservative victories on social issues. Direct democracy has clearly had a con-siderable impact on state taxes and spending, especially in states that have enacted budget and tax limits. These measures have pleased many conservatives, upset liberals, and made life difficult for governors and state legislators. Political scientists, law professors, and lawmakers are often critical of direct legislation.[64] Critics of the initiative and the referendum believe that the Progressives who advocated direct legislation were overly optimistic regarding the abilities of citizens and naively idealistic in thinking that these mechanisms would be safe from manipulation by special interests. Only well-organized interests can gather the appropriate number of signatures and mount the required media campaigns to gain victory. Critics of direct democracy argue that special interests have in fact taken over the process in California, Oregon, and elsewhere.[65] Political consulting firms, for a price, will gather signatures and put nearly anything you want on the ballot. Deceptive pitches are sometimes made to get people to sign petitions. It takes a small fortune to do this, and only well-organized, well-financed, single-interest groups can afford it.[66]

Still another problem with the initiative process is that it can be used to target minorities, as California's limitations on illegal immigrants in 1994 and affirmative action in

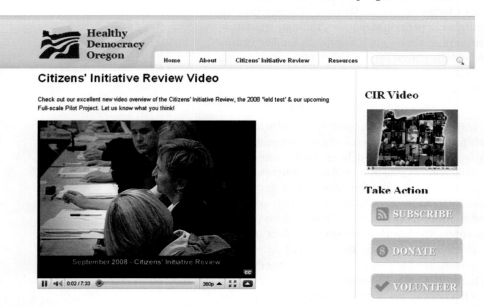

Concerned that voters were lacking quality information on issues going through the initiative process, voters in Oregon formed the Citizens' Initiative Review. A panel of residents reviews the proposed ballots and writes a "Citizens' Statement" detailing their key findings, which is published in Oregon's official Statewide Voter's Pamphlet.

■ *What downside to direct democracy is this panel responding to? Should this solution be adopted in other states?*

1996 did. Similarly, Colorado's controversial Measure 2 in 1992 repealed local ordinances prohibiting discrimination against gays and lesbians and barred the future adoption of such provisions. How far can the majority go in using the initiative process against minorities? The courts have generally reversed part or all of discriminatory initiatives that were successful at the polls, yet such reversals put the courts in the awkward position of opposing a vote of the people. Critics also contend that initiatives and the campaigns around them tend to oversimplify complex policy problems, leaving voters with insufficient information to make informed choices and an inadequate appreciation for the consequences of their choice.

Viewed from another perspective, most of the perceived flaws of the populist processes of direct democracy are also the flaws of democracy. When we vote in an election, we often wish we had more information about issues and candidates. Delegates at constitutional conventions or national party conventions frequently have similar misgivings when they are forced to render yes-or-no votes on complicated issues. So, too, members of state legislatures—especially in the frantic days near the end of their sessions—yearn for more information, more clarity about consequences, and more discussion and compromise than time will permit.

Political scientists Daniel Smith and Caroline Tolbert find that participation in direct democracy also stimulates greater voter turnout, civic engagement, and political efficacy among citizens, and that their impact appears to be greatest at times when no national competitive race is present to stimulate voters.[67] They also note that political parties have seized on initiatives as a means to energize their supporters, divide their opponent's base of support, and raise contributions to the party. Thus, both citizens and political elites are learning political lessons from the initiative process.

Voters throughout the country say citizens ought to have the right, at least occasionally, to vote directly on policy issues. In surveys, both voters and nonvoters say they would be more likely to become interested in politics and vote if some issues appeared along with candidates on their ballots.[68] Californians, who have had to deal with more ballot issues than voters in any other state, continue to say that statewide ballot propositions elections are overall "a good thing for California" (74 percent), even as they acknowledge limits to their own grasp of the process.[69]

The legislative process is never perfect. Even with larger professional staffs, hearings, new technologies, bicameralism, and other distinctive features of constitutional democracy, mistakes are made and defective bills are enacted into law in our legislatures. The Supreme Court has overturned hundreds of laws passed by state legislatures as unconstitutional, and state legislatures often spend much of their time amending or otherwise improving measures they passed in previous years. As a practical matter, however, voters should be at least as skeptical and questioning of the initiative and referendum process as they already are of their state legislators.

CHAPTER **SUMMARY**

24.1 Explain how state legislatures are organized, and describe state legislators and their responsibilities.

All states except Nebraska have a bicameral legislature. In each chamber, the top leadership, including a speaker of the house, is usually selected by the majority party. State legislatures also have committees that focus on certain issue areas, and legislators tend to specialize in areas important to them. A typical state legislator is middle-aged, white, male, and has more education and a higher income than citizens of his or her state. State legislatures have become more diverse in recent decades. Legislators pass policy, provide oversight of how programs are administered, and perform constituency service, working with the resources and institutional structures provided.

24.2 Identify the factors that influence state legislators' voting decisions.

State legislators use many of the same tools for making decisions as members of the U.S. Congress. Political parties are very important in states with competitive party systems. Interest group and constituent concerns weigh heavily for all legislators. Legislators also pay attention to the recommendations of their colleagues, actions taken by other states, and expectations of the federal government.

24.3 Evaluate recent changes in state legislatures.

As a result of legislative reform efforts, most states now have longer annual sessions, larger and more competent staffs, open-meeting laws, and a variety of electronic-age information systems. As they have become more professionalized, they have also had more impact in a variety of policy areas, such as the environment, education, and crime control. Still, most are not as fully professionalized as is the U.S. Congress. Voters in many states are instating term limits as a way of keeping their representatives accountable, ensuring turnover in state legislatures, and encouraging the notion of citizen representation.

24.4 Analyze the controversies over redistricting.

Redistricting is redrawing the lines of legislative electoral districts to reflect changes in the population and conform with Supreme Court rulings regarding one person, one vote. Because political careers can be ruined by redrawn boundaries, redistricting is never easy. Major controversies have arisen over partisan and racially motivated drawing of legislative district lines, and the federal courts are increasingly asked to establish guidelines that will limit such outcomes.

24.5 Evaluate the debate regarding the methods of direct democracy available to some states.

Some states permit voters to place proposed laws or amendments to their state's constitution on the ballot by collecting enough signatures from eligible citizens. Other states allow the legislature to place proposals on the ballot before voters. Supporters of direct democracy like having citizens directly participate in governing themselves. It allows voters to break logjams that might occur in the state government, and it also allows citizens to place limits on state governments that legislatures themselves are unlikely to adopt (like term limits or caps on spending). Opponents argue that the initiative process can be manipulated by small groups with a lot of money, that complex issues are not well suited to simple solutions, and that citizen initiatives sometimes tie the hands of elected officials too much.

CHAPTER **SELF-TEST**

24.1 Explain how state legislatures are organized, and describe state legislators and their responsibilities.

1. In a short essay, describe the typical state legislator including gender, race, age, profession, and political experience. How do you think these demographic factors influence the actions of state legislatures as a whole? Is that result good for the U.S. population? Why or why not?

2. Which is often the most time-consuming aspect of a state legislator's job?
   a. Campaigning
   b. Tending to constituent relations
   c. Attending committee meetings
   d. Researching and writing legislation

3. In a short essay, describe three responsibilities of state legislatures. Consider how they interact with federal and other areas of government, specifically in terms of budgets.

24.2 Identify the factors that influence state legislators' voting decisions.

4. Write a paragraph explaining why retired state legislators are often the most effective lobbyists.

5. In a short essay, describe how lobbyists, interest groups, and party caucuses influence a state legislator's voting decision. Consider the specific desires and influence of each group.

24.3 Evaluate recent changes in state legislatures.

6. Between 1979 and 2009, the number of staffers in state legislatures has gone from _____ to _____.
   a. 17,000; 28,000
   b. 20,000; 35,000

   c. 28,000; 17,000
   d. 35,000; 20,000

7. In a short essay, describe the arguments for and against term limits in state legislatures. Which do you find most compelling?

24.4 Analyze the controversies over redistricting.

8. What is gerrymandering?
   a. Drawing district boundaries to benefit a party, group, or incumbent
   b. Attempting to influence redistricting through the efforts of interest groups
   c. Manipulating data gathered by the U.S. Census Bureau to influence district boundaries
   d. Adjusting district boundaries to give rural and small-town voters more representation than they deserve

9. Why is the drawing of district boundaries often controversial?

24.5 Evaluate the debate regarding the methods of direct democracy available to some states.

10. Which of the following is an element of mandatory referendum?
    a. Citizen review of new government programs
    b. A required period of judicial review for legislation affecting budget policies
    c. A waiting period during which voters must approve legislation before it takes effect
    d. A government program requiring all citizens to participate in some form of direct democracy

11. Are voters sufficiently informed to effectively use direct democracy to shape state policy? How informed do you think voters need to be in order to use direct democracy effectively?

Answers to selected questions: 2. b; 6. a; 8. a; 10. c

mypOliscilab EXERCISES

Apply what you learned in this chapter on MyPoliSciLab.

📖 Read on mypoliscilab.com

eText: Chapter 24

✔ Study and Review on mypoliscilab.com

Pre-Test
Post-Test
Chapter Exam
Flashcards

✳ Explore on mypoliscilab.com

Simulation: You Are Redrawing the Districts in Your State
Timeline: Initiatives and Referendums

KEY TERMS

bicameral legislature, p. 610
unicameral legislature, p. 610
party caucus, p. 615
lobbying, p. 616
lobbyist, p. 616

trustee, p. 617
delegate, p. 618
redistricting, p. 622
gerrymandering, p. 622
malapportionment, p. 622

majority–minority district, p. 624
initiative, p. 624
referendum, p. 625

ADDITIONAL RESOURCES

FURTHER READING

SHAWN BOWLER, TODD DONOVAN, AND CAROLINE J. TOLBERT, EDS., *Citizens as Legislators: Direct Democracy in the United States* (Ohio State University Press, 1998).

WILLIAM M. BULGER, *While the Music Lasts: My Life in Politics* (Houghton Mifflin, 1996).

JOHN M. CAREY, RICHARD G. NIEMI, AND LYNDA W. POWELL, *Term Limits in the State Legislatures* (University of Michigan Press, 2000).

GARY W. COX AND JONATHAN N. KATZ, *Elbridge Gerry's Salamander: The Electoral Consequences of the Reapportionment Revolution* (Cambridge University Press, 2002).

RICK FARMER, ED., *Legislating Without Experience: Case Studies in State Legislative Term Limits* (Lexington Books, 2007).

TYSON KING-MEADOWS, *Devolution and Black State Legislators: Challenges and Choices in the Twenty-First Century* (State University of New York Press, 2006).

THAD KOUSSER, *Term Limits and the Dismantling of State Legislative Professionalism* (Cambridge University Press, 2005).

DAVID B. MAGLEBY, *Direct Legislation: Voting on Ballot Propositions in the United States* (Johns Hopkins University Press, 1984).

ALBERT J. NELSON, *Emerging Influentials in State Legislatures: Women, Blacks, and Hispanics* (Praeger, 1991).

BETH REINGOLD, *Representing Women: Sex, Gender, and Legislative Behavior in Arizona and California* (University of California Press, 2000).

ALAN ROSENTHAL, *Engines of Democracy: Politics and Policymaking in State Legislatures* (CQ Press 2009).

ALAN ROSENTHAL, *Heavy Lifting: The Job of the American Legislature* (CQ Press, 2004).

FRANK SMALLWOOD, *Free and Independent: The Initiation of a College Professor into State Politics* (Greene Press, 1976).

DANIEL A. SMITH AND CAROLINE J. TOLBERT, *Educated by Initiative: The Effects of Direct Democracy on Citizens and Political Organizations in the American States* (University of Michigan Press, 2004).

PEVERILL SQUIRE AND GARY MONCRIEF, *State Legislatures Today: Politics Under the Domes* (Longman, 2010).

PEVERILL SQUIRE AND KEITH E. HAMM, *101 Chambers: Congress, State Legislatures, and the Future of Legislative Studies* (Ohio State University Press, 2005).

SUE THOMAS AND CLYDE WILCOX, EDS., *Women and Elective Office* (Oxford University Press, 1998).

RALPH G. WRIGHT, *Inside the Statehouse: Lessons from the Speaker* (CQ Press 2005). See also *State Legislatures,* published ten times a year by the National Conference of State Legislatures. *Legislative Studies Quarterly* often has articles on state legislatures; it is published by the Legislative Studies Section of the American Political Science Association. *Governing,* published monthly by Congressional Quarterly, Inc., regularly covers state politics and state legislative issues. *Spectrum: The Journal of State Government* is a useful quarterly published by the Council of State Governments.

WEB SITES

www.ncsl.org NCSL provides research, technical assistance, and opportunities to see the exchange of ideas among policy makers.

www.nbcsl.org NBCSL provides educational materials, research, and training programs designed to help legislators and their staff promote the interests of African American constituents.

www.cawp.rutgers.edu CAWP is a leading source of scholarly research and current data about American women's participation in politics and government.

www.nhcsl.org NHCSL provides information to help advocate on behalf of Hispanic communities.

CHAPTER 25

State Governors

Except for the president, governors are the most visible and generally most widely known elected officials in the United States. Governors set the policy agenda in their states, establish spending priorities, advocate for their states at the national and international level, and are generally the most central political figures in their states. Governors make critical policy decisions that directly affect virtually every aspect of the lives of their states' residents—and sometimes governors literally make life and death decisions.

Among the governor's powers is the authority to pardon or commute (lessen the penalty of) criminal sentences or grant a stay (temporary hold) of execution. On January 11, 2003, then Governor George Ryan of Illinois, just two days before leaving office, pardoned four death row inmates and commuted the sentences of every other death row inmate in Illinois (167 at the time) to a life sentence. Ryan, a Republican and stated supporter of the death penalty, had concluded that the death penalty process in his state was flawed and that it could not be conducted in a manner that guaranteed an innocent person would never be executed. Three years earlier, Ryan had declared a moratorium on executions so that the process could be studied.

This remarkable sequence of events was triggered by work done by a group of college journalism students taking a class at Northwestern University in Evanston, Illinois. As part of a class project in 1998, students began investigating the case surrounding the conviction of Anthony Porter. Porter had been convicted and sentenced to death for the murder of two teenagers that occurred in 1982. Porter's case had been appealed and reviewed numerous times, and at one point, he was 48 hours from being executed before a stay was granted. Largely as a result of the investigative work done by the Northwestern students and the evidence it revealed, which provoked another person to confess to the crime, all charges against Porter were dropped and he was released from prison after serving 15 years. Porter's case was not an isolated example— a total of 13 death row inmates had been exonerated based on new evidence during Ryan's tenure as governor. Ryan's life-and-death decisions—celebrated by some and reviled by others—made headlines across the country and around the world. (Unfortunately for former Governor Ryan, he later received national attention for a corruption and bribery conviction for which he was sentenced to serve six and a half years in federal prison.)

Illinois is not the only state to advocate using the powers of the governor to reevaluate use of the death penalty. In May 2010, Ohio Supreme Court Justice Paul E. Pfeifer, one of the authors of Ohio's statute reinstating the death penalty back in the early 1980s when he was a legislator, urged whoever is elected governor to assemble a panel to review the cases of all those currently on Ohio's death row. Pfeifer argued that if those currently on death row were tried for the same crimes today, most would probably not receive the death penalty.[1]

As we will see in this chapter, the importance of the governor has increased substantially in recent decades. States have taken on many new responsibilities and expanded their functions significantly in recent years, elevating governors both within their states and as national political figures. We will examine how governors come into and keep their office, a governor's power and influence in state politics, how the governorship has evolved and been modernized in recent years, how governors interact with other elected state officials, and the rewards of being governor.

CHAPTER **OUTLINE** & CHAPTER LEARNING **OBJECTIVES**

Becoming and Remaining Governor

25.1 Identify the typical pathways by which people attain and retain the governorship.

A Governor's Formal and Informal Powers

25.2 Identify the formal and informal powers of governors, and assess governors' use of these powers to influence policy.

The Job of the Governor: Managing the State

25.3 Evaluate the effectiveness of governors as managers of the state's executive branch.

Assisting the Governor: State Executive Officials

25.4 Outline duties and powers of other top executive officials in state government.

Governors Today: Challenges and Rewards

25.5 Evaluate the challenges and rewards for governors today.

Becoming and Remaining Governor

Each state's constitution and laws spell out the rules of eligibility, tenure, and salary for its governor. Thirty-five states require their governors to be at least 30 years old, and 28 states require candidates to be residents of the state for at least five years immediately preceding the election. Although California, Ohio, Rhode Island, South Dakota, Vermont, Washington, and Wisconsin set the minimum age at 18, the odds against election at age 18 are staggering.[2] In theory, any qualified voter of the state who meets a state's age qualification is eligible for the office of governor; in practice, there are well-traveled career paths to the governor's office.

Most governors are white males approximately 40 to 55 years old. As of early 2010, there have been 32 female governors, nearly half of whom took office in 2000 or later.[3] Most governors were state legislators or held statewide elective office before running for governor. Of the governors in office at the start of 2010, for instance, 21 served in their state legislatures, 9 served as lieutenant governors, and 7 were state attorneys general. In addition, some governors had national governmental experience, including eight who served in the U.S. House of Representatives.[4]

One of the most common paths upward is election to the state legislature, followed by election to a statewide office such as lieutenant governor, secretary of state, or attorney general, followed by a run for governor. Vermont Governor Jim Douglas was elected to the state legislature right out of college and served as secretary of state and state treasurer before becoming governor. Mayors often run for governor; the mayors of Albuquerque, Charlotte, Phoenix, Indianapolis, Las Vegas, and Maui have all run for governor in their states in recent years. In 2010, four governors had been mayors. Although serving in office is certainly helpful for building a political base, it is not essential. Thirteen governors in 2010 had not held previous elective office, although the majority had held some appointed political position.

Two hundred years ago, most states had one- or two-year terms for their governors. Today, all states except New Hampshire and Vermont have four-year terms, and all states except Virginia allow governors to run for more than one consecutive term. Some governors, such as Jim Douglas of Vermont, William Janklow of South Dakota, Roy Romer of Colorado, John Engler of Michigan, Mario Cuomo and George Pataki of New York, Jim Hunt of North Carolina, Mike Leavitt of Utah, and Tommy Thompson of Wisconsin, have been elected to three or four terms as governors, but 35 states now have a two-term limit on governors, and Utah has a three-term limit.[5]

Bill Richardson, the Democratic governor of New Mexico, previously served in the House of Representatives. His second term as governor ends in 2011, and because of terms limits he cannot run for a third.

■ *Do you support limiting governors to two terms, or should successful governors be allowed to continue running for office?*

Governors Under Pressure

Once elected, governors enjoy high visibility in their states. Governors' salaries are certainly higher than the average earnings of U.S. workers: They earn more than $100,000 in 43 states, and salaries range from $212,179 in California to $70,000 in Maine.[6] In addition, governors receive an expense allowance; all but four are provided an executive mansion; 42 have regular access to a state plane or helicopter or both.[7] But these salaries and benefits hardly compare with those of CEOs of major corporations, even though most state governments' revenues and workforces are as large as Fortune 500 companies. Whether they seek the office for the opportunity to serve the public, make history, exercise power, or get a foothold for a run for the Senate or the presidency, nonfinancial incentives are probably dominant for most gubernatorial candidates.

Even as governors have become increasingly important in recent decades, they have also had to deal with the twin problems of rising public expectations and scarcity of resources. People want better schools, uncongested highways, fine universities (with low tuition), a good job market, access to health care, protections for civil rights, low crime, and clean air and water. However, they usually also want their taxes kept as low as possible.

Of the People

AMERICA'S CHANGING FACE

Female Governors

There have been only 32 female governors in all of U.S. history.* But of the 32, nearly half took office in 2000 or later. In 2010, there were six women currently serving as governors. As women have occupied increasingly powerful positions in state legislatures and in lower-level statewide offices, such as lieutenant governor, attorney general, and secretary of state, they have become much more visible as potential candidates for the governorship. African Americans and Hispanics have not made similar gains, however. As of 2010, there was only one Hispanic governor in office, Bill Richardson of New Mexico, and there were two African Americans, Deval Patrick of Massachusetts and David Paterson of New York, who succeeded Eliot Spitzer when he resigned the governorship in early 2008.

Former Arizona Governor Janet Napolitano was named secretary of Homeland Security in 2009.

Female Governors Since 2000

Governor	State	Term of Office
Judy Martz	Montana	2001–2005
Ruth Ann Minner	Delaware	2001–2008
Jane Swift	Massachusetts	2001–2002
Jennifer Granholm	Michigan	2003–
Janet Napolitano	Arizona	2003–2009
Linda Lingle	Hawaii	2003–
Kathleen Sebelius	Kansas	2003–2009
Olene Walker	Utah	2003–2005
Kathleen Blanco	Louisiana	2004–2008
M. Jodie Rell	Connecticut	2004–
Christine Gregoire	Washington	2005–
Sarah Palin	Alaska	2007–2009
Beverly Perdue	North Carolina	2009–
Jan Brewer	Arizona	2009–

SOURCE: "History of Women Governors," Center for American Women and Politics, Eagleton Institute, Rutgers University, January 2007, www.cawp.rutgers.edu/Facts/Officeholders/govhistory.pdf; and *The Book of the States, 2009* (The Council of State Governments), p. 176.

Jennifer Granholm became Michigan's first female governor in 2003.

CRITICAL THINKING QUESTIONS

1. In early 2010, 16 percent of governors were women, the same percentage of women in the U.S. Senate and in the U.S. House of Representatives. Women were more common in state legislatures— approximately 24 percent in 2010.[†] Why might women be more frequently found in state legislatures than in these other offices?

2. Four of the current six female governors are in western or plains states. These states have generally been more likely than other states to elect women to state or national office. Why might that be so?

* The Book of the States, 2009 (The Council of State Governments, 2009), p. 176.
† For more information on women in elected office, see Rutgers University's Center for American Women and Politics Web site, www.cawp.rutgers.edu/.

Former New York Governor Mario Cuomo (who served from 1983 until 1995) used to say he was always running into people who wanted him to expand programs. He would look them in the eye and say, "Now what are you going to give me so that I can pay for it? Do you want to wait longer in line at the motor vehicle office to get your license renewed? Do we stop paving the road in front of your home? Do you mind if we plow the snow less often?" Typically, of course, people requesting additional spending did not want to forgo any of those things, which prompted him to say, "Well, then, I don't understand. Where do I get what I need to do what you want?" Cuomo's point was simple. Given limited resources, elected officials must make choices. They cannot do everything people would like. You must "give to get."[8]

Governors and state legislators face the challenge of administering federally mandated environmental, educational, welfare, and homeland security programs with fewer federal dollars. They have campaigned for the federal government to give more money to the states—without strings. The Republican-controlled U.S. Congress in the late 1990s responded by terminating some underfunded federally mandated programs and shifting a few other federal programs to the states. But in the 2000s, Congress continued to pass legislation that imposed new costs on the states, such as the No Child Left Behind Act of 2002, which some governors say is underfunded.[9]

Reelection

Incumbent governors are typically reelected when they run. Between 1970 and 2004, 74 percent of incumbent governors seeking reelection won.[10] In recent years, incumbents' success has been even greater: In 2006, 25 of 27 incumbents won, for a reelection rate of 93 percent.[11] In 2008, all eight incumbent governors running for reelection won. Incumbent John Corzine lost his bid for reelection in New Jersey in 2009. In 2010, five of the seven Democratic incumbents and all six Republican incumbents running won reelection. The two Democrats who lost were Chet Culver in Iowa and Ted Strickland in Ohio, with Strickland losing by only 2 percentage points. Thus, even while Republicans were winning most of the open seat contests, incumbents from both parties were very successful in holding onto their seats.

Governors' reelection chances may be helped by the insulation of most gubernatorial elections from the sometimes large party swings found in presidential elections. In 34 states, elections for governor are held only in nonpresidential or midterm election years (for example, 2010). Five other states—Kentucky, Louisiana, Mississippi, New Jersey, and Virginia—elect governors in odd-numbered years. Reformers have successfully argued that presidential and gubernatorial elections should be separated so that state elections are not swamped by the tides of national politics. Still, research shows that voting behavior in states can still be affected when national political issues are stressed during a gubernatorial race.[12] Only 11 states hold gubernatorial elections at the same time as presidential elections: governors in New Hampshire and Vermont are elected for two-year terms in all even-numbered years, and nine states elect governors to four-year terms in presidential election years. (See Figure 25–1 for the party affiliations of the governors who held office in 2011.)

Incumbency, however, is not always an advantage for reelection. Governors receive a great deal of public attention—and in Arizona, Alabama, Arkansas, Connecticut, Illinois, New Jersey, and New York, governors have left office in recent years because of personal scandals. Governors also have to make tough decisions, which can antagonize major interests and arouse public criticism. Sometimes governors refuse to run again because they are so unpopular. In 2004, for instance, 3 of 11 incumbent governors decided not to run for reelection even though they were eligible—all 3 had low public approval ratings.[13]

Republican John Kasich, shown here, defeated incumbent Ted Strickland for governor in Ohio. Kasich's victory was one of many for Republicans in 2010, though nearly every other incumbent governor running for re-election won. ■ *Why do you suppose one party can win so many open-seat contests for governor while incumbents running from either party can still hold onto their offices?*

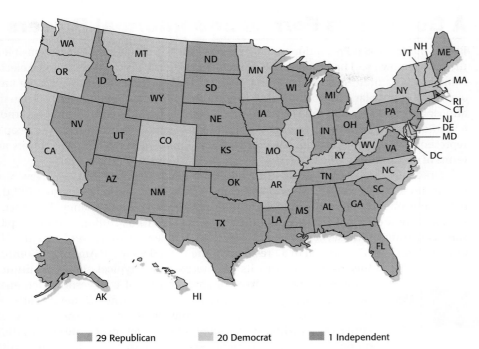

FIGURE 25–1 **Party Control of the Governor's Office, 2011.** After the 2010 elections, Republicans held a majority of governor's offices. ■ *Why does it matter which party controls the governor's office?*

■ 29 Republican　　■ 20 Democrat　　■ 1 Independent

Public anger over taxes and budgets was clearly behind the 2003 California recall election. Gray Davis was widely criticized for having tripled the registration fee, or "car tax," that motorists paid on their vehicles. As future governor Arnold Schwarzenegger said repeatedly in his campaign, "I feel Californians have been punished enough. From the time they get up in the morning and flush the toilet, they're taxed. When they go get a coffee, they're taxed. When they get in their car, they're taxed. When they go to the gas station, they're taxed. When they go to lunch, they're taxed. This goes on all day long. Tax. Tax. Tax. Tax. Tax."[14]

Similarly, in New Jersey in 1993, Governor James Florio was narrowly defeated by Christine Todd Whitman, in part because of a recession, but mostly because Florio's approval ratings had been driven to historic lows after he recommended, and the legislature had enacted, a major tax increase after having promised not to raise taxes during his previous campaign.[15] That tax increase came back to haunt Florio when he ran for U.S. senator in the New Jersey Democratic primary in 2000. His opponent, Jon Corzine, ran ads stressing Florio's role as a big spender and won the primary.

Circumstances often dictate what a governor can or cannot do. The health of the state's economy is a critical factor; incumbents sometimes lose because of a depressed state economy.[16] Their electoral fortunes are also affected by whether voters approve or disapprove of the job the president is doing.[17] The good economic times in the late 1990s plainly helped most governors who ran for reelection; bad economic times hurt them in the early 2000s and again in 2010. Before the 2010 election, Democrats held 29 governorships and Republicans held 21. Following the 2010 election, Republicans emerged with control of 29 governorships, while Democrats held 20. (Rhode Island elected Lincoln Chafee, and Independent who formerly served in the U.S. Senate as a Republican.)

Promises to cut taxes have been effective campaign strategies for several candidates. Many governors in the 1990s, including Christine Todd Whitman of New Jersey and George Pataki of New York, made tax cutting a central part of their campaigns for election and reelection. However, although proposing tax increases can be politically risky, it may not be political suicide for governors.[18] Many other issues can affect governors' prospects for reelection. Governor Jim Doyle of Wisconsin made stem cell research a central issue of his campaign, an issue that has also entered the campaigns in other states.[19] Other issues that have been prominent in recent campaigns are the increasing costs of health insurance, illegal immigration, education quality and funding, and environmental protection.

A Governor's Formal and Informal Powers

LEARNING **OBJECTIVE**

25.2 Identify the formal and informal powers of governors, and assess governors' use of these powers to influence policy.

Before the American Revolution, royal governors were appointed by and responsible to the British crown and had broad powers, including extensive veto power over the elected colonial legislatures. As anti-British sentiment increased, royal governors became more and more unpopular. The position of state governor in the new Republic was born in this atmosphere of distrust. In the 1770s and 1780s, state legislatures elected state governors, a method that ensured that governors would remain under the control of the people's representatives. The early state constitutions also limited governors to few powers and terms of only one or two years.

Gradually, however, the office of governor grew in importance. In New York, the position of chief executive was sufficiently developed and effective by 1787 that it became one of the main models for the proposed U.S. presidency. However, if we compare the formal sources of authority in the U.S. Constitution and in a typical state constitution, we see significant differences. "The executive Power," says the U.S. Constitution, "shall be vested in a President of the United States of America." Compare this statement with its counterpart in a typical state constitution: "The executive department shall consist of a Governor, Lieutenant Governor, Secretary of State, Treasurer, Attorney General," and perhaps other officials. Unlike the president, the governor *shares* executive power with other elected officials. Yet most state constitutions go on to say, "the supreme executive power shall be vested in the Governor, who shall take care that the laws be faithfully executed." Thus, the public looks to the governor as the one state official responsible for executing and enforcing the laws and managing the state administrative system, although the governor's actual authority is often circumscribed.

Governors also enjoy a number of informal powers that stem from such factors as the size of their electoral victory to their job approval rating and how far away the next election is. Political scientists Thad Beyle and Margaret Ferguson have developed a method of measuring both the formal and personal powers of governors, which is reported in Table 25–1.[20] These formal and informal powers are political tools that governors may or may not use to exert real influence in their states. Governors with strong formal powers, for instance, appoint most other top executive officials rather than deal with numerous independently elected executives. Strong governors can succeed themselves for more than one or two terms and have the time to learn their job, carry out major initiatives, and convince legislators that *their* political futures turn in part on cooperation with the governor. Strong governors also have extensive budgetary powers and the ability to veto specific items in bills and budgets passed by the legislature. Governors with high approval ratings from their citizens and/or large electoral mandates also have more potential power than do their less popular counterparts.

A governor's power and influence depend not only on formal authority but also on his or her ability to persuade.[21] This ability, in turn, usually depends on a particular governor's reputation, knowledge of what should be done, and, of course, ability to communicate. Governors usually also benefit from being the leader of their party in the state and from their capacity to draw the attention of state residents through the media, major speeches, and talks around the state. Governors, in short, must have political skills if they are to provide leadership. Yet even the savviest governors need sufficient constitutional authority in order to exert real influence over a state's policies and the administration of its laws.

TABLE

25–1	Rankings of States According to the Formal Powers of the Governor

STRONG

Alaska	Massachusetts
Arkansas	Nebraska
Colorado	New York
Connecticut	Ohio
Iowa	West Virginia

MODERATELY STRONG

Arizona	New Jersey
California	New Mexico
Florida	Oregon
Illinois	Tennessee
Kansas	Utah
Maryland	Vermont
Michigan	Wisconsin
Montana	

MODERATE

Delaware	Mississippi
Georgia	Missouri
Hawaii	New Hampshire
Idaho	North Dakota
Indiana	Pennsylvania
Kentucky	South Dakota
Minnesota	Texas

WEAK

Alabama	Rhode Island
Louisiana	South Carolina
Maine	Virginia
Nevada	Washington
North Carolina	Wyoming
Oklahoma	

SOURCE: Thad Beyle and Margaret Ferguson, "Governors and the Executive Branch" in Virginia Gray and Russell L. Hanson, eds., *Politics in the American States: A Comparative Analysis*, 9th ed (2008).

Most governors have the following constitutional authority:

- To make appointments
- To prepare the state budget
- To veto legislation and to exercise an item veto over appropriations measures
- To issue executive orders
- To command the state National Guard
- To pardon or grant clemency
- To help establish the legislature's agenda

We will next take a closer look at each of these.

Appointive Power

Perhaps a governor's most important job is to recruit talented leaders and managers to head the state's departments, commissions, and agencies.[22] Through recruitment of effective people and prudent delegation of responsibilities to them, a governor can provide direction for the state government.

In most states, the governor is one executive among many, with only limited authority over elected officials, whom the governor can neither appoint nor dismiss. Moreover, if these officials are from a different political party than the governor, they are likely to oppose the governor's recommendations. Governors have greater, yet still limited, power over officials they appoint. Some governors appoint hundreds of key officials; others, such as those in Mississippi, South Carolina, and Texas, have severe restrictions on their appointive power. Moreover, in most states, governors must share their appointive power with the state senate and may remove people only when they have violated the law or failed in their legal duties. State administrators whose programs are supported by federal funds also have a measure of independence from the governor.

Along with appointive power comes a host of challenges. First, salaries for cabinet and agency administrators are modest in many states, especially in the smaller ones, and it is often hard to get candidates to leave better-paying jobs in private industry. Second, powerful politicians may demand that their friends be appointed to certain top posts, and they may threaten to be uncooperative if the governor does not go along with their "suggestions." Finally, relatively high turnover in many state positions often hampers a governor's efforts to carry out programs.

Fiscal and Budgetary Power

A governor's financial planning and budgetary powers are key weapons in getting programs passed. Purchasing, budgeting, and personnel matters are centralized under the governor. When implemented by a strong staff and backed by a strong political base, a governor's fiscal powers are extremely important.

In nearly all states, the governor has responsibility for preparing a budget and presenting it to the state legislature. This takes place every year in 29 states and every second year in 21 states.[23] The art of budget making includes assessing requests from various departments and agencies and balancing them against available resources. Governors and their staffs have to calculate the costs of existing and newly proposed programs and weigh those costs against estimated revenues for the state.

The budget process is similar in most states. In May and June, the governor's budget office, which is called different things in different states, including Office of Management and Budget or Department of Administration, sends request forms to the various executive agencies. From July to October, the agencies complete their detailed requests and send them back for consideration. Their requests are typically higher than the governor's proposed guidelines. The governor's budget chief evaluates all requests, sometimes holds internal administrative hearings, and then makes recommendations to the governor. Finally, the governor presents the recommendations to the legislature at the beginning of the new year. Governors frequently use their annual State of the State Address to present these recommendations and continue to promote them during speeches given throughout the budget process.

Although the governor and chief budget officials may appear to control the budgetary process, considerable budgeting influence remains in the hands of the executive branch agencies. Further, a governor's budget reflects to a very high degree budgetary decisions made throughout the years as well as other factors not easily controlled by governors in the short run. For instance, spending on health care is driven by long-standing eligibility policies, economic cycles that affect how many people qualify for health care, and the rising costs of health care. Spending on prisons is greatly affected by past sentencing practices, among other things. Also, some spending is mandated by the federal government, such as state "matching" dollars in support of federal grants. In summary, governors usually can only tinker with or adjust expenditures at the edges of the overall budget. For example, as much as 80 percent of California's state budget is dictated by factors beyond the governor's control.

The final budget document is presented to the legislature for adoption as an *appropriations measure.* State monies cannot be spent without legislative appropriations. Legislators can, and usually do, make a number of alterations in a governor's budget. Because of this, governors are also forced to anticipate the preferences of each legislative chamber when proposing a budget, or they risk the legislature simply ignoring them and writing their own budget from scratch. Nonetheless, a governor who uses this budget proposal power effectively has an important asset.

In 2007, states spent about 36 percent of their budgets on education, including K–12 schools and higher education institutions. Public welfare, health care, and hospital spending accounted for another 35 percent. Highway spending absorbed another 7 percent of state budgets, and spending on police and corrections took up slightly more than 4 percent. The remaining portion of state spending went to a wide variety of smaller items, such as state parks and recreation facilities, environmental programs, libraries, public health, and general aid to local governments. (Note that these figures represent state spending only; see Chapter 29 for more on state and local spending.)

To pay for these many activities, about half of a state's revenue comes from taxes (approximately 24 percent from sales taxes, 18 percent from personal income taxes, and 3.7 percent from corporate income taxes), while another 30 percent comes from the federal government. The remaining 19 percent comes from fees, bonds, and a variety of other state revenue sources. (See Chapter 29 for more on state and local revenue sources.) When state revenues do not match expenses, governors have to cut or delay programs because every state is required to balance its budget, and states cannot print money as the federal government can.

Veto Power

veto
Rejection by a president or governor of legislation passed by a legislature.

line item veto
The right of an executive to veto parts of a bill approved by a legislature without having to veto the entire bill.

reduction veto
The power of governors in a few states to reduce a particular appropriation.

amendatory veto
The power of governors in a few states to return a bill to the legislature with suggested language changes, conditions, or amendments. Legislators then decide either to accept the governor's recommendations or to pass the bill in its original form over the veto.

Among the most useful gubernatorial powers is the **veto,** the power to reject legislative bills, especially appropriations measures. Michigan Governor Jennifer Granholm vetoed more than 30 bills in her first 18 months in office, including one that would have banned late-term abortions, another that would have created a process for specialty license plates, and another that would have given suburbs more control over the Detroit Water and Sewer Board. Her veto activity led the *Detroit Free Press* to title a story on her tenure, "Granholm Stars in Her Own 'Kill Bill.'"[24]

All state constitutions give governors some veto authority, but in 43 states, governors have the **line item veto,** which permits them to veto individual items in an appropriations bill while signing the remainder of the bill into law. Thus, they can influence the flow of funds to the executive departments and thereby attempt to control their activities. In May 2006, for example, Florida Governor Jeb Bush vetoed $448.7 million from the state's $74 billion budget.[25]

In 12 states, a governor can reduce particular appropriations; this power is called the **reduction veto.** In ten states, governors can exercise what is called an **amendatory veto,** which allows the governor to return a bill to the state legislature with suggested language changes, conditions, or amendments.[26] In this last case, legislators must decide to accept the governor's recommendations or approve the bill in its original form, which in some cases requires a majority vote and in other cases, a three-fifths or super-majority vote.

Governors in Wisconsin have enjoyed particularly powerful veto powers, which at various times have allowed them to delete individual words, phrases, letters, or numbers from a bill allowing them to completely change the bill's meaning. Because it allows governors to delete words and "stitch together" the remaining parts to form a new bill, this power has recently been referred to as the "Frankenstein" veto. However, its overuse has occasionally provoked a backlash among voters. (The *You Will Decide* box on the following page discusses the line item veto further.)

State legislatures can override a governor's veto; in most states, it takes a two-thirds majority of both legislative chambers. Some governors, such as Wisconsin's Tommy Thompson, have vetoed thousands of legislative measures. New York Governor George Pataki vetoed 1,379 provisions the legislature sent him in 1998.[27] Governors on average veto around 4 percent of the bills sent to them, but only approximately 2 percent of gubernatorial vetoes are overridden by legislatures.[28] Most governors believe the veto power should be used sparingly. Indeed, some observers think too-frequent use of the veto is a sign of gubernatorial weakness because an effective governor usually wins battles through negotiations rather than by confronting state legislators.[29]

Legislators in several states have established a *veto session*—a short session following adjournment—so that they can reconsider any measures vetoed by their governor. This is clearly an effort to assert the legislature's check-and-balance authority in relationship to the governor. Most states using veto sessions have legislatures that meet for a limited time; in full-time legislatures, a veto session would be unnecessary.

Executive Orders

One long-standing power of governors is their authority to issue **executive orders,** which have the force of law. Even though executive orders differ from statutes or formal acts passed by the legislature, they have almost the same binding effect. Depending on the state, governors get their authority to issue executive orders from implied powers as chief executive, from specific constitutional grants, or from delegations of authority by their state legislatures. Executive orders supplementing a law are both more detailed and more important than the general guidelines contained in legislation. Governors have issued executive orders during such emergencies as natural disasters and energy crises, in compliance with federal rules and regulations, and to create advisory commissions. However, governors can also use executive orders to make policy. Governor Arnold Schwarzenegger of California, for example, used executive orders in 2006 to promote the use of biofuels, to set up a system to identify high-risk sex offenders, and to promote state contracts with small businesses. State legislators are sometimes angered by sweeping executive orders. They insist that they, not the governor or the courts, should be the primary lawmakers in a state.

Governors do not always have to issue executive orders to change the interpretation of state laws, however. Even though he opposed same-sex marriages, Governor Mitt Romney of Massachusetts reminded local officials in 2004 that they had to follow the state's Supreme Judicial Court decision allowing same-sex marriage of state residents. At the same time, however, he also said he intended to use a 1913 law to prohibit the marriage of same-sex couples from other states. Such marriages would be null and void under his interpretation, he argued, thereby preventing Massachusetts from drawing same-sex couples from across the United States.[30]

Commander in Chief of the National Guard

Emergencies can enhance the authority of an executive because they call for decisive action. As commander in chief of the state's National Guard when it is not in federal service, a governor may use this force when local authorities are inadequate—in case of

executive order
A directive issued by a president or governor that has the force of law.

DECIDE Should Governors Have an Item Veto?

The item veto, which is sometimes called the line item veto, permits governors to nullify parts or items of an appropriations bill without vetoing the entire bill. The legislature may override item vetoes, usually by a supermajority vote. The item veto is available in 43 states, although the provisions vary. Some states only permit governors to veto a specific dollar amount and any language directly associated with that amount, such as "$20,000,000, to be spent by Agency X on construction of a bridge on Highway Y in Town Z." Some states give governors more expansive authority. Governors can nullify not only entire items but also parts of items, including language describing the object and purpose of the expenditure. For instance, the governor could strike out "of a bridge" from the example, or "in Town Z," or every word after "Agency X," all of which would give the governor greater flexibility in using the money appropriated to Agency X.

The main impetus behind the basic item veto was to give governors the power to curtail legislative "pork barrel"

spending—spending on items targeted at individual districts, such as a new public park, a specific road expansion, or a new building at a public university. Such spending items are often bundled together into a single bill. Each item typically benefits only a small minority of state residents and is supported by only a few legislators, but when all the items are bound together, they may secure support from a majority of legislators as enough legislators get a piece of the pie. Of course, what is wasteful "pork barrel" spending to one person is an essential project to another. The criticism against such legislative practices is that the state may end up spending a great deal of money on items that help a small number of people but, from the state perspective, are not worth the costs.

What do you think? Should governors have an item veto? What are the arguments for or against it?

THINKING IT THROUGH

One argument against item vetoes is that they do not accomplish their goals. Research on the effects of item vetoes is inconclusive. They are sometimes associated with lower spending in states, but it is unclear whether the item vetoes are the cause. Most studies find that different states use them at different rates. They are most common in states where the governor faces a legislature controlled by a different political party, suggesting a partisan bias in how governors apply the item veto. They also frequently amount to a very small portion of the state's budget, suggesting that governors use them more for their symbolic value rather than to actually affect state spending.

Another argument against providing item veto authority applies to its expanded versions. Such item vetoes can give enormous, largely unchecked, positive legislative power to the governor. If the governor can nullify language within the bill, not only entire appropriation items (money amounts plus language describing the item), he or she can actually create new legislation without approval from the legislature. As discussed, Wisconsin governors have been doing this sort of "Frankenstein vetoing" for years.

Some argue, in response, that expansive item vetoes are needed to check legislatures, which are including more and more legislation in appropriations bills. Legislatures do this because appropriations bills must eventually be passed, and so they include legislation—sometimes having little to do with spending—that the governor would veto if it stood alone. Expansive item vetoes allow governors to check this effort to push through legislation on the back of the appropriation bills.

Critical Thinking Questions

1. Should all governors have item veto authority? If so, how extensive should the power be—should it permit the item veto to be used in flexible, creative ways, including the striking out of language, not only entire "items"?

2. Your answer to that question probably depends on your answer to another: What is more problematic, executive dominance or legislative dominance? Why?

riots, floods, and other catastrophes. The National Guard played a role in the aftermath of floods in midwestern states, riots and earthquakes in California, fires in Florida, and hurricanes throughout the southeastern states. National Guard troops from Louisiana and Mississippi—joined by troops from 40 other states—were mobilized for search and rescue operations after the devastation and flooding produced by Hurricane Katrina in the Gulf Coast in the summer of 2005.[31]

Congress provides most of the money to operate the National Guard. This fact, along with the supremacy clause of the U.S. Constitution, gives Congress and the president the power to take charge of a state's National Guard even against the wishes of a governor. In 1990, the Supreme Court ruled unanimously that Congress can authorize the president to call National Guard units to active duty and send them outside the United States despite the objections of the governors, several of whom had tried to keep President Ronald Reagan from calling their respective National Guards to training exercises in Honduras.[32] President George W. Bush deployed National Guard troops in Iraq and Afghanistan. More than 250,000 National Guard troops have seen action in these two wars—some serving tours of duty as long as 22 months.[33] States could, if they wished, provide and maintain from their own funds a defense force exempt from being drafted into the armed forces of the United States, but none has done so.

One of the issues surrounding Hurricane Katrina was whether the governor of Louisiana or the president had the authority to direct Louisiana's National Guard response to the disaster. President Bush sought control, but then Democratic Governor Kathleen Blanco resisted. In response, in 2007, Congress altered the 200-year-old Insurrection Act to allow the president to take control of the National Guard for domestic disasters.[34]

Pardon Power

In two-thirds of the states, governors have exclusive and unconditional authority to pardon violators of state law. In the other states, they share this duty with a pardoning board.[35] Except in cases of impeachment or certain specified crimes, the governor may pardon the offender, commute a sentence by reducing it, or grant a reprieve by delaying the punishment. The governor is normally assisted by pardon attorneys or pardon boards that hold hearings and determine whether there are sufficient reasons for a pardon.

Because pardons are usually politically unpopular, some governors issue them only during their final days in office. A Tennessee governor, Ray Blanton (1975–1979), caused considerable controversy and sparked a federal investigation when he pardoned or paroled several dozen convicts just before leaving office in 1979. Critics charged that some of these convicts allegedly "purchased" their releases. Blanton's misuse of his pardon powers created such outrage that his elected successor, Lamar Alexander, was sworn in early and the locks to the governor's office were quickly changed so that Blanton was not able to enter, let alone grant any additional pardons.[36] Yet most pardons are uncontroversial because governors typically administer them with appropriate care.

Similar to a governor's pardon power is the authority to grant a stay of execution in death penalty cases. This is one of the most controversial aspects of executive power in states that permit the death penalty.[37] We opened this chapter with an account of former Illinois Governor George Ryan's use of this power regarding death penalty cases in his state. No other governor has adopted a moratorium, and Texas Governor George W. Bush allowed more than 130 executions during his time in office.

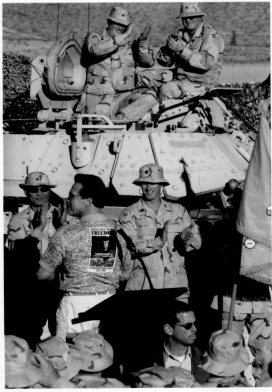

As commander in chief of the state's National Guard when it is not in federal service, a governor may use this force to handle state emergencies such as fires, floods, earthquakes, and other disasters. Here, Governor Arnold Schwarzenegger provides a morale boost for a California National Guard unit. ■ *How does control over the National Guard reflect the distribution of power in federalism?*

Policy-Making Influence

Although governors' formal powers vary widely from state to state, to change public policies, all governors face the challenge of securing the cooperation of many other people and institutions. To enact new legislation, governors may need to bargain with top legislative leaders (often of the opposite party), interest group representatives, local governments (which often lobby for or against legislation and budgets), and the state's bureaucracy (whose expertise is sometimes important in getting legislative support). In some cases, governors need to negotiate with federal agencies for a "waiver," an agreement by a federal agency to permit a state to implement a state law that would otherwise conflict with federal law. Governors must use their formal powers, political strengths, and personal skills to persuade these and other largely independent people and institutions to do what the governor needs them to do, usually by making it clear to such people that it is in their own political interest to do so.

Most governors have many tools at hand in their efforts to persuade. One is their opportunity to focus the public's attention on particular issues, problems, or policy proposals. They can attract more public attention to their views than any single legislator can, although even governors do not have many opportunities to get their message across to the public. Perhaps the most important chances they get are the annual State of the State messages, which they generally deliver to legislatures in the first months of each year. These messages usually highlight certain problems or issues, outline major policy proposals, and sketch the general shape of the executive budget. The effectiveness of such speeches depends not only on the governor's rhetorical skills but also on his or her popularity and reputation for pushing hard and persistently for his or her proposals. It is also essential that the governor's themes resonate with other state officials' views of what is feasible and needed for the times, particularly the current economy and the state's fiscal conditions. All of these speeches given by governors since 2000 are available online at http://www.stateline.org/live/resources/State+Speeches.

The governor's role as party leader may also add to his or her effectiveness in changing policy. Governors can be helpful in raising campaign contributions for state party organizations as well as for state legislators within their own party, usually by giving speeches at major fund-raisers. This kind of help is greatly appreciated and remembered by legislators, who have a much harder time raising large campaign chests because of their lower visibility and more localized networks of supporters. Most legislators also want to help make a governor of their own party successful. Not only are they likely to agree with the governor on many issues, but they may feel that their future reelection chances will be enhanced by a popular governor on their party's ticket.

However, the success of a purely partisan strategy depends in part on whether state legislatures are strongly partisan. In many states, winning legislative coalitions often include members of both political parties. This fluidity of legislative coalitions in states means that successful governors typically must maintain good relationships with many legislators, even those of the opposing party, and thus keep open the possibility of building bipartisan coalitions. Governors new to state politics often learn this lesson the hard way. After his first year in office—a year when he took a very confrontational approach to dealing with legislators—California Governor Arnold Schwarzenegger switched to a more accommodating political style after learning how poorly aggressive tactics worked in state politics:

> I have absorbed my defeat and I have learned my lesson. And the people, who always have the last word, sent a clear message—cut the warfare, cool the rhetoric, find common ground, and fix the problems together. So to my fellow Californians, I say—message received.[38]

Persuasion is time-consuming for governors, so another critical element of policy leadership is their management of time. Governors find it easy to become preoccupied with daily housekeeping tasks and public appearances. Although many governors come to office hoping to introduce new programs and reforms, they often spend most of their time raising money just to keep current programs operating. Some governors are thus viewed as mere "budget balancers" rather than as leaders or shapers of a state's future. Former Vermont Governor Madeleine Kunin recalls that she fixed problems as they happened and yet simultaneously had to define her policy vision for the future. "Finding the time, energy, and perspective to carry out a dual strategy was to be the physical and mental challenge of governing."[39]

Because many governors come to office with impressive legislative and administrative experience, they are more likely to be real executive heads of government, not mere figureheads. Some have initiated creative efforts to expand health insurance coverage, bring more high-technology businesses into their states, increase the quality and accountability of public schools, and make state and local tax systems fairer and more dependable sources of public revenues. Because states are now playing a larger role in many areas of domestic policy in the United States, the policy-making capacities of governors are clearly important to democratic governance in U.S. government as a whole.

Governors and Media Relations

Governors often attempt to shape their influence through aggressive media outreach. Many worked effectively with the media during their gubernatorial campaign and therefore understand their potential. Once in office, however, governors are thrust into a defensive role. Instead of running aggressive advertisements for their campaign, they are now under the media's magnifying glass, subject to scrutiny and investigation by reporters. They are quickly evaluated in light of their campaign promises and in comparison with previous governors.[40]

Past governors have been very aware of the media, with a handful having professional backgrounds in reporting or public relations. For example, former Governors Tom McCall of Oregon and Thomas Kean of New Jersey both had prior experience in public

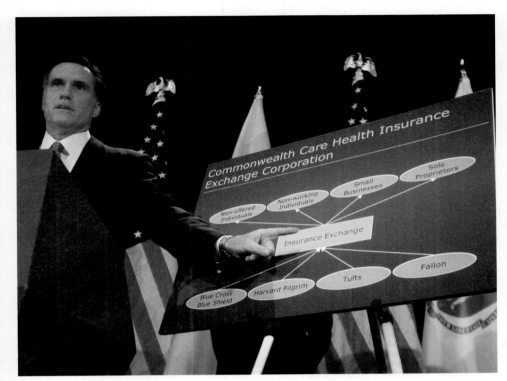

The national health care reform adopted by Congress in 2010 shared many similarities with the state plan Republican Governor Mitt Romney, pictured here, signed into law in Massachusetts in 2006. Those similarities will likely be a political issue if Romney decides to run for president in 2012. ■ *What are the pros and cons of the national government using state policies as blueprints for national policies?*

relations positions—McCall as a journalist and radio announcer and Kean as a state campaign chair for President Ford and a television reporter during the Reagan campaign. Governor Kean notes the importance of communication with the media: "The most important power the governor has is the power of communicating. If that isn't done properly, you lose your power very fast."[41]

Not all governors are effective in dealing with the media, nor do they necessarily enjoy it. As Minnesota's former Governor Jesse Ventura says of the media: "The American media are suffering from very serious problems, and now I've seen them firsthand. They have the most twisted set of biases I've ever seen. As their whipping-boy-of-choice, I've been in a unique position to see what the media have become. There are a few honorable exceptions, but for the most part, they're corrupt, shameless, and irresponsible as hell."[42]

Each governor tends to have a personal style in dealing with the media. Some are very vocal, preferring to host daily radio or television talk shows, while others prefer to avoid the spotlight unless necessary. Governors sometimes request special time on television to explain and make an argument for policy changes. Others become visible by attending community functions, such as building dedications or opening ceremonies. It is especially important for governors to be publicly active as a calming influence during an emergency situation. During a disaster, such as an earthquake, hurricane, or terrorist action, governors have the ability to call out the National Guard and organize official aid groups. To visit, show concern for, and help ameliorate the suffering of involved families can do wonders for a governor's public opinion ratings. Governors must face public scrutiny, yet they can use the media to set and gain support for their agendas.[43]

On April 20, 2010, an explosion on the Deepwater Horizon drilling rig killed 11 workers and triggered a massive oil spill in the Gulf of Mexico. Officials from all levels of government responded, including Louisiana Governor Bobby Jindal, pictured here speaking to local fisherman impacted by the spill. ■ *What role should the local, state, and federal governments have in dealing with environmental disasters? Who should pay the costs of such efforts? Who should make the decisions about what to do?*

The Job of the Governor: Managing the State

LEARNING **OBJECTIVE**

25.3 Evaluate the effectiveness of governors as managers of the state's executive branch.

Governors and their senior staffs are also responsible for managing their state's executive branch, whether by providing strategic planning and vision, initiating policy, settling disputes among different agencies, promoting the state (attracting tourism, exports, and investment), recruiting top state administrative and judicial officials, developing the budget, pulling in federal dollars, or negotiating with the federal government and with nearby states.

Much recent federal legislation, which turns programs over to the states, specifically designates the governor as the chief planning and administrative officer. This role has given governors both more flexibility and more headaches. On one hand, governors can now dispense federal funds as a form of patronage, supporting services and programs for influential professional and local communities. On the other hand, this new intergovernmental relations role requires more time, more staff, and constant negotiations both with the "feds" and with local interest group leaders vying for money or services.

Some reformers have suggested that all state agencies should be accountable to the governor all the time, but others believe that politics should be kept out of the day-to-day operations of a state agency. For example, how much influence should a governor have over the running of the department of corrections in a state? Should public agencies respond to fluctuations in public opinion or to a governor's political mood? Which policy decisions should be made by professionals and experts, and which should be controlled by elected officials or by partisan appointees?

Modernizing State Administrations

Governors in recent years have had more managerial control over their states as a result of the use of modern management techniques: strategic planning, systems analysis, performance measurement and management, customer focus, and sophisticated information technology and budgeting systems. The Pew Center on the States Government Performance Project, mentioned in Chapter 21, provides performance grades for state governments (http://www.pewcenteronthestates.org/gpp_report_card.aspx).[44]

In urban states with competitive party systems, such as New York, Illinois, New Jersey, Pennsylvania, Washington, and California, governors have considerable formal constitutional authority to organize their administrations as they see fit. Even in more rural states, such as South Dakota, scores of agencies have been consolidated into a few comprehensive units as the result of executive orders from the governors.

A few years ago, in the wake of highly publicized scandals, the South Carolina legislature agreed to abolish 75 state boards, folding them into 17 larger executive agencies. This restructuring also gave the governor the authority to hire and fire the directors of most of these agencies.[45] In 2003, Texas enacted a plan to replace 11 health and human services agencies with four departments in order to increase efficiency and improve services.[46]

During the past several decades, various reformers have urged that the governor be made the true manager of the executive branch, by consolidating agencies into a smaller number of more tightly controlled departments, giving the governor greater power to hire and fire senior executives, modernizing state government through better information technology, relying more on private sector contractors to carry out functions previously performed by public agencies, and using performance measures to assess how well contractors and public agencies are achieving their major goals.

However, in some states, reorganization commissions have submitted reports that were filed away and forgotten. Groups that profit from the existing structure will resist change, as will officials who fear loss of jobs or prestige. Also, legislators are sometimes reluctant to approve recommendations that may make a governor too powerful.

Many critics oppose not so much the idea of reorganization as the basic principle of strengthening executive power and responsibility, which has dominated the reorganization movement. Often, they say, there is little evidence to support the adoption of these reforms, and there is a real danger that reorganizers are overlooking basic values in their concern with saving money. Intent on efficiency and economy, reformers often fail to foresee the risks in creating a powerful chief executive where no effective party or legislative opposition exists to keep a strong governor in check.

Effects of Reorganization

Although states have realized large savings through centralized purchasing and modern money management practices, it is difficult to measure the results of consolidating departments, strengthening the governor's control over the executive branch, or establishing an ombudsman office to handle citizen complaints. However, the best-governed states do seem to be those in which the administrative structure has been closely integrated under the governor.

Overall, formal reorganization is not the only way states modify and modernize their governmental structures. Often they change in stages, copying innovations from other states. Certain states, in fact, serve as exporters of innovations. So does the federal government. When the federal government created the Department of Housing and Urban Development, states responded by creating similar departments; when the federal government established the Department of Transportation, so did several of the states; and when the federal government formed special White House-level office for trade, many governors set up their own offices for trade and export responsibilities.

In recent decades, many governors have experimented with management reforms. Mario Cuomo of New York and Pete Wilson of California tried ideas from the private sector, including total quality management (TQM) and performance-based pay initiatives, although public employee labor unions resisted these reforms at the time.[47] More recently, governors have attempted to implement reforms that make state government more accountable on the basis of performance on measurable goals. These reforms typically give state administrators greater flexibility in *how* they manage programs, while they collect more data on the outcomes of public programs and hold the managers accountable for achieving results.[48] However, many agencies have a hard time getting good and timely measures of outcomes or determining precisely how much of an effect their programs have on outcomes compared with the influences of other factors. For instance, discerning the effects of a job training program on employment, distinct from the effects of the economy and demographic changes, is no simple matter.

"Although the analogy between a governor and a private sector chief executive is apt," writes political scientist Thad Beyle, "governors have a distance to go before possessing comparable power of appointment and removal."[49] Many governors do not have the flexibility in hiring and firing personnel that business executives have, and they must share control with various boards, commissions, and elected officials.

In summary, governors can be influential in leading certain reforms and introducing management improvements, but they are rarely as influential and as effective as most citizens assume is the case. All kinds of constitutional, legal, and political restraints put brakes on their attempts to bring about fundamental change. Still, in good economic times, governors are generally able to begin new programs and improve the performance of existing state operations.

Assisting the Governor: State Executive Officials

LEARNING **OBJECTIVE**

25.4 Outline duties and powers of other top executive officials in state government.

Other executive officials elected by the people in most states include the lieutenant governor, secretary of state, attorney general, and treasurer. These offices each have important duties and powers and often constitute rungs on the ladder of political ambition. Many candidates for governor first held one of these other offices in their state. (See Table 25–2 for an inventory of state executive officials.)

Lieutenant Governor

Forty-two states have a lieutenant governor, a post similar to vice president at the national level. In nearly half the states, the lieutenant governor is elected on the same ticket as the

TABLE

25–2	State Executive Officials

Position	Role	Prominence	How Acquired
Lieutenant Governor	Second in command to the governor	Present in 42 states	By popular election in all states
Attorney General	Represents the state before the courts	Present in all 50 states	By appointment in 5 states By popular election in 43 states Elected by the legislature in 2 states
Secretary of State	Publishes the laws; oversees state elections	Present in 47 states	By appointment in 9 states By popular election in 35 states Elected by the legislature in 3 states
Treasurer	Guardian of the state's money	Present in 46 states	By appointment in 7 states By popular election in 35 states Elected by the legislature in 4 states

■ *What is the most common means for selecting executive officials across the states? Why do you suppose that is?*

governor, and in those states, the job is indeed like that of the vice president—the job and its influence depend very much on the discretion of the governor. In 26 states, the lieutenant governor presides over the state senate. The lieutenant governor becomes governor or acting governor in case of the death, disability, resignation, or absence of the governor from the state. Doubtless for this reason, more governors have sprung from this office than from other statewide elective offices. For example, David Paterson assumed the governorship in New York after Governor Eliot Spitzer resigned in the wake of a scandal in 2008.

In states where the governor and lieutenant governor are elected on the same ticket, the lieutenant governor is likely to be given some significant responsibilities. Still, many lieutenant governors have no statutory duties, and in some states, being lieutenant governor is actually a part-time job. Where the lieutenant governor is elected independently of the governor, he or she can sometimes be a member of the opposition party and become a thorn in the side of the chief executive. This is particularly a problem in a state such as Texas, where the state constitution gives the lieutenant governor even greater budgetary powers than the governor.[50]

Although the position of lieutenant governor has worked well in some states, the view persists that lieutenant governors are often in search of job assignments that make them look important. The staffs and cabinets currently growing up around governors put the governor's chief of staff in a position of greater influence than most lieutenant governors. Moreover, many candidates for lieutenant governor seek the post for the name recognition and statewide experience to advance their political careers. In summary, the value to the state of the often-obscure office of lieutenant governor is debatable.[51] You can learn more about the office of lieutenant governor at the National Lieutenant Governors Association Web site at http://www.nlga.us/.

Attorney General

The attorney general—the state's chief lawyer—gives advice to state officials, represents the state before the courts, and in some states, supervises local prosecutors. Some state attorneys general have authority over local prosecutors, and may prosecute cases on their own initiative, although in most states, criminal prosecution remains under the control of the local county prosecutor. Attorneys general have the authority to make sure the state's laws are implemented properly. They work in narcotics enforcement, investigate illegal activities, and often concentrate on laws that protect consumers, the environment, and public safety. They can also issue advisory opinions to state and local officials, and in many cases, review legislation.

In many states, attorneys general have taken the lead as champions of the consumer and protectors of the environment. They often have their own legislative agendas, separate from the governor's. In 1998, 46 state attorneys general settled their lawsuits against the tobacco companies and produced "a new regime of tobacco control," one that required the companies to pay more than $240 million to state governments and the National Association

For the People

GOVERNMENT'S GREATEST ENDEAVORS

Making Government More Ethical

Since the Progressive Era of the 1890s, ethics and corruption in government have been a major political issue. States have made progress throughout the years, but much work remains. Governors are entrusted by voters with the responsibility of running their states honestly and fairly. Earning that trust has been getting harder for governors as continued scandals fuel the concerns of an increasingly skeptical public. In just the last few years, sitting or former governors in South Carolina, New York, Illinois, and North Carolina have faced serious charges regarding legal and ethical violations. A group calling itself Citizens for Responsibility and Ethics in Washington has produced what it calls a report on America's Worst Governors (http://www.citizensforethics.org/worst governors). The group claims to base its evaluations on how well governors abide by their states' ethics, campaign finance, and transparency in government laws.

How can governors respond? Beverly Perdue, the current governor of North Carolina, offers one example. While her predecessor was still being investigated for possible federal corruption charges, Perdue used her

power to issue executive orders to mandate stronger ethics standards for top state officials. Such officials will face longer waiting periods after leaving their posts before they can work as a lobbyist or take a job with a firm their agency regulated. She also requires anyone seeking appointment to a state commission or board to disclose conflicts of interest, previous criminal record, tax problems, or formal grievances filed against them. Perdue was quoted as saying, "The people of North Carolina should rightfully expect and deserve integrity from their public servants."*

Many governors have enacted similar reforms in recent years, hoping to restore

Beverly Purdue, governor of North Carolina.

voter confidence in the governorship regardless of who actually governs. Although efforts like this will not fully eliminate corruption and ethical lapses, they do place the question of ethics higher on a state's agenda. As Governor Perdue's comments suggest, holding our governors and other top officials to the highest ethical standards helps to ensure that our leaders will be guided by what their voters value.

CRITICAL THINKING QUESTIONS

1. What can governors do to help instill a sense of trust in state governments among their citizens?

2. Should governors focus their ethics reform efforts only on the executive branch? What complications arise if governors try to set ethical guidelines for legislators, or vice versa?

3. The framers of the U.S. Constitution were skeptical of government having too much power, but they were also skeptical of too much direct involvement by citizens. How might these considerations affect how open the operations of government should be to public scrutiny?

---

* Perdue was quoted in a news story posted by Cullen Browder, a reporter for WRAL TV in North Carolina, titled "Perdue Tightens Up State Ethics Rules," http://www.wral .com/news/local/politics/story/7360866/.

---

of Attorneys General (http://www.naag.org/) and that imposed new restrictions on the advertising and marketing of tobacco.[52] The lawsuits were largely based on claims that smoking increased the costs of state Medicaid programs. Attorneys general also waged antitrust investigations against corporations such as Microsoft. In California, following allegations of overcharging customers, Attorney General Bill Lockyer filed complaints against four major power companies.[53] New York State's former attorney general, Eliot Spitzer, became a nationally recognized figure through his investigations of Wall Street fraud, Internet fraud, computer chip price fixing, insurance fraud, environmental damages, and other "white collar" crimes, and he used that visibility to build a highly successful campaign for governor in 2006—although he resigned in the wake of his own scandal a year after taking office.[54]

Secretary of State

The secretary of state publishes the laws, supervises elections, licenses professionals, and issues certificates of incorporation. In some states, the secretary issues automobile licenses and registers corporate securities. In states without a Secretary of State these duties are filled by the Lieutenant Governor or some other official. Voters in 35 states elect secretaries of state. In nine states, governors appoint people to this position. In three states, secretaries of state are elected by the legislature. And three states do not have this position at all.

Although all secretaries of state have some duty to oversee state elections, their responsibilities differ greatly from state to state. However, nearly all are implementing the 2002 federal Help America Vote Act, which gave states funding to replace outdated voting equipment and improve the accuracy and accountability of election administration.

Nearly all also share a commitment to increasing voter education and turnout. In 1998, the National Association of Secretaries of State (http://www.nass.org/) launched the "New Millennium Project" to encourage greater participation among young citizens.

Treasurer and Auditor

The treasurer is the guardian of the state's money. Although in some states the job is largely ministerial, state treasurers generally have the responsibility of ensuring that cash is available to meet the obligations of the state and that all available funds are invested to maximize interest return. Treasurers are elected by popular vote in 35 states, elected by the legislature in 4 states, and appointed in 7 states. You can learn more from the National Association of State Treasurers at http://www.nast.net/.

The auditor in most states has two major jobs: to authorize payments from the state treasury and to make periodic audits of officials who handle state money. In Montana, the state auditor serves as insurance commissioner. Before money can be spent, the auditor must sign a *warrant* certifying that the expenditure is authorized by law and that the money is available in the treasury. This job is more accurately called the *preaudit* and is increasingly being assigned to a comptroller appointed by and responsible to the governor. Auditing *after* money has been spent, however, is a job most observers believe should be given to an officer responsible to the legislature. Even advocates of much more centralized administrations believe that the auditor should not be responsible to the governor; however, most auditors are appointed, although in 18 states, they are elected. Learn more online at the National Association of State Auditors, Comptrollers, and Treasurers at http://www.nasact.org/.

Other Officials

Such positions as superintendent of public education, agriculture commissioner, public utilities commissioner, comptroller, and insurance commissioner are less likely to be elected than treasurers or auditors. Putting positions like these on the ballot results in a longer ballot, and voters sometimes pay little attention to them. The proliferation of elected officials also makes it more difficult for governors to manage and lead state government.

As part of the trend toward integrated administration, the duties of elected state officials have generally been limited to those specified in the state constitution. Some important functions have been given to officials appointed by the governor. In many states, the budget director appointed by the governor has a more important role than the elected treasurer or secretary of state. Yet elected officers can often control patronage, attract a following, and thus develop a political base from which to attack the governor's program and administration.

Sometimes progressive and controversial initiatives in state governments come from elected officials. An attorney general in Texas helped design and pass the Texas Open Records Act, one of the broadest and most strictly enforced freedom-of-information statutes in the country. A secretary of state in Massachusetts modernized election laws, helped enact campaign finance laws, and championed conflict-of-interest reforms. A state treasurer in Colorado battled to transfer some of his state's revenue deposits from a few large Denver banks to smaller banks around the state and devised incentives for these banks to lend money to students and small businesses and to support low-income housing and family farms.

Governors Today: Challenges and Rewards

LEARNING **OBJECTIVE**
25.5 Evaluate the challenges and rewards for governors today.

Although the constitutional powers of governors vary from state to state, U.S. citizens evaluate and rate their governors using many of the same criteria they apply to rating presidents.[55] Lamar Alexander, former governor of Tennessee, said a governor needs to "see the state's few most urgent needs, develop strategies to address them, and persuade at least half the people that he or she is right."[56]

Today, a governor is expected to be, among other things, the state's chief policy maker, shaper of the state budget, savvy political party leader, chief recruiter of the best available advisers and administrators, and inspiring renewer of confidence in state

By the People

Who Is Governing Your School?

One of the major areas of policy responsibility for governors is public higher education. In administering the state's higher education system, virtually every governor works with one or more university board or commission. Sometimes each individual campus has a governing board, and sometimes, multiple campuses are part of a system under a single board. Sometimes the members of these boards are appointed, and sometimes, they are elected. In many states, there is a student representative that serves on the board. Find out how your university is governed and who the board members are. In particular, identify whether they have a student member, how the student member is selected, and whether student members have full voting rights.

What issues is your school's governing board currently considering, and do they reflect the priorities of the students? You could organize a forum on campus and invite one or more current board members to field questions from the audience. To prepare, collect survey data from current students regarding their views. If you do not feel your interests are being represented, write a letter to the editor of your local community paper or start a petition drive on campus.

How your school is governed and the decisions the governing board makes can have a dramatic effect on your educational opportunities. If board members come primarily from the business community, they may view the role of colleges as preparing future workers for narrowly focused jobs in industry. Board members with roots in education might place more value on a general liberal arts education rather than training for specific careers. You should seek out this information and then get involved.

CRITICAL THINKING QUESTIONS

1. What are the pros and cons of having a separate board governing higher education, instead of giving this authority to the state department of education?

2. How important is the makeup of the board governing higher education? Should board members be elected by voters or appointed by the governor? How important is student representation on such a board?

---

programs. The governor must also champion the state's interests against the encroachments of federal or local governments and be the state's chief booster to attract business and tourism. In order to be effective, governors are expected to take trips abroad to encourage foreign investment in their states and promote their local products.[57] Thirty-eight states even operate some form of overseas office, including trade mission posts in Harare and Kuala Lumpur.[58] Governors also work with their legislatures to raise revenues for such programs as welfare, education, and economic development. They act as crucial links among the states and between local and the national governments.

No one thinks governors have an easy job. However, most governors earn praise for their leadership, and most enjoy solid public approval ratings.[59] "A governor achieves his personal best by being honest and by staying in touch with the people who elected him to serve them," says Alexander.[60] Former Governor Tom Kean of New Jersey echoed similar thoughts: "I have tried to show during my political career, and especially my years as governor, that responsible government can meet people's needs and bring them together, that government can make a difference in the way we live."[61]

Ultimately, the best governors are ones who have a keen sense of history and their own circumstance. A popular former governor of Utah, the late Scott Matheson, wrote that they have been the men and women who have the right combination of "values for quality service, the courage to stick to their convictions, even when in the minority, integrity by instinct, compassion by nature, leadership by perception, and the character to admit wrong, and when necessary, to accept defeat."[62]

CHAPTER **SUMMARY**

25.1 Identify the typical pathways by which people attain and retain the governorship.

Governors usually have had experience in state government before they reach office, as either legislators, executives, or both. Although most governors are usually white males in their 40s or 50s, more women have become governors in recent decades. Most gubernatorial elections are insulated from national political swings, and at least three out of four governors who run again win reelection. However, most governors cannot remain in office long because of term limits.

25.2 Identify the formal and informal powers of governors, and assess governors' use of these powers to influence policy.

Governors' most important formal powers are their appointive and budgetary powers. They also have veto and pardon powers, they have the power to issue executive orders, and they are commanders in chief of the National Guard. Although differences across states in the formal powers of governors have declined in recent years, substantial differences may still be found.

To be effective, governors must use not only their formal powers but also use their informal powers to draw public attention, lead their party, build and maintain good personal relationships with many officials and institutions, and work well with the media. Governors help set the policy agenda and frame the debate on important public issues.

25.3 Evaluate the effectiveness of governors as managers of the state's executive branch.

During the past generation, reforms in management and organization have strengthened most governorships. Most governors have gained powers that enable them to achieve more of their goals—and they have modernized state government while strengthening their control over the executive branch. Nonetheless, constitutional, legal, and political restraints continue to limit governors' efforts.

CHAPTER **SELF-TEST**

25.1 Identify the typical pathways by which people attain and retain the governorship.

1. Which is one of the most common paths to the governorship?
   a. Serving in the military
   b. Working as an attorney
   c. Being elected to the state legislature
   d. Serving in charitable organizations
2. Why do 75 percent of incumbent governors who seek reelection win?

25.2 Identify the formal and informal powers of governors, and assess governors' use of these powers to influence policy.

3. What is one difference between the federal executive (president) and state executive (governor)?
   a. They are the symbolic heads of their parties.
   b. They share executive power with other officials.
   c. They can veto legislation that has been passed by the legislature.
4. In a short essay, describe three specific formal powers held by governors and compare them across states. Describe how governors can use each of these powers to accomplish their policy goals.
5. In a short essay, describe how governors use their influential position with the media to advance their policy goals, resolve personal scandals, and promote their states.

25.3 Evaluate the effectiveness of governors as managers of the state's executive branch.

6. According to political scientist Thad Beyle, what is one reason governors are not yet as effective as private-sector chief executives in their respective jobs?
   a. State governments are vastly more complex than even large private-sector companies.

25.4 Outline duties and powers of other top executive officials in state government.

In addition to a governor, the voters in most states also elect other statewide officials such as a lieutenant governor, secretary of state, attorney general, and state treasurer. Many of the officials play important political and policy roles in their states, and many current governors previously served in some other statewide elected capacity. State attorneys general have been particularly important in prosecuting fraud, winning major settlements, and other activities in recent years.

25.5 Evaluate the challenges and rewards for governors today.

The job of governor is one of the most important and exacting in U.S. political life. A governor is expected to be the state's chief policy maker, the architect of the state budget, the chief manager of the state administration, and the political and symbolic leader of the state. Specific expectations for governors change over time, especially in response to economic conditions.

   b. Many governors do not have as much flexibility in hiring and firing personnel.
   c. State legislators are more ambitious and self-centered than most employees in private companies.
   d. Many governors have little experience or training in running an organization as large and complex as a state government.
7. Some have suggested giving the governor more direct control over state agencies. Identify one reason for and one against such reform.

25.4 Outline duties and powers of other top executive officials in state government.

8. Which top state official has no statutory duties in many states?
   a. State auditor
   b. Secretary of state
   c. Attorney general
   d. Lieutenant governor
9. In a short essay, compare the duties of three top executive officials in state government. Consider the statutory responsibilities, practical influence, and political roles of each.

25.5 Evaluate the challenges and rewards for governors today.

10. Identify and describe three roles people expect their governors to fill.
11. Imagine you are the governor of your state. In a short essay, identify and describe your most important role, responsibility, and policy goal.
12. U.S. citizens evaluate and rate their governors using many of the same criteria they apply to presidents. In a paragraph, argue what those criteria should be.

Answers to selected questions: 1. c; 3. b; 6. b; 8. d

---

mypⓞliscilab EXERCISES
Where participation leads to action!

Apply what you learned in this chapter with these resources on MyPoliSciLab.

📖—[Read] on **mypoliscilab.com**

   eText: Chapter 25

✔—[Study] and **Review** on **mypoliscilab.com**

   Pre-Test
   Post-Test
   Chapter Exam
   Flashcards

👁—[Watch] on **mypoliscilab.com**

   Video: New York's 2010 Governor's Race
   Video: Wisconsin Governor Seeks to Remove 'Sexting' DA

✳—[Explore] on **mypoliscilab.com**

   Comparative: Comparing Executive Branches
   Simulation: You Are a Governor

KEY TERMS

veto, p. 638
line item veto, p. 638

reduction veto, p. 638
amendatory veto, p. 638

executive order, p. 639

ADDITIONAL RESOURCES

FURTHER READING

THAD L. BEYLE, ED., *Governors and Hard Times* (CQ Press, 1992).

THOMAS M. CARSEY, *Campaign Dynamics: The Race for Governor* (University of Michigan Press, 2000).

DAN T. CARTER, *The Politics of Rage: George Wallace, the Origins of the New Conservatism, and the Transformation of American Politics,* 2d ed. (Louisiana State Press, 2000).

ROBERT S. ERIKSON ET AL., *Statehouse Democracy: Public Opinion and Policy in the American States* (Cambridge University Press, 1993).

ALVIN S. FELZENBERG, *Governor Tom Kean: From the New Jersey Statehouse to the 9–11 Commission* (Rutgers University Press, 2006).

VIRGINIA GRAY AND **RUSSELL HANSON,** EDS., *Politics in the American States: A Comparative Analysis,* 9th ed. (CQ Press, 2007).

MADELEINE M. KUNIN, *Living a Political Life* (Vintage Books, 1995).

BROOKE MASTERS, *Spoiling for a Fight: The Rise of Eliot Spitzer* (Holt, 2007).

SARAH M. MOREHOUSE, *The Governor as Party Leader* (University of Michigan Press, 1998).

ALAN ROSENTHAL, *Governors and Legislatures: Contending Powers* (CQ Press, 1990).

ETHAN G. SRIBNICK, ED., *A Legacy of Innovation: Governors and Public Policy* (Pennsylvania State University Press, 2008).

SUE THOMAS AND **CLYDE WILCOX,** *Women and Elective Office* (Oxford University Press, 1998).

TOMMY G. THOMPSON, *Power to the People: An American State at Work* (HarperCollins, 1996).

T. HARRY WILLIAMS, *Huey Long* (Vintage Books, 1981).

WILLIAM F. WINTER, *The Measure of Our Days: Writings of William F. Winter* (University Press of Mississippi, 2006). See also the quarterly *Spectrum: The Journal of State Government, Governing, State Policy Reports,* and *State Government News.* See also the valuable University of Nebraska Press series on state politics in the individual states, each of which has a chapter on governors.

The National Governors' Association publishes a variety of surveys, reports, and studies, including the weekly *Governors' Bulletin* and the *Proceedings of the National Governors' Association* annual meetings. These and related documents can be purchased by writing to the National Governors' Association, 444 N. Capitol Street NW, Washington, D.C., 20001.

WEB SITES

http://www.stateline.org/ Stateline.org provides news and information on policy and politics in the 50 states.

The following are Web sites for professional associations dedicated to the various top statewide executive branch officials:

www.nga.org/ National Governors Association.

www.nlga.us/ National Lieutenant Governors Association.

www.naag.org/ National Association of Attorneys General.

www.nass.org/ National Association of Secretaries of State.

www.nasact.org/ National Association of State Auditors, Comptrollers, and Treasurers.

Massey Energy Gets $50 Million Verdict Overturned Again

November 13, 2009 00:01 EST

Nov. 13 (Bloomberg) — Massey Energy Co., the fifth-largest U.S. ... after the ... a second time in getting a $50 million jury verdict ... U.S. Supreme Court said West Virginia's highest cou... ... justice should have recused himself.

... West Virginia again reve... ... In Novem...

Judges and Justice in the States

State courts play a major role in how citizens and their government come into contact with each other. Most of the nation's judicial business is conducted by its nearly 30,000 state and municipal judges. Put into perspective, federal courts confront approximately 2 million annual cases, whereas state courts see more than 100 million.[1] State judges preside over most criminal trials, settle most lawsuits between individuals, and administer most estates. They play a vital role in determining who gets what, where, when, and how. Thus, they are crucial in making public policy.

Although federal judges are appointed for life, most state court judges must be elected to either attain or retain their positions. Thus, in many respects, state courts face pressures more similar to other elected officials than do federal judges. This comes with potential advantages and disadvantages that will be discussed in this chapter. However, recent events surrounding campaign contributions to state supreme court candidates have raised some concerns about selecting state judges this way.

One example occurred in West Virginia. In 1998, the Harman Mining Company filed a lawsuit against A.T. Massey Coal Company regarding a contract dispute. In 2002, a state court found in favor of Harman and ordered Massey to pay $50 million in damages. The ruling was appealed to the West Virginia Supreme Court. While the case was pending, Massey's CEO created a nonprofit organization that he used to funnel more than $3 million of his own money to a candidate named Brent Benjamin, who was running for a seat on the state supreme court. Benjamin won the race. *Harman* v. *Massey* finally came before the court in 2007, and the Harman president petitioned for now Justice Benjamin to **recuse** himself from the case—that is, to withdraw from participating in making a ruling to avoid any actual or perceived partiality or bias. Benjamin refused, and in 2008, the court ruled in favor of Massey (thereby overturning the lower court's damage award of $50 million to Harman) by a vote of 3 to 2 with Benjamin voting in the majority. This decision was appealed to the U.S. Supreme Court, which ruled (5 to 4) on June 9, 2009, in *Caperton* v. *A.T. Massey Coal Co.,* that Benjamin should have recused himself. The case was sent back to the West Virginia Supreme Court. Benjamin was replaced on the case by a retired judge, and three other justices who heard the original case were no longer on the court. Massey again won, this time 4-1.[2]

This case pits the principles of freedom for groups and individuals to participate in the electoral process against the desire for an impartial judiciary. How states manage this tension will be a major issue surrounding judicial politics in the coming years.

This tension has been magnified recently because state courts have become more prominent in the political life of their state, and state judges have become embroiled in controversial issues. As the public has pressed for tougher action against criminals, the number of criminal cases processed by the courts has risen, and political debates have developed over standards for sentencing and imprisonment. In civil court, a revolution in tort law—law relating to compensation for injuries to person, reputation, or property—has flooded state courts as more people sue more often about more disputes. This has triggered a backlash so that many states have instituted legislative tort reforms that make it more difficult to bring lawsuits or that limit damage payments. Finally, with the rise of a **new judicial federalism** in many states, judicial interpretations of state constitutions have resulted in controversial rulings in such areas as the right to privacy, public school financing, and equal protection of the law.[3] Thus, what state courts do, how judges make decisions, and how judges are selected have become important political questions.

CHAPTER **OUTLINE**
& CHAPTER LEARNING **OBJECTIVES**

The Structure of State Courts

26.1 Outline the structure of a state court system.

How Judges Are Chosen

26.2 Evaluate the different methods of selecting judges.

The Criminal Justice System

26.3 Describe the roles of the participants in the criminal justice system.

Prisons

26.4 Assess the controversy over the increased use of imprisonment.

Judicial Reform

26.5 Evaluate the proposals and goals of the judicial reform movement.

recuse
To withdraw from participating in making a ruling to avoid any actual or perceived partiality or bias.

new judicial federalism
The practice of some state courts using the bill of rights in their state constitutions to provide more protection for some rights than is provided by the Supreme Court's interpretation of the Bill of Rights in the U.S. Constitution.

The Structure of State Courts

LEARNING **OBJECTIVE**
26.1 Outline the structure of a state court system.

Each state has its own court system, so it is difficult to generalize about them. For convenience, we categorize and discuss state courts as (1) minor courts of limited jurisdiction, (2) trial courts of general jurisdiction, and (3) appellate courts (see Figure 26–1).

Minor Courts

In most states, minor courts handle **misdemeanors**—relatively minor violations of state and local laws—as well as traffic cases and civil suits involving small amounts of money. In some places, they also hold preliminary hearings and set bail for more serious charges. Decisions of the minor courts may be appealed and, in most instances, tried *de novo*—that is, tried all over again without reference to what happened in the minor courts. In most places, these courts are financed and administered by a local government. In cities, these minor courts are known as *municipal courts* and are often divided into traffic courts, family courts, small claims courts, and police courts. Paid *magistrates* trained in the law preside over most of them.

The *justice of the peace* system is being phased out but survives in some states (Arizona, Arkansas, Delaware, Louisiana, Montana, Texas, and Wyoming) and in rural areas; in New York, the justices are called *town justices*. Justices of the peace are elected for short terms, usually two to six years. They need not be trained in the law, and their authority is limited to performing marriages, notarizing papers, handling traffic violations, and hearing misdemeanors, usually those incurring fines less than $200. They also hear minor civil disputes.

Courts handling minor crimes are often so crowded that cases are processed quickly with little individual attention. Although many critics of the legal system contend that judges are too lenient and criminals are back on the streets too quickly, others charge that poor and ignorant defendants often spend days in jail waiting for their cases to go to trial. A new and apparently effective reform is the establishment of *court-watching groups*. In some cities, these groups are sponsored by organizations concerned with seeing that the courts treat fairly those charged with crimes. In other cities, they are supported by those concerned that judges are too easy on defendants. Court watchers make prosecutors, public defenders, and judges more sensitive to the views of the general public.

Trial Courts of General Jurisdiction

Trial courts of **original jurisdiction,** where cases first appear, are called county courts, circuit courts, superior courts, district courts, and common pleas courts. They administer common, criminal, equity, and statutory law. In most states, **felonies** are tried in trial

misdemeanor
A minor crime; the penalty is a fine or imprisonment for a short time, usually less than a year, in a local jail.

original jurisdiction
The authority of a court to hear a case "in the first instance."

felony
A serious crime, the penalty for which can range from imprisonment in a penitentiary for more than a year to death.

FIGURE 26–1 The California State Courts.

■ *How does the state court system compare to the federal court system?*

SOURCE: Guide to California Courts, www.courtinfo.ca.gov/reference/guide.

CALIFORNIA SUPREME COURT
Highest state court; seven justices

COURTS OF APPEAL
Intermediate court; reviews decisions of superior courts; divided into six districts

SUPERIOR COURTS
One in each county; 58 in the state. Each court may have many departments. Decide questions of fact and law.

SMALL CLAIMS	CRIMINAL	CIVIL	JUVENILE
Claims of $2,500 or less.	Felonies: crimes punishable by imprisonment in state facilities.	Disputes where the claim is over $2,500 and cases involving wills, land titles, divorce, child custody, etc.	Correction of offenders under age 18. Protection of abused and neglected minors.

courts; felonies are serious crimes, and the penalty can range from imprisonment in a penitentiary for more than a year to death. Some states maintain separate courts for criminal and civil matters. States generally also have special *probate courts* to administer estates and handle matters related to wills. These courts are all *courts of record* in which trials take place, witnesses testify, and juries render verdicts, although most cases are heard and decided by a judge. *Appellate courts* may review decisions of trial courts; however, most decisions of trial judges are not reviewed and are final. These courts do more than apply the law; they also participate in the never-ending process of shaping the law and public policy.[4]

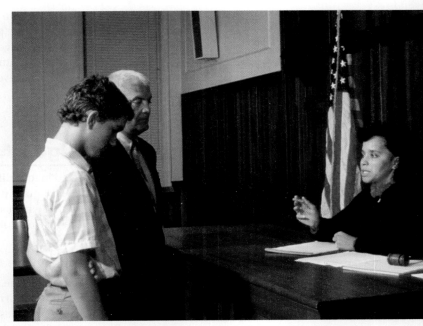

Family court judges deal with the legal issues of minors—children under the age of 18. ■ *What issues might a court-watching group be keeping an eye on in a juvenile court case?*

Appellate Courts

In a few states with relatively smaller caseloads—Delaware, Montana, New Hampshire, Nevada, North Dakota, Rhode Island, West Virginia, and Vermont—trial court decisions are appealed directly to the state supreme court. (In North Dakota, the supreme court can assign cases to a court of appeals composed of three judges chosen from among the trial judges.) Most states, however, have intermediate appeals courts that fit into the system in much the same way that the U.S. Courts of Appeals fit into the federal structure.

All states have a *court of last resort,* usually called the supreme court. In Maine and Massachusetts, the court of last resort is called the supreme judicial court; in Maryland and New York, it is the court of appeals; in West Virginia, it is the supreme court of appeals. And if that is not confusing enough, in New York, the trial courts are called supreme courts. Texas and Oklahoma have two courts of last resort—a supreme court that handles civil matters and a court of criminal appeals. Unless a federal question is involved, state supreme courts are the highest tribunal to which a case may be appealed.

All state judges of all state courts take an oath to uphold the supremacy of the U.S. Constitution, and all state courts have the power of **judicial review.** That is, they may refuse to enforce, and may restrain state and local officials from enforcing, state laws, regulations, or actions if they believe these conflict with the state constitution or the U.S. Constitution. State judges may also declare actions of federal officials or federal laws or regulations to be in conflict with the U.S. Constitution, subject to final review by the U.S. Supreme Court.

State supreme courts have led the way in making judicial decisions available on the Internet. All have Web sites, and nearly all provide access to written opinions and decisions, along with other information, and 10 percent make oral arguments available.[5] The Web site of the National Center for State Courts (www.ncsc.org) provides links to state court Web sites.

State Courts and State Politics

U.S. judges are prominent actors on the political scene, at both the national and state levels. But state courts differ from federal courts in several important ways. State judges are more likely to decide cases involving their legislative and executive branches than the U.S. Supreme Court is to engage in congressional and presidential matters.[6] In addition, state judges are not constrained by the doctrine of federalism when dealing with local units of government. Furthermore, in nine states, the state supreme court can give advisory opinions at the request of the governor or state legislature. An **advisory opinion** is an opinion unrelated to a particular case that gives a court's view about a constitutional or legal issue. An advisory opinion is often requested when there is a question about the constitutionality of a bill or proposal under consideration by the governor and/or legislature.

judicial review

The power of a court to refuse to enforce a law or a government regulation that in the opinion of the judges conflicts with the U.S. Constitution or, in a state court, the state constitution.

advisory opinion

An opinion unrelated to a particular case that gives a court's view about a constitutional or legal issue.

State judges are likely to be part of the state's legal culture, and state judges can claim to be representatives of the people. Most have been educated in the state's law schools.[7] In addition, most state judges serve for limited terms and stand for election. "As elected representatives, like legislators, they feel less hesitant to offer their policy views than do appointed judges."[8] However, they also can be held accountable by voters for their actions.

How Judges Are Chosen

LEARNING **OBJECTIVE**

26.2 Evaluate the different methods of selecting judges.

Judges are selected in four different ways (see Figure 26–2): appointment by the governor, election by the legislature, popular election, or a modified appointment plan known as the Missouri Plan, in which a special commission provides a short list of nominees from which the governor selects one to appoint as judge.

Appointment by the Governor and Election by the Legislature

In Delaware, Hawaii, Maine, New Jersey, New York, and Vermont, judges are appointed by the governor and confirmed by the state senate. In Delaware and Massachusetts, governors select appointees from names submitted by judicial nominating commissions. Election by the legislature is the constitutional practice in South Carolina and Virginia. Even in states that elect judges, a majority "are in fact initially appointed by the governor to fill midterm vacancies, usually occasioned by the retirement or death of sitting judges...and these appointed judges are overwhelmingly favored in their first electoral bids following appointment."[9]

In addition to this formal process of nomination and selection, several informal processes play a role in identifying good candidates for judgeships. Lawyers interested in becoming judges may make their interest known either directly or indirectly to party officials. Leaders of the local bar associations may promote favored members, and various members of the bar may seek out candidates and recruit them. Political leaders and interest groups also participate. Following such suggestions, the candidates go through the formal appointment process.[10]

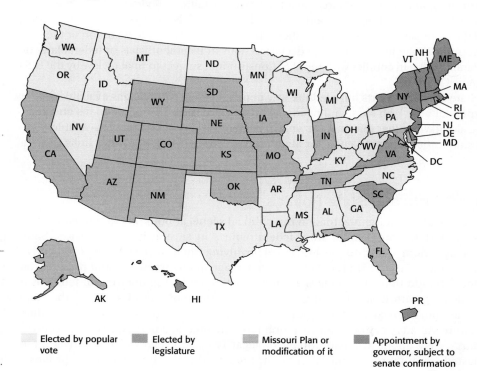

FIGURE 26–2 Method for Selection of Judges of the Court of Last Resort.

■ *Which participants or interests would favor each of these methods of selection, and why?*

SOURCE: *The Book of the States, 2005* (The Council of State Governments, 2005), pp. 318–321.

Legend:
- Elected by popular vote
- Elected by legislature
- Missouri Plan or modification of it
- Appointment by governor, subject to senate confirmation

For the People
GOVERNMENT'S GREATEST ENDEAVORS

Public Funding of Judicial Campaigns

As judicial election campaigns have become more hotly contested and, thus, more controversial, a number of reformers have advocated providing public funding for judicial candidates so that they do not need to raise funds from individuals, companies, or other groups with pending or potential cases coming up in the court. North Carolina has responded with an innovative program of public funding for state supreme court and court of appeals candidates. The program, which first went into effect for the 2004 election cycle, requires potential candidates to first raise a sufficient amount of money from North Carolina registered voters as a way to demonstrate their viability as candidates. Once they qualify, candidates receive a fixed amount of money to run their campaigns. Candidates who accept the funds must abide by spending limits and are barred from accepting any funds from political parties or political action committees (PACs).

One of the most important features of the North Carolina program is the "rescue funds" provision. Because the public funding program is voluntary, potential candidates might be concerned that an opponent might choose not to participate and then greatly outspend those candidates who do participate and must abide by spending limits. To combat this, the North Carolina system provides that candidates who opt into the program will be eligible for additional funds above the spending limit if they find themselves facing an opponent who did not accept public funding and is spending much larger amounts. In 2004 and 2008, 23 of 29 possible candidates participated, and several of those who did not participate chose not to because they were unchallenged. The North Carolina program is being touted as a model for how to help insulate judicial elections from undue influence from campaign contributors. The program has survived challenges that it unduly limits free speech because it is voluntary.

CRITICAL THINKING QUESTIONS

1. What are the pros and cons of public funding for judicial elections? Can states afford to spend public money on campaigns? Can they afford not to?

2. What constitutional issues regarding the First Amendment are raised by public election funding programs?

Popular Election

More than 85 percent of all state and local judges face elections, resulting in a greater number of elections for judges than for state legislators and executive officials. Appellate court judges in eight states face partisan elections, 13 states hold nonpartisan elections, and another 19 states have retention elections for state judges.[11] Nonpartisan judicial elections do not necessarily mean that political parties do not participate. In at least half of the states with nonpartisan judicial elections, parties actively campaign on behalf of candidates. Some states try to isolate judicial elections from partisan politics by holding them separately from other elections.

In 1986, California amended its constitution to forbid political parties from endorsing candidates for judicial office. However, federal courts declared the proposition unconstitutional, and California political parties are once again endorsing judicial candidates. The prevailing view, as Justice Thurgood Marshall observed, was that "the prospect that voters might be persuaded by party endorsements is not a *corruption* of the democratic political process; it *is* the democratic political process."[12]

Until recently, there was little interest in judicial elections, and voter turnout tended to be low. But judicial elections are becoming increasingly spirited. Interest groups focus attention on judges whose decisions they find objectionable. In some states, the death penalty is the issue. In Texas and California, efforts to limit liability lawsuits and damage awards have led to campaign clashes over judicial candidates, with trial lawyers, consumers, and union groups on one side and business interests on the other. In Idaho, one candidate for the supreme court campaigned on a platform stating that the theory of evolution could not be true—and won. An Illinois judge was unseated because of his decisions in abortion cases. Now more than ever, judges have to act like politicians and "feel they are under increasing pressure to be accountable to public opinion."[13]

As judicial elections become more hotly contested, spending in the campaigns has escalated. Between 2000 and 2009, candidate fund raising more than doubled compared with the previous decade, rising from $83.3 million during the 1990s to more than $206 million in the 2000s. Nineteen states set all-time high records for fund raising by high court candidates during the 2000s, and candidates raised more than $45 million collectively in three of the last five election cycles. Nearly half of the money raised during the decade was spent on

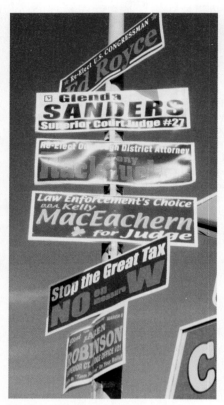

In states with elected judges, campaigns can become very competitive. ■ *What are the advantages and disadvantages of electing judges?*

TV advertising. Parties and interest groups are responsible for 40 percent of all TV advertising spending. A survey conducted in 2001 found that more than 90 percent of elected judges nationwide said they feel pressure to raise money in election years—a figure that jumps to 97 percent of elected high court judges.[14] In many states that elect judges, it is increasingly clear that judicial candidates depend on a small number of law firms, businesses, or special-interest groups, such as the U.S. Chamber of Commerce and the Business Roundtable, for their campaign funds.[15]

Much of the rising cost of judicial campaigns stems from the increased reliance on televised campaign advertising. As recently as a decade ago, most candidates even for state supreme courts did not run TV ads during their campaigns. Those who did generally ran very tame biographical spots focused on their own qualifications and experience. However, as the contests have heated up, so has the advertising. Candidates now routinely face attack ads that are every bit as aggressive as those targeting candidates for other offices. Some examples from 2008 can be found online at http://judicialcampaignoversight. org/2008ads/2008ads1.html.

In response to concerns about the campaigns in judicial elections, most states adopted provisions similar to the American Bar Association's code of judicial conduct that bar judicial candidates from telling the electorate anything about their views on legal and political matters. Some states went even further: the Minnesota Supreme Court, for instance, prohibited judicial candidates from soliciting campaign contributions, declaring their party affiliation, or publicly voicing their positions on controversial issues. However, the U.S. Supreme Court struck down Minnesota's ban on judicial candidates' announcing their positions on controversial legal and political matters as a violation of the First Amendment guarantee of free speech.[16] State and federal courts in Alabama, Georgia, Michigan, Ohio, and other states have also handed down decisions perceived by some as "a roadblock for efforts to curb the increasingly raucous nature of judicial politics."[17] Striking down these limits has contributed greatly to making judicial campaigns look much more like their hotly contested counterparts for legislative and executive offices.

In response to the growing cost of state judicial elections, the American Bar Association, the American Judicature Society, and other organizations are promoting the public financing of state judicial campaigns and elections.[18] Three states—Wisconsin, North Carolina, and New Mexico—provide public financing for some judicial elections. Wisconsin has had publicly financed elections for state supreme court justices since the 1970s; candidates are eligible for $97,000 in state money if they agree to a $215,000 spending limit. The system is paid for through a $1 check-off contribution on income tax returns and has been historically underfinanced. In 2004, North Carolina's Judicial Campaign Reform Act went into effect. Under the Act, all appellate-level judicial races are nonpartisan, and candidates who agree to fund-raising and spending limits receive public financing in the general election.

Minority Representation   The one-person, one-vote rule that applies to legislative elections does not apply to judicial elections.[19] States may create judicial districts so that one judge "represents" many more voters than another judge. Although there is no requirement that states elect judges, if they choose to do so, the federal Voting Rights Act of 1965 applies to these judicial elections.[20]

Because the Voting Rights Act of 1965 forbids any practice or procedure that dilutes the voting power of minorities, it raises a question about the constitutionality of at-large judicial elections. When judges are elected at large for a city or a state, African American and Hispanic candidates sometimes find it difficult to get elected. African American and Hispanic voters tend to be concentrated in the inner cities or in certain geographical areas; thus, their impact is diluted in citywide or statewide elections. For example, in a state in which the population consists of 20 percent African American voters, 20 percent Hispanic voters, and 60 percent white voters, with five judges to be elected on a statewide basis, few if any African American judges or Hispanic judges will be elected. Some Hispanics and African Americans argue that the solution is to divide such a state into five districts, with one judge elected in each district, and draw district lines in such a way that African Americans and Hispanics make up a majority of voters in as many districts as possible, giving them a chance to elect at least one of their own.

Of the People

Women and Minorities on State Supreme Courts

Although state judges were once overwhelmingly white males, that has changed in recent years. A 2008 study found that nearly 12 percent of all state judges were racial or ethnic minorities, and slightly more than half of those minority judges were African American. States with the highest percentages of minority judges include California, Hawaii, Louisiana, Maryland, New Mexico, New York, North Carolina, and Texas. States with the lowest percentages include Alaska, Idaho, Kentucky, Maine, Montana, New Hampshire, North Dakota, South Dakota, Vermont, and Wyoming. Women have become more prominent in state courts as well. In early 2010, the National Association of Women Judges (www.nawj.org) reported that 26 percent of all state judges were women.

CRITICAL THINKING QUESTIONS

1. How might having more women and minorities on the bench affect the decisions of state supreme courts?

2. Should a state change the way it selects judges in order to increase the number of women and minorities on the bench? Why or why not?

Chief Justice Wallace B. Jefferson of Texas was the first African American state supreme court justice in Texas when he was appointed in 2001 by Governor Rick Perry. He was named chief justice in 2004, making him the first African American to hold that post in Texas as well.

SOURCE: Barbara L. Graham, "State Judicial Diversity," *The Book of the States, 2009* (The Council of State Governments, 2009); and The National Association of Women Judges, www.nawj.org.

Merit Selection: The Missouri Plan

Many lawyers and political scientists have argued in favor of a screening process before judges are appointed or elected to ensure that only candidates of merit will be considered. Merit systems are used in 16 states.

One of the oldest merit plans is the Missouri Plan.[21] As used in most states, the **Missouri Plan** provides that when a judicial vacancy occurs, a special *nominating commission* (usually composed of three lawyers elected by the bar, three citizens appointed by the governor, and the chief justice) nominates three candidates.[22] The governor selects one, who then serves as a judge for at least a year. At the next general election, the voters are asked if the appointee should be retained in office. If a majority of the voters agree, the judge serves a new full term (typically 6 to 12 years); if not, another person is selected by the same procedure. At the end of his or her term, an elected judge may ask to have his or her name placed on the ballot, and the voters are again asked whether they want to retain that judge in office.[23] These uncontested elections, in which judges run against their own record, are called **retention elections,** and some require a supermajority vote.

Until recently, retention elections generated little interest and low voter turnout.[24] In the 6,306 judicial retention elections held between 1964 and 2006, fewer than 60 judges were removed by voters, although a few decided not to run when they realized they might fail to be retained.[25] Recently, some state supreme court justices have been vigorously challenged in retention elections, especially when their decisions differed appreciably from the mainstream of public opinion and aroused the hostility of significant special interests. Frequently, the charge was that the judge was "soft on crime." Interest groups have learned that it is relatively easy to target incumbents, and because of constraints on the way judicial candidates are expected to campaign, it is "difficult for targeted judges to defend themselves."[26] One Pennsylvania Supreme Court justice lost a retention race in 2005, and another nearly lost, after a huge voter backlash to a pay raise adopted by the state legislature that increased the salaries of state officials, including judges.

Most voters know little about judges, and what information they have comes from interested parties and persons, especially those who dislike what the judges have done.

Missouri Plan
A system for selecting judges that combines features of the appointive and elective methods. The governor selects judges from lists presented by panels of lawyers and laypersons, and at the end of their term, the judges may run against their own record in retention elections.

retention elections
Elections where judges run uncontested for reelection and voters simply vote for or against keeping them in office.

To provide a more balanced picture, a few states—Alaska, Utah, Colorado, Arizona, and Tennessee—have tried to supply more neutral information about judicial performance. In Colorado, an *evaluation committee* in each judicial district—jointly appointed by the chief justice, governor, president of the senate, and speaker of the house—disseminates information through newspaper supplements, including a final recommendation of "retain" or "do not retain."[27] In Alaska, a judicial council composed of three lawyers, three nonlawyers, and the chief justice provides evaluations that are widely publicized.[28] In Utah, the Judicial Council—consisting of the chief justice, another justice, an appellate court judge, five district court judges, two juvenile court judges, three other lower court judges, a state bar representative, and the state court administrator—certifies incumbents, and this certification, or lack of it, is indicated on the ballot.

Even though contested retention elections are the exception, sitting judges are aware that if they make decisions that offend organized interest groups, they may face opposition the next time their names are placed on the ballot. Whether these pressures threaten the independence of the courts, or are necessary to ensure judicial accountability within our political system in which judges play such an important role, remains a matter of political debate.[29]

Judicial Conduct

Although federal judges hold office during "good behavior"—essentially for life—only Rhode Island's judges have life appointments. In Massachusetts and New Hampshire, judges serve to age 70. In all the other states, they serve for fixed terms ranging from 3 to 15 years.[30] Thirty-seven states and the District of Columbia mandate the retirement of judges at a certain age, usually 70.[31]

The states, rather than the national government, have taken the lead in establishing procedures to judge judges. Each of the 50 states has a board, commission, or court to handle allegations of judicial misconduct. Despite the objections of many judges, these commissions are most often composed of both nonlawyers and lawyers. They investigate complaints and hold hearings for judges who have been charged with improper performance of their duties or unethical or unfair conduct. Establishment of these commis-sions appears to have helped restore public confidence in the state judicial systems.[32] In addition, nonpartisan groups such as the Constitution Project and the Brennan Center for Justice act as watchdog groups because they monitor the operation of and advocate for judicial independence.

The Criminal Justice System

LEARNING **OBJECTIVE**

26.3 Describe the roles of the participants in the criminal justice system.

Justice is handled in the United States by a series of institutions only loosely connected to each other. In addition to judges, there are juries, prosecutors, defense counsels, public defenders, victims, prison officials, and defendants.

The Jury

Although most of us will never be judges or serve as professionals in the administration of justice, all adult citizens have an opportunity—even an obligation—to be jurors. Trial by jury in civil disputes is used less often these days; people make settlements before a trial, elect to have their cases decided by a judge alone, or refer their cases to a mediator or arbitrator. Furthermore, only a small fraction of criminal cases are actually disposed of by a trial before a jury. Still, jury trials, or their possibility, remain a key feature of our justice system.

We have moved from a system in which jury service was restricted to white male property owners to one in which it is the responsibility of *all* adult citizens. But because jury service may be time-consuming and burdensome, many busy people do their best to avoid serving, and today, more time and energy are spent trying to persuade (or coerce) people to serve than in excluding them.

In the past, judges were often willing to excuse doctors, nurses, teachers, executives, and other highly skilled people who pleaded that their services were essential outside the jury room. As a result, juries were often selected from panels consisting in large part of

YOU WILL DECIDE

Should State Judges Be Selected Through Appointment or Popular Election?

After a campaign dubbed eerily similar to one in John Grisham's novel *The Appeal,* sitting Judge Louis Butler lost his bid for a ten-year term to the Wisconsin Supreme Court on April 1, 2008. The state's first and only African American supreme court justice and a former public defender, Butler was appointed to the state's highest court by Governor Doyle in 2004. He was defeated in a close race by Michael Gableman, a circuit county court judge and former prosecutor. Court watchers believe that the election of Gableman will shift the balance of the court from a 4-to-3 court that leaned liberal to a 4-to-3 court leaning conservative. Turnout for the election was approximately 20 percent.

The campaign dismayed nearly everyone in the state. For the second year in a row, third-party groups dominated the race. Although the race was technically nonpartisan, conservative groups, including the state's largest business lobby, an antitax group, and a group advocating traditional families, lined up behind Gableman. The state's largest teachers' union and other liberal organizations backed Butler.

Television ads by these third-party groups were roundly criticized as misleading and undermining the reputation of the court. A controversial ad by Gableman implied that as a public defender, Butler had relied on a technicality to release from prison a convicted child molester who then assaulted another child. Like Butler, the man was black, and the ad ended with a picture of the convicted rapist alongside Butler. In fact, the man was released from prison because he had completed his sentence, not because of Butler's work as a public defender. A watchdog group for judicial elections, the Wisconsin Judicial Campaign Integrity Committee, called the ad "a disgraceful attack" that was "highly offensive and deliberately misleading." Gableman's campaign defended the ad, claiming it was a comparison ad highlighting his career as a prosecutor and Butler's as a public defender.*

What do you think? Should state judges be selected through election? What are the arguments for or against it?

THINKING IT THROUGH

Advocates of an appointive system point to Wisconsin's recent campaign as emblematic of the problems with judicial elections. Contested elections too often generate biased advertisements with incomplete and inaccurate information. Interest groups jump into the fray, hoping to influence the outcome, and their voices drown out those of the candidates. On the bench, judges are supposed to be dispassionate and impartial, making a decision based on the evidence presented. But in a contested campaign, they are pulled into an ideological fray that threatens the independence of the judiciary.

The many uncontested elections are not much better. They are sleepy affairs offering the public no real choice, and incumbent judges are routinely returned to office. In either case, advocates of the appointive method contend that voters are generally uninformed about candidates and not competent to assess legal learning and judicial abilities.

Those who favor judicial elections counter that judges should be directly accountable to the people. When appointed, they may lose touch with the general currents of opinion of the electorate. Moreover, the appointive process gives governors too much power over judges, and merit systems such as the Missouri Plan give too much influence to the bar association, a group with its own interests to protect. Even if judicial elections do not result in the defeat of many sitting judges, elections foster accountability because judges do not want to be defeated and will try to maintain popular support.

Critical Thinking Questions

1. Is judicial accountability an important goal? Or should we put more emphasis on judicial independence? Defend your answer.

2. Which method of selecting judges, appointments or elections, better meets the goals of both accountability and independence? Why?

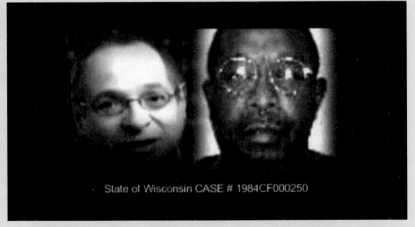

State of Wisconsin CASE # 1984CF000250

A third party ad falsely linking Judge Butler with a convicted rapist, both of whom are African American, was widely criticized.

*Scott Bauer, "Monitoring Group Slams Gableman Ad Featuring Convicted Rapist," *Associated Press,* March 17, 2008.

older people, those who were unemployed or employed in relatively low-paying jobs, single people, and others who were unable to be excused. Most states have reacted to these problems by making it more difficult to be excused. In addition, many states have adopted a "one-day, one-trial" policy, which makes jury service less frequent and less onerous. Because jury trials take more time than bench trials (trials before judges) and cost more, some states use juries of fewer than the standard 12 people for some criminal trials. A few states also permit verdicts by less than a unanimous vote. The U.S. Supreme Court has approved these practices, provided the juries consist of at least six people.[33] However, when deliberating whether to impose the death penalty, a jury must make a unanimous decision.

The Prosecutor

The prosecutor is largely a U.S. invention, one of the few government positions we did not inherit from England. The 2,344 chief prosecutors in the United States (often called *county attorneys* or *district attorneys*) are usually county officials; most are locally elected and subject to little supervision by state authorities. However, in Connecticut, they are appointed by judges, and in New Jersey, by the governor with the consent of the state senate. There are also about 24,000 assistant prosecutors.[34] A prosecutor has "more control over life, liberty, and reputation than any other person in America."[35]

When presented with a case by the police, the prosecutor must decide first whether to file formal charges. He or she may (1) divert the matter out of the criminal justice system and turn it over to a social welfare agency; (2) dismiss the charges; (3) take the matter before a grand jury, which almost always follows the prosecutor's recommendation; or (4) in most jurisdictions, file an **information affidavit,** which serves the same function as a grand jury **indictment.**

A prosecutor who decides not to charge a person accused of some notorious crime is often subject to political pressure and public criticism. But for routine crimes, the prosecutor is politically in a better position to dismiss a charge than the police are. Police are supposed to enforce every law all the time. Of course, it is impossible for them to do so, and they must exercise discretion.[36] But officers who fail to arrest a person alleged to have committed a crime could well be charged with failing in their duty. The prosecutor, however, has more leeway. In fact, the prosecutor is less likely to be criticized for dropping a case because of insufficient evidence than for filing a charge and failing to get a conviction.

information affidavit
Certification by a public prosecutor that there is evidence to justify bringing named individuals to trial.

indictment
A formal written statement from a grand jury charging an individual with an offense; also called a *true bill.*

All citizens have an obligation to serve on juries, and lawyers develop skills in selecting people they think may be sympathetic to their clients. ■ *How does this jury compare to the population at large in terms of race, age, and gender?*

Defense Counsel, Public Defenders, and Others

Many defendants cannot afford the legal counsel to which they are constitutionally entitled. The **assigned counsel system** is the oldest system to provide such defendants with an attorney, and it continues to be used, especially in rural areas. Judges appoint attorneys to represent defendants who cannot afford them. Most such attorneys are paid by the court that appoints them, but sometimes they are expected to do the work **pro bono**—for the public good. Seldom are they given funds to do any investigatory work on behalf of their clients. Some less scrupulous lawyers make their living as assigned counsel; because it is often to their financial advantage to do so, they are quick to plead their clients guilty. They are known contemptuously as members of the "cop-out bar."[37]

Dissatisfaction with the assigned counsel system led to the creation of the **public defender system,** first started in Los Angeles in 1914 and now used in most big cities. Under this system, the government provides a staff of lawyers whose full-time job is to defend individuals who cannot pay. This system provides experienced counsel and relieves the bar of an onerous duty. Critics—including some defendants—protest that because public defenders are paid employees of the state, they are not likely to work as diligently on behalf of their clients as if they were specifically assigned to those clients. But most observers consider the public defender system superior to the assigned counsel system. Steps are being taken to increase the pay of public defenders, protect their independence, and see that they win the confidence of the defendants they represent.

A disproportionate number of prisoners tend to be young, poorly educated black males. ■ *What are some of the factors that cause this pattern? How do you think states should respond?*

Victims and Defendants

When we talk about our criminal justice system, we sometimes forget the two most important parties in any criminal case—the victim of the crime and the person accused of it.

The rights of victims or potential victims are not of the same order as the rights of the accused; the rights of the accused are constitutional rights spelled out in amendments, but nowhere in the Constitution is there any mention of the rights of victims or the public. The framers of the Constitution apparently were much more worried about protecting citizens against the government than about protecting citizens from each other.[38]

In general terms, defendants are likely to be "younger, predominantly male, disproportionately black, less educated, seldom fully employed, and typically unmarried. By the time the sorting process has ended, those sent to prison will consist of an even higher proportion of young, illiterate, black males."[39] Victims, too, tend to be young, black or another minority, and uneducated. A substantial number never report crimes to police and prosecutors—either because of lack of knowledge of what to do or fear of doing it, or, as in the case of rape victims, because they believe they have little chance of proving their attackers guilty. Our system puts the responsibility for prosecuting criminals on the government. In most instances, victims have no role other than as witnesses.

As a result, in recent decades, a victims' rights movement has emerged. The movement originated with liberals (chiefly feminists concerned about the difficulty of winning prosecutions for rape and about the harsh treatment of female witnesses), but it has gained the support of conservatives who consider the judicial system unfair to victims. In the 1984 Victims of Crime Act, Congress authorized federal funds, distributed by the Office of Crime Victims in the Department of Justice, to support state programs compensating victims and providing funds to some victims of federal crimes as well.

Thirty-five states have amended their constitutions to provide for a "victims' bill of rights,"[40] which makes it easier for victims to recover stolen property held in police custody, among other things. Many states also give victims a chance to be heard when prosecutors file formal charges, when judges set bail and impose sentences, and when parole boards consider releasing prisoners. These victims' bills of rights are not without constitutional problems. The introduction of *victim impact statements* by prosecutors seeking the death penalty has been controversial, for instance. The U.S. Supreme Court, after first holding to the contrary, has upheld the right of prosecutors to make victim impact statements to a jury in murder trials citing the personal qualities of the victim and has allowed the jury to consider evidence relating to the murder victim's personal characteristics and the emotional impact of the crime on the victim's family.[41]

assigned counsel system
An arrangement whereby attorneys are provided for people accused of crimes who are unable to hire their own attorneys. The judge assigns a member of the bar to provide counsel to a particular defendant.

pro bono
To serve the public good; a term used to describe work that lawyers (or other professionals) do for which they receive no fees.

public defender system
An arrangement whereby public officials are hired to provide legal assistance to people accused of crimes who are unable to hire their own attorneys.

Plea Bargaining

Only a handful of those accused of committing a crime actually stand trial, and only 5 to 10 percent of those convicted are declared guilty as the result of a formal trial before either a judge or a jury. Most people who go to prison, or who have to pay a criminal fine, do so because they plead guilty.[42] In a common practice called a *plea bargain,* the prosecution offers to reduce the seriousness of the charge and sentence if the defendant will enter a plea of guilty to a lesser crime.

Critics say plea bargaining forces defendants to give up their rights; moreover, they often do not get off much more leniently by pleading guilty to lesser offenses than if they had stood trial on the original charge.[43] Defenders of plea bargaining contend that it works, producing "a result approximating closely, but informally and more swiftly, the results which ought to ensue from a trial, while avoiding most of the undesirable aspects of that ordeal."[44] Many experts and investigators who have looked into the matter have endorsed plea bargaining.

Plea bargaining offers something to all involved. Prosecutors are able to dispose of cases quickly, avoid long and drawn-out trials, eliminate the risk of losing, and build up better conviction records. The accused avoid the danger of being sentenced for more serious charges. Defense attorneys avoid "the dilemma of either incurring the expense of going to trial with a losing case or appearing to provide no service whatsoever to their clients."[45] By being able to handle more clients, they can also make more money. Judges are able to dispose of cases on their dockets more rapidly. In fact, if every case were tried, it would overwhelm the judicial system.

Once the bargain between the prosecutor and the defendant's attorney has been accepted, the matter is taken before a judge, who questions the defendant: "Are you pleading guilty because you are guilty? Are you aware of the maximum sentence for the crime to which you are entering a guilty plea? Were you coerced into pleading guilty or offered anything in return for it? Are you satisfied with the representation afforded by your attorney?" Following appropriate responses, the plea is accepted.[46] As long as defendants know what they are doing and enter into the bargain intelligently, they waive their constitutional rights to trial by pleading guilty and may not back out of the arrangement. Prosecutors must also live up to their side of the bargain.[47]

Sentencing

Due process—the principle of upholding the rights of all those involved, including the prisoner—must be observed in sentencing, which takes place in open court. The prisoner must be present and represented by counsel. In many places, social workers are assigned to help the judge determine the proper sentence. The judge also receives recommendations from the prosecution (and in some jurisdictions from the victim as well), hears the arguments of the defense, and then sets the sentence within the limits prescribed by the state.

The judge sets the sentence, but concerns about sentencing permeate the judicial system. Early in our national history, retribution, deterrence, and protection of society were the primary purposes of sentencing. Then rehabilitation became the major goal, and many people thought it was a more humane approach. The indefinite sentence became popular, motivated by the idea that each prisoner should be considered an individual suffering from an "illness." Each should be diagnosed, a course of treatment should be prescribed, and if and when such experts as psychologists and social workers could certify a "cure," the prisoner should be released.

Most political leaders and many scholars have become disillusioned about our ability to bring about "cures."[48] Others are disillusioned about the deterrent effect of imprisonment. A comprehensive study of rehabilitative efforts inside prisons, although rejecting the conclusion that "nothing works," nonetheless stated, "We do not know of any program or method of rehabilitation that could be guaranteed to reduce the criminal activity of released offenders."[49]

due process
The principle of upholding the rights of all those involved when making a judgment or ruling, including those of the accused or convicted.

Moreover, judges may enjoy considerable discretion in sentencing, and they frequently give different sentences to defendants convicted of the same crime.[50] To reduce such disparities in sentencing, several reforms have been suggested, including establishing more precise legislative standards, creating advisory sentencing councils, and adopting the British practice of allowing appellate courts to modify sentences.

Disillusionment with rehabilitation and disparate sentencing by judges, combined with growing concerns about crime and mounting criticism about alleged judicial leniency, have fueled legislative action for mandatory minimum sentencing requirements and for narrowing judicial discretion.[51] State after state has adopted mandatory prison terms—also known as *determinate sentencing*—for more and more crimes. About half the states have passed so-called three-strikes-and-you're-out laws, which prescribe a mandatory life sentence after three felony convictions.[52]

The Death Penalty

Four years after ruling that death penalty statutes in most states violated the U.S. Constitution, the U.S. Supreme Court in 1976 upheld death penalty statutes in Georgia, Texas, and Florida, holding that the states' revised laws met standards of due process. Today, 35 states allow capital punishment; in the other 15 states, the most severe punishment is a life sentence with no possibility of parole.

Even though most states allow capital punishment, its use varies widely. Since 1976, for example, Texas has executed 457 individuals, and 341 are currently on death row.[53] New Hampshire and Kansas, however, have executed none and have a combined total of 11 inmates currently on death row. Although Illinois still has a statute allowing capital punishment, it has had no executions since 2000, when then-governor Ryan imposed a moratorium on executions (see Chapter 25 opener). The peak in the number of annual executions occurred in 1998, when a total of 98 individuals were executed. Since then, there was a steady decline down to 37 executions in 2008, but it rose again to 52 in 2009.

In December 2007, New Jersey became the first state since 1976 to eliminate the death penalty through an act of the legislature. At the time, there were eight people on death row, but the state had not executed anyone since 1963. In 2008, legislation to abolish the death penalty was introduced in Maryland, Connecticut, Nebraska, Virginia, and Alabama, but it did not pass in any of those states.

Prisons

26.4 Assess the controversy over the increased use of imprisonment.

More people are imprisoned in the United States than in any other country. As of 2008, including juvenile facilities, the United States has more than 2.4 million people behind bars, more than 1.5 million in state and federal prisons, 785,556 in local jails, and nearly 100,000 in juvenile facilities[54] (see Figure 26–3). *Prisons* are for committed criminals serving long sentences. *Jails* are for short-term stays for people awaiting trial and those with sentences of a year or less. "The American inmate population has grown so large that it is difficult to fathom: imagine the combined population of Atlanta, St. Louis, Pittsburgh, Des Moines, and Miami behind bars."[55]

In addition to those in prison or jails, in 2008, more than 5 million adult men and women are on probation or parole. *Probationers* are offenders the courts have placed in community supervision rather than in prison; more than 4.2 million adults were serving probation. *Parolees* are people released after serving a prison term who are under supervision and subject to being returned to prison for rule violations or other offenses; more than 825,000 adults were parolees.[56]

The prison population in the United States has skyrocketed since the 1970s. State and federal prison populations actually declined during the 1960s, but public demands for tougher sentences caused them to climb after 1969. Since 1980, the number of people in prison has more than tripled (see Figure 26–4), although the rate of increase slowed considerably after 1999.

The increase in the prison population has resulted in serious overcrowding. In some states, conditions were so bad that in the 1990s federal judges issued orders calling for either immediate improvement or the release of people being held in conditions that violate the Eighth Amendment prohibition against cruel and unusual punishment. Most states responded to judicial intervention by spending millions to build new prisons and renovate old ones. It costs more than $60,000 to build each cell, and an average of more than $23,000 a year must be spent for each prisoner.[57]

privatization
Contracting public services to private organizations.

recidivist
A repeat offender.

Some cities and counties have even resorted to **privatization,** turning over the responsibility for operating jails to private firms on a contractual basis. Texas has the largest number of inmates in private facilities, and New Mexico has the largest proportion of its inmate population in private prisons (44 percent).[58] Correctional officers strongly oppose privatization and have become a powerful interest group making major contributions to gubernatorial elections.

The high cost of corrections is leading some states to rethink the wisdom of mandatory sentencing. Because half the people in prison and half the trials held are about victimless crimes such as using marijuana, *decriminalization* could substantially reduce the load on the courts and rates of incarceration. Six states, for example, have already repealed statutes on public drunkenness and now consider alcoholism a disease rather than a crime.

States are also considering alternatives for nonviolent offenders such as halfway houses, mental health and drug treatment centers, intensive probation, work release programs, and other community corrections facilities. In 2007, at least six states passed laws designed to shift many more offenders into community-based supervision programs and away from prisons.[59] For example, Nevada expanded eligibility for home confinement, first pioneered in New Mexico in 1983, whereby prisoners serve their time at home while being observed by a variety of monitoring devices.[60] The problem is that these alternative solutions are subject to political attack as being "soft on criminals." Even so, the cost of continued imprisonment is so great that it is prompting state legislatures to convene task forces and to charge corrections departments with researching innovative sentencing options.

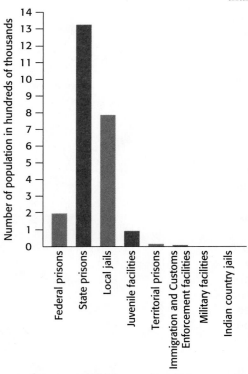

FIGURE 26–3 Total Incarcerated Population at Year-end 2008.

■ *Does the total number of prisoners or their distribution among facilities surprise you?*

SOURCE: U.S. Department of Justice, Bureau of Justice Statistics, "Prisoners in 2008," December 2009.

Finally, states are exploring ways to reduce **recidivism.** Research suggests that "50 percent of offenders will return to prison within three years of release."[61] Reentry programs offer offenders services, such as employment and training programs and substance abuse and mental health treatment, to better prepare them for life outside prison. States have begun to realize that prison growth is not simply a consequence of the crime rate or the state's population. Rather, it is related to state policies regarding criminal justice, including sentencing, the use of community supervision for nonviolent offenders, and failure to reduce parole violations and recidivism.

Judicial Reform

LEARNING **OBJECTIVE**

26.5 Evaluate the proposals and goals of the judicial reform movement.

Crime is a national issue, confronting everyone. The public's attention has been focused on terrorist attacks, drive-by shootings, random killings—especially in schools—and other forms of violence. Yet courts are already overwhelmed by a huge volume of cases. As the American Bar Association observed, "Justice in the United States takes too long, costs too much, and is virtually inaccessible and unaffordable for too many Americans....Our courts are grossly overburdened...and woefully underfunded....The justice system is no longer a 'court of last resort'...but is becoming an emergency room for every social trauma."[62]

We are, many charge, a "litigious society." Dockets are crowded, relief is costly, and delays are common.[63] These problems have led to numerous efforts to improve the administration of justice, in areas including the ways in which judges are selected, the quality of the judicial pool, the way courts operate, and alternative means of dispute resolution and criminal sentencing.

Some reform efforts centered on trying to increase the quality of judges propose increasing their salaries. In most states, judges earn considerably less than most practicing attorneys of the same age and experience. They are unable to earn anything beyond their salaries, and they must be cautious about investments in order to avoid conflicts of interest. Reformers argue that judges should be paid adequately so that they have the financial independence to concentrate on their work and so that successful lawyers will be willing to serve on the bench.

Effective courts also require professional administration. A court can be very large; for example, the court in Hennepin County, Minnesota, has more than 500 employees and 78 judicial officers. Presiding judges are not always given the time or training they need to administer such a system. Training these head judges, reducing their caseloads, and providing additional compensation are some of the recent changes adopted by some states.[64] Advocates of judicial reform also argue that rule-making powers should be given to the state supreme court or its chief justice.

Another way to improve the operation of the courts is to develop alternative methods of resolving disputes. *Alternative dispute resolution* (ADR) procedures serve as alternatives to formal trials. They include mediation, arbitration, conciliation, private judging, and advisory settlement conferences. From time to time, Congress has made grants to encourage states and localities to develop alternative dispute resolution mechanisms, especially for domestic relations issues. ADRs can be part of the established court system or separate from it in neighborhood justice centers or arbitration and mediation forums. Half the states operate arbitration programs as part of their court system.

Despite the disparaging nickname "rent-a-judge," an old practice of hiring private decision makers has been revived. Retired judges and lawyers are paid by the parties involved in the dispute, who agree in advance to abide by the outcome. In some states, appeals courts can review these decisions. Some worry that these alternative practices are drawing the best lawyers into the private system, perhaps resulting in a private system for the rich and a public one for the poor.

Some people have proposed that traffic violations, automobile injury cases, and so-called victimless crimes be handled by some procedure other than a court trial. New York has led the way in removing from the courts minor traffic offenses that do not include serious moving violations; other states are following its lead. Adopting no-fault insurance programs could reduce the large number of cases stemming from automobile accidents.

There is widespread agreement that our justice system, on both the civil and the criminal side, is in recurring crisis. There is less agreement on what to do about it. The problems are complex, the issues are enmeshed in partisan, ideological, and issue politics, and each suggested reform has costs and benefits. Change and reform are likely to come slowly, and perhaps this is as it should be, for our justice system has been created throughout the centuries, built on the accumulated wisdom of the past. How best to administer justice is a question likely to remain on our political agenda.

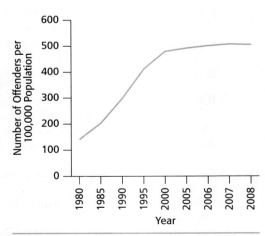

FIGURE 26–4 **Incarceration Rates in Federal and State Jurisdictions.**

■ *What are some of the impacts, on both the prison system and society, of having a high rate of incarceration?*

SOURCE: U.S. Department of Justice, Bureau of Justice Statistics, http://bjs.ojp.usdoj.gov/content/glance/tables/incrttab.cfm.

CHAPTER **SUMMARY**

26.1 Outline the structure of a state court system.

Each state has its own court system. Although the systems vary, they generally include minor courts of limited jurisdiction, trial courts of general jurisdiction, and appellate courts. Each state has a court of last resort, usually called the supreme court. Unless a federal question is involved, state supreme courts are the highest tribunal to which a case may be appealed.

26.2 Evaluate the different methods of selecting judges.

In six states, judges are appointed by the governor and confirmed by the state senate. In a few states, judges are elected by the state legislature. In about half of the states, judges are chosen through a popular election. In the remaining states, judges are chosen through a merit system modeled along the lines of the modified appointment plan known as the Missouri Plan. Most legal reformers and political scientists favor a merit selection system, such as the Missouri Plan, over judicial elections.

26.3 Describe the roles of the participants in the criminal justice system.

Judges, together with jurors, prosecutors, defense counsel, public defenders, and corrections officials, make up a loosely interrelated justice system. Many observers believe that this system is not properly dispensing justice to individual defendants or protecting the public from career criminals. In recent years, more attention has been paid to the rights of victims at both the national and state levels, including amendments to state constitutions giving victims and their families the right to participate in the trial and providing for compensation to victims and their families.

26.4 Assess the controversy over the increased use of imprisonment.

With more than 2 million people in our prisons, the United States has more prisoners than any other country. Imprisonment has been justified as retribution, deterrence, protection of society, and rehabilitation. Disillusionment with rehabilitation and the disparate sentencing by judges has led to the enactment of mandatory minimum sentencing requirements, including three-strikes-and-you're-out legislation. Because of the high cost of imprisonment, states are now considering alternative approaches, including decriminalization, community corrections facilities, and reentry programs.

26.5 Evaluate the proposals and goals of the judicial reform movement.

Judicial reforms are aimed at reducing the crowded dockets and delay that plague courts. Reforms focus on increasing the quality of judges through measures such as higher salaries. Reforms also include improvements in the administration of the court as well as developing alternative methods of resolving disputes.

CHAPTER **SELF-TEST**

26.1 Outline the structure of a state court system.

1. Matching the following terms and definitions.

   a. tort law
   b. misdemeanor
   c. public defender system
   d. indictment

   i. statement charging an individual with an offense
   ii. provides attorneys for those who cannot afford their own
   iii. relating to injuries to person, reputation, or property
   iv. a minor crime

2. If a state does not have an appellate court system, trial court decisions are appealed directly to _____.

3. Using the general outline provided in this chapter, describe how the state court system works.

26.2 Evaluate the different methods of selecting judges.

4. How does a retention election differ from a normal election?

5. Describe which selection method for state judges comes closest to the way U.S. Supreme Court justices are selected.

6. Most state and local judges are elected in some manner. List and explain three benefits and three potential drawbacks of this method of selection.

26.3 Describe the roles of the participants in the criminal justice system.

7. Draw a diagram relating the jury, prosecutor, defense counsel, victim, defendant, and judge to the U.S. justice system. Show how the system works, and detail the specific roles of each actor in the process.

8. Explain how a plea bargain works.

9. Describe both sides of the controversy surrounding mandatory minimum sentencing.

26.4 Assess the controversy over the increased use of imprisonment.

10. Define recidivism. Explain how it relates to the high rates of incarceration in the United States.

11. Write a brief essay exploring some of the possible causes of the high U.S. incarceration rates. What does it say about U.S. society that so many of its citizens are in jail?

26.5 Evaluate the proposals and goals of the judicial reform movement.

12. Write a brief persuasive essay for *one* of the reforms listed in the chapter, detailing and addressing the arguments that could be raised against it.

13. Explain why most judges are unable to earn anything beyond their salaries and must be cautious about investments they make. To help your explanation, use examples (either real or fictitious).

Answers to selected questions: 1. a. iii; b. iv; c. ii; d. i

---

mypoliscilab EXERCISES

Apply what you learned in this chapter on MyPoliSciLab.

Read on mypoliscilab.com

eText: Chapter 26

Study and **Review** on mypoliscilab.com

Pre-Test
Post-Test
Chapter Exam
Flashcards

Watch on mypoliscilab.com

Video: Abuse at Facility for the Mentally Disabled
Video: Pot Possession Now Like Speeding Ticket

Explore on mypoliscilab.com

Comparative: Comparing Judicial Systems

KEY TERMS

recuse, p. 653
new judicial federalism, p. 653
misdemeanor, p. 654
original jurisdiction, p. 654
felony, p. 654
judicial review, p. 655

advisory opinion, p. 655
Missouri Plan, p. 659
retention elections, p. 659
information affidavit, p. 662
indictment, p. 662
assigned counsel system, p. 663

pro bono, p. 663
public defender system, p. 663
due process, p. 664
privatization, p. 666
recidivist, p. 666

ADDITIONAL RESOURCES

FURTHER READING

STEPHEN J. ADLER, *The Jury: Trial and Error in the American Courtroom* (Times Books, 1994).

LAURENCE BAUM, *American Courts: Process and Policy,* 6th ed. (Houghton Mifflin, 2008).

GREG BERMAN AND **JOHN FEINBLATT,** *Good Courts: The Case for Problem-Solving Justice* (New Press, 2005).

MATTHEW BOSWORTH, *Courts as Catalysts: State Supreme Courts and Public School Finance Equity* (State University of New York Press, 2001).

DAVID COLE, *No Equal Justice: Race and Class in the American Criminal Justice System* (New Press, 1999).

SUSAN P. FINO, *The Role of State Supreme Courts in the New Judicial Federalism* (Greenwood Press, 1987).

JULIA FIONDA, *Public Prosecutors and Discretion* (Oxford University Press, 1995).

JOHN B. GATES AND **CHARLES A. JOHNSON,** *The American Courts: A Critical Assessment* (CQ Press, 1991).

MARIE GOTTSCHALK, *The Prison and the Gallows: The Politics of Mass Incarceration in America* (Cambridge University Press, 2006).

JOSEPH R. GRODIN, *In Pursuit of Justice: Reflections of a State Supreme Court Justice* (University of California Press, 1989).

RANDOLPH JONAKAIT, *The American Jury System* (Yale University Press, 2003).

LAURA LANGER, *Judicial Review in State Supreme Courts: A Comparative Study* (State University of New York Press, 2002).

ANN CHIH LIN, *Reform in the Making: The Implementation of Social Policy in Prison* (Princeton University Press, 2000).

CHARLES LOPEMAN, *The Activist Advocate: Policy Making in State Supreme Courts* (Praeger, 1999).

DAVID W. NEUBAUER, *America's Courts and Criminal Justice System,* 8th ed. (Wadsworth, 2004).

DAVID M. O'BRIEN, ED., *Judges on Judging: Views from the Bench* (CQ Press, 2004).

MICHAEL SOLIMINE AND **JAMES WALKER,** *Respecting State Courts: The Inevitability of Judicial Federalism* (Greenwood Press, 2000).

MATTHEW J. STREB, ED., *Running for Judge: The Rising Political, Financial, and Legal Stakes of Judicial Elections* (New York University Press, 2007).

G. ALAN TARR AND **MARY CORNELIA ALDIS PORTER,** *State Supreme Courts in State and Nation* (Yale University Press, 1988).

PAUL B. WICE, *Court Reform and Judicial Leadership* (Praeger, 1995). See also *Judicature: The Journal of the American Judicature Society,* published bimonthly, and its Web site at www.ajs.org.

WEB SITES

www.ncsc.org The National Center for State Courts provides research information and comparative data to support improvement in judicial administration in state courts.

www.nawj.org The National Association of Women Judges advocates for equal justice and access to the courts for women and minorities.

www.brennancenter.org/ The Brennan Center for Justice, a public policy and law institute, is a source for judicial scholarship and advocacy.

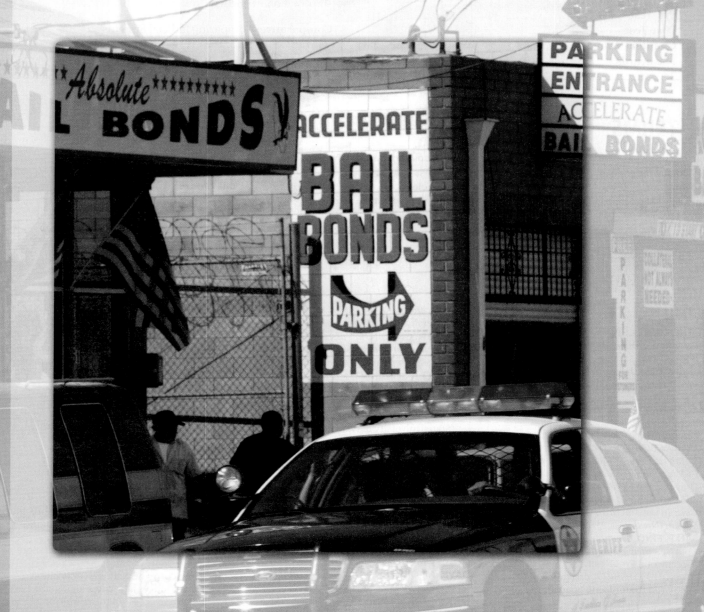

Local Governments and Metropolitics

L ocal governments provide most of the public services ordinary citizens consume on a daily basis. From elementary and secondary schools to traffic lights to electricity and water, we rely on local governments to help us meet our daily needs. One of the major functions provided by local governments are city and county jails. In 2010, National Public Radio (NPR) ran a three-part series on local jails, the system of providing bail for petty offenses, and the powerful bail bondsman lobby that has emerged in recent years.[1]

The NPR story reports that 20 years ago, most defendants accused of petty crimes were released on their own recognizance—meaning they were simply trusted to come to court when required. Today, most defendants are required to post bail or be held in county jails until they can post bail or until their case is resolved. Posting bail requires either making a full cash deposit with the court that is returned to the defendant if they come to court as required, or by paying a bail bondsman a fee—typically 10 percent of the bail level—to post the funds. So, a person arrested and given a bail of $1,000 can either provide the entire amount to the court as a security deposit, which he will get back if he comes to court as required, or he can pay a bondsman $100 (or sometimes more) in a nonrefundable fee and then the bondsman posts the $1,000 deposit. In theory, the bondsman now has the incentive to make sure the defendant comes to court so as not to lose the $1,000 deposit.

In practice, it often does not work that way. NPR found that in Lubbock, Texas, for example, the court routinely only requires a bondsman to pay 5 percent of the total bail amount as a penalty if the defendant does not appear in court. So if the bondsman charges a fee of 10 percent or more, the bondsman makes a profit whether the defendant shows up or not. It turns out that this situation is quite common across the country.

Another consequence of the increasing reliance on bail is a dramatic increase in the number of people housed in city and county jails for extended periods as they await trial because they cannot afford the bail or even the bondsman's 10 percent fee. NPR documented cases that cost county taxpayers thousands of dollars to house defendants accused of stealing a handful of blankets or a single television.

A number of counties have explored alternatives generally called pretrial release programs. Such programs release defendants rather than jail them but provide some sort of monitoring (often including GPS-enabled ankle bracelets) instead of releasing folks on their own recognizance. Broward County, Florida, had a very successful program up and running that cost approximately $7 per day to monitor a defendant, compared with the $116 per day it cost to house them in jail. The program allowed the county to avoid building a new jail at a cost of approximately $20 million as well. However, NPR reports that the same county commissioners that created the program voted two years later to dramatically cut its operations after a local bondsman hired a lobbyist and began making substantial campaign contributions. Pretrial release programs are very unpopular with bondsmen because it substantially reduces their customer base.

This example illustrates two important features to consider when studying local governments. First, local governments make very important decisions that affect citizens in their communities to a great degree. Second, concentrated interests in local communities can have a tremendous impact on local policy making. In the coming pages, we will examine the politics of state and local government and the ways in which these decisions are made.

CHAPTER OUTLINE
CHAPTER LEARNING OBJECTIVES

The Nature of State and Local Relations

27.1 Characterize local government in the United States and the basic relationship between state and local governments.

Counties

27.2 Assess the role of county government.

Towns and Suburbs

27.3 Explain the growth of suburbs and its implications for local governance.

City Government

27.4 Outline the different ways of structuring city government, and describe the functions of mayors.

Central City Politics

27.5 Describe the challenges facing central cities and metro areas.

Metropolitics Today: Meeting the Challenges of Growth and Development

27.6 Evaluate strategies for meeting the various challenges of governance in metropolitan regions.

The Nature of State and Local Relations

27.1 Characterize local government in the United States and the basic relationship between state and local governments.

Local governments vary in structure, size, power, and relationship to one another. Local governments in the United States employ approximately 11.9 million people in more than 89,000 different jurisdictions (see Table 27–1).[2] They are not mentioned in the U.S. Constitution, but in a *constitutional* sense, they all rely on power given to them by the state. That is, most state constitutions create a **unitary system** in which power is vested in the state government, and local units exist only as agents of the state and exercise only those powers expressly given to them by their respective state governments.[3]

Because local governments are typically created by the state and usually have no constitutional authority in their own right, there are fewer obstacles to state interference in local matters than there are to national interference in state matters. State officers participate in local government to a much greater extent than federal officers do in state politics. When doubts arise about the authority of local governments, courts generally decide against them.

Initially, state legislatures had almost unlimited authority over their local governments and ran them pretty much at will. They granted, amended, and repealed city charters; established counties; determined city and county structure; set debt limits; and passed laws for the local units.

But by the end of the nineteenth century, voters had amended or adopted state constitutions that curtailed the power of state legislatures over state local governments. Constitutional provisions determined the structure, and in some cases even the processes, of local governments. **Constitutional home rule** granted constitutional independence to some local units, primarily larger cities, giving them constitutional authority over their form of government and a wide range of other matters. With this protection, state legislatures could no longer determine the structure and powers of these local units.

The extent of state control over local units today varies from state to state and also among the different kinds of local government within each state. At one extreme, local officials merely have to file reports with specified state officials. At the other, state officials have the authority to appoint and remove some local officials, thus exerting considerable control over local affairs. When local governments prove ineffective, state officials may offer them financial assistance with certain strings attached or may even take over responsibilities previously handled locally. The state of Pennsylvania, for instance, took control of Philadelphia's 200,000-pupil school system in 2002 after years of poor achievement and budget problems. Among other things, the state decided to privatize 45 of the city's worst-performing elementary and middle schools, the largest experiment yet in the privatization of public schools.[4] With the passage of the federal No Child Left Behind law in 2002, the federal government extended state involvement in local schools by requiring

unitary system

A constitutional arrangement in which power is concentrated in a central government.

constitutional home rule

State constitutional authorization for local governments to conduct their own affairs.

TABLE

27–1 | Governments in the United States

Type of Government	Number of Governments				
	1967	1977	1987	1997	2007
U.S. government	1	1	1	1	1
State governments	50	50	50	50	50
Local governments	81,248	79,862	83,186	87,453	89,476
County	3,049	3,042	3,042	3,043	3,033
Municipal	18,048	18,862	19,200	19,372	19,492
Township	17,105	16,822	16,691	16,629	16,519
School district	21,782	15,174	14,721	13,726	13,051
Special district	21,264	25,962	29,532	34,683	37,381
Total	**81,299**	**79,913**	**83,237**	**87,504**	**89,527**

■ *The total number of governments has increased since 1967, but which types of governments increased in number, and which decreased?*

SOURCE: For 1967–1997: U.S. Census Bureau, *Statistical Abstract of the United States: 2008*, www.census.gov/compendia/statab. For 2007: U.S. Census Bureau, "2007 Census of Governments," www.census.gov/govs/www/cog2007.html.

states not only to measure schools' progress in meeting standards in reading/language arts, mathematics, and science but also to take corrective action against schools that consistently failed to meet minimal expectations.

Defining Local Government Structures

Before we proceed into the specifics about each level of local government, we will first introduce the big picture. In the United States, a **county** is a local level of government below the state. Counties are used in 48 of the 50 states, and there are on average 62 counties per state. Sub-county governments include **municipalities** and **townships,** which are generally organized around population centers. Because the classification of population centers is a matter of state law, the definition of a city or town varies widely from state to state.

A large city that is a significant economic, political, and cultural center for the region is called a **metropolis.** This metropolis and its adjacent zone of influence, typically one or more closely neighboring cities, is considered a **metropolitan area.** Areas of high population density are considered urban; residential areas—typically within commuting distance of a city—are referred to as suburbs; and rural areas have low population density. (See Figure 27–1.)

Why is there such complexity to local government in this country? The basic pattern was imported from England, as were many of our governmental forms. Over time, new governments were created to take on new jobs when existing units proved either too small or unequal to the task. The past three generations have seen millions of citizens moving from the cities to the suburbs, and then beyond the suburbs to places that were rural only a generation ago. The need to establish and maintain new schools, water and sewage services, law enforcement agencies, roads, and bridges, and the need to meet the many other demands of a sprawling population that have contributed to increasing governmental complexity.

Although our system of local governments is sometimes costly and inefficient, it performs many essential functions and provides opportunities for political officials and citizens to respond, sometimes in innovative ways, to public problems or political views that state and federal governments overlook. Communities have enacted ideas such as

county
The largest local level of government below the state, currently used in 48 states.

municipality
A local level of government within counties that are usually organized around population centers.

township
A local level of government below the county used primarily in 20 northeastern states.

metropolis
A large city or municipality that serves as an economic and cultural center for a region.

metropolitan area
The larger area surrounding a metropolis that is heavily influenced by the metropolis, generally consisting of suburbs and other smaller cities.

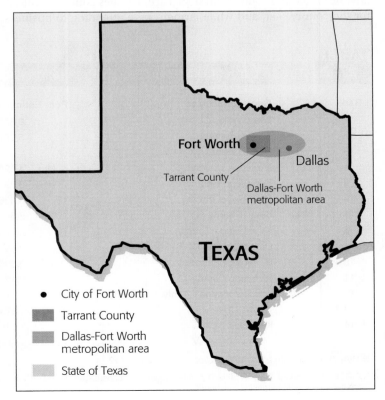

City of Fort Worth

Tarrant County

Dallas-Fort Worth metropolitan area

State of Texas

FIGURE 27–1 Local Government in Fort Worth, Texas.

■ Based on the figure, what are five types of government operating in Fort Worth, Texas?

"living wage" laws (companies doing business with the city must provide their workers enough income for a decent standard of living), public financing programs for election campaigns, and market-based approaches to education reform (such as charter schools and vouchers).[5] National surveys of citizens' views reveal the responsiveness of local governments, which usually come out ahead of both the federal and state governments when people are asked which they trust to perform well in carrying out their responsibilities.[6]

Counties

LEARNING **OBJECTIVE**

27.2 Assess the role of county government.

Counties are the largest jurisdictions within a state and are among the oldest and most stable local governments in terms of their boundaries not changing. Urban and suburban counties have many of the same governmental structures as their rural counterparts, but they are more intertwined with their urban centers. Some suburban counties are better known than any of the cities or municipalities within them—for example, Westchester County, New York; Montgomery County, Maryland; Marin and Orange Counties, California; and Bucks County, Pennsylvania. Some cities, such as Boston, Denver, Baltimore, Philadelphia, San Francisco, and Honolulu, are simultaneously cities and counties; New York City consists of five counties or boroughs—New York (Manhattan), Kings (Brooklyn), Queens, the Bronx, and Richmond (Staten Island). In Louisiana, counties are called *parishes*, whereas in Alaska, they are called *boroughs*. Connecticut and Rhode Island have geographic units called counties, but their counties do not have functioning governments.

There are 3,033 county governments throughout the United States, and they vary in size, population, and functions. Loving County, Texas, for example, had 45 inhabitants in 2009; Los Angeles County, California, had an estimated 9.9 million.[7] Table 27–2 lists the 15 largest counties. Although they represent only 0.5 percent of the 3,033 counties in the United States, more than 48 million people live in them—or 16 percent of the total U.S. population. In fact, more than half the people in the United States live in the most populous 5 percent of all counties.

Counties were originally organized on the idea that the county seat—the town or city where the county government is based—would be no more than a day's journey for anyone within the county's borders. Farm families could pile into their wagons and head for the county seat, and while farmers were attending to business, their families could

TABLE

27–2	The 15 Largest U.S. Counties by Population (2009)	
Rank	**Geographic Area**	**Pop. Estimate July 1, 2009**
1	Los Angeles County, CA	9,848,011
2	Cook County, IL	5,287,037
3	Harris County, TX	4,070,989
4	Maricopa County, AZ	4,023,132
5	San Diego County, CA	3,053,793
6	Orange County, CA	3,026,786
7	Kings County, NY	2,567,098
8	Miami-Dade County, FL	2,500,625
9	Dallas County, TX	2,451,730
10	Queens County, NY	2,306,712
11	Riverside County, CA	2,125,440
12	San Bernardino County, CA	2,017,673
13	Wayne County, MI	1,925,848
14	King County, WA	1,916,441
15	Clark County, NV	1,902,834

■ *Why is the county a useful jurisdiction within a state?*

SOURCE: U.S. Census Bureau, *2009 Population Estimates*, census.gov. Based on Table 7: Resident Population Estimates for the 100 Largest U.S. Counties.

shop and pick up the local gossip. Then they could all get home in time to do the evening chores. Today, of course, we can drive across a whole state or several states in a day.

The traditional functions of counties include law enforcement, highway construction and maintenance, tax collection and property assessment, recording of legal papers, and administration of welfare programs. Until recently, counties were convenient subdivisions that largely carried out policies established elsewhere. During the past generation, however, although counties in a few states have given up some of their responsibilities, in most others, especially in the South, they have taken over from the states such urban functions as transportation, water and sewer operation, and land use planning.[8] Elsewhere, cities are contracting with counties to provide such joint services as employee training, law enforcement, and corrections, and in some instances, cities and counties are merging some governmental functions such as local public education—something we explore further later in this chapter. County governments are least active in the New England states, where the county is often little more than a judicial and law enforcement district; county officials may do some road building but not much else.

County Government

Most counties have limited legislative power. The typical county has a central governing body, variously titled but most frequently called the *county commission* or *board of supervisors*. Most boards have three to seven members, although in very large counties, boards sometimes have several dozen members. They administer state laws, levy taxes, appropriate money, issue bonds, sign contracts on behalf of the county, and handle whatever jobs the state laws and constitution assign to them (see Figure 27–2).

Traditionally, many county boards were composed of the supervisors of townships or other township officials. Now, most of the boards in larger counties are elected from districts. The smaller boards are usually, though not always, elected in at-large elections. (At-large elections are countywide contests, not elections in which each board member is chosen from a different district; usually, the several top vote getters all win seats in at-large elections.) At-large elections make it more difficult for minorities to be elected to office, especially when they are concentrated in a few areas.

The county board shares its powers with a number of other officials, most commonly the sheriff, the county prosecutor or district attorney, the county clerk, the coroner, and the auditor, who are generally elected rather than appointed. Sometimes county treasurers, health officers, and surveyors are also found on the ballot.

Most counties still vest both legislative authority (the power to enact local ordinances and adopt budgets) and executive powers (the administration of policies and the hiring and firing of county employees) in the county commission or board of supervisors. However, an increasing number of counties—more than 40 percent now—assign executive responsibilities to a single individual, and Arkansas, Kentucky, and Tennessee mandate that their counties have a single elected top executive.[9] Some appoint a chief administrative officer who serves at the pleasure of the county commissioners, but the trend is toward an independently elected *county executive*. One recent estimate indicates that more than 700 counties now have elected executives who are responsible for most administrative functions (see Figure 27–3).[10]

County Performance

How well do counties perform? Most adequately perform their traditional duties of assessing property; keeping records; maintaining roads; and administering elections, local courts, and jails.[11] Some struggle with these functions, whereas others have expanded their responsibilities to include child welfare, consumer protection, economic development, water quality, public safety, and employment/training.

Differences in the relative wealth and growth rates of counties likely contribute to differences in performance. Counties rely heavily on their own revenue sources. In 2002, they received only 3 percent of their revenues from the federal government and 33 percent from their states.[12] This means they must rely on their own revenue base to attract

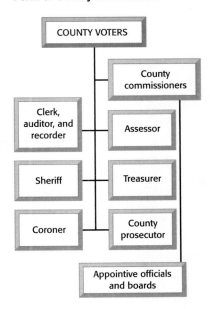

FIGURE 27–2 The Commission Form of County Government.

FIGURE 27–3 The Council with Elected Executive Form of County Government.

professional staff, provide adequate services, and have up-to-date facilities and information systems. This revenue base may be quite weak in many rural and older urban areas.

Yet the trend is toward expanded functions and improved capacity to perform these functions. Their jurisdictional boundaries give counties great potential to solve complex problems difficult to address at the city level or decentralized to local levels of government by the states. The growing professionalization of county workforces and the trend to elect or appoint professional county executives are improving efficiency.

Towns and Suburbs

LEARNING **OBJECTIVE**

27.3 Explain the growth of suburbs and its implications for local governance.

Towns, also called townships, are the basic unit of government smaller than a county in 20 northeastern and midwestern states. The number of towns in the United States has declined as growing municipalities have absorbed them (see Table 27–1). In most states that have them, towns are governed by elected officials typically including a supervisor, town board, and clerk. In New England, citizens do not only vote for members of the town board and other officers; in at least 1,000 towns, they also participate in annual town meetings. The New England town meeting is our most complete example of *direct democracy;* voters participate directly in making rules, passing new laws, levying taxes, and appropriating money. Maine has 209 towns that use a pure town meeting system of democracy,[13] and, according to the Massachusetts Constitution, towns of 6,000 residents or less must adopt a town meeting form of government.[14]

A group of active citizens that provides political and policy-making leadership usually dominates town meetings. Officers elected there perform most of the actual day-to-day governing of the town. Some large towns have adopted a modified *representative* town meeting, electing 50 to 200 town residents to represent their neighborhoods. Yet the open town meeting, at least in small towns in New England, still provides a vital way for people to participate in the policy making of their communities.

During the last half-century, the areas around cities have been the fastest-growing places in the United States (see Figure 27–4). At least 50 percent of U.S. citizens now live in suburban communities. Suburbs have grown up at the expense of cities for a variety of reasons: inexpensive land, lower taxes, cleaner air, more open space for recreational purposes, less crime, and better highways. Resistance to mandatory busing to achieve integrated schools in the 1960s and 1970s contributed to so-called white flight.[15] But it was just as much a matter of class as of race, with middle- and upper-middle-income-level

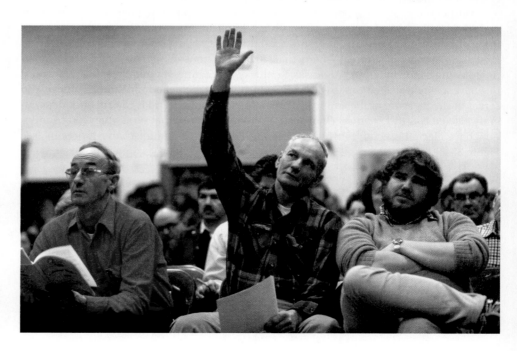

The New England town meeting, like this one in Sandwich, New Hampshire, has long been a celebrated U.S. institution. ■ *How are town meetings examples of direct democracy?*

Percentage of Americans Living in Suburbs and Central Cities at Each Census

■ Suburbs ■ Central cities

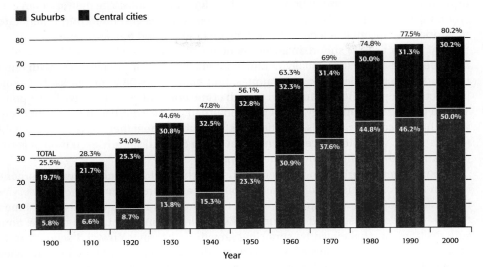

FIGURE 27–4 **Moving to the Suburbs.**

SOURCE: U.S. Census Bureau, *Population Estimates,* factfinder.census.gov.

whites, Asians, and African Americans moving to the suburbs to escape urban crime and to seek more attractive environments in terms of class, religion, race, and lifestyle.[16]

Suburbs have also grown because industries have moved from the central cities in search of cheaper land, lower taxes, and less restrictive building and health codes. Other businesses, including shopping centers, followed the people and the industries. This exodus was accelerated by federal policies promoting interstate highways and mortgages insured by the Federal Housing Administration. Most of the new jobs created in the United States continue to be located in the suburbs or newer cities on the fringes of the central cities. For example, although the St. Louis metropolitan area was fairly compact in 1950, by the end of the twentieth century, it had expanded into 11 counties in both Missouri and Illinois, and high-density areas are now found many miles from the central city (see Figure 27–5). Many of these newer areas are disconnected from other urbanized localities.

The form of suburban government employed by states varies widely. Suburbs have grown in formerly rural townships and in previously unincorporated areas of counties. Smaller municipalities located near larger central cities have also been swallowed up by the growth of suburbs and absorbed by the larger metropolitan area composed of the

FIGURE 27–5 **Map of St. Louis.**
This map shows the expansion of urban areas around St. Louis, Missouri, between 1950 and 2000. Areas are considered urban when their population density exceeds 1,000 people per square mile.
■ *What are some of the factors that account for the urban sprawl seen around St. Louis?*

SOURCE: East-West Gateway Council of Governments— St. Louis, Missouri, http://www.ewgateway.org/pdffiles/ maplibrary/ChangeUA3.pdf.

central city and all its suburban areas. The existing governments of these areas have had to adapt to new, larger populations and their different demands. The metropolitan areas around larger cities usually stretch across several counties and often into other states, presenting significant challenges in planning for land use and transportation.

The major tasks of suburban government are often bound together with those of the metropolis.[17] Larger cities usually maintain an elaborate police department with detective bureaus, crime detection laboratories, and communications networks, but police jurisdiction stops at the city line even though crime does not. Suburbs have fewer police, seldom trained in criminology, so they call on urban police expertise. Intercity highways, which have local access roads, also tie cities and suburbs together. In matters of health, there are often wide differences in services between city and suburb, even though germs, pollutants, and smog do not notice city signposts.

Some larger suburban town governments have begun to resemble city governments, both in the professionalization of elected officials and bureaucracy and in the services that residents of the towns expect to receive. Older suburbs are now experiencing some of the problems long associated with urban disinvestment and population decline. Some suburbs, too, are challenged by sprawling growth that creates crowded schools, traffic congestion, loss of open space, and a lack of affordable housing. Many people believe there is a need for collaborative city–suburb strategies to address sprawl and the structural challenges facing older suburbs and inner cities.

Eminent Domain

Since the founding of the United States, governments have had the power to take private land for public purposes, even without the consent of the landowner. This power, called **eminent domain,** comes from English common law. State and local governments have mostly used eminent domain in cases of clear public need—for instance, the construction of a road or bridge—and tempered it by recognizing a right to just compensation for the landowner, usually paying the market rate for the land.

As discussed in Chapter 15, eminent domain has recently generated some controversy when the Supreme Court ruled that New London, Connecticut's plan to redevelop an older residential neighborhood and turn it over to a private development company to build commercial and residential properties was permissible under the Fifth Amendment's eminent domain provision.[18] This decision generated a lot of criticism in the media, and most states quickly enacted laws revoking or restricting their local governments' powers to use eminent domain for economic development.[19]

City Government

LEARNING **OBJECTIVE**
27.4 Outline the different ways of structuring city government, and describe the functions of mayors.

A city is not merely different real estate; it is also people—men and women living and working together. Aristotle asserted that people came together in the cities for security, but they stayed there for the good life.

Different people define the "good life" differently, yet it often includes these attractions:

- Employment opportunities
- Cultural centers, museums, performing arts centers, and theaters
- Diverse educational institutions
- Entertainment and nightlife
- Professional sports teams
- Wide variety of stores and specialty shops
- Good restaurants
- Diversity of people, architecture, and lifestyles

Although a few cities existed when the U.S. Constitution was written, the nation was overwhelmingly rural in 1787, and seven of ten people worked on farms and clustered mainly in the villages and small towns scattered throughout the 13 states and adjacent

eminent domain
The power a government has to take private land to use for a public purpose.

YOU WILL DECIDE — Does Economic Development Justify Eminent Domain?

One issue raised in the Supreme Court decision of *Kelo* v. *City of New London* (2005) was the question of whether a government may transfer ownership of property from one private owner to another by exercising its power of eminent domain in support of economic development goals.* The city of New London in Connecticut has long suffered from a declining population and high levels of unemployment. When a pharmaceutical corporation began building a large research facility in the city, New London officials decided it would be an excellent opportunity to revitalize the largely run-down area near the corporation's facility by promoting the construction of a hotel, a conference center, a new state park, new residences, and office space. The city set up a private agency to create and implement an ambitious development plan for the area, including acquiring the land needed to put the plan into effect. The development corporation bought many of the parcels of land needed for the plan, but a few landowners refused to sell their land, and the development

corporation, under the city's authority, then exercised the power of eminent domain.

The landowners sued, and the case eventually came before the U.S. Supreme Court, which had to decide whether this use of eminent domain qualified as a "public use" in the federal constitution's "taking clause," which states that private property shall not "be taken for public use, without just compensation."† Most of the landowners suing the city lived on the properties, and no claims were made by the city that these particular properties were blighted or in poor condition. One owner had lived on the property (indeed in the particular house) since her birth in 1918.

What do you think? Should local governments be able to use eminent domain to seize private property for the use of economic development? What are some of the arguments for or against it?

THINKING IT THROUGH

In an opinion written by Justice John Paul Stevens, the Court determined that the taking of these properties was constitutional, even though the properties would in the end be owned, developed, and used by private parties. The reason was that the city's goal was a *public* purpose, to promote economic growth and development, a traditional function of government. Even though some private persons may benefit from the use of eminent domain and the subsequent transfer of property, those facts did not mean the taking of property primarily served private purposes.

Justice Sandra Day O'Connor wrote a dissent arguing that the Court's decision opened the possibility that governments could take property simply because they decided other owners would make more productive use of it. She argued:

> nearly any lawful use of real private property can be said to generate some incidental benefit to the public. Thus, if pre-dicted…positive side effects are enough to render transfer from one private party to another constitutional, then the words 'for public use' do not realistically exclude *any* takings, and thus do not exert any constraint on the eminent domain power.

Further, she wrote, "Nothing is to prevent the State [or City] from replacing any Motel 6 with a Ritz-Carlton, any home with a shopping mall, or any farm with a factory."

Although the case raised many complex questions about the federal constitution, the decision quickly pushed the issue onto the agendas of city councils and state legislatures, which were pressured by the public's (largely negative) reaction to *Kelo* to alter guidelines regarding what local governments may do regarding the taking of land and property in service of economic development goals.**

Critical Thinking Questions

1. Is it ever justifiable for a city or state government to use its eminent domain authority to transfer property from one group of property owners to another to promote economic development in a distressed city or town? Why or why not?

2. If you think this use of eminent domain is justifiable under some circumstances but not others, or only after certain procedures are followed, what should those circumstances or procedures be?

---

*545 U.S. 469 (2005).
†The "takings clause" is found at the end of the Fifth Amendment to the U.S. Constitution and was incorporated into the Fourteenth Amendment to apply to states and localities. The Supreme Court has typically deferred to state and local governments' decisions about what constitutes a "public use."
**For state legislative responses to *Kelo*, see the Web site of the National Conference of State Legislatures, http://www.ncsl.org/?Tabid=17604.

---

territories. These were the indispensable workshops of democracy, the places where democratic skills were developed and political issues were debated.

The United States is now a nation of about 19,492 municipalities, more than 9,000 of which have fewer than 1,000 residents, and only 58 have 300,000 residents or more.[20] Although some small cities or incorporated villages have only a few hundred people, the largest have millions. Three U.S. supercities and their suburbs (New York, Los Angeles, and Chicago) each have populations larger than the total population of the Republic in the 1780s.

A **charter** is to a city what a constitution is to a national or state government. It outlines the structure of the government, defines the authority of the various officials, and provides for their selection. Different structures are not neutral in their impact; they encourage

charter
A city "constitution" that outlines the structure of city government, defines the authority of the various officials, and provides for their selection.

FIGURE 27–6 The Mayor–Council Form of City
Government.

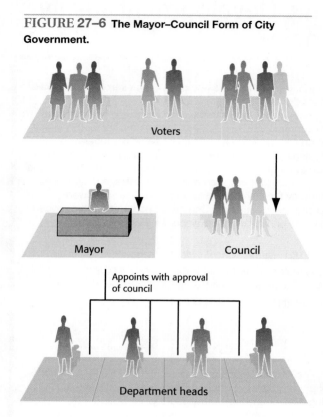

different kinds of participation and responsiveness. Decisions about who gets what, where, and how are shaped by a city's structural arrangements.

The Mayor–Council Charter

The **mayor–council charter** is the oldest type (see Figure 27–6). Under this type of charter, the city council is usually a single chamber. The size of the council varies from as few as 2 members to as many as 50, although 7 is the median size in cities with more than 5,000 people. Most small cities and municipalities use this type of charter. It is also still the most common type in the largest cities, and in medium-sized cities in the East and Midwest.

Many methods are used to select council members: nonpartisan and partisan elections, elections by large and small wards (specific districts in the municipality), or elections from the city at large when the city is not divided into separate geographic districts. Large cities that elect members affiliated with political parties generally choose them by small districts or wards rather than at-large. This arrangement tends to support strong party organizations. Nonpartisan at-large elections make party influence difficult. The larger the election districts, the more likely citywide considerations will affect the selection of council members and the greater the influence of citywide institutions such as local newspapers.

The difference between at-large citywide elections and elections based on small, single-member districts within a city can be significant for racial and ethnic representation on the city council. The at-large system tends to produce councils made up of the city's elite and middle classes. Smaller districts give minorities and the less advantaged a somewhat better chance for representation, especially where neighborhoods have high concentrations of one minority or income group.[21]

The Voting Rights Act of 1965 forbids states and cities with a history of discrimination against minority voters from adopting the at-large system for electing council members if the effect would be to dilute the voting strength of these minorities. In fact, no local government in the 11 former Confederate states can make a change in its voting system without the approval of the U.S. attorney general. But what of cities or counties that have long had at-large elections? Can they be forced to give them up because at-large elections virtually ensure that minorities will never be elected? In a 1980 case, the Supreme Court found that the Constitution forbids only practices adopted or maintained *with the intent to discriminate;* the Court permitted Mobile, Alabama, to keep its seven-decades-old system of choosing city commissioners in at-large elections, even though no black person had ever been elected to the three-person commission, because there was no direct evidence that the system was established with a discriminatory intent.[22] However, Congress rejected this interpretation when it enacted the extension of the Voting Rights Act in 1982. In the revised Act, voters can challenge a voting scheme, such as at-large elections, by demonstrating that the voting arrangements, based on all the evidence presented, were racially discriminatory in their effects regardless of intent.[23]

Weak and Strong Mayor Councils

The powers of the mayor–council form of government vary from charter to charter and even more widely from city to city and mayor to mayor. There are, however, two basic variations of the mayor–council form: the weak mayor council and the strong mayor council.

In cities with the **weak mayor–council form,** mayors are often chosen from members of the elected city council rather than elected directly by the people. The mayor's appointive powers are usually restricted, and the city council as a whole generally possesses both legislative and executive authority. The mayor must usually obtain the council's consent for all major decisions. Often weak mayor–council cities permit direct election by the voters of a number of department heads, such as police chief or controller. In weak mayor–council cities, there is no single administrative head for the city, and power is fragmented. The weak mayor–council plan was designed for an earlier era, when

mayor–council charter
The oldest and most common form of city government, consisting of either a weak mayor and a city council or a strong mayor elected by voters and council.

weak mayor–council form
A form of local government in which the members of the city council select the mayor, who then shares power with other elected or appointed boards and commissions.

cities were smaller and government was simpler. It is ill-suited to large cities, where political and administrative leadership is vital.

Under the **strong mayor–council form,** the mayor is elected directly by the people and given fairly broad appointment powers. The mayor, often with the help of his or her staff, prepares and administers the budget, enjoys almost total administrative authority, and has the power to appoint and dismiss department heads. This system obviously calls for a mayor to be both a good political leader and an effective administrator—qualities not always found in the same person.

Many people believe the strong mayor–council system is the best form of government for large cities because it gives the cities strong political leaders and makes responsive administration possible. Further, by centering authority in the hands of a few individuals, it makes less likely the growth of "invisible government" by people who have power but are not publicly accountable for its use.

The Council–Manager Charter

Reformers in the early 1900s acclaimed the **council–manager plan** (also known as the *city-manager plan*), in which the city council hires a professional administrator to manage city affairs. It was indeed a significant governmental innovation. In 1908, the small city of Staunton, Virginia, appointed a general manager to oversee the city's work. Little note was taken of the step, but the council–manager plan soon became the darling of both reformers and the business elite. They liked the idea that the council would serve as a sort of "board of directors" in the business sense of setting broad policies, while a professional executive would see that these policies were carried out with business-like efficiency (see Figure 27–7).

Under the council–manager charter, the council is usually elected in nonpartisan primaries and elections, either on a citywide basis or by election districts much larger than the wards in mayor–council cities. The council appoints a city manager and supervises the manager's activities. The council still makes the laws and approves the budget, and although it is not supposed to interfere in administration, the council often supervises city government through the manager. The mayor is expected to preside over the council and represent the city on ceremonial occasions, but many mayors in fact do a good deal more than this. The mayor in council–manager cities can sometimes be a strong policy and political leader as well as a dominant influence in exercising political power.[24] This has been the case in cities as different as Cambridge, Massachusetts; San Antonio, Texas; and Colorado Springs, Colorado.

The city manager advises the council on policy and supervises the administration of city business. Because council–manager cities try to attract the best available people, few of their charters require the councils to select managers from among local citizens, nor do they prescribe detailed qualifications. Although council–manager charters seem to call for a nonpolitical city manager who does not make policy but merely carries out policies adopted by the council, and for council members who refrain from interfering with the administration of city affairs, real politics is not so simple. Managers often influence policy, if only informally, and council members get involved in administrative affairs. Indeed, it is often difficult to distinguish clearly between making and applying policy.

Today, more than 3,100 cities located in virtually every state operate under a council–manager charter. In fact, it has become the most popular form of local government in medium-sized cities of more than 10,000 citizens. It is especially popular in California, where approximately 98 percent of the cities use it, as well as in other western and Sun Belt cities. Some of the larger cities operating under a city manager are Dallas, San Antonio, San Jose, Kansas City, Cincinnati, Fresno, Colorado Springs, and Fort Worth.

strong mayor–council form
A form of local government in which the voters directly elect the city council and the mayor, who enjoys nearly total administrative authority and appoints the department heads.

council–manager plan
A form of local government in which the city council hires a professional administrator to manage city affairs; also known as the *city-manager plan*.

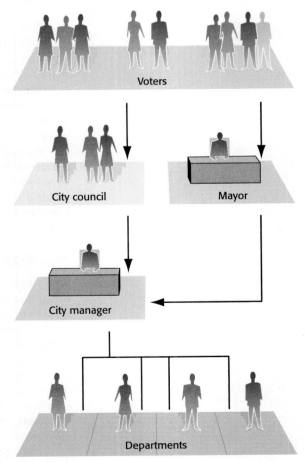

FIGURE 27–7 The Council–Manager Form of City Government.

Of the People

City Councils Are Becoming More Diverse

City councils are becoming more racially and ethnically diverse; the number of people of color serving nearly doubled in the last two decades, in all categories of cities (small, medium, and large), from 7 percent to 13 percent.

During the last decade, Hispanic council membership has increased the most in medium cities, with populations of 70,000 to 199,999—jumping from 0 to 6 percent—and in large cities, with populations of more than 200,000, growing there from 1 percent to 11 percent. During the same time, the percentage of Asian Americans declined from 3 percent to 1 percent.

The representation of women on city councils increased as well. It grew from 21 percent to 25 percent in small cities, from 25 percent to 36 percent in medium-sized cities, and from 33 percent to 36 percent in large cities.

CRITICAL THINKING QUESTIONS

1. What explains the predominance of whites on city councils, as seen in this table?

2. Do you think the representation of women in city councils will continue to increase, stay at present levels, or decline? Why?

Percentage of Council Members

Year	White	African American	Hispanic	Asian	Native American	Other
1979	92	5	1	—	—	—
1989	86	10	1	3	—	1
2001	87	8	3	1	1	1

Percentages may not add to 100 percent because of rounding.

SOURCE: National League of Cities, *Research Brief on America's Cities: The Faces of America's City Councils* (September 2003), available at www.nlc.org. Used by permission.

How has the city-manager plan worked? The literature is mixed, but one empirical study finds no significant difference in the relative efficiency of council–manager versus mayor–council forms of government.[25] Another study found that strategic planning had a greater impact on development policy in council–manager cities compared with mayor–council cities.[26] The study also found that population and median income are stronger influences on developmental policy in mayor–council cities, whereas poverty was a more powerful force on development policy in council-manager systems.

In an effort to become more responsive, some council–manager cities have expanded the size of their councils and abandoned at-large elections for district elections. More than 60 percent of the city-manager cities now also directly elect their mayors to provide greater political accountability and leadership.[27] Some cities have recently moved from a council–manager form of government to a strong mayor–council form, such as San Diego, which switched in 2006.[28]

The Role of the Mayor

Two hundred years ago, the notion of a strong mayor providing vigorous leadership was nonexistent. The need for strong mayoral leadership developed in the late nineteenth century as a means to deal with the social revolution brought on by urbanization, massive waves of immigration, and mounting economic problems of growing cities. In the larger cities, the office of mayor gradually became a key position for political leadership.

The typical mayor is a college graduate, a business or legal professional, and an experienced grassroots politician between 40 and 50 years old. Mayors in the largest cities earn from $90,000 to $216,000 and in middle-sized cities, between $40,000 and $80,000. City managers, chief city administrators, and top appointees sometimes make more than the mayors.

Although most mayors are male, several of the nation's largest cities have had female mayors, including Baltimore, Atlanta, Chicago, Pittsburgh, Houston, Dallas, San Diego, San Antonio, and Portland. As of July 2009, 17.6 percent of municipal governments in the

United States with a population of 30,000 or more were headed by women.[29] Many worked their way up through service on school boards and city councils and in the League of Women Voters. Many African Americans also serve as mayors, especially in larger cities. The first African Americans elected to be mayors in big cities were Carl Stokes of Cleveland and Richard Hatcher of Gary, Indiana, both elected in 1967. Of the 100 largest cities with elected mayors, 39 have had black mayors as of 2007, including six of the ten largest cities in the United States: New York (David Dinkins), Los Angeles (Tom Bradley), Chicago (Harold Washington), Houston (Lee Brown), Philadelphia (Wilson Goode, John Street, and Michael Nutter), and Dallas (Ron Kirk).[30] The National Conference of Black Mayors claims to represent more than 650 black mayors across the United States.[31]

The main job of the mayor is administrative in the broadest sense of the term. Mayors supervise the line agencies—police, fire, public safety, traffic, health, and sanitation—as well as a host of special agencies such as the board of elections, the city planning agency, and commissions that regulate particular occupations and professions. Big-city mayors usually have staffs that carry out typical executive office functions such as human resources, management, budgeting, scheduling, and public relations. In this respect, mayors face the same tasks as corporate executives: coordinating a variety of activities, assigning responsibilities, checking that projects are carried out, finding the ablest people to take charge, and allocating money through control of the budget.

Usually mayors work with the private sector to promote economic opportunities. They try to secure additional jobs, increase the tax base, make the city more attractive to certain kinds of businesses, and coordinate public service expansion with private sector requirements. The private sector undertakes economic development because its success depends on having an educated labor base with appropriate skills, a constant consumer population, stable communities, and increasing property values.

Sometimes a mayor must depend on the party organization to ensure support in the council, as in Chicago, where the huge city council consists of 50 members. Other mayors may have to deal with smaller councils, but they are likely to be weak unless they have enough political support to win cooperation.

Although partisan politics is waning as a feature of city government, mayors as party leaders still often dominate the party's city organizations. Mayors help recruit candidates for office, deal with revolts and opposition within their parties, and represent their parties in Washington or the state capitals. As chief legislators, mayors draw up proposed legislation and also make many specific policies. As chief fund-raisers, mayors bargain for more money for their cities before state and national legislatures.

Mayors often climb the political ladder to run for governor and senator. For example, there were ten current or former mayors running for governor in 2010, and six of them won—in California, Colorado, Connecticut, Tennessee, Rhode Island, and Maine. Seven current or former mayors ran for seats in the U.S. House of Representatives, and five of them won. Current U.S. Senators George Voinovich, Richard Lugar, and Jake Garn had been mayors of Cleveland, Indianapolis, and Salt Lake City, respectively.

Only three presidents had served as mayors—Andrew Johnson, Calvin Coolidge, and Grover Cleveland—and only Cleveland had been mayor of a major city (Buffalo). The most recent former mayor to run for president was Hubert Humphrey in 1968; he lost that election to Richard Nixon, but he had begun his long and otherwise successful political career as mayor of Minneapolis. Former Mayor Rudolph Giuliani of New York City ran for the Republican presidential nomination in 2008 but dropped out quickly after a series of poor finishes in state primaries.

Mayors are expected to help revitalize the economy and attract investors, sports teams, tourists, and conventions. Many mayors,

Michael Bloomberg of New York City seriously considered running as a third-party candidate for U.S. president in the 2008 elections, and the national media closely followed his vacillation and final decision not to run. His name has also been brought up as a potential candidate in 2012. ■ *What would make a mayor a strong presidential candidate?*

such as those in New York, San Francisco, Seattle, Atlanta, Chicago, and Miami, have their own "foreign policies." That is, they play host to foreign dignitaries and business delegations and travel abroad seeking foreign investments as they sing the praises of local exportable goods.[32] It takes courage and missionary zeal to overcome the pessimism and decay that beset most inner cities. But several mayors—including Rudolph Giuliani in New York City and both Richard J. Daley and his son Richard M. Daley in Chicago—succeeded in reducing crime, increasing economic opportunities, and revitalizing downtown businesses and residential areas.

In recent decades, mayors, like presidents and governors, have grown in power and importance. Most cities have altered their charters to give their mayors power to appoint and remove heads of departments, investigate departmental activities, send legislative messages to the city councils, prepare budgets, and veto council ordinances. In other words, mayors have been given a share in policy making, and city administration has been centralized under the mayor's direction.

Central City Politics

LEARNING **OBJECTIVE**

27.5 Describe the challenges facing central cities and metro areas.

Today, most people live in *metropolitan areas,* which include large cities and their suburbs, rather than in the small towns so beloved and often idealized. The U.S. Census Bureau, which counts 363 metropolitan areas, defines a Metropolitan Statistical Area (also called a metro area) as at least one "core" urban area of at least 50,000 people and any adjacent outlying counties "that have a high degree of social and economic integration (as measured by commuting to work) with the urban core."[33]

Approximately 84 percent of U.S. citizens (252 million people) live in metropolitan areas, and 27 percent live in cities of populations greater than 100,000.[34] Between 2000 and 2007, the five fastest-growing large metropolitan areas (of those with a population of more than 1 million) were in the South and the West: Las Vegas, Nevada; Raleigh, North Carolina; Phoenix, Arizona; Austin, Texas; and Riverside, California. All increased their populations by more than 25 percent in only seven years.[35]

In the nineteenth century, masses of new immigrants arrived in the cities from Europe. In the twentieth century, migrants came from rural areas, especially from the South. More recently, this country experienced waves of newcomers from Cuba, Korea, Vietnam, the Philippines, Nicaragua, Haiti, Mexico, and other Latin American countries. Many newcomers settle first in the inner cities—usually in the poorest and most decayed sections—which inevitably puts great stress on the schools and sometimes on community safety as well. Overcrowding and substandard housing in these areas increase health and fire hazards.

Central cities have historically faced a number of problems. They have more "high-cost citizens" (truly needy, handicapped, and senior citizens), and most aging cities have been losing population. They have also lost businesses because land, rents, utilities, operating costs, and taxes are often less expensive in the outer suburbs. Businesses move out of the city to lower their operating costs, and their departure means that cities have smaller tax bases.

The shrinking tax base has made it difficult for cities to raise sufficient revenue from sources such as the property tax. However, the demand for services has not decreased. Many suburban dwellers commute into cities and use city services during the workday but do not pay income taxes in the city. Most of the states have not permitted their cities to raise funds in any meaningful way with a local income tax, which means that cities cannot use the most direct method to make up the lost revenue.[36]

In an effort to recapture part of the tax base that escapes to the suburbs in the evenings, some cities have imposed local payroll or other types of *commuter taxes* to obtain revenue from people who work in the central cities and make frequent use of city facilities yet live in the suburbs. Some city officials say the payroll or commuter tax is an effective way to shift some of the burden to those who benefit from the city but live beyond its borders. But others say it is unlikely to provide significant long-term revenue growth, and they think it encourages even more businesses to leave the city.

For the People

GOVERNMENT'S GREATEST ENDEAVORS

Local Government Discretion

The state government in Arizona passed a series of new laws on immigration in the spring of 2010. Among them is a provision requiring individuals to carry immigration documents with them, allowing local police greater latitude on stopping people suspected of being in the country illegally. Another provision effectively requires local officials to ask someone for proof of legal residence if the police have any suspicion that the person might not be in the country legally.

The catch to these new provisions: Like many state laws, they rely in part on local county sheriffs for enforcement. Clarence W. Dupnik is the sheriff of Pima County, where Tucson is located, and which shares a 123-mile border with Mexico. He has openly stated that he will not enforce the law as he considers it likely to encourage racial profiling, and he feels that enforcing immigration rules is a burden better suited for the federal government. He published an editorial to this effect in *The Wall Street Journal*.*

In contrast, Sheriff Joe Arpaio, his counterpart in Maricopa County, which includes Phoenix, strongly supports the law. In fact, the self-proclaimed "America's Toughest

Sheriff" has engaged in his own crusade to crack down on illegal immigrants for several years before this law was passed.†

Both sheriffs have held their jobs for decades, and both are responding to what they think is right for the citizens of their counties. This is local government in action—responding to citizens and deviating from state policy where they see fit. Depending on your own views regarding legal and illegal immigration, you might applaud the efforts of one of these sheriffs and deplore the efforts of the other, but there is no question that they are exercising what

they feel is the local discretion they have to enforce or not enforce state laws.

CRITICAL THINKING QUESTIONS

1. Should local law enforcement officials have the discretion to enforce some state laws vigorously and others not at all? What are the consequences of your answer?

2. Should dealing with illegal immigrants be primarily a national, state, or local policy problem? Where should policies be set? Which level should pay for them? Who should be charged with implementing those policies?

Sheriff Dupnik has stated he will not enforce the new law.

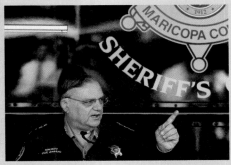

Sheriff Arpaio supports the new law.

*http://online.wsj.com/article/SB10001424052748704342604575222420517514084.html.
†See this National Public Radio story from 2008 at http://www.npr.org/templates/story/story.php?storyId=88002493.

The incidence of child poverty is another problem central cities face. Child poverty is statistically associated with many other problems, such as poor health, infant mortality, stunted growth, low achievement and behavioral problems at school, and future unemployment as a young adult.[37] Poverty is more common among children than adults; in 2008, 19 percent of all children in the United States were estimated to be living in poor households, compared with 12 percent of people between the ages of 18 to 64 and 10 percent of people the age of 65 and older.[38] Child poverty rates are also higher in cities than in suburban or nonmetropolitan areas, but they differ enormously across large cities; Atlanta and Cleveland have some of the highest child poverty rates, nearly *half* of all children in the city, whereas in Seattle and Virginia Beach, fewer than one in eight children were in poor households.[39]

The picture of central cities as being composed exclusively of homeless youth gangs and unemployed masses, however, is misleading. Recently, many of the once-declining central cities have shown signs of rejuvenation and gentrification. **Gentrification** in an area refers to relatively wealthier people buying property in poorer areas of a city and moving there, which results in revitalization of the area and increased property values but is often accompanied by displacing the poor. Cities such as Atlanta, Kansas City, and Newark, which were losing population a decade or two ago, are now gaining new residents. Gentrification and "yuppie" development have attracted some suburbanites to come back to central cities. The reasons for the rebound of many central cities vary from city to city, yet the sustained economic boom

gentrification

A process where relatively wealthier people buy property in poorer areas of a city and relocate there, which results in revitalization of the area and increased property values but is often accompanied by displacing the poor.

Urban renewal has brought new life to the Inner Harbor in Baltimore, Maryland.
■ *How might investment in development and renewal projects pay off for cities in the long run?*

in the 1990s increased local tax revenues, which were then invested heavily in local infrastructure to make cities more appealing. The boom and investment in cities also helped create more jobs.[40]

The Rise of "Edge Cities"

In recent decades, cities have been built on the edges of metropolitan areas. Writer Joel Garreau calls these "edge cities" and suggests that virtually every expanding U.S. city grows in the fashion of Los Angeles, with multiple urban cores.[41] Thus, we have Tysons Corner, Virginia, outside Washington, D.C.; the Perimeter Center at the northern tip of Atlanta's Beltway; the Galleria area west of downtown Houston; and the Schaumburg area northwest of Chicago.

Edge cities have 5 million or more square feet of office space, 600,000 or more square feet of retail space, and more jobs than bedrooms. More often than not, they were empty spaces or farmland only 30 years ago. New freeways appeared first, then a shopping mall or two, and then industrial parks.

Some of the problems of the inner city have caught up with edge cities, just as they have with suburbs: traffic congestion, parking problems, crime, pollution, and urban blight. Political problems have cropped up as well. Most edge cities are in unincorporated areas of counties—that is, they are not part of any city, town, or other municipality—and are subject in varying degrees to be controlled by county governments. Edge cities are sometimes run by "shadow governments"—private owners who set the fees for policing, transportation, and various other services that are normally financed by taxes. There is not much room for government by the people in a community that is essentially a business.

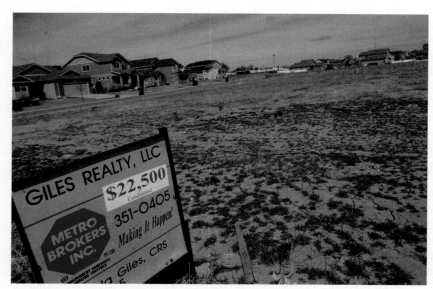

Greeley, Colorado, approximately 50 miles north of Denver, is the core city of what was one of the fastest-growing metro areas in the nation. The area's population grew by 35 percent between 2000 and 2007. However, after the downturn in the housing market in 2007 and 2008, Greeley briefly led the nation in the rate of foreclosures and many recently built homes remain unsold.

Metropolitics Today: Meeting the Challenges of Growth and Development

Until recently, nearly everybody wanted to see his or her city grow. The local newspaper, television stations, radio stations, Chamber of Commerce, union leaders, business community, developers, teachers, and proud citizens worked together to attract new industries. Such industries would bring, they hoped, new jobs, more amenities, increased land values, and more opportunities for young people. The consensus was that a city with a growing population was a healthy one; one with a decreasing population was a sick one.

Local politicians found it risky to oppose economic development and economic growth; those who did feared they would not be reelected. However, beginning about two decades ago, an *antigrowth* movement developed in many cities. There had always been restraints in the wealthy suburbs outside the central cities; in fact, many suburbs were created to escape the growth taking place in central cities. These suburbs adopted building and zoning codes and land use regulations to make it difficult, if not impossible, for industries to be located there and to keep people out who could not afford large houses on large lots. New suburbs were carefully planned to ensure that they would not become too crowded. These zoning regulations were attacked in the courts as strategies to keep the poor and minorities out, but the U.S. Supreme Court ruled in 1977 that as long as zoning rules were racially neutral on their face, they did not violate the Constitution.[42]

LEARNING OBJECTIVE

27.6 Evaluate strategies for meeting the various challenges of governance in metropolitan regions.

Strategies to Govern Metropolitan Regions

Divided executive authority, fragmented legislative power, splintered and noncompetitive political parties, the absence of strong central governments, and the necessity to bargain with national, state, and local officials—all these factors suggest that metro regions are challenges to coherent governance. In some places, fragmentation is especially daunting. The St. Louis metropolitan area, for instance, includes the city of St. Louis, 15 surrounding counties, 274 smaller cities, 107 townships, 136 school districts, and 411 special districts in two states.[43]

At the turn of the twentieth century, reformers were afraid of domination by political bosses. But in the modern metropolis, political machines do not run the central city. Urban bureaucracies may wield a lot of power, but they do not offer metropolitan leadership. Special interests seldom actually control the metropolis, nor does a business elite. Who, then, governs the metropolis? It is typically a "nobody's in charge" arrangement.

Growing fragmentation of government in large metropolitan areas has brought about a variety of reform movements and structural innovations aimed at improving efficiency, effectiveness, and performance. Political scientists and public administration specialists have never been bashful about proposing remedies. Here are the better-known ideas, all of which have been tried somewhere, yet none of which has been adopted nationwide.

Annexation   Annexation is when one (typically large) city absorbs neighboring areas into it. Supporters argue that the resulting larger single government reduces duplication and facilitates solving problems that used to cross municipal borders. In the South, West, and Southwest, large central cities have absorbed adjacent territories. Oklahoma City, for example, added nearly 600 square miles. Houston, Phoenix, San Antonio, El Paso, Colorado Springs, and Kansas City, Missouri, also expanded their boundaries. The now-extended cities serve almost as regional governments.[44]

But annexation has not proved helpful to cities in the Northeast and Midwest because these cities are ringed by entrenched suburban communities that seldom want to be annexed, and state laws make it difficult for the central city to do so against the wishes of the suburbs. Even in such places as the Houston metropolitan area, the annexation option is plagued by legal obstacles and political jealousies.

The Port Authority, jointly headed by the governors of New York and New Jersey, manages much of the transportation infrastructure in the New York City area. Here, Port Authority police officers monitor one of the entrances to the Holland Tunnel.
■ *What are the benefits and challenges in having these services run by a public authority?*

Agreements to Furnish Services The most common solution to the problems of overlapping and duplicating jurisdictions is for the units of government to contract for services. This reform is applauded by many economists, who say it comes close to providing a market that operates according to laws of supply and demand. Most of these agreements call for a few cities to share a single activity. For example, a city may provide hospital services to its neighbors or contract with the county for law enforcement. Especially popular in the Los Angeles area, the contract system is being used with increasing success in many parts of the country. Of course, to be successful, both governments in the contract must agree to its terms.

Public Authorities Public authorities such as the Port Authority in the New York City area and the Tennessee Valley Authority in the South were established to undertake specialized functions in their regions. They have a legal mandate granted by the state (or states) to raise money, hire experts, and take over some city services, such as transportation, water, and housing. The Port Authority of New York and New Jersey built the Twin Towers of the World Trade Center, which were destroyed by the 2001 terrorist attacks. It now shares responsibility with Silverstein Properties for redeveloping the area and for overseeing the operation and security of the bridges and tunnels connecting New York and New Jersey.

Why public authorities? In part because state legislatures sometimes prefer to place important functions outside the reach of mayors and political machines and in part because such authorities have financial flexibility (for example, they may be able to incur debt outside the limits imposed on the city by the state). But most important, many problems are simply too big or cover too wide a geographical area to be handled properly by a city or a group of cities.

Public authorities pose a special problem for mayors. Not only do they remove many of the vital functions of metropolitan government from the mayors' direct control, but even worse, public authorities and special districts constantly come into conflict with local agencies dealing with the same problems in the city.

But if public authorities are a problem for mayors, they are also a temptation. By sponsoring these independent agencies, mayors can sometimes cut down on their administrative load. They can tap other sources of funds and keep city tax rates lower than they would otherwise be. If things go wrong, mayors can say they did not have authority over a certain function and hence cannot be held responsible.

Special Districts Special districts are units of government typically established to provide one or more specific services, such as sewage disposal, fire protection, water supply, or pollution control for a local or regional area. They are often created to enable an existing unit of government to evade tax and debt limits and to spread the tax burden over a wider area than individual municipalities or counties. Many smaller special districts are formed in suburban areas to obtain urban services without having to create a city government or be annexed by one.

Special districts usually have governing boards appointed by officials of other governments or elected by the general public. Special districts are useful for dealing with urgent problems that overlap boundaries of existing government units. Many urban and regional problems defy city and county boundaries, and special districts offer economies of scale that make sense. But critics charge that the rapid increase in the number of special districts during the last 30 years has prevented comprehensive planning. They also lament that few citizens know who runs these special districts, and even fewer know how these officials make decisions.

Regional Coordinating and Planning Councils Nearly all metro regions have some kind of *council of government* (COG). COGs began in the 1950s and were encouraged by the national government. Congress, in fact, mandated that certain federal grants be reviewed by regional planning groups. In essence, these councils bring locally elected officials together. They devote most of their time and resources to physical planning; rarely do they tackle problems of race, poverty, and financial inequities in metro regions. Councils are set up, moreover, in such a way as to give suburbs a veto over virtually any project that would threaten their autonomy. In a few regions, the councils assume operating responsibilities over such regional activities as garbage collection, transportation, and water supply. Critics say these councils rarely provide for creative area-wide governance, yet they serve as an important common ground for elected officials to talk about mutual problems, and they help solve problems in many of the regions.

City–County Consolidations   One traditional means of overcoming the fragmentation of metro regions is to merge the city with the county. This is a pet reform of business elites, the League of Women Voters, and Chambers of Commerce, who view it as a rational, efficient way to simplify administration, cut costs for taxpayers, and eliminate duplication.

More than 30 city–county mergers have taken place. In addition, one city occasionally joins with another, as Sacramento and North Sacramento did in the 1960s. Such mergers can usually be brought about only by a referendum approved by the citizens of the region. Most of the successful ones have taken place in smaller urban areas. Indianapolis, Jacksonville, and Nashville are some of the larger consolidations. The experience of Indianapolis is typical of these consolidations, most of which are in the South and West. In 1970, Indianapolis combined with Marion County to create UNIGOV. This merger required special permission from the legislature. UNIGOV provides many services, but the school systems remain separate, as do the police and sheriff departments. One successful regional merger was the 2000 consolidation of the city of Louisville and Jefferson County, Kentucky.[45]

Many proposed mergers have been rejected by county voters. But it is no longer unusual to find counties running what used to be city jails, zoos, libraries, and similar services. Formal and informal agreements abound as cities and counties remedy overlap and fragmentation by shifting responsibilities for providing specific services among themselves. "City–county functional consolidation in areas such as emergency medical services and natural-disaster planning is growing throughout the United States.... Increasing cooperation is likely to occur in the future as cities and counties struggle to provide more services to a tax-resistant public."[46]

Federated Government   A federated government attempts to take political realities into account by building on existing governments but assigning some crucial functions to an area-wide metro government.[47] One of the few attempts—and there have been only a few—to create a federated government is the Twin Cities Metropolitan Council for the Minneapolis–St. Paul region. This regional organization, established by the legislature in 1967, consists of a 17-member council. Sixteen members are appointed by the governor to represent equal-population districts, while the remaining member is a full-time executive who serves at the pleasure of the governor.

Today, the Metropolitan Council, in essence a new layer of government superimposed on top of existing units, serves as a metropolitan planning, policy-making, and policy-coordinating agency. It reviews applications for federal funds from the region, guides regional planning and development, and opposes local actions that would endanger the overall welfare of the region. It also has taxing authority for the region. The Twin Cities model appears a ready candidate for transfer elsewhere, yet this has happened only in Portland, Oregon.

Portland adopted a bold new charter for the Portland Metropolitan Services District in 1992, which was amended by votes in 2000 and again in 2002.[48] It is a directly elected regional government serving three counties and 24 cities. Its nonpartisan commission members and elected executive officer have an impressive budget and more than 1,200 employees. They oversee waste collection, a zoo, recycling, waste disposal, transportation planning, and regional air and water quality programs, and they constructed Portland's new Convention Center. They have also created a greenbelt around the metro area that preserves extensive open areas.

By the People

MAKING A DIFFERENCE

Community School Boards

The Wake County public school system in North Carolina, which includes the city of Raleigh and the surrounding area, had served for decades as a model of promoting socioeconomic diversity in its schools, in part through a comprehensive system of zoning and busing. However, the program came under increasing criticism from residents in the outlying areas of the county. Several unhappy citizens formed a group they called the Wake Schools Community Alliance (WSCA) and campaigned to get their candidates onto the school board. As one of the founders said, "If you want to change the policy, you have to change the policy makers."*

The WSCA was successful in electing all four of its candidates to open seats on the Wake County school board in October of 2009. By May of 2010, the new school board had officially ended the system's diversity program in favor of a "neighborhood schools" format that critics argue will effectively segregate schools into white wealthy suburban schools and poor black city schools.

Regardless of your views on school zoning and student assignment, the WSCA demonstrated that a small group of motivated citizens can make a huge difference in local politics. Are school board elections in your community partisan or nonpartisan? Are there groups organized to support school board candidates in your community besides political parties? If so, what are their guiding principles? Go to the next public school board meeting, and hear what is on the agenda. Talk to the board members, and express your views. Consider organizing a group to attend and to participate in the board's next meeting. Political officials respond to those who participate, so get involved.

Students try to influence the Wake County school board decision.

CRITICAL THINKING QUESTIONS

1. How much power should elected school board members have to set school policy compared with the power of appointed officials such as superintendents and school principals?

2. Does the WSCA example represent a triumph of local political participation and democracy, or is it an example of those with greater resources shaping policy to fit their needs at the expense of those with fewer resources?

* http://www.newsobserver.com/2009/09/30/118498/wake-diversity-policy-could-be.html.

Community Self-Help Countless people are coming together in their own neighborhoods to tackle common problems or to form neighborhood cooperatives. Some of these self-help groups simply handle baby-sitting arrangements or organize charity events or golf tournaments; others undertake neighborhood crime watches or Little League field construction. Local nonprofit groups in New York have built award-winning apartment complexes amid burned-out inner-city tenements. Other groups have mobilized to bring about storefront revitalization, street improvement, and area beautification programs by initiating farmers' markets, miniparks, and gardens.[49] The contemporary self-help movement is rooted in a past that has long been marked by volunteerism and local associations. In former times, the whole community often rallied when a neighbor's barn burned down; volunteer fire departments emerged out of this tradition.

Many local groups seeking help from city hall or from county officialdom give up after running into a maze of building codes, zoning rules, and countless regulations that inhibit innovation in local government. The alternative to despair is to do it yourself. And this is exactly what is happening at the grassroots level right now. The more successful experiments are watched carefully by the professionals at city hall, and some of the innovations are copied by those in office.

Sometimes progress or justice comes about because some activists take issues to court. Such was the case in bringing in alternative housing for lower-income residents in Mount Laurel, New Jersey. And it was also the case in addressing the fatal effects of toxic dumping by businesses in Woburn, Massachusetts.[50]

The Future of Metropolitan Reorganization

In most metropolitan regions, to combine city and suburbs would be to shift political power to the suburbs. In most northern centers, this would give suburban Republicans more control of city affairs. In other cases, it would enable Democrats to threaten the one-party Republican systems in the suburbs. Under these circumstances, neither Democratic leaders in the central cities nor Republicans in the suburbs show much enthusiasm for metropolitan schemes. African Americans and Hispanics often oppose area consolidation or similar reform proposals that would invariably dilute their political power, often severely.

Some people believe that solutions to metropolitan problems are beyond the capacity of the metropolis itself. They favor a strengthened role for the national government, with special emphasis on ensuring "equity" or on relating services directly to needs. Some advocate reviving federal revenue sharing. Others believe that the job must be done by the states, which hold the fundamental constitutional power. Still others put forward bold proposals to establish regional planning and governance arrangements that would embrace "citistate" areas that include two or more metropolitan clusters, like Baltimore and Washington, D.C.[51]

Today's aging central cities unquestionably face problems: congestion, smog, tension, loss of community, drugs, unsafe streets, neglected children, and visual pollution. They live with racial and ethnic tensions, not only white–black rivalry but rivalry among Latinos, Koreans, and a host of other racial and ethnic groups. Gangs, poverty, broken families, drive-by shootings, and drug-related crimes make life miserable for many who live in the inner cities. Yet is this new? Writers and critics since Thomas Jefferson have projected an unflattering image of the city as a cold, impersonal, and often brutal environment in which crime flourishes and people lose their dignity.

Supporters contend, however, that the big city is not only a place of smog and sprawl; it is the center of innovation, excitement, and vitality. In the last couple of decades, many major cities, including Boston, New York, and Washington, have promoted the redevelopment of run-down areas. In this view, the city offers social diversity and puts less community pressure on the individual to conform. The large

Great public projects at the local level sometimes require great persistence. Frank Lloyd Wright first designed the Monona Terrace Community and Convention Center, to be built on Lake Monona in Madison, Wisconsin, in 1938. However, political controversies, war, and Wright's death in 1959 delayed final approval and funding for the project until 1992, when voters narrowly approved construction, financed by local hotel room taxes and bonds.

community is a meeting place for talent from all around the nation and the world: dancers, musicians, writers, scholars, actors, and business leaders. On the other hand, some critics have charged that redevelopment is *gentrification,* displacing the original lower-income inhabitants with new wealthier residents. The displaced poor then concentrate even more in other blighted neighborhoods.

Some observers dismiss the notion of an "urban crisis." They contend that most city dwellers live more comfortably than ever before, with more and better housing, schools, and transportation. By any conceivable measure of material welfare, the present generation of urban dwellers is better off than other large groups of people anywhere at any time. Most cities, especially in the West and South, are thriving, and many older cities such as Boston, Pittsburgh, and Indianapolis are generally viewed as revived and vital, not decaying.

Throughout history, cities have been threatened by political, social, and environmental catastrophes. Urban decay, in one form or another, has always been with us.[52] Cities thrive because over time they respond to crises and because they are an economic necessity. The economy, transportation systems, past investments, and cultural contributions all make cities inevitable. How well cities survive, and with what mix of people, will depend on the tides of the national economy, the way our regions are organized, the way our social and economic policies are designed, the vision and leadership individual cities muster to build their future, and the degree to which our national leaders promote policies that can help our central cities.[53]

CHAPTER **SUMMARY**

27.1 **Characterize local government in the United States and the basic relationship between state and local governments.**

Local government is big, costly, and overlapping. Local governments in the United States have a variety of jurisdictions and structures, and they perform many essential functions. Because constitutional power is vested in the states, most counties, cities, towns, and special districts are agents of the state, although some local governments are granted constitutional home rule, which gives them greater independence.

27.2 **Assess the role of county government.**

Counties are extremely diverse in their functions, power, and size. They also vary in their structures, which have changed in recent decades. The most common government form at the county level is a board of county commissioners, although larger urban counties are moving to council–administrator or council-elected executive plans.

27.3 **Explain the growth of suburbs and its implications for local governance.**

Suburbs have been the fastest-growing population areas in the United States for several decades. There is no typical suburb. Although many suburbs are homogeneous, the suburban United States is highly heterogeneous. Suburbs are confronting the same

problems as the urban areas they surround. Big cities and their suburbs are now referred to as metropolitan areas and are growing most rapidly in the South and West.

27.4 **Outline the different ways of structuring city government, and describe the functions of mayors.**

The most common government forms at the city level are the mayor–council and council–manager (city-manager) plans. Mayor–council governments generally have a strong mayor elected by voters, although some plans have a weak mayor elected by the council. Council–manager plans appoint a professional administrator. Mayors of major cities play many roles, including administering large city bureaucracies, working with the private sector and even foreign governments to spur economic development, and influencing policy making in the city.

27.5 **Describe the challenges facing central cities and metro areas.**

Inequalities between many central cities and their middle and outer rings of affluent suburbs are increasing. Central cities often struggle with economic hardship, racism, drugs, and crime. Fragmentation and dispersal of political authority in the metropolitan areas often make it difficult to treat their problems.

27.6 Evaluate strategies for meeting the various challenges of governance in metropolitan regions.

A variety of strategies have been used in an effort to solve these problems—annexation, agreements to furnish services, public authorities, special districts, regional coordinating and planning councils, city–county consolidations, federated government, and community self-help programs. Nearly all the strategies for meeting the challenges of growth and economic development involve shifts in political power.

CHAPTER **SELF-TEST**

27.1 Characterize local government in the United States and the basic relationship between state and local governments.

1. Why are there usually fewer obstacles to state interference in local matters than there are to federal interference in state matters?
   a. Local governments have less authority than state legislatures.
   b. Local governments are typically created by state legislatures.
   c. State constitutions often have to be approved every two years.
   d. State governments are often more permissive than local governments to outside influences.
2. What are two or three reasons why a state government may intervene in a local government's jurisdiction?

27.2 Assess the role of county government.

3. Which of the following is *not* a traditional function of counties?
   a. Tax collection
   b. Gathering of census data
   c. Administration of welfare programs
   d. Highway construction and maintenance
4. In a short essay, describe the role of counties in government. Consider their original role, how it has changed over time, and why.

27.3 Explain the growth of suburbs and its implications for local governance.

5. Which of the below is the most significant reason why suburbs have grown?
   a. People wanted to live in smaller communities where they would have more direct control over local government.
   b. The growing middle class grew to dislike the environment of cities.
   c. Traditional cities were unable to meet the growing technological needs of the population.
   d. People wanted to escape deteriorating inner cities.
6. Approximately what percentage of the U.S. population lives in suburban areas?
   a. 10 percent
   b. 25 percent
   c. 50 percent
   d. 80 percent
7. In a short essay, describe suburban governments. Consider their specific responsibilities and how they differ from urban governments.

27.4 Outline the different ways of structuring city government, and describe the functions of mayors.

8. Match the features of city charters on the left with the appropriate type of charter on the right.

   a. The mayor prepares and administers the budget.
   b. The mayor has broad appointment powers.
   c. There is no single administrative head for the city.
   d. Mayors are often chosen from members of an elected city council.
   e. The city council is elected in nonpartisan primaries and elections.
   f. The city council hires a professional administrator to manage city affairs.

   1. Strong mayor–council
   2. Weak mayor–council
   3. Council–manager

9. In a short essay, identify and describe the roles of a mayor in local politics, foreign policy, and economics. Consider the actions of famous mayors such as Rudolph Giuliani, Richard J. Daley, and Harold Washington.

27.5 Describe the challenges facing central cities and metro areas.

10. What percentage of U.S. children was estimated to be living in poverty in 2008?
    a. 5 percent
    b. 12 percent
    c. 19 percent
    d. 24 percent
11. Identify a cause of the current financial problems of many cities.

27.6 Evaluate strategies for meeting the various challenges of governance in metropolitan regions.
12. Which strategy includes residents coming together to form neighborhood cooperatives?
   a. Special districts
   b. Community self-help
c. City–county consolidations
d. Regional coordinating and planning councils
13. In a short essay, describe three strategies to govern metro regions. Consider how they are alike and how they are different. Which do you think would be most effective for the metro area closest to you?

Answers to selected questions: 1. b; 3. b; 5. d; 6. c; 8: a. 1, b. 1, c. 3, d. 2, e. 3, f. 3; 10. c; 12. b

---

mypoliscilab EXERCISES

Apply what you learned in this chapter with these resources on MyPoliSciLab.

📖 **Read** on **mypoliscilab.com**

eText: Chapter 27

✔ **Study** and **Review** on **mypoliscilab.com**

Pre-Test
Post-Test
Chapter Exam
Flashcards

👁 **Watch** on **mypoliscilab.com**

Video: Battling City Corruption

✳ **Explore** on **mypoliscilab.com**

Simulation: You Are the Mayor and Need to Get a Town Budget Passed

KEY TERMS

unitary system, p. 672
constitutional home rule, p. 672
county, p. 673
municipality, p. 673
township, p. 673

metropolis, p. 673
metropolitan area, p. 673
eminent domain, p. 678
charter, p. 679
mayor–council charter, p. 680

weak mayor–council form, p. 680
strong mayor–council form, p. 681
council–manager plan, p. 681
gentrification, p. 685

ADDITIONAL RESOURCES

FURTHER READING

KENNETH D. ACKERMAN, *Boss Tweed: The Rise and Fall of the Corrupt Pol Who Conceived the Soul of Modern New York* (Carroll & Graf, 2005).

GERALD BENJAMIN AND **RICHARD P. NATHAN,** *Regionalism and Realism: A Study of Governments in the New York Metropolitan Area* (Brookings Institution Press, 2001).

FRANK M. BRYAN, *Real Democracy: The New England Town Meeting and How It Works* (Cambridge University Press, 2004).

ADAM COHEN AND **ELIZABETH TAYLOR,** *American Pharaoh: Mayor Richard J. Daley—His Battle for Chicago and the Nation* (Little, Brown, 2000).

PETER DREIER, JOHN MOLLENKOPF, AND **TODD SWANSTROM,** *Place Matters: Metropolitics for the Twenty-First Century* (University Press of Kansas, 2001).

JEFFREY R. HENIG AND **WILBER C. RICH,** EDS., *Mayors in the Middle: Politics, Race, and Mayoral Control of Urban Schools* (Princeton University Press, 2003).

DENNIS R. JUDD AND **TODD SWANSTROM,** *City Politics: Private Power and Public Policy,* 7th ed. (Longman, 2007).

SUZANNE M. LELAND AND **KURT THURMAIER,** EDS., *Case Studies of City–County Consolidation* (Sharpe, 2004).

HENRY J. PRATT, *Churches and Urban Government in Detroit and New York,*

1895–1994 (Wayne State University Press, 2004).

DICK SIMPSON, *Inside Urban Politics: Voices from America's Cities and Suburbs* (Longman, 2004).

RAPHAEL J. SONENSHEIN, *The City at Stake: Secession, Reform, and the Battle for Los Angeles* (Princeton University Press, 2006).

HEATHER ANN THOMPSON, *Whose Detroit? Politics, Labor, and Race in a Modern American City* (Cornell University Press, 2002).

J. PHILLIP THOMPSON, *Double Trouble: Black Mayors, Black Communities, and the Call for a Deep Democracy* (Oxford University Press, 2006).

ROGER VOGEL AND **JOHN J. HARRIGAN,** *Political Change in the Metropolis,* 8th ed.

(Longman, 2007). See also *Governing: The Magazine of States and Localities,* published monthly by Congressional Quarterly; *The National Civic Review,* published by the National Civic League; *The Municipal Yearbook,* published annually by the International City Management Association; and the Web site of the U.S. Conference of Mayors at www.usmayors.org.

WEB SITES

www.naco.org/ The National Association of Counties conducts research, reports on policy initiatives, operates a variety of programs, and represents the interests of county governments in Washington D.C.

www.natat.org/ The National Association of Towns and Townships lobbies in Washington D.C. for policies and programs that help small communities, towns, and suburbs acquire their fair share of federal funding and serve their residents.

www.nlc.org/ The National League of Cities, the oldest national organization representing municipal governments throughout the United States, seeks to strengthen and promote cities as centers of opportunity, leadership, and governance.

www.usmayors.org/ The United States Conference of Mayors is the official nonpartisan organization of cities with populations of 30,000 or more. It lobbies the federal government and provides a forum for the exchange of ideas.

www.icma.org The International City/County Management Association's mission is to create excellence in local governance by developing and fostering professional local government management worldwide

Making State and Local Policy

A t least since the 1983 Nation at Risk Report,[1] which documented a range of short-comings in public education in the United States, state and local governments have been searching for innovative ways to reform education policy. One plan being explored is to provide cash incentives to students for good performance. Roland Fryer Jr., an economist at Harvard University, conducted a major experiment recently to explore whether such incentives would work.[2] Public schools in four different cities—Chicago, Dallas, Washington, D.C., and New York City—participated in the study. Some were randomly assigned to receive no form of payment, whereas others were selected for a variety of payment programs. Some were paid primarily for outcomes, mostly in the form of test scores and grades. Others were paid primarily for behaviors—reading, attending school, participating in class discussions, etc. Although the results were mixed, fairly strong support emerged in favor of providing students with cash benefits for performing tasks that are completely under their control, like reading and attendance. Less success was found for programs focused strictly on grades. Fryer speculates this is because students do not feel they have complete control over grades, and they do not always know which efforts translate into better grades.

Not everyone supports what Fryer is attempting. Psychologists like Edward Deci of the University of Rochester note a number of studies that suggest providing money as an incentive often devalues or diminishes the action itself. Paying someone to perform a task can turn it from something a person intrinsically enjoys into something done for money. Turning learning into work may diminish a student's love of learning or reduce the likelihood of it ever developing in the first place. Fryer and his supporters respond that millions of kids are not learning now for love or any other reason, and if cash incentives work, that it is worth trying. What do you think? Does paying students to perform well teach them to value education, or does it teach them to learn for pay rather than for personal growth? Although Fryer's initial findings look promising, do you think the effect would last over time, particularly if the payments were reduced or eliminated later on? These are the kinds of policy innovations states and localities must consider as they seek to provide the best policies they can for the lowest cost.

Of course, state and local officials constantly wrestle with a wide range of policy decisions and controversies beyond public education. What is the best way to attract business and increase the number of jobs yet encourage environmental quality? How should the state deal with the soaring costs of providing Medicaid? What can be done about traffic congestion? And what role should state and local authorities play regarding terrorism threats?

Mayors, governors, state legislators, county commissioners, judges, union officials, developers, Chambers of Commerce, political party leaders, and citizens strive to develop public policy compromises to such dilemmas. These deliberations receive little media attention compared with decisions made in Washington, D.C., yet the effect of these choices on our day-to-day lives is often equally or perhaps even more important.

This chapter examines some of the policy areas that consume much of the attention and budgets of state and local governments. State and local governments spend most of their budgets on education, welfare and health-related matters, highway and transportation systems, and safety and law enforcement. We will discuss them as well as the issues of planning and regulation.

CHAPTER **OUTLINE**
CHAPTER LEARNING
OBJECTIVES

Public Education

28.1 Outline local, state, and federal government roles in elementary and secondary education.

Higher Education

28.2 Assess the concerns about state funding of higher education.

Social Services

28.3 Describe the role of the state in public assistance programs, and assess the challenges facing state social service programs.

Law Enforcement

28.4 Trace the growth of states' responsibilities for law enforcement.

Planning the Urban Community

28.5 Outline states' tools and priorities for urban planning.

Regulation

28.6 Assess the role of states and communities in regulating and in enforcing compliance with federal and state regulations.

The Importance of State and Local Policy

698 ■ **CHAPTER 28** Making State and Local Policy

Public Education

LEARNING OBJECTIVE

28.1 Outline local, state, and federal government roles in elementary and secondary education.

In ancient Greece, Plato and Aristotle saw education as a vital task of government. Thomas Jefferson, too, was convinced that an educated citizenry was essential to democratic government. But only in the twentieth century did it become generally accepted that government should provide tax-supported education for everyone. Today, free public education for grades 1 through 12 is an established practice in the United States and specifically provided for in many state constitutions. Approximately one-quarter of all state and local government expenditures are for kindergarten–high school (K–12) education.[3]

State and local governments have the primary responsibility for education and provide most of the money to pay for it (see Figure 28–1). Since 1979, overall state funding for education has surpassed local government funding, with the exception of a few states in which revenues for education continue to come primarily from local government. The state role in financing education has increased during the last generation as a result, at least in part, of pressure from state courts to equalize expenditures on education across local school districts. Across the states, spending per student varies widely. The national average in 2006–2007 was $9,683 but ranged from a high of more than $16,163 in New Jersey to a low of $5,706 in Utah.[4]

Administration of Public Education

Unlike most other democracies, which typically administer and fund education at the national level, the basic unit responsible for public elementary and secondary education in the United States is the local school district, and there are slightly less than 14,000 of these.[5] In nearly all districts, voters elect a board of education that sets the school tax rate, appoints a superintendent of schools and other personnel, hires teachers, and runs the schools from kindergarten through grade 12. Each state has a state superintendent of public instruction or commissioner of education. In about a third of the states, this official is popularly elected; in nearly all states, he or she shares authority with a state board of education.

Although actual operation of the public schools is the responsibility of the local community, state officers have important supervisory powers and distribute financial assistance to the communities. State money is distributed according to many formulas, but the trend is toward giving more money to poorer communities to equalize education spending. Many policies are established at the state level, and it is up to local authorities to enforce them. They must ensure that new school buildings meet the minimum specifications set by the state. In some states, officials have the authority to set the course of study in schools—that is, to determine what must be taught and what may not be taught. In several states, especially in the South and Southwest, state authorities determine which textbooks will be used as well, and there is an increasing push in many states to adopt common standards for performance for students.[6]

The Role of the Federal Government in Public Schools

After the former Soviet Union's successful 1957 launch of *Sputnik,* the first satellite put into orbit, Congress responded by providing funding to strengthen mathematics and science education. In 1965, Congress adopted the Elementary and Secondary Education Act, the major federal law dealing with education. The federal government's share in financing local education rose from approximately 2 percent in 1940 to approximately 9.2 percent by 2007.

Through the Department of Education, which was created in 1979, and other agencies, the federal government makes grants to the states for facilities, equipment, scholarships, loans, research, model programs, and general aid at the elementary, secondary, and higher education levels. But federal control over how the money may be spent comes with these federal dollars. Today, federal regulations cover school lunch programs, employment practices, admissions, record keeping, care of experimental animals, and many other matters. Indeed, local school authorities regularly complain that there are more regulations than dollars. With the passage of No Child Left Behind in 2002, and the more recent grant competition developed by the

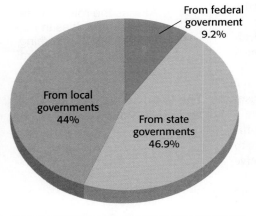

FIGURE 28–1 Spending on Public Elementary and Secondary Schools.

■ *What are some of the implications of the vast majority of public education spending coming from state and local governments rather than the federal government?*

From federal government 9.2%

From local governments 44%

From state governments 46.9%

SOURCE: *Digest of Education Statistics, 2007,* Table 162.

Obama administration called "Race to the Top," the role of the federal government in shaping what schools do has continued to increase.

Educational Controversies

What shall be taught, and who shall teach it, are hotly contested matters. Schools are favorite targets for groups eager to have children taught the "right" things. Of course, little agreement exists on what the "right" things are. Religious groups want family values and morality emphasized, and some want constraints imposed on the teaching of evolution. Others want the schools to teach facts only, without regard for values, especially in areas such as sex education. Labor leaders want students to get the right impression about labor and its role in society. Business leaders are eager for children to see the free enterprise system in a favorable light and want high school graduates who will be well-prepared for increasingly technical jobs. Minorities and women's groups want textbooks to present issues from the perspective they consider correct. Professional educators and civil libertarians try to isolate schools from the pressures of all outside groups—or at least the ones with which they disagree. They say decisions regarding what textbooks should be assigned, what books should be placed in school libraries, and how curricula should be designed are best left to professionals.

There have been many attempts to keep public education relatively free of partisan political influences. For example, local school boards are usually nonpartisan and are often elected when no other partisan races are on the ballot. This separation is strongly supported by parent–teacher associations, the National Education Association, the American Federation of Teachers, and other educational groups. However, education is of such concern to so many people, and there are so many different ideas about how schools should be run, that it can never be fully separated from politics.

Public School Integration   During the 1970s and 1980s, battles were fought in many cities over how to overcome racial segregation in the public schools. In many places, people lived in segregated neighborhoods, which meant that eliminating overt segregation at neighborhood-centered schools would not produce racially diverse schools. One method, which became controversial, was to bus students from one neighborhood to another to achieve racial balance in the schools and overcome the effects of past segregation.

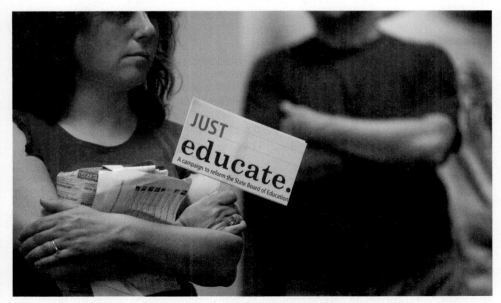

A woman observes a hearing of the Texas State Board of Education, which determines what goes into the textbooks for students in Texas. The decision has far reaching ramifications because what Texas wants ends up in textbooks used all over the country. The Board made a number of controversial changes to their social studies curriculum in 2010 which numerous historians argued were motivated by promoting a conservative ideology rather than accurately reflecting history. ■ *Who should decide what is taught in public schools?*

Of the People

Teachers in the Classroom

Lessons on diversity often start in the classroom. Yet, while the changing face of America has impacted the makeup of students in the classroom, it has had little affect on the teachers, the majority of whom are white and female. According to the most current statistics from the U.S. Census Bureau, the percentage of women in the classroom has actually increased somewhat during the past 20 years in elementary, junior high, and senior high schools.

The large percentage of women in the classroom dates back to the first public schools but also reflects the lack of interest among men in teaching. Salaries for teaching are lower than for comparable jobs requiring a college degree elsewhere in the U.S. economy, in part because public schools are often a target for local budget cuts and in part because women are generally underpaid regardless of their profession.

Minorities have made slightly more progress in becoming public school teachers,

in part because colleges and universities are working harder to recruit minorities to the profession and because public schools are under greater pressure to increase teacher diversity. Although the percentage of minority teachers has risen only slightly during the past two decades, the trend appears to be toward greater representation, especially in junior and senior high schools. When students see the changing face of teaching, they may be more likely to embrace the changing face of diversity in the U.S. economy generally.

Although the U.S. Census Bureau has not followed the percentage of female and minority teachers in private schools as closely, its 2000 figures suggest no difference between the percentage of female teachers in public and private schools but a significantly lower percentage of minority teachers in private schools.

CRITICAL THINKING QUESTIONS

1. What differences might it make in the classroom to have more minority teachers?

2. In what ways may education have to change in order to attract more men to teach in public schools?

Demographic Characteristics of Full-Time Public School Teachers, 2007–2008

SOURCE: National Center for Education Statistics, U.S. Department of Education, "Characteristics of Public, Private, and Bureau of Indian Education Elementary and Secondary School Teachers in the United States: Results from the 2007–08 Schools and Staffing Survey," Table 2 and Table 3, http://nces.ed.gov/pubs2009/2009324/tables.asp.

However, as more middle-class families—many of them white—moved from the cities to the suburbs, busing became an ineffective tool to achieve integration because the courts declined in most cases to require states to integrate cities and suburbs. Racial segregation is still the pattern for the inner-city schools of most large cities in parts of the North, South, and West of the country. Indeed, during the last 15 years, substantial slippage toward segregation has occurred in most of the states that had experienced solid desegregation.[7] In 2009, for the first time, the majority of students in public schools in the South were nonwhite.[8] At the same time, white flight away from the public schools has caused the percentage of students in private schools in the South to double.[9]

Standards and Testing   In 1990, only 14 states had standards for their core curriculum, but now nearly every state has adopted standards for subjects such as mathematics, reading, and science. Some have also adopted "high-stakes testing," tests children must pass to go on to the next grade level or graduate from high school. Advocates of standards and testing argue that such devices are necessary to raise the quality of education provided and to ensure accountability.

Opponents argue, however, that testing is unlikely to produce positive changes in education. Some critics contend that it is unfair and misleading to use standardized tests to measure learning. Minority students and students in districts in impoverished areas may not do well on these tests, and expecting them to do so without addressing inequities in educational resources is counterproductive and unfair. Other critics worry that the use of such tests will force teachers to "teach to the test." Sensitive to the fact that their students will be compared with students in other classes, teachers will devote extensive time to subjects covered on the test, ignore other vibrant topics, and overemphasize test-taking strategies. Not surprisingly, several companies have developed entire sets of textbooks and other curricular materials designed explicitly around the state tests. Finally, some people worry that states will adopt standards that are not very demanding. These critics point out that although states are celebrating gains in state tests, results from a nationwide test given to a sample of students every year show little to no educational improvement.[10]

After much debate and encouragement from George W. Bush, Congress adopted one of the most controversial educational reforms in decades, the No Child Left Behind Act of 2002. A reauthorization of the Elementary and Secondary Education Act, the law requires that, in order to receive federal funds, states must design state standards and annually test children in grades three through eight to determine whether schools are making adequate progress in achieving the standards. Schools that do not make sufficient progress can be identified as "failing" schools, and parents have the right to move their children to another school.

Although the general goals of the No Child Left Behind Act have been embraced, policy makers and educators still struggle with how best to fund and implement the standardized testing. They dislike having their local schools labeled as "in need of improvement" or "failing," and local authorities complain that state and national standards often measure factors beyond the control of a particular school and its staff. "It's really not fair to judge a school whose kids come without having ever read a book, and compare it to a school where kids go to the library and have libraries in their home," says Lynn Stockleg, a middle school teacher in Tulsa, Oklahoma. "It's rather discouraging when you're one of those schools. You know you're working very, very hard and yet your scores are consistently low."[11]

State and local officials have also discovered that complying with the No Child Left Behind Act is far more expensive than originally estimated. One study suggests that fully implementing the requirements of the Act could cost more than $140 billion, yet the federal government has appropriated only a fraction of that amount.[12] State and local officials are seeking more federal funding and more flexibility in implementing the goals of the Act. An independent, bipartisan commission studying the implementation of the Act acknowledged the need for some flexibility but also recommended new requirements because "dramatic improvements" were still needed.[13]

Vouchers Some reformers contend that we will not see real progress in public education until we inject competition into the system by permitting parents to shop for schools the way they shop for goods and services in the economy. One way to do this is to provide parents with a set amount of money—in the form of **vouchers**—they could use to pay for part or all of their children's education in a public or private school of their choice.[14]

Voucher programs have been tried since the mid-1980s in New York, Indianapolis, San Antonio, and Milwaukee. Advocates say vouchers could help the neediest students escape failed schools and get valuable academic preparation at private or religious schools.

Opponents criticize the voucher system, even for public schools, for the negative impact it may have on school reform. Their main contention is that vouchers will badly injure financially struggling public schools by diverting much-needed money. Opponents also argue vouchers would promote "skimming," meaning higher-achieving students would opt out of public schools, leaving behind students who struggle academically and have discipline problems. In rural areas, where few private schools exist, some people fear that vouchers may encourage parents to keep the money under the guise of providing "private" home schooling.

The debate over vouchers has also raised questions about the separation of church and state. Some proponents have argued that voucher programs should include religious schools. More than 80 percent of the students receiving vouchers in places such as Milwaukee and San Antonio attend religious schools, most of them Catholic. Opponents of vouchers for religious schools argue that such an arrangement violates the constitutional separation of church and state. They fear also that in some parts of the country, vouchers would be used for schools that largely exclude racial minorities.

vouchers
Money provided by the government to parents for payment of their children's tuition in a public or private school of their choice.

Secretary of Education Arne Duncan participates in a "Let's Read, Let's Move" event at Columbia Heights Youth Club. Secretary Duncan has led the Obama administration's Race to the Top program, which awards federal money to school systems that adopt reforms the administration hopes will improve public education. ■ *What role should the federal government play in setting education policy?*

In 2002, a divided U.S. Supreme Court ruled that poor children could be granted public money (vouchers) to attend religious schools without violating the separation of church and state provisions in the Bill of Rights. Chief Justice William Rehnquist wrote that his majority opinion was "not an endorsement of religious schooling" but merely a means "to assist poor children in failed schools."[15] Other state courts, however, have ruled that voucher plans violate provisions in state constitutions. In 2004, Colorado's supreme court ruled that the state's voucher program violated the state constitution's requirement for local control of schools. Plaintiffs also charged that the voucher program violated the constitution's provisions regarding the separation of church and state, but the court did not decide that issue.[16] Voters have defeated proposals for school vouchers in several states, including Oregon, Washington, Michigan, California, and Utah. The political movement pushing vouchers has lost some of its steam because of these defeats, the intense opposition of the teachers' unions, and court rulings that said poor families do not have the right to demand vouchers from state and local governments to allow their children to attend better schools.

Charter Schools Another educational reform that provides a publicly funded alternative to standard public schools is the **charter school.** Some states now grant charters to individuals or groups to start schools and receive public funds if they can meet standards specified by law. In exchange for meeting specified learning standards, these schools are exempt from adhering to many of the procedural requirements that must be followed by traditional public schools. Unlike vouchers, which provide funds to the parents, charter schools are under the direct authority of local school boards. There are more than 3,600 charter schools, with more than a million students. Charter schools are the fastest-growing form of choice in K–12 education, and they received a big boost from the federally enacted No Child Left Behind Act, which holds out conversion to charter schools as a possible solution for ineffective traditional public schools.

charter school
A publicly funded alternative to standard public schools in some states, initiated when individuals or groups receive charters; charter schools must meet state standards.

Like privatization in other government services, charter schools are intended to interject the competition of the marketplace into elementary and secondary education. Proponents believe that reducing state and local regulation of charter schools will enable them to improve teacher quality and adopt innovative educational programs. Charter schools generally have more flexibility to hire and fire teachers and are not subject to the collective bargaining arrangements that prevail in many public school systems. Some of their teachers may not have as extensive training as certified teachers in traditional public schools, yet proponents maintain that classroom performance is more important than the undergraduate major of the teacher.

Some charter schools have been very successful. Two "Teach for America" alumni launched a series of charter schools under the name Knowledge Is Power Programs or KIPP. With elementary schools in Houston, New York City, North Carolina, and elsewhere, they have demonstrated effective results. The key to their success is a strict and strong initial commitment by parents and pupils to a philosophy of hard work, longer hours of class time and homework, and no shortcuts. That, coupled with carefully recruited, dedicated teachers, has proved successful.[17]

Another success story is California's first charter school, the Vaughn Street Elementary School, now called the Vaughn Next Century Learning Center. Most of the children at this school speak English as a second language and live in dangerous neighborhoods. In 1993, when the charter school was established, Vaughn Street's pupils' test scores were some of the lowest in the state. Under Principal Yvonne Chan's leadership, test scores have steadily risen, and the school is considered an educational model. Chan attributes these improvements to the greater autonomy of a charter school that allowed her to develop smaller classes, accountability for teachers, and numerous community partnerships.[18]

Some educational activists oppose charter schools. Teachers' unions fear they may lose their collective bargaining position with school boards if charter schools multiply. Other opponents contend that in school systems already strapped for money, it does not make sense to divert funds from struggling schools to such untested experiments. Critics also raise questions about what will be taught in

The 2010 award-winning documentary film, *Waiting for Superman,* explores the state of public education in America. It investigates the practices of successful charter schools to create a model for how America can turn its failing public schools around. ■ *To what degree do you think teachers' compensation should depend on the performance of their students?*

charter schools, the level of teacher competence, and whether religious schools should qualify for public funds as charter schools.

The debate over charter schools is complicated by the fact that they vary widely in quality across the country. A nationwide study of schools conducted by the National Center for Education Statistics within the federal Department of Education found that fourth graders who attended traditional public schools did better in reading and mathematics than their counterparts at charter schools.[19] This led critics of the charter movement to say there is no credible evidence that deregulating public education leads to higher student achievement. Supporters contend that most charter schools enroll students with academic and family problems who are poorly served by traditional public schools. Plainly, there are some excellent and some below-average charter schools. Opponents and supporters agree that good-quality schools must be constructed—one at a time.

Higher Education

Public higher education has generally been provided by states. States support many kinds of universities and colleges, including land-grant universities such as Michigan State University, which were created by the Morrill Act of 1862. In addition, since the end of World War II, there has been a major expansion in the number and size of public *community colleges,* which typically receive funds from local as well as state governments and which allow students to attend the first two years of college or receive a technical education in their own communities.

LEARNING **OBJECTIVE**

28.2 Assess the concerns about state funding of higher education.

Administration of Higher Education

State colleges and universities are governed by boards appointed by the governor in some states and elected by the voters in others. These boards are designed to give public institutions of higher education some independence from state politics, even though many public universities rely heavily on their state legislatures and governors for funding.

With approximately 80 percent of the more than 15 million college students now attending publicly supported institutions, the control and support of higher education have become significant political issues. States have created boards with varying degrees of control over operations and budgets. In addition, governors have tried to impose controls on universities and colleges that many university administrators insist are inappropriate. Yet institutions of higher education have greater independence from political oversight than other tax-supported institutions. Publicly funded colleges and universities usually can control teaching loads, internal procedures, areas of teaching emphasis, hiring and promotion, and the allocation of funds among internal units.

Funding Higher Education

In the twenty-first century, we face questions of access and funding for our colleges and universities. Access to colleges and universities for all students who wish to go has long been the declared goal in many states, but is it desirable? Should students be required to pay higher tuition to cover the cost of their education, or should federal and state governments provide more student aid? What should states do about the underrepresentation of minorities in our colleges and universities? And should illegal immigrants be allowed to attend state colleges at in-state tuition rates?

Tuition at state universities has increased during the last few decades, often at two or three times the rate of inflation. Professors' salaries have not kept pace with tuition increases and have grown only slightly more than the rate of inflation. Although many people agree we need an infusion of new money to update college laboratories, improve libraries, and recruit and keep first-rate college professors, there is little consensus about who should pay for these efforts. The federal government is the chief supplier of student financial aid, and many states are now making major efforts to expand their programs of student aid. Many states, such as Georgia, California, Washington, and Alaska, are investing in programs aimed at keeping top students in their states at state-run as well as independent colleges.

In Illinois, where the state's share of the University of Illinois operating costs has decreased from 38.8 percent to 16.4 percent in the last two decades, staff has been eliminated, faculty have faced salary freezes and unpaid furloughs, student aid has been cut, and classes have been canceled. Parents and teachers protested the cuts to education, but the broke state government has few other options.

Most institutions of higher education—both independent and state-run—receive some kind of government subsidy, through a variety of devices so that students do not pay the full cost of their education. The federal government and most states provide need-based financial assistance in the form of loans and grants, and students with the greatest financial need at the higher-cost institutions are eligible for the most aid. Thus, higher education has what is in effect a limited voucher system; students receive funds and can choose the kind of college or university that best serves their needs. Because of financial aid, we have avoided a *two-track system*—one set of colleges and universities for the poor and another for the rich. Along with students from higher-income families, low-income students can be found in most high-cost independent colleges and universities.

Although states spend 8 to 15 percent of their budgets on higher education, funding for public universities must compete with the rising costs of other state services, notably Medicaid, transportation, elementary and secondary education, and the criminal justice system. In most states, the legislature has an easier time controlling appropriations for higher education on a yearly basis than spending on these other functions. As a result, state funding of public colleges and universities is unstable, rising when state revenues are growing but declining sharply during economic downturns.[20]

With shrinking state budgets in 2009 and 2010, many states' higher education systems have seen dramatic cuts to their budgets. The Center on Budget and Policy Priorities reported in May of 2010 that 41 states had made significant cuts to their higher education budgets.[21] Many states are therefore experimenting with new ways to fund higher education. Some, including New Mexico and West Virginia, have turned to lottery money to fund scholarships for students. Vermont is using lottery revenue to replace some of the state's higher education appropriation from general funds.[22] Colorado adopted a program that gives each undergraduate a voucher to cover some of the costs of attending state public institutions and also gave those institutions more control over setting tuition.[23] As state funds for higher education have declined in many states, public colleges and universities have been allowed to raise tuition levels. Gradually, the burden of paying for college is being shifted from the state to students and their parents, a change that may further reduce access to public higher education for low- and moderate-income families.[24]

Social Services

LEARNING **OBJECTIVE**

28.3 Describe the role of the state in public assistance programs, and assess the challenges facing state social service programs.

What role should state and local governments play in making sure all citizens have their basic housing, health, and nutritional needs met? How important are these social services compared with government's obligation to provide police and fire protection, education, parks and recreation, and other services? For much of our history, human service needs were left to private charities that ran orphanages, old-age homes, hospitals, and other institutions. Philosophically, this reliance on private charity fit well with U.S. notions of limited government and self-reliance. That view changed dramatically during the Great Depression of the 1930s, when poverty, unemployment, and homelessness affected such large numbers of people that the government could no longer act as if these were private matters. Then in the mid-1960s, with President Lyndon Johnson's Great Society agenda, the nation embarked on a second major wave of social service programs, which Johnson called the War on Poverty. Today, we continue to debate whether such programs accomplish their goals and whether alternatives would prove more successful.

YOU WILL DECIDE

Should the Federal Government Encourage Increased State Funding of Higher Education?

As discussed in the chapter, the cost of higher education is rising. Financing higher education is a shared responsibility of students and parents, institutions of higher education, the federal government, and state governments. Yet, state spending on higher education is unstable; it tends to rise when state revenues are growing and decline during economic downturns. Arguing that states need to consistently bear their part of the burden, a proposed measure would require a state to increase spending on higher education each year by an amount equivalent to its average increase during the previous five years. If a state does not maintain this level of increased spending, it would not receive new federal matching funds through the Leveraging Educational Assistance Partnership program, a program that rewards states for supporting low-income students.

What do you think? Should the federal government employ this approach to encourage increased state funding of higher education? What are some of the arguments for or against this?

THINKING IT THROUGH

Supporters of this approach charge that the increased cost of higher education has been borne by students and their parents, institutions of higher education, and the federal government. The cyclical nature of state spending on higher education creates problems for institutions of higher education as well as enrolled students who often must pay higher tuition and fees, even though they too are facing financial challenges. Also, supporters note, during periods of economic growth, state spending increases slowly, and it often takes several years to return to its prerecession level. States need to do their part, supporters declare. "We're pleased that Congress, for the first time, is looking to states and tasking states with some responsibility," said Daniel J. Hurley, director of state relations and policy analysis for the American Association of State Colleges and Universities.[*]

Critics argue that in the long run this requirement would reduce rather than increase state funding for higher education. The National Association of State Budget Officers estimated that between 2008 and 2012, the provision would lead states to spend about 10 percent less than they would otherwise. Critics assume that in order to protect themselves from funding obligations in the future, states would limit increases in appropriations to the smallest amount possible, and they would be discouraged from appropriating large spending increases during periods of economic growth. Opponents also complain that such a provision would constitute unjustified meddling by the federal government into state affairs. The federal government does not provide sufficient funding for higher education to justify this kind of mandate, they observe. "It would set a dangerous precedent for federal intrusion into state policy and appropriations authority," charged RaeAnn Kelsch, Republican legislator from North Dakota and chair of the National Conference of State Legislatures (NCSL) education standing committee.

Critical Thinking Questions

1. Who should pay most of the cost of higher education—students, their parents, the federal government, or state governments?

2. Does the federal government have to cover a larger share of the cost of higher education in order to justify a mandate that state governments maintain a certain level of funding for education over time?

*[*]Sara Hebel, "Disputed Plan Would Let Congress Weigh In on State Budgets for Colleges," *Chronicle of Higher Education*, February 29, 2008, p. 25*

Public Assistance

Pressure to reform the welfare system increased among both Democrats and Republicans in the last decades of the twentieth century. The number of U.S. families on welfare—programs that provide assistance to poor families with children—increased from approximately 600,000 households in 1950 to more than 5 million in the early 1990s, growing 13 times as fast as the general population.[25] Why such growth? Some said this increase occurred because those who were eligible for assistance were finally receiving it. Others charged that "government handouts" robbed recipients of the self-confidence they need to go to work and succeed; in this sense, dependence on welfare is viewed as a curse.

In 1996, fundamental changes were made in welfare policy, including the roles of the federal and state governments. Landmark legislation called **Temporary Assistance for Needy Families (TANF)** replaced the 60-year-old program known as Aid to Families with Dependent Children (AFDC).[26] Under AFDC, states provided monthly cash payments to poor families, largely to single mothers to help them take care of their children. States set different benefit levels, which varied enormously, and states determined whether a smaller or larger proportion of poor families were eligible. The federal government picked

Temporary Assistance for Needy Families (TANF)
A federal welfare reform law that replaced Aid to Families with Dependent Children, the 60-year-old assistance program for poor families with children. This 1996 law strengthened work requirements for recipients, limited the time that families can receive benefits, and gave states flexibility to develop service programs supporting work, marriage, and self-sufficiency.

up most of the costs of AFDC because it matched state spending at rates ranging from one federal dollar for every state dollar spent (in wealthy states such as Connecticut) to about three federal dollars for every state dollar (in low-income states such as Mississippi).

Most of the administrative burdens, however, fell on state and local governments. Every state had a department of human services or welfare that either administered welfare programs directly or, in 13 states, supervised county officials who administered these programs. Administration of AFDC was strictly regulated by federal rules, which were designed to minimize errors and fraud and to ensure that families got the benefits they were entitled to receive given their financial circumstances.

TANF differs from AFDC in several ways. First, it imposes new restrictions on families receiving cash assistance. Welfare is no longer an entitlement for families in financial need. Under most circumstances, adults in the family must work soon after they begin getting benefits, and families may no longer receive benefits indefinitely—most can receive cash assistance for only five years in an adult's lifetime.

Second, TANF expanded the goals of welfare policy. Instead of trying to make it possible for women to care for children rather than work, the program now aims to help parents, most of whom are women, find jobs. Teen parents receiving cash benefits are discouraged from setting up their own households and are required to attend school and live at home with their parents. In addition, states are encouraged to adopt programs that promote marriage and reduce out-of-wedlock births.

Third, states were given greater flexibility in designing and administering welfare policies. States now receive block grants from the federal government and may use these grants to support a wide variety of programs; they need not spend most of their welfare dollars on monthly cash payments to families, as they did under AFDC. Rather, states may spend the grant dollars on services, such as child care for working families, transportation assistance, help in getting and keeping jobs, or programs that promote sexual abstinence among unmarried teens. States are also freed from many of the federal rules they followed when administering AFDC. For instance, they no longer need to use public bureaucracies to administer welfare but may instead use private agencies, even including for-profit corporations and religious institutions.

In exchange for this flexibility, each state must report to the federal government what proportion of its welfare cases (that is, families with able-bodied adults receiving cash assistance) are either working at jobs or engaged in some other work-related activity (such as job search). Each state also files a plan with the secretary of health and human services every two years that describes its TANF program, such as how the state will ensure that recipients engage in work activities within two years of receiving benefits, and the state's goals in preventing and reducing out-of-wedlock pregnancies. Money is distributed to states based on the highest amount of federal funding they received in the years just before TANF was passed. To continue receiving federal funds, states must spend at least 75 percent of the amount they spent in 1994 to ensure that states continue to pay their fair share. Grants to states may also be cut if the states fail to engage enough of their adult cases in work activities. Additional federal funds are available to states as incentives for high performance and as loans if states experience financial hardship.

After TANF was enacted, many states used their flexibility to make major changes in their welfare programs. Some states adopted policies that imposed even stronger restrictions on cash benefits than did the federal law. For example, most states require families with able-bodied adults to participate immediately in work-related activities, not only after two years as required by federal law. Also, 20 states provide no additional benefits to families in which children were born while the family was receiving welfare; 8 states have stricter time limits than the federal law on how long families may receive cash assistance in their lifetimes; and 20 states withdraw all benefits to a family not complying with work requirements even after only one violation.[27]

However, many states have also adopted policies and administrative practices that provide assistance to family heads who seek employment. Nearly all states, with federal help, have greatly increased their spending on child care for low-income working families. Nearly all states also allow families to keep a larger share of the income they receive from jobs than was the case under AFDC. Most states have also increased their provision of employment services to welfare families and those who recently left welfare, including programs that help parents to prepare themselves for jobs, find jobs, train for better jobs, and pay for some of the expenses that go along with work, such as transportation and clothing. Some states have experimented with **workfare** programs designed to help welfare recipients who do not have preschool-aged children develop the self-confidence, skills, and habits necessary for regular employment; many states have developed **responsibility contracts,** requiring recipients to sign a written agreement specifying their responsibilities and outlining a plan for them to obtain work and achieve self-sufficiency.[28]

Partly as a result of the 1996 welfare reform, the number of families receiving welfare has dropped by 63 percent since the law was enacted—from 4.4 million families in August 1996 to 1.7 million families in December 2007.[29] Much evidence also suggests that welfare reform has greatly increased employment rates among low-income single mothers with children, the most common heads of families on welfare. It is widely accepted that welfare reforms have contributed to changes in the sources of income among poor families with children; public cash assistance has declined substantially, while earnings from jobs have grown.

Not all these developments were caused by federal and state welfare reforms. They were doubtless helped by the booming economy of the late 1990s, which created many new jobs.[30] As economic growth slowed after 2000, the employment rate of single mothers declined, and the number of single mothers who neither work nor receive welfare increased. A much larger proportion of the families living in poverty are now *not* receiving welfare benefits. Also, the reforms did not seem to help the hardest cases—typically people with little education, limited skills, and no work experience. Although poverty rates fell in the 1990s, they have since risen, especially among children.[31] One critic who worked in the Clinton administration when federal welfare reform was passed, Georgetown University's Peter Edelman, says: "The main lesson of the 1996 law is that having a job and earning a livable income are two different things."[32]

In early 2006, TANF was reauthorized by Congress, which adopted even more stringent work requirements for people on cash assistance. But it is clear that states are now the prime laboratories for making and implementing social policy.[33] The federal government originally became active in welfare programs because states had been unwilling or unable to tackle these problems on their own. Yet, now the states will determine whether the needs of poor people will be given a higher or lower priority, and how poor families will be treated in bad as well as good economic times.

States, along with the federal government, also provide unemployment benefits distributed to those who are out of work through no fault of their own. Benefit amounts and eligibility requirements vary across the states, though one estimate reports that average benefits are about 36 percent of a worker's former salary.[34] Unemployment benefits are paid for by taxes the federal and state governments levy on employers, which are placed in a state trust fund. If states are not able to cover all of their obligations they can borrow from the federal trust fund, but states must repay those loans. As of April 2010, states had already borrowed nearly $40 billion to help pay for their unemployment programs.[35] Individuals are generally eligible for benefits for 26 weeks, but there are programs available that can extend those benefits up to another 26 weeks if eligibility requirements are met.

Public Health

Prevention and control of disease are major state and local responsibilities. Thousands of local governments—counties, cities, townships, and special health districts—have some kind of public health program. Every state has an agency, usually called a department of health, which administers the state program and supervises local health officials. At the national level, agencies like the U.S. Public Health Service and the Centers for Disease

workfare
A welfare strategy adopted by some states that gives able-bodied adults who do not have preschool-aged children the opportunity to learn job skills that can lead to employment.

responsibility contract
A welfare strategy adopted by some states in which recipients sign a written agreement specifying their responsibilities and outlining a plan for obtaining work and achieving self-sufficiency.

Control and Prevention (CDC) conduct research, assist state and local authorities, and administer federal grants to encourage local agencies to expand their programs.

Every state also administers various federally funded medical benefit programs for the needy and uninsured, such as Medicaid. When it was adopted in 1965, Medicaid was designed as a program to enable states to fund health care for people who were poor and received public assistance. Since then, eligibility has been expanded to include low-income children, pregnant women, families, the disabled, and the elderly.[36] Today, only a minority of Medicaid recipients is on welfare, and two of three live in families with an adult in the workforce. More than half the recipients have family income above the poverty level.[37]

Not to be confused with Medicare—the federal health care program for people over the age of 65—Medicaid now serves more than 55 million people, or 13 percent of the population.[38] States feel some pressure to expand Medicaid to deal with the increasing number of people who are uninsured and to improve the quality of health care provided to poor and low-income people. But these pressures, along with the rising cost of prescription drugs, long-term health care, and other health services, add up to a Medicaid program whose expenditures grow much faster than the rest of the average state budget.

State officials acknowledge that soaring Medicaid spending threatens other policy goals, such as reducing public school class size, increasing public transportation infrastructure, and funding innovative environmental programs. Some have reached into the funds received in settling their suits with tobacco companies, or tapped public employee pension funds, or drained their rainy day reserves in order to meet the requirement in state constitutions that they balance their budgets.[39] Governors around the country pressed President George W. Bush and Congress to increase the federal share of Medicaid's costs, to no avail.

In early 2006, Congress passed the Deficit Reduction Act, which includes many new options for states trying to reduce the growth of Medicaid spending. The Act allows states to develop different benefit packages for different types of Medicaid recipients. For example, Kentucky created four benefit plans designed to address the health needs of particular groups, such as those with mental disabilities who need long-term services, and assigns participants to the plan that best meets their health care needs. The Act also allows states to require some recipients to pay for part of their health care. Idaho now requires beneficiaries to pay a monthly premium of $15 and copayments for using the emergency room. Other states have adopted wellness programs, such as smoking-cessation or weight-loss programs, in the hope that healthier lifestyles will lead to lower health care costs. Citizens who participate in these programs can receive additional health care benefits or bonus points to use for additional wellness activities.[40]

Citizens wait to see a nurse or doctor at a public health clinic. Once all of the federal health care reforms are implemented, every citizen should have health insurance, which should greatly reduce the reliance on free clinics and the expense of emergency room treatments. ■ *Do you think all persons should be required to have health insurance?*

In addition to changes to the Medicaid program, states are experimenting with reforms of the health care system generally. They have tried to expand access to private insurance through small business incentives and tax credits. Some have tried to reform the private insurance marketplace by requiring employers to offer their employees health insurance or pay the state a fee for those who are uninsured. Another reform effort focuses on the "connector model," a quasi-governmental authority or agency that aims to pool—or connect—individuals so that they can buy insurance together at a lower rate.[41] In 2006, Massachusetts reformed its health care system in order to provide insurance coverage to virtually all of its residents.[42] Hawaii has, since 1974, required all employers to provide health care benefits to any employee who works 20 hours a week or more. Although it is hard to make causal claims, Hawaii also has among the lowest insurance premiums for its citizens as well one of the healthiest state populations.[43]

Hoping to increase access to health care for children, in 1997, Congress adopted the State Children's Health Insurance Program, commonly called SCHIP. In this program, the federal government provides matching funds to states to help cover the costs of providing health care to children under the age of 19 who live in families with incomes up to two times the federal poverty line. States can choose to set their own eligibility levels below this level, but they need to receive authorization from the federal government to set it higher, as that would extend coverage to additional children. In 2009, Congress passed and President Obama signed an extension that added more than $30 billion to the program in order to extend coverage to another 4 million children.

In 2010, the U.S. Congress passed and President Obama signed into law a number of reforms to the nation's health care system. Key provisions of that legislation include barring insurance companies from dropping people from coverage when they get sick, allowing younger adults to stay covered under their parent's health insurance plans until age 26, and making it harder for insurance companies to deny coverage to individuals with pre-existing conditions. The plan also creates new insurance exchanges by the year 2014 and requires virtually every person to obtain some form of health insurance coverage or pay a tax or fee if they do not.

A number of states have challenged these reforms in federal court. Earlier in 2010, Virginia passed a law prohibiting any individual from being required to purchase health insurance. Florida, along with seventeen other states, filed a similar lawsuit in federal court challenging the constitutionality of the federal mandate, arguing that it usurps the authority of states to regulate health insurance, thereby infringing on state sovereignty. A number of state legislatures have also taken actions designed to nullify parts of the federal health care reform.

Critics of the various legal challenges pursued by the states counter that the federal government clearly has the authority to tax citizens and regulate health care under the Commerce and Necessary and Proper clauses of the Constitution. They also note that virtually all of the state public officials leading these efforts are Republicans and assert that their motivations are based on partisan politics rather than Constitutional arguments. Most Constitutional scholars think these challenges to the federal law will end up before the U.S. Supreme Court, which they expect to reject the claims of the states.

Law Enforcement

Many state and local government powers stem from their **police powers,** the inherent power of states to use physical force if necessary to protect the health, safety, and welfare of their citizens. This power is among those *not* delegated to the federal government by the Constitution and is instead reserved to the states. On this basis, mayors and governors impose curfews, as they have in some urban riots. Most law enforcement takes place at the local level, but states also have a significant role.

The State Police

In 1835, the famous Texas Rangers were organized as a small border patrol. In 1865, Massachusetts appointed a few state constables to suppress gambling, a job the local police had proved unable or, more probably, unwilling to do. But not until 1905, with the organization of the Pennsylvania State Constabulary, did a state police system come into being. State police became a part of our law enforcement system for a variety of reasons. The growth of urban and metropolitan areas, the coming of the automobile (and the resulting demand for greater protection on the highways and the creation of a mobile force for catching fleeing criminals), and the need for a trained force to maintain order during strikes, fires, floods, and other emergencies all promoted the creation of state police.

The jurisdiction of the state police is generally concentrated on those areas outside of the normal jurisdictions of city police and county sheriffs. That includes enforcing travel laws on state and interstate highways, providing security at the state capitol, and often supporting training and support services for local jurisdictions.

Local and Other Police Forces

At the local level, nearly every municipality maintains its own police force; the county has a sheriff and deputies, and some townships have their own police officers. In fact, there

LEARNING **OBJECTIVE**

28.4 Trace the growth of states' responsibilities for law enforcement.

police powers
Inherent powers of state governments to pass laws to protect public health, safety, and welfare; the national government has no directly granted police powers but accomplishes the same goals through other delegated powers.

By the People

Neighborhood Watch Groups

On March 14, 1964, a woman named Kitty Genovese was raped and murdered in Queens, New York. In the newspaper coverage that followed, it was reported that numerous bystanders witnessed the attack but did nothing to help her. Although these accounts of witness behavior are likely inaccurate,* they are credited with creating the impetus for some of the first neighborhood watch programs designed to get citizens involved in reducing and preventing crimes. In 1972, the National Sheriffs Association began a concerted effort to encourage neighborhood watch programs across the country. USA Freedom Corps, Citizen Corps, and the U.S. Justice Department joined with the National Sheriffs Association in 2002 to launch USAonWatch in an effort to revitalize neighborhood watch programs in the wake of the September 11, 2001, terrorist attacks.

Most neighborhood watch programs focus on having volunteers in a position to observe and report to the police suspected criminal behavior; volunteers are strongly encouraged not to intervene. USAonWatch provides training information and a number of other resources for interested groups and individuals through its Web site at www.usaonwatch.org. Another organization called the National Neighborhood Watch Institute offers signs and other materials for neighborhood watch groups to purchase (www.nnwi.org).

Find out if there are neighborhood watch programs in your community or neighborhood. Many colleges and universities also operate similar volunteer programs, often focused on walking with individuals to and from student centers, libraries, and dorms during late-night hours. Find out if your school has such a program. Consider getting one organized through your student government, campus security, or other organization. As noted above, such programs are not about confronting criminals and escalating a negative situation. Rather, the goal is to prevent such events in the first place by the presence of more people or to be able to quickly call in professional police and security officers.

CRITICAL THINKING QUESTIONS

1. Should citizens actively participate in policing their own neighborhoods, or should the work be left to professional police officers? What are the pros and cons of neighborhood watch programs?

2. Should neighborhood watch participants be required to take training and receive certification? What sort of liability do neighborhood watch participants face if something bad does happen while they are on patrol?

* Jim Rasenberger, "Nightmare on Austin Street," *American Heritage Magazine*, October 2006,

---

are almost 18,000 separate state and local law enforcement agencies in the United States, employing more than 700,000 officers.[44] Local police concentrate on law enforcement and criminal investigation within their local cities, whereas in many counties, sheriffs provide law enforcement outside of incorporated cities. State police, county sheriffs, and local police are all charged with enforcing state and most federal laws. Some cities and counties have further local ordinances that local police enforce as well. In many respects, the police system individuals encounter has more to do with *where* they have committed some act and less to do with *what* they actually did.

State and local governments spend more than $125 billion a year on police protection and correctional or prison institutions.[45] Local governments pay for nearly 70 percent of all police protection costs, including such routine activities as controlling traffic and patrolling neighborhoods but also maintaining court security and preventing juvenile crime. From 1987 to 2003, the number of full-time employees working in local police departments increased by 27 percent, or approximately 135,000 people. The percentage of police officers that were female increased from 7.6 percent to 11.3 percent during the same period.[46] With crime an ever-important issue to many voters, crime control is always on the minds of elected officials.

State police are not the only law enforcement agencies maintained by state governments. There are liquor law enforcement officials, fish and game wardens, fire wardens, detective bureaus, and special motor vehicle police. This dispersion of functions has been criticized, yet each department insists it needs its own law enforcement agency to handle its special problems.

Federal—State Action

The federal government has gradually moved into law enforcement, although local governments still bear the main cost of local law enforcement. Today, for example, it is a federal offense to transport kidnapped individuals or stolen goods across state lines. Taking firearms, explosives, or even information across state lines for illegal purposes is also a federal offense. Federal law enforcement agencies include the Federal Bureau of

Investigation (FBI); the Bureau of Alcohol, Tobacco, Firearms, and Explosives (ATF); and the Drug Enforcement Administration (DEA).

Both violent crime rates and property crime rates have been declining since the early 1990s.[47] Despite these positive trends, politicians in both parties continue to press for government to do more about crime. Some advocate stricter laws regulating guns, whereas others favor more police on the streets or more prisons. Because politicians fear appearing "soft on crime," taking action on crime is almost always a high priority at all levels of government.

Since the September 11, 2001 terrorist attacks on New York City and the Pentagon, every state has designated a homeland security coordinator. These state officials work with the federal Department of Homeland Security to conduct preparedness and training efforts aimed at preventing and dealing with future terrorist attacks. In 2002, the federal government approved funds to train and equip first responders and to prevent bioterrorism.[48] In 2008, federal grants-in-aid to the states for homeland security totaled $1.69 billion.[49]

Although there is a clear need for new and expanded homeland security efforts, few states have the resources to support them. Many local and state officials have complained that most new federal funds are being redirected toward new homeland security concerns such as bioterrorism preparedness, while traditional and basic public safety systems are ignored. This has added to budget shortfalls in most states and has led state and local officials to insist on more federal funds and greater flexibility in how states and localities decide what their priorities are.[50]

Planning the Urban Community

Are our cities good places in which to live and work? Are crime, pollution, garbage, crowded shopping areas, dented fenders, slums and blighted areas, inadequate parks, challenging traffic patterns, and shattered nerves the inevitable costs of urban life?

For at least the first century of the United States' existence, its cities were allowed to grow unchecked. Industrialists were permitted to erect factories wherever they wished. Developers were allowed to construct towering buildings that prevented sunlight from reaching the streets below. Commuters, bicyclists, and pedestrians ended up with transportation systems that rarely met their needs. With increased industrialization and urbanization, political pressures emerged in the late 1800s and early 1900s to reform the city.

Zoning Laws

The most common method of ensuring orderly growth is *zoning*—creating specific areas and limiting property usage in each area. A community may be divided into designated areas for single-family, two-family, or multifamily dwellings; for commercial purposes; and for light or heavy industry. Regulations restrict the height of buildings or require that buildings be located a certain distance apart or a certain distance from the boundaries of the lot.

Zoning regulations help the city or county government coordinate services with land use. Zoning laws also help stabilize property values by preventing, for example, garbage dumps from being located next to residential areas. Day-to-day enforcement is usually the responsibility of a building inspector who ensures that a projected construction project is consistent with building, zoning, fire, and sanitary regulations before granting a building permit. A zoning ordinance, however, is no better than its enforcement. In most cases, a zoning or planning commission or the city council can amend ordinances and make exceptions to regulations, and these officials are often under tremendous pressure to grant exceptions. But if they go too far in permitting special cases, the whole purpose of zoning is defeated.

Zoning is only one kind of community planning. Until recently, city planners were primarily concerned with streets and buildings. Today, most are also concerned with the quality of life. Consequently, planning covers a broad range of activities, including methods to avoid air pollution, improve water quality, and provide for better parks. Planners collect all the information they can about a city and then prepare long-range plans. Can smaller-scale communities be devised within urban centers? Can downtown areas be revitalized, and if so, how? Where should main highways or mass-transit facilities be constructed to meet future needs? Will the water supply be adequate for the population 10, 20, or 50 years

Urban gardens, like this one in Seattle, allow residents to maximize the use of urban spaces, provide for a greener urban environment, and promote greater neighborhood self-sufficiency. ■ *Should local governments do more to encourage these kinds of actions?*

from now? Are hospitals and parks accessible to all? Does the design of public buildings encourage crime or energy waste?

Controlling Growth

Critics of urban and state planning are skeptical whether governors, mayors, or state and local legislators can prevent what they sometimes call the "Los Angelization" of the United States, by which they mean sprawling urban growth without much planning for transportation, environmental protection, or management of water and other resources. Unregulated market forces can cause severe harm to residents, and "politics as usual" does not ensure sensible growth patterns or protect the air, water, and beauty of most states and communities.

Seattle and San Francisco residents voted to limit the height and bulk of downtown buildings in an effort to protect these cities from excessive growth. Maryland and many other states have passed "smart growth" laws aimed at preserving large blocks of contiguous land and ensuring that the necessary roads, sewers, and schools are in place before development proceeds. This legislation is implemented in two ways. The state gives priority funding to development in areas designated by counties as having the proper infrastructure and meeting other guidelines; state funds are also allocated to local governments and private land trusts to purchase the development rights to land "rich in agricultural, forestry, natural, and cultural resources."[51]

A few urban planners recommend looking at European cities such as Paris, where choice neighborhoods in the heart of the city combine elegant six- and seven-story apartment buildings above neighborhood retail stores. A close look at European cities often finds a great number of interior gardens within apartments and meticulously groomed neighborhood parks. A U.S. group called Community Greens helps residents create and share parks in cities across the country.[52] Real estate analyst Christopher Leinberger observed that "walkable urbanism," neighborhoods in which residents can walk to shops, schools, and parks, are now much in demand by a growing segment of the U.S. population.[53]

Obviously, planning and sensible growth depend on public support. They also depend on market forces. No plan will be effective, however, unless it reflects the interests and values of major groups within the community. Planning is clearly a political activity. Different groups view the ends and means of planning differently, and agreements on tough policy options are often hard to reach. Moreover, one of the barriers to successful planning is the general fear of government power. Effective planning therefore requires imaginative collaboration among planners, community leaders, and the popularly elected officials who must bear the responsibility for implementing the plans.[54]

Transportation

Before the automobile, long-distance commercial travel was conducted mainly by canal and railroad. Local roads were built and repaired under the direction of city, township, and county officials. Able-bodied male citizens were required either to put in a certain number of days working on the public roads or to pay taxes for that purpose. By the 1890s, bicycle clubs began to urge the building of hard-surfaced roads, but it was not until the early 1900s and the growing popularity of the automobile that road building became a major industry. This function was gradually transferred from local governments to state governments and the federal government, but counties and townships still have important building and maintenance functions.

Although much of the money comes from the federal government, state and local governments build the highways, public buildings, airports, parks, and recreational facilities. States do the planning, estimate the costs, and arrange for the construction work, even when they receive federal assistance. In order to receive support, however, states

The I-35W bridge spanning the Mississippi River collapsed in Minneapolis during rush hour in the summer of 2007. Paying for the maintenance of transportation infrastructure has become an increasing burden for states. When the federal government passed an economic stimulus package to combat the 2008–2009 recession, funds for transportation repairs were included. ■ *Once roads and bridges are built, who should pay for their maintenance?*

must submit their plans to, and have their work inspected by, the U.S. Department of Transportation (DOT). All federally funded highways must meet DOT standards governing the engineering of the roadbed, employment conditions for construction workers, and weight and load conditions for trucks.

The federal government has supported state highway construction since 1916, and through legislation passed since then, federal aid has increased. Under the Federal Highway Act of 1956, states planned and built the National System of Interstate and Defense Highways. The Eisenhower Interstate System consists of more than 46,000 miles of super-highways linking nearly all cities with a population of 50,000 or more. The federal government paid 90 percent of the cost of this system, with most of the money coming from taxes on gasoline, tires, and trucks that are placed in a trust fund designated for that purpose.

In 2005, Congress passed a $244 billion, five-year authorization of the federal high-way, public transportation, and safety programs. After Interstate 35W bridge collapsed in Minneapolis in August 2007, concerns have been raised about the safety of the nation's transportation infrastructure. In January 2008, the National Surface Transportation Policy and Revenue Study Commission concluded the nation needed to spend $225 billion a year for 50 years to maintain and upgrade surface transportation. Because the current 18.4 cents per gallon federal gas tax has not been increased since 1993 and because the highway transportation fund is expected to face a significant shortfall in fiscal year 2009, the commission recommended an increase in the gas tax to pay for these repairs.[55]

Traffic has become a major problem in recent years—especially in cities such as Boston, Denver, Los Angeles, Seattle, San Francisco, Washington, D.C., and New York. The population is growing and more people own cars, but drivers are also driving more each year. As a result, traffic and congestion have become pressing issues for state governments.[56] Building public transportation systems, increasing road space, or establishing staggered work hours should help; however, transportation policy makers have not found solutions to be simple. Advocates of public transportation point out that even though public transportation is more energy efficient than driving, the federal government provides much less aid to states and localities for mass transit than it does for highways.[57] Adding roads or lanes often leads more people to drive and may ultimately result in new traffic patterns that are no better than the old ones. Staggering work hours is difficult because businesses work most effectively through collaboration, so it is most efficient for workers to be on the job at the same time each day. But with higher gas prices and growing concern over climate change, citizens, businesses, and state and local governments are starting to pursue alternatives to reduce miles driven, and this in turn could reduce traffic congestion.

For the People

Creating Government Efficiency

States spent much of 2009 and 2010 looking for ways to cut their budgets. Much of that involved cuts to programs, but many other efforts were made to reduce operating costs and streamline government operations. "The budget crisis is so severe that it's now possible to do some things that everyone knew were smart but couldn't get done because of political considerations," said John Thomasian, the director of the Center for Best Practices at the National Governors Association.*

A story appearing in *USA Today* described several efforts by states.† For example, Iowa established a centralized purchasing and information technology operation that eliminated 13 separate boards and is projected to save the state $127 million per year. Missouri ended a paid holiday for state workers for the Friday after Thanksgiving, saving $1.2 million a year. Michigan combined ten finance authorities into one as part of a sustained effort that has eliminated more than 300 boards in recent years at a projected savings of more than $3 billion per year. Indiana combined the administration of two large pension funds, producing an estimated savings of $10 million in the first year. Although these kinds of programs alone are not enough to close the budget gaps that states faced at this time, they demonstrate innovative efforts to make state governments operate more efficiently so that they can do more work with less tax money.

Of course, as states eliminate duplication and consolidate operations to achieve greater efficiency, they are also concentrating power and authority into the hands of fewer and fewer top officials. Decisions can be made easier and fewer employees are needed, but mistakes can be compounded. Engineers often design back-up systems and built-in redundancies so that when a primary system fails, a secondary system takes over and minimizes the impact of the first failure.

CRITICAL THINKING QUESTIONS

1. What are the pros and cons of streamlining government programs and operations? In which areas does it make sense to consolidate operations, and in which ones might it be more important to have duplication?

2. How important is efficiency as a goal for government operations? How should we try to measure efficiency in government operations?

*The Center for Best Practices Web site is located at http://www.nga.org/portal/site/nga/menuitem.50aeae5ff70b817ae8ebb856a11010a0/.
†"States Streamline, Reorganize Amid Fiscal Crisis" *USA Today,* March 15, 2010, http://www.usatoday.com/news/nation/2010-03-14-state-budget-cuts_N.htm?POE=click-refer.

Economic Development

Another central priority for governors and mayors, as well as other state and local officials, is providing jobs for their citizens. Governors commonly spend a significant amount of time encouraging companies to relocate within their borders, courting corporate officials, going on trade missions to other countries to promote their states' products, and negotiating favorable tax and other incentives with new businesses. This interest is not new. What is new is the international scope of activities.[58] For example, while in Cuba to sign a deal to export $11 million of his state's wheat, Nebraska Governor Dave Heineman explained that "expanding trade relationships is good for Nebraska and altogether good for America."[59]

States compete with one another because economic development is the key to increasing the tax base that funds government services. But states face a dilemma because satisfying the demands of new businesses can be expensive, and tax incentives can reduce the tax return the new companies will generate. Competition among states has intensified to the point that localities are worried about keeping the jobs they have, not only persuading new companies to move to their area. New York City has offered billions of dollars in incentives to influence several companies not to leave. Critics of these "bidding wars" believe that states should spend tax money on rebuilding infrastructure and strengthening education rather than offering public funds to selected large private companies.

Regulation

LEARNING OBJECTIVE

28.6 Assess the role of states and communities in regulating and in enforcing compliance with federal and state regulations.

States and local communities adopt health and safety regulations on the assumption that the benefits to the general public will outweigh the costs to the individuals and groups being regulated. Thus, laws requiring drivers' licenses, compelling motorists to stop at red lights, mandating seat-belt use, and imposing severe penalties on people caught driving under the influence of alcohol or drugs are intended to protect the safety and freedom of innocent pedestrians and occupants of other motor vehicles. We accept most such laws as both necessary and legitimate.

Environmental Regulation

State and local governments have long been concerned about managing land use and protecting the environment. In such heavily polluted places as Pittsburgh, smoke abatement ordinances were enacted as early as 1860, but aggressive action on air pollution did not come until after World War II.[60]

In the 1950s and 1960s, the federal government's role in environmental regulation was limited to providing state and local governments with grants for research and assistance in developing and implementing their own environmental standards. In the late 1960s and early 1970s, pressure on the federal government to develop and implement national environmental standards increased, particularly with the recognition that air and water pollution does not acknowledge state boundaries. Important legislation dealing with specific environmental problems was adopted in the 1970s, including the Clean Air Act of 1970, the Clean Water Act of 1972, the Safe Drinking Water Act of 1974, the Toxic Substances Control Act of 1976, and the Superfund Act (federal Comprehensive Environmental Response, Compensation, and Liability Act) of 1980. Most of these Acts have been amended one or more times since their initial adoption. In the 1970s, President Nixon created the Environmental Protection Agency (EPA) and gave it primary responsibility for environmental protection programs.

The basic model of environmental regulation has been for the federal government to set national standards for water and air quality. State and local governments are typically put in charge of both implementing standards and monitoring compliance. Yet, because federal environmental grants to states have not increased since the early 1990s, states have come to take on a greater role in expanding legislation and research for environmental programs and to absorb an increasingly large share of the costs. They now pay approximately 80 percent of the costs of federal environmental programs.[61]

One area in which states are increasingly responsible for environmental policy is waste management. Although the Superfund Act cleans up the most contaminated toxic dump sites, state and local policies have been established to cover toxic sites that do not qualify as Superfund sites but still warrant cleanup action.[62] Not unexpectedly, states whose economies are growing have regulated waste management more aggressively than economically hard-pressed states that fear driving industries away with regulations and constraints. But concerns about nuclear waste, acid rain, and hazardous wastes have sparked extensive efforts at regulation within states, as well as court battles with nearby states over the export of unwanted byproducts of energy development.

Another area in which states have become very active is energy use and sustainability. A recent press release by the National Governors Association declares that states are generating new advances in clean energy policy.[63] Many states have been using alternative renewable energy both to cut down on energy costs and to rejuvenate dwindling rural economies. Large-scale wind-energy projects, for example, have been started in New York, Pennsylvania, Colorado, Iowa, Kansas, Texas, and Washington, among other states. As fossil fuel costs became increasingly unpredictable, states started to diversify their approach by investing in biomass, wind, hydroelectric, solar, and geothermal projects. Some states have even implemented innovative tax incentives and "net metering" programs (a practice allowing customers who have solar panels or other personal energy-generating capital to sell their energy back to the overall grid) in order to encourage more individual responsibility. Although none of these tactics has yet become widely accepted, nor is renewable energy expected to soon replace traditional energy sources, they are evidence of active state and local environmental efforts.

Although the EPA has responsibility for the development of national standards, states sometimes take the lead in adopting more demanding standards of environmental protection and pushing the EPA for action. For example, California adopted a law in 2006 "requiring a 25 percent reduction in the state's carbon dioxide emissions by 2020."[64] Although California has the authority to develop its own air quality standards, it has to receive a waiver from the EPA to do so. In late 2007, the EPA denied the state's request for a waiver and blocked California from implementing rules designed to reduce greenhouse gas emissions from cars and trucks. In response, California has sued the EPA, hoping

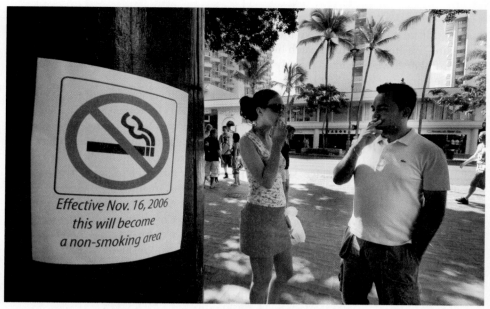

Cities and states often provide their residents with greater health and safety protections than those mandated by the federal government. Many states have passed measures banning smoking in public areas, and some mandate helmet use with bicycles or motorcycles. Often, actions tested at the state level can lead to federal policies. ■ *What are some other examples of states functioning as "laboratories for democracy?"*

to prevent the agency from blocking the rules that it developed and that other states hope to follow. In a press release announcing the lawsuit, Governor Schwarzenegger declared, "It is unconscionable that the federal government is keeping California and 19 other states from adopting these standards. They are ignoring the will of millions of people who want their government to take action in the fight against global warming."[65] In June of 2009, the EPA announced it would grant California's waiver after all.[66]

Working Conditions

Despite expanded federal regulation, state and local governments still have much to say about working conditions.

- *Health and safety legislation:* States require proper heating, lighting, ventilation, fire escapes, and sanitary facilities in work areas. Machinery must be equipped with safety guards. Some standards have also been established to reduce occupation-related diseases. Health, building, and labor inspectors tour industrial plants to ensure compliance with the laws.
- *Workers' compensation:* Today, all states have workers' compensation programs based on the belief that employees should not have to bear the cost of accidents or illnesses incurred because of their jobs. The costs of accidents and occupational diseases are borne by employers and passed on to consumers in the form of higher prices. In the past, employees had to prove that their employers were at fault if they suffered an accident on the job. Today, if people are injured or contract a disease in the ordinary course of employment, they are entitled to compensation set by a prearranged schedule. Workers' compensation is a controversial issue, with employers arguing that employee claims of workplace stress are excessive and will make U.S. firms uncompetitive.
- *Child labor:* All states forbid child labor, yet state laws vary widely in their coverage and in their definition of child labor. Many states set the minimum age for employment at 14. Higher age requirements are normal for employment in hazardous occupations and during school hours. Many of these regulations have been superseded by stricter federal laws.
- *Consumer protection:* The consumer protection movement, which became prominent in the 1960s and 1970s, says consumers should be provided with adequate

safety information and should have their complaints heard. Most states have offices to hear consumer complaints, including lawyers working in the offices of the state attorney general. State governments often establish professional standards and handle complaints about legal and medical services or insurance practices.

Recent state activity to protect consumers has focused on fraud, especially mailed "guaranteed prize schemes," to which millions of people respond. When the prize is not exactly what was promised or the method for selecting winners proves deceptive, people often complain to their state governments. Other areas in which state governments have been active in attempting to protect consumers include charitable solicitations by telephone, long-distance phone service promotions, credit card offers and promotions, and irregularities and fraud in corporations.

The Importance of State and Local Policy

All 50 state governments and more than 86,000 local governments are on the front lines of trying to solve community and regional social problems. They must often work closely with one another and the national government, and this is a frequent source of frustration.[67]

Divided government in Washington, when it occurs, has meant that neither political party could have its way with domestic policy. Presidents Bill Clinton and George W. Bush had different priorities, and the generally divided U.S. Senate has taken a cautious approach on such issues as environmental regulation. Health care reform barely passed a Congress with Democratic majorities in both the House and Senate.

State officials continue to be frustrated with national legislation such as the No Child Left Behind Act and homeland security legislation in recent years that mandates extensive federal requirements into core areas of state and local policy responsibilities yet provides inadequate federal funds to assist in the achievement of these goals.

Innovative governors and state legislators have sponsored important changes in welfare reform, educational testing, transportation, urban planning, and insurance regulation. But the challenges facing state and local officials continue to unfold.

CHAPTER **SUMMARY**

28.1 Outline local, state, and federal government roles in elementary and secondary education.

The federal government's share in financing K–12 education has increased over time but is still low. The influence of the federal government has increased considerably, however, particularly because of the requirements of the No Child Left Behind Act of 2001, a reauthorization of the Elementary and Secondary Education Act. This Act emerged from a reform movement pushing for changes to increase the quality of education, but controversy has developed over the impact of the federal regulations.

28.2 Assess the concerns about state funding of higher education.

State funding of higher education is unstable, rising during periods of economic growth and falling during periods of economic decline. Some public colleges and universities can often raise tuition to make up for lost state revenues, but these tuition increases mean that the burden of paying for higher education shifts to students and their parents.

28.3 Describe the role of the state in public assistance programs, and assess the challenges facing state social service programs.

The national welfare overhaul legislation in 1996 imposed new work requirements and time limits on families receiving cash assistance. It also gave states much greater flexibility in designing and administering programs that serve low-income families with children. The new law established block grants of federal money that must be matched by state funds and focused assistance more on providing employment services, child care, and other forms of noncash services and supports.

States have long sought to eradicate disease and foster practices conducive to a healthy population. The challenges for states today include managing the administration and rising costs of Medicaid and other health care systems.

28.4 Trace the growth of states' responsibilities for law enforcement.

The growth of urban and metropolitan areas and the need for a trained force to maintain order during emergencies led to the creation of the state police.

Additional enforcement agencies have emerged as states have regulated such activities as the sale and use of alcohol, fishing, and hunting. After the September 11 terrorist attacks, state law enforcement agencies took on the additional responsibility of trying to provide for homeland security.

28.5 Outline states' tools and priorities for urban planning.

States attempt to ensure orderly growth through zoning laws and community planning. Transportation is also a major area of state and local government activity. Although the federal government provides financial assistance for the construction of roads, highways, and urban mass transit, the responsibility of planning, building, and maintaining these transportation systems lies with the states. States openly compete with one another in the area of economic development by offering tax incentives, waiving environmental regulations, and giving other enticements to businesses to locate or stay within their boundaries.

28.6 Assess the role of states and communities in regulating and in enforcing compliance with federal and state regulations.

Generally, the federal government sets regulation standards, and states implement them and monitor compliance. Recently, states have taken a more active role in setting environmental regulations regarding waste management, energy use, sustainability, and climate change. State and local governments also set regulations for working conditions that provide protection to employees.

CHAPTER **SELF-TEST**

28.1 Outline local, state, and federal government roles in elementary and secondary education.

1. Do you think the federal government should ensure that the amount spent on education per student does not vary from state to state? Explain your position and respond to one or two likely arguments from those who disagree.
2. Imagine that you are a state commissioner of education in a state that ranks in the bottom 10 percent for educational attainment by students. Write two to three paragraphs explaining how you will resolve the problems in your state's educational system. Anticipate and respond to arguments from those who disagree with your plan.

28.2 Assess the concerns about state funding of higher education.

3. What percentage of a typical state's budget is spent on higher education?
   a. 1 to 7 percent
   b. 8 to 15 percent
   c. 16 to 20 percent
   d. 21 to 25 percent
4. In a short paragraph, explain why you feel that state governments should do more (or less) to fund the higher education of students within their states.

28.3 Describe the role of the state in public assistance programs, and assess the challenges facing state social service programs.

5. Write one or two paragraphs outlining the major differences between AFDC and TANF.
6. Write a paragraph explaining why welfare reform and health care coverage have headed in opposite directions in the last 15 years as far as coverage is concerned.

28.4 Trace the growth of states' responsibilities for law enforcement.

7. Why has there been such a great expansion of people employed in law enforcement in the last 50 years?
8. In one or two paragraphs, tell why it is or is not necessary for different agencies within a state to have their own law enforcement groups. Explain how you would deal with the problems associated with this specialization.

28.5 Outline states' tools and priorities for urban planning.

9. How have cities in the United States tried to prevent uncontrolled growth? List as many means as you can think of. Write a few sentences about which methods you think would be most effective and why.
10. In a paragraph, explain the major points in the evolution of transportation as explained in the chapter.
11. What competing challenges do states face in the pursuit of economic development? What do you think they should do about their dilemma?

28.6 Assess the role of states and communities in regulating and in enforcing compliance with federal and state regulations.

12. In a paragraph, highlight the major points in the development of environmental regulation since the beginning of the twentieth century.
13. In one or two paragraphs, argue whether the growth of federal regulation over the states should continue, and explain why or why not.

Answers to selected questions: 3. b

mypoliscilab EXERCISES
Where participation leads to action!

Apply what you learned in this chapter with these resources on MyPoliSciLab.

📖—│Read on mypoliscilab.com

    eText: Chapter 28

👁—│Watch on mypoliscilab.com

    Video: Suspected Salmonella Outbreak at Texas Plant

✓—│Study and Review on mypoliscilab.com

    Pre-Test
    Post-Test
    Chapter Exam
    Flashcards

KEY TERMS

vouchers, p. 701
charter school, p. 702
Temporary Assistance for Needy Families (TANF), p. 705

workfare, p. 707
responsibility contract, p. 707
police powers, p. 709

ADDITIONAL RESOURCES

FURTHER READING

REBECCA BLANK AND **RON HASKINS,** EDS., *The New World of Welfare* (Brookings Institution Press, 2001).

JASON DEPARLE, *American Dream: Three Women, Ten Kids, and a Nation's Drive to End Welfare* (Viking Penguin, 2004).

R. KENNETH GODWIN AND **FRANK KEMERER,** *School Choice and Tradeoffs: Liberty, Equity, and Diversity* (University of Texas Press, 2002).

VIRGINIA GRAY AND **RUSSELL HANSON,** *Politics in the American States: A Comparative Analysis,* 8th ed. (CQ Press, 2003).

JOHN J. HARRIGAN AND **DAVID NICE,** *Politics and Policy in States and Communities,* 9th ed. (Longman, 2005).

DAVID HURSH, *High-Stakes Testing and the Decline of Teaching and Learning* (Rowman & Littlefield, 2008).

CATHY MARIE JOHNSON, GEORGIA DUERST-LAHTI, AND **NOELLE NORTON,** *Creating Gender: The Sexual Politics of Welfare Policy* (Lynne Rienner, 2007).

NORMAN R. LUTTBEG, *The Grassroots of Democracy: A Comparative Study of Competition and Its Impact in American Cities in the 1990s* (Lexington Books, 1999).

DAVID C. NICE, *Policy Innovation in State Government* (Iowa State University Press, 1994).

MICHAEL A. PAGANO AND **ANN O. M. BOWMAN,** *Cityscape and Capital: The Politics of Urban Development* (Johns Hopkins University Press, 1997).

DAREL PAUL, *Rescaling International Political Economy: Subnational States and the Regulation of the Global Political Economy* (Routledge, 2005).

PAUL E. PETERSON AND **MARTIN R. WEST,** EDS., *No Child Left Behind? The Politics and Practice of School Accountability* (Brookings Institution Press, 2003).

BARRY G. RABE, *Statehouse and Greenhouse: The Emerging Politics of American Climate Change Policy* (Brookings Institution Press, 2004).

DENISE SCHEBERLE, *Federalism and Environmental Policy,* 2d ed. (Georgetown University Press, 2004).

MARK SCHNEIDER, PAUL TESKE, AND **MELISSA MARSCHALL,** *Choosing Schools: Consumer Choice and the Quality of American Schools* (Princeton University Press, 2002).

SANDRA VERGARI, ED., *The Charter School Landscape* (University of Pittsburgh Press, 2002).

JOHN F. WITTE, *The Market Approach to Education: An Analysis of America's First Voucher Program* (Princeton University Press, 1999). See also *Governing: The Magazine of States and Localities,* published monthly by Congressional Quarterly; and the series of excellent books on state government public policy making published by the University of Nebraska Press.

WEB SITES

www.sheriffs.org The National Sheriffs Association is a professional association dedicated to serving the Office of Sheriff and its affiliates through education, training, and information resources.

http://www.grandlodgefop.org/ The Fraternal Order of Police focuses on improving the working conditions of law enforcement officers and the safety of those we serve through education, legislation, information, community involvement, and employee representation.

www.cdc.gov The Centers for Disease Control and Prevention conducts research and disseminates information about health and health related issues facing citizens in the Unites States and throughout the world.

CHAPTER 29

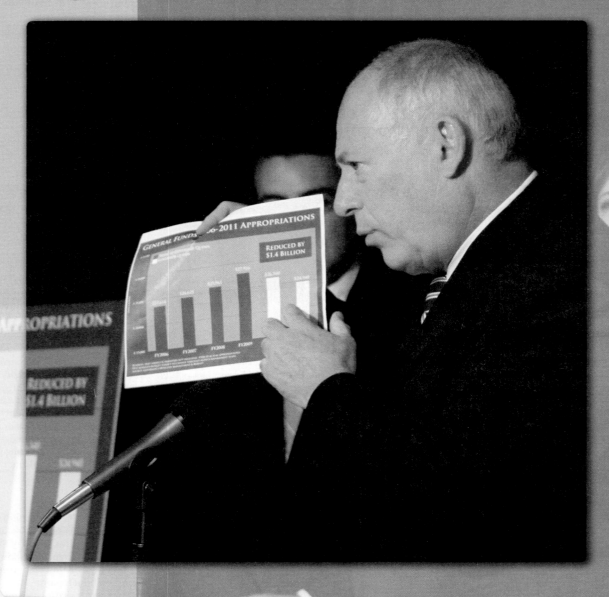

Staffing and Financing State and Local Governments

Passing laws is not easy, but the hardest work sometimes begins after a bill becomes law, as every policy needs qualified people to implement it and funds to pay for it. The states faced significant budgetary shortfalls in 2009 and 2010 resulting from the recession that began in 2008. That produced short-term pressures on states to cut programs, furlough state employees, and raise some taxes and fees. However, the long-term consequences may be even more important.

A report in *The New York Times* in the spring of 2010 described how many states were creating long-term debt problems for themselves as they tried to navigate this budget-tightening period, through such practices as unbalancing budgets, masking debt with account gimmicks, and ignoring the massive number of public workers that will be owed their pensions when they retire.[1] For example, New Hampshire tried to use $110 million from its medical malpractice insurance pool to balance its budget. Colorado has tried to use money from its workers' compensation program for the same purpose. Illinois is trying to defer payments because it is $9 billion behind in paying its bills to vendors. Connecticut is trying to issue new accounting rules, and California forced companies to pay 70 percent of their 2010 corporate income taxes by June. In addition, states face a range of other long-term commitments, with the real ticking time bomb, according to economists Joshua Rauh and Robert Novy-Marx, being future pension obligations states owe. They estimate that states' future pension obligations currently sit at approximately $5.17 trillion, but that states have currently set aside less than $2 trillion to cover those obligations. That leaves a $3.23 trillion hole for states to fill.

The fear is that these practices may create a credit crisis for states similar to what many businesses faced in 2008–2009 and what the country of Greece faced in 2010. States, like businesses, often borrow money to pay for some expenses. For example, states can borrow money for rebuilding roads now and then pay it back over time. This commonly occurs by selling bonds that states promise to repay to investors with some interest. Some economists, such as Kenneth Rogoff and Carmen Reinhart, worry that if states are unable to meet their current and future debt obligations, investors will simply stop purchasing state bonds—essentially creating a credit freeze for states. They write, "When an accident is waiting to happen, it eventually does."

These are major challenges for states. The recent recession has drawn greater attention to these problems. However, the immediate need to balance current budgets (hopefully before the next election) with as little pain as possible works against taking serious steps toward heading off this potential long-term debt crisis that looms ahead for states.

This chapter examines the personnel and fiscal issues faced by state and local governments. It will also discuss the role of state and local employees and the different ways in which they are selected and retained in office, and the reasons governments rely on private agencies instead of their own workforce to perform some functions. The chapter also examines how state and local governments raise the money to pay for their workers and the many services they provide, and it reviews the challenges states and localities face now and in the future as needs increase and funding gets tighter.

Staffing State and Local Governments

LEARNING OBJECTIVE

29.1 Describe the hiring process for public employees, and assess attempts at reform and privatization.

Unlike the federal workforce, which actually has relatively few employees who work directly with citizens, nearly all state and local employees have contact with the public. More than 7.8 million work in elementary, secondary, or higher education; nearly 1 million are police officers and firefighters; and another 800,000 work in state, county, and city hospitals. In addition, 730,000 work as prison guards and corrections officers, and nearly 200,000 work in parks and recreation.[2]

Also unlike the federal government, state and local governments have a large and growing workforce. As of 2008, state and local governments employed about 14.8 million full-time and 4.9 million part-time workers—approximately seven times the number who worked in the federal government.[3] According to the U.S. Bureau of Labor Statistics, state and local governments will continue to grow. By 2016, more than 20.7 million American adults will work in the nation's approximately 89,000 state and local governments. During the same period, the federal government is expected to stay approximately the same size.[4]

Public Employees

More than one-third of the cost of state and local government is employees' salaries. How are these people chosen? A few are elected. A larger number, including many top administrators, are appointed by elected officials. By far the greatest number, however, are typically hired through some kind of **merit system** in which selection and promotion depend on demonstrated performance (merit) rather than political patronage. Although in many jurisdictions it still helps to know the right people and belong to the right party, patronage is not nearly as prevalent as it once was.

Throughout much of the nineteenth century, governments at all levels were dominated by political patronage, a political **spoils system** in which employment was a reward for partisan loyalty and active political support in campaigns and elections. In 1883, Congress passed the Pendleton Civil Service Reform Act, which began to move the federal government from the spoils system to the merit system. Although the Act did not directly affect state and local governments, many of the states began to institute the merit system. In 1939, Democratic Senator Carl Hatch of Arizona pushed through Congress the first Hatch Act, which further promoted the merit principle and limited the political activities of federal, state, and local employees whose salaries were supported with federal funds. Subsequently, state and local governments enacted "little Hatch Acts" that enforced merit principles and restricted the political activities of their employees. Merit testing is now used in most states for hiring or promoting employees. Moreover, under a 1976 Supreme Court decision, states cannot dismiss civil servants for political reasons.[5]

Merit systems are generally administered by an office of state personnel, which prepares and administers examinations, provides lists of job openings, establishes job classifications, and determines salary schedules. It also serves as a board of appeal for employees who are discharged. State personnel offices are concerned with training the already employed, bargaining with labor unions, administering affirmative action programs, and filling top-level executive positions.

However, merit systems increasingly came under attack, particularly in the 1990s. Critics complained that state personnel systems were overly centralized and regulated. State personnel offices used procedures, job descriptions, and tests that often failed to fit the needs of diverse state agencies. Job descriptions were detailed and hard to change, and agency managers were thus prevented from adapting their workforces to changing needs. Procedures for filling jobs involved several levels of bureaucracy, and vacancies took a long time to fill.

Critics also complained that hiring and firing rules deprived responsible officials of authority over their subordinates. They argued that there was so much emphasis on insulating public employees from political coercion that employees enjoyed too much job security. Administrators could not get rid of incompetents. Sometimes, it took months and several elaborate hearings to dismiss public employees unwilling or unable to do their jobs. Also, public managers could not use salaries to reward and retain the best employees because most of the older merit systems permitted only a narrow pay range for any one job. In summary, although merit systems were supposed to emphasize ability and minimize political favoritism, they came to be viewed by many as clumsy, complicated, and unresponsive to the needs of public managers and agencies—and as obstacles to efforts by state and local governments to attract the most skilled people to public sector jobs and reward good performance.

merit system
A system of public employment in which selection and promotion depend on demonstrated performance rather than on political patronage.

spoils system
A system of public employment based on rewarding party loyalists and friends.

Of the People

AMERICA'S CHANGING FACE

The Diverse State and Local Workforce

Like the federal government, state and local governments have become more diverse during the past two decades and will become even more diverse as they add new jobs. Excluding schoolteachers, who are overwhelmingly white and female, the U.S. Census Bureau reports that the state and local workforce is also becoming an employer of choice for minorities. The increasing percentage of Hispanics is largely due to population growth in states such as California, Florida, and Texas, where Hispanic workers are moving into state and local government jobs at high rates.*

Although the percentages of women and minority workers have increased during the past two decades, both groups remain underpaid relative to males and whites. In 2005, males made an average of $44,090 a year, compared with $36,417 for females,

$35,265 for African Americans, and $38,904 for Hispanics. Among high-paid professional jobs, men made approximately $7,000 a year more than women did, in part because men concentrated in the higher-paying professions such as law, finance, and health administration, whereas women tended to concentrate in historically underpaid professions in human services such as child welfare. However, higher rates of pay for men compared to women were also found in all other major occupational categories, such as officials and administrators, technicians, and administrative support workers.

CRITICAL THINKING QUESTIONS

1. Why do you think African Americans make up a larger share of state and local government employees than their percentage in the U.S. population (about 13 percent)?
2. Why do you think Hispanics constitute a smaller share of state and local government employees than their percentage in the U.S. population (approximately 15 percent)?[†]

Percentage of State and Local Government Workers Who Have the Following Characteristics, 1983 and 2007

	1983	2007
Male	60%	55%
Female	40	45
White, Non-Hispanic	76	70
African American	17	18
Asian	n/a	3
Hispanic	5	1

*For 2005 data, see U.S. Equal Employment Opportunity Commission, *Job Patterns for Minorities and Women in State and Local Government* (EEO-4), "2007 Employment Summary by Job Category," http://www.eeoc.gov/eeoc/statistics/employment/jobpat-eeo4/2007/us.html. For earlier data, see U.S. Census Bureau, *Statistical Abstract of the United States: 2008* (U.S. Government Printing Office, 2008), Table 450.

[†]Population figures from U.S. Census Bureau, *Statistical Abstract of the United States: 2008* (U.S. Government Printing Office, 2008), Table 18, www.census.gov/compendia/statab/tables/08s0018.xls.

Reforming Personnel Systems

Criticisms against some aspects of merit systems became more acute as new management philosophies spread among governors and other top state and local government executives. Driven by books such as David Osborne and Ted Gaebler's *Reinventing Government*, by national commissions calling for reform, and by the growing number of governors and public executives with business training or experience, movements grew in many states to reform personnel systems and give public managers greater control over their workforces.[6] In part, the idea was to increase government managers' flexibility in determining how to achieve the goals of government programs, while making managers and their agencies more accountable for achieving measurable results, such as improvements in environmental quality, reductions in the time citizens need to register a vehicle, or increased "customer" satisfaction when using a state park.

Many state governments have in fact deregulated aspects of their personnel systems, especially since the early 1990s.[7] For instance, most states decentralized control over tests and the selection of candidates by reducing the power of state personnel offices and increasing the authority of agencies and managers. Many states also reduced the number of specific job levels and increased the pay ranges that people in particular positions or grades may receive at the discretion of managers. Managers could thus reward high-performing workers. In some states, many of the safeguards in traditional merit systems were eliminated and public managers were given the authority to fire employees who failed to perform well—and the procedures for terminating such employees were simplified.[8]

Georgia and Florida went particularly far in giving managers greater control over employees. In the 1990s, Georgia introduced a merit pay plan, in which employees' salaries were tied to managers' assessments of their performance.[9] The state gave greater control over personnel to operating agencies (as opposed to a single statewide personnel

Sharing Best Practices for Budget Reform

The National Governors Association has developed its Center for Best Practices* to facilitate the communication of effective and innovative developments in state government to governors and their staffs. In early 2010, the center issued a report called "The Big Reset," in which it described ways for governors to push the reset button on how their states operated with an eye toward greater efficiency at a lower cost.[†]

The report offers a number of suggestions for cost savings based on the best practices from across the states. It recommends that states find ways to move nonviolent offenders out of prisons and into some other form of supervised arrangement. In K–12 education, it advocates greater consolidation of school districts and greater use of online materials. The report suggests substantial reductions in pensions and other benefits offered to state employees in order to reduce future spending obligations. In higher education, the report advocates a shift in funding away from enrollments and toward degree completions, noting that only about half of students who begin a four-year college program ever graduate. It suggests pulling resources away from programs that serve very few students, reducing the number of credit hours required for some degrees, allowing high school students to take courses for college credit, and moving more educational content online.

This report represents a concerted effort by thoughtful professionals to help governors manage their states more effectively and with fewer resources. Of course, each of these proposals might save money, but some may be more "costly" than others.

CRITICAL THINKING QUESTIONS

1. What are both the short-term and long-term trade-offs for adopting the various reforms for higher education posed in the report, "The Big Reset"?

2. One of the stronger predictors of a state's economic health is the size of its college-educated workforce. What can states do to increase the number of students who begin and graduate from college?

*Located online at http://www.nga.org/center/.
[†] The report is online at http://www.nga.org/Files/pdf/1002STATEGOVTAFTERGREATRECESSION.PDF.

---

office) so that each agency could tailor its recruitment, selection, and promotion processes to its own needs. Finally, the state required that all newly hired or promoted persons serve "at will," that is, at the discretion of the managers. Employees could be fired for any reason, so long as it was not illegal under federal or state laws such as antidiscrimination statutes. Florida adopted similar reforms.[10]

Although most states did not make changes as extensive as those in Florida and Georgia, more than half the states (such as Arizona, Colorado, Delaware, Idaho, Iowa, Nebraska, South Carolina, Texas, and Vermont) have moved more public employees into at-will positions.[11] It is still unclear what effects the reforms have had. Terminations of employees are easier. Top executives, including governors, probably have more leverage over public employees than before the reforms went into effect.[12] However, whether this greater top-down control has produced more innovation, responsiveness, productivity, or resourcefulness is unknown. Some employee surveys have found declines in employee morale after reforms as well as reports that favoritism in hiring, promotion, and reviews has grown.[13]

The answer probably depends on who gets elected. Some governors—along with their appointees—may use their growing power over public bureaucracies to recruit and promote highly skilled individuals and encourage them to formulate flexible, creative approaches to solving state problems. Other governors and state executives, however, may use their power simply to cut costs, put in their own political supporters, or enforce particular ideological viewpoints in state bureaucracies.[14] Indeed, the most drastic personnel reforms have been pushed by conservative, pro-business governors in states where public employee unions are weak, and the reforms are often accompanied by hostility toward public employees.[15] It is possible that the spread of at-will jobs in some state governments could produce a new form of "spoils" system, if and when governors use their control over state jobs to replace some state employees with ideological allies and intimidate the rest into obedience.

Privatization of Public Services

Rather than relying on their own employees, many state and local governments have "contracted out" public services to private sector organizations, including for-profit corporations as well as nonprofit agencies. This practice, called **outsourcing**, can sometimes have advantages. Private organizations can bring a lot of expertise to public projects. Government agencies, for instance, often contract with information technology consultants to set up new computing systems. Contracting can also give governments flexibility. It allows governments

outsourcing
Contracting of government services to private firms.

to pay only for the completion of a specific project and not be responsible for maintaining a workforce between projects—or a workforce whose skills are not appropriate for later projects. In addition, when governments award contracts competitively—that is, when many private firms seek contracts by submitting bids—there are incentives for suppliers to improve the quality of their services and reduce their costs.

Another reason state governments outsource or "privatize" certain services is that many elected officials distrust their states' own public bureaucracies. In the last two decades, for instance, many state and local governments have privatized major parts of their welfare services. This shift was made possible by federal welfare reforms that gave states the authority to use private organizations to determine eligibility for welfare benefits and to provide services to low-income families.[16] Yet the decision in many states to use this authority was often driven by the belief of legislators and governors that state welfare bureaucracies were unlikely to put welfare reforms into effect.

In Wisconsin, for example, the state's legislature and governor enacted a 1995 welfare reform program called "Wisconsin Works" (also called "W-2") that required Milwaukee to contract with private agencies to implement the new program.[17] The major motivation for turning over the program to private agencies was frustration with the city's welfare bureaucracy; conservative lawmakers in particular believed that public agencies would not implement reforms designed to reduce welfare caseloads and replace cash assistance with a work program. Although Milwaukee's reliance on private agencies has encountered some setbacks and scandals throughout the years, privatization remains in effect. The state uses a fairly sophisticated set of performance measures to control the private contractors.[18] Payments to the private agencies—now mostly nonprofit corporations—are based in part on their record of placing W-2 clients into jobs, getting people into jobs they keep for at least 180 days, finding jobs with good wages, providing job skills training, and moving people with disabilities into programs appropriate for them.[19]

Other states have also privatized major parts of the social service systems. Florida and Arizona have contracted out the administration of all aspects of their welfare-to-work programs.[20] Texas was even more ambitious in its effort to outsource the management of human service programs. It created centralized toll-free call centers where any citizen seeking public assistance could reach private employees with instant computer access to eligibility information about all these programs, as well as the caller's own financial information. These operators could tell each caller whether he or she qualified for a variety of programs, including food stamps, Medicaid, cash assistance, and health insurance for their children. However, five years after the state legislature authorized this vast privatization initiative, the system is reported to be plagued with errors and lost information.[21]

Although these problems in Texas may eventually be resolved, these and other stories about outsourcing show that privatization of social services is often hard to put into practice, as it often demands that public officials exercise quite sophisticated management skills in developing appropriate contracts, finding and evaluating competing contractors, and closely monitoring the quality of services provided by the private agencies. For instance, successful privatization requires the contract between the government and the private company to define that service to the satisfaction of both parties. This task may be feasible in service areas such as garbage collection and snow removal, which can easily be defined and specified in a contract, making them attractive for privatization.[22] However, private contracts may be much more difficult to word when state and local governments want to outsource the wide range of services provided by local police or health departments.

Delegation of emergency and police powers to profit-making corporations also raises many other fundamental questions, particularly those touching on liability and protection of individual rights. A growing number of states, for instance, have outsourced some of their corrections facilities. But stories of prisoner abuse by private contractors have led some state officials to slow or even reverse this movement. Outsourcing also raises fears that private contractors will hire transient or even overseas help at lower pay, undermining merit systems and public employee morale and angering some citizens. Nonetheless, despite all the issues raised by privatization, it is likely to continue or even grow, as cities and states pressed for cash look for ways to cut back on their permanent workforces and rely increasingly on private contractors to provide basic services.

YOU WILL
DECIDE
Should Governments Contract with Faith-Based Organizations?

The expansion of government contracting with private organizations has produced many controversies in recent years, but perhaps the most divisive has surrounded the use of religious or "faith-based" organizations to provide publicly funded services. This is not a new issue, but it took on a new urgency in the wake of President George W. Bush's "Faith-Based and Community Initiative," which promoted greater governmental use of faith-based and community organizations as service providers. Faith-based organizations usually include churches, synagogues, and mosques; nonprofit organizations affiliated with a religious institution; and agencies that clearly incorporate religion in the ways they conduct their operations.

The U.S. Constitution does not allow for public funds to be directly used to support "exclusively religious" activities, such as worship, religious instruction, or proselytizing. Government should also offer and award grants in a neutral manner, favoring neither religion nor nonreligion in choosing contractors. Finally, governments need to ensure that people eligible for the services can exercise real choice between several alternative service providers, including a variety of faith-based and secular organizations.

What do you think? Should government allow or even encourage faith-based organizations to play a larger role in delivering publicly funded social services? What are some arguments for or against this?

THINKING IT THROUGH

Governments must be neutral between faith-based and secular programs, but they are not prohibited from taking steps that would encourage the involvement of faith-based service organizations. They can distribute their contracting notices more widely; they can reduce the size of individual contracts and simplify the process, thereby opening the competition to smaller faith-based and community organizations; and they can even offer training and assistance programs to less experienced organizations in order to expand the pool of service agencies able to compete for government contracts. In fact, a 2005 survey found that more than half of the states engaged in activities designed to affect government partnerships with faith-based social service providers.*

But should governments be doing this? Those who want state and local governments to open contracting processes to faith-based organizations argue that many U.S. citizens are deeply religious, and that service agencies comfortable with religion and religious concerns are more likely to connect with citizens who need help. They sometimes also argue that, despite their lack of professional training, staff in many small faith-based organizations may be more personally committed to their work and compassionate in dealing with clients. Supporters also claim that churches and other congregations are rooted in the community and can therefore help troubled clients find other people and local organizations able to help them connect back into the community.

Those who argue against such efforts dispute many of these claims. In fact, there is not much evidence on either side about the special capacities of faith-based agencies. Opponents argue that it is very difficult to create voucher systems that offer a wide array of faith-based and secular choices, except perhaps in our largest cities, and that it is hard if not impossible for most state and local governments to monitor whether all clients, regardless of their religion, are treated fairly by faith-based programs. Some opponents of contracting with faith-based organizations actually come from religious communities; they argue that getting public money compromises their independent role in society and undermines their charitable mission, which is to serve all people in need, not only those who qualify for public programs.

For more information, see the Pew Forum on Religion and Public Life, pewforum.org.

Critical Thinking Questions

1. Can you think of other possible advantages or disadvantages in using more faith-based organizations to deliver government services?

2. Do you think the advantages are likely to outweigh the disadvantages, or vice versa? If you feel the balance depends on the circumstances, what circumstances are likely to be most important?

*Mark Ragan and David J. Wright, *The Policy Environment for Faith-Based Social Services in the United States: What Has Changed Since 2002?* (Roundtable on Religion and Social Welfare Policy, 2005), p. i, www.religionandsocialpolicy.org/docs/policy/State_Scan_2005_report.pdf.

Paying for State and Local Government

LEARNING **OBJECTIVE**

29.2 Outline sources of revenue for state and local governments and associated issues and constraints.

John Shannon, an authority in the field of public finance, has written that three R's shocked state and local governments from the late 1970s to the early 1990s. The first "R" was the *revolt* of the taxpayers, which started with California's Proposition 13 (which capped property taxes) and quickly became a national phenomenon. The second "R" was the *recession* of the late 1980s and early 1990s, which placed demands on state and local governments to care for the unemployed and needy. And the third "R" was the *reduction* in federal grants, which meant state and local governments were on their own.[23] States had to search for ways to make ends meet and live within their revenue projections.

State revenues grew vigorously from 1993 through mid-2001. However, the recession of 2001–2002 had a substantial impact on state budget revenues. The recession was not severe, yet revenues dropped consistently through mid-2002, and growth remained sluggish until 2004. Meanwhile, the federal government tightened many grants. Although federal grants to the states grew from $286 billion in 2000 to nearly $449 billion in 2007, more than half of the increase was due to increased spending for health care under the Medicaid program for low-income citizens. In 2007, Medicaid alone made up 43 percent of all federal grants to state and local governments.[24]

Although state revenues increased consistently from 2004 through 2007, another drop in revenues was evident by early 2008.[25] Those declines became extreme in 2009 and do not look to be rebounding any time soon (see Figure 29–1).[26] As we have mentioned in other chapters, Medicaid and other health care programs are taking up more and more resources. Transportation and other infrastructure needs have become acute, as highways become more and more congested and aging bridges collapse. And the costs of pension benefits for an aging state and local government workforce are growing rapidly and will continue to do so well into the future.[27] Given the federal government's large deficits and financial struggles, there is also little hope that it will give states more aid, and federal spending on programs that affect the states will likely be cut. In summary, the volatility of state revenues in recent years, combined with the near-continuous growth in demand for resources, creates great challenges for state revenue systems.

Where the Money Comes From

State and local governments get most of their money from taxes. In 2007, they raised 18.8 percent of general revenues from sales taxes, 12.4 percent from personal income taxes, and 16.4 percent from property taxes (see Figure 29–2). Another 20 percent came from federal grants-in-aid, such as federal support for Medicaid, transportation, and welfare-to-work programs. Other revenues came from charges to users of government services—such as tuition from students in public universities and colleges—and from a wide variety of other sources, such as earnings from interest or property sales.[28]

The U.S. Constitution does not dictate where state and local governments are to find revenue; they are free to extract whatever taxes they wish from whomever they wish, as long as their taxing practices meet a few constitutional stipulations and do not conflict with

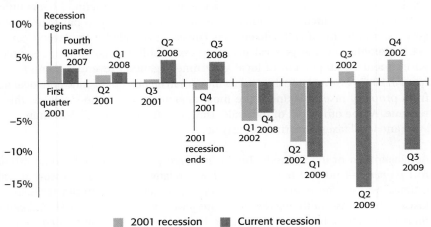

FIGURE 29–1 2001 Recession Compared to Current Recession.

States experienced large revenue decreases in the months following the 2001 recession. This recession has already surpassed those declines, and revenue figures are expected to continue to take a hit. ■ *What are the major differences between the recession in 2001 and the one today?*

SOURCE: "How the Recession Might Change the States," The Pew Center on the States, *State of the States,* February 2010, http://www.pewcenteronthe states.org/uploadedFiles/State_of_the_States_2010.pdf.

FIGURE 29–2 **Percentage of General Revenues Received by State and Local Governments from Major Sources, 2007.**

■ *Based on the major sources of state and local government revenue, why is it that revenue can be so volatile from one year to the next?*

SOURCE: U.S. Census Bureau, *State and Local Government Finances: 2006–07.*

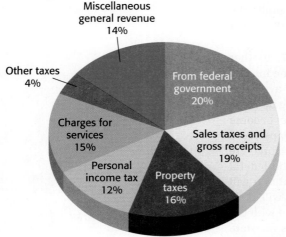

Miscellaneous general revenue 14%

Other taxes 4%

From federal government 20%

Charges for services 15%

Sales taxes and gross receipts 19%

Personal income tax 12%

Property taxes 16%

federal laws. The Constitution has been interpreted to prohibit states from taking the following actions:

1. Taxing exports or imports or levying tonnage duties without the consent of Congress
2. Using taxing powers to interfere with federal operations
3. Discriminating against interstate commerce, unduly burdening it, or taxing it directly
4. Using taxing powers to deprive people of equal protection of the law
5. Depriving individuals of their property without due process

Constitutional lawyers and judges spend much of their time applying these principles to concrete situations. Out of hundreds of disputes, courts have decided that states may collect sales taxes from interstate sales and income taxes from people and corporations within the states, even if the income was earned from interstate business. However, states may not tax the privilege of engaging in interstate commerce or the profits made through interstate transactions that cannot be apportioned to a single state.

State constitutions can and do restrict state legislatures' taxing powers. Certain kinds of property, such as that used for educational, charitable, or religious purposes, are exempt from taxation. State constitutions frequently list the kinds and amounts of taxes that may be collected and from which sources.[29]

Within these constitutional and legal constraints, state and local governments still have considerable flexibility in designing and altering their tax systems. In making these decisions, they may take into account several criteria. A good tax, for instance, may be one that is easy to administer fairly; one that does not burden individuals and corporations with a lot of extra paperwork and activities; one that does not demand enormous and intrusive governmental agencies to ensure compliance; and one that does not allow some people to avoid paying their taxes much more easily than others. A good tax should also distribute financial burdens fairly; that is, it should be at least roughly related to people's or corporations' ability to pay. Governments may also want taxes that are stable or predictable; great uncertainty about future revenues can make it difficult to make basic decisions about budgets and programs. A good tax would also provide what governments need to pay for public programs and be adaptable to changing fiscal needs. We could formulate many other tests as well, but keep these basic criteria in mind as we review the different ways in which state and local governments raise revenues.

The Property Tax

In 1890, economist Edwin Seligman called the property tax "the worst tax known in the civilized world." The tax is not easy to administer, and it sometimes bears little relationship to taxpayers' income or other measures of their ability to pay.[30] In public opinion surveys, a plurality of U.S. citizens has consistently called it the "worst" or "least fair" tax.[31] Nonetheless, the **general property tax** is still a major revenue source for local governments; 23.6 percent of local government general revenues came from property taxes in 2007.[32] New Hampshire earns more than 60 percent of state and local tax revenue from property taxes, making it the most dependent of all the states on this source of revenue. At the other end of the scale, Hawaii and Delaware get less than 15 percent of state and local taxes from the property tax.[33]

general property tax
A tax levied by local and some state governments on real property or personal, tangible property, the major portion of which is on the estimated value of one's home and land.

Administration of the Property Tax   A hundred years ago, wealth primarily consisted of *real property*—land and buildings—that was relatively easy for assessors to value. Their estimate was a good indicator of the property owner's ability to pay taxes. Today, wealth takes many forms—both *tangible* (furniture, jewels, washing machines, rugs, paintings) and *intangible* (stocks, bonds, money in the bank), and it is possible to concentrate a large amount of wealth in the contents of a small rented apartment. The nature of real property has also changed. It no longer consists mainly of barns, houses, and land but rather of large industrial plants, huge retail stores, and office buildings whose value is hard to measure. In addition, property ownership is less likely these days to reflect the ability to pay taxes. An elderly couple with a large house valued at $450,000 may be living on Social Security payments and a small allowance provided by their children. But they must pay higher property taxes than a young couple with two healthy incomes who live in a rented apartment.

Although many communities stipulate that the general property tax be imposed on all property, this is not what actually happens. Significant amounts of real property are exempted from property taxes because they are owned by tax-exempt groups, such as churches, charitable organizations, and colleges. Local governments also often waive the tax as an economic development inducement or for other reasons. As a result, two taxpayers may own similar property, but one is assessed at a higher rate. Intangible personal property is also seldom taxed.

The general property tax is hard to adjust to changing circumstances. It is typically administered by an assessor, whose **assessment** may or may not reflect the real market value of the property. In some states, the assessment is legally required to be a percentage of market value—say, 25 percent. The property tax rate is usually a set amount per $1,000 of assessed valuation or a similar measure. Modern advances in computer record keeping and the use of sophisticated geographic information services have made it easier to keep assessments current. Local and state governments can do very little to change the assessment, but they can raise or lower the tax rates.

A property tax bill typically includes fees or taxes charged by three, four, or more government units, such as the city, county, school board, water utility, and other special districts. The lump-sum payment aspect of the property tax is one reason for its widespread unpopularity and has prompted some places to permit taxpayers to pay their taxes in installments, often collected when homeowners make their monthly mortgage payments to banks, which in turn pay the local government when the property taxes are due.

Property Taxes and Public Education Local reliance on the property tax to support public schools has generated increasing controversy in recent years. The amount of money available to finance education varies tremendously from area to area; rich suburban areas with a high property valuation per pupil can spend much more than poor areas such as the central cities. Reformers have urged the states to take over the financing of public education or at least to assume a greater share of the burden, in order to reduce differences from community to community or to provide enough support to offer an adequate education in all communities. Most states distribute funds to local districts in an attempt to ensure more equitable expenditures, although differences in district expenditures remain large in many states.

assessment
The valuation a government places on property for the purposes of taxation.

Those wanting to reduce differences in expenditures across public school districts have often turned to the courts. As noted in our "For the People" feature in Chapter 22, several state courts have ruled that wide differences between school districts in per-pupil expenditures are inconsistent with the equal protection clause of the Fourteenth Amendment.[34] The California Supreme Court, for example, saw such differences as violating the state constitution.[35] However, in 1973, the U.S. Supreme Court held that there is no federal constitutional requirement that the amount spent per pupil in each school district be the same.[36]

This decision temporarily slowed the push toward equalization of school expenditures, but the controversy remains. School funding cases have been brought in 45 of 50 states, some focusing on a right to an "adequate" education. Adequacy lawsuits usually ask state courts to enforce provisions in state constitutions requiring state governments to guarantee a "sound basic education."[37] The suits claim "all schools must receive the resources [usually some minimum financing per pupil] necessary to provide

Third-grade students at Green Bay Elementary School in North Chicago, Illinois, which has the highest poverty level in its district. ■ *Why do some people argue that funding for public schools shouldn't come primarily from local property taxes?*

students with the opportunity for a meaningful education that enables them to meet challenging new standards."[38] Adequacy suits have been successful in recent years. By early 2010, courts in 28 states had handed down rulings requiring states to remedy either the equity or the adequacy of their education systems; 20 of those rulings were based on adequacy claims.[39]

The Property Tax Revolt   Hostility to the property tax spawned the tax revolts of the last three decades of the twentieth century. The watershed event in the politics of tax cutting was the 1978 passage of California's Proposition 13, which limits increases in property taxes to a maximum of 2 percent each year. Throughout the 1970s, California property taxes had risen dramatically, spurring voters to write this initiative to cut them. Its passage led to similar property tax limitations in other states, but local governments still get nearly three-fourths of their tax revenue from the property tax.[40] In states such as California that have the most stringent limits on the growth of property taxes, the effect has been to shift more of the spending to the state level, where revenues are usually provided by income and sales taxes. Because states usually attach conditions to their aid, local governments then lose control over local programs, such as education. Because the property tax is more stable than most other taxes, when it is limited as a revenue source, the whole state and local tax system becomes more volatile, prone to big declines during recessions and large increases in times of economic growth.

Passage of Proposition 13 made tax reduction an important issue nationwide. It triggered taxing and spending limits in more than a dozen states and helped launch movements for constitutional amendments setting federal spending limits, requiring a balanced federal budget, and **indexing** income tax brackets (automatically adjusting income tax rates to rise with inflation so that, in effect, they remain constant). Tax reduction was not limited to ballot initiatives but spread to state legislatures, most of which reduced income, sales, or property taxes.

Tax cuts are only one way of attempting to curb government spending. States and localities have also adopted various limits that restrict future spending to current levels, hold annual increases to a fixed percentage, or tie them to increases in personal income or inflation.[41] New Jersey was the first state to enact spending limits that applied to both state and local governments. In 1976, it limited growth in state expenditures to the annual percentage increase in per capita personal income and restricted localities to increases of no more than 5 percent without voter approval. As of December 2008, 30 states operated with some sort of tax or expenditure limit.[42]

Property Tax Reform   Despite its weaknesses, the general property tax remains an important source of revenue for local government. Supporters say it is practical and suitable because real property is the chief beneficiary of many local services, such as fire protection. It is also a stable, predictable source of funding, especially important for local governments, because many of their functions—such as police and fire protection, record keeping, and provision of prisons, jails, schools, and libraries—are fairly constant from year to year. This stability can be critical during and after recessions. For instance, state funding of K–12 education dropped substantially during and after the economic slowdown of 2001–2002 because of sharp drops in income and sales taxes. However, local funding of education—most of which came from property taxes—continued to grow in most states between 2002 and 2010, mitigating some of the effects of state cuts.[43]

Communities may correct some of the bad features of the general property tax by improving assessment and administration methods. One reform effort is the *circuit-breaker exemption* (sometimes called a *negative income tax*) by which most states and certain cities give a form of tax relief to lower-income families and the elderly. The idea is to protect family income from property tax overload in the same way an electrical circuit breaker protects a family home from an electrical current overload: "When the property tax burden of an individual exceeds a predetermined percentage of personal income, the circuit breaker goes into effect to relieve the excess financial pressure."[44] The circuit-breaker property tax exemption seems most popular in the Great Lakes and Plains states and least popular in the Southeast, where property tax burdens are low.

indexing
Providing automatic increases to compensate for inflation.

Other Taxes

Although the property tax is the main source of *local* revenue, state and some local governments raise revenues through a wide range of other taxes. Many have been used for several decades, but they have become a larger part of total state and local tax collections since the property tax revolts of the 1970s and 1980s discussed earlier. States and localities seek to diversify their taxes to "spread the pain" of taxes as much as possible (refer back to Figure 29–1).

Sales Taxes   Born during the Great Depression, the **sales tax** is the most important source of revenue for states, which collected more than $352 billion in 2007.[45] The national average for percentage of tax revenues that come from the sales tax is 33 percent, but states like Washington (62 percent), Tennessee (61 percent), Florida and South Dakota (56 percent), and Texas (50 percent) are all well above the national average.[46] Nearly all states impose some kind of general sales tax, normally on retail sales.

Local sales taxes were uncommon until after World War II, but now 35 states allow counties and cities to impose sales taxes. Sales taxes are unpopular with local merchants, who fear they drive business away. In most cases, this is a minor issue that arises only along state borders where consumers can easily drive into another state with a lower sales tax to make purchases.

Sales taxes are easy to administer and produce large amounts of revenue. Many consumers consider them relatively painless because paying a small amount every day means not having to pay a large tax bill all at one time. But labor groups and low-income consumers remain opposed to sales taxes, favoring wider use of the income tax instead. They argue that people with small incomes spend a larger percentage of their budgets on food and clothing than the wealthy do, so sales taxes on these items fall most heavily on those least able to pay. That is why many states exempt necessities—primarily food and medicine—from the sales tax.

Although nearly all states tax some services, none has a broad-based tax on services.[47] It is politically difficult to establish such taxes, as each service industry fights its tax in state

sales tax
A general tax on sales transactions, sometimes exempting food and medicine.

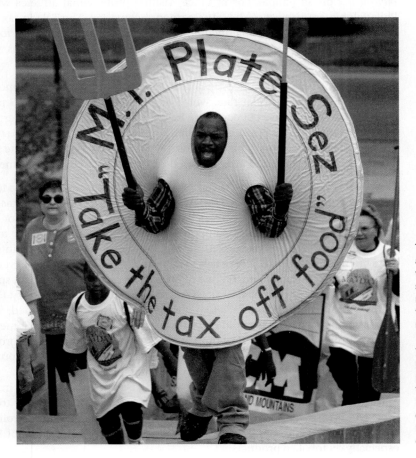

Tennessee legislators considered adopting an income tax in 2001 and 2002 to deal with their state's fiscal crisis. Adding a small personal income tax made sense to many legislators because the state relied very heavily on its sales tax, which was already one of the highest in the nation. However, protests in the summers of both years strengthened opposition to the proposed tax, and Tennessee still does not tax personal income. Some protestors, such as this one, sought relief from the state's very broad sales tax. ■ *What are the trade-offs for a state in relying on a sales tax versus an income tax for its primary source of revenue?*

legislatures and governors' offices. "Expanding the tax base to consumer services is good tax policy," said one economist, "but the service providers rarely see it that way."[48] That may change in the future, however, as the states face greater pressures to find new revenues, and as the U.S. economy continues to shift away from producing goods and toward the provision of an ever-wider array of services. Among the kinds of services currently taxed are cable television, landscaping, income tax preparation, pest control, laundry and dry cleaning, and photocopying.

State and local officials listen with concern to talk about the federal government's imposing a **value-added tax (VAT)** like that used in many western European countries. This tax is imposed on the value added to a product at *each stage* of production and distribution. Should the federal government impose such a tax, state and local officials fear that their ability to use the sales tax will be reduced.

Individual Income Taxes   The state individual, or personal, income tax has been one of the fastest-growing revenue sources for most states in recent decades. Along with the sales tax, it is one of the two largest revenue sources for state government. The individual income tax accounts for approximately 34 percent of all state tax collections, with Oregon (individual income taxes account for 72 percent of its revenues), New York (56 percent), Massachusetts (54 percent), and Virginia (53 percent) well above the national average. By contrast, seven mostly western states—Arizona, Florida, Nevada, South Dakota, Texas, Washington, and Wyoming—do not collect individual income taxes.[49]

Individual income taxes, usually based on federal taxable income, are generally mildly **progressive taxes;** that is, the rate goes up with income. They do not rise as sharply as the federal income tax, however, and seldom are more than 8 percent of taxable income. In the 1990s, many states reduced their highest individual income tax rates.

States generally do not allow local governments to levy income taxes. However, some cities—following the lead of Philadelphia and Toledo—now collect a *wage tax,* and most cities in Ohio as well as cities, towns, and school districts in Pennsylvania levy a similar *payroll tax* on all people. For instance, visiting professional athletes who compete in Philadelphia are subject to the city's earned-income tax. The Toledo tax also applies to corporate profits. A municipal income tax enables hard-pressed cities to collect money from citizens who use city facilities but live in the suburbs. Similar taxes are collected by New York City, Detroit, and Louisville.

Corporate Income and Other Business Taxes   Most states also impose a corporate income tax, usually at a flat rate, which accounts for approximately 6 percent of state taxes.[50] Many states have cut corporate income tax rates or granted generous exemptions as a way to try to attract businesses to their state. States also collect a variety of other kinds of taxes on business activity, including taxes on business assets, corporate franchise taxes, licensing taxes and fees, and taxes imposed when new businesses are formed.

Excise Taxes   Nearly all states tax gasoline, alcohol, and cigarettes; these taxes on specific items are known as **excise taxes.** Because many cities also tax these items, the combined local, state, and federal levies often double the cost of these items for the consumer. Gasoline taxes are sometimes combined with the funds collected for automobile and driver's licenses and are earmarked for highway construction and maintenance. Liquor taxes often consist of both license fees to manufacture or sell alcoholic beverages and levies on their sale or consumption; they are often used for general government spending.

Some states own liquor stores, whose profits go to the state treasury. High taxation of liquor is justified on the grounds that it reduces the amount consumed, falls on an item that is not a necessity of life, and eases the task of law enforcement. Some states, such as North Carolina, set aside part of their alcohol taxes for mental health programs and the rehabilitation of alcoholics. If the tax is raised too high, however, liquor purchases tend to be diverted into illegal channels, and tax revenues fall off.

The rationale for taxing cigarettes is similar. High tobacco taxes in states such as Alaska, New Jersey, and Hawaii, which do not grow tobacco, and low tobacco taxes in tobacco-growing states such as Virginia, North Carolina, and South Carolina, have led to interstate smuggling. Some states levy a general sales tax on top of the excise tax, especially on tobacco products.

value-added tax (VAT)
A tax on the increased value of a product at each stage of production and distribution rather than just at the point of sale.

progressive tax
A tax graduated so that people with higher incomes pay a larger fraction of their income than people with lower incomes.

excise tax
A consumer tax on a specific kind of merchandise, such as tobacco.

Severance Taxes   In several states, **severance taxes** have been a key source of revenue. These are taxes on the privilege of "severing" or removing from the land such natural resources as coal, oil, timber, and gas. In the nation as a whole, severance taxes account for only slightly more than 1 percent of all state taxes. But a few states rely heavily on them. Severance taxes are the main tax source in Alaska, where they make up 50 percent of tax collections, and Wyoming (46 percent); New Mexico, North Dakota, and Oklahoma also get more than 10 percent of their tax revenue from the severance tax.[51] Although 35 states have some type of severance tax, significant revenues from it are not available to most because they do not produce large amounts of natural resources. Tax revenues from severance taxes go up and down with the price of oil, gas, and coal.

The state and local taxes described here do not begin to exhaust the kinds of taxes collected by state and local governments. Admission taxes, stock transfer taxes, inheritance taxes, pari-mutuel taxes, and taxes on utilities and insurance are also common.

Other Sources of Revenue

In addition to taxation, states derive revenue from fees and special service charges. At least 10 percent of the money collected by state and local governments comes from inspecting buildings, recording titles, operating courts, licensing professions, disposing of garbage, and other services. Parking meters have become an important revenue source for some cities. Municipal governments frequently operate water supply and local transit systems. City-operated liquor stores are administered by, and turn a profit in, certain cities in Alaska, Minnesota, North Carolina, and South Dakota. Some states and cities run other business enterprises, such as cable television services, from which they make money (and sometimes lose it, too). North Dakota, for example, operates a state-owned bank. Municipally owned gas and power companies often contribute to city treasuries. In some cases, utility profits are large enough to make other city taxes unnecessary.

As gasoline prices rose to more than $4 per gallon in 2008, some state governments cut their gasoline taxes temporarily to give drivers short-run relief. ■ *Can the regressive nature of excise taxes be justified based on the items taxed being "nonessential" and the fact that the revenue brought in is much needed in the states?*

Legalized Gambling   Recent years have seen a dramatic increase in legalized gambling in the United States. For many years, only Nevada permitted legalized casino gambling, but in 2007, 14 states permitted commercial casinos, 28 had casinos operated by Native American tribes, and 45 permitted racetrack betting.[52] Only Hawaii and Utah do not permit some form of legalized gambling. The spread of casinos was in part a consequence of Native American tribes asserting their right to self-rule on reservations and establishing casinos in states such as California, Michigan, Connecticut, and South Dakota. In addition, gambling companies asserted that prohibitions against land-based casinos did not apply to floating ones, and they promoted gambling on riverboats and dockside casinos.

In 2006, state and local governments received revenues of $5.7 billion from taxes on the operations of casinos and pari-mutuel betting (mostly betting on horse and dog races), up from $3 billion in 1998. Yet states varied greatly in their reliance on this revenue source. In 2007, Nevada and West Virginia received 13.6 and 9.2 percent of their general revenues from gambling, and 20 other states received 2 percent or more of their revenues from these sources.[53]

Lotteries   The District of Columbia, Puerto Rico, and 42 states operate lotteries as a special form of state-sponsored and state-administered gambling that raises money for public purposes.[54] In fact, the Continental Congress ran a lottery to help finance the Revolutionary War. Indeed, all 13 original states used lotteries as a form of voluntary taxation in the 1780s. Lotteries also helped establish some of the nation's earliest colleges, notably Princeton, Harvard, and Yale. In 1964, New Hampshire was the first state to revive the practice in modern times to help balance its budget.

In recent decades, state lotteries have increased in popularity, in part because they increase revenues without raising taxes. Although state-run lotteries provide only 3 percent of what states collect in taxes, they provide essential revenues that would have to be replaced by other sources, all of which are less politically popular.[55] States pay out between 50 and 70 percent of their gross receipts from lotteries in prizes and approximately 6 percent to cover administration costs. The remaining revenues are used for public purposes.

severance tax
A tax on the privilege of "severing" such natural resources as coal, oil, timber, and gas from the land.

States are often ambivalent about legalizing gambling. They get substantial revenues from taxes on gambling, but many voters view the activity as harmful or even sinful. States sometimes express their ambivalence by permitting gambling only in certain places, such as Indian reservations, cruise ships, or riverboats. This cruise ship, docked in South Carolina, travels into international waters before allowing passengers to gamble. ■ *How might the gambling policies in a state be affected by the gambling policies of neighboring states?*

State lotteries generated net profits in excess of $17.7 billion in 2007, up from $8.3 billion in 1993.[56] Many were adopted as a result of a statewide referendum, and states use the revenues for a variety of purposes. About half of the states earmark most or all of their proceeds for education; a significant number of others commit their proceeds to the state general fund. Some states, such as Kansas and Oregon, designate lottery profits for economic development; Minnesota commits part to the environment; Pennsylvania and West Virginia designate senior citizens' programs.

Lottery revenues are not spread evenly across the states. In 2007, approximately 38 percent of all lottery revenues were collected by California, Florida, Michigan, New York, and Texas. In fact, nearly 80 percent of lottery revenue was collected in 15 states—the remaining 27 states with lotteries collected the remaining 20 percent.[57]

Proponents of lotteries identify a popular cause such as education, the environment, or senior citizens as the beneficiaries of lottery profits in hopes of getting popular support for passage of the lottery. Opposition often comes from church groups, which contend that state lotteries are immoral because they are a form of legalized gambling. Proponents counter that churches often raise funds through raffles, bingo, and other games of chance. Opponents also argue that lotteries are a bad investment because they yield a poor rate of return. Proponents respond that tickets are purchased more for their entertainment value than as an investment.

Grants   Grants between governments, usually from higher to lower levels of government, are essential and influential sources of revenue for state and local governments. Federal grants to state governments made up 30 percent of state general revenues in 2007, down slightly from recent years, but up from 26 percent in 1992.[58] The federal government once allocated large sums to cities, but its assistance was only 4 percent of local revenues in 2007. Local governments rely heavily on grants from states, however, which gave them $450 billion in assistance in 2007, or 34 percent of their total revenues.[59]

Most of the growth in federal grants as sources of revenues for state governments has come from Medicaid, a federal program that provides health coverage for low-income individuals. Medicaid accounted for 44 percent of federal grants in 2008, much more than its 30 percent share in 1990.[60] Other major areas of federal assistance include income support (21 percent in 2008), education and training (13 percent), and transportation (11 percent). Overall, federal assistance in the areas of health, social services, and income support is substantial, usually providing most of the funding for these programs at the state level. Outside these areas, however, states receive relatively little federal assistance and fund most functions with their own taxes.

State officials return revenues collected from certain taxes to local governments, often without specifying the purposes for which the money should be used. Local governments receive state and federal grants in a wide range of areas, including education, transportation, corrections, law enforcement, housing, welfare, community development, and health care. Education is particularly dependent on state aid, which grew from 46 percent of total revenues supporting schools in 1992 to a peak of 50 percent in 2001—after which state aid dropped to 48 percent of total education revenues in 2007.[61]

Local governments often see state and federal grants as enhancing the services they provide. Local governments usually need only spend a modest amount of their own revenues on a particular function to qualify for much larger sums of grant money from state or federal governments in support of the same function. But grant money may not

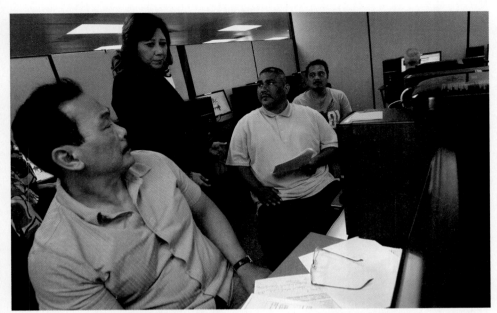

Secretary of Labor Hilda Solis talks with former employees of New United Motor Manufacturing, Inc. (NUMMI) at the company's Remployment Center, where the federal government is providing $19 million in grants to retrain workers. The auto manufacturing company, which closed in 2010, will reopen as production center for Tesla electric cars. ■ *What role should governments play to help businesses and workers adapt to a changing economy?*

be available for some pressing local priorities, or the strings attached to the money may permit state and federal governments to set local priorities. In such cases, are local governments wise to pursue the grants, or should they put their money into their most pressing priorities? Local governments also worry about becoming dependent on grant money now if state or federal money should dry up in the future.

Borrowing Money

State and local governments collect large sums of money to pay for current operating expenses—garbage collection, police protection, and social services. To fund long-term projects for expensive efforts such as building schools, constructing roads, and clearing slums—so-called *capital expenditures*—cities and states often have to borrow money. Because these improvements have long lives and add to the wealth of the community, it is reasonable to pay for them over time. For this purpose, governments issue bonds. Bonds are financial instruments issued by state and local governments and bought by investors. In exchange for a cash payment at the time the bond is issued, the issuing government promises the investor that it will repay the loan with interest over time, usually throughout a long period, such as 20–40 years.

During the early years of the nineteenth century, states and cities subsidized railroad and canal builders. The money for these and other public improvements came from bonds issued by the cities or states and purchased by investors. But the governments often failed to make the payments to investors, and public debts to investors piled up and remained long after the improvements had lost their value. Eventually, governments often defaulted on their obligations to repay. Aroused by the government officials' abuse of their authority, voters insisted on constitutional amendments restricting legislative discretion to borrow money. The power to borrow money for the long term now routinely requires voter approval.

Increasingly important during the last few decades are special-purpose governments or special districts: airport authorities, bridge and highway authorities, water and wastewater districts, public transit authorities, and community college districts. Their creation has led government to turn to *revenue bonds* to help finance their operations. The repayments and dividends due to investors come from tolls and fees charged by the facility. In most cases, revenue bonds do not require voter approval, making it much easier to issue this kind of debt and also to spend more on services such as public transportation.[62]

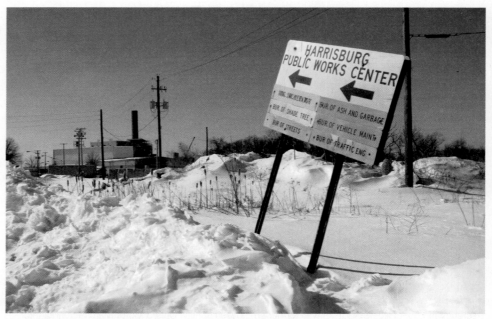

Harrisburg, Pennsylvania sold municipal bonds to help finance city construction projects, but with rising costs and shrinking tax revenue the city has $68 million in debt payments this year that it cannot pay. Its debt was downgraded to five levels below investment grade by Moody's Investors Service, and the city is considering declaring bankruptcy. ■ *What are the potential risks and benefits of selling bonds to pay for major construction projects?*

State and local bonds are attractive to investors because the interest they earn is exempt from federal income tax. State and local governments can borrow money at a lower interest rate than private businesses can, and although credit ratings differ sharply according to economic health, the credit of most cities and states is good. In 2007, for instance, more than 60 percent of the bond ratings for the 85 largest cities were at the two highest possible levels (AAA or AA, which are ratings assigned by Moody's Investors Service).[63] More recent budgetary and economic pressures have likely lowered those ratings somewhat, but thus far, cities continue to be able to find buyers for their bonds fairly easily. Cities with lower ratings also sell bonds, but they need to offer buyers a higher rate of interest; thus, it is more expensive for such cities to borrow money. Most local governments face limits on the general level of debt they can incur, but the sale of bonds is often not covered by such limits. That makes selling bonds an attractive alternative for local governments. However, as discussed in the opener, states need to be careful about maintaining their financial health in order for investors to continue buying their bonds.

State and Local Government Spending

LEARNING OBJECTIVE

29.3 Identify the major expenditures of state and local governments.

State and local governments certainly collect a lot of money through taxes, federal grants, and other sources. Where does the money go? State and local governments spent $2.26 trillion in 2007. More than half of that total went to two functions: health and education. (See Figure 29–3.) Most of the spending on health was disbursed through the Medicaid program, a joint federal–state program that provides medical assistance to low-income families. Three other spending categories were also large, between 7 and 9 percent each: public safety expenditures, which included police, fire protection, and corrections; environment/housing, which encompassed parks and recreation facilities, housing, waste management, and natural resource management; and transportation, which mostly consisted of expenditures on roads and highways. Education spending—including spending on elementary and secondary schools, higher education, and other education programs—varied from 30 to 40 percent of the total spending in different states.

The ways in which state and local governments spend their money have varied over time. Although the percent of state and local expenditures that went to elementary and secondary schools (K–12) is the same today as it was in 1996,[64] other spending priorities have changed. Spending on health grew from 19.8 percent of all state and local expenditures in 1996 to 21.2 percent in 2007, whereas spending on cash assistance dropped from 2.3 percent of the government spending in 1996 to less than 1.0 percent in 2007. Spending on higher education also increased, from 8.5 percent in 1996 to 9.0 percent in 2007.

These patterns of spending and trends point to some of the difficulties state and local governments face in controlling costs. Health programs and elementary and secondary education absorb 45 percent of all state and local spending, yet expenditures for these functions are not easy to cut. Medicaid, for example, is a matching program, in which the federal government provides at least $1 (and sometime up to $3) for every dollar the state spends. As a result, state cuts in Medicaid can produce much larger cuts on total health care spending in a state, including revenues for politically powerful industries, such as hospitals and nursing homes.[65] Elementary and secondary education spending is also hard to control, though for different reasons. It is a mandatory function in nearly all state constitutions, and its primary constituency, parents, is large and includes many middle-class citizens who vote and have intense feelings about the quality of the educational institutions their children attend.

As a result, state and local budget cutting or control must generally focus on the remaining 55 percent. But that too is an increasingly difficult task. Cash assistance payments have been reduced dramatically since the mid-1990s, but now that they represent such a tiny part of the budget, few savings are likely to be found there in the future. Compounding the challenge is the fact that in recent years, prices for the goods and services that state and local governments tend to spend money on, such as transportation, fuel for heating and cooling buildings, road construction materials, health benefits for current and retired employees, and elementary and secondary education, have been increasing faster than general prices overall.[66]

FIGURE 29–3 State and Local Spending, 2006–2007.

■ *Based on the distribution of spending, why do you suppose state and local governments find it so difficult to cut their budgets?*

NOTE: This figure lists vendor payments in health care.

SOURCE: U.S. Census Bureau, *State and Local Government Finances: 2006–07.*

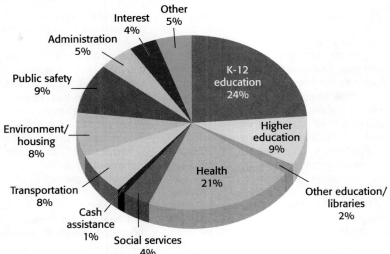

Assessing State and Local Performance

States and localities are where and how most government services are delivered. They are often responsible for delivering on the promises the federal government makes, whether in health care, education, homeland security, economic development, or social services. As the federal government remains focused on war and other national security issues, its budget deficit remains high, and Social Security and Medicare spending grows, states can expect even greater pressure to fill the gaps created by dwindling federal spending for discretionary programs.

In many ways, states have been more responsive than the federal government in recent years to public demands concerning health care coverage, stem cell research, environmental protection, education, and many other issues. However, there are grounds for concern about states' capacities to fund and administer the programs they enact. First, many people worry that state revenue systems do not function well in the new economy. For instance, these systems are better at collecting taxes on goods than on services, on tangible property (such as buildings and land) than on intangible property (such as patents and information), and on businesses whose operations occur in specific locations than on those that are partly virtual and global. In the new economy, however, services, intangible property, and business activities without clear geographic locations are increasingly common. If these trends mean that an increasing number of economic activities such as Internet sales are hard or even impossible to tax, state and local governments may either lose revenues or be forced to raise rates on the activities they can still tax, possibly increasing differences in tax burdens across different businesses and activities and exacerbating inequities. A number of states have responded with efforts to increase the collection of sales taxes on purchases

LEARNING **OBJECTIVE**

29.4 Assess the challenges facing state revenue and management systems.

By the People

Monitoring State Spending

Ask ordinary citizens what, if anything, gets them excited about politics, and very few are likely to say budgets. State budgets are long, dense, and complex documents that are hard even for experts to follow. Yet setting the state's budget every year (or, for some states, every other year) is one of the most important actions a state takes. Remember, states are spending (your) taxpayer money—you should have some idea what they are spending it on.

Every state has a state budget office, and states have gotten much better about providing budget information online. North Carolina, for example, provides a Budgeting 101 link and a Citizens Guide to the state's budget.* New York State's Web site also has a citizen's guide to the budget,† and

California's Department of Finance offers extensive information to citizens online.††

Although citizens can go to individual state government Web sites and hunt for this kind of information, a nonprofit organization called Sunshine Review has established a Web site where anyone can get budget and spending information for any state (http://sunshinereview.org/index.php/Main_Page). This Web site is a wiki Web site in which users can update any element of the site—this is literally government oversight by the people. Find your state on this Web site. What does it say about spending in your state? One of the main missions of Sunshine Review is transparency in government operations. It provides a chart that

reports how easy it is to search state government Web sites for spending information (http://sunshinereview.org/index.php/States_with_spending_online). How open is your state?

CRITICAL THINKING QUESTIONS

1. How easy should it be for citizens to track state spending? Should companies that receive state contracts have some privacy regarding their business dealings with the state?

2. What are the pros and cons of using the Internet and a wiki system like Sunshine Review to keep citizens informed about state spending?

---

* The respective links are http://www.osbm.state.nc.us/ncosbm/budget/budgeting101.shtm and http://www.osbm.state.nc.us/new_content/Citizen_Guide_to_Budget.pdf.

† Located at http://www.budget.state.ny.us/citizen/index.html.

†† Located at http://www.dof.ca.gov/.

---

made by consumers using online retailers like Amazon.com, Overstock.com, and Blue Nile, but the U.S. Supreme Court ruled in 1992 that retailers cannot be forced to collect sales taxes for sales that cross state lines unless they have a physical presence in the state in which the customer resides.[67]

Second, states vary greatly in their fiscal capacities—the economic resources they may tax—and these differences lead to large differences in the extent to which they can meet demands for public programs. For example, states vary in average personal

The new global economy in which services rather than goods are of value, and businesses have online rather than local offices, presents a challenge to state and local governments trying to institute a fair taxing system. ■ *Should states be allowed to collect sales taxes on purchases made online by consumers in their state?*

incomes. In 2008, per capita personal incomes in Mississippi, Utah, and West Virginia were all less than $31,000, whereas in Connecticut, New Jersey, and Massachusetts, they were more than $50,000.[68] Because higher incomes are associated with higher consumption and property values, these income differences affect how easy it is for states to raise revenues not only through income taxes but also through sales and property taxes. States also vary in the natural resources, such as oil, that can be extracted from their lands, differences that in turn affect their abilities to obtain severance taxes.

We can measure state fiscal capacity in many ways, but however we do so, differences are large and also affect state spending on functions such as health care, social services, transportation, and environmental protection.[69] States therefore differ substantially in what they can do for their residents, and many people view these differences as creating inequities in our governmental system. The federal government may attempt to reduce differences by giving larger federal grants-in-aid to low-fiscal-capacity states. However, although some programs, such as Medicaid, provide more generous financial support to relatively poor states, the federal grant system as a whole does not reduce differences in state governments' revenues.[70]

Third, state and local governments also vary greatly in their administrative capabilities. Recall in Chapter 21 where we discussed a 2008 report in *Governing* magazine that rated the performance of states' governments. In that report, only five states won an A or A– grade for their financial management, and only four got an A or A– for managing their employees effectively.[71] What do these differences in state administrative capacity mean? Bad management can mean delays in completing important projects, whereas strong state management capacities can be critically important in implementing challenging new programs.[72]

Although differences remain large, states have improved their management capabilities. As one experienced observer noted in 2008:

> It has been uneven and sometimes halting, but states have been steadily improving their management capacity in most key areas over the past decade or longer. More governors are paying attention to the quality of management, and more are setting measurements of performance, pressuring top managers to meet them, and then reporting the results. Party and ideology seem to have little to do with it; in fact, the language of management reform increasingly seems to unify chief executives when ideology does not.[73]

CHAPTER **SUMMARY**

29.1 Describe the hiring process for public employees, and assess attempts at reform and privatization.

Public employees are largely hired through merit systems. Merit systems have come under attack in recent years, and many states have reformed their personnel systems to give managers greater flexibility and power over employees. The effects of these changes are not yet known, but they may have different effects depending on state leadership.

States have increased their reliance on private sector organizations to deliver many services by "contracting out" or outsourcing. Arguments made in favor of privatization include lower cost and better services, management flexibility, and the unwillingness or inability of state bureaucracies to implement certain programs, such as welfare reform. Privatization, however, is not easy to do. It often requires precisely worded contracts, useful performance measures, and extensive oversight to avoid severe problems of accountability.

29.2 Outline sources of revenue for state and local governments and associated issues and constraints.

State and local governments get most of their money from taxes, although they also raise considerable revenues from federal grants-in-aid and a diverse array

of charges and fees. The national Constitution imposes some constraints on state tax policies, but it also gives state and local governments a lot of flexibility.

The general property tax, despite its unpopularity, remains a major revenue source for public schools. It contributes to inequalities in school funding across communities, but it provides schools and other local functions with a stable, predictable source of revenues. State governments depend heavily on sales taxes, income taxes, excise taxes, and severance taxes. They have recently diversified their revenue sources by turning to such devices as lotteries and other forms of legalized gambling. States also rely increasingly on federal grants-in-aid. However, these grants are concentrated in the health and income support areas, and they do not provide much support for most governmental functions. Intergovernmental grants from states to cities and school districts have increased in importance as local governments have had to deal with rising costs and expectations but limited revenues.

29.3 Identify the major expenditures of state and local governments.

State and local governments spend most of their money on only two functions: health and education. In the last decade, spending on health programs has increased, whereas spending on welfare has declined as a percentage of state and local budgets. Three other spending categories were also large: public safety expenditures, management of housing/environment, and transportation.

29.4 Assess the challenges facing state revenue and management systems.

State revenue and management systems face many challenges in the future, including the problems of raising revenues in a rapidly changing economy and reducing large differences across states in their revenue and management capacities.

CHAPTER **SELF-TEST**

29.1 Describe the hiring process for public employees, and assess attempts at reform and privatization.

1. In one or two paragraphs, explain why state and local governments employ a workforce as large as 20 million people.
2. In a short essay, evaluate the move to merit pay and flexibility in state agencies. Discuss the reasons for the shift and why you feel it has been a positive or a negative change.
3. In a short essay, describe the benefits and problems associated with privatizing government services. Argue for or against further privatization, and discuss whether problems would be reduced if some services were returned to government employees. Why or why not?

29.2 Outline sources of revenue for state and local governments and associated issues and constraints.

4. In a paragraph, discuss and critique the criteria for an effective tax. Add any additional criteria you believe would be useful.
5. Describe the original rationale for property taxes and why that rationale is no longer as tenable as it once was.

6. Imagine that you are a governor and must determine how to finance your state government's operations. Identify which taxes and other revenue sources you will use and which you will not. Defend your choices.

29.3 Identify the major expenditures of state and local governments.

7. Examine Figure 29–3. Write one or two paragraphs explaining where state and local governments spend most of their money, and give your opinion of this distribution. Explain whether you think it should change, how, and why.
8. Assess the idea of tax incentives to attract businesses to a certain locale. In a few sentences, discuss the positive and negative consequences of doing so.

29.4 Assess the challenges facing state revenue and management systems.

9. In a paragraph, explain why some feel that state revenue systems do not function well in the new economy, and show how states may adjust to the new economy.
10. Which challenge do you believe is the most pressing for state governments? In an essay, outline the challenge, its importance, and possible responses to it.

mypoliscilab **EXERCISES**

Apply what you learned in this chapter on MyPoliSciLab.

Read on **mypoliscilab.com**

eText: Chapter 29

Study and **Review** on **mypoliscilab.com**

Pre-Test
Post-Test
Chapter Exam
Flashcards

Watch on **mypoliscilab.com**

Video: California Teacher Layoffs
Video: California Budget Crisis

Explore on **mypoliscilab.com**

Simulation: You Are the Director of Economic Development for Los Angeles

KEY **TERMS**

merit system, p. 722
spoils system, p. 722
outsourcing, p. 724
general property tax, p. 728

assessment, p. 729
indexing, p. 730
sales tax, p. 731
value-added tax (VAT), p. 732

progressive tax, p. 732
excise tax, p. 732
severance tax, p. 733

ADDITIONAL **RESOURCES**

FURTHER READING

GLENN BEAMER, *Creative Politics: Taxes and Public Good in a Federal System* (University of Michigan Press, 1999).

JAMES S. BOWMAN AND **JONATHAN P. WEST,** EDS., *American Public Service: Radical Reform and the Merit System* (CRC Press, 2007).

DAVID BRUNORI, *State Tax Policy: A Political Perspective,* 2d ed. (Urban Institute Press, 2006).

RONALD C. FISHER, *Intergovernmental Fiscal Relations* (Kluwer, 1997).

KATHRYN A. FOSTER, *The Political Economy of Special-Purpose Government* (Georgetown University Press, 1997).

STEVEN D. GOLD, ED., *The Fiscal Crisis of the States: Lessons for the Future* (Georgetown University Press, 1995).

CHARLES T. GOODSELL, *The Case for Bureaucracy,* 4th ed. (Chatham House, 2003).

J. EDWARD KELLOUGH AND **LLOYD G. NIGRO,** *Civil Service Reform in the States* (State University of New York Press, 2006).

ISAAC MARTIN, *The Permanent Tax Revolt: How the Property Tax Transformed American Politics* (Stanford University Press, 2008).

DAVID ALAN NIBERT, *Hitting the Lottery Jackpot: State Governments and the Taxing of Dreams* (Monthly Review Press, 2000).

JOHN E. PETERSEN AND **DENNIS R. STRACHOTA,** EDS., *Local Government Finance: Concepts and Practices* (Government Finance Officers Association, 1991).

HENRY J. RAIMONDO, *Economics of State and Local Government* (Praeger, 1992).

HARVEY S. ROSEN AND **TED GAYER,** *Public Finance,* 8th ed. (McGraw-Hill, 2007).

E. S. SAVAS, *Privatization in the City: Successes, Failures, Lessons* (CQ Press, 2005).

PETER SCHRAG, *California: America's High-Stakes Experiment* (University of California Press, 2008).

RONALD SNELL, *New Realities in State Finance* (National Conference of State Legislatures, 2004).

WEB SITES

www.rockinst.org The Nelson A. Rockefeller Institute of Government seeks to assists states in a non-partisan way as they make fiscal and budgetary policy, along with initiatives in several other areas of state policy making.

www.nast.net National Association of State Treasurers is a professional association of state financial officers that seeks to promote education and the exchange of ideas, build professional relationships, develop standards of excellence and influence public policy for the benefit of the citizens of the states.

www.statelocalgov.net State and Local Government on the Net provides a directory of official websites for state, city, and county governments in the United States.

www.nasbo.org National Association of State Budget Officers is a professional organization that focuses on research, policy development, education, training, and technical assistance for state budget officers.

CONCLUSION

Sustaining Constitutional Democracy

The United States' founding generation fought an eight-year revolution to secure its rights and freedom. First at the Constitutional Convention in 1787 and later in the first Congress, they confronted the challenges of creating a government, writing a Constitution, and drafting a bill of rights that would protect rights to life, liberty, and self-government for themselves and subsequent generations. But they knew, as we also know, that passive allegiance to ideals and rights is never enough. Every generation must become responsible for nurturing these ideals by actively renewing the community and nation of which it is a part.

The framers knew about the rise and decline of ancient Athens. They were familiar with Pericles's funeral oration, which states that the person who takes no part in public affairs is a useless person, a good-for-nothing.[1] According to Pericles and many Athenians, the city's business was everyone's business. Athens had flourished as an example of what a civilized city might be, but it collapsed when greed, self-centeredness, and complacency set in. As time went on, the Athenians wanted security more than they wanted liberty, comfort more than freedom. In the end, they lost it all—security, comfort, and freedom. "Responsibility was the price every man must pay for freedom. It was to be had on no other terms."[2]

If we are to be responsible citizens, we must speak up for what we believe: support for or opposition to particular policies such as the war in Afghanistan, same-sex marriage, health care reform, and more or less regulation of the economy. The exchange of ideas helps produce more-representative policy and better-informed citizens. Our country needs citizens who understand that our well-being is tied to the well-being of our neighbors, community, and country.

More people today live under conditions of greater political freedom than at any previous time. The transition from living under authoritarian rule to shouldering political freedom is often difficult, as evidenced by the efforts to form democratic governments in Russia, Pakistan, and Honduras. Our experience in Iraq and Afghanistan also shows that imposing democracy on societies without the supporting values and institutions is problematic. Throughout history, most people have lived in societies in which a small group at the top imposed its will on others. Today, neither in Castro's Cuba nor in the military regime of North Korea, neither in the People's Republic of China nor in Saudi Arabia, do ordinary people have a voice in the type of decisions we routinely make in the United States: Should we attend college? What kind of employment should we seek? Who should be allowed to enter or leave the country? How much money should be spent for schools, economic development initiatives, health care, or environmental protection? We take for granted the freedom to make such decisions.

Elected leadership and constitutional structures and protections are important, but an active, committed citizenry is equally important. Freedom and obligation go together. Liberty and duty go together. The answer to a nation's problems lies not in producing a perfect constitution or a few larger-than-life leaders. The answer lies in encouraging a nation of attentive and active citizens who will, above and beyond their professional and private ambitions, care about the common concerns of the Republic and strive to make democracy work.

The Case for Government by the People

The essence of our Constitution is that it both grants power to government and withholds power from it. Fearing a weak national government and popular disorder, the framers wanted to strengthen the powers of the national government so that it could carry out its responsibilities, such as ensuring domestic order and maintaining national defense. They also wanted to limit state governments to keep them from interfering with interstate commerce and property rights. Valuing above all the principle of individual liberty, the framers wanted to protect the people from too much government. They wanted a limited government—yet one that could accomplish essential tasks. The solution was to divide up the power of the national government, to make it ultimately responsive, if only indirectly, to the voters.

Most citizens want an efficient and effective government that also promotes social justice. We want to maintain our commitment to liberty and freedom. We want a government that acts for the majority yet protects minorities. We want to safeguard our nation and our streets in a world full of change and violence. We want to protect the rights of the poor, the elderly, and minorities. Do we expect too much from our elected officials and public servants? Of course we do!

Constitutional democracy is a system of checks and balances. Government must balance individual liberties against the collective security needs of society. The questions always are: Which rights of which people are to be protected by what means and at what price to individuals and to the whole society? These questions have arisen again and again in the war on terrorism. The USA PATRIOT Act became law, allowing greater government surveillance and, arguably, security but at the expense of individual liberty. Criticized by both conservatives and liberals, the Act was renewed in 2006 but included some new limitations on government investigations.

Participation and Representation

No political problem is more complicated than working out the proper relationship between voters and elected officials. It is not only a simple matter of ensuring that elected officials do what the voters want them to do. Every individual has a host of conflicting desires, fears, hopes, and expectations, and no government can represent the conflicting desires and expectations of each individual.

Participation

Some propose to bypass this thorny problem of representation by vastly increasing the role of direct popular participation in decision making, through greater use of tools such as the initiative, referendum, or recall.[3] What some regard as the most perfect form of democracy would exist when every person has a full and equal opportunity to participate in all decisions and in all processes of influence, persuasion, and discussion that bear on those decisions. Direct participation in decision making, its advocates contend, will serve two major purposes. First, it will enhance the dignity, self-respect, and understanding of individuals by giving them responsibility for the decisions that shape their lives. Second, direct participation will act as a safeguard against undemocratic and antidemocratic forms of government and prevent the replacement of democracy by dictatorship or tyranny. Interests can be represented, furthered, and defended best by the people they directly concern.

New technologies and new uses of old technologies let governments appeal directly to voters and voters speak directly to public officials. We now have voting by mail in Oregon and other places, and some people advocate voting online. Digital town halls may be next. In the 2008 election, large numbers of voters, especially younger voters, communicated with each other and with the candidates via the Internet. The Internet was also an important fund-raising tool for Barack Obama and will likely grow in importance over time. The Internet is also now an important source of news and political advertising. All of these tools will become a bigger part of communications and interactions between citizens and their government.

Throughout the course of its history, the United States has shifted toward greater direct democracy, and this trend is likely to continue. Suffrage has expanded from only white male property owners being eligible to vote at the time of the founding to all

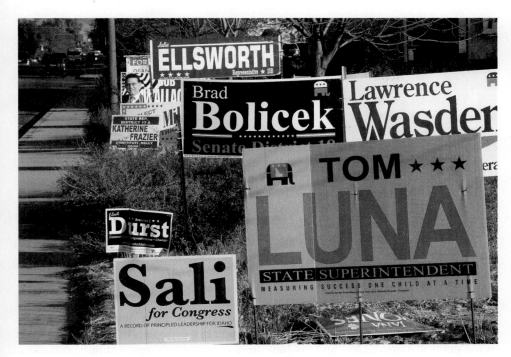

The United States holds more elections for more offices than any other democracy.
■ *Why is participation in the electoral process considered a key component of democracy in America?*

citizens 18 years of age or older being eligible to vote today. The founders designed a system that limited the use of direct representation to the House of Representatives. Today, both the House and Senate are directly elected. Moreover, with the advent of direct primaries, voters decide the nominees for federal office. The initiative and referendum process provides a direct way for citizens to enact or overturn laws and even recall those in government.

However, despite this trend toward increasing direct democracy, we still need elected officials to mediate among factions, build coalitions, and make the compromises necessary for producing policy and action. We also need institutions such as elected legislatures to digest complicated information and conduct impartial hearings to air competing points of view. As a practical matter, people simply cannot spend hours taking part in every decision that affects their lives. Thus, much of the work of government at all levels requires elected representatives.

Representation

Because we must have representatives, who shall represent whom? By electing representatives in a multitude of districts, we can build most minority interests and attitudes into our representative institutions. In the United States, we generally have election processes in which only the candidate receiving the greatest number of votes wins. But there are other ways. For example, Austria and Denmark use proportional representation—a system in which each party running receives the proportion of legislative seats corresponding to its proportion of votes.[4]

Representation can also be influenced by whether there is one party, two, or several. Ours is a strong two-party system that knits local constituencies into coalitions that can elect and sustain national majorities. A major factor in maintaining our two-party system is that single-member legislative districts, such as those for the U.S. Congress and state legislatures, tend to lead to two-party systems. This regularity, called *Duverger's law,* is generally seen as helping to moderate our politics.[5] In contrast, when countries adopt proportional representation, minor parties have greater influence.

Which is better, elected officials who represent coalitions of minorities or officials who represent a relatively clear-cut majority and have little or no obligation to the minority? The answer depends on what you expect from government. A system that represents coalitions of minorities usually reflects the trading, competition, and compromising that must take place in order to reach agreement among the various groups. Instead of acting for a united popular majority with a fairly definite program, either liberal or conservative, the government tries to satisfy all major interests by giving them a voice in decisions and sometimes a veto over actions.

Proponents of this form of representation argue that minority interests must be taken into consideration because the United States has not yet achieved equality in political access and representation. The U.S. Congress and many state legislatures, for example, still contain relatively few women and minorities. Critics also point to the extent of nonvoting and other forms of nonparticipation in politics. Low-income individuals are less well politically organized than upper-income individuals; strong organized groups are biased toward the status quo; a few corporations dominate television and the press; and the two major parties hold a virtual monopoly on party politics, which does not always offer the voters meaningful alternatives.

Critics of this philosophy of representation are concerned that our system of government is catering too much to minority interests with built-in procedures designed to curtail legislative majorities. For example, a Senate rule allows a minority to filibuster and block the will of the majority of senators. More broadly, rulings by the Supreme Court can overturn the will of the majority.[6]

These critics, who believe that governments should be more directly responsive to political majorities, can point to steady improvement in recent years in opening up access to the political system. Election laws have been changed to simplify voter registration, expand and improve voting procedures, and enforce one-person, one-vote standards. Efforts to limit the ability of rich people and well-financed interests to influence elections were cited by Congress as a motivation for passage of campaign finance reform in 2002, and by the Supreme Court in upholding most of that legislation in 2003.[7]

By this point, you undoubtedly appreciate that democracy has to mean much more than popular government and unchecked majority rule. A democracy needs competing politicians with differing views about the public interest. A vital democracy, living and growing, places its faith in the participation of citizens as voters, faith that they will elect not only people who mirror their views but leaders who will exercise their best judgment—"faith that the people will not condemn those whose devotion to principle leads them to unpopular courses, but will reward courage, respect honor, and ultimately recognize right."[8]

The Role of the Politician

Voters today have decidedly mixed views about elected officials. We realize that at their best, politicians are skillful at compromising, mediating, negotiating, and brokering—and that governing often requires these qualities. But we also suspect politicians of being ambitious, conniving, unprincipled, opportunistic, and corrupt.

Still, we often find that individual officeholders are bright, hardworking, and friendly (even though we may suspect they are trying to win our vote). And our liking sometimes turns into reverence after these same politicians die. George Washington, Abraham Lincoln, Dwight D. Eisenhower, and John F. Kennedy are acclaimed today. Harry Truman joked that "a statesman is a politician who has been dead for about ten or fifteen years."[9] Of course, we must put the problem in perspective. In all democracies, people probably expect too much from politicians and, at the same time, distrust those who wield power. Public officeholders tax us, regulate us, and conscript us, after all. We dislike political compromisers and ambitious opportunists—even though we may need such people to get things done.[10] At the same time, individuals can and do make a difference in shaping policy on the local, state, national, and international levels, whether the policy be about drunk driving, early childhood medical care, land mines, or using the courts to influence a policy agenda.

Politics and politicians, including those who work in Washington, are necessary and important to our freedom, security, and prosperity. Although people will disagree about

The U.S. Capitol in Washington, D.C., where both houses of Congress convene. Visitors are allowed to tour the Capitol and even watch Congress in session.

particular policies and processes, there is no disputing the need for government. Political leaders translate the fundamental needs of the people into practical demands on government.

We are fond of saying, "It's all politics." This greatly oversimplified observation implies that things would somehow be improved if we did not have politics and politicians. But politics is the lifeblood of democracy, and without politics, there is no freedom. A nation of subservient followers can never be a democratic one. A democratic nation requires educated, skeptical, caring, engaged, and conscientious citizens who will recognize when change is needed and have the courage to bring about necessary reforms and progress.[11] No matter how brilliant our Constitution or strong our economy, ultimately our system depends on individuals willing to study and speak out on issues, become involved in political parties, and run for and serve in office.

Experience teaches that power wielded justly today may be wielded corruptly tomorrow. It is right and necessary to protest when a policy is wrong or when the rights of other citizens are diminished. Democracy rests solidly on a realistic view of human nature. Criticism of official error is not unpatriotic. Our capacity for justice, as theologian and philosopher Reinhold Niebuhr observed, makes democracy possible. But our "inclination to injustice makes democracy necessary."[12] Democratic politics is the forum where, by acting together, citizens become and remain free.[13]

The ultimate test of a democratic system is the legal existence of an officially recognized opposition. A cardinal characteristic of a constitutional democracy is that it not only recognizes the need for the free organization of opposing views but also positively encourages this organization. Freedom for political expression and dissent is basic—even freedom to speak nonsense so that good sense not yet recognized gets a chance to be heard.[14]

The Importance of Active Citizenship

Crucial to democracy is belief in the free play of ideas. Only when the safety valve of public discussion is available, and when almost any policy is subject to perpetual questioning and challenge, can we be assured that both minority and majority rights will be served. To be afraid of public debate is to be afraid of self-government.

Thomas Jefferson once said, "Were it left to me to decide whether we should have a government without newspapers or newspapers without a government, I should

Education fosters self-confidence in dealing with bureaucracy, is a strong predictor of voting, and provides a knowledge base important to political influence. ■ *In what ways can educated participants have a real impact on our political system and public policies?*

not hesitate for a moment to prefer the latter."[15] Jefferson greatly valued an informed citizenry and had boundless faith in education. He believed that people are endowed with an innate sense of justice; the average person has only to be informed to act wisely. In the long run, said Jefferson, only an educated and enlightened democracy can hope to endure.

Education is one of the best predictors of voting, participation in politics, and knowledge of public affairs. People may not be equally invested or equally willing to invest in democracy, but those who are most attentive—frequently people like you who have gone to college—are more likely to have the willingness and self-confidence to see government and politics as necessary and important.

You now know how to influence public policy and the political process. You have gained an appreciation for the ways individuals and groups can both push and block an agenda. You know that many people choose not to participate in elections or politics, enhancing the power of those who do. Finally, you should also recognize that when individuals combine knowledge with political activity, they expand their influence.

Does political participation by committed individuals bring about constructive change? Remember that in the last half-century, restaurants, motels, and landlords once openly discriminated on the basis of race. Racial segregation in education existed in several states; segregated neighborhoods were a fact of life. Discriminatory practices denied blacks and poor whites access to voting. Women were discriminated against in the workplace and in government. Civil rights legislation and court cases have wrought remarkable changes. This is not to say that we have erased the legacies of racism and other kinds of discrimination from our national life. But as historian Arthur M. Schlesinger Jr. writes, "The genius of America lies in its capacity to forge a single nation from peoples of remarkably diverse racial, religious, and ethnic origins." Schlesinger acknowledges that our government and society have been more open to some than to others, "but it is more open to all today than it was yesterday and it is likely to be even more open tomorrow than today."[16]

Our political system is far from perfect, but it still is an open system and one that has become more and more democratic over time. People *can* fight city hall. People who disagree with policies in the nation can band together and be heard. We know only too well that the American dream is never fully attained. It must always be pursued.

Millions of citizens visit the great monuments in our nation's capital each year. They are always impressed by the memorials to Washington, Jefferson, Lincoln, Franklin D. Roosevelt, and the Vietnam, Korean, and World War II veterans. They are awed by the beauty of the Capitol, the Supreme Court, and the White House. The strength of the nation, however, resides not in these official buildings and monuments but in the hearts, minds, and behavior of citizens. If we lose faith, stop caring, stop participating, and stop believing in the possibilities of self-government, the monuments "will be meaningless piles of stone, and the venture that began with the Declaration of Independence, the venture familiarly known as America will be as lifeless as the stone."[17]

The future of our democracy will be shaped by citizens who care about preserving and extending our political rights and freedoms. Our individual liberties will never be assured unless we are willing to take responsibility for the progress of the whole community, to exercise our determination and belief in democracy. In the words of U.S. poet Archibald MacLeish: "How shall freedom be defended? By arms when it is attacked by arms, by truth when it is attacked by lies, by democratic faith when it is attacked by authoritarian dogma. Always, in the final act, by determination and faith."[18]

ADDITIONAL **RESOURCES**

FURTHER READING

DEREK BOK, *The Trouble with Government* (Harvard University Press, 2001).

RICHARD D. BROWN, *The Strength of a People: The Idea of an Informed Citizenry in America, 1650–1870* (University of North Carolina Press, 1996).

ROBERT A. DAHL, *On Democracy* (Yale University Press, 1998).

AMY GUTMANN AND **DENNIS THOMSON**, *Democracy and Discontent: Why Moral Conflict Cannot Be Avoided in Politics, and What Should Be Done About It* (Belknap Press, 1996).

WEB SITES

www.usa.gov/Contact/Elected.shtml This Web site provides links to contact information for the president and vice president, U.S. senators, U.S. representatives, state governors, and state legislators.

www.constitutionday.us/link_frameset.asp ?url=http://www.constitutioncenter.org/ constitution/ This is an "interactive Constitution" Web site, where you can search the Constitution by keywords or phrases, topics, or court cases.

www.dosomething.org/actnow/ actionguide/how-get-involved-local-politics This Web site provides examples of how to get involved in community politics and includes a link to register to vote in your state.

www.rockthevote.com/ This Web site helps young people register to vote and get involved in politics.

APPENDIX

The Declaration of Independence

Drafted mainly by Thomas Jefferson, this document adopted by the Second Continental Congress, and signed by John Hancock and fifty-five others, outlined the rights of man and the rights to rebellion and self-government. It declared the independence of the colonies from Great Britain, justified rebellion, and listed the grievances against George the III and his government. What is memorable about this famous document is not only that it declared the birth of a new nation, but that it set forth, with eloquence, our basic philosophy of liberty and representative democracy.

IN CONGRESS, JULY 4, 1776

(The unanimous Declaration of the Thirteen United States of America)

PREAMBLE

When, in the course of human events, it becomes necessary for one people to dissolve the political bands which have connected them with another, and to assume, among the powers of the earth, the separate and equal station to which the laws of nature and of nature's God entitle them, a decent respect to the opinions of mankind requires that they should declare the causes which impel them to the separation.

NEW PRINCIPLES OF GOVERNMENT

We hold these truths to be self-evident; that all men are created equal, that they are endowed by their Creator with certain unalienable rights, that among these are life, liberty, and the pursuit of happiness.

That, to secure these rights, governments are instituted among men, deriving their just powers from the consent of the governed.

That whenever any form of government becomes destructive of these ends, it is the right of the people to alter or to abolish it, and to institute new government, laying its foundation on such principles, and organizing its powers in such form, as to them shall seem most likely to effect their safety and happiness. Prudence, indeed will dictate that governments long established should not be changed for light and transient causes; and accordingly all experience hath

shown that mankind are more disposed to suffer while evils are sufferable, than to right themselves by abolishing the forms to which they are accustomed. But when a long train of abuses and usurpations, pursuing invariably the same object, evinces a design to reduce them under absolute despotism, it is their right, it is their duty, to throw off such government, and to provide new guards for their future security.

REASONS FOR SEPARATION

Such has been the patient sufferance of these colonies; and such is now the necessity which constrains them to alter their former systems of government. The history of the present king of Great Britain is a history of repeated injuries and usurpations, all having in direct object the establishment of an absolute tyranny over these states. To prove this, let facts be submitted to a candid world.

He has refused his assent to laws, the most wholesome and necessary for the public good.

He has forbidden his governors to pass laws of immediate and pressing importance unless suspended in their operation till his assent should be obtained; and when so suspended, he has utterly neglected to attend to them.

He has refused to pass other laws for the accommodation of large districts of people, unless those people would relinquish the right of representation in the legislature, a right inestimable to them, and formidable to tyrants only.

He has called together legislative bodies at places unusual, uncomfortable, and distant for the depository of their

public records, for the sole purpose of fatiguing them into compliance with his measures.

He has dissolved representative houses repeatedly, for opposing, with manly firmness, his invasions on the rights of people.

He has refused, for a long time after such dissolutions, to cause others to be elected; whereby the legislative powers incapable of annihilation, have returned to the people at large for their exercise; the state remaining, in the meantime, exposed to all the dangers of invasion from without and convulsions within.

He has endeavored to prevent the population of these states; for that purpose obstructing the laws of naturalization of foreigners, refusing to pass others to encourage their migration hither, and raising the conditions of new appropriations of lands.

He has obstructed the administration of justice, by refusing his assent to laws for establishing judiciary powers.

He has made judges dependent on his will alone for the tenure of their offices, and the amount and payment of their salaries.

He has erected a multitude of new offices, and sent hither swarms of officers to harass our people and eat out their substance.

He has kept among us, in times of peace, standing armies, without the consent of our legislature.

He has affected to render the military independent of, and superior to, the civil power.

He has combined with others to subject us to jurisdiction foreign to our constitution and unacknowledged by our laws, giving his assent to their acts of pretended legislation:

For quartering large bodies of armed troops among us;

For protecting them, by a mock trial, from punishment for any murders which they should commit on the inhabitants of these states;

For cutting off our trade with all parts of the world;

For imposing taxes on us without our consent;

For depriving us, in many cases, of the benefits of trial by jury;

For transporting us beyond seas, to be tried for pretended offenses;

For abolishing the free system of English laws in a neighboring province, establishing therein an arbitrary government, and enlarging its boundaries, so as to render it at once an example and fit instrument for introducing the same absolute rule into these colonies;

For taking away our charters, abolishing our most valuable laws, and altering, fundamentally, the forms of our governments;

For suspending our own legislatures, and declaring themselves invented with power to legislate for us in all cases whatsoever.

He has abdicated government here, by declaring us out of his protection and waging war against us.

He has plundered our seas, ravaged our coasts, burned our towns, and destroyed the lives of our people.

He is at this time transporting large armies of foreign mercenaries to complete the works of death, desolation, and tyranny already begun with circumstances of cruelty and perfidy scarcely paralleled in the most barbarous ages and totally unworthy of the head of a civilized nation.

He has constrained our fellow-citizens, taken captive on the high seas, to bear arms against their country, to become the executioners of their friends and brethren, or to fall themselves by their hands.

He has excited domestic insurrections among us, and has endeavored to bring on the inhabitants of our frontiers the merciless Indian savages, whose known rule of warfare is an undistinguished destruction of all ages, sexes, and conditions.

In every stage of these oppressions we have petitioned for redress in the most humble terms; our repeated petitions have been answered only by repeated injury. A prince whose character is thus marked by every act which may define a tyrant is unfit to be the ruler of a free people.

Nor have we been wanting in attention to our British brethren. We have warned them, from time to time, of attempts by their legislature to extend an unwarrantable jurisdiction over us. We have reminded them of the circumstances of our emigration and settlement here. We have appealed to their native justice and magnanimity;

and we have conjured them, by the ties of our common kindred, to disavow these usurpations, which would inevitably interrupt our connections and correspondence. They, too, have been deaf to the voice of justice and of consanguinity. We must, therefore, acquiesce in the necessity which denounces our separation, and hold them, as we hold the rest of mankind, enemies in war, in peace, friends.

We, therefore, the representatives of the United States of America, in General Congress assembled, appealing to the Supreme Judge of the world for the rectitude of our intentions, do, in the name and by authority of the good people of these colonies, solemnly publish and declare, that these united colonies are, and of right ought to be, free and independent states; that they are absolved from all allegiance to the British crown, and that all political connection between them and the state of Great Britain is, and ought to be, totally dissolved; and that, as free and independent states, they have full power to levy war, conclude peace, contract alliances, establish commerce, and do all other acts and things which independent states may of a right do. And, for the support of this declaration, with a firm reliance on the protection of Divine Providence, we mutually pledge to each other our lives, our fortunes, and our sacred honor.

The Federalist, No. 10, James Madison

THE FEDERALIST, NO. 10, WRITTEN BY JAMES MADISON SOON AFTER THE CONSTITUTIONAL CONVENTION, WAS PREPARED AS ONE OF SEVERAL DOZEN NEWSPAPER ESSAYS AIMED AT PERSUADING NEW YORKERS TO RATIFY THE PROPOSED CONSTITUTION. ONE OF THE MOST IMPORTANT BASIC DOCUMENTS IN AMERICAN POLITICAL HISTORY, IT OUTLINES THE NEED FOR AND THE GENERAL PRINCIPLES OF A DEMOCRATIC REPUBLIC. IT ALSO PROVIDES A POLITICAL AND ECONOMIC ANALYSIS OF THE REALITIES OF INTEREST GROUP OR FACTION POLITICS.

To the People of the State of New York: Among the numerous advantages promised by a well-constructed union, none deserves to be more accurately developed than its tendency to break and control the violence of faction. The friend of popular governments, never

finds himself so much alarmed for their character and fate, as when he contemplates their propensity of this dangerous vice. He will not fail, therefore, to set a due value on any plan which, without violating the principles to which he is attached, provides a proper cure for it.

The instability, injustice, and confusion introduced into the public councils, have, in truth, been the mortal diseases under which popular governments have everywhere perished; as they continue to be the favorite and fruitful topics from which the adversaries to liberty derive their most specious declamations. The valuable improvements made by the American constitutions on the popular models, both ancient and modern, cannot certainly be too much admired; but it would be an unwarrantable partiality, to contend that they have as effectually obviated the danger on this side, as was wished and expected. Complaints are everywhere heard from our most considerate and virtuous citizens, equally the friends of public and private faith, and of public and personal liberty, that our governments are too unstable; that the public good is disregarded in the conflicts of rival parties; and that measures are too often decided, not according to the rules of justice, and the rights of the minor party, but by the superior force of an interested and overbearing majority. However anxiously we may wish that these complaints had no foundation, the evidence of known facts will not permit us to deny that they are in some degree true. It will be found, indeed, on a candid review of our situation, that some of the distresses under which we labor have been erroneously charged on the operations of our governments; but it will be found, at the same time, that other causes will not alone account for many of our heaviest misfortunes; and, particularly, for that prevailing and increasing distrust of public engagements, and alarm for private rights, which are echoed from one end of the continent to the other. These must be chiefly, if not wholly, effects of the unsteadiness and injustice, with which a factious spirit has tainted our public administrations.

By a faction, I understand a number of citizens, whether amounting to a majority of the whole, who are united and actuated by some common impulse of passion, or of interest, adverse to the rights of other citizens, or to the permanent and aggregate interests of the community.

There are two methods of curing the mischiefs of faction: the one, by removing its causes; the other, by controlling its effects.

There are again two methods of removing the causes of faction: the one, by destroying the liberty which is essential to its existence; the other, by giving to every citizen the same opinions, the same passions, and the same interests.

It could never be more truly said, than of the first remedy, that it was worse than the disease. Liberty is to faction what air is to fire, an aliment without which it instantly expires. But it could not be a less folly to abolish liberty, which is essential to political life, because it nourishes faction, than it would be to wish the annihilation of air, which is essential to animal life, because it imparts to fire its destructive agency.

The second expedient is as impracticable, as the first would be unwise. As long as the reason of man continues fallible, and he is at liberty to exercise it, different opinions will be formed. As long as the connection subsists between his reason and his self-love, his opinions and his passions will have a reciprocal influence on each other; and the former will be objects to which the latter will attach themselves. The diversity in the faculties of men, from which the rights of property originate, is not less an insuperable obstacle to an uniformity of interests. The protection of these faculties is the first object of government. From the protection of different and unequal faculties of acquiring property, the possession of different degrees and kinds of property immediately results; and from the influence of these on the sentiments and views of the respective proprietors, ensues a division of the society into different interests and parties.

The latent causes of faction are thus sown in the nature of man; and we see them everywhere brought into different degrees of activity, according to the different circumstances of civil society. A zeal for different opinions concerning religion, concerning government, and many other points, as well of speculation as of practice; an attachment to different leaders ambitiously contending for preeminence and power; or to persons of other descriptions whose fortunes have been interesting to the human passions, have, in turn, divided mankind into parties, inflamed them with mutual animosity, and rendered them much more disposed to vex and oppress each other, than to cooperate for their common good. So strong is this propensity of mankind, to fall into mutual animosities, that where no substantial occasion presents itself, the most frivolous and fanciful distinctions have been sufficient to kindle their unfriendly passions and excite their most violent conflicts. But the most common and durable source of factions, has been the various and unequal distribution of property. Those who hold, and those who are without property, have ever formed distinct interests in society. Those who are creditors, and those who are debtors, fall under a like discrimination. A landed interest, a manufacturing interest, a mercantile interest, a moneyed interest, with many lesser interests, grow up of necessity in civilized nations, and divide them into different classes, actuated by different sentiments and views. The regulation of these various and interfering interests forms the principal task of modern legislation, and involves the spirit of the party and faction in the necessary and ordinary operations of the government.

No man is allowed to be a judge in his own cause; because his interest will certainly bias his judgment, and, not improbably, corrupt his integrity. With equal, nay, with greater reason, a body of men are unfit to be both judges and parties at the same time; yet what are many of the most important acts of legislation, but so many judicial determinations, not indeed concerning the right of single persons, but concerning the rights of large bodies of citizens? And what are the different classes of legislators, but advocates and parties to the causes which they determine? Is a law proposed concerning private debts? It is a question to which the creditors are parties on one side, and the debtors on the other. Justice ought to hold the balance between them. Yet the parties are, and must be, themselves the judges; and the most numerous party, or, in other words, the most powerful faction, must be expected to prevail. Shall domestic manufacturers be encouraged, and in what degree, by restrictions on foreign manufacturers? Are questions which would be differently decided by the landed and the manufacturing classes; and probably by neither with a sole regard to justice and the public good. The apportionment of taxes, on the various descriptions of property, is an act which seems to require the most exact impartiality; yet there is, perhaps, no legislative act, in which greater opportunity and temptation are given to a predominant party to trample on the rules of justice. Every shilling, with which they overburden the inferior number, is a shilling saved to their own pockets.

It is in vain to say, that enlightened statesmen will be able to adjust these clashing interests, and render them all subservient to the public good. Enlightened statesmen will not always be at the helm, nor, in many cases, can such an adjustment be made at all, without taking into view indirect and remote considerations, which will rarely prevail over the immediate interest which one party may find in disregarding the rights of another, or the good of the whole.

The inference to which we are brought is, that the causes of faction cannot be removed; and that relief is only to be sought in the means of controlling its effects.

If a faction consists of less than a majority, relief is supplied by the republican principle, which enables the majority to defeat its sinister views, by regular vote. It may clog the administration, it may convulse the society; but it will be unable to execute and mask its violence under the forms of the Constitution. When a majority is included in a faction, the form of popular government, on the other hand, enables it to sacrifice to its ruling passion or interest, both the public good and the rights of other citizens. To secure the public good, and private rights, against the danger of such a faction, and at the same time to preserve the spirit and the form of popular government, is then the great object to which our inquiries are directed. Let me add, that it is the great desideratum, by which alone this form of government can be rescued from the opprobrium under which it has so long laboured, and be recommended to the esteem and adoption of mankind.

By what means is this object attainable? Evidently by one of two only. Either the existence of the same passion or interest in a majority, at the same time, must be prevented; or the majority, having such coexistent passion or interest, must be rendered, by their number and local situation, unable to concert and carry into effect schemes of oppression. If the impulse and the opportunity be suffered to coincide, we well know that neither moral nor religious motives can be relied on as an adequate control. They are not found to be such on the injustice and violence of individuals, and lose their efficacy in proportion to the number combined together; that is, in proportion as their efficacy becomes needful.

From this view of the subject, it may be concluded, that a pure democracy, by which I mean a society consisting of a small number of citizens, who assemble and administer the government in person, can admit of no cure for the mischiefs of faction. A common passion or interest will, in almost every case, be felt by a majority of the whole; a communication and concert, results from the form of government itself; and there is nothing to check the inducements to sacrifice the weaker party, or an obnoxious individual. Hence, it is, that such democracies have ever been spectacles of turbulence and contention; have ever been found incompatible with personal security, or the rights of property; and have in general been as short in their lives, as they have been violent in their deaths. Theoretic politicians, who have patronized this species of government, have erroneously supposed, that by reducing mankind to a perfect equality in their political rights, they would, at the same time be perfectly equalized and assimilated in their possessions, their opinions, and their passions.

A republic, by which I mean a government in which the scheme of representation takes place, opens a different prospect, and promises the cure for which we are seeking. Let us examine the points in which it varies from pure democracy, and we shall comprehend both the nature of the cure and the efficacy which it must derive from the union.

The two great points of difference, between a democracy and a republic, are, first, the delegation of the government, in the latter, to a small number of citizens, elected by the rest; secondly, the greater number of citizens, and greater sphere of country, over which the latter may be extended.

The effect of the first difference is, on the one hand, to refine and enlarge the public views, by passing them through the medium of a chosen body of citizens, whose wisdom may best discern the true interest of their country, and whose patriotism and love of justice, will be least likely to sacrifice it to temporary or partial considerations. Under such a regulation, it may well happen, that the public voice, pronounced by the representatives of the people, will be more consonant to the public good, than if pronounced by the people themselves, convened for the purpose. On the other hand the effect may be inverted. Men of factious tempers, of local prejudices, or of sinister designs, may by intrigue, by corruption, or by other means, first obtain the suffrages, and then betray the interest of the people. The question resulting is, whether small or extensive republics are most favourable to the election of proper guardians of the public weal; and it is clearly decided in favour of the latter by two obvious considerations.

In the first place, it is to be remarked that, however small the republic may be, the representatives must be raised to a certain number, in order to guard against the cabals of a few; and that however large it may be, they must be limited to a certain number, in order to guard against the confusion of a multitude. Hence, the number of representatives in the two cases not being in proportion to that of the constituents, and being proportionally greatest in the small republic, it follows, that if the proportion of fit characters be not less in the large than in the small republic, the former will present a greater option, and consequently a greater probability of a fit choice.

In the next place, as each representative will be chosen by a greater number of citizens in the large than in the small republic, it will be more difficult for unworthy candidates to practice with success the vicious arts, by which elections are too often carried; and the suffrages of the people being more free, will be more likely to centre in men who possess the most attractive merit, and the most diffusive and established characters.

It must be confessed, that in this, as in most other cases, there is a mean, on both sides of which inconveniences will be found to lie. By enlarging too much the number of electors, you render the representatives too little acquainted with all their local circumstances and lesser interests; as by reducing it too much, you render him unduly attached to these, and too little fit to comprehend and pursue great and national objects. The federal constitution forms a happy combination in this respect; the great and aggregate interests being referred to the national, the local and particular to the state legislatures.

The other point of difference is, the greater number of citizens, and extent of territory, which may be brought within the compass of republican, than of democratic government; and it is this circumstance principally which renders factious combinations less to be dreaded in the former, than in the latter. The smaller the society, the fewer probably will be the distinct parties and interests composing it; the fewer the distinct parties and interests, the more frequently will a majority be found of the same party; and the smaller the number of individuals composing a majority, and the smaller the compass within which they are placed, the more easily will they concert and execute their plans of oppression. Extend the sphere, and you take in a greater variety of parties and interests; you make it less probable that a majority of the whole will have a common motive to invade the

rights of other citizens; or if such a common motive exists, it will be more difficult for all who feel it to discover their own strength, and to act in unison with each other. Besides other impediments, it may be remarked, that where there is a consciousness of unjust or dishonourable purposes, communication is always checked by distrust, in proportion to the number whose concurrence is necessary.

Hence, it clearly appears, that the same advantage, which a republic has over a democracy, in controlling the effects of faction, is enjoyed by a large over a small republic—is enjoyed by the union over the states composing it. Does this advantage consist in the substitution of representatives, whose enlightened views and virtuous sentiments render them superior to local prejudices, and to schemes of injustice? It will not be denied that the representation of the union will be most likely to possess these requisite endowments. Does it consist in the greater security afforded by a greater variety of parties, against the event of any one party being able to outnumber and oppress the rest? In an equal degree does the increased variety of parties, comprised within the union, increase the security? Does it, in fine, consist in the

greater obstacles opposed to the concert and accomplishment of the secret wishes of an unjust and interested majority? Here, again, the extent of the union gives it the most palpable advantage.

The influence of factious leaders may kindle a flame within their particular states, but will be unable to spread a general conflagration through the other states; a religious sect may degenerate into a political faction in a part of the confederacy; but the variety of sects dispersed over the entire face of it, must secure the national councils against any danger from that source: a rage for paper money, for an abolition of debts, for an equal division of property, or for any other improper or wicked project, will be less apt to pervade the whole body of the union than a particular member of it; in the same proportion as such a malady is more likely to taint a particular county or district, than an entire state.

In the extent and proper structure of the union, therefore, we behold a republican remedy for the diseases most incident to republican government. And according to the degree of pleasure and pride we feel in being republicans, ought to be our zeal in cherishing the spirit, and supporting the character of federalists.

The Federalist, No. 51, James Madison

THE FEDERALIST, NO. 51, ALSO WRITTEN BY MADISON, IS A CLASSIC STATEMENT IN DEFENSE OF SEPARATION OF POWERS AND REPUBLICAN PROCESSES. ITS FOURTH PARAGRAPH IS ESPECIALLY FAMOUS AND IS FREQUENTLY QUOTED BY STUDENTS OF GOVERNMENT.

To what expedient, then, shall we finally resort, for maintaining in practice the necessary partition of power among the several departments as laid down in the Constitution? The only answer that can be given is that as all these exterior provisions are found to be inadequate the defect must be supplied, by so contriving the interior structure of the government as that its several constituent parts may, by their mutual relations, be the means of keeping each other in their proper places. Without presuming to undertake a full development of this important idea I will hazard a few general observations which may perhaps place it in a clearer light, and enable us to form a more correct

judgment of the principles and structure of the government planned by the convention.

In order to lay a due foundation for that separate and distinct exercise of the different powers of government, which to a certain extent is admitted on all hands to be essential to the preservation of liberty, it is evident that each department should have a will of its own; and consequently should be so constituted that the members of each should have as little agency as possible in the appointment of the members of the others. Were this principle rigorously adhered to, it would require that all the appointments for the supreme executive, legislative,

and judiciary magistracies should be drawn from the same fountain of authority, the people, through channels having no communication whatever with one another. Perhaps such a plan of constructing the several departments would be less difficult in practice than it may in contemplation appear. Some difficulties, however, and some additional expense would attend the execution of it. Some deviations, therefore, from the principle must be admitted. In the constitution of the judiciary department in particular, it might be inexpedient to insist rigorously on the principle: first, because peculiar qualifications being essential in the members, the primary consideration ought to be to select that mode of choice which best secures these qualifications; second, because the permanent tenure by which the appointments are held in that department must soon destroy all sense of dependence on the authority conferring them.

It is equally evident that the members of each department should be as little dependent as possible on those of the others for the emoluments annexed to their offices. Were the executive magistrate, or the judges, not independent of the legislature in this particular, their independence in every other would be merely nominal.

But the great security against a gradual concentration of the several powers in the same department consists in giving to those who administer each department the necessary constitutional means and personal motives to resist encroachments of the others. The provision for defense must in this, as in all other cases, be made commensurate to the danger of attack. Ambition must be made to counteract ambition. The interest of the man must be connected with the constitutional rights of the place. It may be a reflection on human nature that such devices should be necessary to control the abuses of government. But what is government itself but the greatest of all reflections on human nature? If men were angels, no government would be necessary. If angels were to govern men, neither external nor internal controls on government would be necessary. In framing a government which is to be administered by men over men, the great difficulty lies in this: you must first enable the government to control the governed; and in the next place oblige it to control itself. A dependence on the people is, no doubt, the primary control on the government; but experience has taught mankind the necessity of auxiliary precautions.

This policy of supplying, by opposite and rival interests, the defect of better motives, might be traced through the whole system of human affairs, private as well as public. We see it particularly displayed in all the subordinate distributions of power, where the constant aim is to divide and arrange the several offices in such a manner as that each may be a check on the other—that the private interest of every individual may be a sentinel over the public rights. These inventions of prudence cannot be less requisite in the distribution of the supreme powers of the State.

But it is not possible to give to each department an equal power of self-defense. In republican government, the legislative authority necessarily predominates. The remedy for this inconveniency is to divide the legislature into different branches; and to render them, by modes of election and different principles of action, as little connected with each other as the nature of their common functions and their common dependence on the society will admit. It may even be necessary to guard against dangerous encroachments by still further precautions. As the weight of the legislative authority requires that it should be thus divided, the weakness of the executive may require, on the other hand, that it should be fortified. An absolute negative on the legislature appears, at first view, to be the natural defense with which the executive magistrate should be armed. But perhaps it would be neither altogether safe nor alone sufficient. On ordinary occasions it might not be exerted with the requisite firmness, and on extraordinary occasions it might be perfidiously abused. May not this defect of an absolute negative be supplied by some qualified connection between this weaker department and the weaker branch of the stronger department, by which the latter may be led to support the constitutional rights of the former, without being too much detached from the rights of its own department?

If the principles on which these observations are founded be just, as I persuade myself they are, and they be applied as a criterion to the several State constitutions, and to the federal Constitution, it will be found that if the latter does not perfectly correspond with them, the former are infinitely less able to bear such a test.

There are, moreover, two considerations particularly applicable to the federal system of America, which place that system in a very interesting point of view.

First. In a single republic, all the power surrendered by the people is submitted to the administration of a single government; and the usurpations are guarded against by a division of the government into distinct and separate departments. In the compound republic of America, the power surrendered by the people is first divided between two distinct governments, and then the portion allotted to each subdivided among distinct and separate departments. Hence a double security arises to the rights of the people. The different governments will control each other, at the same time that each will be controlled by itself.

Second. It is of great importance in a republic not only to guard the society against the oppression of its rulers, but to guard one part of the society against the injustice of the other part. Different interests necessarily exist in different classes of citizens. If a majority be united by a common interest, the rights of the minority will be insecure. There are but two methods of providing against this evil: the one by creating a will in the community independent of the majority—that is, of the society itself; the other, by comprehending in the society so many separate descriptions of citizens as will render an unjust combination of a majority of the whole very improbable, if not impracticable. The first method prevails in all governments possessing an hereditary or self-appointed authority. This, at best, is but a precarious security; because a power independent of the society may as well espouse the unjust views of the major as the rightful interests of the minor party, and may possibly be turned against both parties. The second method will be exemplified in the federal republic of the United States. Whilst all authority in it will be derived from and dependent on the society, the society itself will be broken into so many parts, interests and classes of citizens, that the rights of individuals, or of the minority, will be in little danger from interested combinations of the majority. In a free government the security for civil rights must be the same as that for religious rights. It consists in the one case in the multiplicity of interests, and in the other in the multiplicity of sects. The degree of security in both cases will depend on the number of interests and sects; and this may be presumed to depend on the extent of country and number of people comprehended under the same government. This view of the subject must particularly recommend a proper federal system to all the sincere and considerate friends of republican government, since it shows that in exact proportion as the territory of the Union may be formed into more circumscribed Confederacies, or States, oppressive combinations of a majority will be facilitated; the best security, under the republican forms, for the rights of every class of citizen, will be diminished; and consequently the stability and independence of some member of the government, the only other security, must be proportionally increased. Justice is the end of government. It is the end of civil society. It ever has been and ever will be pursued until it be obtained, or until liberty be lost in the pursuit. In a society under the forms of which the stronger faction can readily unite and oppress the weaker, anarchy may as truly be said to reign as in a state of nature, where the weaker individual is not secured against the violence of the stronger; and as, in the latter state, even the stronger individuals are prompted, by the uncertainty of their condition, to submit to a government which may protect the weak as well as themselves; so, in the former state, will the more powerful factions or parties be gradually induced, by a like motive, to wish for a government which will protect all parties, the weaker as well as the more powerful. It can be little doubted that if the State of Rhode Island was separated from the Confederacy and left to itself, the insecurity of rights under the popular form of government within such narrow limits would be displayed by such reiterated oppressions of factious majorities that some power altogether independent of the people would soon be called for by the voice of the very factions whose misrule had proved the necessity to it. In the extended republic of the United States, and among the great variety of interests, parties, and sects which it embraces, a coalition of a majority of the whole society could seldom take place on any other principles than those of justice and the general good; whilst there being thus less danger to a minor from the will of a major party, there must be less pretext, also, to provide for the security of the former, by introducing into the government a will not dependent on the latter, or, in other words, a will independent of the society itself. It is no less certain that it is important, notwithstanding the contrary opinions which have been entertained that the larger the society, provided it lie within a practicable sphere, the more duly capable it will be of self-government. And happily for the *republican cause,* the practicable sphere may be carried to a very great extent by a judicious modification and mixture of the *federal principle.*

The Federalist, No. 78, Alexander Hamilton

THE FEDERALIST, NO. 78, WRITTEN BY ALEXANDER HAMILTON, EXPLAINS AND PRAISES THE PROVISIONS FOR THE JUDICIARY IN THE NEWLY DRAFTED CONSTITUTION. NOTICE ESPECIALLY HOW HAMILTON ASSERTS THAT THE COURTS HAVE A KEY RESPONSIBILITY IN DETERMINING THE MEANING OF THE CONSTITUTION AS FUNDAMENTAL LAW. HAMILTON IS OUTLINING HERE THE DOCTRINE OF JUDICIAL REVIEW AS WE NOW KNOW IT.

We proceed now to an examination of the judiciary department of the proposed government.

In unfolding the defects of the existing Confederation, the utility and necessity of a federal judicature have been clearly pointed out. It is the less necessary to recapitulate the considerations there urged as the propriety of the institution in the abstract is not disputed; the only questions which have been raised being relative to the manner of constituting it, and to its extent. To these points, therefore, our observations shall be confined.

The manner of constituting it seems to embrace these several objects: 1st. The mode of appointing the judges. 2nd. The tenure by which they are to hold their places. 3rd. The partition of the judiciary authority between different courts and their relations to each other.

First. As to the mode of appointing the judges: this is the same with that of appointing the officers of the Union in general and has been so fully discussed in the two last numbers that nothing can be said here which would not be useless repetition.

Second. As to the tenure by which the judges are to hold their places: this chiefly concerns their duration in office, the provisions for their support, the precautions for their responsibility.

According to the plan of the convention, all judges who may be appointed by the United States are to hold their offices *during good behavior;* which is conformable to the most approved of the State constitutions, and among the rest, to that of this State. Its propriety having been drawn into question by the adversaries of that plan is no light symptom of the rage for objection which disorders their imaginations and judgments. The standard of good behavior for the continuance in office of the judicial magistracy is certainly one of the most valuable of the modern improvements in the practice of government. In a monarchy it is an excellent barrier to the despotism of the prince; in a republic it is a no less excellent barrier to the encroachments and oppressions of the representative body. And it is the best expedient which can be devised in any government to secure a steady, upright, and impartial administration of the laws.

Whoever attentively considers the different departments of power must perceive that, in a government in which they are separated from each other, the judiciary, from the nature of its functions, will always be the least dangerous to the political rights of the Constitution; because it will be least in a capacity to annoy or injure them. The executive not only dispenses the honors but holds the sword of the community. The legislature not only commands the purse but prescribes the rules by which the duties and rights of every citizen are to be regulated. The judiciary, on the contrary, has no influence over either the sword or the purse; no direction either of the strength or of the wealth of the society, and can take no active resolution whatever. It may truly be said to have neither FORCE NOR WILL but merely judgment; and must ultimately depend upon the aid of the executive arm even for the efficacy of its judgments.

This simple view of the matter suggests several important consequences. It proves incontestably that the judiciary is beyond comparison the weakest of the three departments of power; that it can never attack with success either of the other two; and that all possible care is requisite to enable it to defend itself against their attacks. It equally proves that though individual oppression may now and then proceed from the courts of justice, the general liberty of the people can never be endangered from that quarter; I mean so long as the judiciary remains truly distinct from both the legislature and the executive. For I agree that "there is no liberty if the power of judging be not separated from the legislative and executive powers." And it proves, in the last place, that as liberty can have nothing to fear from the judiciary alone, but would have everything to fear from its union with either of the other departments, that as all the effects of such a union must ensue from a dependence of the former on the latter, notwithstanding a nominal and apparent separation; that as, from the natural feebleness of the judiciary, it is in continual jeopardy of being overpowered, awed, or influenced by its co-ordinate branches; and that as nothing can contribute so much to its firmness and independence as permanency in office, this quality may therefore be justly regarded as an indispensable ingredient in its constitution, and, in a great measure, as the citadel for the public justice and the public security.

The complete independence of the courts of justice is peculiarly essential in a limited Constitution. By a limited Constitution, I understand one which contains certain specified exceptions to the legislative authority; such, for instance, as that it shall pass no bills of attainder, no *ex post facto laws,* and the like. Limitations of this kind can be preserved in practice no other way than through the medium of courts of justice, whose duty it must be to declare all acts contrary to the manifest tenor of the Constitution void. Without this, all the reservations of particular rights or privileges would amount to nothing.

Some perplexity respecting the rights of the courts to pronounce legislative acts void, because contrary to the Constitution, has arisen from an imagination that the doctrine would imply a superiority to the judiciary to the legislative power. It is urged that the authority which can declare the acts of another void must necessarily be superior to the one whose acts may be declared void. As this doctrine is of great importance in all the American constitutions, a brief discussion of the grounds on which it rests cannot be unacceptable.

There is no position which depends on clearer principles than that every act of a delegated authority, contrary to the tenor of the commission under which it is exercised, is void. No legislative act, therefore, contrary to the Constitution, can be valid. To deny this would be to affirm that the deputy is greater than his principal; that the servant is above his master; that the representatives of the people are superior to the people themselves; that men acting by virtue of powers do not authorize, but what they forbid.

If it be said that the legislative body are themselves the constitutional judges of their own powers and that the construction they put upon them is conclusive upon the other departments it may be answered that this cannot be the natural presumption where it is not to be collected from any particular provisions in the Constitution. It is not otherwise to be supposed that the Constitution could intend to enable the representatives of the people to substitute their *will* to that of their constituents. It is far more rational to suppose that the courts were designed to be an intermediate body between the people and the legislature in order, among other things, to keep the latter within the limits assigned to their authority. The interpretation of the laws is the proper and peculiar province of the courts. A constitution is, in fact, and must be regarded by the judges as, a fundamental law. It therefore belongs to them to ascertain its meaning as well as the meaning of any particular act proceeding from the legislative body. If there should happen to be an irreconcilable variance between the two, that which has the superior obligation and validity ought, of course, to be preferred; or, in other words, the Constitution ought to be preferred to the statute, the intention of the people to the intention of their agents.

Nor does this conclusion by any means suppose a superiority of the judicial to the legislative power. It only supposes that the power of the people is superior to both, and that where the will of the legislature, declared in its statutes, stands in opposition to that of the people, declared in the Constitution, the judges ought to be governed by the latter rather than the former. They ought to regulate their decisions by the fundamental laws rather than by those which are not fundamental.

This exercise of judicial discretion in determining between two contradictory laws is exemplified in a familiar instance. It not uncommonly happens that there are two statutes existing at one time, clashing in whole or in part with each other and neither of them containing any repealing clause or expression. In such a case, it is the province of the courts to liquidate and fix their meaning and operation. So far as they can, by any fair construction, be reconciled to each other, reason and law conspire to dictate that this should be done; where this is impracticable, it becomes a matter of necessity to give effect to one in exclusion of the other. The rule which has obtained in the courts for determining their relative validity is that the last in order of time shall be preferred to the first. But this is a mere rule of construction, not derived from any positive law but from the nature and reason of the thing. It is a rule not enjoined upon the courts by legislative provision but adopted by themselves, as consonant to truth and propriety, for the direction of their conduct as interpreters of the law. They thought it reasonable that between the interfering acts of an equal authority that which was the last indication of its will should have the preference.

But in regard to the interfering acts of a superior and subordinate authority of an original and derivative power, the nature and reason of the thing indicates the converse of that rule as proper to be followed. They teach us that the prior act of a superior ought to be preferred to the subsequent act of an inferior and subordinate authority; and that accordingly, whenever a particular statute contravenes the Constitution, it will be the duty of the judicial tribunals to adhere to the latter and disregard the former.

It can be of no weight to say that the courts, on the pretense of a repugnancy, may substitute their own pleasure to the constitutional intentions of the legislature. This might as well happen in the case of two contradictory statutes; or it might as well happen in every adjudication upon any single statute. The courts must declare the sense of the law; and if they should be disposed to exercise WILL instead of JUDGMENT, the consequence would equally be the substitution of their pleasure to that of the legislative body. The observation, if it prove anything, would prove that there ought to be no judges distinct from that body.

If, then, the courts of justice are to be considered as the bulwarks of a limited Constitution against legislative encroachments, this consideration will afford a strong argument for the permanent tenure of judicial offices, since nothing will contribute so much as this to that independent spirit in the judges which must be essential to the faithful performance of so arduous a duty.

This independence of the judges is equally requisite to guard the Constitution and the rights of individuals from the effects of those ill humors which the arts of designing men, or the influence of particular conjunctures, sometimes disseminate among the people themselves, and which, though they speedily give place to better information, and more deliberate reflection, have a tendency, in the meantime, to occasion dangerous innovations in the government, and serious oppressions of the minor party in the community. Though I trust the friends of the proposed Constitution will never concur with its enemies in questioning that fundamental principal of Republican government which admits the right of the people to alter or abolish the established Constitution whenever they find it inconsistent with their happiness; yet it is not to be inferred from this principle that the representatives of the people, whenever a momentary inclination happens to lay hold of a majority of their constituents incompatible with the provisions in the existing Constitution would, on that account, be justifiable in a violation of those provisions; or that the courts would be under a greater obligation to connive at infractions in this shape than when they had proceeded wholly from the cabals of the representative body. Until the people have, by some solemn and authoritative act, annulled or changed the established form, it is binding upon themselves collectively, as well as individually; and no presumption, or even knowledge of their sentiments, can warrant their representatives in a departure from it prior to such an act. But it is easy to see that it would require an uncommon portion of fortitude in the judges to do their duty as faithful guardians of the Constitution, where legislative invasions of it had been instigated by the major voice of the community.

But it is not with a view to infractions of the Constitution only that the independence of the judges may be an essential safeguard against the effects of occasional ill humors in the society. These sometimes extend no farther than to the injury of the private rights of particular classes of citizens, by unjust and partial laws. Here also the firmness of the judicial magistracy is of vast importance in mitigating the severity and confining the operation of such laws. It not only serves to moderate the immediate mischiefs of those which may have been passed but it operates as a check upon the legislative body in passing them; who, perceiving that obstacles to the success of iniquitous intention are to be expected from the scruples of the courts, are in a manner compelled, by the very motives of the injustice they mediate, to qualify their attempts. This is a circumstance calculated to have more influence upon the character of our governments than but a few may be aware of. The benefits of the integrity and moderation of the judiciary have already been felt in more States than one; and though they may have displeased those whose sinister expectations they may have disappointed, they must have commanded the esteem and applause of all the virtuous and disinterested. Considerate men of every description ought to prize whatever will tend to beget or fortify that temper in the courts; as no man can be sure that he may not be tomorrow the victim of a spirit of injustice, by which he may be a gainer today. And every man must now feel that the inevitable tendency of such a spirit is to sap the foundations of public and private confidence and to introduce in its stead universal distrust and distress.

That inflexible and uniform adherence to the rights of the Constitution, and of individuals, which we perceive to be indispensable in the courts of justice, can certainly not be expected from judges who hold their offices by a temporary commission. Periodical appointments, however regulated, or by whomsoever made, would, in some way or other, be fatal to their necessary independence. If the power of making them was committed either to the executive or legislature there would be danger of an improper complaisance to the branch which possessed it; if to both, there would be an unwillingness to hazard the displeasure of either; if to the people, or to persons chosen by them for the special purpose, there would be too great a disposition to consult popularity to justify a reliance that nothing would be consulted by the Constitution and the laws.

There is yet a further and a weighty reason for the permanency of the judicial offices which is deducible from the nature of the qualifications they require. It has been frequently remarked with great propriety that a voluminous code of laws is one of the inconveniences necessarily connected with the advantages of a free government. To avoid an arbitrary discretion in the courts, it is indispensable that they should be bound down by strict rules and precedents which serve to define and point out their duty in every particular case that comes before them; and it will readily be conceived from the variety of controversies which grow out of the folly and wickedness of mankind that the records of those precedents must unavoidably swell to a very considerable bulk and must demand long and laborious study to acquire a competent knowledge of them. Hence it is that there can be but few men in the society who will have sufficient skill in the laws to qualify them for the stations of judges. And making the proper deductions for the ordinary depravity of human nature, the number must be still smaller of those who unite the requisite integrity with the requisite knowledge. These considerations apprise us that the government can have no great option between fit characters; and that a temporary duration in office which would naturally discourage such characters from quitting a lucrative line of practice to accept a seat on the bench would have a tendency to throw the administration of justice into hands less able and less well qualified to conduct it with utility and dignity. In the present circumstances of this country and in those in which it is likely to be for a long time to come, the disadvantages on this score would be greater than they may at first sight appear; but it must be confessed that they are far inferior to those which present themselves under the other aspects of the subject.

Upon the whole, there can be no room to doubt that the convention acted wisely in copying from the models of those constitutions which have established *good behavior* as the tenure of their judicial offices in point of duration, and that so far from being blamable on this account, their plan would have been inexcusably defective if it had wanted this important feature of good government. The experience of Great Britain affords an illustrious comment on the excellence of the institution.

Year	Candidates	Party	Popular Vote	Electoral Vote
1789	George Washington			69
	John Adams			34
	Others			35
1793	George Washington			132
	John Adams			77
	George Clinton			50
	Others			5
1796	John Adams	Federalist		71
	Thomas Jefferson	Democratic-Republican		68
	Thomas Pinckney	Federalist		59
	Aaron Burr	Democratic-Republican		30
	Others			48
1800	Thomas Jefferson	Democratic-Republican		73
	Aaron Burr	Democratic-Republican		73
	John Adams	Federalist		65
	Charles C. Pinckney	Federalist		64
1804	Thomas Jefferson	Democratic-Republican		162
	Charles C. Pinckney	Federalist		14
1808	James Madison	Democratic-Republican		122
	Charles C. Pinckney	Federalist		47
	George Clinton	Independent-Republican		6
1812	James Madison	Democratic-Republican		128
	DeWitt Clinton	Federalist		89
1816	James Monroe	Democratic-Republican		183
	Rufus King	Federalist		34
1820	James Monroe	Democratic-Republican		231
	John Quincy Adams	Independent-Republican		1
1824	John Quincy Adams	Democratic-Republican	108,740(30.5%)	84
	Andrew Jackson	Democratic-Republican	153,544(43.1%)	99
	Henry Clay	Democratic-Republican	47,136(13.2%)	37
	William H. Crawford	Democratic-Republican	46,618(13.1%)	41
1828	Andrew Jackson	Democratic	647,231(56.0%)	178
	John Quincy Adams	National Republican	509,097(44.0%)	83
1832	Andrew Jackson	Democratic	687,502(55.0%)	219
	Henry Clay	National Republican	530,189(42.4%)	49
	William Wirt	Anti-Masonic		7
	John Floyd	National Republican	33,108(2.6%)	11
1836	Martin Van Buren	Democratic	761,549(50.9%)	170
	William H. Harrison	Whig	549,567(36.7%)	73
	Hugh L. White	Whig	145,396(9.7%)	26
	Daniel Webster	Whig	41,287(2.7%)	14
1840	William H. Harrison	Whig	1,275,017(53.1%)	234
	Martin Van Buren	Democratic	1,128,702(46.9%)	60
1844	James K. Polk	Democratic	1,337,243(49.6%)	170
	Henry Clay	Whig	1,299,068(48.1%)	105
	James G. Birney	Liberty	63,300(2.3%)	
1848	Zachary Taylor	Whig	1,360,101(47.4%)	163
	Lewis Cass	Democratic	1,220,544(42.5%)	127
	Martin Van Buren	Free Soil	291,163(10.1%)	
1852	Franklin Pierce	Democratic	1,601,474(50.9%)	254
	Winfield Scott	Whig	1,386,578(44.1%)	42
1856	James Buchanan	Democratic	1,838,169(45.4%)	174
	John C. Fremont	Republican	1,335,264(33.0%)	114
	Millard Fillmore	American	874,534(21.6%)	8
1860	Abraham Lincoln	Republican	1,865,593(39.8%)	180
	Stephen A. Douglas	Democratic	1,381,713(29.5%)	12
	John C. Breckinridge	Democratic	848,356(18.1%)	72
	John Bell	Constitutional Union	592,906(12.6%)	79
1864	Abraham Lincoln	Republican	2,206,938(55.0%)	212
	George B. McClellan	Democratic	1,803,787(45.0%)	21
1868	Ulysses S. Grant	Republican	3,013,421(52.7%)	214
	Horatio Seymour	Democratic	2,706,829(47.3%)	80
1872	Ulysses S. Grant	Republican	3,596,745(55.6%)	286
	Horace Greeley	Democratic	2,843,446(43.9%)	66
1876	Rutherford B. Hayes	Republican	4,036,571(48.0%)	185
	Samuel J. Tilden	Democratic	4,284,020(51.0%)	184
1880	James A. Garfield	Republican	4,449,053(48.3%)	214
	Winfield S. Hancock	Democratic	4,442,035(48.2%)	155
	James B. Weaver	Greenback-Labor	308,578(3.4%)	
1884	Grover Cleveland	Democratic	4,874,986(48.5%)	219
	James G. Blaine	Republican	4,851,931(48.2%)	182
	Benjamin F. Butler	Greenback-Labor	175,370(1.8%)	
1888	Benjamin Harrison	Republican	5,444,337(47.8%)	233
	Grover Cleveland	Democratic	5,540,050(48.6%)	168

Year	Candidates	Party	Popular Vote	Electoral Vote
1892	Grover Cleveland	Democratic	5,554,414(46.0%)	277
	Benjamin Harrison	Republican	5,190,802(43.0%)	145
	James B. Weaver	Peoples	1,027,329(8.5%)	22
1896	William McKinley	Republican	7,035,638(50.8%)	271
	William J. Bryan	Democratic; Populist	6,467,946(46.7%)	176
1900	William McKinley	Republican	7,219,530(51.7%)	292
	William J. Bryan	Democratic; Populist	6,356,734(45.5%)	155
1904	Theodore Roosevelt	Republican	7,628,834(56.4%)	336
	Alton B. Parker	Democratic	5,084,401(37.6%)	140
	Eugene V. Debs	Socialist	402,460(3.0%)	0
1908	William H. Taft	Republican	7,679,006(51.6%)	321
	William J. Bryan	Democratic	6,409,106(43.1%)	162
	Eugene V. Debs	Socialist	420,820(2.8%)	0
1912	Woodrow Wilson	Democratic	6,286,820(41.8%)	435
	Theodore Roosevelt	Progressive	4,126,020(27.4%)	88
	William H. Taft	Republican	3,483,922(23.2%)	8
	Eugene V. Debs	Socialist	897,011(6.0%)	0
1916	Woodrow Wilson	Democratic	9,129,606(49.3%)	277
	Charles E. Hughes	Republican	8,538,211(46.1%)	254
1920	Warren G. Harding	Republican	16,152,200(61.0%)	404
	James M. Cox	Democratic	9,147,353(34.6%)	127
	Eugene V. Debs	Socialist	919,799(3.5%)	0
1924	Calvin Coolidge	Republican	15,725,016(54.1%)	382
	John W. Davis	Democratic	8,385,586(28.8%)	136
	Robert M. La Follette	Progressive	4,822,856(16.6%)	13
1928	Herbert C. Hoover	Republican	21,392,190(58.2%)	444
	Alfred E. Smith	Democratic	15,016,443(40.8%)	87
1932	Franklin D. Roosevelt	Democratic	22,809,638(57.3%)	472
	Herbert C. Hoover	Republican	15,758,901(39.6%)	59
	Norman Thomas	Socialist	881,951(2.2%)	0
1936	Franklin D. Roosevelt	Democratic	27,751,612(60.7%)	523
	Alfred M. Landon	Republican	16,681,913(36.4%)	8
	William Lemke	Union	891,858(1.9%)	0
1940	Franklin D. Roosevelt	Democratic	27,243,466(54.7%)	449
	Wendell L. Willkie	Republican	22,304,755(44.8%)	82
1944	Franklin D. Roosevelt	Democratic	25,602,505(52.8%)	432
	Thomas E. Dewey	Republican	22,006,278(44.5%)	99
1948	Harry S Truman	Democratic	24,105,812(49.5%)	303
	Thomas E. Dewey	Republican	21,970,065(45.1%)	189
	J. Strom Thurmond	States' Rights	1,169,063(2.4%)	39
	Henry A. Wallace	Progressive	1,157,172(2.4%)	0
1952	Dwight D. Eisenhower	Republican	33,936,234(55.2%)	442
	Adlai E. Stevenson	Democratic	27,314,992(44.5%)	89
1956	Dwight D. Eisenhower	Republican	35,590,472(57.4%)	457
	Adlai E. Stevenson	Democratic	26,022,752(42.0%)	73
1960	John F. Kennedy	Democratic	34,227,096(49.9%)	303
	Richard M. Nixon	Republican	34,108,546(49.6%)	219
1964	Lyndon B. Johnson	Democratic	43,126,233(61.1%)	486
	Barry Goldwater	Republican	27,174,989(38.5%)	52
1968	Richard M. Nixon	Republican	31,783,783(43.4%)	301
	Hubert H. Humphrey	Democratic	31,271,839(42.7%)	191
	George C. Wallace	American Independent	9,899,557(13.5%)	46
1972	Richard M. Nixon	Republican	46,632,189(61.3%)	520
	George McGovern	Democratic	28,422,015(37.3%)	17
1976	Jimmy Carter	Democratic	40,828,587(50.1%)	297
	Gerald R. Ford	Republican	39,147,613(48.0%)	240
1980	Ronald Reagan	Republican	42,941,145(51.0%)	489
	Jimmy Carter	Democratic	34,663,037(41.0%)	49
	John B. Anderson	Independent	5,551,551(6.6%)	0
1984	Ronald Reagan	Republican	53,428,357(59%)	525
	Walter F. Mondale	Democratic	36,930,923(41%)	13
1988	George Bush	Republican	48,881,011(53%)	426
	Michael Dukakis	Democratic	41,828,350(46%)	111
1992	Bill Clinton	Democratic	38,394,210(43%)	370
	George Bush	Republican	33,974,386(38%)	168
	H. Ross Perot	Independent	16,573,465(19%)	0
1996	Bill Clinton	Democratic	45,628,667(49%)	379
	Bob Dole	Republican	37,869,435(41%)	159
	H. Ross Perot	Reform	7,874,283(8%)	0
2000	George W. Bush	Republican	50,456,169(48%)	271
	Al Gore	Democratic	50,996,116(48%)	266
	Ralph Nader	Green	2,767,176(3%)	0
2004	George W. Bush	Republican	60,608,582(51%)	286
	John Kerry	Democratic	57,288,974(48%)	252
	Ralph Nader	Independent	400,924(.35%)	0
2008	Barack Obama	Democratic	66,361,433(53%)	364
	John McCain	Republican	58,024,608(46%)	163

761

GLOSSARY

527 organization A political group organizes under section 527 of the IRS Code that may accept and spend unlimited amounts of money on election activities so long as they are not spent on broadcast ads run in the last 30 days before a primary or 60 days before a general election in which a clearly identified candidate is referred to and a relevant electorate is targeted.

adaptive approach A method used to interpret the Constitution that understands the document to be flexible and responsive to changing needs of the times.

administrative discretion Authority given by Congress to the federal bureaucracy to use reasonable judgment in implementing the laws.

adversary system A judicial system in which the court of law is a neutral arena where two parties argue their differences.

advisory opinion An opinion unrelated to a particular case that gives a court's view about a constitutional or legal issue.

affirmative action Remedial action designed to overcome the effects of discrimination against minorities and women.

amendatory veto The power of governors in a few states to return a bill to legislature with suggested language changes, conditions, or amendments. Legislators then decide either to accept the governor's recommendations or to pass the bill in its original form over the veto.

American dream The widespread belief that the United States is a land of opportunity and that individual initiative and hard work can bring economic success.

amicus curiae brief Literally, a "friend of the court" brief, filed by an individual or organization to present arguments in addition to those presented by the immediate parties to a case.

Annapolis Convention A convention held in September 1786 to consider problems of trade and navigation, attended by five states and important because it issued the call to Congress and the states for what became the Constitutional Convention.

Antifederalists Opponents of ratification of the Constitution and of a strong central government generally.

antitrust legislation Federal laws (starting with the Sherman Antitrust Act of 1890) that try to prevent a monopoly from dominating an industry and restraining trade.

appellate jurisdiction The authority of a court to review decisions made by lower courts.

Articles of Confederation The first governing document of the confederated states, drafted in 1777, ratified in 1781, and replaced by the present Constitution in 1789.

assessment The valuation a government places on property for the purposes of taxation.

assigned counsel system An arrangement whereby attorneys are provided for people accused of crimes who are unable to hire their own attorneys. The judge assigns a member of the bar to provide counsel to a particular defendant.

attentive public Citizens who follow public affairs carefully.

attitudes An individual's propensity to perceive, interpret, or act toward a particular object in a particular way.

autocracy A type of government in which on person with unlimited power rules.

bad tendency test An interpretation of the First Amendment that would permit legislatures to forbid speech encouraging people to engage in illegal action.

bicameralism The principle of a two-house legislature.

bicameral legislature A two-house legislature.

Bipartisan Campaign Reform Act (BCRA) Largely banned party soft money, restored long-standing prohibition on corporation and labor unions use of general treasury funds for electoral purposes, and narrowed the definition of issue advocacy.

budget deficit The condition that exists when the federal government raises less revenue than it spends.

bundling A tactic in which PACs collect contributions form like-minded individuals (each limited to $2,000) and present them to a candidate or political party as a "bundle," thus increasing the PAC's influence.

bureaucracy A form of organization that operates through impersonal, uniform rules and procedures.

bureaucrat A career government employee.

Bush Doctrine A policy by the Bush administration in 2001 that asserts America's right to attack any nation that has weapons of mass destruction that may be used against U.S. interests at home or abroad.

cabinet The advisory council for the president, consisting of the heads of the executive departments, the vice president, and a few other officials selected by the president.

candidate appeal How voters feel about a candidate's background, personality, leadership, ability, and other personal qualities.

candidate expenditure limits Limits on how much money a candidate may spend in support of a campaign for elective office.

capitalism An economic system characterized by private property, competitive markets, economic incentives, and limited government involvement in the production, distribution, and pricing of goods and services.

caucus A meeting of local party members to choose party officials or candidates for public office and to decide the platform.

central clearance Review of all executive branch testimony, reports, and draft legislation by the Office of Management and Budget (OMB) to ensure that each communication to Congress is in accordance with the president's program.

centralists People who favor national action over action at the state and local levels.

charter A city "constitution" that outlines the structure of city government, defines the authority of the various officials, and provides for their selection.

charter school A publicly funded alternative to standard public schools in some states, initiated when individuals or groups receive charters; charter schools must meet state standards.

checks and balances A constitutional grant of powers that enables each of the three branches of government to check some acts of the others and therefore ensure that no branch can dominate.

chief of staff The head of the White House staff.

circuit courts of appeal Courts with appellate jurisdiction that hear appeals from the decisions of lower courts.

civil disobedience Deliberate refusal to obey a law or comply with the order of public officials as a means of expressing opposition.

civil law A law that governs relationships between individuals and defines their legal rights.

civil rights The rights of all people to be free from irrational discrimination such as that based on race, religion, gender or ethnic origin.

civil service Federal employees who work for government through a competitive, not political selection process.

class action suit A lawsuit brought by an individual or a group of people on behalf of all those similarly situated.

clear and present danger test An interpretation of the First Amendment that holds that the government cannot interfere with speech unless the speech presents a clear and present danger that if will lead to evil or illegal acts.

closed primary A primary election in which only persons registered in the party holding the primary may vote.

closed rule A procedural rule in the House of Representatives that prohibits any amendments to bills or provides that only members of the committee reporting the bill may offer amendments.

closed shop A company with a labor agreement under which membership is a condition of employment.

cloture A procedure for terminating debate, especially filibusters, in the Senate.

coattail effect The boost that candidates may get in an election because of the popularity of candidates above them on the ballot.

collective action How groups form and organize to pursue their goals or objectives, including how to get individuals and groups to participate and cooperate. The term has many applications in the various social sciences such as political science, sociology, and economics.

collective bargaining A method whereby representatives of the union and employer determine wages, hours, and other conditions of employment through direct negotiation.

commerce clause The clause in the Constitution (Article 1, Section 8, Clause 1) that gives Congress the power to regulate all business activities that cross state lines or affect more than one state or other nations.

commercial speech Advertisements and commercials for products and services; they receive less First Amendment protection, primarily to discourage flase and misleading ads.

communism A political, social, and economic system based on public ownership of the means of production and exchange. (missing comma after social in text)

concurrent powers Powers that the Constitution gives to both the national and state governments, such as the power to levy taxes.

concurring opinion An opinion that agrees with the majority in a Supreme Court ruling but differs on the reasoning.

confederation A constitutional arrangement in which sovereign nations or states, by compact, create a central government but carefully limit its power and do not give it direct authority over individuals.

conference committee A committee appointed by the presiding officers of each chamber to adjust differences on a particular bill passed by each in different form.

Congressional Budget Office (CBO) An agency of Congress that analyzes presidential budget recommendations and estimates the costs of proposed legislation.

congressional elaboration Congressional legislation that gives further meaning to the Constitution based on sometimes vague constitutional authority, such as the necessary and proper clause.

congressional-executive agreement A formal agreement between the U.S. president and the leaders of other nations that requires approval by both houses of Congress.

Connecticut Compromise The compromise agreement by states at the Constitutional Convention for a bicameral legislature with a lower house in which representation would be based on population and an upper house in which each state would have two senators.

conservatism A belief that limited government ensures order, competitive markets, and personal opportunity.

constituents The residents of a congressional district or state.

Constitutional Convention The convention in Philadelphia, from May 25 to September 17, 1787, that debated and agreed on the Constitution of the United States.

constitutional democracy Government that enforces recognizes limits on those who govern and allows the voice of the people to be heard through free, fair and relatively frequent elections.

Constitutional home rule State constitutional authorization for local governments to conduct their own affairs.

constitutional initiative petition A device that permits voters to place specific amendments to a state constitution on the ballot by petition.

constitutionalism The set of arrangements, including checks and balances, federalism, separation of power, rule of law, due process, and a bill of rights, that requires our leaders to listen, think,

bargain, and explain before they act or make laws. We then hold them politically and legally accountable for how they exercise their power.

content or viewpoint neutrality Laws that apply to all kinds of speech and to all views, not only that which is unpopular or divisive.

contribution limits Limits on how much a single contributor may give to a candidate in an election or period of time.

corporate social responsibility Efforts by corporations to improve their reputations by paying attention to their contributions to the social good.

council-manager plan A form of local government in which the city council hires a professional administrator to manage city affairs; also known as the city-manager plan.

county The largest local level of government below the state, currently used in 48 states.

criminal law A law that defines crimes against the public order.

cross-cutting cleavages Divisions within society that cut across demographic categories to produce groups that are more heterogeneous or different.

crossover voting Voting by a member of one party for a candidate of another party.

de facto segregation Segregation resulting from economic or social conditions or personal choice.

de jure segregation Segregation imposed by law.

dealignment Weakening of partisan preferences that point to a rejection of both major parties and a rise in the number of Independents.

decentralists People who favor state or local action rather than national action.

defendant In a criminal action, the person or party accused of an offense.

delegate An official who is expected to represent the views of his or her constituents even when personally holding different views; one interpretation of the role of the legislator.

delegated (express) powers Powers given explicitly to national government and listed in the Constitution.

deliberation The process where people or elected officials meet together to discuss and consider public matters.

democracy Government by the people, both directly or indirectly, with free and frequent elections.

democratic consensus Widespread agreement of fundamental principles of democratic governance and the values that undergird them.

demography The study of the characteristics of populations.

department Usually the largest organization in government with the largest mission; also the highest rank in the federal hierarchy.

deregulation A policy promoting cutbacks in the amount of federal regulation in specific areas of economic activity.

devolution revolution The effort to slow the growth of the national government by returning many functions to the states.

direct democracy Government in which citizens vote on laws and select officials directly.

direct primary An election in which voters choose party nominees.

discharge petition A petition that, if signed by a majority of the members of the House of Representatives, will pry a bill from committee and bring it to the floor for consideration.

disclosure laws A requirement that candidates specify where the money came from to finance their campaign.

discretionary spending Spending that can be altered by congressional and presidential action.

dissenting opinion An opinion disagreeing with the majority in a Supreme Court ruling.

distributive policy A public policy such as Social Security that provides benefits to all groups in society.

district courts Courts in which criminal and civil cases are originally tried in the federal judicial system.

divided government Governance divided between the parties, especially when one holds the presidency and the other controls one or both houses of Congress.

docket The list of potential cases that reach the Supreme Court.

double jeopardy Trial or punishment for the same crime by the same government; forbidden by the Constitution.

dual citizenship Citizenship in more than one nation.

due process Established rules and regulations that restrain government officials.

due process clause A clause in the Fifth Amendment limiting the power of the national government; a similar clause in the Fourteenth Amendment prohibiting state governments from depriving any person of life, liberty, or property without due process of law.

earmarks Special spending projects that are set aside on behalf of individual members of Congress for their constituents.

economic liberty The belief that individuals should be allowed to pursue their economic self-interest without government restrictions.

economic sanctions Denial of export, import, or financial relations with a target country in an effort to change that nation's policies.

efficacy A sense of self-confidence in being able to produce a desired effect.

electoral college The electoral system used in electing the president and vice president, in which voters vote for electors pledged to cast their ballots for a particular party's candidates.

eminent domain The power of a government to take private property for public use; the U.S. Constitution gives national and state governments this power and requires them to provide just compensation for property so taken.

entitlement program Programs such as unemployment insurance, disaster relief, or disability payments that provide benefits to all eligible citizens.

entitlements Programs such as unemployment insurance, disaster relief, or disability payments that provide benefits to all eligible citizens.

enumerated powers The powers explicitly given to Congress in the Constitution.

environmental impact statement A statement required by federal law from all agencies for any project using federal funds to assess the potential effect of the new construction or development on the environment.

equal protection clause A clause in the Fourteenth Amendment that forbids any state to deny to any person within its jurisdiction the equal protection of the laws. By interpretation, the Fifth Amendment imposes the same limitation on the national government. This clause is the major constitutional restraint on the power of governments to discriminate against persons because of race, national origin, or sex.

equality of opportunity All individuals, regardless of race, gender, or circumstance have the opportunity to participate in politics, self-government, and the economy.

established clause A clause in the First Amendment that states that Congress shall make no law respecting an establishment of religion. The Supreme Court has interpreted this to forbid government support to any or all religions.

ethnicity A social division based on national origin, religion, language, and often race.

ethnocentrism Belief in the superiority of one's nation or ethnic group.

ex post facto law A retroactive criminal law that works to the disadvantage of a person.

excise tax A consumer tax on a specific kind of merchandise, such as tobacco.

exclusionary rule A requirement that evidence unconstitutionally or illegally obtained be excluded from a criminal trial.

executive agreement A formal agreement between the U.S. president and the leaders of other nations that does not require Senate approval.

Executive Office of the President The cluster of presidential staff agencies that help the president carry out his or her responsibilities. Currently, the office includes the Office of Management and Budget, the Council of Economic Advisers, and several other units.

executive order A directive issued by a president or governor that has the force of law.

executive privilege The power to keep executive communications confidential, especially if they relate to national security.

extradition The legal process whereby an alleged criminal offender is surrendered by the officials of one state to officials of the state in which the crime is alleged to have been committed.

faction A term the founders used to refer to political parties and special interests or interest groups.

Federal Election Commission (FEC) A commission created by the 1974 amendments to the Federal Election Campaign Act to administer election reform laws. It consists of six commissioners appointed by the president and confirmed by the Senate. Its duties include overseeing disclosure of campaign finance information, public funding of presidential elections, and enforcing contribution limits.

federal funds rate The amount of interest banks charge for loans to each other.

federal mandate A requirement the national government imposes as a condition for receiving federal funds.

Federal Register An official document, published every weekday, that lists the new and proposed regulations of executive departments and regulatory agencies.

Federal Reserve System The system created by Congress in 1913 to establish banking practices and regulate currency in circulation and the amount of credit available. It consists of 12 regional banks supervised by the Board of Governors. Often simply called "the Fed."

federalism A constitutional arrangement in which power is distributed between a central government and subdivisional governments, called states in the United States. The national and the subdivisional governments both exercise direct authority over individuals.

Federalists Supporters of ratification of the Constitution and of a strong central government.

The Federalist Essays promoting ratification of the Constitution, published anonymously by Alexander Hamilton, John Jay, and James Madison in 1787 and 1788.

felony A serious crime, the penalty for which can range from imprisonment in a penitentiary for more than a year to death.

fighting words Words that by their very nature inflict injury on those to whom they are addressed or incite them to acts of violence.

filibuster A procedural practice in the Senate whereby a senator refuses to relinquish the floor and thereby delays proceedings and prevents a vote on a controversial issue.

fiscal policy Government policy that attempts to manage the economy by controlling taxing and spending.

free exercise clause A clause in the First Amendment that states that Congress shall make no law prohibiting the free exercise of religion.

free rider An individual who does not join a group representing his or her interests yet receives the benefit of the group's influence.

freedom of religion The belief that individuals living in a society should be free to exercise their personal religious convictions without government restrictions.

full faith and credit clause The clause in the Constitution (Article IV, Section 1) requiring each state to recognize the civil judgments rendered by the courts of the other states and to accept their public records and acts as valid.

fundamentalists Conservative Christians who as a group have become more active in politics in the last two decades and were especially influential in the 2000 and 2004 presidential election.

gender gap The difference between the political opinions or political behavior of men and of women.

General Agreement on Tariffs and Trade (GATT) An international trade organization with more than 130 members that seeks to encourage free trade by lowering tariffs and other trade restrictions.

general election Elections in which voters elect officeholders.

general property tax A tax levied by local and some state governments on real property or personal, tangible property, the major portion of which is on the estimated value of one's home and land.

Gentrification A process where relatively wealthier people buy property in poorer areas of a city and relocate there, which results in revitalization of the area and increased property values but is often accompanied by displacing the poor.

gerrymandering The drawing of legislative district boundaries to benefit a party, group, or incumbent.

government The processes and institutions through which binding decisions are made for society.

government corporation A government agency that operates like a business corporation, created to secure greater freedom of action and flexibility for a particular program.

grand jury A jury of 12 to 23 persons, depending on state and local requirements, who privately hear evidence presented by the government to determine whether persons shall be required to stand trial. If the jury believes there is sufficient evidence that a crime was committed, it issues an indictment.

gross domestic product (GDP) The total output of all economic activity in the nation, including goods and services.

hard money Political contributions given to a party, candidate, or interest group that are limited in amount and fully disclosed. Raising such limited funds was harder than raising unlimited soft money, hence the term "hard money."

hard power Reliance on economic and military strength to solve international problems.

Hatch Act A federal statute barring federal employees from active participation in certain kinds of politics and protecting them from being fired on partisan grounds.

heightened scrutiny test This test has been applied when a law classifies based on sex; to be upheld; the law must meet an important government interest.

honeymoon The period at the beginning of a new president's term during which the president enjoys generally positive relations with press and Congress, usually lasting about six months.

horse race A close contest; by extension, any contest in which the focus is on who is ahead and by how much rather than on substantive differences between the candidates.

idealism A theory of international relations that focuses on the hope that nations will act together to solve international problems and promote peace.

impeachment A formal accusation by the lower house of a legislature against a public official; the first step in removal from office.

implementation The process of putting a law into practice through bureaucratic rules or spending.

implied powers Powers inferred from the express powers that allow Congress to carry out its functions.

impoundment Presidential refusal to allow an agency to spend funds that Congress authorized and appropriated.

in forma pauperis A petition that allows a party to file "as a pauper" and avoid paying Court fees.

incremental policy Small adjustments to existing public policies.

incumbent The current holder of elected office.

independent expenditures The Supreme Court has ruled that individuals, groups, and parties can spend unlimited amounts in campaigns for or against candidates as long as they operate independently from the candidate. When an individual, group, or party does so, they are making an independent expenditure.

independent regulatory commission A government agency or commission regulatory power whose independence is protected by Congress.

independent stand-alone agency A government agency that operates outside a traditional government department, but under the president's direct control.

indexing Providing automatic increases to compensate for inflation.

indictment A formal written statement from a grand jury charging an individual with an offense; also called a *true bill*.

individualism The moral, political, and ethical philosophy of life that emphasizes individual rights, effort, and independence.

inflation A rise in the general price level (and decrease in dollar value) owing to an increase in the volume of money and credit in relation to available goods.

information affidavit Certification by a public prosecutor that there is evidence to justify bringing named individuals to trial.

inherent powers The powers of the national government in foreign affairs that the Supreme Court has declared do not depend on constitutional grants but rather grow out of the very existence of the national government.

initiative A procedure whereby a certain number of voters may, by petition, propose a law or constitutional amendment and have it submitted to the voters.

intensity A measure of how strongly an individual holds a particular opinion.

interest group A collection of people who share a common interest or attitude and seek to influence government for specific ends. Interest groups usually work within the framework of government and try to achieve their goals through tactics such as lobbying.

internationalism The belief that nations must engage in international problem solving.

interstate compact An agreement among two or more states. Congress must approve most such agreements.

iron triangle A policy-making instrument composed of a tightly related alliance of a congressional committee, interest groups, and federal department or agency.

isolationism The desire to avoid international engagement altogether.

issue advocacy Promoting a particular position or an issue paid for by interest groups or individuals but no candidates. Much issue advocacy is often electioneering for or against a candidate, avoiding words like "vote for," and until 2004 had not been subject to any regulation.

issue network Relationships among interest groups, congressional committees and subcommittees, and the government agencies that share a common policy concern.

issue-attention cycle The movement of public opinion toward public policy from initial enthusiasm for action to realization of costs and a decline in interest.

Jim Crow laws State laws formerly pervasive throughout the South requiring public facilities and accommodations to be segregated by race; ruled unconstitutional.

joint committee A committee composed of members of both the House of Representatives and the Senate; such committees oversee the Library of Congress and conduct investigations.

judicial activism A philosophy that judges should strike down laws that are inconsistent with norm and values state or implied in the Constitution.

judicial interpretation A method by which judges modify the force of a constitutional provision by reinterpreting its meaning.

judicial restraint A philosophy proposing that judges should strike down the actions of the elected branches only if they clearly violate the literal meaning of the Constitution.

judicial review The power of a court to refuse to enforce a law or a government regulation in the opinion of the judges conflicts with the U.S. Constitution or, in a state court, the state constitution.

justiciable dispute A dispute growing out of an actual case or controversy that is capable of settlement by legal methods.

Keynesian economics An economic theory based on the principles of John Maynard Keynes stating that government spending should increase during business slumps and be curbed during booms.

labor injunction A court order forbidding specific individuals or groups from performing certain acts (such as striking) that the court considers harmful to the rights and property of an employer or a community.

laissez-faire economics A theory that opposes governmental interference in economic affairs beyond what is necessary to protect life and property.

latency Political opinions that are held but not yet expressed.

leadership PAC A PAC formed by an office-holder that collects contributions form individuals other PACs and then makes contributions to other candidates and political parties.

libel Written defamation of another person. For public officials and public figures, the constitutional tests designed to restrict libel actions are especially rigid.

liberalism A belief that government can and should achieve justice and equality of opportunity.

libertarianism An ideology that cherishes individual liberty and insists on minimal government, promoting a free market economy, a non-interventionist foreign policy, and an absence of regulation in moral, economic, and social life.

line item veto Presidential power to strike, or remove, specific items from a spending bill without vetoing the entire package; declared unconstitutional by Supreme Court.

literacy test A literacy requirement some states imposed as a condition of voting, generally used to disqualify black voters in the South; now illegal.

lobbying Engaging in activities aimed at influencing public officials, especially legislators, and the policies they enact.

lobbyist A person who is employed by and acts for an organized interest group or corporation to try to influence policy decisions and positions in the executive and legislative branches.

logrolling Mutual aid and vote trading among legislators.

majority The candidate or party that wins more than half the votes cast in an election.

majority leader The legislative leader selected by the majority party who helps plan party strategy, confers with the other party leaders, and tries to keep members of the party in line.

majority rule Governance according to the expressed preferences of the majority.

majority-minority district A legislative district created to include a majority of minority voters; ruled constitutional as long as race is not the main factor in redistricting.

malapportionment Having legislative districts with unequal populations.

mandate A president's claim of broad public support.

mandatory spending Required spending under the federal budget.

manifest destiny A notion held by nineteenth-century Americans that the United States was destined to rule the continent, from the Atlantic to the Pacific.

manifest opinion A widely shared and consciously held view, such as support for abortion rights or for homeland security.

margin of error The range of percentage points in which the sample accurately reflects the population.

mass media Means of communication that reach the public, including newspapers and magazines, radio, television (broadcast, cable, and satellite), films, recordings, books, and electronic communication.

Mayflower Compact A governing document created by the members of the *Mayflower* to temporarily establish self-government in the Mayflower Colonies in America.

Mayor-council charter The oldest and most common form of city government, consisting of either a weak mayor and a city council or a strong mayor elected by voters and council.

means-tested entitlements Programs such as Medicaid and welfare under which applicants must meet eligibility requirements based on need.

Medicaid A federal program that provides medical benefits for low-income people.

Medicare A national health insurance program for the elderly and disabled.

merit system A system of public employment in which selection and promotion depend on demonstrated performance rather than political patronage.

Merit Systems Protection Board An independent agency that oversees and protects merit in the federal government personnel system.

Metropolis A large city or municipality that serves as an economic and cultural center for a region.

Metropolitan area The larger area surrounding a metropolis that is heavily influenced by the metropolis, generally consisting of suburbs and other smaller cities.

midterm election Elections held midway between presidential elections.

minority leader The legislative leader selected by the minority party as spokesperson for the opposition.

minor party A small political party that persists over time, is often composed of ideologies on the right or left, or is centered on a charismatic candidate. Such a part is also called a *third party*.

misdemeanor A minor crime; the penalty is a fine or imprisonment for a short time, usually less than a year, in a local jail.

Missouri Plan A system for selecting judges that combines features of the appointive and elective methods. The governor selects judges from list presented by panels of lawyers and laypersons, and at the end of their term. the judges may run against their own record in retention elections.

monetary policy Government policy that attempts to manage the economy by controlling the money supply and thus interest rates.

monopoly Domination of an industry by a single company; also the company that dominates the industry.

movement A large body of people interested in a common issue, idea, or concern that is of continuing significance and who are willing to take action. Movements seek to change attitudes or institutions, not just policies.

multilateralism A philosophy that encourages individual nations to act together to solve international problems.

municipality A local level of government within counties that are usually organized around population centers.

name recognition Incumbents have an advantage over challengers in election campaigns because voters are more familiar with them, and incumbents are more recognizable.

national debt The total amount of money the federal government has borrowed to finance deficit spending throughout the year.

national party convention A national meeting of delegates elected in primaries, caucuses, or state conventions who assemble once every four years to nominate candidates for president and vice president, ratify the party platform, elect officers, and adopt rules.

national supremacy A constitutional doctrine that whenever conflict occurs between the constitutionally authorized actions of the national government and those of a state or local government, the actions of the national government prevail.

national tide The inclination to focus on national issues, rather than local issues, in an election campaign. The impact of a national tide can be reduced by the nature of the candidates on the ballot who may have differentiated themselves from their party or its leader if the tide is negative, as well as competition in the election.

nationalism An enduring sense of national identity or consciousness that derives from cultural, historic, linguistic, or political forces.

natural law God's or nature's law that defines right from wrong and is higher than human law.

natural rights The rights of all people to dignity and worth; also called *human rights*.

naturalization A legal action conferring citizenship on an alien.

necessary and proper clause The clause in the Constitution (Article 1, Section 8, Clause 3) setting forth the implied powers of Congress. It states that Congress, in addition to its express powers, has the right to make all laws necessary and proper to carry out all powers the Constitution vests in the national government.

New Jersey Plan The proposal at the Constitutional Convention made by William Paterson of New Jersey for a central government with a single-house legislature in which each state would be represented equally.

new judicial federalism The practice of some state courts using the bill of rights in their state constitutions to provide more protection for some rights than is provided by the Supreme Court's interpretation of the Bill of Rights in the U.S. Constitution.

news media Media that emphasize the news

nondecision A decision not to move ahead with the policy process. In short, it is a decision not to decide.

nongovernmental organization (NGO) A nonprofit association or group operating outside government that advocates and pursues policy objectives.

nonpartisan election An election in which candidates are not selected or endorsed by political parties and party affiliation is not listed on ballots.

normal trade relations Trade status granted as part of an international trade policy that gives a nation the same favorable concessions and tariffs that the best trading partners receive.

North American Free Trade Agreement (NAFTA) An agreement signed by the United States, Canada, and Mexico in 1992 to form the largest free trade zone in the world.

obscenity The quality or state of a work that, taken as a whole, appeals to a prurient interest in sex by depicting sexual conduct in a patently offensive way and that lacks serious literary, artistic, political, or scientific value.

office block ballot A ballot on which all candidate are listed under the office for which they are running.

Office of Management and Budget (OMB) The presidential staff agency that serves as a clearinghouse for budgetary requests and management improvements for government agencies.

Office of Personnel Management (OPM) An agency that administers civil service laws, rules, and regulations.

one-party state A state in which one party wins all or nearly all of the offices and the other party receives only a small proportion of the popular vote.

open primary A primary election in which any voter, regardless of party, may vote.

open rule A procedural rule in the House of Representatives that permits floor amendments within the overall time allocated to the bill.

open shop A company with a labor agreement under which union membership cannot be required as a condition of employment.

opinion of the Court An explanation of a decision of the Supreme Court or any other appellate court.

originalist approach An approach to constitutional interpretation that envisions the document as having a fixed meaning that might be determined by a strict reading of the text of framers' intent.

original jurisdiction The authority of a court to hear a case "in the first instance."

outsourcing Contracting of government services to private firms.

override An action taken by Congress to reverse a presidential veto, requiring two-thirds majority in each chamber.

oversight Legislative or executive review of a particular government program or organization that can be in response to a crisis of some kind or part of routine review.

parliamentary government A form of government in which the legislature selects the prime minister or the president.

partisanship Strong allegiance to one's own political party, often leading to unwillingness to compromise with members of the opposing party.

party caucus A meeting of the members of a party in a legislative chamber to select party leaders and to develop party policy. Called a *conference* by the Republicans.

party column ballot A type of ballot that encourages party-line voting by listing all of a party's candidates in a column under the party name.

party convention A meeting of party delegates to vote on matters of policy and, in some cases, to select part candidates for public office.

party identification An informal and subjective affiliation with a political party that most people acquire in childhood.

party-independent expenditures Spending by political party committees that is independent of the candidate. The spending occurs in relatively few competitive contests and is often substantial.

party registration The act of declaring party affiliation; required by some states when one registers to vote.

patriotism Devotion to one's own country, often seeing it as better or stronger than other countries.

patronage The dispensing of government jobs to persons who belong to the winning political party.

petit jury A jury of 6 to 12 persons that determines quilt or innocence in a civil or criminal action.

plaintiff The party instigating a civil lawsuit.

plea bargain An agreement between a prosecutor and a defendant that the defendant will plead guilty to a lesser offense to avoid having to stand trial for a more serious offense.

pluralism A theory of government holds that open, multiple, and competing groups can check the asserted power by any one group.

plurality The candidate or party with the most votes cast in an election, not necessarily more than half.

pocket veto A veto exercised by the president after Congress has adjourned; if the president takes no action for ten days, the bill does not become law and is not returned to Congress for a possible override.

police powers Inherent powers of state governments to pass laws to protect public health, safety, and welfare; the national government has no directly granted police powers but accomplishes the same goals through other delegated powers.

policy agenda The list of issues that the federal government pays attention to.

policy makers Individuals and groups that make the actual choices to create a public policy.

political action committee (PAC) The political arm of an interest group that is legally entitled to raise funds on a voluntary basis from members, stockholders, or employees to contribute funds to candidates or political parties.

political culture The widely shared beliefs, values, and norms about how citizens relate to government and to one another.

political ideology A consistent pattern of beliefs about political values and the role of government.

political party An organization that seeks political power by electing people to office so that its positions and philosophy become public policy.

political predisposition A characteristic of individuals that is predictive of political behavior.

political science An academic discipline that studies the theory and practice of politics and government. It is one of the socials sciences that use data and methods that overlap with Anthropology, Economics, Geography, History, Psychology, and Sociology.

politician An individual who participates in politics and government, often in the service of a group or political community.

politics The interaction of the people and their government, including citizens, interest groups, political parties, and the institutions of government at all levels. Politics is concerned with who gets what, when, where, and how from government.

poll tax Tax required to vote; prohibited for national elections by the Twenty-Fourth Amendment (1964) and ruled unconstitutional for all elections in *Harper* v. *Board of Elections* (1966).

popular consent The idea that a just government must derive its powers from the consent of the people it governs.

popular sovereignty A belief that ultimate power resides in the people.

power elite A group composed of community, business, and other leaders who determine public policy or block changes in policy without themselves necessarily holding office.

precedent A decision made by a higher court such as a circuit court of appeals or the Supreme Court that is binding on all other federal courts.

preemption The right of a national law or regulation to preclude enforcement of a state or local law or regulation.

preferred position doctrine An interpretation of the First Amendment that holds that freedom of expressions is so essential to democracy that governments should not punish person for what they say, only what they do.

president pro tempore An officer of the Senate selected by the majority party to act as chair in the absence of the vice president.

presidential election Elections held in years when the president is on the ballot.

presidential support score The percentage of times a president wins on key votes in Congress.

presidential ticket The joint listing of the presidential and vice presidential candidates on the same ballot, as required by the Twelfth Amendment.

primary elections Elections in which voter choose party nominees.

prior restraint Censorship imposed before a speech is made or a newspaper is published; usually presumed to be unconstitutional.

privatization Contracting public services to private organizations.

pro bono To serve the public good; a tern used to describe work that lawyers (or other professionals) do for which they receive no fees.

procedural due process A constitutional requirement that governments proceed by proper methods; limits how government may exercise power.

professional associations Groups of individuals who share a common profession and are often organized for common political purposes related to the profession.

progressive tax A tax graduated so that people with higher incomes pay a larger fraction of their income than people with lower incomes.

property rights The rights of an individual to own, use, rent, invest, buy, and sell property.

proportional representation An election system in which each party running receives the proportion of legislative seats corresponding to its proportion of the vote.

prosecutor Government lawyer who tries criminal cases, often referred to as a district attorney or a U.S. Attorney.

prospective issue voting Voting based on what a candidate pledges to do in the future about an issue if elected.

protectionism A policy of erecting trade barriers to protect domestic industry.

public assistance Aid to the poor, "welfare."

public choice Synonymous with "collective action," specifically studies how government officials, politicians, and voter respond to positive and negative incentives.

public defender system An arrangement whereby public officials are hired to provide legal assistance to people accused of crimes who are unable to hire their own attorneys.

public financing laws Laws authorizing grants of government funds to qualifying candidates for elective office, to be used in their campaigns.

public opinion The distribution of individuals preferences for or evaluations of a given issue, candidate, or institution within a specific population.

public policy A specific course of action that government takes to address a problem.

punctuating policy Radical changes to public policy that occur only after the mobilization of large segments of society to demand action.

race A grouping of human beings with distinctive characteristics determined by genetic inheritance.

racial gerrymandering The drawing of election districts so as to ensure that members of certain race are a minority in the district; ruled unconstitutional in *Gomillion* v. *Lightfoot* (1960)

rally point A rise in public approval of the president that follows a crisis as Americans "rally round the flag" and the chief executive.

random sample In this type of sample, every individual has a known and equal chance of being selected.

rational basis test A standard developed by the courts to test the constitutionality of a law; when applied, a law is constitutional as long as it meets a reasonable government interest.

realigning election An election during periods of expanded suffrage and change in the economy and society that proves to be a turning point, redefining the agenda of politics and the alignment of voters within parties.

realism A theory of international relations that focuses on the tendency of nations to operate from self-interest.

reapportionment The assigning by Congress of congressional seats after each census. State legislatures reapportion state legislative districts.

recall A procedure for submitting to popular vote the removal of officials from office before the end of their term.

recall elections A procedure for submitting to popular vote the removal of officials from office before the end of their term.

recess appointment Presidential appointment made without Senate confirmation during Senate recess.

recidivist A repeat offender.

recuse To withdraw from participating in making a ruling to avoid any actual or perceived partiality or bias.

redistributive policy A policy that provides to one group of society while taking away benefits from another through policy solution such as tax increases to pay for job training.

redistricting The redrawing of congressional and other legislative district lines following the census, to accommodate population shifts and keep districts as equal as possible in population.

reduction veto The power of governors in a few states to reduce a particular appropriation.

referendum A procedure for submitting to popular vote measures passed by the legislature or proposed amendments to a state constitution.

regressive tax A tax whereby people with lower incomes pay a higher fraction of their income than people with higher incomes.

regulation A policy that encourages or discourages certain behavior by imposing a legally binding rule. Rules are made through a long process that begins with an act of Congress and ends with issuance of a final rule.

regulatory taking A government regulation that effectively takes land by restricting its use, even if its remains in the owner's name.

reinforcing cleavages Divisions within a society that cut across demographic categories to produce groups that are more heterogeneous or different.

representative democracy Government in which the people elect those who govern and pass laws; also called a *republic*.

reserve powers All powers not specifically delegated to the national government by the Constitution. The reserve power can be found in the Tenth Amendment to the Constitution.

responsibility contract A welfare strategy adopted by some states in which recipients sign a written agreement specifying their responsibilities and outlining a plan for obtaining work and achieving self-sufficiency.

restrictive covenant A provision in a deed to real property prohibiting its sale to a person of a particular race or religion. Judicial enforcement of such deeds is unconstitutional.

retention elections Elections where judges run uncontested for reelection and voters simply vote for or again them in office.

retrospective issue voting Holding incumbents, usually the president's party, responsible for their records on issues, such as the economy or foreign policy.

reverse distributive policy A policy that reduces benefits for all groups such as tax increases in society, often by imposing rules that govern everyone.

revision commission A state commission that recommends changes in the state constitution for action by legislature and vote by the voters.

revolving door An employment cycle in which individuals who work for government agencies that regulate interests eventually end up working for interest groups or businesses with the same policy concern.

rider A provision attached to a bill—to which it may or may not be related—in order to secure its passage or defeat.

right of expatriation The right to renounce one's citizenship.

rule A precise statement of how a law is implemented.

rural Sparsely populated territory and small towns, often associated with farming.

safe seat An elected office that is predictably won by one party or the other, so the success of that party's candidate is almost taken for granted.

sales tax A general tax on sales transactions, sometimes exempting such items as food and drugs.

salience An individual's belief that an issue is important or relevant to him or her.

search warrant A write issued by a magistrate that authorizes the police to search a particular place or person, specifically the place to be searched and the objects to be seized.

selective exposure The process by which individuals screen out messages that do not conform to their own biases.

selective incorporation The process by which provisions of the Bill of Rights are brought within the scope of the Fourteenth Amendment and so applied to state and local governments.

selective perception The process by which individuals perceive what they want in media messages.

senatorial courtesy The presidential custom of submitting the names of prospective appointees for approval to senators from the states in which the appointees are to work.

Senior Executive Service Established by Congress in 1978 as a flexible, mobile corps of senior career executives who work closely with presidential appointees to manage government.

seniority rule A legislative practice that assigns the chair of a committee or subcommittee to the member of the majority party with the longest continuous service on the committee.

separation of powers Constitutional division of powers among the legislative, executive, and judicial branches, with the legislative branch making law, the executive applying and enforcing the law, and the judiciary interpreting the law.

severance tax A tax on the privilege of "severing" such natural resources as coal, oil, timber, and gas from the land.

Shays' Rebellion A rebellion led by Daniel Shays of farmers in western Massachusetts in 1786-1787 protesting mortgage foreclosures. It highlighted the need for a strong national government just as the call for a Constitutional Convention went out.

signing statements A formal document that explains why a president is signing a particular bill into law. These statements may contain objections to the bill and promises not to implement key sections.

single-member district An electoral district in which voters choose one representative or official.

Speaker The presiding officer in the House of Representatives, formally elected by the House but actually selected by the majority party.

special elections Elections in which voters decide on ballet initiatives, vote on statewide constitutional changes or new constitutions, or elect a senator or representative to replace one who has died or resigned.

special or select committee A congressional committee created for a specific purpose, sometimes to conduct an investigation.

split ticket A vote for some of one party's candidates and some of another party's.

social capital Democratic and civil habits discussion, compromise, and respect for differences, which grow out of participation in voluntary organizations.

social contract An agreement whereby individuals voluntarily commit to establish a government that will protect the common interests of all.

social insurance Programs in which eligibility is based on prior contributions to government, usually in the form of payroll taxes.

social safety net The many programs that the federal government provides to protect Americans against economic and social misfortune.

Social Security A combination of entitlement programs, paid for by employer and employee taxes, that includes retirement benefits, health insurance, and support for disabled workers and the children of deceased or disabled workers.

social stratification Divisions in a community among socioeconomic groups or classes.

socialism An economic and governmental system based on public ownership of the means of production and exchange.

socioeconomic status (SES) A division of population based on occupation, income, and education.

soft money Money raised in unlimited amounts by political parties for party-building purposes. Now largely illegal except for limited contributions to state and local parties for voter registration and get-out-the-vote efforts.

soft power Reliance on diplomacy and negotiation to solve international problems.

solicitor general The third-ranking official in the Department of Justice who is responsible for representing the United States in cases before the U.S. Supreme Court.

spoils system A system of public employment based on rewarding party loyalists and friends.

stagflation A combination of an economic slowdown (stagnation) and a rise in prices (inflation).

standing committee A permanent committee established in a legislature, usually focusing on a policy area.

stare decisis The rule of precedent, whereby a rule or law contained in a judicial decision is commonly viewed as binding on judges whenever the same question is presented.

State of the Union Address The president's annual statement to Congress and the nation.

states' rights Powers expressly or implicitly reserved to the states.

statism The idea that the rights of the nation are supreme over the rights of the individuals who make up the nation.

straight ticket A vote for all of one party's candidates.

strict scrutiny test A test applied by the court when a classification is based on race; the government must show that there is a compelling reason for the law and no other less restrictive way to meet the interest.

strong mayor-council form A form of local government in which the voters directly elect the city council and the mayor, who enjoys nearly total administrative authority and appoints the department heads.

substantive due process A constitutional requirement that governments act reasonably and that the substance of the laws themselves be fair and reasonable; limits what a government may be.

suburban An area that typically surrounds the central city, is often residential, and is not as densely populated.

suffrage The right to vote.

Sun Belt The region of the United States in the South and Southwest that has seen population growth relative to the rest of the country and which, because of its climate has attracted retirees.

Supreme Court The court of last resort in the United States. It can hear appeals from federal circuit courts or state high courts.

take care clause The constitutional requirement (in Article II, Section 3) that presidents take care that the laws are faithfully executed, even if they disagree with the purpose of those laws.

tariff A tax levied on imports to help protect a nation's industries, labor, or farmers from foreign competition. It can also be used to raise additional revenue.

tax expenditure A loss of tax revenue due to federal laws that provide special tax incentives or benefits to individuals or businesses.

Temporary Assistance for Needy Families (TANF) A federal welfare reform law that replaced Aid to Families with Dependent Children, the 60-year-old assistance program for poor families with children. This 1996 law strengthened work requirements for recipients, limited the time that families can receive benefits, and gave states flexibility to develop service programs supporting work, marriage, and self-sufficiency.

theocracy Government by religious leaders, who claim divine guidance.

theory of deterrence A theory that is based on creating enough military strength to persuade other nations not to attack first.

think tank A nongovernmental organization that seeks to influence public policy through research and education.

three-fifths compromise The compromise between northern and southern states at the Constitutional Convention that three-fifths of the slave population would be counted for determining direct taxation and representation in the House of Representatives.

township A local level of government below the county used primarily in 20 northeastern states.

trade deficit An imbalance in international trade in which the value of imports exceeds the value of exports.

treaty A formal, public agreement between the United States and one or more nations that must be approved by two-thirds of the Senate.

trust A monopoly that controls good and services, often in combinations that reduce competition.

trustee An official who is expected to vote independently based on his or her judgment of the circumstances; one interpretation of the role of the legislator.

turnout The proportion of the voting-age public that votes, sometimes defined as the number of registered voters that vote.

two-party state A state in which the two major parties alternate in winning majorities.

uncontrollable spending The portion of the federal budget that is spent on previously enacted programs, such as Social Security, that the president and Congress are unwilling to cut.

unemployment The number of Americans who are out of work but actively looking for a job. The number does not usually include those who are not looking.

unicameral legislature A one-house legislature.

unilateralism A philosophy that encourages individual nations to act on their own when facing threats from other nations.

union shop A company in which new employees must join a union within a stated time period.

unitary system A constitutional arrangement that concentrates power in a central government.

universe The groups of people whose preferences we try to measure by taking a sample; also called population.

unprotected speech Libel, obscenity, fighting words, and commercial speech, which are not entitled to constitutional protection in all circumstances.

urban A densely settled territory that is often the central part of a city of metropolitan area.

U.S. attorney general The chief law enforcement officer in the United States and the head of the Department of Justice.

value-added tax (VAT) A tax on the increased value of a product at each stage of production and distribution rather than just at the point of sale.

vesting clause The president's constitutional authority to control most executive functions.

veto A formal decision to reject a bill passed by Congress.

Virginia Plan The initial proposal at the Constitutional Convention made by the Virginia delegation for a strong central government with a bicameral legislature dominated by the big states.

voter registration A system designed to reduce voter fraud by limiting voting to those who have established eligibility to vote by submitting the proper documents, including proof of residency.

voter turnout The proportion of the voting-age public that votes.

vouchers Money provided by the government to parents for payment of their children's tuition in a public or private school of their choice.

weak mayor-council form A form of local government in which the members of the city council select the mayor, who then shares power with other elected or appointed boards and commissions.

weapons of mass destruction Biological, chemical, or nuclear weapons that can cause a massive number of deaths in a single use.

whip The party leader who is the liaison between the leadership and the rank-and-file in the legislature.

white primary A Democratic party primary in the old "one–party South" that was limited to white people and essentially constituted an election; ruled unconstitutional in *Smith* v. *Allwright* (1944).

winner-take-all system An election system in which the candidate with the most votes wins.

women's suffrage The right of women to vote.

workfare A welfare strategy adopted by some states that gives able-bodied adults who do not have preschool-aged children the opportunity to learn job skills that can lead to employment.

World Trade Organization (WTO) An international organization derived from the General Agreement on Tariffs and Trade (GATT) that promotes free trade around the world.

write of certiorari A formal writ used to bring a case before the Supreme Court.

writ of *habeas corpus* A court order requiring explanation to a judge why a prisoner is being held custody.

writ of mandamus A court order directing an official to perform an official duty.

zero-sum games A policy that takes away exactly as much in benefits as another group gains.

NOTES

Introduction

1. Dwight B. Heath, ed., *Mourt's Relation: A Journal of the Pilgrims at Plymouth* (Bedford, MA: Applewood Books, 1963), p. 17.
2. November 11, 1620 on the Julian calendar would be on our present-day Gregorian calendar November 21, 1620.
3. Donald McQuade, Robert Atwan, Martha Banta, Justin Kaplan, David Minter, and Robert Stepto, *The Harper American Literature* (New York: Longman, 1998); John T. Wheelwright, *The Mayflower Pilgrims: Being a Condescension in the Original Wording and Spelling of the Story Written by Gov. William Bradford* (Boston: McGrath-Sherrill Press, 1930).
4. Nathaniel Philbrick, *Mayflower: A Story of Courage, Community, and War* (New York: Penguin Group, 2006), p. 42.
5. Ibid, p. 352.
6. Michael Kammen, *Mystic Chords of Memory: The Transformation of Tradition in American Culture* (New York: Vintage Books, 1993).
7. Louis Hartz, *The Liberal Tradition in America* (New York: Harcourt, Brace, and World, Inc., 1955), pp. 48–49.
8. Crispin Gill, *Mayflower Remembered: A History of the Plymouth Pilgrims* (New York: Taplinger Publishing, 1970), p. 155; Michael Kammen, *Mystic Chords of Memory: The Transformation of Tradition in American Culture* (New York: Vintage Books, 1993), p. 64.
9. Michael Kammen, *Mystic Chords of Memory: The Transformation of Tradition in American Culture* (New York: Vintage Books, 1993).
10. Mayflower Compact (1620), http://avalon. law.yale.edu/17th_century/mayflower.asp (accessed February 9, 2010).
11. Louis Hartz, *The Liberal Tradition in America* (New York: Harcourt, Brace, and World, Inc., 1955), p. 63; see also Jack Citrin, "Political Culture," in Peter H. Schuck and James Q. Wilson, eds., *Understanding America: The Anatomy of an Exceptional Nation* (New York City, NY: Public Affairs, 2008), pp. 147–148.
12. Jack Citrin, "Political Culture," p. 162.
13. Ibid, p. 170.
14. Benjamin M. Friedman, "The Economic System," in Peter H. Shuck and James Q. Wilson, eds., *Understanding America: The Anatomy of an Exceptional Nation* (New York: Public Affairs, 2008), p. x.
15. See Roger Smith, *Civic Ideals: Conflicting Visions of Citizenship in U.S. History* (Michigan: Book Crafters, 1997).
16. Carl J. Richard, *The Founders and the Classics: Greece, Rome, and the American Enlightenment* (Harvard University Press, 1995).
17. "Essex Result," *The Founders' Constitution*, April 29, 1778, http://press-pubs.uchicago. edu/founders/documents/v1ch4s8.html (accessed December 1, 2009).
18. John Locke, "The Second Treatise of Civil Government," http://www.constitution. org/jl/2ndtreat.htm (accessed May 20, 2010) (Chapter 7, Section 87, 2nd Treatise).
19. "Locke's Political Philosophy," *Stanford Encyclopedia of Philosophy*, November 9, 2005, http://plato.stanford.edu/entries/locke-political/ (accessed December 1, 2009).

20. Louis Hartz, *The Liberal Tradition in America*, pp. 60–61.
21. John Locke, "The Second Treatise of Civil Government," http://www.constitution. org/jl/2ndtreat.htm (accessed May 20, 2010) (Chapter 7, section 87, 2nd Treatise).
22. Frederick G. Whelan, *Hume and Machiavelli: Political Realism and Liberal Thought* (Lanham: Lexington Books, 2005), p. 43.
23. Jean-Jacques Rousseau, "The Social Contract," http://www.constitution.org/jjr/socon_03.htm (accessed May 20, 2010).
24. Peter H. Shuck and James Q. Wilson, eds., *Understanding America: The Anatomy of an Exceptional Nation* (New York, NY: Public Affairs, 2008), p. x.
25. The Declaration of Independence (1776).
26. James Madison, "The Federalist #10," in *The Federalist Papers* (New York: Penguin Books, 1987), p. 3.
27. James Madison, "The Federalist #51," in *The Federalist Papers* (New York: Penguin Books, 1987), p. 1.
28. We do not enter here into the famous debate in the philosophy of science about "normal science," "paradigm shifts," etc. Rather, we aspire to produce a text that details the foundation of what we do and do not know about the subject. See Thomas Kuhn, *The Structure of Scientific Revolutions*, 2d ed. (Chicago: University of Chicago Press, 1970), p. 1.
29. Robert Post, 2009, "Debating Disciplinarity," *Critical Inquiry*, 35 (Summer): 749–770.
30. Horace Mann, quoted in Gregory J. Fritzburg, "Schools Can't Do It Alone: A Broader Conception of Equality of Education," www.newhorizons.org/strategies/multicultur al/fritzberg.htm (accessed October 30, 2009). This quote is from Mann's Twelfth Annual Report as Secretary of Massachusetts State Board of Education, http://www.tncrimlaw. com/civil_bible/horace_mann.htm (accessed May 20, 2010).

Chapter 1

1. David Boaz, "The Man Who Would Not Be King," *CATO Institute*, February 20, 2006, www.cato.org/pub_display.php?pub_id= 5593 (accessed November 30, 2009).
2. Al Gore, speech delivered on December 13, 2000, www.cnn.com/ELECTION/2000/transcripts/ 121300/t651213.html.
3. Aristotle, *Politics* (Oxford University Press, 1998); and George Huxley, "On Aristotle's Best State," *History of Political Thought*, 6 (Summer 1985), pp. 139–149.
4. John Locke, *Two Treatises of Government and a Letter Concerning Toleration* (Yale University Press, 2003); and Virginia McDonald, "A Guide to the Interpretation of Locke the Political Theorist," *Canadian Journal of Political Science*, 6 (December 1973), pp. 602–623.
5. Thomas Hobbes, *Leviathan* (Oxford University Press, 1998); and Frank M. Coleman, "The Hobbesian Basis of American Constitutionalism," *Polity*, 7 (Autumn 1974), pp. 57–89.
6. Charles de Montesquieu, *The Spirit of the Laws* (Cambridge University Press, 1989);

and E. P. Panagopoulos, *Essays on the History and Meaning of Checks and Balances* (University Press of America, 1986).
7. *Reitman v. Mulkey*, 387 U.S. 369 (1967).
8. David B. Magleby, *Direct Legislation: Voting on Ballot Propositions in the United States* (Johns Hopkins University Press, 1984), p. 119.
9. Sheri Berman, "Civil Society and the Collapse of the Weimar Republic," *World Politics*, 49, No. 3 (April 1997), pp. 410–429.
10. Seymour Martin Lipset, "The Social Requisites of Democracy Revisited," *American Sociological Review*, 59 (1994), pp. 1–22.
11. For a discussion of the importance for democracy of such overlapping group memberships, see David Truman's seminal work, *The Governmental Process*, 2d ed. (Knopf, 1971).
12. Lesli J. Favor, *The Iroquois Constitution: A Primary Source Investigation of the Law of the Iroquois* (Rosen, 2003), p. 60.
13. Joyce Appleby, "The American Heritage: The Heirs and the Disinherited," *Journal of American History*, 74 (December 1987), p. 808.
14. Kevin Butterfield, "What You Should Know About the Declaration of Independence," *St. Louis Post-Dispatch*, July 4, 2000, p. F1.
15. Richard L. Hillard, "Liberalism, Civic Humanism, and the American Revolutionary Bill of Rights, 1775–1790," paper presented at the annual meeting of the Organization of American Historians, Reno, NV, March 26, 1988.
16. Robert W. Hoffert, *A Politics of Tensions: The Articles of Confederation and American Political Ideas* (University Press of Colorado, 1992); see also Merrill Jensen, *The Articles of Confederation: An Interpretation of the Social-Constitutional History of the American Revolution, 1774–1781* (University of Wisconsin Press, 1970).
17. *The Federalist*, No. 40.
18. Quoted in Charles L. Mee Jr., *The Genius of the People* (Harper & Row, 1987), p. 51.
19. Charles A. Beard, *An Economic Interpretation of the Constitution of the United States* (Macmillan, 1913).
20. Robert Brown, *Charles Beard and the Constitution: A Critical Analysis of "An Economic Interpretation of the Constitution"* (Princeton University Press, 1956).
21. Declaration of Congress, February 21, 1787; and Worthington C. Ford et al., eds., *Journals of the Continental Congress, 1774–1789*, 32 (Washington, DC, 1904–1937), p. 74.
22. Seymour Martin Lipset, "George Washington and the Founding of Democracy," *Journal of Democracy*, 9 (October 1998), p. 31.
23. David O. Stewart, *The Men Who Invented the Constitution: The Summer of 1787* (Simon & Schuster: NY, 2007).
24. See the essays in Thomas E. Cronin, ed., *Inventing the American Presidency* (University Press of Kansas, 1989); see also Richard J. Ellis, ed., *Founding the American Presidency* (Rowman & Littlefield, 1999).
25. David McKay, *American Politics and Society* (Wiley-Blackwell: Malden, MA, 2009); see also Saul Cornell "Aristocracy Assailed: The Ideology of Backcountry Anti-Federalism," *Journal of American History*, 76 (March),

p. 1156, www.jstor.org/stable/pdfplus/
2936593.pdf.

26. Charles A. Beard and Mary R. Beard, *A Basic History of the United States* (New Home Library, 1944), p. 136.

27. W. B. Allen and Gordon Lloyd, eds., *The Essential Antifederalist* (University Press of America, 1985), pp. xi–xiii.

28. See Herbert J. Storing, ed., abridgment by Murray Dry, *The Anti-Federalist: Writings by the Opponents of the Constitution* (University of Chicago Press, 1985).

29. On the role of the promised Bill of Rights amendments in the ratification of the Constitution, see Leonard W. Levy, *Constitutional Opinions* (Oxford University Press, 1986), Chapter 6.

Chapter 2

1. www.nationmaster.com.

2. *District of Columbia* v. *Heller*, 554 U.S. ___ (2008).

3. *McDonald* v. *Chicago*, ___ U.S. ___ (2010).

4. Sanford Levinson, *Constitutional Faith* (Princeton University Press, 1988), pp. 9–52.

5. Richard Morin, "We Love It—What We Know of It," *The Washington Post National Weekly Edition* (September 22, 1997), p. 35.

6. Alexander Hamilton, James Madison, and John Jay, in Clinton Rossiter, ed., *The Federalist Papers* (New American Library, 1961).

7. Quoted in Alpheus T. Mason, *The Supreme Court: Palladium of Freedom* (University of Michigan Press, 1962), p. 10.

8. Hamilton, Madison, and Jay, *The Federalist Papers.*

9. Ibid.

10. Ibid.

11. Justice Brandeis dissenting in *Myers* v. *United States*, 272 U.S. 52 (1926).

12. Charles O. Jones, "The Separate Presidency," in Anthony King, ed., *The New American Political System*, 2d ed. (AEI Press, 1990), p. 3.

13. Morris P. Fiorina, "An Era of Divided Government," *Political Science Quarterly* 107 (1992), p. 407.

14. David R. Mayhew, *Divided We Govern: Party Control, Lawmaking, and Investigations, 1946–1990* (Yale University Press, 1991), p. 4; see also James A. Thurber, ed., *Divided Democracy: Presidents and Congress in Cooperation and Conflict* (CQ Press, 1991).

15. Charles O. Jones, *Separate but Equal Branches: Congress and the Presidency* (Chatham House, 1995).

16. Judith A. Best, *The Choice of the People? Debating the Electoral College* (Rowman & Littlefield, 1996).

17. Michael Rothfeld and Patrick McGreevy, "Meg Whitman Sets Record Spending Pace in Campaign for Governor," *Los Angeles Times*, March 22, 2010.

18. James Risen and Eric Lichtblau. "Bush Lets U.S. Spy on Callers Without Courts," *New York Times*, December 16, 2005.

19. Hamilton, Madison, and Jay, *The Federalist Papers.*

20. See Alec Stone Sweet, Wayne Sandholtz, and Neil Fligstein, *The Institutionalization of Europe* (Oxford University Press, 2001); Alec Stone Sweet, *Governing with Judges: Constitutional Politics in Europe* (Oxford University Press, 2000); and Anne-Marie Slaughter, Alec Stone Sweet, and J.H.H. Weiler, *The European Court and National Courts—Doctrine, Jurisprudence: Legal Change in Its Social Context* (Hart, 1998).

21. *Marbury* v. *Madison*, 5 U. S. 137 (1803).

22. Dumas Malone, *Jefferson the President: First Term, 1801–1805* (Little, Brown, 1970), p. 145.

23. J. W. Peltason, *Federal Courts in the Political Process* (Random House, 1955).

24. Richard E. Neustadt, *Presidential Power* (Free Press, 1990), pp. 180–181.

25. *Marabury* v. *Madison*, 5 U.S. 137 (1803).

26. *Brown* v. *Board of Education*, 347 U.S. 483 (1954).

27. *Griswold* v. *Connecticut*, 381 U.S. 479 (1965).

28. *Texas* v. *Johnson*, 491 U.S. 397 (1989).

29. *United States* v. *Eichman*, 496 U.S. 310 (1990).

30. John A. Clark and Kevin T. McGuire, "Congress, the Supreme Court, and the Flag," *Political Research Quarterly* 49 (1996), pp. 771–781.

31. Senate Joint Resolution 12, 109th Congress, 2d session.

32. Ann Stuart Diamond, "A Convention for Proposing Amendments: The Constitution's Other Method," *Publius* 11 (Summer 1981), pp. 113–146; and Wilbur Edel, "Amending the Constitution by Convention: Myths and Realities," *State Government* 55 (1982), pp. 51–56.

33. Russell L. Caplan, *Constitutional Brinksmanship: Amending the Constitution by National Convention* (Oxford University Press, 1988), p. x; see also David E. Kyvig, *Explicit and Authentic Acts: Amending the U.S. Constitution, 1776–1995* (University Press of Kansas, 1996), p. 440.

34. Samuel S. Freedman and Pamela J. Naughton, *ERA: May a State Change Its Vote?* (Wayne State University Press, 1979).

35. Kyvig, *Explicit and Authentic Acts*, p. 286; and *Dillon* v. *Gloss*, 256 U.S. 368 (1921).

36. Mark R. Daniels, Robert Darcy, and Joseph W. Westphal, "The ERA Won—at Least in the Opinion Polls," *P.S.: Political Science and Politics* (Fall 1982), p. 583.

37. National Organization for Women, www.now.org/issues/economic/eratext.html.

38. Janet K. Boles, *The Politics of the Equal Rights Amendment: Conflict and Decision-Making Powers* (Longman, 1979), p. 4.

39. Gilbert Y. Steiner, *Constitutional Inequality: The Political Fortunes of the Equal Rights Amendment* (Brookings Institution Press, 1985), p. 64; see also Mary Frances Berry, *Why the ERA Failed: Politics, Women's Rights, and the Amending Process of the Constitution* (Indiana University Press, 1986).

Chapter 3

1. For further historical background, see Samuel J. Beer, *To Make a Nation: The Rediscovery of American Federalism* (Harvard University Press, 1993).

2. See "Eyes on the Road: States Crack Down on Texting While Driving," *State Health Notes*, 29, 523 (September 15, 2008), available at ncsl.org/default.aspx?tabid=14662.

3. William H. Stewart, *Concepts of Federalism* (Center for the Study of Federalism/University Press of America, 1984); see also Preston King, *Federalism and Federation*, 2d ed. (Cass, 2001).

4. Morton Grodzins, "The Federal System," in *Goals for Americans: The Report of the President's Commission on National Goals* (Columbia University Press, 1960).

5. Thomas R. Dye, *American Federalism: Competition Among Governments* (Lexington Books, 1990), pp. 13–17.

6. Michael D. Reagan and John G. Sanzone, *The New Federalism* (Oxford University Press, 1981), p. 175.

7. William H. Riker, *The Development of American Federalism* (Academic Press, 1987), pp. 14–15. Riker contends not only that federalism does not

guarantee freedom but also that the framers of our federal system, as well as those of other nations, were animated not by considerations of safeguarding freedom but by practical considerations of preserving unity.

8. U.S. Census Bureau, *Statistical Abstract of the United States* (Government Printing Office, 2007), p. 487.

9. Charles Evans Hughes, "War Powers Under the Constitution," *ABA Reports*, 62 (1917), p. 238.

10. *Gibbons* v. *Ogden*, 22 U.S. 1 (1824).

11. *Reno* v. *Condon*, 528 U.S. 141 (2000).

12. *Champion* v. *Ames*, 188 U.S. 321 (1907).

13. *Caminetti* v. *United States*, 242 U.S. 470 (1917).

14. *Federal Radio Commission* v. *Nelson Brothers*, 289 U.S. 266 (1933).

15. See Jesse Choper, *Judicial Review and the National Political Process* (University of Chicago Press, 1980); and John T. Noonan Jr., *Narrowing the Nation's Power: The Supreme Court Sides with the States* (University of California Press, 2002).

16. See Michael S. Greve, *Real Federalism: Why It Matters, How It Could Happen* (American Enterprise Institute, 1999).

17. *Printz* v. *United States*, 521 U.S. 898 (1997); see also *New York* v. *United States*, 505 U.S. 144 (1992).

18. See *Franchise Tax Board of California* v. *Hyatt*, 538 U.S. 488 (2003).

19. *California* v. *Superior Courts of California*, 482 U.S. 400 (1987).

20. David C. Nice, "State Participation in Interstate Compacts," *Publius*, 17 (Spring 1987), p. 70; see also *Interstate Compacts and Agencies*, Council of State Governments (Author, 1995), for a list of compacts by subject and by state with brief descriptions.

21. *McCulloch* v. *Maryland*, 4 Wheaton 316 (1819).

22. Joseph F. Zimmerman, "Federal Preemption Under Reagan's New Federalism," *Publius*, 21 (Winter 1991), pp. 7–28.

23. Oliver Wendell Holmes Jr., *Collected Legal Papers* (Harcourt, 1920), pp. 295–296.

24. See, for example, *United States* v. *Lopez*, 514 U.S. 549 (1995).

25. *Seminole Tribe of Florida* v. *Florida*, 517 U.S. 44 (1996).

26. *Alden* v. *Maine*, 527 U.S. 706 (1999); *Kimel* v. *Florida Board of Regents*, 528 U.S. 62 (2000); *Vermont Agency of Natural Resources* v. *United States ex rel. Stevens*, 529 U.S. 765 (2000).

27. George Will, "A Revival of Federalism?" *Newsweek* (May 29, 2000), p. 78.

28. *United States* v. *Morrison*, 529 U.S. 598 (2000).

29. The term "devolution revolution" was coined by Richard P. Nathan in testimony before the Senate Finance Committee, quoted in Daniel Patrick Moynihan, "The Devolution Revolution," *New York Times* (August 6, 1995), p. B15.

30. John E. Chubb, "The Political Economy of Federalism," *American Political Science Review*, 79 (December 1985), p. 1005.

31. Donald F. Kettl, *The Regulation of American Federalism* (Johns Hopkins University Press, 1987), pp. 154–155.

32. See Paul J. Posner, *The Politics of Unfunded Mandates: Whither Federalism?* (Georgetown University Press, 1998).

33. *Restoring Confidence and Competence*, Advisory Commission on Intergovernmental Relations (Author, 1981), p. 30.

34. Aaron Wildavsky, "Bare Bones: Putting Flesh on the Skeleton of American Federalism," in *The Future of Federalism in the 1980s* (Advisory Commission on Intergovernmental Relations, 1981), p. 79.

35. Peterson, *Price of Federalism*, p. 182.

36. Dye, *American Federalism*, p. 199.

37. John J. DiIulio Jr. and Donald F. Kettl, *Fine Print: The Contract with America, Devolution, and the Administrative Realities of American Federalism* (Brookings Institution Press, 1995), p. 60.

38. John Kincaid, "Devolution in the United States," in Nicolaidis and Howse, eds., *The Federal Vision* (Oxford, 2002), p. 144.

Chapter 4

1. Wesley G. Pippert, "You Could View This as a Racist Concept," *United Press International* (February 23, 1982).

2. Richard Severo, "Dr. King and Communism: No Link Ever Established," *New York Times* (October 22, 1983).

3. *New York Times*, "Tagliabue Is Firm on '93 Bowl Shift" (December 8, 1990).

4. MSNBC, "A More Perfect Union: Full Transcription of Obama's Speech on Race as Prepared for Delivery," March 18, 2008, http://www.msnbc.msn.com/id/23690567/ (accessed December 7, 2009).

5. "CNN Election Center 2008," November 11, 2009, http://www.cnn.com/ELECTION/2008/results/polls/#USP00p1 (accessed May 20, 2010).

6. David B. Magleby, J. Quin Monson, and Kelly D. Patterson, *Dancing Without Partners: How Candidates, Parties, and Interest Groups Interact in the Presidential Campaign* (Rowman & Littlefield, 2007); David B. Magleby, ed., *The Change Election: Money, Mobilization, and Persuasion in the 2008 Federal Elections* (Temple University Press, 2011).

7. Robert D. Putnam, "Bowling Alone: America's Declining Social Capital," *Journal of Democracy*, 6 (January 1995), pp. 65–78; see also Robert D. Putnam, *Bowling Alone: The Collapse and Revival of American Community* (Simon & Schuster, 2000); and Robert D. Putnam, "Bowling Together," *The American Prospect*, 13 (February 2002), p. 20.

8. Joe Rospars, Obama for America new media director, interview by David Magleby, January 28, 2009.

9. Dan Morgan, "An End to the Day of High Cotton? GOP Constituents Caught in Battle Over Subsidies," *Washington Post* (March 8, 2005), p. A1. Remnants of mercantilism persist today in policies such as farm subsidies.

10. Clinton Rossiter, *Conservatism in America* (Vintage Books, 1962), p. 72.

11. Bernard Bailyn, *The Ideological Origins of the American Revolution* (Belknap Press, 1967); Gordon S. Wood, *The Creation of the American Republic, 1776–1787* (University of North Carolina Press, 1969); and Jack Citrin, "Political Culture," in Peter H. Schuck and James Q. Wilson, eds., *Understanding America: The Anatomy of an Exceptional Nation* (New York: Public Affairs, 2008), pp. 160–161.

12. Peter H. Shuck and James Q. Wilson, eds., *Understanding America: The Anatomy of an Exceptional Nation* (New York: Public Affairs, 2008), p. 629.

13. See Ronald Dworkin, *Taking Rights Seriously* (Harvard University Press, 1977).

14. The Pew Research Center for the People & the Press, "Independents Take Center Stage in Obama Era," http://people-press.org/report/?pageid=1519 (accessed December 3, 2009).

15. *Marbury* v. *Madison*, 5 U.S. 137 (1803).

16. "A Nation Challenged: Excerpts from President's Speech: 'We Will Prevail' in War on Terrorism," *New York Times* (November 9, 2001), p. B1.

17. World Values Survey, 2004, margaux. grandvinum.se/SebTest/wvs/index_html.

18. World Values Survey, "WVS 2005–2008 Wave Data Files," *World Values Survey Association*, 2009.

19. Robert Coles, *The Political Life of Children* (Atlantic Monthly Press, 1986).

20. Fred I. Greenstein, *Children and Politics* (Yale University Press, 1965).

21. Raymond E. Wolfinger and Steven Rosenstone, *Who Votes?* (Yale University Press, 1980).

22. Peter H. Shuck and James Q. Wilson, "Looking Back," in Peter H. Schuck and James Q. Wilson, eds., *Understanding America: The Anatomy of an Exceptional Nation* (New York: Public Affairs, 2008), p. 630.

23. Rachel X. Weissman, "The Kids Are All Right—They're Just a Little Converged," *American Demographics*, 20 (December 1998), pp. 30–32.

24. Jeremy Rifkin, *The European Dream* (Penguin, 2005).

25. Alberto Alesina and Edward Glaeser, *Fighting Poverty in the U.S. and Europe: A World of Difference* (Oxford University Press, 2004).

26. *New York Times*, "Bloomberg Spent $102 Million to Win 3rd Term" (November 27, 2009), http://cityroom.blogs.nytimes.com/2009/11/27/bloomberg-spent-102-million-to-win-3rd-term/ (accessed December 7, 2009).

27. Jonathan P. Hicks, "Bloomberg Outspent Himself: $78 Million in '05 Versus $74 million in '01," *New York Times* (December 6, 2005), at http://www.nytimes.com/2005/12/06/nyregion/metrocampaigns/06mayor.html (accessed December 8, 2009).

28. Open Secrets, www.opensecrets.org/politicians/summary.php?cid=N000099548 cycle=2002 (accessed April 13, 2010); and Chris Cillizza, "Corzine Defeats Forrester to Become Governor," *Washington Post* (November 9, 2005), p. A18.

29. Tina Susman and Mark Z. Barabak, "New York's Bloomberg Spent Big, for Small Return," *Los Angeles Times* (November 6, 2009), http://www.latimes.com/news/nationworld/nation/la-na-bloomberg6-2009nov06,0,2043342.story (accessed November 11, 2009).

30. Glen Justice, "Advocacy Groups Reflect on Their Role in the Election," *New York Times* (November 5, 2004), p. A1.

31. When adjusted using the consumer price index (CPI1), the percentage of households earning more than $75,000 a year has risen from 10.1 percent in 1970 to 22.6 percent in 1999. U.S., Census Bureau, *Statistical Abstracts of the United States, 2001* (U.S. Government Printing Office, 2001), Table 661; see also Julia Isaac, "Economic Mobility of Black and White Families," *Economic Mobility Project*, Brookings Institution, November 2007.

32. See Michael B. Katz, *The "Underclass" Debate* (Princeton University Press, 1993); Theodore Dalrymple, *Life at the Bottom: The Worldview That Makes the Underclass* (Dee, 2001); and Charles A. Murray, *The Underclass Revisited* (AEI Press, 1999).

33. The Pew Research Center for the People & the Press, "Huge Racial Divide Over Katrina and Its Consequences," *Press Release*, September 8, 2005, available at people-press.org/reports/pdf/255.pdf (accessed May 20, 2010).

34. Bailyn, *Ideological Origins*.

35. Robert A. Dahl, "Liberal Democracy in the United States," in William Livingston, ed., *A Prospect of Liberal Democracy* (University of Texas Press, 1979), p. 64.

36. Ibid., pp. 59–60.

37. *Citizens United v. FEC* 558 U.S. ___ (2010).

38. "Breakdown of the Final Bailout Bill," *Washington Post* (September 28, 2008), http://www.washingtonpost.com/wp-dyn/content/article/2008/09/28/AR2008092800900.html (accessed December 10, 2009).

39. Carl Hulse and David M. Herszenhorn, "House Rejects Bailout Package, 228-205; Stocks Plunge," *New York Times* (September 29, 2008), http://www.nytimes.com/2008/09/30/business/30bailout.html?scp=1&sq=House%20Rejects%20Bailout%20Package,%20228-205;%20Stocks%20Plunge&st=cse (accessed April 13, 2010) and http://www.nytimes.com/2008/09/30/business/30bailout.html?adxnnl=1&adxnnlx=1260464575-BTAstaQVqKIBTkP1Sxgf4Q (accessed December 10, 2009).

40. The Department of the Treasury, "Financial Regulatory Reform: A New Foundation Rebuilding Financial Supervision and Regulation," June 17, 2009, http://www.house.gov/apps/list/hearing/financial svcs_dem/testimony_treasury.pdf (accessed December 10, 2009).

41. Dan Balz and Haynes Johnson, *The Battle for America 2008: The Story of an Extraordinary Election* (New York: Viking Penguin, 2009), p. 57.

42. Quoted in David Brooks, "Need a Map? The Right," *Washington Post* (October 31, 1999), p. B1.

43. David B. Magleby, *The Outside Campaign* (Rowman & Littlefield, 2001).

44. David B. Magleby, J. Quin Monson, and Kelly D. Patterson, *Dancing Without Partners: How Candidates, Parties, and Interest Groups Interact in the Presidential Campaign* (Maryland: Rowman & Littlefield, 2007); see also David B. Magleby and J. Quin Monson, eds., *The Last Hurrah? Soft Money and Issue Advocacy in the 2002 Congressional Elections* (Washington, DC: Brookings Institution Press, 2003); David B. Magleby, J. Quin Monson, and Kelly D. Patterson, eds., *Dancing Without Partners: How Candidates, Parties, and Interest Groups Interact in the New Campaign Finance Environment* (Washington, DC: Brookings Institution Press, 2005); and David B. Magleby and Kelly D. Patterson, eds., *War Games: Issues and Resources in the Battle for Control of Congress* (Washington, DC: Brookings Institution Press, 2007).

45. Michael Luo, "Huckabee Lays Out His Claim as an 'Authentic Conservative,'" *New York Times* (November 27, 2007), http://www.nytimes.com/2007/11/27/us/politics/27adbox.html?_r=1&scp=1&sq=Huckabee%20Lays%20Out%20His%20Claim%20as%20&st=cse (accessed April 13, 2010).

46. Edison Media Research/Mitofsky International Entrance Poll, January 3, 2008.

47. David E. Campbell and J. Quinn Monson, "The Case of Bush's Reelection: Did Gay Marriage Do It?" in David E. Campbell, ed., *A Matter of Faith: Religion in the 2004 Presidential Election* (Brookings Institution Press, 2007), pp. 120–141.

48. Jonathan Rauch, "The Accidental Radical," *National Journal* (July 26, 2003), pp. 2404–2410.

49. Kathleen Day, *S&L Hell: The People and the Politics Behind the $1 Trillion Savings and Loan Scandal* (Norton, 1993).

50. Jon Hilsenrath, Serena Ng, and Damian Paletta, "Worst Crisis Since '30's, With No End Yet in Sight," http://online.wsj.com/article/SB122169431617549947.html (accessed May 20, 2010).

51. Sylvia Nasar, "Even Among the Well-Off, the Rich Get Richer," *New York Times* (March 5, 1992), p. A1.

52. Irving Howe, *Socialism and America* (Harcourt, 1985); and Michael Harrington, *Socialism: Past and Future* (Arcade, 1989).

53. Daniel Yergin and Joseph Stanislaw, *The Commanding Heights: The Battle Between*

Government and the Marketplace That Is Remaking the Modern World (Simon & Schuster, 1998).

54. Charles Murray, *What It Means to Be a Libertarian* (Broadway Books, 1997).

55. Alec MacGillis, "The Libertarian Surprise: Ron Paul," *Washington Post* (December 16, 2007), http://www.washingtonpost.com/wp-dyn/content/article/2007/12/15/AR2007121501314.html (accessed April 27, 2010).

56. *American National Election Study: 1990,* Center for Political Studies, University of Michigan; and *Post-Election Survey,* April 1991.

57. Earl Black and Merle Black, *The Rise of Southern Republicans* (Belknap Press, 2002).

Chapter 5

1. Lev Grossman, Viveca Novak, and Eric Roston, "Campaign '04: Technology: What Your Party Knows About You," *Time Magazine* (October 18, 2004), http://www.time.com/time/magazine/article/0,9171,995394-1,00.html (accessed March 8, 2010).

2. Senator Charles Schumer from an NPR story by Mara Liasson, "GOP Bets on Get-Out-Vote Campaign for Win," October 6, 2006, http://www.npr.org/templates/story/ story.php?storyId=6211237 (accessed March 8, 2010).

3. Albert Einstein, quoted in Laurence J. Peter, *Peter's Quotations* (Morrow, 1977), p. 358.

4. Alexis de Tocqueville, *Democracy in America,* edited by J. P. Mayer, translated by George Lawrence (Doubleday, 1969), p. 278. Originally published 1835 (Vol. 1) and 1840 (Vol. 2).

5. See John Lewis Gaddis, *Surprise, Security, and the American Experience* (Harvard University Press, 2005).

6. This excludes the Japanese attack on the U.S. territory of Hawaii in 1941 and other attacks on U.S. embassies or territories.

7. Food and Agriculture Organization of the United Nations, "Statistical Appendix," *Food Outlook,* 1 (June 2007), www.fao.org/docrep/010/ah864e/ah864e14.htm (accessed May 20, 2010).

8. Alexis de Tocqueville, *Democracy in America,* translated by Henry Reeve, www.netlibrary.com, p. 153.

9. Harold Hongju Koh, "On American Exceptionalism," *Stanford Law Review,* 55 (May 2003), p. 1481.

10. U.S. Census Bureau, *Statistical Abstract of the United States: 2010* (U.S. Government Printing Office).

11. Arthur C. Paulson, *Realignment and Party Revival: Understanding American Electoral Politics at the Turn of the Twenty-First Century* (Westport, 2000), p. 46.

12. U.S. Census Bureau of the Census, www.census.gov/population/cen2000/tab01.pdf (accessed March 3, 2006).

13. Richard E. Cohen, "Census Data Shows 11 House Seats Could Shift," *National Journal* (December 23, 2009), http://www.nationaljournal.com/njonline/no_20091223_2521.php (Accessed May 20, 2010).

14. Robert S. Erikson, Gerald C. Wright, and John P. McIver, *Statehouse Democracy: Public Opinion and Policy in the American States* (Cambridge University Press, 1993).

15. *Statistical Abstract: 2010,* p. 18.

16. Holly Idelson, "Count Adds Seats in Eight States," *Congressional Quarterly Weekly Report,* 48 (December 29, 1999), p. 4240.

17. John M. Broder, "Term Waning, Gov. Davis Reflects on the Battle Lost," *New York Times* (November 12, 2003), p. A12.

18. *Statistical Abstract: 2010,* p. 36.

19. Ibid.

20. Ibid.

21. U.S. Census Bureau, "2006–2008 American Community Survey 3-Year Estimates," http://factfinder.census.gov/ (accessed March 1, 2010).

22. David R. Harris and Jeremiah Joseph Sim, "Who is Multiracial? Assessing the Complexity of Lived Race," *American Sociological Review* (August 2002), p. 615.

23. *Statistical Abstract: 2010,* p. 25.

24. Ibid.

25. U.S. Census Bureau, "Projections of the Population and Components of Change for the United States: 2010 to 2050," *U.S. Department of Commerce,* http://www.census.gov/population/www/projections/summary tables.html (accessed May 20, 2010).

26. See James Meader and John Bart, "The More You Spend, the Less They Listen: The South Dakota U.S. Senate Race," in David B. Magleby and J. Quin Monson, eds., *The Last Hurrah? Soft Money and Issue Advocacy in the 2002 Congressional Elections* (Brookings Institution Press, 2004), p. 173; see also Elizabeth Theiss Smith and Richard Braunstein, "The Nationalization of Local Politics in South Dakota," in David B. Magleby and J. Quin Monson, eds., *Dancing Without Partners: How Candidates, Parties, and Interest Groups Interact in the New Campaign Finance Environment* (Center for the Study of Elections and Democracy, 2005), pp. 241–242.

27. Tom Cole, "About Tom Cole," 2008, http://www.cole.house.gov/about/biography.shtml. (accessed May 20, 2010).

28. Henry J. Kaiser Family Foundation, "Race, Ethnicity, and Healthcare Issue Brief," http://www.kff.org/minorityhealth/upload/7977.pdf (accessed March 1, 2010).

29. Robert D. Ballard, "Introduction: Lure of the New South," in Robert D. Ballard, ed., *In Search of the New South: The Black Urban Experience in the 1970s and 1980s* (University of Alabama Press, 1989), p. 5; and *Statistical Abstract: 2008,* p. 449.

30. *Statistical Abstract: 2010,* p. 447. Constant 2007 dollars.

31. Ibid., p. 458.

32. *Statistical Abstract: 2010,* p. 447.

33. *Statistical Abstract: 2010,* p. 148.

34. *Statistical Abstract: 2010,* p. 145.

35. *Statistical Abstract: 2010,* p. 13.

36. Jeremy D. Mayer, *Running on Race* (Random House, 2002), pp. 4, 297; see also Mark R. Levy and Michael S. Kramer, *The Ethnic Factor: How America's Minorities Decide Elections* (Simon & Schuster, 1973); and Mark Stern, "Democratic Presidency and Voting Rights," in Lawrence W. Mooreland, Robert P. Steed, and Todd A. Baker, eds., *Blacks in Southern Politics,* (Praeger, 1987), pp. 50–51.

37. For 1984–2000, see Harold W. Stanley and Richard G. Niemi, *Vital Statistics on American Politics, 2000–2001* (CQ Press, 2001), p. 122; for 2004, see Harold W. Stanley and Richard G. Niemi, *Vital Statistics on American Politics, 2005–2006* (CQ Press, 2006), p. 124.

38. BBC News, "The U.S. Election in Figures," http://news.bbc.co.uk/2/hi/americas/us_elections_2008/7715914.stm (accessed November 7, 2008).

39. *Statistical Abstract: 2010,* p. 25.

40. See Earl Black, "Presidential Address: The Newest Southern Politics," *Journal of Politics* (August 1998), pp. 595–607.

41. Stanley and Niemi, *Vital Statistics on American Politics, 2009–2010,* pp. 53–54.

42. Ibid.

43. Anne E. Kornblut, "For Bill Clinton, Echoes of Jackson in Obama Win," *Washington Post* (January 26, 2008).

44. BBC News, "The U.S. Election in Figures," http://news.bbc.co.uk/2/hi/americas/us_elections_2008/7715914.stm (accessed November 7, 2008).

45. Matt Barreto, Rodolfo O. de la Garza, Jongho Lee, Jaesung Ryu, and Harry P. Pachon, "Latino Voter Mobilization in 2000," Tomás Rivera Policy Institute (2000), pp. 4–5, www.trpi.org/PDFs/Voter_mobiliz_2.pdf; see also Richard E. Cohen, "Hispanic Hopes Fade," *National Journal* (February 2, 2002).

46. *Statistical Abstract: 2010,* p. 25.

47. Rodney Hero, F. Chris Garcia, John Garcia, and Harry Pachon, "Latino Participation, Partisanship, and Office Holding," *PS: Political Science and Politics,* 33, No. 3 (September, 2000), pp. 529–534.

48. *Statistical Abstract: 2010,* p. 46.

49. Michael Hoefer, Nancy Rytina, and Christopher Campbell, "Estimates of the Unauthorized Immigrant Population Residing in the United States: January 2008," Department of Homeland Security, http://www.dhs.gov/xlibrary/assets/statistics/publications/ois_ill_pe_2008.pdf (accessed February 2010).

50. *Statistical Abstract: 2008,* p. 13.

51. Tom Squitieri, "Redistricting Falls Short of Hispanics' Hopes," *USA Today* (August 27, 2002), p. 11A.

52. Andrew L. Aoki and Don T. Nakanishi, "Asian Pacific Americans and the New Minority Politics," *PS: Political Science and Politics* (September 2001), p. 605.

53. Ibid.

54. *Statistical Abstract: 2010,* p. 148.

55. Ibid., p. 47.

56. Ibid., p. 44.

57. "The Foreign-Born Population in the United States: 2003," http://www.census.gov/prod/2004pubs/p20-551.pdf, p. 1.

58. Leni Yahil, *The Holocaust: The Fate of European Jewry* (Oxford University Press, 1990).

59. Stephen C. LeSuer, *The 1838 Mormon War in Missouri* (University of Missouri Press, 1987), pp. 151–153.

60. John Conway, "An Adapted Organic Tradition," *Daedalus,* 117 (Fall 1988), p. 382. For an extended comparison of the impact of religion on politics in the United States and Canada, see Seymour Martin Lipset, *Continental Divide: The Values and Institutions of the United States and Canada* (Routledge, 1990), pp. 74–89.

61. John F. Kennedy, address delivered to the Greater Houston Ministerial Association on September 12, 1960, millercenter.virginia.edu/scripps/diglibrary/prezspeeches/kennedy/index.html.

62. Taylor Branch, *Parting the Waters: America in the King Years, 1954–1963* (Simon & Schuster, 1988), p. 3.

63. Ronald Inglehart and Wayne E. Baker, "Looking Forward, Looking Back: Continuity and Change at the Turn of the Millennium," *American Sociological Review* (February 2000), pp. 29, 31.

64. Kenneth D. Wald and Allison Calhoun-Brown, *Religion and Politics in the United States,* 5th ed. (New York: Rowman and Littlefield, 2006), p. 9.

65. Pew Forum on Religious and Public Life, "Eastern, New Age Beliefs Widespread Many Americans Mix Multiple Faiths," December 2009, http://pewforum.org/newassets/images/reports/multiplefaiths/multiplefaiths.pdf (accessed February 18, 2010).

66. The Pew Forum on Religion and Public Life, *U.S. Religious Landscape Survey,* February 2008, p. 7, http://religions.pewforum.org/pdf/report-religious-landscape-study-full.pdf (accessed February 24, 2010).

67. William H. Flanigan and Nancy H. Zingale, *Political Behavior of the American Electorate,* 11th ed. (CQ Press, 2006), p. 141.

68. *Statistical Abstract: 2010,* p. 61.

69. Ibid.

70. Ibid.

71. *Statistical Abstract: 2010,* pp. 18, 59; see also www.thearda.com/mapsReports/reports/selectState.asp.

72. The Association of Religion Data Archives, "Southern Baptist Convention," 2000, http://www.thearda.com/Denoms/D_1087_d.asp (accessed February 22, 2010).

73. Ibid.

74. American Religion Data Archive, "Jewish Estimate—Number of Adherents," www.thearda.com/mapsReports/maps/map.asp?state=101&variable=20; ARDA; and "Metro Area Membership Report," www.thearda.com/mapsReports/reports/metro/5602_2000.asp.

75. CNN, "Exit Polls: Results," www.cnn.com/ELECTION/2000/results (accessed September 1, 2006).

76. Pew Forum on Religion and Public Life, "Voting Religiously" November 5, 2008, http://pewresearch.org/pubs/1022/exit-poll-analysis-religion (accessed February 19, 2010).

77. *2000 American National Election Study* (Center for Political Studies, 2000); *2004 American National Election Study* (Center for Political Studies, 2004); and *2008 American National Election Study* (Center for Political Studies, 2008). Post-election surveys often overestimate the vote and that appeared to be especially the case in the 2004 National Election Study. See Morris Fiorina and Jon Krosnick, "*Economist/You Gov Internet Presidential Poll,*" www.economist.com/media/pdf/Paper.pdf; and Michael P. McDonald and Samuel Popkin, "The Myth of the Vanishing Voter," *American Political Science Review,* 95 (2001), pp. 963–974.

78. "Presidential Vote by Religious Affiliation and Race," msnbc.com (accessed November 7, 2008).

79. James West Davidson, William E. Gienapp, Christine Leigh Heyrman, Mark H. Lytle, and Michael B. Stoff, *Nation of Nations* (McGraw-Hill, 1990), pp. 833–834.

80. Margaret C. Trevor, "Political Socialization, Party Identification, and the Gender Gap," *Public Opinion Quarterly,* 63 (Spring 1999), p. 62.

81. *Statistical Abstract: 2006,* p. 263; Sue Tolleson-Rinehart and Jyl J. Josephson, eds., *Gender and American Politics* (Sharpe, 2000), pp. 77–78; and Center for American Women and Politics, "Gender Differences in Voter Turnout," 2009, http://www.cawp.rutgers.edu/fast_facts/voters/documents/genderdiff.pdf (accessed February 18, 2010).

82. Sue Tolleson-Rinehart and Jyl J. Josephson, *Gender and American Politics,* pp. 232–233; see also Cindy Simon Rosenthal, ed., *Women Transforming Congress* (University of Oklahoma Press, 2002), pp. 128–139.

83. Paul Steinhauser, "Men's Support Gives Palin Edge in Latest Poll," *CNN,* September 9, 2008, http://www.cnn.com/2008/POLITICS/09/09/palin.poll (accessed March 1, 2010).

84. Barbara C. Burrell, *A Woman's Place Is in the House: Campaigning for Congress in the Feminist Era* (University of Michigan Press, 1994).

85. Marjorie Connelly, "The Election; Who Voted: A Portrait of American Politics, 1976–2000," *New York Times* (November 12, 2000), p. D4.

86. *Statistical Abstract: 2006,* p. 247; and CNN, "U.S. President National Exit Poll," 2004, http://www.cnn.com/ELECTION/2004/pages/results/states/US/P/00/epolls.0.html (accessed February 18, 2010).

87. CNN, "Obama's Election Redraws America's Electoral Divide," November 5, 2008, http://www.cnn.com/2008/POLITICS/11/05/election.president/index.html (accessed February 18, 2010).

88. Diane L. Fowlkes, "Feminist Theory: Reconstructing Research and Teaching About American Politics and Government," *News for Teachers of Political Science* (Winter 1987), pp. 6–9; see also Sally Helgesen, *Everyday Revolutionaries: Working Women and the Transformation of American Life* (Doubleday, 1998); Karen Lehrman, *The Lipstick Proviso: Women, Sex, and Power in the Real World* (Anchor/Doubleday, 1997); Tanya Melich, *The Republican War Against Women: An Insider's Report from Behind the Lines* (Bantam Books, 1998); and Virginia Valian, *Why So Slow? The Advancement of Women* (MIT Press, 1998).

89. Arlie Russell Hochschild, "There's No Place Like Work," *New York Times* (April 20, 1997), p. 51.

90. The Pew Research Center, *Gay Marriage a Voting Issue, but Mostly for Opponents,* February 27, 2004, www.people-press.org/reports/display.php3?ReportID=204; and Alexis Simendinger, "Why Issues Matter," *National Journal* (April 1, 2000), based on data from a Pew Center Poll conducted March 15–19, 2000.

91. *Statistical Abstract: 2010,* p. 450.

92. *Statistical Abstract: 2010,* p. 451.

93. U.S. Census Bureau, "Men's and Women's Earnings by State: 2008 American Community Survey," http://www.census.gov/prod/2009pubs/acsbr08-3.pdf (accessed February 22, 2010).

94. Catalyst, "Women in Law in the U.S.," September 2009, http://www.catalyst.org/publication/246/women-in-law-in-the-us (accessed February 18, 2010).

95. Princeton Review, *Best 290 Business Schools: 2008 Edition* (Random House, 2007).

96. Alliance for Board Diversity, "New Report Finds Little Change in Diversity on Corporate Boards," Press release, January 17, 2008.

97. Catherine Rampell, "As Layoffs Surge, Women May Pass Men in Job Force," *New York Times* (February 5, 2009), http://www.nytimes.com/2009/02/06/business/06women.html.

98. Catherine Rampell, "Women Now a Majority in American Workplaces," *New York Times* (February 5, 2010), p. A10.

99. Anna Quindlen, "Some Struggles Never Seem to End," *New York Times* (November 14, 2001), p. H24.

100. "Gay and Lesbian Families in the U.S.," Urban Institute, http://www.urban.org/publications/1000491.html.

101. Adam Clymer, "Senate Expands Hate Crimes Law to Include Gays," *New York Times* (June 21, 2000), p. A1.

102. David Masci, "The Future of Marriage," *CQ Researcher Online,* 14, No. 17 (May 7, 2004), pp. 397–420.

103. U.S. Census Bureau, "Unmarried-Partner Households by Region and Sex of Partners: 2007," *Statistical Abstract of the United States: 2010* (Washington, D.C.), p. 55.

104. U.S. Census Bureau, "Table MS-2. Estimated Median Age at First Marriage, by Sex: 1890 to the Present," January 2009, http://www.census.gov/population/socdemo/hh-fam/ms2.csv (accessed February 23, 2010).

105. CIA World Factbook, "Country Comparison: Total Fertility Rate," 2009, https://www.cia.gov/library/publications/the-world-factbook/rankorder/2127rank.html (accessed February 23, 2010).

106. United Nations Statistics Division, "Social Indicators," unstats.un.org/unsd/demographic/products/socind/childbr.htm.

107. The census stopped releasing divorce data in 1998, possibly because several states stopped providing it.

108. *Statistical Abstract: 2010,* p. 94.

109. *General Social Survey (GSS) 1972–2009 Cumulative Codebook,* http://publicdata.norc.org:41000/gss/documents//BOOK/2008%20GSS%20Codebook.pdf.

110. Thomas Jefferson to P. S. du Pont de Nemours, April 24, 1816, in Paul L. Ford, ed., *The Writings of Thomas Jefferson* (Putnam, 1899), Vol. 10, p. 25.

111. *Statistical Abstract: 2010,* p. 146.

112. *Statistical Abstract: 2008,* p. 146.

113. *Statistical Abstract: 2010,* p. 149.

114. Herbert McClosky and John Zaller, *The American Ethos: Public Attitudes Toward Capitalism and Democracy* (Harvard University Press, 1984), p. 261.

115. Raymond E. Wolfinger, Fred I. Greenstein, and Martin Shapiro, *Dynamics of American Politics,* 2d ed. (Prentice Hall, 1980), p. 19.

116. Thomas Jefferson, "Autobiography," in Adrienne Koch and William Peden, eds., *The Life and Selected Writings of Thomas Jefferson* (Modern Library, 1944), p. 38.

117. Harold W. Stanley and Richard G. Niemi, *Vital Statistics on American Politics, 2007–2008* (CQ Press, 2008), p. 374–375.

118. Stanley Fischer, "Symposium on the Slowdown in Productivity Growth," *Journal of Economic Perspectives,* 2 (Fall 1988), pp. 3–7.

119. Peter J. Nicholson, "The Rich Are Not Getting Much Richer; No, It's the Very, Very Rich," *Globe and Mail* (January 5, 2008), p. 17A.

120. *Statistical Abstract: 2010,* p. 455.

121. U.S. Census Bureau, http://www.census.gov/hhes/www/poverty/threshld/thresh09.html.

122. *Statistical Abstract: 2010,* http://www.census.gov/prod/2008pubs/p60-235.pdf (accessed March 4, 2010), p. 13.

123. Ibid.

124. *Statistical Abstract: 2010,* p. 457.

125. *Statistical Abstract: 2006,* p. 464.

126. Parker, Jennifer, "Obama Clinches Democratic Nomination," *ABC News,* January 3, 2008, http://abcnews.go.com/Politics/Vote2008/story?id=4987177&page=1 (accessed February 18, 2010).

127. U.S. Department of Commerce, Bureau of Economic Analysis, "Real Gross Domestic Product, 1 Decimal" (February 28, 2008), research.stlouisfed.org/fred2/data/GDPC1.txt.

128. Daniel Bell, *The Coming of Post-Industrial Society: A Venture in Social Forecasting* (Basic Books, 1973), p. xviii.

129. *Statistical Abstract: 2010,* p. 392.

130. *Statistical Abstract: 2010,* p. 427.

131. *Statistical Abstract: 2010,* p. 392.

132. Gabriel A. Almond, G. Bingham Powell, Jr., Russell J. Dalton, and Kaare Strøm, eds., *Comparative Politics Today: A World View,* 9th ed. (Pearson Longman, 2008), p. 54.

133. Seymour Martin Lipset, *Continental Divide: The Values and Institutions of the United States and Canada* (Routledge, 1990), p. 170.

134. Ibid.

135. Population Division of the Department of Economic and Social Affairs of the United Nations Secretariat, *World Population Prospects: The 2008 Revision,* http://esa.un.org/unpp (accessed March 2, 2010).

136. Susan A. MacManus, *Young v. Old: Generational Combat in the 21st Century* (Westview Press, 1996), pp. 48–49, 174–176, 245.

137. Nicholas L. Danigelis, Stephen J. Cutler, and Melissa Hardy, "Population Aging, Intracohort Aging, and Sociopolitical Attitudes," *American Sociological Review,* 72 (October 2007), p. 816.

138. CIRCLE, "Youth Turnout Rate Rises to at Least 52%," Center for Information and Research on Civic Learning and Engagement, November 7, 2008, http://www.civicyouth .org/?p=323.

139. CNN, "Exit Polls: Results," www.cnn.com/ ELECTION/2008/results/polls.main/ (accessed November 5, 2008).

140. Carl N. Degler, *Out of Our Past: The Forces That Shaped Modern America*, 3d ed. (Harper & Row, 1984), p. 322.

141. http://www.rockthevote.com/about/ press-room/press-releases/rock-the-vote- registers.html (accessed November 6, 2008).

Chapter 6

1. Peter Slevin, "Key Democrat Feels the Heat After Voting for House Plan," *Washington Post* (August 10, 2009), http://www.washingtonpost .com/wp-dyn/content/article/2009/08/09/ AR2009080902428.html (accessed May 21, 2010).

2. "Stop! The Size and Power of the State Is Growing, and Discontent Is on the Rise," *The Economist* (2010), pp. 10–18.

3. Nate Silver, "Tea Party Nonpartisan Attendance Estimates: Now 300,000+ Tea Party Attendance Estimate," *FiveThirtyEight,* April 16, 2009, http://www.fivethirtyeight.com/2009/04/tea- party-nonpartisan-attendance.html, retrieved June 16, 2009 (accessed February 24, 2010).

4. Tea Party Express, "About," 2010, http:// www.teapartyexpress.org/about/ (accessed February 22, 2010).

5. Our Country Deserves Better, "Campaigns," 2010, http://www.ourcountrydeservesbetter .com/campaigns (accessed February 22, 2010).

6. Kate Zernike, "Palin Assails Obama at Tea Party Meeting," *New York Times,* February 6, 2010, http://www.nytimes.com/2010/02/07/us/ politics/08palin.html (accessed February 22, 2010).

7. FreedomWorks, "About," 2008, http://www .freedomworks.org/about/about-freedom- works (accessed February 22, 2010).

8. Michael Sokolove, "Dick Armey Is Back on the Attack," *New York Times,* November 8, 2009, http://www.nytimes.com/2009/ 11/08/ magazine/08Armey-t.html (accessed February 22, 2010).

9. Michael Sokolove, "Dick Armey Is Back on the Attack."

10. Michael Sokolove, "Dick Armey is Back on the Attack."

11. Adam Nagourney, Jeff Zeleny, Kate Zernike, and Michael Cooper, "G.O.P. Used Energy and Stealth to Win Seat," *New York Times* (January 21, 2010).

12. James Madison, *The Federalist,* No. 10, November 23, 1787, in Isaac Kramnick, ed., *The Federalist Papers* (Penguin, 1987), pp. 122–128.

13. See Robert Dahl, *Who Governs?* (Yale University Press, 1961).

14. Center for Responsive Politics, "Microsoft Corp: Donor Profile," http://www.opensecrets.org/ orgs/summary.asp?ID=D000000115&Name= Microsoft+Corp (accessed May 21, 2010).

15. Gabriel A. Almond, G. Bingham Powell, Jr., Russell J. Dalton, and Kaare Strøm, *Comparative Politics Today,* 9th ed. (Pearson Longman, 2008), p. 70.

16. Minimum wage data compiled from International Labour Organization, Working Time Database, Minimum Wages Database, www.ilo.org/travaildatabase/servlet/minimu mwages (accessed May 21, 2010); minimum wage rates converted to American dollars per hour based on a 40-hour workweek.

17. Change to Win, "About Us," 2010, http:// www.changetowin.org/about-us.html (accessed March 15, 2010).

18. Office of Labor Management Standards, Union Reports, and Constitutions, http://www.dol .gov/olms/regs/compliance/rrlo/lmrda.htm (accessed May 21, 2010).

19. AFL-CIO, "About Us: Union Facts," www.aflcio .org/aboutus/faq/ (accessed May 21, 2010).

20. U.S. Bureau of Labor Statistics, www.bls. gov/cps/cpsaat40.pdf (accessed May 21, 2010).

21. Service Employees International Union, "Letters from President Andy Stern to SEIU Members: Where Do We Go from Here?," December 17, 2009, http://www.seiu.org/2009/12/letter-from- president-andy-stern-to-seiu-members-where- do-we-go-from-here.php (accessed February 24, 2010).

22. Brian C. Mooney, "Nation's Two Biggest Unions to Wait on Presidential Endorsement," *Boston Globe* (September 11, 2003), p. A3.

23. Alison Grant, "Labor Chief Sees Anti-Union Efforts Growing Bolder," (Cleveland) *Plain Dealer* (November 22, 2005), p. C1.

24. James MacGregor Burns and Stewart Burns, *A People's Charter: The Pursuit of Rights in America* (Knopf, 1991).

25. Chris W. Cox, "Who We Are, and What We Do," National Rifle Associaton, www. nraila.org/About/ (accessed May 21, 2010).

26. Laura Longhine, "Display Cases," *Legal Affairs,* November 2005, http://www.legalaffairs .org/issues/November-December-2005/ scene_longhine_novdec05.msp (accessed March 15, 2010).

27. The American Israel Public Affairs Committee, "What is AIPAC?," http://www.aipac.org/about_ AIPAC/default.asp (accessed February 22, 2010).

28. National Education Association, http://www .nea.org/home/1704.htm (accessed March 2, 2010).

29. See Mancur Olson, *The Logic of Collective Action* (Harvard University Press, 1971).

30. Kenneth J. Arrow, "A Difficulty in the Concept of Social Welfare," *Journal of Political Economy,* 58 (August), pp. 328–346; see also David Austen-Smith and Jeffrey S. Banks, "Social Choice Theory, Game Theory, and Positive Political Theory," *Annual Review of Political Science,* 1 (June), pp. 259–287.

31. Robert Salisbury, "Interest Representation: The Dominance of Institutions," *American Political Science Review,* 78 (March 1984), p. 66.

32. V. O. Key, Jr., *Public Opinion and American Democracy* (Knopf, 1961), pp. 504–507.

33. Daniel Stone, "The Browning of Grass Roots: How Astroturfing Is Taking Over Local Activism," *Newsweek,* August 20, 2009, http://www.newsweek.com/id/212934 (accessed April 29, 2010).

34. http://bipac.net/bipac_public/initial.asp (accessed May 21, 2010); see also David B. Magleby, Anthony Corrado, and Kelly D. Patterson, *Financing the 2004 Election* (Brookings Institute Press, 2006); and David B. Magleby, J. Quin Monson, and Kelly Patterson, *Electing Congress: New Rules for an Old Game* (Pearson Prentice Hall, 2007).

35. Andrew Chadwick, "Digital Network Repertoires and Organizational Hybridity," *Political Communication,* 24 (July–September 2007), p. 284.

36. R. Kenneth Godwin, *One Billion Dollars of Influence: The Direct Marketing of Politics* (Chatham House, 1988).

37. David B. Magleby, J. Quin Monson, and Kelly Patterson, *Electing Congress: New Rules for an Old Game* (Prentice Hall, 2006); see also David B. Magleby, J. Quin Monson, and Kelly D. Patterson, *Dancing Without Partners: How Candidates, Parties, and Interest Groups Interact in the Presidential Campaign* (Rowman & Littlefield, 2007); and David B. Magleby and Kelly D. Patterson, eds., *The Battle for Congress: Iraq, Scandal, and Campaign Finance in the 2006 Election* (Paradigm, 2008).

38. The *Federal Register* is published every week- day. You can find it at the library or on the Internet at www.gpoaccess.gov.

39. Lucius J. Barker, "Third Parties in Litigation: A Systemic View of the Judicial Function," *Journal of Politics,* 29 (February 1967), pp. 41–69; and Jethro K. Lieberman, *Litigious Society,* rev. ed. (Basic Books, 1983).

40. Gregory A. Caldeira and John R. Wright, "Organized Interests and Agenda Setting in the U.S. Supreme Court," *American Political Science Review,* 82 (December 1988), pp. 1109–1127; see also Gregory A. Caldeira and John R. Wright, "*Amici Curiae* Before the Supreme Court: Who Participates, When, and How Much?" *Journal of Politics,* 52 (August 1990), pp. 782–806.

41. Lee Epstein and C. K. Rowland, "Debunking the Myth of Interest Group Invincibility in the Courts," *American Political Science Review,* 85 (March 1991), pp. 205–217.

42. Robert D. McFadden, "Across the U.S., Protests for Immigrants Draw Thousands," *New York Times* (April 10, 2006), p. A14; and Anna Gorman and J. Michael Kennedy, "The Immigration Debate," *Los Angeles Times* (April 11, 2006), p. A11.

43. Judy Keen and Martin Kasindorf, "From Coast to Coast, 'We Need to Be Heard,' " *USA Today* (May 2, 2006), p. 3A.

44. See Kenneth Klee, "The Siege of Seattle," *Newsweek* (December 13, 1999), p. 30.

45. League of Conservation Voters, "Key Races of the 2004 Congressional Election Cycle," www.lcv.org/campaigns/2004-congressional/ (accessed May 21, 2010).

46. Ethan Bronner, *Battle for Justice: How the Bork Nomination Shook America* (Norton, 1989), pp. 50–55.

47. Hugh Heclo, "Issue Networks and the Executive Establishment," in Anthony King, ed., *The New American Political System* (American Enterprise Institute, 1978).

48. David Mayhew, *Congress: The Electoral Connection* (Yale University Press, 1974), p. 45.

49. John R. Wright, "Contributions, Lobbying, and Committee Voting in the U.S. House of Representatives," *American Political Science Review,* 84 (June 1990), pp. 417–438.

50. Dan Eggen, "Expecting Final Push on Health Care Reform, Interest Groups Rally for Big Finish," *Washington Post,* February 28, 2010, http://www.washingtonpost.com/wp-dyn/ content/article/2010/02/27/AR2010022703253 .html (accessed April 29, 2010).

51. *McConnell v. Federal Elections Commission,* 124 S. Ct. 621 (2003).

52. For evidence of the impact of PAC expenditures on legislative committee behavior and legislative involvement generally, see Richard L. Hall and Frank W. Wayman, "Buying Time: Moneyed Interests and the Mobilization of Bias in Congressional Committees," *American Political Science Review,* 84 (September 1990), pp. 797–820.

53. Federal Election Commission, "Number of Federal PACs Increases," Press Release, March 9, 2009, http://www.fec.gov/press/press2009/ 20090309PACcount.shtml (accessed May 21, 2010).

54. Ibid.

55. Open Secrets, "Business Associations," July 13, 2009, http://www.opensecrets.org/pacs/

industry.php?txt=N00&cycle=2008 (accessed March 17, 2010).

56. Amy Keller, "Leadership PACs 'Not Sinister,' FEC Told," *Roll Call* (February 27, 2003).

57. Open Secrets, opensecrets.org/pacs/lookup2 .asp?strid=C00344234&cycle=2008 (accessed May 21, 2010).

58. Paul Krugman, "Toward One-Party Rule," *New York Times* (June 27, 2003), p. A27.

59. J. Quin Monson, "Get On TeleVision vs. Get On the Van: GOTV and the Ground War in 2002," in David B. Magleby and J. Quin Monson, eds., *The Last Hurrah* (Brookings Institution Press, 2004), p. 108.

60. David B. Magleby and Nicole Carlisle Smith, "Party Money in the 2002 Congressional Elections," in David B. Magleby and J. Quin Monson, eds., *The Last Hurrah* (Brookings Institution Press, 2004), p. 54; David B. Magleby and Eric A. Smith, "Party Soft Money in the 2000 Congressional Elections," in David B. Magleby, ed., *The Other Campaign* (Rowman & Littlefield, 2003), pp. 34–35; Mariane Holt, "The Surge in Party Money," in David B. Magleby, ed., *Outside Money* (Rowman & Littlefield, 2000), p. 36; and David B. Magleby, "Conclusions and Implications," in David B. Magleby, ed., *Outside Money* (Rowman & Littlefield, 2000), p. 214.

61. *Federal Election Commission* v. *Wisconsin Right to Life Inc.*, 551 U.S._ (2007).

62. *Citizens United* v. *Federal Election Commission*, 558 U.S. ___ (2010).

63. Allan Cigler, "Interest Groups and Financing the 2008 Election," in David B. Magleby and Anthony Corrado, ed., *Financing the 2008 Election* (Brookings Institution Press, forthcoming), pp. 29–32.

64. Ruth Marcus, "Labor Spent $119 Million for '96 Politics, Study Says; Almost All Contributions Went to Democrats," *Washington Post* (September 10, 1997), p. A19.

65. Kate Zernike, "Kerry Pressing Swift Boat Case Long After Loss," *New York Times* (May 28, 2006), p. A1.

66. Internal Revenue Code, Title 26, frwebgate. access.gpo.gov/cgi-bin/getdoc.cgi?dbname= browse_usc&docid=Cite:+26USC501 (accessed May 21, 2010).

67. Nicholas Confessore, "Bush's Secret Stash," *Washington Monthly*, 36 (May 2004), pp. 17–23.

68. Center for Responsive Politics, "527 Committees: Top 50 Federally Focused Organizations," http://www.opensecrets.org/ 527s/527cmtes.php?level=c&evele=1008 (accessed November 8, 2008).

69. David B. Magleby, "How the 2008 Elections Were Financed," in David B. Magleby, ed. *The Change Election: Money, Mobilization, and Persuasion in the 2008 Federal Elections*, pp. 41–45.

70. David B. Magleby, "How the 2008 Elections Were Financed," pp. 41–45.

71. David B. Magleby, "How the 2008 Elections Were Financed," p. 41.

72. E. J. Dionne, Jr., "Fear of McCain-Feingold," *Washington Post* (December 3, 2002), p. A25.

73. The Campaign Legal Center, "Interveners Urge Supreme Court to Sustain BCRA in Its Entirety," www.campaignlegalcenter.org/ press-814.html (accessed May 21, 2010).

74. David B. Magleby and Kelly D. Patterson, "Campaign Consultants and Direct Democracy: Politics of Citizen Control," in James E. Thurber and Candice J. Nelson, eds., *Campaign Warriors: The Role of Political Consultants in Elections* (Brookings Institution Press, 2000).

75. Ronald Reagan, "Remarks to Administration Officials on Domestic Policy," December 13, 1988, *Weekly Compilation of Presidential Documents*, 24 (December 1988), pp. 1615–1620.

76. Sylvia Tesh, "In Support of Single-Interest Politics," *Political Science Quarterly*, 99 (Spring 1984), pp. 27–44.

77. Legislative Resource Center's Lobbying Section, telephone interview, April 7, 2004.

Chapter 7

1. E. E. Schattschneider, *Party Government* (Holt, Rinehart and Winston, 1942), p. 1.

2. See Scott Mainwaring, "Party Systems in the Third Wave," *Journal of Democracy* (July 1998), pp. 67-81.

3. Joseph A. Schlesinger, *Political Parties and the Winning of Office* (University of Michigan Press, 1994).

4. Robert R. Alford and Eugene C. Lee, "Voting Turnout in American Cities," *American Political Science Review* 62 (September), pp. 809–810.

5. Gary W. Cox and Mathew D. McCubbins, *Legislative Leviathan: Party Government in the House* (University of California Press, 1993).

6. David W. Brady and Craig Volden, *Revolving Gridlock: Politics and Policy from Carter to Clinton* (Westview Press, 1998); James A. Thurber, ed., *Divided Democracy: Cooperation and Conflict Between the President and Congress* (CQ Press, 1991); James A. Thurber, ed., *Rivals for Power: Presidential–Congressional Relations* (CQ Press, 1996); Charles O. Jones, *Separate but Equal Branches: Congress and the Presidency* (Chatham House, 1995), Chapters 5 and 6; and Jon R. Bond and Richard Fleisher, *The President in the Legislative Arena* (University of Chicago Press, 1990).

7. *California Democratic Party et al.* v. *Jones*, 120 S. Ct. 2402 (2000).

8. George Skelton, "California Open Primaries? Give Them a Chance," *Los Angeles Times*, February 11, 2010, http://articles.latimes.com/ 2010/feb/11/local/la-me-cap11-2010feb11 (accessed March 29, 2010).

9. Adam Nagourney, "Obama Takes Iowa in a Big Turnout as Clinton Falters; Huckabee Victor," *New York Times*, January 4, 2008, p. A1.

10. Peverill Squire, "The Iowa Caucuses, 1972–2008: A Eulogy," *The Forum* 5, No. 4, Article 1, pp. 2–5, www.bepress.com/forum/vol5/iss4/art1.

11. Gabriel A. Almond, G. Bingham Powell, Jr., Russell J. Dalton, and Kaare Strøm, *Comparative Politics Today: A World View*, 9th ed. (Pearson Longman, 2008), pp. 81, 89.

12. For an analysis of the potential effects of different electoral rules in the United States, see Todd Donovan and Shawn Bowler, *Reforming the Republic: Democratic Institutions for the New America* (Prentice Hall, 2004).

13. William H. Riker, "The Two-Party System and Duverger's Law: An Essay on the History of Political Science," *American Political Science Review* 76 (December 1982), pp. 753–766. For a classic analysis, see E. E. Schattschneider, *Party Government* (Holt, Rinehart and Winston, 1942).

14. Maurice Duverger, *Party Politics and Pressure Groups* (Nelson, 1972), pp. 23–32.

15. Steven J. Rosenstone, Roy L. Behr, and Edward H. Lazarus, *Third Parties in America: Citizen Response to Major Party Failure*, 2d ed. (Princeton University Press, 1996); see also Xandra Kayden and Eddie Mahe, Jr., *The Party Goes On: The Persistence of the Two-Party System in the United States* (Basic Books, 1985), pp. 143–144. The Republican Party, which started as a third party, was one of the two major parties by 1860, the year Republican Abraham Lincoln won the Presidency; see Lewis L. Gould, *Grand Old Party: A History of the Republicans* (Random House, 2003), pp. 3–17.

16. Dean Lacy and Quin Monson, "The Origins and Impact of Voter Support for Third-Party Candidates: A Case Study of the 1998 Minnesota Gubernatorial Election," *Political Research Quarterly* 55(2), pp. 409–437.

17. On the impact of third parties, see Howard R. Penniman, "Presidential Third Parties and the Modern American Two-Party System," in William J. Crotty, ed., *The Party Symbol* (Freeman, 1980), pp. 101–117; see also Frank Smallwood, *The Other Candidates: Third Parties in Presidential Elections* (University Press of New England, 1983).

18. Benjamin Franklin, George Washington, and Thomas Jefferson, quoted in Richard Hofstadter, *The Idea of a Party System* (University of California Press, 1969), pp. 2, 123.

19. For concise histories of the two parties, see Jules Witcover, *Party of the People: A History of the Democrats* (Random House, 2003); and Gould, *Grand Old Party*.

20. See V. O. Key, Jr., "A Theory of Critical Elections," *Journal of Politics* 17 (February 1955), pp. 3–18; Walter Dean Burnham, *Critical Elections and the Mainsprings of American Politics* (Norton, 1970), pp. 1–10; and E. E. Schattschneider, *The Semisovereign People: A Realist's View of Democracy in America* (Holt, Rinehart and Winston, 1975), pp. 78–80.

21. William E. Gienapp, *The Origins of the Republican Party, 1852–1856* (Oxford University Press, 1987).

22. Gould, *Grand Old Party*, p. 88.

23. Ibid.

24. David W. Brady, "Election, Congress, and Public Policy Changes, 1886–1960," in Bruce A. Campbell and Richard Trilling, eds., *Realignment in American Politics: Toward a Theory* (University of Texas Press, 1980), p. 188.

25. L. Sandy Maisel, *Parties and Elections in America: The Electoral Process* (Rowman & Littlefield, 2002), pp. 48–49.

26. Gerald Pomper, "Classification of Presidential Elections," *Journal of Politics* 29 (August 1967), p. 538.

27. Earl Black and Merle Black, *The Rise of Southern Republicans* (Belknap Press, 2003).

28. See Byron E. Shafer, *The End of Realignment: Interpreting American Electoral Eras* (University of Wisconsin Press, 1991).

29. Michael F. Meffert, Helmut Norpoth, and Anirudh V. S. Ruhil, "Realignment and Macropartisanship," *American Political Science Review* 95 (December 2001), pp. 953–962.

30. "NAAS Survey: State Voter Registration Figures for the 2008 General Election," http:// www.naas.org (accessed November 8, 2008).

31. See http://www.teaparty.org/about.php.

32. Kate Zernike and Megan Thee-Brenan, "Poll Finds Tea Party Backers Wealthier and More Educated," *New York Times*, April 14, 2010, http://www.nytimes.com/2010/04/15/us/ politics/15poll.html (accessed May 12, 2010).

33. "Scott Brown to Skip Tea Party Rally in Boston with Sarah Palin," *The Huffington Post*, April 12, 2010, http://www.huffingtonpost .com/2010/04/12/scott-brown-to-skip-tea- p_n_533961.html (accessed May 12, 2010); and Kirk Johnson, "Utah Delegates Oust Three-Term G.O.P. Senator over Race," *New York Times*, May 8, 2010, http://www.nytimes.com/2010/ 05/09/us/politics/09utah.html (accessed May 12, 2010).

34. Zernike and Thee-Brenan, "Poll Finds Tea Party Backers Wealthier and More Educated."

35. Ibid.

36. V. O. Key, Jr., *Political Parties and Pressure Groups*, 5th ed. (International, 1964); see also Marjorie Randon Hershey, *Party Politics in America*, 12th ed. (Longman, 2006).

37. Federal Election Commission, "National Party Activity Summarized," press release, October 30, 2006, www.fec.gov/press/press2006/20061030party/20061030party.html.

38. Hershey, *Party Politics in America.*

39. David B. Magleby, J. Quin Monson, and Kelly D. Patterson, "The Lingering Effects of a Night Spent Dancing," in David B. Magleby, J. Quin Monson, and Kelly D. Patterson, eds., *Dancing Without Partners: How Candidates, Parties, and Interest Groups Interact in the Presidential Campaign* (Lanham, MD: Rowman & Littlefield, 2007), pp. 163–167; and David B. Magleby, ed., *The Change Election: Money, Mobilization, and Persuasion in the 2008 Federal Election* (Temple University Press, 2011).

40. David B. Magleby, "How the 2008 Election Was Financed," in David B. Magleby, ed., *The Change Election: Money, Mobilization, and Persuasion in the 2008 Federal Elections* (Temple University Press, 2011).

41. The early Republican efforts and advantages over the Democrats are well documented in Thomas B. Edsall, *The New Politics of Inequality* (Norton, 1984); and Gary C. Jacobson, "The Republican Advantage in Campaign Finances," in John E. Chubb and Paul E. Peterson, eds., *New Direction in American Politics* (Brookings Institution Press, 1985), p. 6; see also David B. Magleby and Kelly D. Patterson, "Rules of Engagement: BCRA and Unanswered Questions," in David B. Magleby and Kelly D. Patterson, eds., *The Battle for Congress: Iraq, Scandal, and Campaign Finance in the 2006 Election* (Paradigm, 2008), pp. 33–36.

42. David C. King, "The Polarization of American Political Parties and Mistrust of Government," in Joseph S. Nye, Philip Zelikow, and David C. King, eds., *Why People Don't Trust Government* (Harvard University Press, 1997); and National Election Study, "Important Difference in What Democratic and Republican Parties Stand For, 1952–2000," www.umich.net/nes/edu/nesguide/toptable/tab2b_4.htm.

43. Kelly D. Patterson, *Political Parties and the Maintenance of Liberal Democracy* (Columbia University Press, 1996), pp. 30–31.

44. Tom Shales, "Bush, Bringing the Party to Life; From the New Nominee, a Splendid Acceptance Speech," *The Washington Post*, August 19, 1988, p. C1.

45. Jonathan Martin, "Republicans Rejects 'Purity Test," *Politico*, January 29, 2010, http://dyn.politico.com/printstory.cfm?uuid=7CE131F9-18FE-70B2-A87EC11BCD6EFFFE (accessed March 29, 2010).

46. See James L. Gibson, Cornelius P. Cotter, John F. Bibby, and Robert J. Huckshorn, "Assessing Party Organizational Strength," *American Journal of Political Science* 27 (May 1983), pp. 193–222; see also Cornelius P. Cotter, James L. Gibson, John F. Bibby, and Robert Huckshorn, *Party Organizations in American Politics* (University of Pittsburg Press, 1989).

47. Paul S. Herrnson, *Party Campaigning in the 1980s: Have the National Parties Made a Comeback as Key Players in Congressional Elections?* (Harvard University Press, 1988), p. 122.

48. *Marbury* v. *Madison*, 1 Cranch 137 (1803).

49. See Angus Campbell, Philip E. Converse, Warren E. Miller, and Donald E. Stokes, *The American Voter* (University of Chicago Press, 1960); Norman A. Nie, Sidney Verba, and John R. Petrocik, *The Changing American Voter*, enlarged ed. (Harvard University Press, 1979); and Warren E. Miller and J. Merrill Shanks, *The New American Voter* (Harvard University Press, 1996).

50. Campbell et al., *The American Voter*, pp. 121–128.

51. Ibid.

52. Bruce E. Keith et al., *The Myth of the Independent Voter* (University of California Press, 1992).

53. Nine percent of all voters were Pure Independents in 1956 and 1960; Keith et al., *The Myth of the Independent Voter*, p. 51. In 1992, the figure was also 9 percent; *1992 National Election Study* (Center for Political Studies, University of Michigan, 1992).

54. David B. Magleby and Candice J. Nelson, *The Money Chase: Congressional Campaign Finance Reform* (Brookings Institution Press, 1990), p. 16.

55. David B. Magleby, ed., *Outside Money: Soft Money and Issue Advocacy in the 1998 Congressional Elections* (Rowman & Littlefield, 2003); and David B. Magleby, ed., *The Other Campaign: Soft Money and Issue Advocacy in the 2000 Congressional Elections* (Rowman & Littlefield, 2003).

56. Jonathan S. Krasno and Daniel E. Seltz, *Buying Time: Television Advertising in the 1998 Congressional Elections*, report of a grant funded by the Pew Charitable Trusts (1998).

59. *Colorado Republican Federal Campaign Committee* v. *Federal Election Commission*, 518 U.S. 604 (1996).

58. Sidney M. Milkis, "Parties Versus Interest Groups," in Anthony Corrado, Thomas E. Mann, and Trevor Potter, eds., *Inside the Campaign Finance Battle: Court Testimony on the New Reforms* (Brookings Institution Press, 2003), p. 44.

59. "Comparative Data," in the Ace Electoral Knowledge Network Database, http://aceproject.org/epic-en (accessed March 30, 2010).

60. Ndubisi Obiorah, *Political Finance and Democracy in Nigeria* (Center for Law and Social Action, 2004).

61. Paul S. Herrnson, *Party Campaigning in the 1980s* (Harvard University Press, 1988), pp. 80–81.

Chapter 8

1. Priscilla L. Southwell and Justin Burchett, "Survey of Vote-by-Mail Senate Election in the State of Oregon," *PS: Political Science & Politics* 30 (1997), p. 53.

2. David B. Magleby, "Participation in Mail Ballot Elections," *Political Research Quarterly* 40 (1987), p. 81.

3. Paul Gronke, Eva Galanes-Rosenbaum, and Peter A. Miller, "Early Voting and Turnout," *PS: Political Science & Politics* 40 (2007), pp. 639–645.

4. http://elections.gmu.edu/Early_Voting_2008_Final.html.

5. Robert Coles, *The Political Life of Children* (Atlantic Monthly Press, 2000), pp. 24–25; see also Stephen M. Caliendo, *Teachers Matter: The Trouble with Leaving Political Education to the Coaches* (Greenwood Press, 2000).

6. Caliendo, *Teachers Matter*, pp. 16–17.

7. James Garbarino, *Raising Children in a Socially Toxic Environment* (Jossey-Bass, 1995).

8. Gabriel A. Almond and Sidney Verba, eds. *The Civic Culture Revisited* (Little Brown, 1980), p. 13.

9. J. L. Glanville, "Political Socialization or Selection? Adolescent Extracurricular Participation and Political Activity in Early Adulthood," *Social Science Quarterly* 80 (1999), p. 279.

10. National Association of Secretaries of State, *New Millennium Project, Part I: American Youth Attitudes on Policies, Citizenship, Government, and Voting* (Author, 1999); and "Political Interest on the Rebound Among the Nation's Freshmen," Higher Education Research Institute, Fall 2003, www.gseis.ucla.edu/heri/03_press_release.pdf.

11. Margaret Stimmann Branson, "Making the Case for Civic Education: Educating Young People for Responsible Citizenship," paper presented at the Conference for Professional Development for Program Trainers, Manhattan Beach, Calif., February 25, 2001.

12. B. Bradford Brown, Sue Ann Eicher, and Sandra Petrie, "The Importance of Peer Group ("Crowd") Affiliation in Adolescence," *Journal of Adolescence* 9 (March 1986), pp. 73–96.

13. Kenneth Feldman and Theodore M. Newcomb, *The Impact of College on Students*, Vol. 2 (Jossey-Bass, 1969), pp. 16–24, 49–56; see also David O. Sears and Nicholas A. Valentino, "Politics Matters: Political Events as Catalysts for Preadult Socialization," *American Political Science Review* 91 (March 1997), pp. 45–65.

14. Daniel B. German, "The Role of the Media in Political Socialization and Attitude Formation Toward Racial/Ethnic Minorities in the U.S.," in Robert F. Farnen, ed., *Nationalism, Ethnicity, and Identity: Cross National and Comparative Perspective* (Transaction, 2004), p. 287.

15. James G. Gimpel, J. Celeste Lay, and Jason E. Schuknecht, *Cultivating Democracy: Civic Environments and Political Socialization in America* (Brookings Institution Press, 2003), p. 127 (see Chapter 5).

16. Robert D. Putnam, "The Rebirth of American Civic Life," *Boston Globe*, March 2, 2008, p. D9.

17. For a general discussion of political knowledge, see Michael Delli Carpini and Scott Keeter, *What Americans Know About Politics and Why It Matters* (Yale University Press, 1996).

18. *The 2000 National Election Study*, Center for Political Studies, University of Michigan; see also the NES Guide to Public Opinion and Electoral Behavior, www.umich.edu/nes/nesguide/nesguide.htm.

19. Erikson and Tedin, *American Public Opinion*, p. 304.

20. *The 2004 National Election Study* (Center for Political Studies, University of Michigan, 2004).

21. http://www.gallup.com/poll/111664/Gallup-Daily-Obama-Continues-Outpace-McCain.aspx (accessed November 7, 2008. Note: We removed the "no opinion" and percentaged the other categories to sum to 100 percent.

22. Thomas D. Snyder, Sally A. Dillow, and Charlene M. Hoffman, "Number of Persons Age 18 and Over, by Highest Level of Education Attained, Age, Sex, and Race/Ethnicity: 2005," *Digest of Education Statistics 2007* (U.S. Government Printing Office, 2008), p. 24.

23. Peverill Squire, "Why the 1936 *Literary Digest* Poll Failed," *Public Opinion Quarterly* 52 (Spring 1988), pp. 125–133.

24. Ibid., p. 128.

25. Quoted in Hadley Cantril, *Gauging Public Opinion* (Princeton University Press, 1944), p. viii.

26. John G. Geer, *From Tea Leaves to Opinion Polls: A Theory of Democratic Leadership* (Columbia University Press, 1996).

27. Norman J. Ornstein and Amy S. Mitchell, "The Permanent Campaign: The Trend Toward Continuous Campaigning Stems from Advances in Technology and the Proliferation of Public Opinion Polls," *World and I* 12 (January 1997): 48–55.

28. "Do You Approve or Disapprove of the Way George W. Bush Is Handling the Situation with Iraq?" CBS News and *New York Times* Poll, May 3, 2003; and May 20, 2004, www.pollingreport.com/iraq2.htm.

29. CBS News and *New York Times*, "Looking Ahead to the General Election," www.cbsnews.com/htdocs/pdf/apr08b_genelec.pdf.

30. Gallup, "Gallup Daily: Obama Job Approval," http://www.gallup.com/poll/113980/gallup-daily-obama-job-approval.aspx (accessed April 16, 2010).

31. Lawrence R. Jacobs and Robert R. Shapiro, *Politicians Don't Pander* (University of Chicago Press, 2000), p. 3.

32. Robert S. Erikson and Kent L. Tedin, *American Public Opinion: Its Origins, Content, and Impact*, 6th ed. (Longman, 2001), pp. 272–273. On the centrality of the reelection motive, see David R. Mayhew, *Congress: The Electoral Connection* (Yale University Press, 1974).

33. http://www.nytimes.com/2008/11/03/us/politics/03Campaign.html?hp (accessed November 7, 2008).

34. Nicole B. Ellison, Charles Steinfield, and Cliff Lampe, "The Benefits of Facebook 'Friends': Social Capital and College Students' Use of Online Social Network Sites," *Journal of Computer-Mediated Communication* 12 (2007), Art. 1.

35. Data from the American National Election Studies, Center for Political Studies, University of Michigan, 1948-2004, www.electionstudies.org/studypages/download/datacenter_all.htm.

36. *The 2008 National Election Study.*

37. Julie Bosman, "More Hiring and Advertising Ahead for Paul as the Donations Pour In," *New York Times*, December 18, 2007.

38. Frank R. Parker, *Black Votes Count: Political Empowerment in Mississippi After 1965* (University of North Carolina Press, 1990), p. 3.

39. Bernard Grofman and Lisa Handley, "The Impact of the Voting Rights Act on Black Representation in Southern State Legislatures," *Legislative Studies Quarterly* 16 (February 1991), pp. 111–128.

40. International Institute for Democracy and Electoral Assistance, "Voter Turnout from 1945 to Date: A Global Report on Political Participation," www.idea.int/voter_turnout/index.html.

41. Raymond E. Wolfinger and Steven J. Rosenstone, "The Effect of Registration Laws on Voter Turnout," *American Political Science Review* 72 (March 1978), p. 41.

42. Ibid., p. 24.

43. Raymond E. Wolfinger and Steven J. Rosenstone, *Who Votes?* (Yale University Press, 1980), pp. 78, 88.

44. Federal Election Commission, "The Impact of the National Voter Registration Act on Federal Elections 1999–2000," www.fec.gov.

45. See Raymond E. Wolfinger and Ben Highton, "Estimating the Effects of the National Voter Registration Act of 1993," *Political Behavior* (June 1998), pp. 79–104; and Raymond E. Wolfinger and Jonathan Hoffman, "Registering and Voting with Motor Voter," *PS: Political Science & Politics* (March 2001), pp. 85–92.

46. Quin Monson and Lindsay Nielson, "Mobilizing the Early Voter," paper presented at the annual meeting of the Midwest Political Science Association, Chicago, Ill., April 3–6, 2008; and Michael P. McDonald and Thomas Schaller, "Voter Mobilization in the 2008 Presidential Election," in David B. Magleby, ed., *The Change Election: Money, Mobilization, and Persuasion in the 2008 Federal Elections* (Temple University Press, 2011).

47. U.S. Census Bureau, "Voting and Registration in the Election of November 2004," www.census.gov/prod/2006pubs/p20-556.pdf.

48. The Early Voting Information Center, "Absence and Early Voting Laws," www.earlyvoting.net/ states/abs/aws.php (accessed October 14, 2008).

49. For a discussion of the differences in the turnout between presidential and midterm elections, see James E. Campbell, "The Presidential Surge and Its Midterm Decline in Congressional Elections, 1868-1988," *Journal of Politics* 53 (May 1991), pp. 477–487.

50. David E. Rosenbaum, "Democrats Keep Solid Hold on Congress," *New York Times*, November 9, 1988, p. A24; Louis V. Gerstner, "Next Time, Let Us Boldly Vote as No Democracy Has Before," *USA Today*, November 16, 1998, p. A15; and Michael P. McDonald and Thomas Schaller, "Voter Mobilization in the 2008 Presidential Election," in David B. Magleby, ed., *The Change Election: Money, Mobilization, and Persuasion in the 2008 Federal Elections* (Temple University Press, 2011), p. 89.

51. Data from Curtis Gans, "President Bush, Mobilization Drives Propel Turnout to Post-1968 High; Kerry, Democratic Weakness Shown," *Center for Voting and Democracy*, November 4, 2004, www.fairvote.org/reports/csae2004electionreport.pdf.

52. Wolfinger and Rosenstone, *Who Votes?*, p. 102.

53. For a discussion of mobilization efforts and race, see Jan Leighley, *Strength in Numbers? The Political Mobilization of Racial and Ethnic Minorities* (Princeton University Press, 2001).

54. http://www.cnn.com/ELECTION/2008/results/ polls (accessed November 6, 2008).

55. U.S. Census Bureau, "Reported Voting and Registration by Race, Hispanic Origin, Sex, and Age Groups: November 1964 to 2008," *Voting and Registration*, July 2009, http://www.census.gov/hhes/www/socdemo/voting/publications/historical/index.html (accessed April 29, 2010).

56. Ibid.

57. Howard W. Stanley and Richard G. Niemi, *Vital Statistics on Politics, 1999–2000* (CQ Press, 2000), pp. 120–121; and Harold W. Stanley and Richard G. Niemi, *Vital Statistics on Politics, 2005–2006* (CQ Press, 2006), pp. 124–125.

58. http://www.cnn.com/ELECTIONS/2008/results/ polls (accessed November 6, 2008).

59. http://www.cnn.com/ELECTIONS/2008/results/ polls (accessed November 6, 2008).

60. http://www.time.com/time/politics/article/0,8599,1708570,00.html (accessed April 16, 2010); and Heather Smith, Rock the Vote Executive Director, interview with David B. Magleby (March 25, 2009).

61. The Center for Information & Research on Civic Learning and Engagement, "Turnout by Education, Race, and Gender and Other 2008 Youth Voting Statistics," November 2008, http://www.civicyouth.org/?p=324 (accessed April 21, 2010).

62. David B. Magleby, ed., *The Change Election: Money, Mobilization, and Persuasion in the 2008 Federal Elections* (Temple University Press, 2011).

63. http://www.cnn.com/ELECTIONS/2008/results/ polls (accessed November 6, 2008).

64. U.S. Census Bureau, "Voting and Registration in the Election of November 2000," www.census.gov/prod/2002pubs/p20-542.pdf.

65. Christopher R. Ellis, Joseph Daniel Ura, and Jenna Ashley-Robinson, "The Dynamic Consequences of Nonvoting in American National Elections," *Political Research Quarterly* 59 (June 2006), pp. 232–233.

66. Austin Ranney, "Nonvoting Is Not a Social Disease," *Public Opinion* (October–November 1983), pp. 16–19.

67. Sidney Verba, "Would the Dream of Political Equality Turn Out to Be a Nightmare?" *Perspectives on Politics* 4 (December 2003), pp. 667–672.

68. E. E. Schattschneider, *The Semisovereign People* (Dryden Press, 1975), p. 96.

69. Stephen Earl Bennett and David Resnick, "The Implications of Nonvoting for Democracy in the United States," *American Journal of Political Science* 84 (August 1990), pp. 771–802.

70. David B. Magleby, Candice J. Nelson, and Mark C. Westlye, "The Myth of the Independent Voter Revisited" Working Paper 10-01, Center for the Study of Elections and Democracy, Brigham Young University, January 2010. http://csed.byu.edu/Assets/Magleby%20Nelson%20Westlye%202010.pdf].

71. Ibid.

72. http://www.whitehouse.gov/history/presidents/ (accessed November 8, 2008).

73. David Menefee-Libey, *The Triumph of Campaign-Centered Politics* (Chatham House/Seven Bridges Press, 2000).

74. J. Merrill Shanks and Warren E. Miller, "Policy Direction and Performance Evaluation: Complementary Explanations of the Reagan Elections," *British Journal of Political Science* 20 (1990), pp. 143–235; and Warren E. Miller and J. Merrill Shanks, "Policy Direction and Performance Evaluation: Comparing George Bush's Victory with Those of Ronald Reagan in 1980–1984," paper presented at the annual meeting of the American Political Science Association, Atlanta, Ga., August 31–September 2, 1989.

75. Amihai Glazer, "The Strategy of Candidate Ambiguity," *American Political Science Review* 84 (March 1990), pp. 237–241.

76. Robert S. Erikson and David W. Romero, "Candidate Equilibrium and the Behavioral Model of the Vote," *American Political Science Review* 84 (December 1990), p. 1122.

77. Morris P. Fiorina, *Retrospective Voting in American National Elections* (Yale University Press, 1981).

78. Cable News Network. "Exit Polls Election 2000," www.cnn.com/ELECTION/2000/results/index.epolls.html (last accessed July 12, 2008).

79. Gerald H. Kramer, "Short-Term Fluctuations in U.S. Voting Behavior, 1896–1964," *American Political Science Review* 65 (March 1971), pp. 131–143; see also Edward R. Tufte, "Determinants of the Outcomes of Midterm Congressional Elections," *American Political Science Review* (September 1975), pp. 812–826; and Andrew E. Busch, *Horses in Midstream: U.S. Midterm Elections and Their Consequences* (University of Pittsburgh Press, 1999).

80. John R. Hibbing and John R. Alford, "The Educational Impact of Economic Conditions: Who Is Held Responsible?" *American Journal of Political Science* 25 (August 1981), pp. 423–439; and Morris P. Fiorina, "Who Is Held Responsible? Further Evidence on the Hibbing-Alford Thesis," *American Journal of Political Science* (February 1983), pp. 158-164.

81. David B. Magleby, "Electoral Politics as Team Sport: Advantage to the Democrats," in John C. Green and Daniel J. Coffey, eds., *The State of the Parties: The Changing Role of Contemporary American Parties* (Rowman & Littlefield, 2011).

82. Ryan L. Claasen, David B. Magleby, J. Quin Monson, and Kelly D. Patterson, "At Your Service: Voter Evaluations of Poll Worker Performance," *American Politics Research* 36 (July 2008): 612–634.

Chapter 9

1. David B. Magleby, "Adaptation and Innovation in the Financing of the 2008 Elections," in David B. Magleby and Anthony Corrado, eds.,

Financing the 2008 Election (Brookings Institution Press, 2010), Table 1–3.

2. Anthony Corrado, "Fund-raising Strategies in the 2008 Presidential Campaign," in James Thurber and Candice J. Nelson, eds., *Campaigns and Elections American Style* (Boulder, CO: Westview Press, 2009), p. 114.

3. U.S. Census Bureau, "Number of Elected Officials Exceeds Half Million—Almost All Are with Local Governments," press release, January 30, 1995.

4. U.S. Senate, www.senate.gov/general/ contact_information/senators_cfm.cfm.

5. Associated Press, "Voters Retain State Term Limits," November 4, 2008, http://www .kxmb.com/News/293253.asp (accessed November 6, 2008).

6. *U.S. Term Limits Inc. v. Thornton*, 514 U.S. 799 (1995).

7. For an insightful examination of electoral rules, see Bernard Grofman and Arend Lijphart, eds., *Electoral Laws and Their Political Consequences* (Agathon Press, 1986).

8. New York State Board of Elections, "2009 Election Results: 23rd Congressional District," December 15, 2009, http://www.elections .state.ny.us/NYSBOE/Elections/2009/Special/ 23rdCDSpecialVoteResults.pdf (accessed May 19, 2010).

9. Arend Lijphart, "The Political Consequences of Electoral Laws, 1945–85," *American Political Science Review* 84 (June 1990), pp. 481–495; see also David M. Farrell, *Electoral Systems: A Comparative Introduction* (Macmillan, 2001).

10. There was one faithless elector in 2000 from the District of Columbia who abstained rather than cast her vote for Al Gore in order to protest the lack of congressional representation for Washington, D.C. See www.cnn.com/ 2001/ALLPOLITICS/stories/01/06/electoral .vote/index.html. The electoral college vote in 2004 had one faithless elector, an elector from Minnesota who voted for John Edwards instead of John Kerry.

11. As noted, one of Gore's electors abstained, reducing his vote from 267 to 266; www.cnn .com/2001/ALLPOLITICS/stories/01/06/ electoral.vote/index.html.

12. Paul D. Schumaker and Burdett A. Loomis, *Choosing a President: The Electoral College and Beyond* (Seven Bridges Press, 2002), p. 60; see also George Rabinowitz and Stuart Elaine MacDonald, "The Power of the States in U.S. Presidential Elections," *American Political Science Review* 80 (March 1986), pp. 65–87; and Dany M. Adkison and Christopher Elliott, "The Electoral College: A Misunderstood Institution," *PS: Political Science and Politics* 30 (March 1997), pp. 77–80.

13. See, for example, David R. Mayhew, *Congress: The Electoral Connection* (Yale University Press, 1974); Richard F. Fenno, Jr., *Home Style: House Members in Their Districts* (Little, Brown, 1978); and James E. Campbell, "The Return of Incumbents: The Nature of Incumbency Advantage," *Western Political Quarterly* 36 (September 1983), pp. 434–444.

14. Gary King and Andrew Gelman, "Systemic Consequences of Incumbency Advantage in U.S. House Elections," *American Journal of Political Science* 35 (February 1991), pp. 110–137.

15. Alan I. Abramowitz, "Economic Conditions, Presidential Popularity, and Voting Behavior in Midterm Congressional Elections," *Journal of Politics* 47 (February 1985), pp. 31–43; see also Gary C. Jacobson, *The Politics of Congressional Elections,* 5th ed. (Addison-Wesley, 2001), pp. 146–153.

16. See Edward R. Tufte, *Political Control of the Economy* (Princeton University Press, 1978); see also his "Determinants of the Outcomes of Midterm Congressional Elections," *American Political Science Review* 69 (September 1975), pp. 812–826. For a more recent discussion of the same subject, see Jacobson, *Politics of Congressional Elections,* pp. 123–178.

17. Alan I. Abramowitz and Jeffrey A. Segal, "Determinants of the Outcomes of U.S. Senate Elections," *Journal of Politics* 48 (1986), pp. 433–439.

18. David B. Magleby and Kelly D. Patterson, eds., *The Battle for Congress: Iraq, Scandal, and Campaign Finance in the 2006 Election* (Paradigm, 2008).

19. Rhodes Cook, "Congress and Primaries: Looking for Clues to a Tidal Wave," *The Wall Street Journal,* July 24, 2008, http://blogs.wsj .com/political perceptions/2008/07/24/ Congressional-Primaries-looking-for-clues-to-tidal-wave/.

20. Linda L. Fowler and Robert D. McClure, *Political Ambition: Who Decides to Run for Congress* (Yale University Press, 1989); and Paul S. Herrnson, *Congressional Elections: Campaigning at Home and in Washington,* 5th ed. (CQ Press, 2007), p. 45.

21. Kathleen Hall Jamieson, *Everything You Think You Know About Politics…and Why You're Wrong* (Basic Books, 2000), p. 38.

22. For a discussion of different explanations of the impact of incumbency, see Keith Krehbiel and John R. Wright, "The Incumbency Effect in Congressional Elections: A Test of Two Explanations," *American Journal of Political Science* 27 (February 1983), p. 140.

23. Harold W. Stanley and Richard G. Niemi, *Vital Statistics on American Politics 2009–2010* (CQ Press, 2010), pp. 45–47.

24. "Financial Activity of Senate and House General Election Campaigns," Federal Election Commission, http://www.fec.gov/press/ press2009/2009Dec29Cong/4gen08.pdf.

25. Candice J. Nelson, "Spending in the 2000 Elections," in David B. Magleby, ed., *Financing the 2000 Election* (Brookings Institution Press, 2002), pp. 28–30.

26. Jonathan S. Krasno, *Challengers, Competition, and Reelection: Comparing Senate and House Elections* (Yale University Press, 1994), p. 2.

27. Alan I. Abramowitz, "Explaining Senate Election Outcomes," *American Political Science Review* 82 (June 1988), pp. 385–403.

28. Ben Smith, "Obama Clears Field for Gillibrand in New York," *Politico,* May 15, 2009, http://www.politico.com/blogs/bensmith/ 0509/Obama_clears_field_for_Gillibrand_in_ New_York.html (accessed April 28, 2010.)

29. David B. Magleby, "More Bang for the Buck: Campaign Spending in Small State U.S. Senate Elections," paper presented at the annual meeting of the Western Political Science Association, Salt Lake City, Utah (March 30–April 1, 1989).

30. Scott Shepard, "Politicians Already Looking to 2008 Election," *Austin (Texas) American-Statesman,* February 6, 2005; and Associated Press, "Former Bush Aide: 2008 Democratic Nomination Belongs to Hillary," April 30, 2005.

31. Susan Saulny, "Thompson Enters Race from 'Tonight Show' Couch," *New York Times,* September 6, 2007, p. A23.

32. Arthur Hadley, *Invisible Primary* (Prentice Hall, 1976).

33. "State by State Summary 2004 Presidential Primaries, Caucuses, and Conventions," www.thegreenpapers.com/P04/tally.phtml.

34. The descriptions of these types of primaries are drawn from James W. Davis, *Presidential Primaries,* rev. ed. (Greenwood Press, 1984),

Chapter 3. See pp. 56–63 for specifics on each state (and Puerto Rico). This material is used with the permission of the publisher.

35. Paul T. David and James W. Caesar, *Proportional Representation in Presidential Nominating Politics* (University Press of Virginia, 1980), pp. 9–11.

36. See Rhodes Cook, *Race for the Presidency: Winning the 2004 Nomination* (CQ Press, 2004), p. 5; see also the Republican National Committee, www.rnc.org.

37. Nelson W. Polsby and Aaron Wildavsky, *Presidential Elections: Strategies and Structures of American Politics,* 11th ed. (Rowman & Littlefield, 2004), p. 110.

38. The Green Papers, *The Green Papers, 2004 Presidential Primaries, Caucuses, and Conventions: New York Republican,* www.thegreenpapers.com/P04/NY-R.phtml.

39. Costas Panagopoulos, "Election Issues 2004 in Depth," *Campaigns & Elections* (May 2004), p. 48.

40. Lesley Clark, "DNC Votes to Strip Florida of Delegates: Florida's Status as a Key Presidential Prize Is in Doubt, with National Democratic Party Leaders Rejecting a State Plan to Hold an Early Primary," *Miami Herald,* August 26, 2007; see also "Campaign Briefing: On the Trail," *Newsday,* December 2, 2007, p. A3.

41. Jill Zuckman, "McCain Wins Nomination: Huckabee Steps Aside as Ex-Rival Targets Democrats," *Chicago Tribune,* March 5, 2008.

42. Federal Election Commission, "2004 Presidential Primary Dates and Candidates Filing Deadlines for Ballot Access," May 26, 2004, www.fec.gov.

43. *California Democratic Party et al., Petitioners* v. *Bill Jones, Secretary of State of California et al.,* 530 U.S. 567 (2000).

44. David Redlawsk and Arthur Sanders, "Groups and Grassroots in the Iowa Caucuses," in David B. Magleby, ed., *Outside Money in the 2000. Presidential Primaries and Congressional Elections,* in *PS: Political Science and Politics* (June 2001), p. 270; see also Iowa Caucus Project 2004, www.iowacaucus.org.

45. Perry Bacon, Jr., "Clinton Blames MoveOn for Caucus Losses," *The Washington Post,* blog.washingtonpost.com/the-trail/2008/04/ 19/clinton_blames_moveon_for_cauc.html.

46. "Stunner in N.H.: Clinton Defeats Obama," January 9, 2008, www.msnbc.msn.com/ id/22551718/.

47. The viewership of conventions has declined as the amount of time devoted to conventions dropped. In 1988, Democrats averaged 27.1 million viewers and Republicans 24.5 million. By 1996, viewership for the Democrats was 18 million viewers on average; for the Republicans, it was 16.6 million. See John Carmody, "The TV Column," *The Washington Post,* September 2, 1996, p. D4. Viewership figures improved somewhat in 2000: Democrats averaged 20.6 million viewers and Republicans 19.2 million. See Don Aucoin, "Democrats Hold TV Ratings Edge," *The Boston Globe,* August 19, 2000, p. F3; and Jim Rutenberg and Brain Stelter, "Conventions, Anything but Dull, Are a TV Hit," *New York Times,* September 6, 2008.

48. Barry Goldwater, speech to the Republican National Convention accepting the Republican nomination for president, July 16, 1964, www.washingtonpost.com/wp-srv/politics/ daily/may98/goldwaterspeech.htm.

49. Acceptance speech at the 1980 Convention, July 17, 1980, http://www.nationalcenter .org/ReaganConvention1980.html.

50. Jeff Fishel, *Presidents and Promises* (CQ Press, 1984), pp. 26–28.

51. Joe Von Kanel and Hal Quinley, "Exit Polls: Obama Wins Big Among Young, Minority Voters," *CNN Politics.com*, November 4, 2008, http://www.cnn.com/2008/POLITICS/11/04/exit.polls/ (accessed April 28, 2010).

52. Sam Reed, "Washington State's February 19, 2008 Presidential Primary," www.secstate.wa.gov/elections/pdf/2008PP/PP%20MFQ%20Updated%20August%202007%20Final.pdf.

53. Richard Wagner, "Ballot Access News," www.ballot-access.org/2008/020108.html.

54. North Carolina State Board of Elections, "Fact Sheet: Running for President of the United States of America," http://www.sboe.stak.nc.us/GetDocument.aspx?id=308.

55. Commission on Presidential Debates, www.debates.org/pages/news_040617_p.html.

56. Ralph Nader, "Open the Debates for Third-Party Candidates Like Bob Barr, Cynthia McKinney, and Me," *U.S. News and World Report*, September 22, 2008, http://www.usnews.com/articles/opinion/2008/09/22/nader-open-the-debates-for-third-party-candidates-like-bob-barr-cynthia-mckinney-and-me.html (accessed March 18, 2010).

57. "The Great Ad Wars of 2004," *New York Times*, November 11, 2004, www.polisci.wisc.edu/tvadvertising/Press_Clippings/Press_Clipping_PDFs/110104%20NYTIMES_AD_GRAPHIC.pdf.

58. University of Wisconsin–Madison and the Brennan Center for Justice at NYU School of Law, "Political Advertising Nearly Tripled in 2000 with Half-a-Million More TV Ads," press release, March 14, 2001; David B. Magleby, "Elections as Team Sports: Spending by Candidates, Political Parties, and Interest Groups in the 2008 Election Cycle," in David B. Magleby, ed., *The Change Election: Money, Mobilization, and Persuasion in the 2008 Federal Elections* (Temple University Press, 2011).

59. Robert S. Erikson, "Economic Conditions and the Presidential Vote," *American Political Science Review* 83 (June 1989), pp. 567–575. Class-based voting has also become more important. See Robert S. Erikson, Thomas O. Lancaster, and David W. Romers, "Group Components of the Presidential Vote, 1952–1984," *Journal of Politics* 51 (May 1989), pp. 337–346.

60. David B. Magleby, "Elections as Team Sports: Spending by Candidates, Political Parties, and Interest Groups in the 2008 Election Cycle," in David B. Magleby, ed., *The Change Election: Money, Mobilization, and Persuasion in the 2008 Federal Elections*, p. 9.

61. John C. Fortier and Norman J. Ornstein, "The Absentee Ballot and the Secret Ballot: Challenges for Election Reform," *University of Michigan Journal of Law Reform* 36 (Spring 2003), pp. 483–517.

62. Jerrold G. Rusk, "The Effect of the Australian Ballot Reform on Split Ticket Voting: 1876–1908," *American Political Science Review* 64 (December 1970), pp. 1220–1238.

63. Fortier and Ornstein, "The Absentee Ballot and the Secret Ballot."

64. Lewis L. Gould, *Grand Old Party: A History of the Republicans* (Random House, 2003), p. 236.

65. David B. Magleby and Candice J. Nelson, *The Money Chase: Congressional Campaign Finance Reform* (Brookings Institution Press, 1990), pp. 13–14.

66. http://www.opensecrets.org/pres08/summary.php?cycle=2008&cid=N00009638 (accessed November 6, 2008).

67. Anthony Corrado, Thomas E. Mann, Daniel R. Ortiz, and Trevor Potter, eds., *The New Campaign Finance Sourcebook* (Brookings Institution Press, 2005).

68. *Davis* v. *FEC.* 128 S.Ct. 2759. (2008).

69. Elizabeth Drew, *The Corruption of American Politics: What Went Wrong and Why* (Carol, 1999), pp. 7–8.

70. Gould, *Grand Old Party*, pp. 389–391; and Jules Witcover, *Party of the People: A History of the Democrats* (Random House, 2003), pp. 589–590.

71. Anthony Corrado, "Money and Politics: A History of Campaign Finance Law," in *Campaign Finance Reform: A Sourcebook* (Brookings Institution Press, 1997), p. 32.

72. See Senate Committee on Governmental Affairs, "1997 Special Investigation in Connection with the 1996 Federal Election Campaigns," http://hsgac.senate.gov/sireport.htm.

73. *Buckley* v. *Valeo*, 424 U.S. 1 (1976).

74. David B. Magleby and Eric A. Smith, "Party Soft Money in the 2000 Congressional Elections," in David B. Magleby, ed., *The Other Campaign: Soft Money and Issue Advocacy in the 2000 Congressional Elections*, p. 29, 38; and David B. Magleby and Nicole Carlisle Squires, "Party Money in the 2002 Congressional Elections," in David B. Magleby and J. Quin Monson, eds., *The Last Hurrah? Soft Money and Issue Advocacy in the 2002 Congressional Elections* (Brookings Institution Press, 2004), pp. 44–5, Figure 2–2. http://hsgac.senate.gov/sireport.htm.

75. David B. Magleby and Nicole Carlisle Squires, "Party Money in the 2002 Congressional Elections," in *The Last Hurrah?* p. 45, Figure 2–2.

76. *McConnell* v. *Federal Election Commission*, 540 U.S. 93 (2003).

77. Corrado, Mann, Ortiz, and Potter, *The New Campaign Finance Sourcebook*, p. 79.

78. David B. Magleby, ed., *The Last Hurrah* (Brookings Institution Press, 2004), pp. 44–45.

79. Ibid., p. 46.

80. *McConnell* v. *Federal Election Commission*.

81. *Buckley* v. *Valeo*, Footnote 52.

82. *Federal Election Commission* v. *Wisconsin Right to Life, Inc.*, 551 U.S. 449 (2007).

83. *Citizen's United* v. *Federal Election Commission*, 558 U.S. (2010).

84. See Joseph A. Pika, "Campaign Spending and Activity in the 2000 Delaware U.S. Senate Race," in David B. Magleby, ed., *Election Advocacy: Soft Money and Issue Advocacy in the 2000 Congressional Elections* (Center for the Study of Elections and Democracy, Brigham Young University, 2001), pp. 51–61.

85. Magleby, *Dictum Without Data*, p. 12.

86. Kate Snow, "Obama Could Get 'Swift Boated,'" *ABC News*, April 19, 2008, abcnews.go.com/Politics/story?id=4688386.

87. David B. Magleby, ed., *The Change Election: Money, Mobilization, and Persuasion in the 2008 Federal Elections* (Provo, UT: Center for the Study of Elections and Democracy).

88. David B. Magleby, "Change and Continuity in the Financing of Federal Elections," in David B. Magleby, Anthony J. Corrado, and Kelly D. Patterson, eds., *Financing the 2004 Elections* (Brookings Institution Press, 2006), p. 15.

89. Bipartisan Campaign Reform Act of 2002, 107th Cong., 1st sess., H.R. 2356.

90. Corrado, Mann, Ortiz, and Potter, *The New Campaign Finance Sourcebook*, pp. 74–76.

91. David B. Magleby, ed., *Dancing Without Partners Monograph*, csed.byu.edu/Publications/DancingwithoutPartners.pdf, p. 53.

92. Federal Election Commission, "FEC Reports on Congressional Financial Activity for 2000," press release, May 15, 2001; Federal Election Commission, "Congressional Candidates Spend $1.16 Billion During 2003–2004," press release, June 9, 2005; and Federal Election Commission, "Congressional Candidates

Raised $1.42 Billion in 2007–2008," press release, December 29, 2009.

93. *Colorado Republican Federal Campaign Committee* v. *Federal Election Commission*, 518 U.S. 604 (1996).

94. BCRA does allow candidates to pay themselves out of their campaign funds, something that helps less-affluent candidates run. But given the high cost of campaigns, such a strategy is often not going to be helpful to winning the election.

95. Federal Election Commission, "2000–2001 Financial Activity of Senate and House General Election Campaigns," www.fec.gov; and Federal Election Commission, "1999-2000 Financial Activity of Senate and House General Election Campaigns," www.fec.gov.

96. New Jersey Election Law Enforcement Commission, "Candidate Disclosure Report," http://www.elec.state.nj.us/ELECReport/StandardSearch.aspx.

97. Jose Antonia Vargas, "Campaign.USA: With the Internet Comes a New Political 'Clickocracy,'" *The Washington Post*, April 1, 2008, p. C01.

98. U.S. Census Bureau, *Statistical Abstract of the United States: 2006* (U.S. Government Printing Office, 2006), p. 267.

99. Federal Election Commission, herndon1.sdrdc.com/fecimg/srssea.html; see also FEC, "Congressional Candidates Spend $1.16 Billion During 2003–2004," press release, June 9, 2005, www.fec.gov/press/press2005/20050609candidate/20050609candidate.html.

100. Rick Hampson, "Former Banker Was Big Spender," *USA Today*, November 9, 2000, p. A9.

101. See Todd Donovan and Shawn Bowler, *Reforming the Republic: Democratic Institutions for a New America* (Prentice Hall, 2004).

102. Curtis B. Gans, director, Committee for the Study of the American Electorate, personal communication, September 22, 2004.

103. The President's Commission for a National Agenda for the Eighties, in *A National Agenda for the Eighties* (U.S. Government Printing Office, 1980), p. 97, proposed holding four presidential primaries, scheduled approximately one month apart.

Chapter 10

1. Evan Tracey and CMAG as quoted in Alan Fram, "The Influence Game: Drug Lobby's Health Care Win," *Associated Press*, March 29, 2010, http://www.tnsmi-cmag.com/Publications/PR_20100329.pdf (accessed May 3, 2010).

2. Katharine Q. Seelye, "Competing Ads on Health Care Plan Swamp the Airwaves," *New York Times*, August 15, 2009, http://www.nytimes.com/2009/08/16/health/policy/16ads.html?_r=1 (accessed May 3, 2010).

3. Michael Scherer, "Top 10 Health-Care-Reform Fight Ads," *TIME*, August 19, 2009, http://www.time.com/time/specials/packages/article/0,28804,1917490_1917489_1917470,00.html (accessed May 3, 2010).

4. Source Watch, "Coalition for Health Insurance Choices," *Source Watch*, http://www.sourcewatch.org/index.php?title=Coalition_for_Health_Insurance_Choices (accessed May 6, 2010).

5. Darrell M. West, Diane Heith, and Chris Goodwin, "Harry and Louise Go to Washington: Political Advertising and Health Care Reform," *Journal of Health Politics, Policy and Law* 21(1) (1996), pp. 35–68.

6. Alan Fram, "Harry and Louise Back on TV, for Health Overhaul," *Associated Press*, July 16, 2009, http://abcnews.go.com/Business/story?id=8103244&page=1 (accessed May 6, 2010).

7. Husna Haq, "Why Americas Oppose the Healthcare Reform Bill," *The Christian Science Monitor*, March 19, 2010, http://www .csmonitor.com/USA/Politics/2010/0319/ Why-Americans-oppose-the-healthcare-reform-bill (accessed May 6, 2010).

8. William Rivers, *The Other Government* (Universe Books, 1982); Douglas Cater, *The Fourth Branch of Government* (Houghton Mifflin, 1959); Dom Bonafede, "The Washington Press: An Interpreter or a Participant in Policy Making?" *National Journal*, April 24, 1982, pp. 716–721; and Michael Ledeen, "Learning to Say 'No' to the Press," *Public Interest* 73 (Fall 1983), p. 113.

9. Leslie G. Moeller, "The Big Four: Mass Media Actualities and Expectations," in Richard W. Budd and Brent D. Ruben, eds., *Beyond Media: New Approaches to Mass Communication* (Transaction Books, 1988), p. 15.

10. Pew Research Center for the People & the Press, "Far More Voters Believe Election Outcome Matters," questionnaire, May 9, 2006, http://people-press.org/reports/ print.php3?PageID=802. One service that e-mails customized news and reminders to subscribers is infobeat.com.

11. See Doris A. Graber, "Say It with Pictures: The Impact of Audiovisual News on Public Opinion Formation," paper presented at the annual meeting of the Midwest Political Science Association, April 1987, Chicago; and Benjamin I. Page, Robert Y. Shapiro, and Glenn R. Dempsey, "What Moves Public Opinion?" *American Political Science Review* 76 (March 1987), pp. 23–43.

12. U.S. Census Bureau, *Statistical Abstract of the United States: 2010* (U.S. Government Printing Office, 2010), pp. 693–694.

13. Pew Project for Excellence in Journalism, "Overview," *The State of The News Media: 2010*, http://www.stateofthemedia.org/2010/ overview_key_findings.php (accessed March 2, 2010).

14. Ibid.

15. Leigh Holmwood, "Barack Obama Speech Watched by 38.4M Americans," *The Guardian*, September 2, 2008, http://www.guardian.co.uk/ media/2008/sep/02/tvratings.democrats2008 (accessed March 29, 2010).

16. Jeffrey W. Koch, "Campaign Ads' Impact on Voter Certainty and Knowledge of Candidates' Ideological Positions," 2003, *American Political Science Association*, http://www.allacademic .com//meta/p_mla_apa_research_citation/ 0/6/2/4/8/pages62486/p62486-1.php (accessed March 30, 2010).

17. David B. Magleby, "Adaptation and Innovation in the Financing of the 2008 Elections," in David B. Magleby and Anthony Corrado, eds., *Financing the 2008 Election* (Brookings, forth-coming).

18. Journalism.org, "Local TV," March 15, 2004, http://www.stateofthemedia.org/ 2004/ narrative_localtv_contentanalysis.asp? cat=2&media=6 (accessed May 26, 2010); see also, Marc Fisher, "TV Stations Offer a Clear Picture of Indifference," *The Washington Post*, September 26, 2000, p. B1.

19. Alliance for Better Campaigns, *Political Standard* 4 (March 2001), p. 6.

20. *Statistical Abstract of the United States: 2010*, p. 694.

21. *Statistical Abstract of the United States: 2010*, p. 694.

22. Mediamark Research Inc., "Mediamark Research Inc. Releases MediaDay Study," press release, June 25, 2007, http://www.mediamark .com/ PDF/Mediamark%20Research%20Inc% 20Releases%20MediaDay%20Study.pdf, (accessed April 2, 2008).

23. Robert J. Duffy, Kyle L. Saunders, and Joshua Dunn, "Colorado: Democrats Expand Their Base and Win Unaffiliated Voters," in David B. Magleby, ed., *The Change Election: Money, Mobilization, and Persuasion in the 2008 Federal Elections* (Temple University Press, 2011).

24. National Public Radio, "Morning Edition: About the Program," *NPR*, 2010, http:// www.npr.org/templates/story/story.php? storyId=5003 (accessed April 23, 2010).

25. Paul Farhi, "Limbaugh's Audience Size? It's Largely Up in the Air," *The Washington Post*, March 7, 2009, http://www.washingtonpost .com/wp-dyn/content/article/2009/03/06/ AR2009030603435.html (accessed April 30, 2010).

26. *Statistical Abstract of the United States: 2010*, p. 696.

27. Newspaper Association of America, "Readership," http://www.naa.org/ TrendsandNumbers/Readership.aspx (accessed March 30, 2010).

28. Nat Ives, "Publishers: Why Count Only People Who Pay?" *Advertising Age*, November 12, 2007, p. 8.

29. National Public Radio, "Extra! Extra! We Still Want News," *On the Media* (transcript), March 28, 2008, at http://www.onthemedia.org/ transcripts/2008/03/28/05, accessed April 3, 2008; and Noam Cohen, "Craig (of the List) Looks Beyond the Web," *New York Times*, May 12, 2008, C1.

30. *The Washington Times*, "Circulation Declines Are Getting Steeper," http://www.washingtontimes .com/news/2009/apr/28/circulation-declines-are-getting-steeper/ (accessed May 26, 2010).

31. Stephanie Clifford, "Newsweek on Block as Era of the Newsweekly Fades" *New York Times*, May 5, 2010, http://www.nytimes.com/2010/ 05/06/business/media/06newsweek.htm (accessed May 14, 2010).

32. Arthur L. Norberg and Judy E. O'Neill, *Transforming Computer Technology: Information Processing for the Pentagon, 1962–1986* (Johns Hopkins University Press, 1996).

33. Boutell.com, "WWW FAQS: How Many Web Sites Are There?," http://www.boutell.com/ newfaq/misc/sizeofweb.html (accessed May 26, 2010).

34. Domain Tools, "Domain Counts & Internet Statistics," http://www.domaintools.com/ internet-statistics/ (accessed May 26, 2010).

35. Alex Mindlin, "Web Passes Papers as a News Source," *New York Times*, January 4, 2009, http://www.nytimes.com/2009/01/05/business/ media/05drill.html (accessed March 30, 2010).

36. Pew Internet & American Life Project, *Teens and Technology*, July 27, 2005, www .pewinternet.org/pdfs/PIP_Teens_Tech_ July2005web.pdf (accessed May 12, 2006).

37. Amanda Lenhart, Sousan Arafeh, Aaron Smith, and Alexandra McGill, "Writing, Technology, and Teens," *Pew Internet & American Life Project*, April 2008, http://www.pewinternet.org/ Reports/2008/Writing-Technology-and-Teens/ 04-The-Lives-of-Teens-and-Their-Technology/ 05-Many-teens-go-online-daily .aspx?r=1 (accessed May 26, 2010); and Amanda Lenhart, "Teens and Social Media: An Overview," *Pew Internet & American Life Project*, April 10, 2009, http://isites.harvard.edu/fs/docs/icb.topic603902 .files/Teens%20Social%20Media%20and %20Health%20-%20NYPH%20Dept %20Pew% 20Internet.pdf (accessed May 26, 2010).

38. Cass Sunstein, *Republic.com* (Princeton University Press, 2001), pp. 73–75.

39. http://www.edisonreserach.com/twitter_ usage_2010.php (accessed June 10, 2010)

40. Time.com, "How Facebook Is Redefining Privacy," (accessed June 10, 2010).

41. http://blog.nielsen.com/nielsenwire/global/ facebook-and-twitter-post-large-year-over-year-gains-in-unique-users/ and http://blog.nielsen.com/nielsenwire/global/ led-by-facebook-twitter-global-time-spent-on-social-media-sites-up-82-year-over-year/ (accessed June 10, 2010).

42. Pew Research Center for the People & the Press, "Key Audiences Now Blend Online and Traditional Sources," August 17, 2008, http://people-press.org/report/?pageid=1352 (accessed April 22, 2010).

43. Pew Research Center for the People & the Press, Survey Reports, "Bottom-Line Pressures Now Hurting Coverage, Say Journalists" May 23, 2004, http://people-press.org/reports/display .php3?PageID=826 (accessed May 26, 2010).

44. See Robert A. Rutland, *Newsmongers: Journalism in the Life of the Nation, 1690–1972* (Dial Press, 1973).

45. David Paul Nord, *Communities of Journalism* (University of Illinois Press, 2001), pp. 80–89.

46. Quoted in Frank Luther Mott, *American Journalism*, 3d ed. (Macmillan, 1962), p. 412.

47. During the 1930s, members of Congress on one network alone made more than 1,000 speeches. See Edward W. Chester, *Radio, Television, and American Politics* (Sheed & Ward, 1969), p. 62.

48. Frances Perkins, quoted in James MacGregor Burns, *Roosevelt: The Lion and the Fox* (Harcourt, 1956), p. 205.

49. CBS News, "Abuse of Iraqi POWs by GIs Probed: 60 Minutes II Has Exclusive Report on Alleged Mistreatment," April 28, 2004, http://www .cbsnews.com/stories/2004/04/27/60II/ main614063.shtml (accessed April 23, 2008).

50. Dana Priest, "CIA Holds Terror Suspects in Secret Prisons," *The Washington Post*, November 2, 2005, p. A01.

51. Fred Emery, *Watergate: The Corruption of American Politics and the Fall of Richard Nixon* (Touchstone, 1995).

52. Bob Woodward and Carl Bernstein, *All the President's Men* (Simon & Schuster, 1994).

53. Mark Felt, John D. O'Connor, and W. Mark Felt, *A G-Man's Life: The FBI, Being 'Deep Throat' and the Struggle for Honor in Washington* (Public Affairs Press, 2006).

54. Martin Peers, "Murdoch Wins His Bid for Dow Jones," *The Wall Street Journal*, August 1, 2007, p. A1.

55. News Corporation, home page, http://www .newscorp.com/index.html (accessed April 3, 2008).

56. Gannett Company, "Company Profile," www.gannett.com/about/company_profile .htm (accessed April 22, 2010); and "Gannett Company, Inc: Company Information," *New York Times*, http://topics.nytimes.com/ topics/news/business/companies/gannett_ company/index.html (accessed April 22, 2010).

57. Tribune Company, "About Tribune," http:// www.tribune.com/ (accessed April 22, 2010).

58. Neilsen Company, "2010 Media Industry Facts," http://blog.nielsen.com/nielsenwire/press/ nielsen-fact-sheet-2010.pdf (accessed May 26, 2010); and "FCC Issues 12th Annual Report to Congress on Video Competition," press release, February 10, 2006, hraunfoss.fcc.gov/edocs_ public/attachmatch/DOC-263763A1.pdf (accessed May 11, 2006).

59. Seth Schiesel, "FCC Rules on Ownership Under Review," *New York Times*, April 3, 2002, p. C1.

60. Donna Britt, "Janet's 'Reveal' Lays Bare an Insidious Trend," *The Washington Post*, February 4, 2004, p. B1.

61. Cecilia Kang, "Super Bowl Fine Is Voided," *The Washington Post*, July 22, 2008, http://www.washingtonpost.com/wp-dyn/content/article/2008/07/21/AR2008072100904.html (accessed April 23, 2010).

62. Shanto Iyengar, Mark D. Peters, and Donald R. Kinder, "Experimental Demonstrations of the 'Not-So-Minimal' Consequences of Television News Programs," *American Political Science Review* 76 (December 1982), pp. 848–858.

63. Ibid.; Maxwell E. McCombs and Donald L. Shaw, "The Agenda-Setting Function of the Mass Media," *Public Opinion Quarterly* 36 (1972), pp. 176–187; Maxwell E. McCombs and Sheldon Gilbert, "News Influence on Our Pictures of the World," in Jennings Bryant and Dolf Gillman, eds., *Perspectives on Media Effects* (Erlbaum, 1986), pp. 1–15; and Iyengar and Kinder, *News That Matters*.

64. Quoted in Michael J. Robinson and Margaret A. Sheehan, *Over the Wire and on TV: CBS and UPI in Campaign '80* (Russell Sage Foundation, 1983), p. xiii.

65. ABC News, http://abcnews.go.com/US/story?id=92498&page=1 (accessed May 26, 2010).

66. David B. Magleby, *Direct Legislation: Voting on Ballot Propositions in the United States* (Johns Hopkins University Press, 1984).

67. Rush Limbaugh, *See, I Told You So* (Pocket Books, 1993), p. 326.

68. Rick Lyman, "Multimedia Deal: The History; 2 Commanding Publishers, 2 Powerful Empires," *New York Times*, March 14, 2000, p. C16.

69. David Broder, "Beware of the 'Insider' Syndrome: Why Newsmakers and News Reporters Shouldn't Get Too Cozy," *The Washington Post*, December 4, 1988, p. A21; see also Broder, "Thin-Skinned Journalists," *The Washington Post*, January 11, 1989, p. A21.

70. Daniel p. Moynihan, "The Presidency and the Press," *Commentary* 51 (March 1971), p. 43.

71. See, for example, Jack Dennis, "Preadult Learning of Political Independence: Media and Family Communications Effects," *Communication Research* 13 (July 1987), pp. 401–433; and Olive Stevens, *Children Talking Politics* (Robertson, 1982).

72. Elihu Katz and Paul Lazarsfeld, *Personal Influence: The Part Played by People in the Flow of Mass Communications* (Free Press, 1955).

73. See Angus Campbell, Philip E. Converse, Warren E. Miller, and Donald E. Stokes, *The American Voter* (Wiley, 1960).

74. Pew Research Center for the People & the Press, Survey Reports, "News Audiences Increasingly Politicized," June 8, 2004, http://people-press.org/reports/display.php3?ReportID=215 (accessed May 26, 2010).

75. Paul Lazarsfeld, Bernard Berelson, and Hazel Gaudet, *The People's Choice: How the Voter Makes Up His Mind in a Presidential Campaign*, 3d ed. (Columbia University Press, 1968); and Bernard Berelson, Paul Lazarsfeld, and William McPhee, *Voting: A Study of Opinion Formation in a Presidential Campaign* (University of Chicago Press, 1954).

76. Stuart Oskamp, ed., *Television as a Social Issue* (Sage, 1988); James W. Carey, ed., *Media, Myths, and Narratives: Television and the Press* (Sage, 1988).

77. Times Mirror Center for the People and the Press, "Times Mirror News Interest Index," press releases, January 16 and February 28, 1992.

78. opensecrets.org, "Swift Boat Veterans for Truth, 2004 Election Cycle," http://www.opensecrets.org/527s/527events.php?id=61 (accessed May 26, 2010).

79. David B. Magleby, J. Quin Monson, and Kelly D. Patterson, *Dancing Without Partners: How Parties, Candidates, and Interest Groups Interact in the 2004 Presidential Campaign* (Rowman & Littlefield, 2007), pp. 24–25.

80. Paul T. David, Ralph M. Goldman, and Richard C. Bain, *The Politics of the National Party Conventions* (Brookings Institution Press, 1960), pp. 300–301.

81. David B. Wilkerson, "McCain Speech's TV Audience Edges Obama's," *The Wall Street Journal*, September 5, 2008, http://www.marketwatch.com/story/mccain-speech-outdraws-tv-audience-for-obama (accessed June 21, 2010).

82. Frank I. Lutz, *Candidates, Consultants, and Campaigns* (Blackwell, 1988), Chapter 7.

83. Larry J. Sabato, "Gerald Ford's 'Free Poland' Gaffe—1976," *The Washington Post*, www.washingtonpost.com/wp-srv/politics/special/clinton/frenzy/ford.htm (accessed May 9, 2006).

84. CBS News, "CBS News Video Contradicts Clinton's Story: CBS' Sharyl Attkisson Was on Bosnia Trip—And Got a Warm, Sniper-Free Welcome," http://www.cbsnews.com/stories/2008/03/24/eveningnews/main3964921.shtml (accessed April 23, 2008).

85. Perry Bacon, Jr., and Shailagh Murray, "Opponents Paint Obama as an Elitist," *The Washington Post*, April 12, 2008, p. A04.

86. Larry J. Sabato, *The Rise of Political Consultants* (Basic Books, 1981).

87. See Thurber and Nelson, *Campaign Warriors: Political Consultants in Elections* (Brookings, 2000).

88. Quoted in Sabato, *Rise of Political Consultants*, p. 144.

89. John R. Zaller, *The Nature and Origins of Mass Opinion* (Cambridge University Press, 1992).

90. Shanto Iyengar and Donald R. Kinder, *News that Matters: Television and American Opinion* (University of Chicago Press, 1987), p. 2.

91. Thomas E. Patterson, *The Mass Media Election: How Americans Choose Their President* (Praeger, 1980), Chapter 12.

92. John H. Aldrich, *Before the Convention* (University of Chicago Press, 1980), p. 65; see also Patterson, *Mass Media Election*.

93. John Foley et al., *Nominating a President: The Process and the Press* (Praeger, 1980), p. 39. For the press's treatment of incumbents, see James Glen Stovall, "Incumbency and News Coverage of the 1980 Presidential Election Campaign," *Western Political Quarterly* 37 (December 1984), p. 621.

94. Stephen Ansolabehere and Shanto Iyengar, *Going Negative: How Political Advertisements Shrink and Polarize the Electorate* (Free Press, 1995).

95. John G. Geer, *In Defense of Negativity: Attack Ads in Presidential Campaigns* (University of Chicago Press, 2006); and Richard R. Lau, Lee Sigelman, and Ivy Brown Rovner, "The Effects of Negative Political Campaigns: A Meta-Analytic Reassessment," *Journal of Politics* 69 (November 2007), pp. 1176–1209.

96. William Glaberson, "A New Press Role: Solving Problems," *New York Times*, October 3, 1994, p. D6.

97. Patterson, *Mass Media Election*, pp. 115–117.

98. Michael Traugott, Benjamin Highton, and Henry E. Brady, *A Review of Recent Controversies Concerning the 2004 Presidential Election Exit Polls*, March 10, 2005, http://elections.ssrc.org/research/ExitPollReport031005.pdf; see also Michael Traugott, "The Accuracy of the National Preelection Polls in the 2004 Presidential Election," *Public Opinion Quarterly* 69 (Special Issue 2005), pp. 642–654.

99. Lewis Wolfson, *The Untapped Power of the Press* (Praeger, 1985), p. 79.

100. Lloyd Cutler, "Foreign Policy on Deadline," *Foreign Policy* 56 (Fall 1984), p. 114.

101. Michael B. Grossman and Martha Joynt Kumar, *Portraying the President* (Johns Hopkins University Press, 1981), pp. 255–263; and Fredric T. Smoller, *The Six o'Clock Presidency: A Theory of Presidential Press Relations in the Age of Television* (Praeger, 1990), pp. 31–49.

102. Stephen Hess, *Live from Capitol Hill!* (Brookings Institution, 1991), pp. 62–76; and Timothy E. Cook, *Making Laws and Making News* (Brookings Institution, 1989), pp. 81–86.

103. Susan Heilmann Miller, "News Coverage of Congress: The Search for the Ultimate Spokesperson," *Journalism Quarterly* 54 (Autumn 1977), pp. 459–465.

104. See Stephen Hess, *Live from Capitol Hill: Studies of Congress and the Media* (Brookings Institution Press, 1991), pp. 102–110.

105. Richard Davis, "Whither the Congress and the Supreme Court? The Television News Portrayal of American National Government," *Television Quarterly* 22 (1987), pp. 55–63.

106. For a discussion of the Supreme Court and public opinion, see Thomas R. Marshall, *Public Opinion and the Supreme Court* (Unwin Hyman, 1989); and Gregory Caldiera, "Neither the Purse nor the Sword: Dynamics of Public Confidence in the Supreme Court," *American Political Science Review* 80 (December 1986), pp. 1209–1228.

107. For a discussion of the relationship between the Supreme Court and the press, see Richard Davis, "Lifting the Shroud: News Media Portrayal of the U.S. Supreme Court," *Communications and the Law* 9 (October 1987), pp. 43–58; and Elliot E. Slotnick, "Media Coverage of Supreme Court Decision Making: Problems and Prospects," *Judicature* (October–November 1991), pp. 128–142.

108. Times Mirror Center, "Campaign '92," *Times Mirror*, January 16, 1992.

109. Quoted in Herbert Schmertz, "The Making of the Presidency," *Presidential Studies Quarterly* 16 (Winter 1986), p. 25.

Chapter 11

1. Evan Bayh, "Why I'm Leaving the Senate," *New York Times*, February 25, 2010, p. D8.

2. Charles Warren, *The Making of the Constitution* (Little, Brown, 1928), p. 195.

3. *Bush* v. *Vera*, 517 U.S. 952 (1996).

4. See David B. Magleby, *Last Hurrah? Soft Money and Issue Advocacy in the 2002 Elections* (Brookings Institution Press, 2004).

5. See Citizens Against Government Waste at www.cagw.org for the latest information on earmarks.

6. R. P. Fairfield, *The Federalist Papers* (Doubleday, 1961), p. 160.

7. See Roger H. Davidson and Walter J. Oleszek, *Congress and Its Members*, 10th ed. (CQ Press, 2005).

8. For discussion of the modern Speakership, see Barbara Sinclair, "House Majority Party Leadership in an Era of Legislative Constraint,"

in Roger H. Davidson, ed., *The Postreform Congress* (St. Martin's Press, 1992), pp. 91–111; and Ronald M. Peters, Jr., ed., *The Speaker: Leadership in the U.S. House of Representatives* (CQ Press, 1995).

9. For an insightful set of essays on Senate leadership, see Richard A. Baker and Roger H. Davidson, eds., *First Among Equals: Outstanding Senate Leaders of the Twentieth Century* (CQ Press, 1991).

10. Sarah A. Binder and Steven S. Smith, *Politics or Principles? Filibustering in the United States Senate* (Brookings Institution Press, 1997).

11. Helen Dewar, "Senate Filibuster Ends with Talk of Next Stage in Fight," *Washington Post*, November 15, 2003, p. A9.

12. Joel D. Aberbach, *Keeping a Watchful Eye: The Politics of Congressional Oversight* (Brookings, 1991).

13. "Résumé of Congressional Activity, 105th Congress," *Congressional Record*, Daily Digest, January 19, 1999, p. D29.

14. Davidson and Oleszek, *Congress and Its Members*, p. 307.

15. Sarah A. Binder, Thomas E. Mann, and Molly Reynolds, *One Year Later: Is Congress Still the Broken Branch?* (Brookings Institution Press, 2008).

16. For a history of the early Congresses, see James Sterling Young, *The Washington Community, 1800–1828* (Columbia University Press, 1966).

17. Davidson and Oleszek, *Congress and Its Members*, p. 30.

18. Nelson Polsby, "The Institutionalization of the U.S. House of Representatives," *American Political Science Association* (March 1968), pp. 144–168.

19. Herbert Asher, "The Learning of Legislative Norms," *American Political Science Review* 67 (June 1973), pp. 499–513.

20. See the case studies in Richard F. Fenno, Jr., *Senators on the Campaign Trail: The Politics of Representation* (University of Oklahoma Press, 1996), p. 331; see also Benjamin Bishin, "Constituency Influence in Congress: Does Subconstituency Matter?" *Legislative Studies Quarterly* (August 2000), pp. 389–415.

21. Statistics from congressional Web sites (www.senate.gov; www.house.gov); see also the Library of Congress Web site (thomas.loc.gov).

22. Bill Bradley, *Time Present, Time Past: A Memoir* (Knopf, 1996), Chapter 4.

23. From a 1999 CBS survey reported in "Poll Readings," *National Journal*, October 9, 1999, p. 2917.

24. Richard E. Cohen, "Vote Ratings," *National Journal*, February 21, 2005, p. 426.

25. Joseph I. Lieberman, *In Praise of Public Life* (Simon & Schuster, 2000), p. 109.

26. Catherine Richert, "Party Unity: United We Stand Opposed," *Congressional Quarterly Weekly*, January 14, 2008, p. 143.

27. *CQ Weekly*, January 11, 2010, p. 117.

28. Senate S. 1, *Honest Leadership and Open Government Act of 2007*, passed September 14, 2007.

Chapter 12

1. Adriana Lins de Albuquerque, Alicia Cheng, and Sarah Gephart, "A Year in Iraq and Afghanistan," *New York Times*, January 9, 2010, p. B10.

2. The story of Obama's decision was detailed by the *Washington Post* in an article by Anne E. Kornblatt, Scott Wilson, and Karen DeYoung, "Obama Pressed for a Faster Surge: Afghan Review a Marathon," December 6, 2009, p, A1.

3. Alexander Hamilton, James Madison, and John Jay, *The Federalist Papers* (Bantam Classic, 2003), pp. 426–427.

4. See Paul C. Light, *Vice Presidential Power* (Johns Hopkins University Press, 1984).

5. Richard Pious, *The American Presidency* (Basic Books, 1978).

6. This history of presidential powers draws heavily on Sidney M. Milkis and Michael Nelson, *The American Presidency: Origins and Development, 1976–2000*, 4th ed. (CQ Press, 2003).

7. See Al Kamen, "For Bush, the Fun Begins at Recess," *Washington Post*, June 29, 2007, p. A19; for a scholarly argument about this power, see the paper by Michael B. Rappaport, "The Original Meaning of the Recess Appointments Clause," October 6, 2004, at http://ssrn.com/abstract=601563.

8. See Phillip J. Cooper, "George W. Bush, Edgar Allan Poe, and the Use and Abuse of Presidential Signing Statements," *Presidential Studies Quarterly* 35 (September 2005), pp. 515–532.

9. Letter from Abraham Lincoln to his Illinois law partner W. H. Herndon, February 15, 1848, *in Abraham Lincoln, Speeches and Writings, 1832–1858* (Library of America, 1989), p. 175.

10. Miles A. Pomper, "Bush Hopes to Avoid Battle with Congress over Iraq," *Weekly*, August 31, 2002, p. 2251.

11. Louis Fisher, *Congressional Abdication on War and Spending* (Texas A&M University Press, 2000), p. 184.

12. Raoul Berger, Executive Privilege: *A Constitutional Myth* (Harvard University Press, 1974).

13. Mark J. Rozell, "The Law: Executive Privilege—Definition and Standards of Application," *Presidential Studies Quarterly* (December 1999), p. 924.

14. *United States v. Nixon*, 418 U.S. 683 (1974).

15. *Clinton et al. v. New York City et al.*, 524 U.S. 417 (1998).

16. See Bradley H. Patterson Jr., *The White House Staff: Inside the West Wing and Beyond* (Brookings Institution Press, 2000).

17. See Irving Janis, *Groupthink* (Houghton Mifflin, 1982).

18. For the views on presidents and the White House staff of a highly placed White House aide in several administrations, see David Gergen, *Eyewitness to Power: The Essence of Leadership, Nixon to Clinton* (Touchstone, 2000).

19. See Shelley Lynne Tomkins, *Inside OMB: Politics and Process in the President's Budget Office* (Sharpe, 1998).

20. See Paul C. Light, *The President's Agenda: Domestic Policy Choice from Kennedy Through Clinton* (Johns Hopkins University Press, 1999).

21. *United States v. Curtiss-Wright Export Corp.*, 299 U.S. 304 (1936).

22. Richard E. Neustadt, *Presidential Power and the Modern Presidents* (Free Press, 1991).

23. The phrase "power to persuade" is from Richard Neustadt, *Presidential Power and the Modern Presidents: The Politics of Leadership from Roosevelt to Reagan* (Free Press, 1990), p. 7.

24. Clea Benson, "Presidential Support: The Power of No," *CQ Weekly*, January 14, 2008, p. 132.

Chapter 13

1. Alexander Hamilton, James Madison, and John Jay, *The Federalist Papers* (Bantam Classic, 2003), p. 427.

2. See Stanley Elkins and Eric McKitrick, *The Age of Federalism* (Oxford University Press, 1993), pp. 50–51.

3. See John A. Rohr, *To Run a Constitution: The Legitimacy of the Administrative State* (University of Kansas Press, 1986).

4. Paul C. Light, *A Government Ill Executed: The Decline of the Federal Service and How to Reverse It* (Harvard University Press, 2008), Chapter 7.

5. Donald Kettl, *Leadership at the Fed* (Yale University Press, 1986).

6. James Fesler and Donald Kettl, *The Politics of the Administrative Process* (Chatham House, 1991).

7. See Paul C. Light, *Thickening Government* (Brookings Institution Press, 1995).

8. See Terry M. Moe, "The Politics of Structural Choice: Toward a Theory of Public Bureaucracy," in Oliver E. Williamson, ed., *Organization Theory: From Chester Barnard to the Present and Beyond* (Oxford University Press, 1990), pp. 140–162.

9. For an analysis of the use and abuse of the civil service system in the early twentieth century, see Stephen Skowronek, *Building a New American State* (Cambridge University Press, 1982).

10. See Jeanne Ponessa, "The Hatch Act Rewrite," *CQ Weekly*, November 13, 1993, pp. 3146–3147.

11. Theodore J. Lowi, Jr., *The End of Liberalism*, 2d ed. (Norton, 1979).

12. Eric Pianin, "EPA Aims to Change Pollution Rules," *The Washington Post*, December 5, 2003, p. A2.

13. Morris P. Fiorina, "Flagellating the Federal Bureaucracy," *Society* (March–April 1983), p. 73.

14. Alexander Hamilton, James Madison, and John Jay, *The Federalist*, ed. Benjamin Fletcher Wright (Cambridge, MA: Harvard University Press, 1961), p. 451.

Chapter 14

1. *Citizens United* v. *Federal Election Commission*, 558 U.S. ___ (2010).

2. *Austin* v. *Michigan Chamber of Commerce*, 494 U.S. 652 (1990).

3. Robert Barnes and Anne Kornblut, "It's Obama vs. the Supreme Court, Round 2, Over Campaign Finance Ruling," *The Washington Post*, March 11, 2010.

4. Roy P. Fairfield, ed., *The Federalist Papers* (Johns Hopkins University Press, 1981), p. 227.

5. Jerome Frank, *Courts on Trial: Myth and Reality in American Justice* (Princeton University Press, 1949), pp. 80–103; see also Martin Shapiro, *Courts* (University of Chicago Press, 1981); and Robert P. Burns, *A Theory of the Trial* (Princeton University Press, 1999).

6. Many of these workload statistics can be found in the Supreme Court's 2009, *Year-End Report on the Federal Judiciary* (U.S. Government Printing Office, December 31, 2009).

7. Fairfield, *The Federalist Papers*, p. 228.

8. Harold W. Chase, *Federal Judges: The Appointing Process* (University of Minnesota Press, 1972); and Sheldon Goldman, *Picking Federal Judges: Lower Court Selection from Roosevelt Through Reagan* (Yale University Press, 1997).

9. See David M. O'Brien, "Ironies and Disappointments: Bush and Federal Judgeships," in Colin Campbell and Bert A. Rockman, eds., *The George W. Bush Presidency* (CQ Press, 2004), pp. 133–157; and Brannon P. Denning, "The Judicial Confirmation Process and the Blue Slip," *Judicature* (March–April 2002), pp. 218–226.

10. Russell Wheeler, "Judicial Nominations in the First Fourteen Months of the Obama and Bush

Administrations," *Governance Studies at Brookings* (April 7, 2010).

11. Scott E. Graves and Robert M. Howard, *Justice Takes a Recess: Judicial Appointments from George Washington to George W. Bush* (Lexington Books, 2009).

12. Lisa M. Holmes and Roger E. Hartley, "Increasing Senate Scrutiny of Lower Federal Court Nominees," *Judicature* (May–June 1997), p. 275.

13. George Watson and John Stookey, "Supreme Court Confirmation Hearings: A View from the Senate," *Judicature* (December 1987–January 1988), p. 193; see also John Massaro, *Supremely Political: The Role of Ideology and Presidential Management in Unsuccessful Supreme Court Nominations* (State University of New York Press, 1990).

14. Barbara A. Perry and Henry J. Abraham, "A 'Representative' Supreme Court? The Thomas, Ginsburg, and Breyer Appointments," *Judicature* (January– February 1998), pp. 158–165.

15. Donald Santarelli, quoted in Jerry Landauer, "Shaping the Bench," *The Wall Street Journal*, December 10, 1970, p. 1.

16. Lee Epstein, Jeffrey A. Segal, Harold J. Spaeth, and Thomas G. Walker. *The Supreme Court Compendium: Data, Decisions, and Developments* (CQ Press, 2007), figures updated by the authors.

17. Tony Mauro, "The Supreme Court as Quiz Show," *Recorder* (December 8, 1993), p. 10.

18. Joyce O'Connor, "Selections from Notes Kept on an Internship at the U.S. Supreme Court" (Fall 1988), *Law, Courts, and Judicial Process* 6 (Spring 1989), p. 44.

19. Forrest Maltzman, James F. Spriggs III, and Paul Wahlbeck, *Crafting Law on the Supreme Court: The Collegial Game* (Cambridge University Press, 2000).

20. Charles Evans Hughes, *The Supreme Court of the United States* (Columbia University Press, 1966), p. 68.

21. Daniel M. Berman, *It Is So Ordered: The Supreme Court Rules on School Segregation* (Norton, 1986), p. 114; and David M. O'Brien, *Storm Center: The Supreme Court in American Politics*, 7th ed. (Norton, 2005), pp. 262–272.

22. *Brown* v. *Board of Education of Topeka*, 347 U.S. 483 (1954).

23. *Citizens United* v. *Federal Election Commission*, 558 U.S. ___ (2010).

24. William H. Rehnquist, quoted in John R. Vile, "The Selection and Tenure of Chief Justices," *Judicature* (September–October 1994), p. 98.

25. David Danelski, "The Influence of the Chief Justice in the Decisional Process of the Supreme Court," in Thomas P. Jahnige and Sheldon Goldman, eds., *The Federal Judicial System: Readings in Process and Behavior* (Holt, Rinehart and Winston, 1968), p. 148.

26. O'Brien, *Storm Center*, Chapter 3.

27. Artemus Ward and David L. Weiden, *Sorcerers' Apprentices: 100 Years of Law Clerks at the United States Supreme Court* (New York University Press, 2006); and Todd C. Peppers, *Courtiers of the Marble Palace: The Rise and Influence of the Supreme Court Law Clerk* (Stanford University Press, 2006).

28. Lincoln Caplan, *The Tenth Justice: The Solicitor General and the Rule of Law* (Knopf, 1987); and Rebecca Mae Salokar, *The Solicitor General: The Politics of Law* (Temple University Press, 1992).

29. Gregory A. Caldeira and John R. Wright, "Organized Interest and Agenda Setting in the U.S. Supreme Court," *American Political Science Review* 82 (December 1988), p. 1110; and Donald R. Songer and Reginald S.

Sheehan, "Interest Group Success in the Courts: *Amicus* Participation in the Supreme Court," *Political Research Quarterly* 46 (June 1993), pp. 339–354.

30. *Grutter* v. *Bollinger*, 539 U.S. 306 (2003); Neal Devins, "Explaining Grutter v. Bollinger," *University of Pennsylvania Law Review*, 152, No. 1 (November 2003).

31. Paul M. Collins, Jr., *Friends of the Supreme Court: Interest Groups and Judicial Decision Making* (Oxford University Press, 2008).

32. Caldeira and Wright, "Organized Interest and Agenda Setting," *American Political Science Review* 82 (December 1988), p. 1118; and Songer and Sheehan, "Interest Group Success in the Courts," *Political Research Quarterly* 46 (June 1993).

33. Gerald N. Rosenberg, *Hollow Hope: Can Courts Bring About Sound Change?* (University of Chicago Press, 1991).

34. J. W. Peltason, *Fifty-Eight Lonely Men: Southern Federal Judges and School Desegregation* (University of Illinois Press, 1971); and Gary Orfield and Chungmei Lee, *Brown at 50: King's Dream or Plessy's Nightmare* (Civil Rights Project, Harvard University, 2004).

35. See Benjamin N. Cardozo, *The Nature of the Judicial Process* (Yale University Press, 1921)—a classic.

36. William O. Douglas, quoted in O'Brien, *Storm Center*, p. 184.

37. *Citizens United* v. *Federal Election Commission*, 558 U.S. _____ (2010), C. J. Roberts concurring.

38. Lee Epstein, Jeffrey A. Segal, Harold J. Spaeth, and Thomas G. Walker, *The Supreme Court Compendium: Data, Decisions, and Developments*, 4th ed. (CQ Press, 2007). Data through 2005–2006 Supreme Court term.

39. See Keith Perine, "Precedent Heeded, but Not Revered on High Court," *CQ Weekly*, November 28, 2005, pp. 3180–3184.

40. *Gonzales* v. *Carhart*, 550 U.S. 124 (2007).

41. Ex parte *McCardle*, 74 U.S. 506 (1869).

42. See Shawn Francis Peters, *Judging the Jehovah's Witnesses* (University of Kansas Press, 2002); Clyde Wilcox, *Onward, Christian Soldiers? The Religious Right in American Politics* (Westview Press, 1996); Mark Tushnet, *The NAACP's Legal Strategy Against Segregated Education, 1925–1950* (University of North Carolina Press, 1987); and Karen O'Connor, *Women's Organizations' Use of the Court* (Lexington Books, 1980).

43. J. W. Peltason, "The Supreme Court: Transactional or Transformational Leadership," in Michael R. Beschloss and Thomas E. Cronin, eds., *Essays in Honor of James MacGregor Burns* (Prentice Hall, 1988), pp. 165–180; and Valerie Hoekstra, *Public Reactions to Supreme Court Decisions* (Cambridge University Press, 2003).

44. *Planned Parenthood* v. *Casey*, 505 U.S. 833 (1992).

45. Edward White, "The Supreme Court of the United States," *American Bar Association Journal* 7 (1921), p. 341.

Chapter **15**

1. *Roper* v. *Simmons*, 543 U.S. 551 (2005).

2. *Graham* v. *Florida*, ___U.S.___ (2010).

3. Justice Felix Frankfurther, dissenting in *United States* v. *Rabinowitz*, 339 U.S. 56 (1950).

4. Jeffrey Smith, *War and Press Freedom* (Oxford University Press, 1999); and David Cole, *Enemy Aliens: Double Standards and Constitutional Freedoms in the War on Terrorism* (New Press, 2003).

5. *Hamdan* v. *Rumsfeld*, 548 U.S. 557 (2006).

6. Josh White and William Branigin, "Hamdan to Be Sent to Yemen," *The Washington Post*, November 25, 2008.

7. *Boumediene* v. *Bush*, 553 U.S. _____ (2008).

8. *Felker* v. *Turpin*, 518 U.S. 651 (1996); *Winthrow* v. *Williams*, 507 U.S. 680 (1993); *McCleskey* v. *Zant*, 499 U.S. 467 (1991); and *Stone* v. *Powell*, 428 U.S. 465 (1976).

9. *Barron* v. *Baltimore*, 7 Peters 243 (1833).

10. *Gitlow* v. *New York*, 268 U.S. 652 (1925).

11. Richard C. Cortner, *The Supreme Court and the Second Bill of Rights: The Fourteenth Amendment and the Nationalization of Civil Liberties* (University of Wisconsin Press, 1981).

12. *Witters* v. *Washington Department of Services for the Blind*, 474 U.S. 481 (1986); and *Locke* v. *Davey*, 540 U.S. 712 (2004).

13. *Wallace* v. *Jaffree*, 472 U.S. 38 (1985).

14. *Everson* v. *Board of Education of Ewing Township*, 333 U.S. 203 (1947).

15. *Lemon* v. *Kurtzman*, 403 U.S. 602 (1971).

16. *Capital Square Review Board* v. *Pinette*, 515 U.S. 753 (1995).

17. *Allegheny* v. *ACLU*, 492 U.S. 573 (1989).

18. *Bowen* v. *Kendrick*, 487 U.S. 589 (1988); *Lee* v. *Weisman*, 505 U.S. 577 (1992); *Board of Education of Kiryas Joel Village School District* v. *Grumet*, 512 U.S. 687 (1994); and *Zelman* v. *Simmons-Harris*, 536 U.S. 629 (2002).

19. *Mitchell* v. *Helms*, 530 U.S. 793 (2000).

20. *Agostini* v. *Felton*, 521 U.S. 74 (1997).

21. *Employment Division of Human Resources of Oregon* v. *Smith*, 494 U.S. 872 (1990).

22. *Church of Lukumi Babalu Aye* v. *City of Hialeah*, 508 U.S. 520 (1993).

23. *Brown* v. *Hartlage*, 456 U.S. 45 (1982).

24. *New York Times Company* v. *United States*, 403 U.S. 670 (1971).

25. Ibid., *Near* v. *Minnesota*, 283 U.S. 697 (1930).

26. *Hazelwood School District* v. *Kuhlmeier*, 484 U.S. 260 (1988).

27. *New York Times* v. *Sullivan*, 376 U.S. 254 (1964).

28. *Hustler Magazine* v. *Falwell*, 485 U.S. 46 (1988).

29. Potter Stewart, concurring in *Jacobellis* v. *Ohio*, 378 U.S. 184 (1964).

30. *Miller* v. *California*, 413 U.S. 15 (1973).

31. *Young* v. *American Mini Theatres*, 427 U.S. 51 (1976); *Renton* v. *Playtime Theatres, Inc.*, 475 U.S. 41 (1986); and *City of Los Angeles* v. *Alameda Books, Inc.*, 535 U.S. 425 (2002).

32. *Barnes* v. *Glen Theatre, Inc.*, 501 U.S. 560 (1991); and *City of Erie* v. *Pap's A.M.*, 529 U.S. 277 (2000).

33. *Chaplinsky* v. *New Hampshire*, 315 U.S. 568 (1942).

34. *Cohen* v. *California*, 403 U.S. 115 (1971).

35. *Wisconsin* v. *Mitchell*, 508 U.S. 476 (1993).

36. *44 Liquormart, Inc.* v. *Rhode Island*, 517 U.S. 484 (1996); and *Thompson* v. *Western States Medical Center*, 535 U.S. 357 (2002).

37. *Branzburg* v. *Hayes*, 408 U.S. 665 (1972).

38. *Federal Communications Commission* v. *Pacifica Foundation*, 438 U.S. 726 (1978).

39. *United States* v. *Playboy Entertainment Group*, 529 U.S. 803 (2000); and *Denver Area Educational Television* v. *Federal Communications Commission*, 518 U.S. 727 (1996).

40. *Reno* v. *American Civil Liberties Union*, 521 U.S. 844 (1997).

41. *Ashcroft* v. *ACLU*, 542 U.S. 656 (2004).

42. *Walker* v. *Birmingham*, 388 U.S. 307 (1967).

43. *Madsen* v. *Women's Health Center*, 512 U.S. 753 (1994); *Schenck* v. *Pro-Choice Network*, 519 U.S. 357 (1997); and *Hill* v. *Colorado*, 530 U.S. 703 (2000).

44. *First English Evangelical* v. *Los Angeles County*, 482 U.S. 304 (1987); see Richard A. Epstein, *Taking: Private Property and the Power of Eminent Domain* (Harvard University Press, 1985).

45. *Lucas* v. *South Carolina Coastal Commission*, 505 U.S. 647 (1992).
46. *Tahoe-Sierra Council, Inc.* v. *Tahoe Regional Planning Agency*, 535 U.S. 302 (2002).
47. *Kelo* v. *City of New London*, 545 U.S. 469 (2005).
48. *United States* v. *554 Acres of Land*, 441 U.S. 506 (1979).
49. *Mathews* v. *Eldridge*, 424 U.S. 319 (1976), restated in *Connecticut* v. *Doeher*, 501 U.S. 1 (1991).
50. *Meyer* v. *Nebraska*, 262 U.S. 390 (1923).
51. *Griswold* v. *Connecticut*, 381 U.S. 479 (1965).
52. Philip B. Kurland, *Some Reflections on Privacy and the Constitution* (University of Chicago Center for Policy Study, 1976), p. 9. A classic and influential article about privacy is Samuel D. Warren and Louis D. Brandeis, "The Right to Privacy," *Harvard Law Review* (December 15, 1890), pp. 193–220.
53. *Roe* v. *Wade*, 410 U.S. 113 (1973).
54. *Planned Parenthood of Southeastern Pennsylvania* v. *Casey*, 505 U.S. 833 (1992).
55. *Stenberg* v. *Carhart*, 530 U.S. 914 (2000).
56. *Gonzales* v. *Carhart*, 550 U.S. 124 (2007).
57. *Bowers* v. *Hardwick*, 478 U.S. 186 (1986).
58. *Lawrence* v. *Texas*, 539 U.S. 558 (2003).
59. But see *Washington* v. *Chrisman*, 445 U.S. 1 (1982); and compare *Georgia* v. *Randolph*, 126 547 U.S. 103 (2006).
60. *Katz* v. *United States*, 389 U.S. 347 (1967).
61. *California* v. *Hodari D.*, 499 U.S. 621 (1991).
62. *Bond* v. *United States*, 529 U.S. 334 (2000).
63. *Terry* v. *Ohio*, 392 U.S. 1 (1968).
64. *Hiibel* v. *Sixth Judicial District of Nevada*, 542 U.S. 177 (2004).
65. *Minnesota* v. *Dickerson*, 508 U.S. 366 (1993).
66. *Almeida-Sanchez* v. *United States*, 413 U.S. 266 (1973); *United States* v. *Ortiz*, 422 U.S. 891 (1975); *United States* v. *Arvizu*, 534 U.S. 161 (2002); and *United States* v. *Flores-Montano*, 541 U.S. 149 (2004).
67. *United States* v. *Ramsey*, 431 U.S. 606 (1977).
68. *Mapp* v. *Ohio*, 367 U.S. 643 (1961).
69. Senate Committee on the Judiciary, the Jury, and the Search for Truth: The Case Against Excluding Relevant Evidence at Trial, Hearing Before the Committee, 104th Cong., 1st sess. (U.S. Government Printing Office, 1997).
70. *United States* v. *Leon*, 468 U.S. 897 (1984); and *Arizona* v. *Evans*, 514 U.S. 1 (1995).
71. *Miranda* v. *Arizona*, 384 U.S. 436 (1966); but see *Yarborough* v. *Alvarado*, 541 U.S. 652 (2004).
72. *Dickerson* v. *United States*, 530 U.S. 428 (2000).
73. *United States* v. *Enterprises, Inc.*, 498 U.S. 292 (1991).
74. *J. E. B.* v. *Alabama ex rel T. B.*, 511 U.S. 127 (1994); *Batson* v. *Kentucky*, 476 U.S. 79 (1986); *Powers* v. *Ohio*, 499 U.S. 400 (1991); *Hernandez* v. *New York*, 500 U.S. 352 (1991); and *Georgia* v. *McCollum*, 505 U.S. 42 (1990).
75. *Ewing* v. *California*, 538 U.S. 11 (2003).
76. *Benton* v. *Maryland*, 395 U.S. 784 (1969); see also *Kansas* v. *Hendricks*, 521 U.S. 346 (1997).
77. *Graham* v. *Collins*, 506 U.S. 461 (1993).
78. Death Penalty Information Center, "Facts About the Death Penalty," February 25, 2010, www.deathpenaltyinfo.org/documents/ FactSheet.pdf.
79. Barry Scheck, Peter Neufeld, and Jim Dwyer, *Actual Innocence: Five Days to Execution and Other Dispatches from the Wrongly Convicted* (Doubleday, 2000); and Timothy Kaufman-Osborn, *From Noose to Needle: Capital Punishment and the Late Liberal State* (University of Michigan Press, 2002).
80. Death Penalty Information Center, "Innocence and the Death Penalty," May 2, 2008, www .deathpenaltyinfo.org/article.php?did=412# inn-yr-rc.
81. *Atkins* v. *Virginia*, 536 U.S. 304 (2002).

82. *Roper* v. *Simmons*, 543 U.S. 551 (2006).
83. *Kennedy* v. *Louisiana*, 554 U.S. _____ (2008).
84. *Baze* v. *Rees*, 553 U.S. _____ (2008).
85. *Schenck* v. *United States*, 249 U.S. 47 (1919).
86. "Congress Extends PATRIOT Act, No New Protections," *The Washington Post*, February 25, 2010.
87. Louis Fisher, *Religious Liberties in America: Political Safeguards* (University Press of Kansas, 2002).

Chapter 16

1. NewsHour Online, "Supreme Court Revisits Race in Public Schools," December 4, 2006, www.pbs.org/newshour/bb/law/july-dec06/ scotus_12–04.html.
2. "How the Racial-Tiebreaker Case Began," *Seattle Times*, June 28, 2007.
3. *Parents Involved in Community Schools* v. *Seattle School District, No. 1*, 551 U.S. 701 (2007).
4. Andrew Hacker, *Two Nations: Black and White, Separate, Hostile, Unequal* (Scribner, 1992).
5. *Slaughter-House Cases*, 83 U.S. 36 (1873).
6. Ex Parte *Milligan*, 71 U.S. 2 (1866).
7. *Korematsu* v. *United States*, 323 U.S. 214 (1944).
8. Ex Parte *Quirin*, 317 U.S. 1 (1942).
9. *Reid* v. *Covert*, 354 U.S. 1 (1957).
10. *Boumediene* v. *Bush*, 553 U.S. _____ (2008)
11. *Matxhews* v. *Diaz*, 426 U.S. 67 (1976); and *Shaughnessy* v. *United States ex rel. Mezei*, 345 U.S. 206 (1953).
12. *Demore* v. *Kim*, 538 U.S. 510 (2003).
13. *Zadvydas* v. *Davis*, 533 U.S. 678 (2001).
14. *Yick Wo* v. *Hopkins*, 118 U.S. 356 (1886); *Kwong Hai Chew* v. *Colding*, 344 U.S. 590 (1953); *Zadvydas* v. *Davis*, 533 U.S. 678 (2001); *Rasul* v. *Bush*, 542 U.S. 466 (2004); and *Hamdi* v. *Rumsfeld*, 542 U.S. 507 (2004).
15. *Foley* v. *Connelie*, 435 U.S. 291 (1978); *Ambach* v. *Norwick*, 441 U.S. 68 (1979); *Cabell* v. *Chavez-Salido*, 454 U.S. 432 (1982).
16. *Plyler* v. *Doe*, 457 U.S. 202 (1982).
17. *Slaughter-House Cases*, 83 U.S. 36 (1873); and *Civil Rights Cases*, 109 U.S. 3 (1883).
18. *Plessy* v. *Ferguson*, 163 U.S. 537 (1896).
19. *Brown* v. *Board of Education of Topeka*, 347 U.S. 483 (1954); and *Brown* v. *Board of Education of Topeka*, 349 U.S. 294 (1955).
20. *Gomillion* v. *Lightfoot*, 364 U.S. 339 (1960).
21. Taylor Branch, *Parting the Waters: America in the King Years, 1954–1963* (Simon & Schuster, 1988); see also Harris Wofford, *Of Kennedys and Kings: Making Sense of the Sixties* (Farrar, Straus, & Giroux, 1980).
22. See Charles Whalen and Barbara Whalen, *The Longest Debate: A Legislative History of the 1964 Civil Rights Act* (Mentor, 1985); and Hugh Davis Graham, *The Civil Rights Era* (Oxford University Press, 1990).
23. David Remnick, *The Bridge: The Life and Rise of Barack Obama* (Knopf, 2010).
24. Ellen Carol Du Bois, *Feminism and Suffrage: The Emergence of an Independent Women's Movement in America, 1848–1869* (Cornell University Press, 1978); and Joan Hoff-Wilson, "Women and the Constitution," *News for Teachers of Political Science* (Summer 1985), pp. 10–15.
25. Susan M. Hartmann, *From Margin to Mainstream: American Women and Politics Since 1960* (Temple University Press, 1989); and Susan Gluck Mezey, *In Pursuit of Equality: Women, Public Policy, and the Federal Courts* (St. Martin's Press, 1992).
26. *United States* v. *Virginia*, 518 U.S. 515 (1996); see also Philippa Strum, *Women in the Barracks: The VMI Case and Equal Rights* (University Press of Kansas, 2002).

27. *Meritor Savings Bank, FBD* v. *Vinson*, 477 U.S. 57 (1986).
28. *Oncale* v. *Sundowner Offshore Services*, 523 U.S. 75 (1998); *Faragher* v. *City of Boca Raton*, 524 U.S. 775 (1998); and *Burlington Industries* v. *Ellerth*, 524 U.S. 742 (1998).
29. U.S. Census Bureau, "Texas Becomes Nation's Newest Majority-Minority State, Census Bureau Announces," August 11, 2005, www.census.gov/Press-Release/www/ releases/archives/population/005514.html.
30. Randal C. Archibald, "Arizona Enacts Stringent Law on Immigration," *New York Times*, April 23, 2010.
31. Celia W. Dugger, "U.S. Study Says Asian Americans Face Widespread Discrimination," *New York Times*, February 29, 1992, p. 1, reporting on U.S. Civil Rights Commission, *Civil Rights Issues Facing Asian Americans in the 1990s* (U.S. Government Printing Office, 1992).
32. *Takao Ozawa* v. *United States*, 260 U.S. 178 (1922).
33. *Korematsu* v. *United States*, 323 U.S. 214 (1944).
34. Won Moo Hurh, *Korean Immigrants in America* (Fairleigh Dickinson University Press, 1984).
35. Antonio J. A. Pido, *The Filipinos in America: Macro/Micro Dimensions of Immigration and Integration* (Center for Migration Studies of New York, 1986).
36. Harold L. Hodgkinson, *The Demographics of American Indians: One Percent of the People, Fifty Percent of the Diversity* (Institute for Educational Leadership/Center for Demographic Policy, 1990), pp. 1–5.
37. "Assimilation, Relocation, Genocide: The Trail of Tears," *Indian Country Diaries*, PBS, November 2006, www.pbs.org/indiancountry/ history/trail.html.
38. *Morey* v. *Doud*, 354 U.S. 459 (1957); and *Allegheny Pittsburgh Coal Co.* v. *County Commission*, 488 U.S. 336 (1989).
39. *City of Cleburne, Texas* v. *Cleburne Living Center*, 473 U.S. 432 (1985); *Heller* v. *Doe*, 509 U.S. 312 (1993); and *Romer* v. *Evans*, 517 U.S. 620 (1996).
40. *San Antonio School District* v. *Rodriguez*, 411 U.S. 1 (1973).
41. *Frontiero* v. *Richardson*, 411 U.S. 677 (1973).
42. *San Antonio School District* v. *Rodriguez*, 411 U.S. 1 (1973); and Douglas Reed, *On Equal Terms: The Constitutional Politics of Educational Opportunity* (Princeton University Press, 2001).
43. Matthew Bosworth, *Courts as Catalysts: State Supreme Courts and Public School Finance Equity* (State University of New York Press, 2001).
44. Sandra Day O'Connor, in *Kimel* v. *Florida Board of Regents*, 528 U.S. 62 (2000).
45. Ibid.
46. *Romer* v. *Evans*, 517 U.S. 620 (1996).
47. European Union and LGBT Rights, International Lesbian and Gay Association Europe, http:// www.ilga-europe.org/europe/guide/european_ union/european_union_and_lgbt_rights.
48. Mexico City Passes Gay Union Law," BBC News, November 10, 2006, http://news.bbc.co.uk/ 2/hi/6134730.stm.
49. International Lesbian and Gay Association, www.ilga.org.
50. Leon F. Litwack, *Trouble in Mind: Black Southerners in the Age of Jim Crow* (1998), p. 227, as cited in James W. Fox, Jr., "Intimations of Citizenship: Repressions and Expressions of Equal Citizenship in the Era of Jim Crow," *Howard University Law Journal* (Fall 2006).
51. Harold W. Stanley, *Voter Mobilization and the Politics of Race: The South and Universal Suffrage, 1952–1984* (Praeger, 1987).
52. Abigail M. Thernstrom, *Whose Votes Count? Affirmative Action and Minority Voting Rights* (Harvard University Press, 1987), p. 15.

53. *Smith* v. *Allwright*, 321 U.S. 64 9 (1944).
54. *Gomillion* v. *Lightfoot*, 364 U.S. 339 (1960).
55. *Harper* v. *Virginia Board of Elections*, 383 U.S. 663 (1966).
56. Thernstrom, *Whose Votes Count?* For a contrary view, see Bernard Grofman, Lisa Handley, and Richard G. Niemi, *Minority Representation and the Quest for Voting Equality* (Cambridge University Press, 1992).
57. *Morse* v. *Republican Party of Virginia*, 517 U.S. 116 (1996).
58. Northwest Austin Municipal Utility District Number One v. Holder, 557 U.S. ____ (2009)
59. *Shaw* v. *Reno*, 509 U.S. 630 (1993).
60. *Civil Rights Cases*, 109 U.S. 3 (1883).
61. *Plessy* v. *Ferguson*, 163 U.S. 537 (1896).
62. *Heart of Atlanta Motel* v. *United States*, 379 U.S. 421 (1964).
63. Darryl Van Duch, "Plagued by Politics, EEOC Backlog Grows," *Recorder* (August 18, 1998), p. 1; and David Rovella, "EEOC Chairman Casellas: 'We Are Being Selective,'" *National Law Journal* (November 20, 1995), p. 1.
64. *Shelley* v. *Kraemer*, 334 U.S. 1 (1948).
65. *Sweat* v. *Painter*, 339 U.S. 629 (1950).
66. *Brown* v. *Board of Education of Topeka*, 347 U.S. 483 (1954); see also J. W. Peltason, *Fifty-Eight Lonely Men: Southern Federal Judges and School Desegregation* (University of Illinois Press, 1971), p. 248.
67. *Brown* v. *Board of Education of Topeka*, 349 U.S. 294 (1955).
68. *Freeman* v. *Pitts*, 503 U.S. 467 (1992); and *Missouri* v. *Jenkins*, 515 U.S. 70 (1995).
69. See Gary Orfield, Susan E. Eaton, and the Harvard Project on School Desegregation, *Dismantling Desegregation: The Quiet Reversal of Brown* v. *Board of Education* (New Press, 1996).
70. Raymond Hernandez, "NAACP Suspends Yonkers Leader After Criticism of Usefulness of School Busing," *New York Times*, November 1, 1995, p. A13.
71. Gary Orfield and Chungmei Lee, *Brown at 50: King's Dream or Plessy's Nightmare?* (Civil Rights Project, Harvard University, 2004), http://www.civilrightsproject.ucla.edu/research/reseg04/brown50.pdf; see also Charles Clotfelter, *After Brown: The Rise and Retreat of School Desegregation* (Princeton University Press, 2004).
72. Richard Kahlenberg, *All Together Now: Creating Middle-Class Schools Through Public School Choice* (Brookings Institution Press, 2003).
73. John Marshall Harlan, dissenting in *Plessy* v. *Ferguson*, 163 U.S. 537 (1896).
74. *University of California Regents* v. *Bakke*, 438 U.S. 265 (1978); see also Howard Ball, *The Bakke Case* (University Press of Kansas, 2000).
75. *Gratz* v. *Bollinger*, 539 U.S. 244 (2003).
76. *Grutter* v. *Bollinger*, 539 U.S. 306 (2003).
77. Scott Jaschik, "Michigan Votes Down Affirmative Action," *Inside Higher Education* (November 8, 2006), www.insidehighered.com/news/2006/11/08/Michigan.
78. *Hopwood* v. *Texas*, 518 U.S. 1016 (1996).
79. James Farmer, quoted in Rochelle L. Stanfield, "Black Complaints Haven't Translated into Political Organization and Power," *National Journal* (June 14, 1980), p. 465.
80. Orfield and Lee, *Brown at 50;* and Clotfeler, *After Brown.*
81. D'Vera Cohn, "Hispanic Growth Surges Fueled by Births in U.S.," *The Washington Post*, June 9, 2005, p. A1.
82. Gary Orfield, "Separate Societies: Have the Kerner Warnings Come True?" in Fred R. Harris and Roger W. Wilkins, eds., *Quiet Riots: Race and Poverty in the United States—The Kerner*

Report Twenty Years Later (Pantheon, 1988), p. 103; see also Nicholas Lehmann, *The Promised Land* (Knopf, 1991).
83. William J. Wilson, *The Truly Disadvantaged: The Inner City, the Underclass, and Public Policy* (University of Chicago Press, 1987), esp. Chapter 5; and Kevin Phillips, *The Politics of Rich and Poor* (Random House, 1995).
84. Gary Orfield and Carole Ashkinaze, *The Closing Door: Conservative Policy and Black Opportunity* (University of Chicago Press, 1991), pp. 221–234.

Chapter 17

1. http://www.whitehouse.gov/blog/09/04/21/A-Call-to-Service.
2. The original types of public policy were developed by Theodore J. Lowi, "American Business, Public Policy, Case Studies, and Political Theory," *World Politics* 16 (1964), pp. 677–715.
3. See Paul C. Light, *Artful Work: The Politics of Social Security Reform* (Random House, 1985), for a discussion of redistributive policy.
4. Quoted in Gabriel Almond, G. Bingham Powell, Jr., Russell J. Dalton, and Kaare Strom, *Comparative Politics Today: A World View* (Longman, 2008), p. 171.
5. William Greider, "The Education of David Stockman," *Atlantic* (1981), p. 296.
6. John Kingdon, *Agendas, Alternatives, and Public Policies* (Little, Brown, 1984), p. 3.
7. Anthony Downs, "The 'Issue-Attention Cycle,'" *Public Interest* 28 (Summer 1972), p. 38.
8. James L. True, Bryan D. Jones, and Frank R. Baumgartner, "Punctuated-Equilibrium Theory: Explaining Stability and Change in Public Policymaking," in Paul A. Sabatier, ed., *Theories of the Policy Process* (Westview Press, 2007), p. 157.
9. Hugh Heclo, "Issue Networks and the Executive Establishment," in A. King, ed., *The New American Political System* (American Enterprise Institute, 1978), pp. 87–124.
10. Lester Salamon and Michael Lund, "The Tools Approach: Basic Analytics," in L. Salamon, ed., *Beyond Privatization: The Tools of Government Action* (Urban Institute Press, 1989).
11. See Paul C. Light, *A Government Ill Executed: The Decline of the Federal Service and How to Reverse It* (Harvard University Press, 2008).
12. See Cornelius Kerwin, *Rulemaking: How Government Agencies Write Law and Make Policy* (CQ Press, 2003).
13. See Kingdon, *Agendas, Alternatives, and Public Policies,* for a description of the policy-making process.

Chapter 18

1. Office of Management and Budget, *Budget of the U.S. Government, Fiscal Year 2009, Analytical Perspectives* (U.S. Government Printing Office, February 2008), p. 298.
2. Ibid., pp. 245, 332.
3. For a discussion of the budgetary cycle, see Allen Schick, *The Federal Budget: Politics, Policy, Process*, rev. ed. (Brookings Institution Press, 2000).
4. Efforts at past tax reform are described in Jeffrey H. Birnbaum and Alan S. Murray, *Showdown at Gucci Gulch: Lawmakers, Lobbyists, and the Unlikely Triumph of Tax Reform* (Vintage Books, 1988); see also Timothy J. Conlan, Margaret T. Wrightson, and David R. Beam, *Taxing Choices: The Politics of Tax Reform* (CQ Press, 1990).

5. The debate over Keynes and his economic theories is still alive in the United States. See Donald E. Moggridge, *Maynard Keynes: An Economist's Biography* (Routledge, 1992).
6. *United States* v. *E. C. Knight Co.*, 156 U.S. 1 (1895).
7. On the origins of the Federal Trade Commission and the role of Louis D. Brandeis, see Thomas K. McCraw, *Prophets of Regulation* (Belknap Press, 1984), Chapter 3.
8. For a useful history of airline deregulation, see Steven A. Morrison and Clifford Winston, *The Evolution of the Airline Industry* (Brookings Institution Press, 1995).
9. On Southwest Airlines and its longtime chief executive Herb Kelleher, see Kevin Freiberg and Jackie Freiberg, *Nuts!* (Bard Press, 1996).

Chapter 19

1. Sheryl Gay Stolberg, Jeff Zelny, and Carl Hulse, "Vote on Health Care Today Caps a Journey Back from the Brink," *New York Times*, March 21 2010, p. A.1.
2. Michael B. Katz, *In the Shadow of the Poorhouse: A Social History of Welfare in America* (Basic Books, 1986).
3. This history draws heavily on Theda Skocpol's research on the subject, starting with "America's First Social Security System: The Expansion of Benefits for Civil War Veterans," *Political Science Quarterly* 108 (Winter 1993), pp. 64–87.
4. These numbers can be found at the Department of Health and Human Services Web site, aspe.hhs.gov/poverty/07poverty.shtml.
5. Gertrude Schaffner Goldberg and Eleanor Kremen, eds., *The Feminization of Poverty: Only in America?* (Greenwood Press, 1990).
6. See, for example, Margaret Weir, "Political Parties and Social Policymaking," in Margaret Weir, ed., *The Social Divide: Political Parties and the Future of Activist Government* (Brookings Institution Press, 1998).
7. Self-employed workers must cover both amounts, and many state and local government workers are not required to participate.
8. Martha Derthick, "No More Easy Votes for Social Security," *Brookings Review* 10 (Fall 1992), pp. 50–53.
9. For a pessimistic view of the viability of Social Security, see Neil Howe and Richard Jackson, "The Myth of the 2.2 Percent Solution," www.cato.org/dailys/7–21–98.html. Robert D. Reischauer of the Brookings Institution testified before the House Committee on Ways and Means on November 19, 1998, that Social Security will start running deficits by 2021 and that by 2032, "reserves will be depleted."
10. See Theda Skocpol, *Protecting Soldiers and Mothers: The Political Origins of Social Policy in the United States* (Belknap Press, 1992), Chapter 9, for a history of the Act.
11. Lyndon Johnson, speech at the University of Michigan, May 1964, in *Congress and the Nation, 1965–1968: A Review of Government and Politics During the Johnson Years* (CQ Press, 1969), Vol. 2, p. 650.
12. William J. Clinton, acceptance speech, Democratic National Convention, Chicago, July 6, 1992.
13. Robert Pear, "Judge Rules States Can't Cut Welfare," *New York Times*, October 14, 1997, p. A1.
14. Centers for Medicare and Medicaid Services, "Health Accounts," www.cms.hhs.gov.
15. http://www.cms.hhs.gov/NationalHealth ExpendData/downloads/highlights.pdf.
16. U.S. Census Bureau, www.census.gov.

Chapter 20

1. See Lee Feinstein, "Darfur and Beyond: What Is Needed to Prevent Mass Atrocities," *Council on Foreign Relations*, January 2007.

2. Condoleezza Rice, quoted in Glenn Kessler, "Rice Lays Out Case for War in Iraq," *The Washington Post*, August 16, 2002, p. A1.

3. See Joseph Nye, *Soft Power: The Means to Success in World Politics* (Public Affairs, 2005).

4. See Glenn Kessler, "U.S. Decision on Iraq Has Puzzling Past: Opponents of War Wonder When, How Policy Was Set," *The Washington Post*, January 12, 2003, p. A1, for a detailed history of the increasing interest in Iraq.

5. Remarks to the United Nations, September 12, 2003.

6. See Jason H. Campbell and Michael E. O'Hanlon, "The State of Iraq: An Update," *New York Times*, March 9, 2008, p. A28.

7. For more information, visit the Peace Corps Web site, www.peacecorps.gov. For a useful study of the Peace Corps, see Elizabeth Cobbs Hoffman, *All You Need Is Love: The Peace Corps and the Spirit of the 1960s* (Harvard University Press, 1998).

8. For a fascinating history of U.S. intelligence operations, see Christopher Andrew, *For the President's Eyes Only: Secret Intelligence and the American Presidency from Washington to Bush* (HarperCollins, 1995). See also Rhodri Jeffreys-Jones, *The CIA and American Democracy*, 2d ed. (Yale University Press, 1998).

9. National Commission on Terrorist Attacks on the United States, *The 9/11 Commission Report* (Norton, 2004), p. 12.

10. *Public Papers of the Presidents, Dwight D. Eisenhower* (U.S. Government Printing Office, 1960), pp. 1035–1040.

11. P. W. Singer, "Winning the War of Words: Information Warfare in Afghanistan," *Brookings Analysis Paper No. 5*, October 2001.

12. "U.S. Foreign Aid Spending Since World War II," *Public Perspective* 8 (August–September 1997), p. 11.

13. Gallup Poll, May 2000, www.gallup.com.

14. See Sebastian Mallaby, "Why So Stingy on Foreign Aid?" *The Washington Post National Weekly Edition*, July 3, 2000, p. 27.

15. See Robert Kagan, "The Kerry Doctrine," *The Washington Post*, August 1, 2004, p. B7, for this argument.

16. Gary Hufbauer and Jeffrey J. Schott, "Economic Sanctions and Foreign Policy," *PS: Political Science and Politics* 18 (Fall 1985), p. 278.

17. John Prados, *The President's Secret Wars: CIA and Pentagon Covert Operations Since World War II* (Morrow, 1986); and Daniel Patrick Moynihan, *Secrecy: The American Experience* (Yale University Press, 1998).

Chapter 21

1. Data are for end of year, 2008. Taken from the *Bureau of Justice Statistics Summary of the Total Correctional Population*, http://bjs.ojp .usdoj.gov/index.cfm?ty=tp&tid=11.

2. John Holahan et al., "Which Way for Federalism and Health Policy?" *Health Affairs*, Web Exclusive (July 2003), pp. W3, 317–319, content.healthaffairs.org/cgi/reprint/hlthaff .w3.317v1.pdf.

3. Calculated from 2005 data in U.S. Bureau of Transportation Statistics, *National Transportation Statistics*, Appendix A–Modal Profiles, Highway Profile, www.bts.gov/publications/national_ transportation_statistics/ html/table_ highway_profile.html.

4. U.S. Census Bureau, *Statistical Abstract of the United States: 2010* (U.S. Government Printing Office, 2010), Table 269, http://www.census.gov/ compendia/statab/2010/tables/10s0269.pdf.

5. All spending data taken from the U.S. Census Bureau, *Statistical Abstract of the United States: 2010* (U.S. Government Printing Office, 2008), Tables 418, 457, and 651, http://www.census .gov/compendia/statab/.

6. Suho Bae and Robert Ward, "Long-Term Trends in State and Local Revenues and Expenditures," *Rockefeller Institute Fiscal Brief* (May 2008), www.rockinst.org.

7. U.S. Census Bureau, *Statistical Abstract of the United States: 2010* (U.S. Government Printing Office, 2010), Table 449, http://www.census.gov/ compendia/statab/2010/tables/10s0449.pdf.

8. U.S. Census Bureau, *Statistical Abstract of the United States: 2010* (U.S. Government Printing Office, 2010), Table 450, http://www.census.gov/ compendia/statab/2010/tables/10s0450.pdf.

9. Robert S. Lynd and Helen M. Lynd, *Middletown* (Harcourt, 1929). See also their analysis of Muncie ten years later in *Middletown in Transition* (Harcourt, 1937).

10. Floyd Hunter, *Community Power Structure* (University of North Carolina Press, 1953). For a reassessment and rebuttal of Hunter's findings, see M. Kent Jennings, *Community Influentials: The Elites of Atlanta* (Free Press, 1964).

11. Clarence N. Stone, *Regime Politics: Governing Atlanta 1946–1988* (University Press of Kansas, 1989).

12. Robert A. Dahl, *Who Governs? Democracy and Power in an American City* (Yale University Press, 1961).

13. See Peter Bachrach and Morton S. Baratz, "Two Faces of Power" *American Political Science Review* 56, no. 4 (1962): 947–952 and (1962 APSR); and Clarence N. Stone, "Systemic Power in Community Decision Making: A Restatement of Stratification Theory" *American Political Science Review* 74, no. 4 (1980): 978–990.

14. Rufus P. Browning, Dale Rogers Marshall, and David H. Tabb, *Protest Is Not Enough: The Struggle of Blacks and Hispanics for Equality in Urban Politics* (University of California Press, 1984).

15. See the interesting study of San Jose, California, by Phillip J. Troustine and Terry Christensen, *Movers and Shakers: The Study of Community Power* (St. Martin's Press, 1982). See also Clarence N. Stone, *Regime Politics: Governing Atlanta, 1946–1988* (University Press of Kansas, 1989).

16. See, for example, Peter Bachrach and Morton S. Baratz, *Power and Poverty: Theory and Practice* (Oxford University Press, 1970); Matthew A. Crenson, *The Un-politics of Air Pollution: A Study of Non-Decisionmaking in the Cities* (Johns Hopkins University Press, 1971); and John Gaventa, *Power and Powerlessness: Quiescence and Rebellion in an Appalachian Valley* (University of Illinois Press, 1980).

17. Bryan D. Jones and Lynn W. Bachelor, *The Sustaining Hand: Community Leadership and Corporate Power*, 2d ed. (University Press of Kansas, 1993), p. 254. See also Stone, *Regime Politics*.

18. Daniel J. Elazar, *American Federalism: A View from the States*, 3rd ed (Harper and Row, 1984).

19. Tobacco-Free Kids, November 2009, http://www.tobaccofreekids.org/research/ factsheets/pdf/0097.pdf.

20. Orzechowski and Walker, *The Tax Burden on Tobacco: Historical Compilation* 2004 (Author, 2005).

21. Stone, *Regime Politics*, p. 232.

22. For a detailed analysis of how W. R. Grace and Beatrice Foods had to rely on law firms to fight legal actions surrounding their operations in Woburn, Massachusetts, see Jonathan Harr, *A Civil Action* (Vintage Books, 1996). See also Alan Rosenthal, *The Third House: Lobbyists and Lobbying in the States*, 2d ed. (CQ Press, 2001).

23. See Clive S. Thomas and Ronald J. Hrebenar, "Interest Groups in the States," in Virginia Gray, Russell L. Hanson, and Herbert Jacob, eds., *Politics in the American States* (CQ Press, 1999), pp. 122–158.

24. For a list of state lobbying laws, see National Council of Nonprofit Associations, *State Lobbying Laws*, www.ncna.org/_uploads/ documents/live//Lobby_Regulations_Chart.xls.

25. For a general discussion of ethics reform and enforcement efforts, see *Spectrum: The Journal of State Government* (Winter 1993).

26. On various efforts to improve ethical practices and professionalism in the state legislatures and the limits of these efforts, see Alan Rosenthal, *Drawing the Line: Legislative Ethics in the States* (University of Nebraska Press, 1996).

27. For information on state lobbying laws, see the database maintained by Center for Ethics in Government of the National Conference of State Legislatures, www.ncsl.org/programs/ ethics/database.htm.

28. Diane D. Blair, *Arkansas Politics and Government* (University of Nebraska Press, 1988), p. 118.

29. Richard L. Cole and John Kincaid, "Public Opinion on U.S. Federal and Intergovernmental Issues in 2006: Continuity and Change," *Publius* 36, no. 3 (Summer 2006), pp. 453–454.

30. http://www.gallup.com/poll/122915/ trust-state-government-sinks-new-low.aspx.

31. http://pewresearch.org/pubs/1569/trust-in-government-distrust-discontent-anger-parti-san-rancor.

32. Peter Slevin "Obama Administration to Buy Illinois Prison for Guantanamo Detainees" *The Washington Post*, December 16, 2009.

33. Paul Peterson, *City Limits* (University of Chicago Press, 1981), p. 124. See also the useful discussion of the challenge of covering state legislative politics in Browne and VerBurg, *Michigan Politics and Government*, pp. 242–245.

34. M. Jae Moon, "The Evolution of E-Government Among Municipalities: Rhetoric or Reality?" *Public Administration Review* 62, no. 4 (July/August 2002), pp. 424–433.

35. Ibid., p. 18–20.

36. Joseph F. Zimmerman, *The New England Town Meeting: Democracy in Action* (Praeger, 1999).

37. Victor S. DeSantis and David Hill, "Citizen Participation in Local Politics: Evidence from New England Town Meetings," *State and Local Government Review* (Fall 2004), pp. 166–173.

38. See, for example, Daniel Kemmis, *The Good City and the Good Life* (Houghton Mifflin, 1995); and David L. Kirp, John P Dwyer, and Larry A. Rosenthal, *Our Town: Race, Housing, and the Soul of Suburbia* (Rutgers University Press, 1997).

39. Eugene F. Rivers III, "High-Octane Faith," in E. J. Dionne Jr., ed., *Community Works: The Revival of Civil Society in America* (Brookings Institution Press, 1998), p. 61.

40. Karen Rowley, *GulfGov Reports: Response, Recovery, and the Role of the Nonprofit Community in the Two Years Since Katrina and Rita* (Rockefeller Institute of Government and Public Affairs Research Council of Louisiana, 2007), p. v.

41. For the efforts of a big-city mayor and his team of advisers, see Buzz Bissinger, *A Prayer for the City* (Random House, 1997). See also the example of Milwaukee's mayor, John O. Norquist, *Wealth of Cities* (Addison-Wesley, 1998).

42. Iris J. Lav and Phillip Oliff, *Federal Grants to States and Localities Cut Deeply in Fiscal Year 2009 Federal Budget* (Center on Budget and Policy Priorities, February 4, 2008).

43. Donald J. Boyd, "What Will Happen to State Government Finances in a Recession?" *Rockefeller Institute Fiscal Report* (Rockefeller Institute of Government, January 30, 2008), p. 17.

44. The Pew Center on the States, *One in 100: Behind Bars in America 2008* (Pew Charitable Trusts, 2008), p. 14.

45. Nelson A. Rockefeller, *The Future of Federalism* (Harvard University Press, 1962), p. 9.

Chapter 22

1. Gerald Benjamin, "The Functions of State Constitutions in a Federal System," paper presented at the American Political Science Association Round Table (Washington, D.C., 1984).

2. John Adams, quoted in Judith S. Kaye, "Federalism's Other Tier," *Constitution* 3 (Winter 1991), p. 50.

3. Christopher W. Hammons, "State Constitutional Reform: Is It Necessary?" *Albany Law Review* 64 (2001), pp. 1328–1334.

4. *The Book of the States, 2009* (Council of State Governments, 2009), Table 1.1, p. 12.

5. Steve Geissinger, "Changing the Constitution Is a Powerful Government-Reform Tool Avoided by Officials," *Alameda (Calif.) Times-Star*, November 9, 2003, p. C1.

6. South Dakota Constitution, Article XI, Section 8.

7. Alabama Constitution, Amendment 383 (1901).

8. Donald S. Lutz, "Toward a Theory of Constitutional Amendment," in Sanford Levinson, ed., *Responding to Imperfection: The Theory and Practice of Constitutional Amendment* (Princeton University Press, 1995), pp. 237–274.

9. *The Book of the States, 2009*, Table 1.1, p. 12; and John Kincaid, "State Constitutions in the Federal System," *Annals of the American Academy of Political and Social Science* 496 (March 1988), p. 14.

10. *The Book of the States, 2009*, Table 1.1, p. 12.

11. *Indiana v. Gerschoffer*, 763 N.E.2d 960 (2002).

12. *Anchorage Police Department Employees Association v. Anchorage*, 24 P.3d 547 (2001).

13. *American Academy of Pediatrics v. Lungren*, 490 P.2d 797 (1997).

14. Kaye, "Federalism's Other Tier," p. 54.

15. See, for example, Matthew Bosworth, *Courts as Catalysts: State Supreme Courts and Public School Finances Equity* (State University of New York Press, 2001); and Charles Lopeman, *The Activist Advocate: Policy Making in State Supreme Courts* (Praeger, 1999).

16. *Michigan v. Long*, 463 U.S. 1032 (1983); "Our Judicial Federalism," *Intergovernmental Perspective* 15 (Summer 1989), pp. 8–15; and William M. Wiecek, "Some Protection of Personal Liberty: Remembering the Future," and Kermit L. Hall, "Mostly Anchor and Little Sail: The Evolution of American State Constitutions," in Paul Finkelman and Stephen E. Gottlieb, eds., *Toward a Usable Past: Liberty Under State Constitutions* (University of Georgia Press, 1991), pp. 371–417.

17. Deborah Baker, "Canvassing Board Certifies Amendment Election," *Santa Fe New Mexican*, October 14, 2003, p. A1.

18. *The Book of the States, 2007*, p. 4.

19. *The Book of the States, 2009*, p. 3.

20. Fred Keeley, "California Dreamin': An On-Time Budget," *Sacramento Bee*, July 17, 2005.

21. *The Book of the States, 2005*, p. 17.

22. *The Book of the States, 2009*, pp. 3–4.

23. Tip H. Allen, Jr., "The Enduring Traditions of the State Constitutions," in Dale Krane and Stephen D. Shaffer, eds., *Mississippi Government and Politics: Modernizers Versus Traditionalists* (University of Nebraska Press, 1992), pp. xx–xxv.

24. *The Book of the States, 2002* (Council of State Governments, 2002), p. 14.

25. David B. Magleby, "Direct Legislation in the American States," in David Butler and Austin Ranney, eds., *Referendums Around the World: The Growing Use of Direct Democracy* (AEI Press, 1994), p. 225.

26. California Commission on Campaign Financing, *Democracy by Initiative: A Summary of the Report and Recommendations of the California Commission on Campaign Financing* (Center for Responsive Government, 1992), p. 25.

27. *Amador Valley Joint Union High School District v. State Board of Equalization*, 22 Cal. 3d 208 (1978), quoted in Eugene C. Lee, "The Revision of California's Constitution," *CPS Brief: A Publication of the California Policy Seminar* 3 (April 1991), p. 1.

28. *The Book of the States, 2007*, p. 3; see also Magleby, "Direct Legislation," p. 251.

29. *The Book of the States, 2009*, p. 3.

30. G. Alan Tarr, *Understanding State Constitutions* (Princeton University Press, 2000), p. 158; and Thomas Gais and Gerald Benjamin, "Public Discontent and the Decline of Deliberation: A Dilemma in State Constitutional Reform," *Temple Law Review* 68, No. 3 (1995), pp. 1292–1300.

31. Ibid., pp. 160–161.

32. Gerald Benjamin and Thomas Gais, "Constitutional Conventionphobia," in Burton C. Agata and Eric Lane, eds. *State Constitutions: Competing Perspectives* (Hofstra Law and Policy Symposium, 1996), Vol. 1, p. 69; Tarr, *Understanding State Constitutions*, p. 25; and *The Book of the States, 2005*, p. 17.

33. Caleb Nelson, "A Re-Evaluation of Scholarly Explanations for the Rise of the Elective Judiciary in Antebellum America," *American Journal of Legal History* 37, No. 2 (1993), p. 221.

34. Elder Witt, "State Supreme Courts: Tilting the Balance Toward Change," *Governing* (August 1988), p. 33.

35. G. Alan Tarr, keynote address, Conference on State Constitutional Reform, May 4, 2000, www .camlaw.rugers.edu/statecon/keynote.html.

36. Lee, "Revision of California's Constitution," p. 7; see also Lutz, "Toward a Theory of Constitutional Amendment," pp. 355–370.

37. "State of Rhode Island General Assembly," www.rilin.state.ri.us/studteaguide/RhodeIsland History/chapt9.html.

38. Re Jan Ruggiero, Director of Elections, Elections Division, Office of the Secretary of State, Providence, RI, www.state.ri.us.

39. Common Cause of Rhode Island, "Separation of Powers," www.commoncauseri.org/news.

40. State of Hawaii Statewide Election Summary Report, November 4, 2008, http://hawaii.gov .elections/results/2008/general/files/ histatewide.pdf.

41. Beryl E. Pettus and Randall W. Bland, *Texas Government Today* (Dorsey Press, 1979), pp. 34–36; see also Janice C. May, "Texas Constitutional Revision and Laments," *National Civic Review* (February 1977), pp. 64–69.

42. B. Drummond Ayres, Jr., "Alabama Governor Set for Tough Race," *New York Times*, February 27, 2002, p. A16.

43. Albert E. McKinley, "Two New Southern Constitutions," *Political Science Quarterly* 18 (September 1903), pp. 480–511.

44. For more information, go to the Web site of the Alabama Citizens for Constitutional Reform, www.constitutionalreform.org.

45. Associated Press, "Constitution Work May Come in 2003," *Montgomery (Ala.) Advertiser*, December 11, 2002, www. montgomeryadvertiser.com.

46. Editorial, "Constitutional Count, House Sending Clear Message: People Can't Be Trusted," *Birmingham (Ala.) News*, March 21, 2002, p. A20.

47. Manuel Roig-Franzia, "Vote Opens Old Racial Wounds; School Segregation Remains a State Law as Amendment Is Defeated," *The Washington Post*, November 28, 2004, p. A1.

48. See, for instance, the Web site of Alabama Citizens for Constitutional Reform, www.constitutionalreform.org.

49. *The Book of the States, 2005*, pp. 3–9.

Chapter 23

1. *Crawford v. Marion County Election Board*, 553 U.S. 181 (2008).

2. U.S. Constitution, Article I, Section 4.

3. U.S. Constitution, Article II, Section 2.

4. Alexander Hamilton, James Madison, and John Jay, *The Federalist Papers*, No. 59.

5. U.S. Constitution, Article IV, Section 4.

6. Akkhil Reed Amar, *America's Constitution: A Biography* (Random House, 2006), pp. 422–423.

7. Larry N. Gerston and Terry Christensen, *Recall! California's Political Earthquake* (Sharpe, 2004).

8. Data taken from Project Vote: http://www. projectvote.org/images/publications/ Felon%20Voting/felon_voting_laws_by_ state_Sept_11_2008.pdf.

9. The Council of State Governments, *The Book of the States 2007*, Vol. 39 (Author, 2007), pp. 293–295.

10. U.S. Census Bureau , *Statistical Abstract of the United States: 2001* (U.S. Government Printing Office, 2001), p. 26.

11. U.S. Election Assistance Commission, "The Impact of the National Voter Registration Act, 2005–06," http://www.eac.gov/assets/1/Page/ NVRA_Reports_and_Data_Sets_2006–2005.pdf

12. Cynthia Rugeley and Robert A. Jackson, "Getting on the Rolls: Analyzing the Effects of Lowered Barriers on Voter Registration," *State Politics and Policy Quarterly* 9(1): 56–78.

13. Benjamin Highton and Raymond E. Wolfinger, *Political Behavior* 20 (June 1998), pp. 94–97.

14. Raymond E. Wolfinger and Steven J. Rosenstone, *Who Votes?* (Yale University Press, 1980), p. 130.

15. R. Michael Alverez, Delia Bailey, and Jonathan N. Katz, "The Effect of Voter Identification Laws on Turnout," *Caltech/MIT Voting Technology Project*, working paper no. 57 (October 2007), www.vote.caltech.edu/media/documents/wps/ vtp_wp57.pdf.

16. U.S. Census Bureau, *Statistical Abstract of the United States: 2010*, Table 409, http://www .census.gov/compendia/statab/2010/tables/ 10s0409.pdf.

17. For a brief overview of the Voting Rights Act, see U.S. Department of Justice, Civil Rights Division, Voting Section, "Introduction to Federal Voting Rights Laws," www.usdoj.gov/crt/voting/intro/ intro.htm.

18. Barney Warf, "Voting Technologies and Residual Ballots in the 2000 and 2004 Presidential Elections," *Political Geography* 25 (June 2006), p. 533.
19. Election Data Services, Inc., *2006 Voting Equipment Study* (Election Data Services, 2006), p. 4.
20. Ibid.
21. Brennan Center Task Force on Voting System Security, *The Machinery of Democracy: Protecting Elections in an Electronic World* (Brennan Center for Justice, New York University School of Law, 2006).
22. R. Doug Lewis, "2006 Elections: Successful Implementation and Continuing Issues," *The Book of the States 2007* (Council of State Governments, 2007), pp. 277–279.
23. Paul S. Herrnson et al., *Voting Technology: The Not-So-Simple Act of Casting a Ballot* (Brookings Institution Press, 2008), pp. 91–110.
24. Ryan L. Claasen, David B. Magleby, J. Quin Monson, and Kelly B. Patterson, "At Your Service: Voter Evaluations of Poll Worker Performance," *American Politics Research* (forthcoming).
25. David B. Magleby, "Participation in Mail Ballot Elections," *Western Political Quarterly* 40 (March 1987), pp. 79–91.
26. Priscilla Southwell, "Five Years Later: A Re-Assessment of Oregon's Vote by Mail Electoral Process" (2003), and Paul Gronke, "Ballot Integrity and Voting by Mail: The Oregon Experience" (2005), both available at www.sos.state.or.us/executive/policy-initiatives/vbm/execvbm.htm.
27. The Early Voting Information Center at Reed College, "Absentee and Early Voting Laws: Summary Table (last updated, February 21, 2008)," www.earlyvoting.net/states/abslaws.php. Absentee ballots for all states are available at www.justvote.org.
28. Washington Secretary of State's Office Report available online at http://www.sos.wa.gov/elections/absentee_stats.aspx.
29. Early Voting Information Center, "Absentee and Early Voting Laws."
30. Data taken from: http://elections.gmu.edu/early_vote_2008.html.
31. Comment by Bryan Jones of the University of Washington, quoted in Neil Modie, "Obama Big Winner in Washington Caucus," *Seattle Post-Intelligencer*, February 10, 2008.
32. Lewis, "2006 Elections," pp. 284–285.
33. For information on the 2008 primaries and the relationship between party and the vote, see the exit poll data available at "Election Center 2008: Primaries and Caucuses," CNNPolitics .com, www.cnn.com/ELECTION/2008/.
34. Thomas M.Carsey, *Campaign Dynamics: The Race for Governor*, Chapter 8 (University of Michigan Press, Ann Arbor, MI, 2000).
35. Thomas M. Carsey and Gerald C. Wright. "State and National Factors in Gubernatorial and Senatorial Elections" (1998), *American Journal of Political Science* 42(3): 994–1002; see also James E. Campbell "Presidential Coattails and Midterm Losses in State Legislative Elections" (1986), *American Political Science Review* 80(1): 45–63.
36. National Conference of State Legislatures historical trends on ballot measures, http://www.ncsl.org/default.aspx?tabid=20114#historical.
37. David B. Magleby, *Direct Legislation: Voting on Ballot Propositions in the United States* (Johns Hopkins University Press, 1984), Chapters 7–9.
38. David B. Magleby, "Campaign Spending and Referendum Voting," paper presented at the

annual meeting of the Western Political Science Association, Albuquerque, NM, March 1994.
39. *Financing California's Statewide Ballot Measures: Receipts and Expenditures Through December 31,1998* (California Secretary of State, 1998), p. 2.
40. National Conference of State Legislatures, "Recall of State Officials" March 21, 2006, http://www.ncsl.org/default.aspx?tabid=16581.
41. California Secretary of State Kevin Shelly, www.ss.ca.gov/elections/elections_recall_faqs .htm#20.
42. See Gerston and Christensen, *Recall.*
43. California Voter Foundation, www.calvoter .org/voter/elections/archive/recall/index.html (accessed June 15, 2006).
44. National Conference of State Legislatures, "Recall of Local Officials," http://www.ncsl .org/Default.aspx?TabId=16540.
45. National Conference of State Legislatures, "Campaign Finance Reform: An Overview," February 5, 2008, www.ncsl.org/programs/legismgt/about/campfin.htm.
46. U.S. Supreme Court ruling in *Citizens United* v. *Federal Election Commission* (2010).
47. Ian Urbina "24 States' Laws Open to Attack After Campaign Finance Ruling" *New York Times,* January 22, 2010, http://www.nytimes.com/2010/01/23/us/politics/23states.html.
48. Edward D. Feigenbaum and James A. Palmer, *Campaign Finance Law 2002* (U.S. Federal Election Commission, 2002), Chart 2-A. For more information on campaign finance laws, see www.fec.gov.
49. The Supreme Court decision is *Randall et al.* v. *Sorrell et al.*, No. 04–1528 (2006).
50. Secretary of State and Commission on Governmental Ethics and Election Practices, *2008 Candidate Guide: Running for Office in Maine*, pp. 39–41, mainegov-images.informe .org/ethics/pdf/2008_candidate_guide.pdf.
51. Other "clean money" states include Arizona, Connecticut, and Vermont, see www .publicampaign.org/where. For an assessment of the effects of two of these programs, see U.S. Government Accountability Office, *Campaign Finance Reform: Early Experiences of Two States That Offer Full Public Funding for Political Candidates*, GAO-03–453 (U.S. Government Accountability Office, 2003).
52. See remarks by Michael Malbin in *Rockefeller Institute of Government*, "Can and Should NYC's Campaign Reforms Be Extended to State Offices?" (Rockefeller Institute of Government, April 25, 2007).
53. Michael Malbin and Thomas Gais, *The Day After Reform: Sobering Campaign Finance Lessons from the American States* (Rockefeller Institute Press, 1998), pp. 65–70.
54. See Maine Citizens for Clean Elections, "Clean Election Supporters Call for Full Restoration of Clean Election Fund," www.mainecleanelections.org.
55. For example, see the North Carolina Voters for Clean Elections Web site, http://www.ncvce .org/index.php?page=ncjudicialprogram.
56. John F. Bibby, *Politics, Parties, and Elections in America*, 5th ed. (Wadsworth, 2003).
57. Mike Royko, *Boss: Richard J. Daley of Chicago* (Dutton, 1971).
58. Melvin G. Holli, *The American Mayor: The Best and the Worst Big-City Leaders* (Pennsylvania State University Press, 1999).
59. According to Todd Taylor, executive director, Utah Democratic Party, these requirements are intended to promote gender equity; personal communication, November 18, 1998.
60. The Web site for the National Republican Party is http://www.gop.com, and the Web site for

the National Democratic Party is http:// www.democrats.org/. State party links are available on these Web sites or are easily located with an Internet search of the party name and the state name of interest.
61. See Cornelius P. Cotter, James L. Gibson, John F. Bibby, and Robert J. Huckshorn, *Party Organizations in America* (Praeger, 1984).
62. Ronald E. Weber, ed., *American State and Local Politics: Directions for the21st Century* (Chatham House, 1999), p. 174.
63. U.S. Election Assistance Commission, "Voter Registration and Turnout 2000," www.eac.gov.
64. U.S. Department of Commerce, *Statistical Abstract of the United States: 2006* (October 2005), p. 264; and Greg McDonald, "Primary Turnout May Prolong Downtrend," stateline.org (accessed September 17, 2002).
65. Michael McDonald, United State Elections Project, http://elections.gmu.edu/voter_turnout.htm.
66. Donald P. Green and Alan S. Gerber, *Get Out the Vote* (Brookings Institution Press, 2004), p. 9.
67. For a discussion of coordinated campaigns, see Paul Herrnson, "National Party Organizations and the Postreform Congress," in Roger Davidson, ed., *The Postreform Congress* (St. Martin's Press, 1992), pp. 65–67.
68. See Cotter et al., *Party Organizations in America.*
69. New Jersey Election Law Enforcement Commission, *The 2005 Assembly Election: New Trends on the Horizon?* (Author, September 2006), p. 19.
70. Malbin and Gais, *The Day After Reform*, pp. 145–152.
71. New Jersey Election Law Enforcement Commission, *The 2005 Assembly Election: New Trends on the Horizon?* (September 2006), p. 19.
72. See Bruce E. Keith, David B. Magleby, Candice J. Nelson, Elizabeth Orr, Mark C. Westlye, and Raymond E. Wolfinger, *The Myth of the Independent Voter* (University of California Press, 1992), p. 52.
73. The Field Poll, "Voters Very Dissatisfied with State Budget Negotiations. Blame Davis and Both Parties in the Legislature. Three in Four Fear the State Is Seriously Off on the Wrong Track," www.field.com/ fieldpollonline/sub-scribers/RLS2074.pdf.
74. The Field Poll, "How Schwarzenegger's History and Characteristics Helps and Hurts Him in His Bid to Become Governor," www.field.com/fieldpollonline/subscribers/RLS2083.pdf.
75. Stephen Ansolabehere and James M. Synder, Jr., "The Incumbency Advantage in U.S. Elections: An Analysis of State and Federal Offices," March 15, 2002, web.mit.edu/polisci/research/representation/incumb_advantage_elj.pdf.
76. Malcolm E. Jewell and David M. Olson, *Political Parties and Elections in American States,* 3d ed. (Dorsey Press, 1988), p. 121; and William H. Flanigan and Nancy H. Zingale, *Political Behavior of the American Electorate*, 8th ed. (CQ Press, 1994), p. 195.
77. Flanigan and Zingale, *Political Behavior of the American Electorate*, 8th ed., (CQ Press, 1994), p. 171.
78. Thomas M. Carsey, *Campaign Dynamics: The Race for Governor* (University of Michigan Press, 2000).
79. James Sample, Lauren Jones, and Rachel Weiss, *The New Politics of Judicial Elections, 2006* (Justice at Stake Campaign, 2006).
80. Willis D. Hawley, *Nonpartisan Elections and the Case for Party Politics* (Wiley, 1973), pp. 81–82; see also Brian F. Schaffner, Matthew Streb, and Gerald Wright, "Teams Without Uniforms: The Nonpartisan Ballot in State and Local

Elections," *Political Research Quarterly* 54 (March 2001), pp. 7–30.

81. Susan Welch and Timothy Bledsoe, "The Partisan Consequences of Nonpartisan Elections and the Changing Nature of Urban Politics," *American Journal of Political Science* 30 (February 1986), pp. 128–139.

82. Gerald C. Wright and Tracy Osborn, "Party and Roll Call Voting in the American Legislature," paper presented at the Midwest Political Science Association Meeting, Chicago, 2002.

83. Gerald C. Wright and Brian F. Schaffner, "The Influence of Party: Evidence from the State Legislatures" (2002), *American Political Science Review* 96(2): 367–379.

84. The major cases are: *Baker* v. *Carr* (1962), *Reynolds* v. *Sims* (1963), and *Wesberry* v. *Sanders* (1963).

85. Gary W. Cox and Jonathan N. Katz, *Elbridge Gerry's Salamander: The Electoral Consequences of the Reapportionment Revolution* (Cambridge University Press, 2002).

86. National Conference of State Legislatures, "2008 Partisan Composition of State Legislatures," www.ncsl.org/statevote/partycomptable2008.htm.

87. U.S. Census Bureau, *Statistical Abstract of the United States: 2010*, Table 400, http://www.census.gov/compendia/statab/2010/tables/10s0400.pdf.

88. Pamela M. Prah, "First Salvos Prepared for Statehouse Redistricting Battles," stateline.org, August 24, 2006, www.stateline.org/live/details/story?contentId=136505.

89. Bill Mears, "Texas Redistricting Reaches High Court," CNN, February 28, 2006, www.cnn.com/2006/LAW/02/28/scotus.texas/. The Supreme Court decision was *League of United Latin American Citizens et al.* v. *Perry, Governor of Texas et al.*, No. 05–204 (2006).

90. Kevin Duggan, "GOP Map Cast Aside," *Fort Collins Coloradoan*, December 2, 2003, http://coloradoan.com/news/coloradoanpublishing/Legislature2004/redistricting/120203_ruling.html.

91. The classic work here is V. O. Key, *Southern Politics in State and Nation* (Knoph, 1949; reprinted by the University of Tennessee Press).

92. Terrel L. Rhodes, *Republicans in the South: Voting for the State House, Voting for the White House* (Praeger, 2000), p. 88.

Chapter 24

1. National Conference of State Legislatures, http://www.ncsl.org/default.aspx?tabid=14843.

2. Ralph G. Wright, *Inside the Statehouse: Lessons from the Speaker* (CQ Press, 2005), p. 227.

3. For a useful look at Nebraska's unique legislature, see Jack Rodgers, Robert Sittig, and Susan Welch, "The Legislature," in Robert D. Miewald, ed., *Nebraska Government and Politics* (University of Nebraska Press, 1984), pp. 57–86.

4. *The Book of the States, 2009* (Council of State Governments, 2009), Table 3–3, p. 87

5. Peverill Squire and Keith E. Hamm, *101 Chambers: Congress, State Legislatures, and the Future of Legislative Studies* (Ohio State University Press), Table 4–1, p. 102.

6. Richard A. Clucas, "Exercising Control: The Power of State House Speakers," paper presented at the annual meeting of the Western Political Science Association, Los Angeles, March 1998; see also Malcolm E. Jewell and Marcia Lynn Whicker, *Legislative Leadership in the American States* (University of Michigan Press, 1997).

7. *The Book of the States, 2005* (The Council of State Governments, 2005), pp. 136–137.

8. Wayne L. Francis, *The Legislative Committee Game: A Comparative Analysis of 50 States* (Ohio State University Press, 1989).

9. *The Book of the States, 2009*, Table 3–23, p. 140.

10. Alan Rosenthal, *Legislative Life: People, Process, and Performance in the States* (Harper & Row, 1981), pp. 112–113.

11. See Peverill Squire, "Uncontested Seats in State Legislative Elections," *Legislative Studies Quarterly* 35 (February 2000), pp. 131–146.

12. Richard G. Niemi, Lynda W. Powell, William D. Berry, Thomas M. Carsey, and James M. Snyder, Jr., "Competition in State Legislative Elections, 1992–2002," in Michael P. McDonald and John Samples, eds., *The Marketplace of Democracy: Electoral Competition and American Politics* (Brookings, 2006).

13. Alan Rosenthal, "The Legislative Unraveling of Institutional Fabric," in Carl E. Van Horn, ed., *The State of the States*, 3d ed. (CQ Press, 1996), p. 118.

14. Gary F. Moncrief, Peverill Squire, and Malcolm E. Jewell, *Who Runs for the Legislature?* (Prentice Hall, 2000).

15. Frank Smallwood, *Free and Independent: The Initiation of a College Professor into State Politics* (Greene Press, 1976), p. 223.

16. The *Book of the States, 2007* (The Council of State Governments, 2007), p. 80.

17. See Sue Thomas, *How Women Legislate* (Oxford University Press, 1994); see also Lesley Dahlkemper, "Growing Accustomed to Her Face," *State Legislatures* (July–August 1996), pp. 37–45; and Kathleen Dolan and Lynne Ford, "Change and Continuity Among Women State Legislators" *Political Research Quarterly* 50 (March 1997), pp. 137–151.

18. "Former State Legislators in Congress," National Conference of State Legislatures, www.ncsl.org/statefed/fsl.htm.

19. For fascinating comparative data, see *Inside the Legislative Process: A Comprehensive Survey by the American Society of Legislative Clerks and Secretaries* (National Conference of State Legislatures, 1998).

20. Wayne L. Francis, *The Legislative Committee Game: A Comparative Analysis of 50 States* (Ohio State University Press, 1989).

21. Keith E. Hamm, Ronald D. Hedlund, and Nancy Martorano, "Measuring State Legislative Committee Power: Change and Chamber Differences in the 20th Century," *State Politics and Policy Quarterly* 6 (2006): 88–111.

22. Gerald C. Wright and Tracy Osborn, "Party and Roll Call Voting in the American Legislature," paper presented at the annual meeting of the 2002 Midwest Political Science Association, April 2002.

23. Boris Shor and Nolan McCarty, "The Ideological Mapping of American Legislatures," working paper, http://home.uchicago.edu/~bshor/research/votesmart.pdf.

24. Keith E. Hamm and Gary F. Moncrief, "Legislative Politics in the States," in Virginia Gray et al., *Politics in the American States*, 7th ed. (CQ Press, 1999), p. 184.

25. Anthony J. Nownes, Clive S. Thomas, and Ronald J. Hrebenar, "Interest Groups in the States" in Virginia Gray and Russell L. Hanson, eds., *Politics in the American States*, 9th ed. (CQ Press, 2008).

26. Lobbying strategies are outlined in Jay Michael and Dan Walters, *The Third House: Lobbyists, Power, and Money in Sacramento* (Berkeley Public Policy Press, 2001). Other lobbying realities are discussed in Tom Loftus, *Art of Legislative Politics* (CQ Press, 1994), Chapter 10; and Alan Rosenthal, *Drawing the Line: Legislative Ethics in the States* (University of Nebraska Press, 1996).

27. Thomas Frank, "Ex-Legislators Use Contacts," *The Denver Post*, July 5, 1996, p. 16A; see also Loftus, *Art of Legislative Politics*.

28. Joel A. Thompson and Gary F. Moncrief, eds., *Campaign Finance in State Legislative Elections* (CQ Press, 1998).

29. Frank Smallwood, *Free and Independent* (Greene Press, 1976), p. 165; see also Alan Rosenthal, *The Third House: Lobbyists and Lobbying in the States*, 2d ed. (CQ Press, 2001); and "State Legislators Mix Public and Private Business, Study Says," *New York Times*, May 21, 2000, p. 26.

30. David D. Kirkpatrick, "States Take Lead on Ethics Rules for Lawmakers," *New York Times*, January 1, 2007, p. A1.

31. Adam Nossiter, "New Louisiana Governor Pierces Brazen Style of Business as Usual," *New York Times*, February 28, 2008, p. A1.

32. Charles Mahtesian, "The Ethics Backlash," *Governing* (October 1999), pp. 39–41.

33. Quote appears in the documentary film by Paul Stekler, "Last Man Standing: Politics, Texas Style" (Midnight Films, 2004).

34. John E. Brandl, *Money and Good Intentions Are Not Enough: Or, Why a Liberal Democrat Thinks States Need Both Competition and Community* (Brookings Institution Press, 1998), p. 58.

35. Alan Rosenthal, "The Legislative Institution: In Transition and at Risk," in Carl E. Van Horn, ed., *The State of the States*, 2d ed. (CQ Press, 1993), pp. 136–137; see also Alan Ehrenhalt, "An Embattled Institution," *Governing* (January 1992), pp. 28–33; and Karen Hansen, "Our Beleaguered Institution," *State Legislatures* (January 1994), pp. 12–17.

36. Rosenthal, "The Legislative Institution," p. 144.

37. See, for example, Christopher Conte, "Laptop Legislatures," *Governing* (November 1999), p. 36.

38. "Size of State Legislative Staff: 1979, 1988, 1996, 2003, and 2009," National Conference of State Legislatures, http://www.ncsl.org/default.aspx?tabid=14843.

39. Carrie Koch, "A Room for a View," *State Legislatures* (May 1997), pp. 32–34.

40. http://www.pewcenteronthestates.org/uploadedFiles/Grading-the-States-2008.pdf.

41. Rich Jones, "The State Legislatures," in *The Book of the States, 1992–1993* (The Council of State Governments, 1992), p. 125.

42. Michael Janofsky, "Idaho Legislature Repeals Term-Limit Law, Undoing Voter Approved Measure," *New York Times*, February 2, 2002, p. A11; see also Wayne Hoffman, "The Battle Over Term Limits," *State Legislatures* (May 2002), pp. 25–29.

43. Janofsky, "Idaho Legislature," p. A11.

44. See Daniel B. Wood, "The Term-Limit Movement of the '90s Stalls," *Christian Science Monitor*, April 27, 2004, p. A1.

45. www.washingtonpost.com/wp-srv/politics/elections/2006/or.html.

46. See John M. Carey, Richard G. Niemi, and Lynda W. Powell, *Term Limits in the State Legislatures* (University of Michigan Press, 2000).

47. Thad Kousser, *Term Limits and the Dismantling of State Legislative Professionalism* (Cambridge University Press, 2005), p. 203.

48. Jack Quinn et al., "Redrawing the Districts, Changing the Rules," *The Washington Post National Weekly Edition*, April 1, 1991, p. 23.

49. Gordon E. Baker, *The Reapportionment Revolution* (Random House, 1966), p. 47.

50. *Baker* v. *Carr*, 369 U.S. 186 (1962).

51. *Wesberry* v. *Sanders*, 376 U.S. 1 (1964).

52. *Reynolds* v. *Sims*, 377 U.S. 533 (1964).

53. *Brown* v. *Thomson*, 103 S.Ct. 2690 (1983).

54. Gary W. Cox and Jonathan N. Katz, *Elbridge Gerry's Salamander: The Electoral Consequences*

of the Reapportionment Revolution (Cambridge University Press, 2002).

55. *Shaw* v. *Reno*, 509 U.S. 630 (1993); *Abrams* v. *Johnson*, 138 L.Ed. 2d 285 (1997). For a summary of state and federal judicial cases on drawing legislative district lines, see *Redistricting Case Summaries from the '90s* (National Conference of State Legislatures, 1998); see also Ronald E. Weber, "Emerging Trends in State Legislative Redistricting," *Spectrum: The Journal of State Government* 75 (Winter 2002), pp. 13–15; and additional updates can be found at the National Conference of State Legislatures Web site, www.ncsl.org.

56. *League of United Latin American Citizens* v. *Perry*, 399 F. Supp. 2d 756 (2006); and *Davis* v. *Bandemer*, 478 U.S. 109 (1986).

57. See Spencer C. Olin, *California's Prodigal Sons: Hiram Johnson and the Progressives, 1911–1917* (University of California Press, 1968).

58. Teri Renner, "Local Initiative and Referendum in the United States," www.iandrinstitute.org/Local%20I&R.htm.

59. A comprehensive list is available in *The Book of the States, 2009*, pp. 343–347.

60. *The Book of the States, 2009*, p. 339.

61. John G. Matsusaka, "2008 Ballot Propositions" in *The Book of the States, 2009*, p. 337.

62. David B. Magleby, "Ballot Initiatives and Intergovernmental Relations," paper presented at the annual meeting of the Western Political Science Association, Los Angeles, March 1998, p. 2.

63. Ibid., p. 13.

64. See, for example, Eugene C. Lee, "The Initiative Boom: An Excess of Democracy," in Gerald C. Lubenow and Bruce E. Cain, eds., *Governing California* (Institute of Governmental Studies, University of California, 1997), pp. 113–136; see also David S. Broder, *Democracy Derailed: Initiative Campaigns and the Power of Money* (Harcourt, 2000). But see Zolton L. Hajnul, Elisabeth R. Gerber, and Hugh Louch, "Minorities and Direct Legislation: Evidence from California Ballot Proposition Elections," paper presented at the annual meeting of the American Political Science Association, Washington, D.C., September 1–3, 2000; see also Elisabeth Gerber, *The Populist Paradox* (Princeton University Press, 1999).

65. See Peter Schrag, *Paradise Lost: California's Experience, America's Future* (New Press, 1998); see also the decidedly negative appraisal offered by Richard Ellis, *Democratic Delusions: The Initiative Process in America* (University Press of Kansas, 2002).

66. David B. Magleby and Kelly D. Paterson, "Consultants and Direct Democracy," *PS: Political Science and Politics* 31 (June 1998), pp. 160–161; see also Broder, *Democracy Derailed*.

67. Daniel A. Smith and Caroline J. Tolbert, *Educated by Initiative: The Effects of Direct Democracy on Citizens and Political Organizations in the American States* (University of Michigan Press, 2004).

68. Thomas E. Cronin, *Direct Democracy: The Politics of the Initiative, Referendum, and Recall* (Harvard University Press, 1989).

69. Michael G. Hagen and Edward L. Lascher, Jr., "Public Opinion About Ballot Initiatives," paper presented at the annual meeting of the American Political Science Association, Boston, September 3–6, 1998.

Chapter 25

1. "Death Row Cases Should Be Reviewed, Justice Says," *Columbus Dispatch*, May 15, 2010.

2. *The Book of the States, 2009* (The Council of State Governments, 2009), p. 187.

3. Ibid., p. 176.

4. The National Governors Association (http://www.nga.org/) publishes a short biography of every current governor, available online at http://www.nga.org/Files/pdf/BIOBOOK.pdf.

5. National Governors Association Current List of Governors' Political Affiliations and Terms of Office, http://www.nga.org/Files/pdf/GOVLIST.PDF.

6. *Book of the States*, p. 176.

7. Ibid, p. 188.

8. *The Book of the States, 2009*, p. 188.

9. This story is adapted from Robert S. McElvaine, *Mario Cuomo: A Biography* (Scribner, 1988), pp. 337–338; see also the assessment of Governor Pete Wilson's turbulent first years as governor of California in Robert Reinhold, "The Curse of the Statehouse," *The New York Times Magazine*, May 3, 1992, pp. 27–28, 54, 58–59.

10. Paul Foy, "Utah Governor Defies No Child Left Behind Act," *Associated Press*, May 2, 2005.

11. Thad L. Beyle, "2004 Gubernatorial Elections," *Spectrum: The Journal of State Government* (Winter 2005), p. 12.

12. Thad L. Beyle, "Race to Spend Money," *State News* (January 2008), p. 14.

13. Thomas M. Carsey, *Campaign Dynamics: The Race for Governor* (University of Michigan Press, 2000), Chapter 8.

14. Beyle, "2004 Gubernatorial Elections," p. 12.

15. Charlie LeDuff, "The California Recall: The Governor-Elect," *New York Times*, October 9, 2003, p. A33.

16. See Thomas M. Carsey, *Campaign Dynamics: The Race for Governor* (University of Michigan Press, 2000), Chapter 6 for a detailed account of this race.

17. Economic conditions may be more important in gubernatorial elections in some states than in others. See Michael Ebeid and Jonathan Rodden "Economic Geography and Economic Voting: Evidence from the U.S. States," *British Journal of Political Science* 36, No. 3 (July 2006), pp. 527–547.

18. Thomas M. Carsey and Gerald C. Wright, "State and National Factors in Gubernatorial and Senate Elections," *American Journal of Political Science* 42(3) (1998): 994–1002.

19. Richard F. Winters, "The Politics of Taxing and Spending," in Virginia Gray, Russell Hanson, and Herbert Jacob, eds., *Politics in the American States: A Comparative Analysis*, p. 329.

20. Kathleen Gallagher, "Doyle Will Give Keynote Speech at Stem Cell Summit," *Milwaukee Journal Sentinel*, June 6, 2006.

21. Thad Beyle and Margaret Ferguson, "Governors and the Executive Branch" in Virginia Gray and Russell L. Hanson, eds., *Politics in the American States: A Comparative Analysis*, 9th ed. (CQ Press, 2008).

22. In some cases, a governor's style and strategy alienate legislators. See, for example, Charles Mahtesian's analysis of Minnesota's Jesse Ventura, "Can He Govern?" *Governing* (May 2000), pp. 36–42. In contrast, Governor Bruce Babbitt worked effectively even with a legislature controlled by the opposition party. See David R. Berman, *Arizona Politics and Government* (University of Nebraska Press, 1998), pp. 116–117.

23. For a lighthearted commentary by a member of Governor Pete Wilson's Electronic Commerce Advisory Council, see Stewart Alsop, "Helping the Governor Figure Out E-Commerce," *Fortune*, June 8, 1998, p. 269.

24. Ronald K. Snell, "Annual and Biennial Budgeting: The Experience of State

Governments" (National Conference of State Legislatures, 2004), www.ncsl.org/programs/fiscal/annlbien.htm.

25. Kathleen Gray, "Granholm Stars in Her Own 'Kill Bill,'" *Detroit Free Press*, April 26, 2004, p. A1.

26. John Kennedy and Jason Garcia, "Governor's Veto Pen Leaves Heavy Mark," *Orlando Sentinel*, May 26, 2006.

27. Daniel C. Vock, "Governors Enjoy Quirky Veto Power," Stateline.org, April 24, 2007, www.stateline.org/live/printable/story?contentId=201710.

28. Cited in a profile of New York in *Governing* (February 1999), p. 66.

29. Thad L. Beyle, "Being Governor," in Carl E. Van Horn, ed., *The State of the States*, 3d ed. (CQ Press, 1996), p. 89.

30. But see Governor Tommy Thompson's defense of using frequent vetoes, *Power to the People: An American State at Work* (HarperCollins, 1996), and the view of one of his main critics in the Wisconsin legislature, Tom Loftus, *The Art of Legislative Politics* (CQ Press, 1994), Chapter 5. On the varied effectiveness of the line item veto as a tool for fiscal responsibility, see Glenn Abney and Thomas P. Lauth, "The Item Veto and Fiscal Responsibility," *Journal of Politics* 59 (August 1997), pp. 882–892. On how a governor's rash use of the line item veto can infuriate legislators, see Mahtesian, "Can He Govern?," p. 40.

31. Katie Zezima, "Obey Same-Sex Marriage Law, Officials Told," *New York Times*, April 25, 2004, p. A15.

32. Martha Derthick, "Where Federalism Didn't Fail," *Public Administration Review* (December 2007), p. 41; see also Kathleen Murphy, "Katrina Sets Record in State-to-State Help," Stateline.org/live/ViewPage.action?siteNodeId=136&languageId=1&contentId=53077 (accessed September 9, 2005).

33. *Perpich et al.* v. *Department of Defense*, 110 L.Ed. 312 (1990).

34. John Gramlich, "Governors May Regain Sole Control Over Guard," Stateline.org, December 17, 2007, www.stateline.org/live/printable/story?contentId=265258 (accessed September 17, 2010); see also Jennifer Nedeau, "National Guard Sacrifices Hit Home," Stateline.org, December 17, 2007, www.stateline.org/live/printable/story?contentId=211236.

35. "Governors Lose in Power Struggle Over National Guard ," Stateline.org, http://www.stateline.org/live/details/story?contentId=170453.

36. Kavan Peterson, "Governors Shy from Clemency Power," Stateline.org, January 30, 2003, www.stateline.org/live/printable/story?contentId=15145.

37. Ryan Alessi and Jack Brammer, "Fletcher Pardons 9," *Lexington (Ky.) Herald-Leader*, August 30, 2005.

38. For background on this controversy, see Jonathan Alter, "The Death Penalty on Trial," *Newsweek*, June 12, 2000, pp. 26–34.

39. Willoughby, *The State of the States*, p. 137.

40. Kunin, *Living a Political Life*, p. 382.

41. Beyle, "The Governors," pp. 224–226.

42. Thomas H. Kean, quoted in Barbara Salmore and Stephen Salmore, *New Jersey Politics and Government* (University of Nebraska Press, 1998), p. 136.

43. Jesse Ventura, *I Ain't Got Time to Bleed* (Signet Press, 2000), pp. 296–297.

44. Beyle, "The Governors," pp. 224–226.

45. http://www.pewcenteronthestates.org/initiatives_detail.aspx?initiativeID=36072.

46. Alan Ehrenhalt, "Reinventing Government in the Unlikeliest Place," *Governing* (August 1993), pp. 7–8.

47. "Two New Agencies Launch Under Reorganization," *Associated Press,* August 31, 2004.

48. Jonathan Walters, "Fad Mad," *Governing* (September 1996), p. 49.

49. Dall Forsythe, ed., *Quicker, Better, Cheaper? Managing Performance in American Government* (Rockefeller Institute Press, 2001), especially Chapters 12–16.

50. Beyle, "Being Governor," p. 106.

51. See the discussion of Governor George W. Bush and his relationship with his lieutenant governor in Jonathan Walters, "The Taming of Texas," *Governing* (July 1998), p. 20; see also "The Future of the Texas Lieutenant Governor," *Comparative State Politics* (October 1995), pp. 21–24.

52. But see Charles N. Wheeler III, "Why Illinois Still Needs Lieutenant Governor's Position," *Illinois Issues* (September 1994), pp. 6–7.

53. Martha Derthick, "Federalism and the Politics of Tobacco," *Publius* (Winter 2001), p. 47.

54. For additional information on the Office of the Attorney General, State of California, visit www.caag.state.ca.us.

55. For Eliot Spitzer's career before he won the governorship, see Brooke A. Masters, *Spoiling for a Fight: The Rise of Eliot Spitzer* (Times Books, 2006).

56. See Thad L. Beyle, "Enhancing Executive Leadership in the States," *State and Local Government Review* (Winter 1995), pp. 18–35; and Thad L. Beyle, "The Governors," in Virginia Gray, Russell Hanson, and Herbert Jacob, eds. *Politics in the American States: A Comparative Analysis,* 7th ed. (CQ Press, 1999), pp. 191–231.

57. Lamar Alexander, *Steps Along the Way: A Governor's Scrapbook* (Nelson, 1986), p. 112. Similar views can be found in former Vermont Governor Madeleine M. Kunin's memoir, *Living a Political Life* (Vintage Books, 1995).

58. See Earl H. Fry, *The Expanding Role of State and Local Governments in U.S. Foreign Policy* (Council on Foreign Relations Press, 1998); see also, for example, Alan Johnson, "Taft Shows He's Up to the Job on Foreign Grounds," *Columbus (Ohio) Dispatch,* February 14, 2000.

59. *The Book of the States, 1998–1999* (The Council of State Governments, 1998), p. xxiii.

60. Professor Thad L. Beyle at the University of North Carolina at Chapel Hill tracks state polls on governors' job performances and finds that Democratic, Republican, and Independent governors alike all averaged approximately 60 percent public approval in the 1990s.

61. Alexander, *Steps Along the Way,* p. 141.

62. Thomas H. Kean, *The Politics of Inclusion* (Free Press, 1988), p. 248.

63. Scott Matheson with James Edwin Kee, *Out of Balance* (Peregrine Smith Books, 1986), p. 186; see also the reflections of another popular western governor in Cecil Andrus and Joel Connelly, *Cecil Andrus: Politics Western Style* (Sasquatch Books, 1998).

Chapter 26

1. National Center for State Courts, *Examining the Work of State Courts, 2006* (National Center for State Courts, 2005), p. 22.

2. The same Massey coal company owned the mine at which a major explosion took place in April of 2010 that killed 29 workers.

3. See Michael Solimine and James Walker, *Respecting State Courts: The Inevitability of Judicial Federalism* (Greenwood Press, 2000); and Matthew Bosworth, *Courts as Catalysts:* *State Supreme Courts and Public School Finance Equity* (State University of New York Press, 2001).

4. Lynn Mather, "Policy Making in State Trial Courts," in John B. Gates and Charles A. Johnson, eds., *The American Courts: A Critical Assessment* (CQ Press, 1991), pp. 119–157.

5. Patrick Schmidt and Paul Martin, "To the Internet and Beyond: State Supreme Courts on the World Wide Web," *Judicature* 84 (May–June 2001), pp. 314–325.

6. Robert F. Williams, "In the Supreme Court's Shadow: Legitimacy of State Rejection of Supreme Court Reasoning and Results," *South Carolina Law Review* 56 (Spring 1984), p. 353.

7. Harry P. Stumpf and John H. Culver, *The Politics of State Courts* (Longman, 1992), pp. 8–11.

8. Hans A. Linde, "Observations of a State Court Judge," in Robert A. Katzmann, ed., *Judges and Legislators: Toward Institutional Comity* (Brookings Institution Press, 1988), p. 118.

9. Philip L. Dubois, "State Trial Court Appointments: Does the Governor Make a Difference?" *Judicature* 69 (June–July 1985), pp. 20–21.

10. Charles H. Sheldon and Nicholas P. Lovrich, Jr., "State Judicial Recruitment," in John B. Gates and Charles A. Johnson, eds., *The American Courts: A Critical Assessment* (CQ Press, 1991), pp. 172–173.

11. See American Judicature Society, www.ajs.org/js/judicialselectioncharts.pdf.

12. Thurgood Marshall, in *Renne* v. *Geary,* 501 U.S. 312 (1991).

13. "Judges Say Political Influence Threatens Independence of Judiciary," *(Yankton, S.D.) Press and Dakotan,* www.pressandakotan.com/stories/101797/judges.html. [AU: Please check this link as it didn't open for me; also, is "*(Yankton, S.D.)*" correct as set?]

14. Adam Skaggs, "Buying Justice: The Impact of Citizens United on Judicial Elections," report for the Brennan Center for Justice, 2010, http://www.brennancenter.org/page/-/publications/BCReportBuyingJustice.pdf?nocdn=1.

15. Michael Scherer, "The Making of the Corporate Judiciary," *Mother Jones* (November 2003), p. 72.

16. *Republican Party of Minnesota* v. *White,* 536 U.S. 765 (2002).

17. William Glaberson, "Court Rulings Curb Efforts to Rein in Judicial Races," *New York Times,* October 7, 2000, p. A8.

18. See Justice at Stake Campaign, Brennan Center for Justice at New York University Law School, and National Institute on Money in State Politics, *The New Politics of Judicial Elections* (Justice at Stake Campaign, 2001); and American Bar Association, Standing Committee on Judicial Independence, *Public Financing of Judicial Campaigns: Report of the Commission on Public Financing of Judicial Campaigns* (American Bar Association, 2002).

19. *Wells* v. *Edwards,* 409 U.S. 1095 (1973).

20. *Chisom* v. *Roemer,* 501 U.S. 400 (1991); and *Houston Lawyers' Association* v. *Texas Attorney General,* 501 U.S. 419 (1991); see also Tracy Thompson, "The New Front in the Battle for Civil Rights: Judgeships," *The Washington Post National Weekly Edition,* December 18, 1989, p. 34.

21. J. W. Peltason, *The Missouri Plan for the Selection of Judges* (University of Missouri Studies, 1945). The plan was previously known as the Nonpartisan Plan for the Selection of Judges or the Kales Plan until it was called the Missouri Plan by this monograph.

22. Beth M. Henschen, Robert Moog, and Steven Davis, "Judicial Nominating Commissioners: A National Profile," *Judicature* 73 (April–May 1990), pp. 328–334.

23. Philip L. Dubois, "The Politics of Innovation in State Courts: The Merit Plan of Judicial Selection," *Publius* 20 (Winter 1990), p. 40.

24. Warren K. Hall and Larry T. Aspin, "What Twenty Years of Judicial Retention Elections Have Told Us," *Judicature* 70 (April–May 1987), pp. 340–347; and Susan B. Caron and Larry C. Berkson, *Judicial Retention Elections in the United States* (American Judicature Society, 1980).

25. Larry T. Aspin, "Trends in Judicial Retention Elections, 1964–2006," *Judicature* 90 (March–April 2007), p. 210; and "Evaluating the Performance of Judges Standing for Retention," *Judicature* 79 (January–February 1996), pp. 190–195.

26. Traciel Reid, "The Politicization of Retention Elections," *Judicature* 83 (September–October 1999), p. 68.

27. Thomas E. Cronin and Robert D. Loevy, *Colorado Politics and Government* (University of Nebraska Press, 1993), pp. 251–253.

28. "The Need for Judicial Performance Evaluations for Retention Elections," *Judicature* 75 (October–November 1991), p. 124.

29. Henry Weinstein, "Forum Airs Questions of Jurist Independence," *Los Angeles Times,* November 22, 1998, p. A18.

30. *The Book of the States, 2007* (The Council of State Governments, 2005), p. 256.

31. Jeffrey Shaman, Steven Lubet, and James Alfini, *Judicial Conduct and Ethics,* 3d ed. (Lexis, 2000), Sec. 15.07.

32. Jolanta Juskiewicz Perlstein and Nathan Goldman, "Judicial Disciplinary Commissions: A New Approach to the Discipline and Removal of State Judges," in Phil Dubois, ed., *The Analysis of Judicial Reform* (Lexington Books, 1982), pp. 93–106.

33. *Burch* v. *Louisiana,* 441 U.S. 130 (1979); and *Ballew* v. *Georgia,* 435 U.S. 223 (1978). See Reid Hastie, Steven D. Penrod, and Nancy Pennington, *Inside the Jury* (Harvard University Press, 1983), for a study showing that nonunanimous verdicts are more likely to bring convictions than those requiring unanimity. Federal courts often use juries of fewer than 12 for civil cases. For federal criminal trials, the Supreme Court still requires both the common-law jury of 12 and unanimous verdicts.

34. *Prosecutors in State Courts, 2005* (U.S. Department of Justice, Bureau of Justice Statistics, 2002), www.ojp.usdoj.gov/bjs/pub/pdf/psc05.pdf.

35. Robert H. Jackson, quoted in Jack M. Kress, "Progress and Prosecution," *Annals of the American Academy of Political and Social Science* (January 1976), p. 100.

36. William K. Muir, *Police: Streetcorner Politicians* (University of Chicago Press, 1977).

37. Charles E. Silberman, *Criminal Violence, Criminal Justice* (Random House, 1978), p. 303.

38. Jay Livingston, *Crime and Criminology* (Prentice Hall, 1992), p. 474.

39. Silberman, *Criminal Violence,* p. 218; see also David Cole, *No Equal Justice: Race and Class in the American Criminal Justice System* (New Press, 1999).

40. National Victims Constitutional Amendment Passage, www.nvcap.org/stvras.htm.

41. *South Carolina* v. *Gathers,* 490 U.S. 805 (1989); and *Payne* v. *Tennessee,* 501 U.S. 808 (1991).

42. *Felony Sentences in State Courts, 2002* (U.S. Department of Justice, Bureau of Justice Statistics, 2004).

43. Thomas M. Uhlman and N. Darlene Walker, "A Plea Is No Bargain: The Impact of Case Disposition on Sentencing," *Social Science Quarterly* 60 (September 1979), pp. 218–234; see also Malcolm M. Feeley, *The Process Is the Punishment* (Russell Sage, 1979).

44. Thomas Church, Jr., "Plea Bargains, Concessions and the Courts: Analysis of a Quasi-Experiment," *Law and Society Review* 14 (Spring 1976), p. 400. For a contrary view, see National Advisory Commission on Criminal Justice Standards and Goals, *Report of the Task Force* (U.S. Government Printing Office, 1979).

45. Church, "Plea Bargains," p. 400.

46. Jonathan D. Casper, *American Criminal Justice: The Defendant's Perspective* (Prentice Hall, 1972), pp. 52–53. Abraham S. Goldstein, *The Passive Judiciary: Prosecutorial Discretion and the Guilty Plea* (Louisiana State University Press, 1981), is critical of judges for not supervising plea bargains more actively.

47. *Santobello* v. *New York,* 404 U.S. 257 (1971).

48. Henry N. Pontell, *A Capacity to Punish* (Indiana University Press, 1985).

49. Lee Sechrest, Susan O. White, and Elizabeth D. Brown, eds., *The Rehabilitation of Criminal Offenders: Problems and Prospects* (National Academy of Sciences, 1979), pp. 3–6.

50. John Hagan and Kristin Bumiler, "Making Sense of Sentencing: A Review and Critique of Sentencing Research," in Alfred Blumstein et al., eds., *Research on Sentencing* (National Academy Press, 1983), Vol. 2; and Susan Welch, Michael Combs, and John Gruhl, "Do Black Judges Make a Difference?" *American Journal of Political Science* 32 (February 1988), pp. 126–135.

51. William B. Eldridge, "Shifting Views of the Sentencing Functions," *Annals of the American Academy of Political and Social Science* (July 1982), pp. 104–111.

52. The Supreme Court upheld these laws in *Ewing* v. *California,* 538 U.S. 11 (2003).

53. Data for this section comes from the Death Penalty Information Center, www.deathpenaltyinfo.org.

54. Bureau of Justice Statistics, "Prisoners in 2008," December 2010, Table 9, http://bjs.ojp.usdoj .gov/index.cfm?ty=pbdetail&iid=1763.

55. Eric Schlosser, "The Prison-Industrial Complex," *Atlantic,* December 1998, p. 52.

56. Bureau of Justice Statistics, "Probation and Parole in the United States, 2006," December 2007.

57. "One in 100: Behind Bars in America 2008," Pew Center on the States, February 2008, www.pewcenteronthestates.org/ uploadedFiles/One%20in%20100.pdf.

58. William J. Sabol, Heather Couture, and Paige M. Harrison, *Prisoners in 2006* (Bureau of Justice Statistics, 2007).

59. Alison Lawrence, "State Sentencing and Corrections Legislation, 2007 Action, 2008 Outlook," National Conference of State Legislatures, January 2008, p. 4, www.ncsl.org/ print/cj/07sentencingreport.pdf.

60. Barbara Fink, "Opening the Door on Community Corrections," *State Legislatures* (September 1984), pp. 24–31.

61. Lawrence, "State Sentencing and Corrections Legislation," p. 7.

62. Quoted in Associated Press, "ABA 'Public Jurist' Considers Reforms in Legal System," December 1993.

63. Franklin M. Zweig et al., "Securing the Future for America's State Courts," *Judicature* 73 (April–May 1990), pp. 297–298.

64. *The Book of the States, 2007,* p. 251.

Chapter 27

1. The story is available online at http://www .npr.org/templates/story/story.php?storyId=12 2954677.

2. Employment data available at U.S. Census Bureau, "2006 Public Employment Data: Local Governments," ftp2.census.gov/govs/apes/ 06locus.txt.

3. *Hunter* v. *City of Pittsburgh,* 208 U.S. 161 (1907).

4. Brian Gill, Ron Zimmer, Jolley Christman, and Suzanne Blanc, *State Takeover, School Restructuring, Private Management, and Student Achievement in Philadelphia* (RAND Corporation, 2007), p. xi.

5. On the living wage, see Oren M. Levin-Waldman, *The Political Economy of the Living Wage: A Study of Four Cities* (Sharpe, 2004). One successful city campaign reform is found in New York City; for information on the New York City Campaign Finance Board and its pro-grams, see www.nyccfb.info. Also see Rockefeller Institute, "Can and Should NYC's Campaign Finance Reforms Be Extended to State Offices," www.rockinst.org/search/ SearchResults.aspx?bodytext=campaign% 20finance&title=campaign%20finance. On charter schools and cities, see Paul S. Grogan and Tony Proscio, *Comeback Cities: A Blueprint for Urban Neighborhood Revival* (Westview Press, 2000), Chapter 9.

6. Richard L. Cole, John Kincaid, and Andrew Parkin, "Public Opinion on Federalism in the United States and Canada," *Publius* 32 (Fall 2002), Tables 1 and 7.

7. Data obtained from U.S. Census Bureau, "State and County Quickfacts," quickfacts.census .gov/qfd/.

8. An excellent overview of counties is Donald C. Menzel, ed., *The American County: Frontiers of Knowledge* (University of Alabama Press, 1996).

9. National Association of Counties, "An Overview of County Government," www.naco.org/ Content/NavigationMenu/About_Counties/ County_Government/A_Brief_Overview_of_ County_Government.htm.

10. See County Executives of America, "Access Government: County Executives Map," www.countyexecutives.org/accessgov/ countymap.htm.

11. For an assessment of the county performance in certain administrative and fiscal functions, see Katherine Barrett and Richard Greene, with Michele Mariani, "Grading the Counties 2002: A Management Report Card," *Governing* (February 2002), www.governing.com/gpp/ 2002/gp2intro.htm.

12. National Association of Counties, "An Overview."

13. Maine Municipal Association, http://www .memun.org/public/local_govt/government .htm.

14. See Amendment LXXXIX of the Massachusetts Constitution.

15. See this 1978 article in Time Magazine (http://www.time.com/time/magazine/ article/0,9171,912178,00.html) and this 2004 article in U.S. News (http://www.usnews .com/usnews/news/articles/040322/ 22after.htm).

16. For a history of suburban development, see Rosalyn Baxandall and Elizabeth Ewen, *Picture Windows: How the Suburbs Happened* (Basic Books, 2000).

17. See Paul G. Lewis, *Shaping Suburbia: How Political Institutions Organize Urban Development* (University of Pittsburgh Press, 1996).

18. *Kelo* v. *City of New London,* 125 S. Ct. 2655 (2005).

19. National Conference of State Legislatures, "Eminent Domain," www.ncsl.org/programs/ natres/EMINDOMAIN.htm.

20. National League of Cities "Cities 101," http://www.nlc.org/about_cities/cities_101/ 138.aspx.

21. Susan Welch, "The Impact of At-Large Elections on the Representation of Blacks and Hispanics," *The Journal of Politics* 52(4) (1990): 1050–76.

22. *Mobile* v. *Bolden,* 446 U.S. 55 (1980).

23. *Rogers* v. *Lodge,* 458 U.S. 613 (1982); and *Thornburg* v. *Gingles,* 478 U.S. 30 (1986).

24. For the experience of one mayor in a council–manager city, see the memoir by Cambridge, Massachusetts, Mayor Barbara Ackermann, *"You the Mayor?" The Education of a City Politician* (Auburn, 1989).

25. Kathy Hayes and Semoon Chang, "The Relative Efficiency of City-Manager and Mayor–Council Forms of Government," *Southern Economic Journal* 57(1) (1990): 167–177.

26. Richard C. Feiock, Moon-Gi Jeong, and Jaehoon Kim, "Credible Commitment and Council–Manager Government: Implications for Policy Instrument Choices," *Public Administration Review* 63(5) (2003): 616–625.

27. See James H. Svara and Associates, *Facilitative Leadership in Local Government: Lessons from Successful Mayors and Chairpersons in the Council–Manager Form* (Jossey-Bass, 1994).

28. See San Diego's official Web site, http:// www.sandiego.gov/mayortransition/.

29. Center for American Women and Politics, Eagleton Institute of Politics, Rutgers, The State University of New Jersey, "Women Mayors in U.S. Cities 2009," http://www.cawp .rutgers.edu/fast_facts/levels_of_office/ Local-WomenMayors .php.

30. Joint Center for Political and Economic Studies, "Black Big-City Mayors, 2002–2007," www .jointcenter.org/current_research_and_policy_ activities/political_participation.

31. http://ncbm.org/2009/04/our-mission/.

32. See Earl H. Fry, *The Expanding Role of State and Local Governments in U.S. Foreign Affairs* (Council on Foreign Relations, 1998), especially Chapter 4.

33. U.S. Census Bureau, "Metropolitan and Micropolitan Statistical Areas," www.census .gov/population/www/estimates/metroarea .html.

34. U.S. Census Bureau, "Population and Percent Distribution by Core Based Statistical Area (CBSA) Status for the United States, Regions, and Divisions: 2000 and 2007," Population Division, Table 11, www.census.gov/ population/www/estimates/metro_ general/2007/CBSA-EST2007–11.xls.

35. U.S. Census Bureau, "Annual Estimates of the Population of Metropolitan and Micropolitan Statistical Areas: April 1, 2000 to July 1, 2007," Table 1.

36. The legal constraints on Baltimore, for exam-ple, are outlined in David Rusk, *Baltimore Unbound: A Strategy for Regional Renewal* (Abell Foundation/Johns Hopkins University Press, 1996).

37. These associations are particularly strong for children who live in very poor households during several years and when they are very young. See Jeanne Brooks-Gunn and Greg

J. Duncan, "The Effects of Poverty on Children," *Future of Children* 7 (Summer/Fall 1997), pp. 55–71.

38. National Center for Children in Poverty, "Basic Facts About Low-Income Children," http://www.nccp.org/publications/pub_892.html.

39. U.S. Census Bureau, *Income, Poverty, and Health Insurance Coverage in the United States: 2005* (U.S. Government Printing Office, 2006), pp. 15–16.

40. D'Vera Cohn, "A New Millennium for America's Cities," *The Washington Post National Weekly Edition*, October 30, 2000, p. 34.

41. Joel Garreau, *Edge City* (Doubleday, 1991).

42. *Arlington Heights* v. *Metropolitan Housing Development Corp.*, 429 U.S. 252, 97 S.Ct. 555, 50 L.Ed.2d 450 (1977).

43. Updated information on which counties are included in Metropolitan Statistical Areas is published by the U.S. Office of Management and Budget and is available through the U.S. Census Bureau Web site at www.whitehouse.gov/omb/bulletins/fy2007/b07-01.pdf. Once the counties in an MSA are identified, the Census Bureau's "Governments Integrated Directory (GID)" Web site can produce a list of all governments within those counties, see harvester.census.gov/gid/gid_02/options.html. The latest data available, as of April 2008, are from the 2002 survey of governments. A complete survey of local governments is conducted every five years, so the next available survey will be for 2007.

44. David Rusk, former mayor of Albuquerque, makes this case well in *Baltimore Unbound* and in *Cities Without Suburbs*, 2d ed. (Woodrow Wilson Center Press/Johns Hopkins University Press, 1995).

45. See Suzanne M. Leland and Kurt Thurmaier, eds., *Case Studies of City–County Consolidation* (Sharpe, 2004); and Jered B. Carr and Richard C. Feiock, eds., *City–County Consolidation and Its Alternatives* (Sharpe, 2004).

46. Ellen Perlman, "Polite Tenacity," *Governing* (November 2000), pp. 34, 214.

47. See Myron Orfield, *Metropolitics: A Regional Agenda for Community and Stability* (Brookings Institution Press, 1997); and Manuel Pastor, ed., *Regions That Work: How Cities and Suburbs Can Grow Together* (University of Minnesota Press, 2000).

48. The metro government Web site is located at http://www.oregonmetro.gov/ and a link to the charter itself is located at http://www.oregonmetro.gov/index.cfm/go/by.web/id=629.

49. See E. J. Dionne, Jr., ed., *Community Works: The Revival of Civil Society in America* (Brookings Institution Press, 1998).

50. See David L. Kirp et al., *Our Town: Race, Housing, and the Soul of Suburbia* (Rutgers University Press, 1997); and Jonathan Harr, *A Civil Action* (Vintage Books, 1996).

51. See the recommendation often prescribed by a major proponent of regionalism, Neal R. Peirce, in Charles Mahtesian, ed., "The Civic Therapist," *Governing* (September 1995), pp. 24–27; see also Dreier, Mollenkopf, and Swanstrom, *Place Matters*, Chapter 7.

52. "The End of Urban Man? Care to Bet?" *The Economist*, December 31, 1999, pp. 25–26.

53. See the thoughtful recommendations in Robert J. Waste, *Independent Cities: Rethinking U.S. Urban Policy* (Oxford University Press, 1998); but also see Clarissa Rile Hayward, "The Difference States Make: Democracy, Identity, and the American City," *American Political Science Review* 97 (November 2003), p. 501.

Chapter **28**

1. The report is archived by the National Commission on Excellence in Education at http://www2.ed.gov/pubs/NatAtRisk/index.html.

2. For more information on the study, see Amanda Ripley (2010), "Should Kids Be Bribed to Do Well in School?," *Time Magazine*, April 8, 2010, http://www.time.com/time/nation/article/0,8599,1978589-1,00.html.

3. U.S. Census Bureau, *Statistical Abstract of the United States: 2008* (U.S. Government Printing Office, 2008), Table 422, "State and Local Governments—Revenue and Expenditures by Function: 2004."

4. *Digest of Education Statistics, 2009*, "Total and Current Expenditures per Pupil in Fall Enrollment in Public Elementary and Secondary Education, by Function and State or Jurisdiction: 2006–2007," Table 183, http://nces.ed.gov/programs/digest/d09/tables/dt09_183.asp.

5. *Digest of Education Statistics, 2009*, "Number of Public School Districts and Public and Private Elementary and Secondary Schools: Selected Years, 1869–70 Through 2007–08," Table 86, http://nces.ed.gov/programs/digest/d09/tables/dt09_086.asp.

6. "Governors, State School Superintendents Propose Common Academic Standards" *The Washington Post*, March 11, 2010, http://www.washingtonpost.com/wp-dyn/content/article/2010/03/10/AR2010031000024.html?referrer=emailarticle.

7. See Gary Orfield and Chungmei Lee, *Brown at 50: King's Dream or Plessy's Nightmare* (Harvard Civil Rights Project, 2004); see also Gary Orfield, Susan E. Eaton, and the Harvard Project on School Desegregation, *Dismantling Desegregation: The Quiet Reversal of Brown v. Board of Education* (New Press, 1996).

8. "A New Diverse Majority: Students of Color in the South's Public Schools" Southern Education Foundation report, http://www.sefatl.org/pdf/New Diverse Majority.pdf.

9. "The Next Fight: Resegregation" *USA Today*, May 18, 2010, http://www.usatoday.com/news/opinion/forum/2010-05-19-column19_ST_N.htm.

10. Peter Harkness, "State and Localities: Test, but Verify," *CQ Weekly*, March 26, 2007, p. 882.

11. Quoted in "Statewide Student Tests," *State Legislatures*, February 2004, p. 33; see also Dewayne Matthews, "No Child Left Behind: The Challenge of Implementation," *The Book of the States, 2004* (The Council of State Governments, 2004), pp. 493–496; and June Kronholz, "Bush's Education Law Gets an Incomplete," *The Wall Street Journal*, September 1, 2004, p. A6.

12. William J. Mathis, "The Cost of Implementing the Federal No Child Left Behind Act: Different Assumptions, Different Answers," *Peabody Journal of Education* 80, No. 2 (2005), pp. 90–119.

13. Michael Sandler, "Commission Recommends Broad Changes to 2002 Education Law," *CQ Weekly*, February 19, 2007, p. 552. For a discussion of recommendations by state legislatures, see "Joint Statement of the National Conference of State Legislatures and the American Association of School Administrators on ESEA Reauthorization," National Conference of State Legislatures, www.ncsl.org/statefed/NCSLAASAJoint Statement.htm.

14. C. Eugene Steuerle, Van Doorn Ooms, George Peterson, and Robert D. Reischauer, eds., *Vouchers and the Provision of Public Services*

(Brookings Institution Press, 2000); see also "Colorado Adopts Statewide School Vouchers," *State Legislatures*, July–August 2003, p. 7.

15. William H. Rehnquist, quoted in Richard Rothstein, "Failed Schools? The Meaning Is Unclear," *New York Times*, July 3, 2002, p. A14.

16. Jon Sarche, "Public School Vouchers Unconstitutional, Colorado Supreme Court Says," *Associated Press*, June 28, 2004.

17. See, for example, "Report Cards for the Knowledge Is Power Program," *U.S. News & World Report Online*, April 29, 2008, www.usnews.com/blogs/on-education/2008/4/29/report-cards-for-the-knowledge-is-power-program.html.

18. www.irvine.org/leadershipAwards/recipients/yvonneChan.shtml.

19. Diana Jean Schemo, "Study of Test Scores Finds Charter Schools Lagging," *New York Times*, August 23, 2006; see also the National Center for Education Statistics, U.S. Department of Education, *The Nation's Report Card: America's Charter Schools*, nces.ed.gov/nationsreportcard/pdf/studies/2005456.pdf.

20. Michael S. McPherson and Morton Owen Schapiro, "Funding Roller Coaster for Public Higher Education," *Science*, November 14, 2003, p. 1157.

21. "An Update on State Budget Cuts," Center on Budget and Policy Priorities, May 25, 2010, http://www.cbpp.org/cms/index.cfm?fa=view&id=1214.

22. Paula Pant, "U. Colorado Explores Options in Funding," *University Wire*, January 18, 2007.

23. Karin Fischer, "Colorado's 'Noble Experiment,'" *Chronicle of Higher Education*, July 15, 2005, p. 29.

24. See Christine Walton and Julie Davis Bell, "New Ways to Fund Higher Ed," *State Legislatures*, December 2003, pp. 28–31; see also John Buntin, "Setting Colleges Free," *Governing* (September 2003), pp. 18–22.

25. "Recipients and Families 1936–2001," Administration for Children and Families, www.acf.hhs.gov/news/stats/3697.htm.

26. R. Kent Weaver, *Ending Welfare as We Know It* (Brookings Institution Press, 2000).

27. On state policies, see Office of Family Assistance, Administration for Children and Families, U.S. Department of Health and Human Services, *Temporary Assistance to Needy Families: Sixth Annual Report to Congress* (Office of Family Assistance, 2004), Chapter 12.

28. See Rebecca Blank and Ron Haskins, eds., *The New World of Welfare* (Brookings Institution Press, 2001); Isabel V. Sawhill et al., *Welfare Reform and Beyond: The Future of the Safety Net* (Brookings Institution Press, 2002); and Carol W. Weissert, ed., *Learning from Leaders: Welfare Reform Politics and Policy in Five Midwestern States* (Rockefeller Institute Press, 2000).

29. Data on number of families on Temporary Assistance for Needy Families from the U.S. Administration for Children and Families, "TANF Families," Excel spreadsheet, April 8, 2008, available at www.acf.hhs.gov/programs/ofa/data-reports/caseload/2007/20074_caseloadreport.xls.

30. For an extensive review of studies on the effects of welfare reform, see Rebecca Blank, "Evaluating Welfare Reform in the U.S.," *Journal of Economic Literature*, December 2002, pp. 1105–1166.

31. Sharon Parrott and Arloc Sherman, "TANF at 10: Program Results Are More Mixed Than Often Understood," Center on Budget and Policy Priorities, August 17, 2006.

32. Peter Edelman, "The True Purpose of Welfare Reform," *New York Times*, May 29, 2002, p. A21.

33. See, for example, David Hage, *Reforming Welfare by Rewarding Work: One State's Successful Experiment* (University of Minnesota Press, 2004); and Courtney Jarchow and Jack Tweedie, "Welfare and Wedding Vows," *State Legislatures*, April 2003, pp. 24–28.

34. "Are unemployment benefits no longer temporary?". The Washington Post. March 9, 2010. http://www.washingtonpost.com/wp-dyn/content/article/2010/03/08/AR2010030804927.html.

35. Center on Budget and Policy Priorities, "Introduction to Unemployment Insurance" (updated April 16, 2010) http://www.cbpp.org/cms/index.cfm?fa=view&id=1466

36. "Issue Brief: Medicaid Redesigned: State Innovations in Health Coverage and Delivery," National Governors Association Center for Best Practices, March 27, 2008.

37. Dennis G. Smith, Janet G. Freeze, Susan N. Hill, and Lyn R. Killman, "The Future of Medicaid," in *The Book of the States, 2006* (The Council of State Governments, 2006), p. 491.

38. "Issue Brief: Leading the Way: State Health Reform Initiatives," National Governors Association Center for Best Practices, July 11, 2007; see also "Issue Brief: Medicaid Redesigned: State Innovations in Health Coverage and Delivery," National Governors Association Center for Best Practices, March 27, 2008.

39. David S. Broder, "States in Fiscal Crises," *The Washington Post National Weekly Edition*, May 27, 2002, p. 4

40. "Issue Brief: Medicaid Redesigned."

41. "Issue Brief: Leading the Way."

42. The program is detailed on the state's Web site at: http://www.mass.gov/?pageID=mg2subtopic&L=4&L0=Home&L1=Resident&L2=Health&L3=Health+Care+Reform&sid=massgov2.

43. "In Hawaii's Health System, Lessons for Lawmakers," *New York Times*, October 16, 2009, http://www.nytimes.com/2009/10/17/health/policy/17hawaii.html.

44. Law Enforcement Statistics, Bureau of Justice Statistics, www.ojp.usdoj.gov/bjs/lawenf.htm.

45. *Statistical Abstract of the United States: 2008* (U.S. Government Printing Office, 2008), Table 429, "State and Local Governments—Expenditures and Debt by State: 2004."

46. Data from the Bureau of Justice Statistics, "Local Police" link at http://bjs.ojp.usdoj.gov/index.cfm?ty=tp&tid=71.

47. Bureau of Justice Statistics, State-Level Crime Trends Database, http://bjsdata.ojp.usdoj.gov/dataonline/Search/Crime/State/RunCrimeStatebyState.cfm.

48. Jodi Wilgoren, "New Terror Alert Brings No Change in States' Security," *New York Times*, May 25, 2002, p. A11.

49. *Statistical Abstract of the United States: 2009* (U.S. Government Printing Office, 2008), Table 516, "Homeland Security Grants by States/Territories, 2007 and 2008," https://www.census.gov/compendia/statab/2010/tables/10s0516.pdf.

50. See Amy C. Hughes, "State Emergency Management: New Realities in a Homeland Security World," *The Book of the States, 2004* (The Council of State Governments, 2004), pp. 485–488.

51. Larry Morandi, "Growing Pains," *State Legislatures*, October–November 1998, pp. 24–28.

52. www.communitygreens.org/ExistingGreens/existinggreens.htm.

53. Neal Peirce, "Walkability = Livability = Billions," *The Washington Post Writers Group*, December 16, 2007, www.citistates.com/peirce.

54. See Robert B. Albritton, "Subsidies: Welfare and Transportation," in Virginia Gray, Herbert Jacob, and Kenneth Vines, eds., *Politics in the American States: A Comparative Analysis*, 7th ed. (CQ Press, 1999); and E. J. Dionne, Jr., ed., *Community Works: The Revival of Civil Society in America* (Brookings Institution Press, 2000).

55. Colby Itkowitz, "Panel's Proposal to Raise Gas Taxes Finds Little Support on Capitol Hill," *CQ Weekly*, January 21, 2008, p. 209.

56. But see Michele Mariani, "Transit's High-Tech Route," *Governing* (May 2004), pp. 60–67; and Rob Gurwitt, "Connecting the Suburban Dots," *Governing* (October 2003), pp. 36–40.

57. Colby Itkowitz, "Mass Transit, Road Repair Vie for Federal Dollars," *CQ Weekly*, March 24, 2008, p. 772.

58. Darel Paul, *Rescaling International Political Economy: Subnational States and the Regulation of the Global Political Economy* (Routledge, 2005).

59. James C. McKinley, Jr., "For U.S. Exporters in Cuba, Business Trumps Politics," *New York Times*, November 12, 2007, p. A3.

60. For a discussion of the evolution of environmental policy in a particularly interesting place, see Charles O. Jones, *Clean Air: The Policies and Politics of Pollution Control* (University of Pittsburgh Press, 1973).

61. R. Steven Brown, "State Environmental Expenditures, 2005–2008," The Environmental Council of the States, March 2008.

62. Jeff Dale, "Realistic Redevelopment," *State Legislatures*, February 1999, pp. 28–31.

63. "States Leading the Way in Advancing Clean Energy," National Governors Association, May 6, 2010, http://www.nga.org/portal/site/nga/menuitem.6c9a8a9ebc6ae07eee28aca9501010a0/?vgnextoid=6611dfdd9b868210VgnVCM1000005e00100aRCRD&vgnextchannel=759b8f2005361010VgnVCM1000001a01010aRCRD.

64. Felicity Barringer and William Yardley, "Bush Splits on Greenhouse Gases with Congress and State Officials," *New York Times*, April 4, 2007, p. A1.

65. http://gov.ca.gov/press-release/8400/.

66. http://gov.ca.gov/press-release/12608/.

67. See Donald F. Kettl, "Federalism, Anyone?" *Governing* (February 2004), p. 14.

Chapter 29

1. "State Debt Woes Grow Too Big to Camouflage," *New York Times*, March 29, 2010.

2. Figures include full-time employees. Calculated from U.S. Census Bureau, "State and Local Government Employment and Payroll Data, 2008," http://www.census.gov/govs/apes/.

3. U.S. Census Bureau, "State and Local Government Employment and Payroll Data, 2008," http://www.census.gov/govs/apes/.

4. U.S. Bureau of Labor Statistics, "Employment Outlook: 2006–2016," *Monthly Labor Review* (November 2007), p. 7, www.bls.gov/opub/mlr/2007/11/art1full.pdf.

5. *Elrod* v. *Burns*, 427 U.S. 347 (1976).

6. "David Osborne and Ted Gaebler," *Reinventing Government: How the Entrepreneurial Spirit Is Transforming the Public Sector* (Addison-Wesley, 1992); see also "National Commission on the State and Local Public Service" ["Winter Commission"], *Hard Truths/Tough Choices: An Agenda for State and Local Reform* (Rockefeller Institute of Government, 1993).

7. Steven W. Hays and Jessica E. Sowa, "A Broader Look at the 'Accountability' Movement: Some Grim Realities in State Civil Service Systems," *Review of Public Personnel Administration* 26 (June 2006), pp. 107–108.

8. Jerrell Coggburn, "Personnel Deregulation: Exploring Differences in the American States," *Journal of Public Administration Research and Theory* 11, No. 2 (2001): 223–244.

9. J. Edward Kellough and Lloyd G. Nigro, "Pay for Performance in Georgia State Government: Employee Perspectives in Georgia Gain After 5 Years," *Review of Public Personnel Administration* 22 (Summer 2002), pp. 146–166; and Stephen E. Condrey, "Reinventing State Civil Service Systems," *Review of Public Personnel Administration* 22 (Summer 2002), pp. 114–124.

10. James S. Bowman, Marc G. Gertz, Sally C. Gertz, and Russell L. Williams, "Civil Service Reform in Florida State Government: Employee Attitudes 1 Year Later," *Review of Public Personnel Administration* 23 (December 2003), pp. 286–304.

11. Hays and Sowa, "A Broader Look," pp. 107–108.

12. Bowman et al., "Civil Service Reform," pp. 291, 294.

13. Kellough and Nigro, "Pay for Performance," pp. 151, 154–155.

14. Hays and Sowa, "A Broader Look," pp. 115–116; see also Condrey, "Reinventing State Civil Service Systems," pp. 119–121.

15. Coggburn, "Personnel Deregulation"; and Hays and Sowa, "A Broader Look," pp. 113–114.

16. Pamela Winston et al., "Privatization of Welfare Services: A Review of the Literature," report submitted to the Department of Health and Human Services, Assistant Secretary for Planning and Evaluation (Mathematica Policy Research, Inc., May 2002), pp. 3–6, www.mathematica-mpr.com/PDFs/privatization.pdf.

17. For a description of the enactment and early years of W-2, see Thomas Kaplan, "Wisconsin's W-2 Program: Welfare as We Might Come to Know It?," in Carol S. Weissert, ed., *Learning from Leaders: Welfare Reform Politics and Policy in Five Midwestern States* (Rockefeller Institute Press, 2000), pp. 77–113.

18. See http://www.dwd.state.wi.us/dwd/employers.htm.

19. See Wisconsin Department of Workforce Development, "Performance Standards for the 2006–2009 W-2 and Related Programs Contract," dwd.wisconsin.gov/w2/contracts/20062009/pdf/appendix_b1.pdf. For an update on Wisconsin's W-2 program in Milwaukee, see Karen Gardiner, Mike Fishman, Mark Ragan, and Tom Gais, "Local Implementation of TANF in Five Sites: Changes Related to the Deficit Reduction Act," final report prepared for the U.S. Administration for Children and Families, Office of Planning, Research, and Evaluation, March 31, 2008.

20. Winston et al., "Privatization," p. 11.

21. Robert T. Garrett, "Texas' Welfare Privatization Efforts Snagged," *The Dallas Morning News*, April 6, 2008, www.dallasnews.com/sharedcontent/dws/dn/latestnews/stories/040708dntexcallcenters.3b22a5b.html.

22. See Reason Public Policy Institute, a pro-privatization think tank, at www.privatization.org.

23. John Shannon, "The Deregulation of Fiscal Federalism," in Thomas R. Swartz and John E.

Peck, eds., *The Changing Face of Fiscal Federalism* (Sharpe, 1990), p. 31.

24. U.S. Census Bureau, *Statistical Abstract of the United States: 2008* (U.S. Government Printing Office, 2000), Table 419.

25. Lucy Dadayan and Robert B. Ward, "State Tax Revenue Weakens Still Further, While Costs Rise Sharply," *State Revenue Report*, No. 71 (Rockefeller Institute Press, March 2008); and Donald J. Boyd and Lucy Dadayan, "State Revenue Flash Report: Sales Tax Declines in Most States," *Rockefeller Institute Fiscal Features* (Rockefeller Institute Press, May 1, 2008).

26. "State of the States 2010," Pew Center for the States, http://www.pewcenteronthestates.org/uploadedFiles/State_of_the_States_2010.pdf.

27. Don Boyd, "State Finances: Solid Recovery but Challenges Ahead," *The Book of the States, 2006* (The Council of State Governments, 2006), pp. 340–342.

28. U.S. Census Bureau, *State and Local Government Finances: 2006–2007*, Table 1, http://www2.census.gov/govs/estimate/07slsstab1a.xls.

29. For a recent discussion of state and local tax issues, see Katherine Barrett, Richard Greene, Michele Mariani, and Anya Sostek, "The Way We Tax: A 50-State Report," *Governing* (February 2003), pp. 11–40.

30. For a brief history of the property tax, see Dennis Hale, "The Evaluation of the Property Tax: A Study of the Relation Between Public Finance and Political Theory," *Journal of Politics* 47 (May 1985), pp. 382–404; see also C. Lowell Harris, ed., *The Property Tax and Local Finance* (Academy of Political Science, 1983).

31. Richard L. Cole, John Kincaid, and Andrew Parkin, "Public Opinion on Federalism in the United States and Canada in 2002," *Publius* 42 (Fall 2002), Table 4.

32. U.S. Census Bureau, *State and Local Government Finances: 2007*, http://www2.census.gov/govs/estimate/07slsstab2a.xls.

33. Calculations based on data from U.S. Census Bureau, *Statistical Abstract of the United States: 2008* (U.S. Government Printing Office, 2008), Table 428, www.census.gov/compendia/statab/tables/08s0428.xls.

34. See Roy Bahl, David L. Sjoquist, and W. Loren Williams, "School Finance Reform and Impact on Property Taxes," *Proceedings of the Eighty-Third Annual National Tax Association Conference, 1990* (National Tax Association, Tax Institute of America, 1991), pp. 163–171.

35. *Serrano* v. *Priest*, 5 Cal. 3d ed. 487, 96 Cal. Rptr. 601 (1971).

36. *San Antonio Independent School District* v. *Rodriquez*, 411 U.S. 1 (1973).

37. Michael A. Rebell, "Poverty, 'Meaningful' Educational Opportunity, and the Necessary Role of the Courts," *North Carolina Law Review* 85 (2007), p. 1501.

38. Michael A. Rebell, "Equal Opportunity and the Courts," *Phi Delta Kappan* 89 (February 2008), www.pdkintl.org/kappan/k_v89/k0802reb.htm.

39. For the most recent information on such litigation, see www.schoolfunding.info.

40. Calculation based on data from U.S. Census Bureau, *Statistical Abstract of the United States: 2008* (U.S. Government Printing Office, 2008), Table 441.

41. Suho Bae and Thomas Gais, "The Effectiveness of State-Level Tax and Expenditure Limitations (TELs)," *Rockefeller Institute Fiscal Brief*, April 15, 2007, www.rockinst.org/WorkArea/showcontent.aspx?id=11804.

42. "State Tax and Expenditure Limits, 2008," National Conference of State Legislatures, http://www.ncsl.org/default.aspx?tabid=12633.

43. "Time Series Chart of U.S. Government Spending, Local Spending on Education," usgovernmentspending.com, http://www.usgovernmentspending.com/downchart_gs.php?chart=20-local&state=US&local=s.

44. J. Richard Aronson and John L. Hilley, *Financing State and Local Governments*, 4th ed. (Brookings Institution Press, 1986), p. 138; see also U.S. Advisory Commission on Intergovernmental Relations, *Property Tax Circuit-Breakers: Current Status and Policy Issues* (U.S. Government Printing Office, 1975); and Steven D. Gold, "Circuit-Breakers and Other Relief Measures," in C. Lowell Harris, ed., *The Property Tax and Local Finance* (Academy of Political Science, 1983), pp. 119–132.

45. U.S. Census Bureau, *State and Local Government Finances: 2007*, http://www2.census.gov/govs/estimate/07slsstab1a.xls.

46. Calculations based on data in U.S. Census Bureau, *Statistical Abstract of the United States: 2008* (U.S. Government Printing Office, 2000), Table 439, www.census.gov/compendia/statab/tables/08s0439.xls.

47. Michael Mazerov, "Expanding Sales Taxation of Services: Options and Issues," *Center on Budget and Policy Priorities*, June 19, 2003.

48. Katherine Barrett and Richard Greene, "Growth and Taxes," *Governing* (January 2008), p. 24.

49. Based on 2005 data from U.S. Census Bureau, *Statistical Abstract of the United States: 2008*, Table 439. www.census.gov/compendia/statab/tables/08s0439.xls.

50. Ibid.

51. Ibid.

52. Pamela M. Prah, "States Scramble for Gambling Jackpot," Stateline.org, September 12, 2007, www.stateline.org/live/details/story?contentId=239294.

53. "For the First Time, A Smaller Jackpot," Fiscal Studies report from the Rockefeller Institute, September 21, 2009, http://www.rockinst.org/pdf/government_finance/2009-09-21-No_More_Jackpot.pdf.

54. Prah, "States Scramble."

55. Rockefeller Institute Press, forthcoming.

56. "For the First Time, A Smaller Jackpot," Fiscal Studies report from the Rockefeller Institute, September 21, 2009, http://www.rockinst.org/pdf/government_finance/2009-09-21-No_More_Jackpot.pdf.

57. Ibid.

58. U.S. Census Bureau, *State and Local Government Finances: 2007*, http://www2.census.gov/govs/estimate/07slsstab1a.xls.

59. Ibid.

60. U.S. Census Bureau, *Statistical Abstract of the United States: 2010*, Table 420.

61. Suho Bae and Thomas Gais, "Fiscal Report: K–12 Education Spending by State and Local Governments," *Rockefeller Institute Policy Brief*, June 25, 2007; see also U.S. Census Bureau, "Public Education Finances, 2007," July 2009, http://www2.census.gov/govs/school/07f33pub.pdf.

62. Kathryn A. Foster, *The Political Economy of Special-Purpose Government* (Georgetown University Press, 1997); and Robert L. Bland and Wes Clarke, "Budgeting for Capital Improvements," in Roy T. Meyers, ed., *Handbook of Government Budgeting* (Jossey-Bass, 1999), pp. 653–677.

63. U.S. Census Bureau, *Statistical Abstract of the United States: 2010* (U.S. Government Printing Office, 2008), Table 434, https://www.census.gov/compendia/statab/2010/tables/10s0434.pdf.

64. Data on state and local government finances for these and other years are available at U.S. Census Bureau, *State and Local Government Finances*, www.census.gov/govs/www/estimate.html.

65. James W. Fossett and Courtney E. Burke, *Medicaid and State Budgets in FY 2004: Why Medicaid Is So Hard to Cut* (Rockefeller Institute Press, July 2004), www.rockinst.org/WorkArea/showcontent.aspx?id=6592.

66. Lucy Dadayan and Robert B. Ward, "State Tax Revenue Weakens Still Further, While Costs Rise Sharply," *State Revenue Report* (Rockefeller Institute Press, March 2008), pp. 10–12, www.rockinst.org/WorkArea/showcontent.aspx?id=14556.

67. Declan McCullagh, "More States Propose Internet Sales Taxes" CNET News, March 8, 2010, http://news.cnet.com/8301-13578_3-10465658-38.html.

68. U.S. Census Bureau, *Statistical Abstract of the United States: 2010* (U.S. Government Printing Office, 2010), Table 665, https://www.census.gov/compendia/statab/2010/tables/10s0665.pdf.

69. Yesim Yilmaz et al., "Measuring Fiscal Disparities Across the U.S. States," *Assessing the New Federalism: Occasional Paper No. 74* (Urban Institute, 2006); and The Lewin Group and the Rockefeller Institute of Government, *Spending on Social Welfare Programs in Rich and Poor States*, final report prepared for the Department of Health and Human Services, Assistant Secretary for Planning and Evaluation (DHHS/ASPE, 2004).

70. Yilmaz et al., "Measuring Fiscal Disparities," p. 24; and Lewin and Rockefeller, *Spending*, p. 24.

71. See "Grading the States, 2008," *Governing* (March 2008).

72. Lawrence M. Mead, *Government Matters: Welfare Reform in Wisconsin* (Princeton University Press, 2004).

73. Peter Harkness, "Management Matters," *Governing* (April 7, 2008), www.governing.com/articles/0804hark.htm.

Conclusion

1. Thucydides, *History of the Peloponnesian War*, translated by Benjamin Jowett (Prometheus Books, 1998).

2. Edith Hamilton, *The Echo of Greece* (Norton, 1957), p. 47.

3. For a book advocating more direct democracy, see Ted Becker and Christa Daryl Slaton, *The Future of Teledemocracy* (Praeger, 2000); for a contrary view, see Richard J. Ellis, *Democratic Delusions: The Initiative Process in America* (University Press of Kansas, 2002).

4. For an extensive list of countries that use some form of proportional representation, see ACE The Electoral Knowledge Network, "Comparative Data: Electoral Systems," aceproject.org/epic-en/es.

5. For more on the relationship between electoral institutions and party systems, see Maurice Duverger, *Political Parties: Their Organization and Activity in the Modern State* (Wiley, 1954).

6. *Lawrence* v. *Texas*, 539 U.S. 558 (2003).

7. The Campaign Legal Center, www.campaignlegalcenter.org/BCRA.html; and *McConnell* v. *FEC*, 124 S. Ct. 619 (2003).

8. John F. Kennedy, *Profiles in Courage* (Pocket Books, 1956), p. 108.

9. Harry S. Truman, impromptu remarks before the Reciprocity Club, Washington, D.C., April 11, 1958, as reported by the *New York World-Telegram*, April 12, 1958, p. 4, www.bartleby .com/73/1405.html.

10. These books will give you insight into the life of public officeholders: Bill Clinton, *My Life* (Knopf, 2004); Harry Reid and Mark Warren, *The Good Fight* (Putnam Adult, 2008); George Tenet, *At the Center of the Storm: My Years at the CIA* (HarperCollins, 2007); and Alan Greenspan, *The Age of Turbulence* (Penguin, 2007).

11. See Kareem Abdul-Jabar and Alan Steinberg, *Black Profiles in Courage* (Morrow, 1996).

12. Reinhold Niebuhr, *The Children of Light and the Children of Darkness* (Scribner, 1944), p. xi.

13. See Bernard Crick, *In Defense of Politics*, rev. ed. (Pelican Books, 1983); and Stimson Bullitt, *To Be a Politician*, rev. ed. (Yale University Press, 1977).

14. See Nat Hentoff, *Free Speech for Me—but Not for Thee: How the American Left and Right Relentlessly Censor Each Other* (Harper Perennial, 1993).

15. Thomas Jefferson, letter to Edward Carrington, January 16, 1787, in Thomas Jefferson Randolph, ed., *Memoir, Correspondence, and Miscellanies, from the Papers of Thomas Jefferson*, 2d ed., Vol. 2 (Carvill, 1830), Letter 43. Available online from Project Gutenberg at www.gutenberg.org/files/16782/16782-h/ 16782-h.htm.

16. Arthur M. Schlesinger, Jr., *The Disuniting of America* (Norton, 1993), p. 134.

17. John W. Gardner, *Self-Renewal*, rev. ed. (Norton, 1981), p. xiv.

18. In George Field, ed., *Famous Words of Freedom*, (Freedom House, 1955).

CREDITS

Photo Credits

INTRODUCTION: 2: The Granger Collection, New York; **6:** The Granger Collection, New York; **7:** The Granger Collection, New York; **11:** Courtesy Central Asian Institute

CHAPTER 1: 16: Saul Loeb/AP Photo; **18:** Jim Young/Reuters/Corbis; **19:** Corbis Digital Stock; **20:** Lee Marriner/AP Photo; **21:** zumawire westphotos/Newscom; **23:** Cristobal Herrara/AP Photo; **25:** M. Spencer Green/AP Photo; **26:** Tsvangirayi Mukwazhi/AP Photo; **29:** Bettmann/Corbis; **31:** Getty Images/Liaison; **34:** *(left)* Ian Wagreich/UPI; **34:** *(right)* Bettmann/ Corbis; **37:** Bettmann/Corbis

CHAPTER 2: 42: Mark Wilson/Getty Images; **44:** Massimo Borchi/Corbis; **45:** Bettmann/ Corbis; **49:** Joe Raedle/Getty Images; **50:** Jason DeCrow/AP Photo; **52:** The Granger Collection, New York; **55:** U.S. Senate/AP Photo; **58:** Image Works/Time & Life Pictures/Getty Images; **61:** AP Photo

CHAPTER 3: 76: Tony Avelar/The Christian Science Monitor/Getty Images; **79:** Damian Dovarganes/AP Photo; **82:** Johnny Crawford/ The Image Works; **83:** nagelstock/Alamy; **85:** Aaron D. Allmon II/U.S. Air Force via Getty Images; **86:** *(top)* Carl D. Walsh/Aurora; **86:** *(bottom)* Joe Raedle/Getty Images; **88:** Michael Smith/ Newscom; **90:** Jonathan Nourok/Getty Images; **91:** Thomas Wright/ University of Florida/IFAS/AP Photo; **92:** Dream Pictures/Getty Images; **94:** Alex Wong/Getty Images; **95:** Ed Kashi/Corbis; **96:** Yael Swerdlow/AP Photo

CHAPTER 4: 104: Bettmann/Corbis; **107:** Paul Conklin/Photoedit; **109:** Madalyn Ruggiero/ AP Photo; **113:** Newscom; **114:** *(left)* Ellen McKnight/Alamy; **114:** *(right)* Bebeto Matthews/ AP Photo; **115:** *(top)* Mario Tama/Getty Images; **115:** *(bottom)* Bettmann/Corbis; **117:** Chris Kleponis/Newcom; **119:** Jacquelyn Martin/AP Photo; **120:** Tim Sloan/AFP/Getty Images; **122:** Will Powers/AP Photo

CHAPTER 5: 128: David Grossman/Alamy; **132:** *(top)* Panoramic Images/Getty Images; **132:** *(bottom)* Corbis; **134:** Eric Draper/ AP Photo; **136:** *(left)* Patti McConville/Getty Images; **136:** *(right)* Mary Ann Chastain/AP Photo; **138:** Doug Benc/Getty Images; **140:** *(top)* Mark Leffingwell/Getty Images; **140:** *(bottom)* Michael Reynolds/EPA/Corbis; **143:** Carlos Barria/Reuters/Landov; **145:** *(top)* David J. Phillip/AP Photo; **145:** *(bottom)* Arthur Hochstein/Time Life Pictures/Getty Images; **149:** Elizabeth Crews; **151:** William Thomas Cain/ Getty Images

CHAPTER 6: 156: Harrison McClary/Reuters/ Landov; **159:** Morteza Nikoubazl/Reuters/ Landov; **162:** *(top)* Emmanuel Dunand/Getty Images; **162:** *(bottom)* Teri Stratford/Six-Cats Research Inc.; **163:** *(top)* Matthew Staver/ Bloomberg via Getty Images; **163:** *(bottom)* Stephanie London, Courtesy AIPAC; **166:** Photo by Ian Wagreich. Courtesy of U.S. Chamber of Congress; **167:** Al Grillo/AP Photo; **168:** Nick Ut/AP Photo; **170:** *(top)* Photo by Steven Halperson/Tisara Photography. Courtesy Lewis-Burke Associates, LLC; **170:** *(bottom)* UPI/ Landov; **176:** Teri Stratford/Six-Cats Research Inc. **180:** Janet Hostetter/AP Photo

CHAPTER 7: 184: Jim Young/Landov; **187:** Billy Suratt/Auma Press/Corbis; **189:** *(top)* Newscom; **189:** *(bottom)* Reiner Jensen/Corbis; **193:** Library of Congress; **195:** © 2008 Jupiter Images/Getty Images; **196:** Ed Reinkel/AP Photo; **197:** Sean Gardner/Reuters/Landov; **199:** Pablo Martinez Monsivais/AP Photo; **201:** Terry Gilliam/AP Photo; **205:** Scott Audette/Reuters/Landov;

CHAPTER 8: 212: Tim Boyles/Getty Images; **214:** Mark Humphrey/AP Photo; **215:** Lynn Avedisian; **218:** *(top)* Suzanne Dechillo/ The New York Times/Redux; **218:** *(bottom)* Bettmann/Corbis; **221:** Teri Stratford/Six-Cats Research Inc.; **223:** Jeff Widener/AP Photo; **224:** Damian Dovarganes/ AP Photo; **228:** Tom Olmscheid/AP Photo; **231:** Getty Images; **233:** *(top)* AP Photo; **233:** *(bottom)* AFL-CIO 2010; **235:** Teri Stratford/Six-Cats Research Inc.

CHAPTER 9: 240: Mark Weber/Landov; **244:** Marla Brose/Albuquerque Journal/AP Photo; **248:** Ben Margot/AP Photo; **255:** Mark Wilson/ Newscom; **256:** William Thomas Cain/Getty Images; **257:** Carlos Barria/Landov; **261:** to come; **263:** Teri Stratford/Six-Cats Research Inc.; **266:** Getty Images; **270:** Richard Clement/Landov

CHAPTER 10: 276: Shannon Stapleton/Corbis; **277:** Jim Sulley/Wirepix/The Image Works; **281:** *(top)* Bettmann/Corbis; **281:** *(bottom)* UPI/ Bettmann/Corbis; **282:** *(top)* Courtesy of Wikipedia.com/Zuma Press; **282:** *(bottom)* Philadelphia Inquirer/MCT/Landov; **284:** Liu Jin/AFP/Getty Images; **286:** Adam Rountree/ AP Photo; **289:** *(top)* Rick Bowmer/AP Photo; **289:** *(bottom)* Joe Raedle/Getty Images; **291:** Matthew Healey/UPI/Landov; **293:** Mike Theiler/UPI/Landov

CHAPTER 11: 298: AJ Mast/AP Photo; **300:** Jessica Kourkounis/The New York Times/Redux; **302:** Moses Olmos/Newscom; **304:** *(top)* Joe Burbank/MCT/Landov; **304:** *(bottom)* Win McNamee/Getty Images; **305:** Alexander Nemenov/AFP/Getty Images; **307:** *(top)* Sgt. James L. Haprer Jr./ USAF/AFP/Newscom; **307:** *(bottom)* Ron Sachs/ Newscom; **309:** *(top)* Paul Sakuma/AP Photo; **309:** *(bottom)* U.S. Senate Historical Office; **311:** Shawn Thew/EPA/Landov; **312:** Martin H. Simon/Corbis; **316:** Scott J. Ferrell/Getty Images; **317:** Mark Wilson/Getty Images; **319:** Tim Sloan/AFP/Getty Images; **320:** Adam Larkey/ABC via Getty Images

CHAPTER 12: 324: Tim Wimborne/Reuters/ Landov; **326:** J. Scott Applewhite/AP Photo; **327:** *(top)* Leif Skoogfors/Corbis; **327:** *(bottom)* EPA/ STR/Landov; **328:** ptsphotoshot/Newscom; **330:** AP Photo; **332:** UPI/Landov; **333:** *(top)* Ric Francis/AP Photo; **333:** *(bottom)* Cecil Stoughton/ Corbis; **334:** Behrouz Mehri/Getty Images; **335:** Kyodo via AP Photo; **336:** Smithsonian American Art Museum, Washington D.C./Art Resource; **338:** Greg Mathieson/Landov; **340:** *(left)* Karin Cooper/ CBS/AP Photo; **340:** *(right)* Alex Wong/ Getty Images; **341:** Win McNamee/Reuters/Getty Images; **342:** Newscom; **344:** Dirck Halstead/ Getty Images

CHAPTER 13: 350: Saul Loeb/AFP/Getty Images; **352:** The Granger Collection, New York; **355:** Sinclair Stammers/Photo Researchers; **357:** *(top)* Dennis Cook/AP Photo; **357:** *(bottom)* Evan Vucci/AP Photo; **359:** *(top)* Bizuayehu Tesfaye/AP Photo; **359:** *(bottom)* Manuel Balce Ceneta/AP Photo; **360:** Charles Rex Arbogast/AP Photo; **363:** *(top)* David Glass/AP Photo; **363:** *(bottom)* Gerald Herbert/AP Photo; **364:** JP Greenwood/ Getty Images; **367:** *(top)* Mark Wilson/Getty Images; **367:** *(bottom)* Gerald Herbert/AP Photo; **369:** Alan Singer/CBS Television

CHAPTER 14: 374: Alex Wong/Getty Images; **377:** Morgan Smith, The Texas Tribune; **382:** Alex Wong/Getty Images; **383:** *(top)* Clary/UPI/ Corbis; **383:** *(bottom)* Chip Somodella/Getty Images; **384:** *(top left)* Brendan Smialowski/ Getty Images; **384:** *(top right)* Mark Wilson/Getty Images; **384:** *(bottom)* Stephen Crowley/The New York Times/Redux; **385:** Stephen Crowley/ The New York Times/Redux; **391:** David Hume Kennerly/Getty Images; **392:** Bill O'Leary/The Washington Post; **393:** Jay Reeves/AP Photo

CHAPTER 15: 400: Robert Caplin/AP Photo; **406:** Peter Yates/ Time Life Pictures/Getty Images; **408:** *(top)* Carl Iwasaki/Getty Images; **408:** *(bottom)* Charles Tasnadi/AP Photo; **409:** Chris Seward/The News & Observer/AP Photo; **410:** Michael Porro/Getty Images; **411:** *(top)* Nick Ut/AP Photo; **411:** *(bottom)* Michael Caulfield/Getty Images; **412:** Don Emmert/ AFP/Getty Images; **413:** Jessica Hill/AP Photo; **414:** Andres Leighton/AP Photo; **416:** Alex Wong/Getty Images; **417:** Nancy G. Fire Photography, Nancy Greifenhagen/Alamy; **418:** Mike Derer/AP Photo; **419:** Bettmann/Corbis

CHAPTER 16: 428: Kevin P. Casey/The New York Times/Redux; **430:** Richard Ellis/Getty Images; **432:** Corbis; **434:** *(top)* Kidwiler Collection/Diamond Images/Getty Images; **434:** *(bottom)* Laurie P. Winfrey/Woodfin Camp; **435:** *(top)* Francis Miller/Time & Life Pictures/ Getty Images; **435:** *(bottom)* Bettmann/Corbis; **437:** Rick D'Elia/Corbis; **438:** Tim Sloan/AFP/ Getty Images; **442:** Rich Pedroncelli/AP Photo; **444:** National Conference of State Legislators; **446:** William Thomas Cain/Getty Images; **448:** Bettmann/ Corbis; **450:** Danny Moloshok/AP Photo; **451:** AP Photo

CHAPTER 17: 458: Bob Daemmrich/The Image Works; **460:** Jason Reed/Reuters/Corbis;

461: Rebecca Cook/Reuters/Landov; 464: Eric Lee/Lawrence Bender Prods./The Kobal Collection; 468: AP Photo; 470: Peter Andrews/Landov; 471: M.L. Suckley/FDR Library/AP Photo; 474: (top) USCG/Landov; 474: (bottom) Carolyn Kaster/AP Photo

CHAPTER 18: 478: UPI/Landov; 481: (left) AP Photo; 481: (right) Paul Sakuma/AP Photo; 485: AFP/Getty Images; 487: M. Spencer Green/AP Photo; 488: Topham/The Image Works; 489: (top) Jose Fuste Raga/Corbis; 489: (bottom) Chris Sattlberger/Getty Images; 490: Brian Lee/Corbis; 491: Rick Wilking/Reuters/Landov; 494: (top) Konrad Steffen/University of Colorado/Reuters/Landov; 494: (bottom) Don Emmert/AFP/Newscom; 496: Landon Nordeman/Getty Images

CHAPTER 19: 500: J. Scott Applewhite/AP Photo; 502: Alamy; 503: Matthew Cavanaugh/Corbis; 505: Bob Daemmrich/The Image Works; 506: Peter Hvizdak/The Image Works; 508: Dennis MacDonald/Photoedit; 509: David Buffington/Getty Images; 510: Bonnie Kamin/Photoedit; 513: Darron Cummings/AP Photo; 514: Brett Flashnick/AP Photo; 515: (top) Larry Downing/Reuters/ Landov; 515: (bottom) KIPP Foundation/Ethan Pines Photography; 518: Chao Soi Cheong/AP Photo

CHAPTER 20: 522: Beatrice Mategwa/ Reuters/Corbis; 524: Lee Jin Man/ AP Photo; 526: Digital Globe/Reuters/Landov; 527: Karl Schumacher/AFP/Getty Images; 528: Joe Raedle/Getty Images; 529: Baz Ratner/ Reuters/Landov; 530: Bob Strong/ Reuters/ Corbis; 531: (top) J. Scott Applewhite/AP Photo; 531: (bottom) Chris Hondros/Getty Images; 532: UPI; 534: Sean Heasley/Corbis; 535: Patrick D. McDermott/Landov; 537: Geert Vanden Wijngaert/AP Photo; 539: American Red Cross; 541: Patrick Gelly/The Image Works; 540: T. Campion/Corbis Sygma

CHAPTER 21: 546: Rich Pedroncelli/AP Photo; 548: (left) Bill Ross/Corbis; 548: (center) Richard T. Nowitz/Corbis; 548: (right) Alamy; 550: Alamy; 551: Stan Honda/AFP/Getty Images; 554: Alamy; 555: Julia Malokie/AP Photo; 557: David Greedy/Getty Images; 560: James D. Wilson/Woodfin Camp & Associates; 562: Chicago Tribune/MCT/Landov

CHAPTER 22: 566: Elise Amendola/AP Photo; 573: Elaine Thompson/AP Photo;

CHAPTER 23: 582: Tracy A. Woodward/The Washington Post/Getty Images; 584: Library of Congress; 587: McCain Library and Archives, University of Mississippi; 589: Marcio Jose Sanchez/AP Photo; 591: AP Photo; 592: Bill Pugliano/Getty Images; 598: Eric Engman/Getty Images; 600: Charlie Neibergall/AP Photo; 602: Sue Ogrocki/AP Photo

CHAPTER 24: 608: Tom Olmscheid/AP Photo; 611: Aurelia Venture/Newscom; 614: Joshua Lott/Reuters/ Landov; 622: Harry Cabluck/AP Photo

CHAPTER 25: 630: John Zich/AFP/Getty Images; 632: Courtesy Scott Merrick; 633: (top) John Froschauer/AP Photo; 633: (bottom) John L. Russell/AP Photo; 634: David Kohl/AP Photo; 641: Damian Dovargenes/AP Photo; 643: (top)

Chitose Suzuki/ AP Photo; 643: (bottom) Gerald Herbert/AP Photo; 647 Raleigh News Observer/MCT/Landov

CHAPTER 26: 652: Teri Stratford/Six-Cats Research Inc.; 655: Billy E. Barnes/Photoedit; 658: Tony Freeman/ Photoedit; 659: Photo by Robert Laughon Jr.; 662: Tony Gutierrez/AP Photo; 663: Scott T. Baxter/Photodisc/Getty Images

CHAPTER 27: 670: David McNew/Getty Images; 676: Farrell Grehan/Corbis; 683: Corbis; 685 both: Ross D. Franklin/AP Photo; 686: (top) Richard Cummins/Superstock; 686: (bottom) Chris Hoffman/Newscom; 688: Justin Lane/epa/ Corbis; 690: Ethan Hyman/The News & Observer; 691: Farrell Grehan/Corbis

CHAPTER 28: 696: © Samantha Contis; 699: Bob Daemmrich/Alamy; 701: Sarah L. Voisin/The Washington Post via Getty Images; 702: Byron Purvis/AdMedia/Newscom; 704: Chicago Tribune/MCT/Landov; 708: Tim Boyle/ Getty Images; 712: Kevin R. Morris/ Corbis; 713: Craig Lassig/Corbis; 716: Ronen Zilberman/AP Photo

CHAPTER 29: 720: Charles Cherney/AP Photo; 729: AP Photo; 731: Mark Humphrey/AP Photo; 733: Charles Rex Arbogast/AP Photo; 734: Mark Wilson/Getty Images; 735: Aric Crabb/Bay Area News Group/The Contra Costa Times/AP Photo; 736: Bloomberg via Getty Images

CONCLUSION: 742: Kevin Fleming/Corbis; 745: David R. Frazier/The Image Works; 747: Tim Graham/Getty Images; 748: Cassy Muronaka/ Photoedit

Text Credits

INTRODUCTION: 10: From "Obama More Popular Abroad Than at Home, Global Image of U.S. Continues to Benefit" July 2010, by Pew Global Attitudes Project. Copyright (c) 2010 by Pew Global Attitudes Project, a project of the Pew Research Center. Reprinted with permission.

CHAPTER 1: 24: From "Obama More Popular Abroad Than at Home, Global Image of U.S. Continues to Benefit" July 2010, by Pew Global Attitudes Project. Copyright (c) 2010 by Pew Global Attitudes Project, a project of the Pew Research Center. Reprinted with permission. 32: From Maps.com. Copyright (c) by Maps.com. Reprinted by permission.

CHAPTER 2: 54: From "Obama More Popular Abroad Than at Home, Global Image of U.S. Continues to Benefit" July 2010, by Pew Global Attitudes Project. Copyright (c) 2010 by Pew Global Attitudes Project, a project of the Pew Research Center. Reprinted with permission.

CHAPTER 3: 80: From "Obama More Popular Abroad Than at Home, Global Image of U.S. Continues to Benefit" July 2010, by Pew Global Attitudes Project. Copyright (c) 2010 by Pew Global Attitudes Project, a project of the Pew Research Center. Reprinted with permission. 83: From GETTING CURRENT: RECENT DEMOGRAPHIC TRENDS IN METROPOLITAN AMERICA by William H. Frey, Alan Berube, Audrey Singer and Jill H. Wilson. Copyright (c)

2010 by William H. Frey, Alan Berube, Audrey Singer and Jill H. Wilson. Reprinted by permission of The Brookings Institution.

CHAPTER 4: 121: From "Obama More Popular Abroad Than at Home, Global Image of U.S. Continues to Benefit" July 2010, by Pew Global Attitudes Project. Copyright (c) 2010 by Pew Global Attitudes Project, a project of the Pew Research Center. Reprinted with permission.

CHAPTER 5: 131: From "Obama More Popular Abroad Than at Home, Global Image of U.S. Continues to Benefit" July 2010, by Pew Global Attitudes Project. Copyright (c) 2010 by Pew Global Attitudes Project, a project of the Pew Research Center. Reprinted with permission. 144: From "Data Points: Gender in the 2008 Election" by U.S. News Staff from U.S. NEWS AND WORLD REPORT, November 6, 2008. Copyright (c) 2008 by U.S. News and World Report Licensing. Reprinted by permission of Wright's Media.

CHAPTER 6: 164: From "Obama More Popular Abroad Than at Home, Global Image of U.S. Continues to Benefit" July 2010, by Pew Global Attitudes Project. Copyright (c) 2010 by Pew Global Attitudes Project, a project of the Pew Research Center. Reprinted with permission.

CHAPTER 7: 190: From "Obama More Popular Abroad Than at Home, Global Image of U.S. Continues to Benefit" July 2010, by Pew Global Attitudes Project. Copyright (c) 2010 by Pew Global Attitudes Project, a project of the Pew Research Center. Reprinted with permission. 191: From GUIDE TO U.S. ELECTIONS, 6e, Vol. 1. Copyright (c) 2010 by CQ Press. Reprinted with permission. 203: From VITAL STATISTICS ON AMERICAN POLITICS, 2009-2010 by Harold W. Stanley and Richard G. Niemi. Copyright (c) 2010 by Stanley and Niemi. Reprinted by permission of CQ Press.

CHAPTER 8: 217: From "Senate Legislative Process a Mystery to Many: Political Knowledge Update," January 28, 2010 by Pew Research Center for the People and Press, a Project of the Pew Research Center. Copyright (c) 2010 by Pew Research Center. Reprinted with permission. 234: From GLOBAL OPINION TRENDS 2002–2007: A RISING TIDE LIFTS MOOD IN THE DEVELOPING WORLD by Pew Global Attitudes Project. Copyright (c) 2007 by Pew Global Attitudes Project, a project of the Pew Research Center. Reprinted with permission.

CHAPTER 9: 246: From VITAL STATISTICS ON AMERICAN POLITICS, 2007-2008 by Harold W. Stanley and Richard G. Niemi. Copyright (c) 2008 by Stanley and Niemi. Reprinted by permission of CQ Press. 247: From "Obama More Popular Abroad Than at Home, Global Image of U.S. Continues to Benefit" July 2010, by Pew Global Attitudes Project. Copyright (c) 2010 by Pew Global Attitudes Project, a project of the Pew Research Center. Reprinted with permission. 248: From VITAL STATISTICS ON AMERICAN POLITICS, 2009-2010 by Harold W. Stanley and Richard G. Niemi. Copyright (c) 2010 by Stanley and Niemi. Reprinted by permission of CQ Press.

CHAPTER 10: 278: From "Obama More Popular Abroad Than at Home, Global Image of U.S.

INDEX

COURSE EXAM

Introduction: Government by the People

1. Who is considered to be the architect of the Constitution?
   a. Thomas Jefferson
   b. George Washington
   c. John Adams
   d. James Madison

2. How did the Mayflower Compact become an important model for government in America?

3. Which philosopher wrote that people once lived in a state of nature but could enter into self-government through a social contract?

   a. David Hume
   b. John Locke
   c. Jean-Jacques Rousseau
   d. Thomas Hobbes

4. For which of the terms is the following definition most appropriate? "The belief that the authority and legitimacy of government is based in the consent and authority of the individuals living within its boundaries."
   a. Pure democracy
   b. Popular sovereignty
   c. Individualism
   d. Freedom of speech

Part I Constitutional Principles

Chapter 1: Constitutional Democracy
Identify the philosophical principles on which our democratic republic is based.

5. All of the following aspects of direct democracy were added *after* the constitution was signed EXCEPT:
   a. Direct primary elections of U.S. Senators
   b. Initiative process for enacting legislation
   c. Referendum on issues put forward by legislatures
   d. Recall of state government leaders
   e. Direct election of members of the House of Representatives

6. Some societies are better positioned to maintain a healthy democracy than are others. List and describe at least three of the conditions that lead to a strong democracy.

7. Which of the following is NOT a distinct element of the Constitution?
   a. Federalism
   b. Economic equality
   c. Bicameralism
   d. Bill of rights
   e. Separation of powers

8. In what ways did the Articles of Confederation differ from our current constitution?

9. What is the three-fifths compromise, and what social conditions led to the compromise? What parts of the country did the two different sides of the issue represent?

Chapter 2: Constitutional Foundations
Describe the creation and adoption of the Constitution and the Bill of Rights, and identify the process for Amendments.

10. How has new technology and the media changed the system of checks and balances established by the Constitution?

11. The decision in the Supreme Court case *Marbury v. Madison* established which of the following?
    a. The Supreme Court's right to review acts of the national legislature
    b. The Supreme Court as the main interpreter of the Constitution

    c. That Marbury was entitled to his commission and Madison should have delivered it to him
    d. That the proper court could issue a writ of mandamus, even against so high an official as the secretary of state
    e. All of the above

12. Describe the two methods for proposing amendments to the U.S. Constitution and why you think that only one of these have been used thus far.

13. Which of the following applications of checks and balances has been used the most widely?
    a. Vetoes
    b. Judicial review
    c. Impeachment
    d. Confirmation

Chapter 3: American Federalism
Explain federalism in America, and analyze the relationship between the federal and state and local governments.

14. Define federalism and explain the ways governments at different levels can share power in different kinds of federalism.

15. Which one of the following is NOT an advantage of federalism?
    a. It checks the growth of tyranny.
    b. It encourages experimentation.
    c. It allows unity without uniformity.
    d. It encourages holding elected officials accountable through a division of power.
    e. It keeps government closer to the people.

16. What is the difference between delegated or express powers and implied powers? List some of both types.

17. A decentralist would agree with which one of the following statements?
    a. For the sake of national well-being, more power should be given to the federal government.
    b. Any question about whether the states have given a particular function to the central government or have reserved it for themselves should be resolved in favor of the states.
    c. The devolution revolution should be defeated.

d. Presidents Abraham Lincoln and Franklin Roosevelt had a correct understanding of the balance in power between the states and federal government.

e. The national government is an agent of the people, not the states.

18. Which of the following is one of the three types of federal grants currently given?
   a. Welfare grant
   b. Income equalization grant
   c. Categorical-formula grant
   d. Revenue sharing grant
   e. Education grant

19. Historically, how had federalism been used to retain slavery, segregation, and discrimination? Provide arguments for and against retaining federalism given these patterns. Are there examples of states having laws today that treat people differently?

The Big Picture

20. Compare and contrast the originalist approach to interpreting the U.S. Constitution with the adaptive approach.

21. Explain how the system of federalism addressed the framers' concerns over the power of the new federal government.

Part II The Political Process

Chapter 4: Political Culture and Ideology
Explain the role of political culture and ideology in American government.

22. Name five of the shared values that contribute to American political culture.

23. Which of the following is NOT one of the characteristics of the rule of law?
   a. Laws should apply to the present and future, not punish something someone did in the past (Prospectivity).
   b. Laws should be specifically designed to promote different outcomes for particular groups or individuals in society (Specificity).
   c. Valid laws are made by those in legitimate power through popular consent (Authority).
   d. Valid laws cannot be kept secret and then enforced (Publicity).
   e. Laws must be enforced impartially and with fair processes (Due Process).

24. Explain the conflict in values between a *competitive economy* and an *egalitarian society*.

25. Which of the following political ideologies is most likely to advocate affirmative action programs?
   a. Social conservative
   b. Contemporary liberal
   c. Libertarian
   d. Traditional conservative
   e. A and B

26. Which of the following political ideology(ies) is most likely to oppose government programs like those implemented in the New Deal of the 1930s?
   a. Contemporary liberal
   b. Libertarian
   c. Traditional conservative
   d. B and C
   e. All of the above

Chapter 5: The American Political Landscape
Describe how American social and economic differences affect political beliefs and policy preferences.

27. What is the difference between a reinforcing cleavage and a cross-cutting cleavage? Give some examples of each.

28. Define political socialization.

29. True or False: Religion has been an important catalyst for political change in the United States.

30. All of the following are true about women in the United States EXCEPT:
   a. Women are more likely to oppose violence in any form.
   b. There are serious income inequalities between men and women.
   c. The number of women in Congress reached new highs in the 1990s.
   d. Women are more likely to vote for female candidates.

Chapter 6: Interest Groups
Evaluate the efforts of different kinds of interest groups to influence elections and legislation.

31. Describe and give examples of four techniques interest groups use to exert influence.

32. The AFL-CIO is what type of interest group?
   a. Foreign Policy
   b. Public-Sector
   c. Ideological or Single-Issue
   d. Business
   e. Labor

33. Which piece of legislation doubled the allowed individual contribution limits and banned soft money?
   a. The Bipartisan Campaign Reform Act (BCRA)
   b. The Sherman Antitrust Act (SAT)
   c. The Elections and Campaigning Amendment (ECA)
   d. The Restoring Trust in Election Financing Act (RTEFA)
   e. The Federal Election Campaign Act of 1971 (FECA)

34. How do cross-cutting interests affect interest groups' influence?

35. Which of the following is NOT one of the functions of a lobbyist?
   a. Help members of Congress overcome party differences
   b. Help prepare legislation and testify before legislative hearings
   c. Provide information for decision makers in all branches of government
   d. Contribute a large share of the costs of campaigns
   e. Help educate and mobilize public opinion

Chapter 7: Political Parties
Explain the role of political parties, and assess the need for parties in American government.

36. Describe why third parties have difficulty obtaining support in the United States.

37. Which of the following does NOT mark a time of major partisan realignment?
    a. The Civil War
    b. The Progressive Era
    c. The New Deal
    d. Vietnam and the Great Society
    e. Jackson and grassroots democracy

38. Which of the following is a feature of a parliamentary system rather than the U.S. party system?
    a. Winner-take-all
    b. Ideological parties
    c. Single-member districts
    d. Two dominant parties
    e. Candidate-centered campaigns

39. Discuss why some believe political parties are dying in the United States.

Chapter 8: Public Opinion, Participation, and Voting
Explain differences in opinions and rates of participation, and evaluate the importance of public opinion and participation in a democracy.

40. Which of the following is considered the most powerful agent of political socialization?
    a. Peers and friends
    b. Mass media
    c. Religious background
    d. Ethnic background
    e. Family

41. Define a random sample and explain what measures are taken when selecting a random sample to ensure it is representative of the population as a whole.

42. Generally, which of the following types of elections has the highest turnout?
    a. Primary election
    b. Midterm election
    c. Presidential election
    d. Special election
    e. Off-year election

43. Compare and contrast voting on the basis of party with voting on the basis of candidates.

44. Briefly describe some of the problems involved with counting Florida's ballots after the 2000 presidential election and what has been done to correct them.

Chapter 9: Campaigns and Elections
Compare and contrast the elections for president and Congress, and describe how elections have changed over time.

45. Compared with proportional representation, single-member districts typically:
    a. Encourage more participation of minor parties.
    b. Accurately reveal divisions in voter preferences.

c. Establish a clear winner.
    d. Lead to greater ideological extremism.
    e. None of the above

46. Partisan gerrymandering is:
    a. The negative advertising between parties during elections.
    b. The process of drawing district boundaries to benefit a certain party.
    c. The support a congressional candidate receives from a popular president of the same party.
    d. When members of Congress vote along strict party lines.

47. List and explain three key advantages incumbents enjoy in elections.

48. The Bipartisan Campaign Reform Act did all of the following EXCEPT:
    a. Ban soft money.
    b. Index contribution limits to inflation.
    c. Restrict the way 527 groups communicate with voters.
    d. Limit the amount candidates can spend on their own campaigns.
    e. Provide a new definition for "electioneering communications."

49. Identify and discuss the strengths and weaknesses of one potential reform for the presidential primary system and one potential reform for the presidential general election system.

Chapter 10: The Media and U.S. Politics
Describe the evolution of the media and evaluate its impact on public opinion, elections, and government.

50. Americans' number one news source is which of the following?
    a. Television
    b. Newspapers
    c. Radio
    d. Internet
    e. Magazines

51. What is investigative journalism? Discuss the role it played in two events in U.S. history.

52. All of the following limit media influence EXCEPT:
    a. Selective exposure
    b. Needs of viewers and listeners
    c. Audience fragmentation
    d. Growth of the Internet
    e. Selective perception

53. What has been the impact of television on candidates and elections?

54. How do presidents influence the media in order to push their agenda and reach their goals?

The Big Picture

55. How does America's two party system affect elections and the decisions of voters?

56. What are the primary arguments for and against strong campaign finance laws?

Chapter 11: Congress
Identify the legislative powers of Congress, and compare and contrast the House of Representatives and the Senate.

57. Which of the following is NOT an advantage incumbents enjoy?
    a. Franking privilege
    b. Greater access to the media
    c. Greater access to money
    d. More able to run as agent of change
    e. More visibility

58. Congressional regulation on semi trucks traveling across the country would be justified by which of the following enumerated powers?
    a. The power to raise, make, and borrow money
    b. The power to regulate interstate commerce
    c. The power to unify and expand the country
    d. The power to prepare and declare war
    e. The power to create monopolies

59. Compare and contrast the "delegate" and "trustee" approaches to representation.

60. Which of the following is NOT one of the types of congressional committees?
    a. Authorizing
    b. Oversight
    c. Budget
    d. Constitution
    e. Appropriations

61. Describe the roles of both the Speaker of the House and the Senate president.

Chapter 12: The Presidency
Identify the powers of the president for leading the nation.

62. Which of the following is NOT a presidential power given by the Constitution?
    a. The power to appoint judges
    b. The power to assume the role of commander in chief
    c. The power to declare war
    d. The power to be negotiate treaties
    e. The power to take care that the laws are faithfully executed

63. Discuss George Washington's and Franklin Delano Roosevelt's individual impacts on the Office of the Presidency.

64. Which power of the president did Congress curtail?
    a. The power to issue executive orders
    b. The executive privilege
    c. The use of signing statements
    d. The line item veto
    e. The use of impoundment

65. Which of the following has been said to most significantly enlarge presidential powers over time?
    a. Economic or foreign crises
    b. The power to appoint federal judges
    c. The line item veto
    d. Increasing use of signing statements

Chapter 13: The Federal Bureaucracy
Describe the role of the federal bureaucracy in implementing the laws.

66. With regard to the federal bureaucracy, all of the following are mandated in the Constitution EXCEPT:
    a. Current Representatives and Senators cannot hold executive branch positions.
    b. The president has complete authority to nominate senior government officers.
    c. The president has power to fill vacancies in the bureaucracy when the Senate is in recess.
    d. The president has power to create departments of government.
    e. The president is responsible to supervise the work of members of the bureaucracy.

67. Identify and explain key differences between independent regulatory commissions and independent stand-alone agencies.

68. Which of the following is NOT a part of the process for selecting presidential appointees?
    a. Selection of appointee by the White House Presidential Personnel Office
    b. The White House clearance process
    c. Review and hearing in a House committee
    d. Review and hearing in a Senate committee

69. The primary responsibility of all organizations in the federal bureaucracy is:
    a. Executing or implementing the laws
    b. Establishing entitlement programs and other services
    c. Responding to national disasters
    d. Overseeing the quality of goods produced within the United States
    e. Providing a check to the power of the president

70. In what ways can the president and Congress oversee and control the bureaucracy?

Chapter 14: The Judiciary
Explain the role of the courts in the system of checks and balances, and evaluate the challenges for judicial independence.

71. What does it mean that the federal judiciary is a passive and reactive branch?

72. In which of the following cases would the Supreme Court have original jurisdiction?
    a. A case involving a serial killer
    b. A case involving mass corporate fraud
    c. A case involving two states
    d. A case involving the governor of Texas
    e. A case involving a Tennessee church

73. Compare and contrast judicial activism and judicial restraint.

74. Which of the following is NOT one of the necessary steps the Supreme Court takes in making a judgment?
    a. Briefing the case
    b. Holding the oral argument
    c. Meeting in conference
    d. Reviewing public opinion
    e. Writing the opinion

The Big Picture

75. To what degree is the Supreme Court given policy-making power by the Constitution? What are the pros and cons of a Supreme Court that exerts strong influence over policy?

76. What are the strengths and weaknesses of a strong federal bureaucracy? What institutions are in place to control the federal bureaucracy, and do they do they do an adequate job?

Part IV Individual Rights and Liberties

Chapter 15: Civil Liberties
Describe the individual liberties protected in the Bill of Rights, and evaluate the limitations on these rights.

77. Which of the following is a correct definition of civil liberties?
    a. Constitutional protections of all persons against governmental restrictions on the freedoms of conscience, religion, and expression
    b. The constitutional rights of all persons to due process and the equal protection of the laws
    c. The constitutional right not to be discriminated against by governments because of race, ethnic background, religion, or gender
    d. Rights that are granted by governments and may be subject to conditions or restrictions
    e. All of the above

78. Which of the following kinds of speech is protected under the First Amendment?
    a. Libel
    b. Obscenity
    c. Fighting words
    d. Commercial speech
    e. Hate speech

79. What is the difference between procedural due process and substantive due process?

80. Which of the following court cases re-affirmed a woman's right to abort a pregnancy?
    a. *Roe* v. *Wade*
    b. *Planned Parenthood* v. *Casey*
    c. *Stenberg* v. *Carhart*
    d. *Bowers* v. *Hardwick*
    e. *Lawrence* v. *Texas*

Chapter 16: Civil Rights
Explain how Congress and the Supreme Court have expanded and protected civil rights.

81. Which one of the following is NOT a requirement for naturalization?
    a. Be over the age of 18
    b. Be able to read, write, and speak English

c. Understand and demonstrate an attachment to the history, principles, and form of government of the United States
    d. Be lawfully admitted for permanent residence and have resided in the United States for at least 7 years
    e. Possess a good moral character

82. Name two specific rights that are derived from national citizenship in the United States.

83. Which amendment to the Constitution contains the equal protection clause?
    a. 5th
    b. 13th
    c. 14th
    d. 15th
    e. 19th

84. Explain the difference between *de jure* segregation and *de facto* segregation.

85. If the Supreme Court decides that a law is subject to strict scrutiny because it creates a suspect classification, which of the following must the government prove in order to justify that classification?
    a. That the classification serves a compelling government interest.
    b. That the classification rationally distinguishes between visible characteristics of people.
    c. That there is no less restrictive way to accomplish the government interest.
    d. A and C
    e. All of the above

The Big Picture

86. What are the primary arguments for and against affirmative action policies?

87. Why is free speech important to the survival of democracy? Are there situations where the right to free speech ought to be limited? Explain.

Part V The Politics of National Policy

Chapter 17: The Policy Process
Identify the steps in the policymaking process.

88. Which of the following is a redistributive policy?
    a. Social Security
    b. Education funding
    c. Interstate highway system

d. Air traffic control
    e. Welfare

89. Which one of the following is NOT a necessary step in making public policy?
    a. Deciding to act
    b. Designing a political implementation strategy

c. Setting the agenda of problems to be addressed
d. Deciding how much to do
e. Deciding who will deliver the goods or services

90. Compare and contrast incremental policy and punctuating policy. Give examples of each.

91. In recent years, the federal government has become more dependent on *third-party government*. Which one of the following is NOT a source of *third-party government*?
a. State and local governments
b. Colleges and universities
c. Private businesses
d. Charities
e. The State Department

92. How can private citizens affect public policy?

Chapter 18: Making Economic Policy
Describe the federal government's tools for making economic policy.

93. Explain the difference between fiscal policy and monetary policy and how each can influence the nation's economy.

94. The acronym CPI means:
a. Child Protection Initiative
b. Consumer Price Index
c. Contraction Predicted Inflation
d. Commodity Price Index
e. None of the above

95. The largest source of tax revenue for the federal government is:
a. Payroll taxes
b. Corporate income taxes
c. Excise taxes
d. Individual income taxes
e. Estate taxes

96. Which organization oversees the budget process on behalf of the president?
a. Office of Management and Budget
b. Congressional Budget Office
c. Internal Revenue Service
d. Presidential Budget Office
e. Federal Reserve

97. Explain how changes in the federal funds rate can affect the economy.

98. The Fair Labor Standards Act of 1938 regulated labor in which of the following areas?
a. Wages and hours
b. Child labor
c. Industrial safety and occupational health
d. Both A and B
e. All of the above

Chapter 19: Making Social Policy
Trace the evolution of social policy, and describe the government's recent challenges in protecting Americans from hardship.

99. What are entitlements? Name two examples of entitlement programs.

100. All of the following are programs instituted under President Lyndon Johnson's Great Society EXCEPT:
a. Food Stamps
b. Medicare
c. Medicaid
d. Social Security
e. Housing Assistance

101. List five of the major provisions of the Patient Protection and Affordable Health Care Act.

102. How has the federal government attempted to set higher standards for public education, and what challenges has it faced?

Chapter 20: Making Foreign and Defense Policy
Describe the tools of foreign policymaking, and evaluate the status of America's current foreign policy interests.

103. Describe the contrasting theories of realism and idealism as they apply to foreign policy.

104. Which one of the following exemplify isolationism in foreign policy?
a. The Iraq War
b. Obama's decision to send more troops to Afghanistan
c. Obama's vote against the Iraq War
d. The War on Terror
e. All of the above

105. Which one of the following is the most important intelligence unit?
a. Federal Bureau of Investigation
b. Bureau of Intelligence and Research
c. Defense Intelligence Agency
d. Central Intelligence Agency
e. National Security Agency

106. What is the difference between soft power and hard power?

107. Which of the following is a type of hard power?
a. Conventional diplomacy
b. Foreign aid
c. Economic sanctions
d. Public diplomacy
e. Image building

The Big Picture

108. What are the ways the federal government can influence the nation's economy? What are the pros and cons of governmental involvement in the economy?

109. Define redistributive social policy. What are the arguments for and against increasing wealth redistribution?

Part VI State and Local Government

Chapter 21: State and Local Politics
Identify the range of policy programs administered by state and local governments, and analyze the influences on state and local politics.

110. Explain the theory of pluralism in local politics.

111. Citizens have the greatest trust in which of the following levels of government?
    a. National
    b. State
    c. Local
    d. Intra-state
    e. The amount of trust is roughly the same for all levels

112. Which of the following is NOT a central concern for state and local governments?
    a. Inner city poverty
    b. Education
    c. Health care
    d. A strong military
    e. Environmental regulation

113. What are some of the factors that restrain newspapers from holding local officials accountable?

Chapter 22: State Constitutions
Compare and contrast the U.S. Constitution with state constitutions.

114. What does it mean to say that a constitution is like a straitjacket, and what factors lead to straitjacket constitutions?

115. Which of the following is NOT a way that state constitutions can be amended?
    a. Legislative proposal
    b. Revision commission
    c. Constitutional initiative petition
    d. Constitutional convention
    e. U. S. Supreme Court decision

116. Explain why some states might require supermajorities to change their state constitutions.

117. If a state supreme court rules that a U.S. constitutional provision outlining the rights of gun owners is more limited than previously believed, this would be an example of:
    a. Judicial interpretation
    b. New judicial federalism
    c. Strict constitutionalism
    d. Constitutional literalism
    e. None of the above

Chapter 23: Parties and Elections in the States
Assess the importance of parties and elections at the state level.

118. An election that is held to fill a vacant office or address a one-time issue is called a:
    a. General election
    b. Primary election
    c. Recall election
    d. Provisional election
    e. Special election

119. According to the Constitution, who is primarily responsible for determining who may vote?
    a. Congress
    b. The federal courts
    c. State governments
    d. Town councils
    e. The electoral college

120. Explain the meaning of the term *office block ballot*. Does it typically encourage a straight ticket vote or a split ticket vote?

121. Explain the difference between a *closed primary* and an *open primary*.

122. Following the national census, state legislatures are constitutionally required to realign congressional district boundaries to make them equal in population. This is called:
    a. Reapportionment
    b. Redistricting
    c. Disclosure
    d. Voter mobilization
    e. Electoral adjustment

Chapter 24: State Legislatures
Describe the functions of state legislatures and evaluate their responsiveness to the people.

123. Which of the following traits would NOT be typical of a state legislator?
    a. White
    b. Male
    c. Lawyer
    d. Lower income
    e. All of these traits are typical

124. Which of the following is an example of an elected official acting as a trustee?
    a. Voting for a canal because his or her neighbors all support it
    b. Voting for a tax increase even though her or his constituents all strongly oppose it
    c. Voting for an immigration bill after being pressed by friends
    d. Voting for the new seatbelt law because it is popular
    e. All of the above

125. What are the pros and cons of term limits?

126. Which of the following is an example of malapportionment in legislative districts?
    a. Drawing a district that excludes all Democrats
    b. Excluding all African Americans from a district
    c. Drawing a district that is not contiguous
    d. Neighboring districts that vary greatly in population
    e. All of the above

127. What is direct democracy and what are its strengths and weaknesses?

Chapter 25: State Governors
Explain how governors use their formal and informal powers to influence public policy.

128. Which of the following is NOT true of a typical state's governor?
    a. The executive power is fully vested in him or her
    b. Has the power to make appointments
    c. Has the power to veto legislation
    d. Commands the state National Guard
    e. Can pardon or grant clemency to criminals

129. Explain what a line item veto is.

130. Which one of the following is typically second in command to the governor?
    a. Attorney general
    b. Lieutenant governor
    c. Secretary of state
    d. Treasurer
    e. Senate president

131. What are some of the challenges facing current governors?

Chapter 26: Judges and Justice in the States
Describe the judicial system at the state level, and evaluate the differences across the states in judicial selection and sentencing.

132. Describe the functions of the three main kinds of state courts—minor courts, trial courts, and appellate courts.

133. Which of the following is NOT one of the ways that state judges are chosen?
    a. Appointment by the governor
    b. Election by the legislature
    c. Popular election
    d. Appointment by the president
    e. The Missouri plan

134. Explain how a *retention election* works.

135. An *information affidavit* is a certification that there is enough evidence to justify bringing named individuals to trial. Who is responsible for submitting an information affidavit?
    a. Judge
    b. Trial jury
    c. Public prosecutor
    d. Grand jury
    e. Public defender

136. Explain how an *assigned counsel system* works.

137. Describe three proposals for reforming the state judicial system.

Chapter 27: Local Governments and Metropolitics
Identify the functions of local governments, including counties, cities, towns, and special districts.

138. Explain why New England town meetings are the most complete demonstration of direct democracy in the United States.

139. What is the informal definition of a *metropolitan area*?
    a. A large city
    b. A large city and its suburbs
    c. The suburbs surrounding a large city
    d. A large city and its suburbs, as well as neighboring towns that use the same public transportation systems

140. Why is the concept of *eminent domain* controversial?

141. A *township* is a level of local government beneath the county that is primarily used in which region of the United States?
    a. Northwest
    b. Southwest
    c. Northeast
    d. Southeast

142. List and describe three strategies for governing metropolitan regions.

Chapter 28: Making State and Local Policy
Evaluate the importance of state and local governments in implementing policy.

143. In the United States, the responsibility for administering public education is constitutionally reserved to:
    a. The federal government
    b. State governments
    c. Private individuals
    d. All of the above
    e. None of the above

144. Explain the term *voucher*.

145. On what Constitutional grounds are some states challenging the recent national health care reform law, and on what Constitutional grounds does the the federal government respond?

146. Explain three general purposes for enacting and enforcing zoning laws.

147. Give two examples of how states are taking the lead in setting responsible environmental policy.

Chapter 29: Staffing and Financing State and Local Governments
Describe the challenges for state and local governments in organizing resources, raising funds, and managing expenditures.

148. Public employment that is structured so that selection and promotion depend primarily on political patronage is called:
    a. The spoils system
    b. The merit system
    c. Outsourcing
    d. Competitive bureaucracy
    e. Professional civil service

149. Which of the following is the states' largest source of revenue?
    a. Sale of state properties
    b. Federal grants

c. Charges for government services
d. Taxes
e. Tuition at state universities

150. Explain why property taxes are often controversial.

151. A tax graduated so that people with higher incomes pay a larger fraction of their income than people with lower incomes is called a(n):
   a. Excise tax
   b. Value-added tax
   c. Progressive tax
   d. Sales tax
   e. Severance tax

152. Why do states differ in fiscal capacity (the economic resources they can tax)?

The Big Picture

153. What are the arguments for and against higher salaries for state legislators?

154. Explain the four different ways in which state judges are selected.

155. Explain the arguments for and against giving state governors the power of the line item veto.

Conclusion: Sustaining Constitutional Democracy

156. Duverger's law is best described as:
   a. An observation that single-member legislative districts tend to lead to two-party systems
   b. A law proposed by Sen. Duverger (R-GA) prohibiting proportional representation in the U.S.
   c. A doctrine of political science equating democracy with economic prosperity
   d. A rule designating the procedure for the formation of House committees
   e. An observation that district lines tend to be drawn to maximize incumbent party strength

157. Why is active citizenship crucial for democracy?

ANSWERS

1. D

2. The Mayflower Compact became a model of how a group could unite under a unanimous agreement of self-government. The compact illustrated how the governed could be a legitimate source of government. Some say that it created the "seeds" of the American constitutional government and the written constitution.

3. B

4. B

PART I Constitutional Principles

5. Answer: E

6. High levels of education (an educated citizenry), a relatively prosperous and stable economy with a fairly equitable distribution of wealth, private ownership of property, a market economy, social stability (meaning peaceful relationships between different subgroups within a country), widely shared ideals of democracy (one person, one vote; freedom of speech; majority rule; and freedom of assembly) despite differing ideological views.

7. B

8. The Articles of Confederation lacked a strong executive and an independent judiciary. Under the Articles of Confederation, Congress had no direct authority over citizens. It could not levy taxes, regulate trade between states or with other nations, or prevent states from taxing each other's goods or issuing their own currencies. State governments could overturn national laws in practice. The Constitution reversed all of these characteristics.

9. The three-fifths compromise dealt with the method of counting slaves for the purpose of apportioning seats in the House of Representatives. Southern slave states wanted to count all slaves in their population, while northern free states did not want them to be included. With the three-fifths compromise, each slave would be counted as three-fifths of a person when determining apportionment of seats. This quelled the desires of both sides by maintaining a balance of power. The compromise also included a provision to eliminate the importation of slaves, which occurred in 1808.

10. Presidents have increased their power due to their ability to appeal directly to millions of people and to receive immediate access to public opinion. Interest groups are able to target thousands of letters and calls at members of Congress, to orchestrate campaigns to write letters to editors, and to organize and mobilize on the Internet. Nongovernmental institutions, such as special-interest groups and the press, have greater independence and influence. Wealthy individuals are able to bypass political parties and carry their message directly to the public.

11. E

12. Amendments can be proposed by a two-thirds vote of both houses of Congress or by a convention called by Congress at the request of the legislatures in two-thirds of the states. The latter method has never been used. Reasons for this may include that there are no specific directions in the Constitution for how delegates to such a convention would be selected or for the scope of amendments that may be considered by the convention once it is in session. Also, it may be more difficult to organize state legislatures in order to propose calling a convention.

13. A

14. Federalism is a constitutional arrangement in which power is distributed between a central government and subdivisional governments, called states in the United States. The national and subdivisional governments both exercise direct authority over individuals. The ways that governments at different levels can share power include:
    - Dual federalism: a limited list of powers are given to the national government, and the rest are reserved to the states.
    - Cooperative federalism: stresses intergovernmental relationships in delivering governmental goods and services.
    - Marble cake federalism: a mixed set of responsibilities where all levels of government engage in a variety of issues and programs (as opposed to dual federalism).
    - Competitive federalism: all levels of government compete with each other over ways to put together packages of services and taxes.
    - Permissive federalism: the states' share of power depends on the permission and permissiveness of the national government.
    - New federalism: the power of the federal government is limited in favor of the broad powers reserved to the states.

15. D

16. Delegated, or express, powers are powers explicitly given to the national government through statements in the Constitution. Implied powers are powers inferred from the express powers that are given to Congress in the Constitution. Express powers include the powers to declare war and to create post offices, while implied powers include the power to create banks.

17. B

18. C

19. State and national governments have disagreed often on civil rights and civil liberties issues. Thus, even when the national government outlawed slavery, segregation, and discrimination, states in which these new laws were not popular did not enforce these federal laws. Federalism also can create inconsistent laws among states that can create problems for people moving between states or for expanding businesses. Despite these potential problems, federalism has many advantages, including decentralization of power, and preventing the growth of tyranny. It also encourages experimentation in lower levels of government that might be adopted elsewhere. Finally, it keeps government closer to the people so that it can better engage more citizens in the governing process. There are laws today permitting same-sex marriage or civil unions in some states and not others.

20. Those who use an originalist approach to constitutional interpretation read the document literally and understand the words to mean what they meant at the time they were ratified. The adaptive approach is one through which the Constitution is seen as an evolving document that should be understood in light of society's norms and values.

21. The framers wanted a central government strong enough to address their concerns over the economy and international relations, but they also wanted government that was responsive to the diverse needs of state citizens. Federalism does both by providing the benefits of a strong central government balanced by smaller state governments that are closer to the people.

PART II The Political Process

22. Liberty, Equality, Individualism, Respect for the Common Person, Democratic Consensus—including majority rule and popular sovereignty, Justice and the Rule of Law, Patriotism, Optimism, Idealism.

23. B

24. A competitive economy allows individuals to reap large rewards for their initiative and hard work, while the goal of an egalitarian society is for everyone to earn a decent living. Conflicts between these value systems include whether or not people should be allowed to fail, or whether the success of some should be allowed to come at the expense of others.

25. B

26. D

27. Reinforcing cleavages are differences that reinforce each other and serve to polarize society. Cross-cutting cleavages pull the same people in different directions, thereby offsetting the polarizing effect of social and economic differences between people. An example of reinforcing cleavages includes the division between Northern and Southern Italy. American diversity has typically been considered more cross-cutting because most people fit it into several different social groups.

28. The process by which we develop our political attitudes, values, and beliefs.

29. True

30. D

31. Interest groups exert influence on policy by mobilizing the public, by executing mass mailings, and by contacting government directly about proposed rules and regulations. They may also influence rulemaking by making it difficult to enforce regulations and rules. Interest groups also exert influence by initiating lawsuits and by filing amicus curiae briefs for cases in which they are not directly involved.

32. E

33. A

34. Cross-cutting interests reduce and stabilize the influence of interest groups, which typically prevents any one group from assuming a commanding role in politics.

35. A

36. Third parties have difficulty obtaining support in the U.S. because our system of elections involves single-member districts and a winner-take-all system. These methods do not offer any incentive for a smaller third party to form, as it is unlikely that they would be able to obtain a plurality of votes. Also, our presidential system, where the head of government is not part of the legislative branch, makes development of a third party less likely.

37. D

38. B

39. Some claim that increased use of TV, radio, the Internet, and telephones have strengthened the role of candidates while reducing the role of parties in educating and mobilizing voters.

40. E

41. A random sample is a sample in which each person in the population or group has an equal and known chance of being selected into the sample. Random-digit dialing, in which a computer generates phone numbers to include in a sample, can gather random samples. Similarly, exit polls target randomly selected voters leaving the polls to predict election results.

42. C

43. Citizens vote most often for a candidate from their preferred party. Voters use party identification as a way to more easily make decisions when they do not have detailed information on individual candidates. Alternatively, citizens may vote on the basis of a candidate when that candidate has made an appeal directly to voters.

44. Punch-card ballots had "hanging chads" or punches that did not completely perforate the card. Also, some counties in Florida used "butterfly ballots" on which the candidates' names were staggered on opposite sides of the ballot with the punch holes in a straight line in the middle of the ballot. Some voters complained these made it difficult to tell which candidate went with which punch. In order to fix these problems, Florida enacted legislation to modernize the voting process, to purchase more than $30 million worth of touchscreen machines, and to establish minimum standards for polling places and voting machines. On a federal level, the Congress passed the Help America Vote Act (HAVA) in 2002. This provided $3.9 billion of federal funds to modernize voting processes and to mandate that states keep accurate voter registration lists. Also under HAVA, if there is uncertainty surrounding a person's voter registration, he or she can cast a provisional ballot.

45. C

46. B

47. Incumbents typically enjoy better name recognition and greater visibility than challengers. Also, incumbents can reference their efforts on behalf of their constituents during their recent time in office, and they typically have access to greater funds than challengers. Finally, incumbents' district boundaries have usually been drawn in a way that benefits them.

48. D

49. Potential answers include:
    - National Presidential Primary is simple, direct, and representative, likely drawing a larger turnout. It may enhance the role of showmanship and be much more expensive, hurting less well-known candidates.
    - Regional Primaries may bring more coherence to the election process and encourage emphasis on regional issues. However, they are expensive, and they give an advantage to candidates from the region with the first primary, thus increasing polarization in some areas of the country.

- Direct Popular Election would give each voter the same weight (one person, one vote), so each voter would feel that his or her vote counts. Also, this would grant more legitimacy to the winner. Direct Popular Elections may undermine federalism, encourage unrestrained majority rule and political extremism, and hurt the most populous and competitive states.
- National Bonus Plan adds 102 more electors awarded on a winner-take-all basis. This method would avoid elections being decided by the House and ensure that president that wins popular vote wins the presidency. However, this plan is more complicated and requires a runoff if there is no winner.
- District System (candidate who wins each district gets that district's vote) increases representation from the current system because a candidate that is strong in some areas of a state but not others can still win some of the electoral votes. Otherwise, this system is similar to the electoral college.

50. A

51. In addition to reporting the news, journalists sometimes actually investigate emerging stories. Investigative reporters will reveal their findings to the public, which often has political consequences. For example, the reports on the torture of Iraqi prisoners at Abu Ghraib by U.S. soldiers in 2004, as well as the reports on Dana Priest's 2005 investigation of secret CIA prisons where suspected terrorists were held and interrogated, held enormous political and legal consequences. Reporters Jack Anderson, Robert Woodward, and Carl Bernstein's investigation of the attempted burglary at the Democratic National Committee headquarters in the Watergate building revealed the political corruption of the Nixon White House and reelection committee, ultimately leading to the former president's resignation.

52. D

53. Since the increased use of television during campaigns, candidates have become more focused on image and visibility. Mistakes made by candidates are more likely to be problematic for candidates with increased visibility and media coverage. Television has also made election issues more accessible to the public, but it has also contributed to the increased costs of campaigning. Furthermore, election night reporting has dampened voter turnout in western states because results from eastern states have already been counted and announced on television before some western voters get to the polls.

54. Presidents use the media to set the agenda and to push certain legislation. Presidents hold news conferences or may leak certain information and news to reporters. Any event that the president attends or activity he engages in is newsworthy.

55. The U.S. two-party system presents voters with candidates that are typically more centrist than might be the case with a multi-party system. In a winner-take-all system as we have in the U.S., voters who favor third party candidates might be less likely to vote, given that they know their favored candidate has little chance of winning the election.

56. One of the arguments against strong campaign finance laws is a concern with constitutionally protected free speech. Since candidates for office must spend money to convey their message, restricting the amount of money they can spend restricts their speech. Alternatively, proponents of strong campaign finance laws argue that they help to reign in well-financed special interests and allow individual citizens to affect campaigns through their contributions.

PART III Policy-Making Institutions

57. D

58. B

59. Delegates determine what their constituency wants and then acts accordingly. Trustees act and vote according to their own opinions of what is best for their constituency, state, and nation.

60. D

61. The Speaker of the House is the most powerful leader on Capitol Hill. This position is always filled by a member of the majority party. The Speaker has the power to rule on questions of parliamentary procedure, to recognize members who rise to speak, to appoint members to temporary committees, to reorganize House committees, to name committee chairs, to appoint allies to leadership posts, and to reduce the size of committee staffs. The president of the Senate is also the vice president of the United States but has little actual influence over Senate proceedings, only voting when there is a tie. The President pro tempore is generally the most senior member of the majority party in the Senate and acts as chair in the absence of the vice president. Often his or her senatorial responsibilities are delegated to junior members of the majority party.

62. C

63. George Washington established the legitimacy and authority of the presidency. He provided an example of how the president could carry out the duties assigned to him in the Constitution. His most important contribution was likely his resignation from office after serving for two terms. Franklin Roosevelt was most likely the first president to fully use the powers of the presidency as well as to dominate Congress. He also set a precedent of personal communication with American citizens.

64. E

65. A

66. D

67. Independent regulatory commissions are independent in the sense that they do not report to the president. Thus, these commissions are more insulated from politics, though the commissioners are appointed by the president and approved by Congress. Independent stand-alone agencies are independent from any department, but they report directly to the president.

68. C

69. A

70. Presidents control federal bureaucracy through the powers of appointment, reorganization, and budgeting. They can also influence the bureaucracy by mobilizing public opinion and support from Congress. The main ways Congress can control the bureaucracy is through formulating budgets, appropriating funds, confirming personnel, authorizing new programs, conducting investigations and hearings, and terminating agencies.

71. The Supreme Court cannot choose what issues will be brought to it. It can only address issues outside parties choose to litigate.

72. C

73. Judicial activism is the philosophy that judges should strike down laws that are inconsistent with norms and values stated or implied in Constitution. Judicial restraint is the philosophy that judges should strike down the actions of the elected branches only if they clearly violate the literal meaning of the Constitution.

74. D

75. The Constitution gives the Supreme Court the power to hear cases and controversies. It cannot take up issues that are not brought to it. It also cannot enforce its decisions. It must rely on the executive to do that. This keeps the Court, whose members are unelected, from having too much latitude to change policy, but it can also make it possible for the elected branches and the public to ignore unpopular rulings, even those that may protect minority rights.

76. A strong federal bureaucracy can provide expertise in implementing policy. But if the bureaucracy is too strong, it might frustrate the will of the elected branches. The president maintains a check on the bureaucracy through the power to appoint senior officials, and Congress maintains the power to appropriate funds as well as to create and eliminate bureaucratic agencies, with the president's cooperation.

PART IV Individual Rights and Liberties

77. A

78. E

79. Procedural due process mainly limits the executive and judicial branches because they apply the law and review its application. Substantive due process mainly limits the legislative branch because it actually creates and enacts laws.

80. B

81. D

82. The rights to use the navigable waters of the United States and protection on the high seas, to assemble peacefully and petition for redress of grievances, to vote if qualified to do so under state laws and have your vote counted properly, and to travel throughout the United States.

83. C

84. Officially sanctioned segregation is *de jure* segregation. Segregation that arises as a result of social and economic conditions such as housing patterns is *de facto* segregation.

85. D

86. One of the primary arguments in favor of affirmative action, particularly in education, is the need to promote diversity. One of the arguments against it is that the Fourteenth Amendment prohibits racial discrimination and while affirmative action programs may seek to promote diversity, they do so by discriminating based on race.

87. Democracy requires that citizens have the right to convey their ideas to each other, to their representatives, and to the country as a whole. Thus, free speech is essential for a healthy democracy. There are some instances in which free speech might not be protected, such as when it poses an immediate danger to national security or is judged to be obscene.

PART V The Politics of National Policy

88. E. Of the programs mentioned, only welfare takes money from one group and gives it exclusively to another group.

89. B. While B might be part of a president, party, or group's calculation when attempting to influence policy, it is not necessary in making public policy.

90. Incremental policy consists of small changes to existing policy, such as increasing funding to colleges by a few hundred dollars, whereas punctuating policy is more radical and can only occur after mobilization of large segments of society. An example of punctuating policy would be a health care bill that makes purchasing health insurance mandatory.

91. E

92. There are many possible ways for citizens to affect public policy, including joining interest groups, writing letters, sending e-mails, confronting legislators at community meetings, and even running for office.

93. Fiscal policy means using federal spending and taxation to stimulate or slow the economy. Monetary policy means manipulating the supply of money in the economy to smooth periods of growth and recession.

94. B

95. D

96. A

97. Increasing the federal funds rate increases the costs for money and credit, thus slowing the economy. Lowering the federal funds rate makes money more accessible for investment and growth, thus stimulating the economy.

98. D

99. Entitlements are programs under which the government provides benefits to all eligible citizens, regardless of need such as disaster relief or disability payments.

100. D

101. Provisions of the Patient Protection and Affordable Health Care Act include: most Americans will be required to purchase health insurance starting in 2014; insurance companies will be prevented from denying coverage for any reason; insurance companies will extend coverage under parents' plans for young Americans up through the age of 26; the Medicaid program will be extended to all poor Americans under 65; and individual Americans will pay a tax on "Cadillac" insurance plans.

102. Congress has enacted legislation concerning public education, including the Elementary and Secondary Education Act (1965) and the No Child Left Behind Act (2002). However, states have not always been favorable to such efforts, particularly when the federal laws require them to meet higher standards without sufficient resources.

103. Realism assumes that nations will act out of self-interest, while idealism is open to the idea that nations will work together to solve international problems.

104. C

105. D

106. Soft power relies on diplomacy to solve international problems, while hard power relies on economic and military strength.

107. C

108. There are a variety of ways in which the government can influence the nation's economy, including increasing or decreasing government spending, raising or lowering taxes, changing the federal funds rate, and increasing or lowering trade barriers. Some argue that government involvement improves economic growth and promotes a strong economy. Others argue that government regulation stifles competition and the potential for private industry to succeed.

109. Redistributive policies take benefits away from one group in society and provide benefits to another group in society. One argument in favor of such programs is that they provide benefits to those who truly need them. Opponents might argue that such programs penalize those who succeed by taxing them to redistribute benefits.

PART VI State and Local Government

110. A theory of government that holds that open, multiple and competing groups can check the asserted power of any one group.

111. C. Polling shows that citizens are most trustful in local government.

112. D. Military strength is a concern of the federal government.

113. Owners of newspapers are often friends with local officials, and they recognize that speaking well of their town and officials is ultimately to their benefit if it brings expansion.

114. "Constitutions as straitjackets" refers to constitutions being very detailed; hence they are like straitjackets imposed on the present by the past. Constitutions become more detailed as amendments are passed, often in an attempt to reign in the power of corrupt legislators.

115. E. The Supreme Court has no power to directly enact an amendment on a state constitution. Their rulings may in effect change state law but their rulings do not amend constitutions.

116. Some states may be concerned that their constitutions are too easily changed. Amendments that only garner a bare majority might not be in the best interest of the state. With a higher bar for amending the document, groups would be forced to appeal to a greater segment of the state's population.

117. A. Judicial interpretation is a method by which judges modify the force of a constitutional provision by reinterpreting its meaning.

118. E

119. C

120. An office block ballot is a ballot on which all candidates are listed under the office for which they are running. This type of ballot typically encourages a split ticket vote.

121. A closed primary is a primary election in which only persons registered in the party holding the primary may vote. An open primary is a primary election in which any voter, regardless of party, may vote.

122. B

123. D. The typical state legislator is financially well-off.

124. B. All other answers involve the legislator acting in response to constituent pressure.

125. Having term limits prevents professional politicians serving in the legislature, but it leads to an amateur legislature and gives increased power to lobbyists.

126. D. Malapportionment refers to having districts with unequal populations.

127. It refers to the initiative process where citizens are able to place issues directly on a state-wide ballot. It brings the political process closer to the people, but it can be manipulated by special interests and uninformed citizens.

128. A. In contrast to the president, governors typically have to share executive power with other officers.

129. Line item veto is the right of an executive to veto parts of a bill approved by a legislature without having to veto the entire bill.

130. B

131. Governors are expected to be the state's chief policy maker, shaper of the state budget, savvy political party leader, chief recruiter of the best available advisers and administrators, and inspiring leader who renews public confidence in state programs.

132. Minor trial courts handle minor violations of state and local laws and, in some cases, the preliminary hearings for more serious offenses. Major courts are typically courts of general jurisdiction hearing civil and criminal cases. Appeals courts handle challenges to outcomes of trial courts.

133. D

134. A sitting judge runs *uncontested* for reelection: Voters simply vote in favor or against keeping her or him in office.

135. C

136. An arrangement whereby attorneys are provided for people accused of crimes who are unable to hire their own attorneys. The judge assigns a member of the bar to provide counsel to a particular defendant.

137. Efforts to reform state courts include some that focus on increasing judicial quality, improving professional administration, and developing alternative methods to resolve disputes.

138. Voters participate directly in making rules, passing new laws, levying taxes, and appropriating money.

139. B

140. Eminent domain is controversial because it places individual landowners' interests at odds with state and local governments' interests. It allows the government to take private land for public purposes, even when the landowner does not give consent, as long as the owner is paid the fair market value. Many people have different views of what important public purposes would justify governments exercising this power.

141. C

142. Strategies to govern metropolitan areas include annexation, agreements to furnish services, public authorities, special districts, regional coordinating and planning councils, city-county consolidations, and federated government.

143. B

144. Money provided by the government to parents for payment of their children's tuition in a public or private school of their choice.

145. Some states challenge the federal government's efforts at health-care reform as exceeding their authority under the commerce clause and infringing on the states' power under the Tenth Amendment. Proponents argue that the federal government has regulatory authority due to its impact on interstate commerce and to provide for the general welfare.

146. For the local government to coordinate services and land use; to stabilize property values; to maintain standards of sanitation; to maintain public safety; to improve quality of life in the community.

147. States have become active in protecting the environment through waste management, controlling auto emissions, and promoting responsible energy use and sustainability.

148. A

149. D

150. Property taxes bear little relationship to a taxpayers' income or other measures of their ability to pay. Real property cannot always be easily converted into money with which to pay the tax. Exemptions sometimes create situations where two taxpayers with similar property pay different tax rates. Assessments may or may not reflect the actual market value of the property. Most property taxes require a lump-sum payment that could be difficult for some taxpayers to meet.

151. C

152. States differ in average personal incomes. Average personal income is often correlated with consumption and property values, which affect the amount of money a state can raise through sales taxes and property taxes. States also have different amounts of natural resources, which affect the amount they can collect in severance taxes.

153. Opponents of raising state legislators' salaries argue that professional politicians do not necessarily do a good job. Proponents argue that legislators work longer hours on more complicated and demanding work than most citizens realize.

154. State court judges are determined in several ways throughout the U.S. including gubernatorial appointment, election by the state legislature, popular election, and merit-selection plans.

155. Some argue that a line item veto would give governors unchecked power that could frustrate the will of the legislature. Others argue this power is needed to check legislatures which are including more and more legislation in their appropriations bills.

156. A

157. Active citizenship is crucial because democracy derives its power from the governed. Thus, in order to ensure that majority and minority rights are protected, the public must take an active role in governing whether through voting, voter mobilization and lobbying, and/or running for office. Active citizenship also ensures that policies are adequately discussed and debated before they are implemented.